The Eating Disorders

Medical and Psychological
Bases of
Diagnosis and Treatment

The Eating Disorders
Medical and Psychological Bases of Diagnosis and Treatment

Edited by
Barton J. Blinder, M.D., Ph.D.
Department of Psychiatry and Human Behavior
College of Medicine, University of California, Irvine
Director, Eating Disorders Program and Research Studies

Barry F. Chaitin, M.D.
Department of Psychiatry and Human Behavior
College of Medicine, University of California, Irvine
Clinical Director, University Service, Capistrano-by-the-Sea Hospital

Renée S. Goldstein, Ph.D.
Department of Psychiatry and Human Behavior
College of Medicine, University of California, Irvine

PMA PUBLISHING CORP.
New York

NOTICE: The editors, contributors, and publisher of this work have made every effort to ensure that the drug dosage schedules and/or procedures are accurate and in accord with the standards accepted at the time of publications. Readers are cautioned, however, to check the product information sheet included in the package of each drug they plan to administer. This is particularly important in regard to new or infrequently used drugs. The publisher is not responsible for any errors of fact or omissions in this book.

Library of Congress Cataloging in Publication Data

The Eating disorders.

    Includes bibliographies and index.
      1. Eating disorders.   I. Blinder, Barton J..
II. Chaitin, Barry F.   III. Goldstein, Renée. [DNLM:
1. Appetite Disorders — diagnosis. 2. Appetite
Disorders — therapy.   WM 175 E1475]
RC552.E18E285   1988   616.85'2   88-15251
ISBN 0-89335-300-0

Printed in the United States of America

Dedication

The editors dedicate this volume to Hilde Bruch, M.D., and Albert Stunkard, M.D., whose scientific contributions and educational endeavors have enriched the field.

Contributors

ELLIOTT M. BLASS, PH.D.
Department of Psychology, The Johns Hopkins
    University
Baltimore, Maryland

BARTON J. BLINDER, M.D., PH.D
Department of Psychiatry and Human Behavior,
    University of California Irvine
University Service, Capistrano by the Sea Hospital
Dana Point, California

JOHN E. BLUNDELL, PH.D., F.B.PS.S.
Department of Psychology, The University of Leeds
United Kingdom

BARRY F. CHAITIN, M.D.
Department of Psychiatry and Human Behavior,
    University of California Irvine
University Service, Capistrano by the Sea Hospital
Dana Point, California

ROWAN T. CHLEBOWSKI, M.D., PH.D.
Department of Medicine, Division of Medical
    Oncology, Harbor UCLA Medical Center
UCLA School of Medicine
Torrance, California

JEAN DENSMORE-JOHN, M.D., R.D.
Nutritionist in Private Practice
Clinical Nutrition Consultants of Santa Barbara
Santa Barbara, California

KATHERINE DIXON, M.D.
Psychiatric Centers at San Diego
San Diego, California

ADAM DREWNOWSKI, PH.D.
Human Nutrition Program, School of Public
    Health, The University of Michigan
Ann Arbor, Michigan

MICHAEL H. EBERT, M.D.
Department of Psychiatry, Vanderbilt University
Nashville, Tennessee

DANIEL M.A. FREEMAN, M.D.
Private Practice
Jenkintown, Pennsylvania

A. GERTLER, M.A.
Rishon Le-Zion Mental Health Community Clinic
Israel

JAMES GIBBS, M.D.
The Edward W. Bourne Behavioral Research
    Laboratory, Department of Psychiatry, The New
    York Hospital-Cornell Medical Center
White Plains, New York

I. LEE GISLASON, M.D.
Department of Psychiatry and Human Behavior,
    Child Study Center, University of California Irvine
UCI Medical Center
Orange, California

STANLEY GOODMAN, M.D.
Private Practice
Irvine, California

RICHARD A. GORDON, PH.D.
Department of Psychology, Bard College
Annandale-on-Hudson, New York

HARVEY E. GWIRTSMAN, M.D.
Neuropsychiatric Institute, University of California
	Los Angeles
Los Angeles, California

JENNIFER HAGMAN, M.D.
Department of Psychiatry and Human Behavior,
	University of California Irvine, UCI Medical
	Center
Orange, California

ROBERT HAMPTON, III, M.D.
Private Practice
Balboa, California

PHYLLIS HENDERSON, M.D.
Department of Psychiatry
Loma Linda University Medical Center
Loma Linda, California

MARION HETHERINGTON, V. PHIL.
Department of Psychiatry and Behavioral Sciences,
	The Johns Hopkins University School of Medicine
Baltimore, Maryland

ANDREW J. HILL, PH.D.
Department of Psychology, The University of Leeds
United Kingdom

LEIGH-ANN HOHLSTEIN
Laboratory of Clinical Science, Section of Clinical
	Studies, National Institute on Alcohol Abuse
Bethesda, Maryland

L.K. GEORGE HSU, M.D.
Department of Psychiatry, School of Medicine,
	Western Psychiatric Institute and Clinic,
	University of Pittsburgh
Pittsburgh, Pennsylvania

GLYNN ISAAC, PH.D. (DEC.)
Department of Anthropology, Peabody Museum,
	Harvard University
Cambridge, Massachusetts

DOUGLAS G. KAHN, M.D.
Department of Psychiatry and Human Behavior,
	University of California Irvine
College of Medicine
Newport Beach, California

WALTER H. KAYE, M.D.
Department of Psychiatry, University of Pittsburgh
Pittsburgh, Pennsylvania

DEAN D. KRAHN, M.D.
Department of Psychiatry, Veterans Administration
	Medical Center
Minneapolis, Minnesota

SHELDON Z. KRAMER, PH.D.
Department of Psychology, Assistant Clinical
	Training Director of Clinical Psychology, U.S.
	International University, San Diego
Medical Consultant and Trainer of Family Therapy,
	Department of Psychiatry, U.S. Navy, San Diego
San Diego, California

JAMES R. KUECHLER, M.D.
Department of Psychiatry and Human Behavior,
	University of California Irvine
Muirlands Medical Center
El Toro, California

C. RAYMOND LAKE, M.D., PH.D.
Departments of Psychiatry and Pharmacology,
	Uniform Services, University of Health Sciences
Bethesda, Maryland

FELIX E.F. LAROCCA, M.D., F.A.P.A.
BASH Treatment and Research Center, Deaconess
	Hospital
St. Louis, Missouri

PIERRE LEICHNER, M.D.
Director, Community Psychiatric Center, Douglas
	Hospital
Verdun, Quebec, Canada

ALLAN S. LEVINE, PH.D.
Neuroendocrine Research Laboratory, Veterans
	Administration Medical Center
Minneapolis, Minnesota

RONALD LIEBMAN, M.D.
Department of Psychiatry, Temple University
	School of Medicine
Philadelphia, Pennyslvania

NADINE A. LEVINSON, D.D.S.
Department of Psychiatry and Human Behavior,
  University of California Irvine
Laguna Niguel, California

DAVID L. MARGULES, PH.D.
Department of Psychology, Temple University
Philadelphia, Pennsylvania

ROLF MEERMAN, M.D., PH.D.
Lecturer of Psychiatry at the University of Munster,
  School of Medicine and Medical Director,
  Psychosomatic Hospital Bad Pyrmont
Bad Pyrmont, West Germany

JAMES E. MITCHELL, M.D.
Department of Psychiatry, University of Minnesota
Minneapolis, Minnesota

JOHN E. MORLEY, M.D.
Veterans Administration Medical Center
Sepulveda, California

CHRISTIANE NAPIERSKI, M.D.
Department of Psychiatry, University of Munster
Munster, West Germany

RICHARD L. PYLE, M.D.
Department of Psychiatry, University of Minnesota
Minneapolis, Minnesota

BARBARA J. ROLLS, PH.D.
Department of Psychiatry and Behavioral Sciences,
  The Johns Hopkins University School of Medicine
Baltimore, Maryland

PETER ROY-BYRNE, M.D.
Biological Psychiatry Branch, National Institute of
  Mental Health
Bethesda, Maryland

S. MARK SACHER, D.O.
Department of Psychiatry and Human Behavior,
  University of California Irvine
UCI Medical Center
Orange, California

JOHN SARGENT, M.D.
Center for Psychosomatic and Eating Disorders,
  Philadelphia Guild Guidance Clinic
Philadelphia, Pennsylvania

TIMOTHY SCHALLERT, M.D.
Psychology Department, Institute for Neurological
  Sciences, University of Texas at Austin
Austin, Texas

JEANNE SEPT, PH.D.
Department of Anthropology, Indiana University
Bloomington, Indiana

JAMES C. SHEININ, M.D.
Division of Endocrinology and Metabolism,
  Department of Medicine, Michael Reese
  Hospital and Medical Center, University of
  Chicago, Pritzker School of Medicine
Chicago, Illinois

DAVID C. SIBLEY, M.D.
Private Practice
Brea, California

LAWRENCE D. SPORTY, M.D.
Department of Psychiatry and Human Behavior,
  University of California Irvine Medical Center
Orange, California

MARC H. STOLAR, M.D.
Private Practice
Tustin, California

CARL I. THOMPSON, PH.D.
Department of Psychology, Wabash College
Crawfordsville, Indiana

WALTER VANDEREYCKEN, M.D.
University Psychiatric Center
Kortenberg, Belgium

B. TIMOTHY WALSH, M.D.
Department of Psychiatry, College of Physicians &
  Surgeons, Columbia University
New York, New York

C. PHILIP WILSON, M.D.
Private Practice
New York, New York

JOSEPH L. WOOLSTON, M.D.
Child Study Center, Yale University
New Haven, Connecticut

Contents

Preface

This volume is the result of a major effort to approach the concept of a medical text for the eating disorders directed to the health professions. Our forebearers – E.L. Bliss and C.H. Branch, *Anorexia Nervosa: Its history, psychology, and biology,* (1960); M.R. Kaufman and M. Heiman, *Evolution of psychosomatic concepts; anorexia nervosa: a paradigm,* (1964); H. Thoma, *Anorexia nervosa,* (1967); H. Bruch, *Eating disorders; obesity, anorexia nervosa, and the person within,* (1973); R.A. Vigersky, *Anorexia nervosa,* (1977); P. Dally, *Anorexia nervosa,* (1979); A.H. Crisp, *Anorexia nervosa: let me be,* (1980); P.E. Garfinkel and D.M. Garner, *Anorexia nervosa: a multidimensional perspective,* (1982); P.S. Powers and R.C. Fernandez, *Current treatment of anorexia nervosa and bulimia,* (1984); D.M. Garner and P.E. Garfinkel, *Handbook of psychotherapy for anorexia nervosa and bulimia,* (1985); A.E. Anderson, *Practical comprehensive treatment of anorexia nervosa and bulimia,* (1985) – have contributed immensely to heightening historical perspectives emphasizing predominately clinical features, providing epidemiologic focus and documenting the vissicitudes of various treatment approaches.

Our aim is to present the beginnings of a comprehensive psychobiologic curriculum for the eating disorders; to foster the education and encourage the interest of the widest possible readership in general medicine, psychiatry, psychology, nutritional science and nursing; and promote both the highest level of informed treatment of patients who suffer from eating disorders and advance the research contributions to our basic clinical knowledge.

This work can serve also as an organized reference for clinicians and researchers with the hope of promoting cross-fertilization between the neurobiologic studies of appetite and eating, and clinical practice.

Conveyed in the sections and chapters of this book are the exciting advances in knowledge, diagnostic concepts and clinical accumen over the past decade that contain the promise of comprehensive treatment in the future.

There is expanded coverage in the text to include rumination and pica; special interests: oncology, eating disorders in the menstrual cycle, eating disorders and affective disorders, and eating disorders and other psychiatric conditions. Treatment techniques described in the text emphasize a broad coverage of principles directed toward the rehabilitation of the patient in the direction of competence, self-awareness and self-regulation.

The hope of the editors and contributors to this volume is to stimulate teaching and research in the eating disorders over the next decade and to establish the guidelines of a pertinent curriculum.

Barton J. Blinder, M.D., Ph.D.
Barry F. Chaitin, M.D.
Renée Goldstein, Ph.D.

Acknowledgements

The editors wish to express their heartfelt gratitude to Susan Hemington for her wit, good humor, and perserverence in the collection and preparation of the manuscripts. A multi-authored text creates unusual logistical problems and Ms. Hemington proved herself equal to the challange. It is fair to say that this project could not have been successfully completed without Ms. Hemington's exceptional assistance. Professor Gordon Globus was continually supportive of the project and provided encouragement and advice. Our administrator, Jeanne Reiss is to be thanked for her skill in creating and maintaining an harmonious work environment. Last, but not least, the administration and staff of Capistrano-by-the-Sea Hospital are to be commended for the creation of an exemplary clinical environment in which we were able to learn from our patients and formulate some of the questions which this volume, hopefully, addresses.

The Eating Disorders

*Medical and Psychological
Bases of
Diagnosis and Treatment*

Section I

Neurobiologic Foundations of Appetite and Eating: Basic and Applied Studies

John E. Morley

he regulation of appetite and eating is an extremely complex process. The decision to eat or not to eat is based on the interaction of a variety of external and internal cues. Overriding all else is the availability of food: During a famine there are few fat people! Food availability interacts with social attitudes and the knowledge of the value of the available foodstuffs. Thus, survival for the moose on the shores of Lake Superior depends on the knowledge that it needs to graze not only on the high-energy-containing deciduous leaves but also on aquatic plants to obtain its salt requirements. The central role of social mores in the regulation of feeding is demonstrated by the sharing of food as a gesture of peace by the hunter-gatherer and typified by the modern business lunch. The next process in the decision to eat involves the hedonic qualities (sight, smell, and taste) of the food. We all have eaten our fill in a restaurant but found it impossible to refuse those extra calories we clearly don't need when the waiter wheels the dessert cart in front of us. The applied studies in this section deal predominantly with the factors enhancing or decreasing the acceptability of a particular food.

Thus, with the increasing affluence of a society, overeating becomes a natural way of life. At first this is accepted as a just reward for hard work, as in Isaiah 55:2: "...and let your soul delight itself with fatness." However, with time, the organism becomes aware that gluttony and obesity are just as detrimental to species survival as was the marasmic status. This leads to the

need to develop a variety of inhibitory systems to decrease food intake.

Basic animal studies have tended to concentrate on these inhibitory factors, and this is reflected by the general content of the chapters in this section on basic studies. Early studies spent much time debating the role of different absorbed nutrients as appetite regulator. This led to the development of a variety of "appetostat" theories in which various authors vied to establish their nutrient (eg, glucose, fatty acids, amino acids, or purines) as the factor responsible for inhibiting feeding (the Holy Grail Hypothesis).

More recently it has become clear that a variety of gastrointestinal hormones that are released during a meal are capable of decreasing food intake. Whether these peptide hormones are true satiety agents or merely produce a mild state of aversion if being hotly debated. However, it seems reasonable to suggest that in the end it will prove to be an interaction of these hormones and the physicochemical properties of the absorbed nutrients that leads to the termination of a single meal. In addition, the state of glycogen repletion or depletion of the liver, the production of energy (heat) by tissues such as brown fat, and the effect of fat depots on the circulating concentration of fatty acids and insulin all appear to be capable of modulating feeding.

Finally, all this information needs to be coordinated, and the organism has to make the decision whether to eat. This integrative process appears to take place within the central nervous system (predominantly but not entirely in the hypothalamus). There is growing evidence

1

that this integrative process involves a variety of neurotransmitters (monoamines, neuropeptides, prostaglandins, and amino acids) interacting on a backdrup of hypothalamic interneurons. The putative role of these neurotransmitters is discussed in two of the chapters in the basic studies section.

If after reading the chapters on the Neurobiologic Foundations of Appetite and Eating the neophyte is left somewhat bemused by the multitude of factors involved and theories invoked to explain them, heart can perhaps be taken from the words of the English philosopher, Emerson Pugh: "If the human brain were so simple that we could understand it, we would be so simple that we couldn't." The chapters in this section clearly demonstrate that despite the tremendous progress in our knowledge of the neurobiologic foundations of appetite in the last decade, we are just emerging from medieval times, hopefully to enter the Renaissance Period of insights into appetite regulation. Despite our present limitations, I believe that the future development of viable treatment modalities for eating disorders will be based in the knowledge gained from the neurobiologic foundations of appetite and eating.

Chapter 1

The Development of Feeding Behavior

Elliott M. Blass

Feeding is unique among mammalian behaviors. It is the only behavior that can be practiced successfully in total isolation yet almost always occurs in a social mileau. The meal is a setting for intense social interactions, for joy, and for pain. The meal has become incorporated into religious and national festivals such as the Passover seder or Thanksgiving dinner. It has become an integral part of Western and Eastern cultures alike in the form of coffee breaks and other social interactions.

Feeding is also unique in the sense that it changes developmentally. Mammalian infants cannot feed alone, and they derive their sustenance from breast or bottle. Over time the infants' repertoire of ingesta eaten and of consummatory motor patterns expands from their limited base of suckling milk, and the adult ingestive profile of independent feeding and drinking emerges. The social aspect of group feeding continues, however, and this serves as an opportunity for cultural transmission.

Things can go awry in feeding settings, however, and pathology can develop. If the feeding history is sufficiently traumatic and the other aspects of the psychosocial mileau are not sufficiently supportive, pathology is presented as in anorexia nervosa, bulimia, severe obesity, and other behavioral disorders.

There are major difficulties in identifying the causes of feeding disorders, however. Among the stumbling blocks are lack of time, lack of proper experimental control, and documentation of aberrant feeding situations.

Animal studies circumvent some of these problems. Accordingly, this chapter focuses on the development of feeding in animals, mostly laboratory rats. In this chapter I will document the physiological bases of early ingestive behavior, especially suckling, and the influences that the suckling setting can exert on future noningestive and ingestive behaviors.

SUCKLING

Developmental psychobiologists have come to appreciate the richness and complexity of the suckling act only during the past decade [2,3,4,5]. What appeared at first to be a simple reflex [6] is now appreciated to be under the influence of diverse physiological, social, and experiential factors. Moreover, the influence of these factors changes during development. It is now appreciated that suckling *cannot* be equated with feeding [4,7]; that the earliest determinants of suckling—more specifically, nipple attachment—are social [8], not physiological; and that internal factors start to exert their influences at about two weeks of age in developing rats [2,3,4,5]. Yet even after physiological factors come into play, they do so against the background of social deprivation until weaning is almost complete [8]. During the postnatal period [9], indeed even prenatally [10], the stimulus that will elicit nipple attachment and milk withdrawal is infuenced by various experiences. In short, as will be more fully documented, the nest setting offers a remarkably rich opportunity for conditioning and learning that are influential during and beyond the nursing period [11].

During the first 10 to 12 days after birth, nipple attachment appears to be an end in and of itself. Rats remain attached to a nonlactating dam for up to 12 hours without milk delivery [12]. Attachment latencies are not influenced by deprivation very much [13]. Indeed, rats younger than 12 days of age continue to suckle despite receiving up to 22% of their body weight in infusions through a tongue cannula [14] or by actually withdrawing milk from the milk-laden nipples of dams that had not nursed their own young overnight [15]. This is a remarkable testimony to the lack of adultlike control over milk intake. Rats that obtain these large volumes of milk detach from the nipple only after milk has refluxed into the nares from the bloated stomach and caused respiratory distress. This changes by Day 15, when normal amounts of milk are taken (ie, within the volume of milk found in the stomachs of rats continuously with their dam [14,15]).

Even though volume intake does not appear to be determined by internal factors in rats younger than 15 days of age, the rate at which milk is ingested via suckling is. Cramer and Blass [15] confirmed earlier reports of Houpt and her colleagues [16,17] that demonstrated differential intake according to differential deprivation length. Cramer and Blass [15] showed that this differential intake was directly related to the frequency with which rats shifted from nipple to nipple after each milk letdown, with more deprived rats shifting more frequently. This is an important infantile strategy, because it allowed deprived pups to sample more nipples before the ducts constricted, thereby making milk unavailable until the next letdown. Thus, there is control over ingestive activity in the sense that increased deprivation leads to increased nipple-shifting, yielding additional opportunities to obtain milk, and this is probably under vagal control [18]. However, given that a rat is attached to a nipple, then deprivation does not seem to affect the likelihood of extracting the available milk in rats younger than two weeks of age.

Deprivation to suckling infants is very different than adult deprivation. Until rats are about 25 days of age, it is lack of suckling opportunity per se that determines responsivity to the internal signals affecting rate of intake. By Day 25, it is the energetic consequence of deprivation that allows the physiological signals to gain control in older rats. Cramer and Blass [8] studied six groups of rats. One group was deprived of maternal contact and suckling for eight hours. Another group was not deprived. The remaining groups had different components of privation imposed during the eight-hour period. One group was deprived of suckling and its con-

comitant nutritional and hydrational benefits by living with a thelectomized (nipples surgically removed) female that was maintained in a maternal state. These animals, therefore, enjoyed maternal contact during privation. Another group was allowed to suckle a maternal female whose nipples were sutured, preventing milk letdown. A third group was deprived of female contact but received three, intubations (2% of body-weight) of "half and half creamer" to help offset the caloric deficit encountered during suckling abstinence. The final group was allowed to suckle nonnutritively and also received the three preloads. As can be seen from figure 1, nonnutritive suckling *per se* was sufficient to cause levels of milk intake in 15-day-old rats that did not differ from those of nondeprived rats. Intake was not due to energy or caloric deficit, because intubation did not reduce intake. Much the same holds true for Day 20 rats. It is clear that contact without suckling opportunity (thelectomized dam) was not enough to ward off the consequences of privation. By Day 25 missed suckling opportunities exerted rather little effect on milk derived from suckling. The critical factor appears to be the lost nutrients, because the preloads fully restored intake to baseline levels. In short, for suckling rats younger than two weeks of age, nipple attachment appears to be the motivating factor as a determinant of the highly specialized suckling act [19]. By two weeks, physiological controls of gastric distention [14], cholecystokinin, and dehydration [20] are operative. These controls in rats 15 and 20 days of age affect both the frequency of nipple shifting as well as volume intake. They appear to become activated in the context of the animals having been separated from the dam and *not* because of physiological consequences of separation. By Day 25 the factors affecting intake from the nipple appear to be similar to those affecting both feeding away from the dam and adult feeding.

Privation affects motivational as well as consummatory systems. According to Amsel et al [21], infant rats' running speed accurately reflects the quality of the maternal interaction that is awaiting the infant at the end of a runway. That is, rats run fastest when allowed to suckle nutritively, slower for nonnutritive suckling, and slower yet to only establish contact. Stoloff and Blass [22] showed that 2- or 24-hour deprived 17-day-old rats prefer to suckle rather than eat, even if the suckling is nonnutritive. By Day 21 suckling is preferred to eating a liquid diet only if the nipple is lactating, and by Day 28 feeding is always preferred over suckling. These results are in complete accord with the Cramer and Blass [8] findings concerning milk intake determinants in rats during the weaning period.

Thus, in rats, at least, a prolonged period of suckling

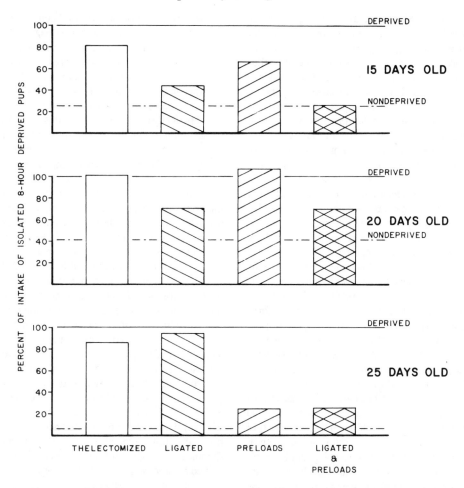

Figure 1.1 Percentage of intake of 8 hr. suckling-deprived rats by rats in different privation conditions

is strongly favored by the infant, even after it has started feeding and drinking independently and even at an age when rats are often weaned in the laboratory (Day 21). The implications of this protracted period of contact are of considerable interest, because during this period the infant much prefers the odors of its mother to that of other female or male rats [23]. This contact during the late weaning and early juvenile stage provides the unique biological opportunity for the infant to learn from its mother directly and indirectly about various facets of the environment in which it is about to enter independently. I will shortly return to this issue of what is learned in the next setting, but first a discussion of infantile feeding is in order.

FEEDING DURING DEVELOPMENT

The first hint that adultlike ingestive behavior could be obtained in suckling infants was provided by Wirth and Epstein [24], who observed increased water and milk intake in dehydrated rats that were held to a tube that delivered a continuous flow of liquid. This has been extended by Bruno [25], who observed increased water intake in rats that could initiate drinking by lowering their heads onto a fluid-soaked mat and drink in a very warm test chamber. In the interim, however, Hall and his colleagues [26,27,28] demonstrated that under certain conditions of high ambient temperature and deprivation, and when the infant rat pups' limited motoric capacity is taken into account, feeding could occur. Remarkably, feeding in 1-to 9-day-old rats had many of the major characteristics of normal adult feeding. That is, it was sensitive to the factors that enhanced food intake as well as to those that decreased it. Specifically, intake of a liquid diet, whether infused through an anterior mouth cannula or taken from a moist mat at 33°-34°C; eating a mash diet directly from the floor of a 34°C container; or ingesting sucrose were all linearly enhanced by privation [26-28]. Moreover, as feeding progressed, pups showed a progressive sequence of satiety similar to that of adults, suggesting that satiety mechanisms were in place for the feeding system at a time when they did not appear to affect intake derived from suckling. These behaviors could only be obtained in rats that were tested in the heat. When milk was infused into the mouths of pups kept at room temperature, the pups allowed the milk to dribble out of their mouths.

This feeding had another salient characteristic of adult ingestive behavior: Johanson and Hall [29] observed that 1-day-old rats receiving milk through an anterior cannula (it opened into the rostral portion of the lower jaw) became extraordinarily activated, displaying a wide variety of postures that even included lordosis. The researchers capitalized on the fact that these pups also did a lot of thrusting upward along the sides of the container. They placed a paddle on the wall of the test container and trained infant rats to push the paddle to obtain food. The increased operant rate was contingent upon the animals' receiving food for their efforts. Yoked control rats did not increase operant rate. Moreover, when tested with two paddles in the cage, the rats tracked a reversal of the rewarded paddle, showing further the properties of a motivated behavioral system. Clearly, major facets of the ingestive system are in place before ever being used by the animal under natural circumstances. Indeed, if the system were used, it would probably be lethal to the animal given the immaturity of the gastrointestinal tract. These data can be taken as another example of motor systems being fully available before their use. This is a conservative evolutionary approach that provides a safe margin of error for meeting early feeding demands [30]. Another phylogenetic interpretation may shed greater light on the evolutionary significance of suckling behavior. I will return to this issue after discussing learning that may occur in the nest.

LEARNING THROUGH MOTHER-INFANT CONTACTS

In addition to Johanson and Hall's demonstration of instrumental learning by Day-1 rats, there have been a number of demonstrations of both instrumental and classical learning outside of the nest area. Moran, Schwartz, and Blass [31], for example, used the major features of the Johanson and Hall technique to demonstrate that Day-3 rats would push a lever to obtain electrical stimulation to the medial forebrain bundle (MFB). It is of considerable interest that the rats in the Moran et al study behaved similarly to those studied by Johanson and Hall in terms of the broad spectrum of activities that were elicited by MFB stimulation.

Classical conditioning has also been obtained away from the nest. Johanson and her colleagues [32,33] demonstrated that rats would come to prefer an otherwise aversive odor if that odor was paired with the delivery of food to the mouth. Thus, both classical and instrumental conditioning can be obtained in infant rats, and the parameters of this conditioning have been elucidated by Rudy and Cheattle [34]. It is remarkable that these animals that bear only the slightest physical, sensory, and motoric similarity to adults differ only subtly in their abilities to be conditioned under the right circumstances.

It turns out that the right circumstances are exactly the ones that are present in the nest. The nest is kept warm by the dam, and she vigorously activates her pups on her return to the nest to nurse. In fact, according to Shair et al [35], the EEG indicates an awake state only at the initiation of suckling and after a milk letdown, when rat pups exhibit the hyperextension response for milk withdrawal and then shift to another nipple. Thus, the circumstances necessary for conditioning away from nest and dam are routinely present in the nest itself. The infant can be reeily conditioned under these circumstances. Brake [36] for example, has shown that Day-10 rats will come to prefer an odor that is specifically paired with milk delivery through a nipple. Pedersen and Blass [10] and Pedersen et al [9] demonstrated that prenatal and postnatal stimulation, the latter mimicking that which is delivered by the dam to her nestlings, determines the stimuli that will elicit suckling. Prenatal conditioning, both appetitive and aversive, have been reported by Smotherman [37] and Stickrod et al [38] in a series of remarkable experiments. Indeed, according to DeCasper and Feifer [39] human infants appear to respond to their mothers' voices on the basis of having heard them in utero.

There is now considerable indirect evidence that classical conditioning during the nesting period determines the expression of vital behaviors during adulthood. Alberts [40], in an extensive series of studies on huddling behavior, demonstrated that after two weeks of age, huddling occurs in albino rats with animals bearing a familiar scent, and that this scent becomes familiar by virtue of the infants' contact with the dam. Also, Leon [23] demonstrated that infant rats learn about certain characteristics of the mother during the weaning period by virtue of an attraction to the potent odor of the dams' bacteria-rich excreta. Likewise, Galef and Clark [41,42] found that rats, at weaning, ate the foods that adult rats, especially the mother, ate. This is a very important finding in the context of feeding ontogeny. Galef and Clark [42] discovered that familiarity with safe foods was conferred by virtue of the infants' obtaining information concerning that food via suckling and possibly by eating the mother's excreta. The weanlings learned about poisonous foods by following adults to the feeding station and observing avoidance by the adults, who spilled and contaminated the poisoned food by urinating on it. Thus, the bond formed during development appears to have allowed the infants to venture from the nest to learn about the features of the external world in low-risk setting accompanied by the adults. It is important to note that the infants are *not* learning how to eat. Hall's [43] experiments had shown first that infants reared away from the dam ate normally upon their very first presentation of food, and as indicated above, the feeding system according to Johanson and Hall [27] is functional, albeit normally unavailable, during infancy.

PHYLOGENETIC CONSIDERATIONS

Precocity of feeding, even on the day of birth, in otherwise altricial mammals is remarkable. It may simply represent an example of a complex behavioral system being available before it is called upon (ie, to ensure its availability when the mother can no longer guarantee sufficient calories for growth because of the increased litter biomass) [7,30]. I find it difficult to envisage, however, how this would be selected phylogenetically, especially given the fact that the immature gastrointestinal system could not handle food directly ingested from the environment. I would like to speculate that this early feeding system represents the regression of a phylogenetically older system of infantile ingestion that has become subserved to the phylogenetic suckling system as the sole mechanism of infantile ingestion.

The question presents itself, therefore, as to why has suckling evolved. It requires extensive morphological, physiological, hormonal, and behavioral modifications on the part of the mother and the young. Nursing is extremely costly to the mother. She endures a hyperphagia that is so severe that it can not be exaggereated by ventromedial hypothalamic destruction [44]. She is also markedly hyperdipsic and expends considerable metabolic energy converting food to milk for the young. The hyperphagia and especially the hyperdipsia are particulalry noteworthy, because mothers make themselves more vulnerable to predators to obtain sufficient food and water, and this vulnerability is exaggerated when moving about saddled with an infant. Obviously, these risks had to be offset by phylogenetic gains in inclusive fitness. The remarkable abilities of newborn altricial mammals to be conditioned at birth, indeed in utero, raise the possibility that altricial mammals may use the suckling period to learn from the dam about the rules of the external world in a relatively protected setting. (It also allows for rapid growth because of the low energy

expenditure by nested animals with very few physiological heat-producing obligations or capacities). That such learning takes place has been documented [11,40]. The means through which these experiences can enhance inclusive fitness are just now starting to be appreciated [45].

The hypothesis can be stated specifically. A protracted period of contact between mother and offspring has evolved that increases inclusive fitness. Central to this is the infants' ability to form associations between intrinsically rewarding maternal features (eg, warmth, milk) and her arbitrary features (eg, odor, sound, color, and behavior patterns). This association is positive and causes infantile patterns of behavior that maintain maternal proximity. Through this proximity, the mother teaches her young before and during the weaning process [41,42,46]. She does *not* teach *how* to eat, for example, so much as *what and where (and whom)* to eat. The infant, therefore, benefits from parental experience rather than discovering major environmental traps directly, at considerable risk.

This invites speculation on the mandatory phylogenetic changes for nursing and suckling to have evolved. Recent paleontological literature suggests that certain reptilian groups lived in relatively close contact with their young [47,48], a trait that is seen in today's crocodillians. Accordingly, one means of encouraging a prolonged contact is to reduce thermal capacity and regress body size so that, relative to adults, the surface-to-mass ratio is high, leaving the infant in a state in which body contact is necessary to ensure normothermia. These alterations in themselves are not sufficient to ensure protracted contact. The situation is abetted, over time, by making the mother the infants' exclusive food source. There is a problem here. Given that the starting point is the reptile with its well-developed (at birth) dentition, digestive system, and behavioral response systems for procuring food, then morphologial, physiological, and behavioral regression is in order. My thesis is that this has been achieved over the course of phylogenetic time. The suckling response is unique; the digestive system can only handle mother's milk, and the mammalian dentition emerges slowly. One may add to this the change in articulation that allowed for a more complex facial neuromusculature to ensure the seal on the nipple for milk withdrawal, and the pieces are all in place for protracted infant contact with the mother. The parallel changes in maternal morphology and hormonal and physiological controls attendant to the nursing setting completes the picture. Accordingly, one possible means of viewing feeding systems, at least in infant rats, is as a vestige of an earlier system that became increasingly less available, so that the infant could form a bond with the mother that allows it to learn from her in a low-risk set-

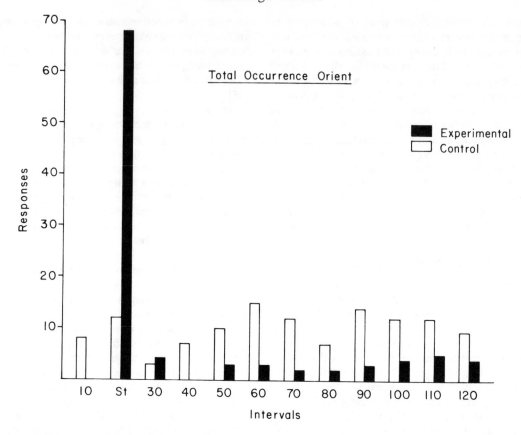

Figure 1.2 Total number of orient responses by experimental (filled histograms) and control human infants 2-48 hours old

ting. These phylogenetic and ontogenetic considerations regarding conditioning and affective relationships predict that human infants should also extract certain features from the charged nursing setting. I turn to this issue now.

CONDITIONING DURING HUMAN INFANCY

Pioneer work in this area has come from the laboratory of Lipsitt [49] at Brown University. Lipsitt demonstrated under a variety of circumstances that infants can modify rooting and orienting behaviors that are rewarded with the presentation of sweet solutions. From Sameroff's [50] studies, we learn that infants can modify their suckling rate during the first week of life in order to have sucrose injected into the mouth via a special nipple. Despite these and other unquivocal demonstrations of instrumental behavior in human infants during the first postnatal week [51]. there have not been unequivocal demonstrations of classical conditioning. With Judith Ganchrow and Jacob Steiner of the Hebrew University in Jerusalem, I attempted to obtain

classical conditioning in infants 2 to 48 hours of age [52]. We accomplished this by stroking the infant's forehead for ten seconds every two minutes and immediately following this delivery of 0.2cc of 0.037M sucrose solution within ten seconds. The infants avidly accepted the sucrose, making sucking movements and orienting toward the source of delivery. Over the course of conditioning trials, the infants came to make many orient and suck responses during the stroking period itself. This is shown in figure 2, where the number of orient responses of the experimental and control infants are presented for each ten-seconds bin of the two-minute trails. Control infants were treated in a manner identical with that of experimental infants except that a 10-, 20-, or 30-second delay was interposed between stroking and sucrose delivery. These data demonstrate the capacity of the newborn human infant to be classically conditioned in an appetitive setting that has certain characteristics of the nursing setting. Moreover, when extinction was instituted, seven of the eight experimental infants cried, whereas only one of sixteen control infants did so. This suggests that the experimental infants were responding to the violation of the predicitive relationship and not strictly to the withdrawal of sucrose.

DISCUSSION

These data have made it clear that conditioning in nonhuman mammals can readily take place in the nest situation. Conditioning occurs when certain features of the mother, such as her arousing qualities, her touch, and warmth stimulate the infant in a highly predictive and biologically significant setting. Through this, affectional systems are formed, behavioral patterns are developed, and biologically significant information is acquired. In humans, and presumably in nonhuman mammals, sometimes things go wrong, and in humans, clearly identifiable syndromes of pathology develop. I am not claiming that the etiology of these problems can be attributed necessarily to faulty nursing. I do suggest, however, that the learning capabilities in the infant have been selected for, and that opportunities are present to acquire harmful patterns of coping during suckling and early stages of mother-infant interactions. That is, the phylogenetically old associational mechanism may lead the individual to formulate an appropriate affectional bond with an inappropriately behaving parent. To maintain the bond, the proximity-seeking behavior of the child is expressed pathologically to seek inappropriate rewards. During normal development, normal and presumably adaptive patterns are obtained from a stable and supportive setting that is marked by physiological pleasure and contact comfort [53]. In the pathological setting, presumably through the same processes, the same physiological stimuli may be associated with parenting patterns that are highly inappropriate. To the extent that the etiology of behavioral feeding disorders such as marked obesity, anorexia nervosa, and bulimia are poorly understood, it behooves us to assess the earliest feeding histories of these patients to see if classes of ineffectual or harmful parenting emerge.

ACKNOWLEDGEMENT

Research from the author's laboratory was supported by a grant in aid of research AM 18560 from the National Institute of Arthritis Metabolism and Digestive Diseases and research scientist MH00524 from the National Institute of Mental Health.

REFERENCES

1. Rozin P. The selection of food by rats, humans and other animals. In Rosenblatt JS, Hinde RA, Shaw E, Beer C, eds. Advances in the study of behavior, vol 6. New York: Academic Press, 1976:21-76.

2. Blass EM, Hall WG, Teicher MH. The ontogeny of suckling and ingestive behaviors. In Sprague JM, Epstein AN, eds. Progress in psychobiology and physiological psychology, vol. 8. New York: Academic Press, 1979:243-300.

3. Blass EM, Teicher MH. Suckling. Science, 1980;210:15-22.

4. Hall WG, Williams CL. Suckling isn't feeding, or is it? A search for developmental continuities. In Rosenblatt JS, Hinde RA, Beer C, Busnell MC, eds. Advances in the study of behavior, vol 13. 1983;219-254.

5. Drewett RF. The development of motivational systems. Prog Brain Res, 1978; 48:407-417.

6. Teitelbaum P. The use of operant methods in the assessment and control of motivational states. In Honig WK, ed. Operant behavior: areas of research and application. New York: Appleton-Cenutury-Crofts, 1966:

7. Hall WG. The ontogeny of feeding in rats: I. Ingestive and behavioral responses to oral infusions. J Comp Physiol Psychol, 1979; 93:977-1000 (b).

8. Cramer CP, Blass EM. Nutritive and non-nutritive determinants of milk intake of suckling rats. Behav Neurosci, 1986, 99:578- 582.

9. Pedersen PE, Williams CL, Blass EM. Activation and odor conditioning of suckling behavior in three day old albino rats. J Exp Psychol An Behav Proc, 1983; 4:329-41.

10. Pedersen PE, Blass EM. Prenatal and postnatal determinants of the first suckling episode in albino rats. Dev Psychobiol, 1982; 15:349-55.

11. Rosenblatt JS. Olfaction mediates developmental transition in the altricial newborn of selected species of mammals. Dev Psychobiol, 1983; 16:347-76.

12. Cramer CP, Blass EM, Hall WG. The ontogeny of nipple-shifting behavior in albino rats: Mechanisms of control and possible significance. Dev Psychobiol, 1980; 13:165-80.

13. Cramer CP, Blass EM. The contribution of ambient temperature to suckling behavior in rats 3-10 days of age. Dev Psychobiol, 1982; 15:339-48.

14. Hall WG, Rosenblatt JS. Suckling behavior and intake control in the developing rat pup. J Comp Physiol Psychol, 1977; 91:1232-47.

15. Cramer CP, Blass EM. Mechanisms of control of milk intake in suckling rats. Am J Physiol, 1983; 245(2):R154-9.

16. Houpt KA, Epstein AN. Ontogeny of controls of food intake in the rat. GI fill and glucoprivation. Am J Physiol, 1973; 225:58-66.

17. Houpt KA, Houpt TR. Effects of gastric loads and food deprivation on subsequent food intake in suckling rats. J Comp Physiol Psychol, 1975; 88:764-72.

18. Lorenz DN. Effects of gastric firing and vagotomy on ingestion, nipple attachment, and weight gain by suckling rats. Dev Psychobiol, 1983; 16:469-84.

19. Blass EM, Beardsley W, Hall WG. Age-dependent inhibition of suckling by cholecystokinin. Am J Physiol, 1979; 236:E567-70.

20. Bruno JP, Craigmyle L, Blass EM. Dehydration inhibits suckling behavior in weanling rats. JCPP, 1982; 96:405-15.

21. Amsel A, Letz R, Burdette DR. Appetitive learning and extinction in 11-day-old rat pups. Effects of various reinforcement conditions. J Comp Physiol Psychol, 1977; 91:1156-67.

22. Stoloff ML, Blass EM. Changes in appetitive behavior in weanling age rats: Tranisitions from suckling to feeding behavior. Dev Psychobiol, 1983; 16:439-54.

23. Leon M. Dietary control of maternal pheromone in the lactating rat. Physiol Behav, 1975; 14:311-19.

24. Wirth JB, Epstein AN. Ontogeny of thirst in the infant rat. Am J Physiol, 1976; 230:188-98.

25. Bruno J. Development of drinking behavior in pre-weanling rats. J Comp Physiol Psychol, 1981; 95:1016-27.

26. Hall WG, Bryan TE. The ontogeny of feeding in rats: II. Independent ingestive behavior. J Comp Physiol Psychol, 1980; 746-56.

27. Johanson IB, Hall WG. The ontogeny of feeding in rats. III. Thermal determinants of early ingestive responding. J Comp Physiol Psychol, 1980;94:977-92.

28. Hall WG, Bryan TE. The ontogeny of feeding in rats. IV. Taste development as measured by intake and behavioral responses to oral infusions of sucrose and quinine. J Comp Physiol Psychol, 1981; 95:240-51.

29. Johanson IB, Hall WG. Appetitive learning in 1-day-old-rat pups. Science, 1979; 205:419-20.

30. Anokhin PK. Systemogenesis as a general regulator of brain development. Himwich WA, Himwich WA, eds. In The developing brain. New York: American Elsevier, 1964:

31. Moran TH, Schwartz GJ, Blass EM. Organized behavioral responses to lateral hypothalamic electrical stimulation in infant rats. J Neurosci, 1983; 3:10-19.

32. Johanson IB, Teicher MJ. Classical conditioning of an odor preference in 3-day-old rats. Behav Neur Biol, 1980; 132-36.

33. Johanson IB, Hall WG. Appetitive conditioning in neonatal rats: Conditioned orientation to novel odor. Dev Psychobiol, 1979; 15:379-97.

34. heatle MD. Ontogeny of association learning: Acquisition of odor aversions by neonatal rats. In Spear NE, Cambell BA, eds. Ontogeny of learning and memory. New Jersey: Hillsdale, Erlbaum, 1979:

35. Shair H, Brake S, Hofer M. Suckling in the rat: Evidence for patterned behavior during sleep. Behav Neurosci, 1984; 98:366-70.

36. Brake SC. Suckling infant rats learn a preference for a noval olfactory stimulus paired with milk delivery. Science, 1981; 211:506-508.

37. Smotherman WP. Odor aversion learning by the rat fetus. Physiol Behav, 1982; 29:767-71,

38. Stickrod G, Kimble DP, Smotherman WP. In utero taste/odor aversion conditioning in the rat. Physiol Behav, 1982; 28:5-7.

39. DeCasper AJ, Fifer WP. Of human bonding: Newborns prefer their mother's voices. Science, 1980; 208:1174-76.

40. Alberts JR. Ontogeny of olfaction: Reciprocal roles of sensation and behavior in the development of perception. In Aslin Rn, Alberts JR, Petersen MR, eds. The development of perception: psychobiological perspectives. New York: Academic Press; 321-357.

41. Galef BG, Clark MM. Mother's milk and adult presence: Two factors determining initial dietary selection by weanling rats. J Comp Physiol Psych, 1972; 78:213-19.

42. Galef BG, Clark MM. Mother's milk: A determinant of the feeding preference of weanling rats. J Comp Physiol Psych, 1972; 78:213-19.

43. Hall WG. Weaning and growth of artificially reared rats. Science, 1975; 190:1313-15.

44. Kennedy GC. Ontogeny of mechanisms controlling food and water intake. In Code CF, ed. Handbook of physiology, section 6: alimentary canal. Washington, DC: American Physiological Society, 1967:337-352.

45. Holmes WB, Sherman PW. The ontogeny of kin recognition in two species of ground squirrels. Amer Zool, 1982: 22:491-517.

46. Rheingold HR. Maternal behavior in the dog. In Rheingold HR, ed. Maternal behavior in mammals. New York: John Wiley, 1963:169-202.

47. Mossman DJ, Sajeant WAS. The footprints of extinct animals. Sci Am, 1983; 248:74-85.

48. Horner JR. The nesting behavior of dinosaurs. Sci Am, 1984; 250:130-137.

49. Lipsit LP. Infant learning: The blooming, buzzing confusion revisited. In Meyer ME, ed. Second western symposium on learning: early learning. Bellingham, Washington: Western Washington State College, 1971:

50. Sameroff AJ. The components of suckling in the human newborn. J Experi Child Psychol, 1968; 6:607-23.

51. Papousek H. Experimental studies of appetitional behavior in human newborns and infants. In Stevenson HW, Hess EH, Rheingold HL, eds. Early behavior: comparative and developmental approaches. New York: John Wiley & Sons, 1967:

52. Blass EM, Ganchrow JR, Steiner JE. Classical conditioning in newborn humans 2-48 hours of age. Infant Behav Develop, 1984; 7:223-35.

53. Blass EM, Kehoe P. Behavioral characteristics of emerging opiate systems in newborn rats. In Krasnegoz N, Blass EM, Hofer M, Smotherman, W (eds.). Perinatal Behavioral Developement: A Psychobiological Perspective. New York: Academic Press 1987:61-82.

Chapter 2

Neurotransmitter Regulation of Appetite and Eating

John E. Morley, Allen S. Levine and Dean D. Krahn

The regulation of feeding is an extremely complex process involving a variety of peripheral inputs including the hedonic qualities of food, neuronal and hormonal signals from the gastrointestinal tract, the physicochemical qualities of absorbed food, the state of glycogen stores in the liver, the status of the organism's fat stores, and possibly the activity of brown adipose tissue. In addition to these internal cues, external cues such as the availability and types of food, and psychological factors in higher animals and cultural factors (eg, the need to eat only kosher foods), in humans also play a role. In the feeding literature, the classical approach to handling this excess of regulatory factors has been to stress the importance of one or another factor while ignoring the potential interplay of multiple factors. Further, there has been a marked tendency to underemphasize the mechanism(s) by which these factors are integrated within the central nervous system. While this underemphasis of central factors was perhaps a natural response to the practical difficulties involved in studying central mechanisms of appetite control, these central factors have contined to be slighted despite the emergence of technologies that make central studies feasible.

With the recent discovery of the existence of multiple neurotransmitters (more than 55 have now been identified), it is becoming possible to dissect the neurochemical messengers responsible for integrating the multiple peripheral signals concerning the status of the energy stores of the organism. It has become convenient to artificially divide the control of feeding into a *peripheral satiety system* and a *central feeding system*. In this chapter we will concentrate on the role of neurotransmitters as integrators of the central feeding system.

There are three major families of neurotransmitters: amino acids, eg, gamma-aminobutyric acid (GABA); amines, eg, catecholamines and serotonin; and neuropeptides. The concentrations of neurotransmitters in the brain range from micromolar (μM) to fentomolar (fM). The critical functional concentration of a neurotransmitter, however, is that existing in the synapse. Because synaptic neurotransmitter levels are not measureable, it is not possible to clearly establish which concentration of any neurotransmitter is physiological as opposed to pharmacological. The behavioral effect of any specific neurotransmitter is highly dependent on the anatomical site at which it is released (eg, norepinephrine increases feeding when infused into the paraventricular nucleus but decreases feeding when injected into the lateral hypothalamus).

Studies using lesioning and stimulation of various areas of the central nervous system have placed the soul of appetite regulation in the hypothalamus. Simplistically, the hypothalamus can be perceived as a powerful computer responsible for integrating all of the inputs concerning the nutrient status of the organism and making the output decision of whether or not the organism should feed. From a teleological point of view, one might postulate that an older system (developed when food was scarce) would be the feeding drive system(s) ordering the organism to eat whenever food was available. In transition from times of famine to feast, organisms developed a secondary satiety system responsible for attempting to restrain the unbridled feeding system. Thus, feeding is thought to be dependent on the balance between a feeding initiation system and a feeding cessation (or satiety) system. A large number of neurotransmitters have been identified as being capable of initiating or inhibiting feeding. At the outset it should be stressed that it is not well delineated at this time whether these represent true satiety factors or nonspecific disruptors of behavior (including food intake).

If the hypothalamus is likened to a computer, the neurotransmitters can be thought of as computer chips. The release of a neurotransmitter into a specific area represents the release of a prepackaged set of information, which sets in motion a variety of neuronal impulses leading to the switching on of a number of closely related behaviors. The most simple example of a peptide regulating two closely related species-preserving functions is seen in a shellfish, the *Pleurobranchea*. This mollusk has a voracious appetite and devours anything up to one-third its size that comes in its vicinity. This habit of eating everything would have resulted in extinction of this species, because everytime it laid eggs, it would have eaten them. Nature, therefore, endowed this shellfish with an interesting peptide hormone called the egg-laying hormone [1]. About 15 minutes after injecting this mollusk with egg-laying hormone, it stops eating and shortly after that it lays its eggs. This dual function of the egg-laying hormone in producing satiety as well as egg laying demonstrates the potential advantages of a single substance regulating two closely related functions.

HISTORICAL BACKGROUND

Historically, the understanding of a central feeding system began with the studies of Heatherington and Ranson [2], who in 1940 demonstrated that lesions of the ventromedial hypothalamus (VMH) resulted in obesity. Later, electrical stimulation of this area was shown to inhibit feeding and a variety of catabolic responses, leading to the designation of the VMH as the satiety center. In 1951, Anand and Brobeck [3] showed that destruction of the lateral hypothalamus (LH) produced aphagia and weight loss. Electrical stimulation of the lateral hypothalamus was then shown to increase feeding and to initiate a variety of anabolic responses. It was then suggested that the LH was the feeding center.

It has subsequently been realized that these original anatomical studies represented a great oversimplification of the true situation [4]. Ablation and electrical

Table 2.1 Anatomical site involved in feeding

Site	Lesion	Electrical Stimulation
Ventromedial Hypothalamus	Increases feeding	Decreases feeding
Paraventricular Nucleus	Increases feeding	?
Dorsomedial Nucleus	Increases feeding	?
Lateral Hypothalamus	Decreases feeding	Increases feeding
Striatum	Decreases feeding	?
Globus Pallidus	Decreases feeding	?
Midbrain Tegmentum	Decreases feeding	Facilitates feeding

stimulation studies have shown that a variety of central nervous system areas are involved in feeding regulation (Table 1). In addition, it appears that in many instances, the fibers coursing through the area are mainly responsible for appetite regulation. The satiety center is associated with two major pathways—a serotonergic pathway originating in the raphe nuclei of the pontine-midbrain area and then coursing through the VMH (the median raphe nuclei tracts) and the ventral adrenergic bundle, which passes through the perifornical area in the vicinity of the ventral hypothalamus. The LH is associated with the dopaminergic nigrostriatal tract. Apart from feeding, these tracts also appear to be associated with the reward or pleasure centers of the brain.

The association of tracts of neurochemical specificity with lesions having specific effects on feeding suggested a new route for investigating feeding control. In 1962, in a pioneering article in the American Journal of Physiology, Grossman showed that intrahypothalamic injection of norepinephrine (NE) induced vigorous feeding and that acetylcholine inhibited feeding [5]. Subsequently elegant studies by Leibowitz at the Rockefeller University in New York have clearly established that alpha-adrenergic stimulation in the area of the paraventricular nucleus (PVN) and VMH stimulated feeding, and ß-adrenergic stimulation in the LH inhibits feeding [6].

In 1976 and 1977 a series of studies by Blundell, Coscina and Hoebel and their colleagues were published demonstrating that depletion of brain serotonin by either neurotoxins (eg, 5,6 hydroxytryptamine) or serotonin synthesis depletors resulted in hyperphagia and obesity [7]. Earlier studies in 1971 had demonstrated that local injections of serotonin into the brain decreased feeding [8]. However, it is now recognized

Table 2.2 Neurotransmitters that play a putative role in feeding regulation

	Increase Feeding	Decrease Feeding
Monoamines	Norepinephrine (α- agonists)	Norepinephrine (ß) Serotonin
Amino Acids	GABA (muscimol)	GABA
Peptides	Opioid peptides Neuropeptide Y Galanin	Corticotropin Releasing Factor Neurotensin Bombesin Calcitonin Calcitonin Gene- Related Peptide Somatostatin Thyrotropin Releasing Hormone Cyclo-histidyl Proline Diketopiperazine Cholecystokinin
Miscellaneous	Endogenous benzodiazepines Acetylcholine	Adenosine Acetylcholine Prostaglandins

that while serotonin 5-HT$_{1A}$ inhibits food intake, the 5-HT$_{1B}$ serotonin receptor enhances feeding [51].

A number of studies have shown that destruction of dopaminergic and other catecholaminergic fibers with the neurotoxin 6-hydroxydopamine can lead to hypophagia and weight loss. Morley et al [9] found that the dopamine agonist, bromergocriptine, stimulated feeding at low doses after central administration and inhibited it at higher doses, which are associated with stereotypic behaviors.

In a classical study in 1976, Grandison and Guidotti showed that direct injection of ß-endorphin into the VMH initiated feeding [10]. This study, coupled with the studies by Holtzman at Emory University showing that the opioid antagonist, naloxone, decreased feeding [11], led to the concept that endogenous opioid peptides were involved in initiating feeding. In 1977, Vijayan and McCann found that centrally administered thyrotropin-releasing hormone and somatostatin inhibited feeding after central injection [12]. Subsequently, a large number of neuropeptides have been shown to inhibit feeding after central administration [13]. Table 2 lists the neurotransmitters that appear to be involved in the central regulation of appetite.

In 1980, in an attempt to bring some order to the rapidly proliferating field of feeding inhibiting and initiating neurotransmitters, Morley [4] postulated the concept of a central satiety cascade in which a dopamine-opioid interaction was responsible for the initiation of feeding and that this interaction was held in check by a variety of inhibitory and disinhibitory neurotransmitters. This cascade system would be similar to the well-recognized biological cascades for clotting and complement fixation. Despite the fact that the original model was an oversimplification, this model has aided us and others in the design of further experiments that attempt to unravel the complexities of central regulation of appetite.

CURRENT STUDIES

Norepinephrine

A variety of studies have shown that norepinephrine has a facilitatory effect on enhancing food intake when injected into the central nervous system [6]. The primary site for norepinephrine-induced eating appears to be the paraventricular nucleus [6]. This norepinephrine-induced feeding is mediated through alpha-adrenergic receptors [6]. Norepinephrine increases in feeding are due to an increase in meal size rather than in meal frequency and to create a preference for carbohydrate-rich foodstuffs [6]. The facilitatory effects of centrally administered norepinephrine on feeding requires an intact vagus [14], and corticosterone has been shown to be an essential humoral factor for norepinephrine-induced feeding to occur [15].

The potential physiological role of norepinephrine in feeding has been suggested by studies showing that spontaneous and deprivation-induced feeding are associated with increased turnover of endogenous norepinephrine and down-regulation of alpha-adrenoreceptors in the paraventricular nucleus [16]. Further, Myers and McCaleb [17] have shown that infusion of nutrients into the duodenum inhibits synaptic release of norepinephrine from medial hypothalamic sites.

Lesions of the paraventricular nucleus result in hyperphagia rather than decreased eating while attenuating norepinephrine-induced eating [18]. This suggests that the norepinephrine-induced feeding is secondary to inhibition of the release of a satiety factor in this nucleus.

Besides the evidence for an alpha-adrenergic feeding system in the paraventricular nucleus, it has been shown that norepinephrine injected into the lateral hypothalamus decreases feeding, and lesions of the ventral norepinephrinergic bundle cause mild hyperphagia [6]. Myers and McCaleb [17] found that duodenal nutrient infusion enhanced synaptic norepinephrine release from lateral hypothalamic sites. These and other studies have led Leibowitz [6] to suggest there may be a ß-adrenergic satiety system in the region of the perifornical bundle.

Serotonin

A variety of studies have suggested, but not proved, that serotonin functions as a satiety agent [7]. Serotonin agonists and drugs that potentiate serotonin actions (eg, fenfluramine), decrease feeding, whereas serotonergic antagonists and the serotonergic neurotoxins (5,6 and 5,7 dihydroxytryptamine) enhance feeding.

Studies by Blundell and Latham [19] have shown that drugs which enhance serotonin release or block serotonin uptake have specific effects on the meal pattern. These serotonergic stimulants decrease meal size without affecting the initiation of feeding or the meal frequency. Serotonin results in a decrease in carbohydrate and/or caloric intake while preserving or even potentiating protein intake [20]. Serotonin inhibits norepinephrine-induced feeding, and like norepinephrine, appears to exert its major action in either the paraventricular nucleus or the VMH. Recently it has been suggested that some of the effects of serotonin stimulators may be mediated through peripheral effects resulting in a slowing of gastric emptying [21].

Phenylethylamine and Amphetamine

The structures of many of the more widely used anorectic drugs in humans are closely related to the ß-phenylethylamine nucleus (eg, amphetamines, diethylpropion). Multiple studies have demonstrated that amphetamine inhibits eating while leading to hyperactivity and stereotypy. Amphetamine's anorectic effect appears to be mediated predominantly in the area of the lateral hypothalamus [6]. At present the general consensus is that amphetamine produces its effect by releasing catecholamines in the perifornical area resulting in stimulation of the ß-adrenergic satiety system [6].

Peripheral administration of high doses of phenylethylamine inhibits feeding, but the specificity of this effect is unclear [22]. Interest in the possibility of a phenylethylamine satiety system was recently stimulated by the study of Paul et al [23] at the National Institute of Mental Health. They demonstrated that there are highly specific amphetamine receptors in the central nervous system. The endogenous ligand for the "amphetamine receptor" appears to be phenylethylamine. In their studies, they found that the anorexic potency of a variety of phenylethylamine derivatives are related to their ability to bind to the phenylethylamine receptor.

Gamma-amino Butyric Acid (GABA), the Benzodiazepine Receptor and Purines

GABA has a dual action on food intake [24,25]. When administered centrally, the GABA analog, muscimol, stimulates food intake. This effect is present after local minor injections of GABA or its analog into the cell bodies of the nucleus dorsalis raphe, the paraventricular nucleus, and the ventromedical nucleus. Norepinephrine-induced feeding is inhibited by GABA antagonists, suggesting that the alpha-adrenergic feeding system may operate through stimulation of GABA

releases, which inturn inhibits the release of a major satiety factor. On the other hand, GABA injected into the nigrostriatal tracts inhibits feeding possibly by reducing dopaminergic transmission from the substantia nigra. Thus, it appears that the universal inhibitory neurotransmitter GABA elevates appetite by inhibiting the satiety center and its connections and decreases food intake by inhibiting the lateral hypothalamic dopaminergic system.

A number of studies have shown that benzodiazepines enhance feeding in rats [26]. Benzodiazepine-induced feeding has been shown to involve interactions with serotonergic, opioid, and GABAergic mechanisms.

Levine and Morley [27] have shown that the purine, inosine, suppresses diazepam-induced feeding. 7-methylinosine, which *in vitro* fails to bind to the benzodiazepine-binding site, had no effect on starvation-induced eating, whereas other purines that bind to the diazepam receptor decreased feeding in this paradigm. This led to the suggestion that purines may represent endogenous substances that regulate food intake through interactions with the benzodiazepine receptor. However, the finding that centrally administered adenosine (which doesn't interact with benzodiazepine receptor) is a more potent inhibitor of feeding than inosine suggests that the central purinergic regulation of feeding may be independent of an interaction with the diazepam receptor. Recently, Agren et al [28] found elevated xanthine levels in the CSF are associated with poor appetite in depressed patients, suggesting a link between purines and appetite in humans.

Opioid Feeding Systems

Opioid antagonists have been shown to decrease feeding under a variety of conditions in a large number of species, including humans [29]. There is some evidence to suggest that opioid antagonists preferentially decrease fat intake [30]. A variety of studies have shown that exogenous opiates are capable of increasing food intake in rats and mice, and recently we have found that butorphanol tartrate increases feeding in humans [29 and unpublished observation].

Evidence exists that a variety of endogenous opioids including ß-endorphin, D-ala-leu-enkephalin and dynorphin increase feeding in rats after central administration [31,32,33]. Studies in our laboratory with the endogenous kappa opioid receptor ligand, dynorphin-(1-17) and a variety of exogenous kappa opiates has suggested that the dynorphin-kappa opioid receptor plays a major role in modulation of feeding [33]. In addition, measurements of ir-dynorphin levels in the central nervous system have demonstrated that they are altered in a variety of situations in which feeding is initiated.

Other studies have, however, suggested a role for other opioid receptors in appetite regulation. Thus, analogous to the findings for the role of opioid receptors in analgesia, it appears that multiple opioid receptors may be involved in appetite regulation, each producing an effect on different aspects of feeding and acting at different anatomical sites. Finally, it should be pointed out that the effect of opioids on feeding appears to be modulated by the prevailing glucose levels, adrenal secretions, the time of the day, and whether the animal is tested in a home or in a foreign cage.

Neuropeptide Y

Neuropeptide Y (NPY) is the most potent orexigenic agent yet identified [52]. It produces a highly specific increase in carbohydrate ingestion. Chronic administration leads to weight gain. It has been suggested that it may play a roll in the pathogenesis of bulimia.

Other Neuropeptides

In contrast to the opioid peptides and NPY, most other neuropeptides appear to inhibit rather than stimulate feeding. Whether or not this ability of neuropeptides to suppress feeding after central administration represents a true satiety effect or a nonspecific disruption of behavior is a subject of intense debate at the present time (*vide infra*).

Calcitonin is a potent inhibitor of feeding after central administration [34]. It appears to produce its satiating effects by inhibiting calcium uptake at the hypothalamic level [35]. Recently, Rosenfeld et al [36] showed that the calcitonin gene is processed differently in the central nervous sytem, giving rise to calcitonin gene-related peptide (CGRP). Studies in our laboratory have shown that CGRP suppresses feeding after central administation in rats; that this effect is less potent than CGRP on a molar basis, and that CGRP produces a conditioned taste aversion.

Besides inhibiting feeding after peripheral administration, bombesin, a tetradecapeptide originally isolated from the skin of frogs, also decreases feeding when centrally administered [37,38]. It also induces marked grooming, slows gastric emptying, and decreases gastric acid secretion. The site of action of bombesin on feeding appears to be in the lateral hypothalamus.

The role of cholecystokinin (CCK) in feeding after central administration in the rat is somewhat unclear, but the effect appears to be minor. However, infusion of CCK into the ventricles of sheep decreases feeding, and infusion of antisera to CCK-8 into the left ventricle of sheep resulted in a significant increase in feeding [39]. These data suggest that there may be marked species differences in the site of action of CCK on feeding.

Porte and Woods [40] have found that centrally infused insulin decreases feeding in baboons in contrast to its peripheral effect of increasing feeding, probably secondary to the hypoglycemia that insulin produces peripherally. They have suggested that insulin serves as the key body adiposity signal to the central nervous system. Their feeling is based, in part, on the impressive correlation between the degree of adiposity and plasma insulin levels and the presence of immunoreactive insulin in the CSF. Recently, an insulin-like peptide, Insulin Growth Factor, has also been shown to decrease food intake after central administration [41].

Among the other peptides postulated to decrease feeding by a central mechanism are thyrotropin-releasing hormone and its metabolite, cyclohistidyl proline diketropiperazine; corticotropin-releasing factor and its homologue, sauvagine; and neurotensin.

CONTROVERSIES AND FUTURE DIRECTIONS

Two major controversies in the role of central neurotransmitters in feeding have already been alluded to, namely, the specificity of the effect and the problem of species diversity.

Specificity of Effect

It has been suggested that almost anything found in the vicinity of the kitchen sink will decrease feeding in the rat, presumably by inducing sickness rather than physiological satiety. Most of the studies conducted on the effects of neurotransmitters on feeding have been pharmacological in nature, and there is little data concerning the specificity of these effects. Thus, at present, the conclusion that these agents represent physiological satiety substances is tenuous. However, their distribution in sites within the central nervous system known to be involved in feeding regulation and the obvious requirements for multiple neurotransmitters to regulate the complexities of feeding suggests that some of these agents will eventually turn out to be satiety coordinators.

Because much controversy revolves around whether or not these agents cause "sickness," it needs to be pointed out that, unlike the human, the rat cannot be asked whether or not it is sick. Also, the rat does not display emesis. The available paradigms for discerning "sickness" in the rat all have many problems [42]. Further, any of us who have gorged ourselves, as was the custom of the ancient Romans, clearly realize that there is a continuum between the sensations of satiety, abdominal discomfort, nausea, and eventually vomiting. Thus, although we need to avoid exaggerating the role of the neurotransmitters in feeding regulation until it is better defined, we need to realize that many of these will turn out to be involved in feeding regulation and that the present neuropharmacological studies represent important first steps in the ultimate teasing out of the complexities of feeding regulation within the central nervous system.

We would like to suggest that the following criteria represent the ultimate proof of the role for a neurotransmitter in feeding: (1) The neurotransmitter produces its effect in one or more localized sites, and the concentration required to produce the effect at that site is less than that necessary to produce the effect after intraventricular administration. (2) Discrete lesions of the same site result in the obliteration of the feeding effect. (3) There is some degree of behavioral specificity after injection into a localized site of action. (4) Concentrations or turnover of the neurotransmitter or its receptors alter in the specific site of action during states of altered satiety. At present, only norepinephrine (alpha-agonist properties) and possibly serotonin come close to meeting these criteria.

Species Diversity

It is becoming abundantly clear that the rat is not necessarily a universal model for the understanding of feeding behavior. Thus, although the opiate antagonist, naloxone, deceases feeding in many species from wolves and humans to mice, it is ineffective at doing so in the racoon and the Chinese hamster. To further illustrate the complexities of the situation, naloxone's effects are severely attenuated in neonatal and very old rats. Similarly, the opiate agonist, butorphanol tartrate, while increasing feeding in the rat, decreases feeding in the guinea pig. We have already alluded to similar species diversity of responsiveness to CCK. Further, the effects of opiate agonists on feeding display a marked circadian rhythm, producing an increase in feeding during the daytime but often decreasing feeding at night. Thus, for full understanding of the effects of a neurotransmitter, the test conditions and the species used in testing a neurotransmitter are of paramount importance.

CURRENT HYPOTHESES AND POSSIBLE CLINICAL APPLCIATIONS

The Central Satiety Cascade

Bearing in mind the caveats presented in the previous section, we have found it useful to develop a malleable matchstick diagram of neurotransmitter interactions in feeding as an aid to remembering the putative interactions occuring in the hypothalamus and to help in the design of future pharmacological experiments [4]. Neurotransmitter interactions can somewhat artificially be divided into those that occur in the paraventricular nucleus (and/or VMH) and those that occur in the region

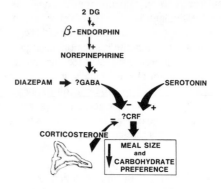

PARAVENTRICULAR NUCLEUS AND VENTROMEDIAL HYPOTHALAMUS

Figure 2.1 Interactions of neurotransmitters modulating feeding in the paraventricular and ventromedial hypothalamus. 2-DG = 2-deoxyglucose; GABA = gamma-amino butyric acid; CRF = corticotropin releasing factor.

of the lateral hypothalamus.

The major defined system in the paraventricular nucleus is that involved with the norepinephrine (alpha-agonist) increase in meal size (figure 1). Norepinephrine release is stimulated by ß-endorphin from the arcuate nucleus [31], which in turn may be released by 2-deoxyglucose [43]. Vagal inputs (not shown) from the periphery would modulate norepinephrine release to integrate central and peripheral mechanisms. Norepinephrine itself stimulates GABA release, which in turn inhibits the release of a satiety factor responsible for the inhibitory effect of the PVN-VMH. Release of this satiety factor would be stimulated by serotonin. One possible candidate for this satiety factor is corticotropin-releasing factor (CRF), which besides inhibiting feeding, is inhibited by norepinephrine and stimulated by serotonin [44].

In the lateral hypothalamus the major interaction appears to be the close relationship between dynorphin

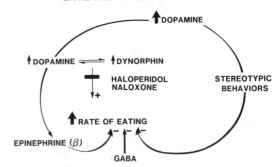

LATERAL HYPOTHALAMUS

Figure 2.2 Interactions of nurotransmitters modulating feeding in the lateral hypothalamus.

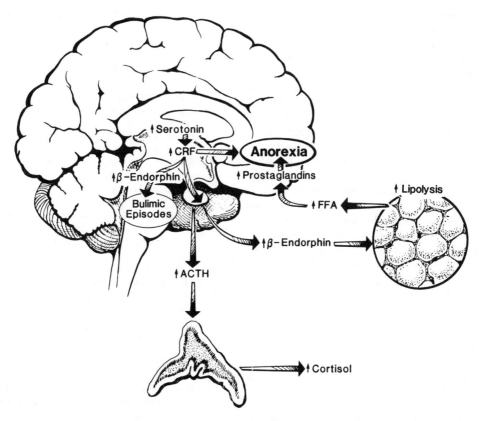

Figure 2.3 Hypothesized model for neurotransmitter abnormalities in anorexia nervosa. FFA = free fatty acids.

and dopamine, which is responsible for stimulating feeding (figure 2). This system is held in check by satiety inputs from the PVN/VMH. These may include CRF, ß-agonist, CGRP, and bombesin. The understanding and localization of this system is far less well established than the PVN/VMH interrelationships.

Stress and Feeding

Numerous studies in the wild have shown that when animals are under stress (eg, birds during boundary disputes), they indulge in displacement eating. Using the mild tail pinch model of stress-inducing eating in the rat, a number of groups have provided evidence that this behavior is dependent on the activation of endogenous opioids and the dopaminergic system [45]. Overall the primary behavior appears to be stereotypic chewing with eating being an epiphenomenon. Recently it has been shown that when a small mouse is defeated by a larger mouse, the smaller mouse displays stress-induced eating which is naloxone reversible [46].

CRF is a 41 amino acide peptide, which appears to fulfill Hans Selye's criteria for the central mediator of the "general adaptation to stress" syndrome. Centrally administered CRF causes decreased feeding and increased grooming activity [47]. Because patients with anorexia nervosa have an overactive hypothalamic-pituitary adrenal axis, the possibility that CRF represents a biological substrate for some of the manifestations of anorexia nervosa needs to be considered (figure 3). If CRF levels are elevated in patients with anorexia nervosa, then the bouts of binge eating in some of these patients could be explained by excessive CRF production releasing ß-endorphin from the arcuate nucleus. Further, it has been reported that administration of naloxone to patients with anorexia nervosa results in a paradoxical weight gain without increase in appetite [48]. This could be secondary to inhibition of the effects of circumlating ß-endorphin producing lipolysis.

Development of New Pharmacological Agents

As we obtain more exciting information concerning the neurotransmitters involved in appetite regulation, this should lead to an increasingly sophisticated ability to create agonists and antagonists that will turn out to be useful in the treatment of obesity or anorectic states. Preliminary observations showing this have been reported in the studies of Atkinson [49] who has shown that a long-acting opioid antagonist, naltrexone, produces a mild decrease in weight in obese females. However, subsequent studies have produced disappointing results as far as the use of opiate antagonists in obesity are concerned [53]. In view of the potent nature of kappa agonists in increasing feeding it is possible that the development of a selective kappa opioid antagonist may lead to an even more potent anorectic agent. In addition, these basic studies have clearly shown that appetite regulation is multifactorial, and therefore, multiple clinical approaches need to be developed rather than expecting one agent to turn out to be the universal panacea. Finally, with our increasingly sophisticated knowledge of neurotransmitters, we will begin to recognize specific syndromes of obesity and anorexia for which we can tailor specific treatments. An early example of this was the young boy reported by Dunger et al [50] who had a syndrome characterized by increased endogenous opioid activity and was obese.

REFERENCES

1. Davis WJ, Mpitsos GJ, Pinneo JM. The behavioral hierarchy of the mollusk, Pleurobranchea. II. Hormonal suppression of feeding associated with egg laying. J Comp Physiol, 1974; 95:225-43.
2. Heatherington AW, Ranson SW. The spontaneous activity and food intake of rats with hypothalamic lesions. Am J Physiol, 1942; 136:609-17.
3. Anand BK, Brobeck JR. Hypothalamic control of food intake in rats and cats. Yale J Biol Med, 1952; 24:123-40.
4. Morley JE. The neuroendocrine control of appetite: The role of the endogenous opiates, cholecystokinin, TRH, gamma-amino butyric acid and the diazepam receptor. Life Sci, 1980; 27:355-68.
5. Grossman SP. Direct adrenergic and cholinergic stimulation of hypothalamic mechansisms. Am J Physiol, 1962; 303:872-82.
6. Leibowitz SF. Neurochemical systems of the hypothalamus in control of feeding and drinking behavior and water and electrolyte excretion. In Morgane P, Panksepp J, eds. Handbook of the hypothalamus, vol. 3. New York: Marcel-Decker, 1980: 299-437.
7. Blundell JE. Serotonin and feeding. In Esmon WB, ed. Serotonin in health and disease, vol. 5, New York: Spectrum, 1979: 403-50.
8. Goldman HW, Lehr D, Friedman F. Antagonist effects of alpha and beta-adrenergically coded hypothalamic neurons on consummatory behavior in the rat. Nature, 1971; 231:453-54.
9. Morley JE, Levine AS, Grace M, Kneip J. Dynorphin-(1-13), dopamine and feeding in rats. Pharmacol Biochem Behav, 1982; 16:701-05.
10. Grandison L, Guidotti A. Stimulation of food intake by muscimol and beta endorphin. Neuropharmacology, 1977; 16:533-36.
11. Holtzman SG. Behavioral effects of separate and combined administration of naloxone and d-amphetamine. J Pharmacol Exp Ther, 1974; 189:5160.
12. Vijayan E, McCann SM. Suppression of feeding and drinking activity in rats following intraventricular injection of thyrotropin releasing hormone (TRH). Endocrinology, 1977; 100:1727-30.
13. Morley JE, Levine AS. The central control of appetite. Lancet, 1983; i:398-401.
14. Sawchenko PE, Gold RM, Leibowitz SF. Evidence for vagal involvement in the eating elicited by adrenergic stimulation of the paraventricular nucleus. Brain Res, 1981; 225:249-69.
15. Leibowitz SF, Roland CR, Hor L, Squillari V. Noradrenergic feeding elicited via the paraventricular nucleus is dependent upon circulating corticosterone. Physiol Behav, 1984.
16. Jhanwar-Aniyal M, Fleisher F, Levin BF, Leibowitz SF. Impact of food deprivation on hypothalamic αa-drenergic receptor activity and nonrepinephrine turnover in rat brain. Soc Neurosci Abstr, 1982; 8:711.
17. Myers RD, McCaleb ML. Feeding: Satiety signal from intestine triggers brain's noradrenergic mechanisms. Science, 1980; 209:1035-7.
18. Leibowitz SF, Hammer NJ, Chang K. Feeding behavior induced by central norepinephrine injection is attenuated by discrete lesions in the hypothalamic paraventricular nucleus. Pharmacol Biochem Behav, 1983; 19:945-50.
19. Blundell, JE, Latham CJ. Effect of pharmacological agents on micro-and macro-structure of feeding behavior: Implications for the analysis of drug action. In Bray GA, ed. Recent Advances in Obesity research, II. London: Newman, 1978:
20. Wurtman JJ, Wurtman RJ. Fenfluramine and fluoxetine spare protein consumption while suppressing calorie intake by rats. Science, 1977; 198:1178-80.
21. Davies, RF, Rossi III J, Panksepp J, Bean NJ, Zolovick, AJ. Fenfluramine anorexia: A peripheral locus of action. Physiol Behav, 1983; 30:723-30.
22. Dourish CT. Phenylethylamine-induced anorexia in the albino rat. In Hoebel BG, Novin D, eds. Neural Basis of feeding and reward. Brunswick, ME: The Haer Institute, 1982: 543-49.
23. Paul SM, Hulihan-Giblin B, Skolnick P. (+)-Amphetamine binding to rat hypothalamus: Relation to anorexic potency of phenylethylamines. Science, 1982; 218:487-90.
24. Panksepp J, Bishop P, Rossi III J. Neurohumoral and endocrine control of feeding. Psychoneuroendocrinology, 1979; 4:89-106.
25. Morley JE, Levine AS, Kneip J. Muscimol induced feeding: A model to study the hypothalamic regulation of appetite. Life Sci, 1981; 29:1213-18.
26. Cooper SJ. Benzodiazepines as appetite enhancing compounds. Appetite, 1980; 1:7-19.
27. Levine AS, Morley JE. Purinergic regulation of food

intake. Science, 1982; 217:79-9.

28. Agren H, Nikalsson F, Hallgren R. Brain purinergic activity linked with depressive symptomatology: Hypoxanthine and xanthine in CSF of patients with major depressive disorders. Psychiat Res, 1983; 9:179-89.

29. Morley JE, Levine AS, Yim GKW, Lowy MT. Opioid modulation of appetite. Neurosci Biobehav Res, 1983; 7:281-305.

30. Marks-Kaufman R, Kanarek RB. Morphine selectively influences macronutrient intake in the rat. Pharmacol Biochem Behav, 1980; 12:427-30.

31. Leibowitz SF, Hor L. Endorphinergic and α-noradrenergic systems in the paraventricular nucleus: Effects on eating behavior. Peptides, 1982; 3:421-8.

32. Tepperman FS, Hirst M. Effect of intrahypothalamic injection of [D-Ala^2, D-Leu^5] enkephalin on feeding and temperature in the rat. Eur J Pharmacol, 1983; 96:243-9.

33. Morley JE, Levine AS. The involvement of dynorphin and the kappa opioid receptor in feeding. Peptides, 1983; 4:797-800.

34. Freed WJ, Perlow MJ, Wyatt RD. Calcitonin: Inhibitory effect on eating in rats. Science, 1979; 206:85-92.

35. Levine AS, Morley JE. Reduction of feeding in rats by calcitonin. Brain Res, 1981; 222:187-91.

36. Rosenfeld M, Mermod JJ, Amara SG, et al. Production of a novel neuropeptide encoded by the calcitonin gene via tissue specific RNA processing. Nature, 1983; 304-129-35.

37. Gibbs J, Kulkosky PJ, Smith GP. Effects of peripheral and central bombesin on feeding behavior of rats. Peptides, 1981; 2:179-83.

38. Morley JE, Levine AS. Bombesin inhibits stress-induced eating. Pharmacol Biochem Behav, 1981; 14:149-51.

39. Della-Fera MA, Baile CA, Schneider BS, Grinker JA. Cholecystokinin-antibody injected in cerbral ventricles stimulates feeding in sheep. Science, 1981; 212:687-9.

40. Porte D Jr, Woods SC. Regulation of food intake and body weight by insulin. Diabetologia, 1981; 20:274-80.

41. Tannenbaum GS, Guyda HJ, Posner BI. Insulin-like growth factors: A role in growth hormone negative feedback and body weight regulation. Science, 1983; 220:777-9.

42. Billington CJ, Levine AS, Morley JE. Are peptides truly satiety agents? A method of testing for neurohormonal satiety effects. Am J Physiol, 1983; 245:R920-6.

43. Lowy MT, Maickel RP, Yim GKW. Naloxone reduction of stress-related feeding. Life Sci, 1980; 26:2113-8.

44. Buckingham JC. Corticotropin releasing factor. Pharmacol Rev, 1980; 31:253-74.

45. Morley JE, Levine AS, Rowland NE. Stress induced eating. Life Sci, 1983; 32:2169-82.

46. Teskey GC, Kavaliers M, Hirst M. Aggression and defeat induce opioid analgesic and ingestive responses in mice. Fed Proc, 1984; 43:2709A.

47. Morley JE, Levine AS. Corticotropin releasing factor, grooming and ingestive behavior. Life Sci, 1982; 31:1459-64.

48. Moore R, Mills IH, Forster A. Naloxone in the treatment of anorexia nervosa: Effect on weight gain and lipolysis. J Roy Soc Med, 1981; 74:129-31.

49. Atkinson RL. Naltrexone for weight loss in obesity. Abstracts Fourth Int Cong on Obesity, 1983; 30A:81.

50. Dunger DB, Leonard JV, Wolff OH, Preece MA. Effect of naloxone in a previously undescribed hypothalamic syndrome: A disorder of the endogenous opioid peptide system. Lancet, 1980; i:1277-80.

51. Dourish CT, Huston PH, Kennett GA, Curzon A. 8-OH-DPAT-induced hyperphagia: its' neural basis and possible therapeutic relevance. Appetite, 1986; 7(suppl):127-145.

52. Morley JE, Levine AS, Gomell BA, Kneip J, Grace M. Studies on the effect of neuropeptide Y on ingestive behaviors in the rat. Am J Physiol, 1987; 252:R599-609.

53. Mitchell JE, Morley JE, Levine AS, Hutsukami D, Gannon M, Pfohl D. High-dose naltrexone therapy and dietary counselling for obesity. Biol Psychiat, 1987; 22:35-42.

Chapter 3

Energy Balance and Opioid Receptors: Epsilons in the Periphery Promote Conservation; Kappa and Delta in the CNS Permit Expenditures

David L. Margules

Opium arrests life, anesthetises. Well being comes from a kind of death. Without opium I am cold, I catch cold, I do not feel hungry. I am impatient to impose what I invent. When I smoke I am warm, I do not know what colds are, I am hungry. My impatience disappears." "Opium leads the organism towards death in euphoric mood. The tortures arise from the process of returning to life against one's wish. A whole spring-time excites the veins to madness, bringing with it ice and fiery lava.

Jean Cocteau
Opium, The Diary of a Cure

OVERVIEW

In this chapter I present evidence that requires the revision and extension of my 1979 opioid theory [1] of the conservation of energy. Opioid peptides participate not only in hibernation-like phenomena that conserve energy, but also in the most intense of energy expenditures including arousal from hibernation and migration. The 1979 theory [1] did not propose a role for opioids in energy expenditure. Instead it focused on the many energy-conserving actions of morphine. Recent measurements of metabolic weight loss show that morphine, as predicted by the 1979 theory reduces the rate of such losses. Moreover this conservatory action can be blocked by an opioid antagonist that *does not* enter the brain. Therefore, the energy-conserving action of morphine must be localized to the body rather than to the brain. The body's opioid peptide responsible for energy conservation appears to be the specific ligand, beta endorphin. Also identified are the specific receptors where beta-endorphin acts to conserve energy; these receptors are known as the epsilon set. Apparently the epsilon receptors in the body act, more or less continuously to conserve energy until they receive either a kappa-receptor-mediated message or delta-receptor-mediated message from the brain that permits the expenditure of energy.

The evidence for kappa receptor control is based on two experiments: In one, a specific kappa agonist is shown to promote energy expenditure in a dose-related fashion. In the other, an energy-expending effect of morphine is unmasked by blocking morphine's conservatory actions in the body with an opioid antagonist that does not enter the brain. Additional experiments demonstrate that the unmasked energy-expending effect of morphine can be blocked by a specific kappa receptor antagonist that acts in the brain. The brain's kappa opioid system for the expenditure of energy contributes to arousal from hibernation, reproduction, and other calorically expensive activities. In addition we have preliminary evidence that delta opioid receptors in the brain contribute to the linear running and perseverance involved in migration. Other aspects of migration such as social group formation may also involve opioids.

The revised theory has implications for understanding the eating disorders. Anorexia nervosa can be understood as an excess of kappa or delta receptor activity in the brain. Some forms of obesity can be understood not only in terms of excessive epsilon activity in the body but also in terms of insufficient kappa and/or delta receptor activity in the brain. The new theory can account for the excessive dynorphin reported to be present in the pituitary glands of obese mice. Such an accumulation could occur because of an inability of obese mice to release this peptide from storage sites. This idea is compatable with the well known supersensitivity of obese mice to drugs that block kappa-type opioid receptors in the brain. The theory also gives rise to an alternative explanation for the increase in feeding caused by kappa agonists in lean rodents. These increases may not be a direct effect of such drugs but secondary to caloric shortages produced by the increases that these drugs induce in metabolic weight loss.

The naturally-occurring opioid peptides have a major integrative role in energy balance [1,2,3]. I have presented evidence that some of these peptides, such as beta endorphin act to promote the conservation of energy [1]. In this chapter I discuss evidence that this action occurs primarily from epsilon receptors located in the periphery [4]. I also present evidence that other opioid peptides such as dynorphin act at kappa receptors in the brain to promote the expenditure of energy [4]. Moreover met-enkephalin acting at delta receptors in the brain may contribute to migration-like behavior of sufficient duration and intensity to allow very long and difficult journeys to be sustained until completion. Thus peptides that have a short form of the met-enkephalin sequence may contribute to the active rather than passive adaptation to famine. *These three types of opioid peptides work together to accomplish the delicate balance between conservation, expenditure, and behavioral adaptation to famine.*

They do this by coordinating a series of adaptive changes in many organ systems. For example, in man, morphine or beta-endorphin induces passivity, lowers respiratory rate and volume, lowers body temperature, reduces motor activity, induces constipation, reduces reactivity to sensory stimuli of arousal including pain, and reduces sexual urges [1]. The changes induced by morphine or beta-endorphin share a common theme: All of them move the organism toward the death-like state of hibernation. An organism faced with seasonal food shortages has two basic choices: hibernate or migrate. Reptiles and amphibians are cold blooded. They conserve energy by becoming stuporous in the cold.

In contrast, relatively few mammals deal with food shortages by means of stupor. Instead most mammals have developed the energy-expending process of migration as a viable alternative. Migration requires extensive coordination of sensory information by the brain, whereas hibernation requires much less sensory processing.

The movement toward migration has encouraged the development of complex and sophisticated brain mechanisms capable for example, of navigation. In this chapter I present evidence that hibernation and migration have different opioid substrates. The more primitive one employing epsilon opioid receptors underlies hibernation. One way of studying these components uses opioid antagonists that block opioid receptors. For example, low doses of naloxone prematurely arouse Turkish hamsters from hibernation [5]. Thus, hibernation may represent a opioid-induced energy conservation. According to the theory presented here, hibernation may involve epsilon receptors. Energy conservation induced by beta endorphin also occurs in certain less-intense and less-prolonged forms, including sleep [6] and the psychological state known as learned helplessness [7,8]. The opioid receptors that contribute to learned helplessness are located in the brain [8] and these may be epsilon receptors.

In this chapter I extend the opioid theory of energy conservation to include certain cases of opioid-induced increases in energy expenditure that previously could not be incorporated by the theory. These effects of dynorphin do not occur at epsilon receptors. Instead, a new receptor known as the kappa receptor has evolved to handle dynorphin. Kappa receptors can be stimulated selectively by opiate drugs such as U50,488H or non-selectively by drugs such as morphine, which also stimulate epsilon receptors at similar doses. Kappa receptors may be blocked selectively by the kappa receptor antagonist MR2266. Naloxone or naltrexone may also be used to block kappa receptors, usually at doses higher than those that block epsilon receptors.

U50,488H increases reactivity to pain [9] in mice as well as increasing metabolic weight loss [4]. This suggests that opioid peptides that contain the leu-enkephalin sequence (i.e. dynorphin) act at kappa receptors involved in promoting arousal from cold-induced stupor. This would allow the organism to expend massive amounts of calories necessry for example to arouse itself from hibernation and/or to create an offspring. Delta receptors have evolved to handle certain short met-enkephalin like opioids. Although it is difficult to selectively stimulate delta receptors, FK33824 is one of the better substances available at present for this purpose.

ENERGY EXPENDITURE

Met-enkephalin-containing peptides may participate in the sustenance of the motivational urge to migrate, thus allowing it to last long enough to complete trips of thousands of miles. Migration represents one of the most prolonged states of energy expenditure known. As such, it must involve its own kind of euphoria, for otherwise the organism would be distracted and would fail to persevere. Met-enkephalin may also participate in less-intense and less-prolonged states of energy expenditure such as arousal from sleep and certain learned behaviors [7]. Recently we reported that a met-enkephalin analogue FK33824 produces linear running in mice with obliviousness to environmental stimuli and undirectional movement. We showed that this migration like running was mediated by opioid receptors in the CNS [16,31]. These may be delta receptors concerned with certain aspects of migration such as navigation and perseverence.

Arousal from hibernation and migration are not the only massive energy-expending actions that involve opioid activity. Withdrawal from opiates precipitates a violent syndrome of energy-expending action, including lacrimation, vomiting, hyperthemia, diarrhrea, ejaculation, increased respiration, sweating, etc. The overreaction is due, in part, to hyperactivity in a brain pathway known as the ventral noradrenergic bundle. The evidence for this assertion is based on experiments employing selective lesions of this bundle made with 6-hydroxydopamine. The lesions deplete hypothalamic norepinephrine and also substantially reduce the symptoms of the withdrawal syndrome [10]. The ventral noradrenergic bundle contains a cotransmitter, dynorphin, released along with norepinephrine [11]. This suggests that the release of both excessive norepinephrine and excessive dynorphin contributes to the violence of the withdrawal syndrome. Accordingly, drugs that inhibit either transmitter should attenuate the withdrawal syndrome. This includes drugs like clonidine, an alpha 2 agonist, that already are known to attenuate the abrupt withdrawal symptoms [12]. This should also hold true for MR2266, a kappa receptor antagonist. Perhaps the combination of MR2266 and clonidine would be a supereffective treatment for the attenuation of the withdrawal syndrome.

Naturally, many opioids have the capacity to attenuate this syndrome in morphine-tolerant animals by restorating high levels of opioid receptor occupation.

Dynorphin is no exception to this rule [13]. This could be explained if dynorphin or some related metabolite could occupy opioid receptors other than kappa during the state of withdrawal. Most conservative scientists agree that beta endorphin acts at epsilon, mu, and delta receptors. Perhaps dynorphin also acts at various opioid receptors. Furthermore there are subtypes of both mu and kappa receptors. All of these receptor types and subtypes occur in great numbers throughout the body and brain in remarkably diverse tissues including lung, gut, many endocrine glands, genitals, and also the central and peripheral divisions of the nervous system. Such complexity makes it difficult to unravel opioid functions. Certain theoretical considerations may provide a framework helpful in this endeavor.

HIBERATION MIGRATION AND BREEDING

From an evolutionary point of view it appears that the met-enkaphalin-containing opioid peptides evolved before the leu-enkaphalin-containing peptides. This was shown by demonstrations [14] in the South African clawed toad, *Xenopus laevis,* that neither of its two pro-enkephalin genes codes for a leu-enkephalin sequence. In constrast, the human proenkephalin gene contains the code for this sequence, as do the genes of other vertebrates that diverged from *X. laevis* some 350 million years ago. *X. laevis,* in common with most amphibians comes out of its hibernation-like behavior by absorbing heat from the environment rather than generating heat internally. This raises the possibility that the evolution of the gene coding for leu-enkephalin contributed to the capacity of organisms to generate all the heat necessary to arouse themselves from their cold induced stupor. Later in evolution with warm blooded animals, migration becomes an important adaptive response to famine. This may be connected with evolution of genes coding for met-enkephalin and the delta opioid receptor. Migration often brings animals together in groups, whereas hibernation is a solitary activity. This suggests that the met-enkephalin-coding gene may contribute to the social bonding associated with migration.

At the end of migration or hibration, animals often engage in seasonal breeding behavior to insure the reproduction of the species. Beta-endorphins of hypothalamic origin participate in the menstrual cycle. It is responsible for slowing down the luteinizing hormone (LH) pulse frequency from one an hour to one every five or six hours. This is necessary for the luteal phase of the cycle to occur. In contrast, naloxone is an effective stimulant for the release of LH at all times of the estrus cycle of rats. Moreover, chronic naloxone in primates accelerates the LH pulse frequency so that the ordinary slow luteal pulse frequency (one very five or six hours) is speeded up to the faster rate of the follicular phase (one very hour).

Interestingly, leu-enkephalin also stimulates the release of LH [17]. It is not yet clear whether this is due to an action at kappa receptors. There also are some indications that delta-type opioid receptors may contribute to the increased amplitude of the LH pulse seen during the luteal phase of the cycle. Thus, beta endorphin could act at epsilon receptors to inhibit LH pulse frequency and delta receptors to increase LH pulse amplitude. This complicates the situation. Nevertheless, the LH stimulative action of leu-enkephalin fits the current theory quite well. Apparently, a balance occurs between the LH pulse-inhibiting action of epsilon receptors and the LH pulse-stimulating action of kappa receptors that modulates the pulsatile release of gonadotrophin-releasing hormone from the arcuate nucleus, thereby exerting a major influence on the menstrual cycle in females [18].

In males sexual desire is similarly influenced, at least insofar as beta-endorphin suppresses libido, and naltrexone increases the low libido of the male Zucker obese rat (fa/fa) sufficiently to turn this sexual "dud" into a sexual "stud" [3]. These lines of evidence suggest that the energy-expending activities regulated by opioid peptides include reproduction in both females and males.

WEIGHT LOSS: PERIPHERAL AND CENTRAL RECEPTOR SITES OF ACTION

Metabolic weight loss is another energy-expending activity regulated by opioid peptides. We used metabolic weight loss as a model system to establish the roles of epsilon and kappa receptors. Henry et al [4], made measurements of metabolic weight loss in mice under the influence of various doses of morphine or U50,488H, a selective kappa receptor agonist. This work helped establish that opioid receptors participate in energy expenditure. All animals lose weight over time because of the cost of metabolic processes: heat production, muscle activity, and the generation of CO_2 and gaseous H_2O. This weight loss can be measured by the use of a computer-controlled balance capable of weighing live animals accurately to the nearest 10 mg [4]. By effectively trapping urine and feces in a granulated clay bedding weighed along with the animal, we were able to obtain weight loss values that correlated highly with other measures of metabolism such as oxygen consumption. Our findings were as follows: Morphine produced a dose-related decrease in the rate of metabolic weight loss (figure 1). Neither DAGO nor morphiceptin, fairly specific mu receptor agonists, had this effect.

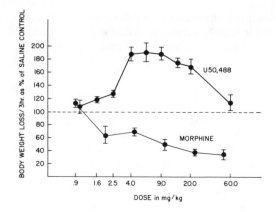

Figure 3.1 Opioid receptors: an epsilon set in the body acts to conserve energy until a kappa set in the brain permits energy expenditure.

These findings directly confirm the opioid theory of conservation. They also eliminate the mu receptor as a possible site and leave two possibilities: delta or epsilon receptors. The energy-conserving action of morphine had some specificity, because it was completely blocked by the opioid antagonist, naltrexone, at low doses. Naltrexone does not usually block delta receptors at low doses. Thus, by a process of elimination we are left with epsilon receptors as the most likely candidates for morphine's energy-conserving action.

The evidence for the kappa-receptor-induced increase in energy expenditure is more straightforward. U50,488H increased metabolic weight loss in a dose-related manner (figure 1). The shape of the dose-response curve was an inverted U function. At the maximum effective dose (between 4 and 9 mg/kg U50,488H produced a doubling of the metabolic weight loss. This action of U50,488H was blocked by 6 mg/kg of MR2266, a specific kappa receptor antagonist, but it was only slightly reduced (from 190 to 170% of saline controls) by 6 mg/kg of naltrexone. This indicates that the U50,488H-induced increase in metabolic weight loss has some specificity; it is blocked selectively by kappa opioid receptor antagonists.

In order to obtain information about the site of these opioid actions, we decided to antagonize their actions with an opioid antagonist that does not enter the brain known as MR2663BR (naltrexone methobromide). This substance had no effect on the U50,488H-induced increase in metabolic weight loss [4]. This suggests that U50,488H increases metabolic weight loss by actions at kappa receptors located in the brain. In contrast, MR2663BR completely reversed the direction of metabolic weight loss for the morphine-injected mice, producing a $151\% \pm 13$ increase over saline controls [4]. Thus, the combination of morphine plus MR2663BR revealed, or unmasked, an effect just like that of U50,488H. This could be due to kappa receptor activity. In support of this idea, the increase in metabolic weight loss induced by morphine plus MR2663BR was completely blocked by the kappa receptor antagonist MR2266 (6 mg/kg) [4]. These results suggest that morphine has two antagonistic actions: a peripheral energy-conservation effect at epsilon receptors, and a central energy-expenditure effect at kappa receptors. Apparently the conservation action is large enough to completely mask the expenditure action, and this explains why morphine alone produces a decrease in metabolic weight loss. Blockade (by means of MR2663BR) of the peripheral opioid receptors, however, allows the central kappa action of morphine to manifest itself without opposition from the peripheral epsilon system. In order to test further the idea of antagonism between these two systems, we showed that increasing amounts of morphine caused increasing inhibition of metabolic weight loss induced by a constant amount of U50,488H [4].

OBESITY AND ANOREXIA NERVOSA

These results have important implications for understanding obesity and anorexia nervosa. They suggest the following scenario: The periphery contains a opioid system (epsilon type) for energy conservation that functions only to conserve and store calories. It cannot engage in caloric expenditure unless a message comes from the brain to allow this. The brain message involves, in part, a kappa-type and/or delta type opioid receptor for energy expenditure. In obesity there may be either insufficient central kappa or delta opioid message for expenditure and/or too much peripheral epsilon message for conservation. This suggests that the treatment of obese subjects with a combination of a kappa agonist and a peripheral antagonist such as MR2663BR would optimize their chances of losing weight. This prediction is quite counter-intuitive from the point of view of the literature indicating that kappa agonists stimulate feeding [19]. Yet, from the data reported here, kappa agonists should work as an anti-obesity treatment. In support of this possibility, kappa agonists increase urination [20] and also increase metabolic weight loss [4].

The theory described above also has implications for the treatment of anorexia nervosa. Here the problem may be too much kappa or delta message of expenditure from the brain and/or an insufficient opioid message of conservation in the periphery. The theory predicts that treatment with drugs that block kappa receptors, such as MR2266 should help anorexics to eat more. They could further be encouraged to eat with a form of opioid that activated epsilon receptors in the periphery alone. Some evidence already exists that anorexia nervosa does indeed have an opioid component [21]. Finally, our recent work with delta receptors in the brain suggests that the well known sloth of the obese may be due in part to a lack of delta opioid receptor activity. Moreover, hyperactivity of delta receptors in the brain could contribute to behavioral hyperactivity in anorexia nervosa.

The theory has implications for understanding genetic obesity, which has been identified most definitively in mutant rodents (ob/ob mice and fa/fa rats). These animals are heavily biased toward energy conservation. They seek and accumulate excessive calories. Moreover, their efforts at energy expenditure and reproduction are marginal. In this chapter, I review evidence that this bias toward energy conservation is due, in part, to the combination of excessive activity from beta-endorphin systems, diminished activity from dynorphin systems and diminished activity from met-enkephalin systems. Some evidence supports this hypothesis in one subgroup of the human population, obese hirsute women, who have excessive beta-endorphin in their blood [22]. Other forms of human obesity have not been investigated extensively.

The changes responsible for environmental obesity are likely to be more subtle than those involved in genetic obesity. Nevertheless, the opioid mechanism involved in environmental obesity may be fundamentally the same as that of genetic obesity. In support of this idea, an opioid peptide involvement was established in ordinary rats that had their obesity induced by a highly palatable diet [23]. Thus, the opioid theory of obesity has been extended to an environmental type of obesity. If this work can be extended to humans, it would expand considerably the possible role of opioids in the etiology of obesity. This has proved difficult to accomplish. Most of our information is on the genetic forms of obesity. These forms involve relatively long-lasting changes in opioid peptides that should induce relatively long-lasting changes in the opioid receptors.

RECEPTOR SENSITIVITIES AND REGULATION IN OBESITY

I will now consider new evidence on the question of receptor subsensitivity and supersensitivity underlying opioid actions in obese mutants. Three precursors for opioid peptides have been identified: pro-opiomelanocortin, pro-enkephalin, and pro-dynorphin. Members of all three families occur in excess in the pituitary of genetically obese rodents [24,25] and beta-endorphin occurs in excess in their blood [26]. Beta-endorphin in the pituitary, for example, becomes elevated as early as four weeks of age in obese mice (C57BL/6J *ob/ob*) [26,27] and remains elevated throughout their lifespan [27]. In old age the pituitary beta-endorphin levels reach new highs [27]. Leu-enkephalin in the posterior pituitary also rises sharply between the ages of five weeks and three months in the *ob/ob* mouse [28]. These genetically obese mutants therefore represent an animal model with a lifetime of multiple opioid excesses. Other peptide excesses, such as hyperinsulinemia, often induce a decrease (downregulation) in the binding of the peptide by its receptors. Therefore, opioid excesses should produce similar changes. Conversely, opioid shortages should induce an upregulation in opioid receptors. Indeed, upregulation of mu receptors from chronic treatment with naltrexone has been demonstrated [29]. Is this true for opioid peptides in the genetically obese? If so, certain opioid receptor types should show such upregulation. Conversely, other opioid receptor types should show downregulation if their ligand is in excess supply.

This raises two interesting possibilities for receptor changes in the obese mice. Kappa receptors in the brain may be upregulated in response to a shortage of dynorphin. This hypothesis is based on the assumption that obese mice have accumulated opioid peptides such as dynorphin in storage sites instead of releasing them. There is no direct evidence in support of this hypothesis. However, indirect evidence indicates that obese mice are supersensitive to the feeding- and drinking-increasing action of a kappa agonist [25,26]. Such supersensitivity is compatible with upregulation of kappa receptors. The situation with the epsilon receptors in the body should be quite the opposite. We know that beta-endorphin in obese mice is released from storage, because we find beta-endorphin in excess in the blood. This should lead to a downregulation of epsilon receptors in the periphery. This hypothesis remains to be tested.

A large body of evidence shows that genetically obese rodents have substantial supersensitivity to opioid antagonists including naloxone, naltrexone, and MR2266 [24,25]. Their feeding and drinking behavior, for example, is suppressed by opioid antagonists at doses one tenth of those required to do this in lean controls [24]. In other words, they are supersensitive to the symptoms of the withdrawal syndrome precipitated by an opioid antagonist. The withdrawal syndrome also occurs spontaneously in subjects that have developed tolerance to morphine after the effects of an opiate such as morphine wears off.

We have shown [30] that obese mice have an exaggerated set of symptoms to withdrawal from morphine compared with their lean controls. For example, obese mice lose more body weight than lean mice. Ordinarily female obese mice (five to six months old) gain 0.16 g/day compared with 0.002 g/day for lean controls. Withdrawal from morphine abolished their gain and produced a dose-related loss in body weight in the obese

mice. The lean mice had to be in withdrawal from doses of morphine five times greater than those of the obese mice in order to show the same effect on body weight loss.

The obese mice also showed sharper drops in food and water intake due to morphine withdrawal than the lean mice. This effect was particularly dramatic for the drop in water intake, which dropped so steeply that the obese mice, who ordinarily take about 1.3 ml of water for every gram of food eaten, lost this polydipsia entirely and required only 0.8 ml of water for each gram of food. The abnormally high water- to-food ratio of obese mice was restored to the level of lean mice by withdrawal from morphine. The restoration was a linear function of the log of the dose of morphine that the mice were being withdrawn from (1 to 16 mg/kg). Thus, the *ob/ob* mouse has both supersensitivity to withdrawal from morphine and supersensitivity to the withdrawal precipitated by opioid antagonists. This data has encouraged us to embark on a major investigation of receptor-binding characteristics (affinity and number) in obese and lean rodents. We hope to characterize upregulation and downregulation for the various receptor types and test some of the predictions of this revised theory of opioid function in the conservation and expenditure of energy.

HETEROGENIETY OF RECEPTOR TYPES

The idea of differential and sometimes opposite reactions in receptors for different opioid types has an important parallel with the glucocorticoid system of obese mice. We have shown that genetically obese mice (ob/ob) are hypersensitive to glucocorticoid-induced stimulation of feeding but dramatically insensitive to glucocorticoid-induced losses in body weight [32]. These different actions of glucocorticoids would act in tandem to promote obesity. Steroids as well as peptides have significant roles in the etiology of obesity and anorexia. Moreover there appears to be the same heterogeniety of steroid receptor types, particularly in glucocorticoid receptor types as there is in opioid receptor type. We have found reduced binding and activation of glucocorticoid receptor complexes in whole brain liver, cerebral cortex, hippocampus and hypothalamus of genetically obese and diabetic mice (mdb/mdb) as compared to their lean control [33].

REFERENCES

1. Margules DL. Beta-endorphin and endoloxone: Hormones of the autonomic nervous system for the conservation or expenditure of resources and bodily energy in anticipation of famine or feast. Neurosi Biobehav Rev, 1979; 3:155-62.

2. Margules DL. Obesity and the development of the diffuse neuroendocrine system. Intnl J of Obesity, 1980; 4:296-303.

3. Margules DL. Opioid and antiopioid actions in the survival and reproduction of individuals. In Steven J. Cooper, ed. Theory in psychopharmacology, vol 1. New York: Academic Press, 1981: 177-195.

4. Henry LJ, Walker J, Margules DL. Opposite effects of opiate agonists on metabolic weight loss in mice. Neuropeptides, 1985; 5:327-330.

5. Margules DL, Goldman B, Finck A. Hibernation: an opioid-dependent state? Brain Res Bull, 1979; 4:721-4.

6. Ott D, Inoue K, Arndt S. Beta-endorphin level in CSF rises substantially during natural sleep. Neuropeptides (in press).

7. Whitehouse WG, Walker J, Margules DL, Bersh PJ. Antiopioid drugs overcome the learned helplessness effect but impair otherwise competant escape performance. Physiol and Behav, 1983; 30:731-4.

8. Whitehouse WG, Blustein JE, Walker J, Bersh PJ, Margules DL. Shock controllability and opioid substrates of escape performance and nociception: differential effects of peripheral and centrally acting naltrexone. Behav Neurosci, 1986; 99:717-733.

9. Ramabadran K. Hyperalgesic effect of the selective kappa opioid agonist, U-50488H in mice. Japan, J Pharmacol, 1983; 33:1289-92.

10. Lewis MJ, Costa JL, Jacobowitz DM, Margules DL. Tolerance, physical dependence and opioid-seeking behavior: dependence on dienncephalic norepinephrine. Brain Research, 1976; 107:156-65.

11. Miller MJ, Miller MH, Czlonkowski A, Herz A. Contrasting interactions of the locus coeruleus as compared to the ventral noradrenergic bundle with CNS and pituitary pools of vasopression, dynorphin and related opioid peptides in the rat. Brain Research, 1984; 198:243-52.

12. Gold MS. Clonidine blocks acute opiate-withdrawal symptoms. Lancet, 1978; 8090:599-602.

13. Lee NM, Smith AP. Possible regulatory function of dynorphin and its clinical implications. Trends in Pharmacological Sciences, 1984; 5:108-10.

14. Martins GJM, Herbert M. Polymorphism and absence of Leu-enkephalin sequences in proenkephalin genes in *Xenopus laevis*. Nature, 1984; 310:251-4.

15. Sugiyama K, Furuta H. Histamine release induced by dynorphin (1-13) from rat mast cells. Jap J Pharm, 1984; 35:247-52.

16. Margules DL. Central and peripheral opioid peptides in learned helplessness, feeding, drinking, and obesity; male and female running behavior; and immuno-competance. In Genazzani AR, Muller EE, eds. Central and peripheral endorphins: Basic and clincial aspects. New York: Raven Press (in press).

17. Leadem CA, Kalra SP. The effects of various opiate agonists on LH and prolactin secretion in ovariectomized rats. Abstract of the 65 Annual Meeting, Endocrine Society. San Antonio, 1983: 163.

18. Ferin M. Endogenous opioid peptides and the menstrual cycle. Trends in Neurosciences, 1984; 7:194-6.

19. Morley JE, Levine AS. Dynorphin - (1-13) induces spontaneous feeding. Life Sciences, 1981; 29:1901-3.

20. Rathburn RC, Kattan RW, Leander JD. Effects of mu- and kappa-opioid receptor agonists on urinary output in mice. Pharm Biochem and Behavior, 1983; 19:863-6.

21. Gillman MA, Lichtigfeld EJ. Opioid involvements in anorexia nervosa. South African Medical Journal, 1984; 65:4.

22. Givens JR, Wiedemann E, Andersen RN, Kitabchi AE. Beta-endorphin and beta-lipotropin plasma levels in hirsute women: correlation with body weight. J Clin Endocr Metab, 1980; 50:975-6.

23. Mandenoff A, Fumeron F, Apfellbaum M, Margules DL. Endogenous opiates and energy balance. Science, 1982; 215:1537.

24. Margules DL, Moisset B, Lewis MJ, Shibuya H, Pert CB. Beta-endorphin is associated with overeating in genetically obese mice (ob/ob) and rats (fa/fa). Science, 1978; 202:988-91.

25. Ferguson-Segall M, Flynn JJ, Walker J, Margules DL. Increased immunoreactive dynorphin and leu-enkephalin in posterior pituitary of obese mice (ob/ob) and supersensitivity to drugs that act at kappa receptors. Life Sciences, 1982; 31:2233-38.

26. Recant L, Voyles NR, Luciano M, Pert CB. Naltrexone reduces weight gain, alters "beta endorphin," and reduces insulin output from pancreatic islets of genetically obese mice. Peptides, 1980; 1:309-13.

27. Garthwaite TL, Martinson DR, Tseng LF, Hagen TC, Menshan LA. A longitudinal profile of the genetically obese mouse. Endocrinology, 1980; 107:671-80.

28. Rossier J, Rogers J, Shibasaki T, Guillemin R, Bloom FE. Opioid peptides and alpha MSH in genetically obese mice (ob/ob) during development. Proc Soc Natl Acad Sci, USA, 1980; 77:666-9.

29. Tempel A, Gardner EL, Zukin RS. Visualization of opiate receptor upregulation by light microscopy autoradiography. Proc Nat Acad Sci USA, 1984; 81:3893-7.

30. Flynn JJ, Walker J, Margules DL. Exaggerated weight loss in genetically obese (ob/ob) mice by withdrawal from morphine. In Leong Way E, ed. Endogenous & exogenous opiate agonists and antagonists. New York: Pergamon Press, 1980: 525-528.

31. Calcagnetti, DJ, Flynn JJ, Margules DL. Opioid-induced linear running in obese (ob/ob) and lean mice. Pharm Biochem and Behav, 1987; 26-743-47.

32. McGinnis R, Walker J, Margules DL. Genetically obese (ob/ob) mice are hypersensitive to glucocorticoid stimulation of feeding but dramatically resist glucocorticoid-induced weight loss. Life Sciences, 1987; 40:1561-70.

33. Webb ML, Flynn JJ, Schmidt TJ, Margules DL, Litwak G. Decreased glucocorticoid binding and receptor activation in brain of genetically diabetic (mdb/mdb) mice. J Steroid Biochem, 1986; 25:649-57.

Supported in part by a research grant from the National Science Foundation BNS 8216104.

Chapter 4

Long-Term History of Human Diet

Glynn Ll. Isaac and Jeanne M. Sept

INTRODUCTION

A walk down a supermarket aisle these days takes a city-dweller past an amazing array of foods stocking the shelves. Faced with many packages boldly labled "LOW IN SODIUM," "NO CHOLESTEROL," or even "100% NATURAL," a hungry consumer might well pause to reflect. Is there, in fact, a "natural" diet for humans?

Supermarkets and packaged foods, of course, are 20th century additions to the human lifestyle, and the refined, cellophaned diets typical of industrialized societies fall at one atypical edge of the wide dietary range of people today. Most human societies now depend on agricultural products as staple food sources; the particular crops and animals they tend vary with local environmental conditions. Societies in the humid tropics, for instance, often rely on local root crops, while groups in cooler temperate climates generally depend on domestic grains, or more rarely, dairy products.

But these domestic foods that support much of the world's population today have only joined the human dietary repertoire relatively recently; agriculture and animal husbandry were not developed until 10,000 years ago. Today there are still a few groups that prefer a hunting and gathering lifestyle to a farming one, but before 10,000 years ago, and actually during 99% of the human past, people lived solely on wild foods that they gathered or hunted. Whether or not such wild foods can be regarded as the "natural foods" for people, they certainly represent the starting point of human dietary development.

This paper briefly reviews current knowledge of the ancient diets of humans and looks at ways in which modern human diets differ from those of the past. Our perspective of human dietary history is based on information from both the present and the past, and the following sections summarize how different sources of evidence contribute to what is definitely known, what is probable, and what is as yet uncertain about the history of human diet. Even seen from many angles, an overall narrative of human dietary history is incomplete; but what *is* known can nevertheless offer an important perspective on the background to human dietary choices today.

RANGE OF NONINDUSTRIAL HUMAN DIETS COMPARED WITH PRIMATES

A review of the subsistence habits of nonindustrial societies today, such as that done by Gaulin and Konner [1], highlights the incredible variety of human dietary patterns. They range from isolated examples of hunting and gathering populations to a range of food producers dependent solely on domestic stock or agricultural staples to survive. In the face of this dietary diversity, there is little agreement on what an ideal diet for all people should consist of, or even on how to gauge "acceptable" diets [2]. For instance, Young and Scrimshaw [3] and many others [4] discuss the variable nutritional

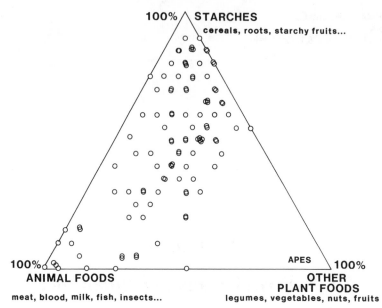

Figure 4.1 Diet composition of 117 non-industrial human societies, in relation to diet composition of apes: proportions of animal foods, starches, and other plant foods. (Data taken from Gaulin and Konner, 1977) [1]

needs of human populations with different geographical, cultural, and genetic backgrounds. However, it is safe to conclude that many very different dietary mixes allow humans to grow, thrive, and multiply.

While humans range from being almost completely carnivorous, as the Eskimo groups in northern temperate and arctic regions, to largely vegetarian, as the San hunter-gatherers in southern Africa [5], the majority of societies effectively balance their diet as an omnivorous mix between meat and vegetables. Most people in most societies depend on plant foods as the main reliable source of calories, and many plant food staples are also good sources of high-quality protein, such as wheat, nuts, and legumes. However others, like manioc and rice, are not and require either supplementary proteins or amino acids to support nutritionally balanced diets [6,7]. Some groups get protein supplements from vegetable greens [8] or by eating suites of plant foods with amino acid complements such as maize and beans [9]. However, such protein balance is easily achieved by eating animal (or insect) foods in a mix with plant foods, and this is the most common dietary pattern, as illustrated in figure 1.

Humans often try to maximize the amount of animal foods that they eat, giving the impression that they would like more meat and fat then they get. Hayden [5] and Speth and Spielman [10] have recently noted this apparent preoccupation with meat and fat among people of many different societies. Lipids, in particular, emerge as a scarce, crucial resource for hunter-gatherers and many food producing groups, probably

because humans require essential fatty acids for a number of metabolic functions, and lipids are a concentrated source of energy that can balance some of the high costs of protein metabolism. Yet lipids are rare in most plant foods except seeds, and nondomestic animals tend to be quite lean, with only their bone marrow offering a hunter much in the way of fats [11,12].

In addition to craving meat or fat, most humans seem to have "sweet teeth," and will fill up on naturally occurring sugars —honey and ripe fruits— when they are available. Honey, especially, seems to elicit great enthusiasm and energetic search efforts from a number of foraging groups [5]. However, wild ripe fruits are rarely passed by and are particularly common snack foods among hunter-gatherer groups.

But regardless of fruit's temptations, the largest contributions that plant foods make to modern human diets come in the form of starches. For today's hunter-gatherer populations, tubers are among the most common staple plant foods and are generally quite starchy. And the main staple crops of groups that practice agriculture tend to be much more starchy than their wild counterparts [13], particularly the seed crops such as the wheat and maize that support large populations in western Europe and the Americas, and the rice and millets grown widely in Africa and Asia. Starchy root crops, such as yams, manioc, and potatoes, are also staples over large parts of the tropics [6].

Where there are plant foods, there are also structural carbohydrates, and long hours of preparation are necessary to reduce the bulk of most plant foods. As a re-

Table 4.1 Classes of food eaten by human groups and examples of non-human primates.
Key: Importance in diet. ● = very minor; + = minor; X = moderately important (> 15%); X = predominant
(>40% or 50%)

	PRIMATES:			HUMANS:				
	Baboon	Gorilla	Chimp	Hunter-Gatherers		Agri-Horticulture		Pastoralists
				warm-temperate tropical	cold-temperate arctic	dry tropics temperate	humid tropics	
Fruits	X	+	X	X	o	+	X	+
Seeds, Nuts	X	o	+	X	+	+	+	+
Leaves, Shoots, shallow Roots	X	X	+	+		+	X	o
Grains	+			X		X	+	+
Tubers	+			X	o	X	X	+
Animal	o		X	X	X	X	X	X
meat, fat, insect M	M	M	M	M	M	M	M	
fish F				F	F	F	F	
dairy D						D		D

sult, the diets of even the most eclectic of nonindustrial peoples, and particularly those of nomadic hunter-gatherers, have a much higher fiber content than the more refined and meaty diets of western supermarket denizens [14].

At the same time, almost all human groups are subject to periodic food shortages. For hunters and gatherers this occurs to a greater or lesser extent on a regular seasonal basis—often during dry seasons when both plant and animal foods are restricted [15,16]. For food producers such shortages obviously occur less often, especially if foods are stored in any way. But when they do happen, because of drought or crop pests, for instance, food shortages tend to be severe for agriculturalists because of high population densities, and they can produce famine.

Comparing the range of nonindustrial human diets with the feeding habits of other primates [1,17] emphasizes that many of these general features of human diets are actually quite distinctive. As summarized in table 1, the bulk of the diets of our closest natural relatives, the apes, is composed of fruits and leaves, with modest intermittent supplements from the flesh of small animals and insects. Humans stand out for several reasons:

1. the much higher proportion of *animal food* they eat;
2. their focus on *starchy* plant foods, particularly grains and tubers (foods rarely, if ever, touched by apes); and
3. their use of cooking and *preparation* techniques that help reduce the fibrous bulk of these foods and

make some, such as grains, more palatable.

Figure 1 emphasizes how distinct the range of nonindustrial human dietary patterns is compared with other primates along two dimensions: in terms of plant food starches—rather than sugars—as sources of carbohydrates, and animal foods—rather than leaves—as primary sources of protein. However, these modern differences between the diets of humans and other primates were not nearly as pronounced during the course of prehistory. The next section summarizes what is known about the human dietary past from the fossil and archaeological records.

EVIDENCE OF PREHISTORIC HUMAN DIETS

Before considering what human ancestors ate, it is useful to summarize who they were and where they lived. Figure 2 presents a simplified "time line" chart of some of the key features of dietary evidence relating to the human fossil record. Note that while the modern human species *Homo sapiens* has only been around for the last 40,000 years, the time line presented here begins with fossil samples roughly ten million years old.

1. Abundant fossils of ape-like quadrupedal primates have been found from the early Miocene time period in areas that were once forested and tropical. Paleontologists are reluctant, as yet, to choose between these fossil ape species to pick a particular human ancestor, but several of them could be likely candidates.

2. Between the Miocene period and the subsequent

Plio-Pleistocene there is a four to five million year gap in the record of hominoid fossils, but biochemical evidence suggests that this is the time during which the human lineage separated from the African apes.

3. From the period around four million years ago, paleontologists have found a number of fossils in Africa that can be placed squarely on the human family tree: creatures that walked upright on two legs and had ape-sized brains and distinctive teeth—members of the genus *Australopithecus.*

4. The first fossils that can definitely be placed in the human genus *Homo* have been found in African sediments roughly two million years old; early *Homo* resembled contemporary Australopithecines in many ways but had a distinctly larger brain.

5. By one million years ago Australopithecines are no longer present in the fossil record, and the only surviving human-like creature was *Homo erectus,* a larger-brained descendent of the early *Homo,* fossilized in sediments throughout the Old World tropics and lower temperate latitudes.

6. For the next million years the human lineage spread throughout the Old World and slowly evolved larger brains until, by 150,000-100,000 years ago, human ancestors resembled extremely robust and sturdy versions of modern humans, with brains as large as ours today. They are referred to as "archaic" *Homo sapiens,* or neanderthals.

7. After 125,000 years ago, human populations underwent a fairly swift biological shift that can be called the "loss of robusticity" transition. Human skeletons became much less muscular, with more slender limb bones; subtle changes also occurred in pelvic shape and the boney architecture of the skull. Current genetic and fossil evidence [46,47] suggests that this transition from archaic to modern *Homo sapiens* first took place in Africa, and that fully modern human populations spread from Africa to other parts of the world. After 30,000 years ago, all human populations were fully modern.

For the oldest of these stages the fossil bones themselves provide the only evidence of diet, and this kind of evidence is also available for the entire prehistoric re-

cord.* Fossil jaws and teeth, in particular, can be examined from the perspective of comparative studies of the biomechanics of jaw function and the relationships between diet and dental anatomy in primates. In contrast to the Miocene hominoids that had dental patterns basically similar to those of living apes [18,19], the Australopithecines had a distinct "megadont" adaptation of very large, thickly-enameled cheek teeth and massive chewing musculature relative to their body size [20]. Such dental apparatus is apparently suited to heavily masticated diets, including foods that require either strong crushing or long periods of sustained chewing [21,22]. The later Australopithecines that branched off the human lineage, such as *A. robustus,* developed these characters to an extreme, having only tiny front teeth, but sporting huge molars and premolars with thickly enameled crowns, often worn flat. Even young juvenile robust Australopithecines show heavy wear on their huge milk molars [21].

Early specimens of *Homo,* on the other hand, have relatively larger incisors and much smaller cheek teeth than the robust Australopithecines, and the subsequent species *Homo erectus* and *H. sapiens* continue the trend of allometrically reduced post-canine dentition [20]. This suggests that *Homo* had shifted to a diet of foods requiring less oral preparation than the foods of Australopithecines—perhaps foods that were less fibrous, or foods that were prepared, before ingestion, by the use of fire (eg, singed to remove tough coats or cooked) or other technology (eg, shredded or pounded).

New studies of the microscopic wear patterns on the teeth of these fossils are beginning to provide additional evidence of dietary habits. Walker [20] and others have found that the teeth of Australopithecines and early *Homo* show no signs of the bone-chewing or grass-eating that produce distinctive wear patterns on the teeth of other animals; instead these fossils show wear patterns that most resemble wear on the teeth of largely frugivorous primates, like the chimpanzee. The one specimen of *Homo erectus* so far examined has unusual (for a primate) microscopic scratches on its molars that may have been caused by eating roots or other foods covered with sand grains from the soil.

Archaeologists seek telltale bits of ancient equipment used in the food quest and have collected a record of

---

* In addition to clues from the morphology and biomechanical properties of fossil bones, under favorable circumstances the composition of ancient bones can give some indication of what the animal ate. For instance, the ratio of plant food to meat in the diet can be reflected in the relative proportion of strontium in that individual's bones. Similarly, eating certain foods like maize or legumes gives a distinctive isotopic composition to the bones of the consumer (eg, stable carbon and nitrogen isotopes). Techniques to determine the trace element and isotopic composition of ancient bones as an indicator of ancient diets have been most successfully applied to bones from recent time periods, to trace the development of agriculture, for instance [43,44]. However, researchers are now also planning to analyze the composition of fossil bones from our earliest ancestors as well [45].

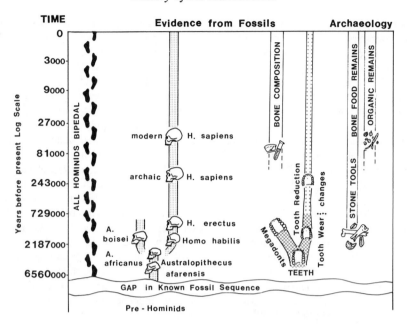

Figure 4.2 Time-line of the available evidence used to infer prehistoric diet: the fossil record and the archaeological record.

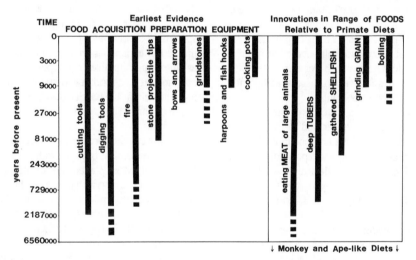

Figure 4.3 Stages in the history of human diet: innovations in food acquisition and preparation equipment, and innovations in dietary range.

changing subsistence technology that spans about two million years. In many cases they have also found the refuse from ancient meals associated with tools. Figure 3 summarizes features of this long record.

The earliest technology we have evidence for is associated with *Homo habilis*. Simple, but effective, sharp-edged stone flakes were used as cutting tools for meat and plant foods. This is evident from diagnostic microwear "polish" preserved on the tool edges [23]. Stones were also used as hammers, or pounders. Broken ani-

mal limb bones that were used as digging implements have been found at archaeological sites at Olduvai Gorge, Tanzania, and at Swartkrans, in southern Africa [24,25], suggesting that hominids were already digging up underground bulbs or tubers. Wooden digging implements were probably in more general use than bone ones, but because wood does not survive as well as bone, we lack direct evidence of this.

By modern standards, the pace of technological development during most of the Pleistocene was very slow [26,27], and many of the tools and devices used to acquire or process foods first appear in the archaeological record only very recently, after the emergence of modern *Homo sapiens.* Examples of very recent technological inventions include bows and arrows, and spear throwers (atlatl); stone sickles used to harvest cereals; grindstones, commonly used to grind seeds; and storage and cooking devices such as pottery or ovens.

Faunal and floral remains found in association with tools at archaeological sites can also be an important source of information about prehistoric human diets. For instance, many of the bones of large ungulates found at the early archaeological sites in east Africa have cut marks on them inflicted by stone tools, which were used to slice off meat [28,29]. Cut marks provide additional evidence that by two million years ago eating meat from large animals was a part of ancestral human subsistence to a degree unknown in any living ape or monkey, although it is still unclear whether animals were actually hunted during this early time period or whether meat was obtained by scavenging [30,31,32,48].

The use of fire is not firmly documented in the archaeological record until 500,000 years ago, although it may go back some 1,400,000 years. Because cooking can significantly alter the palatability and toxicity of foods, especially plant foods, prehistoric human diets before the use of fire could well have been more restricted than modern hunter-gatherer diets [33]. For example, many legumes could not be used as a major food source until detoxified by cooking.

The earliest archaeological remains of intensive shellfish and fish consumption are found in two 100,000-year-old sites, one in the north and one in the south of Africa [34]. Aquatic foods were most probably not eaten much before this period, but shellfish and fish have since become dietary staples in many parts of the world. Stretches of coast in many areas of North America, Australia, and Africa, for instance, are still mounded with the shellfish middens left at recent archaeological sites. While the shells are conspicuous, fish were often the main food eaten at these sites. Catching fish in quantity requires sophisticated tools, such as nets, hooks and lines, or harpoons, that were only invented during the last 20,000 years.

It is difficult to document the prehistoric consumption of plant foods. Human ancestors undoubtedly ate ripe fruits and some greens, just as most humans and nonhuman primates do today, but it is important to determine at what point starches came to be such a distinctive staple in human diets. At any time human ancestors could have easily gathered shallow bulbs and corms low in starches, as baboons do with paws alone in many parts of Africa [35,36]. Digging tools found at early sites [25] suggest that by two million years ago deeper underground foods had become accessible to prehistoric human populations as well, but it is still uncertain at what point in prehistory human populations began to systematically harvest the vast, and probably starchy, stores of deeply buried tubers common in dry habitats that sustain many hunter-gatherer populations today.

Documenting the consumption of seeds is slightly easier. While Jolly [37] suggested that seed-eating may have been a very early adaptation in the course of human dietary history, no evidence of eating hard seeds is present on any of the early fossil teeth so far examined [22]. It is also not known whether prehistoric populations could have gotten much nutritional benefit from eating any amount of raw cereal grains. The first archaeological indications of seedy prehistoric diets come with the appearance of equipment roughly 20,000 years ago—grindstones to process seeds, and stone "sickle blades" used to harvest grasses—followed by wild cereal grains themselves preserved at archaeological sites, all very late in prehistory relative to long-term dietary adaptations.

In many parts of the world the archaeological record documents significant changes in prehistoric human diets that occurred at about the same time that seeds became staples. These changes to so-called "broad-spectrum" subsistence systems 20,000 years ago were marked by expanding breadth of hunter-gatherer diets as different groups used new types of technology to procure and process food. It was in such settings that farming and animal husbandry developed in a number of different parts of the world shortly after 10,000 years ago [6].

The advent and spread of food production, especially farming economies, brought with it rapid changes for human diet. Most plants were domesticated for their seeds or roots, and so with widespread farming came the strong human dependence on dependable starch staples such as cereals and tubers, as well as legumes. Food production also allowed people to focus more intensively on the production and consumption of a few staples, for better or for worse, losing much of the diet breadth that is characteristic of most hunter-gatherers that anthropologists have observed. The shift to farming had a variety of profound interlinking effects. Some of the changes are ones that we still feel positive about: the adoption of more settled ways of life; living in sturdy houses; having more possessions and wealth; forming the large-scale cooperative societies that we associate with civilization. But not all changes were for the better. In some instances, overcrowding and unbalanced, monotonous diets produce disease and malnutrition levels among food producers that are unknown among hunter-gatherer populations [38,39].

Table 4.2 Tracing feeding patterns back from the present

Stage	Years ago	Food Acquisition Technology and Its Implications	Notes
IV	0	Development of bulk food transport, global trade networks. Use of fossil fuels. Processed, packaged foods.	Great diversity in feeding patterns, both within and between societies. Diverse diet for both rich and poor.
III	2000	Beginning of farming and its spread. Cereal, root and legume crops become staple foods for many societies	Starch staples become common — for many individuals, most nourishment is derived from just a few kinds of crops.
II	10,000	Development of cooking pots. Development of seed- and grain-grinding equipment. Development of equipment for getting more animal foods (nets, traps, bows, arrows, etc.).	Most populations were sustained by a wide variety of plant and animal foods.
I	30,000	Control and use of fire. Gathering and hunting in cooperating groups. Development of carrying devices (bags, baskets, trays). Development of digging tools, spears, knives.	Dietary patterns in this period are poorly understood. They probably include more meat than any primate eats today, yet were dominated mainly by plant foods. Powerful chewing was important.
0	2,000,000	Primate-like condition, probably with fruit and leaves as the predominate foods.	Individuals move to where food is, then feed and move on.

HUMAN DIET, PAST AND PRESENT

Table 2 summarizes the main stages in food acquisition and diet that probably characterized the human past, beginning with a period over two million years ago during which our ancestors had feeding patterns probably similar to those of several primates today. While the increasing use of technology in food acquisition through time paces dietary changes, the manner in which dietary patterns were causally linked to technological developments is still imperfectly understood. Still, clear changes in human diets can be traced over the last two million years, with the rate of change strongly accelerating in the very recent past with the development of food production.

Ultimately, the starting point for the trajectory of change must have been a fiber-rich fruit and leaf diet, as is commonly eaten by monkey and apes. The first steps away from this, taken by our ancestors two or three million years ago, added meat, and probably (starchy?) tubers, to the diet. Then for a very long time human ancestors undoubtedly ate varied, fiber-rich diets that combined proportions of starches, meats, nuts, fruits, and some leaves. Some of the genetically controlled physiological differences between modern humans and apes [40,41,4] are, in fact, probably linked to the long-term history of such distinct, human dietary patterns.

Such varied, diverse diets remain characteristic of most human groups today [49]. However, since the invention of agriculture, and since the soaring rise of technology, some humans have begun to eat different, less-balanced diets. Many of the world's poor are obliged by circumstance to eat mainly starch, while in cities the affluent populations can choose novel gastronomic patterns impossible for our ancestors, such as fiber-free diets or fat-rich diets coupled with inactive lifestyles. With these extremes, in spite of human physiological flexibility, health problems may arise that are linked to eating patterns unique in the long-term history of human diets [42]. Given this situation, archaeologists, anthropologists, and zoologists cannot say "this is what one should eat," but they can show which modern diets are most different from the range of patterns that were normal in the long-term past.

REFERENCES

1. Gaulin SJC, Konner M. On the natural diet of primates, including humans. In Wurtman RJ, Wurtman JJ, eds. Nutrition and the brain, vol 1. New York: Raven Press, 1977: 1-86.
2. Mann AE. Diet and human evolution. In Harding RSO, Teleki G, eds. Omnivorous primates. New York: Columbia University Press, 1981: 10-37.
3. Young VR, Scrimshaw NA. Genetic and biological variability in human nutrient requirements. Am J Clin Nutr, 1979; 32:486-500.
4. Walcher DN, Kretchmer N, eds. Food, nutrition and evolution: Food as an environmental factor in the genesis of human variability. New York: Masson Pub, 1981.
5. Hayden B. Subsistence and ecological adaptations of modern hunter-gatherers. In Harding RSO, Teleki G, eds. Omnivorous primates. New York: Columbia UP, 1981: 344-421.
6. Harris DR. The prehistory of human subsistence: a speculative outline. In Walcher DN, Kretchmer N, eds. Food, nutrition and evolution. New York: Masson Pub, 1981: 15-35.
7. Haas JD, Harrison GG. Nutritional anthropology and biological adaptation. Annual Review of Anthroplogy, 1977; 6:69-101.
8. Fleuret A. The role of wild forage plants in the diet; a case study from Lushoto, Tanzania. Ecology of Food and Nutrition, 1979; 8:87-93.
9. Kies C, Fox HM. Inter-relationships of leucine with lysine, tryptophan, and niacine as they influence the protein value of cereal grains for humans. Cereal Chem, 1972; 49:223.
10. Speth J, Spielman KA. Energy source, protein metabolism, and hunter-gatherer subsistence strategies. Journal of Anthropological Arch, 1983; 2:1-31.
11. Allen CE, Mackey MA. Compositional characteristics and the potential for change in foods of animal origin. In Beitx DC, Hansen RG, eds. Animal products in human nutrition. New York: Academic Press, 1982: 199-224.
12. Ledger HP. Body composition as a basis for a comparative study of some East African mammals. Symp Sool Soc Lond, 1968; 21:289-310.
13. Harris RS. Effects of agricultural practices on foods of plant origin. In Harris RS, Karmas E, eds. Nutritional evaluation of food processing. Westport Connecticut: Avi, 1975: 33-57.
14. Van Soest PJ. Some physical characteristics of dietary fibres and their influence on the mocrobial ecology of the human colon. Proc Nutr Soc. 1984; 43:25-33.
15. Wilmsen EN. Seasonal effects of dietary intake on Kalahari San. Fed Proc, 1978; 37:65-72.
16. Stini WA. Body composition and nutrient reserves in evolutionary perspective. In Walcher DN, Kretchmer N, eds. Food, nutrition and evolution. New York: Masson, 1981: 107-20.
17. Harding RSO, Teleki G, eds. Omnivorous primates: Gathering and hunting in human evolution. New York: Columbia UP,1981:
18. Kay RF. Diets of early Miocene African hominoids. Nature, 1977; 268(5621):628-30.
19. Kay RF. The nut-crackers - a new theory of the adaptations of the Ramapithecinae. American Journal of Physical Anthropology, 1981; 55:141-51.
20. Walker A. Diet and teeth: dietary hypotheses and human evolution. Phil Trans Roy Soc Lond, 1981; B 292:57-64.
21. Grine, FE. Trophic differences between 'gracile' and 'robust' Australopithecines: a scanning electron microscope analysis of occlusal events. So Afr J Sci, 1981; 77:203-30.
22. McHenry H. Relative cheek tooth size in Australopithecus. AJPA, 1984; 64(3):297-306.
23. Keeley LH, Toth N. Microwear polishes on early stone tools from Koobi Fora, Kenya. Nature, 1981; 293:464-5.
24. Leakey MD. Olduvai Gorge, vol 3. Cambridge: University Press, 1971:
25. Brain CK. The Swartkrans site: stratigraphy of the fossil hominids and a reconstruction of the environment of early Homo. In Proc ler Congres Int Paleontologie Humaine, vol 2: L'Homo erectus et la place de l'homme de Tautavel parmi les hominides fossiles. Paris: CNRS, 1982: 676-706.
26. Isaac GLI. Chronology and the tempo of cultural change in the Pleistocene. In Bishop WW, Miller J, eds. Calibration of hominid evoluation. Edinburgh: Scottish Academic Press: 381-430.
27. Isaac GLI. Aspects of human evolution. In Bendall DA, ed. Evolution from molecules to men. Cambridge: University Press, 1983: 509-43.
28. Bunn HT. Archaeological evidence for meat-eating by Pleio-Pleistocene hominids from Koobi Fora dn Olduvai Gorge. Nature, 1981; 291:574-7.
29. Potts R, Shipman P. Cutmarks made by stone tools on bones from Olduvai Gorge, Tanzania. Nature, 1981; 291:577-80.
30. Isaac GLI, Crader D. To what extent were early hominids carnivorous?: An archaeological perspective. In Harding RSO, Teleki G, eds. Omnivorous primates. New York: Columbia UP, 1981: 37-103.
31. Isaac GL. Bones in contention. In Clutton-Brock J, Grigson C, eds. Animals and archaeology, vol 1: Hunters and their prey. BAR Int, Series 163, 1983: 3-20.
32. Shipman P, Rose J. Early hominid hunting, butchering and carcass-processing behaviors: approaches to the fossil record. J Anthrop Arch, 1983; 2:57-98.
33. Stahl A. Hominid dietary selection before fire. Curr Anthrop, 1984; 25(2):151-68.
34. Clark JD. The cultures of the Middle Palaeolithic/Middle Stone Age. In Clark JD, ed. Cambridge history of Africa, vol 1: From the earliest times to c.500

BC. Cambridge: University Press, 1982: 248-341.

35. Hamilton III WJ, Buskirk RE, Buskirk WH. Omnivory and utilization of food resources by Chacma baboon, *Papio ursinus.* Am Nat, 1978; 112(987):911-24.

36. Post DG. Feeding behavior of yellow baboon (*Papio cynecephalus*) in the Amboseli National Park, Kenya. Int J Primatol, 1982; 3(4):403-30.

37. Jolly CJ. The seed-eaters: a new model of hominid differentiation based on a baboon analogy. Man, 1970; 5/1:2-26.

38. Cassidy CM. Nutrition and health in agriculturalists and hunter-gatherers: a case study of two prehistoric populations. In Jerome RF, Pelto GH, eds. Nutritional anthropology, contemporary approaches to diet and culture. Pleasantville, NY: Redgrave, 1980: 117-45.

39. Cohen MN, Armelagos GJ, eds. Paleopathology at the Origins of Agriculture. New York: Academic Press, 1984.

40. Chivers DJ, Hladik CM. Morphology of the gastrointestinal tract in primates: comparisons with other mammals in relation to diet. J Morph, 19;80; 166:337-86.

41. Sibley RM. Strategies of digestion and defecation. In Townshead CR, Catlaw P, eds. Physiological ecology: an evolutionary approach to resource use. Oxford: Blackwell Sci Publ, 1981: 109-39.

42. Eaton SB, Konner M. Paleolithic nutrition, a consideration of its nature and current implications. New Engl J Med, 1985; 312(5):283-9.

43. Van Der Merwe NJ. Carbon isotopes, photosynthesis, and archaeology. American Scientist, 1982; 70:596-606.

44. Schoeninger MJ: Diet and the evolution of modern human form in the Middle East. AJPA, 1982; 58:37-52.

45. Ambrose SH, DeNiro MJ. Reconstruction of African human diet using bone collagen carbon and nitrogen isotope ratios. Nature, 1986; 319:321-324.

46. Cann RL, Stoneking M, Wilson AC. Mitochrondrial DNA and human evolution. Nature, 1987; 325:31-36.

47. Rightmire, GP. *Homo sapiens* in sub-Saharan Africa. In Smith RH, Spencer F, eds. The origins of modern humans. New York: Alan Liss, 1984; 294-325.

48. Blumenschine, R. Characteristics of an early hominid scavenging niche. Current Anthropol. in press; 28(4).

49. Messer E. Anthropological perspectives on diet. Ann Rev Anthropol, 1984; 13:205-49.

Chapter 5

Animal Models of Eating Disorders: Hypothalamic Function

Timothy Schallert

INTRODUCTION

One of the oldest and most investigated models of food intake disorders is the hyperphagia response to electrical stimulation of the lateral hypothalamic area (ESLH) in sated animals [1]. For decades researchers have been concerned with the possibility that under natural conditions, individual differences in the level of activity of neurons in the LH could override other mechanisms of satiety and contribute significantly to daily food intake and body weight. Particularly attractive was the implication that ESLH might yield a rough approximation of some relatively high level of activity present in the LH of people who eat to excess. Based on the animal research, some clinicians have gone so far as to use ESLH to locate and destroy "feeding sites" in obese humans [2].

ESLH has been the focus of controversy for the last twenty years. The purpose of this chapter is to summarize the background leading up to this controversy, to review the key issues critically, and to outline the current status of ESLH as an animal analog of bulimic behavior.

HISTORICAL BACKGROUND

In 1943, Brugger [3] found that macroelectrode stimulation of the perifornical area of the LH elicited intense eating of both edible and inedible objects in most cats he tested, and in two of them the stimulation resulted in consumption of edible substances exclusively. In 1949 Hess [4] reported gnawing, biting, and eating responses to ESLH, but it was not until Anand and Brobeck reported that aphagia resulted from the destruction of this same area in rats and cats [5] that reference to a LH center for feeding became prevalent.

In the middle 1950s, Larsson [6], Smith [7], and Miller [8] reported that ESLH of specific points reliably initiated either feeding or drinking in nondeprived animals, and that interruption of the ESLH resulted in a cessation of the stimulation-induced responses. These investigators suggested that the elicited behaviors genuinely reflected the triggering of distinct neural systems or motivational states normally active during deprivation-induced behaviors. Miller and his collaborators [9,10] spent the next decade conducting research that they believed strongly supported this hypothesis. They reported that with the onset of electrical current, mildly thirsty (but not hungry) rats, which were known to be stimulation-induced eaters, would not only actively seek edible objects but would also terminate drinking behavior to engage in food-seeking and eventually feeding behavior. Furthermore, the animals receiving ESLH learned new responses or emitted responses, which had been previously reinforced with food, to gain access to the appropriate goal object, a finding confirmed by others [11].

Miller was concerned that a nonspecific gnawing reflex was being aroused and that the animals might have been responding merely because it would be more reinforcing to chew on a solid substance rather than on nothing at all. However, he showed that water-deprived rats switched from drinking water to lapping milk with ESLH onset, suggesting to him that hunger was the predominant incentive [9]. Miller also predicted that the offset of the current might function as a reward, just as in conventional appetitive behaviors [9]. In support of this prediction, he found that sated rats learned to press a bar or to choose that arm of a T-maze that turned off the current stimulating an LH eating site.

The strength of the motivation to engage in a feeding response to ESLH was indicated by studies showing that rats ate to the point of obesity with frequent applications of the electrical stimulus [12], and tolerated shock [13] or quinine additives [14] to gain access to food during the stimulation.

Misher and Brooks [15] found that stimulation of LH sites that supported stimulation-induced eating also increased the output of gastric acid. This was expected, because gastric activation was known to increase during food deprivation. Stimulation at sites not arousing well-defined feeding responses did not alter gastric acidity. Later, others [16,17] reported that the frequency of stomach contractions increased during and immediately following stimulation of positive but not negative feeding sites.

The well-known antiappetite drug, d-amphetamine, raised the current threshold for stimulation of eating [9,18]. Moreover, free, or intragastric, feeding inhibited stimulation-induced eating, whereas drinking, or intragastric watering, inhibited only stimulation-induced drinking [19]. Thus, ESLH-induced behaviors appeared to be affected appropriately by factors known to influence deprivation-induced behaviors. By 1970, nearly all investigators enthusiastically supported the compelling view that stimulation-induced behaviors reflected the activation of neural system specific to deprivation-induced feeding behaviors [20-22].

CONTROVERSIES

This view, commonly called the "specificity" interpretation of ESLH [23], was challenged aggressively by Valenstein et al [24]. After reviewing the literature pertaining to stimulation-induced behavior and compiling histological results from their own laboratory, they noted that there was extensive overlap of hypothalamic sites at which stimulation yielded widely divergent behaviors [24-26]. They proposed that this lack of anatomical specificity had gone undiscovered because researchers had commonly allowed animals in their experiments to experience a preferred goal object throughout all training sessions, thereby precluding the emergence of less-preferred behaviors.

In an influential series of experiments, they showed that initial performance of either eating, gnawing, or drinking behaviors elicited by ESLH was, in most cases, subject to change without manipulation of stimulation parameters [27]. For example, stimulation-induced eaters might gradually switch to drinking following the removal of food, and in subsequent competition tests, the new behavior (drinking) would be displayed as readily and as vigorously as eating. In fact, when the initial goal object was returned, each of the two stimulation-induced behavior patterns were displayed in most instances. It appeared, then, that behaviors elicited by ESLH were considerably more plastic than was generally accepted and that no circumscribed area of the rat hypothalamus could be identified with electrically-elicited eating or drinking behaviors.

Although the results of Valenstein and his co-workers [24] were consistent with viewing the hypothalamic stimulation as nonspecific in action, the potential contribution of separate but spatially intertwined LH systems could not be ruled out [28,29]. Mogenson and Morgan, even before the work of Valenstein et al [27] conducted similar experiments but had concluded that the LH contained interdigitated and partially overlapping integrative-control systems for both feeding and drinking [30,31; see also 93]. When Mogenson found that the delivery of an electrical stimulus could elicit a single behavior in pretests but a second behavior following various environmental manipulations, he merely inferred that the neural circuit of the first behavior was being influenced to a greater degree initially by the stimulation, after which the influence somehow changed to equally affect the neural circuit of both behaviors. He suggested that the opportunity to engage in a second behavior could directly affect the sensitivity of the LH through an impingement of corresponding peripheral afferents on a select neural system. Indeed, there had been many examples in the literature of studies showing changes in the threshold for stimulation-induced feeding, drinking, or reinforcement brought about by such peripheral influences as deprivation, stomach overloading, appetite whetting, or drugs [9,19,30,32,33].

Wise [34] also countered with the objection that circuits for feeding and drinking appeared to have different elicitation thresholds even before any modification attempts, and that the prolonged stimulation procedure used by Valenstein et al [27] perhaps involved the gradual increase in sensitivity of a system whose intermeshed fibers were initially silent to the original stimulation. He argued that had Valenstein et al [27] varied their current levels to begin with, they might have produced switching of behaviors without the further training trials.

The conclusion of Wise [34] was based primarily on the finding that a simple altering of the intensity of ESLH caused a complete behavior replacement. However, Valenstein and his colleagues [35-37] pointed out that Wise had confounded the effects of shifting stimulation intensity with those of removing the initially favored object in this procedure. They found that if the rats were subjected to varying intensities of stimulation during competition trials, a nonpreferred behavior would not be elicited unless the originally selected goal object was removed. Moreover, the new behavior would then only gradually emerge, a result which Valenstein and his colleagues saw as incompatible with the hypothesis that two separate drives were simultaneously competing for satisfaction during ESLH. Furthermore, repeated stimulation in the absence of any goal object would not subsequently produce a change in behavioral tendency [36].

Wise [38] then amended his original viewpoint. Incrementing movable electrodes in 0.113-mm steps, he showed that once a particular behavior from a certain testing site was established in a given rat, any threshold changes brought about by continued stimulation were usually transferred to a range of other positive sites discovered in that animal. A carryover of threshold to remote sites indicated that the neural changes underlying this effect were not peculiar to a single LH locus, as his earlier hypothesis [34] required. Although this confirmed the position of Valenstein et al [24] that frequent stimulation produces some kind of developing tendency in an animal to respond in a particular way, rather than a change in the threshold of neural tissues surrounding the electrode tips, Wise nevertheless continued to view ESLH and food deprivation as essentially similar [39]

Valenstein et al [24] suggested that repeated discharging of a behavior in response to electrical stimulation gradually provides the reinforcement to continue the behavior or to engage in instrumental tasks that are rewarded by the opportunity to elicit the behavior. Any modification of the behavior was seen as related to the reinforcement derived from engaging in a different prepotent behavior.

This assumption of behavior-generated reinforcement was the cornerstone of Valenstein's position from the beginning, and was essential to the "nonspecificity" view of ESLH. Cagguila [40] rejected this assumption and favored the specificity hypothesis, because he found that the first behavior to be reliably evoked by the stimulation was not always the first one tested. However, because Valenstein et al believed that the stimulation-related reinforcing feedback only gradually affected behavior, they did not insist that the preferred ESLH- induced response be established immediately.

The nonspecificity hypothesis did not explain the factors that influenced the occurrence of the initially evoked behavior or the variables that differentially prejudiced the evocation of one of two equally reinforced responses. Valenstein and his colleagues [24,41] could not influence the induction of a particular behavior by imparting selective deprivation conditions on an animal before the first testing experience. They also could not affect the relative frequency of one established stimulation- induced behavior over another in competition testing merely by providing previous experience in a test chamber distinctly associated with the opportunity to display that behavior without ESLH. Valenstein and his colleagues [25,41] briefly noted that the physical proximity of the food or water to the animal at the moment of stimulation seemed to be important in determining which behavior would be exhibited. However, this interpretation was made in the absence of systematic comparisons between the stimulation-induced animals (which were thought by most investigators to resemble hungry/thirsty animals [42]) and animals that were simultaneously deprived of both food and water. It seems likely that if food- plus water-deprived rats had been placed in an environment where a disproportionate balance of food or water existed, response probabilities even without ESLH would have been influenced by physical proximity to the goal object.

Mogenson [30] and Milgram et al [43] were able to find a small percentage of rats whose initial behavioral preference could not be switched despite many modification sessions, a finding to which Valenstein et al [24,27] also admitted. Valenstein et al emphasized the rarity of this effect, while Mogenson and Milgram et al used this finding to marshal support for stimulation specificity. Valenstein et al [24] further argued that these rare cases of specificity may have occurred because unscored behaviors such as tail preening sometimes developed during the modification sessions and thus precluded the possible emergence of target behaviors.

Some investigators tried to limit the modifiability of behavioral tendency through the use of small-diameter electrodes. Miller [44] expected to obtain greater specificity with the smaller electrodes, but instead found it extremely difficult to elicit any observable behaviors at all. According to Valenstein et al [24] with smaller electrodes, the likelihood of obtaining a specific stimulus-bound behavior was greatly decreased; but if a response was elicited, a second response could be obtained. Others [45,46] did observe some apparently static behaviors by reducing the surface area of the electrode tips. The anatomical correlates compared quite favorably to the extensive maps of Olds et al [47] who used even smaller electrodes and low current levels but unfortuately made no attempt to modify the behaviors elicited.

The largest effort to discredit the specificity view included a series of studies in search of dissimilarities between behavior elicited by ESLH and behavior caused by deprivation of food or water. For example, Valenstein and his colleagues found that rats displaying stimulation-bound eating of one kind of food would not readily switch to another food when the first food was removed, though the second was the familiar home cage chow [48]. They and many others [49] reasoned that food-deprived rats should eat the chow in this situation. In the same study [48] the rats would not readily switch from eating standard laboratory pellets to eating powdered chow after removal of the pellets. Again, "these animals certainly did not behave like hungry animals" [50]. However, it was never clear whether the behavior of these stimulation-induced eaters was to be compared to severely food-deprived, to mildly food-deprived or, according to an overlapping systems hypothesis, to food-and-water deprived animals.

There were two features in the study just described that should have weakened its impact in the literature. First, a palatable food had been replaced by less-preferred laboratory pellets in the first situation, and in the second situation, the texture of familiar pellets was changed to powder. Second, water was always available during the competition trials. It should not have been surprising that most of the animals immediately, and all of them eventually, switched to drinking when the preferred food substance was removed. This would be expected of food-and-water deprived animals as well.

In another paper, it was reported that sated rats, which were pretrained under water deprivation to drink from both a water dish and a water bottle and were subsequently exposed to the water bottle alone during ESLH, would not always switch to drinking from the water dish when the bottle was removed during later stimulation tests [51]. Again, however, Valenstein et al failed to emphasize that food was available and that large quantities of it were usually ingested during these later tests. It remained possible that a feeding system had been stimulated simultaneously with a drinking system.

It was further shown that stimulation-induced drinkers preferred a 30% glucose solution to water in a two-choice situation, while the reverse was true for the same animals when they were water deprived [51,52]. However, these animals were called "stimulus-bound drinkers" rather than "stimulus-bound eaters/drinkers," which others found inappropriate. In fact, rats deprived of food alone or of both food and water preferred a sweet solution to water [39,53]. Moreover the concentration of sucrose required to maintain a consistent feeding bout was found to be related to pulse frequency of ESLH in much the same way as it was known to be related to the level of food deprivation [54,55].

Valenstein and Phillips [56] found that rats reared from birth on a liquid diet alone later displayed stimulus-bound eating of solid food pellets when mature but would not display stimulus-bound eating of the familiar liquid diet despite multiple stimulation sessions in the absence of any other goal objects. Although this was taken as evidence that ESLH could produce a behavior that was topographically similar to, yet fundamentally different from, a deprivation-induced behavior, in some respects the results of this particular study were quite puzzling. One might have asked, for example, why the rats in this study ignored the familiar liquid diet during ESLH when earlier studies describing stimulus-bound behavior had indicated clearly that rats would ingest a variety of liquid foods in response to electrical stimulation [9,12,14,33,44,57].

Moreover, because many researchers had left the impression that it was relatively easy to compel animals to switch from eating to drinking during ESLH [24,27,30,38], there remained the question of why the rats in this study neither drank water nor ate the liquid food when the solid pellets were removed. It may have been relevant that the screening procedure of Valenstein and Phillips required that all animals not displaying stimulation-induced eating of food pellets be discarded even before beginning testing with the liquid diet. It was possible that in doing so they had discarded animals that would have consumed the liquid diet during test sessions, had they been given the opportunity.

Valenstein and his colleagues [24,50,58,59] often concluded that it seemed unnecessary to assume that ESLH reflects the neural substrate for specific regulatory behaviors. They proposed that their nonspecificity hypothesis facilitated a more realistic discussion of stimulation-induced behavior. Because ESLH sometimes produced gnawing, grooming, object carrying, food shuffling, tail preening, and general activity, they argued that it was therefore cumbersome to handle the view that the LH contained neural components directly associated with the motivation to perform all of these behaviors [24]. Likewise, the apparent paradox that animals would turn on stimulation of that same electrode site that elicited hunger or thirst did not demand the additional postulation of an overlapping reinforcement system [9,60], if one simply assumed that ESLH did not activate hunger or thirst. However, Bergquist [61] felt strongly the opposite way. He found it difficult to conceive of what kind of single organismic state or mood could possibly be commonly related to such a diverse list of behaviors without referring to distinct overlapping systems. Again, there could be no consensus without additional data.

In a further elaboration of his belief that misinterpretations occurred with the view that stimulation-induced behaviors were comparable to the deprivation-induced behaviors, Valenstein [50,58,62] began to emphasize that the behaviors executed by hypothalamically stimulated rats were pre-formed and species- specific. Thus, Valenstein [58] stated that many of the behaviors evoked by hypothalamic stimulation could be better understood by an analysis of the prepotent responses of the species. By itself, this line of reasoning also was unconvincing. However, Valenstein [50,63] went on to make the more influential argument that a variety of species-specific behaviors (including eating or drinking) could be evoked without deprivation by low (presumably stimulating) doses of pentobarbital [64] or non-injurious pain and stress [65-69]. Though this evidence was still indirect, it was important in that it served as a reminder that it was possible for ingestive behavior to emerge from recognized forms of disorganized behavioral activation. However, it had not been disputed that both specific and nonspecific sources of eating existed. Most investigators remained opposed based on the functional reputation of the hypothalamus, the lack of definitive conflicting data, and the specificity of chemical stimulation, which appeared better established than electrical stimulation [61,70,71]. Nevertheless, additional converts entered Valenstein's camp following the demonstration by Antelman and Szechman that tail pinching caused eating and gnawing in some animals [72]. Then Koob et al [73] reported that animals subjected to tail pinching learned to turn into that arm of a T- maze in which there was wood to gnaw, an effect that partially paralleled the well-known work of Coons et al with ESLH [10]. Though the analogous experiment with feeding was never conducted, these data gave Valenstein's view sufficient plausibility that even some of the ardent proponents of the specificity interpretation were no longer so certain, and the controversy seemed to stalemate.

TOWARD RESOLUTION

As noted in the previous section, the key to Valenstein's position was the idea, adapted from Glickman and Schiff [74], that the actual display of a behavior during ESLH is reinforcing, and for this reason it is repeated increasingly over subsequent stimulation sessions. For example, as an animal is permitted to eat during ESLH, the eating response gradually strengthens, because eating during activation is reinforcing. It follows that stimuli associated with eating (such as a lever or a goal box) would acquire secondary reinforcement properties (and that gastric activity would increase in anticipation of an eating reaction). A similar proposal was later expressed by Herrnstein [75] to explain the development of "displacement" or related behaviors for which the reinforcer is not obvious. Therefore, to begin to build a bridge between Valenstein's work and the traditional view of ESLH, it was necessary to study the behavior of animals *before* they had the opportunity to eat during stimulation. In all previous experiments, the behavior of stimulation-bound eaters was examined only after they were screened for eating during stimulation (and usually following extensive eating experience during ESLH).

The following experiment was conducted to address this conditioning issue directly [1]: Before any screening, rats were allowed access to familiar food-related odors (but not the food itself) through a small opening at the end of one arm of a T- shaped enclosure. A control odor unrelated to food was present at the other arm. Upon placing their snouts near either opening, the animals activated one of two photocell circuits, which recorded responses and time spent investigating each odor source. It is well known, of course, that food-deprived rats readily approach stimuli related to food [76-80]. Moreover, food odors are pleasant to food-deprived people but become neutral or unpleasant with satiety [81]. The question raised was whether the food odors would be attractive during stimulation to these animals, which had never been given the opportunity to eat during ESLH and thus would not have experienced the putative reinforcement derived from rating during ESLH.

As expected, when the rats were simply food deprived, they appeared highly attracted to the food odors, spending a large percentage of time investigating the region of the enclosure from which the odors emanated and little time at the control region. Also as expected, when the rats were not food deprived and were not subjected to ESLH, they spent little time at either end of the enclosure. However, in the critical test, when the rats received ESLH but were not food deprived, they became very active but appeared unattracted to the food odors, spending little time investigating the food odor region of the enclosure. This same stimulation induced vigorous eating in later screening tests. Only following extensive stimulation-bound feeding experience did it induce great attraction for the food odors. A control condition ruled out the possibility that ESLH excluded orientation to food odors by, for example, inducing behavior incompatible with odor- investigating responses. When animals received ESLH in the prescreening test while also food deprived, they still appeared highly attracted to the food odors.

Thus, if testing is done before stimulation-induced eating is allowed, food deprivation, but not ESLH alone, yields approach and investigation of food odors. These data are most consonant with the view that ESLH is a nondirected, but directable, activator of behavior [82,94]. Oral manipulation of materials encountered in the environment may reduce the level of cerebral activation by interrupting the long bouts of forward locomotion, rearing reactions, head movements, and postural adjustments forced on the animal by ESLH. If food, for example, is available, eating is channeled by "feedback reinforcement." Eventually with experience the condition caused by ESLH becomes difficult to distinguish from the condition caused by food deprivation (perhaps even from the animal's perspective; see 1,95).

What indication is there that various oral behaviors have a common type of deactivating effect in the brain? Vanderwolf and his colleagues [83-86] have shown in electrophysiological analyses that behavioral activation, including the type produced by ESLH in the absence of goal objects (so-called type-1 behaviors such as forward locomotion, head movements, rearing, turning, and postural adjustments), is associated with a major source of cerebral activation (a noncholinergic, possibly serotonergic, ascending input). When an animal engages in so- called type-2 behavior (including chewing, licking, grooming, or gnawing) the type-1 source of cerebral activation is inhibited. What remains, or what replaces the type-1 source, is a second source (involving a cholinergic input), which appears to be identical to that associated with complete immobility (a behavior that presumably is impossible to achieve during ESLH). This is not meant to imply that a forcibly-induced uninterrupted train of type-1 cerebral activation necessarily is aversive or that type-2 cerebral activation is reinforcing. However, as a step toward understanding stimulation-bound eating, it is important to identify neural correlates shared by the behaviors initially induced by ESLH and then to compare these with neural correlates shared by eating and other behaviors likely to emerge with chronic stimulation.

CONCLUSION

It has been difficult for many to accept the possibility that ESLH does not (at least at first) simulate neural conditions present during nutritional or hydrational deficits. This difficulty stems in part from a misunderstanding about the concept of homeostasis. A long-established working view in the field of food and fluid intake has been that behavior and physiology are tightly regulated, perhaps by some shared "homeostatic" mechanism in the brain. It was believed that eating, even excessive eating, ought to reflect a change in this mechanism. However, it is critical to realize that behavior can fluctuate relatively independent of homeostatic processes, especially those that protect the brain. Homeostasis is the label Cannon gave to Bernard's physiological processes that evolved to keep the internal environment stabilized against the many forces of nonphysiological equilibrium that would otherwise destroy the fragile cells therein [87]. Homeostasis can correct for behavioral fluctuations, but neither Bernard nor Cannon emphasized that behavior is elicited directly by deviations in the internal environment. Indeed, their point was that homeostatic mechanisms evolved to free the organism from moment-to-moment behavioral maintenance of energy or fluid balance. Obvious examples of the adaptive features of this separation include learned avoidance of a dangerous water hole, and weight regulation despite socially facilitated excessive eating. It is helpful to keep this relationship in mind when developing animal models of feeding disorders. Disorders characterized by aberrations in eating behavior should be distinguished from those in which the primary problem is related to physiological mechanisms of weight regulation [96,97]. ESLH may be a useful method for studying some forms of binge eating, because excessive eating and learning are the predominant features. Moreover, the stimulus, the environment, and the history of the animal can be precisely controlled. However, any animal model is an experimental compromise [88]. It is far from clear how well ESLH resembles some of the conditions underlying eating disorders in people [89-92,98].

REFERENCES

1. Schallert T. Reactivity to food odors during hypothalamic stimulation in rats not experienced with stimulation-induced eating. Physiol Behav, 1977; 18:1061-66.

2. Quaade F, Vaernet K, Larsson S. Stereotaxic stimulation and electrocoagulation of the lateral hypothalamus in obese humans. Acta Neurochirurgica, 1974; 30:111-7.

3. Brugger M. Fresstrieb als hypothalamisches symptom. Helv physiol pharmac acta, 1943; 1:183-98.

4. Hess WR. Das zwischenhirn: Syndrome, lokalisationen, Functionen. Basel: Schwabe, 1949.

5. Anand BK, Brobeck JR. Hypothalamic control of food intake in rats and cats. Yale J of Biol Med, 1951;

24:123-40.

6. Larsson S. On the hypothalamic organization of the nervous mechanisms regulating food intake. Acta Physiol Scand, 1955; 32:1-40.

7. Smith OA. Stimulation of lateral and medial hypothalamus and food intake in the rat. Anat Rec, 1956; 124:363-4.

8. Miller NE. Experiments on motivation; studies combining psychological, physiological, and pharmacological techniques. Science, 1957; 126:1271-8.

9. Miller NE. Some motivational effects of brain stimulation and drugs. Fed Proceed, 1960; 19:846-54.

10. Coons EE, Levak M, Miller NE. Lateral hypothalamus: Learning of food-seeking response motivated by electrical stimulation. Science, 1965; 150:1320-1.

11. Mendelson J, Chorover SL. Lateral hypothalamic stimulation in satiated rats, T-maze learning for food. Science, 1965; 149:559-61.

12. Steinbaum EA, Miller NE. Obesity from eating elicited by daily stimulation of hypothalamus. Am J Physiol, 1965; 209:1-5.

13. Morgane PJ. Distinct "feeding" and "hunger" motivating systems in the lateral hypothalamus of the rat. Science, 1961; 133:887-88.

14. Tenen SS, Miller NE. Strength of electrical stimulation of lateral hypothalamus, food deprivation, and tolerance for quinine in food. J Comp Physiol Psychol, 1964; 58:55-62.

15. Misher A, Brooks FP. Electrical stimulation of the hypothalamus and gastric secretion in the albino rat. Am J Physiol, 1966; 211:403-6.

16. Glavcheva L, Manchanda SK, Box B, Stevenson JAF. Gastric motor activity during feeding induced by stimulation of the lateral hypothalamus in the rat. Canad J Physiol Pharmacol, 1972; 50:1091-98.

17. Ball GG. Vagotomy: Effect on electrically elicited eating and self-stimulation in the lateral hypothalamus. Science, 1974; 194:484-5.

18. Stark P, Totty CW. Effects of amphetamines on eating elicited by hypothalamic stimulation. J Pharmacol Exper Ther, 1967; 158:272-8.

19. Devor MG, Wise RA, Milgram NW, Hoebel BG. Physiolgocial control of hypothalamically elicited feeding and drinking. J Comp Physiol Psychol 1970; 73:220-32.

20. Miller NE. Commentary. In Valenstein ES, ed. Brain stimulation and motivation. Glenview, Ill: Scott, Froesman, & CO, 1973.

21. Mogenson GJ. Hypothalamic limbic mechanisms in the control of water intake. In Epstein AN, Kissileff, HR, Stellar E, eds. The neuropsychology of thirst. Washington DC: VH Winston & Sons, 1973.

22. Wise RA, Erdmann E. Emotionality, hunger, and normal eating: Implications for interpretation of electrically induced behavior. Behav Biol, 1973; 8:519-31.

23. Mogenson GJ. Changing views of the role of the hypothalamus in the control of ingestive behaviors. International Symposium at Calgary (Karger, Basel), 1974: 268-293.

24. Valenstein ES, Cox VC, Kakolewski JW. Reexamination of the role of the hypothalamus in motivation. Psychol Rev, 1970; 77:16-31.

25. Valenstein ES, Cox VC, Kakolweski JW. The hypothalamus and motivated behavior. In Trapp J, ed. Reinforcement and Behavior. New York: Academic Press, 1969.

26. Cox VC, Valenstein ES. Distribution of hypothalamic sites yielding stimulus-bound behavior. Brain, Behav Evol, 1969; 2:359-76.

27. Valenstein ES, Cox VC, Kakolewski JM. Modification of motivated behavior elicited by electrical stimulation of the hypothalamus. Science, 1968; 169:1119-21.

28. Grossman SP. Eating or drinking elicited by direct adrenergic or cholinergic stimulation of hypothalamus. Science, 1960; 132:301-2.

29. Grossman SP. Role of the hypothalamus in the regulation of food and water intake. Psychol Rev, 1975, 82:200-24.

30. Mogenson GJ, Morgan CW. Effects of induced drinking on self-stimulation of the lateral hypothalamus. Exper Brain Res, 1967; 3:111-6.

31. Mogenson, GJ. Stability and modification of consummatory behavior elicited by electrical stimulation of the hypothalamus. Physiol Behav, 1971; 6:225-60.

32. Coons EE, Cruce JAF. Lateral hypothalamus: Food current intensity of maintaining self-stimulation of hunger. Science, 1968; 159:1117-9.

33. Hoebel BG. Feeding and self-stimulation. Ann New York Acad Sci, 1969; 157:758-78.

34. Wise RA. Hypothalamic motivational systems: Fixed or plastic neural circuits? Science, 1968; 162:377-79.

35. Cox VC, Valenstein ES. Effects of stimulation intensity on behavior elicited by hypothalamic stimulation. J Comp Physiol Psychol, 1969; 69:730-3.

36. Valenstein ES, Cox VC, Kakolewski JW. The hypothalamus and motivated behavior. In Tapp J, ed. Reinforcement and behavior. New York: Academic Press, 1969.

37. Valenstein ES, Cox VC, Kakolewski JW. Hypothalamic motivational systems: Fixed or plastic neural circuits? Science, 1969; 163:1084.

38. Wise RA. Individual differences in effects of hypothalamic stimulation: The role of the stimulation locus. Physiol Behav, 1971; 6:569-72.

39. Wise RA. Lateral hypothalamic electrical stimulation: Does it make animals "hungry"? Brain Res, 1974; 67:187-209.

40. Cagguila AR. Stability of behavior produced by electrical stimulation of the rat hypothalamus. Brain Behav Evol, 1969; 2:343-58.

41. Valenstein ES, Cox VC. The influence of hunger, thirst, and previous experience in the test chamber of stimulus-bound eating and drinking. J Comp Physiol Psychol, 1970; 70:189-99.

42. Hoebel BG. Feeding: Neural control of intake. Ann Rev Physiol, 1971; 33:533-59.

43. Milgram NW, Devor M, Server AC. Spontaneous changes in behaviors induced by electrical stimulation

of the lateral hypothalamus in rats. J Comp Physiol Psychol, 1971; 75:491-9.

44. Miller NE. Chemical coding of behavior in the brain. Science, 1965; 148:328-38.

45. Roberts WW. Are hypothalamic motivational mechanisms functionally and anatomically specific. Brain Behav Evol, 1969; 2:317-42.

46. Huang YH, Mogenson GJ. Neural pathways mediating drinking and feeding in rats. Exper Neurol, 1972; 37:269-86.

47. Olds J, Allan WS, Briese E. Differentiation of hypothalamic drive and reward centers. Am J Physiol, 1971; 221:368-75.

48. Valenstein ES, Cox VC, Kakolewski JW. The motivation underlying eating elicited by lateral hypothalamic stimulation. Physiol Behav, 1968; 3:969-71.

49. Watson PJ, Short MA, Hartman DF. Re-emergence of hypothalamically elicited eating following change in food. Physiol Behav, 1979; 23:663-7.

50. Valenstein ES. History of brain stimulation: Investigations into the physiology of motivation. In Valenstein ES, ed. Brain Stimulation and Motivation. Glenview, Ill: Scott, Foresman, & Co. 1973: 168.

51. Valenstein ES, Kakolewski JW, Cox VC. A comparison of stimulus-bound drinking and drinking induced by water deprivation. Commun Behav Biol, 1968; 2:227-33.

52. White SD, Wayner MJ, Cott A. Effects of intensity water deprivation, prior water ingestion, and palatability of drinking evoked by lateral hypothalamic electrical stimulation. Physiol Behav, 1970; 5:611-19.

53. Strouthes A, Volo AM, Unger T. Hunger, thirst, and their interactive effects on the rat's drinking in a saccharin-water choice. Physiol Behav, 1974; 13:153-7.

54. Grill HJ, Coons EE. The CNS weighting of external and internal factors in feeding behavior. Behav Biol, 1976; 18:563-9.

55. Booth DA. Taste reactivity in starved, ready to eat, and recently fed rats. Physiol Behav, 1972; 8:901-8.

56. Valenstein ES, Phillips AG. Stimulus-bound eating and deprivation from prior contact with food pellets. Physiol Behav, 1970; 5:279-82.

57. Hoebel BG, Teitelbaum P. Hypothalamic control of feeding and self-stimulation. Science, 1962; 135:375-7.

58. Valenstein ES. Commentary. In Valenstein ES, ed. Brain Stimulation and Motivation. Glenview, Ill: Scott, Foresman & Co, 1973.

59. Valenstein ES. Invited comment: Electrical stimulation and hypothalamic function: historical perspective. In Epstein AN, Kissileff HR, Stellar E, eds. The Neuropsychology of Thirst. Washington, DC: VH Winston & Sons, 1973.

60. LeMagnen J. Body energy balance and food intake: a neuroendocrine regulatory mechanism. Physiol Rev, 1983; 63:314-86.

61. Bergquist EH. Role of the hypothalamus in motivation: An examination of Valenstein's reexamination. Psychol Rev, 1972; 79:542-6.

62. Phillips AG, Cox VC, Kakolewski JW, Valenstein ES.

63. Valenstein ES. Behavior elicited by hypothalamic stimulation. Brain Behav Evol, 1969; 2:295-316.

64. Jacobs BL, Farel PB. Motivated behavior produced by increased arousal in the presence of goal objects. Physiol Behav, 1971; 6:473-6.

65. Barfield RJ, Sachs RD. Sexual behavior: Stimulation by painful electric shock to the skin in male rats. Science, 1968; 161:392-4.

66. Black SL, Vanderwolf CH. Thumping behavior in the rabbit. Physiol Behav, 1969; 4:445-9.

67. Cagguila AR, Eibergen R. Copulation of virgin male rats evoked by painful peripheral stimulation. J Comp Physiol Psychol, 1969; 69:414-9.

68. Siegel PS, Brantley JJ. The relationship of emotionality to the consummatory response of eating. J Exp Psychol, 1951; 42:304-6.

69. Siegel PS, Siegel HS. The effect of emotionality on the water intake of the rat. J Comp Physiol Psychol, 1949; 42:12-6.

70. Singer G, Montgomery RB. Specificity of chemical stimulation of the rat brain and other related issues in the interpretation of chemical stimulation data. Pharmacol Biochem Behav, 1973; 1:211-21.

71. Beideman LR, Goldstein R. Specificity of carbachol in the elicitation of drinking. Psychon Sci, 1970; 20:261-2.

72. Antelman SM, Szechtman H. Tail pinch induces eating in sated rats which appears to depend on nigrostriatal dopamine. Science, 1975; 189:731-3.

73. Koob GF, Fray PJ, Iversen SD. Tail-pinch stimulation: Sufficient motivation for learning. Science, 1976; 194:637-39.

74. Glickman SE, Schiff BB. A biological theory of reinforcement. Psychol Rev, 1967; 74:81-109.

75. Herrnstein RJ. The evolution of behaviorism. Amer Psychol, 1977; 32:593-603.

76. Bindra D. The interrelated mechanisms of reinforcement and motivation, and the nature of their influence on responses. In Levine DH, ed. Nebraska symposium on motivation. Lincoln: University of Nebraska Press, 1970.

77. Fantl L, Schuckman H. Lateral hypothalamus and hunger: Responses to a secondary reinforcer with and without electrical stimulation. Physiol Behav, 1957; 2:355-7.

78. Sheffield FD. New evidence on the drive-induction theory of reinforcement. In Haber RN, ed. Current research in motivation. New York: Holt, Rinehart, and Winston, 1966.

79. Tapp JT. Activity, reactivity and the behavior-directing properties of stimuli. In Tapp JT, ed. Reinforcement and behavior. New York: Academic Press, 1969.

80. Ackil JE, Weese GD, Frommer GP. Responses induced by stimuli that predict lateral hypothalamic stimulation. Physiol Psychol, 1982; 10:129-144.

81. Cabanac M. Physiological role of pleasure. Science, 1971; 173:1102-7.

82. Mittleman G, Valenstein ES. Ingestive behavior

evoked by hypothalamic stimulation and schedule-induced polydipsia are related. Science, 1984; 224:415-7.

83. Vanderwolf CH. The role of the cerebral cortex and ascending activating systems in the control of behavior. In Satinoff E, Teitelbaum P, eds. Handbook of behavioral neurobiology, vol 6. New York: Plenum, 1983.

84. Whishaw IQ, Schallert T. Hippocampal RSA (Theta), apnea, bradycardia and effects of atropine during underwater swimming in the rat. Electroenceph Clin Neurophysiol, 1977; 42:389-96.

85. Schallert T, De Ryck M, Teitelbaum P. Atropine stereotypy as a behavioral trap: A movement subsystem and electroencephalographic analysis. J Comp Physiol Psychol, 1980; 94:1-24.

86. Whishaw IQ, Bland BH, Robinson TE, Vanderwolf CH. Neuromuscular blockade: The effects on two hippocampal RSA (Theta) systems and neocortical desynchronization. Brain Res Bull, 1976; 1:573-81.

87. Schallert T, Hsiao S. Homeostasis and life. Behav Brain Sci, 1979; 2:118.

88. Schallert T, Whishaw IQ. Bilateral cutaneous stimulation of the somatosensory system in hemidecorticate rats. Behav Neurosci, 1984; 98:518-40.

89. Hudson JI, Harrison GP, Jonas JM, Yurgelun-Todd D. Family history study of anorexia nervosa and bulimia. Brit J Psychiat, 1983; 142:133-8.

90. Wurtman RJ. Nutrition: The changing scene. Lancet, 1983; 1:1145-7.

91. Herzog DB, Copeland PM. Eating disorders. New Engl J Med, 1985; 313:295-303.

92. Piran N, Kennedy S, Garfinkle PE, Owens M. Affective disturbance in eating disorders. J Nerv Ment Dis, 1985; 173:395- 400.

93. Morley JE, Levine AS. The pharmacology of eating behavior. Ann Rev Pharmacol Toxicol, 1985; 25:127-46.

94. Mittleman G, Castaneda E, Robinson TE, Valenstein ES. The propensity for nonregulatory ingestive behavior is related to differences in dopamine systems: Behavioral and biochemcial evidence. Behav Neurosci, 1986; 100:213-20.

95. Fray PJ, Robbins TW. Stress-induced eating: Rejoinder. Appetite, 1980; 1:349-53.

96. Flier JS, Cook KS, Usher P, Spiegelman OM. Severely impaired adipsin expression in genetic and acquired obesity. Science, 1987; 237:405-08.

97. Ruderman AJ. Dietary restraint: A theoretical and empirical review. Psychol Bull 1986; 99:247-62.

98. Rosenthal NE, Hefferman MM. Bulimia, carbohydrate craving, and depression: A central connection? In Wurtman RJ, Wurtman JJ, eds. Nutrition and the brain. New York: Raven Press, 1986.

Chapter 6

Adjusting Food Intake to Meet Homeostatic Demands: Implications for Anorexia Nervosa

Carl I. Thompson

INTRODUCTION

All living organisms continually monitor and adjust a multitude of internal variables in order to keep their biological processes operating at consistent and optimal levels. The 19th- century physiologist Bernard paid cogent tribute to the significance of a stable internal environment when he noted that "The constancy of the 'milieu interieur' is the condition of a free and independent existence" [1]. Early in the present century, Cannon introduced the word "homeostasis" to refer to the complex biological responses necessary to maintain a steady state in the body [2].

Food intake plays an essential role in homeostasis. Virtually all of an organism's functions ultimately depend on food, and a multitude of biological and psychological factors exert an influence on feeding and metabolic activity. These include hormonal level, body temperature, neurotransmitter activity, fluid levels, metabolic fuel reserves, past experience, psychological mood, and others. All of these factors have specific requirements for optimal function, and all of them exert some influence on food intake to achieve this end.

Under ideal conditions, the needs of different bodily functions place compatible demands on the food control system, and the consequences of food intake resulting from these demands are almost uniformly beneficial. This ideal does not always hold, however, and

homeostasis often involves compromise. In a situation where a food-deprived individual wishes to lose weight, for example, or when eating causes gastrointestinal disturbance, there is pressure both to eat and to abstain. The amount of food consumed in such cases reflects the combined effects of all feeding pressures, both positive and negative, acting on the individual at that moment, and this can be seen as an attempt to maximize overall function in accord with current needs and resources.

Anorexia nervosa is an example of a disorder in which different needs make conflicting demands on the food intake system. On the one hand, body weight drops so low that death from starvation may be imminent, and there is an urgent need for additional metabolic fuel. On the other hand, a number of powerful factors can act to inhibit feeding. Some of these inhibitory factors may be primary to anorexia nervosa, and others are a secondary consequence of starvation. Nevertheless, they all act to inhibit food consumption and weight gain.

The remainder of this chapter provides an overview of some of the factors known to exert a controlling influence on food intake, with particular reference to those that may play a role in the symptomatology of anorexia nervosa. These include osmotic pressure, body temperature, gastric emptying rate, food palatability, learned food aversions, zinc availability, and cognitive determinants. Other factors could have been included in this list, but those presented here will serve to illustrate the concept that homeostatic constraints may limit food intake, even in individuals whose body weights are critically low. Each factor is discussed in two parts: The first summarizes its role in feeding, and the second explores possible implications for anorexia nervosa.

FACTORS INFLUENCING FOOD INTAKE

Osmotic Pressure

Water is required for the metabolism of most foods, and the regulation of food and water intake are closely related. Ingestion of hypertonic foods causes the movement of extracellular fluid into the stomach, and if this shift becomes excessive, the organism protects itself from further loss by decreasing its food intake. This protective mechanism is particularly noticeable under conditions of total water deprivation, which drastically reduces eating in most species [3]. Also, concentrated foods, regardless of their caloric content, are more filling than foods with lower osmotic pressure [4]. Overhydration affects food intake in an opposite manner, so that increased eating occurs following dilution of plasma salts or excessive water loading [5].

The duodenum is particularly sensitive to changes in osmotic pressure. Hypertonic stimulation in this area reflexively triggers release of enterogastrone, a hormone that slows the rate of gastric emptying [6] and reduces hunger [7]. These actions both protect against further fluid loss.

Osmotic Pressure and Anorexia

Rapid changes in body fluid levels are typical of malnutrition [8], and anorexic patients are often severely dehydrated. The abuse of diuretics, which occurs commonly in anorexia nervosa, can by itself lower weight by as much as 10 kg [9]. Partial diabetes insipidus, leading to excessive loss of body water through the urine, is also common in anorexia nervosa [10]. To the extent that dehydration is present, anorexic patients are subject to a compensatory pressure to avoid food to protect against further fluid loss. Until re-hydration is achieved, efforts to increase food intake operate in opposition to this osmotic defense mechanism.

Body Temperature

Regulation of body temperature has a high priority for warm- blooded animals, and a variety of mechanisms ensure that temperature stays within narrow limits. During heat stress, for example, mammals may sacrifice needed water to lower their body temperatures through evaporative heat loss.

Food consumption generates a considerable amount of heat. This occurs not only because heat is released by the chemical activity of digestion, but also because feeding causes a sympathetic activation of brown fat [11]. This tissue, which is specialized for heat production, is very sensitive to alterations in nutritional state, undergoing rapid increases in weight and thermic activity after even a single meal [12]. Food is refused when body temperature is elevated, which helps to avoid additional thermal stress, and food intake increases when mammals encounter a cooler environment [13].

Several years ago Brobeck [14] formulated a "thermostatic" theory of food intake regulation, which suggested that maintenance of a stable and optimal body temperature is so important for survival that it forms an essential basis for making the decision whether or not to eat. One component of this theory is that a rise in body temperature serves as a satiety signal. Recent investigations have suggested that the thermogenesis caused by dietary activation of brown fat may be part of such a signal. Meals are terminated quickly if they generate a high respiration rate in brown fat, whereas meals that induce a lower rate of brown fat activity continue for a longer period of time [15].

Body Temperature and Anorexia

A common symptom of anorexia nervosa is decreased basal temperature. Patients complain of constant chilliness, and their extremities are often cold and blue. In one study of 100 anorexic patients, 80 had rectal temperatures of 96.6 degrees F or below, and some had temperatures as low as 93.0 degrees [16]. This reduced temperature may reflect a last-ditch effort to apportion metabolic fuel that ordinarily would be spent on heat production to other functions critical for life [17], although in extreme cases hypothermia itself becomes life-threatening for anorexics.

Normally, one would expect an unequivocal pressure to increase thermogenesis, and therefore food intake, in response to reduced body temperature. In anorexia nervosa, however, there is an impaired ability to activate heat loss mechanisms when temperature rises too far, and any heat source, internal or external, can rapidly produce hyperthermia. Wakeling and Russell [18] have reported that when one forearm is immersed in warm water, anorexic patients develop an abnormally high, and subjectively uncomfortable, elevation in central body temperature before peripheral vasodilatation begins, and even then the response progresses very slowly. This reduced ability to dissipate excess heat disappears after patients gain weight. It probably reflects an effort to conserve needed water by minimizing evaporative heat loss, because normal subjects who become dehydrated also exhibit abnormally slow vasodilatation in response to heat [19].

A rapid rise in body temperature during feeding, coupled with an impaired ability to dissipate excessive heat, may trigger a premature satiety signal in some anorexic patients. Wakeling and Russell [18] have reported that ingestion of a meal causes the temperatures of anorexic patients to quickly reach or surpass those of normal controls, whose temperatures remain constant during feeding. When otherwise-normal subjects lose weight from food deprivation, an unusually large meal is required to produce satiety, and hunger reappears rapidly. In contrast, subjects with anorexia nervosa feel full after consuming a 400-calorie lunch, and postprandial satiety persists as long, or longer, than it does in controls who eat a similar meal [20].

Gastric Emptying

Several converging lines of evidence suggest that gastric emptying rate may serve an important function in the control of food intake. Appetite typically is reduced when there is a reduction in the rate that food leaves the stomach. Thus, the anorectic drug fenfluramine, which reduces meal size and prolongs the duration of satiety [21], produces a profound inhibition of gastric emptying in rats [22]. In addition, tolerance to the gastric slowing produced by fenfluramine follows a time course that closely matches tolerance to its anorectic effects.

A number of factors can act to slow gastric emptying. One is simply the presence of hypertonic food [6,23]. This causes the release of enterogastrone, which in turn slows passage into the duodenum of any remaining stomach contents [24]. Other factors that reduce gastric clerarance rate include strenuous physical exercise [25], high environmental temperature [26], and an excessive accumulation of body fat [27].

Moderately increased gastric clearance rates are associated with increased food intake, but if the emptying rate becomes too rapid, an opposite effect occurs. This is particularly evident after damage to the vagus nerve, which causes a disorder known as the "dumping syndrome" in man. The premature emptying of food into the duodenum after vagotomy is accompanied by epigastric discomfort, early satiety, and nausea. Patients usually learn to avoid it by taking small, frequent meals [28].

Gastric Emptying and Anorexia

Recent evidence suggests that abnormal gastric clearance rates may contribute to the accelerated onset of satiety often reported by patients with anorexia nervosa. In otherwise healthy humans, low body weight tends to be associated with moderately rapid gastric clearance and an associated increase in appetite. However, the gastric clearance rates of patients with anorexia nervosa are often abnormally slow, typically requiring more than twice the usual time [29]. This disturbance may be primary to anorexic symptoms in some patients, because abnormally slow emptying rates have been reported to persist even after significant weight gain [29]. In other patients, reduced clearance rates may be secondary to dehydration[23] and strenuous exercise [25], which slow gastric emptying and are common symptoms of anorexia nervosa.

An occasional anorexic patient may exhibit a greatly accelerated rate of gastric emptying. Dubois [29] reported that one of his patients, out of a group of 15, exhibited an abnormally rapid gastric clearance, with rates in various test situations ranging from two to eight times faster than control values. This is reminiscent of the so-called "dumping syndrome" seen after vagotomy [28], and it raises the possibility that some anorexic patients may suffer from a vagal abnormality.

Food Palatability

Palatability is an important determinant of food intake, and a reduction in the sense of taste causes a corresponding reduction in appetite. Thus, gustatory deafferentation causes a decrease in both food intake and feed efficiency, and the body weights of rats that are deprived of their sense of taste will drop even when the diet remains unchanged [30].

Other things being equal, the less pleasant a food tastes, the more satiating it is. When rats are restricted to a diet that has been made unpalatable by the addition of a disliked taste, body weights may drop substantially [31], whereas a diet of highly palatable foods will elevate energy intake and induce obesity [32].

Palatability influences food intake and utilization through its effect on the "cephalic" phase of digestion. Cephalic reflexes, which are triggered by the sensory aspects of a meal, serve to ready the gastrointestinal tract to move and absorb food, prepare the viscera to metabolize and store nutrients, and provide the organism with immediate feedback about the ultimate postingestional consequences of food [33]. Included among these reflexes are changes in gastric motility and in the secretions of saliva, gastric juices, pancreatic enzymes, and insulin. One example of a potential consequence for body weight is that the better a food tastes, the greater the peak insulin release during the first minutes following meal onset [34]; this in turn delays the onset of satiety and increases the proportion of a meal that is stored as fat.

Sweet foods usually taste less pleasant after a meal. Cabanac [35] has called this phenomenon "alliesthesia," meaning "changed sensation," and he has reported that normal subjects rate sweet tastes as less pleasurable after ingesting a glucose solution than they do when they are hungry.

Food Palatability and Anorexia

Anorexic individuals exhibit a severe reduction in their sense of taste. Compared with controls, they have difficulty both in differentiating a test solution from water and in correctly identifying a taste quality as bitter, sour, sweet, or salty [36]. Food intake drops when the sense of taste is impaired [30], and hypogeusesthesia probably contributes to the lowered body weight of anorexia nervosa.

Patients with anorexia nervosa also experience less alliesthesia than controls after a meal. This defect appears to be independent of their reduced body weight, because differences between anorexic patients and controls persist even after any contribution of body weight is statistically removed by covariance analysis [20]. It also seems unlikely that the reduced alliesthesia of anorexic patients is due to a lower satiety level following a glucose preload, because evidence indicates that anorexic individuals feel just as full as controls immediately after a meal [20]. Interestingly, the absence of any decrease in postmeal taste sensation appears to be related to a tendency for anorexic patients to overestimate their own body size. Garfinkel and his associates [20] reported that impaired alliesthesia occurred more often in anorexics who overestimated their body size than in those who did not (see Chapters 10 and 11 in this book). This suggests a pervasive self-perceptive deficit.

Learned Food Aversions

Taste preferences decrease rapidly for foods associated with illness, and learned food aversions are adaptive in helping the organism avoid poisons and correct dietary deficiencies [37]. There is a biological predisposition to associate tastes with any feeling of malaise that develops within a few hours after ingesting food, regardless of whether the food actually caused the disorder [38].

Numerous treatments have been demonstrated to initiate a taste aversion. For example, hypotensive agents produce a conditioned aversion to tastes with which they are paired in rats [39], and human cancer patients exhibit a diminished taste preference for foods eaten immediately before receiving a chemotherapy treatment in which nausea is a side effect [40]. Damage to the vagus nerve causes an abnormally rapid rate of gastric emptying and, because of the ensuing malaise, rats develop an aversion to new foods consumed after vagotomy [41].

A learned association with malaise causes the abandonment of many diets that lack an essential nutrient or that are eaten during a long-term illness. In rats, the decline in food intake during terminal cancer is accompanied by an aversion specific to the diet consumed during tumor growth, and food consumption increases immediately if a different diet is introduced [42]. Similarly, rats fed a diet that lacks an essential nutrient such as thiamine soon avoid that diet, preferentially selecting almost any available novel food rather than continuing to eat the diet that is deficient [43].

Learned Food Aversions and Anorexia

Many of the conditions necessary to acquire taste aversions are present in anorexia nervosa. Food consumption produces unpleasant physiological sensations and affective responses in many patients, and feelings of being bloated or nauseated are often reported [44]. Whereas control subjects usually feel more "relaxed" after a test meal, anorexic patients describe themselves as more nervous, tense, depressed, and irritable [20]. Anorexic individuals consistently suffer from low blood pressure [45] and disturbances in gastric emptying [29]. These symptoms are of interest in light of experimental studies that have demonstrated a tendency to avoid foods associated with hypotensive drugs [39] or vagotomy [41].

Nutrition deficits involving zinc, copper, and total iron-blinding capacity are common in anorexia nervosa [36]. It may be that these deficiencies initiate dietary aversions that contribute to the reduced intake of anorexia patients.

Zinc Availability

Zinc is an essential element in humans and animals. It is important for the function of some 70 metalloenzymes, which play key roles in RNA and DNA activity, protein synthesis, energy metabolism, and vitamin utilization [46]. Zinc deficiency has been associated with impaired appetite, taste loss, growth retardation, gastrointestinal malfunction, dermatitis, depression, decreased sexual activity, impaired immune function, delayed puberty, and an increased level of circulating corticosteroids [47-50].

There is growing concern that there may be a chronic borderline zinc deficiency in the United States. In a recent study of 22 self-selected diets in the United States, 18 contained less than the minimum daily requirement of zinc [51]. Sandstead [52] reviewed the status of zinc nutrition in middle and upper income families in the United States and concluded that zinc deficiency is common, due primarily to poor eating habits and lack of meat in the diet. Individuals at particularly high risk for zinc deficiency include diabetics, those undergoing rapid growth, people on prolonged intravenous therapy, and those suffering from gastrointestinal disorders or in chronically debilitated states [53]. Corticosteroids cause an increase in urinary zinc excretion [54], and stress of any kind will magnify a borderline zinc deficiency.

Zinc Availability and Anorexia

Numerous symptoms are common to both zinc deficiency [47-50] and anorexia nervosa. Included among these are impaired appetite, growth retardation, taste loss, gastrointestinal malfunction, delayed puberty, low sexual activity, and depression.

As noted above, borderline zinc deficiency may be present in a sizable portion of the population. The nutritional impairment associated with anorexia nervosa magnifies this risk, because weight loss lowers zinc stores, and depressed appetite reduces zinc intake. Additional factors that might predispose anorexic patients to a zinc deficiency include poor glucose tolerance [16], gastrointestinal abnormalities [29], and onset of anorexic symptoms at a time normally associated with rapid physical growth.

At least one clinical study has provided direct evidence for a zinc deficiency in anorexia nervosa. In a study of 30 patients, Casper and associates [36] reported that plasma zinc levels and taste acuity were significantly depressed compared with control levels. After several weeks of treatment, which included zinc supplementation, patients exhibited increased plasma zinc levels and weight gains. Taste function also improved substantially, although it still was abnormal.

The clinical symptoms of zinc deficiency may be less readily apparent in anorexic patients than in normals, since an abnormally low metabolic rate in anorexic patients [55] probably reduces tissue requirements for zinc. However, Casper's [36] data suggest that zinc supplementation may be a useful adjunct to teatment, since patients in this study usually regained their appetite within a few days after treatment began. The possibility that insufficient zinc contributes to the symptoms of anorexia nervosa needs further investigation.

Cognitive Factors

Physiological stability usually receives the focus of attention in any discussion of homeostasis, but psychological equilibrium is equally vital to the organism. All of an organism's functions are interrelated in an inseparable manner. Many, if not all, physiological changes affect psychological state, and cognitive processes exert a direct effect on physiological function.

Cognitive factors play an important role in determining what weight levels should be maintained. This is especially true in societies where good food is plentiful, but obesity is considered unattractive. Our national preoccupation with dieting and a lean figure sometimes leads to behaviors that conflict with optimum physiological function. Nisbett [56] has marshaled evidence that obese people who perceive themselves as over-

weight share many behavioral and physiological similarities with organisms that are semistarving, including emotional lability, increased levels of plasma free fatty acids, low interest in sex, and reduced energy. He suggests that this occurs because most obese individuals persistently try to maintain a weight below that dictated by purely physiological considerations, and in this sense, are "starving." In these cases homeostatic balance requires a trade-off between the benefits associated with increased social acceptance and the reduced function resulting from an inadequate supply of easily available metabolic fuel.

Cognitive Factors and Anorexia

There is little question that cognitive factors play an important motivational role in the dogged pursuit of thinness that is characteristic of anorexia nervosa. Anorexia is overrepresented in the upper social classes [57], where the sociocultural pressures for women to maintain a thin shape are especially compelling [58]. The likelihood of developing anorexia also is high among dance and modeling students [59], whose careers often demand thin figures.

The adoration of thinnness in our culture mitigates against the recognition of low body weight as a disorder and provides a source of reward for the anorexic individual. In one study of college females, only 5%, throught that they were too thin, even though 38% were statistically underweight [60]. Branch and Eurman [61] found that at least half of a sample of friends and relatives of anorexic females "admired" the "patients' appearance" and "envied" their "self-control and discipline" around food.

Patients with anorexia nervosa are abnormally dependent on cognitive factors in determining when they feel full. Garfinkel and his associates [20] found that the feeling of satiety following a standard test lunch persisted much longer in anorexic patients than in controls when the lunch appeared to contain many calories, but not when the caloric content appeared low. This unusual reliance on cognitive factors may be fostered in part by an impaired sensitivity to other satiety cues. For example, anorexic patients are less accurate than controls in estimating the amount of food given them through a stomach tube [62], and they often complain of feeling unable to rely accurately on internal sensations as a cue to stop eating.

CONCLUSIONS

For most healthy individuals, a drop in body weight triggers a set of compensatory events that work in synchrony toward rapid recovery of the lost weight. Hunger increases, edible substances are actively sought, food utilization becomes more efficient, and satiety is difficult to attain.

A different picture is presented by patients with anorexia nervosa. Although these individuals exhibit some of the expected weight-gain responses, such as increased feed efficiency, others are notably absent. In fact, the net sum of homeostatic pressures often leads to a downward spiral of weight loss that can persist to the point of starvation.

Numerous factors can reduce food intake, and several of these may contribute to the symptoms seen in anorexic patients. In this chapter we have discussed evidence that decreased food consumption occurs in response to a loss of body fluids, a rise in body temperature, an abnormally slow (or precipitous) rate of gastric emptying, a diminished capacity to taste food, dietary aversions triggered by illness or nutrient deficiency, low zinc availability, and cognitive pressures to avoid food or lose weight. All of these phenomena may operate to some degree in anorexia nervosa.

Given the variety of factors that contribute to reduced intake and the awareness that these inhibitory mechanisms can be activated by multiple means, one would expect to find many differences among anorexic patients in the spectrum of inhibitory pressures that are present, the degree to which they operate, and the extent to which they are primary or secondary to the disorder. Concerning this last point, some causes of decreased food intake may be both primary and secondary to anorexia. An example of this would be a patient whose low food intake is aggravated by a dehydration that derives both from a partial diabetes insipidus (primary dehydration) and from an abuse of diuretics (secondary dehydration). Another example would be an individual in whom reduced intake follows an imparied taste function that is due both to a defect in the gustatory system and to a zinc deficiency resulting from inadequate intake. It is becoming increasingly clear that anorexia nervosa is not a single disorder. Unraveling its mysteries will require a multifaceted approach.

REFERENCES

1. Bernard C. Les Phenomenes de la Vie, vol 1. Paris: Librarie J-B Bailliers et Fils, 1878.
2. Cannon WB. Organization for physiological homeostasis. Physiol Rev, 1929; 9:399-431.
3. Cizek LJ, Nocenti MR. Relationship between water and food ingestion in the rat. Am J Physiol, 1965; 208:615-20.
4. Schwartzbaum JS, Ward HP. An osmotic factor in the regulation of food intake in the rat. J Comp Physiol Psychol, 1958; 51:555-60.
5. Lal H, Zabik J. Increased food consumption in thirsty rats after water satiation: Inhibition by salts. Psychon Sci, 1970; 20:131-2.
6. Hunt JN, Pathak JD. The osmotic effects of some simple molecules and ions on gastric emptying. J Physiol, 1960; 154:254-69.
7. Ehman GK, Albert DJ, Jamieson JL. Injections into the duodenum and the induction of satiety in the rat. Can J Psychol, 1972; 25:147-66.
8. Pertschuk MJ, Crosby LO, Mullen JL. Nonlinearity of weight gain and nutrition intake. In Darby PL, Garfinkel PE, Garner DM, Coscina DV, eds. Anorexia nervosa: Recent developments in research. News York: Alan R Liss Inc, 1983:301-10.
9. Crisp AH. Some aspects of the psychopathology of anorexia nervosa. In Darby PL, Garfinkel PE, Garner DM, Coscina DV, eds. Anorexia nervosa: Recent developments in research. New York: Alan R Liss Inc, 1983:15-28.
10. Vigersky RA, Loriaux DL. Anorexia nervosa as a model of hypothalamic dysfunction. In Vigersky RA, ed. Anorexia nervosa. New York: Raven, 1977:109-21.
11. Himms-Hagen J. Nonshivering thermogenesis. Brain Res. Bull, 1984; 12:151-60.
12. Glick Z, Teague RJ, Bray GA. Brown adipose tissue: Thermic response increased by a single low protein high carbohydrate meal. Science, 1981; 213:1125-7.
13. Thompson CI. Controls of Eating. New York: SP Medical & Scientific Books, 1980:18-29.
14. Brobeck JR. Food intake as a mechanism of temperature regulation. Yale J Biol Med, 1948; 20:545-52.
15. Glick Z. Inverse relationship between brown fat thermogenesis and meal size: The thermostatic control of food intake revisisted. Physiol Behav, 1982; 29:1137-40.
16. Silverman JA. Medical consequences of starvation; The malnutrition of anorexia nervosa: Caveat Medicus. In Darby PL, Garfinkel PE, Garner DM, Coscina DV, eds. Anorexia Nervosa: Recent developments in research. New York: Alan R Liss Inc, 1983:293-9.
17. Rothwell NJ, Stock MJ. Effect of chronic food restriction on energy balance, thermogenic capacity, and brown-adipose-tissue activity in the rat. Biosci Rep, 1982; 2:543-9.
18. Wakeling A, Russell GFM. Disturbances in the regulation of body temperature in anorexia nervosa. Psychol Med,. 1970; 1:30-9.
19. Grande F, Mongale JE, Buskirk ER, Taylor HL. Body temperature responses to exercise in man on restricted food and water intake.J Appl Physiol, 1959; 14:194-8.
20. Garfinkel PE, Moldofsky H, Garner DM, Stancer HC, Coscina DV. Body awareness in anorexia nervosa: Disturbances in "body image" and "satiety." Psychosom Med, 1978; 40:487-98.
21. Davies RF, Rossi J III, Panksepp J, Bean NJ, Zolovick AJ. Fenfluramine anorexia: A peripheral locus of action. Physiol Behav, 1983; 30:723-30.
22. Rowland N, Carlton J. Inhibition of gastric emptying by peripheral and central fenfluramine in rats: Correlation with anorexia. Life Sciences, 1984; 34:2495-9.
23. Hunt JN, Stubbs DF. The volume and energy content

of meals as determinants of gastric emptying. J Physiol London, 1975; 245:209-25.

24. Grossman MI. Gastrointestinal hormones. Physiol Rev, 1950; 30:33-90.

25. Ramsbottom N, Hunt JN. Effect of exercise on gastric emptying and gastric secretion. Digestion, 1974; 10:1-8.

26. Kraly FS, Blass EM. Increased feeding in rats in a low ambient temperature. In Novin D, Wyrwicka W, Bray GA, eds. Hunger: Basic mechanisms and clinical implications. New York: Raven Press, 1976:77-87.

27. Lavigne ME, Wiley ZD, Meyer JH, Martin P, MacGregor IL. Gastric emptying rates of solid food in relation to body size. Gastroenterology, 1978; 74:1258-60.

28. Roberts K. The dumping syndrome. In Thompson C, Berkowitz D, Polish E, eds. The stomach. New York; Grune and Stratton, 1967:426-9.

29. Dubois A, Gross HA, Ebert MH, Castell DO. Altered gastric emptying and secretion in primary anorexia nervosa. Gastroenterology, 1979; 77:319-23.

30. Jacquin MF. Gustation and ingestive behavior in the rat. Behav Neurosci, 1983; 97:98-109.

31. Keesey RE, Boyle PC. Effects of quinine adulteration upon body weight of LH-lesioned and intact male rats. J Comp Physiol Psychol, 1973; 84:38-46.

32. Sclafani A. Dietary Obesity. In Stunkard AJ, ed. Obesity. Philadlephia; Saunders, 1980:166-81.

33. Powley TL. The ventromedial hypothalamic syndrome, satiety, and a cephalic phase hypothesis. Psychol Review, 1977; 84:89-126.

34. Louis-Sylvestre J, Le Magnen J. Palatibility and preabsorptive insulin release. Body Energy Regulation and the Stimulation to Eat. Nurosci Biobehav Rev, Supp, 1980; 4:43-6.

35. Cabanac M. Physiolgoical role of pleasure. Science, 1971; 173:1103-7.

36. Casper RC, Kirschner B, Sandstead HH, Jacob RA, Davis JM. An evaluation of trace metals, vitamins, and taste function in anorexia nervosa. Am J Clin Nutr, 1980; 33:1801-8.

37. Barker LM, Best MR, Domjan M, eds. Learning Mechanisms in Food Selection. Waco Texas; Baylor University Press, 1977:1-632.

38. Rozin P, Kalat JW. Specific hungers and poison avoidance as adaptive specializations of learning. Psychol Rev, 1971; 78:459-86.

39. Kresel JJ, Barofsky I. Conditioned saccharin aversion development following administration of hypotensive agents. Physiol Behav, 1979; 23:733-6.

40. Bernstein IL. Webster MW. Learned taste aversions in humans. Physiol Behav, 1980; 25:363-6.

41. Bernstein IL, Goehler LE. Vagotomy produces learned food aversions in the rat. Behav Neurosci, 1984; 97:585-94.

42. Bernstein IL, Sigmundi RA. Tumor anorexia: A learned food aversion? Science, 1980; 209-416-8.

43. Rogers W, Rozin P. Novel food preferences in thiamine deficient rats. J Comp Physiol Psychol, 1966; 61:1-4.

44. Garfinkel PE, Garner DM. The multidetermined nature of anorexia nervosa. In Darby PL, Garfinkel PE, Garner DM, Coscina DV, eds. Anorexia nervosa: Recent developments in research. New York; Alan R Liss, Inc, 1983:3-14.

45. Schwabe AD, Lippe BM, Chang RJ, Pops MA, Yager J: Anorexia nervosa. Ann Intern Med, 1981; 94:371-81.

46. Kirchgessner M, Roth HP, Weigand E. Biochemical changes in zinc deficiency. In Prasad AS, ed. Trace Elements in human health and disease, Vol1, New York; Academic Press, 1976:181-7.

47. Fernandes G, Nair M, Onoe K, Tanaka T, Floyd R, Good RA. Impairment of cell-mediated immunity functions by dietary zinc deficiency in mice. Proc Natl Acad Sci, 1979; 76:457-61.

48. Prasad AS. Role of zinc in humans. In Risby TH, ed. Ultratrace metal analysis in biolgoical sciences and enviornment. Washington, DC; American Chemical Society, 1979:197-229.

49. Gordon EF, Bond JT, Gordon RC, Renny MR. Zinc deficiency and behavior: A developmental perspective. Physiol Behav, 1982; 28:893-7.

50. Gordon EF, Gordon RC, Passal DB. Zinc Metabolism: Basic, clinical, and behavioral aspects. Pediat, 1981; 99:341-9.

51. Wolf WR, Holden J, Green FE. Daily intake of zinc and copper from self-selected diets. Fed Proc. 1977; 36:1175.

52. Sandstead HH. Zinc nutrition in the United States. Am J Clin Nutr, 1973; 26:1251-60.

53. Henkin RI, Marshall JR, Meret S. Maternal-fetal metabolism of copper and zinc at term. Am J Obstet Gynecol, 1971; 110-131-4.

54. Flynn A, et al. Zinc deficiency with altered adrenocortical function and its relation to delayed healing. Lancet, 1973; 1:789.

55. Moshang T, Parks JS, Baker L, Vaidya V, Utiger R, Bongiovanni AM, Snyder P. Low serum triiodothyronine in patients with anorexia nervosa. J Clin Endocrin Metabol, 1975; 40:470-3.

56. Nisbett RE. Hunger, obesity and the ventromedial hypothalamus. Psychol Rev, 1972; 79:433-53.

57. Kendall RE, Hall DJ, Hailey A, Babigan HM. The epidemiology of anorexia nervosa. Psychol Med, 1973; 3:200-3.

58. Bruch H. The Golden Cage. Cambridge: Harvard University Press, 1978:22-37.

59. Garner DM, Garfinkel PE. Olmsted MP. An overview of sociocultural factors in the development of anorexia nervosa. In Darby PL, Garfinkel PE, Garner DM, Coscina DV, eds. Anorexia nervosa: Recent developemnts in research. New York; Alan R Liss Inc, 1983:65-82.

60. Gray SH. Social aspects of body image: Perception of normalcy of weight and affect of college undergraduates. Percept Motor Skills, 1977; 45:1035-40.

61. Branch CHH, Eurman LJ. Social attitudes toward patients with anorexia nervosa. Am J Psychiatry, 1980; 137:631-2.

62.   Coddington RD, Bruch H. Gastric perceptivity in nor-
       mal, obese, and schizophrenic subjects. Psychosomat-
       ics, 1970; 11:571-9.

Chapter 7

Gastrointestinal Peptides
and the Limitation of Meal Size

James Gibbs

Research into the physiological mechanisms controlling food intake has a long and varied history. Two major theories have dominated this research until recently. One proposed a role for glucose metabolism in meal initiation (the "glucostatic hypothesis") [1], and the other proposed roles for hypothalamic hunger and satiety "centers" in body weight regulation [2,3]. In spite of decades of experimental work, however, so many inconsistencies, conflicts, and gaps persist in each of these theories that new tactics have evolved.

One of the fastest growing of these new tactics is the attempt to determine whether gastrointestinal peptides are decisive in ending a meal. The logic here is that, since a wide variety of peptides are rapidly released into blood by ingested food as it stimulates the stomach and small intestine, some of these peptides might act as negative feedback signals to stop eating—in other words, they might function as "satiety signals."

Even before synthetic or highly purified peptides became available, several studies suggested that crude or partially purified gut extracts might decrease food intake [4-7]. In 1972, three gut hormones had become available in relatively pure form: gastrin, from gastric mucosa; secretin; and cholescystokinin (CCK), from duodenal mucosa. We began to test each of these peptide hormones to determine if they would decrease food intake.

CHOLECYSTOKININ AS A PARADIGM FOR A SATIETY SIGNAL

Secretin and gastrin failed to decrease food intake, but the initial results using CCK were striking. Intraperitoneal injections of a 10% pure preparation of CCK caused a large and clearly dose-related inhibition of solid food intake [8] (figure 1).

It was apparent that the rats in these early tests with CCK were not incapacitated in any obvious way. Further inspection revealed that CCK was not preventing or delaying the approach to food when it was offered at the beginning of each test. Instead, it was shortening the duration of the test meal—a characteristic consistent with a satiety action [9].

In a series of follow-up studies, we then put CCK through several tests of behavioral specificity. It reduced liquid food intake even more effectively than it reduced solid food intake, demonstrating that the reduction did not represent an impairment of specific motor movements involved in grasping and chewing solid food. CCK did not change core body temperature. CCK failed to reduce water intake when rats were water deprived; it did, however, produce the characteristic potent dose-related reduction of liquid food intake when the same rats were food deprived. This behavioral dissociation argues powerfully against the possibility that some subclinical malaise or slight discomfort is the mechanism of action of CCK [8].

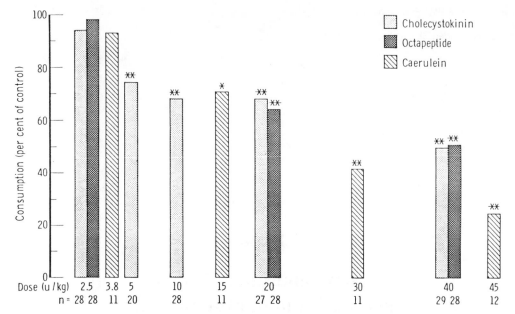

Figure 7.1 Consumption of solid food (expressed as a percent of control consumption) during the first 30 minutes following intraperitoneal injection of impure cholecystokinin (lighter bars), the synthetic C-terminal octapeptide of cholecystokinin (darker bars), or caerulein (hatched bars). Each substance produced a dose-related suppression of food intake. One unit of impure cholecystokinin is equivalent to approximately 0.05 μg of the synthetic octapeptide in biological activity. Doses of caerulein were calculated by assuming that it was 15 times as potent by weight as impure cholecystokinin (A. Anastasi, personal communication). Mean control intakes ranged from 2.8-4.3g. Statistical differences from control intakes after vehicle injection of 0.15 M NaCl: *p < 0.01; p < 0.001.

Because only an impure extract containing CCK had been employed in the initial tests, we next sought evidence for chemical specificity. Systemic injections of the biologically active synthetic C-terminal octapeptide of CCK (CCK-8) and the related decapeptide ceruletide produced inhibitory effects on food intake that were similar to those produced by the original impure preparation (figure 1). Desulfated CCK-8, a biologically weak analogue, did not inhibit food intake [10]. Large doses of gastrin, chemically similar to CCK, were also ineffective.

In an attempt to determine the potency of CCK, we next prepared rats with chronic indwelling gastric cannulas that could be temporarily opened at a test meal to allow the rapid drainage of all of an ingested liquid food. When rats were first tested with the gastric cannulas open, the results were surprising—feeding was virtually continuous for hours [11]. Thus, under these test conditions, when little or no food accumulated in the stomach or stimulated the small intestine, satiety was absent. This fact made a test of CCK's presumed satiety action even more interesting, because CCK originates in the small intestine. The results of the test were clear, and can be seen in figure 2. CCK inhibited sham feeding, demonstrating its potency in a situation in which there was no gastric distention and food stimula-

tion of the small intestine was absent or minimal [10].

Additional persuasive evidence that the inhibition of sham feeding by CCK represented a state of satiety appeared in this test. CCK not only inhibited sham feeding, but it elicited the fixed sequence of behaviors that normally characterize the end of a meal in rats: grooming, locomotion and rearing, and finally resting [12].

The results of tests with CCK in rats were encouraging enough to lead to investigations in other species. CCK, administered systemically, has been examined for a satiety-like action in mice [13-15], chickens [16], rabbits [17], sheep [18], pigs [19], and rhesus monkeys [20]. The success of this last study led to tests in humans. Under double-blind conditions, slow intravenous infusions of CCK produced reductions of meal size ranging from 15% to 50% in lean men and women [21,22] and in obese men [23]. These infusions, all in the low-nanogram-dose range, failed to produce any evidence of toxicity or significant side effects. Thus, the results of objective tests in rats, indicating that CCK was producing satiety, not malaise, predicted the subjective experience of humans, who reported that they felt normal satiety, not malaise [24].

The peripheral and central routes that exogenous CCK uses when it produces the behavioral and subjective state of satiety are incompletely known. It is known

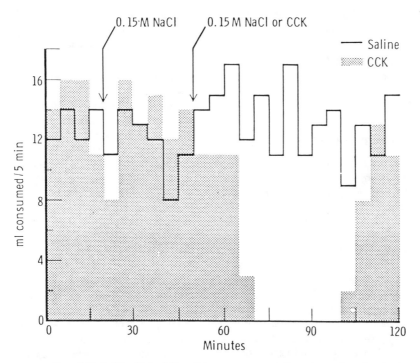

Figure 7.2 Sham consumption of diluted liquid food (in ml) by one representative rat on a day when impure cholecystokinin was injected intraperitoneally in a dose of 40 units- kg^{-1} (shaded area) and on an adjacent day when equivolumetric vehicle (0.15 m NaCl) was injected (line). Cholecystokinin produced a rapid, complete, and transient inhibition of food intake.

that the full action of peripherally-administered CCK-8 is crucially dependent on the subdiaphragmatic vagus [25,26] and that the important elements of this vagal requirement are gastric [25] and afferent [27]. Based on studies in rhesus monkeys, McHugh has suggested that the satiety effect of exogenous CCK is indirect and dependent on the peptide's inhibition of gastric emptying and a resultant gastric distention [28]. Such an indirect action of circulating CCK on the stomach might then be mediated by gastric vagal afferents to the brain stem.

An outline of important brain areas mediating the satiety action of systemically-injected CCK in the rat may now be emerging. Within the brain stem, electrolytic lesions of the area postrema-nuclear tractus solitarius (the latter a target for vagal afferents) may attenuate the effect of intraperitoneally administered CCK [29]. Within the diencephalon, lesions of the paraventricular nucleus (a target for nucleus tractus solitarius afferents) [29] (JN Crawley, personal communication) or the dorsomedial nucleus [30] also attenuate the effect of intraperitoneally administered CCK. Finally, observations of injections of low concentrations of CCK-8 into the fourth ventricle [31], overlying the nucleus tractus solitarius, into the third ventricle (E Stellar, personal communication) or directly into the paraventricular nucleus [32] suggest that these injections may mimic actions of

neuronal CCK, perhaps in nucleus tractus solitarius and paraventricular nucleus. At this point, however, these observations remain only suggestions. Baile and his colleagues, based on extensive work since 1979, have produced strong support for their conclusion that central CCK is primarily responsible for satiety in sheep [33].

There is another major area of ignorance in the CCK puzzle. Does the satiety action of exogenous CCK have physiological meaning? No one has produced the critical evidence needed to decide whether endogenous CCK exerts a limiting effect on meal size under normal conditions in animals or humans. It is known that apparently low doses of exogenous CCK-8 (50ng-kg^{1} in rats) [34] (30ng- kg^{-1} in humans) [21] inhibit food intake. But this is not critical evidence, because reliable radioimmunoassays that agree on the absolute levels of the multiple circulating forms of CCK in human or rat plasma are required to allow comparisons with levels achieved after such doses of exogenous CCK. These radioimmunoassays are not available at present. Furthermore, the straightforward measurement of circulating CCK levels may provide incomplete information. It seems extremely unlikely the CCK could be the only satiety signal, and much more likely that it would interact with other satiety signals released by the action of food on the surface of the gut. In fact, Moran and McHugh have demonstrated striking potentiation of the satiating effect of a low dose (4ng- kg^{-1}-min^{-1}) of CCK-8 by gastric distention in the rhesus monkey [35]. Thus, it will be hazardous to categorize satiety candidates as pharmacological or physiological until the important candidates are identified and their interactions are quantified.

OTHER PUTATIVE SATIETY PEPTIDES

Bombesin (BBS) is one of several peptides isolated from amphibian skin by Erspamer and his colleagues during the 1970s (for review, see reference 36). This research effort has proved to be of great importance, because families of peptides closely resembling the amphibian ones have been identified throughout the mammalian gut and brain [37,38]. We found that intraperitoneal injections of BBS produced effects on food intake in rats that were remarkably similar to those of CCK. BBS caused rapid, large, dose-related inhibitions that were behaviorally specific and without obvious side effects [39,40]. Gastrin-releasing peptide (GRP), a mammalian counterpart of amphibian BBS, had similar effects in rats [41], in mice [42], and in baboons [43]. In the one test to date in humans, an intravenous infusion of BBS (4 ng/kg^{-1}-min^{-1}) decreased meal size without producing significant side effects [44].

Because the satiety characteristics of BBS were so remarkably similar to those of CCK, we tested the effect of subdiaphragmatic vagotomy on BBS-induced satiety. In contrast to its blockade of CCK-induced satiety, vagotomy did not alter the satiety potency of BBS [45]. This dissociation demonstrated that the mechanisms of action of the two peptides are different; BBS does not produce satiety in rats solely by releasing endogenous CCK. Collins and his colleagues [46], using the CCK antagonist proglumide, have obtained independent results supporting this conclusion. In addition, Bellinger and Bernardis showed that dorsomedial hypothalamic lesions significantly attentuated the suppression of feeding by CCK, but not by BBS [30].

Although we now know that the mechanism of action of BBS on food intake is different from that of CCK, we do not know what the mechanism is. Furthermore, no endocrine or neural ablation has been shown to block its action. Presently, we are combining vagal and spinal disconnections in an attempt to block the satiety effect of peripherally-injected BBS.

In the late 1950s, shortly after pure pancreatic glucagon became available, it was administered to human volunteers in attempts to reduce the subjective sense of hunger [47] and to produce weight loss [48]. Both attempts were successful. These early results in humans have been followed up by animal studies showing that the inhibition by glucagon was specific for food intake and did not reduce water intake, and that, like CCK and BBS, glucagon exerted its satiety-like action during the last portion of the meal, without altering the initial rate of feeding [49].

Martin and Novin, in the earliest search for a mechanism of action for glucagon, found that hepatic-portal infusions of this peptide produced a dose-related inhibition of food intake [50]. VanderWeele and his colleagues showed that subdiaphragmatic vagotomy blocked glucagon-induced satiety [51,52]. Geary and Smith found that selective hepatic vagotomy blocked the effect, whereas selective gastric or selective coeliac vagotomy did not [53]; Bellinger and Williams, however, failed to modify the inhibitory action of glucagon on feeding by a presumed complete liver denervation [54].

As is well known, the major effect of glucagon at the liver is glycogenolysis. Although this seemed the obvious choice for a hepatic mechanism of action, Geary and Smith [55] demonstrated clear evidence against this possibility: They showed that glucagon produced a marked hepatic vein hyperglycemia (via hepatic glycogenolysis) when it was injected just before sham feeding, but that it failed to have any effect on sham feeding. Thus, hepatic vein hyperglycemia is not sufficient as a mechanism of action for glucagon-induced satiety.

Strong evidence that the satiety action of exogenous glucagon reflects a physiological action of the endogenous hormone came from the study of Langhans et al [56], when they demonstrated that the acute administration of antiglucagon antibodies to rats produced a large increase in meal size. If this result can be replicated, and the specificity of the antibody can be shown under the behavioral test conditions, the results will constitute the strongest evidence yet supporting a physiological role for any putative satiety signal.

Other peptides that have been shown to reduce food intake under some circumstance in at least one species include somatostatin [57,58], calcitonin [59,60], pancreatic polypeptide [61,62,42], and thyrotropin-releasing hormone [63-66]. The available evidence supporting a true satiety role for any of these peptides fails to meet the standards applied above to CCK, BBS, and pancreatic glucagon.

CONCLUSION

Three peripheral peptides—cholecystokinin, bombesin, and pancreatic glucagon—produce potent inhibitions of food intake and exert constellations of behavioral effects in several species, which make each one a serious candidate for a physiological role in regulating meal size. Cholecystokinin is by far the most thoroughly investigated candidate. Nevertheless, in no case has a physiological role for any of the three peptides been demonstrated, and in no case is the mechanism of action understood. In the setting of this volume, a final caution deserves emphasis: How the limiting effect of these peptides on experimental meal size might relate to the deranged controls of feeding behavior and body weight seen in patients with eating disorders remains intriguing, but almost entirely unknown.

ACKNOWLEDGMENTS

The author was supported by Research Scientist Development Award MH70874. I thank GP Smith for a critical reading and J Magnetti for careful preparation of this chapter.

REFERENCES

1. Mayer J. Glucostatic mechansims in regulation of food intake. New Engl J Med, 1953; 249:13-16.

2. Anand BK, Brobeck JR. Hypothalamic control of food intake. Yale J Biol Med, 1951; 24:123-40.

3. Brobeck JR, Tepperman J, Long CNH. Experimental hypothalamic hyperphagia in the albino rat. Yale J Biol Med, 1943; 15:831-53.

4. Maclagan NF. The role of appetite in the control of body weight. J Physiol, 1937; 90:385-94.

5. Ugolev AM. The influence of duodenal extracts on general appetite. Doklady Akademii Nauk SSSR, 1960; 133:632-4.

6. Schally AV, Redding TW, Lucien HW, et al. Enterogastrone inhibits eating by fasted mice. Science, 1967; 157:210-1.

7. Sjodin L. Influence of secretin and cholecystokinin on canine gastric secretion elicited by food and by exogenous gastrin. Acta Physiol Scan, 1972; 85:110-7.

8. Gibbs J, Young RC, Smith GP. Cholecystokinin decreases food intake in rats. J Comp Physiol Psychol, 1973; 84:488-95.

9. Booth DA. Conditioned satiety in the rat. J Comp Physiol Psychol, 1972; 81:457-71.

10. Gibbs J, Young RC, Smith GP. Cholecystokinin elicits satiety in rats with open gastric fistulas. Nature, 1973; 245:323-5.

11. Young RC, Gibbs J, Antin J, et al. Absence of satiety during sham feeding in the rat. J Comp Physiol Psychol, 1974; 87:795-800.

12. Antin J, Gibbs J, Holt J, et al. Cholecystokinin elicits the complete behavioral sequence of satiety in rats. J Comp Physiol Psychol, 1975; 89:784-90.

13. Parrott RF, Batt RAL. The feeding response of obese mice (genotype, ob/ob) and their wild-type littermates to cholecystokinin (pancreozymin). Physiol Behav, 1980; 24:751-3.

14. McLaughlin CL, Baile CA. Obese mice and the satiety effects of cholecystokinin, bombesin and pancreatic polypeptide. Physiol Behav, 1981; 26:433-7.

15. Strohmayer AJ, Smith GP. Cholecystokinin inhibits food-intake in genetically-obese (C57BL-6J-ob) mice. Peptides, 1981; 2:39-43.

16. Savory CJ, Gentle MJ. Intravenous injections of cholecystokinin and caerulein suppress food intake in domestic fowls. Experientia, 1980; 36:1191-2.

17. Houpt TR, Anika SM, Wolff NC. Satiety effects of cholescystokinin and caerulein in rabbits. Am J Physiol, 1978; 235:R23-8.

18. Grovum WL. Factors affecting the voluntary intake of food by sheep. 3. The effect of intravenous infusions of gastrin, cholecystokinin and secretin on motility of the reticulo-rumen and intake. Br J Nutr, 1981; 45:183-201.

19. Anika SM, Houpt TR, Houpt KA. Cholecystokinin and satiety in pigs. Am J Physiol, 1981; 240:R310-8.

20. Gibbs J, Falasco JD, McHugh PR. Cholecystokinin decreased food intake in rhesus monkeys. Am J Physiol, 1976; 230:15-8.

21. Kissileff HR, Pi-Sunyer FX, Thornton J, et al. Cholecystokinin-octapeptide (CCK-8) decreases food intake in man. Am J Clin Nutr, 1980; 34:154-60.

22. Stacher G, Steinringer H, Schmierer G. Cholecys Personal communication, 1984.

95. Singh NN. Aversive control of rumination in the mentally retarded. J Prac Approach Develpm Hand 1979; 3:2-6.

96. Singh NN, Manning PJ, Angell MJ. Effects of an oral hygiene punishment procedure on chronic rumination and collateral behaviors in monozygous twins. J Appl Behav Anal 1982; 15:309-14.

97. Wolf MM, Birnbrauer J, Lawler J, Williams T. The operant extinction, reinstatement and re-extinction of vomiting behavior in a retarded child. In Ulrich R, Statnik T, Mabry J, eds. Control of Human Behavior: From Cure to Prevention, vol 2. Glenview, Ill: Scott, Forseman, 1970: pp. 146-149.

98. Barmann BC. Use of contingent vibration in the treatment of self-stimulatory hand-mouthing and ruminative vomiting behavior. J Behav Ther Exp Psychiat 1980; 11:307-11.

99. Davis WB, Weiseler NA, Hanzel TE. Contingent music in management of rumination and out-of-seat behavior in a profoundly mentally retarded institutionalized male. Mental Retardation 1980; 18:43-4.

100. Daniel WH. Management of chronic rumination with a contingent exercise procedure employing topographically dissimilar behavior. J Behav Ther and Exp Psychiat 1982; 12(2):149-52.

101. Duker PC, Seys DM. Elimination of vomiting in a retarded female using restitutional overcorrection. Behav Ther 1977; 8:255-7.

102. Becker JV, Turner SM, Sajwaj TE. Multiple behavioral effects of the use of lemon juice with a ruminating toddler-age child. Behav Mod 1978; 2:267-78.

103. Galbraith DA, Bryick RJ, Rutledge JT. An aversive conditioning approach to the inhibition of chronic

vomiting. Canad Psychiat Assn J 1970; 15:311-3.

104. Greenspan S. Personal communication, 1984.

105. Bkubder BJ.Rumination: A benign disorder? Int J Eating Disorders 1986; 5:385-6.

106. Amarnath RD, Abe-92.

35. Moran TH, McHugh PR. Cholecystokinin suppresses food intake by inhibiting gastric emptying. Am J Physiol, 1982; 242:R491-7.

36. Erspamer V, Melchiorri P. Active polypeptides: from amphibian skin to gastrointestinal tract and brain of mammals. Trends Pharmacol Sci, 1980; 1:391-5.

37. McDonald TJ, Jöurnvall H, Nilsson G, et al. Characterization of a gastrin releasing peptide from porcine non-antral gastric tissue. Biochem Biophys Res Commun, 1979; 90:227-33.

38. Walsh JH, Wong HC, Dockray GJ. Bombesin-like peptides in mammals. Fedn Proc, 1979; 38:2315-9.

39. Gibbs J, Fauser DJ, Rowe EA, et al. Bombesin suppresses feeding in rats. Nature, 1979; 282:208-10.

40. Gibbs J. Effect of bombesin on feeding behavior. Life Sci, 1985; 37:147-53.

41. Stein LJ, Woods SC. Gastrin releasing peptide reduces meal size in rats. Peptides, 1982; 3:833-5.

42. McLaughlin CL, Baile CA. Obese mice and the satiety effects of cholecystokinin, bombesin and pancreatic polypeptide. Physiol Behav, 1981; 26:433-7.

43. Figlewicz DP, Stein LJ, Woods SC, et al. Acute and chronic gastrin-relasing peptide decreases food intake in baboons. Am J Physiol, 1985; 248:R578-83.

44. Muurahainen NE, Kissileff HR, Thornton J, et al. Bombesin: another peptide that inhibits feeding in man. Soc Nuerosci Abstr, 1983; 9:183.

45. Smith GP, Jerome C, Gibbs J. Abdominal vagotomy does not block the satiety effect of bombesin in the rat. Peptides, 1981; 2:409-11.

46. Collins S, Walker D, Forsyth P, et al. The effects of proglumide on cholecystokinin-, bombesin-, and glucagon-induced satiety in the rat. Life Sci, 1983; 32:2223-9.

47. Stunkard AJ, VanItallie TB, Reis BB. The mechanism of satiety: effect of glucagon on gastric hunger contractions in man. Proc Soc Exper Biol & Med, 1955: 89:258.

48. Schulman JL, Carleton JL, Whitney G, et al. Effect of glucagon on food intake and body weight in man. J Appl Physiol, 1957; 11:419-21.

49. Geary N, Smith GP. Pancreatic glucagon and postprandial satiety in the rat. Physiol Behav, 1982; 28:313-22.

50. Martin JR, Novin D. Decreased feeding in rats following hepatic-portal infusion of glucagon. Physiol Behav, 1977; 19:461-6.

51. Martin JR, Novin D, VanderWeele DA. Loss of glucagon suppression of feeding after vagotomy in rats. Am J Physiol, 1978; 234:E314-8.

52. VanderWeele DA, Geiselman PJ, Novin D. Pancreatic glucagon, food deprivation and feeding in intact and vagotomized rabbits. Physiol Behav, 1979; 23:155-8.

53. Geary N, Smith GP. Selective hepatic vagotomy blocks pancreatic glucagon's satiety effect. Physiol Behav,

1983; 31:391-4.

54. Bellinger LL, Williams FE. Liver denervation does not modify feeding responses to metabolic challenges or hypertonic NaC1 induced water consumption. Physiol Behav, 1983; 30:463-70.

55. Geary N, Smith GP. Pancreatic glucagon fails to inhibit sham feeding in the rat. Peptides, 1982; 3:163-6.

56. Langhans W, Ziegler V, Scharrer E, et al. Stimulation of feeding in rats by intraperitoneal injection of antibodies to glucagon. Science, 1982; 218:894-6.

57. Lotter EC, Krinsky R, McKay JM, et al. Somatostatin decreases food intake of rats and baboons. J Comp Physiol Psychol, 1981; 95:278-87.

58. Levine AS, Morley JE. Peripherally administered somatostatin reduces feeding by a vagally mediated mechanism. Pharmacol Biochem Behav, 1982; 16:897-902.

59. Perlow MJ, Freed WJ, Carman JS, et al. Calcitonin reduces feeding in man, monkey and rat. Pharmacol Biochem Behav, 1980; 12:609-12.

60. Freed WJ, Perlow MJ, Wyatt RJ. Calcitonin: inhibitory effect on eating in rats. Science, 1979; 206:850-2.

61. Malaisse-Legae F, Carpentier JL, Patel YC, et al. Pancreatic polypeptide: a possible role in the regulation of food intake in the mouse. Experientia, 1977; 33:915-7.

62. Gates RJ, Lazarus R. The ability of pancreatic polypeptide (APP and BPP) to return to normal the hyperglycemia, hyperinsulinemia and weight gain of New Zealand obese mice. Hormone Res, 1977; 8:189-202.

63. Vijayan E, McCann SM. Suppression of feeding and drinking activity in rats following intraventricular injection of thyrotropin releasing hormone (TRH). Endocrinology, 1977; 100:1727-30.

64. Morley JE, Levine AS. Thyrotropin releasing hormone suppresses stress induced eating. Life Sci, 1980; 27:1259-61.

65. Konturek SJ, Tasler J, Jaworek J, et al. Comparison of TRH and anorexigenic peptide on food intake and gastrointestinal secretions. Peptides, 1981; 2 (Suppl 2):235-40.

66. Morley JE, Levine AS, Kniep J, et al. The effect of vagotomy on the satiety effects of neuropeptides and naloxone. Life Sci, 1982; 30:1943-7.

Applied Studies

Chapter 8

Descriptive and Operational Study of Eating in Humans

John E. Blundell and Andrew J. Hill

INTRODUCTION

The most fundamental research on feeding is directed toward mechanisms responsible for the initiation, maintenance, and termination of eating. This enterprise can be partitioned into investigations of the control of caloric intake, selection of foods and nutrients, and the distribution of eating episodes. This body of research helps to provide explanations for disordered eating, whether represented by overingestion or underingestion of calories, aberrant preferences and selection of food, or abnormal sizes or patterns of eating episodes. In turn, investigations of mechanisms and causes of eating disorders depend on the accurate and reliable monitoring of the target behavior, namely, eating.

A number of methods are available for the measurement of this activity. However, eating cannot be properly represented simply as a block of behavior detached from the sensations and feelings evoked by food or the responses that accompany ingestion. Eating is certainly an act of behavior, but it achieves meaning because it is embedded in a context of mental events and physiological happenings.

Eating can perhaps be viewed most profitably as a part of a broader bio-psychological system [1,2]. For this reason the descriptive and operational study of eating should include ways of assessing the accompanying attitudes, feelings, sensations, experiences, motivations, and cognitions together with certain physiological responses. This chapter provides an inventory of techniques and procedures used to research and analyze normal and disordered eating. The review is accompanied by critical comment on the nature of the research devices and on certain of the mechanisms that they have revealed. This assembly of procedures represents the basic instruments for the experimental study of eating in humans in the laboratory, clinic, or natural environment.

THE STRUCTURE OF EATING BEHAVIOR

Clinicians and researchers frequently need to know not only the total amount of food ingested (grams, calories, joules) by clients or subjects, but also the temporal distribution of eating. This forces an assessment of the structure of eating behavior. In turn, this can be carried out at the macro or micro level of analysis (or at certain intermediate stages).

On one hand, eating can be viewed as an activity distributed over very long periods of time, the study of which can reveal large-scale patterns or trends. On the other hand, a fine-grain analysis reveals how tiny individual acts are assembled in a nonarbitrary fashion into the complex behavioral sequence that constitutes the familiar act of eating. Indeed, eating is such a commonplace act that it is easy to overlook the fact that it represents a well-organised sequence of individual movements.

It is clear that investigation of mechanisms responsible for eating requires the analysis of micro-events as well as the study of large-scale, long-term trends in consumption. Consequently, the structure of eating involves monitoring consumption over months and sometimes years as well as the recording of events occurring within a single meal.

Naturally, different types of procedures are required for these distinctive tasks. The principle division is between direct and indirect techniques. Direct measurement of behavioral events is possible over short intervals of time, while long-term assessment usually depends on indirect recording of food intake. One other distinction is between monitoring in a free natural environment with attendant problems of control and precision and measuring in artificial laboratory or clinic situations where accuracy is clearly easier to achieve. The particular limitations of data collected under these different circumstances presents researchers with the dilemma of assigning importance to either the (relatively) inaccurate recording under natural circumstances or the (very) accurate recording in unnatural situations. This review deals with both sets of conditions.

The Dietary Study of Individuals

Many of the methods for surveying individual and group dietary practices are long established and have been extensively detailed and reviewed elsewhere [3-6]. The methods described in this chapter refer only to the food intake of the individual and should be distinguished from those designed to give more general information about populations, institutions, or families. The information they provide is particularly useful when complementing data from other techniques.

Individual dietary studies fall into two basic categories:

1. *Recording present intake.* This may be done in two ways. Subjects may maintain detailed diary records of all food eaten, describing the quantities in terms of household measurements or by estimation. Alternatively, all the ingredients used in the preparation of the food when cooked may be precisely weighed, together with an wastage at the end of the meal. Obviously, while the latter is the more precise method, it requires a great deal of effort on behalf of the participant and frequent supervision by the researcher. Both methods also suffer from the handicap of constantly drawing attention to the process of selection and consumption of the food. Procedures involving a high level of self-monitoring may therefore impose their own influence on the behavior under study and alter subjects' normal eating habits. This occurs with obese individuals [7] and may also influence the extreme patterns characteristic of anorexia nervosa and bulimia nervosa.

2. *Recording past intake.* The techniques used to aid the subject to remember and describe their previous intake differ largely in the duration of the recall period. The most common procedure elicits an inventory of the food eaten over the previous 24 hours, either by asking subjects to note the foods on a checklist or by detailing the meals together with estimated amounts of food. This recall maybe extended over a period of three days or up to a week. Alternatively, an estimate of the subjects' "usual dietary intake" or "diet history" maybe obtained by cross-checking the 24-hour recall in an interview where questions relating to purchasing, likes and dislikes, and food uses supplement the recall data. The subsequent direct recording of food intake for a short period or use of multiple 24-hour records may be used as additional cross-checks.

Generally, recall techniques are quick and inexpensive and do not require specialist supervision. Their cost-effectiveness, however, may vary according to the required accuracy of the study. Many more 24-hours records are needed to establish accurately protein or fat intake than to describe energy intake [8]. Dietary recall is also liable to the "flat slop syndrome"—a tendency to overreport low levels and underreport high levels of consumption, a consideration particularly important in cases of disordered eating.

Finally, mention should be made of the uses of tables of food composition. These texts are frequently used to convert dietary data into caloric or nutritional composition, and there is some controversy about the accuracy of this procedure [3,4]. Paul and Southgate [9] say of their own revision of McCance and Widdowson's The Composition of Foods, the values are of "representative samples" of the foods and as such may reflect the "average composition of the food." Isolated samples may therefore be of a quite different composition. Data from large groups of people should have intrinsic accuracy, but in studies of individuals, accuracy may be improved by extending the period of study and thereby increasing the size of the food sample consumed.

Obervational Studies

Many studies on human eating use as the dependent variable some portion of the act of consumption or a particular sample that reflects the quantity of food eaten. However, one apparently uncomplicated procedure for describing eating behavior is to observe and subsequently classify the entire sequence of behavior. This strategy is commonly used by ethologists [10] for the study of animal behavior, but has been extended for use in humans—particularly children [11]—and provides both a qualitative and quantitative account of the expressed behavior. In principle, because behavior is recorded in its totality, the strategy used should be a powerful tool for describing feeding in man.

Behavior may be monitored in naturalistic settings (cafes, restaurants, refectories, or homes) or in the laboratory under controlled conditions. Analysis can be done on "live" behavior or carried out from video recordings. In general, the observational method frequently makes use of some form of sampling. Event sampling requires that every occurrence of a specified event during the course of the observational period is recorded. Time sampling means that whatever event is occurring at specified (brief) intervals during the observational period is monitored. For eating behavior, which normally spans a relatively short period of time (usually a meal), a number of significant events (taking a bite, pausing, swallowing, etc.) are continuously recorded by an observer. It is necessary to check the accuracy of the ratings of this observer by comparing them (coefficient of concordance) with an independent observer rating the same sequence. This is a necesssary requirement, since even events such as taking a bite of food, which can be defined fairly unambiguously, may be recorded differently by two independent observers. This is particularly important when the onset and termination of an event is recorded as well as the overall frequency of events. Consequently, although the observational method is apparently uncomplicated, its interpretation is hindered by a number of methodological pitfalls and its use must be governed by clear methodological principles.

In studies of eating behavior the main variables extracted from the behavior sequence are listed below:
1. Meal duration
2. Total number of mouthfuls (or bites)
3. Average mouthful size
4. Duration of each mouthful
5. Number of chews per mouthful
6. Mouthfuls per meal
7. Chews per meal
8. Mouthfuls per minute
9. Amount per minute
10. Number of noneating episodes during the meal
11. Intermouthful interval

Certain of these variables refer to the frequency of specific events (eg, taking a mouthful of food), whereas others refer to the rate of expression of behavior. Alterations in these variables have been used in attempts to detect differences between particular groups of individuals, eg, obese and normal weight [12], between foods varying in preference value [13], between drugs with different neurochemical profiles [14], and to assess the development of satiation during the course of a meal [15,16].

Studies using observational methods have been the subject of two critical reviews [17,18]. Over the years the main theoretical focus of attention has been the attempt to use the observational procedure to define an obese eating style. No general agreement has been reached on this issue—probably due as much to difficulties in defining obese and normal as to problems associated with descriptions of style. Used carefully, observational procedures can be sensitive research devices. Owing to the considerable variability in qualitative eating profiles between individuals, the procedures function best in within- group rather than between-group research designs.

Techniques Using Specialized Apparatus

During the last 20 years a number of specialized devices have been developed or adapted to improve the sensitivity, accuracy, or reliability of measuring food consumption. Most provide continuous monitoring of intake. Some are designed for liquid rather than solid food, and others allow a degree of food choice. Some demand a somewhat unnatural eating response, while others attempt to allow unhindered eating to take place. No device is perfect; they all have strengths and weaknesses.

1. *Liquid food reservoirs and pumps.* Automated devices for continuous monitoring of the food intake of animals have been used in experiments for more than 40 years. The first of this type of monitoring apparatus for humans appears to have occurred about 20 years ago [19]. The device was used to facilitate feeding of a patient with carcinoma of the lip. Flexible tubing connected a mouthpiece to a reservoir containing a liquid diet, with a valve and pump inserted into the circuit. When the patient depressed a button, the pump was activated and a fixed amount of the diet (7.4 ml) was delivered through the mouthpiece. Every activation of the pump was recorded and the time of the event was automatically printed to provide a continuous record of liquid intake. The patient used the device coninuously for 17 days, taking in 2,000 to 3,500 kcals per day, usually in three or four distinct meals. This study demonstrated that drinking liquid provided a pattern of intake suitable for investigations of mechanisms contolling food consumption.

More recently a number of studies have been carried out using variations of the reservoir-type of apparatus in which liquid food is either sucked [20] or pumped at a steady rate during the depression of a button [21]. The technique has been used to investigate the effectiveness of oral and intragastric feeding on intake [21,22], the effects of preloads [23] and caloric dilution [24] on meal size, the hyperphagic and hypophagic responses to stress in normal and obese subjects [25], the onset of biological satiation [26], and the effect of drugs on voluntary intake [27]. The technique certainly provides an objective method for studying certain parameters of ingestion, but the dependence of the procedure on liquid food with consequent restriction of variety of taste and texture obviously limits the extent to which results can be generalized to more natural eating circumstances and situations. In summary, the technique scores high for internal validity, but somewhat lower for external validity.

2. *Automatic monitoring via eating utensils (BITE).* The major disadvantage of the reservoir system—limiting the variety of foods that can be monitored—is directly confronted by the development of a device for continuous monitoring of the consumption of solid and semisolid foods. The technique is based on recognition that human eating is composed of a sequence of contacts between the mouth and the eating utensil and that the number of contacts is proportional to the amount consumed. Therefore, by continuously monitoring these contacts it becomes possible to track the temporal course of food consumption.

The system operates through specially constructed spoons and forks [28] with handles that contain miniaturized telemetering equipment. Each portion of food placed in the mouth with the utensil makes a contact that permits a current to flow through the circuit. The passage of current constitutes a signal that is telemetered to recording equipment by a battery-powered transmitter within the utensil. Consequently, the technique is not encumbered by wires. The device is known as a Bite-Indicating Telemetering Eatometer, or BITE. Studies with a nontelemetering prototype of BITE have shown that the device provides good records of two parameters: the number of bites and the interbite interval. In fact, since the test food used was a semisolid yogurt, the bite actually refers to a spoonful of yogurt. The data indicated large individual differences in the interbite internal (pauses between mouthfuls) and that in most subjects interbite intervals were larger in the last quarter of the meal than the first, which in turn, means that subjects tended to slow the rate of ingestion during the consumption of this yogurt.

Studies on the most sophistocated version of this bite, or mouthful-measuring, technique have not yet been published. Moreover, it remains to be shown that the device can provide an accurate record of the eating of semisolid foods with a fork similar to the way in which it monitors the consumption of a thick liquid (yogurt) with a spoon. In addition, the value of the technique will be lessened if it is discovered that mouthfuls or bites (mouth-utensil contacts) vary in size during the course of a meal. It is also not yet clear if bite or interbite intervals give a valid response to changes in palatability of food, motivation to eat, or the operation of satiation mechanisms. At the moment, the full potential of this system is unknown, but it could prove useful in certain clinical settings or, as seems more likely, in studies on the consumption of new products manufactured by food companies.

3. *Monitoring of intake via the plate.* In attempting to measure intrameal events by analyzing the structure of eating behavior (eg, mouthfuls and intervals) the BITE procedure sacrifices the requirement to monitor changes in the actual weight of food being eaten. Another technique adopts the alternative approach—that is, accurate measurement of alterations in the weight of food being eaten while ignoring the physical elements of eating behavior. This is achieved by the continuous weighing of the subject's plate (or other vessel) with a concealed electronic balance on which the plate rest. The device is called the Universal Eating Monitor (UEM), and it can be used with either solid food on plates or liquid foods such as soups in dishes.

This technique should combine the accurate monitoring of intake found with the reservoir method with the advantage of being able to cope with normal solid foods. Therefore, in the first description and test of the procedure, a comparison was made between foods cut up into pieces and placed on a plate and the same foods liquified in a blender and served in a bowl [29]. The test foods were yogurt, apples, bananas, tofu (bean curd), and soy nuts. For the solid, chewable version of the meal the fruit and tofu were cut into small disks and mixed with the yogurt and soy bean (powder form). For the liquid meal all the elements were blended together in stages.

The foods were served on a plate or bowl placed on a panel set into a table and covered by a cloth. Beneath the panel was an electronic weighing instrument that was connected to a digital computer. Readings of the weight of the plate were made and stored every three seconds during the course of the meal and for some time afterward. From these readings a cumulative intake curve (weight of food removed from plate over time) was plotted. This curve is the major parameter of eating provided by this technique.

For the initial investigation with the technique, intake of the two types of foods was measured following either three or six hours of food deprivation. Results indicated that total amount consumed did not vary with the length of deprivation, nor did it depend on the consistency of the food. However, differences were apparent in the rate of ingestion. The liquified food was eaten faster (108 g/min) than the solid food (71 g/min). Differences were also apparent in the initial rate of consumption and in the rate of deceleration. The initial rate was higher for the liquified food (148.7 g/min) than for the solid food (95.6 g/min), and the rate of deceleration was greater (8.6 g/min compared with 1.9 g/min). Accordingly, the negatively accelerated intake curve, regarded by some as an indicator of biological satiation [26], was displayed only with the liquified version of the food.

The pilot study with the technique illustrated that it could accurately and precisely track intake of both liquid and solid food. Moreover, the subtle differences in the cumulative intake curves for the two diets indicated that the device is sensitive to at least some of the factors influencing overall food consumption.

More recently the device has been used to evaluate the effect of the gut hormone cholecystokinin (CCK-8) on eating [30]. It was found that CCK-8 significantly reduced the total amount of food consumed (average decrease 125.5 g) and shortened the duration of the meal by 2.6 minutes. Although the food used in this study was a liquified blend of yogurt and fruit, the cumulative intake curve did not reveal any effect of CCK-8 on either the rate of ingestion or on the shape of the curve. Consequently, CCK-8 shortened this somewhat artificial meal without changing the rate of eating.

This alteration in amount consumed and duration of the meal show that the technique can be usefully employed and may be particularly valuable in investigating the effects of potential anorexic substances. The accurate readout of adjustments in the weight of liquid consumed is similar to that which could be obtained with the reservoir method: The great advantage of this technique, however, is that the food can be eaten normally from a bowl instead of being sucked or pumped through a pipe. In addition, the continuous tracking of intake by the computer gives the cumulative curve a sensitivity to certain factors influencing different processes underlying consumption.

4. *Food dispensing machines.* Many of the techniques now used to study human eating derived from strategies used to monitor feeding patterns in animals. The use of pellet dispensers and eatometers have been instrumental in understanding the effects of pharmacological manipulations on feeding behavior in animals [31]. This principle has subsequently been taken up for the study of the effect of anorectic drugs on food intake in humans [32,33].

The solid-food dispenser is basically a commerical food vending machine modified to provide small food units (quarter sandwiches) with weight, nutrient content, and calorific value that are accurately controlled. The removal of each food unit from the dispenser can be monitored, and consequently, a cumulative record can be obtained of the subject's behavior (feeding profile) and the weight of food consumed (calorie intake).

Some advantages of this device are that it uses common solid foods that are likely to be regularly consumed, and the act of eating does not have to be specially modified. The resolving power of the device—or its capacity to detect subtle or small adjustments in intake—is obviously restricted by the size of the individual food units. Consequently, the sensitivity to mild intrameal influences is much lower than in the UEM and in comparable animal eatometers in which the individual units are tiny (45 mg) pellets. However, the solid food dispenser can detect alterations in eating profiles induced by drugs with anoretic properties and can be used to compare temporal patterns of hunger ratings and food intake [34].

One further major advantage of this type of device is that it can be used to monitor not only food intake but also food selection. By stocking the machine with items varying in macro-nutrient composition, it becomes possible to measure protein and carbohydrate intakes separately and also to assess a subject's preference for particular nutrients or tastes. This strategy has been used to evaluate the effect of serotonin manipulations on nutrient selection in normal subjects [35] and to measure the suppression of carbohydrate craving in obese people [36].

5. *Monitoring of chewing and swallowing—the edogram.* The methods described have attempted to track human eating in two ways—either by monitoring and measuring the volume or weight of food as it is consumed, or by detecting and recording the actual behavior of subjects as they eat. The analysis of behavior can focus on the macrostructure or microstructure of eating. Of course, the structure of behavior can be recorded and analyzed using observational methods, but the special feature of the edogram is that it provides an automated and objective method for describing the microstructure of eating, particularly the rate of chewing, duration of chewing between successive swallowing movements, and intrameal pauses without chewing.

The initial work with this technique was carried out by Pierson and Le Magnen [37], and the edogram was composed from the electromyographic recordings of masseter muscles together with the record of swallowing movements. In more recent studies, swallowing—or deglutition—has been measured by changes in pressure in a balloon resting on the Adam's apple and kept in place by an elastic collar, while chewing has been measured by a strain gauge that monitors jaw movements [38,39].

The standardized test food used in these studies is normally a number of small open sandwiches—a 4-cm square piece of bread covered with a distinctively flavored food. Consequently, this procedure provides a sensitive technique for the continuous monitoring of the important elements that make up eating behavior. In addition, since the test food is composed of small consumable units of known weight, volume, and caloric value, the procedure allows continuous tracking of caloric intake. Consequently, the technique combines some of the best aspects of BITE and UEM. With a sensitive device such as this it becomes possible to describe the way in which eating behavior and food intake is influenced by such variables as palatability of the food, level of deprivation, and body weight of the subjects, and to detect the changes in structure of eating that take place during the course of a meal (as long as the meal is composed of the standard food units).

In an initial study using normal weight subjects, increasing the palatability of the food items (assessed by visual analogue rating scales) brought about an increase in meal size and meal duration. That is, subjects ate more of the foods they preferred. Less obvious was the finding that the more palatable the food, the less time subjects spent chewing it. It was also shown that chewing time per food unit and the interval between food units increased from the beginning to the end of the meal [38]. This reduction in the rate of eating across the course of a meal has been observed in other investigations and reflects the decline in appetite, or the development of satiation, as the meal proceeds [40]. Interestingly, in a subsequent study comparing eating patterns of lean and obese subjects, neither eating rate nor any other parameter changed during the course of the meal in obese subjects [39]. A more recent investigation indicates that eating parameters appear to be influenced similarly by food deprivation and palatability [41]. When strong deprivation (15 hours) and high palatability are combined, their effects are generally additive, not synergistic. The sensitivity of the edogram with the food unit system permitting the consumption of single and mixed-flavor meals means that this technique is a valuable tool for investigating the functional relationships between factors influencing food intake.

THE MEASUREMENT OF TRAITS

The terms "trait" and "state" have been borrowed from the study and measurement of personality. They distinguish those individual characteristics that are enduring from those that are more short-lived. A "trait," which may reflect ability, temperament, or motivation, is an underlying feature that contributes to behavior and remains relatively stable over time. "States," on the other hand, are short-term and especially liable to change. For example, the level of anxiety experienced at any given time if composed of both state and trait anxiety [42]. Similarly, eating can be seen to reflect long-term relatively stable characteristics (traits) and short-term moment- to-moment influences (states).

The description and measurement of what we shall call "eating traits" are invariably carried out using some form of questionnaire. Little will be said here about the processes involved in questionnaire design or about the variety of rating or weighting technique subsumed under this method. This information is available elsewhere [43]. The intention is to outline the uses of questionnaires and to describe some of those most frequently used. The review of "eating traits" may be organized into three categories: (1) food habits, (2) dieting, restraint, and attitudes to weight, and (3) eating attitudes and behavior.

Food Habits

There have been many published accounts of the food habits and eating habits of groups of people, particularly of younger people [44-48]. In general, the methods used are broad surveys encompassing intake diaries and detailed questionnaires. The type of information that these questionnaires are designed to provide include the following:

1. Food consumption data—often complementary to that of intake diaries.
2. Details of purchasing—amount of money spent, where brought, where consumed.
3. Classification of foods eaten—health foods, fast foods, confectionary, and alcohol consumption.
4. Structure of food intake—meal frequency, missed meals, structuring of meals, snacking, dieting to lose weight.
5. Food preferences and dislikes.

The last category, food preferences and dislikes, has been the focus of special investigation under the auspices of the American Armed Forces [49]. The procedure elicited ratings of preference for a large sample of foods (375) from a large sample of respondents (nearly 4,000), together with estimates of the frequency of consumption of each item. The items were then grouped into food classes and hierarchies of preference plotted both within each class and between classes. Items appearing very low in the hedonic scale, and so generally disliked, could be identified as could those particularly liked.

This information has not only been used for institutional menu planning, but has been used to characterize the preferences of particular groups within the general population. Differences in preferences have been described between white and black personnel, between overweight and underweight individuals [50], and between men and women [51]. These data are of particular value for industrial food service systems, because they describe the average tendencies of particular classes of people. However, this type of survey procedure, designed to reveal the patterns of food choice of specific groups, offers little information concerning individual profiles of preference, In addition, the findings will be limited to the nature of the population being studied (eg, US Armed Forces personnel) and the types of products (culturally defined foods) available.

Dieting, Restraint, and Attitudes to Weight

Questionnaire surveys of attitudes toward weight show dissatisfaction with present weight to be prevalent in late- adolescent girls; in one instance, 80% gave their desired weight as lower than their present weight [52]. In a separate study, over half the sample (females aged 14 to 20) said they had felt fat at some time, and about a third had actively dieted to lose weight [53]. The frequency of dieting together with the variety of effects that restricting food intake may have on physiological, psychological, and behavioral parameters [2], means that the assessment of attitudes about dietary restriction is of considerable social importance.

The first method to go beyond the simple question, "Are you on a diet?", was a short rating scale devised by Herman and Mack [54]. It consisted of five questions relating to dieting, eating behavior and associated emotions, and short-term weight change. The rating scale was regarded as measuring the factor of "dietary restraint". The score achieved on this set of questions was found to predict the outcome of behavioral studies in the laboratory. In various experiments the food consumption of subjects classified as highly concerned with dieting (highly restrained) was markedly different from that of low-restraint subjects.

At about the same time, Pudel et al. [55] developed a 40-item questionnaire that identified people of normal weight who remained at that weight by restricting their food intake—the so-called "latent obese." Unfortunately however, this questionnaire has never been published in English. Herman et al later extended the restraint questionnaire to ten items in length but of essentially similar content [56]. While this version of the restraint questionnaire has been widely used, concern has been expressed about the combination of questions relating to eating behavior with those concerning weight

changes. Factor analyses of responses to the restraint questionnaire have consistently yielded two, although not necessarily unrelated, factors—dietary concern and weight fluctuation [57-59]. These have been found to differ from each other in their relationship with variables such as weight status, self-consciousness, and social anxiety. However, Herman and Policy [60] have argued in response that body weight changes are symptomatic of, and are an integral part of, a concern with dieting. In this regard, it seems surprising that no account is taken of subjects' "success" in dieting and that the present state of weight loss or gain is ignored. The latter factor may constitute one of the state variables that interacts with the trait variable of restraint to determine the behavioral outcome of experiments.

Criticism has come from another direction, with Ruderman [61] arguing that the questionnaire has a different meaning for normal weight and overweight individuals. The obese typically score higher (ie, show more restraint) than normal-weight subjects, and there is evidence that they may use different constructs in doing so. However, although these psychometric analyses are informative and provide useful notes of caution about the use of the questionnaire, they do not undermine the principles of this scale. Nor should they be seen as invalidating the concept of restraint (recently further developed by Herman and Polivy) [62].

An alternative measure of restraint has been devised by Stunkard [63]. The questionnaire items were initially a combination of Herman's longer restraint scale, a translation of Pudel et al's latent-obesity questionnaire, together with a number of new items. Factor analysis of a large number of responses, validation, and a second factor analysis left a questionnaire containing 58 items within a three-factor structure. The principal factors have been termed "cognitive restraint," "tendency toward disinhibition" or "emotional lability" and "perceived hunger." Further assessments of reliability and validity have caused the authors to revise the questionnaire and to change or omit a number of items [64]. Most notably, the four items relating to weight fluctuation in Herman's revised scale have been omitted in this revision.

The final 51-item questionnaire has also changed slightly in the interpretation of the three factors. Factor 1 is now seen as "cognitive control leading to behavioral restraint in eating," while factor 2 is a more general dimension of "disinhibited eating," indicative of a susceptibility to disinhibition of restraint [65]. Factor 3 remains as "susceptibility to hunger."

It remains to be seen how useful the three-factor structure of this questionnaire will be. The score on factor 1 will be particularly useful in the quantification of the trait of dietary restaint. As such it may become more

Table 8.1 Published questionnaires assessing eating attitudes and behaviors

Test	Number and type of items	Variables measured	Target population and other comments
Anorectic Attitude Scale (66)	63 items, self-rated on a 4-point scale (scored 1-4)	Factor analysis: Denial Psychosexual immaturity Loss of appetite Interpersonal control Thin body ideal Hypothermia Compulsivity Hyperactivity Purgatives	Anorexic nervosa Unbalanced number of items per category, ranging from 2-19
Anorectic Behavior Scale (68)	22 items, observer-rated No/Not sure/Yes (scored 0-2)	Behaviors arranged under categories: Resistance to eating Disposing of food Activity	Anorexia nervosa
Binge Eating Scale (69)	16 items, self-rated on a 4-point scale (scored 0-3)	Severity of binge-eating problems	Binge eaters; only obese subjects considered during development
Binge Scale Questionnaire (70)	9 items, self-rated, choice of 3 or 4 alternatives (scored 0-2,3)	Severity of binge-eating	Binge eaters; subjects of many weight groups used during development
Eating Attitudes Test (73)	40 items, self-rated on a 6-point scale (scored 0-3)	Severity of anorexia nervosa/symptom index	Anorexia nervosa although has been used with nonclinical populations
Eating Attitudes Test — Revision (74)	26 items, self-rated on a 6-point scale (scored 0-3)	Factor Analyzed: Dieting Bulimia and food preoccupation Oral control	Anorexia nervosa
Eating Behavior Inventory (71)	26 items, self-rated on a 5-point scale (scored 1-5)	Measure of behaviors implicated in weight loss	Overweight subjects in a behavioral weight program
Eating Disorder Inventory (67)	64 items, self-rated on a 6-point scale (scored 0-3)	Predetermined subscales: Drive for thinness Bulimia Body dissatisfaction Ineffectiveness Perfectionism Interpersonal distrust Interoceptive awareness Maturity fears	Anorexia nervosa both"restrictors" and "bulimics;" has also been used with other weight and feeding disordered populations
Master Questionnaire (72)	56 items, self-rated, True/False (scoring unspecified)	Cluster and factor analyses: Hopelessness Physical attribution Motivation Stimulus control Energy balance knowledge	Obesity; authors express some reservations about internal consistency

widely used as a clinical and research tool than Herman's revised restraint questionnaire. At present, the trait of restraint appears to be a powerful predictor of behavior, and its measurement has considerable theoretical and practical significance.

Eating Attitudes and Behavior

Questionnaire assessments of an individual's eating behavior and associated attitudes have more frequently arisen from the need to objectively describe the characteristics of disordered eaters or people with weight problems. Most of the individual items are intended to indicate deviations from normal attitudes or behavior, although no existing catalogue of "normal" eating attitudes and behavior exists. A range of scales and tests are currently available, which have been validated and tested for reliability to varying degrees. These scales are set out in table 1, where some details are given of the source of each questionnaire, it's extent, completion and scoring, what it measures, and the target subject group.

The questionnaires differ from each other on a number of parameters, which in turn influences the information revealed. This confers a degree of uniqueness on each individual technique. Thus, two questionnaires each designed to describe features of anorexia nervosa may disclose different aspects of the condition. For example, questionnaires may be completed by the subjects themselves or by an outside oberver. Both methods have inherent drawbacks. Self-report questionnaires are open to any bias in the subjects' style of response and even to deliberately inaccurate reporting. Observer-rated judgments reflect the theoretical assumptions of the observer, and there is often a need for prolonged observation before a representative judgement can be made. Secondly, questionnaires differ in their scope. They range from ones that measure a single factor, say severity, to those that are multidimensional in structure, quantifying a series of independent factors or providing information under a diverse series of headings. Thirdly, questionnaires differ in their usage. They may simply form the assessment part of a research enterprise and, as such, numerically identify individuals or groups of subjects. Alternatively, their function may be to quantify attitudes or behaviors that are important for diagnosis, and when shared with the individual, act as a basis for therapeutic intervention. It is essential that these general characteristics of questionnaires be considered before choosing between existing methods or constructing a new questionnaire.

The influence of these features can be seen in the individual tests. For example, The Anorectic Attitude Scale [66] describes nine categories of attitudes typical of anorexia nervosa. The eight factors that make up the Eating Disorder Inventory [67], again originally developed for use with anorexia nervosa patients, are markedly different from those in the Anorectic Attitude Scale. Part of this difference lies in the EDI's broad description of patients' behavioral and cognitive patterns. This makes the questionnaire viable for use with other groups of disordered eaters, eg, normal-weight bulimics. The Anorectic Attitude Scale, on the other hand, is more closely related to diagnostic features of anorexia nervosa and is thus limited in application. Slade's [68] Anoretic Behavior Scale, while dealing with the same

population, provides completely different information. Here the presence or absence of behaviors typical of anorexics are observer-rated. In addition, it is particularly selective, dealing with only three categories of behavior, a feature that may limit its usefulness outside a clinical environment.

The Binge Eating Scale [69] is designed to show the severity of binge eating problems. However, its utility is limited by being derived from the study of only obese subjects. While many features of binge eating are shared by people of all weight categories, the validity for non-obese people should be demonstrated before it can be more extensively used. In contrast, the Binge Scale Questionnaire [70] was developed with subjects of varying weights. Containing only nine items, however, it is the most brief of the questionnaires described.

The Eating Behavior Inventory [71] and the Master Questionnaire [72] address characteristics of obesity. The published version of the Master Questionnaire, as acknowledged by the authors, requires revalidation with different groups of obese subjects in a variety of treatment settings to show its potential. The Eating Behavior Inventory was designed to assess behavior implicated in weight loss for use in a behavioral weight-loss program. Each behavior is scored for its "inappropriateness" (in facilitating weight control), and a persons' training program is tailored to the behavior measured in the inventory.

Garner and Garfinkel's Eating Attitudes Test [73] and its revision [74] are undoubtedly the most widely used of the questionnaires. The adopted format, a series of statements requiring the subject to indicate the personal relevance of each, enables the questionnaire to function in a number of ways. It can provide a scale of severity of anorexia nervosa, distinguishing anorexic patients from recovered anorexics and normal subjects [73]. The revised version can distinguish the bulimic and restricter subtypes [74]. As previously described, patients' responses may play an important role during therapeutic intervention. Alternatively, this test may be used in nonclinical populations to study the development of anorexia in high-risk subjects [75] or to screen groups of subjects [76]. A note of caution regarding this latter function, however, has been made on methodological grounds [77], and it is acknowledged that tests such as the EAT and EDI should accompany clinical judgements rather than replace them [67].

MEASUREMENT OF STATES INFLUENCING EATING

The previous section has reviewed ways of measuring long-term, fairly stable and enduring dispositions that influence eating behavior; the habits, cognitions, and attitudes that form part of a person's lifestyle and that tend to characterize the relationship to food. This section will deal with a collection of factors that are labile and that show marked shifts over short periods of time. These factors fluctuate around eating episodes and constitute a set of variables that influence food consumption in the short-term; They do not remain at stable levels over long periods of time. In most cases they not only help to determine food intake but are themselves influenced by the amount and composition of the food consumed. In this way they represent measurable indices of the moment-to-moment tendency to eat.

Ratings of Hunger and Satiety

Before the methods used to quantify experiences of hunger and satiety are discussed, it is appropriate to describe the background to the use of such assessments. A brief glance at the literature indicates the high degree of acceptance that experiences of hunger and satiety play a central role in the control of eating. There is, however, less agreement about the source of such experiences. To what extent are hunger and satiety subjective expressions of physiological need? How dependent are they on the prominence of somatic sensations? To what extent are these experiences set apart from immediate physiological state by conditioning [78,79]? It appears that these experiences do not have universally accepted identities [40], and the data generated from different assessment methods may be conflicting and misleading. Furthermore, the way in which experimental subjects use the term "hunger" may differ from the manner intended by the experimenter. Thus, in declaring a feeling of hunger, a person may be referring to local sensations in the body, the passage of time since the last meal, the presence of salient cues associated with eating, or they may be making an attribution to justify the imminent act of eating [40].

Additional problems include the presumed relationship between such ratings and food intake. Often the correlation between hunger ratings and food consumption is low [80,81], and in certain cases these two measures can be completely dissociated [34]. One reason for this is that these ratings are influenced by variables other than those signaling physiological depletion or repletion. Hunger ratings have been found to vary according to the "apparent" rather than "real" caloric value of food [82]. They may also vary according to the individual's preference for the food being consumed [83]. Even non-food- oriented beliefs can adjust ratings of hunger after food deprivation [84]. Consequently quantifying the subjective experience of hunger is not a simple issue, as often presumed.

The two most common rating methods are fixed-point scales and visual-analogue scales. Fixed-point scales are quick and simple to use, and the data they provide are easy to analyze. However, the scales can vary greatly in complexity. At their most simple they are numerical indications of the presence or absence of hunger [85]. Scales with a wider response range may have every point extensively defined to ensure that the subject understands the meaning of the scale [86]. Alternatively, the scale may have as many as 100 divisions with only a few points anchored by words [87]. The tendency has been for different research groups to construct their own scale, which is unique not only in the number of points used but also in definition of the measured variable. Thus, Jordan and his co-workers often used nine-point scales [20,21], while others have used seven-point scales [88]. In considering the appropriate number of points to be included in this type of scale, the freedom to make a wide range of possible responses (multiple-point scales) has to be balanced against the precision and reliability of the device (scales with few points). Hodson and Greene [87] found that responses on 100-point scales of hunger and enjoyment of food were related to behavioral and physiological parameters, while the same variables measured on five-point scales were not. It therefore seems likely that scales with an insufficient number of fixed points may be insensitive to certain changes in subjective experience.

A variant of fixed-point scales are graphic-ratings scales, or scales with points marked on a straight line. A study of their use in expressing pain, however, reveals some of the deficiencies shared by all fixed-point methods. The distribution of ratings was found to be influenced by a variety of factors, including the familiarity of patients with the scales, the nature of the experiment, the orientation of the line (horizontal or vertical), how the line was graduated, and by the fixed points themselves [89].

One way of overcoming some of the failings of fixed-point scales is to abolish the points completely. Thus, visual-analogue scales are horizontal lines (often 10 cm long), unbroken and unmarked except for word anchors at each end [32]. The user of the scale is instructed to mark the line at a point that most accurately represents the intensity of the subjective feeling at that time. The experimenter measures the distance to that mark in millimetres from one end, thus yielding a score of 0 to 100. By doing away with all the verbal labels except the end definitions, visual-analogue scales have retained the advantages of fixed- point scales while avoiding the effects on the mid-range of the distribution of either descriptive terms or preferred numbers [89]. Indeed, in a direct comparison of the two methods, it was found that the visual-analogue scale was as accurate and reliable as a fixed-point scale but more sensitive in registering the intensity of chronic pain [90]. However, this would appear to be the case only if the scale is 10 cm or more in length [91].

Visual-analogue scales are not, however, entirely devoid of abnormalities in their distribution of responses. For example, Bond and Lader [92] found that responses on a number of mood visual-analogue scales showed evidence of results being skewed to the positive end and of a peak at the center on a number of scales. Much of this deviation from a normal distribution is a result of using bipolar scales (eg, tired/alert; hungry/satiated) rather than unipolar scales (eg, very tired/not at all tired; very hungry/not at all hungry). The latter require subjects to make their assessment only on a single construct, rather than on a compound of two, which may vary independently and differently for different subjects. The formulation of scales with hunger and satiety at opposite ends probably lead to errors that may be exaggerated when attempts are made to define points along this artificial continuum [93]. Subjects may be unable to reliably discriminate between the points when referring to their own personal experience [94].

One particularly revealing way of using visual-analogue scales in the study of experiences accompanying eating has been to administer scales of hunger and other experiences at particular times before, during, and after a meal. This method of "temporal tracking" has disclosed previously unpredicted effects of physiological and sensory manipulations. Thus, ratings of hunger return to control levels during eating after being lowered by anorectic drugs before eating [95]. In addition, the palatability of food influences hunger ratings when the food is seen, during the first part of the meal, and two hours after the food was eaten [83].

Bodily Sensations

Certain bodily sensations are well associated with states of hunger and satiety. Commonplace experience associates gastric motility with hunger and gastric fullness with satiation. However, experimental evidence shows only a "weak and inconsistent influence" of gastric motility on hunger ratings [96]. Furthermore, while sensations originating from the area of the stomach may be particularly prominent, they form only one component of a range of accompanying sensations.

The first systematic study of premeal and postmeal bodily sensations was conducted using a checklist format [97]. A range of sensations was described and localized according to various bodily areas: the stomach, mouth, throat and head, together with more general physical sensations. Subjects read through the lists and recorded the presence of sensations at various times before, at the beginning of, and at the end of a meal. These records allowed changes in the incidence and location of the sensations to be plotted and were successful in describing clear shifts in sensory experience.

A similar methodology was employed in a study of the premeal and postmeal bodily sensations experienced by anorexic nervosa patients [98]. Again, the technique was successful in revealing a difference in response, but on this occasion the patients differed from a control group in the variability of their response. There appeared to be a greater variation in the way the anorexics perceived the gastric component after eating. Gastric sensation was either absent, present as bloating, or alternated with no sensation.

Bodily sensation checklist data presented as frequency counts have been used to compare the effects of anorectic drugs before and after meals [81], to compare the percentages of subjects experiencing a sensation within particular groups [99], and to provide statements of variability in response [98]. However, data conforming to a nominal scale obviously has limitations. An alternative method therefore has been to scale the intensity of each individual sensation in order to provide data on an interval scale. This permits the reporting of a greater range of response than assessing presence or absence of a sensation. Factor analysis and cluster analysis of such ratings have yielded a complex set of sensation clusters, the structure of which changes before and after a meal [100]. However, further analysis of this type is necessary, under a range of experimental conditions, before the most meaningful components can be extracted.

An obvious way of reducing the complexity involved with multiple sensations is to monitor and rate the salience of a single sensation. Indeed, this has been viewed as a way of describing hunger and satiety and has taken the form of requesting subjects to report the presence of a (any) hunger or satiety sensation [101]. Alternatively, the sensation may be specified and, for example, satiety described as ratings of gastric fullness. There are two problems with this type of strategy, however. First, the distillation of a complex experience such as satiety into a single sensation may be conceptually erroneous. Second, the use of psychophysical methods for scaling an experience like satiety may be misleading. A psychophysical procedure really requires a firm physical or physiological parameter varying along a dimension in order to calibrate the subjective sensation. Even cross-modal matching, requiring subjects to match their feeling of gastric fullness to the length of a tape measure [102], does not increase the power of the technique.

A further problem is that while psychophysical procedures have been shown to be accurate for visual and auditory sensations, somatic sense modalities are known to be perceptually vague and to have concomitant aversive qualities that may influence the scaling of intensity [103]. The separation of an affective dimension of a sensation from the dimension of intensity is recognized in the study of pain sensations [104,105] and has been incorporated into methods of measurement. Moreover, the independence of these dimensions has been demonstrated experimentally [106,107]. A description of the affective nature of bodily sensations, in addition to that of their strength, would more fully define the sensations characteristic of energy depletion and repletion.

Taste Hedonics

As with bodily sensations, taste stimuli have clearly distinguishable qualities. A taste stimulus may be judged according to its intensity (strength) and to its hedonic (pleasantness) properties. However, little will be said here about taste sensitivity. It is known that people vary in their ability to perceive particular tastes. The reasons for this are various and include adrenal cortical insufficiency [108], diabetes [109], cancer [110], taste bud pathology [111], nutrition [112], and age [113]. The methodological issues concerning taste sensitivity have been extensively reviewed elsewhere [114]. Instead, attention will be directed to the description of taste hedonics and in particular to short-term changes in hedonics.

One way of ordering the pleasantness of a range of solutions is to present the subject with a series of paired comparisons [115,116]. The subject is simply required to say which of the pair is preferred. A forced-choice requirement may also be imposed, whereby the subject must indicate a preference for one over the other and is not allowed to make judgements of equality. The presentation of all the possible pairings from a series of stimulus concentrations allows preference to be expressed on a scale against concentration.

The rank ordering of sitmuli is an extension of the paired- comparison method and arranges the three or more stimuli in order of preference or pleasantness. The subject should be allowed to "back-check" and taste solutions encountered earlier to make accurate judgements. One way of displaying these data is to tabulate the number of subjects who ranked each solution as the most pleasant [117].

The methods described have the disadvantage that the pleasantness of a solution is defined relative to other solutions. The scaling is ordinal; in other words, no absolute value of pleasantness is obtained. This may be remedied by rating pleasantness by assigning some type of physical value to each stimulus. Magnitude estimation requires subjects to make their estimates of pleasantness on a ratio scale. Category scaling, which is more common, provides intervals of pleasantness. The most common example of the latter is the nine-point hedonic scale and is usually attributed to Peryam and Pilgrim [118]. It is still widely used [119] and provides a range of response from 1—"extremely unpleasant" or "as unpleasant as anything ever tasted,"—to 9—"extremely pleasant" or "as pleasant as anything ever tasted,"—with 5 being defined as "neutral" or "neither pleasant nor unpleasant." While this is the standard hedonic scale, there are numerous others, which differ in the number of categories and wording used. Visual-analogue scales may even be used, anchored by words such as "like—dislike" [120].

The usual way of eliciting hedonic responses to a taste is to present a range of concentrations of the taste stimulus and to plot hedonic appreciation as a function of increasing concentration. The parallel measurement of intensity enables detection and recognition thresholds to be computed and has shown taste stimuli to have unforeseen hedonic properties even when they are apparently undetectable. Moreover, these so-called "expectancy ratings" (the procedural details mean that the subject usually knows what modality they are tasting even though they can't taste the individual solution) differ according to weight status [121]. It may be that adult-onset obese subjects differ from juvenile-onset or never-obese subjects in how they anticipate the pleasurable quality of a taste. Further study is required to amplify this matter. However, it does point to the crucial role of methodology in this type of research. Accurate assessments of the hedonic properties of taste sitmuli share a number of methodological features with descriptions of intensity. For example, the subjects' mouth should be untainted by prior ingestion or smoking for some specified time (eg, previous two hours). Subjects should be provided with a neutral mouthwash (eg, tap water) between each trial, the presentation of stimuli carefully counterbalanced, and the study conducted double-blind (ie, without either subject or experimenter aware of the identity of each stimulus).

Data collected in this fashion have shown three important properties of taste hedonics. First, the relationship between pleasantness and the concentration of a solution is different to that of intensity [122]. Second, this relationship varies from subject to subject, with two characteristic pleasantness- concentration profiles emerging [123,124]. Type-I responders show a decrease in preference for very sweet stimuli, while type-II responders show a monotonic rise in pleasantness as sweetness increases. These two profiles do not simply reflect the hedonic patterns of obese and normal-weight subjects. The relationship between weight and taste perception is not a simple one. Both types of responders are found in all weight categories, but there is evidence that a greater proportion of the obese are type-I responders [123]. However, this categorization only applies to the hedonic response to a sweet taste, not to any other taste modality [121].

Third, subjects' hedonic response to a sweet stimulus depends in part on their physiological or nutritional state. *Alliesthesia*, a word coined by Cabanac [125] and meaning "changed sensation," describes the dependence of hedonic experience on the internal milieu. It is best shown by the decrease in pleasantness of a sweet solution after ingestion of a nutritive glucose meal. This is an example of negative alliesthesia [126]. The opposite, positive alliesthesia, or increase in pleasantness, has been shown following injected insulin, but it is much less robust and limited to a short period over half an hour after administration [127].

The methods used to describe this shift in hedonic appreciation are extensions of those previously detailed. There are two basic methods. In one, a range of concentrations of a sweet solution are tasted and rated on a numerical hedonic scale (often using only five points). The range of solutions (normally five different concentrations) covers a broad spectrum of sweetness. Ratings are made twice, once before the load and again 45 or 60 minutes later. The alternative method is to track on the same scale the pleasantness of a single moderately sweet solution. The standard solution is rated first before ingestion of the load and at regular intervals after ingestion (as frequently as every three minutes to every 15 minutes) for the next hour. Although alliesthesia appears consistent and replicable, the hedonic shift itself may be fairly small so that data are often plotted as cumulative changes in order to emphasize the response.

Research into the mechanisms underlying alliesthesia has prompted a shift away from a simple interpretation in order to account for the hedonic changes brought about by noncaloric sweeteners such as cyclamate [128] and mannitol [129], and has led to the introduction of mediating physiological features such as putative duodenal osmotic receptors [129]. The real importance of alliesthesia is its likely functional properties; that is, the decline in preference in the sweet taste modality leading to decreased food intake and so being part of the process of satiation [130]. The consumption of real foods has indeed been shown to produce alliesthesia to a sweet solution, and solid foods are more effective in this regard than liquid foods [131]. However, two notes of caution should be made here. First, although there is evidence that loads of different nutrient composition (eg, high in protein), reduce the pleasantness of a sweet taste [132], the reasoning behind alliesthesia is that the

hedonic value of a taste serves as an indicator of the physiologic need for the substrate signified by the taste. A high protein load should therefore alter subjective preferences for savory stimuli [133]. It is necessary to show that alliesthesia is related to nutritional needs and is not simply a particular phenomenon relating to changes in pleasantness of sweet solutions. Second, experiments that study changes in taste hedonics following the consumption of real foods confound comparisons across treatments by not controlling for the overall macronutrient composition of the load or its fiber content. Changing the nature of the dietary fiber in a food may effect physiological and subjective response [93]. Indeed, other factors may be involved in the development of alliesthesia in these circumstances [134].

Food Preferences

Apart from the total amount of food eaten, the most obvious factor that distinguishes between the eating patterns of individuals or groups is the type of food eaten. It is normally supposed that the type of food selected is determined by subjective preferences. Indeed, the expressed preference for a food is one of a handful of factors that strongly predict the nature and quantity of food consumed [135]. In other words, disclosing preferences about particular foods appears to correlate with actual food consumed. Consequently, an instrument for assessing food preferences could be profitable used in clinical and commercial situations. Surprisingly, food preferences are only rarely assessed in investigations of mechanisms controlling feeding.

Certain techniques are frequently used in the sensory evaluation of foods and beverages [136]. However, it should not be assumed that taste preferences and food preferences are identical. The preference for a food is not simply the sum of the preferences for the individual tastes that make up that food; other qualities may be crucial including odor, texture, temperature, specific culturally-derived influences, and metabolic and neurochemical effects. Food preference is a multidimensional composite of all these factors [133].

The most simple technique that is sensitive to short-term changes in preference is a checklist of basic food items. The subjects' task is to check the items that they would like to eat, considering each one independently of the others. The overall score constitutes a range of food preferences. In addition, the food items may be ranked in order of preference to give a hierarchy of preference. Alternatively, the frequency of checking of food items may be compared between two or more predetermined categories such as high calorie-low calorie or high protein-high carbohydrate. Fluctuations in recorded food preferences can therefore reveal aberrant or idiosyncratic eating patterns such as salt preference, carbohydrate craving, or meat avoidance. Variants of this check-list method often include hedonic scales or visual- analogue scales associated with each item. On these, subjects may indicate how pleasant they find each food item, or they may give an estimate of the amount of each item they think they would like to eat.

The methods described have been used to investigate whether particular preferences are associated with changes in hunger and satiety. For example, the number of both high-protein and high- carbohydrate foods selected from a checklist has been found to decrease after a meal, high-protein foods showing the largest decrease in selection, while the selection of low-calorie foods do not decrease [83,95]. This type of checklist has also been used to disclose the relationships between neurotransmitter alterations brought about by various drugs and preferences for foods rich in protein and carbohydrate [81]. Interestingly, changes in the checklist recording of nutrient- specific items was noted for a dose of one drug (fenfluramine) that exerted no measureable effect on food intake or subjective hunger. A food preference checklist is a sensitive device. Assessments of the pleasantness of checklist food items, and of the quantities of each that subjects think they could eat, are also capable of distinguishing the satiating effects of soups of different caloric densities [101]. Rating the pleasantness of a range of foods has yielded a particularly stable laboratory phenomenon—sensory specific satiety. This refers to the decline in pleasantness of foods eaten in large quantities compared with those not eaten [137] (see Chapter 10, this volume).

An alternative to the checklist methods of quantifying preference is provided by a forced-choice procedure. In this subjects are obliged to choose only one of a pair of food items, the one they would most like to eat. The items are included on the basis that they are representative of specified categories (eg, high protein-high carbohydrate). The presentation of a list of all possible pairings of items from category A versus items from category B affords a measure of the relative preference of A over B and also provides a hierarchy of preference of the individual items used. This forced-choice procedure has been used to describe how the distribution of carbohydrate versus protein food choices changes before and after eating [95] and to give additional weight to evidence of the superior satiating capacity of protein over carbohydrate.*

Although many of the examples given of the use of food preference assessments are based on nutritional comparisons, foods vary according to many other parameters. The methods described are suitable for other classifications (eg, sweet versus savory). Indeed, it is likely that the relative importance of these parameters changes according to physiological or environmental circumstances. Described above are basic methods that may be tailored to suit the purposes of individual studies. It is also important to acknowledge that the mode of presentation of the food item may influence the response and that a real food may be perceived as more pleasant, or at least differently, to a food name [138].

Lastly, some comment should be made about the relationship between food preference measures and food consumption. It is interesting to note that the relationship between the dislike of a food item and nonuse is stronger than that between liking for and consumption [139]. This may be because food dislikes are better understood and the mechanisms involved in their acquisition more easily identifiable. Thus a food-rejection taxonomy may be developed [140], and nausea identified as a potent instigator of dislike [141]. It appears to be far less easy to describe food likes or preferences in a similar way [142]. Considering the attention that is now being directed to mechanisms controlling the selection of foods in addition to the control of total calories, the measurement of food preferences will figure more prominently in future investigations.

Salivation

The secretion of saliva is, like a range of other physiological processes, an involuntary accompaniment to eating. However, what makes salivation of particular interest in the present context is its capacity to be conditioned to the arrival of food and to anticipate eating. These anticipatory responses are known as cephalic reflexes and are sensitive to the sight and smell of food [143,144]. Functionally they act to prepare the digestive system to receive food [145]. A number of findings have prompted this physiological response to be viewed as a reliable index of appetite. First, it is apparently uncontaminated by the cognitive and methodological variables that influence pencil-and-paper ratings. Second, anticipatory salivation is modulated by palatability and deprivation and correlates significantly with ratings of hunger and food appeal [88; see 146 for review]. In addition, one characteristic distinguishes salivation from the other cephalic reflexes—the ease of measurement.

There are three basic measurement techniques. The most widely used is the SHP (Strongin, Hinsie and Peck) method [147].One to three preweighed dental rolls are placed under the tongue and left there for a short period of time (eg, two minutes). They are then collected and placed in a sealed container to be weighed

---

* Hill AJ, Blundell JE. The relationship between protein intake, ratings of hunger and satiety and food preferences. Paper presented to the Eating Habits Symposium, Sussex University, UK. April, 1984.

at the end of the experiment. Normally, two or three measures are taken, with a suitable period between each, to establish an accurate mean level of response. In contrast to this procedure, which requires very little specialized equipment, the Lashley suction cup monitors saliva flow rate from a single group of salivary glands. This device takes the form of a plastic cup positioned unilaterally or bilaterally over Stensen's duct and held to the inside of the cheek by negative pressure, which draws the saliva to a recording device [148]. The advantage of this method is that it is very accurate and may be used to provide continuous records of saliva flow over a relatively long period of time, such as an hour [149]. However, both methods suffer from being intrusive and somewhat uncomfortable. The alternative is to collect the total salivary output from the mouth. This may be done by suction using a dental fluid ejector continuously or at the end of a timed period [150], or by simply voiding the accumulated secretions into a preweighed specimen jar [144,148]. The latter method may be further distinguished by whether it was "working" (subjects move their mouth and jaw in a continuous chewing motion) or "quiet" (no movement).

Comparisons of these methods have shown them to be significantly intercorrelated, and it has been concluded that, "considerations other than greater precision may be used to dictate the choice of an appropriate procedure" [148]. One of the major considerations is the design of the experiment. There are two basic ways in which salivation is studied. One way is to measure salivation in a range of subjects and to correlate it with another variable such as weight or dieting status. The other method, and more commonly used, is to establish a baseline of responding and to compare this with the level of salivation elicited by a food-related stimulus or some experimental manipulation. The stimulus used in "stimulus-induced salivation" may be the sight or smell of real food, a food word, or thinking about food.

Stimulus-induced salivation (SIS) does not lack sensitivity. For example, a low dose (10 mg) of an anorectic drug (amphetamine) reduced SIS while leaving hunger ratings unaffected [151]. In addition to deprivation and palatability [88], SIS has also been shown to be influenced by body weight [152], by dieting to lose weight [153], and is even dependent on the time of day [146]. Indeed, it appears that salivation is a supersensitive response. This may account for the inconsistent relationship found between salivation and hunger ratings in studies varying in methodology and experimental design [154]. It remains to be confirmed whether salivation represents a global index of hunger or appetite. Other studies suggest a more specific role for salivation. For example, Blundell and Freeman [155] found the degree of salivation brought about by particular odors

could be modified by prior administration of a nutritional load. In particular, a glucose load selectively suppressed subsequent salivation to a sweet (honey-flavored) odor. This finding indicates that SIS may be used as a measure of alliesthesia and of sensory-specific satiety. The influence of the macronutrient composition of particular loads awaits investigation.

OTHER TECHNIQUES

There are a few techniques which either do not fit easily into one of the previous sections or whose characteristics are sufficiently specialized to warrant separate consideration. Research on feeding in young children is one area in which original methods of study have been developed. The consideration of multiple attributions in preference and food choice is another. Some of the techniques used in these two areas are described below.

Working With Young Children

Indications of the taste and food preferences of young children (less than 4 years of age) have in the past relied on food selection and food intake as their sole measures [156,157]. More recently however, experimental strategies have been developed that have enabled researchers to study these issues in more detail, either by careful observation or by harnessing the child's developing but limited verbal skills.

The first of these originated in an attempt to describe the facial expressions of newborn babies to various tastes and odors. In a study of 3- to 7-day-old infants, Steiner [158] found patterns of gustofacial responses characteristic of the basic taste modalities. He found the responses to a sweet taste to be typified by retracted mouth corners, a "smiling" expression and vigorous sucks and licking. In contrast, the responses to a sour taste included lip pursing, nose wrinkling, and blinking. Bitter tastes and a number of smells also had their own associated responses. Research into the origin and nature of these responses has shown them to occur in premature babies, in neonates before their first feeding, and even in babies born without a cerebral cortex. Steiner concludes that this discrimination of stimuli in hedonic terms, ie, pleasant or aversive, has biological significance in conveying information about the acceptability of a food. Whatever their origin or function, these gustofacial reflexes clearly have potential as nonverbal indicators of preference. Moreover, their stability is typified by their endurance into adulthood.

A method for obtaining food preference data from slightly older children has been devised by Birch [159]. She uses three cartoon drawings of faces that describe three categories of hedonic response: like, dislike, and neutral. The children (age range from 2 years and older) first spend time learning the meaning of the faces; the smiling face signifies someone who had "just eaten something liked", while the face with the down-turned mouth is of someone who had "just eaten something disliked." Having learned these categories, the children are presented with a cup containing small pieces of food and are asked to taste the food. They are then asked whether they liked it, disliked it, or whether it was just okay, and to put the cup in front of the face showing the appropriate response. Having completed this for a number of foods the child's attention may be focused on the individual categories and questions such as, "Tell me the food you liked the best," to elicit a rank order of preferences for the foods in each category. This method has been used to study a range of cognitive and social factors that contribute to food preferences. The foods chosen by peers, foods followed by a contingent reward, and the social rules governing the appropriateness of foods at particular times of day have all been shown to influence the expressed liking for foods by children [160-162].

Multidimensional Analyses

As research has progressed, it has become apparent that many processes are under the control of a group of influences rather than a single controlling factor. This being so, a complete account of the antecedents of a behavior cannot be made without dealing with multiple sources of information. Thus, the determinants of what is chosen to be eaten in a single meal will include not only physiological needs and the nutritional content of the food, but also pleasantness, taste, perceived health value of the food, and even its price [163]. Procedures have been developed specifically to describe the interplay of two or more such determinants. These techniques had their origins in the study of psychophysics and in the analysis of factors making up personality. In the present context they have been used to analyze taste preference and to describe the relationship between food beliefs and food intake.

Multidimensional scaling is a mathematical technique that plots individual sitmuli according to ratings made on scales of the perceived attributes of foods or tastes. The plots can be regarded as maps, which are two-dimensional graphical representations using the two most important attributes as axes. In the resulting spatial arrangement, the closer the individual stimuli (foods or tastes), the more similar they are in terms of those qualities. There are many ways in which the stimuli may be rated. Schiffman [164] gives four examples of the way "preference space" may be described. Stimuli may be rated according to their similarity, according to which of a pair of stimuli is preferred, the de-

gree to which one is preferred over another, or according to their ratings over a large range of attributes. A related procedure—the response surface method—has been used to determine preferences for combinations of fatty and sweet substances [165]. It has been demonstrated that preferences for sweetness and dietary fat combined in a complex food system are interdependent.

The technique used in studies of food beliefs and of the ways people construe foods has many features in common with multidimensional scaling, although the theoretical background is quite different. The basic instrument, the repertory grid, originated in the study of personal constructs [166]. Fundamental to this theory is the idea that people have cognitive features that are shaped by, and in turn determine, the world in which they live. These features, or constructs, may be shared by many people or be relatively uncommon, and they may vary in their complexity and stability. In the present context, the idea is that particular perceived qualities of food, eg, how fattening it is, determine selection and consumption. The repertory grid provides a format within which a range of foods (elements) may be assessed along a range of individually-relevant properties (constucts) and be portrayed graphically in a way similar to that for multidimensional scaling.

One use of multidimensional analyses has been to examine the hierarchy of constructs for individual subjects. The structure of these food belief systems may then be related to other aspects of the subject's background or be used to distinguish the subject from others [167,168]. Interestingly, measures afforded by such an analysis have been found to be significantly correlated with the frequency of intake of the foods mentioned, so establishing a link between food beliefs and usage [167]. A second way is to average the grids of a group of individuals and to compare the conceptual structure of one group with that of another. A common basis for comparison has been that of weight, with obese and slim 10-year-olds differing in their conceptions of energy density, tastiness, and preference [169]. Weight differences are not always apparent, however, as obese and normal-weight adults were found not to differ in their perception of a variety of soft drinks [170]. Variables such as restraint may prove to be more potent in this regard.

It is important to recognize that multidimensional scaling procedures are in the relatively early stages of development for use in this area of research. The power of these techniques to derive orderly relations from a complex network of interrelated variables suggests that they will have an increasingly important role to play in determining the relative importance of multiple variables influencing the processes controlling food selection and consumption.

POSTSCRIPT

This chapter has brought together various procedures used to measure and monitor eating behavior applicable to a wide variety of circumstances. In compiling this battery of techniques it has been necessary to include instruments devised to measure aspects of subjective experience as well as overt behavior. Together these provide research tools for investigating mechanisms underlying normal and abnormal eating in quite different situations and over distinctive spans of time. The techniques stand as a testimony to the inventiveness and technical skill of researchers. In addition, they illustrate clearly that the understanding of eating and its disorders proceeds not only by the advancement of good ideas but also through the development of instruments for the precise and reliable description of the basic phenomena under study.

REFERENCES

1. Blundell JE. Biogrammar of feeding: pharmacological manipulations and their interpretations. In Cooper SJ, ed. Progress in theory in psychopharmacology. London: Academic Press, 1981:233-76.

2. Blundell JE, Hill AJ. Biopsychological interactions underlying the study and treatment of obesity. In Christie MJ, Mellett P, eds. The psychosomatic approach: contemporary practice of whole-person care. Chichester: Wiley, 1986:113-38.

3. Keys A. Dietary survey methods. In Levy R, Rifkind B, Dennis B, Ernst N, eds. Nutrition, lipids and coronary heart disease. New York: Raven Press, 1979:1-23.

4. Marr JW. Individual dietary surveys: purposes and methods. World Rev Nutr Dietet, 1971; 13:105-64.

5. Nesheim RD. Current methods for assessing food intake. In Selvey N, White PL, eds. Nutrition in the 1980s: Constraints on our knowledge. New York: Liss, 1981:49-57.

6. Roberge AG, Sevigny J, Seoane N, et al. Dietary intake data: usefulness and limitations. Prog Food Nutr Sci, 1984; 8:27-42.

7. Wing RR, Carrol C, Jeffery RW. Repeated observation of obese and normal subjects eating in the natural environment. Addict Behav, 1978; 3:191-6.

8. Balogh M, Kahn HA, Medalie JH. Random repeat 24-hour dietary records. Am J Clin Nutr, 1971; 24:304-10.

9. Paul AA, Southgate DAT. McCance and Widdowson's The Composition of Foods. 4th ed. London: HMSO, 1978:31

10. Tinbergen EA, Tinbergen N. Early childhood autism—an ethological approach. Z Tierpsychol, 1972; 10:1-53.

11. Hutt SJ, Hutt C. Direct Observation and Measurement of Behavior. Illinois; CC Thomas, 1970.

12. Hill SW, McCutcheon NB. Eating responses of obese and non-obese humans during dinner meals. Psychosom Med, 1975; 37:395-401.

13. Hill SW. Eating responses of humans during dinner meals. J Comp Physiol Psychol, 1974; 86:652-7.

14. Blundell JE, Latham CJ, McArthur RA, et al. Structural analysis of the actions of amphetamine and fenfluramine on food intake and feeding behavior in animals and man. Curr Med Res Opinion, 1979; 6:34-54.

15. Adams N, Ferguson J, Stunkard AJ, et al. The eating behavior of obese and non-obese women. Behav Res Ther, 1978; 16:225-32.

16. Rogers PJ, Blundell JE. Effect of anorexic drugs on food intake and the microstructure of eating in human subjects. Psychopharmacol, 1979; 66:159-65.

17. Stunkard AJ, Kaplan D. Eating in public places: a review of the direct observation of eating behavior. Int J Obesity, 1977; 1:89-101.

18. Spitzer L, Rodin J. Human eating behavior: a critical review of studies in normal weight and overweight individuals. Appetite, 1981; 2:293-329.

19. Hashim SA, Van Itallie TB. An automatically monitored food dispensing apparatus for the study of food intake in man. Fed Proc, 1964; 23:82-4.

20. Jordan HA, Weiland WF, Zebley SP, et al. Direct measurement of food intake in man: a method for the objective study of eating behavior. Psychosom Med, 1966; 28:836-42.

21. Jordan HA. Voluntary intragastric feeding: oral and gastric contributions to food intake and hunger in man. J Comp Physiol Psychol, 1969; 68:498-506.

22. Spiegel TA, Jordan HA: Effects of simultaneous oral-intragastric ingestion on meal patterns and satiety in humans. J Comp Physiol Psychol, 1978; 92:133-141.

23. Walike BC, Jordan HA, Stellar E. Preloading and the regulation of food intake in man. J Comp Physiol Psychol, 1969;327-33.

24. Spiegel TA. Caloric regulation of food intake in man. J Comp Physiol Psychol, 1973; 84:24-37.

25. Meyer JE, Pudel V. Experimental studies on food-intake in obese and normal weight subjects. J Psychosom Res, 1972; 16:305-8.

26. Pudel VE, Oetting M. Eating in the laboratory: behavioral aspects of the positive energy balance. Int J Obesity, 1977; 1:369-86.

27. Hoebel BG. Brain reward and aversion systems in the control of feeding and sexual behavior. Neb Symp Motiv, 1974; 22:49-112.

28. Moon RD. Monitoring human eating patterns during the ingestion of non-liquid foods. Int J Obesity,1979; 3:281-8.

29. Kissileff HR, Klingsberg G, Van Itallie TB. Universal eating monitor for continuous recording of solid or liquid consumption in man. Am J Physiol, 1980; 238:14-22.

30. Pi-Sunyer X, Kissileff HR, Thornton J, et al. C-terminal octapeptide of cholecystokinin decreases food intake in obese men. Physiol Behav, 1982; 29:627-30.

31. Blundell JE, Latham CJ, Leshem MB. Differences be-

tween the anorexic action of amphetamine and fenfluramine: possible effects on hunger and satiety. J
Pharm Pharmacol, 1976; 28: 471-7.

32. Silverstone T, Fincham J. Experimental techniques for
the measurement of hunger and food intake in man for
use in the evaluation of anorectic drugs. In Garattini
S, Samanin R, eds. Central mechanisms of anorectic
drugs. New York: Raven Press, 1978:375-82.

33. Silverstone T, Fincham J, Brydon J. A new technique
for the continuous measurement of food intake in
man. Am J Clin Nutr, 1980; 33:1852-5.

34. Trenchard E, Silverstone JT. Naloxone reduces the
food intake of normal human volunteers. Appetite,
1983; 4:43-50.

35. Wurtman JJ, Wurtman RJ. Suppression of carbohydrate consumption as snacks and at mealtimes by DL-
fenfluramine or tryptophan. In Garattini S, Samanin
R, eds. Anorectic agents—mechanisms of action and
tolerance. New York: Raven Press, 1981:169-82.

36. Wurtman JJ, Wirtman RJ, Growden JH, et al. Carbohydrate craving in obese people: suppression by treatment affecting serotoninergic transmission. Int J Eating Disorders, 1981; 1:2-15.

37. Pierson A, Le Magnen J. Etude quantitative du pro-
cessus de régulation des ésesponses alimentaires chez
l'homme. Physiol Behav, 1969; 4:61-7.

38. Bellisle F, Le Magnen J. The analysis of human feeding patterns: the edogram. Appetite, 1980; 1:141-50.

39. Bellisle F, Le Magnen J. The structure of meals in
humans: eating and drinking patterns in lean and
obese subjects. Physiol Behav, 1981; 27:649-58.

40. Blundell JE. Hunger, appetite and satiety—constructs
in search of identities. In Turner M, ed. Nutrition and
lifestyles. London: Applied Science Publishers,
1979:21-42.

41. Bellisle F, Lucas F, Amrani R, et al. Deprivation, pal-
ability and the micro-structure of meals in human subjects. Appetite, 1984; 5:85-94.

42. Spielberger CD. The nature and measurement of
anxiety. In Spielberger CD, Diaz-Guerrero R, eds.
Cross-Cultural Anxiety. New York: Wiley, 1976:3-12.

43. Oppenheim AN. Questionnaire Design and Attitude
Measurement. London: Heinemann, 1966.

44. Bender AE. Food preferences of males and females.
Proc Nutr Soc, 1976; 35:181-9.

45. Greger JL, Divilbiss L, Aschenbeck SK. Dietary habits of adolescent females. Ecol Food Nutr, 1979; 7:312-
8.

46. Huenemann RL, Shapiro LR, Hampton MC, et al. A
longitudinal study of gross body composition and body
conformation and their association with food and activity in a teen-age population. Am J Clin Nutr, 1966;
18:325-38.

47. Jakobovits C, Halstead P, Kelley L, et al. Eating habits and nutrient intakes of college women over a thirty-
year period. J Am Dietet Assoc, 1977; 71:405-11.

48. Truswell AS, Darnton-Hill I. Food habits of adolescents. Nutr Rev, 1981; 39:73-88.

49. Meiselman HL, Waterman D. Food preferences of en-
listed personnel in the Armed Forces. J Am Dietet
Assoc, 1978; 73:621-9.

50. Meiselman HL, Wyant KW. Food preferences and
flavor experiences. In Solms J, Hall RL, eds. Criteria
of food acceptance: How a man chooses what he eats.
Zurich; Forster, 1981:144-52.

51. Wyant KW, Meiselman HL. Sex and race differences
in food preferences of military personnel. J Am Dietet
Assoc, 1984; 84:169-75.

52. Dwyer JT, Feldman JJ, Seltzer CC, et al. Adolescent
attitudes toward weight and appearance. J Nutr Educ,
1969; 1:14-19.

53. Nylander I. The feeling of being fat and dieting in a
school population. Acta Socio-Med Scand, 1971; 1:17-
26.

54. Herman CP, Mack D. Restrained and unrestrained
eating. J Pers, 1975; 43:647-60.

55. Pudel VE, Metzdorff M, Oetting MX. Zur persoehn-
lichkeit adipoeser in psychologischen tests uner
beruecksichtigung latent fettsuenchtiger. Zeitschrift
fur Psychosomatische Medizin und Psychoanalyse,
1975; 21:345-50.

56. Herman CP, Polivy J, Pliner P, et al. Distractibility in
dieters and non dieters: an alternative view of "exter-
nality". J Pers Soc Psychol, 1978; 36:536-48.

57. Blanchard FA, Frost RO. Two factors of restraint:
concern for dieting and weight fluctuation. Behav Res
Ther, 1983; 21:259-67.

58. Drewnowski A, Riskey D, Desor JA. Feeling fat yet
unconcerned: self-reported overweight and the restraint scale. Appetite, 1982; 3:273-9.

59. Lowe MR. Dietary concern, weight fluctation and
weight status: further explorations of the restraint
scale. Behav Res Ther, 1984; 22:243-8.

60. Herman CP, Polivy J. Weight change and dietary concern in the overweight: are they really independent?
Appetite, 1982; 3:280-1.

61. Ruderman AJ. The restraint scale: a psychometric investigation. Behav Res Ther, 1983; 21:253-8.

62. Herman CP, Polivy J. A boundary model for the regulation of eating. In Stunkard AJ, Stellar E, eds. Eating and its disorders. New York: Raven Press,
1984:141-56.

63. Stunkard AJ. "Restrained eating": what it is and a new
scale to measure it. In Cioffi LA, et al, eds. The body
weight regulatory system: normal and disturbed mechanisms. New York: Raven Press, 1981:243-51.

64. Stunkard AJ, Messick S. The Three-Factor Eating
Questionnaire to measure dietary restraint, disinhibition and hunger. J Psychosom Res, 1985; 29:71-83.

65. Herman CP, Polivy J. Restrained eating. In Stunkard
AJ, ed. Obesity. Philadelphia: Saunders, 1980:208-25.

66. Halmi KA, Goldberg SC, Casper RC, et al. Pretreatment predictors of outcome in anorexia nervosa. Br J
Psychiat, 1979; 134:71-8.

67. Garner DM, Olmstead MP, Polivy J. Development
and validation of a multidimensional Eating Disorder
Inventory for anorexia nervosa and bulimia. Int J Eating Disorders, 1983; 2:15-34.

68. Slade PD. A short anorexic behavior scale. Br J Psychiat, 1973; 122:83-5.

69. Gormally J, Black S, Daston S, et al. The assessment of binge eating severity among obese persons. Addictive Behav, 1982; 7:47- 55.

70. Hawkins RC, Clement PF. Development and construct validation of a self-report measure of binge eating tendencies. Addictive Behav, 1980; 5:219-26.

71. O'Neil PM, Currey HS, Hirsch AA, et al. Development and validation of the Eating Behaviour Inventory. J Behav Assessment, 1979; 1:123-322.

72. Straw MK, Straw RB, Mahoney MJ, et al. The Master Questionnaire: preliminary report on an obesity assessment device. Addictive Behav,1984; 9:1-10.

73. Garner DM, Garfinkel PE. The Eating Attitudes Test: an index of the symptoms of anorexia nervosa. Psychol Med, 1979; 9:273-9.

74. Garner DM, Olmstead MP, Bohr Y, et al. The Eating Attitudes Test: psychometrtic features and clinical correlates. Psychol Med, 1982; 12:871-8.

75. Button EJ, Whitehouse A. Subclinical anorexia nervosa. Psychol Med, 1981; 11:509-16.

76. Mann AH, Wakeling A, Wood K, et al. Screening for abnormal eating attitudes and psychiatric morbidity in an unselected population of 15-year-old schoolgirls. Psychol Med, 1983; 13:573-80.

77. Williams P, Hand D, Tarnopolsky A. The problem of screening for uncommon disorders — a comment on the Eating Attitudes Test. Psychol Med, 1982; 12:431-4.

78. Booth DA. Satiety and appetite are conditioned reactions. Psychosom Med, 1977; 39:76-81.

79. Stunkard AJ. Satiety is a conditioned reflex. Psychosom Med, 1975; 37:383-7.

80. Silverstone JT, Stunkard AJ. The anorectic effect of dexamphetamine sulphate. Br J Pharmacol Chemother, 1968; 33:513- 22.

81. Blundell JE, Rogers PJ. Effects of anorectic drugs on food intake, food selection and preferences and hunger motivation and subjective experiences. Appetite, 1980; 1:151-65.

82. Wooley OW, Wooley SC, Dunham RB. Can calories be perceived and do they affect hunger in obese and non obese humans? J Comp Physiol Psychol, 1972; 80:250-8.

83. Hill AJ, Magson LD, Blundell JE. Hunger and palatability: tracking ratings of subjective experience before, during and after the consumption of preferred and less preferred food. Appetite, 1984; 5:361-71.

84. Brehm ML, Back KW, Bogdonoff MD. A physiological effect of cognitive dissonance under stress and deprivation. J Abnorm Soc Psychol, 1964; 69:303-10.

85. Beecher HK. Quantitative study of the effect of a narcotic on hunger. In Beecher HK, ed. Measurement of subjective responses. Quantitative effects of drugs. New York: Oxford University Press, 1959:352-63.

86. Durrant ML, Royston P. The long-term effect of energy intake on salivation, hunger and appetite ratings, and estimates of energy intake in obese patients. Psychosom Med, 1980; 42:385-95.

87. Hodson RJ, Greene JB. The saliva priming effect, eating speed and the measurement of hunger. Behav Res Ther, 1980; 18:243-7.

88. Wooley SC, Wooley OW. Salivation to the sight and thought of food: a new measure of appetite. Psychosom Med, 1973; 35:136-42.

89. Scott J, Huskisson EC. Graphic representation of pain. Pain, 1976; 2:175-84.

90. Joyce CRB, Zutshi DW, Hrubes V, et al. Comparison of fixed interval and visual analogue scales for rating chronic pain. Europ J Clin Pharmacol, 1975; 8:415-29.

91. Revill SI, Robinson JO, Rosen M, et al. The reliability of a linear analogue for evaluating pain. Anaesthesia, 1976; 31:1191- 9.

92. Bond A, Lader M. The use of visual analogue scales in rating subjective feelings. Br J Med Psychol, 1974; 47:211-8.

93. Haber GB, Heaton KW, Murphy D, et al. Depletion and disruption of dietary fiber. Effects on satiety, plasma-glucose and serum- insulin. Lancet, 1977; ii:679-82.

94. Shapiro MB. The single variable approach to assessing the intensity of the feeling of depression. Europ J Behav Anal Modif, 1975; 1:62-70.

95. Blundell JE, Hill AJ. Analysis of hunger: interrelationships with palatability, nutrient composition and eating. In Van Itallie, TB, ed. Recent advances in obesity research, vol 4. London: Libbey, 1985:199-206.

96. Stunkard AJ, Fox S. The relationship of gastric motility and hunger. A summary of the evidence. Psychosom Med, 1971; 33:123- 34.

97. Monello LF, Seltzer CC, Mayer J. Hunger and satiety sensations in men, women, boys and girls; a preliminary report. Ann NY Acad Sci, 1965; 131:593-602.

98. Garfinkel PE. Perception of hunger and satiety in anorexia nervosa. Psychol Med, 1974; 4:309-15.

99. Monello LF, Mayer J. Hunger and satiety sensations in men, women, boys and girls, Am J Clin Nutr, 1967; 20:253-61.

100. Mather P. Covert nutrient supplementation and normal feeding in man and rat: experimentation and simulation. [MSc Thesis], UK; University of Birmingham, 1977.

101. Fuller J. Human appetite and body size control. The roles of individual differences and food dependencies in human appetite and body size control processes. [PhD Thesis], UK: University of Birmingham, 1980.

102. Teghtsoonian M, Becker E, Edelman B. A psychophysical analysis of perceived satiety: its relation to consumatory behavior and degree of overweight. Appetite, 1981; 2:217-29.

103. Chapman CR. Pain and perception: comparison of sensory decision theory and evoked potential methods. In Bonica JJ, ed. Pain. New York: Raven Press, 1980:111-42.

104. Melzack R. The McGill Pain Questionnaire: major properties and scoring methods. Pain, 1975; 1:277-99.

105. Reading AE, Newton JR. A card sort method of pain

assessment. J Psychosom Res, 1978; 22:503-12.

106. Johnson JE, Rice VH. Sensory and distress components of pain: implications for the study of clinical pain. Nursing Res, 1974; 23:203-9.

107. Gracely RH, McGrath P, Dubner R. Validity and sensitivity of ratio scales of sensory and affective verbal pain descriptors: manipulation of affect by diazepam. Pain, 1978; 5:19-29.

108. Henkin RI, Gill JR, Bartter FC. Studies on taste thresholds in normal man and in patients with adrenal cortical insufficiency: the role of adrenal cortical steroids and of serum sodium concentration. J Clin Invest, 1963; 42:727-35.

109. Hardy SL, Brennand CP, Wyse BW. Taste thresholds of individuals with diabetes mellitus and of control subjects. J Am Dietet Assoc, 1981; 79:286-9.

110. De Wys WD. Changes in taste sensation in cancer patients: correlation with caloric intake. In Kare MR, Maller O, eds. The chemical senses and nutrition. New York: Academic Press, 1977:381-9.

111. Henkin RI, Schechter PJ, Hoye R, et al. Idiopathic hypogeusia with dysgeusia, hyposmia anddysosmia. JAMA, 1971; 217:434-40.

112 Bertino M, Beauchamp GK, Engelman K. Long-term reduction in dietary sodium alters the taste of salt. Am J Clin Nutr, 1982; 36:1134-44.

113. Cowart BJ. Development of taste perception in humans: sensitivity and preference throughout the life span. Psychol Bull, 1981; 90:43-73.

114. Meiselman HL. Human taste perception. In Furia TE, Bellanca N, eds. Fenaroli's handbook of flavor ingredients, 2nd ed. vol 1. Cleveland: CRC Press, 1975:12-43.

115. Lawson WB,Zeidler A, Rubenstein A. Taste detection and preferences in diabetics and their relatives. Psychosom Med, 1979; 41:219-27.

116. Pangborn RM. Individual variation in affective responses to taste stimuli. Psychon Sci, 1970; 21:125-6.

117. Chappell GM. Flavor assessment of sugar solutions. J Sci Food Agric, 1953; 4:346-50.

118. Peryam DR, Pilgrim FJ. Hedonic scale method of measuring food preferences. Food Technol, 1957; 11(9):9-14.

119. Rodin J, Moskowitz HR, Bray GA. Relationship between obesity, weight loss, and taste responsiveness. Physiol Behav,1976; 17:591- 7.

120. Trant AS, Serin J, Douglass HO. In taste related to anorexia in cancer patients? Am J Clin Nutr, 1982; 36:45-58.

121. Malcolm R, O'Neill PM, Hirsch AA, et al. Taste hedonics and thresholds in obesity. Int J Obesity, 1980; 4:203-12.

122. Moskowitz HR, Kluter RA, Westerling J, et al. Sugar sweetness and pleasantness: evidence for different psychological laws. Science, 1974; 184:583-5.

123. Johnson WG, Keane TM, Bonar JR, et al. Hedonic ratings of sucross solutions: effects of body weight, weight loss and dietary restriction. Addictive Behav, 1979; 4:231-6.

124. Thompson DA, Moskowitz HR, Campbnell RG. Taste and olfaction in human obesity. Physiol Behav, 1977; 19:335-7.

125. Cabana CM. The physiological role of pleasure. Science, 1971; 173:1103-7.

126. Cabanac M, Duclaux R. Obesity: absence of satiety aversion to sucrose. Science, 1970; 168:496-7.

127. Briese E, Quijada M. Positive alliesthesia after insulin. Experientia, 1979; 35:1058-9.

128. Wooley OW, Wooley SC, Dunham RB. Calories and sweet taste: effects on sucrose preference in the obese and non-obese. Physiol Behav, 1972; 9:765-8.

129. Cabanac M, Fantino M. Origin of olfacto-gustatory alliesthesia: intestinal sensitivity to carbohydrate concentration. Physiol Behav, 1977; 18:1039-45.

130. Blundell JE, Rogers PJ. Hunger and appetite — a biopsychological perspective. In Cairella M, Jacobelli A, Papalia D, eds. Obesity. Rome: Societa Editrice Universo, 1980:99-119.

131. Scherr S, King KR. Sensory and metabolic feedback in the modulation of taste hedonics. Physiol Behav, 1982; 29:827-32.

132. Fantino M. Role of sensory input in the control of food intake. J Autonom Nerv System, 1984; 10:347-58.

133. Hill AJ, Blundell JE. Nutrients and behaviour: research strategies for the investigation of taste characteristics, food preferences, hunger sensations and eating patterns in man. J Psychiat Res, 1982/3; 17:203-12.

134. Kissileff HR, Gruss LP, Thornton J, et al. The satiating efficiency of foods. Physiol Behav, 1984; 32:319-32.

135. Pilgrim FJ, Kamen JM. Predictors of human food consumption. Science, 1963; 139:501-2.

136. IFT Sensory Evaluation Division: Sensory evaluation guide for testing food and beverage products. Food Technology, 1981; 35:50- 9.

137. Rolls BJ, Rolls ET, Rowe EA, et al. Sensory specific satiety in man. Physiol Behav, 1981; 27:137-42.

138. Booth DA. Appetite and satiety as metabolic expectancies. In Katsuki Y, Soto M, Takagi SF, Oomura Y, eds. Food intake and chemical senses. Tokyo: University of Tokyo Press, 1977:317-30.

139. Randall E, Sanjur D. Food preferences — their conceptualization and relationship to consumption. Ecol Food Nutr, 1981; 11:151-61.

140. Fallon AE, Rozin P. The psychological bases of food rejections by humans. Ecol Food Nutr, 1983; 13:15-26.

141. Pelchat ML, Rozin P. The special role in nausea in the acquisition of food dislikes by humans. Appetite, 1982; 3:341-51.

142. Rozin P. Preference and affect in food selection. In Kroeze, JHA, ed. Preference behavior and chemoreception. London: Information Retrieval, 1979:289-97.

143. Sjostrom L, Garellick G, Krotkiewski M, et al. Peripheral insulin in response to the sight and smell of food. Metabolism, 1980; 29:901-9.

144. Sahakian BJ, Lean MEJ, Robbins TW, et al. Salivation and insulin secretion in response to food in non-obese men and women. Appetite, 1981; 2:209-16.

145. Powley TL. The ventromedial hypothalamus syndrome, satiety, and a cephalic phase hypothesis. Psychol Rev, 1977; 84:89-126.

146. Wooley OW, Wooley SC. Relationship of salivation in humans to deprivation, inhibition and the encephalisation of hunger. Appetite, 1981; 2:331-50.

147. Peck R. The SHP test, an aid in the detection and measurement of depression. Arch Gen Psychiat, 1959; 1:35-40.

148. White KD. Salivation: a review and experimental investigation of major techniques. Psychophysiol, 1977; 14:203-12.

149. Pangborn RM, Chung CM. Parotid salivation in response to sodium chloride and monosodium glutamate in water and in broths. Appetite, 1981; 2:380-5.

150. Klajner F, Herman CP, Polivy J, et al. Human obesity, dieting, and anticipatory salivation to food. Physiol Behav, 1981; 27:195- 8.

151. Wooley OW, Wooley SC, Williams BS. Salivation as a measure of appetite: studies of the anorectic effects of calories and amphetamine. In Novin D, Wyrwicka W, Bray G, eds. Hunger: Basic mechanisms and clinical implications. New York: Raven Press, 1976:421-9.

152. Wooley S, Wooley OW, Dunham R. Appetitive salivary responses: a study of obese-normal differences. In Howard A, ed. Recent advances in obesity research, vol 1. London: Newman, 1975:253.

153. Herman CP, Polivy J, Klajner F, et al. Salivation in dieters and non-dieters. Appetite, 1981; 2:356-61.

154. Sahakian BJ. Salivation and appetite: commentary on the forum. Appetite, 1981; 2:386-9.

155. Blundell JE, Freeman DG. Sensitivity of stimulus-induced salivation (SIS), hunger ratings and alliesthesia to a glucose load: SIS as a measure of specific satiation. Appetite, 1981; 2:373-5.

156. Davis CM. Self-selection of diets by newly-weaned infants. Am J Dis Child, 1928; 36:651-79.

157. Desor JA, Maller O, Turner RE. Taste in acceptance of sugars by human infants. J Comp Physiol Psychol, 1973; 84:495-501.

158. Steiner JE. Human facial expressions in response to taste and smell stimulation. Adv Child Devel Behav, 1979; 13:257-95.

159. Birch LL. Dimensions of preschool children's food preferences. J Nutr Educ, 1979; 11:77-80.

160. Birch LL. Effect of peer model's food choices and eating behaviors on preschoolers' food preferences. Child Devel, 1980; 51:489-96.

161. Birch LL, Birch D, Marlin DW, et al. Effects of instrumental consumption on children's food preference. Appetite, 1982; 3:125- 34.

162. Birch LL, Billman J, Richards SS. Time of day influences food acceptability. Appetite, 1984; 5:109-16.

163. Lau D, Hanada L, Kaminskyj O, et al. Predicting food use by measuring atittudes and preference. Food Product Development, 1979; 13:66-72.

164. Schiffman SS. Preference: a multidimensional concept. In Kroeze JHA, ed. Preference behavior and Chemoreception. London: Information Retrieval, 1979:163-79.

165. Drewnowski A, Greenwood RC. Cream and sugar: human preferences for high-fat foods. Physiol behav, 1983; 30:629-33.

166. Bannister D, Fransella F. Inquiring man. The theory of personal constructs. Harmondsworth; Penguin, 1971.

167. Bell AC, Stewart AM, Radford AJ, et al. A method for describing food beliefs which may predict personal food choice. J Nutr Educ, 1981; 13:22-6.

168. Worsley A. Thought for food: investigations of cognitive aspects of food. Ecol Food Nutr, 1980; 9:65-80.

169. Worsley A, Peters AJ, Worsley AJ, et al. Australian 10-year-olds' perceptions of food. III. The influence of obesity status. Int J Obesity, 1984; 8:327-41.

170. Drewnowski A, Grinker JA, Hirsch J. Obesity and flavor perception: multidimensional scaling of soft drinks. Appetite, 1982; 3:361-8.

Chapter 9

The Effect of Psychopharmacological Agents on Appetite and Eating

Marc H. Stolar

INTRODUCTION

Many medications increase or decrease appetite and/or weight. Some of these have been tested in anorexia nervosa and bulimia. To date, no well-controlled, large-scale studies with successful results have been replicated. In general, there is as yet, no accepted medication for the treatment of anorexia or bulimia (see Chapter 42, this volume).

This chapter reviews medications that influence weight and/or appetite, including some that have been given to patients with eating disorders. The presentation is chronological, dealing first with medications generally used before 1970, second during the 1970s and third after the 1970s. Therefore, the text is divided into three sections.

Rather than separating medications by whether they increase or decrease appetite or weight, I have retained chronology as the standard within each section. Those that increase appetite could help patients with restrictive anorexia, and those that decrease appetite could help with bulimia.

SECTION I: MEDICATIONS USED BEFORE 1970

Insulin

One of the earliest medications used for eating disorders was insulin. A review in 1946 indicated insulin's use in 1942 in small doses before meals, without success. Some patients seemed to respond to deep insulin shock with increased appetite and weight, though there was no change in personality. Insulin was also of no value in ambulatory subjects. The authors felt treatment with insulin should be followed by psychotherapy to be successful. They also felt that since patients with anorexia did not respond to insulin as schizophrenics did, anorexia was not a form of schizophrenia [1].

In 1960, Dally and Sargant proposed the combination of modified insulin and large doses of chlorpromazine. They found modified insulin alone was of little value. Twenty anorectic patients were given varying doses of chlorpromazine, up to 1000 mg per day, and remained on bed rest until regaining their normal weight. They were also given modified insulin therapy, starting with five units and progressively increasing the dosage until the patient was sweaty and drowsy. They were then given a large meal, and precautions were taken to avoid hypoglycemia. The dose range was 40 to 80 units, with the average being 60. When weight was regained, medication was stopped and psychotherapeutic work was begun. The combined treatment yielded an average weight gain of 4.4 lb per week, compared with treatment by other methods, which yielded an average gain of 1.3 lb per week [1]. Crisp, in 1965, disagreed with this program on the basis that most of those patients were already hungry. He was concerned that insulin use might lead to bulimia [2].

In 1966, Dally and Sargant performed a follow-up study on some of the patients who received insulin in their 1960 study. The method was as described above, and the patients were compared with patients on bed rest and high-calorie diets. Patients receiving insulin and chlorpromazine gained twice as much weight as the non-medication group. There were no adverse reactions to the insulin. It was felt that most of the effect was due to the antipsychotic actions of the drug and that insulin alone was not much more effective than bed rest alone [3]. In 1967, Dally reported that weight was gained with this program, but there was no difference in final outcome between the methods of weight gain that were compared. That is, follow-up indicated that weight may have been gained rapidly with this treatment, but the weight was not necessarily maintained over several years. He felt that insulin and chlorpromazine were certainly not a cure [4].

Chlorpromazine

Chlorpromazine, an antipsychotic medication, often produces weight gain as one of its side effects. A study in 1958 of 73 chronic schizophrenics showed increases in weight and appetite. After discontinuing the drug, patients began losing weight. Some have suggested that the medication lowers metcholic rate, and thus weight gain occurs. Possibly, these schizophrenic patients' behavior became more organized with the antipsychotic drugs and they were better able to eat and care for their nutritional needs [5].

Other studies have shown weight gain in crossover, placebo- controlled comparisons. One study also found more weight gain with chlorpromazine than with promazine and more weight gain with promazine than with either placebo or phenobarbital. Another comparison showed a greater increase in weight with chlorpromazine than with triflupromazine and mepazine. The largest absolute gain occurred early and averaged 1.4 to 5 lb in 12 weeks in these several studies. Again, weight returned to previous levels after stopping the drug. Mechanisms suggested in these studies include fluid retention, effect on appetite regulatory mechanisms in the brain, and changes in food consumption. However, if the medication were directly stimulating the brain, appetite and weight gain would be dose related, a result not found [6].

As noted above, Dally and Sargant used insulin and chlorpromazine in their program. The dose of chlorpromazine used was up to 1000 mg a day. They felt that improvement in weight may have been related to fluid retention, but they also attributed it to better acceptance of treatment. One side-effect was hypotension. The combination of the two drugs was more effective than either insulin or chlorpromazine alone [1].

In 1965, Crisp gave 400 to 600 mg of chlorpromazine a day, without insulin, accompanied by a 3,000-calorie diet and supportive psychotherapy. Initially, all but 2 of 21 subjects returned to normal weight. At the time of follow-up, two had died, and 15 of the remaining 19 had normal weight. Eleven of these had normal eating behavior [7].

In another report, Crisp discussed possible mechanisms for chlorpromazine's actions, including increased calmness with decreased activity, leading to decreased energy expenditure or increased carbohydrate intake as a second possibility. He also noted that the medication has other effects, such as amenorrhea, galactorrhea, and hypothermia, which may be mediated by the hypothalamus. These phenomena also occur in anorexia. He postulated that chlorpromazine may affect the appetite by acting on the hypothalamus [7].

In 1966, Dally and Sargant reported rare complications from the chlorpromazine. Extrapyramidal symptoms occurred in 9 of 50 patients, and all nine responded to decreased antipsychotic medication or the addition of antiparkinsonian drugs. Five had one grand mal seizure, and occasional pitting edema occurred. Rashes, sleepiness, blurred vision, dry mouth, and jaundice were reported also. Bulimia developed in 45% of the patients [3].

Other mechanisms of drug action have been suggested. Chlorpromazine may increase fat deposition [8], increase fluid intake secondary to dry mouth [9], or change the utilization of certain foods as a consequence of changes in the basal metabolism rate [9]. Food intake is increased in animals following chlorpromazine injection into the lateral hypothalamus [10].

Not all the reports on chlorpromazine and anorexia nervosa are positive. Roland surveyed 30 cases in the literature in 1970 and found five in whom the medication was of little help [11]. Russell reported on seven patients in whom the drug was not effective without an overall treatment plan for weight gain [12].

Gross, at the Cleveland Clinic, preferred not to use the medication for several reasons. The drug increases the danger of orthostatic hypotension, and anorectics usually already have low blood pressure. Also anorectic patients have abnormal liver function and liver function tests, and neuroleptics may affect the liver. Additionally, the extrapyramidal symptoms of tightness in the throat and difficulty in swallowing may increase the anorexia. Further, anorectics may have seizures during initial refeeding, and antipsychotics decrease the seizure threshold. He suggested neuroleptic treatment for only a few weeks to encourage acceptance of therapy and the weight gain. He uses 25 to 50 mg three to four times a day for inpatients and 10 to 20 mg three to four times a day for outpatients [13].

Amitriptyline

In 1964, a letter to the editor of The Lancet reported on 30 female patients taking amitripyline for four months. They developed voracious appetites with an apparent increase in carbohydrate intake. Weight increased as much as 28 lb in four to five weeks. Fat deposits increased, and breasts became large and tender. Some patients thought they were pregnant [14].

Paykel and associates in 1973 studied 51 depressed patients aged 26 to 60 treated with 100 to 150 mg amitriptyline daily. Most gained weight rapidly during the first three months. The authors noted that this could relate to recovery from depression. The average weight gain almost doubled after three months in comparison to the initial three-month period. Additionally, craving for carbohydrates increased significantly during the second and sixth months on the medication compared to no medication. The carbohydrate craving in the second month was significantly related to medication dose and not to hypoglycemia, as faintness or dizziness were not present. Overall weight gain was not related significantly to dose. Subjects withdrawn from the drug lost the excess weight that had been gained. Carbohydrate craving was associated with a higher growth-hormone response to exogenous insulin, that is, to hypoglycemia. This suggests that amitriptyline may alter hypothalamic sensitivity to glucose, indicating a central mechanism of drug action [15].

Nakra et al in 1977 tested Paykel's hypothesis that hypoglycemia induces weight gain. Six nondepressed healthy volunteers were given 50 mg amitriptyline twice a day for 28 days. Blood was obtained for fasting glucose and fasting blood insulin before the study and on days 14 and 28 of the study. During the study, amitriptyline levels were measured to determine compliance. Subjects were weighed weekly and asked to report changes in appetite, eating habits, and side effects. There was no significant weight gain, and only two reported increased appetite. The latter was especially in the evening and included excessive cravings for sweets. There was no significant difference in glucose tolerance curves, fasting or peak insulin, or glucose/insulin ratio curves. The authors felt these results did not support the hypothesis that hypoglycemia and hyperinsulinemia are responsible for the weight gain during amitriptyline therapy [16].

Nakra and his colleagues discussed several other possible mechanisms for the effect noted. Weight gain was not attributed to lifting of mood, because mood remained improved after medication was stopped, but the weight that had been gained was subsequently lost.

Amitriptyline could have a central effect on weight-regulating mechanisms. Others have postulated that the drug inhibits nonepinephrine and blocks alpha-adrenergic receptors, leading to a relative increase in beta-adrenergic effect. This would lead to sitmulation of beta-adrenergic receptors in the pancreas, with a subsequent increase in insulin. The insulin would produce hypoglycemia and hunger.

Needleman and Waber, in 1977, studied five females and one male aged 11 to 17 who had severe aversion to food, cold extremities, weight loss greater than 20%, and in the females, amenorrhea. They were given 75 to 150 mg amitriptyline daily. Socialization and mood improved, and extremities became warmer. Weight gain occurred between 6 to 12 days after treatment was commenced. Both patients and staff reported improved eating behavior and attitude toward food. Three subjects discontinued the medication and continued to gain weight. The authors suggested that the improvement of both appetite and temperature regulation may be mediated by the hypothalamus [17].

Kendler (1978) suggested that an abnormal body weight set point occurs in the eating disorders and that the set point is altered by the various medications that affect appetite and weight. The weight set point would produce increased appetite and decreased satiety until an increased body weight is reached. He reported on a patient given amitriptyline whose appetite increased within eight days, resulting in weight gain. Over the next seven weeks she gained 1 kg a week and was rarely satisfied by large amounts of high-calorie foods. When the medication was stopped, weight gain continued to more than 25% over her ideal weight, despite the return of the depressed mood. Hunger persisted and was associated with lack of satiety. Kendler suggested that the patient's body weight set point may have been altered by the drug [18].

On the other hand, others have reported that amitriptyline was ineffective in inducing weight gain. In one study of 80 patients taking 50 to 200 mg a day of the drug, some still needed hospital admission and coercion to put on weight. Another patient, who had lost more than 30 kg and was given a six-month trial of tryptophan and amitriptyline, had minimal response.

As with all medications, amitriptyline has side effects. These include sedation, tachycardia, and postural hypotension, in addition to dry mouth. If the patient quenches this thirst with high-calorie liquids and/or increases total fluid intake, weight gain may occur.

Clomipramine

Clomipramine is widely used in Europe but is not yet available in the United States. In one report, treatment with 50 mg at bedtime yielded increased appetite and more appropriate eating habits but produced no weight gain. Beaumont (1973) reported that its use in anorexia was first suggested in 1969 in a study of four patients in whom weight was restored to normal levels with treatment for about ten weeks. In 1971 that group was enlarged to ten cases. Another study reported that the drug antagonized fenfluramine- induced anorexia. Some studies used the intravenous form of this drug [19]. As clomipramine is a very selective inhibitor of serotonin uptake. Katz and Walsh (1978) suggested using the intravenous form after tryptophan priming, which decreases hepatic conversion of the drug to the demethylated metabolite. The demethylated compound is a weaker inhibitor of serotonin reuptake [20].

In 1980 Lacey and Crisp gave 50 mg of clomipramine or a placebo to 16 female anorectics at bedtime until they reached their target weights. They were also on bed rest, 2,600 calories a day, twice-weekly weighings, and individual psychotherapy. Half of the group was medicated, and the other half received a placebo. Hunger was significantly greater in the group receiving clomipramine. No significant difference in weight gain occurred between the two groups. The medicated group, however, tended to maintain their body weight better after leaving the trial than the placebo-treated group [10].

Studies show that clomipramine affects hypothalamic hormones, influences the neurotransmitters thought to be involved in food intake regulation, and may increase insulin peripherally by direct action on the pancreas, as is suggested for amitriptyline. It is chemically similar to chlorpromazine, which may have a direct effect on hypothalamic hunger-regulating mechanisms. Perhaps clomipramine may decrease anxiety about eating and reduce obsessional intrapsychic conflicts about weight [10].

Others

Other medications affect appetite and weight. Simmonds' disease (pituitary cachexia) is rare but can be confused with anorexia. In both there is loss of weight, gynecological disturbance, low basal metabolism rate, hypotension, and bradycardia. ACTH and cortisone were used in treating five patients with anorexia as an adjunct to other therapy, with mood and appetite improvement being the target symptoms for the drugs. Three of the patients received both ACTH and cortisone. In one case, cortisone was administered for seven days immediately after nine days of ACTH treatment; the other two patients took the drugs simultaneously. Two received only cortisone. One patient (described as "uncooperative") who one took the drugs immediately in sequence had no benefit; two had improved appetite, weight, and attitude with cortisone; and two benefited

from ACTH. One had depression as a side effect and all five had mild to moderate generalized edema, which was controlled by potassium chloride. Two of three who had ACTH reported insomnia and nocturnal restlessness. Weight gain in one was 15 lb over one month and in another 15 lb over two months [21].

Other drugs have been tried with little or no success, or results have not been replicated. Reserpine has been used in anorexia, but the doses that produced increased appetite also produced depression. Thyroid has been tried with little effect. Benzedrine sulfate was given to two patients with depressive symptoms and was of no help. Sulfa drugs and vitamin B_{12} have also been tried without success.

Thioridizene was given to a 12-year-old female with a three-month history of obsessive eating habits and weight loss, who had been tried on chlorpromazine with some weight gain. She received 800 mg daily and in two months gained 9 lb. Gross, at the Cleveland Clinic, prefers thioridizine to chlorpramazine because orthostatic hypotension occurs more often with the latter and because thioridizine has some antidepressant effect [13].

Fifty-three obese patients were treated with an appetite-reducing product made of hydrophilic granules called Prefil, which is intended to decrease appetite by bulk. The granules are 60% dietary fibers (vegetable gum) and swell in the stomach, creating a sense of fullness and satiety when taken with water before eating a meal. Six of 26 patients had side effects (three had abdominal discomfort; two had nausea, and one had headache) [22].

Four anorectic patients were treated with glycerol. In a starvation state, glycerol turnover and conversion to glucose increases and a higher proportion of glucose is derived from glycerol. Thus, administration of glycerol to anorectics would provide a source of glucose, remove excess fatty acids, and assist repletion of carbohydrate stores. The patients tested maintained their weight and, according to family, improved in their acceptance of food [23].

A 21-year-old woman with anorexia had been ineffectively treated with the beta-blocker propranolol. She was then given the alpha- blocker phenoxybenzamine, which produced weight gain. When the drug was stopped because of nausea and postural hypotension, weight loss resumed. Treatment was recommenced at a lower dose and weight gain recurred. Theoretically, decreased norepinephrine levels would decrease satiation—that is, increase appetite [24].

SECTION II: MEDICATIONS USED DURING THE 1970s

Cyproheptadine

Cyproheptadine is an antiserotonergic, antihistaminergic agent, often used for allergy. Chemically it is similar to LSD and the phenothiazines. It also has anticholinergic and sedative effects. In 1962, Lavenstein et al studied 28 asthmatic children taking cyproheptadine compared with chlorpheniramine in a double-blind protocol. Those receiving cyproheptadine showed a marked increase in appetite and weight. They appeared to have exogenous obesity and not fluid retention. The authors felt this was not an antihistamine effect, since the chlorpheniramine is equally potent in that respect. The median weight gain on cyproheptadine was more than twice that on chlorpheniramine. Four times as many children had increased appetite, as reported by parents and patients, with cyproheptadine as with the other drug. Appetite and weight returned to normal when the drug was stopped. The children also had an increase in linear growth, which is common in children with obesity due to increased food intake. Appetitive effects were unrelated to decreases in allergic symptoms, which occurred with both drugs [25].

Bergen, in 1964, followed up on this study. Hospitalized chronically asthmatic children were given either cyproheptadine or placebo for 15 weeks in a double-blind study. Again, cyproheptadine produced increased weight and appetite. Carbohydrate tolerance tests showed no significant differences between the groups. When the drug was discontinued, appetite and weight decreased again. They found no symptoms of hypoglycemia as well as no change in glucose tolerance tests. The authors theorized that cyproheptadine stimulates lipogenesis through stimulation of the hexose monophosphate shunt or stimulation of growth hormone secretion [26].

Chakrabarty et al (1967) administered cyproheptadine to cats and measured food intake, glucose utilization, and EEG. Glucose utilization decreased in cats that had exhibited hunger behavior. EEG changes occurred in the feeding centers but not in the satiety centers of treated animals. They suggested that cyproheptadine has a chronic hypoglycemic effect and that decreases in glucose utilization induce both increases in food intake and hypothalamic feeding center activity. They suggest that glucose utilization, not blood glucose, influences the brain centers explaining why previous studies failed to find a correlation between blood glucose and appetite increase [27].

In 1969, Noble further pursued this line of thinking by measuring the effect of cyproheptadine in comparison to placebo on appetite and weight in healthy underweight adults. Both appetite and weight increased significantly. Drowsiness was a common transient side effect. Most patients were female, and appetite was self-rated. Again, weight gain appeared as exogenous obesity. There was no evidence of hyperadrenocorticism, water retention, or hypothyroidism [28].

In 1970, Benady described the first report of cyproheptadine treatment as adjunct therapy in anorexia nervosa. A 12-year-old female was 4 ft 11 in and weighted 56 lb 13 oz. She gained 18 lb in two months taking chlorpromazine, bed rest, and twice weekly psychotherapy. After initial treatment with Mellaril, she was switched to cyproheptadine and gained an average of 1-1/4 lb a week over six months. No side effects were noted. After nine months, she doubled her initial weight measured 2-1/2 years previously at age 12, and six months later she had lost only 10 lb, and her periods had returned [29].

Goldberg and his colleagues (1979) compared liquid cyproheptadine and placebo in a double-blind study of anorectics. One subgroup responded positively to treatment. This group had a history of birth delivery complications, a 41% to 52% weight loss from normal and a history of previous outpatient treatment failure. The researchers felt this drug could be more useful in a more severe form of the illness. No complications were noted [30]. The effect of the drug on attitudes was explored in a different group of patients. Fear of becoming fat was reduced (though not to normal) in the medicated group but not with placebo. Cyproheptadine also reduced resistance to eating, but the placebo had a mild effect on resistance as well [31].

Halmi et al (1983) compared amitriptyline, cyproheptadine, and placebo in the treatment of 57 anorectic females. Cyproheptadine induced weight gain and reduced depression without complicating side effects. The mechanism of action of cyproheptadine is unknown. In treated adults, serum amylase is increased and fasting blood sugar is decreased. Affects on the pancreas and on cell permeability to glucose have been postulated [33].

Side effects of the medication have been rare. However, drowsiness, dizziness, apprehension, rash, and dry mouth can occur. Occasionally, agitation, confusion, and visual hallucinations appear. Contraindications include glaucoma and predisposition to urinary retention. Patients should not concurrently use alcohol or CNS depressants, and the effect of concurrent antidepressant medication is unknown.

Lithium

Weight gain is one of the most prominent side-effects of lithium. In one study on seven patients, a substantial weight gain occurred in all initially with a leveling off over the next one to six years. Weight gain was attributed to improved general health and better appetite and diet in people no longer suffering severe, debilitating depressive disorder. The weight gain seemed to be increased fat and solid tissue, while total body water was constant. The authors suggested patients reach the weight they would have obtained if they had not been ill, and they postulated that weight gain is related to drug effects on mood [34]. However, lithium treatment also increases weight in rats, suggesting that its action may not be related to relief from psychosis [35].

Further study shows a correlation between number of fat cells initially and subsequent weight gain with lithium tratment. There was, however, no correlation with fat cell size. Thus, patients with weight problems before using the drug tended to develop more weight problems on the medication than patients without previous weight problems. Lithium may directly stimulate deposition of fat in cells and thus those with more cells gain weight. This could occur through inhibition of adenyl cyclase activity and thus lower lipolysis [36].

The same authors also found a weak correlation between appetite increase and weight gain following lithium treatment. In this study, no link to previous history of infant obesity was observed. Nearly all patients reported increased thirst, and weight gain was correlated with liquid intake. There was no difference in weight gain by gender, diagnosis (unipolar versus bipolar depression) or improvement of mood [37].

In preliminary findings on two anorectics given lithium, Barcai reported significant weight gain in six weeks, lasting for one year. Both reported increases in food intake. No metabolic investigations were done [38].

Treatment of euthymics with either lithium or placebo induced weight gain only in patients taking the drug. Since mood control could not be related to drug action in this study, the authors suggested that lithium affects weight directly [39].

Amphetamine

The most frequently used drug for weight reduction is amphetamine. It is a stimulant, euphoriant, and anorectic. It causes peripheral sympathominetic action and in large doses can produce a paranoid psychosis similar to paranoid schiziphrenia. The neurotransmitters dopamine and norepinephrine seem to be involved in its action.

Most of the literature on amphetamine involves its mechanisms of actions and the influence of other drugs on amphetamine-induced anorexia. Amphetamine decreases eating at times and increases it at other times. It changes the rate of feeding, latency (time before onset of feeding), meal number, and selection of food.

The effectiveness of amphetamine in appetite reduction may be increased by administration two hours after meals. Amphetamine mobilizes fats from deposits. Amphetamine should be used only early in the course of treatment, when temptation is maximal [40].

Metoclopramide

Often patients with anorexia complain of discomfort after eating and with refeeding. These symptoms include fullness, bloating, epigastric pain, regurgitation, nausea, heartburn, and vomiting. These symptoms may be related to delayed gastric emptying. Metoclopramide (Reglan) is an antiemetic that can alleviate these symptoms.

In 1977, Moldofsky et al published a preliminary report on the use of Reglan for relief of dyspepsia in anorectics. In follow-up after three to six months, patients were free of dyspepsia while taking 10 mg at bedtime. Two patients had depressive symptoms while on the drug, but these ceased when the medication was discontinued [41].

Saleh and Lebwohl (1980) reported on five female and two male anorectics with moderate to severe gastrointestinal symptoms. Seven normal-weight people with minor GI problems served as controls. Normally, 55% or less of an ingested meal will remain in the stomach 90 minutes after ingestion. Six of the seven anorectics had greater than 85% of their meal remaining (mean was 90%) compared with mean of 42% retained in the normal controls, indicating delayed gastric emptying in the anorectics. After being given Reglan, the mean for the anorectics decreased to 64% retention, with five of the seven having a significant reduction of meal retention, indicating a facilitation of gastric emptying. One month of taking the medication yielded a significant increase in weight and marked improvement of GI symptoms, mostly in tolerance to meals, postprandial epigastric pain, excessive belching, vomiting, and satiety. Two patients had no change in gastric emptying but still gained weight, indicating that the increase in weight was not related to gastric emptying. No side effects or untoward reactions were noted [42].

Metoclopramide increases lower esophageal sphincter tone, antral gastric contractions, and the rate of gastric emptying. It also relaxes the duodenal cap, which prevents pyloric regurgitation. It does not affect gastric enzyme secretions and potentiates acetylcholine action. It makes gastric contractions more effective. The mechanism of action is through blockade of dopamine receptors, particularly in the brainstem. By blocking dopamine, metoclopramide inhibits gastric acid secretion and gastric relaxation.

Another consequence of the inhibition of dopamine by metoclopramide is increased prolactin secretion leading to galactorrhea, cardiac arrhythmias, and increased incidence of breast cancer. Thyrotropin and aldosterone may be increased. Central side-effects occur in about 10% of those under treatment and include somnolence, lassitude, dizziness, faintness, nervousness, anxiety, and lethargy. Extrapyramidal symptoms may occur (metoclopramide should not be given concurrently with a neuroleptic, except with caution). Tardive dyskinesia may also follow its use, but there is no significant antipsychotic or tranqulizing effect at the dose recommended and use within two weeks of treatment with a monoamine oxidase inhibitor, tricyclic antidepressant, or sympathomimetic is not recommended. Absolute contraindications include pheochyromocytoma and organic intestinal obstruction and perforation. Relative contraindications are Parkinson's disease, CNS depressant treatment, and procaine or procainamide sensitivity. Dose should be decreased in renal disease.

Fenfluramine

Fenfluramine (Pondimin), like amphetamine, produces anorexia but is not believed to be a stimulant. The two drugs are structurally similar. Fenfluramine acts via serotonergic pathways. Kirby and Turner (1976) suggest the drug has peripheral infleunces on glucose metabolism, which may be important in the weight loss accompanying treatment. Fenfluramine increases glucose uptake into skeletal muscle in addition to its central effects. The authors felt the central changes in neurotransmitters and behavior (sedation) may be occurring through the hypothalamus, causing neuroendocrine changes, and indirectly influencing peripheral metabolism [43].

Jespersen and Scheel-Kruger, in 1973, looked at drugs that affect serotonin and studied their effects on the anorexia produced by fenfluramine. The serotonin-blockers methergoline and methysergide and the serotonin-reuptake inhibitor chlorimipramine were used. Methergoline antagonized the anorectic effect of fenfluramine, but methysergide did not antagonize the anorexia significantly. The authors felt this may be due to a difference in antiserotoninergic potency (10 to 30 times) between methergoline and methysergide. Chlorimipramine produced dose-related antagonism to femfluramine's anorexia-inducing activity [44].

Wurtman et al (1981) studied 24 obese people who stated that they had excessive appetite for carbohydrates. They were given fenfluramine, tryptophan (serotonin percursor), or placebo. Fenfluramine significantly reduced carbohydrate snacking in six of nine tested as well as for the entire group. The authors concluded that carbohbydrate snacking can sometimes be diminished by treatments, which are thought to enhance serotonin neurotransmission. The timing of the snacks was not changed by the drug and there was no significant weight loss. The doses used in this study are below those generally used to produce anorexia [45].

Fenfluramine and its main metabolite inhibit glyceride synthesis and increase glucose utilization. The drug may promote a wasting of calories leading to weight loss by a peripheral mechanism [43]. Fenfluramine hastens the end of an initial episode of eating, thereby decreasing food intake. It could be involved in the satiety mechanism via its effects on serotonergic pathways. Decreasing serotonin seems to increase food intake and, as shown by fenfluramine, increasing serotonin decreases food intake. Other studies suggest that Pondimin works by enhancing lipolysis or causing the release of hormones. Fenfluramine effects the size of the meal and the rate of intake.

Phenytoin

Green and Rau studied phenytoin (Dilantin) and its effect in eating disorders. In 1974, ten patients with compulsive eating were treated with phenytoin. All but one had an abnormal EEG, suggesting a possible neurological dysfunction. Nine of these ten were treated successfully. The authors suggested that compulsive eating may be a neurological disturbance with psychodynamic factors determining whether patients become anoretic, obese, or maintain normal weight. All the patients believed they were fat and had used amphetamine unsuccessfully in the past in attempting to overcome their compulsive eating [47].

In 1977 Green and Rau reported on 31 patients. They defined compulsive eating as eating episodes that were irregular, unpredictable, ego-dystonic, involving large amounts of food eaten "against the eater's will," accompanied by guilt, an aura at times, and mild depersonalization. Fourteen of these 31 had abnormal EEGs, and the authors noted the similarity between these episodes and some types of seizure activity, insofar as symptom complex. Twenty-six of the 31 were given phenytoin. Nine patients responded positively with reduced eating, while 17 didn't respond or had an inadequate trial. It is noteworthy that of 12 patients with abnormal EEGs, six had a positive response and only three of 14 with normal EEGs had a positive response. Four who had responded to phenytoin, including one with a normal EEG, were then put on a double-blind study of phenytoin versus placebo with a crossover for four months. All responded to the drug [48].

Wermuth et al in 1977 reported on 19 people in a 12-week, double-blind, crossover study comparing placebo and phenytoin in treating severe binge eating. When subjects were given placebo and then the drug, the number of binges decreased while on the drug compared with pretreatment and on placebo. However, when patients were given the drug first, the number of binges decreased from the pretreatment period but this pattern was not reversed when the subjects were switched to placebo. The EEG was abnormal in 7 of 19. There was no consistent change in weight or the intensity of the binges. EEG abnormalities did not correlate with treatment response, and the same was true for phenytoin levels, weight, frequency of binges, night eating, frequent snacking, eating continuously during the day, eating at regular meals, and postbinge vomiting. Binges of one hour or less were associated with a good response, but a history of anorexia was associated with no improvement. The action of the drug terminates soon after it is discontinued. The authors noted that the effect on binges is similar to the effect on seizures in that the frequency of the binges was decreased but not the intensity. Binge activity was lowered even at low serum levels of phenytoin [49].

Weiss and Levitz (1976) reported one case of unsuccessful treatment with phenytoin in bulimia [50].

Others

Other medications were suggested in the 1970s for treating eating disorders or were described to affect weight and/or appetite.

Johanson and Knorr (1977) suggested using L-Dopa for the treatment of anorexia nervosa. They noted similarities in behavior between anorectics and patients with Parkinson's disease, and they suggested that anorexia nervosa may have a dopaminergic component. Nine patients (eight females and one male) were given the drug and five of the nine gained weight while on the medication. The drug seemed well tolerated, though several had black urine and several noted significant hair loss [51].

Pizotifen is an antiserotonergic, antihistaminergic agent structurally similar to cyproheptadine and the tricyclic antidepressants. It has weak anticholinergic activity and is used for prophylactic treatment of vascular headaches (though it is of no value in acute attacks). With the usual dose of 1-1/2 to 3 mg daily, drowsiness, appetite increase, and weight gain have occurred, though in most, these effects are mild and tend to decrease with prolonged therapy. In one study of four anorectic patients, Pizotifen was helpful. It had a mild hypoglycemic effect, probably not due to a change in peripheral utilization of glucose, but perhaps to inhibition of glycogenolysis or gluconeogenesis in the liver. Other side-effects included bradycardia, hypotension, mydriasis, epileptiform seizures, muscle spasms, miosis, and hypotonia. Weight gain was 2 to 10 kg, mostly in the first few weeks. Appetite was described as voracious, and sweets were craved. Weight gain may be due to fluid retention or endocrine effects [52].

Rats injected intraventricularly with parachlorophenylalanine (PCPA) showed hyperphagia primarily in the daytime. This chemical decreases brain serotonin, thus supporting the concept that decreased brain serotonin leads to overeating and increased body weight. The effect was dose related. PCPA decreases serotonin by inhibiting tryptophan hydroxylase [53].

Zimelidine was developed as an antidepressant that inhibited serotonin reuptake (therefore increasing the effect of serotonin). A placebo-controlled, double-blind, crossover study on overweight nondepressed people was done. Of 18 women who completed the study, more weight was lost with the medication than with placebo and, according to self-rating, appetite was also reduced. Sleep disturbance occurred with the drug. Weight loss averaged 2.5 kg, which is comparable to marketed appetite suppressants [54]. Another study of the antidepressant efficacy of Zimelidine showed that of 15 patients, 13 lost weight and two gained. The average loss was less than 1 kg but was significant [55].

SECTION III: MEDICATIONS USED AFTER THE 1970s

Monoamine-Oxidase Inhibitors (MAOI)

As with other antidepressants, early reports suggested that MAOI, in combination with amitriptyline, increased hunger and cravings for sweet foods. This combination of drugs increases norepinephrine levels, intensifies beta-adrenergic effects, increasing insulin release, causing hypoglycemia, and leads to hunger.

More recently, studies have been done with the MAOI isocarboxazid and phenelzine. One study was done on depressed patients, some of whom exhibited hyperphagia and weight gain (at least 5 lb) as symptoms of their depression before treatment. These patients had rapid, early, and virtually complete cessation of overeating and weight loss on isocarboxazid. Other patients in the same trial who initially had poor appetite and weight loss as presenting symptoms, showed a tendency to increased appetite, but the change was gradual, not rapid as above, and was not significant [56].

Two reports appeared concerning the use of phenelzine and its effect on appetite. One patient with agoraphobia had increased appetite within two weeks after initiation of treatment and increased weight after six. When the phenelzine was discontinued, appetite returned to normal shortly thereafter [57]. Another patient gained 20 kg in four months. Weight gain terminated when the drug was discontinued [58].

Cholecystokinin (CCK)

Cholecystokinin (CCK) is normally released when food enters the duodenum and causes animals to stop eating. In man, slow infusion increases food intake but rapid infusion, as shown in one study, decreases it by 12%, with 96% of the decrease occurring in the first eight minutes. With the slow infusion, food intake was increased by 22%. The CCK used in this study was only 20% pure [59].

Genetically obese mice have increased beta-endorphin and decreased CCK. Food intake increases with morphine or beta-endorphin administration. Opiates play a role in regulating stress-induced feeding, and CCK blocks that action. Faris et al hypothesized that CCK directly antagonizes endogenous opiates. They tested this by observing the effect of CCK on shock-induced analgesia in the front paw of rats. They found CCK blocks the analgesia and suggested that it may block other opiate-mediated behaviors, such as feeding [60].

Benzodiazepines

Early studies on benzobiazephine (BZDZ) showed that it induces eating behavior. Thus, high doses of Librium and Valium countered amphetamine-induced anorexia in humans. Increases in weight have been reported in animals as well. Even satiated animals will increase food intake when given BZDZ, suggesting they may be able to override the normal control of feeding. It may be that BZDZ- induced hyperphagia is controlled by endogenous opiates as recent evidence suggests that naloxone decreases diazepam-induced hyperphagia in satiated animals, even at low doses [61].

Endogenous Opiates and Opiate Antagonists

Opiates have been reported to both increase and decrease feeding behavior. The research is in its early stages, but most of the evidence suggests that endogenous opioids induce obesity in animals by increasing appetite.

Naloxone and naltrexone are the opiate antagonists studied. Naloxone decreases diazepam-induced hyperphagia in satiated animals, possibly by inducing early satiety so feeding terminates sooner, by decreasing incentives to eating (visual, gustatory, olfactory, thermal stimuli) or the rewards of food and/or palatability of food. It reduces food intake in food-deprived rats as well. Mild pinching of rats (stress) promotes eating, and naloxone can reverse this effect, suggesting that the eating is mediated by endogenous opiates. It is possible that opiates are released strictly for analgesia and the increased food intake is an ancillary effect. Less likely, the animals may eat to obtain analgesia from some element of the food (Zioudrou et al found "exorphins" in casein and gluten, which bind to opiate receptors [72]).

McCarthy et al in 1981 studied the effect of naloxone on food intake in rats, rabbits, and cats and compared it with the known anorectic agents fenfluramine and diethylproprion. Naloxone produced dose-related decreases in food consumption in all three species [46].

Moore et al found that when naloxone was administered intravenously over a five-week period to anorectics who were also on an antidepressant, weight gain occurred [62].

Lowy and Yim (1981) studied the effect of naltrexone in food-deprived rats and found that it decreased the feeding that normally follows food deprivation by 47% compared with control. This effect occurred independently of suppression of water intake [63].

Sternbach and co-workers, in 1982, gave naltrexone to clonidine-detoxified opiate addicts as part of their drug treatment program. Several had decreased appetite and weight loss, with the loss regained after the drug was stopped [64]. They indicated that Hollister reported decreased food intake in six of ten nonaddicted, normal subjects given the medication [73]. Naltrexone has few side-effects and no known abuse potential compared with amphetamines [64].

Others

Apomorphine stimulates dopamine receptors. Intraperitoneal administration of apomorphine to food-deprived rats decreased food consumption during the first half hour. Pimozide, a dopamine blocker, reversed this effect, reportedly without affecting food intake itself. These findings suggest that dopaminergic neurons mediate the effect of apomorphine on food intake in rats and that dopamine inhibits feeding behavior [65]. Morphine is reported to increase feeding at times and decrease it at other times.

Antelman and Szechtman in 1975, investigated the effect of dopamine blockers on eating induced by tail pinching in rats. Haldol and spiroperidol significantly blocked about 50% of the behaviors at various doses, and pimozide about 60%. Each produced moderate ptosis in most and discontinuous lurching movements (more with spiroperidol), which may be similar to human extrapyramidal symptoms [66].

One preliminary report exists on the effect of dopamine blockers on eating behavior in humans. A male anorectic who was taking pimozide for a month gained weight, and his obsession with weight disappeared, as did his bradycardia and overactivity [67].

Tryptophan is a precursor of serotonin. When tryptophan is administered to rats, both food intake and meal size decrease. These phenomena occur even in food-deprived animals, in whom there was more time between meals, with little effect on the rate of eating. The action on meal size occurs only in the first few hours after administration and the latency (time beween administration and start of meal) was not affected. Also, reduction of meal frequency is absent. These results resemble those that occur with other drugs believed to affect serotonin metabolism, but do not suggest whether the mechanism is central or peripheral (influence on gastric emptying or gut motility) [68].

Wurtman et al administered fenfluramine, tryptophan, and placebo to 24 obese subjects with carbohydrate craving. Tryptophan did not significantly modify eating patterns for the group as a whole. Brain uptake of tryptophan is increased when given before meals and with some carbohydrates, and its uptake is suppressed by high-protein meals. However, neither of the conditions for increasing tryptophan uptake into the brain were met in this study [45].

Methysergide (Sansert) is used to prevent migraine headaches, possibly through serotonin antagonism. Weight gain and fluid retention are associated with the commonly used dosage [69]. Sansert may influence serotonin in the gut, and serotonin may influence satiety by a peripheral mechanism. Ninety-eight percent of the body's serotonin is in the gut, not the brain [70].

Clonidine, an alpha-adrenergic agonist, was given intramuscularly to monkeys. Food intake increased significantly, and all but two gained weight by the end of one week. Substantial decreases in food intake occurrred in most during drug withdrawal, and there was weight loss back to baseline by the seventh day after withdrawal. Previous reports have stated that the injection of the drug into the lateral hypothalamus of satiated rats greatly increased food intake [71].

Gamma-aminobutyric acid (GABA) has been implicated in the mechanism of action of benzodiazephines, and bicuculline is a GABA antagonist. GABA may be involved in the feeding induced by norepinephrine and beta-endorphins, since these effects are partially blocked by bicuculline, which also decreases benzodiazepine-induced hyperphagia. Bicuculline itself has been reported to both increase and decrease food intake. Benzodiazepine, opiate, CCK, GABA, and bicuculline effects on eating may be linked.

Since the original writing of this chapter, more literature has appeared on medications in the treatment of the eating disorders. The field is getting even more specific as these papers deal with trials of the drugs in the eating disorders, not just descriptions of effects on weight and/or appetite as the early literature did.

Some case reports on the use of imipramine, carbamazepine, sodium valproate, alprazolam and nomifensine have been published. Additionally, further case reports can be added to the review above for medications such as lithium, phenytoin, phenelzine, tranytlcypromine, methylamphetamine, fenfluramine and isocarboxazid.

We have also reached the stage where double-blind, placebo-controlled studies are being done. Mianserin has been studied for treatment of bulimia nervosa and

lithium for anorexia nervosa.

Hughes et al showed a 91% decrease in binge frequency with desipramine compared with a 19% increase with placebo. Crossover yielded 84% decrease for those originally on placebo. 69% of the 22 patients had complete abstinence. Results persisted at one month follow-up [74].

Pope and Hudson also studied 22 bulimics with imipramine versus placebo. The medication significantly reduced binge frequency and 90% at follow-up continued doing well [75].

Mitchell and Groat used amitriptyline in 32 female, bulimic outpatients and compared it to placebo in double-blind conditions. 150 mg at bedtime was associated with considerable improvement in eating behavior as well as a significant antidepressant effect. There was a minimal, concurrent behavior modification program as well [76].

Walsh and his group studied 20 normal weight bulimics. Nine were treated with phenelzine and eleven were given placebo in a double-blind trial. Phenelzine significantly reduced the number of binges per week. Five of the nine with medication stopped beinging completely and the other four decreased by at least 50%. No one on placebo stopped completely and only two of eleven reduced by 50% or more [77].

Halmi randomly assigned 72 anorectics in a double-blind study to receive cyproheptadine, amitriptyline or placebo. Those with bulimia had worse results with cyproheptadine than placebo or amitriptyline where as the nonbulimics did significantly better with cyproheptadine [78].

CONCLUSION

Many medications are available with side-effects that include influence on weight and/or appetite. Those that increase appetite could be helpful in treating anorexia nervosa, and some have been tested to that end. Others decrease appetite and may be helpful in alleviating bulimic symptoms. Research has begun in that direction. Thus far, no single medication, nor any combination of drugs, has been definitively successful in treating the eating disorders.

Some medications have been tried to no avail. Others await their turn. A look to the immediate future indicates that opiate antagonists and agonists, MAOI, CCK, and benzodiazepines may give some hope for treatment of these illnesses. Further, these compounds may provide more knowledge of the basics of appetite and weight regulation, that could lead to medications for amelioration of the eating disorders some time in the distant future.

Work in this area is extremely important, since even temporary relief of symptoms can produce improved health for the patient, more effective psychotherapeutic work, and possibly a cure for the eating disorders.

REFERENCES

1. Dally PJ, Sargant W. A new treatment of anorexia nervosa. Br Med J, 1960; 1:1770-3.

2. Crisp AH. A treatment regime for anorexia nervosa. Br J Psychiatry, 1965; 112:505-12.

3. Dally P, Sargant W. Treatment and outcome of anorexia nervosa. Br Med J, 1966; 2:793-5.

4. Dally PJ. Anorexia nervosa-long-term follow up and effects of treatment. Journal of Psychosomatic Research, 1967; 11:151-5.

5. Planansky K. Changes in weight in patients receiving a "tranquilizing" drug. Psychiatr Q, 1958; 32:289-303.

6. Klott CJ, Caffey EM. Weight changes during treatment with phenothiazine derivatives. Journal of Neuropsychiatry, 1960; 2:102-8.

7. Crisp AH. Clinical and therapeutic aspects of anorexia nervosa- a study of 30 cases. Journal of Psychosomatic Research, 1965; 9:67-78.

8. Paykel ES, Mueller PS, de la Vegne PM. Drugs causing weight gain. Br J Psychiatry, 1973; 123:501, and summarized in Br Med J, 1974; 1:168.

9. Kalucy RS. Drug-induced weight gain. Current Therapeutics August, 1981; 127-40.

10. Lacey JH, Crisp AH. Hunger, food intake and weight: The impact of clomipramine on a refeeding anorexia nervosa population. Postgraduate Medical Journal, 1980; 56 (Suppl 1):79-85.

11. Roland CV Jr. Anorexia nervosa: A survey of the literature and review of 30 cases. Int Psych Clinics, 1970; 7:37-137.

12. Russell GFM. General management of anorexia nervosa and difficulties in assessing the efficacy of treatment. In Vigersky RA, ed. Anorexia Nervosa. New York: Raven Press, 1977; 277-289.

13. Gross M, ed. An in-hospital therapy program in anorexia nervosa: A comprehensive approach. Lexington, Mass: The Collamore Press, 1982; 91-101.

14. Arenillas L. Amitriptyline and body weight. Lancet Feb, 1964; 22:432-3.

15. Paykel ES, Mueller PS, de la Vergne PM. Amitriptyline, weight gain and carbohydrate craving: A side effect. Br J Psychiatry, 1973; 123:501-7.

16. Nakra BRS, Rutland P, Verma S, et al. Amitriptyline and weight gain: A biochemical and endocrinological study. Curr Med Res Opin, 1977; 4:602-6.

17. Needleman HL, Waber D. The use of amitriptyline in anorexia nervosa. In Vigersky RA, ed. Anorexia Nervosa. New York: Raven Press, 1977: 357-62.

18. Kendler KS. Amitriptyline-induced obesity in anorexia nervosa: A case report. Am J Psychiatry, 1978; 135:1107-8.

19. Beaumont G. Clomipramine (Anafranil) in the treatment of pain, enuresis and anorexia nervosa. J Int Med Res, 1973; 1:435-7.

20. Katz JL, Walsh BT. Depression in anorexia nervosa. Am J Psychiatry, 1978; 135:507.

21. Greenblatt RB, Barfield WE, Clark SL. The use of ACTH and cortisone in the treatment of anorexia nervosa. Journal of the Medical Association of Georgia, 1951; July:299-301.

22. Valle-Jones JC. The evaluation of a new appetite-reducing agent (Prefil) in the management of obesity. British Journal of Clinical Practice, 1980; 34:72-4.

23. Caplin H, Ginsburg J, Beaconsfield P. Glycerol and treatment of anorexia. Lancet, 1973; 1:319.

24. Redmons DE Jr, Swann A, Heninger GR. Phenoxybenzamine in anorexia nervosa. Lancet, 1976; 2:307.

25. Lavenstein AF, Dacaney EP, Lasagna L, et al. Effect of cyproheptadine on asthmatic children. Study appetite, weight gain and linear growth. JAMA, 1962; 180:912-6.

26. Bergen SS Jr. Appetite stimulating properties of cyproheptadine .Amer J Dis Child, 1964; 108:270-3.

27. Chakrabarty AS, Pillai RV, Anand BK, et al. Effect of cyproheptadine on the electrical activity of the hypothalamic feeding centres. Brain Res, 1967; 6:561-9.

28. Noble RE. Effect of cyproheptadine on appetite and weight gain in adults. JAMA, 1969; 209:2054-5.

29. Benady DR. Cyproheptadine hydrochloride (Periactin) and anorexia nervosa: A case report. Br J Psychiatry, 1970; 117:681-2.

30. Goldberg SC, Halmi KA, Eckert ED, et al. Cyproheptadine in anorexia nervosa. Br J Psychiatry, 1979; 134:67-70.

31. Goldberg SC, Eckert ED, Halmi KA, et al. Effects of cyproheptadine on symptoms and attitudes in anorexia nervosa. Arch Gen Psychiatry, 1980; 37:1083.

32. Halmi KA, Eckert ED. Falk JR. Cyproheptadine, an antidepressant and weight-inducing drug for anorexia nervosa. Psychopharmacology Bulletin, 1983; 19:103-5.

33. Drash A, Elliott J, Langs H, et al. The effect of cyproheptadine on carbohydrate metabolism. Clinical Pharmacology and Therapeutics, 1966; 7:340-6.

34. Kerry RJ, Liebling LI, Owen G. Weight changes in lithium responders. Acta Psychiatr Scand, 1970; 46:238-43.

35. Plenge PK, Mellerup ET, Rafaelsen OJ. Weight gain in lithium- treated rats. International Pharmacopsychiatry, 1973; 8:234-8.

36. Vendsborg PB, Bach-Mortensen N, Rafaelsen OJ. Fat cell number and weight gain in lithium treated patients. Acta Psychiatr Scan, 1976; 53:355-9.

37. Vendsborg PB, Bech P, Rafaelsen OJ. Lithium treatment and weight gain. Acta Psychiatr Scand, 1976; 53:139-47.

38. Barcai A. Lithium in adult anorexia nervosa. A pilot report on two patients. Acta Psychiatr Scand, 1977; 55:97-101.

39. Peselow ED, Dunner DL, Fieve RR, et al. Lithium carbonate and weight gain. J Affect Dis, 1980; 2:303-10.

40. Penick SB, Stundard AJ. The treatment of obesity. Advances in Psychosomatic Medicine, 1972; 7:217-28.

41. Moldofsky H, Jeuniewic N, Garfinkel PE. Preliminary report on metoclopramide in anorexia nervosa. In Vigersky, RA, ed. Anorexia Nervosa. New York: Raven Press, 1977: 373-5.

42. Saleh JW, Lebwohl P. Metoclopramide-induced gastric emptying in patients with anorexia nervosa. American Journal of Gastroenterology, 1980; 74:127-32.

43. Kirby MJ, Turner P. Do "anorectic" drugs produce weight loss by appetite suppression? Lancet, 1976; 1(7959):566-7.

44. Jespersen S, Scheel-Krueger J. Evidence for a difference in mechanism of action between fenfluramine- and amphetamine- induced anorexia. J Pharm Pharmac, 1973; 25:49-54.

45. Wurtman JJ, Wurtman RJ, Growdon JH, et al. Carbohydrate craving in obese people: suppression by treatments of affecting seroninergic transmission. Int J Eating Disorders, 1981; 1:2-15.

46. McCarthy PS, Dettmar PW, Lynn AG, et al. Anorectic actions of the opiate antagonist naloxone. Neuropharmacology, 1981; 20:1347- 9.

47. Green RS, Rau JH. Treatment of compulsive eating disturbances with anticonvulsant medication. Am J Psychiatry, 1974; 134:428-32.

48. Green RS, Rau JH. The use of diphenylhydantoin in compulsive eating disorders: Further studies. In Vigersky RA, ed. Anorexia Nervosa. New York: Raven Press, 1977: 377-82.

49. Wermuth BM, Davis KL, Hollister LE, et al. Phenytoin treatment of the binge-eating syndrome. Am J Psychiatry, 1977; 134:1249-53.

50. Weiss T, Lievitz L. Diphenylhydantoin treatment of bulimia. Am J Psychiatry, 1976; 133:1093.

51. Johanson AJ, Knorr NJ. L-dopa as treatment for anorexia nervosa. In Vigersky RA, ed. Anorexia Nervosa, New York: Raven Press, 1977; 363-72.

52. Speight TM, Avery GS. Pizotifen (BC-105): A review of its pharmacological properties and its therapeutic efficacy in vascular headaches. Drugs, 1972; 3:159-203.

53. Breisch ST, Zemlan FP, Hoebel BG. Hyperphagia and obesity following serotonin depletion by intraventricular p- chlorophenylalanine. Science, 1976; 192(4237):382-5.

54. Simpson RJ, Lawton DJ, Watt MH, et al. Effect of zimelidine, a new antidepressant, on appetite and body weight. Br J Clin Pharmac, 1980; 10:96-8.

55. Aberg A, Holmberg G. Preliminary clinical test of zimelidine (H 102/09), a new 5-HT uptake inhibitor. Acta Psychiatr Scand, 1979; 59:45-58.

56. Davidson J. Turnbull C. Loss of appetite and weight associated with the monoamine oxidase inhibitor isocarboxazid. Journal of Clinical Psychopharmacology, 1982; 2:263-6.

57. Pohl R. Anorgasmia caused by MAOIs. Am J Psychiatry, 1983; 140:510.

58. Christenson R. MAOIs Anorgasmia and weight gain. Am J Psychiatry, 1983; 140:1260.

59. Studevant RAL, Goetz H. Cholecystokinin both stimulates and inhibits human food intake. Nature, 1976; 261:713-5.

60. Faris PL, Komisaruk BR, Watkins LR, et al. Evidence for the neruopeptide cholecystokinin as an antagonist of opiate analgesia. Science, 1983; 219:310-2.

61. Cooper SJ. Minireview: Benzodiazepine-opiate antagonist interactions in relation to feeding and drinking behavior. Life Sci, 1983; 32:1043-51.

62. Moore R, Mills IH, Forster A. Naloxone in the treatment of anorexia nervosa: Effects of weight gain and lipolysis. Journal of the Royal Society of Medicine, 1981; 74:129-31.

63. Lowy MT, Yim GKW. The anorexic effect of naltrexone is independent of its suppressant effect on water intake. Neuropharmacology, 1981; 20:883-6.

64. Sternbach HA, Annitto W, Potash ALC. et al. Anorexic effects of naltrexone in man. Lancet, 1982; 1:388-9.

65. Barzaghi F, Groppetti A, Mantegazza P, et al. Reduction of food intake by apomorphine: A pimozide-sensitive effect. J Pharm Pharmac, 1973; 25:909-11.

66. Antelman S, Szechtman H. Tail pinch induces eating in sated rats which appears to depend on nigrostriatal dopamine. Science, 1975; 189:731-3.

67. Plantley F. Pimozide in the treatment of anorexia nervosa. Lancet, 1977; 1:1105.

68. Latham CJ, Blundell JE. Evidence for the effect of tryptophan on the patterns of food consumption in free feeding and food deprived rats. Life Sci, 1979; 24:1971-8.

69. Graham JG. Methysergide for the prevention of headache. N Engl J Med, 1964; 270:67-72.

70. Blundell JE. Is there a role for serotonin (5-hydroxy-tryptamine) in feeding? International Journal of Obesity, 1977; 1:15-42.

71. Schlemmer RJ Jr, Casper RC, Narasimachari N, et al. Clonidine induced hyperphagia and weight gain in monkeys. Psychopharmacology, 1979; 61:233-4.

72. Ziovdrov C, Streaty RA, Klee, WA. Opioid peptides derived from food proteins. The exorphins. J Biol Chem, 1979; 254(7):2446-9.

73. Hollister LE, Johnson K, Boukhabza D et al. Adverse effects of naltrexone in subjects not dependnet on opiates. Drug Alc Dep, 1981; 8(1):37-41.

74. Hughes PL, Wells LA, Cunningham CJ et al. Treating bulimia with desipramine. A double-blind, placebo-controlled study. Arch Gen Psychiatry, 1986; 43:182-6.

75. Pope HG Jr, Hudson JI, Jonas JM et al. Bulimia treated with imipramine: A placebo-controlled, double-blind study. Am J Psychiatry, 1983; 140:554-8.

76. Mitchell JE, Groat R. A placebo-controlled, double-blind trial of amitriptyline in bulimia. J Clin Psychopharmacol, 1984; 4:186-93.

77. Walsh BT, Stewart JW, Roose SP et al. Treatment of bulimia with phenelzine. A double-blind, placebo-con-

trolled study. Arch Gen Psychiatry, 1984; 41:1105-9.

78. Halmi K, Eckert E, LaDu TJ et al. Anorexia nervosa.
     Treatment efficacy of cyproheptadine and amitripty-
     line. Arch Gen Psychiatry, 1986; 43:177-81.

Chapter 10

Palatability and Preference: Basic Studies

Barbara J. Rolls and Marion Hetherington

The hedonic response to a food, or its palatability, is probably the most important influence on both the amount eaten and the type of food selected. This review will consider the way that foods come to be considered as palatable or unpalatable, and how such responses can be modified. The implications of this type of work will be discussed in relation to anorexia nervosa and bulimia nervosa.

EARLY FOOD PREFERENCES

Taste preferences may start to develop even before birth. The peripheral taste system becomes functional during gestation, and the fetus swallows amniotic fluid that contains fluctuating amounts of sugars, salts, urea, and citric acid. It is possible that this intrauterine experience significantly affects the behavior of the neonate [1], who when first tested within hours of birth shows a preference for sweet solutions [2]. Neonates respond with different facial expressions to sweet, sour, bitter, and salty tastes [3]. There is some indication that they dislike salty, bitter, and sour tastes, although this dislike is not as clear as the liking for sweet tastes [4]. Because sweet substances are usually nutritious, while harmful substances may taste bitter, it has been suggested that newborn infants may possess some innate nutritional wisdom. That these preferences do not always guide ingestion in young children is indicated by the high incidence of poisoning, where poisons are often bitter substances such as aspirin [5].

How are the primitive responses of infants translated into food likes and dislikes when the first exposure to foods other than milk occurs? Davis [6] analyzed the food selection of newly weaned infants in an attempt to answer this question. These babies, aged from 6 to 11 months at the start of the study, had little experience of the food offered and were protected from adult influences. At mealtimes they were presented with a variety of natural nutritious foods. There was no indication that "instinct" influenced initial choices. The babies tasted everything, including spoons, trays, and paper. After this initial sampling, definite likes and dislikes emerged. Despite food preferences, in the long term the infants selected a varied and balanced diet and grew at normal rates and maintained good health. Davis concluded that there must be an innate automatic mechanism, of which appetite is part, that aids good nutrition. However, she had offered the infants only wholesome foods; as long as they consumed a variety of items it would have been difficult not to eat a balanced diet. We will see later that there does appear to be a mechanism that ensures that a varied diet is consumed.

THE IMPORTANCE OF EARLY EXPOSURE TO FOODS

Although innate factors may initially ensure that the mother's milk is consumed and after weaning would promote the consumption of a varied diet, experiences with foods and the environment constantly exert a modifying effect on food preferences. Such experience can be an important modulator of even innate food preferences. Beauchamp and Moran [7] assessed taste preferences in infants at birth and at six months of age by allowing brief ad libitum ingestion of sucrose solutions and water. At six months of age, 27% of the babies had been fed sweetened water by their mothers. The results showed that the experience of consuming sweetened water maintained the preference for sucrose, while the absence of this experience led to a depression of the preference.

In an experiment on the introduction of new foods to families of different national origin living in Israel, the children were more likely to try new recipes than the adults [8]. Muto et al (1969) [9] found that American children, who had more experience with a variety of spices than Japanese children, liked a greater variety of spices. Since children may be more willing to try new foods, and since early experience is likely to be an important determinant of adult preferences, children should be exposed to as broad a range of nutritious foods as possible.

SOCIAL INFLUENCES ON CHILDREN'S FOOD PREFERENCES

The food preferences of preschool children are influenced primarily by two factors, namely familiarity and sweetness. Familiarity was the more important influence in those under 4 years, and sweetness was most important in those over 4 years [10]. Social influences can, however, alter food preferences. Children, especially the very young, are affected by what the mother and other respected adults choose. This influence is greater if the adult eats the food rather than just offers it to the child [11]. Stories of heroes eating particular foods [12] or association of foods with positive role models on the television can also increase liking [13].

Other children have a powerful influence on the food choices of preschool children. Birch [14] assessed the vegetable preferences of children aged approximately 3 to 5 years and then arranged seating at lunch according to this assessment. A target child who preferred vegetable A was seated with three or four other children who preferred vegetable B. They were allowed to choose between the preferred and the nonpreferred vegetable. The target child chose first on the first test day and on the subsequent three test days the peers chose first. It was found that the target child followed the example set by the other children and showed a significant shift from his preferred vegetable on day 1 to his nonpreferred vegetable on day 4 (table 1). The 3- to 4-year-olds were more affected by peers than the 4- to 5-years-olds. The procedure produced relatively long-term effects in that

Table 10.1 Proportion of initially nonpreferred vegetables that were chosen first each test day.*

	Day			
	1	2	3	4
Target children (N = 17)	0.12	0.41	0.59	0.59
Peers (N = 48)	0.15	0.20	0.16	0.15

*Influenced by their peers, the target children showed a significant shift from choosing their preferred food on day 1 to choosing their nonpreferred food by day 4 (14).

the shifts in preference persisted after the test in most of the children. In a subsequent study it was found that such shifts in preference can generalize to other foods that the children regard as similar [15]. Mere exposure to advertisements for nutritious foods, or to children with different cultural backgrounds, or indeed education of parents to eat nutritious foods *with* their children could significantly alter children's preferences.

USE OF FOOD TO CONTROL CHILDREN'S BEHAVIOR

Children's food preferences can be affected by the context in which foods are presented. From an early age food becomes a powerful manipulator of behavior. The use of food as rewards or associating them with adult attention can cause a change in preference for those foods. Birch et al [16] found that a food that was initially neither liked nor disliked became more preferred relative to seven other snack foods if the child received the food every time he performed well, or when an adult gave the child extra attention. Just giving the child the food in a nonsocial situation or familiarity with the food did not alter initial preference. The shifts in preference persisted for at least six weeks after the termination of the experiment. The practical implications of this finding are that if we are trying to limit intake of particular foods such as sweets, they should not be used as rewards nor should they be associated with a situation where children receive a lot of positive adult attention. Although nonsweet foods are not usually used to reward behavior, it is possible to increase preference for these foods [16]. Thus, positive contexts could be used to increase preference for foods that are not initially highly preferred but are nutritionally desirable.

In some situations the use of food to control behavior can lead to decreased preference. One frequent parental response to a child not eating a nutritious but unpopular food is to make another desired activity depend on consumption of this food. For example, a parent may say, "Eat your peas, and then you can go out to play," or "Drink your milk and then you can watch television." This type of parental manipulation can adversely affect children's food preferences. In a recent study children were allowed a particular play activity after they had consumed a fruit juice that was neither liked nor disliked at the start of the study. Over the three weeks of the study the preference for the juice the children were "bribed" to drink decreased compared with the other juices. Forcing children to consume foods may, in the long term, be counterproductive, since the nutritious food may be liked even less. Perhaps this is because the child perceives, "If she has to give me a reward for drinking or eating this, I must not like it," [17].

The use of foods to control children's behavior is a widespread practice. For example, an American survey of 2,000 households found that nearly 60% of the mothers stated that they used foods as rewards or treats or withheld sweet food as punishment [18]. The prevalence of forcing children to consume food to gain access to desired activities has not been assessed, but it seems likely that this practice is widespread. Although the use of foods to control behavior can have marked effects on food choices, most parents are probably misusing this powerful nutritional tool. Using highly preferred, probably sweet foods, to reward children enhances innate or already established preferences, while forcing children to eat nutritious foods makes it even less likely that they will be consumed in the future.

CONDITIONING OF FOOD AVERSIONS AND PREFERENCES

Thus far, the importance of early experience with foods on the establishment of food preferences has been stressed. While it is undoubtedly important to train children in good eating habits, it would be maladaptive for early habits to be rigidly maintained, because in the face of a changing food source or of physiological changes this could lead to malnutrition. That preferences change in adults is illustrated by the widespread consumption of coffee, alcoholic beverages, and chili, which are aversive to children [19,20]. Despite the willingness to expand and adapt feeding habits, the influence of culture, much of which is instilled at an early age, is very persistent. Immigrant groups tend to retain, often at great expense, the cuisine of their home countries. Indeed, they resist full-scale adoption of the cuisine of the new country, even after several generations [19].

Food Dislikes

Although cultural influences constitute one of the major determinants of food habits, there are a number of chance events that may alter preferences. One way

foods may come to be disliked is through association with aversive consequences. When a food is sampled, there is an unusual learning mechanism that helps animals to decide whether it is safe. Normally if we are to learn that events are associated with one another, they must occur in close temporal proximity. However, food-associated learning appears to be different. When a food is ingested, it takes some time for its metabolic consequences to be felt. Appropriately, animals have a predisposition to associate food-related cues with the consequences of ingestion, even if these consequences are not felt for minutes or even hours after eating. For example, the taste of a food consumed just before a bout of nausea or vomiting may be aversive subsequently [21].

In a systematic study Garb and Stunkard [22] found that 38% of all subjects had had at least one food aversion at some time. Eighty-seven percent of these aversions were referred to a gastrointestinal upset, and 83% of such upsets were thought to be caused by food. One association between food and illness was enough to produce an aversion that lasted many years. This persistence is characteristic of food aversions and points to their survival value. Aversions were found to develop with delays of up to six hours between tasting and illness. Novel and previously disliked foods were particularly likely to be associated with the illness. Again emphasizing the importance of early influences on feeding habits, the onset of taste aversions was most common between the ages of 6 and 12 when the prevalence was 30%; it then fell steadily to 6% after the age of 60.

That nausea can have profound effects on food preferences has also been demonstrated experimentally in patients receiving chemotherapy or radiotherapy for cancer. Children who had eaten a new, well-liked flavor of ice cream just before nausea-producing chemotherapy did not want that flavor of ice cream in subsequent sessions, whereas children who had tasted the ice cream previously but who were not made nauseous did want the ice cream [23]. J.C. Smith (personal communication) has described similar aversions to fruit drinks consumed by adults before nausea-producing radiotherapy.

The full significance of acquired aversions to the development of food preferences remains to be evaluated. It has been said that the time to feed children "junk" food is when they are ill [5], but it is not clear how significant this would be in influencing food choices, since food aversions are very taste specific. There have, however, been some reports of obese people being conditioned to dislike some high-energy foods after they had been associated with noxious odors [24]. Since many people develop taste aversions, especially children, more research is needed to determine how learned food aversions could be put to use to beneficially modify food preferences.

Food dislikes may develop for many reasons other than taste aversion learning. Foods may be avoided because they cause allergies or intolerance or are supposed to have other detrimental effect such as cardiovascular disease, obesity, cancer, etc. Some potential foods may be rejected without ever being sampled because of cultural or religious associations and taboos, which lead to strong disgust reactions [19].

Learning About the Satisfaction Derived from Foods

Positive associations such as the consumption of foods by respected individuals or the use of foods as rewards can, as we have seen, affect food preferences. Foods can also come to be preferred because they have beneficial postingestive consequences. If hungry individuals eat foods that satisfy their hunger, at subsequent meals the preference for these foods increases at the stage where ingestion previously produced optimum satiety. In a series of studies in which the starch content of foods was varied, Booth et al [25,26] found that such conditioning of food pleasantness was related to the metabolic effects of the foods even when subjects were unaware of differences in energy density. Conversely, when subjects were satiated or approaching satiety, the consumption of energy-dense starch-enriched foods led to a decrease in the subsequent attractiveness of that food. Such learning about the satiety value of foods depends on the sensory properties of foods. Thus Booth found that after the initial pairing of a particular flavor with a particular energy density, in the next test in which pairings of energy density and flavor were altered, subjects ate amounts appropriate to the original flavor, regardless of the current energy value.

Booth [25] also found that the appearance of foods affects estimates of energy content. He had subjects estimate the energy density and satisfaction that would be derived from eating snack foods with misleading appearance in relation to real energy content. People who had never sampled these foods were seriously misled as to the energy content, but their estimations improved after three experiences of eating the foods. Even so, the rank ordering of the foods according to energy density was not as good as a random ranking, even in very experienced consumers of the products.

Booth's experiments show that the sensory properties of foods may lead people to select foods inappropriate for the satisfaction of needs. Such inappropriate selection could lead to overconsumption, since there is a tendency to "clean the plate" or to finish portions of food [27]. The energy and nutritional composition

should be clearly labeled on packages, and consumers should be educated to use this information. Clearly, they cannot rely entirely on innate nutritional wisdom or on experience gained from consuming foods to ensure that they select appropriately.

FAMILIARITY AND FOOD PREFERENCE

In her self-selection studies in newly weaned infants, Davis [6] found that the children tried most of the foods presented. In the post-weaning period it would be adaptive to be predisposed to trying new foods. However, this period when everything will be sampled does not last long, and by the time children are two years of age, familiarity with foods becomes a major determinant of preference. Birch and Marlin [28] found that when 2-year-olds were given variable amounts of exposure to novel cheeses or fruits, preference became an increasing function of exposure frequency. It should be remembered from the discussion above that the quality of the exposure to foods will also be important, so that repeatedly eating food in a negative context will not increase preference. In the natural environment, the variety of factors that combine to form the signature of an individual's food preferences will be extraordinarily complex.

Exposure to foods can also exert a modifying effect on adults' food preferences. Pliner [29], under the guise of having subjects detect bitterness in completely novel fruit drinks, presented three different juices either 20, 10, or 5 times. With each tasting they rated the pleasantness of the drink. Although the subjects were unaware that drinks were repeatedly presented and thought they were getting 35 different drinks, they showed a strong effect of exposure on liking (figure 1).

The exposure effects contrast with the phenomena described in subsequent sections (alliesthesia and sensory-specific satiety), where consumption decreased the liking for a food in a meal. Stang [30] also found that repeatedly tasting spices such as cinnamon, garlic salt, etc. decreased the rated pleasantness. It is possible that exposure only increases the liking for novel foods. When foods are already in the food repertoire, repeated consumption will lead to decreased liking. Both responses to foods would have adaptive value. Wariness of new foods would help to protect an individual from the consequences of ingesting poisons. As foods are sampled and found to be safe, this neophobia would disappear. The adaptive value of decreased pleasantness as foods are consumed would be in promoting the consumption of a varied diet.

ALLIESTHESIA

The hedonic response or liking for particular foods depends not only on past experience with foods but also

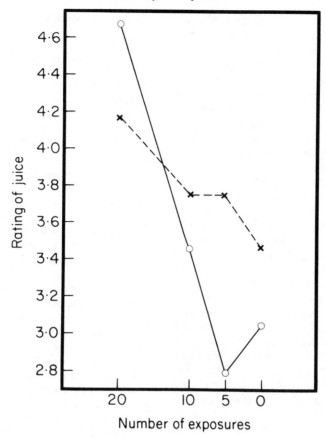

Figure 10.1 Mean liking for novel fruit juices as a function of exposures and session (24 subjects for data point). Session 1 (0———0); Session 2 (X---------X). The results show a strong exposure effect so that the more frequently a juice was tested, the better it was liked (29).

varies within an individual depending on the state of repletion. Cabanac [31] called this changing response to foods alliesthesia, which is derived from the Greek for "changed sensation." He suggested that the internal state was the main influence on alliesthesia, so that, for example, the requirement of an organism for a particular food or nutrient would determine the pleasantness of its taste. This need is thought to depend not only on meal-to-meal fluctuations in nutrients, but also on the long-term state of over-repletion (obesity) or depletion (dieting or anorexia). The effects of body weight on hedonic responses to foods will be considered later.

In the early experiments on alliesthesia sweet solutions were tasted and rated before and after 50g of glucose were given either orally or intragastrically. After these preloads of sugar, the sweet solutions became gradually less pleasant to taste over 45 to 60 minutes [31]. Food-related smells, such as that of oranges, also became less pleasant, but salty tastes were unaffected by a sugar preload, and sweet tastes were unaffected by a salt preload that decreased the pleasantness of salty

solutions [32]. Because of the slow time course of the hedonic changes, and because they occurred with intragastric loads, it was thought that sensory stimulation by the preloads at the oropharyngeal level had little influence on the changes, which were presumed to be due to an alteration in physiological need for particular substances. The receptors that detect such changes in need are thought to be in the duodenum, since glucose produced a more intense and more rapid change in the hedonic response when tubed directly into the duodenum than when tubed into the stomach. Postabsorptive changes seem not to be involved in alliesthesia in that intubation of mannitol, a nonabsorbed sugar, into the stomach reduced the pleasantness of a sweet solution, whereas injections of glucose into the superior mesenteric artery were without effect [33].

Let us consider what effect, if any, alliesthesia might have on food selection. Cabanac did not observe changes in the pleasantness of sweet solutions until 20 minutes after the glucose load. It seems unlikely that such slow changes would have a major influence on either food selection or food intake within most meals. Booth et al [34] concluded that gastrointestinal or post-absorptive effects of glucose do not affect food intake until about 15 minutes after consumption. They suggest that during the first 20 minutes of a meal, reactions to the oral qualities of foods would be a major influence on intake. Cabanac and Fantino [35] did not experimentally relate the hedonic changes to subsequent food intake or selection, so it is not clear how important alliesthesia is in such regulatory behavior. Although it should be noted that the changes found after glucose ingestion were not highly specific in that, for example, meat and fish smells were affected. Duclaux et al [36] also found that after ad libitum consumption of a mixed meal (eg, ham, bread, french-fried potatoes, milk, orange), all food-related odors tested 15 to 120 minutes after the meal decreased in pleasantness with a maximal change after 60 minutes.

Since there is little evidence concerning the role of alliesthesia in food selection, let us consider the broader issue of whether the postabsorptive consequences of eating are likely to affect food selection. For example, it is possible that changes in blood glucose or insulin following eating could affect food choices. Mayer-Gross and Walker [37] found that preference for 30% sucrose solutions was related to blood glucose level in a group of schizophrenics treated with large doses of insulin. They postulated that this effect was due to changes in the perception of the sweet taste. Recently, Spitzer and Rodin [38] have questioned whether ingestion of fructose or glucose, which have different effects on plasma glucose and insulin, have different effects on food intake and food selection in a subsequent meal 2- 1/4 hours later. They found that whereas total food intake was related to the effects of the sugars on plasma glucose, there were no differences in the proportions of carbohydrate, protein, or fat selected. The differences in plasma glucose between subjects in this study would have been much smaller than in the insulin therapy study, but nevertheless this data does not support the notion that meal-to-meal food selection will be based on physiological need for particular nutrients. Furthermore, Scherr and King [39] found that changes in the pleasantness of sweet and nonsweet foods following meals of real foods depended on the energy content of the meal and not on the type of nutrients in the meal. Perhaps alterations in the selection of nutrients are only apparent when either very severe or chronic deficiencies or excesses of nutrients or metabolites occur. This cannot be decided until more well-controlled studies of food selection have been conducted in humans in relation to physiological changes.

SENSORY-SPECIFIC SATIETY

Shortly after Cabanac suggested that the pleasantness or palatability of food depends on its physiological usefulness, his suggestion was challenged. Wooley et al [40] found that ingestion of a noncaloric sweet solution of cyclamate was just as effective after 15 minutes in decreasing the pleasantness of 20% sucrose as was glucose. This suggested that the sensory properties of the preload or meal are an important influence on the changing hedonic response.

In a series of experiments using real foods, we have assessed the effect of eating on the change in the pleasantness of some sensory properties (eg, taste, appearance, smell, and texture) of foods. One aim of our experiments was to determine whether the hedonic changes reported by Cabanac [31] after fixed preloads of solutions were also seen with consumption of real foods. If such changes were seen, then how long did they persist, and how would they affect subsequent food intake? Would pleasantness changes be specific to a food that was consumed, or would eating decrease the pleasantness of all foods? Are both the sensory properties of foods and the post-absorptive effects involved in the changing response?

Our standard procedure was to invite young adults of normal body weight who were unaware of the aims of the experiment to come to the laboratory for lunch. They were tested alone in cubicles, and before the start of the meal they tasted and rated the pleasantness of the sensory properties of foods. In the first experiment [41] 24 subjects rated the taste of eight foods (cheese on cracker, sausage, chicken, walnuts, bread, raisins, banana, cookies). After this initial rating they were given a plate of either cheese on crackers or sausages and instructed to eat as much as they liked. Two minutes after the end of the meal subjects rerated the taste of the eight foods. It was found that the liking for the food eaten decreased significantly more than for the foods not eaten. We then tested whether these hedonic changes were related to the amounts of particular foods that would be eaten subsequently in a meal by giving the subjects an unexpected second course of either the food they had just eaten, or a food that they had not eaten. During this second course subjects ate significantly more if given a different food than if given the same food. It was found that the change in liking for the foods over the first course correlated with the amount that would be eaten in the second course. These results indicate that the changes in pleasantness of the taste of food that occur during eating are very rapid, and as such will be an important determinant both of food selection in a meal and of the amount eaten.

In a related experiment [42] we have looked at the changes in the hedonic response to foods over a four-

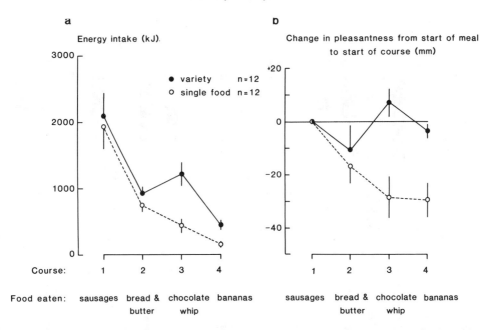

Figure 10.2 (a) A paired comparison of the mean (± SEM) energy intake in each course by subjects when given the plain and varied meals. Data for course 1 are from subjects given sausages in the plain meal; for course 2, from subjects given bread and butter; for course 3, from subjects given chocolate desert; and for course 4, from subjects given bananas. (b) A paired comparison of the mean (± SEM) change in pleasantness of the taste of foods from the start of the meal to the start of the course in which that food was eaten. Data collected as in figure 2(a). Changes in pleasantness before a food was eaten predicted the intake of that food in the following course (42).

course meal that consisted of two savory courses (ie, foods that were not sweet) followed by dessert and fruit. In this experiment, we determined whether, in a meal with very varied food, the specific decreases in the pleasantness of foods already eaten gave way to a more general satiety after several courses, so that all foods became unpleasant. We also determined whether food intake in successive courses in a meal was related to changes in pleasantness that had already occurred in the meal.

Forty-eight male and female subjects of normal weight were tested twice at lunch time. On one occasion they were given a varied meal consisting of four successive courses, which were sausages, bread and butter, chocolate whipped dessert, and bananas. On the other occasion they were given a plain meal that consisted of just one of the four foods offered repeatedly in the four courses. Subjects rated the pleasantness of the taste of eight foods (figure 3) at the start and end of each course. They were allowed to eat as much as they liked in each course. The way in which the hedonic response to the taste of food changed during this four-course meal is shown in figure 2a. To avoid the effect of individual preferences on the results, data is shown only for the same subjects eating the same food in a particular course. For example, the pleasantness ratings for course three are

just for the 12 subjects that had chocolate whip in the plain meal. Thus changes in the plain meal, when subjects had already had two courses of whip, can be compared with the varied meal, when they had already eaten sausages and bread and butter. In the plain meal the pleasantness of the taste of the foods showed a consistent decline with time, whereas there was little change in the pleasantness of the uneaten foods in the varied meal. It was found that these pleasantness changes correlated significantly with the amount of a particular food that was eaten in the subsequent course (figure 2b). The relative lack of change in the pleasantness of foods that had not yet been eaten in the varied meal may explain how variety in the diet stimulates food intake.

The way in which eating a particular food can affect the pleasantness of its taste and that of other noneaten foods was shown most clearly for the plain meals when the same food had been offered in the four courses. The changes in pleasantness from the start of the meal to the end of the fourth course are shown in figure 3 for each type of plain meal. It can be clearly seen that the pleasantness of the eaten food showed the largest decline. There were, however, some interactions between foods, so that some of the uneaten foods decreased in pleasantness more than other uneaten foods. The basis of this interaction appeared to be that consumption of

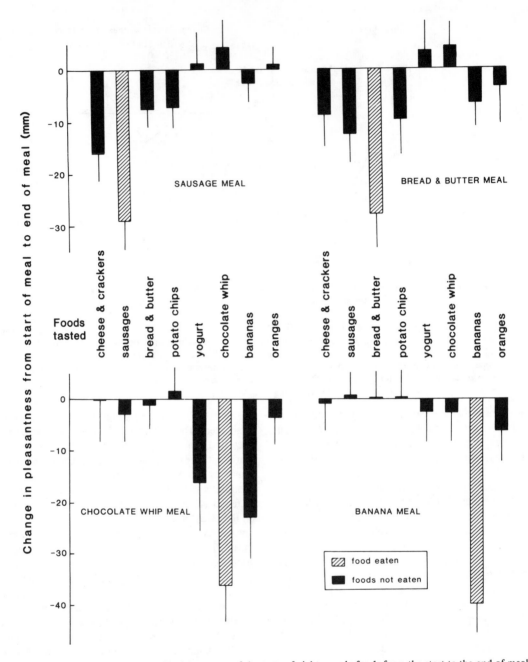

Figure 10.3 Mean (± SEM) changes in pleasantness of the taste of eight sample foods from the start to the end of meals in which just one food was eaten throughout, showing data for these four different plain meals separately. The eaten foods (hatched bars) declined the most in pleasantness (42).

sweet foods caused some decline in the pleasantness of other sweet foods but had little effect on savory foods, whereas the consumption of savory foods decreased the pleasantness of other savory foods and not sweet foods. The savory foods were higher in fat content than the

sweet foods, so it is not clear whether such interactions take place just on the basis of differences in flavor, or whether energy or even specific macronutrients may also be involved.

These changes in palatability that occur during eating explain why there is a tendency to eat a variety of

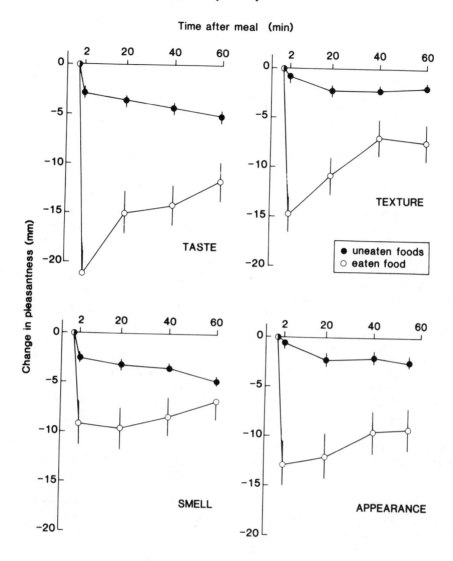

CHEESE ON CRACKER

Figure 10.4 Changes in the pleasantness of the taste of nine foods (uneaten foods were consomme, tomato soup, orange jello, raspberry jello, tomato segment, orange segment, orange drink, and chocolate bar) from before to 2, 20, 40, and 60 minutes after a meal of cheese on crackers. Within two minutes after the meal, the pleasantness of all the sensory properties of the eaten food had decreased significantly more than for the uneaten foods. We call these changes "sensory specific satiety."

foods in a meal (recall the infants described by Davis [6]). As a particular food is consumed, the pleasantness of its taste and the desire to eat it will decline, but the taste of noneaten foods, particularly those that are very different from the eaten food, will remain pleasant. Thus, to maintain palatability at a high level there will be a tendency to switch between foods. Since the best way to ensure that a good balance of nutrients is consumed is to eat a variety of foods, the hedonic shifts that occur during a meal will have an important adaptive advantage.

EVIDENCE THAT THE SENSORY PROPERTIES OF FOODS AFFECT PLEASANTNESS CHANGES

The changes in pleasantness following ingestion of sugar solutions developed slowly over an hour [31]. On the other hand we found that marked changes occurred two minutes after eating a food to satiety. To determine the time course of the changes following real foods, we (V. Burley, M. Hetherington, P. van Duijvenvoorde, and B. Rolls) conducted on experiment in which subjects rated nine foods (cheese on cracker, orange jello, raspberry jello, tomato soup, consomme, orange drink, tomato segment, orange segment, and chocolate) and then ate as much cheese on cracker as they liked, and rerated the pleasantness of the nine foods at 2, 20, 40, and 60 minutes after the meal. We also wanted to know whether sensory properties other than the taste of food were affected by eating, so subjects rated the pleasantness of texture, smell, appearance, and taste at these time intervals.

The results are shown in figure 4. For all of the sensory properties there was a bigger increase in the pleasantness of the eaten food than of the noneaten foods. The changes tended to be greatest at two minutes after the meal, with a gradual recovery in pleasantness over the hour after eating. It is clear from this data that the largest changes in the hedonic response to foods occur before most of the meal will have been absorbed. It is possible that the presence of some food in the gut could have contributed to the changes, but if the physiological usefulness of the food were the major influence on palatabililty, the change in the eaten food should have continued to decline after two minutes. Instead we saw a very rapid decline in the pleasantness of foods, indicating that the major influence on the hedonic response to foods comes from the sensory properties of foods. Whether this is due to decreased sensitivity to foods just consumed or to a cognitive knowledge that enough of a particular food has been consumed is not yet clear.

Another way to determine the importance of the physiological usefulness of foods for hedonic responses is to compare the effects of nutritive and nonnutritive foods. Wooley et al [40] compared nutritive and nonnutritive sweet solutions, but there has been no equivalent experiment using real foods. We (V. Burley, M. Hetherington, P. van Duijvenvoorde, A. Haddon, S. Pickering, and B. Rolls) developed a very low-energy density tomato soup, which was well matched in its sensory properties to high-energy tomato soup. On two separate occasions subjects came to the laboratory at lunchtime, and after rating the pleasantness of the taste of tomato soup and eight other foods, they ate as much as they liked of high-calorie soup in one test, and low-calorie soup in the other test. The subjects ate similar amounts of the two soups in terms of weight (low-calorie 237g; high calorie 297g), which meant that they consumed a mean of 17 kcal in the low-energy meal and 146 kcal in the high-energy meal. None of the subjects was aware of the differences in energy density, and there was no indication of compensation for the missing calories in the low calorie meal, either during the meal, or in a second course of cheese on crackers offered one hour later. Furthermore, both soups had similar effects on hunger over the hour after eating. It can be seen in figure 5 that both soups had similar effects on the change in pleasantness of the taste of tomato soup. Thus, the sensory properties of foods are a major influence on the changes in pleasantness that follow eating a particular food. This is not to say that the energy consumed is not also important. It seems likely that when a lot of food is consumed, there could be a point when subjects are so replete no food will taste pleasant. Because of the importance of the sensory properties of foods for changing hedonic responses, we have called such changes "sensory-specific satiety."

THE INFLUENCE OF VARIETY IN THE DIET ON FOOD INTAKE

Providing a wide variety of foods may be a good way of ensuring that a balance of nutrients is consumed, and if satiety is specific to a food that has been eaten, the selection of further foods and additional eating may occur if a wide variety of foods is readily available. We tested this proposition in a series of experiments. In the first experiment [42], subjects were offered a four-course meal consisting of foods very different in the sensory properties, energy density, nutrient composition (sausages, bread and butter, chocolate whip, and bananas). Figure 3 shows when the same food was eaten in a particular course in both the variety and the single-food conditions, the variety enhanced intake in courses three and four, and this was probably because the foods eaten declined in pleasantness, whereas those not eaten remained unchanged. The mean intake data for all the subjects is shown in figure 6. It indicates that in the varied meal the weight of food eaten was increased by 44% and the energy intake by 60%. In another study when normal-weight subjects were offered successive courses of four kinds of sandwiches, they ate a third more (p < 0.001) than if offered the same kind throughout. Also, if three yogurts that differed in flavor, texture, and color were offered in succession, significantly more (p < 0.01) was consumed than if one yogurt was offered, even if that single yogurt was the favorite [43].

The sensory properties of foods that could contribute to the sensory-specific component of satiety and the enhancement of intake by variety include taste, smell, color, shape, texture, and temperature. To determine to what extent some of these different sensory properties of foods can contribute to sensory-specific satiety and to the increase in food intake caused by variety, we

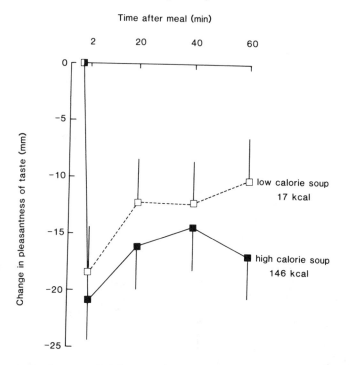

Figure 10.5 The changes in the pleasantness of the taste of tomato soup from before eating to 2, 20, 40, or 60 minutes after eating were similar whether the tomato soup eaten in the meal provided 17 kcal or 146 kcal. This indicates that the sensory properties of the food eaten, rather than its physiological effects, have the most important influences on the hedonic changes that follow a meal.

separately manipulated the flavor, color, or shape of foods but kept the nutrient composition constant.

VARIATIONS IN FLAVOR

The flavor of food most readily affects palatability. The pleasantness of both the taste and the smell of foods decreases as they are consumed, so it seemed a reasonable prediction that changing just the flavor (taste and smell) of food would affect the amount eaten in a meal consisting of successive courses. Having found that intake was enhanced when yogurts that differed in flavor, texture, and appearance were presented in succession, we conducted a similar study in which three flavors of yogurt were offered, but the texture and appearance were kept constant. Although the flavors (raspberry, strawberry, and cherry) were distinguishable, there was no increase in the intake in the variety condition compared with intake of just the favorite flavor [43]. In another study [44] we altered just the flavor of chocolates (orange-, mint-, and coffee-flavored Matchmakers, Rowntree Mackintosh Ltd) and again found no enhancement of intake in the variety condition. Although the foods used in these studies were distinctive in flavor, they had strong background flavors coming from either the yogurt or chocolate and all were sweet. Recall that we found the consumption of one sweet food can decrease the palatability of other sweet foods. In our next experiment, we tested whether a more fundamental difference in flavor could lead to an enhancement of intake. We used cream cheese sandwiches flavored with salt, curry powder, or lemon essence and saccharin, and found a 15% enhancement of intake (see figure 7) when the three flavors were presented in succession compared with the intake of the favorite flavor (p<0.05) [45,46]. Thus changes in the flavors of foods presented in a meal can lead to an enhancement of intake, but it appears that the contrast in flavor, if not accompanied by changes in appearance or texture, must be large before this enhancement is seen.

VARIATIONS IN COLOR

We found that sensory-specific satiety occurred for the appearance of foods as well as for the taste, so we predicted that changes in appearance could lead to an enhancement of food intake in a meal. In a study in which school children were offered Smarties (Rowntree Mackintosh Ltd), the only variable was the color of the coating on these chocolates (green, yellow, pink, violet). Subjects were tested three times, with the favorite color

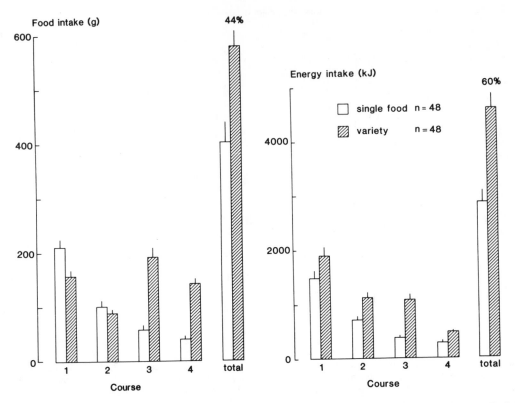

Figure 10.6 Mean (± SEM) energy intake and mean (± SEM) weight of food eaten by subjects in each course and the total intake by sugjects given a plain or varied meal, Subjects ate significantly more when given the varied meal than when given the plain meal (42).

presented in four successive courses, with four different colors presented in succession, and with the four colors presented simultaneously in four successive courses. Subjects consumed the same total amount in all four conditions, so the variety of colors was without effect on intake. When just one color was presented, the subjects had rated the pleasantness of all four colors before and after eating the single color. The decrease in the pleasantness of the color eaten was significantly greater (p<0.001) than for the colors not eaten [45,46]. Thus, the taste of foods that differ only in color is less appealing after they had been consumed than before eating. It seems likely that such subjective changes would affect the choice of foods to be consumed subsequently and would encourage switching between foods of different colors.

VARIATIONS IN SHAPE

Changes in the shape of food affect both the appearance and the feel of the food in the mouth. To determine whether shape is an important influence on feeding, we assessed the effect of offering a variety of shapes of pasta on food intake and subjective responses to

foods. Subjects were tested twice—once with just the favorite shape repeatedly presented, and once with three different shapes presented in three successive courses. There was a significant enhancement (14%, p<0.025) of intake with the variety of shapes (see figure 8). When just one shape was presented, the pleasantness of the food eaten decreased more than that of the foods not eaten [45,46]. This could explain why the variety of shapes increased energy intake.

STUDIES ON THE SIMULTANEOUS PRESENTATION OF A VARIETY OF FOODS

There have been several studies in which different foods were presented simultaneously rather than in successive courses. Pliner et al [47] offered three different snack foods (pizza, sausage rolls, and pork and shrimp egg rolls) either together or singly and found that subjects ate significantly more of these bite-sized snacks when all three were available than when just one was available (19.4 versus 15.8 pieces). They suggested that this effect was mediated by differential decreases in palatability, since palatability declined more rapidly

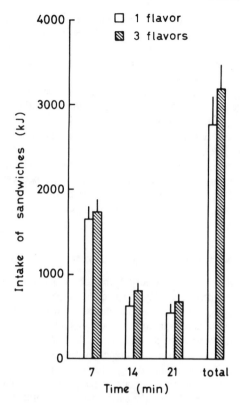

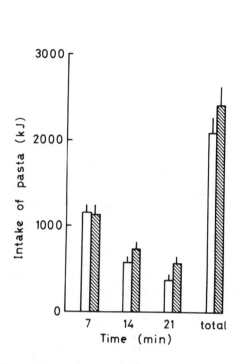

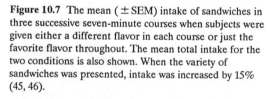

Figure 10.7 The mean (± SEM) intake of sandwiches in three successive seven-minute courses when subjects were given either a different flavor in each course or just the favorite flavor throughout. The mean total intake for the two conditions is also shown. When the variety of sandwiches was presented, intake was increased by 15% (45, 46).

Figure 10.8 The mean (± SEM) amount of pasta consumed in three successive seven-minute courses when subjects were given either a different shape in each course or just the favorite shape throughout. The mean total intake for the two conditions is also shown. When the variety of shapes was presented, intake was increased by 14% (45, 46).

when only one food was available than when three foods were available. Although in this study it was not possible to eliminate the possibility that variety enhanced intake because subjects always had access to a preferred food, results from a subsequent well-controlled study also indicated that the simultaneous presentation of foods (bread with five different spreads) led to greater intake than when any one of the foods was presented alone [48,49]. The mixed meal was more palatable than any single flavor condition, even the most preferred. As in previous studies, meal size and duration were increased. Water was freely available, and it was consumed between the different foods, probably to rinse the mouth and to optimize sensory stimulation.

PALATABILITY, VARIETY, AND CONTROL OF BODY WEIGHT

Because satiety is relatively specific to foods that have been eaten, more is consumed during a varied meal than

in a monotonous one. The more different foods are, the greater will be the enhancement of intake by variety. The flavor and shape of foods can affect both the amount of food eaten and the subjective responses to foods, whereas the color of foods is probably an important factor in diet selection. This has implications for diet control as well as for how to continually stimulate the palate. An implication for dieting is that limiting the variety of the sensory aspects of foods that are readily available (while maintaining adequate nutritional content) will help reduce intake. On the other hand, variation in as many sensory aspects of foods as possible will stimulate the palate and enhance appetite.

There is some evidence that the variety and palatability of the diet can influence long-term food preferences and also body weight. Studies of the effects of the consumption of monotonous army rations indicate that repeated presentation of some foods can lead to a persistent decrease in the pleasantness of these foods

[50,51]. For example, there was no recovery to initial pleasantness of canned meats for three to six months after the end of the experiment. Staple foods and foods of initial high palatability declined much less in palatability with repeated presentation. Decreases in palatability were associated with decreased consumption of the particular foods, but total food intake was not reported [50,51]. Moskowitz [52] has confirmed that foods have time preference curves. These indicate that foods not consumed for about three months are highly desired, but those eaten the day before are not desired at all. Foods such as meat and shellfish, foods with a heavy fat content, or foods that carry the meal such as the entree, have very steep curves and are greatly desired if not eaten for a long period, but recent consumption eliminates the desire for such foods. Items that do not carry the meal and do not have a high fat or protein content, such as bread, salad, potatoes, and some desserts have a much flatter function and can be eaten every day with no loss in preference. It appears that decreases in palatability can extend beyond a meal to affect general acceptability, at least of some foods.

Body weight maintenance may depend to some extent on the availability of a varied and palatable diet. In studies of the effects of consumption of a monotonous liquid diet, it was found that both obese people [53] and normal-weight individuals [54] voluntarily restricted intake and lost weight. There is also some evidence that if diets that are freely available are very varied and palatable, there may be excessive weight gain. In a hospital setting, the provision of a plentiful and varied supply of palatable food led to overeating and weight gain over three- to six-day periods in both obese [55] and normal-weight subjects [56].

It is difficult to conduct long-term controlled studies on the effects of variety and palatability on body weight in humans. It is therefore worth briefly considering the animal literature. In recent years there have been a number of reports of obesity in rats given free access to a variety of palatable high-energy foods [57,58]. In most of these studies the obesity could be due to the high palatability of the foods and their high energy content as well as the variety in the sensory properties of the foods.

We [59] examined whether variety per se is an important factor in the devleopment of obesity by using foods of similar energy density and nutrient composition. We looked at both the successive and the simultaneous presentation of three different foods (cookies, crackers, chocolate). To control for the possibility that an increase in body weight might be due simply to ingestion of a favorite food, which would be available in the variety conditions, control groups of rats were continuously offered just one of the experimental foods. The results are shown in figure 9. All rats offered the palatable foods were hyperphagic compared with chow-fed controls. Rats given the simultaneous but not the successive variety diet were more hyperphagic than the other groups fed palatable foods, and they showed significantly greater body weight and fat gains. Thus, the effect of variety on food intake can extend beyond a single meal and contribute to the development of obesity. It seems likely that in affluent Western societies where there is continual stimulation of appetite by both successive and simultaneous variety within and between meals, there will be little opportunity to compensate for overeating due to variety without consciously limiting intake.

OBESITY AND HEDONIC RESPONSES TO FOODS

It has been suggested [60] that obese and normal-weight individuals differ in the cues that control their feeding behavior. Obese individuals may rely more on external cues associated with food such as palatability than do normal-weight individuals. Palatability affects the amount eaten in all subjects, with foods high in palatability consistently being eaten in greater quantity than those of lower palatability. Changes in palatability have a larger effect on the eating by obese people than that by normal-weight individuals in that obese subjects consume larger quantities of palatable foods and smaller quantities of less palatable foods than do the normal weight subjects [61]. From these findings it would be predicted that obese subjects might respond more to the prolonged palatability provided by a varied meal. However, Pliner et al [47] did not find any effect of body weight on consumption in their experiment, where a choice of palatable foods was offered.

Herman and Polivy [62] have shown that normal-weight individuals, who must constantly restrain their eating and diet to control body weight (many individuals with eating disorders score high on dietary restraint) [63], show many of the same eating behaviors that characterize the obese. It is therefore worth examining the response of these individuals to choice and variety in the diet. As with the obese, these "restrained" eaters did not increase intake with additional choice in a single presentation [47]. Rolls et al [43] found, however, that when a succession of distinctive flavors of yogurt were offered, the female subjects (primarily restrained eaters) showed a greater enhancement of intake by variety than did male subjects (primarily unrestrained nondieters). Clearly, the responses of individuals to variety and palatability will require further analysis if we are to understand whether these factors have an impor-

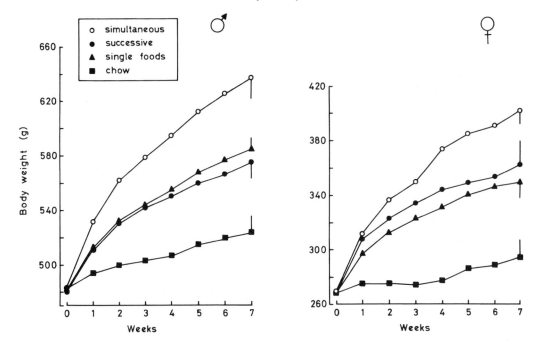

Figure 10.9 Mean (± SEM) body weights of male and female rats in each dietary condition over a seven- week period. The availability of a simultaneous variety of foods led to obesity (59).

tant role in the etiology of obesity.

Cabanac [64] has suggested that the physiological usefulness of foods is important, not only in the short-term regulation of food intake, but also in the control of body weight. When people are at their normal body weight, or "set point," they experience normal alliesthesia or decreased liking for sweet solutions after sweet preloads. However, when there is a decrease in body weight due to dieting or underfeeding, alliesthesia is absent so that sweet foods will remain pleasant and more food will be eaten, which will tend to restore body weight. Thus, as a result of negative energy balance, the threshold for satiety signals may be increased or internal satiety signals may be ignored. The difference between normal and obese individuals will be in the body weight at which the set point is fixed. Although Cabanac's hypotheses have remained controversial because of some failures to replicate his data [65], the idea of exploring hedonic responses to food by obese subjects, or indeed, by subjects who have any problems with food intake or body weight, should be pursued further.

EATING DISORDERS AND RESPONSES TO FOOD

Although it is believed that eating disorders are associated with an inability to respond normally to internal cues related to hunger and satiety, few studies have directly tested this hypothesis. Coddington and Bruch [66] found that patients with anorexia nervosa were less accurate than a normal control group in judging the quantities of intragastric food loads. While differences in stomach motility and gastric contractions associated with hunger have not been found between anorexics and normals, not all anorexic patients associate gastric contractions with hunger [67]. Interpretation of these findings is complicated, because it is not clear how important gastric sensations are in controlling intake in normal-weight individuals and by the fact that anorexics may normally feel more bloated than normals because they have slowed gastric emptying [68].

Few studies have looked at the responses of patients with eating disorders to food and eating. Garfinkel [69] reasoned that since part of the disturbed eating in anorexia could be due to an inability to recognize internal sensations, it would be of interest to compare the sensations associated with hunger and satiety in anorexic and normal subjects. By administering a self-rating questionnaire before and after a standard meal, he found that anorexic patients perceived hunger in a manner similar to the controls, but they were more preoccupied with thoughts of food, had a stronger urge to eat, and were more anxious when hungry. After the test meal, satiety differed in the anorexics, in that they did not describe it in terms of gastric fullness as did the controls. Those patients who learned to deal with this lack of satiety by relying on external cues, such as set portion

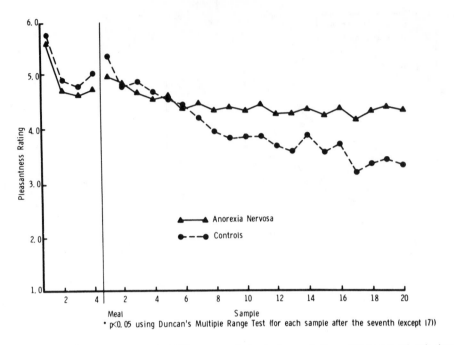

* p<0.05 using Duncan's Multiple Range Test (for each sample after the seventh (except 17))

Figure 10.10 The pleasantness of the taste of a 20% sucrose solution before and after a 400-kcal test lunch. Anorexic subjects did not show the decline in the pleasantness of the taste of sucrose seen in the normal-weight subjects after the meal (71).

sizes, were the most likely to show an improvement in their condition. When Garfinkel's experiment was performed in 1974, there was no distinction between anorexic and bulimic patients. Recent work [70] indicates that future experiments should distinguish between these patient populations. Before a test meal, bulimic patients reported less hunger and greater fullness than both anorexic and control subjects, and this difference persisted after a standard liquid meal of 400 calories. Anorexic patients reported greater fullness than controls both before and after the meal, and this could be due to delayed gastric emptying. Also, both anorexic and bulimic subjects reported more feelings of being bloated both before and after the meal. As in the Garfinkel study [69], ratings of hunger did not differ between the anorexics and normals.

It is not known whether patients with eating disorders can distinguish between meals of different energy density. Garfinkel et al [71] examined differences between anorexics and normals in response to two equicaloric meals that subjects perceived as differing by about 100 to 125 calories. Changes in fullness over the 20 minutes after the meal were the same in both groups after the low-connotation meal so that satiety decreased at 20 minutes, but after the high-connotation meal, satiety decreased in the normals but stayed high in the anorexics. Thus, it appears that in the anorexics there is a sub-

stantial cognitive component influencing satiety, so that if they believe they have eaten a lot, they remain full for a prolonged period. The clearance of these meals from the stomach was not determined.

Although it is clear that patients with eating disorders show aberrant responses to some foods, ie, carbohydrate and fat avoidance [72], there have been few studies in which responses to specific foods have been assessed. Although anorexics and normals do not differ in their sensitivity to sucrose [73], anorexics differ from normals in that they do not show a decrease in the pleasantness of sucrose after eating a meal (figure 10) [71].

Recently we have conducted a series of experiments on the ability of eating disordered and dieting subjects to display sensory-specific satiety [74]. This was achieved by tracking their hedonic responses to specific foods before and after test meals and by comparing their responses to those of normal-weight, non-dieting control subjects. The procedure used was to invite inpatients and outpatients being treated for anorexia and bulimia nervosa at the Johns Hopkins Eating and Weight Disorders Clinic to participate in the experiments. Also, normal-weight and overweight dieting and normal-weight, non-dieting women were recruited from the local student population. Three different experiments were conducted with a similar basic procedure. Subjects came to the laboratory around lunchtime either fasted (Experiment 1) or having had a small standard breakfast, and rated hunger, fullness, thirst, desire to eat, prospective consumption (amount they thought they could eat), fear of becoming fat and depression on visual analog scales. In addition, they rated the pleasantness of the appearance, smell, texture and taste of nine sample foods on scales marked at one end with not at all pleasant and on the other extremely pleasant. Following these ratings, the subjects were given either cottage cheese (low-caloric food) or cheese on crackers (high calorie food) and asked to eat all of the food as a fixed load (Experiment 3) or as much as they wanted (Experiments 1 and 2). After consuming this first course test meal, subjects were then asked to re-rate the subjective and sensory variables as before at 2 mintues (Experiment 2) and at 20, 40 and 60 minutes after the first course (Experiments 1 and 3). In all of the experiments after the post-meal ratings had been made, a self-selection meal consisting of a variety of foods was offered to the subjects with the instruciton to eat as much of the food as they wanted. Two minutes after completing this second course, a final set of subjective and sensory ratings was completed.

Although the experiments were designed to answer three different questions: Experiment 1 the effect of fasting on subjective and sensory ratings and food intake, Experiment 2 the influence of *ad libitum* consumption of a high or low-calorie food on these variables and Experiment 3 the effect of preloads on hunger, appetite, satiety and food intake, the results of the experiments yielded consistent trends. Initial ratings of hunger were lower in the bulimic and anorectic groups and fullness significantly higher in the anorectic subjects prior to the test meals, relative to all of the other subjects. Desire to eat and food intake were consistently lower in the anorectic subjects, whereas there was a tendency for the bulimic subjects to binge on the foods available in the self-selection meal. Typically, the anorectic subjects responded to a high-calorie or low-calorie first course in the same way, by eating less than all of the other subjects in the second course. However, the bulimic subjects tended to eat more after the high-calorie food and less after the low-calorie food, suggesting a counter-regulatory pattern of control [75].

Importantly, anorectic individuals demonstrated clear sensory-specific satiety, regardless of the caloric content of the first course test meal and whether the meal was consumed freely or consumed as a fixed load. Bulimics, in contrast, failed to report a decline in the pleasantness of the eaten food relative to the uneaten foods, suggesting an absence of sensory-specific satiety. The finding that anorectic subjects displayed sensory-specific satiety indicates that these subjects are capable of reporting a decrease in the pleasantness of food with

consumption, which is not in agreement with the findings of other researchers [71,73]. However, there are at least two possible explanations of this discrepancy. Firstly, the methodologies employed in the studies are different and the discrepant conclusions may reflect differences between the assessment of solutions in hedonic analyses compared to actual foods. This may be a result of different processes operating between tasting solutions and responding to real foods which are not only different on a sensory level, but which differ in their perceived effects on body weight, particularly in eating disordered subjects. Secondly, the reported decline in the pleasantness of the eaten food may be attributable to cognitive satiety rather than sensory-specific satiety per se. This means that the strong decline in pleasantness may indicate a reluctance to continue eating the food by the individual, rather than the development of satiety to the sensory characteristics of the foods.

The bulimic subjects failed to report sensory-specific changes in the pleasantness of the foods regardless of the amount of food consumed or its caloric content. One possible explanation for this, is that since almost half of the bulimics admitted to having binged on the available food, hedonic responses may, like food intake [76], be different when the subject is bingeing relative to non-binge episodes of eating. This possible explanation needs to be tested systematically by tracking hedonic responses to foods during normal meals compared to binge eating episodes. However, paucity of information about the responses of patients with eating disorders to food and to eating seems surprising until it is recognized that we are only beginning to understand the factors that influence eating in normal subjects. Few experimental paradigms have been found to produce similar findings in different laboratories. In our own studies of eating in normal subjects, we have described some fundamental influences on intake, which have proved highly replicable and robust. For example, sensory-specific satiety, or the decrease in the pleasantness of the taste of a food that has been eaten, appears to be an inbuilt mechanism that helps to ensure that a variety of foods is consumed. The experiments of Davis [6] in which newly weaned infants selected varied meals indicated that sensory specific satiety may be present. Also, Birch (figure 11) has recently found that 3- to 4-year-old children show sensory specific satiety. It seems likely that in anorexia nervosa, the cognitive control of food intake that will restrict meals to safe, perhaps monotonous, diets may override the usual tendency to switch between foods. In cases of obesity and bulimia nervosa the opposite may be true, since the problem may be based on eating many varied, high-energy foods. It is hoped that by gaining understanding of how normal individuals control food intake and selection, this knowledge can be applied to in-

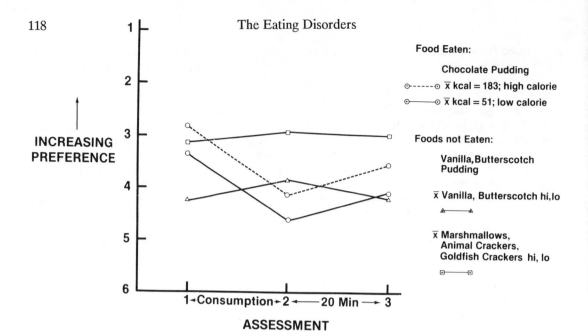

Figure 10.11 Three- to four-year-old children rated their preference for chocolate, vanilla, and butterscotch pudding; marshmallows; animal crackers; and goldfish crackers before and 2 and 20 mintues after eating 4 oz of high- or low-calorie chocolate pudding. The children showed sensory-specific satiety in that the preference for the eaten food declined, whereas the uneaten foods were not affected. As in adults the biggest changes were seen two minutes after eating and were similar following the high- and low-energy meals (L.L. Birch, unpublished).

fluencing the food choices of individuals with disordered eating.

ACKNOWLEDGMENTS

The author's experiments were supported by the Medical Research Council of Great Britain. The collaboration of V.J. Burley, E.T., Rolls, E.A. Rowe, and P.M. van Duijvenvoorde is gratefully acknowledged.

REFERENCES

1. Mistretta CM, Bradley RM. Taste in utero: theoretical considerations. In Weiffenbach JM, ed. Taste and development: The genesis of sweet preference. Bethesda, MD: DHEW, 1977:51-64.

2. Desor JA, Maller O, Turner R. Taste in acceptance of sugars by human infants. J Comp Physiol Psychol, 1973; 84:496-501.

3. Steiner JE. Facial expressions of the neonate infant indicating the hedonics of food-related chemical stimuli. In Weiffenbach JM, ed. Taste and development: The genesis of sweet preference. Bethesda, MD: DHEW, 1977:173-188.

4. Desor JA, Maller O, Andrews K. Ingestive responses of human newborns to salty, sour, and bitter stimuli. J Comp Physiol Psychol, 1975; 89:966-970.

5. Engen T. The origin of preferences in taste and smell. In Kroeze JHA, ed. Preference behaviour and chemoreception. London: Information Retrieval, Ltd, 1980:263-274.

6. Davis CM. Self selection of diet by newly weaned infants. An experimental study. Am J Dis Child, 1928; 36:651-79.

7. Beauchamp GK, Moran M. Dietary experience and sweet taste preference in human infants. Appetite, 1982; 3:139-52.

8. Bavly S. Changes in food habits in Israel. J Am Diet Assoc, 1966; 48:488-95.

9. Muto S, Muzuno K, Kobayashi Y. Dietary patterns of Japanese and American preschool children in Tokyo. J Am Diet Assoc, 1969; 55:252-6.

10. Birch LL. Dimensions of preschool children's food preferences. J Nutr Ed, 1979; 11:77-80.

11. Harper LV, Sanders KM. The effect of adult's eating on young children's acceptance of unfamiliar foods. J Exper Child Psychol, 1975; 20:206-14.

12. Duncker K. Experimental modification of children's food preferences through social suggestion. J Abnorm Social Psychol, 1938; 33:489-507.

13. Rodin J. Social and immediate environmental influences on food selection. Int J Obesity, 1980; 4:364-70.

14. Birch LL. Effects of peer models' food choices and eating behavior on preschoolers' food preferences. Child

Devel, 1980; 51:489-96.

15. Birch LL. Generalization of a modified food preference. Child Devel, 1981; 52:755-8.

16. Birch LL, Zimmerman SI, Hind H. The influence of social-affective context on the formation of children's food preferences. Child Devel, 1980; 51:856-61.

17. Birch LL, Birch D, Marlin DW, Kraemer L. Effects of instrumental consumption on children's food preference. Appetite, 1982; 3:125-34.

18. Eppright ES, Fox HM, Fryer BA, et al. Eating behavior of preschool children. J Nutr Ed, 1969; Summer:16-19.

19. Rozin Pl. Acquisition of food preferences and attitudes to food. Int J Obesity, 1980; 4:356-63.

20. Cines BM, Rozin P. Some aspects of the liking for hot coffee and coffee flavor. Appetite, 1982; 3:23-4.

21. Barker LM, Best MR, Domjan M, eds. Learning mechanisms in food selection. Baylor, Texas: Baylor University Press, 1977:

22. Garb JL, Stunkard AJ. Taste aversions in man. Am J Psychiatry, 1974; 131:1204-7.

23. Pelchat ML, Rozin P. The special role of nausea in the acquisition of food dislikes by humans. Appetite, 1982; 3:341-51.

24. Morganstern KP. Cigarette smoke as a noxious stimulus in self-managed aversion therapy for compulsive eating: technique and case illustration. Behav Ther, 1974; 5:255-61.

25. Booth DA. Momentary acceptance of particular foods and processes that change it. In Solms J, Hall RL, eds. Criteria of food acceptance — How man chooses what he eats. Zurich; Foster-Verlag, 1981:49-68.

26. Booth DA, Mather P, Fuller J. Starch content of ordinary food associatively conditions human appetite and satiation, indexed by intake and eating pleasantness of starch-paired flavours. Appetite, 1982; 3:163-84.

27. Krassner HA, Brownell KD, Stunkard AJ. Cleaning the plate: food left over by overweight and normal weight persons. Behav Res Therapy, 1979; 17:155-6.

28. Birch LL, Marlin DW. I don't like it; I never tried it: effects of exposure on two-year-old children's food preferences. Appetite, 1982; 3:353-60.

29. Pliner P. The effects of mere exposure on liking for edible substances. Appetite, 1982; 3:283-90.

30. Stang DJ. When familiarity breeds contempt, absence makes the heart grow fonder: effects of exposure and delay on taste pleasantness ratings. Bull Psychol Soc, 1975; 6:273-5.

31. Cabanac M. Physiological role of pleasure. Science, 1971; 173:1103-7.

32. Cabanac M, Duclaux R. Specificity of internal signals in producing satiety for taste stimuli. Nature, 1970; 227:966-7.

33. Pruvost M, Duquesnel J, Cabanac M. Injection of glucose into the superior mesenteric artery in man, absence of negative alliesthesia in response to sweet stimuli. Physiol Behav, 1973; 11:355-8.

34. Booth DA, Campbell AT, Chase A. Temporal bounds of post-ingestive glucose induced satiety in man. Nature, 1970; 288:1104-5.

35. Cabanac M, Fantino M. Origin of olfacto-gustatory alliesthesia: intestinal sensitivity to carbohydrate concentration? Physiol Behav, 1977; 18:1039-45.

36. Duclaux R, Feisthauer J, Cabanac M. Effects of eating a meal on the pleasantness of food and nonfood odors in man. Physiol Behav. 1973; 10:1029-33.

37. Mayer-Gross W, Walker JW. Taste and selection of food in hypoglycaemia. Brit J Exp Path, 1946; 27:297-305.

38. Spitzer L, Rodin J. Effects of fructose and glucose preloads on subsequent food intake. Appetite, 1987; 8:135-145.

39. Scherr S, King KR. Sensory and metabolic feedback in the modulation of taste hedonics. Physiol Behav, 1982; 29:827-32.

40. Wooley OW, Wooley SC, Dunham RB. Calories and sweet taste: effects of sucrose preference in the obese and nonobese. Physiol Behav, 1972; 9:765-8.

41. Rolls BJ, Rolls ET, Rowe EA, Sweeney K. Sensory specific satiety in man. Physiol Behav,1981; 27:137-42.

42. Rolls BJ, van Duijvenvoorde P, Rolls ET. Pleasantness changes and food intake in a varied four course meal. Appetite, 1984; 5:337-348.

43. Rolls BJ, Rowe EA, Rolls ET, et al. Variety in a meal enhances food intake in man. Physiol Behav, 1981; 26:215-21.

44. Rolls BJ, Rolls ET, Rowe EA. The influence of variety on human food selection and intake. In Barker LM, ed. Psychobiology of human food selection. Westport, Conn: AVI Publishing Co, 1982:101-122.

45. Rolls BJ, Rowe EA, Rolls ET. How sensory properties of foods affect human feeding behavior. Physiol Behav, 1982; 29:409-17.

46. Rolls BJ, Rowe EA, Rolls ET. How flavour and appearance affect human feeding. Proc Nutr Soc, 1982; 41:109-17.

47. Pliner P, Polivy J, Herman CP, Zakalusny I. Short-term intake of overweight individuals and normal weight dieters and non-dieters with and without choice amongst a variety of foods. Appetite, 1980; 1:203-13.

48. Bellisle F, Le Magnen J. The analysis of human feeding patterns: the edogram. Appetite, 1980; 1:141-50.

49. Bellisle F, Le Magnen J. The structure of meals in humans: eating and drinking patterns in lean and obese subjects. Physiol Behav, 1981; 17:649-58.

50. Schutz JG, Pilgrim FJ. A field study of monotony. Psych Rep, 1958; 4:559-65.

51. Siegel PS, Pilgrim FJ. The effect of monotony on the acceptance of food. Am J Psychol, 1958; 71:756-9.

52. Moskowitz HR. Mind, body and pleasure: An analysis of factors which influence sensory hedonics. In Kroeze, JHA, ed. Preference behavior and chemoreception, London: Information Retrieval, Ltd. 1979;131.

53. Hashim SA, Van Itallie TB. Studies in normal and obese subjects with a monitored food dispensing device. Ann NY Acad Sci, 1965; 131:654-61.

54. Cabanac M, Rabe EF. Influence of a monotonous food on body weight regulation in humans. Physiol Behav, 1976; 17:675-8.

55. Porikos KP, Booth TB, Van Itallie TB. Effect of covert nutritive dilution on the sponstaneous food intake of obese individuals: a pilot study. Am J Clin Nutr, 1977; 30:1638-44.

56. Porikos KP, Hesser MF, Van Itallie TB. Caloric regulation in normal weight men maintained on a palatable diet of conventional foods. Physiol Behav, 1982; 29:293-300.

57. Sclafani A, Springer D. Dietary obesity in adult rats: similarities to hypothalamic and human obesity syndromes. Physiol Behav, 1976; 17:461-71.

58. Rolls BJ, Rowe EA, Turner RC. Persistent obesity in rats following a period of consumption of a mixed, high energy diet. J Physiol, 1980; 298:415-27.

59. Rolls BJ, van Duijvenvoorde PM, Rowe EA. Variety in the diet enhances intake in a meal and contributes to the development of obesity in the rat. Physiol Behav, 1983; 31:21-7.

60. Schachter S. Some extraordinary facts about obese humans and rats. Am Psychol, 1971; 26:129-44.

61. Pliner P. Influence of psychological (exogenous) and endogenous factors in the regulation of nutritional uptake. In Katzen HM, Mahler RJ, eds. Advances in modern nutrition, vol 2: Diabetes, obesity, and vascular disease. Washington, DC: Hemisphere Publishing Corp, 1978:551-573.

62. Herman CP, Polivy J. Anxiety, restraint, and eating behavior. J Abnorm Psychol, 1975; 84:666-72.

63. Fairburn CG, Cooper PJ. The clinical features of bulimia nervosa. Brit J Psychiatry, 1984; 144:238-46.

64. Cabanac M. Sensory pleasure. Quart Rev Biol, 1979; 54:1-29.

65. Leon GR, Roth L. Obesity: psychological causes, correlations, and speculations. Psych Bull, 1977; 34:117-39.

66. Coddington RD, Bruch H. Gastric perceptivity in normal, obese and schizophrenic subjects. Psychosomatics, 1970; 11:571-9.

67. Silverstone JT, Russell GFM. Gastric hunger contractions in anorexia nervosa. Brit J Psychiat, 1967; 113:257-63.

68. Dubois A, Gross HA, Ebert MH, Castell DO. Altered gastric emptying and secretion in primary anorexia nervosa. Gastroenterology, 1979; 77:319-23.

69. Garfinkel PE. Perception of hunger and satiety in anorexia nervosa. Psychol Med, 1974; 4:309-15.

70. Robinson RG, Tortosa M, Sullivan J, et al. Quantitative assessment of psychologic state of patients with anorexia nervosa, or bulimia: response to caloric stimulus. Psychosom Med, 1983; 45:283-92.

71. Garfinkel PE, Moldofsky H, Garner DM, et al. Body image awareness in anorexia nervosa: disturbances in "body image" and "satiety". Psychosom Med, 1978; 40:487-98.

72. Crisp AH. The possible significance of some behavioural correlates of weight and carbohydrate intake. J Psychosom Res, 1967; 11:117-31.

73. Lacey JH, Stanley PA, Crutchfield M, Crisp AH. Sucrose sensitivity in anorexia nervosa. J Psychosom Res, 1977; 21:17-21.

74. Hetherington M, Rolls BJ. Sensory-specific satiety and food intake in eating disorders. In Walsh BT, ed. Eating behavior in eating disorders. Washington, DC: American Psychiatric Press, Inc., in press.

75. Herman CP, Polivy J. A boundary model for the regulation of eating. In Stunkard AJ, Stellar E, eds. Eating and its disorders. New York: Raven Press, 1985;141-156.

76. Kissileff HR, Walsh BT, Kral JG, Cassidy SM. Laboratory studies of eating behavior in women with bulimia. Physiol Behav, 1986; 38:563-570.

Chapter 11

Physiological Basis of Food Preferences in Eating Disorders

Adam Drewnowski

Both cognitive and physiological factors determine taste preferences and dietary choices in humans. Food intake may be primarily determined by hunger and metabolic status of the organism, but it is also influenced by nutritional beliefs and attitudes toward weight and dieting [1]. This delicate balance between human behavior and metabolism is disturbed in eating disorders, where a conscious denial of calories can override the body's metabolic needs. Dramatic weight loss seen in anorexia nervosa is often associated with the rejection of specific foods, most often fats, starches and sweet desserts—a phenomenon often described as "carbohydrate phobia" [2].

Anorexia nervosa is also characterized by a variety of metabolic and neuroendocrine dysfunctions, including amenorrhea, hypothyroidism, hypotension, and increased adrenal activity [3]. Some of these changes are the likely consequence of metabolic starvartion resulting from the relentless pursuit of extreme thinness, since many neuroendocrine abnormalities are reversed following weight regain [4]. However, certain symptoms of the anorectic syndrome have been attributed to a basic primary hypothalamic disorder [5]. For example, amenorrhea occurs in at least one third of anorectic patients before any weight loss has occurred, and it may persist after the return to normal body weight, suggesting that some disturbances in the hypothalamic-pituitary-ovarian axis are not fully accounted for by the mal-nourished state [6]. Furthermore, indirect evidence has linked anorexia nervosa to affective disorders. It has been suggested that mood swings and the binge-purge cycles that are common in anorectic patients are the result of hypothalamic fluctuations in alpha-noradrenergic function and therefore susceptible to pharmacological intervention [7]. Treatment studies of anorexia nervosa with antidepressants have been conducted to eveluate this hypothesis [6].

Central neurotransmitter mechanisms may influence eating behaviors and weight status in different ways. Psychopharmacological studies [7,8] have examined the role of adrenergic, dopaminergic, serotonergic, and opiate receptor systems in the regulation of caloric intake and in the selection of specific macronutrients in the rat. Studies on the noradrenergic system in the medial hypothalamus suggest that chemical blockade of noradrenergic activation or irreversible damage in this area produces, in the rat, a variety of symptoms similar to those of anorectic patients [7]. These symptoms include a decrease in total food intake, a reduction in meal size and rate of eating, a disturbed diurnal pattern of eating, and hyperactivity. In contrast, medial hypothalamic injections of norepinephrine are likely to cause a rebound toward overeating of a carbohydrate-rich diet. The abnormally large eating response of satiated rats following medial hypothalamic injections of norepinephrine have been compared to bulimic episodes shown by anorectic patients [7,9]. Compulsive binge eating of sugar and fat-containing foods may also be linked to abnormal function of the endogenous opioid system. Animal studies have documented that exogenous opiate agonists increase the consumption of palatable diets, while opiate antagonists suppress intake and prevent dieting-induced obesity in the laboratory rat. Sensory studies suggest further that opiates may be involved in mediating the pleasure response to sugar and possibly fat [10], explaining perhaps the uncontrollable cravings for sweet taste often reported by patients with eating disorders.

Clinical studies of eating disorders have only recently began to focus on the interaction between metabolic and behavioral variables underlying food palatability and diet selection [1,11-13]. Because neuroendocrine disorders, physiological factors, and the overriding obsession with food and dieting are so closely intertwined, it is difficult to assess their precise contribution to dietary restriction and other abnormalities of eating behavior. However, there is indirect evidence that binge-purge or binge-starvation cycles have a physiological as well as a psychological basis. While binge eating may be viewed as a periodic breakdown of dietary restraint, it may be that cravings for sweet-tasting foods are metabolically determined. Preferences for sweet taste may be influenced by body-weight status, a range of physiological variables, or adipose tissue metabolism [12]. The patient, aware of abnormal craving for sweets, may use fasting or purging in a conscious attempt to regulate a grossly disturbed physiological mechanism [7].

It is worth noting that "carbohydrate phobia" and starch avoidance is not a permanent trait. Forbidden foods such as ice cream, cookies, and desserts are typically consumed to excess during binge eating episodes shown by up to 50% of anorectic patients [14]. During such episodes, large amounts (>2,000 kcal) of easily ingested and usually sweet-tasting foods are consumed in a short space of time. The sensation of satiety is reportedly absent, and eating is accompanied by breathlessness, sweating, racing pulse, and other symptoms of sympathetic activiation. Bulimic episodes are generally terminated by abdominal pain, sleep, social interruption or self-induced vomiting, and are followed by guilt and depression and by prolonged periods of severely restrictred dieting [15,16].

MALNUTRITION AND TASTE

The diet of anorectic patients is typically low in calories, but it includes often excessive amounts of green vegetables, salads, and fruits, sometimes supplemented by daily vitamins [2,17]. Protein intake is generally adequate, but fats and carbohydrates, including sweets and desserts are strictly avoided. Consumption of a relatively high-protein diet produces an unusual type of malnutrition. Extreme emaciation follows from caloric restriction, but protein metabolism is relatively preserved. Russell [2] studied hospitalized patients, including four men, with severe anorexia nervosa to assess the relative importance of protein and calorie malnutrition to the disease state. Weight regained by subjects was primarily fat, indicating that only a small amount of protein depletion had to be corrected by refeeding. The typical diet of anorectic patients has been reported as low in carbohydrate but adequate in both protein and fat [2].

Although the typical diet is not vitamin deficient, it may lack trace minerals, especially copper and zinc. Trace metals, including zinc, cooper, and nickel are thought to have a role in normal taste and smell, and zinc deficiency can depress appetite and facilitate abstinence from food. This possibility was explored in a study [17] of 30 hospitalized women, all meeting Feighner's criteria for anorexia nervosa. Trace metals, vitamins, and other biochemical parameters were measured in an attempt to relate them to taste function, biochemical changes, and clinical signs of the disorder. Plasma and urinary zinc in anorectic patients were moderately lower than in normal controls. The majority of anorectic patients had subnormal taste acuity for bitter and sour substances; taste acuity for salt and sweet was less disturbed. However, taste recognition scores failed to correlate with plasma zinc levels. Appetite was suppressed but not absent unless the patient totally abstained from food, indicating that the role of zinc during total abstinence from food should be further investigated. Nutritional therapy including zinc supplementation and concommitant psychotherapy was reported to improve the patients' emotional well-being and led to substantial weight gain [17].

PERCEPTION OF INTERNAL STATES

The palatability of a given food often depends on the internal states of hunger and satiety [1]. In fact, satiety occurring within a meal has been operationally defined as the point at which food stops tasting good [18]. Anorectic patients are reported to show normal awareness of hunger, but often show disturbances in satiety. These may include postprandial sensation of nausea, distension, and bloating, tense and irritable moods, as well as cognitive preoccupation with food [19,20]. Studies on the relationship between sensations of hunger and gastric distension or gastric motility [21-22] reported that although most anorectic patients correctly identified stomach contractions, some did not interpret them as hunger. One clinical study [22] compared the rates of gastric emptying in ten anorexic patients and in 12 healthy volunteers fed a sample meal of cornflakes, milk, and sugar. Anorectic patients showed significantly slower gastric emptying and their perception of extreme fullness may well reflect abnormal gastrointestinal function. Attitudinal studies [23] have shown that eating disorder patients tend to dislike calorie dense foods—that is foods rich in fat. It may be that such foods, which delay gastric emptying even further, cause acute discomfort to the anorectic patient.

The perception of satiety is likely to have a cognitive component [1]. In a study of 26 anorectic women and 16 controls, Garfinkel et al [20] provided the subjects with meals that were viewed as either high or low calorie, although the meals were in fact identical (400 kcal). Anorectics reported feeling fuller than normals premeal, and they stayed fuller longer after eating the high-calorie-connotation meal. The findings that the expectation of satiety affects the perception of internal state are generally consistent with comparable data obtained for normal-weight and obese individuals [1].

RESPONSIVENESS TO SWEET TASTE

Scientific studies on taste responsiveness have primarily focused on the perception of sweetness and the reported pleasantness of sweet solutions [11]. In contrast to the extensive literature on the role of sweet taste in human obesity [24], there are relatively few studies on the responsiveness to sweet taste of extremely underweight individuals [12]. Previous studies of threshold detection, stimulus recognition, and magnitude estimation of sweetness intensity have generally failed to show differences in sensory function between obese and normal-weight individuals [24,25]. In a study of six anorectic patients and six age-matched controls [26], sensitivity to the sweet taste of sucrose was examined using a two-alternative forced-choice method. Anorectic patients appeared to show a lower taste sensitivity for 0.175% sucrose, but this difference was not statistically significant. Patients gaining weight on a high-calorie, high-carbohydrate diet appeared to show lower sensitivity to sucrose than patients maintaining a stable weight on a low-calorie diet. The study found no major differences in sensory function between anorectic patients and controls, concluding that small differences in the threshold detection of sweet taste may be a consequence of sucrose avoidance in both anorectic and dieting individuals [26].

Studies on the hedonics of sweet taste have generally shown that the pleasure response to sweetness can be influenced by changes in metabolic status [24]. One measure thought to link the subject's taste responsiveness with internal state is the test commonly known as the satiety aversion to sucrose [27]. In early applications of this test, normal-weight subjects were reported to find sweet solutions less pleasant after ingesting 100 ml of concentrated glucose solution. Glucose preloading was assumed to result in "satiety," causing a temporary aversion to the sweet taste of sucrose [27]. Dieting individuals at below-normal body weight reportedly failed to show the satiety aversion to sucrose, which returned following weight regain. Early studies on obese subjects showed that the obese rated sweet solutions as equally pleasant both before and after the ingestion of glucose preload [28], although this finding was not confirmed by other investigators [11,24]. There has been, however, some agreement that sustained caloric deprivation or sustained weight loss do lead to enhanced pleasantness ratings for sweet stimuli. Formerly obese patients, or overweight teenage girls following several weeks of weight reduction, showed higher preference ratings for sweetened KoolAid or sweet milkshakes [29,30]. Since reponsiveness to sweet taste is affected by the long-term metabolic status of the organism, it has been thought to serve as a behavioral measure of a physiological "set-point" [27].

A few recent studies have suggested that the relationship between preferences for sweet taste and body weight status may be more complex. One study [31] compared responses to sucrose preloads in underweight, normal-weight, and dieting moderately overweight subjects (at 10% or more above ideal body weight). Overweight subjects rated sucrose solutions higher at the outset than did the other groups, but there were no differences among subjects in the change of pleasantness ratings of 20% and 40% sucrose solutions before and after ingesting 400 ml of 20% sucrose. The authors concluded that contrary to Cabanac's hypothesis, the magnitude of postingestive change in itself cannot be considered a valid indicator of whether an individual is at set point [31].

Anorectic patients who are substantially below normal body weight, and so presumably below "set point," might be expected to show an absence of satiety aversion to sucrose. Garfinkel et al [20] tested 26 anorectic patients and 16 normal-weight volunteers for responsiveness to 20% sucrose solutions presented both before and at three-minute intervals for an hour following a 400 kcal meal. Following repeated sampling, anorectic patients showed slightly higher pleasantness ratings for sucrose compared with normal volunteers and were thought not to show the normal satiety aversion to sucrose. It is worth noting that the failure to develop satiety aversion to sucrose was closely related to disturbances in body image as measured using the anomorphic lens technique [20,32].

A follow-up study [33] addressed the issue of the stability of satiety aversion to sucrose following weight regain. Sixteen of 26 original anorectic patients and 13 of 16 original controls were tested one year after the original study. Subjects consumed each of two lunches on two days, one appearing high in calories and one low in calories, although the meals were of equal caloric value (400 kcal). A 20% sucrose solution was tasted before and after the meal. No change was found in the magnitude of satiety aversion to sucrose following the consumption of either meal, and no difference in the development of sucrose aversion was found in either group. The failure of anorectic individuals to show an aversion to sucrose appeared stable from year to year and significant weight gain seemed to have no effect. Clearly, responsiveness to sweet taste, as tracked by the present technique, is not as closely linked to indices of body weight as previously thought. However, other congitive variables may be involved: In both groups of subjects, overestimators of body size, compared with underestimators, failed to show satiety aversion to sucrose [33].

COMPLEX TASTE STIMULI

Because the scientific study of taste preferences has been based largely on model systems that do not resemble real foods, there is growing concern that laboratory results may not be applicable to real-life situations [34-36]. For example, patterns of response to sweetness or saltiness cannot be extrapolated from water solutions to the more complex apricot nectar or tomato juice [36,37]. More investigators now urge that studies on taste perception and preferences be conducted with suprathreshold stimuli that are more representative of foods commonly encountered in the diet. Such studies would examine the potential contributions to food preference of sensory factors other than the four tastes, and would focus on aspects of food texture, consistency, and flavor, which have remained largely unexplored in clinical research [35]. In particular, despite growing evidence that eating disorder patients dislike not carbohydrate but fat, very little is known about the psychophysics or the hedonics of fat perception or about human preferences for fat-containing foods [12,13].

Sensory studies of complex food-like stimuli require the use of procedures that are capable of mapping sensory space and describing taste preference of individual subjects. Such procedures, originally developed for marketing research studies, include multidimensional scaling [38,39], used for product positioning in the marketplace; unfolding techniques, used to examine

criteria underlying judgements of preference [40]; and response surface methodology, which maps consumer preferences as a function of perceived stimulus attributes [12,13].

For our sensory stimuli, we used a range of commercially available dairy foods, sweetened with different amounts of sucrose. Preliminary studies on the taste of dairy products reveled that sweetness/sourness and the butter fat content were the key aspects of taste sensation. Normal-weight subjects identified cream cheese and sweetened condensed milk as highly preferred, while buttermilk and skim milk ranked lowest on the list. To determine whether the liking for these high-fat foods was the consequence of stimulus sweetness or its fat content, we developed a simplified system of milk products for further investigations of the sensory space [13].

The subjects were asked to rate the perceived intensity of sweetness, fatness, and creaminess of 20 different mixtures of milk, cream, and sugar, and assigned an overall hedonic rating to each sample. As expected, intensity estimates increased as logarithmic functions of sucrose or fat concentration, and no mixture phenomena were observed. Fat levels did not affect the judgment of sweetness, while estimates of creaminess were independent of sugar levels. In contrast, hedonic responses to sweetness were strongly modulated by the fat content of the samples tested. Sucrose in heavy cream was rated as much more palatable than the same amount of sucrose in skim milk. In fact, of all 20 samples, the favorite was heavy cream mixed with safflower oil ($>50\%$ fat w/w) and sweetened with only 10% sucrose [13].

Tests of this procedure with normal-weight, obese, and stabilized reduced-obese subject populations [41] have shown that taste and hedonic responsiveness are not affected by short-term changes in metabolic status, such as overnight fasting. Long-term nutritional status was more important: Obese patients disliked sweetness and preferred high-fat foods, while reduced-obese patients showed enhanced preferences for both sugar and fat.

Additional studies [42] suggest that anorectic patients at below- normal body weight dislike the oral sensation of fat. In contrast to obese patients who greatly preferred fat to sugar, anorectic patients preferred intense sweetness over fat. These changes in taste responsiveness were reliably linked to the measure of body mass index (weight/height^2), and it is tempting to speculate that they are metabolically determined [12]. Among potential metabolic antecedents of this behavioral response are insulin levels, adipose cell size, or lipoprotein lipase activity [41]. The contribution of the

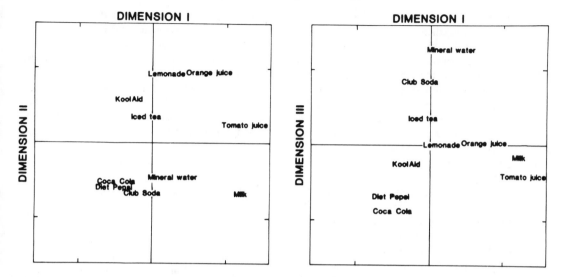

Figure 11.1 A three-dimensional MDS solution of the perceptual space for a variety of soft drinks achieved by the SINDSCAL program. Dimension I: naturalness; Dimension II: taste; Dimension III: sweetness.

endogenous opioid system also deserves further study.

an aversion [44].

ATTITUDINAL FACTORS AND DEVELOPMENT OF AVERSIONS

Nausea and self-induced vomiting, which are prevalent among anorectic women, may play a role in the development of food aversions. The acquisition of taste aversion among 260 female and 257 male college students was the focus of one study [43] conducted using questionnaires or written interviews. The mean number of aversions reported was 0.8 per person; one or more aversions was reported for 65% of the subjects. Females were more likely to report aversions than males (70.3% versus 60.5%), and aversions were more likely to form with less-familiar, less-preferred foods. One fourth of the aversions were to alcoholic beverages, and 29% of aversions generalized to related foods.

A similar study [44] of three groups of subjects with eating and drinking disorders included anorectic/bulimic women, chronic alcoholics, and college students who were heavy users of alcohol. The anorectic population included seven women diagnosed as anorectic, two diagnosed as bulimic, and ten with both disorders. Among the anorectic women, 29% reported one or more aversions; and among those suffering from both disorders, 80% reported one or more aversions. Overall, 58% reported one or more aversions. While college students reported strength of aversion-forming nausea at 4 on a 5-point scale, subjects with eating disorders reported a 4.7 rating. However, no subject reported that self-induced vomiting was a specific cause of

COGNITIVE STRUCTURE

Dieting obese and anorectic patients are likely to differ in terms of their attitudes toward food and dieting. Whereas the reduced obese typically overeat calorie-dense foods and eventually regain body weight, the behavior of anorectic patients is greatly influenced by "cognitive structure" that includes self-image and nutritional attitudes and beliefs. Although they are severely emaciated, anorectic patients often report that they are eating enough calories to maintain what they insist is a normal state of health and body weight. Total elimination of starches or fats from the anorectic diet [2] may be the direct result of the patients' distorted beliefs regarding the nutritional or caloric value of different foods. Misperceptions of anorectic individuals regarding their body size or body image have been investigated in some detail [32], but little data are available on perceptual distortions with regard to foods [23].

Quantitative techniques borrowed from marketing research studies permit the mapping of preference space for a variety of food items. The major premise of a mathematical technique known as multidimensional scaling (MDS) is that judgements of psychological similarity between pairs of items reflect the location of the items in perceptual space, whose chief dimensions correspond to the principal features of the scaled items [38,39]. The technique can therefore be used to map mental spaces for food stimuli and to examine potential differences in "point of view" among individuals or groups of individuals.

One study employing these techniques has been carried out with anorectic patients. The data are preliminary and should be regarded solely as a demonstration of the new methodology. The subjects were 12 normal-weight individuals (mean weight, 145 lb), four obese subjects (mean weight, 393 lb), and a group of seven young women hospitalized for anorexia nervosa (mean weight, 92 lb). The study employed direct proximity judgements to provide an estimate of the degree of perceived similarity among different food items—in this case, soft drinks, presented verbally by brand name. The subjects were also asked to rate each item along a number of adjective scales and to indicate a degree of preference for each item, using the standard nine-point hedonic preference scale [39]. MDS of proximity matrices provided a three-dimensional solution that is summarized in the two panels of Figure 1. It can be seen that the subjects distinguished between the different soft drinks on the basis of three sensory attributes: (1) naturalness, (2) taste, and (3) sweetness and calories. Dimension I ("naturalness") distinguished between fruit juices and carbonated beverages, while Dimension II correlated with the concepts of "taste". Dimension III represented the concepts of sweetness and calories and discriminated between club soda and mineral water and the sweetened and more caloric soft drinks.

Table 11.1 Simple correlations between self-reported preference ratings and bipolar adjective scales as a function of subject group

	Preference ratings		
	Normal-weight (n=12)	Obese (n=4)	Anorectic (n=7)
Artificial - Natural	0.87*	0.56	0.45
Dry - Sweet	-0.03	0.09	-0.55
Low calorie - High calorie	0.09	0.19	-0.31
Tasteless - Intense taste	0.46	0.75*	0.07

NOTE: * denotes $p < .05$

Although the subjects did not differ in their perceptions of the beverages, self-reported preference ratings differed among the groups. As seen in Table 1, the preferences of normal-weight subjects correlated with the concept of naturalness (Dimension I), while obese individuals preferred those soft drinks that were more intensely flavored (Dimension II). Anorectic patients showed no distinct preferences: Their ratings were generally lower throughout, with calorie-free diet soda and mineral water reported as the most preferred items.

The data suggest that the three groups of subjects tend to use different criteria in determining their food preferences. It remains to be seen whether the patterns of food preference are the cause or merely the result of disordered eating and abnormal body weight. Prospective studies of cognitive structure following weight regain should provide information as to whether taste preferences and food choices in eating disorders are affected by physiological varaible and body weight status.

REFERENCES

1. Drewnowski A. Cognitive structure in obesity and dieting. In Greenwood MRC, ed. Obesity: contemporary issues in clinical nutrition. New York: Churchill Livingstone 1983:
2. Russell GFM. The nutritional disorder in anorexia nervosa. J Psychosom Res, 1967; 11:141-9.
3. Brown GM. Neuroendocrine abnormalities in psychosocial dwarfism and anorexia nervosa. In Van Praag HM, Dekker M, eds. Handbook of biological psychiatry, part III: Brain mechanisms and abnormal behavior, genetics, and neuroendocrinology. New York: 1980:
4. Sherman BM, Halmi KA. The effect of nutritional rehabilitation on hypothalamic-pituitary function in anorexia nervosa. In Vigersky RA, ed. Anorexia Nervosa. New York: Raven Press, 1977:
5. Mawson AR. Anorexia nervosa and the regulation of intake: A review. Psychol Med, 1974; 4:289-308.
6. Halmi KA. Anorexia nervosa. In Grahame-Smith DG, Hippius H, Winokur G, eds. Psychopharmacology, vol 1, part 2, clinical psychopharmacology. Amsterdam: Excerpta Medica, 1982:
7. Leibowitz SF. Hypothalamic noradrenergic system: Role in control of appetite and relation to anorexia nervosa. In New directions in anorexia nervosa. Proceedings of the Fourth Ross Conference on Medical Research, 1982:
8. Leibowitz SF. Hypothalamic catecholamine systems in relation to control of eating behavior and to mechanisms of reward. In Hoebel BG, Novin D, eds. The neural basis of feeding and reward. Brunswick, ME: Haer Institute, 1982:
9. Leibowitz SF, Hor L. Endorphinergic and alpha-noradrenergic systems in the paraventricular nucleus: Effects on eating behavior. Peptides, 1982; 3:421-8.
10. Blass EM. Opioids, sugar and the inherent taste of sweet: broad motivational implications. In Dobbing J, ed. Sweetness. Springer-Verlag, Berlin, 1987.
11. Drewnowski A, Gruen R, Grinker JA. Carbohydrates, sweet taste and obesity: Changing consumption patterns and health implications. In Lineback DR, Inglett GE, eds. Basic symposium on food carbohydrates. New York: AVI Publishing, 1982:
12. Drewnowski A, Greenwood MRC, Halmi KA. Carbohydrate or fat phobia: Taste responsiveness in ano-

rexia nervosa. Fed Proc, 1984; 43(3):475.

13. Drewnowski A, Greenwood MRC. Cream and sugar: Human preferences for high-fat foods. Physiol Behav, 1983; 30:629-33.

14. Russell GFM. Bulimia nervosa: An ominous variant of anorexia nervosa. Psychol Med, 1979; 9:429-48.

15. Casper RC, Eckert ED, Halmi KA, et al. Bulimia: Its incidence and clinical importance in patients with anorexia nervosa. Arch Gen Psychiat, 1980; 37:1030-5.

16. Garfinkel PE, Moldofsky H, Garner DM. The heterogeneity of anorexia nervosa: Bulimia as a distinct subgroup. Arch Gen Psychiat, 1980; 37:1036-40.

17. Casper R, Kirschner B, Sandstead H, et al. An evaluation of trace metals, vitamins, and taste function in anorexia nervosa. Am J Clin Nutr, 1980; 33:1801-8.

18. Rolls BJ, Rowe EA, Sweeney K. Sensory specific satiety in man. Physiol Behav, 1981; 271:137-42.

19. Garfinkel PE. Perception of hunger and satiety in anorexia nervosa. Psychol Med, 1974; 4:309-15.

20. Garfinkel PE, Moldofsky H, Garner DM, et al. Body awareness in anorexia nervosa: Disturbances in "body image" and "satiety." Psychosom Med, 1978; 40:487-98.

21. Holt S, Ford MJ, Grant S, et al. Abnormal gastric emptying in primary anorexia nervosa. Br J Psychiatry, 1981; 139:550-2.

22. Russell DM, Freedman ML, Feighlin DHI, et al. Delayed gastric emptying and improvement with domperidone in a patient with anorexia nervosa. AM J Psychiatry, 1983; 140(9):1235-6.

23. Drewnowski A, Pierce B, Halmi KA. Fat aversion in eating disorders. Appetite (in press).

24. Grinker J. Obesity and sweet taste. Am J Clin Nutr, 1978; 31:1078-87.

25. Grinker JA, Hirsch J, Smith D. Taste sensitivity and susceptibility to external influence in obese and normal-weight subjects. J Personal Soc Psychol, 1972; 22:320-5.

26. Lacey JH, Stanley PA, Crutchfield SM. Sucrose sensitivity in anorexia nervosa. J Psychosom Res, 1977; 21:17-21.

27. Cabanac M. Physiological role of pleasure. Science, 1971; 173:1103-7.

28. Cabanac M, Duclaux R. Obesity: Absence of satiety aversion to sucrose. Science, 1970; 168:496-7.

29. Grinker JA, Price J, Greenwood MRC. Studies of taste in childhood obesity. In Novin D, Wyrwicka W, Bray GA, eds. Hunger: Basic mechanisms and clinical implications. New York: Raven Press, 1976:

30. Rodin J, Moskowitz, Bray GA. Relationship between obesity, weight loss, and taste responsiveness. Physiol Behav, 1976; 17:391-7.

31. Gilbert DG, Hagen RL. Taste in underweight, overweight, and normal-weight subjects before, during, and after sucrose ingestion. Addictive Behaviors, 1980; 5:137-42.

32. Garner DM, Garfinkel PE, Moldofsky H. Perceptual experiences in anorexia nervosa and obesity. Can Psychiat Assoc J, 1978; 23:249-63.

33. Garfinkel PE, Moldofsky H, Garner DM. The stabil-

ity of perceptual disturbances in anorexia nervosa. Psychol Med, 1979; 9:703-8.

34. Moskowitz HR, Kluter RA, Westerling J, et al. Sugar sweetness and pleasantness: Evidence for different psychophysical laws. Science, 1974; 184:583-5.

35. Moskowitz HR. Taste and food technology: Acceptability, aesthetics and preference. In Carterette EL, Friedman MP, eds. Handbook of perception, vol VIA, tasting and smelling. New York: Academic Press, 1978:

36. Pangborn RM, Pecore SD. Taste perception of sodium chloride in relation to dietary intake of salt. Am J Clin Nutr, 1982; 35:510-20.

37. Witherly SA, Pangborn RM, Stern JS. Gustatory responses and eating duration of obese and lean adults. Appetite, 1980; 1:53-63.

38. Schiffman SS, Musante G, Conger J. Application of multidimensional scaling to ratings of foods for obese and normal-weight individuals. Physiol Behav, 1979; 23:1-9.

39. Drewnowski A, Grinker JA, Hirsch J. Obesity and flavor perception: Multidimensional scaling of soft drinks. Appetite, 1982; 3:361-8.

40. Birch LL. Preschool children's food preferences and consumption patterns. J Nutr Ed, 1979; 11:189-92.

41. Drewnowski A, Brunzell JB, Sande K, et al. Sweet tooth reconsidered: taste responsiveness in human obesity. Physiol Behav, 1985; 35:617-622.

42. Drewnowski A, Halmi, KA, Pierce B, Gibbs J, Smith GP. Taste and eating disorders. Am J Clin Nutr, 1987; 46:442-50.

43. Logue AW, Ophir I, Strauss KE. The acquisition of taste aversions in humans. Behav Res Ther, 1981; 19:319-33.

44. Logue AW, Logue KR, Strauss KE. The acquisition of taste aversions in humans with eating and drinking disorders. Behav Res Ther, 1983; 21:275-89.

Section II

Clinical Entities

Barton J. Blinder, Barry F. Chaitin, and Renée Goldstein

The purpose of this section is to provide a systematic and careful delineation of diagnostic considerations and clinical features of the eating disorders.

Increased case detection and clinical reporting of the eating disorders in the past decade has led to recognition of the need for studies based on controlled and accurate observations of developmental features, epidemiology, clinical phenomena, family interactive patterns, and sociocultural influences.

From the earliest clinical descriptions of anorexia nervosa by Morton (1689), Gull (1873), and Lesegue (1873) and suggestive bulimic features reported in certain patients by Abraham (1916) and Wulf (1932), paradoxes and obscurities have abounded, clouding a clear understanding of the subtle interactions of eating, nutrition, and behavior. To advance beyond stereotypic conceptions we must broaden our understanding of the eat

ing disorders for different ages, genders, and cultural groups. We must also be more aware of the psychobiologic significance of appetite and eating disturbances in other medical and psychiatric disorders.

Medical and dental complications of eating disorders must be recognized to fully comprehend the symptoms of psychological and physical impairment that determine the clinical presentation of patients and pose both acute danger and possible chronic handicap. Studies of potential specificity of CNS neurotransmitters and neuroendocrine regulatory defects may define subgroups of patients with anorexia nervosa and bulimia and enable us to identify them with clinical and laboratory findings. A broadened clinical perspective along with increasing public and professional interests will promote research to define more specific therapeutic interventions in the future.

Chapter 12

Prevalence and Incidence Studies of Anorexia Nervosa

Pierre Leichner and A. Gertler

Epidemiology has been defined as, "the field of science dealing with the relationships of the various factors which determine the frequencies and distributions of a disease or a physiological state in a human community," [1]. This form of information can have multiple purposes. First, the study of demographic variables associated with the prevalence and/or incidence of anorexic nervosa may lead to a better understanding of the etiological factors associated with the onset of this disorder. This information can also be used in planning preventive strategies. Second, of particular importance during this period of economic constraint, this information may be required to justify the need for adequate treatment facilities to health care administrators.

In this chapter we will focus primarily on the prevalence of anorexia nervosa and the various demographic variables that have been shown to be associated with this disorder. We will only comment briefly on outcome studies as they might affect prevalence rates.

Our objectives are to provide the reader with the following:

1. A thorough updated review of published epidemiological studies of anorexia nervosa,
2. Information in a tabular form that will allow the reader to obtain a chronological view of the literature and to note the important features of each referenced study,
3. A review of the problems inherent in previous work, and,

4. Directions for future work.

HISTORICAL CONSIDERATIONS

It has become clear from previous reviews of the history of this disorder that accurate clinical descriptions have been available since the early 1870s. However, as London [2] has pointed out, it is also possible that until the early 1900s many anorexics may have been misdiagnosed as suffering from "chlorosis" (hypochromic anemia) or amenorrhea. In any case, until the early 1910s this disorder was felt to be quite rare and was recognized as requiring psychological treatment primarily. In 1914 the description by Bliss and Branch of a patient with anterior pituitary damage and weight loss ushered in a new era for the diagnosis and treatment of anorexia nervosa [3]. For the next three decades this illness was seen as a primary endocrine illness and patients were likely to be treated by endocrinologists. The illness was still felt to be rare. However, in the absence of the identification of a causative primary endocrine disturbance and with the increasing body of literature from psychiatrists regarding psychological etiologies, the diagnosis and treatment of anorexia nervosa gradually shifted back to mental health professionals over the last three decades. This trend has persisted to the degree that the diagnosis of anorexia nervosa has now been clearly outlined in the Diagnostic and Statistical Manual of Mental Disorders of the American Psychiatric Association of Mental Disorders (DSM III) [4], and its management is now primarily carried out in mental health care settings.

Although it would appear that the psychological and behavioral symptomatology of anorexia nervosa has remained constant throughout the years, it was only in 1972 that specific diagnostic criteria were first spelled out [5]. This occurred as part of the general movement in American psychiatry to attempt to standardize diagnoses as reflected by the DSM III [4]. Before this development the majority of epidemiologic work had depended on case reports and the significant description of larger cohorts of patients by a few recognized experts in the field [3,6]. These works have been of great importance in providing the foundation for our understanding of this disorder, but they could not address the prevalence issues accurately and may have in fact been somewhat misleading, because they may have reflected the features of a selected sample of anorexics.

More recently this introduction of diagnostic criteria and the increased awareness for the need to develop reliable and valid questionnaires have resulted in an increasing number of epidemiological studies, using questionnaires and structured interviews of general and student population. These studies are leading some to the realization that anorexia nervosa may well be part of a continuum of eating disorders and that it exists in mild and moderate forms as well. Adding to this view are surveys of the attitudes of the general adolescent population toward food and eating, which have shown that large numbers of today's young people possess unhealthy attitudes toward food and maladaptive eating behaviors.

COMMON LIMITATIONS OF THE SURVEYS REVIEWED

A number of common limitations were shared by several of the epidemiological studies reviewed. These should be kept in mind in interpreting the data presented in the following tables:

1. The lack of standarized criteria for case recognition, particularly before 1970,
2. The variability of the methodology used to identify cases,
3. The tendency of hospital case register studies to identify only the most severely ill and only those able to obtain appropriate treatment,
4. The tendency that anorexic patients have in denying or hiding their symptoms, thus often delaying recognition and treatment,
5. The limitation of overly specific criteria leading to the exclusion of mild to moderate forms of the disease,
6. The lack of adequately defined geographical populations being studied.

PREVALENCE OF ANOREXIA NERVOSA

The information regarding the incidence and prevalence of anorexia nervosa is presented in three tables that are divided according to the type of population studied. Table 1 presents the finding of studies relating to the incidence of anorexia nervosa in the general population. These studies were carried out between 1930 and 1983. The majority before 1980 relied primarily on the case registers of hospitals for identifying anorexic patients. Those conducted since 1970 have relied more often on questionnaires designed to identify symptomatology as outlined in the DSM III [4]. Although the case register studies were conducted in different countries (eg, Sweden, Switzerland, United States, Scotland, and Britain) they show remarkably similar trends over time. Thus, it seems that the incidence of severe cases of anorexia nervosa coming to the attention of health care professionals before 1960 was 0.24 to 0.45 per 100,000 population per year, and this has increased to 0.45 to 1.6 per 100,000, after 1960. Although most of the studies suffer from the limitations outlined before, the similar ranges of these figures and the generally increasing trend found by all investigators support the impression that anorexia nervosa is being treated in increasing numbers in hospitals in North America and Europe.

This impression, however, is challenged by the 0.1 per 100,000 population overall lifetime prevalence found by Robins et al in a yet unpublished recent large-scale survey in the United States. This finding may not be that surprising if one observes that Robins and his collaborators only surveyed populations aged 18 or older and strictly applied the DSM III criteria. Thus, many of the younger and mild to moderate cases were excluded from this figure. Indeed, their observation stands in contrast with the survey conducted by Pope [10] recently among women shoppers in the United States, which reported a prevalence of 0.7%.

The prevalence of anorexia nervosa in the general medical population is reviewed in table 2. Data presented there reviews findings carried out during 1974 to 1979. Interpreting this information is considerably limited because of significant differences between the methods of case recognition and between the medical programs from which case were identified. Of historical interest is the interesting speculation by Loudon [2] that perhaps many of the female patients that presented to hospitals during the 18th and early 19th centruies who were diagnosed as suffering from chlorosis or amenorrhea were possibly anorexic. Indeed, the clinical description of chlorosis and the demographic variables associated with the illness (eg, upper socioeconomic-class females) were suspiciously similar to that of anorexia

Table 12.1 Incidence of Anorexia Nervosa in the General Population

Approximate Period Surveyed	Incidence/100,000 Population Per Year	Population Base (N=anorexic cases)	Method of Recognition	Authors and Date of Publication
1931-1960 1951-1960	0.24R 0.45	Women hospitalized for anorexia nervosa in departments of internal medicine, pediatrics, gynecology in a defined area in South Sweden (N=94)	Case registers and interviews with patients or families, questionnaires and psychological test.	Theander (1970) (6)
		General Population	Case registers	Kendell et al (1973) (7)
1960-1969 1965-1971 1966-1969	0.37 0.66 1.6	Camberwell, Lon. (N=8) Monroe Country, N.Y. (N=24) N.E. Scotland (N=30)		
1960-1969 1970-1976	0.35 0.64	Monroe County, USA White population (N=53)	Psychiatric case registers and hospital records	Jones et al (1980) (8)
1956-1975 1956-1958 1963-1965 1973-1975	 0.38 0.55 1.12	Admissions to pediatric and psychiatric clinics in a defined region in Switzerland (N=65)	Case histories	Willi and Grossman (1983) (9)
1980 	 0.1 0.05 0.08	18 or older general population (N=6) Overall lifetime prevalence male lifetime prevalence female lifetime prevalence New Haven, Baltimore, St.Louis	Diagnostic interview schedule (DIS) and DSM III diagnostic classification	Robins (1984) Unpublished manuscript

nervosa. In addition, a recent study [14] has also shown that a significant percentage of women coming to amenorrhea clinics in departments of gynecology have anorexia nervosa. Hence, although it is impossible to estimate the exact proportion of patients who had anorexia nervosa during those years and were treated for chlorosis or amenorrhea, it is probable that a significant percentage of these patients were anorexic. Of transcultural interest is the study carried out by Buhrich [12] suggesting a relatively low prevalence of anorexia nervosa among psychiatric patients in Malasia, perhaps secondary to different sociocolutral pressures.

Table 3 reviews some more recent studies conducted primarily in student populations. Of these the best known and most quoted study is that of Crisp et al [15] conducted among English school girls in private and public schools. In this work Crisp and his collaborators made a great effort to identify unequivocal cases of anorexia nervosa. The majority of teachers in these schools met with the authors to identify current and past cases. This case spotting also involved checking the medical records of the students before accepting the diagnosis. In doubtful cases, additional interviews were conducted. The compreheansive (public) schools were very large, hence the information accepted was only for the current school year, and there was less detail then that in the independent schools (private). The diagnostic criteria allowed the inclusion of only severe cases of anorexia nervosa, that is, only patients who had lost at least 30% of their body weight. Thus, 27 cases were identified. In the comprehensive schools only one case was identified. The overall prevalence was 0.25% with a range of 0.05%

Table 12.2 Prevalence of Anorexia Nervosa in Medical Hospital Population

Approximate Period Surveyed	Prevalence (%)	Population Base (N=anorexic cases)	Method of Recognition	Authors and Date of Publication
1972	5.6	Japaneses adolescents with school maladjustment and psychosomatic disorders (N=13)	Not specified	Ikemi et al (1974) (11)
1774-1818	0.9--4.6* with chlorosis and/or amenorrhea	Female medical admissions to various dispensaries *(possible anorexics)	Case registers	London (1980) (2)
1760-1840	1.4- 5.1	Outpatient admissions for various hospitals, England	Case registers	
1953-1979	0.05	Patients attended by 17 psychiatrists (N=30) Malaysia	Questionnaire given to 17 psychiatrists who recorded their patients	Buhrich (1981) (12)
1976-1977	0.28	Outpatients in 35 medical institutions in Japan (N=267)	Hospital charts and a list of symptoms similar to DSM III	Suematsu et al (1983) (13)
	0.88	Inpatients in 35 medical institutions in Japan (N=157)		

in the public schools to 1.05% in the girls over age 16 in private schools. Due to the severity of the diagnostic criteria used in this study, milder cases were probably excluded. Other surveys have reported figures in the range to 0 to 4.2% among high school and college students. These studies may not have used as strict a procedure as Crisp et al [15], and this may account for their slightly more elevated prevalence rates. Alternatively, since these studies are also more recent, they may reflect an increase in the prevalence of the disease.

Further evidence regarding the influence of sociocultural factors has been provided by prevalence studies of anorexia nervosa in special groups. These results are presented in table 4. The table represents findings of studies carried out from 1978 to 1983. Professional dancers, modeling students, and dieticians were surveyed. Prevalence estimates were relatively high, ranging from 1.4% to 7.6%, the higher prevalences being among the more competitive professional dance student groups. This observation, along with similar trends observed by Smith [22] and Yates [23] among athletes points to the perfectionism, rigid self- discipline, high performance expectations, high competitiveness, high tolerance of physical pain, and viewing one's body as an instrument to reach a goal, as common factors that may lead the vulnerable individual to anorexia nervosa.

STUDIES USING THE EATING ATTITUDES TEST (E.A.T.)

The results of previous studies using the E.A.T. are presented in table 5. The E.A.T. is a 40-item questionnaire developed by Garner and Garfinkel [24] to assess the broad range of symptom areas associated with anorexia nervosa, including food preoccupation, body image for thinness, dieting, slow eating, clandestine eating, social pressure to gain weight, vomiting, and laxative abuse. Subjects respond on a five-point scale ranging from "very often" to "never" on how well the item applies. The E.A.T. score is then calculated according to a method outlined by Garner and Garfinkel. The scale in the original study had an internal reliability coefficient of 0.94 and overall validity coefficient of 0.72. In that study the mean E.A.T. scores of patients with anorexia nervosa were significantly higher than that of normal controls, obese women, and recovered anorexics. This report, along with subsequent work using dance and music students [20], has encouraged several

Table 12.3 Prevalence of Anorexia Nervosa in Student Populations

Approximate Period Surveyed	Prevalence (%)	Population Base (N=total number surveyed)	Method of Recognition	Authors and Date of Publication
1972-1974	0.46	Independent sector (private) schools for girls in England (N = 9605)	Clearcut cases of primary anorexia nervosa recognized in school records by teaching staff and discussed with consultants	Crisp et al (1976) (15)
	0.17	Girls under 16		
	1.05	Girls over 16		
	0.05	Comprehensive (public) schools (N = 2786)		
	0.25	Overall		
1975		Female students at Edinburgh University (N = 3139)	Questionnaire about different diseases	Sheldrake et al (1976) (16)
	2.0	arts (N = 1249)		
	1.3	social science (N = 871)		
	2.3	professional studies (N = 471)		
	1.3	science (N = 548)		
1979		Students in high schools in Johannesburg, 16 years and older (N = 1246)	Measurements of the body size and weight	Ballot et al (1981) (17)
	2.9	Overall		
	4.0, 2.6	Two coeducational provincial schools		
	1.9	Working class schools		
	3.7	Girls-only school		
	0.0	Two private schools		
	4.8	One private school		
1983		Students from three schools: two colleges and one high school (female N = 544)	Questionnaire using the DSM III criteria	Pope et al (1984) (18)
	1.0-4.2	USA		

other investigators to use the E.A.T. to study the prevalence of maladaptive eating behaviors among general populations at high risk (high school and college students). The precentages of students with E.A.T. scores in the anorexic range have tended to be higher than the percentages obtained from the stricter prevalence studies of students reported in table 3. This is not surprising, because the E.A.T. may indeed report false positives as well as mild and moderate forms of the disorder. Button and Whitehouse [25] studying a population of 578 English college students, found that 6.3% of the female students aged 16 to 22 scored in the anorexic range. Follow-up interviews identified only one of these students as suffering from the severe syndrome, while the rest suffered from "subclinical anorexia." Another British study conducted by Mann et al [29] among a population of 15-year-old English schoolgirls found 6.9% of these students to score in the anorexic range. On further interviewing these students, no full anorexic syndrome was discovered. However, a number of these girls suffered from a partial syndrome. Mann then pointed out that despite the satisfactory sensitivity and specificity of the E.A.T. when using the recommended cut score in populations where the prevalence is small, significant numbers of noncases will be identified. In a study comparing anorexic patients and bulimic patients, Srikameswaran [27] revealed that the mean scores of both these groups of patients were equally high. These concerns regarding false positives were further substantiated by a large-scale survey conducted by Leichner et al [30] among 4,649 Canadian high school and college students aged 12 to 20. These investigators found higher mean E.A.T. scores in their population than both previous British studies. Accordingly, they also found a

Table 12.4 Prevalence of Anorexia Nervosa in Special Groups

Approximate Period Surveyed	Prevalence (%)	Population Base (N=total number surveyed)	Method of Recognition	Authors and Date of Publication
1977	5.4	Professional dance students in Canada (N=112)	E.A.T. and diagnostic criteria of Feighner	Garner and Garfinkel (1978) (19)
1979		Professional dance students in Canada (N=183)	E.A.T. and diagnostic interview	Garner and Garfinkel (1980) (20)
	6.0	Overall		
	7.6	More competitive setting (N=103)		
	3.8	Less competitive setting (N=80)		
	3.5	Modeling students (N=56)		
1981		Members of the British Dietetic Association (N=760)	Questionnaire	Morgan and Mayberry (1983) (21)
	2.0	Age 20-24		
	1.4	Age 25-29		
	4.7	Age 30-34		
1983	0.7	Women shoppers in USA (N=300)	Questionnaire based on DSM III	Pope et al (1984) (10)

higher percentage (22.0%) of females scoring in the anorexic range. Interestingly, the majority of females scoring in this range had a weight problem related to being overweight rather than underweight. It would then appear that the E.A.T. scale used alone would identify a large number of individuals with maladaptive attitudes toward food and maladaptive patterns of eating who may be suffering from mild or moderate forms of anorexia nervosa, bulimia, or obesity. Leichner et al [30] then made an attempt to increase the specificity of their survey by combining the high E.A.T.'s scores with percentage weight deviation from the median. They thus identified 0.11% of the males and 0.75% of females who scored in the anorexic range as well as had a percent weight deviation of 20% or less from median. These numbers are similar to those identified by Crisp et al [15]. Using a weight deviation of -4% to less than -19% from median, another 0.95% of males and 4.2% of females were identified. The majority of this population may be mild to moderate cases of anorexia. These numbers are in keeping with the numbers suggested in the less-stringent student population prevalence studies. Further development of the scale in terms of cutting scores as well as the addition of some other items and information regarding height and weight may further increase its specificity. Further work is also needed in studying the eating patterns of patients with psychiatric and medical disorders that might affect eating (eg, depression and diabetes).

DEMOGRAPHIC VARIABLES

Sex

Table 6 reviews the sex distribution among anorexic patients from 1932 to 1980. The majority of these studies were based on populations of anorexics who were in treatment. Only the study by Robins, which reported sex prevalence rates among the 18-or-older general population, found no significant differences between the sexes. Unfortunately, their overall prevalence rate was also much lower than that in many other studies, suggesting that their criteria may have been excessively strict. The range of male percentages in the other studies was from 0% to 29.2%, with the majority of studies from 3.9% to 14%. It would therefore seem fair to conclude that most patients being treated for severe anorexia nervosa are female. Except for the study by Robins, there does not seem to be any significant trend suggesting that the proportion of males has been increasing. However, since the overall prevalence of the illness

Table 12.5 Results of Studies Using the Eating Attitude Test (E.A.T.)

Mean E.A.T. Score	Population Description (N=total number surveyed)	Authors and Date of Publication
58.9	Anorexia nervosa (N=33) x age = 22.5	Garner and Garfinkel (1979) (24)
15.6	Normal controls (N=59) x age = 21.8	
16.5	Obese (N=16)	
11.4	Recovered anorexia nervosa (N=9) (Canada)	
25.6	Dance students (N=183) x age = 18.6	Garner and Garfinkel (1980) (20)
13.7	Music students (N=35) x age = 15.2	
15.4	Normal control students (N=81) Canada x age = 21.5	
7.6	English college studies (N=132) Age = 16-22	Button and Whithouse (1981) (25)
12.0	Female (N=446) Age = 16-22 6.3% in anorexic range (Britain)	
49.8	Female respondents to an advertisement in a popular women's magazine (N=499) 89% in anorexic range (England)	Fairbun and Cooper (1982) (26)
58.1	Anorexia nervosa (N=22) x age = 20.2	Srikameswaran et al (1984) (27)
59.6	Bulimia (N=17) x age = 21.5	
17.0	Control (N=44) x age = 20.6 Canada	
11.4	Consecutive female attenders (younger than 40) of a family planning clinic (N=669) 6.0% in anorexic range (England)	Cooper and Fairbun (1983) (28)
9.6*	English 15-year-old school girl (N=262) *E.A.T. (26 items) 6.9% in anorexic range (Britain)	Mann et al (1983) (29)
	Canadian high school and College students (N=4649)	Leichner et al (1984) (30)
17.5	Males (N=2297)	
23.5	Females (N=2404)	
	5.7% of males in anorexic range; 22.3% of females in anorexic range (Canada)	

The Eating Disorders

Table 12.6 Demographic Variables for Anorexia Nervosa—Sex

Approximate Period Surveyed	Percentage of males	Population (N=anorexic cases)	Method of Recognition	Authors and Date of Publication
1930-1953	11.0	Case reports USA (N=473)	Literature review	Bliss and Branch (1960 (3)
1932-1952	10.5	Anorexic patients attending the Maudsley Hospital England (N=38)	Hospital records	Kay and Leigh (1954) (31)
1942-1964	14	In and outpatients, USA (N=43)	Psychological evaluation	Bruch (1966) (32)
1962-1973	7.5	Anorexics admitted to a London Hospital (N=173)	Interviews with families	Crisp and Toms (1972) (33)
1966-1969 1960-1969 1965-1974	6.7 29.2 0.0	General population Scotland (N=30) Monroe county— anorexic patients drawn from general population (N=24) Anorexic patients drawn from general population (N=8)	Case registers Case registers Case registers	Kendell et al (1973) (7)
1960-1974	9.5	Patients from three hospitals, USA (N=42)	Weight loss without organic cause—15% at least	Warren and Vande Wiele (1973) (34)
1966-1972	4.3	Anorexics attending a Student Health Center, England (N=23)	Psychiatric assessment	Duddle (1973) (35)
1920-1972	6.4	Anorexics from hospital population, USA (N=94)	Charts from general and psychiatric hospitals	Halmi (1974) (36)
1959-1966	7.3	Anorexics in metabolic unit, London, (N=41)	Diagnostic criteria for anorexia nervosa	Morgan and Russell (1975) (37)
1956-1975 1956-1969 1970-1975	4.9 3.6 5.7	Patients treated in the United Birmingham Hospitals (N=206)	Records of general practitioners and psychiatrists, checked according to criteria for anorexia nervosa	Husan and Tibbetts (1977) (38)
1960-1969 1970-1976	27.0	Monroe County, New York (N=53) (1960-69 N=22) (1970-76 N=31)	Diagnosed anorexics from psychiatric case registers and hospital records	Jones et al (1980) (8)

Table 12.6 Demographic Variables for Anorexia Nervosa—Sex (continued)

1953-1979	6.7	Anorexic patients attended by 17 psychiatrists, Malaysia (N = 30)	Questionnaires given to 17 psychiatrists for their patients	Buhrich (1981) (12)
1958-1976	4.5	Anorexic patients treated in different settings, Norway (N = 133)	Diagnostic interviews	Basse and Eskeland (1982) (39)
1977	4.2	Anorexic patients in insitute of psychiatry, Copenhagen (N = 24)	Feighner's criteria in judgements of two psychiatrists	Fichter et al (1982) (40)
1970-1981	3.9	Anorexic referrals to clinics (N = 276)	Diagnostic interviews	Garfinkel and Garner (1982) (41)
1966-1981	14.0	Hospitalized anorexic patients Canada (N = 50)	Hospital chart analysis	Dongier and Samy (42) (1983)
1956-1975	0.0	Case reports of anorexic patients in a region in Switzerland (N = 65)	Hospital registers	Willi and Grossmann (1983) (9)
1977-1982	7.0	Anorexics treated in Phipps service, Baltimore (N-140)	DSM III	Andersen and Mickalide (1983) (43)
1976-1977	5.4	Patients identified as anorexics in 35 medical institutions, Japan (N = 316)	According to list of symptoms and hospital charts	Suematsu et al (1983) (13)
1980	31.0	18 or older general population (N = 6)	Diagnostic interview schedule (DIS) and DSM III diagnostic classification	Robins (1984) Unpublished manuscript

seems to be increasing, the actual number of males with anorexia nervosa has also been increasing at a similar rate as females. This observation may suggest that the factors felt to be causative may have increased in quantity but have not changed in quality over the past few decades. Andersen [43] has challenged these observations by suggesting that male anorexics tend to be misdiagnosed more often than female anorexics. Reasons that may account for this may include the fact that for many years the distinctive physiological symptom of amenorrhea was felt to be crucial in the diagnosis of anorexia nervosa, thus leading clinicians not to include this diagnosis in the differential of emaciated males. Also males

have been known to seek medical attention less often than females [43]. As these patients already tend to avoid medical attention, it may be that males are even stronger in this resistance and hence less often noted.

Age

Information regarding the variable of age is summarized in table 7. This table presents the findings of studies carried out from 1932 to 1982. Again, this data reflects the age of onset of cases that have reached the attention of health care professionals. Among this population it would appear fairly safe to conclude that is the majority of cases, onset is during the early teens and

Table 12.7 Demographic variables for Anorexia Nervosa—Age

Approximate Period Surveyed	Age	Population (N-anorexic cases)	Method of Recognition	Authors and Date of Publication
1932-1952	Age of onset: five patients >16 three patients <35 70% before age 26	Anorexic patients attending Maudsley Hospital (N=34)	Hospital records	Kay and Leigh (1954) (31)
1881-1952	Range 31-85 average age 21-1/2 years	Case reports U.S.A. (N=245)	Literature review	Bliss and Branch (1960) (3)
1942-1964	Onset: females 11-28 males 12-14	In and out patients, U.S.A. (N=43)	Psychological evaluations	Bruch (1966) (32)
1931-1960	Onset: range 11-26; for 85% range 13-20; 10% (nine cases) at age 21 or after three cases over age 25; one at age 34; five cases before age 13	All females admitted to hospital for anorexia nervosa from a well defined region in south Sweden (N=94)	Case registers; interviews; questionnaires	Theander (1970) (6)
1960-1971	Range 10-26 mean 13:	Patients admitted to three hospitals U.S.A. (N=42)	Weight loss of at least 15% without organic cause	Warren and Vande Wiele (1973) (34)
1966-1969	27 females between age 15-34	Anorexic patients drawn from general population register (N=44) Scotland	Case registers	Kendell et al (1973) (7)
1960-1969	Eight females 15 three females 34 mean age 22.2, median between 15-19	Anorexic patients drawn from general population, Monroe County (N=24)	Case register	Kendell et al (1973) (7)
1965-1971	Seven between 15-34 mean age 21.6	Anorexic patients drawn from general population Camberwell (N=8)	Case registers	
1920-1972	Onset: 13% over age 25 8% before age 10; 31% between age 10-15 47% between age 16-25	Anorexic patients from hospital population U.S.A. (N=94)	charts from general and psychiatric hospitals	Halmi (1974) (36)
1959-1966	Range 12.8-47, mean 21.5, onset between 11-40 mean 15.3=3.14	Anorexics admitted to a metabolic unit, London, (N=41)	Diagnostic criteria for anorexic nervosa	Morgan and Russell (1975) (37)
1960-1969	males females 0-14 2 9 (56%) 15-24 4 3 25-34 - 2 15-34 - 2 35-44 - 2	Anorexic patients drawn from register—Monroe County, New York (N=53)	Psychiatric case register records	Jones et al (1980) (8)
1970-1976	0-14 1 10 (34%) 15-24 1 15 (52%) 25-34 - 3 35-44 - 1			

Table 12.7 Demographic variables for Anorexia Nervosa—Age (continued)

Approximate Period Surveyed	Age	Population (N-anorexic cases)	Method of Recognition	Authors and Date of Publication
1953-1979	Age 10-14 1 case 15-20 11 females 1 male 21- 25 13 females 1 male 26-30 3 females	Patients attended by 17 psychiatrists Malaysia (N = 27)	Questionnaire given the 17 psychiatrists for their patients	Bhurich (1981) (12)
1977	Range 13-29	Anorexic patients in an inpatient ward in institute of psychiatry, Copenhagen	Feighner's criteria and judgement of two psychiatrists	Fichter et al (1982) (40)
1970-1975 1976-1981	Age of onset 12-18 Age of onset 19-22	Referrals to program Canada (N = 287)		Garfinkel and Gardner (1982) (41)
1976-1977	Onset — mid teens to early twenties, 5.4% (17 patients) over age 31	Anorexic patients in 35 medical institutions, Japan (N = 316)	List of symptoms applied to hospital charts	Suematsu et al (1983) (13)
1966-1981 1966-1976 1972-1981	14.2 mean age 13.5 years average 15 years average	Patients hospitalized Canada (N = 50)	Hospital chart analysis	Dongier and Samy (1983) (42)
1956-1975 1956-1958 1963-1965 1973-1975	General average age of onset 16.9 Average age of onset 16.9 Average age of onset 16.9 Average age of onset 16.8	Patients from most clinics in a Swiss region (N = 65)	Case histories	Willi and Grossmann (1983) (9)
1981	Range 20-34	Members of the British Dietetic Association (N = 760)	Questionnaire about common gastrointestinal diseases	Morgan and Mayberry(1983) (21)
1963-1978	Age range 15-44, mean 24.6; Age at onset 11-12, mean 14.0	Anorexic patients treated in three hospitals, Germany (N = 21)	Files, diagnosed according to Feighner's criteria	Steinhausen and Glanville (1983) (45)
1977-1982	Range 18-47, average 29.2; six cases between age 18 to 26	Male anorexics treated in Phipps service, U.S.A. (N = 10)	DSM III	Anderson and Michalide (1983) (43)
1980	18-44 no consistent trend	18 or older general population (N = 6)	Diagnostic interviews schedule (DIS) DSM III	Robins (1984) Unpublished

Table 12.8 Demographic Variables for Anorexia Nervosa—Socioeconomic Variables

Approximate Period Surveyed	Social Class	Population (N=anorexic cases)	Method of Recognition	Authors and Date of Publication
1962-1964	I = 14, II = 23, III, IV = 6 (II-includes 3 males) III, IV-includes females)	In- and outpatients USA (N = 34)	Psychological evaluation	Bruch (1966) (32)
1956-1975	II = 3, III = 5	Anorexics treated in United Birmingham Hospitals (N = 8)	Records of general practitioners, and psychiatrists, checked according to criteria for anorexia	Hasan and Tibbetts (1977) (38)
1959-1966	I, II = 65.9% (17.9% in general population)	Anorexics admitted to a metabolic unit London (N = 41)	Diagnostic criteria for anorexia nervosa	Morgan and Russell (1975) (37)
1961-1969	II, III > IV, V not statistically significant	Female anorexics drawn from general population, Scotland (N = 38)	Case registers	Kendell et al (1973) (7)
1960-1969	No statistically significant difference in distribution from general population	Anorexics drawn from general population, Monroe County, (N = 24)		
1965-1969	I = 3, II = 2 high significant upper class bias	Anorexics drawn from general population Camberwell (N = 8)		
1960-1969	44.4% upper class (N = 24)	Monroe County, New York	Case registers	Jones et al (1980) (8)
1970-1976	I = 5, II = 14, III = 10 (N = 29)	Anorexics drawn from general population record (N = 53)		
1953-1979	I, II = 12, III = 13, IV, V = 2 (I, II 2 males)	Anorexic patients attended by 17 psychiatrists, Malaysia (N = 27)	Questionnaire given to 17 psychiatrists for their patients	Buchrich (1981) (12)
1962-1972	I, II = 50%, III, IV, V = 50%	Male anorexics in St. George Hospital, England (N = 12)	Interviews with families	Crisp and Toms (1972) (33)
1963-1978	I, II = 5%, III = 81%, IV, V = 14%	Patients treated in three hospitals in West Germany (N = 21)	Files, diagnosed according to Feighner's criteria	Steinhausen and Granville (1983) (45)
1966-1981	No difference	Patients hospitalized Canada (N = 50)	Hospital chart analysis	Dongiers and Damy (1983) (42)
1970	I and II	Referred female cases of anorexia nervosa, England (N = 25)	Questionnaire	Russell (1972) (46)
1970-1981		Referrals to special program	Diagnostic interviews	Garfinkel and Garner (1982) (41)

Table 12.8 Demographic Variables for Anorexia Nervosa—Socioeconomic Variables (continued)

Approximate Period Surveyed	Social Class	Population (N=anorexic cases)	Method of Recognition	Authors and Date of Publication
1970-1975 1976	I, II = 70.6%, III, IV = 29.4% I, II = 52.0%, III, IV = 48.0%			
1977-1982	Two-third of professional managerial social classes	Male anorexics treated in Phipps Service, Baltimore (N = 10)	DSM III	Anderson and Mickalide (1983) (43)
1976	I, II = 50%, III = 27%, IV, V = 23%	Patients treated in a London Hospital (N = 56)	Interviews with families	Kalucy et al (1977) (47)

early 20s. Individual case reports have suggested a possible range from 7 years to 85 years of age [3]. It is difficult from this information to assess whether the age of onset of anorexic nervosa has indeed been increasing recently as has been suggested by Garfinkel and Garner [41]. The occurrence of anorexia nervosa in older women has been well documented by Bliss and Branch [3] in their review of cases from 1818 to 1952. Hence, older presentations are not a new phenomenon. Whether there is a true increase in the incidence of anorexia nervosa in the older population or whether this increase reflects the "coming out of the closet" of older patients is difficult to assess. It is probable that the increasing information through the media and popular press has caused a greater awareness of the disease among patients and health care professionals. And this may also be leading to the diagnosis of mild to moderate cases of anorexia nervosa that previously might have been tolerated by health care professionals and families [44]. Arguing for a true increase in the incidence of anorexia nervosa in the older age-group is what would seem to be an increase in the sociocultural pressures on women in all ages to become slim and maintain youthful figures.

Socioeconomic Status

Information regarding the distribution of the socioeconomic status of the families of anorexic patients is summarized in table 8. This table presents the findings of studies carried out from 1942 to 1982. Although overall the figures presented tend to indicate a preponderance of upper social classes, it is also clear from the earliest reports that significant numbers of anorexics came from lower socioeconomic backgrounds. Several authors have expressed their opinion that the disorder

is spreading across the social groups. However, it is difficult from the information available to know whether this is a true change. In fact, the study by Jones et al [8] reported finding a higher percentage of upper social class patients between 1970 and 1976 (73%) than between 1960 and 1969 (44.4%). In order to explain a change in the distribution of the illness, one would have to assume that factors implied as being associated with anorexia nervosa such as attitudes and practices of child rearing, attitudes toward sexuality, food, body weight, high achievement orientations, and the availability of food are becoming more similar across the classes. Although this is quite possible, it is equally likely that the high preponderance among the upper social economic class may have been a reflection of the different ability that these parents and patients had in recognizing the illness and their ability to seek out professional expertise. Recently the amount of information distributed to the public as well as the number of treatment facilities available have increased. These factors, along with improved diagnostic skills among health care professionals, may be contributing to the evening-out of the distribution among socioeconomic groups. For example, an emaciated youth from a lower socioeconomic class may have previously been diagnosed as malnourished, whereas now increased sensitivity to anorexia nervosa may allow for appropriate detection. Also of support to this trend was the observation by Leichner et al [30] that there were no significant differences between the numbers of students who scored in the anorexic range in the various socioeconomic classes. More comprehensive studies of the patterns of referrals to clinics and general population surveys are required to monitor these trends.

Table 12.9 Educational Status of Anorexics

Approximate Period Surveyed	Education	Population (N=anorexic cases)	Method of Recognition	Authors and Date of Publication
1931-1960	65% (61 patients) more than elementary education; almost 40% matriculation level 17% academic education; high correlation between socio-ecocomic status of parents and the level of education	Female patients from a defined region in south Sweden (N=94)	Hospital archives and interviews of patients or families and questionnaires and psychological tests	Theander (1970) (6)
1959-1966	61% high academic achievements; 32% higher education	Anorexic patients admitted to a metabolic unit (N=41)	Diagnostic criteria for anorexic nervosa	Morgan and Russell (1975) (37)
1956-1975	Significantly more often attended upper level high schools than average	Female anorexics hospitalized in most clinics in a Swiss region (N=6)	Case histories	Willi and Grossmann (1983) (9)
1966-1972	All did well academically	Anorexic patients attended at Student's Health Center Manchester (N=23)	Psychiatric assessment criteria by Dally (69)	Duddle (1973) (35)
1970	Boarding school education	Diagnosed cases of anorexia nervosa, England (N=25)	Questionnaire and clinical interviews	Russell (1972) (46)
1970-1972	72% above average scholastic performance; 26% average; 8% below average	Anorexics from general psychiatric hospitals, USA (N=94)	Charts and diagnostic criteria by Feighner	Halmi (1974) (36)
1980	No consistent patterns	18 or older general population USA (N=9.543)	Diagnostic interview schedules (DIS) and DSM III classification	Robins (1984) unpublished

Educational Status

Information regarding the level of education of anorexic patients is sumamrized in table 9. This table presents the findings of studies carried out from 1931 to 1980. The methods of measuring the level of education in these samples were diverse. Nevertheless, there seemed to be an almost unanimous finding that these patients were more successful than average in their education. This observation may be interpreted to indicate high intelligence, high self-expectations, a high drive toward perfection, and/or high wish to please others (in particular parents). Again, further work is necessary to elucidate these features in the context of the general population surveys.

Sibship

The information regarding sibship is summarized in table 10. This table presents the findings of studies carried out from 1942 to 1981. From this review there would appear to be some trend favoring an association between anorexia nervosa and being first or second children. Five out of nine studies in the table found 25% to 50% of anorexic patients to be firstborn. Only children tended not to be included, thus perhaps minimizing these figures. Three studies found 32% to 40% of anorexic patients to be second children. In trying to explain this finding, one might speculate that firstborn children may be expected to carry more responsibility within the family. They may also be the ones on which the parents

Table 12.10 Sibship

Approximate Period of Survey	Sibship	Population (N=anorexic cases)	Method of recognition	Authors and Date of Publication
1931-1960	15% (14 patients) only child; 25% (24 patients) first born; 29% (27 patients) youngest of two or more—0.8 of them 6 years after their next oldest sibling; 31% (29 patients) middle; 20 patients had only sisters; 21 patients had only brothers; number of sisters and brothers equal in this group	Female patients from a defined area in south Sweden (N=94)	Hospital archives and interviews of patients or families questionnaire and psychological tests	Theander (1970) (6)
1942-1964	Eight patients were only children; 17 (37%) were oldest; 11 were middle; seven youngest	In and outpatients U.S.A. (N=43)	Psychological evaluation	Bruch (1966) (32)
1956-1975	Five patients—first born; four patients—second born; one patient—youngest of three	Male patients treated in United Birmingham Hospitals (N=10)	Records of general practitioners and psychiatrists checked according to criteria of anorexia nervosa	Hasan and Tibbetts (1977) (38)
1956-1975	No specific birthrank in majority of patients, girls predominated	Females hospitalized in most clinics in a Swiss region (N=65)	Case histories	Willi and Grossmann (1983) (9)
1962-1972	Seven first born, five second born	Male patients in a London hospital (N=13)	Interviews with families	Crisp and Toms (1972) (33)
1966-1972	Four only children	Anorexic patients attended at Student's Health Center, Manchester (N=23)	Psychiatric assessment (criteria by Dally 69)	Duddle (1973) (35)
1966-1981	Birth rank 2.37	Hospitalized patients Canada (N=50)	Hospital chart analysis	Dongier and Samy (1982) (42)
1970	Second born in family	Diagnosed cases of anorexia nervosa, England (N=25)	Questionnaire—clinical interviews	Russell (1972) (46)
1920-1972	40% first born, 32% second; 19% third, 17% fourth or later	Anorexic patients from general and psychiatric hospitals, USA (N=94)	Charts and diagnostic criteria by Feighner	Halmi (1974) (36)

Table 12.11 Race

Approximate Period Surveyed	Race	Population (N=anorexic cases)	Method of Recognition	Authors and Date of Publication
1953-1979	19 Chinese 8 Indians 1 Malayan 2 Eurasians	Patients referred to psychiatrists Malaysia (N = 30)	Reports on questionnaires	Buhrich (1981)(12)
1960-1971	40 white 1 black 1 Chinese	Patients admitted to three hospitals USA (N = 42)	Weight loss of at least 15% without organic cause	Warren and Vande Wiele (1973) (34)
1980-1981	4 blacks	Consultations to specialty clinic Canada (N = 120)	Diagnostic interviews	Garfinkel and Garner (1982) (41)
1976-1977	Japanese	Outpatients and inpatients in 35 medical institutions (N = 424)	Hospital charts and a list of symptoms similar to DSM III	Suematou et al. (1983) (13)
1980	Lower in blacks	18 or older general population USA (N = 9.543)	Diagnostic interview schedule (DIS) and DSM III criteria	Robins (1984) unpublished

project their first expectations. The combination of high parental expectations and family responsibilities may be associated with this disorder. Unfortunately, it is difficult to interpret the importance of these observations, because none of the studies compared these statistics with those of the general population.

Race

Information regarding race is summarized in table 11. The table presents the findings of studies and case reports carried out from 1953 to 1981. It appears clearly that the prevalence of anorexia nervosa in the black population in the Untied States was relatively low. Until 1984, only 11 cases were presented in various scientific publications. Garfinkel and Garner [41], who did not have any referrals of blacks until 1979, reported four cases out of 120 since then. Pumariega et al [48] reported two cases referred to him in six months. These authors raised the question of whether the incidence of anorexia nervosa was rising in the black population. Incidence could be seen as rising because of increased awareness regarding anorexia nervosa or the increasing use of the health care system by blacks [48]. Alternatively, it could also be due to socioculutral changes. Attitudinal differences toward body weight between white and black populations were studied by Huememann et

al [49] in 1966 in California High Schools. They found that black girls differed from white and Chinese in relation to their body size. Black girls were more satisfied with their figures. Many of them considered themselves about right or even a little too thin. They were more realistic in estimating their body size than other ethnic groups. Nevertheless, there was a steady increase with age in the number who thought they were too fat. The importance of sociocultural factors was also highlighted by Ikemi et al [11], who suggested that westernization of Japan and changes in the traditional family system has been associated in the increase of anorexia nervosa in that country.

Outcome Studies

Although most epidemiological studies do not take the influence of outcome into consideration, it is likely that as more comprehensive treatment programs strive for a more global improvement of the patient than just weight restoration, the number of patients recognized as suffering from the disorder and various stages of treatment will increase.

The problems with outcome studies have been well reviewed by Garfinkel and Garner [41]. They are in many ways similar to the ones outlined with epidemiological studies in this chapter. Overall, Garfinkel and

Garner's review of long-duration evaluations shows "that over 40% of patients have recovered and 30% are considerably improved at follow-up. However at least 20% are unimproved or seriously impaired and 9% have died as a result of the illness" (pg.329, 41). It is becoming evident that those patients who are unimproved or only partially improved need long-term treatment. The implications of this are that if the number of referrals to specialty clinics increases at a rate greater than that of complete cures, the number of patients known with this disorder and in treatment is bound to increase until a certain steady-state is achieved. This phenomenon may in part explain why the point prevalence of these disorders is increasing in treatment centers.

CONCLUSIONS

A significant amount of work has been done since the late 1800s regarding the epidemiology of anorexia nervosa. Changes in medical interest and sociocultural changes have influenced the quantity and the quality of this work. The last decade has seen an increased sophistication and interest in these studies. In the light of reviewing this work where would appear to be two consistent findings. First, despite various methodologies, almost all studies point to an increase in the number of patients presenting for treatment to mental health care professionals. The degree to which this may reflect an increase in the incidence of this disorder is yet to be established. Repeated work using improved criteria and validified questionnaires may further clarify this question. Second, most patients presenting to health care professionals are female. There is little convincing evidence to argue that this is primarily due to a biological factor. Rather, the evidence seems to favor the influence of specific sociocultural factors on women. The influence of other variables discussed in this chapter are less convincingly established and may in fact be in flux. That these factors may be changing is not surprising if one considers the important role of sociocultural factors in influencing the symptomatology of mental disorders. Hence, as cultural pressures for slimness further spread across all socioeconomic classes and into underdeveloped countries, one might expect further changes. Finally, recent works using validated questionnaires in general student populations clearly highlight the high rate of maladaptive eating patterns among today's youth. The rates of possible mild to moderate cases of anorexia nervosa identified through these methods is alarming.

DIRECTION FOR FUTURE WORK

Work remains to be done in the following areas:
1. The development of better screening procedures for the general population. Further validation studies of the instruments used in the identification and assessment of eating disorders are required. Further refinements aimed at increasing their specificity will greatly help to more accurately determine the prevalence of this disorder in the general population.
2. General population surveys. Most of the work that has been published up to now has focused on the high-risk groups of female high school students and college students. Yet it is becoming evident that this disorder also occurs among the male population and the older general population in significant numbers. More comprehensive studies are required in these groups.,
3. The development of prospective studies. All the work that has been reviewed in this chapter concerns primarily retrospective studies. Prospective studies are needed to verify our understanding of the significant etiological factors for these disorders. Repeated surveys of the general population with closer follow-up of those identified at high risk are needed.
4. Preventive measures. Preventive programs need to be developed in the context of evaluation instruments to measure their impact in terms of the incidence of anorexia nervosa. A more aggressive approach is needed in high schools and colleges to correct maladaptive eating patterns based on insufficient knowledge of the risk associated with the excessive valuing of slimness. The media generally need to be continuously informed and warned of the potential damages that some of their advertising practices can lead to an needs to be further encouraged to be more critical of the material they present to the public.

REFERENCES

1. Dorland's illustrated medical dictionary, 24th edition, Philadelphia: WB Saunders Company, 1965:499.
2. London ISL. Chlorosis, anaemia and anorexia nervosa. Br Med J, 1980; 281:20-7.
3. Bliss, EL, Branch CHH. Anorexia nervosa: Its history, psychology and biology. New York: Paul B. Hoeber Inc, 1960.
4. Diagnostic and statistical manual of mental disorders, third edition. The American Psychiatric Association, 1980.
5. Feighner JP, Robins E, Guze SB, et al. Diagnostic criteria for use in psychiatric research. Arch Gen Psychiatry, 1972; 26:59-63.
6. Theander S. Anorexia nervosa: A psychiatric investigation of 94 female patients. Acta Psychiatr Scand (Suppl), 1970; 214:1-189.

7. Kendell RE, Hall DJ, Hailey A, et al. The epidemiology of anorexia nervosa. Psychol Med, 1973; 3:200-3.

8. Jones DJ, Fox MM, Babigian HM, et al. Epidemiology of anorexia nervosa in Monroe Country, New York: 1960-1976. Psychosom Med, 1980; 42:551-8.

9. Willi J, Grossmann S. Epidemiology of anorexia nervosa in a defined region of Switzerland. Am J Psychiatry, 1983; 140:564-7.

10. Pope Jr, HG, Hudson JI, Yurgelun Todd D. Anorexia nervosa and bulimia among 300 suburban women shoppers. Am J Psychiatry, 1984; 141:292-4.

11. Ikemi Y, Ago Y, Nakagawa S, et al. Psycosomatic mechanism under social changes. Japan J Psychoson Res, 1974; 18:15-24.

12. Buhrich N. Frequency of presentation of anorexia nervosa in malaysia. Australia NZ J Psychiatry, 1981; 15:153-5.

13. Suematsu H, Koboki T, Aoki H et al. Statistical studies on the clinical picture of anorexia nervosa. Horumon to RMSLO, 1983; 27:693-6.

14. Holmberg N, Nylander L. Weight loss in secondary amenorrhea. Acta Obstet Gynec Scand, 1971; 50:241-6.

15. Crisp AH, Palmer RL, Kalucy RS. How common is anorexia nervosa? A prevalence study. Br J Psychiatry, 1976; 128:549-54.

16. Sheldrake P, Cormack M, McGuire J. Psycosomatic illness, birth order and intellectual preference-II women. J Psychosom Res, 1976; 20:45-9.

17. Ballot NS, Delaney NE, Erskine PJ, et al. Anorexia nervosa—a prevalence study. S Afr Med J, 1981; 27:992-3.

18. Pope HG, Hudson JI, Yurgelum - Todd D, et al. Prevalence of anorexia nervosa and bulimia in three student populations. Int J Eating Disorders, 1984; 3:3:45-51.

19. Garner DM, Garfinkel PE. Socio-culutral factors in anorexia nervosa. Lancet, 1978; 674.

20. Garner DM, Garfinkel PE. Socio-cultural factors in the development of anorexia nervosa. Psychol Med, 1980; 10:647-56.

21. Morgan GJ, Mayberry JF. Common gastrointestinal diseases and anorexia nervosa in british dietitians. Public Health, 1983; 97:166-70.

22. Smith NJ. Excessive weight loss and food aversion in athletes simulating anorexia nervosa. Pediatrics, 1980; 66:139-42.

23. Yates A, Leehey K, Shisslak CM. Running - an analogue of anorexia? N Engl J Med, 1983; 308:251-5.

24. Garner DM, Garfinkel PE. The eating attitudes test: An index of the symptoms of anorexia nervosa. Psychol Med, 1979; 1:1-7.

25. Button EJ, Whitehouse A. Subclinical anorexia nervosa. Psychol Med, 1981; 11:509-16.

26. Fairburn CG, Cooper PJ. Self-induced vomiting and bulimia nervosa; an undetected problem. Br Med J. 1982; 289:1153-5.

27. Srikameswaran S, Leichner P, Harper D. Sex role idealogy among women with anorexia nervosa and bulimia. Intl Journal of Eating Disorders, 1984; 3:3:39-43.

28. Cooper PJ, Fairbun CG. Binge eating and self-induced vomiting in the community: A preliminary study. Br J Psychiatry, 1983; 142:139-44.

29. Mann AH, Wakeling A, Wood K, Monck E, Dobbs R. Szmuckler G. Screening for abnormal eating attitudes and psychiatric morbidity in an unselected population of 156 year old school girls. Psychol Med, 1983; 13:573-80.

30. Leichner P, Arnett J, Rallo JS, et al. An epidemiologic study of maladaptive eating attitudes in a Canadian school age population. Int J Eating Dis, 1986; 5:969-982.

31. Kay DWK, Leigh D. The natural history treatment and prognosis of anorexia nervosa, based on a study of 38 patients. J Ment Sci, 1954; 100:411-31.

32. Bruch H. Anorexia nervosa and its differential diagnosos. J Nerv Ment Dis, 1966; 141:555-66.

33. Crisp AH, Toms DA. Primary anorexia nervosa or weight phobia in the male: Report on 13 cases. Br Med J. 1972; 1:334-8.

34. Warren MP, Vande Wiele RL. Clinical and metabolic features of anorexia nervosa. Am J Obstet Gynecol, 1973; 117:435-49.

35. Duddle M. An increase of anorexia nervosa in a university population. Br J Psychiatry, 1973; 123:711-2.

36. Halmi Kh. Anorexia nervosa, demographic and clinical features in 94 cases. Psychosom Med, 1974; 36:18-26.

37. Morgan HG, Russell GFM. Value of family background and clinical features as predictors of long-term outcome of anorexia nervosa; four year follow-up study of 41 patients. Psychol Med,1975; 5:355-71.

38. Hasan MK, Tibbetts RW. Primary anorexia nervosa (weight phobia) in males. Postgrad Med J, 1977; 53:146-51.

39. Bassoe HH, Eskeland I. A prospective study of 133 patients with anorexia nervosa; treatment and outcome. Acta Psychiatr Scand, 1981; 65:127-33.

40. Fichter MM, Doerr P, Pirke KM, et al. Behavior attitude, nutrition and endocrinology in anorexia nervosa. Acta Psychiat Scand, 1982; 66:429-44.

41. Garfinkel PE, Garner DM. Anorexia nervosa - a multidimensional perspective. New York: Brunner/Mazel, 1982:329.

42. Dongier S, Samy M. Anorexia nervosa: A study of 50 hospitalized cases. Psychosomatic Medicine. Krakowski A, Kimball CP, eds. New York: Penum Press, 1983:143-160.

43. Anderson AE, Mickalide AD. Anorexia nervosa in the male: An under-diagnosed disorder. Psychosomatics, 1983; 24:12.

44. Hinkle LE, Redmont R, Plummer N, et al. II. An explanation of the relation between symptoms, disability and serious illness in Nuo homogeneous groups of men and women. J Public Health, 1960; 50:1327-36.

45. Steinhausen HC, Glanville K. A long term follow-up of adolescent anorexia nervosa. Acta Psychiatr Scand,

1983; 68:1-10.

46. Russell JAO. Psychosocial aspects of weight loss and amenorhea in adolescent girls. Psychosomatic Medicine in Obstetrics and Gynaecology. Third International Congress. London, 1971: 593-595 (Karger, Bartel 1972).

47. Kalucy RS, Crisp AH, Lacey JH, et al. Prevalence and prognosis in anorexia nervosa. Aust NZJ Psychistry, 1977; 11:251-7.

48. Pumariega AJ, Edwards P, Mitchell CB. Anorexia nervosa in black adolescents. J Am Soc Child Psychiatry, 1984; 23:111-14.

49. Huenemann KL, Shapiro LR, Hampton MC, et al. A longitudinal study of gross body composition and body conformation and their association with food and activity in a teen-age population; Views of teen-age subjects on body conformation, food and activity. Am JH Clin Nutr, 1966; 18:325-38.

Chapter 13

A Sociocultural Interpretation of the Current Epidemic of Eating Disorders

Richard A. Gordon

The eating disorders, anorexia nervosa and bulimia, have attracted considerable interest and attention in recent years. The professional literature on them has grown tremendously since the mid-1970s, including a number of books and articles as well as the emergence of a major journal devoted to their study [1-9]. In addition, numerous international conferences on anorexia nervosa and bulimia have been held since 1977, and specialized hospital units, outpatient centers, and lay self-help groups specifically devoted to their treatment have multiplied throughout the United States and in many countries of Western Europe. It appears that the increased interest in eating disorders has occurred all over the industrialized world, as substantial numbers of cases have been reported on in Eastern Europe, Japan, and the Soviet Union [5,10-13,82]. Most observers agree that this dramatic surge in professional and lay interest is a response to a significant increase in the frequency of these disorders over the past two decades, a phenomenon that will be more specifically documented below. Given the practical and theoretical importance of the current epidemic of these disorders, the need to account for the increase in their frequency is a pressing one.

Most authorities in the field of eating disorders appear to agree that the recent increase in eating disorders is most probably explicable in sociocultural and historical terms. Thus, Bruch [14], one of the best known clinical interpreters of anorexia nervosa, with many years of experience, has written of a "sociocultural epidemic." Putting the case even more strongly, Schwartz et al [15] have suggested that the eating disorders have become the present instance of what Kluckholn [16] has described as a particular society's "pet" mental disorder.

In this chapter, it will be argued that the eating disorders have become a central focus for the linkage between culture and psychopathology in our time, and in fact that these disorders are expressing issues pertaining to gender, selfhood, and autonomy that have assumed particular significance in the cultural milieu of the late 20th century Western world. In order to articulate these notions, a general conception of the nature of a "pivotal" mental disorder will be used, and that is Devereux's [17,18] concept of an "ethnic disorder." Devereux's ideas have been in the literature for about 30 years now, but have been little used.

THE CONCEPT OF ETHNIC DISORDER

The notion of ethnic disorder was first presented by Devereux in his challenging essay on normality and abnormality [17], and it was elaborated further in a later essay [18]. The term "ethnic" as used by Devereux does not carry its usual implication of a highly homogeneous cultural group (such as the various "ethnic groups" that comprise the United States' population), but rather is synonymous with the looser notion of "pertaining to a particular culture."

The most general definition of an ethnic disorder is that it is a particular pattern of psychopathology that is intimately related to the character—that is, the common attitudes, conflicts, and strivings—of a people. Furthermore, it is a focal expression for the core psychological tensions, conflicts, and contradictions of a culture, and is intimately connected with prevailing cultural values. It is entirely possible that one and the *same* psychiatric disorder can be an ethnic disorder in one culture and an "idiosyncratic" disorder in another. From the standpoint of the analysis of "epidemics" of psychopathology, this is tantamount to the statement that a disorder can be rare in one culture, but epidemic to another, owing to its linkage with central processes in the latter.

The following list of the central properties of an ethnic disorder represent a distillation of the wide-ranging considerations that Devereux raised in his two essays on the subject:

1. The disorder occurs frequently within the culture in question and is one of the common psychiatric conditions within the culture.
2. The disorder is expressed in varying degrees of severity and in borderline, "subclinical," forms that fall in the midrange of a continuum between normative cultural behaviors at one end and diagnosable clinical psychopathology at the other.
3. The dynamic conflicts underlying the symptoms are central and pervasive in the culture but are of sufficient intensity in certain individuals to arouse psychological defenses and precipitate symptoms.
4. The symptomatology of the disorder is a final common pathway for the expression of a diverse spectrum of underlying psychopathology.
5. The symptoms in clinical cases represent the extremes of normative behaviors within the culture, which are exploited by the individual as ready-made modes of psychological defense.
6. The disorder itself is a culturally sanctioned pattern of being "crazy" or psychologically deviant and is modeled by influential social figures and agencies.
7. The symptoms simultaneously affirm and negate cultural values and norms. As a result, the societal response to the disorder is an ambivalent one and individuals with symptoms are both punished and rewarded by members or agencies within the culture.

EATING DISORDERS AS ETHNIC DISORDERS

In the following discussion, a variety of clinical and research evidence will be used to argue that anorexia nervosa and bulimia readily fulfill each of the criteria for an ethnic disorder as outline. Throughout the discussion, particular attention will be given to the issue of the recent apparent increase in the incidence of these disorders.

1. First, *the disorder manifests itself relatively frequently within the society in question.* Because of its intimate linkages with the psychological dynamics, values, and behavior patterns of the culture, an ethnic disorder will be relatively prevalent among other psychiatric patterns in the society. In fact, in Devereux's view, the concept of an ethnic disorder enables one to understand "the absence, or at least the extreme infrequency of a certain syndrome in a given society, in which different syndromes proliferate; the variations, determined by the culture, in the incidence and proportion of various syndromes; and finally, the fact that in a given society the full range of all known psychiatric disorders is rarely oberved," [19].

There seems to be little question that both anorexia nervosa and bulimia have become increasingly prevalent in the Western world. A number of studies indicate that the frequency of anorexia nervosa increased substantially in the United States and the United Kingdom from the late 1960s through the early 1980s [20-22,83]; in general, these studies indicated that the rates of the disorder in the general population increased by a factor of at least two. However, the absolute number of anorexic patients as indicated by these surveys was still small, on the order of 15 cases per million population. A clearer perspective on the epidemic nature of the phenomenon comes from an examination not of the general population, but of the population at risk for the disorder—namely, adolescent females. For example, Jones et al [20], in a survey of Monroe County, New York, found that the rate of cases for females in the 15 to 24 age-group during the period 1970 to 1976 increased by 400% over that for the period 1960 to 1969. In surveying a university population in England, Duddle [23] found a steady increase in cases presenting themselves to the university health center, starting with no cases in 1966 and 1967 and increasing to 13 cases in 1972. Crisp et al [21] estimated the prevalence in adolescent females enrolled in independent schools in England in the mid-1970s to be approximately one severe case for every 100 students, more than 100 times the prevalence in the general population at the time of the survey. This was the rate for a secondary school population, and it is likely if college students were included, the prevalence rates would be larger, perhaps owing to the fact that many cases of anorexia nervosa begin during the college years [7]. Unfortunately, prevalence data for anorexia nervosa in college populations, with the exception of the study of Duddle [23], are lacking at this point.

It should be pointed out that all of the studies cited above used rigorous diagnostic criteria, and therefore the prevalence rates are based on only severe cases that have come to the attention of medical authorities. This undoubtedly results in an underestimation of the extent of the problem. A more accurate picture of the prevalence of anorexic symptoms in the culture at large would be gained from efforts to identify symptoms in nonclinical populations and to include mild cases in one's prevalence figures (see section 2).

For normal-weight bulimia, the case for a high and probably increasing prevalence is even more striking. For example, Halmi and her colleagues found that among summer school students at the State University of New York at Purchase, roughly 13% of a random sample of course registrants met the DSM III criteria for bulimia [22]. Pope and Hudson [24] also surveyed a college population and found the percentage of studnets who at one time in their lives fulfilled the DSM III criteria for bulimia to be on the order of 15%. The latter authors also conducted a study on a shopping mall in suburban Boston and found the lifetime prevalence of bulimia among a random sample of female shoppers, varying widely in age, to be approximately 10%, and among subjects between the ages of 13 and 20, the prevalence was around 17% [25]. When more stringent criteria for bulimia than those of the DSM III are employed (for example, at least one binging and purging episode per week), the percentage of women in various studies drops substantially, but it still varies from between 2% to 5% [26,27]. Pope and Hudson, in a review of the recent epidemiological literature, suggest that even if conservative diagnostic criteria are employed, the number of women suffering from bulimia in the United States falls somewhere between one and three million [26]. It is also important to note that in both studies in which respondents varied widely in age, a lifetime history of bulimia or active bulimia tended to be heavily concentrated in the younger subjects, indicating that the high rate of reported bulimia is probably a relatively recent phenomenon [24,25]. Corroborating this was a study by Pyle et al [84] that found a threefold increase in the prevalence of clinical bulimia among freshmen at two midwestern universities from 1980 to 1983.

As to the relative prevalence of these disorders among other psychiatric problems, Duddle [23], in the survey discussed, found that the number of cases of anorexia nervosa presenting themselves in 1972 [13] was comparable to the number of common psychiatric disorders presenting in the same year (for example, 21 cases of "depressive neurosis"). A survey by Stagler and

Printz [28] of a university population indicated a DSM III diagnosis of bulimia in 4% of the students who sought treatment, which the authors suggest is a conservative estimate of the prevalence of the disorder in the population. The authors were surprised at the fact that the percentage of reported bulimia was on the order of magnitude of other common psychiatric problems in their sample, the most frequent of which was mild depression (dysthymic disorder), present in 15% of their study sample.

Of course, there is always the possibility that reported increases in the frequency of a disorder are due to a greater awareness of it or improved diagnostic criteria. While space does not permit a full discussion of this issue, suffice it to say that the consistency of the available data, the overwhelming impression of clinical professionals, and a number of other considerations make such an interpretation unlikely [15]. We can reasonably conclude, then, anorexia and bulimia meet the first criterion of an ethnic disorder, and that is that they are now common and becoming increasingly so.

2. *An ethnic disorder is expressed in both varying degrees of severity and in borderline, "subclinical," forms.* To quote Devereux [18] directly, "A fairly reliable indication of whether a given psychological derangement is an ethnic (and not an idiosyncratic) neurosis is the frequency with which such cases are diagnosed as 'borderline,' 'ambulatory,' or 'mixed,' or as 'hyphenated'." According to Devereux, the reason for this proliferation of borderline cases is that the disorder in question is so intimately linked with culturally pervasive psychological and behavioral trends that the symptomatic behaviors associated with the disorder tend to merge and blur with "normal" behavior within the culture. It is the proliferation of borderline, subclinical, cases that most strikingly illustrates the pervasiveness of an ethnic disorder in a culture.

The existence of a spectrum of anorexic and bulimic conditions, and in particular the existence of "subclinical" forms of these disorders, has been well documented. An important early study was that of Nylander [29], who investigated dieting behavior among Swedish adolescents. Nylander reported that the majority of the 1,241 women surveyed reported "feeling fat" at least some of the time, and that dieting was highly prevalent, particularly among the older secondary school women. More importantly, nearly 10% of the study sample reported at least three symptoms of clinical anorexia nervosa, the most common of which were fatigue, increased interest in food, depression, chilliness, constipation, anxiety, and amenorrhea. Nylander proposed, as a result of these findings, that the syndrome of anorexia nervosa occurs on a continuum, with the clinically identified cases representing the extreme end. Furthermore, "most cases of anorexia nervosa are incipient and/or mild and never come to medical attention but are spontaneously cured with increasing maturity" (p 25).

A more recent study by Button and Whitehouse [30] led to similar conclusions. The authors administered the Eating Attitudes Test, a scale developed by Garner and Garfinkel [31] for the purpose of identifying anorexic-like attitudes towards food, to 578 students at a College of Technology in England. A total of 28 female students (6.3% of the total female sample) scored in the "anorexic range" of the scale, and subsequent individual interviews revealed that these students were experiencing many of the clinical symptoms of anorexia nervosa, such as significant weight loss, hyperactivity, obsessive calorie-counting, and so forth. Particularly striking was the fact that roughly 40% of this high-scoring group of students were using self-induced vomiting as a weight-loss technique, a rate comparable to populations of clinically diagnosed anorexics. At the same time, few of them manifested the full spectrum of anorexic symptoms, particularly emaciation, and in fact only one fulfilled stringent diagnostic criteria for the disorder. The authors concluded, therefore, that anorexia nervosa occurs along a continuum of severity, and that most of their weight-preoccupied students should be considered as having "subclinical" cases of the disorder. In their words, "Cases of anorexia nervosa (fulfilling strict diagnostic criteria) may, therefore, be regarded as very much the tip of the iceberg with respect of excessive weight concern among young females," [p515].

The findings of Nylander and Button and Whitehouse are consistent with the results of studies by Garner and Garfinkel [31] and Thompson and Schwartz [32], who also found in separate investigations that eating disorder symptoms were prevalent in student populations, even though individuals manifesting the symptoms had not sought help for their problems and had not therefore been identified clinically.

A study by Garner et al [33] found that within a group of "weight-preoccupied" college females, as determined by the Eating Disorder Inventory, one subgroup closely resembled clinical anorexics along most dimensions, while a second subgroup resembled the anorexics only in their weight preoccupation, but were otherwise less pathological. In a subsequent study of self-induced vomiting in a non-clinical sample, roughly 10 percent resembled clinical bulimics on the EDI, 43 percent had elevated scores on weight-preoccupation scales, and the remaining 47 percent were in the normal range [85]. The authors made the important point that we should not assume that all weight-preoccupied subjects have the same psychopathology as clinical anorexics or

bulimics. On the whole, however, most of the research discussed in this section strongly suggests that the symptoms of anorexia and bulimia do occur along a continuum of severity and that the disorder is manifested in a spectrum of milder, subclinical forms.

3. *The psychological conflicts underlying the symptoms are central and pervasive in the culture, but are of sufficient intensity in the patient to arouse psychological defenses and precipitate symptoms.* Devereux [18] put it this way:

> The underlying conflict of the psychosis or neurosis is also present in the majority of normal people. The conflict in the neurotic or the psychotic is simply *more intense* than it is in other people. In short the patient is *like* everyone —but more intensely so than anyone else. [p216]

Presumably because of the idiosyncrasies of personal experience and learning, certain individuals experience particularly intense versions of a common cultural conflict, and these individuals are at elevated risk to succumb to the disorder.

It has been suggested by a number of writers that anorexic and bulimic patients suffer from extreme versions of conflicts regarding identity, self-esteem, and autonomy that have become pervasive among women in the industrialized societies [34-37]. The linkage of these conflicts to recent historical transformations in women's roles and identity suggests one reason why the epidemic increase in eating disorders has affected mainly women, while the percentage of male anorexics appears to have remained relatively constant [20]. While the relatively small number of male anorexics and bulimics suffer from similar conflicts in identity and autonomy [38,39], the relative rarity of these disorders in men is a consequence of the fact that these issues have not been historically central for male adolescents. However, some recent speculations regarding a possible analogue of anorexia nervosa in middle-aged men—the "obligatory running syndrome," which also appears to result from conflicts regarding personal identity, self-esteem, and autonomy—suggest that the psychology of eating disorders may not be limited to women but may in fact represent a core set of psychosocial issues that are of fundamental significance for both sexes in modern industrial societies [40].

The case for the relationship between the eating disorders and psychosocial conflicts in women has been made by a number of authors. Garfinkel [41], for example, has pointed out that anorexic symptoms express both the desire for thinness, itself a consequence of powerful cultural pressures, and the competitive strivings for success among middle-class young women. Garfinkel stresses the linkage of achievement pressures in women with the striving for beauty and suggests that these cultural pressures may force some adolescent girls into a position where they believe weight control is equal to self-control, and this is equal to beauty and success. Garner and Garfinkel [31] have also done some important empirical studies on these issues, which suggest, among other things, that greater competitive pressure on women, when combined with a demand for thinness, is associated with a greater incidence of eating pathology.

Bruch [1,14] also points to the competitive and ambitious strivings of anorexic patients. Bruch, however, taking a somewhat more dynamic point of view, suggests that these striving for specialness and autonomy cover over underlying feelings of helplessness, inefficacy, and emptiness. While Bruch's discussion proceeds for the most part on the individual level, she has referred in her more recent writings [14] to a "sociocultural epidemic" of anorexia nervosa, presumably as a consequence in part of cultural changes that have made these conflicts widespread among women. More specifically, in her last paper [42] she suggests that the radical shift in social expectations for female achievement have made these conflicts between dependency and autonomy extremely pervasive in the culture, and thus, these changes can be said to be partly responsible for the increased frequency of anorexic disorders.

The author who has perhaps been most explicit about the relationships between the conflicts experienced by anorexic patients to these social and historical issues is the Italian psychiatrist, Mara Selvini Palazolli [37]. In an important monograph, Palazolli described the anorexic as an adolescent who turns against her body because it symbolizes her feelings of passive exploitation by others and her sense of being dominated and controlled by others, particularly her mother. These feelings of being a passive "succubus," as she puts it, are exaggerations of normative "existential" characteristics of female puberty, but they are particularly painful for the anorexic, because they conflict sharply with her temperamental "elan vital, a passionate though suppressed love of life, a 'sthenic spur' which alone explains her heroic defence reaction" [p67].

Palazolli [37] suggests that the particular intrapsychic conflicts experienced by the anorexic, which on an individual level originate in her early experience in her family, both reflect and magnify recent cultural pressures on women associated with a drastic shift in role expectations. Thus, modern women are expected to have careers and to adopt traditionally "masculine" values that permeate the universities, the professions, and the business world. At the same time they are under increas-

ing pressure to maintain traditional female role orientation, that is to say, to be attractive and fashionable, as well as continuing to carry out the tasks of childbearing and motherhoood. These highly stressful pressures are experienced by the majority of women in the culture, but come to a head in the woman who develops anorexia nervosa. The chief reason for this lies in the family of the anorexic, whose parents, themselves conflicted between the traditional and the modern, provide a milieu in which such an identity crisis can easily become acute.

Although cast somewhat differently, a similar argument about psychosocial gender-identity conflicts in normal-weight bulimics was presented by Bokind-Lodahl [35]. Boskind-Lodahl emphasized the extent to which her bulimic patients (mostly college-aged women) experience an acute conflict between their intellectual talents and achievement motivation on the one hand, and their intense socialization to traditional female role expectations on the other.

There are also some empirical studies that lend support that eating disordered patients are troubled by sex-role conflicts [43,44]. These studies have used the Bem Sex-Role Inventory, a scale that measures a subject's identification with culturally stereotypic masculine and feminine traits. For example, Sitnick and Katz [44] examined sex roles in a group of anorexic patients (both hospitalized and nonhospitalized) in comparison with healthy controls in college and graduate school. They found that while the anorexics did not differ from the controls on measures of stereotypically defined "feminine" traits, they scored significantly lower than the controls on "masculine" trait scales. The authors' interpretation of these findings is that anorexic women have been unable to integrate such traditionally "masculine" strivings in a period of rapid sociocultural change, in which such traits as aggressive self-reliance have become "particularly essential for optimal functioning for a woman in Western society" [p82].

To sum up, clinical interpretations as well as a limited amount of empirical evidence suggest that eating disordered patients suffer from an acute version of a psychological conflict that has become pervasive among women in our culture in our time. Due to sweeping changes in our culture that have accelerated over the past two decades, women are expected to be independent, assertive achievers, and at the same time to fulfill traditional expectations to be attractive and to play a nurturant and largely supportive (and subordinate) social role [45]. The synthesis of these two contradictory roles, or what Dyrenforth et al [46] call "the divergent axes of nurturance and assertion," has turned out, as the latter authors suggest, to be easily incorporated as an ideal, but more difficult to realize in practice. As a number of writers suggested, thinness has become the symbol for the achievement of this synthesis [46,47], thus suggesting one reason why anorexic and bulimic disorders have become the symptom of choice during the present historical period.

While these issues have affected most young women in Western societies, the individual who becomes anorexic or bulimic is particularly vulnerable to them for a variety of reasons—the idiosyncrasies of her family experience, which have been particularly conflictual with respect to the issue of female identity, temperamental factors, and a number of other possible reasons [7]. The point is that these sociocultural factors are such that virtually all young women in the culture have become vulnerable to eating disorders; however, only those with particular individual vulnerabilities ultimately become patients.

4. *The symptomatology of the disorder is a vehicle for the expression of a diverse spectrum of underlying psychopathology.* While an ethnic disorder expresses a nuclear cultural conflict, the symptoms also constitute a "final common pathway" for the expression of a spectrum of idiosyncratic personal distress and individual psychopathology. Devereux [17] points out that a number of psychiatric revisionists have suggested that many of the hysterical patients treated by Breuer and Freud in the late years of the 19th century were actually suffering from borderline schizophrenia or some other nonhysterical psychiatric disorder. In his view, these rediagnoses, if accurate, indirectly illustrate the point that by virtue of its linkage with common cultural conflicts and behaviors, an ethnic disorder can serve as a "mask" for a variety of psychopathological conditions. Thus, in the 19th century, the typical quasisomatic, quasineurolgoical symptoms of hysterical conversion disorders were consistent with a cultural model of how "nervous" people behave, as well as the culturally acceptable expression of distress by women in thr form of somatic illness. Consequently, a variety of underlying psychological difficulties, including depression, repressed aggression or sexuality, characterological problems or even psychotic disorganization could be expressed in the form of hysterical conversion symptoms [48].

Support for this notion of a final common pathway for eating disorders derives from a number of studies that document the psychiatric heterogeneity of these conditions. For example, in an intensive personality study using psychological testing of six patients with severe cases of anorexia nervosa, Bram et al [49] found that two patients had a borderline personality organization, one had a schizoid personality disorder, one had a hysterical personality, and two had no identifiable personality disorder. Johnson [50], referring to work done by Swift and Stern [51], reports that bulimic and anorexic patients tend to be characterized by one of three types of underlying psychopathology: a classic borderline personality organiation, with impulsive, unstable, explosive, acting-out tendencies; a "false-self" type of personality, who, like the classic anorexic described by Bruch, shows a superficially "good" and compliant adaptation, but who suffers from a sense of inner emptiness and underlying deprivation; and an "identity-conflicted" group who manifest various classical symptoms of neurotic anxiety and depression. These groups may be seen as varying along a dimension of greater to lesser degrees of psychological disorganization, respectively. Johnson points out that these diverse psychopathologies have been prevalent in clinical populations for some time, but in previous historical periods would most likely not have manifested eating-disordered symptoms but rather some other culturally patterned syndrome. For example, the patient in the latter group (identity-conflicted, neurotic), in the latter half of the 19th century, would have been likely to present hysterical conversion symptoms, such as Freud's famous patient Dora [52,53]. Similarly, Johnson [50] suggests that the borderline patient, as late as a decade ago in the "era of The Exorcist," would be likely to appear at the clinic as "possessed," not bulimic.

5. *The symptoms represent extremes of normative behaviors and values within the culture, which are exploited by the individual as ready-made modes of psychological defense.* As Devereux suggests [17], obsessive-compulsive personality traits are extensions of culturally normative preoccupations with cleanliness, order, and control that are common in industrial societies, particularly those governed by the ethos of capitalism. In a non-Western context, the symptoms of the Malaysian "running amok" syndrome are an exaggeration of the heroism prized in the ancient Malay warriors, and the symptoms of Amok are almost literally depicted in Malaysian epics. The continuity of the symptoms with culturally normative behaviors results in an ethnic disorder being readily imitable and easily learned and in fact is what makes the symptoms so readily available as acceptable modes of defense against psychological conflict. As has been pointed out earlier, the 19th century hysterical woman was merely using an exaggeration of the then culturally regnant concept of the "frailty of woman" in the service of a defense against her own undoubtedly intense psychological conflicts [54,55].

It has now become almost commonplace in the literature on eating disorders that behaviors that are central to anorexia nervosa—fanatical dieting and the relentless pursuit of thinness—are modeled directly by powerful influences within the culture and represent the extremes of the dieting behavior and concern with thinness that have become increasingly prevalent in the industrialized affluent societies in the 20th century [1,7,15]. The most visible of these influences has been the marketing of the ideal of thinness by the fashion industry. Even a casual view of the best-known fashion magazines such as *Vogue* and *Cosmopolitan* makes it abundantly clear that the anorectic body type is not an isolated pathological aberration but has become an idealized standard of beauty and high fashion in Western societies. The trend toward increasingly greater degrees of thinness has been documented systematically by Garner et al [56]. These authors determined empirically that the shape and weight of two standards of beauty—the Playboy centerfold and the Miss America winner—have shown a consistent trend toward lower weight and toward a "tubular" versus an "hourglass" shape over the past two decades. In their studies of ballet students, Garner and Garfinkel [7] have shown that the pressure to be thin in and of itself results in an increased incidence weight preoccupation and eating disorder symptomatology.

The contemporary idealization of thinness is the product of a historical evolution over the past century, an epoch that Bennett and Gurin [47] have dubbed aptly, "The Century of Svelte." The latter authors, in their excellent book on dieting, have traced this historical development, beginning with the "femme fatale" of the 19th century, to the "flapper" of the 1920s, and finally to the extreme of the "Twiggy" body that emerged in the late 1960s and has become the standard of the late 20th century. They argue that the evolution of the image of the thin female had a great deal to do with the emergence of the politically and sexually liberated woman. Thinness at once implied mobility, both physical and social, and also a disengagement of female sexuality from the functions of childbearing and childrearing, the latter being typically associated with maternal plumpness. While thinness originally took on symbolic value for women as a sign of freedom from traditional constraints and oppressions, it was soon exploited by a profit-oriented fashion industry, which played upon a set of motivations in women that conflicted sharply with emerging ideals of female assertiveness and independence—namely, the traditional desire to be beautiful and sexually attractive. Thus, the meanings of thinness were highly suited to express the psychological conflicts regarding female identity discussed earlier.

A direct consequence of this cultural preoccupation with thinness has been the ubiquitous efforts at dieting and weight-control among middle- and upper-class women. Surveys in the 1960s of high school students have shown that 65% to 80% of high school females wanted to weigh less, and 60% reported having actively dieted at some time during the survey [57]. In the study previously alluded to, Garner et al [56] found that the number of diet articles in womens' magazines grew by about 50% during the 1970s compared with the 1960s. Furthermore, the number of popular diet books and fad diets have proliferated tremendously in recent years, and a booming diet and weight-loss industry, which has received sanction and status from warnings against the dangers of obesity from the medical industry, now reaps large profits from fat-conscious consumers [47]. As pointed out earlier, many cases of anorexia nervosa, particularly those of moderate, "subclinical" degrees of severity, can probably be understood as extensions of this culturally normative relationship between the pursuit of extreme thinness and dieting [29,33].

In addition to the pursuit of thinness through dieting, a further phenomenon that may well be related to the increase in anorexic disorders is the growing preoccupation in contemporary culture with exercise. In particular, we have witnessed a virtual explosion in pursuit of such activities as jogging and aerobic exercise during the past 15 years, a phenomenon that began in America but which has proliferated throughout the industrialized world [58]. The relationship of the latter to anorexic disorders has been explored in a recent paper by Epling et al [59], who demonstrated in laboratory animals that under certain circumstances, a positive feedback loop is established between reduced food intake and increased physical activity, with the two mutually amplifying each other. The result is a pattern of self-starvation coupled with increased physical activity that resembles anorexia nervosa—a pattern that the authors dub "activity anorexia."

Rather than seeing the jogging and exercising engaged in by the anorexic as a consequence of her desire to lose weight, which is the traditional view, Epling et al [59] emphasize that compulsive exercising may also be one *antecedent* of the disorder. This notion has been borne out by a growing awareness of an increasing problem of anorexic disorders among athletes [60], as well as a recent study of a group of anorexic patients in Australia, which indicated that a substantial number of cases of anorexia nervosa were initially "triggered" by excessive levels of exercise, and not (in these cases) dieting [61]. Epling et al [59] further suggest that the reason anorexic disorders are so much more common in women is that, unlike physical exercise, dieting is sex-typed, for the reasons we have elucidated. Therefore, the *combination* between diet and exercise, which is in their view the cause of self-starvation, is much more likely to occur in women than in men.

Summing up, some of the primary symptoms of anorexic disorders, an obsession with thinness and a fanatical devotion to dieting and exercise, are clearly extensions and exaggerations of behaviors and ideals that have become normative and positively valued among middle-class Westerners. Furthermore, these behaviors are ideally suited to serving as defenses against the modal psychosocial conflicts that we discussed above. Through the pursuit of thinness, the anorexic is able to find a pathological symbolic resolution of the historical dilemma that rages within her on a psychic level: how to achieve autonomy, assertiveness, and power and at the same time fulfill traditional expectations of femininity. Stringent dieting and a severe exercise regimen—behaviors that have many of the general characteristics of obsessive-compulsive rituals—provide her with a powerful sense of autonomy, self-control, and achievement in the face of tormenting inner conflicts and feelings of powerlessness and worthlessness, of being a "nothing," [14].

6. *The disorder itself is a culturally sanctioned mode of being "crazy" or psychologically deviant, and is modeled by significant influences within the culture.* Devereux suggests that the symptoms are implicitly sanctioned by the society as templates for deviant behavior and as an acceptable way to discharge tension and be "crazy." Essentially, the culture provides a directive to the effect of "Don't go crazy, but if you do, you should behave as follows."

Devereux is not explicit about the processes by which these templates for deviant behavior are communicated, but presumably they would be transmitted by processes of vicarious learning that have been well-described by contemporary social-learning theorists [62]. Bandura's research has shown that complex behaviors can be acquired through simple observational learning, especially if the person who is imitated (the"model") is a figure of high prestige or social power or if the learner observes that the model's behavior itself results in reinforcement. Thus, the communication of an ethnic disorder would be enhanced if it was modeled by figures of high prestige or visibility in the culture, or by peers or other socially influential figures who themselves are observed to receive positive reinforcement of their symptomatic behavior.

In the contemporary world, the mass media, entertainment figures, and advertising are potent and influential vehicles for the communication and modeling of cultural prescriptions [63]. The influence of the media has been particularly in evidence in the case of anorexia and bulimia. As has already been pointed out, many of the most influential fashion models have manifested a blatant rendition of the anorexic body type. In addition, a number of well-known and widely admired entertainment figures have been known to

have, or have openly admitted to having eating disorders. A case in point is that of Jane Fonda, whose confession of a 21-year history of bulimia have been widely publicized recently, including in her own semi-autobiographical writings [64]. While it was clearly not her intention to do so, it is possible that the public admission of an eating disorder by such an influential role model—particularly one who has been so explicitly involved with the struggle on the part of women to synthesize traditional and new ideals—may well have given some sanction to certain women to engage in this form of weight control.

In addition, there have been an increasing number of often sensationalized descriptions of eating disorders in the mass media. A survey conducted by the author indicated that articles about anorexia nervosa and bulimia in womens' magazines increased dramatically from 1974 to 1983 [65]. Some of the titles of these articles suggest the context of social imitation, competition, and contagion in which a number of anorexic disorders begin (eg, "My Sister and I Tried to Outdiet Each Other with Some Pretty Scary Results"). The highly paradoxical character of anorexic disorders in an affluent culture (ie, self-starvation in the midst of plenty, or the dramatic excesses of consumption and purification of the binge-purge cycle) undoubtedly contributes further to the fascination that they generate in the public. While the ostensible purpose of many of these articles is to provide information to the public (some of them are explicitly formulated as warnings), it is at least possible that such literature has functioned as a double-edged sword by glamorizing experimentation with extreme dieting (eg, characterizing anorexics as "golden girls") or self-induced vomiting as a weight-control technique. This is not to say that such publicity would be a sufficient cause of either disorder, but only to suggest that such influences could serve as "triggers" in an already predisposed individual [15].

A particularly dramatic example of a virtually overt "prescription" of the symptoms is to be found in the case of one of the most notorious and yet widely disseminated fad diets, the "Beverly Hills" diet [66]. *The Beverly Hills Diet* was on the *New York Times* best seller list for several months, and in addition to numerous adherents, attracted a great deal of attention and criticism from medically oriented writers [67]. Wooley and Wooley [68], in a devastating critique of this book, suggest that:

The *Beverly Hills Diet* marks the first time an eating disorder—anorexia nervosa—has been marketed as a cure for obesity. It is a case of one disease being offered as a cure for another...Judy Mazel offers us an unwitting translation of the anorexic's delusional system into the jargon of pop culture and pseudo-science...The popularity of her diet can be seen as yet another symptom of a weight-obsessed culture. But it is also a form of direct training in anorexic behavior, which should be of great concern at a time when eating disorders constitute a virtual epidemic among young women (p7).

According to Wooley and Wooley, Mazel has written a virtual handbook for the psychology of starvation. Repeatedly, it advances the characteristic anorexic misconception that undigested food in the alimentary/gastrointestinal system, which gives rise to the phenomenal sensation of "fullness," is the equivalent to "being fat." The virtual obsession with every mouthful of food (as evidenced by complicated charts scheduling every morsel of intake), the magical investment in the scale, the suggestion of hyperactivity associated with reduced food intake ("three little grapes and you're ready to run a mile"), the association of hunger and an empty stomach with feelings of moral purity—these reflect essential themes of the anorexic's psychology. Furthermore, the book virtually advocates bulimia as a way of life, with its argument that dieting makes binge-eating possible so long as it is followed by appropriate drastic reduction in intake, and also the tacit encouragment to eat foods that lead to purging. To use Wooley and Wooley's forceful characterization, it represents "the Mass Marketing of Anorexia Nervosa."

Finally, some mention needs to be made of the possible role of peer influences in the modeling of anorexic and bulimic symptoms, factors that have been relatively neglected in the literature on eating disorders. More specifically, dieting among women, and perhaps particularly among female adolescents, frequently occurs in a highly competitive context [69,70]. The observation of the powerful reinforcements that result from the achievement of thinness through starvation dieting could potentially make such radical methods of weight control compellingly atttractive to a vulnerable adoelscent. Moreover, the observation that others can achieve a "special" status (see next section) and receive admiration for their "control" further serves to heighten the attractiveness of "being anorexic". Anecdotal clinical reports also suggest that bulimic methods of weight control can be acquired through peer influence. It is frequently mentioned in the clinical literature that experimentation with self-induced vomiting as a technique of weight control is often initiated on hearing about it or even receivng instruction in the method from a friend [3,71].

7. *The symptoms of an ethnic disorder simultaneously affirm and negate cultural values and norms, and therefore evoke a highly ambivalent social response.*

As a result, the patient with an ethnic disorder assumes simultaneously an elevated and a denigrated status. Devereux (1980a) suggests that the relationship of an ethnic disorder to societal values and norms is a highly paradoxical one. On the one hand, to the extent that the symptoms are extremes of positively valued behaviors, the disorder itself may take on an exalted status. In fact, "numerous ethnic symptoms are readily mistaken for socially approved behavior."

On the other hand, the symptoms of an ethnic disorder have a tendency to negate and undermine the values of the society in which it occurs. To the extent that the disorder reflects such a rebellion, it will typically be met with controlling and punitive social responses. Yet, the response to the negative aspects of an ethnic disorder may be an ambivalent one. To the extent that the rebellion represented by the behavior of the deviant may express values that people in the society secretly aspire to, the behavior of the disordered individual may meet with secret approval and admiration. As Devereux [17] put it, the symptoms enable the individual "to be antisocial in a socially approved and sometimes even prestigious manner" (p31).

These paradoxical characteristics apply readily to the case of eating disorders, particularly to anorexia nervosa. First, her refusal to eat in her project to rid herself of every last vestige of body fat represents a fundamental negation of the ethic of consumption in an affluent social milieu. The extreme contradiction posed by this refusal of plentiful supplies needs to be viewed in the context of the middle- or upper-class socioeconomic status of the families of most anorexics [72]. While it may well not be her intention to do so, it would appear that refusing to eat seems like the most dramatic and fundamental negation of her parents' typical economic success and social advantages that she could possibly have devised. Second, in achieving such extreme thinness, along with the typical consequences of amennorhea and the diminishment of secondary sexual characteristics, she has in effect regressed to a prepubertal state, there by negating her adult status. The particular rebellion implied in this retreat from adulthood must be understood in the context of the high standards for performance, achievement, and appearance that frequently characterize the families of anorexics [73,74].

However, the anorexic manifests a kind of obstinate willfulness in the pursuit of her starvation diet, somewhat reminiscent of the characteristic defiance of the hysterical woman in the 19th century [54]. The most obvious manifestation and consequence of this is the power struggle that she typically gets into over her eating with both family and hospital staff [7,75]. In some instances, this has led to overtly punitive treatment regimens, for example the advocacy of the use of a "switch" by the mother to enforce compliance from her daughter [76]. While such drastic measures may be interpreted as an understandable response to a patient with a life-threatening disease who stubbornly denies her illness and resists treatment, there is also a sociopolitical "subtext" to these interactions between (predominantly) male physicians and female patients, similar perhaps to the sexual politics of the interaction between 19th-century physicians and hysterical patients so lucidly described by Smith-Rosenberg [54].

Despite the concern that her emaciated state evokes, along with the controlling and sometimes punitive responses elicited by her determined efforts to starve herself, there is evidence that the anorexic patient also meets with a certain degree of admiration and approval for her behavior, responses that can only serve to reinforce her condition. In a study that throws light on this phenomenon, Branch and Eurman [77] reported distributing a questionnaire to families and friends of a number of students with anorexia nervosa. While the authors found considerable concern with their patients' weight loss, they also "found that the anorectic patient meets with more approval than disapproval from family and friends." In describing the patient, the words "slender," "neat," "well-groomed," and "fashionable" were used much more frequently than the words "skinny," "emaciated," and "haggard." Furthermore, a number of respondents expressed admiration for the control and discipline exhibited by the patient in her rigorous dieting, an attitude that was epitomized by the comment of one patient's friend, "She is victorious."

Branch and Eurman [77] were particularly alarmed that such support for her behavior from her immediate social milieu would work directly against efforts at treatment. Their findings suggest that anorexics, despite being perceived as ill, have something of an exalted status in our society as well—a consequence of her "achievement" of the extreme of certain cultural ideals. This study demonstrates that these include not only thinness but also the virtues of self-discipline and self-control. Mackenzie [78] has suggested that these latter traditional "Protestant" values are undergoing a renewed affirmation among the middle and upper classes in the advanced industrial societies, for whom a reconstituted "puritanism" seems to be functioning as an antidote to the excesses and loss of standards of behavior in societies governed by an ethos of limitless consumption and an "anything-goes" morality.

As suggested by Garfinkel and Garner [7], the idealization of emaciation associated with an illness has an historical precedent, and that is the romanticization of the thin and frail figure of the tubercular patient in the 19th century. Sontag [79] has pointed out that the tubercular appearance was associated with cultural refinement, sensitivity, and creativity, and because of this the disease had a certain elevated status. For somewhat different reasons, anorexia nervosa appears to have also become such a "classy" disease, not only because it has been typically associated with wealth and social status, but because of the way in which it both affirms and negates contemporary cultural ideas.

Perhaps because the bulimic suffers from loss of control during eating binges, and also because her purging behavior is seen as "gross" or "disgusting," her status may not be quite as elevated as the anorexic. However, recent popular literature, as well as observations on college campuses, suggest that it is also becoming "in," or fashionable, to be bulimic. In addition, there is a way in which the social response to a bulimic may even be more powerfully reinforcing than the reaction to anorexia. Because bulimia is typically a closely guarded secret [80], the individual is able to maintain control over the weight without anyone knowing about her methods. Since she does not become emaciated like the restricting anorexic, and because at the same time she is able to maintain her weight at or perhaps somewhat below her normal level, she may be typically complimented for "how good she looks," and yet no one will question her or be in a position to attempt to impose control over her eating patterns.

CONCLUSION

Using Devereux's conceptualization of an "ethnic disorder," this chapter has suggested that anorexia nervosa and bulimia are expressing central identity conflicts that have become virtually normative among adolescent and young adult women in the present historical period in Western cultures. It has been suggested that these disorders serve as a final common pathway for the expression of a spectrum of individual distress and psychopathology, by virtue of the continuity of the symptoms with highly prevalent cultural practices (dieting and exercise). Furthermore, it appears that the eating disorders have become standardized and widely imitated models for the expression of psychological distress and deviance. Because of their linkage with positive cultural values such as physical attractiveness, control, and autonomy they have assumed a glamorous status, although, like any form of psychopathology, the social response they evoke is an ambivalent one.

While anorexia nervosa was first identified as a medical disorder in the 16th century, it was probably a relatively rare condition until recently, despite the disproportionate amount of attention that it received in the psychiatric literature [6]. From Devereux's standpoint, it could be argued that anorexia nervosa did not become a true ethnic disorder until the recent past, during which there was a convergence between cultural values and psychosocial issues on the one hand, and the psychopathology of the disorder on the other. Perhaps only when this confluence takes place is an epidemic of psychopathology possible.

Finally, while the emphasis in this chapter has been on sociocultural factors, there is no intention of negating the role of biological factors in eating disorders. Such factors are most likely of considerable significance in understanding why specific individuals are predisposed to the disease, and they undoubtedly must be considered in understanding the disease process itself [7,81]. However, it is the author's opinion that sociocultural factors such as those discussed in this paper are critical to an understanding of why these disorders have increased in frequency and become one of the most central psychiatric problems in our time.

ACKNOWLEDGMENT

The author would like to thank the administration of Bard College for their support and for release time to conduct the initial research for this paper.

REFERENCES

1. Bruch H. Eating disorders: Obesity, anorexic nervosa, and the person within. New York: Basic Books, 1973.
2. Bemis K. Current approaches to the etiology and treatment of anorexia nervosa. Psychol Bull, 1978; 85:593-617.
3. Boskind-White M, White WC. Bulimarexia. New York: WW Norton, 1983.
4. Cauwels J. Bulimia: The binge-purge compulsion. New York: Doubleday, 1983.
5. Crisp AH. Anorexia nervosa: Let me be. London: Academic Press, 1981.
6. Darby L, ed. Anorexia nervosa: Recent developments in research. New York: Alan R. Liss, 1983.
7. Garfinkel PE, Garner DM. Anorexia nervosa: A multidimensional perspective. New York: Brunner Mazel, 1982.
8. The International Journal of Eating Disorders, vols 1-3. New York: Van Norstrand Rheinhold. 1982-1984.
9. Sours JA. Starving to death in a sea of objects. New York: Jason Aronson, 1979.
10. Kasperlik-Zaluska A, Migdalska D, Kazubska M, Wisniewska-Wozniak T. Clinical, psychiatric, and endocrinological correlations in 42 cases of anorexia nervosa. Psychaitria Polska Warsaw, 1981; 15:355-63.
11. Korkina MV, Marilov VV. The contemporary state of the problem of anorexia nervosa. Journal of Neuropathology and Psychiatry (Soviet Union) 1978;

110:574-83.
12. Nogami Y, Yabana F. On Kibarashi-gui Binge-Eating. Folia Psychiatr Neurol Jpn, 1977; 31:159-66.
13. Totani R. Anorexia nervosa. Jpn J Clin Med, 1982; 6:1363-70.
14. Bruch H. The golden cage. New York: Vintage Books, 1978.
15. Schwartz DM, Thompson MG, Johnson CL. Anorexia nervosa and bulimia: the socio-cultural context. Int J Eating Disord, 1982; 1:20-35.
16. Kluckholn C. Mirror for man. New York: McGraw-Hill, 1954:
17. Devereux G. Normal and abnormal, 1956. In Devereux G. Basic Problems of ethnopsychiatry. Chicago: University of Chicago Press, 1980:3-71.
18. Devereux G.1965. Schizophrenia: An ethnic psychosis, or schizophrenia without tears. In Devereux, G. Basic Problems of ethnopsychiatry. Chicago: University of Chicago Press, 1980:214- 236.
19. Kendall RE, Hall DJ Hailey A, et al. The epidemiology of anorexia nervosa. Psychol Med, 1973; 3:200-3.
20. Jones DJ, Fox MM, Babigan HM, et al. Epidemiology of anorexia nervosa in Monroe County, New York: 1960-1976. Psychosom Med, 1980; 42:551-8.
21. Crisp AH, Palmer RL, Kalucy RS. How common is anorexia nervosa? a prevalence study. Br J Psychiatry, 1976, 128:549-54.
22. Halmi KA, Falk Jr, Schwartz E. Binge-eating and vomiting: a survey of a college population.
23. Duddle M. An increase in anorexia nervosa in a university population. Br J Psychiatry, 1973; 128:211-2.
24. Pope HG, Hudson JI. Prevalence of anorexia nervosa and bulimia among three student populations. Int J Eating Disord, 1984; 3:45- 51.
25. Pope HG, Hudson JI, Yurgelun-Todd D. Anorexia nervosa and bulimia among 300 suburban women shoppers. Am J Psychiatry, 1984; 141:292-4.
26. Pope HG, Hudson JI. New hope for binge eaters. New York: Harper and Row, 1984.
27. Pyle RL, Mitchell JE, Eckert ED, et al. The incidence of bulimia in freshman college students. Int J Eating Disord, 1982; 2:75-85.
28. Stagler RS, Printz AM. DSM III: Psychiatric diagnosis in a University population. Am J Psychiatry, 1980; 137:937-40.
29. Nylander I. The feeling of being fat and dieting in a school population. Acta Socio-Medica Scandinavia, 1971; 1:17-26.
30. Button EJ, Whitehouse A. Subclinical anorexia nervosa. Psychol Med, 1981; 11:509-16.
31. Garner DM, Garfinkel PE. The eating attitudes test: an index of the symptoms of anorexia nervosa. Psychol Med, 1979; 9:273-9.
32. Thompson MG, Schwartz DM. Life adjustment of women with anorexia nervosa and anorexic-like behavior. Int J Eating Disord, 1982; 1:47-59.
33. Garner DM, Olmsted MP, Garfinkel PE. Does anorexia nervosa occur on a continuum? Int J Eating Disord, 1983; 2:11-20.

34. Bardwick J. In transition. New York: Holt Rhinehart, and Winston, 1978.

35. Boskind-Lodahl M. Cinderella's stepsisters: a feminist perspective on anorexia nervosa and bulimia. Signs: A Journal of Women in Culture and Society, 1976; 2:342-56.

36. Chernin K. The obsession. New York: Harper and Row, 1981.

37. Palazolli, MS. Self-starvation. New York: Jason Aronson, 1978.

38. Crisp AH, Burns T. The clinical presentation of anorexia nervosa in the male. Int J Eating Disord, 1983; 2:5-11.

39. Herzog DB, Norman DK, Gordon C, Pepose M. Sexual conflict and eating disorders in 27 males. Am J Psychiatry, 1984; 141:989-90.

40. Yates A, Leehey K, Shisslak C. Running: an analogue of anorexia? New Eng J Med, 1983; 308:251-5.

41. Garfinkel PE, Some recent observations on the pathogenesis of anorexia nervosa. Can J Psychiatry, 1981; 26:218-22.

42. Bruch H. Four decades of eating disorders. In Garner DM and Garinkel PE. Handbook of Psychotherapy for Anorexia Nervosa and Bulimia. New York: Guilford Press, 1985:7-18.

43. Dunn PK, Ondercin P. Personality variables related to compulsive eating in college women. J Clin Psychol, 1979; 37:43-9.

44. Sitnick T, Katz JL. Sex role identity and anorexia nervosa. Int J Eating Disord, 1984; 3:81-99.

45. Baker-Miller J. Toward a new psychology of women. Boston: Beacon Press, 1976.

46. Dyrenforth SR, Wooley OW, Wooley SC. A woman's body in a man's world: a review of findings on body image and weight control. In Kaplan JR. A woman's conflict: The special relationship between women and food. Englewood Cliffs: Prentice Hall, 1980:31-57.

47. Bennett W, Gurin J. The dieter's dilemma. New York: Basic Books, 1982.

48. Reichard S. A re-examination of 'studies in hysteria'. Psychoanalytic Quarterly, 1956; 25:155-77.

49. Bram S, Eger D, Halmi KA. Anorexia nervosa and personality type: a preliminary report. Int J Eating Disord, 1983; 2:67-73.

50. Johnson C. Bulimia: a psychoeducational approach. Lecture at Second Annual Conference of the Center for the Study of Anorexia and Bulimia, New York: November, 1983.

51. Swift WJ, Stern S. The psychodynamic diversity of anorexia nervosa. Int J Eating Disord, 1982; 2:27-35.

52. Freud S. Dora. New York: Collier Books, 1962.

53. Erikson E. Insight and responsibility. New York: WW Norton, 1964.

54. Smith-Rosenberg C. The hysterical woman: Sex roles in 19th century America. Social Research, 1972; 39:652-75.

55. Fairburn WRR. Observations on the nature of hysterical states. Br J Med Psychol, 1951; 27:105-25.

56. Garner DM, Garfinkel PE, Schwartz D. Cultural expectations of thinness in women. Psychol Rep., 1980; 47:483-91.

57. Wooley SC, Wooley OW. Anorexia and obesity. In Brodsky AM, Hare-Mustin RT, eds. Women and psychotherapy. New York: The Guilford Press, 1980:135-158.

58. Shaping Up: The worldwide fitness boom. Newsweek, International Edition, 1984 Sept 10:34-38.

59. Epling WF, Pierce WD, Stefan L. A theory of activity based anorexia. Int J Eating Disord, 1983; 3:27-46.

60. Smith N. Excessive weight loss and food aversion in athletes simulating anorexia nervosa. Pediatrics, 1980; 66:139-42.

61. Beumont PJV, Touyz SW, Hook S. Excessive exercise in anorexia nervosa. Presented at Third International Conference of Eating Disorders, Swansea, Wales, September, 1984.

62. Bandura A. Social learning theory. General Learning Press, 1971.

63. Brown R. (ed.) Children and television. Beverly Hills: Sage Publication, 1976.

64. Fonda J, McCarthy M. Women coming of age. New York: Simon and Schuster, 1984.

65. The number of articles reported in the *Reader's Guide* increased from a total of two in 1972 to 14 in 1983. Some representative selections are: Ramsey J. Anorexia Nervosa: dying of thinness. MS. 5:103-6; When dieting goes wild, *U.S. News and World Report,* 1978 85:62; Conley B. My Sister and I tried to out-diet each other with some pretty scary results. *Glamour,* 1979; 77:38ff; Stein B. Dangerous eat-and purge disorder called bulimia strikes young women. *People* 1981; 16:47-8.

66. Mazel J. The Beverly Hills diet. New York: Macmillan, 1981.

67. Mirkin GB, Shore RN. The Beverly Hills diet: dangers of the newest weight loss fad. JAMA, 1981; 246:2235-7.

68. Wooley OW, Wooley S. The Beverly Hills eating disorder: the mass marketing of anorexia nervosa. Int J Eating Disord, 1982; 1:57-68.

69. Dwyer JT, Feldman J, Myer J. The social psycology of dieting. Journal of Health and Social Behavior, 1970; 11:269-87.

70. Rodin J, Silberstein L, Striegel-Moore R. Women and weight: A normative discontent. In the Nebraska Symposium of Motivation, vol 32. Lincoln: University of Nebraska Press, 1985:1268-307.

71. Gandour MJ. Bulimia: clinical description, assessment, etiology, and treatment. Int J Eating Disord, 1984; 3:3-38.

72. Askevold F. Social class and psychosomatic illness. Psychother Psychosom, 1982; 38:256-9.

73. Kalucy RS, Crisp AH, Harding B. A study of 56 families with anorexia nervosa. British Journal of Medical Psychology, 1977; 50:381-9.

74. Garfinkel PE, Garner DM, Rose J, et al. A comparison of characterics in the families of patients with anorexia nervosa and normal controls. Psychol Med,

1983; 13:821-8.

75. Minuchin S, Rosman BL, Baker L. Psychosomatic families: Anorexia nervosa in context. Cambridge: Harvard University Press, 1978.

76. Blue R. The use of punishment in treatment of anorexia nervosa. Psychological Reports, 1979; 44: 743-6. Cited in Garfinkel and Garner, 1982: 251.

77. Branch CHH, Eurman LJ. Social attitudes toward patients with anorexia nervosa. Am J Psychiatry, 1980; 137:631-2.

78. Mackenzie M. The distrust of pleasure in affluent societies: anthropology and the concept of culture in eating disorders. Paper presented at Third International Conference on Anorexia and Related Disorders. Swansea, Wales: September, 1984.

79. Sontag S. Illness as metaphor. New York: Farrar, Struass, and Giroux, 1978.

80. Herzog D. Bulimia: the secretive syndrome. Psychosomatics, 1982; 23:481-7.

81. Hsu LKG. The etiology of anorexia nervosa. Psychol Med, 1983; 13:231-8.

82. Faltus F. Anorexia nervosa in Czechoslovakia. Int J Eating Disord, 1986; 5:581-585.

83. Szmuckler G, McCance C, McCrone L et al. Anorexia nervosa: a psychiatric case register study from Aberdeen. Psychol Med, 1986; 16:49-58.

84. Pyle R, Halvorson P, Neuman P et al. The increasing prevalence of bulimia in freshman college students. Int J Eating Disord, 1986; 5:631-648.

85. Olmsted M, Garner DM. The significance of self-induced vomiting as a weight-control method among non-clinical samples. Int J Eating Disord, 1986; 5:683-700.

Chapter 14

Family Structure of Interpersonal Relationships in the Eating Disorders

Sheldon Z. Kramer

Much of the early and current literature on bulimia and related eating disorders implicitly assumed or openly postulated a linear model of development and treatment. The linear model includes all the therapeutic methodologies that focus on the individual patient. Traditionally, these approaches attended to the medical-neurological, psychodynamic, and behavioral aspects of the disorder.

Minuchin et al [1] discuss the differences between the linear and systems model; they state that:

> the system model posits a circular movement of parts that affect each other. The system can be activated at any number of points and feedback mechanisms are operative at many points. The activation and regulation of the system can be done by system members or by forces outside the system. In the linear model, the behavior of the individual is seen as sparked by others. It presumes an action and a reaction, a stimulus and a response, or a cause and effect. In the systems paradigm, every part of a system is seen as organizing and being organized by other parts. An individual's behavior is both caused and causative. A beginning or an end are defined only by arbitrary framing and punctuating. The action of one part is simultaneously the interrelationship of other parts of the system.

Sluzki [2] discusses how the emphasis on systems-oriented approaches reflects its main concern with patterns of symptom maintenance in contrast to the process of symptom production. Sluzki states:

> The hypothesis about the patterns of symptom maintenance is drawn through observing and probing the interactional context of the symptoms in the present. This view is based on the premise that, regardless of their ultimate origin, symptoms or conflicts of any sort can only persist if they are maintained by ongoing interactional patterns. (p. 275)

An important issue is the emphasis on familial interactions and styles. Sluzki adds:

> The guiding question is how the interpersonal matrix composed of the behaviors of all the participants, supports the symptomn rather than what caused the symptom to appear. The why in a symptom is therefore by-passed, in favor of the explanation of how, that is, of those behaviors of each and all the participants that contribute at present to the persistence of maintenance of the symptomatic behavior. (p. 274)

Sluzki elaborates on how his position departs radically from traditional psychiatric thinking. He discusses how the systemic paradigm will take focus away from the process of symptom production (ie, why did the symptom occur?) to the patterns of symptom maintenance (how is the symptom maintained?). He states:

> That persisting symptoms and patterns may lose ties with the collective conflict that triggered or anchored them in their origin. It could even be proposed, within this paradigm, that many collectively maintained symptoms do not have a discernible triggering conflict at all, and that their existence is the result of random phenomena that became anchored progressively by all the participants of the collective, as the symptoms-maintaining patterns became organizing principles for the group: they insure family rituals routines, they introduce order, they become cherished markers of collective identity. (p. 275)

Sluzki [2] states that the systemic paradigm requires a shift in epistemology that gave birth to the field of family therapy.

Clinicians and researchers have been trying to distinguish different subtypes of anorexic patients. The focus of study has been dividing those anorexics who continuously restrict their food intake in contrast with those who have clear-cut episodes of self-induced vomiting to prevent digestion of food. This latter description is associated with bulimia [3-7]. There has also been a population of patients identified who have bulimia but maintain a relatively normal weight [7-12]. There is little systematic research in comparing these subtypes with one another. This chapter will focus on current theories and empirical research regarding familial interactions and relationships as well as general systemic factors on the maintenance of eating disorders. More specifically, this chapter will review the current knowledge regarding the family structure of interpersonal relations and how familial patterns manifest themselves in the anorexic subtypes.

ANOREXIC FAMILY SYSTEMS

Family therapists have approached the problem of anorexia nervosa as reflecting a specific type of family interactive style [1,13-19]. On the surface, anorexic families appear to have a perfect, ideal environment that reflects a calm, orderly demeanor between family members. However, when anorexic families are more closely observed, their interactions appear superficial and empty. There is seldom any expression of affection or warmth [19]. When feelings are expressed, they are usually overintellectualized [18,20]. Family members

do not take a specific stand on an issue, and therefore, it is easy to get confused as to who is expressing a position [21]. Anorexic families have a low tolerance for watching others in the family suffer. As a consequence, offspring are extremely sheltered [18]. Parental dyads appear secure, although there may be underlying dissatisfactions and tensions; these feelings are usually submerged and not discussed [17-20]. Bruch [20] suggests that the parents of anorexics appear to have loveless marriages. There is a tendency for the parents to put high expectations on their anorexic offspring to overcompensate for their own frustrations in one another. There are also descriptions of how the anorexic unites her parents by remaining ill [22].

Yager [23], in a review article on family issues and anorexia, describes how anectodal reports of parental personality styles as well as parent-child interactions show a great amount of variability. Mothers' relationships with daughters are reported by some to be overinvolved, by others to be ambivalent, and by still others to be rejecting. Yager cites studies where there are reports of "normal" relationships between parents and their children. Despite these contradictory observations noted between mother-child interactions, some general consistent themes do emerge. Anorexic mothers tend to foster ambitions for high achievement in their daughters. Mothers are said to overly invest themselves in their daughters because of feelings of frustration in their own career goals. Mothers of anorexics are involved socially, but they have a lack of intimate friends. Many times, the anorexic daughter is mother's confidant [20]. Because of underlying dissension in the marital dyad, mothers turn to their daughters to fulfill their empty lives [24]. The overinvolvement between mothers and anorexic daughters reflects difficulty with mothers separating from their own mothers [19,24]. With the overinvolvement between mother and anorexic daughter, there are also reports of lack of warmth and understanding in this relationship [19,25].

There are also wide variations in father-daughter dyads. Some descriptions of anorexic fathers depict them as kind and affectionate, while others report passive, ineffectual, and weak behaviors; in addition, they are peripheral to the family [26,27]. There are descriptions of father and daughter coalitions, however; it should be noted that these patterns have been described more in anorexic bulimic (patients who are currently showing a combination of anorexic and bulimic symptoms or have a history of one symptom while currently manifesting the other) and normal-weight bulimic families (Schwartz RC, Psychologist, Family Systems Program, Chicago Institute for Juvenile Research and Department of Psychiatry, University of Illinois, College of

Medicine, Chicago, Illinois, personal communication, 1982).

Taipale et al [24] report alcoholism and infantile behavior in fathers of anorexics and bulimics. Twenty-five percent of the fathers of 120 anorexics showed signs of depression at the beginning and near the end of treatment. The anorexic's father's depression being more visible at the end of treatment supports the notion of family homeostasis in anorexia and bulimia. Crisp et al [13] compared degrees of neuroticism of parents of anorexic patients with a control group before and after weight gain of their daughters. It was found that when their anorexic daughters' weight returned to normal, there was an increase in psychological turmoil in the parents. This finding was especially evident in the bulimic subjects.

Systems concepts regarding anorexic families have been most clearly delineated by Minuchin et al [1]. Minuchin and his coresearchers have postulated a group of family system characteristics that reflect the transactional dynamics of "psychosomatic families" of patients with juvenile onset diabetes mellitus, bronchial asthma, and anorexia nervosa. One such characteristic is *enmeshment*, a transactional style where family members are overinvolved with and overresponsive to one another. Each member develops poorly differentiated perceptions of one another and of themselves. Family members intrude on each other's thoughts, feelings, activities, and communications. There is extreme sensitivity among family members and minor upsets are responded to rapidly. Shifting alliances among family members are also observed. In some enmeshed families, one parent enlists a child's participation in a coalition against the other parent. This reflects a blurring of generational boundaries. This pattern hinders separation and individuation of family members. At times in the family life cycle it is necessary for a family to be enmeshed. For example, when an infant is born, there is a mutual overinvolvement between the parents and the newborn; however, if this extreme closeness continues to occur as the child grows, it delays the natural growth of independence within the child. A child growing up in an enmeshed family learns that loyalty to her family is of primary importance, and she may act in a manner to get approval from others as opposed to seeking self-approval. The parents in an enmeshed family are hypervigilant with regard to all the girl's activities. The anorexic girl's body seems to belong to the whole family, because so much energy is focused on it.

Another characteristic of the anorexic family is *overprotectiveness*, in which members have an extremely high concern for one another. Nurturant and protective responses are sought and supplied most of the time. Critical remarks are usually softened by soothing responses. Parental control over the children is the norm in the anorexic family. In addition, anorexic children can be very overconcerned and protect their parents.

The third main characteristic is *rigidity;* these families tend to deny the need for change, and they preserve accustomed patterns of interaction and behaviors. Efforts at changing the family system by any member initiates a reverberation throughout that system to maintain the status quo and prevent change from occurring. The rigidity can be especially seen when the family cycle usually points to a need for accommodation to a natural change such as when an adolescent is requesting more independence. In anorexic families, it is found that family members insist on retaining accustomed methods of interaction. Because issues that threaten change are not allowed to surface, these families remain in an extreme state of prolonged submerged stress; however, they present themselves as normal except for their offspring's medical problems.

The fourth transactional pattern is *avoidance of conflict and lack of conflict resolution.* There is low tolerance for overt conflict within the family. Any discussion involving differences of opinion and issues of autonomy and control are avoided. Some eating disordered families deny the existence of any problems and are highly invested in concensus and harmony. Other psychosomatic families disagree openly, but constant interruptions and subject changes are used as a way to deflect or diffuse conflict. The resolution of these conflicts would require some degree of individual autonomy, which is gravely lacking in these families. Consequently, there is no utilization of any methods that can lead to the negotiation of differences. Problems are left unresolved and are perpetuated by avoidance maneuvers.

A fifth system characteristic is the role that the child or identified patient plays in the family's pattern of avoiding conflict. Viewed from a transactional point of view, the identified patient acts as a regulator in the family system. Often, in psychosomatic families, the symptomatic child is involved in parental conflict in different ways.

The typical patterns of child-parental overinvolvement are triangulation, parent-child coalition, and detouring. In the first two patterns, triangulation and parent-child coalitions, the spouses are in conflict with each other, and the identified patient is openly pressed to ally with one parent against the other. In *triangulation,* the child or identified patient is put in a position of splitting her loyalites to both her parents. She will not be able to express herself without siding with one parent against the other. In a *parent-child coalition,* the child tends to move into a stable coalition with one parent against the other. The third child-parent overinvolvement is *detouring.* In this pattern, both the spouses unite and blame or scapegoat their sick child. This maneuver serves to deflect any sign of marital strife or even minor differences.

Minuchin's psychosomatic family model assumes that family structure does not independently cause a particular disorder. Organ dysfunction is present and the child or identified patient is physiologically vulnerable. This model includes a perspective that focuses on a biopsychosocial model of the development of a disease process. However, the paradigm focuses predominantly on familial influences.

In the case of anorexic families and psychosomatic families in general, it is characteristic that focus is on bodily functions. In families with an anorexic child, the whole family often has a special concern with such matters as eating, table manners, diets, and food fads (Minuchin, p. 61) [1]. Family interactional styles influence the child's health by acting as a catalyst in the production and maintenance of psychophysiological processes.

In order to test the generality of the above observations on the anorexic family as well as on psychosomatic families in general, a formal controlled study of these assumptions was conducted by Minuchin[1]. Forty-five families were studied. Three psychosomatic groups were included; eleven families with anorexics, ten families with asthmatics, and nine families with psychosomatic diabetic children were included. Two control groups were also used. Eight families were included where diabetes was under medical control; however, this group manifested behavioral problems. In addition, seven families with "normal" behavior or nonpsychosomatic diabetes were included in the study.

Minuchin and his colleagues set up a standardized interactive task for each family. Each session was videotaped and at a later time scored by independent raters on operationalized constructs of enmeshment, overprotectiveness, conflict avoidance, and rigidity. In general, the results of this part of the study indicated that the more dysfunctional families were more extreme on the above dimensions compared with the normal control groups. In addition, the anorexic families showed the most extreme patterns compared with the dysfunctional family contrast groups.

A second part of the study involved setting up live family diagnostic interview where the interviewer first induced stress in the marital dyad beyond its usual tolerance level and then brought only their psychosomatic offspring into the room. This task was set up to be able to observe systematically the role that the child played in detouring parental conflict. The results indicated that the parents of the psychosomatics tended to be more extreme on avoiding conflict and indeed used detouring mechanisms on to the child more often than did the contrast groups. The anorexic groups appeared to be the most extreme in diffusing conflict and by focusing on their offspring.

It should be noted that the above reported research study does not describe in detail how the transactional constructs were operationalized or rated. In addition, no statistical analyses were reported. In sum, although Minuchin and his colleagues describe their controlled research, this major study remains largely an anecdotal account of the psychosomatic family. Without a detailed critical account of how the transactional constructs were operationalized, rated, and statistically analyzed, one cannot scientifically objectively judge the outcome of the results.

Minuchin and colleagues also conducted a simultaneous physiological experiment with a sample of the diabetic children and their families during the live family diagnostic interview. Before these experiments it was found that the children who had exacerbations in their diabetic conditions showed a higher degree of free fatty acids (FFA) in their blood. FFA can be used as a biological marker for emotional arousal. During the live diagnostic family sessions, blood samples were drawn from both the parents and the diabetic child. As the interviewer induced conflict in the marital dyad, there were increases in the FFA level in both spouses; however, when the diabetic child entered the interview room, the parents' FFA levels decreased, and the child's increased. In fact, it was reported that the child's FFA level continued to increase after the induced stress in the marital couple subsided. Overall, the psychosomatic groups showed a greater significance of sensitivity to family conflict compared with the contrast groups.

These results were said to give further evidence of the role of the psychosomatic child in the context of his family. It is suggested that these physiological results support the concepts of parental protectiveness and reinforce family homeostasis. With the psychosomatic child's FFA level continuing to rise after the marital stress was alleviated, it was suggested that the psychosomatic symptom is maintained within the family system dealing with unresolved family conflict.

Although the above physiological study reinforces the psychosomatic family paradigm, the study can be criticized due to the small number of subjects. In addition, diabetics were used to generalize these patterns with anorexic families as well as all psychosomatic families in general. This indeed may not be the case. Other physiological studies within a systemic paradigm are needed to show further evidence of the interrelationship between psychosomatic illness and family dysfunction.

Selvini-Palazzoli [17], an Italian psychiatrist, worked with anorexic families at the Milan Center of Family

Studies. She observed family system characteristics similar to those described by Minuchin. She reports that communication patterns are extremely faulty; family members discount messages sent by others. The parents are described as unwilling to take responsibility or a leadership role; each parent tends to blame faulty decisions on the other. Blame can radically be shifted from one member to another. For example, mothers are said to blame their inability to help with decision-making on her overinvolvement with taking care of the children. All decisions are viewed as "for the good" of another (p. 209). Selvini-Palazzoli states that each parent feels victimized and views his or her position in the family as a personal sacrifice to the family. She describes the children in this family acting as a buffer for parental disharmony. She calls this state of affairs a "three way matrimony" (p. 211). The child is said to be more focused on her parents than her own individual development. When the anorexic child attempts to separate, the parents act to block this out to aid in maintaining homeostatis processes.

BULIMIC FAMILIES

Although there have been many anecdotal reports on family systems characteristics of the anorexic, there is a paucity of literature on bulimic family systems.

Schwartz [28] reports a family therapy case of an identified patient who is a 17-year-old normal-weight bulimic female. This reported case is a part of an outcome study of family therapy with bulimics. Schwartz reports that the bulimic families' structure was not hidden, unlike many anorexic families. He states that one could observe the distress in the family through the open criticism toward the identified patient. The mother and the identified patient, at times, would form a coalition against the father. At other times, coalitions shifted with the identified patient and father allied against the mother. It is interesting to note that Schwartz' description of more open criticism in bulimic families has also been reported in families of drug addicts and abusers. But drug-abusing families show more detouring-attacking mechanisms instead of the detouring-protecting patterns in the anorexic restricter families [29]. It is easy to understand how parents could be more overprotective with a daughter who appears like a skeleton as opposed to a self-indulgent child. Both detouring-attacking and detouring-protective processes serve as homeostatic mechanisms to deflect marital tensions. Although some similarities exist between drug abuse and the bulimic family populations, these need to be further researched.

Lemberg and Bohanske [30] contrasted the anorexic restricter, anorexic-bulimic, and normal-weight bulimic family system with one another. Their observation

through case study suggests that anorexic-bulimic families are more conflict ridden than the conflict-avoidant pattern in the restrictor anorexic population. They categorize the anorexic-bulimic families as more disjointed and less cohesive. In addition, they view the family structure as being more chaotic. In contrast, with the anorexic-restricter group, the anorexic-bulimic's symptoms are less protective of family conflict, but more a "protest." The bulimic behavior is depicted as a symptom that reflects the general chaos in the system and the lack of system response to the developmental needs of the adolescent or young adult. Lemberg and Bohanske state that the anorexic bulimic patients remain enmeshed in the chaotic family process whether living in or out of the home. They also state that the family's chaos is reflected in the finding that the families are unavailable because of divorce, distance, or general family discord. Lemberg and Bohanske also compare the normal-weight bulimic to the restricter anorexic and the anorexic-bulimic groups. They state that the family system model appears less applicable in the normal-weight bulimic groups. They state that, although unresearched, bulimic symptoms in normal-weight individuals appear to occur in patients who have good premorbid family adjustment. However, they state that these women are currently under psychological stress that is related to the young adults' developmental period and not to the family of origin's system. He concludes that bulimic behavior appears to be activated more in the social context with conflict around intimacy and peer relations. This concept contradicts the family systems notion that the bulimic symptom is embedded in the family context and helps the family to maintain a homeostatic equilibrium. Thus, Lemberg and Bohanske appear to be extending some bulimic symptomatology to reflect individual psychopathology that is separate from the family system.

Gawelek [31], in her case study of five binge-purgers, found the daughters to perceive their families as "ideal," but relationships were conflicted and strained. There were also reports of more open conflict with the mother [18,31,32]. In contrast with the anorexic, the bulimic rebels during her development, with increased dissension at adolescence. In contrast, anorexics are cited as harboring repressed hostile feelings toward the mother, although, on the surface, mother-daughter relations appear to be nonproblematic or conflicting.

Hicks [33] studied 24 bulimic women who met DSM III criteria for bulimia through a questionnaire and semistructured interviews. One of the main goals in the study was to investigate the bulimic perceptions of their family of origin. The average age of the women was 28.25 years. Although all the women met DSM II criteria for bulimia, five of the subjects had anorexia during their adolescence. The majority of subjects reported their parents' marriage as unhappy, frustrated, and full of unresolved conflicts. There was evidence of stable coalitions between mother and daughter against father or some third person, usually a grandparent. Although there was overinvolvement between mother and daughter, the relationships were cited as highly ambivalent. There were reports of conflict-avoidance patterns between mother and daughter; however, there were also reports of open fighting and expressions of conflict without resolution. Fathers were perceived as unavailable and uninvolved with home life. Fathers were described as being unavailable in terms of work involvements, alcoholic abuse, and physical or psychological ailments. Fathers were also reported to be prone to outbursts of temper as well as actual incidents of physical abuse. There were some instances that daughters reported being fearful of their fathers. Some of the subjects in Hicks' sample felt they had to cater to their father's narcissistic needs. Overall, women were mixed in their description of childhood closeness with their fathers. Although fathers were reported as being unavailable, descriptions of paternal figures indicate a strong presence in the lives of bulimics (p. 156).

Other researchers cited fathers of bulimics as possessing a high degree of obsessionality and problems with impulse control [22]. While fathers of anorexics are seen as peripheral to the system, the same studies indicate the binge-purger's father may be the object of "hero worship" [8]. He is similar to the anorexic father who places high value on achievement. Gawelek [31] also reports an emotional closeness between bulimic women and their fathers. The closeness in their relationships are remembered in childhood; however, bulimics perceive their fathers to be more distant and peripheral with the onset of puberty.

Hicks [33] reports that leaving home for bulimics was wrought with difficulties; often these would be times when severe binge-purge episodes would occur. Many of the subjects reported that there was an increase of turmoil in their parents' marriage when they left home resulting, at times, in separation or divorce. Other subjects reported increased psychiatric symptoms in the parents, usually with the father who showed an increase in alcohol consumption and affective disorders.

Hicks also reported sibling relationships of bulimics as being highly competitive, usually with brothers.

Roots, et al [45] in their recent book entitled *Bulimia: A Systems Approach to Treatment*, anecdotally describes three types of bulimic families that they have observed clinically: the perfect family, the overprotective family and the chaotic family. The perfect and the overprotective families reflect the anorexic restricter family found in Minuchin's early research. On the other hand, the chaotic family has characteristics similar to their anorexic restricter counterparts such as enmeshment and lack of conflict resolution. However, the chaotic bulimic families have been observed to have more inconsistent rules and greater expression of open anger and conflict.

EMPIRICALLY BASED STUDIES ON FAMILY SYSTEMS OF ANOREXICS AND BULIMICS

Empirical-controlled studies on family systems and eating disorders are scarce. Sonne [34] cites Sabovich's study that systematically examined anorexic's parents' dependency, insecurity, boundary difficulties, and maladaptive management of sexual and aggressive impulses through the use of psychological measures. Sabovich matched the sample of anorexic parents with other parents of emotionally disturbed outpatient and inpatient girls. Results suggested that the parental dyad of anorexics exhibited more insecurity, dependency, and difficulty with impulse management compared with all other contrast groups.

Sonne [34] also reported a study by Sonne and Goldstein using the same populations as Sabovich. The research explored the extent of overinvolvement exhibited between family members in a simulated interaction. The simulation involved each parent role playing with his or her daughter as if she were in the room. Parental communications were coded for "acknowledgment," "direction," or "projection" of the child's inner state. Mothers of anorexics pointed to a communication pattern of high direction and low acknowledgment compared with mothers in the contrast groups. Anorexic fathers showed a mixture of roles including a passive-peripheral role, and at times, a more active, subtly intrusive role.

Another empirical study by Sonne [34] investigated transactions in family systems that had an anorexic offspring. She focused mainly on studying the pattern of enmeshment and conflict avoidance patterns in these families. Her sample included 11 anorexic female inpatients, five of other inpatient emotionally disturbed adolescents, and 27 outpatient emotionally disturbed teenagers. In order for the subjects to be included in the study, both mothers and fathers needed to participate in the research. The interactions focused on mother-daughter and father-daughter dyads. These dyadic interactions involved a discussion of a problem area that was of mutual concern. The interactions were tape recorded, and the session was transcribed on paper. The transcription was then coded on the degree of intrusiveness, evasion, and disagreement. The results were the opposite of those hypothesized. Anorexic families showed less intrusive or enmeshed behaviors compared with the other contrast groups. This was due to low parental intrusion; however, anorexic adolescents were seen as equal or more controlling toward parents contrasted to the other adolescent comparison groups. In addition, the anorexics made more inferences about their parents' feelings, attitudes, opinions, motives, or behaviors without checking out if these perceptions were valid. Anorexic families in this study did show a significantly higher conflict-avoidant pattern in mother-daughter interaction compared with contrast groups. However, the characteristics of conflict avoidance between father-daughter dyads was not significantly different from comparison groups. Sonne noted that anorexic adolescents in part tried more than controls to engage their fathers in a more personal interaction. However, compared with controls, anorexic fathers tended to distance themselves from their daughters when they tried to push for more involvement. Overall, there was a more diversified transactional pattern between father and anorexic daughters as compared to mother-anorexic dyadic sequences.

Sonne's results of less enmeshment in anorexic adolescents contradicts Minuchin's findings. She discusses these results and offers explanation. She states that the operationalized behavior she used perhaps did not truly match up with the construct of enmeshment. In addition, her control groups differed from Minuchin's; they were composed of other emotionally disturbed adolescents in comparison with Minuchin's use of other psychosomatic physically ill and "normal" groups. Another confounding variables was the emphasis on conflict in experimental interactions. Consequently, Sonne thought this may have actually produced a tendency for the dyad to increase the avoidance of conflict, thus, creating an illusion of harmony. However, it is in this writer's opinion that the dyad was not stressed enough to see the enmeshed patterns become amplified. It should be noted that Minuchin actually induced a crisis in the family for change to occur. At these times, one could clearly see the enmeshed and conflict avoidance patterns in these families.

Sonne [34] compared a subset of her anorexic patients who were additionally bulimic and compared them with the other anorexic restricters. Results indicated three of the four anorexic nonrestricters showed patterns of both high intrusion and high disagreements with their mothers. No correlation between bulimic symptoms and level of disagreement were apparent. Sonne hypothesizes that the pattern of greater intrusion and conflict may be evidence of extreme ambivalence with both dependency and hostility being acted out. In addition, the greater ambivalence in the bulimic group may lead to a greater amount of conflict expression without resolution.

Yager [23], in a preliminary pilot study, compared more than 30 anorexic and anorexic-bulimic patients, age 20, using the Family Environment Scale. When he administered the test separately to each parent and patient, each person reported a very different family environment. However, these data were not statistically analyzed.

Garner et al [35] compared groups of 59 restricter and nonrestricter anorexics with normal-weight bulimics on a family assessment scale that measures task accomplishments, role performance, communication, affective expression, affective involvement, control, and value and norms. They report an extremely high similarity on all of the subscales for both the anorexic-bulimic and normal-weight bulimic groups. The scores on the family measures, except for role performance, indicated more severe pathology in both the bulimic groups compared with the anorexic restricter group.

Strober [36] administered two family measures to the parents of anorexic and anorexic-bulimic patients. Each set of parents jointly completed the Moos Family Environment Scale (FES) [37] for the purpose of describing family patterns before the onset of their daughter's eating disorder. The parents also completed the Locke Wallace short marital adjustment test [38].

On the FES, anorexic-bulimic families showed significantly higher levels of conflictual interactions and expressions of negativity among members; in contrast, anorexic families were associated more with greater cohesion (ie, mutual support and concern among family members) and organization (ie, clarity of structure, rules, and division of responsibilities). On the marital adjustment scale, disharmony was found in both groups; however, significantly higher levels were reported by parents of anorexic-bulimics compared with anorexics.

Strober matched his two samples on age (x years = 15.7) and duration of illness (x months = 11.9). However, he did not match his samples with a normal control groups. If one compares Strober's findings with the normative data for normal families cited in the FES manual, there are contradictions that exist between Strober's results and the majority of system theorists' observations of anorexic families. Anorexic families perceived themselves as significantly higher on cohesiveness than anorexic-bulimics; however, anorexic-bulimics scored lower on the cohesiveness scale when compared with FES normal family groups. According to Minuchin's theory, dysfunctional or symptomatic families would be seen on the extremes of the cohesiveness dimension. Minuchin labels extremely high cohesion as enmeshment and extremely low cohesion as disengagement. Both of these extremes are considered dysfunctional. Functional normal families are cited as having a balance on the enmeshment-disengagement continuum. Therefore, one can conclude that Strober's results showed that the anorexic-bulimic families were more disengaged. This finding contradicts Minuchin's theory as anorexic families are viewed as all enmeshed or extremely cohesive.

Another contradiction between Minuchin's structural theory and Strober's research findings is that on the FES conflict scale (extent to which the open expressions of anger, aggression, and conflictual interactions are characteristic of the family) is that both anorexic and anorexic-bulimic groups are seen as higher than normals on this dimension. According to Minuchin's theory, all anorexic families would be more extreme on conflict avoidance than functional-normal families.

A critical evaluation of Strober's study shows several confounding variables. Family measures were administered and analyzed from only the parents' perspective; different scores could have been obtained if the identified patient's responses were analyzed, since her perception of her family could be markedly dissimilar from her parents'. In addition, parents were asked to fill out the FES retrospectively, before their daughters' symptoms. Since the mean time between onset of symptoms and hospitalization was 11.9 months, perceptions of the family environment could have been distorted. Another weakness of Strober's study was the absence of a normal matched control group. This would be important in order to more fully understand and illuminate theoretical notions between functional and dysfunctional families.

Another weakness of Strober's study is the use of only the FES to measure family structure. Epstein et al state that the instrument is a research-oriented assessment tool and therefore may not be applicable to clinical populations [39].

Kramer [40] studied the family systems characteristics of anorexic restricters, anorexic-bulimic, and normal-weight bulimic and compared them with a normal-weight control group. Two paper and pencil tests were used in the study, including the Family Environment Scale [37] and the Structural Family Interaction Scale [41]. In addition, an eating behavior survey was employed to assess the degree of bulimia and/or anorexia nervosa as well as other miscelleanous behaviors. An overall sample of 60 family triads consisting of mother, father, and daughters were used in the study. Eight anorexics, 20 anorexic-bulimics, 18 normal-weight bulimics, and 14 controls were included in the sample. The groups were matched on age (mean = 20 years), socioeconomic status (mean family income = $35,000), and family size (mean = five members). All of the subjects met criteria for the diagnosis of eating disorders as defined by the DSM III (modification in anorexic restricter

group had to be at least 15% below normal weight using insurance charts). Anorexic bulimics and normal-weight bulimics were also matched on severity of symptoms. All binged and vomited at least once a day. Most of the eating disordered subjects had been in some type of individual treatment in the past, but most of the samples were no longer currently engaged in therapy. All eating disordered subjects were recruited from outpatient therapists and self-help groups in the Southern California area.

Kramer [40] found that, in general, all the eating disorder groups were more similar than different on family systems characteristics. In addition, the eating disorder groups showed more dysfunctional family patterns than a normal control group. The anorexic-bulimic group yielded more dysfunctional patterns than the other contrast groups. Anorexic-bulimics perceived more mother overprotection, father overprotection, mother neglect, and less flexibility, mother-child conflict resolution and independence compared with anorexics, normal-weight bulimics, and controls. Anorexic restricters perceived the least parent management and the greatest triangulation maneuvers (each parent actively trying to get their daughter to be in coalition against the other parent) compared with anorexic-bulimic, normal-weight bulimic, and control groups. Another finding was that the general ordering of the contrast groups, in terms of the most to the least family dysfunction were the following: anorexic-bulimic, normal-weight bulimic, anorexic, and controls.

Kramer's study also yielded significant correlation coefficients suggesting that a relationship does exist between the type, severity, frequency, and/or set of bulimic symptoms and family systems variables. For example, Kramer found that the rapid intake of food was associated with the higher family rigidity and achievement orientations. In addition, the greater the amount of foods eaten during the binge, the less the family flexibility; and the greater the family's intellecutal orientation, the greater the frequency of self-induced vomiting. These findings may reflect how bulimic symptomatology helps to maintain chronic predictable patterns in the family system for homeostatic purposes. In addition, bulimic symptoms may represent a rebellion on the daughter's behalf to try to escape from family control and embedded values such as achievement and intellectualization. In addition, bulimic symptoms could be viewed as the daughter's manner in which she deals with her ambivalence over dependence versus independence.

Overall, Kramer's findings were consistent with Minuchin's psychosomatic paradigm. His findings also extend Minuchin's family systems model to include an-

Table 14.1 Summary of the Eating Disorder and Family Characteristics From Different Researchers

Researcher	Anorexics	Anorexic-Bulimics	Normal-Weight Bulimics
Boskind-Lodahl (1976)	Father pressures for high achievement Less involvement with father	—	Father pressures for achievement Father is worshipped as hero figure
Minuchin (1978)	Extremes on: Enmeshment Overprotection Conflict avoidance Rigidity Parent-child coalition Triangulation Detouring (Protective)	No different than anorexics	—
Gawelek (1979)	No rebellion during adolescence Conflict avoidance especially with mother	—	High control — rebels during adolescence Conflict expression, especially with mother
Sonne (1981)	Less enmeshment compared with other psychiatric groups Greater conflict avoidance compared with other psychiatric groups Fathers more peripheral	More enmeshment or high intrusion High levels of disagreements	—
Strober (1981)	Exteme on cohesion, and organization Less conflict, and expression	Less cohesion Less organization More conflict expression	—
Hicks (1982)	—	—	Stable coalition between mother and daughter — although relationship; highly ambivalent Distant fathers — both conflict avoidant and open conflict expressed (Sample — mixture of normal-weight bulimics and anorexic-bulimics)
Lemberg (1982)	More cohesion More conflict avoidance More rigidity	Less cohesive (but enmeshed) More conflict expression More chaos	Good pre-morbid Family adjustment
Schwartz (1982)	Conflict avoidance More mother-child coalition	—	Conflict expression without resolution More father-child coalition
Yager (1982)	No significant difference between anorexics and anorexic- bulimics	—	—
Kramer (1983)*	Less parent management and more triangulation compared with anorexic bulimic, normal-weight bulimic, and normal controls	More mother overprotection, father overprotection, mother neglect, rigidity (less flexibility), less mother-child conflict resolution, less independence compared with anorexics, normal-weight bulimics, and normal controls	
Garner and Garfinkel (1985)	Overall less severe family pathology	Both anorexic-bulimics and normal-weight bulimics bulimics greater family pathology	

Table 14.1 Summary of the Eating Disorder and Family Characteristics From Different Researchers (continued)

Researcher	Anorexics	Anorexic-Bulimics	Normal-Weight Bulimics
Kog, et al., (1985)** Humphrey (1986)		Anorexic-Bulimics greater isolation, detachment, conflict, less involvement compared to normal controls	
Casper (1986)		Anorexic-Bulimics greater intrusion compared to anorexic restrictors	
Root, et al.***			

*Overall, all eating disorder groups in general are more similar than different and all eating disorder groups in general are greater than normal controls. All results taken from Daughter's Perception of Her Family System.

**No consistant pattern profile among eating disorder groups.

***All eating disordered groups similar in enmeshment, triangulating, and lack of conflict resolution—bulimic families consist of perfect and protective configurations that are similar in anorexic restrictors. However some bulimic families have more chaos—less organization and more open conflict.

orexic subtypes; bulimic families, in general, are more dysfunctional in interactive style than the anorexic restricter family type.

Kog, et al [42] investigated Minuchin's psychosomatic family model through a pilot study of 10 families with both anorexic and bulimic patients. They utilized a series of in vivo standardized interactional tasks. The families were rated through paper and pencil measures as well as observational data via videotape. The researchers measured enmeshment, rigidity, overprotection and lack of conflict resolution.

The preliminary results of the Kog, et al study was that they did not find a specific or consistent interactional pattern. However, it should be noted that the subjects were heterogeneous including age ranges of young teenagers (mean age - 16) through young adults (mean age - 20). In addition, they studied mild and severe cases of eating disorder symptoms. Kog, et al criticize Minuchion's paradigm as being limited conceptually and methodologically.

Humphrey [43] compared patterns of family reactions in 16 bulimic-anorexic and 24 non-distressed family triads. The study used paper and pencil tests including the Family Environment Scale (FES) and the Family Adaptability and Cohesion evaluation scale (FACES). Each individual of the family triads including father, mother and daughter were tested. Results indicated that the bulimic-anorexic families experienced greater isolation, detachment, conflict, less involvement and support than did controls. The author concluded that bulimic-anorexic families seemed more hostile, and chaotic than they did overprotective, and over-involved

as had been reported for anorexic restricter families.

Casper [44] compared anorexic bulimics to anorexic restricters. Her preliminary results indicated that the anorexic bulimic families were more intrusive compared to the anorexic restricter group.

CONCLUSIONS

In summary, there are contradictory findings and observations between anorexic subtypes and family interactive styles. Table 1 gives a summary of all the eating disorders groups and corresponding family systems characteristics from different research previously discussed.

Many factors contribute to the variability of findings across eating disorder groups. Many studies have limited generalizability because of the small numbers in their sample. In addition, many studies recruit subjects who volunteered; therefore, subjects may have not been a true representation of all anorexics and bulimics. Many of the bulimics are secretive about their eating behavior, and those bulimics may be different from ones who are studied. Another problem when trying to synthesize and integrate findings between different studies is whether the subjects are inpatients or outpatients. Hospitalized patients may show different family characteristics (ie, more chaotic patterns) compared with non-hospitalized patients. A similar issue has to do with comparing studies that use subjects with varying degrees of severity of symptomatology. For example, Garner's study showing more equal extreme dysfunction in both anorexic-bulimic and normal-weight bulimic compared with restricter anorexics is inconsistent with Kramer's study where there were more similarity between all anorexic subtype groups on family characteristics as well as the anorexic-bulimic group showing the greatest degree of family dysfunction. The sample that Garner used appeared to be eating disordered groups that were more chronic and severe in their symptoms. Another limitation on issues of generalizability is due to age difference in samples studied. For example, Minuchin's sample was mainly composed of young adolescent females. In other studies (ie, Garner, Kramer, Kog), the mean age was significantly higher.

Another methodological problem that adds to difficulty in assessing family systems is that many studies use self-report measures that involve individual member's perceptions of their family functioning. One's perception of one's family organization could be very different from researchers who used observational data (ie, Minuchin).

Patterns of research such as Kog, et al need to be continued. Research is needed to break down many confounding variables to distinguish family system characteristics of anorexic subtypes from one another. Future studies could focus on comparing inpatient and outpatient populations, different age-groups, as well as intact and broken families with one another. Last, it would be highly desirable, although quite cumbersome, to design a study to assess the family structure through the use of videotape. Independent raters could score the family on a number of dependent variables and compare these results to self-report measures. This would allow family researchers to see if paper and pencil measures correlate with observations of family structure. The would also control for reporter bias and social desirability as confounding variables. In addition, it would give a great deal more validity to the assessment tools.

REFERENCES

1. Minuchin S, Rosman BL, Baker L. Psychosomatic families: Anorexia in context. Cambridge, MA: Harvard University Press, 1978:
2. Sluzki CE. Process of symptom production and patterns of symptom maintenance. Journal of Marital and Family Therapy, (July) 1981:
3. Beaumont P, George G, Smart D. 'Dieter's and 'vomiters and purgers' in anorexia nervosa. Psychological Medicine, 1976; 6:617-22.
4. Beaumont PJV. Further categorization of patients with anorexia nervosa. Australian and New Zealand Journal of Psychiatry, 1977; 11:223-6.
5. Casper AC, Eckert ED, Halmi KA, Goldberg SC, Dabis JM. Bulimia: Its incidence and clinical importance in patients with anorexia nervosa. Archives of General Psychiatry, 1980; 37:1030-5.

6. Garfinkel PE, Moldofsky H, Garner DM. The heterogeneity of anorexia nervosa: Bulimia as a distinct subgroup. Archives of General Psychiatry, 1980; 37:1036-40.
7. Russell GFM. Bulimia nervosa: an ominous varient of anorexia nervosa. Psychological Medicine, 1979; 9:429-48.
8. Boskind-Lodahl M. Cinderella's stepsisters: A feminist perspective on anorexia nervosa and bulimia. Journal of Women in Culture and Society, 1976; 2(2):342-56.
9. Halmi KA, Falk JR, Schwartz E. Binge eating and vomiting; a survey of a college population. Psychological Medicine, 1981; 11:697-706.
10. Herzog DB. Bulimia: The secretive syndrome. Psychosomatics, 1982; 23:5:481-7.
11. Johnson CL, Stuckey MK, Lewis LD, Schwartz DM. Bulimia: A survey of 316 cases. International Journal of Eating Disorders, 1982; 2(1):
12. Mitchell JE, Pyle RL. The bulimic syndrome in normal weight individuals: A review International Journal of Eating Disorders, 1982; Winter,
13. Crisp AH, Hading B, McGuinness B. Anorexia nervosa: psychoneurotic characteristics of parents' relationship to prognosis. Journal of Psychosomatic Research, 1974; 18:167-73.
14. Kalucy RS, Crisp AH, Harding B. A study of 56 families: Anorexia nervosa. British Journal of Medical Psychology, 1977; 47:349-61.
15. Liebman R, Minuchin S, Baker L. An integrated treatment program for anorexia nervosa. American Journal of Psychiatry, 1974; 131:432-6.
16. Rosman BL, Minuchin S, Liebman R. Family lunch session: An introduction to family therapy in anorexia nervosa. American Journal of Orthopsychiatry, 1975; 45:846-53.
17. Selvini-Palazzoli. Self-starvation: From individual to family therapy in the treatment of anorexia nervosa. Neww York: Jason Aronson, 1978:
18. Sours JA. Starving to death in a sea of objects: The anorexia nervosa syndrome. New York: Jason Aronson, 1980:
19. Wold P. Family structure in three cases of anorexia nervosa: The role of the father. American Journal of Psychiatry, 1973; 130:1394-7.
20. Bruch H. Eating disorders: Obesity, anorexia nervosa and the person within. New York: Basic Books, 1973:
21. Bruch H. The golden cage. Cambridge, MA: Harvard University Press, 1978:
22. Crisp AH, Kalucy RS, Lacy JH, Harding B. The long-term prognosis in anorexia nervosa; some factors predictive of outcome. In Vigersky L (Ed.) Anorexia Nervosa. New York: Raven Press, 1977:
23. Yager J. Family issues in the pathogenesis of anorexia nervosa. Psycosomatic Medicine, 1982; 44(1):
24. Taipale V, Tuimi O, Auhee N. Anorexia nervosa: An illness of two generations. Acto paldopsychiatrics, 1971; 38:21-5.
25. Guiora A. Dysorexia, a psychopathological study of an-

orexia and bulimia. American Journal of Psychiatry, 1967; 124:39.

26. Sours JA. The anorexia nervosa syndrome. International Journal of Psychoanalysis, 1974; 55:567-79.

27. Bemis KN. Current approaches to the etiology and treatment of anorexia nervosa. Psychological Bulletin of the American Psychological Association, 1978; 85(3):593-617.

28. Schwartz RC. Bulimia and family therapy: A case study vol. 2, The International Journal of Eating Disorders, Autumn 1982; 1:75-82.

29. Stanton DM, Fodel TC. The family therapy of drug abuse and addiction. New York: Guilford Press, 1982:

30. Lemberg R, Bohanse J. The "Psychosomatic family" revisited: A consideration of anorexia nervosa, bulimia nervosa, and bulimia as distinct clinical syndromes. Presented at American Association for Marriage and Family Therapy, 40th Annual Conference, Dallas, Texas: 1982.

31. Gawelek N. The binge-purger: A descriptive study. (Dissertation). Boston University, 1979:

32. Boskind-Ladahl M, White W. The definition and treatment of bulimarexia in college women-a pilot study. Journal of the American College Health Associates, 1970;

33. Hicks CF. Family and cultural factors in the development of eating disorders: A study of feminine identity in twenty-four bulimic women. (Dissertation). University of Massachusetts, 1982:

34. Sonne JL. Anorexia nervosa: an examination of family transactions. (Dissertation). Los Angeles: University of California, 1981:

35. Garner DM, Garfinkel PE, O'Shaughnessy MN. The validity of the distinction between bulimia with and without anorexia nervosa. Am J Psychiatry, 1985; 142:5.

36. Storber M. The significance of bulimia in juvenile anorexia nervosa: An exploration of possible etiological factors. International Journal of Eating Disorders, 1981; 1:

37. Moos RH. The family environmental scale. Palo Alto, CA: Consulting Psychologists Press, 1974:

38. Locke HJ, Wallace KM. Short marital adjustment and prediction tests: Their reliability and validity. Marriage and Family Living, 1959; 21:251-5.

39. Walsh ed. Normal families. New York: Guilford Press, 1982:

40. Kramer SZ. Bulimia and related eating disorders: a family systems perspective (Dissertation). Ann Arbor, Michigan: California School of Professional Psychology-San Diego, University Microfilms International, 1983:

41. Perosa LM. The development of a questionnaire to measure Minuchin's structural family concepts and the application of this psychosomatic family model to learning disabled families. (Dissertation). Ann Arbor, Michigan: State University of New York at Buffalo. University Microfilms International, 1980:

42. Kog E, Vandereycken W, Vertonnen H. Towards a Verification of the Psychosomatic Model: A Pilot Study of Ten Families with an Anorexic/Bulimia Nervosa Patients, International Journal Eating Disorders, Vol.4, 1985; 4:525-538.

43. Humphrey L. Family Relations in Bulimic-Anorexic and Non-Distressed Families, The International Journal of Eating Disorders, Vol. 5, 1986; 2:223-232.

44. Casper R. Preliminary Results Reported at Second International Conference on Eating Disorders, New York, 1986.

45. Root MP, Fallon P, Freidrich WN. Bulimia: A Systems Approach to Treatment. Penguin Books, 1986.

Chapter 15

Experimental Body Image Research in Anorexia Nervosa Patients*

Rolf Meermann, Christiane Napierski, and Walter Vandereycken

SUMMARY

The significance of the disturbed body image as a psychopathological phenomenon in anorexia nervosa patients is quite evident to clinicians. It appears to be difficult to assess this disturbance in a more objective way.

The studies on body image perception discussed here make use of objective psychometric methods of measurement: image marking procedure, visual size estimation apparatus, distorting photograph technique, and video distortion. The results of these studies are presented and the following methodological problems are discussed: reliability, validity, experimental situation, and selection of subjects.

Furthermore, our own experimental data on 52 anorexic patients as well as 210 control subjects, studied with three different perceptual tasks, are presented.

BODY IMAGE DISTURBANCES IN ANOREXIA NERVOSA

"In its most literal sense body image refers to the body as a psychological experience and focuses on the individual feelings and attitudes towards his own body. It is concerned with the individual's subjective experiences with his body and the manner in which he has organized these experiences" [1]. The concept of body image is applied to a wide range of pathology especially in the field of neurology and psychiatry. Its notion has become a central theme in the conceptualization of anorexia nervosa which Bruch [2], as early as 1962, defined as a "perceptual and conceptual disturbance or disorder of body image". This aspect of the syndrome has even become a major diagnostic criterion according to DSM-III [3]. Therefore it is no wonder that a great number of researchers have attempted to assess this phenomenon in a more objective way. Several studies have been done on the determination of body image in anorexia nervosa, especially with regard to the accuracy of perception of one's own body dimensions.

The studies on body image perception to be discussed here make use of objective psychometric methods of measurement, which orientate themselves to the different methods and procedural rules laid down by experimental (ie, empirical) psychology, in particular perceptual psychology. The investigations are intended to quantify the clinically observable distortions in self-perception that anorectic patients show and in so doing to make them comparable. In this respect, one can talk of an approach that could just as well be regarded to belong to the field of experimental psychopathological research and—as in the case of evaluative followup stu-

* This study has been supported by grant DFG Me 716/1-2 of the Deutsche Forschungsgemeinschaft for R.M.

Table 15.1 **Object and results of studies, which use so-called "objective" methods of measurement to research the body image of anorexia nervosa patients. (AN = Anorexia nervosa patients; BN = Bulimia nervosa; NC = Normal controls)**

No.	Authors	Object of study	Summary of results
1.	Gallwitz (1965)	Is the Photo Distortion Method useful in trying to gain insights into the body self-image and attitude towards one's own body?	AN show stronger emotional involvement, resistence + greater discrepancy between ideal and real body image.
2.	Slade and Russell (1973a)	Do AN overestimate their body-shape more than NC?	AN overestimate versus NC; NC estimate relatively exactly with tendency to underestimate high; positive intercorrelation of perception-indices indicate good intertest-reliability + a general factor g of body-perception.
	(1973b)	Are ANs distortions of body perception a function of a general perceptive disturbance?	Perception of body image and perception of objects are relatively independent of one another; AN's disturbance of body perception can't be caused by a general factor of perceptive disturbance.
	(1973c)	Do AN overestimate their own body height? Do AN overestimate other women's bodies as well?	Exact estimation of height by AN; overestimation of own body more pronounced than that of female model.
	(1973d)	Does the erroneous perception of own body depend on weight and status of illness?	AN: overestimation is being reduced by weight-increase and correlates with unfavorable prognosis upon release.
3.	Crisp and Kalucy (1974a)	Degree of dependency of perception of own body on body weight before and after restoration of normal weight in AN.	AN as well as NC overestimate their body; lesser overestimation correlates with good prognosis; after carbohydrate rich meal overestimation in AN, but not in NC.
	(1974b)	Degree of dependency of perception of own body on meals given shortly before testing in AN.	
4.	Askevold (1975)	Description of various aspects of the Image Marking Method as a procedure for measuring the body image.	Overestimation in AN; difference between real- and estimated measurement especially pronounced in those body regions, in which patients experienced their symptoms.
5.	Garner et al. (1976)	Hypotheses: a) AN and obese overestimate their body compared with controls, b) AN and obese show feelings of own ineffectivity, c) Disturbances of self-perception relative to feelings of ineffectivity, duration of illness, degree of weight loss.	With Photo Distortion Method relative overestimation in AN; and absolute overestimation in NC; all subjects overestimate when using the Visual Size Estimation Apparatus; AN prove to be more introverted than NC; Overestimation in AN correlates with neuroticism and lack of self control, but not with duration of illness and weight loss.
6.	Garfinkel et al (1977)	Report on course of illness in AN with respect to clinical characteristics, disturbances of self-perception and effectiveness of various types of therapy.	Overestimation in AN correlates with bad clinical values and unfavorable prognosis.
7.	Button et al. (1977)	Are overestimations specific for AN or are self-perception disturbances rather the rule than the exception? Does the exactness of body-estimations increase with weight gain? Does the extent of overestimation relate to a bad prognosis?	No differences between AN + NC estimations; body weight- increase does not correlate with overestimations; overestimation relates to vomiting and early recidivation; sign. correlations between Body Perception Indices suggests a general factor g of body perception.
8.	Fries (1977)	Are the Visual Size Estimation Apparatus and the Anorectic Behavior Rating Scale useful in diagnosing "true" anorexia nervosa.?	AN and patients with a secondary amenorrhea overestimate in comparison with NC; weight has no effect on estimations; positive correlations between extent of perceptual disturbance and the Anorectic Behavior Rating Scale.
9.	Goldberg et al. (1977)	Are there any links between characteristics of AN before treatment and later increase in body weight as a result of the therapy?	Overestimation correlates with denial of illness and resistance to increase of body weight.

Table 15.1 Object and results of studies, which use so-called "objective" methods of measurement to research the body image of anorexia nervosa patients. (AN = Anorexia nervosa patients; BN = Bulimia nervosa; NC = Normal controls) (continued)

No.	Authors	Object of study	Summary of results
10.	Pierloot and Houben (1978)	Do AN overestimate their own body? How high is the divergence between the estimations of various body regions with different measuring techniques?	Partially significant overestimation in AN; greater individual variability in AN's estimations; no significant correlations of overestimations with personality traits nor with the variability of estimations.
11.	Wingate and Christie (1978)	Hypothesis: AN overestimate their body; there is an inverse relationship between the extent of overestimation.	AN overestimate more than NC; there is an inverse relationship between the extent of overestimation and ego- strength.
12.	Garfinkel et al. (1978)	Hypotheses: Body image disturbances in AN are related to the visual and gustatory perception of meals. They decrease when watching own mirror-image. As opposed to NC, AN show no saturation-aversion to cane sugar. There is a correlation between disturbances of body iamge and lack of saturation-aversion.	Tendency toward greater over-estimation and more interindividual variability of estimations in AN; in AN lack of influence of external cues on estimations; in AN no aversion to cane sugar; no clues to a possible relation between disturbances of body-image and individual weight-loss; overestimation relate to lack of saturation-aversion in AN.
13.	Garfinkel et al. (1979)	Replication study to establish long-time-stability of body image disturbances found in AN.	Overestimation lead to bad clinical evaluation and unfavorable prognosis.
14.	Ben Tovim (1979)	Body percpetion in AN.	All subjects overestimate; AN overestimate more than ND; inverse relationship between decreased exactness of self- perception and actual body width.
15.	Strober et al. (1979)	Characterization of peculiarities of the body image in first-episode AN during the acute and recuperative period with the help of various measuring methods.	No significant differences between AN and control group: all overestimate; possible significant intercorrelation between the AN's and the control group's Body Perception Indices; possible correlation between vomiting and estimation as well as between estimations and weight at AN's commitment to hospital.
16.	Casper et al. (1979)	Relationship between distortion of body image, weight gain during treatment, and selected characteristics of AN.	No significant difference between AN and NC, both groups overestimate; in AN relationship between overestimation and lesser weight-gain, more pronounced denial of illness, psychosexual immaturity and earlier therapeutic failures.
17.	Meermann (1983)	Comparison of body perception in age-matched anorectic patients and ballet- and gymnastic pupils	With Video Distortion Technique AN and NC underestimate their own body* and those of a female display dummy. With Image Marking Method and with Body Image Screening Scale AN and NC overestimate the most of the body-dimensions, significant for AN in the estimates of the hips, lower abdomen, thigh and frontal and lateral calf. No significant differences between AN and NC in the estimation of the display dummy.
18.	Freeman et al. (1984)	Does the body-perception of restricting AN and of BN differ from that of other groups of patients? Does food-intake influence body perception? Which psychological variables does body perception correlate with?	Restricting AN and BN overestimate more strongly and show more variation than those of the two control groups. Food intake has no influence on body perception. All subjects chose a slimmer ideal. BN showed the most difference between ideal and real body estimation. Positive correlations are found between the real- and ideal-estimations and the scores on the Beck's Depression Inventory and the depression scale of the MMPI.

Table 15.1 Object and results of studies, which use so-called "objective" methods of measurement to research the body image of anorexia nervosa patients. (AN = Anorexia nervosa patients; BN = Bulimia nervosa; NC = Normal controls) (continued)

No.	Authors	Object of study	Summary of results
19.	Napierski and Meermann (1985)	Changes in body perception in AN during the therapeutic process. Which psychological variables does body perception correlate with?	With Video Distortion Technique AN underestimate* at three points in time. Definite overestimation of nearly all body measurements in Image Marking Method. No uniform trend during course of therapy: increase as well as decrease of estimated measures of own body. With Body Image Screening Scale overestimation of dimensions of own body and that of a display dummy at three points in time. Correlations between overestimation and duration of illness, number of therapeutic failures, lowest weight at time of first treatment, unusual handling with foods and sexual anxieties.
20.	Tipton and Adams (1983)	Comparison of body perception and satisfaction with own body between BN and three NC groups.	BN overestimate their measurements significantly when compared with NC. No significant differences between the experimental groups with regard to dissatisfaction with their appearance.
21.	Touyz et al. (1984/1985)	Comparison on AN's and NC's estimations of the following: - subjective real-image - wished for ideal-image - most aversive self-image - normative image of a model - female model	Subjective real-image: AN show stronger tendency to overestimate and larger SD. Ideal-image: AN and NC chose slimmer image, more pronounced in AN than in NC. Most aversive self-image: endomorphic figure in nearly all AN and NC. An underestimate normative picture of the model by 16% to 20%, NC by 5%. When confrontated with model, AN showed stronger underestimation than NC.
22.	Norris (1984)	Comparison of body perception indices (BPIs) of AN, BN, emotionally disturbed women and NC; Influence of mirror-confrontation on estimations (Pre-/Post-BPIs).	Pre-BPIs of NC lower than in other three groups (ns); NC show tendency to underestimate. Post-BPIs in comparison to Pre-BPIs in AN significant reduced, also reduced in BN (ns) but hardly any reduction in NC. Significant correlations between post-BPIs and positive course of therapy in AN and BN. No significant correlation between BPIs and duration of illness, age, or degree of weight loss.
23.	Ben-Tovim and Crisp (1984)	Reliability of measurements of body perception and relationship between actual body measurements and estimations	NC: correlations between estimations from first and second measurement (after 1 hour) = around 0.82 to 0.96, estimations of first and second measurement (after 14 days) = 0.79 to 0.95. No significant correlation between estimated distances and actual width of body. Estimated distances larger than actual distances and following a body-configuration.

*Underestimation seems to be due to the method of the Video Distortion Technique and by neglecting the objective standard (the undistorted video picture of the subject) and comparing only mean-differences, AN deliver significant overestimation in comparison with their control group.

dies—to the field of comparative psychotherapeutic research [4-8,40]. The underlying hypotheses, the methodology, and the results of all studies on body image perception in anorexia nervosa using objective psychometric methods of measurement are summarized in tables 1, 2, and 3.

It is often assumed that the denial of illness and the weight phobia, which are typical features of anorexia nervosa, are reflected in the patient's overestimation of her own body size. Such an overestimation would then be a characteristic and even diagnostic sign of anorexia nervosa. This assumption, however, could not yet be validated.

Table 1 shows that experimental studies of body image perception in anorectic and comparison groups have produced conflicting results. Only few studies reported a significant overestimation in anorexia nervosa patients in comparison with their control groups (study no. 5, 9, 10, 11, 12, 17, 21 and 22 on table 1). In other investigations the anorexia nervosa patients show both underestimation and overestimation, while some normal controls, schizophrenic, and obese patients, pregnant women, ballet, and gymnastic pupils also show the tendency to overestimate their own body size.

Despite of the advantages of experimental procedure and the quantifiable results they produce, a direct comparison of the results is virtually impossible because of the important methodological shortcomings and the diversity of methods chosen for measuring body image perception [8].

METHODOLOGICAL PROBLEMS IN BODY IMAGE ASSESSMENT

The main methodological problems encountered concern the reliability, the validity, the experimental situation, and the selection of subjects.

Reliability

Reliability refers to the internal consistency, stability, and repeatability of a procedure. A test or method is reliable to the extent to which the same results can be reproduced each time it is applied under the same conditions. Reliability is especially critical, since it determines the upper limit on the potential validity or accuracy of the measure.

Visual Size Estimation Apparatus. The Visual Size Estimation Apparatus (VSEA) or movable caliper technique [15] consists of two lights mounted on a horizontal bar in such a way that they can be moved to indicate perceived widths of specific regions. In a darkened room, subjects are asked to estimate the dimensions of various body regions and these data are then compared with the actual dimensions resulting in a Body Perception Index (B.P.I.), ie, the perceived size multiplied by 100 and then divided by the actual size.

Halmi et al [16] had 86 female pupils estimate—among other things—the width of their face, chest, waist, and hips as well as their body depth using the VSEA. They regarded the estimations for the various bodily dimensions as test recurrences with a tendency toward over- or underestimation. They determined the retest reliability for the test results of the five measures by intercorrelating the estimates. These intercorrelations varied from 0.38 to 0.65, which is not high enough for the reliability coefficient. However, they were high enough to make the presumption that the measurements of the five areas of the body assess the same underlying dimension. For this reason, Halmi et al [16] determined the mean value for each subject for each of

the five estimates, and, by applying the Spearman-Brown prophecy formula, they were able to establish a reliability coefficient of 0.84 for their test. Other authors also determined the intercorrelations for their subjects' estimates using the VSEA and obtained values from 0.25 to 0.94 [15,17,18].

Ben-Tovim and Crisp [19] calculated coefficients of reliability between initial estimates made by 11 normal females (face, chest, waist, hips) and their estimates after 60 minutes and after 14 days. The coefficients of test-retest reliability were very high and significant (range from 0.82 to 0.96 and from 0.79 to 0.95).

Thus, the reliability of this method appears to be rather variable.

Image Marking Method. With this method [20], the subject stands before a sheet of paper mounted on a wall and is instructed to mark the points that correspond to dimensions of specific body regions with a pencil. Pierloot and Houben [18] established intercorrelations of 0.30 to 0.61 for anorexia nervosa patients when using the Image Marking Method (IMM), and from 0.52 to 0.75 for normal controls. Strober et al [21] gained intercorrelations of 0.51 to 0.72 for subjects using the same test.

Our own results [22-24,8] for 262 subjects in table 5 reports with the IMM appear to be rather equivocal, and its utility rests on further studies of reliability and validity.

Distorting Photograph Technique. This method [25] involves the subject's estimation of her size using a projected photograph of the body, which can be distorted along the horizontal axis with an anamorphic lens.

Garfinkel et al [26,27] correlated the results of numerous trials using this method: estimates made before and after a high-calorie meal correlated highly in the case of anorexia nervosa patients ($r = 0.90$, $p = 0.001$); for normal controls the correlation coefficient was $r = 0.51$, $p = 0.02$. The following correlation coefficients were found for estimates before and after a low-calorie content meal: $r = 0.86$, ($p = 0.001$) for anorexia nervosa patients and $r = 0.86$ ($p = 0.001$) for normal controls. The anorexia nervosa patients' results also showed the following correlation coefficients: $r = 0.75$ ($p = 0.003$) after a week and $r = 0.56$ ($p = 0.02$) after a year. In the case of the normal controls, however, these correlation coefficients were $r = 0.14$ (ns) after one week and $r = 0.39$ (ns) after one year [27]. The absence of data on this method obtained by other researchers makes it difficult to judge its repeatability.

Video Distortion Method. Allebeck et al [28] proposed the use of a television system for body image research. One may modify a videomonitor (or camera) so that subjects can adjust the proportions of their body picture on the screen. This technique has only recently

Table 15.2 Demographical characteristics of examined samples (Legend: in= inpatient/ out= out-patient/ f= female/ m=male/ n= neurotic/ h= healthy/ nw= normal weight/ ep= eating problems)

Study No.	Experimental Group — No. of subjects and special features	Age (years) x, (SD)	Height (cm) x, (SD)	Weight (kg) x, (SD)	Control Group — No. of subjects and special features	Age (years) x, (SD)	Height (cm) x, (SD)	Weight (kg) x, (SD)
1	10 AN f	16-30	–	–	none of their own			
2a	13 AN f	19.79 (5.78)	160.2 (9.95)	40.76 (5.65)	20 NCf	25.0 (4.71)	163.0 (8.31)	60.25 (3.08)
	1 AN m	–	–	–				
2b	12 AN f in	20.6	157.0	40.22	see Study No. 2a			
2c	9 AN f	–	–	–	see Study No. 2a			
2d	10 AN f	–	–	–	see Study No. 2a			
3	4 AN f in				none			
	5 AN f in	ca. 21	65 in.	–	6 NC f	–	65.6 in	–
4	15 AN f in 21, 18, 37,16, 7, 13 psychosomatically ill	over 18			20 NC f (Physiotherapists)	over 18		
5	18 AN f in	20.7	161.9	42.8	16 f "thin" without ep	20.6	159.9	40.7
	16 obese f	20.8	164.3	85.3	16 NC f	20.8	163.3	56.0
					16 n	20.6	159.3	53.9
6	27 ANp f	20.4	–	–	none			
	1 ANp m	–	–	–				
7	20 AN f	23.86 (7.23)	159.7 (4.42)	41.23 (4.59)	16 NC f	23.06 (3.13)	166.0 (5.78)	57.24 (4.88)
8	14 AN f (data of Study No. 2)	19.79 (5.78)	160.2 (9.95)	40.76 (5.65)	see Study No. 2			
	21 AN f	20.8	–	78.5	22 NC f	24.3	–	93.7
	17 f with sec. amenorhoe	–	–	82.8 (18.7%)				
9	44 AN f in	20.18 (5.38)	159.8 (5.96)	33.7 (4.65)	none			
10	31 AN f in	20.92 (3.89)	162.0 (0.07)	40.99 (6.75)	20 n f in	21.15 (3.84)	165.0 (0.05)	57.94 (7.21)
11	15 AN f in	20.8	160.9	43.2	15 NC f	20.8	164.3	54.84
					15 NC f	17.4	158.2	53.02
12	26 AN f in	20.8 (0.7)	162.9 (1.2)	42.4 (1.9)	16 NC f without ep	21.8 (0.9)	164.1 (1.3)	55.80 (1.3)
13	16 AN f out	21.8 (0.86)	162.6 (1.34)	47.5 (2.3)	16 NC f without ep	22.4 (0.98)	163.5 (1.4)	56.3 (1.61)
14	8 AN in	19.7 (3.6)	161.1 (7.5)	43.3 (5.9)	11 girls	15.4 (0.5)	164.8 (5.2)	53.7 (0.5)
					11 mothers of girls	44.9	161.4	57.5

No.	Patient group	Age	Height	Weight	Control group	Age	Height	Weight
15	18 AN f	14.77 (1.01)	160.1 (6.45)	36.17 (3.7)	24 nurses	23.2 (4.4)	166.2 (4.2)	62.2 (5.4)
16	79 AN f	—	—	—	24 patients nw, f	15.1 (1.3)	162.9 (5.9)	50.5 (8.8)
–					86 girls	10–18	—	— (3.4)
17	36 AN f in	18.86 (4.18)	166.3 (6.4)	46.4 (6.86)	44 Nc f	20–40	—	—
					35 Ballet-&Gymnastic pupils	18.11 (3.3)	166.7 (6.99)	55.0 (8.7)
18	19 Abstainers	23.7 (6.3)	162.0 (5.6)	41.0 (6.0)	15 NC	22.5 (3.4)	165.5 (4.2)	57.0 (7.4)
	27 BN	24.1 (4.8)	166.8 (6.9)	51.9 (10.6)	9 psychiatric patients	27.3 (3.4)	165.0 (6.4)	53.8 (9.6)
19	16 AN	—	—	—	none	—	—	—
20	11 BN	—	—	—	12 "dieters"	—	—	—
					12 "restrained NC"	—	—	—
					12 NC (age-matched)	—	—	—
21	15 AN f	19.06 (5.2)	161.0 (7.01)	44.5 (7.4)	15 NC	20.8 (5.8)	166.0 (7.0)	57.9 (4.7)
22	12 AN f	16.8 (13–20)	—	71%(norm) (65–77%)	12 emotional disturbed f	16.7 (13–20)	—	102% 95–108%
	12 BN	18.9 (16–23)	—	105% (88–120%)	12 NC f	16.4 (13–20)	—	99% 94–106%
23	see Study No. 14				11 NC f	27.2 (10.7)	163.7 (5.3)	59.6 (0.3)

Table 15.3 Employed methods of measurement and details of testing-procedure

Study No.	Tests	Test Trials	Adjustments	Estimations of			
				Object	Ideal	Mirror-Confr.	Own body parts
1	Photo Distortion Technique (Gottschalk, 1954)	1	?	no	yes	no	Head
2a	VSEA, Anthropometer	1	4	no	no	no	Head, chest, waist, hips
2b	- as 2a -	1	4	yes	no	no	- as 2a -
2c	- as 2a plus Visual Height Estimation	1	4	Model	no	yes	- as 2a plus body height -
2d	- as 2a -	7 to 18	4	no	no	no	- as 2a -
3	VSEA	4	4	no	no	no	Head, shoulder, waist, hips, thighs
4	IMM	1	1	no	no	no	Shoulder, waist, hips, B- height
5	Adjustable Distorting Photograph Technique, VSEA, EPI, Rotter's Locus of Control Scale	1	2	Vase Model	yes	yes	Photo of body in bikini face, chest, waist, hips
6	- as 5a -			no	no	no	Face, chest, hips, waist, stomach-deep
7	VSEA, Anthropometer	1	2	no	no	no	Face, chest, hips, waist
8	VSEA, Anthropometer, Anorectic Behavior Rating Scale	1	4				Face, chest, waist, hips, arm length, body depth
9	VESA, Slade's Anorectic Behavior Scale, Anorectic Attitude Scale, Hopkins Symptom Check List, Psychiatric Rating Scale	?	?	yes	no	no	
10	IMM, VSEA, Anthropometer, Corrected VSEA, MMPI, Rorschach, Andriesen Question.		1 / 2	no	no	yes	Face, shoulders, waist, hips
11	IMM, MMPI	1	1	no	no	no	Shoulders, hips, waist, B-height
12	Adjustable Distorting Photograph Technique	2 (7 days)	2	Vase	yes	yes	Photo of whole body
13	- as 12 -						
14	VSEA, Anthropometer, Slade's Anorectic B. Scale	1	2	no	no	no	Face, chest, waist, hips
15	IMM, Body Distortion Questionnaire, Body-Concept- Scale	2(6 month)	1	no	no	no	Shoulders, waist, hips
16	VSEA, Anthropometer, Anorectic Attitude Scale	1	4	yes	no	no	Face, chest, hips, waist, length of arm and foot

#	Method						Body parts/view
17	IMM, Anthropometer, Video Distortion Technique, Body Image Screening Scale, Anorexic Nervosa Inventar zur Selbstbeurtei-lung	1	6	model-dummy	no	no	Head, shoulders, waist, hips, frontal thigh + calf, lateral head, chest-back, abdomen-back, lower abdomen-posterior, lateral thigh and calf, view of head, whole body frontal and lateral
18	Video Distortion Technique (two Monitors), Eating Attitudes Test, BDI, Hunger & Satiety Scale, MOOS Menstrual Distress Questionnaire, MMPI, Anorexic Rating Scales, Mosher Guilt Inventories	2	2	no	yes	no	Frontal view of body, lateral view of body
19	- as 17 -	2-4					
20	Polaroid photograph with video-setup	1	1	no	yes	no	Lateral view of body
21	Polaroid photograph with video-setup	1	2	model	yes	no	Frontal + lateral view of body
22	Movable Light Line	2	4	no	no	yes	Head, waist, hips, thighs
23	VSEA	3 (1 hour, 14 days)	?	no	no	no	Head, chest, waist, hips

VSEA = Visual Size Estimation Apparatus; IMM = Image Marking Method

Table 15.4 Correlation between body perception indices for various dimensions

Author	Method	Body Dimensions	Anorexic N	patients range	Normal N	Controls Range
Halmi et al (1977)	VSEA	Face, chest, waist, hips	–	–	86	.38 to .65
Slade and Russell (1973)	VSEA	"	14	.72 to .93	20	.37 to .79
Button et al (1977)	VSEA	"	20	.52 to .81	16	.66 to .88
Goldberg et al (1977)	VSEA	"	44	.47 to .85	–	–
Pierloot and Houben(1978)	VSEA Corr.	"	31	.29 to .59	20	.25 to .81
	VSEA	"	20	.25 to .59	20	.38 to .59
	IMM	Chest, waist, hips	31	.30 to .61	20	.52 to .75
Strober et al (1979)	IMM	"	18	.51 to .66	24	.49 to .72
Meerman (1983)	IMM	Face, chest, waist, hips	36	.35 to .79	35	.19 to .84

(Corr.) VSEA = (Corrected) Visual Size Estimation Apparatus; IMM = Image Marking Method

Table 15.5 Reliability Analysis of the Image Marking Method*

	Body Frontal					Body Sagittal				
	Cronbach's Alpha	F-Prob. Between Measures		Nonadditivity		Cronbach's Alpha	F-Prob. Between Measures		Nonadditivity	
Groups		F	P	F	P		F	P	F	P
39 NC	0.787	33.2	0.0	27.0	0.00	0.556	7.9	0.00	17.1	0.00
52 AN	0.810	32.8	0.0	17.2	0.00	0.856	15.9	0.00	16.4	0.00
34 SCH	0.712	30.4	0.0	0.1	0.78	0.771	5.2	0.00	9.1	0.00
35 BAL	0.752	42.3	0.0	0.5	0.50	0.815	15.7	0.00	3.3	0.07
30 NC	0.785	18.0	0.0	1.4	0.20	0.714	3.5	0.01	0.6	0.44
32 DEP	0.869	4.9	0.0	0.7	0.40	0.878	6.2	0.00	3.8	0.05
40 OB	0.772	26.1	0.0	5.6	0.02	0.860	6.8	0.00	15.2	0.00

NC = Normal Controls; AN = Anorexic nervosa patients; SCH = Schizophrenics; BAL = Ballet-pupils; DEP = depressed patients; OB = obese patients.
*From Meermann, Napierski and Vandereycken (1986) (8)

Table 15.6 Reliability Analysis of the Video Distortion Technique*

Groups	Head			Body Frontal			Body Sagittal		
	Cronbach's Alpha	F-Prob. Between Measures		Cronbach's Alpha	F-Prob. Between Measures		Cronbach's Alpha	F-Prob. Between Measures	
		F	P		F	P		F	P
39 NC	0.900	12.58	0.0	0.945	12.51	0.0	0.926	9.55	0.00
52 AN	0.892	20.39	0.0	0.967	13.76	0.0	0.961	3.64	0.00
34 SCH	0.868	10.56	0.0	0.910	10.64	0.0	0.952	4.94	0.00
35 BAL	0.866	32.07	0.0	0.895	28.78	0.0	0.913	29.44	0.00
30 NC	0.896	14.79	0.0	0.939	22.25	0.0	0.886	8.31	0.00
32 DEP	0.895	4.56	0.0	0.891	8.92	0.0	0.880	2.76	0.02
40 OB	0.927	26.74	0.0	0.943	14.52	0.0	0.921	4.61	0.00

NC = Normal Controls; AN = Anorexic nervosa patients; SCH = Schizophrenics; BAL = Ballet = pupil; DEP = depressed patients; OB = obese patients
*From Meermann, Napierski and Vandereycken (1986) (8)

been applied to anorexia nervosa patients first by our own research group in Munster [22] and later by other investigators [23,29]. The latter researchers found a high retest reliability of 0.91 for eating disorder patients (anorexia nervosa and bulimia nervosa) and of 0.83 for control subjects.

Table 6 shows the degree of reliability we have obtained using the video distortion method [8,22,30].

Generally speaking, the anorectic patients' estimations of body dimensions seem to remain relatively congruent despite the use of different test measures. This would appear to favor the hypothesis that their body size estimations represent a relatively stable phenomenon that can be measured fairly satisfactorily using the test methods discussed so far.

Validity

The validity of a test is the degree of accuracy with which the test actually measures the characteristics it states to measure. A test is valid when its results permit a direct and accurate conclusion as to the degree of the characteristics to be measured. The term validity is a general term for different specific types of validity that a test can have. The most widely used form of validity is the *convergent validity*, which is determined by correlating the results with other independent assessments of the same or a similar characteristic.

Garner et al [31], Strober et al [21] and Meermann [22,30] used this form of validity by correlating the results gained by different self-rating scales with each other. Garner et al [31] determined the following values for the correlation coefficients when they correlated the mean scores of their subjects' self-ratings using the photo distortion technique and their VSEA-scores: $r=0.50$ ($p<0.05$) for anorexia nervosa patients and $r=0.44$ ($p<0.05$) for obese patients. No significant correlations worth noting were determined for the control groups.

Research by Strober et al [21] could not determine any noteworthy correlations between the results of their subjects in the Image Marking Method, the Draw-a-Person-Test, and the Body Distortion Questionnaire. Other studies found that the degree of body overestimation encountered among anorectic subjects correlated with a number of psychopathological and prognostic variables (see Table 7) such as neuroticism and lack of self-control or external-control orientation [18,31], interoceptive disorders [27], denial of illness and poor response to in-patient treatment [33,34], and vomiting [17,21,29]. Table 8 shows the correlative relationship we found in one of our studies [8,24].

Experimental Situation

A direct comparison of the results of different studies is not only complicated by the variety of methods used,

but also by the differences in setting and test execution. Variables such as the time of day, the time span since the last meal, motivation and instruction, the subjects' clothing during the estimation procedure, the sex of and the familiarity with the researcher, technical differences in the apparatus used, etc, can all have an influence on the subjects' performance:

Button et al [17] mentioned the possiblity that the lack of similarity between their results with the VSEA and those of Slade and Russell [15] could well be the result of different test conditions and influences such as behavior and sex of the researcher, type of instruments used, or even different lighting. In the study of Wingate and Christie [35] using the VSEA, the subject could not record her estimates directly but had to communicate with the researcher, who handled the apparatus. It is quite possible that results have been influenced, for example, by the time that elapsed between the subject's decision, her saying "stop" and the researcher's reaction, which actually stopped the movable caliper device. Furthermore, some authors fail to give a detailed description or to discuss the clothes their subjects are wearing at the time of estimation, even though this variable might be of special importance considering the emotional involvement of the subject and the tactile sensations experienced during the marking of the body regions to be estimated.

Even though some studies were able to show that the body image of anorexics is relatively stable and independent of external stimuli, the question remains, to what extent factors like time of day, testedness of the subject, or the time since the contents of the last meal before the experiment contribute to the high level of variability within the experimental groups.

The person as well as the behavior of the experimenter definitely are some further important influential factors. Especially with these tests of body perception and with mostly female anorectics, an experimenter of the opposite sex could arouse emotional reactions like shame or exhibitionistic actions that could influence the situation considerably. Other psychological influences on the part of the experimenter such as attitude and sensitivity toward the subject, patience, and verbal as well as nonverbal behavior might be of influence. Another thing that must not be neglected is the well-known Rosenthal effect concerning the expectations of the experimenter. Furthermore, the set of instructions given at the beginning of the experiment play an important role. With body image tests, it is necessary to clarify whether the subjects' estimations should be of a perceptive nature or of an objective one, that is, should the instructions be given in such a way, as to induce estimation of the body regions according to their actual size

Table 15.7a Correlations between body perception and psychopathological data in anorectic patients.

	N AN	Method	Face	Chest	Waist	Hips	Investigators
Activity	44	VSEA	-0.21	-0.93	-0.21	-0.16	Goldberg et al (1977)
	12	IMM		Composite score body frontal = -0.70*			Meermann and Napierski (1983)
				Composite score body sagittal = -0.62*			
Premorbid hyperactivity	44	VSEA	0.41*	0.28	0.52*	0.62*	Goldberg et al (1977)
Denial of illness	44	VSEA	0.28	0.19	0.45*	0.45*	Goldberg et al (1977)
	81	VSEA		Composite score = 0.48*			Casper et al (1979)
Hunger	44	VSEA	0.45*	0.45*	0.48*	0.56*	Goldberg et al (1977)
Loss of appetite	81	VSEA		Composite score = 0.47*			Casper et al (1979)
Psychosexual immaturity	44	VSEA	0.32*	0.37*	0.51*	0.53*	Goldberg et al (1977)
	81	VSEA		Composite score = 0.44			Casper et al (1979)
Ego strength	15	IMM	—	-0.69**	-0.75**	-0.69**	Wingate and Christie (1978)
External control	19	VSEA		Composite score = 0.40			Pierloot and Houben (1978)
Emotional immaturity (FPI)	8	IMM		Composite score = 0.94*			Meermann and Napierski (1983)
Therapeutic failure	52	IMM		Composite score body frontal = 0.47**			
				Composite score body sagittal = 0.61**			
	81	VESA		Composite score = 0.25*			Casper et al (1979)

Table 15.7b Correlations between body perception and psychopathological data in anorectic patients.

	N AN	Method	Head	Body Frontal	Body Sagittal	Investigator
Duration of illness	52	Video	—	0.72**	0.67**	Meermann and Napierski (1983)
Therapeutic failure	42	"	0.64*	0.84*	0.77**	"
Denial of illness	12	"	0.70**	—	—	"
Sexual fear	8	"	—	0.85*	0.83*	"
Unusual handling with food	12	"	0.70**	—	—	"
Negative effects on eating	12	"	—	—	0.69*	"
Typical female self-description	8	"	—	0.75*	-0.91*	"
Global clinical score	28	DPT		0.67**		Garfinkel et al (1977)
Neuroticism (EPI)	18	DPT		0.57**		Garner et al (1976)
Extroversion (EPI)				0.34		
Lack of self-control				0.47*		
Total I-E score				0.35		

IMM = Image Marking Method; VSEA = Visual Size Estimation Apparatus; Video = Video-Distortion Technique; DPT = Distorting Photograph Technique; * = p < 0.05; ** = p < 0.01

From Naperski, Meermann and Vandereycken (1986)(8)

Table 15.8 Correlations between overestimation and other variables in anorexia nervosa*

	Image Marking Method Body Frontal/Sagittal		Video Distortion Technique Head	Body Frontal/Sagittal	
Duration of illness	—	—	—	0.72**(a)	0.67**(a)
Prior therapeutic failures	0.47**(a)	0.61**(a)	0.64*(b)	0.84**(b)	0.77**(b)
Admission weight	-0.49*(a)	-0.49*(a)	—	- 0.70**(b)	-0.62*(b)
Unusual handling with food	—	—	0.70**(b)	—	—
Hyperactivity	-0.70*(b)	-0.62*(b)	—	—	—
Denial of illness	—	—	0.70**(b)	—	—
Fear of sexuality	—	—	—	0.85*(c)	0.83*(c)
Emotional immaturity	0.94*(c)	—	—	—	—

a = 52 patients; b = 12 patients; c = 8 patients
*p = < 0.05; ** p = < 0.01
*From Meermann, Napierski and Vandereycken (1986) (8)

(eg, "Please try to estimate the breadth of your shoulders as accurately as possible") or should the instruction rather refer to the feeling the subject has of her body (eg, "Please indicate, how wide this part of your body feels to you")? Unfortunately, only in very few studies is there any indication of which nature the instructions were. Also most studies left equally unanswered the question of whether any influences of pharmacological medication on the test-outcome can be ruled out.

But even in the case of the best possible standardization, there always remain the intraindividual psychological characteristics of the subject such as attitude toward and foreknowledge of the study and the tests involved. Unenthusiastic and unmotivated patients, who fail to see the meaning of the examination, will probably produce less meaningful estimations than those who see an opportunity for some self-experience in this procedure. The amount of foreknowledge will also influence the results of the estimations, especially if the patient has to fear institutional consequences such as endangering a planned release. Button et al [17] draw attention to the fact that the subject's being informed about the hypotheses and already published findings on body perception could influence anorectic patient's estimates.

In conclusion, researchers must be well aware of the many methodolgoical pitfalls and should pay careful attention to the standarization of the research procedure.

Selection of Subjects

An important methodological shortcoming of body image research concerns the size and composition of the patient and control groups. Few studies have a sufficiently large sample from which to draw methodologically sound conclusions with regard to the overall population. A decisive factor, which has only been taken into account in recent studies, is the age of the controls.

Halmi et al [16] showed how important the subjects' age is for the exactitude of their bodily perception. They proved that the subject's age and their tendency to overestimate their bodily dimensions correlated negatively; their findings were based on the results of 86 subjects of normal weight, who were both physically and mentally healthy and aged between 10 and 18 years. Askevold [20] also points out that body perception could be dependent on age, as the body image changes parallel to physical and mental development. With regard to this last point, it is important to note that several studies found no significant difference in the estimation of bodily dimensions among their samples [17,31,34,36]. These results rectify the original results by Slade and Russell [15] where the control subjects were significantly older than the anorexia nervosa patients.

When selecting the control group, little attention has been paid to variables such as socioeconomic status, intelligence [18], eating behavior or adherence to diets [34,37,38], or psychopathology [21,31,35]. Akevold [15] forwarded the opinion that intelligence and education have no influence on the estimation of one's own body size. But it remains to be clarified to what extent a differentiated body perception and its transformation into estimates is dependent on cognitive development.

As to the composition of the patient group, many studies lack such relevant demographic data as actual weight, duration of illness, stage of treatment or diagnostic criteria (eg, Feighner criteria [39], DSM-III, exclusion of bulimia nervosa or latent obese patients, etc) used to select the patients. Moreover, the heterogeneity of anorexia nervosa is generally not taken into account when analysing the results of the studies. Research has shown that the estimates of body size were not homogenous within the anorexia nervosa patient's groups. On the contrary, they seemed to be influenced

Table 15.9 Correlations between body-perception and weight of anorexia nervosa patients.

	N-Xn	Body Parts Face	Chest	Waist	Hips	Comp. Score	Investigation
Assessment weight	10	-0.21	0.41**	-0.36	-0.29*	–	2
	11	0.33	0.67**	0.56**	0.45*	–	7
Total weight loss	21	–	–	–	–	0.21	8
Pretreatment weight	11	-0.17	0.44*	0.01	0.24	–	7
Admission weight	81	–	–	–	–	-0.24*	16
Amount of weight gain	10	0.25*	0.30**	0.32**	0.34**	–	2
since admission	11	0.33	0.67**	0.56**	0.45*	–	7
	44	-0.31	-0.40	-0.57	-0.55	–	9
	81	–	–	–	–	-0.39*	16
Proportion of weight gain by the time of 1st assessment	11	0.33	0.66**	0.57**	0.46	–	7
Follow-up index:	15	-0.55*	-0.28	-0.51*	-0.61**	(when underweight)	7
	10	-0.26	0.13	-0.05	0.15	(when normal w.)	2
	9	0.28	0.68*	0.45	0.47	(on admission)	2
		0.88**	0.72*	0.40	0.57	(average during admission)	
		0.73*	0.63*	0.48	0.67*	(at discharge)	2

No 2 = Slade & Russell 1973; No 7 = Garfinkel et al. 1977; No 8 = Fries 1977; No 9 = Goldberg et al. 1977; No 16 = Casper et al. 1979

$*p = 0.05$
$**p = 0.01$

by factors such as regular or occasional vomiting [17], the degree of illness denial, and resistance to previous treatment that had failed [33].

DISCUSSION

Body image is an extremely complex phenomenon including the schematic representation of parts of the body and personal views (cognitive constructs) as well as subjective experiences of bodily functions, and it seems to be profoundly influenced by the individuals's emotional states. Therefore self-estimation of body sizes can be seen only as a crude measure of the whole complex body image. Experimental studies, on the other hand, might be more useful if the many methodological problems discussed are taken into account.

Slade [40] made group comparisons across studies: (a) in terms of averaged values for anorectic and control groups by using all available studies, and (b) in terms of both the number of individuals overestimating body size and also the number of studies producing significant versus nonsignificant group comparisons. The main conclusions of these comparisons and other specific results of the experimental studies can be summed up as follows:

1. Anorexia nervosa patients tend to overestimate the dimensions of their own body more than non-anorectics do, and they display a large variability of etimates.
2. Because overestimation occurs also in some non-anorectic individuals, it cannot be seen as specific for anorectics and thus lacks clear-cut diagnostic value.
3. While using size-estimation methods (like the Image Marking Procedure, the Visual Size Estimation procedure, and similar techniques) the modal tendency for most groups under investigation is one of overestimation; the trend of individual's estimations using image-distorting methods (like the Distorting Photograph Technique or the Video-Distortion Technique) is toward an underestimation of body size.
4. Comparing different subgroups of eating disorders, patients with bulimia and/or vomiting show a greater tendency to overestimate their own body size than restricting anorexics.

From the results of the experimental studies it can be deduced that the body image concept in its currently researched form (difference between subjective estimations and objective body measurement) needs to be refined. The use of the Body Perception Index (BPI) as a measure of accuracy of self-perception rests on the assumption that the actual body width is being estimated

and that individuals who estimate 100% correct actually have an undistorted body image. But studies show that a 100% correct estimation of one's own "objective" body size apparently is not the norm and that, on the contrary, a certain tendency to overestimate appears physiologically and psychologically sensible. The observation that dimensions of the head, it being one of the "most significant" parts of the body, are mostly overestimated by normal people as well, is in accordance with this hypothesis. The exact experimental basis of self-estimations of body widths remains uncertain.

The methods used to determine body image appear to measure the manifold components of body image with a different degree of sensitivity, reliability and validity. Slade [40] discussed three different hypotheses that could explain the differences in experimental results:

1. The "threshold-difference hypothesis" suggests that the "size-estimation" methods (IMM, VSEA) have lower thresholds for identifying tendencies of overestimation than the methods working with the distortion of the image of the individual.
2. The "state-trait hypothesis" suggests that the "size-estimation" methods measure another, but related, aspect of the body image than the "image-distortion" methods. While the first mentioned techniques possibly reflect a fluid state of body-size sensitivity (which is strongly dependent on situative affective/emotional factors), the second group of methods possibly reflects a relatively fixed cognitive attitude to body size.
3. In the case of anorexia nervosa "size-estimation" techniques possibly reflect "a nonspecific-setting condition of weight sensitivity," ubiquitous in nearly all females of the Western society, whereas the "image-distortion" techniques may reflect an "negative reinforcing factor for weight-loss control."

At present none of these hypotheses can be verified. Also it has not yet been answered conclusively whether or to what extent the large overestimation found in many patients with anorexia nervosa is a conditioned factor, a secondary result of the physical emaciation, or psychological compensatory mechanism in the sense of an avoidance of cognitive dissonance. Of significant interest remains the fact that pronounced body image disturbances in the sense of overestimation appear to be associated with a more pronounced psychopathology and increased risk of therapeutic failure. For future studies on the body image, an increase in the range of data is to be encouraged in three directions:

1. A more exact demographic and clinical description of the sample being studied ("hard" data concerning the illness).

2. An increase in the methods used for measuring body image (at least two perceptual methods and also self-rating scales or questionnaires to measure the patient's degree of satisfaction with her body, the subjective experience of her appearance, etc).

3. The development of other techniques not only to assess body image but also to influence it in a therapeutic sense, for instance by self-image confrontation or video feedback/video playback [41,43].

REFERENCES

1. McRea CW, Summerfield AB, Rosen B. Body image: A selective review of existing measurement techniques. Br J Med Psychol, 1982; 55:225-33.

2. Bruch H. Perceptual and conceptual disturbances in anorexia nervosa. Psychosom Med, 1962; 24:187-94.

3. American Psychiatric Association. Diagnostic and statistical manual of mental disorders, third edition (DSM-III). Washington, DC: American Psychiatric Association, 1980.

4. Garfinkel PE, Garner DM. Anorexia nervosa. A multidimensional prespective. New York: Brunner/Mazel, 1982:

5. Garner DM, Garfinkel PE. Measurement of body image in anorexia nervosa. In: Vigersky R, ed. Anorexia nervosa. New York: Raven Press, 1977; 27-30.

6. Hsu LK. Is there a disturbance in body image in anorexia nervosa? J Nerv Ment Dis, 1982; 170:305-7.

7. Meermann R, Fichter MM. Storungen des Korperschemas (body-image) bei psychischen Erkrankungen. Methodik und experimentelle Ergebnisse bei anorexia nervosa. Psychother Psychosom Med Psycho, 1982; 32:162-9.

8. Meermann R, Napierski C, Vandereycken W. Methodological problems of body image research in anorexia nervosa patients. Acta Psychiat, Belg, 1986; 86:42-51.

9. Slade D. Awareness of body dimensions during pregnancy: an analogue study. Psychol Med, 1977; 7:245-52.

10. Gallwitz A. Versuch einer experimentellen Erfassung des body image bei weiblichen Magersuchtigen. In: Meyer JE, Feldmann J, eds. Anorexia nervosa. Stuttgart: Thieme, 1965:

11. Norris DL. The effects of mirror confrontation on self-estimation of body dimensions in anorexia nervosa, bulimia and two control groups. Psychol Med, 1984; 14:835-42.

12. Tipton CR, Adams HE. The assessment of body image in bulimics and normals. Paper presented at the World Congress on Behavior Therapy. Washington, DC: 1983;

13. Touyz SW, Beumont PJ, Collins JK, McCabe M, Jupp J. Body shape perception and its disturbance in anorexia nervosa. Br J Psychiatry, 1984; 144:167-71.

14. Touyz SW, Beumont JV, Collins JK, McCabe M, Jupp J. Body image disturbance in anorexia nervosa. In: Pichot P, Berner P, Wolf R, Thau K, eds. Psychiatry, the state of the Art, volume 4: Psychotherapy and psychosomatic medicine. New York: Plenum Press, 1985:

15. Slade PD, Russell GF. Awareness of body dimensions in anorexia nervosa: Crosssectional and longitudinal studies. Psychol Med, 1973; 3:188-99.

16. Halmi KA, Goldbert SC, Cummingham S. Perceptual distortion of body image in adolescent girls: Distortion of body image in adolescence. Psychol Med, 1977; 7:253-7.

17. Button EJ, Fransella F, Slade PD. A reappraisal of body perception disturbance in anorexia nervosa. Psychol Med, 1977; 7:235-43.

18. Pierloot RA, Houben ME. Estimation of body dimensions in anorexia nervosa. Psychol Med, 1978; 8:317-24.

19. Ben-Tovim DI, Crisp AH. The reliability of esitmates of body width and their relationship to current measured body size among anorexic and normal subjects. Psychol Med, 1984; 14:843-6.

20. Askevold F. Measuring body image: Preliminary report on a new method. Psychother Psychosom, 1975; 26:71-7.

21. Strober M, Goldenberg I, Green J, Saxon J. Body image disturbances in anorexia nervosa during the acute und recuperative phase. Psychol Med, 1979; 9:695-701.

22. Meermann R. Experimental investigation of disturbance in body image estimation in anorexia nervosa patients, and ballet- and gymnastic pupils. Intl Journal of Eating Disorders, 1983a; 2:91-100.

23. Meermann R. Body image disturbances in anorexia nervosa: Some diagnostic and therapeutic implications. In: Minsel WR, Herff W, eds. Research on psychotherapeutic approaches. Frankfurt: Peter Lang, 1983b:230-236.

24. Napierski C, Meermann R, Vandereycken W. Video-ounterstützende Verlaufsdiagnostik von Körperschemastörungen. In: Hartwich P, Badura HO, eds. Möglichkeiten und Grenzen der Audiovision in Psychiatrie, Psychotherapie und Psychosomatik, Aachen, 1985; 68-103.

25. Glucksman ML, Hirsch J. The response of obese patients to weight reduction: The perception of body size. III. Psychosom Med, 1969; 31:1-17.

26. Garfinkel PE, Moldofsky H, Garner DM, Stancer HC, Coscina DV. Body awareness in anorexia nervosa: Disturbances in body image and satiety. Psychosom Med, 1978; 40:487-98.

27. Garfinkel PE, Moldofsky H, Garner DM. The stability of perceptual disturbances in anorexia nervosa. Psychol Med, 1979; 9:703-8.

28. Allebeck P, Hallberg D, Espmark S. Body image: an apparatus for measuring disturbances in estimation of size and shape. J Psychosom Res, 1976; 20:583-9.

29. Freeman RJ, Thomas CDE, Solyom L, Hunter MA. A modified video camera for measuring body image distortion: technical description and reliability. Psychol Med, 1984; 14:411-6.

30. Meermann R. Methodological problems in body image research. International Conference on Anorexia ner-

vosa and related disorders. Wales, England: University College Swansea 03.-07.09.1984:

31. Garner DM, Garfinkel PE, Stancer HC, Moldofsky H. Body image disturbances in anorexia nervosa and obesity. Psychosom Med, 1976; 38:327-37.

32. Garfinkel PE, Moldofsky H, Garner DM. The outcome of anorexia nervosa: Significance of features, body image and behavior modification. In: Vigersky RA, ed. Anorexia nervosa. New York: Raven Press, 1977; 315-330.

33. Goldberg SC, Halmi KA, Casper R, Eckert E, Davis JM. Pretreatment predictors of weight gain in anorexia nervosa. In: Vigersky R, ed. Anorexia nervosa. New York: Raven Press, 1977:

34. Casper RC, Halmi KA, Goldberg SC, Eckert ED, Davis JM. Disturbances in body image estimation as related to other characteristics and outcome in anorexia nervosa. Br J Psychiatry, 1979; 134:60-6.

35. Wingate BA, Christie MJ. Ego strength and body image in anorexia nervosa. J Psychosom Res, 1978; 22:201-4.

36. Crisp AH, Kalucy RS. Aspects of the perceptual disorder in anorexia nervosa. Br J Med Psychol, 1974; 47:349-61.

37. Fries H. Studies on secondary amenorrhea, anorectic behavior and body image perception: Importance for the early recognition of anorexia nervosa. In: Vigersky R. ed. Anorexia nervosa. New York: Raven Press, 1977:

38. Ben-Tovim DI, Whitehead J, Crisp AH. A controlled study of the perception of body width in anorexia nervosa. J Psychosom Res, 1979; 23:267-72.

39. Feighner JP, Robins E, Guze SB, Woodruff RS, Jr. Winokur G, Munoz R. Diagnostic criteria for use in psychiatric research. Arch Gen Psychiatry, 1972; 26:57-63.

40. Slade PD. A review of body image studies in anorexia nervosa and bulimia nervosa. J Psychiat Res, 1985; 19:255-65.

41. Vandereycken W, Meermann R. Anorexia nervosa: A clinician's guide to treatment. New York: Walter de Gruyter and Co, 1984:

42. Meerman R, Vandereycken W. Body image disturbances in eating disorders from the viewpoint of experimental research. In: Pirke KM et al, eds. Psychobiology of bulimia nervosa. Berlin, New York: Springer 1987, in press.

43. Vandereycken W, Probst M, Meermann R. An experimental video-confrontation procedure as a therapeutic technique and a research tool in the treatment of eating disorders. In: Pirke KM et al, eds. Psychobiology of bulimia nervosa. Berlin, New York: Springer 1987, in press.

Chapter 16

Transcultural Perspectives on Eating Disorders

Daniel M.A. Freeman

It is commonplace that one man's meat is another man's poison. Since the fact of cultural variability is well known, this paper will not attempt to catalogue the range of eating phenomena that illustrate the diversity of human experience. Rather, we will focus on three seemingly bizarre and to us almost unthinkable phenomena and attempt to illuminate the human function of each. We will consider a practice of forcing preadolescent boys to orally ingest the semen of older youths on a regular basis over a period of years, the eating of portions of the bodies of one's dead relatives, and a conviction that one's dead relative is likely to return as a ghost and attempt to eat you. The three examples lead to very different sequelae in terms of eating and emotional disorders.

For the past 25 years cultural anthropologists and psychoanalysts have been fruitfully collaborating in interdisciplinary colloquia at American Psychoanalytic Association conventions. The examples are drawn from this collaboration and material presented at these colloquia in 1971, 1982, and 1983. The data for the first two examples were gathered by anthropologists Gilbert H. Herdt and Fitz J.P. Poole, and the data for the third by my wife and I, an anthropologist and child psychoanalyst husband-and-wife team.

FORCED INGESTION OF FELLATED SEMEN

In the early 1970s, Herdt studied a hitherto isolated tribe in the remote Eastern Highlands of Papua, New Guinea, whose members believe that oral insemination is essential for boys to grow into men [1,2]. He explored Sambia observations concerning human physiology that led to concepts of human nature and of maleness and femaleness that are very different from our own. These concepts are the basis of Sambia beliefs and ritual practice.

Sambia men have come to regard women with awe and to perceive themselves as having been born incomplete and weak. They observe that powerful forces are alive within women, as the waxing and waning of menstrual cycles dramatizes the periodicity of an active energy that empowers woman's fecundity. The woman's menstrual blood organ appears to be self-activating and internally self-sustaining. Unlike warriors, who are endangered when they lose blood in battle, women are seemingly unaffected by their blood loss, possessing an apparently great natural power to generate and regenerate blood. Blood is seen as a source of vitality and fuel for endurance; hence, women are seen as innately healthier than men. It is noted that women also have the power to bear children, whereas every man is incomplete until he attains a wife who can bear him a child.

Sambia men experience themselves as having something missing, and perceive femaleness to be inherently more powerful. They regard masculine strength and masculinity not as natural endowments but rather as attributes they must constantly strive to attain. Their assumption is that femaleness is fundamental and that the vitality of all beings stems from a female aspect. Maleness emerges from femaleness, but only as a result of years of ritual effort. This is not a reality with which men are comfortable, and they seek to deny and compensate for it. In their rituals, they create secret male counterparts for the female functions of nursing and menstruation. For example, each month at the time of their wives' menstruation, Sambian men secretly induce painful nosebleeding by thrusting sharp canes up their nostrils. Women are seen as steadfast like the Earth itself, harkening back to the mother who was the central figure of the boy's childhood [1].

Sambian men are very concerned about the overwhelming influence that such powerful mothers have on their young developing sons. Fathers keep at a distance and do not have an active role in the boys' rearing in early childhood. They then fear that the boy has been feminized and made soft by the years of close contact with his mother. The boy must be separated from her and masculinized by being submitted to rituals that will turn him into a man. Semen is the masculinizing fluid that will counteract all of the feminine substances and influences and assure the development and maintenance of masculinity.

Sambian boys are taken from their mothers between ages 7 and 10 and initiated into the male cult. Thereafter, for the next 10 to 15 years, they have contact only with males and engage in fellatio on a daily basis. Elders teach that semen is absolutely essential. From the latter part of childhood until puberty, boys should ingest as much semen as possible. Then the young initiates are transformed, with the assistance of ritual, into older youths, and they become the fellated partners for a new group of ritual novices. Both young fellating boys and older fellated youths must absolutely avoid women on pain of severe punishment. They are warned that females are contaminating and their menstrual blood polluting and potentially lethal. Participation in prescribed fellatio activities and required avoidance of women continue until marriage. Even casual conversations between boys and girls are blocked and forbidden.

The earlier prolonged nurturant dependency on mother contributed a core of oral optimism, which will be valuable for the future warrior; but then it is necessary to masculinize him into unflinching bravery in preparation for brutal murderous warfare and to separate him from his soft dependent cravings. The onset of the initiation rites is frightening and traumatic [2]. Purging, beating, and nose-bleeding are used to rid the boy of his physical contamination by women. Then the important masculinizing ingestive rites begin. Herdt recognized that the oral insemination had to be understood as an ingestive rite within initiation and that it had no permanent long-term effect on adult sexual preference for heterosexuality.

The idea of fellatio is first introduced to the novices with the explanation that all grown men "ate the penis" in the past and it was this that resulted in their having grown big. They are told that it is urgent for them to similarly ingest semen; otherwise their bodies will remain small and ugly. The boys are frightened and initially experience shame and revulsion. They are told that ingestion of semen is equivalent to the ingestion of maternal breast milk. It is explained that the mothers' food that they received in the past was inadequate and that was the reason for their past retarded development. The ingestion of nutritive and masculinizing semen will allow them to complete their development as a man [1]. Against the background of an increase in dependent longings arising from their abrupt separation from their mothers and the traumatic initiation they are experiencing, an oral dependent regression occurs, and the vast majority of Sambia boys fall in line with the pattern of oral semen ingestion that is constrained by cultural requirement. They are aware of being in an invidious state of subordination as sexual objects who are being treated like a woman or wife, and they do express some fears of becoming pregnant from fellatio, but they are comforted by the notion that semen is "our breast milk" and see themselves as likened to an infant being fed by its mother. Ultimately, indeed, their bodies and penises do start to grow as promised, they attain puberty, and they progress to a new stage of being bachelor pubescent youths who are fellated by a new group of young initiates.

What are the fantasies of the older youths who are fellated? Initially they are afraid; they fear that being fellated will lead to a loss and depletion of the very semen they have been working to accumulate. They fear a depletion of their vital strength. On the other hand, they wish to move forward toward manhood, have an obligation to conform, are able to eat masculinizing foods that help maintain their level of semen, are eager to transcend the subservient position they have been in as fellators, and now for the first time will have an ejaculatory erotic outlet.

After puberty, all youths cease being fellators. After marriage, some transiently continue to be fellated by young boys during the adjustment to their new marriage. But by the time their first child is born, virtually all Sambia men are exclusively heterosexual.

During their years of fellatio, young novices and older youths don't think of themselves as attracted only or primarily to males. They continue to be interested in and excited by women's bodies but are forbidden access to them. They deride anal intercourse, which is known to be practiced by other tribes, and do not practice it.

Fellatio is clearly regarded as an erotically gratifying genital activity by older youths and adult males. They do not seem, however, to pay attention to the specific gender of the mouth that does the sucking or to think of it as specifically a male mouth when the fellator is a young boy. In the most sacred of all Sambia myths, which is recounted by those who have attained full manhood, the ancestral father offers the services of his young son as a fellator to his older adolescent son to appease the sexual desires of his adolescent son so that the youth will not overthrow the father and take possession of the father's wife as a sexual object. The young boy's mouth is perceived as a surrogate gratifying orifice to serve as a sexual outlet and to forestall oedipal confrontation during adolescence until the youth has married and attained an acceptable heterosexual outlet of his own [1].

There is also an oral level to the fantasies that are experienced by the fellated youths and adult males. For example, men report having to withdraw from the nursing situation because they feel jealous as they observe the baby sucking the breast. The older men recreate this situation when they get their adolescent sons to be the "breast feeders" and their young initiate sons to be the sucklings who suckle on the older youths' "breasts." The difference is that now the youths and older males experience the fantasy of themselves being the potent woman. But they continue to be jealous of the nurslings who are ingesting all of the good "milk" that creates strength and potency.

On the surface, Sambia fellatio appears to be "homosexual" because it occurs between males. The preferred sexual object for almost all Sambia initiates, youths, and adult males is, however, a woman. The enforced separation of initiates from their mothers does not take away their fantasy that it is a woman's breast that they wish to suckle. Youths are coerced temporarily to use a surrogate orifice, but their true interest is in obtaining a woman. Thus although this ritually enforced behavior occurs between members of the same sex, it might better be described as pseudo-homosexual.

The orally oriented component of the fellatio has an interesting counterpart in our own culture. Blos [3] described a pseudo-heterosexual pattern focused primarily on oral fellatio wishes in a group of delinquent girls. Arrested at a preadolescent level and experiencing extreme ambivalence in their relationships with their mothers, they became prostitutes whose true goal was to be cuddled and breast-fed by the penis of a safer (male) kind of person than the mother that they longed for but feared. Their behavior as prostitutes appeared manifestly to be heterosexual but was actually oral and pseudo-heterosexual. Their true goal was to receive good mother's milk ingested by fellatio as they suckled at the man's breast/penis.

All phenomena observed in other cultures may have counterparts in the fantasies or fears of some individuals within our own culture. These fantasies may be acted out or portrayed symbolically in dreams. At other times we see patients whose presenting symptomatology represents a defense against such fantasies.

Traumatic initiation into a cult of ritualized enforced fellatio might seriously disrupt the emotional development of boys in another culture and result in not only severe psychophysiologic eating disturbances but also serious psychopathology. Within the context of Sambia culture, there are transient reactions of fear, disgust, and shame but not lasting psychopathology. The boys emerge from their role as fellators determined ever after to be dominant penetrators (in their relations with women and especially in warfare) and never again to be put into a subservient passive position.

The eating phenomena that we will be considering in this paper are all related in one way or another to issues of separation and mourning. It has often been noted that mourning includes a regressive oral incorporative component. The mourner seeks to take into himself those aspects of the departed that he cherishes and treasures and wishes to hold onto and lock forever within the "locket" of his heart. The young Sambia boy who has abruptly been separated from his mother and has lost forever his world of childhood pleasures seeks regressively to orally introject the good milk of his lost "good mother." The male world and the initiatory process in which he becomes immersed redefine for him the connotations of "good mother" and "bad mother," but emotionally he seeks to deal with his loss through typical mourning introjective processes.

The next example will be one in which there is an oral biting rather than oral sucking response in the mourning process.

EATING PORTIONS OF THE BODIES OF ONE'S DEAD RELATIVES

If the idea of forcing young boys to perform fellatio and ingest semen is not confusing or upsetting enough to the Western observer or reader, let us now turn to the funerary idea of eating pieces of the bodies of one's dead relatives. Poole studied a New Guinea tribe whose members regularly carry out this (and a number of other) cannibalistic practices. He directly witnessed funerary cannabalistic rites on 11 occasions [4].

All societies struggle to find answers to the eternal questions of birth, life, and death, and they seek to establish ideologies that explain the relationship between the mortal biological individual and the enduring continuity and perpetuity of society and the cosmos. Many societies choose to emphasize the recurrences and the repetitions of life experiences and have developed a cyclical concept of time rather than a concept of time as a linear, unidirectional, irreversible highway. They note that birth follows death just as death follows birth and that springtime follows winter as regularly as waves beat in sequence on the shore. From such a perspective, historical lives are transcended by an eternal cosmological order. The promise of continuity and rebirth becomes a negation of the apparent finality of death with its consequent threat of rupture and discontinuity. The Bimin-Kuskusmin view death as a rebirth into a collectivity of ancestral spirits, which in turn is the source of fertility and substance out of which new generations of babies will be born. The dead and the living are thus connected in an eternal regenerative cycle, with a continuity between the clan collectivities of the ancestral world and the fetuses of those yet to be born [5].

As people age and become elders, they are seen not as approaching a point of finality but rather as moving toward ancestorhood and immortality. Therefore, even as their bodily faculties wane, they are seen as progressively gaining in ritual and spiritual power. When they die, various relatives are required to eat prescribed pieces of their corpse. This includes lower belly fat (from the area adjacent to the genitalia) and bone marrow. In addition, the wife of a deceased man, if she is still within her childbearing years, is expected to eat a tiny raw fragment of flesh from her dead husband's penis, while the husband who is still sexually and ritually active is obliged to eat a small raw fragment of flesh from his dead wife's vagina. When paramount ritual elders die, portions of their raw heart tissue and uterus are also eaten [4,5]. Such mortuary cannibalism is seen as ensuring both the safe passage of the departed relative's spirit to the ancestral world and the recycling of his or her ritual and procreative strength.

The reader may be aghast in trying to imagine such practices. It may be quite understandable that people would want to develop a concept of societal and cosmic regenerative continuity, but why do it in this way? Indeed, Poole observed that Bimin-Kuskusmin children of age 4 or 5 became terrified after witnessing their parents engaged in such cannibalism, avoided their parents, shrieked in their presence, and recounted nightmares concerning creatures whose features resembled their parents and who were smeared with blood or other organs. He also found that many adults whom he interviewed and who admitted to having participated in such socially proper cannibalistic practices acknowledged considerable ambivalence, horror, and disgust at their own acts. Many reported that they had not been able to engage in the act, had not completed it, had vomited or even fainted, or had hidden the prescribed morsel and had lied about consuming it [4]. This act is therefore a very difficult one even for many Bimin-

Kuskusmin, despite the fact that it is only one of several forms of socially sanctioned or nonsanctioned forms of cannibalism that occur in their society. In Bimin-Kuskusmin culture, cannibalism is at times perceived as being an inhuman ghoulish nightmare and at other times perceived as a sacred moral duty. On the field of battle, fully initiated men may consume certain parts of the bodies of slain enemy warriors in order to defile, express contempt, and preclude accession to ancestorhood by the enemy. All adult men and women also participated in complex acts of ritual cannibalism during the Great Pandanus Rite, which occurred about once every generation. An enemy male and enemy female were sacrificed through prolonged torture, and portions of their bodies were eaten by all Bimin-Kuskusmin adults. The purpose was to gain the strength attained by the victims through their agony of prolonged tortured suffering and thereby strengthen the fertility and growth of both humans and pandanus trees. At the same time, this cannibalistic act would nullify the threat of enemy warriors and enemy witchcraft. In addition to these socially sanctioned and ritually prescribed forms of anthropophagia, there are other cannibalistic acts of witches and emotionally disturbed individuals that are viewed with horror and disgust as barbaric and inhuman.

All of this further emphasizes the question as to why cannibalism should be chosen as the means to achieve these ends. Poole's data gives us some excellent clues as to the origin of oral aggressive impulses during Bimin-Kuskusmin infancy and early childhood [6,7].

The Bimin-Kuskusmin focus a great deal of attention and concern on the well-being of infants. They are hypervigilant, closely monitoring the mother's care for her child and watching for possible interactive problems. Poole has described almost compulsive divinations and constant attention to subtle features of behavior, through which they monitor dyadic aspects of the physical, psychological, social, and spiritual maturation of infants, watching for possible aberrant development. It is the mother's responsibility to calm her infant with gentle fondling, cradling, warming, and nursing, and by speaking to it frequently with affection. It is feared that she may harm the infant by neglect, through erratic behavior, or by exposing the infant to emotional outbursts. Her angry thoughts and feelings and her anxieties can be harmful to the infant, so it is emphasized that she must control her fear and anger when the infant is unruly. She must especially try to guard the infant against extreme emotional displays and protect the infant from being startled or frightened. Ideally, it is expected that nursing will be permissive and that a child will never be punished. Yet it is feared and reported that there are women who neglect, overcontrol, and physically abuse heir infants in private and who desire to cause discomfort and misfortune. Most feared of all is the Taman witch, who appears indistinguishable on the surface, but s driven by insatiable sexual and cannibalistic impulses and is unable to either produce or adequately nourish normal offspring [8].

The infant is almost always in bodily contact with its mother for the first two years and is nursed on and beyond demand. The father is absent because of residential segregation, and there is a strict postpartum sex taboo until the child is fully weaned at age 3 to 4 years.

It is the mother's responsibility to actively stimulate the infant as much as possible without provoking any form of anger and rage. Illness in the infant is seen as occurring when self-centeredness in the infant goes too far or when the encompassment within the dyadic relationship with mother becomes too oppressive. The feared illnesses are various states of infantile anger and rage. These result from prenatal resentment and negative feelings in the mother toward the unborn child and from postnatal treatment of the child. Urgent ritual intervention by father and a change in the mother's care for the child become essential; otherwise such an illness will have a fatal outcome. In addition to harm arising from actual abuse, neglect, or hostile impulses in the mother, it is recognized that frustration provoked by the mother's control of the infant's behavior can be a source of infantile rage. Rage can arise from the ways in which the infant is restricted, isolated, constrained in its explorations, and forced to breast-feed beyond its desire [6].

A mother is expected to stimulate her infant son's penis, leading to erections, to promote growth and strength. In turn, she is expected to get him to stimulate her breasts, producing hardening of her nipples, to induce copious lactation. It is explicitly recognized that there is a sexual connotation to such mutual stimulation, but it is seen as a playful one only. If the mother is responsible, she will try to ensure that the limits of "infantile lust" are not exceeded, by only occasionally and gently rubbing the penis, and by discouraging her son's manipulating her breast at such times. She is supposed to cover her breasts when stimulating the penis in the ritually prescribed manner and often does so ostentatiously as a display to an ever-watchful public that she is acting properly in caring for her son.

But some mothers are believed to stimulate their sons beyond the bounds of "infantile lust" to satisfy their own sexual desires, to the detriment of their child. Poole notes that these "erotic" acts are often somewhat rough. He reports that the mother's stimulation of the penis may involve pulling, pinching, and twisting in a manner that frequently causes struggling and crying in the infant child. In turn, he reports having treated many women whose nipples had been bruised and lacerated by their infants. Such injuries to the mother's nipples are seen as deliberate, as retaliation for "penis rubbing," or as revenge related to the mother's attempts to frustrate and control the child [6,7].

An additional trauma occurs in the middle of the first year of life when the infant experiences stranger anxiety. Fearful that her presence may increase the fear to such an extent that the infant is driven to a frenzied state of uncontrollable tremors, the mother withdraws when the child experiences stranger anxiety. Only later in infancy will the mother remain with the child in the threatening situation and seek to calm it by offering comfort with respect to the specific object of fear [6].

From these descriptions it is clear that Bimin-Kuskusmin mothers are expected to stimulate their infants almost to the point of overload and rage without going over that threshold—while simultaneously making efforts to calm and control them almost to the point of being oppressively overgratifying and frustratingly overcontrolling. It is clear from the hypervigilant concerns of other members of this society that a significant number of mothers go beyond these bounds, some through immaturity and inexperience and others acting out hostile destructive impulses and lust. In these instances, oral aggressive and hostile destructive impulses, confusingly sadomasochistically linked to erotic impulses, are stirred up in the infant. Some women who are driven by base desires and a quest to destroy all vestiges of masculinity in their sons are identified as witches.

Though the roots of oral aggressive and erotic impulses go back to the mother-child interaction in infancy, the final consolidation of the child's fantasies concerning cannibalism occurs at age 4 or 5 when he discovers that his own parents perform cannibalistic acts. As has already been mentioned, some children react with terror at this time, avoid their parents, shriek in their presence, and recount terrifying cannibalistic nightmares.

In view of the apparently wide range of mother-infant experiences, it is not surprising that while oral aggressive impulses can be successfully directed into ritually sanctioned channels for most members of Bimin-Kuskusmin society, aberrant individuals may manifest various forms of indiscriminate and insane cannibalism. The most deviant individuals are those who have suffered the most erratic outbursts and sadomasochistic abusive experiences. They are reported to either die in infancy or to become deranged beasts, devoid of all vestiges of proper personhood, who are excluded from society.

Developmental experiences can, therefore, result in a recognized form of psychopathologic eating disorder. More commonly, however, the oral impulses are sublimated into a socially integrative sacred form of ritual obligation. Oral introjective mechanisms are operative in

Bimin-Kuskusmin funerary cannibalism, as in all forms of mourning, as the mourner takes inside and identifies with the positive attributes of the departed. Ritual obligation and sacred moral responsibility require that mature Bimin-Kuskusmin participate in an act that assures regenerative continuity and fertility for their society, no matter how personally distasteful the required act is. Though oral aggressive impulses had a place in their feelings earlier in their lives, most are now reticent and uncomfortable about engaging in such an act even when they are convinced that it is essential and obligatory.

In our own culture, we can see a conflict over a somewhat similar issue in anorexia nervosa, where every effort may be focused on an urgent determination to conquer a dangerous ravenous oral aggressive impulse.

Both Sambia and Bimin-Kuskusmin practices exemplify eating behaviors that for us would be extremely conflictual, but which serve constructive socially and emotionally adaptive functions in these societies. Recently our society has adopted a practice not totally dissimilar from that of Bimin-Kuskusmin tradition when we transplant organs of recently deceased individuals to promote life within the bodies of the living.

Next we will consider a severe acute eating disorder, which is recognized as a dangerous form of psychopathology within its own culture yet occurs in at least 85% of the members of the society. Kiowa Apache Ghost Sickness is an illness that occurs when a mourner fears that he is about to be attacked and devoured by the ghost of the departed.

THE FEAR OF BEING EATEN BY A GHOST

My wife and I worked with the Plains Apache or Kiowa Apache Indians in Oklahoma in 1964 and 1965 [9-12]. Since Apaches always had an intense fear of ghosts, death traditionally evoked elaborate ritual defenses. Despite the cultural changes of the past century, Ghost Sickness remains remarkably prevalent.

It is believed that after death the vital force or animating spirit of an individual, including his good qualities and the controls that had regulated his behavior, departs for an afterworld in the sky or heaven. His impulses, evil tendencies, yearnings, and rage are thereby released, and become dangerous and all but unpredictable. The precipitate of these evil tendencies can furnish motive power for a ghost that may seek to return to spread terror and sickness among the living [13]. The proper destination of the ghost is an afterworld located under a mythological northern lake. However, lonesome feelings in the mourner or loneliness in the ghost may cause the ghost to remain nearby, grieving at the severance of relationships, "stingy" for his posses-

sions, jealous of those who remain behind, and wanting to take along those who have been close to him. Lonesome feelings in the mourner may cause his mind to wander out of his body; and loneliness in the ghost may cause him to return. The ghost is a mirror image of the mourner's feelings of loss and deprivation [10].

The Ghost Sickness attack is often preceded by hypersalivation and fear of swallowing one's saliva for a period of several days. Suddenly, the afflicted mourner is grasped by terror as he hears a sound and knows that the ghost of the deceased relative is coming up behind him. If he turns part way to look back over his shoulder he will be paralyzed by the touch of deadness and twisted into a spasmodic, right-sided palsy as the ghost tries to pull him toward him. Most dangerous of all is to catch a glimpse of the face and biting mouth of the ghost, which fortunately are usually enveloped in shadow. It is anticipated that the ghost will be possessed by biting rage derived from a previous traumatic abandonment that all Apaches experienced in early childhood.

The entire right side of the afflicted individual is twisted and shaking violently. He is hyperventilating, massively hypersalivating, terrified that if he swallows his saliva it will choke him and stop up his breathing, and terrified of a conflict between his wish for reunion and fear of oral incorporative engulfment. The oral phenomena commonly include tightening in the mouth, biting of the tongue if he tries to speak, air swallowing, choking, inability to eat or drink, and vomiting to get rid of any saliva inadvertently swallowed. The mouth and face are twisted as though the ghost had grabbed hold of the victim's mouth and pulled it toward the right. The right arm and leg are in a spastic posture resembling tetany or resembling what would be an effeminate mannerism in our culture.

The victim of the attack feels that he is choked by his spit and that his breathing is blocked (commonly caused by esophageal spasm, diaphragmatic spasm, and hyperventilatory apnea). Ultimately he may lapse into unconsciousness by a vasovagal mechanism as a result of the hyperventilation followed by breath holding and straining. The spastic shaking followed by unconsciousness creates an epileptiform picture but these are not epileptic seizures.

Longing for reunion, yet terrified of cannibalistic engulfment, the mourner becomes panicked as the ghost starts to pull him and as a portion of his body becomes paralyzed by the touch of deadness. The symptoms represent dissociative, conversion, and psychophysiologic phenomena as he struggles with feelings of loss and regressive oral incorporative impulses as well as active restitutive attempts as he struggles against fragmentation and loss of sense of self.

But this is a *normative* mourning reaction for Apaches, until their early 30s, in response to the death of a parent or relative who has been a key parent substitute. Eighty-five percent of Apache adults report having experienced at least a partial syndrome at the time of mourning, involving cannibalistic fantasies and concomitant gastrointestinal psychophysiological reactions. (The true lifetime prevalence is probably even higher because some individuals were interviewed in their early 20s before they had outgrown the vulnerable period for Ghost Sickness, and because there is reticence to discuss ghost fears, since the malevolence of ghosts used to be thought to be related to witchcraft). Sixty-nine percent of adults report that these cannibalistic features were accompanied by overt ghost fears. In 46%, the ghost fears and cannibalistic fantasies were sufficiently intense to cause a *severe* eating disturbance. Fifteen percent developed the full-blown "Ghost Sickness" reaction including all of the previous features plus an actual attack and twisting by the ghost, right-sided spasmodic palsy and epileptiform spells. Our interest will focus on the cannibalistic and gastrointestinal responses common to both the partial and full-blown Ghost Sickness syndromes.

Both the ghost and the idealized image of the departed's good qualities (which becomes the spirit that goes to the sky world) represent intrapsychic images of the parent that became established early in life. Despite the disruptive nature of the acute Ghost Sickness attack, the splitting off and projection of "bad" aspects of the ghost serve an important function. They helps in purify the "good" image of the parent, thereby facilitating selective identification with the good qualities. This is an essential part of mourning. The mourner's family and the entire community rally to his assistance, and with the help of healing ceremonies, the regression is usually brief and recovery rapid. Interestingly, after the early 30s, Ghost Sickness rarely occurs, and the mourning process shifts to a pattern similar to that experienced by adolescents and adults in our culture. A much more detailed analysis of Apache child development and the intrapsychic processes underlying this particular form of mourning reaction has been presented in previous papers [9,10].

Actual acts of cannibalism were unknown but much feared among these Apaches. They are very much concerned with issues of biting animals and man-eating monsters [14]. They continue to be extremely afraid of bears, for example, though hundred of years have passed since their migration to their present location where bears are unknown. Dreams of biting animals and biting monsters are so common that Apaches often awaken hypersalivating and choking, and traditionally would induce vomiting prophylactically each morning to get rid of any saliva inadvertently swallowed during such dreams while they were sleeping. Cannibalistic fears are explicit in some of the dreams, such as dreams of an attacking biting face coming at them or dreams of being forced to eat human flesh. Apaches would not eat the flesh of any animal that in fact or fantasy was perceived to be a man-eater for fear that they would be turned into such a monster. Actual cannibalistic acts were said to occur only when starvation drove someone insane.

Why would children grow up with a cultural expectation that the ghost of their parent or key parent substitute would come back and attempt to devour them? It is easier to understand the loneliness of the bereaved and his wish for and fear of reunion with the departed. Why such an explosion of conflict about the mourner's own ingestive impulses and terror that he, in turn, was about to be devoured?

We should briefly mention that the child was socialized in a world in which biting bogeys and myths concerning biting monsters were used as warnings to shape his behavior. Children were even warned in the mythology that if they went too far, they might get into a situation where a relative or someone they trusted turned out to be a cannibal. At times, a cloth or frying pan painted with a scary face with a biting mouth would be used to frighten a wayward child. However, these data leave unanswered our question as to why there should have been such a focus on biting and devouring and how the developing Apache child came to expect and fear such an attack from key nurturant figures if death removed the loved one's rational controls.

The critical determinants in Apache child development occurred during the second year of life. An abrupt traumatic displacement and rejection of the nursling in the midst of the rapprochement subphase of separation-individuation [10,15] had a decisive impact on personality development and altered the course of the entire life cycle.

After the first year of life, which was permissive but inconsistent in a way that focused the infant's dependence on the nurturant relationship with its mother, there was a sudden interruption of this relationship with a shift of the primary caretaking role from parents to grandparents. This slowed the rate of progression through the life cycle and prolonged each of the subsequent stages of development. Because a substitute relationship of special privilege was available with the grandparents (who had matured and were much more emotionally available for a child-rearing role than the parents were), the traumatic disruption in the midst of separation-individuation did not lead to a permanent arrest, and development resumed.

Of particular importance in the Apache life cycle was a prolongation of adolescence through the 20s, which made Apaches well suited for their raiding and hunting equestrian way of life. Their high degree of adaptability and success in exploiting their environment depended on the initiative, daring, and assertiveness of the adolescent and young adult warrior-hunter. The late teens and twenties were a period of intense activity, freedom, and license. Youths did not marry before age 30. Psychological maturation was even further delayed. Initial marriages were unstable and temporary, and true stability and deepening attachment to one's spouse developed only with an advance of years [16].

During the childbearing period of the teens and 20s, adolescent parents were emotionally unprepared for the full weight of parental responsibility. They were neither physically nor emotionally available for the task of caring for children. While men were away hunting and on the warpath, women in the active stage of life were engaged in the hard labor of tanning hides, making clothing and teepees, moving camp and preparing food, in addition to responsibilities of caring for infants. Continuing adolescent conflicts made them inadequately emotionally available to their children. However, subsequent emotional maturation enabled both men and women to later fill critical child-rearing roles.

It was within the special privilege and reciprocity of the relationship with the grandparents that the child gradually recovered from his rejection by his mother. But then it was in relation to the death of these substitute nurturing figures that ghost fears were most likely to occur. It was the loving nurturing grandparent that paradoxically might be the most likely to be feared as a potentially malevolent and cannibalizing ghost.

Favoritism and rejection of children were present in extreme forms. The youngest child was favored, pampered, and believed to be smartest and best. The special position of a youngest child enhanced the uniqueness of the relationship to mother during infancy but led to the severity of the fall when a younger sibling came along. The harshness of the rejection was made possible by the parent's concepts of the child [11] and was intensified by the mother's inability to tolerate the child's rage after the abrupt weaning and realignment of family relationships. The life cycle was conceptualized as a series of separate compartments rather than as a progressive evolution, with the child being viewed as an occupant of a separate category from an adult. Since the child was not thought of developmentally in terms of a linear progression toward adulthood, and since his qualities were conceived of as innate rather than acquired, the parent would simply react to an overall impression of the child's inherent goodness or badness. The rejection was abrupt and harsh. The child was initially either "poisoned" by pepper or other bitter-tasting material being put on the nipple or abruptly taken away from his mother. Sub-

sequently, as his turmoil and rage mounted and as he tried to get back to her, he was angrily pushed away with comments like, "You crazy kid!! *Get* away!"

Apache mythology vividly portrays the chaotic feelings and emotional turbulence of the rejected child which are later regressively revived in Ghost Sickness at the time of mourning [12,14]. The child is portrayed as turning into a cannibalizing water monster. In one myth a starving Apache turns into a water monster when he eats a strange egg. He then demands that young children be thrown into his pool for him to devour. The people around the child also seem to turn into cannibalizing monsters. Even grandparents who offer help are feared as possible deceivers who may really be cannibals. When the emotionally "starving" child does receive food, he is afraid to eat and is afraid that something or someone is trying to fatten him up in order to devour him. This projection derives from his own cannibalistic rage and impulse to attack and devour both his mother's breast and the fattened baby who is receiving her attention. Mothers are warned that if they fall asleep (withdraw) while nursing a child, they will be attacked by a waterdog lizard (the angry, biting, rejected child), who will eat through their breast into their heart and kill them. When a sibling and grandparent try to rescue Water Boy, Water Boy scratches and bites at them as he accuses them, "You threw me away!" They patiently try to restrain and calm him and explain to him that it is not they who rejected him and that they are trying to save him. Gradually he calms down within his new relationships, yet he continues to have impulses (portrayed by coyote in the mythology) to cannibalize his younger sibling and fears that his younger sibling will take his food away from him. Apaches used to consider it a delicacy to eat the "clabber" or congealed milk from inside the stomach of a freshly slaughtered calf or fawn. The ultimate wish was not only to recover mother's milk stolen by the younger sibling but also to orally introject the lost mother in order to deal with the separation from her.

Oral introjective identificatory processes are the normal mechanisms utilized by a child at this stage to deal with separation from mother. By establishing a stable internal representation of mother the child is able to be reassured of her continuing existence and her continuing emotional availability even when they are separated from each other. Because the separation in Apaches was abrupt and traumatic rather than gradual and masterable, it is not surprising that this process of dealing with separation through identification was disrupted [10]. Feelings about both oneself and mother remain flooded with aggression. The Apaches and closely related Navajos have stories of mythological figures swallowing either a porcupine or horned toad but then being unable to assimilate and ultimately being killed by what they have swallowed. In various versions it could either choke off your breath, penetrate your heart, or cause you to swell up until your belly bursts open. Because of the suffusion of all of the child's feelings and relationships with biting rage, the process of separating by gradually establishing a stable internal representation of mother is impossible. Instead of completing the process of separation and individuation at this stage, the child is left with dangerous cannibalistic impulses and with fears of cannibalistic danger from those around him. Though his process of development gradually continues in the context of his new relationships, unresolved fears from the past may be reactivated in Ghost Sickness at the time of the death of a key nurturant figure.

We can now understand how it could be that a mourner would fear that his departed loved one would seek to attack and destroy him. The child's memories of parental and grandparental figures are ambivalent including both loving and sadistic features. There are two components of the image of the departed, a good side, which includes the positive memories of both infancy and the later experiences with the grandparent, and a bad side, which includes the chaotic memories from the time when the hitherto nurturant mother suddenly turned on the child and the universe suddenly seemed to be engulfed in danger and rage. It is not the loving portion of the image of the parent/grandparent that is feared; rather, it is the part of the composite image that derived from the chaos and biting fantasies at the time of the child's rapprochement rejection.

As we have already mentioned, the regressive splitting apart of these two images at the time of mourning facilitates the purification of the good parent image and selective identification with these good qualities. With the aid of their family and the entire community (who fill a supportive role similar to that originally played by the grandparent), the attack of Ghost Sickness is relatively brief, and the mourning process is successfully concluded.

Similar ghost phenomena occur, at times, in children from North American and European cultures. They are particularly common in those Mediterranean cultures where access to the world of spirits is valued as part of folk healing traditions. The author has treated Southern Italian adolescents suffering from a Ghost Sickness syndrome that appeared nearly identical to the Apache Ghost Sickness syndrome, and children of North European extraction who have had frightening ghost experiences that were similar in many regards. Little Red Riding Hood feared that her sweet old grandmother could turn into a wolf that would try to devour her.

A brief chapter does not do justice to the richness and complexity of any one of the cultures summarized, nor does it allow us to consider intrapsychic and interpersonal mechanisms in detail. These examples of practices and human responses that contrast sharply with those of our own culture may, however, offer a perspective on our assumptions about normative and pathologic phenomena.

One man's meat indeed can be another man's poison. Practices that may be meaningfully integrated into the total life experience and world view of one culture may be traumatically dystonic in another setting. We have also seen that some reactions may be so disruptive that even though they are "normative" (in the sense that they occur in the vast majority of individuals), they are still regarded as psychopathology even within their own culture.

Although all humans share common biological mechanisms, each culture shapes the developmental experiences of its children in its own unique way. No normative or pathological meaning can be imputed to phenomena apart from their cultural context. We have seen that regular fellatio between Sambia males cannot be considered homosexual in our usual meaning of that word, though it continues over a period of years. It is an enforced transient ritualized substitute, first for the nurturant mother and later for the still-unavailable heterosexual partner. The preferred object is a woman. Sambia men turn to heterosexuality as soon as heterosexuality is permitted.

For most Bimin-Kuskusmin adults, the eating of small portions of the body of one's dead relative does not gratify a conscious cannibalistic impulse. Rather, it is a repugnant ritual necessary to honor and perpetuate the spirit and substance of the dead and to promote fertility and continuity of the living.

Though Kiowa Apache Ghost Sickness involves a regressive fragmentation and dissociative loss of boundaries accompanied by severe cannibalistic fears and gastrointestinal phenomena, it serves an adaptive purpose in the course of mourning. The splitting off and projection of the image of the ghost with all of its aggressive components facilitates purification and identification with those idealized portions of the image of the departed that become internalized in the course of the mourning process.

Even an extremely dystonic eating practice, such as enforced ingestion of semen by young boys or required ingestion of parts of the dead body of one's relative, need not necessarily lead to an eating disorder. By contrast, a mere fantasy of being attacked by a ghost can lead to a severe disorder. We have also seen that neither the intensity and severity of Ghost Sickness nor the prolonged 10-to15-year span of ritualized fellatio have any prognostic implication for long-term outcome. Clearly, patterns of child rearing, ritual practice, and reactive eating and emotional disorders can each only be understood in their cultural context.

REFERENCES

1. Herdt GH. Guardians of the flutes. New York: McGraw-Hill, 1981.
2. Herdt GH. Fetish and fantasy in Sambia initiation. In Herdt GH, ed. Rituals of manhood. Berekley: University of California Press, 1982: 44-97.
3. Blos P. On adolescence. New York: Free Press of Glencoe, 1962: 230-44.
4. Poole FJP. Cannibals, tricksters, and witches: anthropophagic images among Bimin-Kuskusmin. In Brown P, Tuzin D, eds. The ethnography of cannibalism. Washington: Society of Psychological Anthropology, 1983: 6-32.
5. Poole FJP. Symobols of substance: Bimin-Kuskusmin models of procreation, death, and personhood. Mankind, 1984; 14:191-216.
6. Poole FJP. Coming into social being: cultural images of infants in Bimin-Kuskusmin folk psychology. In White G, Kirkpatrick J, eds. Person, self, and experience: Exploring pacific ethnopsychologies. Berkeley: University of California Press, 1985: 183-242.
7. Poole FJP. Folk models of eroticism in mothers and sons: aspects of sexuality among Bimin-Kuskusmin. Unpublished paper.
8. Poole FJP. Tamam: Ideological and sociological configurations of "witchcraft" among Bimin-Kuskusmin. Social Analysis, 1981; 8:58-76.
9. Freeman DMA. Adolescent crises of the Kiowa Apache Indian male. In Brody Ed, ed. Minority group adolescents in the United States. Baltimore: Williams & Wilkins, 1968: 157-204.
10. Freeman DMA, Foulks EF, Freeman PA. Ghost sickness and superego development in the Kiowa Apache male. In Muensterberger W, Esman AH, Boyer LB, eds. The psychoanalytic study of society. New Haven: Yale University Press, 1976: 123-77.
11. Freeman PA. Kiowa Apache concepts and attitudes towards the child. In Papers in anthropology. Norman: Department of Anthropology, University of Oklahma, 1971; 12,1:90-160.
12. Freeman DMA. Mythological portrayal of developmental processes and major intrapsychic restructuralizations. In Boyer LB, eds. The psychoanalytic study of society. New York: Psychohistory Press, 1981: 319-40.
13. Opler ME, Bittle WE. The death practices and eschatology of the Kiowa Apache. Southwestern Journal of Anthropology, 1961; 17:383- 94.
14. McAllister JG. Kiowa Apache tales. In Boatright MC, ed. The sky is my tipi. Dallas: Southern Methodist University Press, 1949; 22:1-141.
15. Mahler MS, Pine F, Bergman A. The psychological birth of the human infant, Symbiosis and Individuation. New York: Basic Books, 1975.
16. McAllister JG. Kiowa Apache social organization. In Eggan F, ed. Social anthropology of North American tribes. Chicago: University of Chicago Press, 1937: 96-169.

Chapter 17

New Neuroendocrine Findings in Anorexia Nervosa and Bulimia

Harry E. Gwirtsman, Leigh Anne Hohlstein, and Peter Roy-Byrne

Anorexia nervosa is a disorder in which a patient deliberately loses weight and fails to maintain a minimal normal weight for his age and height. Bulimia nervosa is a disorder characterized by recurrent episodes of binge eating, often followed by purging of the food by vomiting. Both anorexia nervosa and bulimia are associated with pervasive endocrine dysfunction, including amenorrhea, oligomenorrhea, and thyroid disturbances. Early endocrine studies in anorectics demonstrated that the pituitary-ovarian axis showed abnormal regulation, with luteinizing hormone (LH) rhythms reverting to an immature prepubescent pattern. No studies of pituitary-ovarian function in normal-weight bulimics have yet been published. The advent of new technologies and pharmacologic challenges have made it possible to examine the hypothalamo-pituitary-adrenal (HPA) and hypothalamo-pituitary-thyroid (HPT) endocrine axes in greater detail. Inasmuch as these endocrine disturbances may parallel or reflect perturbations in mood, appetite, and behavior, they may have relevance to the etiologies of these illnesses.

HYPOTHALAMO-PITUITARY-ADRENAL (HPA) AXIS

Corticotropin-releasing factor (CRF) and thyrotropin-releasing hormone (TRH) are released by neurons in the hypothalamus and enter the pituitary portal system in the infundibulum, where they are trans-ported to the anterior pituitary gland. Here they act upon receptors on the pituicytes to cause the release of adrenocorticotropic hormone (ACTH) and thyrotropin (TSH) respectively. Neurotransmitters appear to exert effects upon CRF, with serotonin and acetylcholine being stimulatory for the most part, and norepinephrine producing a tonic inhibitory effect [1,2,3]. Cortisol itself exerts both positive and negative feedback on ACTH, and possibly, also on CRF release. Much less is known about the neurotransmitter relationships with TRH, but the thyroid hormones thyroxine (T_4) and triiodothyronine (T_3) exert feedback inhibition on TSH and possibly also on TRH. Elevated glucocorticoids also inhibit TSH release, and it has been speculated that hyperactivity of the HPA axis can cause a diminution of activity in the HPT axis [4].

In normal individuals there is a diurnal rhythm for cortisol, with an increasing number of secretory episodes occurring between 2 and 8 AM, resulting in a peak plasma level at approximately 8 AM. Then there is a gradual decline in plasma levels and secretory episodes throughout the day, leading to a nadir at approximately midnight and 2 AM [5-7]. Normally, cortisol is cleared by renal mechanisms and has an approximate half-life in plasma of 60 minutes [6]. Studies by Boyar and Doerr demonstrated that the diurnal curve in patients with low-weight anorexia is reset at a higher level and is distorted, with a more pronounced peak and loss of the

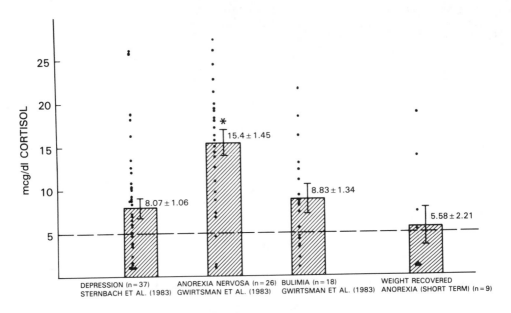

4 P.M. POST DEXAMETHASONE CORTISOL IN DEPRESSION, ANOREXIA NERVOSA, AND BULIMIA.

Figure 17.1 Underweight anorexic patients (AN) demonstrate the least amount of suppression to dexamethasone, with only 3 of 26 patients showing suppression below 5 mcg/dl. After short-term weight recovery, AN demonstrate more complete suppression, but a significant fraction still do not suppress. Depressives and bulimics demonstrate similar rates of nonsuppression.

nadir. Boyar felt that delayed degradation and abnormal metabolism of cortisol to tetrahydro-cortisone was the cause of this diurnal distortion, since the half-life of cortisol is prolonged to about 90 minutes in anorexia [8,9]. However, subsequent data from his own lab and by Doerr have shown that patients with anorexia show persistence of secretory bursts into the late evening, and overall, the cortisol production rate is increased in anorexia [6,9]. However, when anorexics regain weight, the diurnal cortisol pattern begins to return to normal [9,10].

In summary, then, the studies have demonstrated elevated plasma cortisols, elevated 24-hours mean plasma cortisol [7,8,11,12], distortion of the circadian cortisol rhythm, and prolonged plasma half-life of cortisol in anorexia nervosa [6-9,12]. These changes are precisely what is seen with pure protein-calorie malnutrition (PCM), and therefore probably represent an artifact of low weight or starvation [14-16]. However, there may be some differences between anorexia nervosa and pure malnutrition. First of all, the 24-hour output of urinary free cortisol (UFC) is elevated in the low-weight state of anorexia nervosa and returns to normal following weight recovery [10], while the UFC appears to be normal in malnutrition and shows no change after refeeding. This conclusion may be premature, because the excretion of free cortisol is dependent on glomeru-

lar filtration rates (GFR), and GFR may show a greater reduction in malnutrition than in anorexia. Secondly, cortisol production rate is elevated in anorexia nervosa, while it is diminished in PCM [15-17]. Furthermore, the cortisol production rate appears to decrease when patients with anorexia nervosa regain their weight, but it increases with weight recovery in PCM [10,15]. Thus, in this one parameter of cortisol metabolism, anorexics show an abnormality not seen in pure malnutrition. It is of interest that cortisol production rate and UFC are also increased in depressives [5,18], and this manifestation of HPA dysregulation in anorexia nervosa may be more closely related to the psychiatric condition than the physical state.

Efforts to perturb the HPA axis have been used in an attempt to assess its integrity in anorexia nervosa. Exogenous ACTH stimulation of the adrenal gland results in exaggerated cortisol responses in anorexics [11,19] similar to that seen in depressed patients, whereas this effect does not occur in pure malnutrition [14,15]. Metyrapone blocks the final step in cortisol synthesis from its precursor steroids. This produces a fall in cortisol levels. Such an acute drop should feed back upon the pituitary gland and produce an increase in the pituitary production of ACTH and possibly of CRF. The ACTH response to metyrapone administration is entirely normal in anorexia and in malnutrition. Thus, the

Table 17.1 Hypothalamic-Pituitary-Adrenal Axis I

	Anorexia Nervosa	Protein-Calorie Malnutrition	Depression
Basal Levels			
Plasma Cortisol	elevated	elevated	elevated
24-hour Mean Plasma Cortisol	elevated	elevated	elevated
24-hour Mean Plasma Cortisol, after Weight Recovery	normal	normal	—
Circadian Rhythm of Cortisol	preserved but distorted	—	very distorted
Metabolism			
Cortisol Production Rate (PPR) Relative to Body Size	increased	normal	increased
Change in PPR Compared with Low Weight	decreased	increased	—
Half-life of Cortisol in Plasma	increased	increased	normal
24-hour Excretion of Unconjugated ("free") Cortisol (UFC)	increased	increased	increased
Stimulation Studies			
ACTH and Cortisol Response to Metyrapone	normal	normal	normal
Cortisol Response to ACTH Stimulation	probably exaggerated	probably normal	probably normal
Suppression Studies			
Cortisol Response to Dexamethasone	Most have non-suppression	All have non-suppression	40% have non-suppression
Dexamethasone Suppression after Weight Gain	most suppress	normal	—

pituitary appears to respond normally to feedback regulation by the adrenal gland, ie, a drop in cortisol production by the adrenal gland in both anorexia and malnutrition, and the adrenal gland is probably hyperresponsive to signals from the pituitary in anorexia.

Dexamethasone is a highly potent synthetic glucocorticoid. It may be given as a single dose to suppress production of ACTH and CRF, mimicking the feedback inhibition by cortisol. This is known as the dexamethasone suppression test (DST). The general strategy is to give dexamethasone at 11 PM or midnight during the nadir of cortisol secretion, and in sufficient doses to suppress the HPA axis. Serum cortisol is sampled at 8 AM on Day 2. An extensive body of literature in psychiatry has demonstrated that the 4 PM and 11 PM time points on Day 2 have diagnostic utility in affective disorders, especially major depressive disorder with melancholia. A high percentage of control subjects, when given 1 or 2 mg dexamethasone PO at 11 PM, show complete suppression of cortisol to levels less than 2 mcg/dl, and this suppression lasts at least 24 hours. However, depressives and patients with other psychiatric disorders will show escape from suppression, usually at the 4 PM or 11 PM

time points. Figure 1 shows the 4 PM postdexamethasone cortisol in patients with anorexia nervosa, bulimia, weight-recovered anorexics, and a comparison group of patients with major depression. All patients were tested using the same RIA assay with an intraassay coefficient of variability of 16.2% and a sensitivity of 1 mcg/dl. Patients with low-weight anorexia nervosa show significantly higher cortisols than depressives and bulimics (ANOVA, one-way $F=8.56$, $p=0.04$), and fewer patients with low-weight anorexia nervosa suppress. However, following weight restoration, this difference disappears. It is of note that in PCM, dexamethasone does not suppress the HPA axis, but after refeeding, suppressibility returns to normal [15]. These relationships are summarized in table 1.

Based upon these findings, we divided our sample of low-weight anorexics and normal-weight bulimics to further investigate the relationship between weight and the DST. Figure 2 demonstrates clearly that in low-weight anorexia nervosa, bulimia nervosa, and obesity, lower weight patients show significantly more nonsuppression than higher weight patients. An emerging lit-

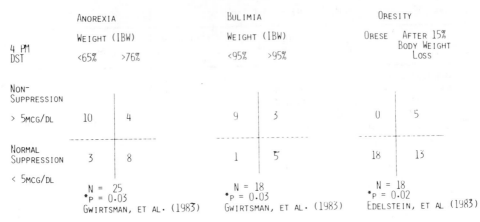

*Fisher Exact Test

Figure 17.2 When anorexics and bulimics are divided into groups based upon weight, they appear to have different responses to dexamethasone. Anorexics below 65% of ideal body weight (IBW) and bulimics below 95% of IBW suppressed less frequently than their slightly heavier counterparts. This has also been found in obese subjects. In these populations weight was an important determinant of DST nonsuppressibility, but degree of depression was not.

erature is beginning to examine this issue in normal volunteers and depressed patients. Thus far, two studies have asserted that the HPA axis becomes disinhibited when normal volunteers lose weight by dieting [20,21], and four of seven studies have found a positive relationship between dexamethaxone nonsuppression and history of weight loss in depressives [20-26].

Thus, in patients with both low-weight anorexia and normal-weight bulimia nervosa, a number of studies have demonstrated nonsuppressibility of cortisol in response to dexamethason [8,9,12,27-31]. The relationship of this biological parameter with mood state is an important one and has been inadequately investigated. In underweight anorexics [28] we failed to find an association between the presence of depression and DST nonsuppresison. In normal-weight bulimics, we found that 5/22 (23%) of our sample met criteria for DSM III major depressive disorder, but again there was no consistent relationship with DST abnormalities. Additionally, there was no significant relationship between DST and duration and severity of illness, menstrual abnormalities, T3 and T4 results, family history, previous history of primary anorexia nervosa, or treatment response with antidepressant. Edelstein et al [32] also failed to find any coincident mood changes with weight loss in her obese subjects who converted to abnormal DSTs. In weight-recovered anorexic patients, a number continue to show nonsuppression [27,33]. It is interesting to speculate that dexamethasone nonsuppressibility in this group may be more related to their psychiatric condition than their physical state, since patients with pure malnutrition do not suppress either, but all recover after refeeding [15,16].

HYPOTHALAMO-PITUITARY-THYROID (HPT) AXIS

It has been known for some time that patients with anorexia nervosa show clinical signs of hypothyroidism, including cold intolerance, constipation, low basal metabolism rate (BMR), bradycardia, elevated carotene, and slowed deep tendon reflexes. As mentioned before, the HPT axis is an endocrine cascade system with T4 and T3 as its final end product. These hormones act to inhibit TSH and possibly also TRH [4]. The control of TSH secretion is complex and controversial and may also involve other hormones and neurotransmitters. It has been found that electrical stimulation of the anterior hypothalamus, TRH, estrogens, and possibly norepinephrine enhance the secretion of TSH, whereas periphypothalamic lesions, somatostatin, dopamine, hypercortisol states, exogenous steroids, and possibly growth hormone (GH) [34] exert inhibitory effects on TSH release [4,35]. The effects of serotonin on the HPT axis are still unclear, but there is some evidence that this neurotransmitter may be inhibitory [36].

TRH itself is found in multiple brain regions such as the pineal, the amygdala, and other limbic areas, and may be transported through the CSF to act upon the anterior pituitary [4]. Exogenous TRH also releases prolactin in normals [4] and causes abnormal secretion of GH in anorexia, chronic liver disease, mental depression, acromegaly, hypothyroidism [36], and bulimia nervosa [31,37], but not in volunteers. These differential effects and some animal data imply that TRH may be modifying the pituitary directly and also indirectly via monoaminergic pathways. In disease states that affect the integrity of such pathways, the direct stimulatory effect of TRH on the pituitary becomes unmasked [36].

Basal chemical indices of thyroid function have been well studied and there is agreement that serum total T_4 is low normal in anorexia nervosa [36,38,39-43], but free T_4 is normal [36]. T_3 is in the hypothroid range, [36,38,41,44] even lower than in myxedema [41]. It appears as if T_3 but not T_4 is extremely sensitive to nutritional state, as studies of experimental starvation in normal volunteers and obese patients [45,46] demonstrate marked decreases in T_3, and the low T_3 seen in anorexia nervosa and PCM is corrected following weight gain [42,44,47]. One study has demonstrated rises of T_3 into the hyperthyroid range in anorexics during weight gain [41]. Reverse T_3, or rT_3, is a metabolically inactive isomer of T_3 that has been found to be elevated in anorexia nervosa [35,48], experimentally starved controls, obese individuals [48] PCM, and other disease states [47]. It is thought that tissue conversion of T_4 to T_3 is routed to rT_3 as a peripheral adaptation to starvation, which returns to normal following nutritional rehabilitation [32,35,46,48].

Baseline TSH levels in anorexia nervosa are in the normal range [35,38,40,42,43,49] and do not seem altered in starved controls or overweight patients [45,48]. In normal weight bulimics, baseline T_3 and T_4 concentrations are in the normal range [31,37]. Basal TSH levels in 11 female and three male bulimics that we studied were normal at 2.0 ± 0.1 u$^{U/L}$ and 1.6 ± 0.5 u$^{U/L}$ respectively. One other study [37] found one of six patients had mildly elevated basal TSH levels.

TSH has a circadian rhythm in normals [4,50] with a peak occurring during or after the onset of sleep and a nadir in the late afternoon. Both indirect [44] and direct (Gwirtsman, Kaye, and Gold, unpublished observations) measurement of these circadian rhythms indicate a loss of the nighttime surge in anorexia nervosa, with a general resetting of the curve upwards. Although these data are still preliminary and require replication, it is interesting that in animals, both hypothyroidism and hypothalamic lesions can abolish this TSH periodicity [4], implying that such dysregulation in anorexia nervosa may reflect hypothalamic dyscontrol.

The TRH stimulation test (TST) looks at the responsivity of the pituitary gland to maximal stimulation by the hypothalamic tripeptide TRH. The TST has been found to be blunted in a sizable perentage of patients with affective disorder. A normal response to TRH is a surge of TSH release from the pituitary reaching a peak at approximately 30 minutes and attaining a magnitude of 10 to 15 ng/ml over the baseline level. This peak minus baseline difference is known as the Δ Max TSH. Generally a Δ Max TSH of less than 5 to 7 ng/ml is considered a blunted response to TRH. In clinical hypothyroidism the TSH response to TRH is exaggerated, and when this is due to disease in the hypothalamus, the peak response of Δ Max TSH is often delayed [4,40]. Several investigators have looked at this response in small samples of anorectic patients, and some show a normal curve [40,43,49], but most demonstrate a delayed response [35,38,42-44,53]. Occasionally the TSH response has been blunted [34,35,42]. These changes are not due to hypothyroidism but are probably related to hypothalamic dysfunction, perhaps a deficiency of TRH [44,49]. It should be noted that, while some studies suggest that acute starvation of volunteers [51] and obese patients [52] diminishes the TSH response to TRH, other studies have failed to find this [45,48].

Following weight gain, many anorexia patients develop a more rapid response of Δ Max TSH and fewer blunted responses are seen [35,41], but some continue to be abnormal. Additionally, underweight anorexics demonstrate pathological GH increases to TRH [34,53]. These GH responses appear to be related in an inverse fashion to the blunted TSH response [34] and only partially correct with weight gain [42]. Such pathological changes are not specific to anorexia nervosa. Prolactin responses to TRH remain normal in anorexia at low weight and following weight recovery [42]. TST abnormalities and clinical characteristics of anorexia nervosa such as depression have not been studied to our knowledge.

In normal-weight bulimia nervosa TSH responses to TRH have been found to be blunted in eight of ten females in one study [31] and one of six patients in another investigation [37]. In our sample of 18 bulimics, TST abnormalities were not related systematically to duration and severity of illness, menstrual abnormalities, T_3 and T_4, past history of anorexia nervosa, family history, presence of major depressive disorders, or treatment response to antidepressants. There was a trend for patients with blunted TSH responses to TRH to be lower weight than those with normal responses (N=10, p=0.09).

HPA AND HPT RELATIONSHIPS

In order to assess the relationship between the HPA and HPT axes, it is important to perform tests relating to both of these axes in anorexia nervosa and bulimia nervosa. In depressed patients 70% to 80% of patients demonstrate either a DST or TRH abnormality, and 30% to 40% have a disturbance on both tests [53,54] (figure 3). We are unaware of any studies that examine this relationship in anorexics or in malnourished patients. However, in a small sample of bulimic patients who weighed 95% $\pm$ 2.4% of ideal weight by (range 83% to 111%) by Metropolitan Life Insurance tables, we found that all subjects had either a DST or TRH ab-

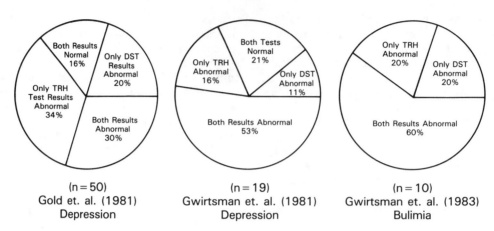

Thyrotropin releasing hormone (TRH) test and dexamethasone suppression test
(DST) abnormalities in unipolar depression and bulimia.

Figure 17.3 Two studies agree that neuroendocrine abnormalities are commonly found in depression. Only 16% to 21% of depressed individuals had no abnormality on either the TRH or DST. In ten normal-weight bulimics, the same degree of neuroendocrine dysfunction can be demonstrated. All of the bulimics had either a TRH or DST abnormality, and 6 of 10 were abnormal on both tests.

normality and six of ten or 60%, had both tests abnormal. Our bulimia nervosa patients had signs and symptoms of depression, usually meeting criteria for dysthymic disorder, but only three had symptoms that were severe enough to classify as major depressive disorder. The data collected thus far are preliminary and are insufficient to allow us to attribute the cause of the more endocrinologically disturbed patients to severity of their depressions. Similarly, there were no consistent relationships between menstrual abnormalities, nor history of anorexia nervosa, and the double DST and TST abnormality. Perhaps the neuroendocrine aberrations in these bulimic patients are related more to the behaviors of bingeing and vomiting. Studies are now underway in this laboratory to determine if this is so.

NEUROENDOCRINE-ADRENERGIC SYSTEM RELATIONSHIPS

The adrenergic system has been studied extensively in eating disorders and will be reviewed in the chapter by Kaye et al. Several studies of urinary 3-methoxy-4-hydroxy-phenylglycol (MHPG) agree that this parameter is low in underweight anorexia nervosa patients [28,55,56,57] and returns to normal with refeeding [56,57]. CSF levels of norepinephrine are normal in underweight and refed anorectics but decline in the long-term weight recovered phase [58]. Defining the relationships between the adrenergic system and the HPA and HPT axes is important in enhancing our understanding of the biophysiology of eating disorders. One

study [28] demonstrates a direct relationship between DST nonsuppression and lowered MHPG in underweight anorexia nervosa. In order to explore the relationship between neuroendocrine dysfunction and the adrenergic system in normal-weight bulimia nervosa, our patients received methylphenidate stimulation tests (MST) and urinary MHPG was measured. Additionally, they were treated for their disorder with adrenergic agents.

Twenty-four hour urine MHPG was collected, preserved, and measured by methods previously described [59]. Specimens were only used for MHPG analysis if total urine volume was greater than 1,000 ml/24hours or urine creatinine was greater than 15mg/kg [60]. Low MHPG is less than 1,027 mcg/24hours for normal women [61]. The MST involves the administration of an oral amphetamine-like compound, which can have a rapid, though time-limited, mood-elevating effect on depressed patients. Seven bulimic patients were given 10 to 20 mg methylphenidate orally in open trial, and mood ratings were done before and one and two hours after the administration of the drug.

The results are as follows: Bulimics had normal mean MHPG (N=10, MHPG=1,308.7 ± 151.4 SEM) but showed a bimodal distribution, with five subjects having distinctly low MHPG (mean=808 ± 59 SEM) and five subjects having normal MHPG (mean=1,642 ± 109 SEM). These two subgroups were significantly different (T=5.81 p<0.001 df=8). The two subgroups discriminated by MHPG did not differ according to DST results, ideal body weight, or clinical variables. However,

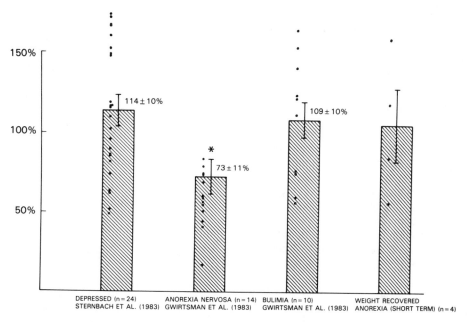

24-HOUR URINE MHPG IN DEPRESSION, ANOREXIA NERVOSA, AND BULIMIA

Figure 17.4 Although 24-hour urine MHPG is distinctly low in underweight anorexics, this represents only the absolute value of MHPG. When MHPG is corrected for body weight, it comes up to the normal range. Weight-recovered AN women show normal urinary MHPG, as do depressives and bulimics. Subgroups of patients have decreased urinary output of MPGH (not shown).

we did find a correlation between MHPG and TSH response to TRH (r=0.83, p=0.05). This is in contrast to the inverse correlation found in another study of depressed patients [62] and the failure to find any correlation in a sample of depressed female patients [63]. This suggests that bulimics do not merely represent a subgroup of affective disorder but may have a more distinct psychobiological identity. Figure 4 shows the MHPG values in bulimics, anorexics, and a comparison group of depressives. It is evident that anorexics have lower absolute values of MHPG (ANOVA, one-way, F=8.58 p<0.05), but this is problematic, since these values have not been corrected for percent body weight. When this is done, MHPG for underweight anorexic subjects comes up into the normal range.

Sixteen bulimics were treated with medication, two had maprotiline, nine were on tranylcypromine, two had imipramine (IMI), and three were given desipramine (DMI). Fourteen of these had depression ratings, and of these, 8 of 14, or 57%, had a definite antidepressant response [64]. Five of ten, or 50%, had a >50% improvement in binge frequency, and these patients also improved in their depression ratings (t=-2.56 p=0.034.). It was also found that patients tended to have more mood improvement with tricyclics than with nontricyclic compounds (t=2.3 p=0.038).

Four of seven patients had a definite mood-elevating effect after receiving methylphenidate. Measures of appetite were not done. This agrees with another study that demonstrated clear euphoriant effects on mood with intravenous methylamphetamine [65]. Neither urine MHPG, MST, nor treatment response to antidepressants, either adrenergic or nonadrenergic, was related in any systematic fashion to DST results. TST results could also not be consistently related to any adrenergic measure except for MHPG, and as previously mentioned, numbers were often too small to permit adequate statistical analysis. The only endocrinological parameter that predicted improvement in bulimic symtoms was the presence of normal menstrual periods (t=-3.0 p=0.024). This agrees with another study done on anorexics demonstrating a correlation between outcome and return of menses [66].

It is probably not surprising that significant relationships between adrenergic and neuroendocrine parameters did not emerge in this preliminary study, inasmuch as the sample size is small, bulimia nervosa is probably a heterogeneous disorder, and the tests done are probably neither extraordinarily specific for a single neurotransmitter, nor do they necessarily represent CNS function adequately. However, the lack of a relationship between the HPA axis and tests of adrenergic function may be quite significant in bulimia nervosa, since a direct relationship is noted in anorexia nervosa [33] and in depressives [67]. Further studies looking at neuroendocrine-neurotransmitter relationships in eating disordered individuals are being undertaken in our laboratory in order to examine whether more complex system interactions will have some diagnostic specificity.

CLINICAL CONCLUSIONS

1. The dexamethosone suppression test is not useful diagnostically in patients with low-weight anorexia nervosa, since it is almost always positive regardless of mood.

2. In patients with anorexia nervosa who are weight recovered, and in normal-weight bulimics, the dexamethasone suppression test may have limited diagnostic utility. However, more study is needed here, because a definite relationship between DST nonsuppressibility and mood state has not been established.

3. The TST probably adds little diagnostically to the diagnosis of normal-weight bulimia, since most patients who are acutely ill and in the hospital will show blunted responses, regardless of mood state or family loading for affective disorder.

4. Relationships between the adrenergic system and neuroendocrine tests in eating disorders are complex and appear to be different from those found in depressives.

5. Although many bulimics appear to respond to standard antidepressant medications with improvements in mood and eating patterns, neither neuroendocrine measures nor tests of noredrenertic function predict such responses in any systematic fashion.

REFERENCES

1. Sachar EJ, Asnis G, Halbreich V, et al. Recent studies in the neuroendocrinology of major depressive disorders. Psychiatry Clin North Am, 1980; 3:313-26.

2. Balfour DJK, Benwell MEM. Betamethasone-induced pituitary- adrenocortical suppression and brain 5-hydroxytryptamine in the rat. Psychoneuroendocrinol, 1979; 4:83-6.

3. Jones MT, Hillhouse E, Burden J. Secretion of corticotropin releasing hormone in vitro. In: Martini L, Ganong WF, eds. Frontiers in neuroendocrinology: vol 4. New York: Raven Press, 1976:

4. Vagenakis AG. Regulation of TSH secretion. In: Clinical neuroendocrinology: A pathophysiological approach. Tolis G. ed. New York: Raven Press, 1979; 329-43.

5. Sachar EJ. Twenty-four-hour cortisol secretory patterns in depressed and manic patients. Prog Brain Research, 1975; 42:81-91.

6. Walsh BT, Katz JL, Levin J, Kream J, et al. Adrenal activity in anorexia nervosa. Psychosom Med, 1978; 40:499-505.

7. Boyar RM, Hellman LD, Roffwarg H, Katz J, Zumoff B, et al. Cortisol secretion and metabolism in anorexia nervosa. New Engl J Med, 1977; 296:190-3.

8. Boyar RM. Anorexia nervosa. Circadian rhythm of plasma hormones. 1977; 295:1069.

9. Doerr P, Fichter M, Pirke KM, et al. Relationship between weight gain and hypothalamic pituitary adrenal function in patients with anorexia nervosa. J Steroid Biochem, 1981; 13:529-37.

10. Walsh BT, Katz JL, Levin J, Kream J, et al. The production rate of cortisol declines during recovery from anorexia nervosa. J Clin Endocr Metab, 1981; 53:203-5.

11. Danowski TS, Livstone E, Gonzales AR, et al. Fractional and partial hypopituitarism in anorexia nervosa. Hormones, 1972; 3:105- 18.

12. Bethge H, Nagel AM, Solbach HG, et al. Disturbance of cortisol regulation of adrenocortical function in anorexia nervosa, parallels to endogenous depression and Cushings syndrome. Mater Med Nordmark, 1970; 22:204-14.

13. Walsh BT. Endocrine disturbances in anorexia nervosa and depression. Psychosom Med, 1982; 44:85-91.

14. Rao KSJ, Srikantia SG, Gopalan C. Plasma cortisol levels in protein-calorie malnutrition. Arch Dis Childhood, 1968; 43:365.

15. Smith SR, Bledsoe T, Chhetri MK. Cortisol metabolism and the pituitary adrenal axis in adults with protein calorie malnutriton. J Clin Endocr Metab, 1975; 49:43-52.

16. Alleyne GAO, Young VH. Adrenocortical function in children with severe protein calorie malnutrition. PCM Clin Sci, 1967; 33:189- 200.

17. Walsh BT. The endocrinology of anorexia nervosa. Psychiatric Clin of North Am, 1980; 3:299-312.

18. Carroll BJ, Curtis GC, Mendels J. Neuroendocrine regulation in depression: I. Limbic system adrenocortical dysfunction. Arch Gen Psychiatry, 1976; 33:1039-44.

19. Warren MP and Vande Wiele PL. Clinical and metabolic features of anorexia nervosa. Amer J Obstet Gynec, 1973; 117:435-49.

20. Berger M, Pirke KM, Doerr P, Krieg C, Von Zerssen D. Influence of weight loss on the dexamethasone suppression test. Arch of Gen Psychiatry, 1983; 40:585-6.

21. Yerevanian BI, Bachiewicz GJ, Iker HP, Privitera MP. The influence of weight loss on the dexamethasone suppression test. Psychiatry Research, 1984; 12:155-60.

22. Abou-Saleh MJ, Millin P, Coppen A. Dexamethasone suppression test in depression. Neuropharmacology, 1983; 22:549-50.

23. Targum S. Reported weight loss and the dexamethasone suppression test. Psychiatry Research, 1983; 9:173-4.

24. Nasr SJ, Pandey G, Altman EG, et al. Symptom profile of patients with positive DST. A pilot study. Bio-

logical Psychiatry, 1983; 18:571-4.

25. Kline MD, Beeber HP. Weight loss and the dexamethasone suppression test. Arch Gen Psychiatry, 1983; 40:1034-5.

26. Gwirtsman HE, Roy-Byrne P, Gitlin MJ, et al. Reported weight loss and dexamethasone nonsuppression in depressed patients. J Aff Dis, 1985; 9:193-6.

27. Halmi KA, Sherman BM. Prediction of treatment response in anorexia nervosa. In: Biological psychiatry today. Amsterdam: Elsevier/North Holland Biomedical Press, 1979; 609-614.

28. Gerner RH, Gwirtsman HE. Abnormalities of dexamethasone suppression test and urinary MHPG in anorexia nervosa. Am J Psychiatry, 1981; 138:650-3.

29. Hudson JI, Laffer PS, Pope HG. Bulimia related to affective disorder by family history and response to the DST. Am J Psychiatry, 1982; 139:685-7.

30. Hudson JI, Pope HG, Jonas JM, et al. HPA Axis hyperactivity in bulimia. Psychiatry Res, 1983; 8:111-7.

31. Gwirtsman HE, Roy-Byrne P, Yager J, et al. Neuroendocrine abnormalities in bulimia. Am J Psychiatry, 1983; 140:559-63.

32. Edelstein CK, Roy-Byrne P, Fawzy FI, et al. Effects of weight loss on the dexamethasone suppression test. Am J Psychiatry, 1983; 140:338-41.

33. Gwirtsman HE, Gerner RH. Neurochemical abnormalities in anorexia nervosa: similarities to affective disorders. Biol Psychiatry, 1981; 16:991-5.

34. Macaron C, Wilber JF, Green O, et al. Studies of growth hormone (GH), TSH, and PRL secretion in anorexia nervosa. In: Psychoneuroendocrinology, 1978; 3:181-5.

35. Leslie RDG, Isaacs AJ, Gomez J, et al. Hypothalamic-pituitary- thyroid function in anorexia nervosa. Brit Med J, 1978; 2:526-28.

36. Collu R. Abnormal pituitary hormone response to thyrotropin releasing hormone: an index of central nervous system dysfunction. In: Tolis G, ed. Clincial neuroendocrinology: A pathophysiological approach. New York: Raven Press, 1979:129-37.

37. Mitchell JE, Bantle JP. Metabolic and endocrine investigations in women of normal weight with the bulimia syndrome. Biol Psychiatry, 1983; 18(3):355-64.

38. Moshang TJR, Utiger RD. Low triiodothyronine euthyroidism in anorexia nervosa. In: Vigersky RS, ed. Anorexia nervosa. New York: Raven Press, 1977: 263-70.

39. Burman KD, Vigersky RA, Loriaux DL, Strum D, Djuh YY, et al. Investigations concerning thyroxine deiodinative pathways in patients with anorexia nervosa. In Vigersky RA, ed. Anorexia nervosa. New York: Raven Press, 1977; 255-61.

40. Moshang T, Parks JS, Baker L, Vaidya V, et al. Low serum triiodothyronine in patients with anorexia nervosa. J Clin Endocr Metab, 1975; 40:470-3.

41. Moore R, Mills H. Serum T_3 and T_4 levels in patients with anorexia nervosa showing transient hyperthyroidism during weight gain. Clin Endocrinology, 1979; 10:443-9.

42. Casper RC, Frohman LA. Delayed TSH release in anorexia nervosa following injection of TRH. Psychoneuroendocrinology, 1982; 7:59- 68.

43. Miyai K, Yamamoto T, Azukizawa M, Ishibashi K, Kumahara Y. Serum thyroid hormones and thyrotropin in anorexia nervosa. J Clin Endocr Metab, 1975; 40(2):334-8.

44. Croxson MS, Ibbertson HK. Low serum triiodothyronine (T3) and hypothyroidism in anorexia nervosa. J Clin Endocr Metab, 1977; 44:167-74.

45. Portnay GI, O'Brian JT, Bush J, et al. The effect of starvation on the concentration and binding of thyroxine and triiodothyronine in serum and on the response to TRH. J Clin Endocr Metab, 1974; 39:191-4.

46. Vagenakis AG, Burger A, Portnay M, et al. Diversion of peripheral thyroxine metabolism from activiating to inactivating pathways during complete fasting. J Clin Endocr Metab, 1975; 41:191-4.

47. Chopra IJ, Chopra V, Smith SR, et al. Reciprocal changes in serum concentration of 3,3',5' triiodothyronine (reverse T3) and 3,3'5-triiodothyronine (T3) in systemic illnesses. J Clin Endocr Metab, 1975; 41:1043-9.

48. Vagenakis A. Thyroid hormone metabolism in prolonged experimental starvation in man. In: Vigersky RA, ed. Anorexsia Nervosa. New York: Raven Press, 1977; 243-53.

49. Lundberg PO, Walinder J, Werner I, et al. Effects of thyrotopin- releasing hormone on plasma levels of TSH, FSH, LH, and GH in anorexia nervosa. Europ J Clin Invest, 1972; 2:150-3.

50. Azukizawa M, Pekary AE, Hershman JM, et al. Plasma thryotropin, thyroxine, and triiodothyromine relationships in man. J Clin Endocr Metab, 1978;l 43:533-42.

51. Vinik AI, Kalk WJ, McLaren H, et al. Fasting blunts the TSH response to synthetic TRH. J Clin Endocr Metab, 1976; 45:509-11.

52. Carlson HE, Drenick EJ, Chopra IJ, et al. Alterations in basal and TRH stimulated serum levels of thyrotropin, prolactin, and thyroid hormones in starved obese men. J Clin Endocr Metab, 1977; 45:707-13.

53. Gold MS, Pottash ALC, Extein I, et al. Diagnosis of depression in the 1980s. JAMA, 1981; 245:1562-4.

54. Sternbach H, Gwirtsman H, Gerner RH. Biological tests in the diagnosis and treatment of affective disorders. In: Shah NS, Donald AG, eds. Psychoneuroendocrine dysfunction in psychiatric and neurologic illness: Influence of psychopharmacological agents. New York: Plenum Press, 1984: 383-98.

55. Halmi KA, Dekirminjian H, Davis JM, et al. Catecholamine metabolism in anorexia nervosa. Arch Gen Psychiatry, 1978; 35:458-60.

56. Gross HA, Lake CR, Ebert MH, et al. Catecholamine metabolism in primary anorexia nervosa. J Clin Endocr Metab, 1979; 49(6):805-9.

57. Abraham SF, Beumont PJV, Cobbin DM. Catecholamine metabolism and body weight in anorexia nervosa. Brit J Psychiatry, 1981; 138:244-7.

58. Kaye WH, Ebert MH, Raliegh M, et al. Abnormalities

in CNS monoamine metabolism in anorexia nervosa.
Arch Gen Psychiatry, 1984; 41:350-5.

59. Dekirminjian H, Maas JN. An improved procedure of
3-methoxy-4- hydroxy phenylglycol determination by
gas liquid chromatography. Annual Biochem, 1970;
35:113.

60. Edwards DJ, Spiker DG, Neil JF, et al. MHPG excretion in depression. Psychiatry Research, 1980; 2:295.

61. Dekirminjian H. National psychopharmacology
laboratory, Knoxville Tenn, 1981.

62. Davis KL, Hollister LE, Mathe AA, et al. Neuroendocrine and neurochemical measurements in depression. Am J Psychiatry, 1981; 138:1555-62.

63. Sternbach HA, Kirstein L, Pottash ALC, et al. The
TRH test and urinary MHPG in unipolar depression.
J Aff Disorders, 1983; 5:233-7.

64. Roy-Byrne P, Gwirtsman H, Edelstein CK, et al. Eating disorders and antidepressants. J Clin Psychopharmacology, 1983; 3:60-1.

65. Ong YL, Checkley SA, Russell FM. Suppression of
bulimic symptoms with methylamphetamine. Brit J
Psychiat, 1981; 143:288-93.

66. Falk JR, Halmi KA. Amenorrhea in anorexia nervosa:
Examination of the critical body weight hypothesis.
Biol Psychiatry, 1982; 17(7):799-806.

67. Jimerson DC, Insel TR, Reus VI, et al. Increased
plasma MHPG in dexamathasone resistant depressed
patients. Arch Gen Psychiatry, 1983; 40:173-6.

Chapter 18

Disturbances in Brain Neurotransmitter Systems in Anorexia Nervosa: A Review of CSF Studies

Walter H. Kaye, Michael H. Ebert, and C. Raymond Lake

INTRODUCTION

Patients with anorexia appear to have characteristic disturbances of appetite, neuroendocrine function, motor activity, and mood. Since CNS neurotransmitters modulate these systems, it is logical to try to determine whether disturbances of brain chemistry occur in anorexia nervosa. Two major problems, however, have limited progress in investigating brain neurochemistry in anorexia nervosa. First, the technology available to explore brain neurochemistry in living human subjects is limited. Perhaps the best available method is to measure concentrations of brain neurochemicals in CSF. It is difficult, however, to correlate CSF neurochemical values with disturbances of specific brain pathways. Second, while abnormalities of CSF neurochemicals have been found in underweight anorectics, these abnormalities may be secondary to malnutrition or contribute to weight loss and aberrant behavior. Studying anorectics after weight recovery may be one way of circumventing such problems and identifying possible trait disturbances. Despite these problems, a number of CSF studies have been carried out, and in fact, offer some insights into pathophysiolgoic processes in anorexia nervosa. This chapter will review CSF studies to date in anorexia nervosa and discuss the implications of these findings.

BACKGROUND

The possibility of neurotransmitter disturbance in the brains of patients with anorexia nervosa has been argued for the past decade. Mawson [1] hypothesized that central catecholamine pathways might be involved in anorexia nervosa. Barry and Klawans [2] suggested that increased activity of dopamine might theoretically account for much of the pathophysiology of this disorder, while Redmond et al [3] suggested that excessive norepinephrine activity might be contributory. Other authors [4,5] have reviewed the possibility of brain dysfunction in anorexia nervosa.

The inacessibility of the brain to clinical investigations has made it difficult to prove or disprove theories. Measuring levels of neurochemicals in the CSF is one of the few techniques available for looking directly at brain neurotransmitter metabolism. A major difficulty with CSF studies is that measurements of neurochemicals in CSF are thought to reflect the sum contributions of various brain and spinal cord regions. There is no method presently available to relate changes in CSF neurochemical concentrations to specific brain regions, but CSF studies remain the best available technique to estimate brain neurotransmitter activity.

The past decade of research has generated an immense amount of data about physiologic disturbances in underweight patients with anorexia nervosa. Abnormalities exist in practically every endocrine system measured; these include the cortisol [6-8], gonadotropic [9-12], thyroid [13-15], growth hormone [16,17], and water regulation [18,19] systems. These disturbances are not due to primary pituitary dysfunction, but appear to reflect hypothalamic dysregulation. Many of the neurochemicals discussed in this paper have been implicated in the hypothalamic regulation of one or more of the neuroendocrine abnormalities mentioned. The neurochemistry of endocrine regulation is complex, and interested readers are referred to reviews [20,21].

Disturbances of mood have been described in anorexia nervosa [22], as well as in their family members [23]. The relationship of severity of dysphoria to anorexia nervosa, however, is not clear, as it is not certain whether dysphoria is primarily associated with malnutrition or whether there is an underlying trait-related mood disorder. The monoamines, as well as certain neuropeptides such as the opiates, have been implicated in mood regulation in humans. Whether disturbances of these systems do, in fact, contribute to alterations of mood in anorexia nervosa, seems a reasonable hypothesis, but is not proved.

Patients with anorexia nervosa manifest a paradoxical attitude toward food. Anorectics are often obsessed with food, have an appetite, and a desire to eat. They are, however, at the same time, terrified of eating and gaining weight. Little is known about the neurochemistry of appetite regulation in anorexia nervosa and whether disturbances of the neurochemistry modulating appetite produce these ambivalent food-related behaviors. The past decade has produced some understanding of the neurotransmitter systems that modulate appetite in animals. Again, the monamines, the opiates, and a number of other neuropeptides have been implicated in appetite regulation [24].

Several groups have now found that underweight anorectics have a decrease in sympathetic nervous system (SNS) activity as measured by decreased plasma norepinephrine and decreased urinary MHPG. The CNS regulates the SNS and contributes some proportion of MHPG to the pool of peripheral MHPG, CSF norepinephrine and MHPG values often correlate with peripheral measures of norepinephrine and MHPG. Overall, it would seem reasonable to expect underweight anorectics to also have decreased CSF, norepinephrine, and MHPG, although this has not occurred in the few studies published.

Neurochemical abnormalities could be caused by weight loss or be the cause of weight loss in anorexia nervosa. The options available to determine cause and effect of neurochemical abnormalities in anorexia nervosa are limited. Prospective investigations of then neurochemistry of a population at risk for anorexia are not feasible because of the low prevalence of the illness. Studies of acutely ill anorectics are complicated by the quagmire of cause and effect. Even though CSF neurochemical abnormalities in this group may not answer the question of cause and effect, they certainly suggest abnormal brain function. These findings give clues as to which systems are most disturbed during weight loss and malnutrition. Specific disturbances can be further characterized by new generations of pharmacologic challenge studies designed to explore individual neurotransmitter systems.

Another option is to study anorectics after long-term weight recovery. If some system continued to be disturbed after weight recovery, this might serve as a clue to trait-related abnormalities in anorexia nervosa. We have found disturbances of norepinephrine and serotonin (5-HT) in anorectics studied months after weight restoration. Whether these findings are related to continued symptoms or whether recovery depends on alterations in specific systems occurring is unclear.

CSF studies remain a rather controversial and relatively infrequently performed procedure, particularly as a research tool in anorexia nervosa. These studies have proved to be safe in our patients. There have been no harmful side-effects aside from a 15% incident of post-lumbar headache, rarely lasting more than two or three days and responding to bed rest.

CNS MONAMINE DISTURBANCES

Methodologic difficulties exist with measuring monamines in CSF. The monoamines serotonin and dopamine cannot be reliably measured in CSF. Rather, investigators measure concentrations of the serotonin metabolite, 5-hydroxyindoleacetic acid (5-HIAA) and of the dopamine metabolite, homovanillic acid (HVA) in CSF. These metabolites are thought to reflect the turnover of serotonin and dopamine respectively in brain [25].

Both norepinephrine and its major metabolite, MHPG, can be measured in CSF. Since a substantial portion of free MHPG in human CSF is derived from plasma [26], CSF MHPG is not an accurate reflection of brain norepinephrine turnover. It is unclear whether CSF norepinephrine concentrations adequately reflect brain norepinephrine metabolism because of rapid reuptake of norepinephrine by brain neurons [27,28] and because brainstem norepinephrine centers contribute disproportionately large amounts of norepinephrine to lumbar CSF [29]. All monoamine systems have multiple pathways in the brain so that if alterations are found

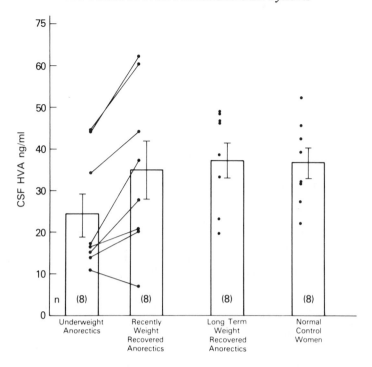

Figure 18.1 Mean ($\pm$ SEM) concentrations of HVA in CSF for each group of anorectics and normal controls. Underweight anorectics had a significant increase (t = 3.77, p < .01) in CSF HVA after weight restoration.

in CSF measurements, the source(s) of these disturbances are uncertain.

Monoamine Precursors

All of the monamines are derived from neutral amino acid precursors. Tryptophan is the precursor of 5-HT, and tyrosine is the precursor of dopamine and norepinephrine. It is thought that all neutral amino acids compete for one transport site at the blood brain barrier [30], therefore, the uptake of any one neutral amino acid depends on the concentration in blood of the other neutral amino acids.

Several groups have found that underweight anorectics had normal concentrations of monamine precursor amino acids in their blood [31,32]. The ratios of the amino acid precursors to the other neutral amino acids are also normal in underweight anorectics [31]. Others, however, have found that underweight anorectics have decreased concentrations of amino acid precursors. In underweight anorectics, Coppen et al [33] found low total and free plasma tryptophan, and Gerner et al [34] found significantly lower concentrations of CSF tyrosine than controls. Because of these conflicting findings, it remains unclear whether decreased availability of monoamine precursors contribute to CSF monoamine disturbances in underweight anorectics.

Brain Serotonin and Dopamine Metabolism: Basal CSF Concentrations

Only two studies [31,34] report basal CSF concentrations of 5-HIAA and HVA in underweight anorectics. Both groups found that underweight anorectics had basal concentrations of 5-HIAA and HVA that were similar to healthy controls. Gerner and associates [34] only measured these metabolites in underweight anorectics and controls. Our laboratory [31] measured these metabolites in underweight anorectics, and again in the same patients after weight restoration. We found that seven of eight patients studied as underweight anorectics showed an increase in CSF HVA (figure 1) and 5-HIAA (Figure 2) after weight recovery. Because of the small number of subjects and the large variance, it is only apparent that CSF HVA and 5-HIAA were decreased in underweight anorectics when the same subjects were compared while underweight and after weight recovery. We also measured these metabolites in a group of anorectics who had been weight recovered for a mean of 20 months and found that this group had values of CSF 5-HIAA and HVA that was also similar to controls.

Underweight anorectics have neuroendocrine disturbances that tend to normalize with weight recovery. CSF concentrations of dopamine and 5-HT metabolites have a similar pattern. Could abnormalities in CNS

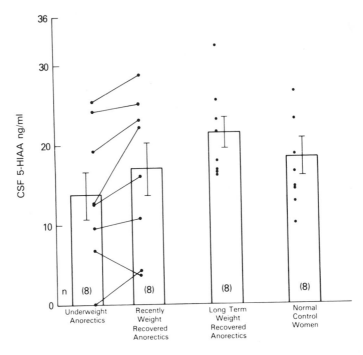

Figure 18.2 Mean (± SEM) concentrations of 5-HIAA in CSF for each group of anorectics and normal controls. Underweight anorectics had a significant increase (t = 2.42, p < .05) in CSF 5-HIAA with recent weight recovery. Long-term weight recovered anorectics had significantly elevated CSF 5-HIAA concentrations compared with the underweight anorectics (t = 2.58, p = .02).

dopamine and 5-HT pathways account for then neuroendocrine disturbances found in underweight anorectics? Central 5-HT and dopamine pathways modulate some of the neuroendocrine systems that are disturbed in underweight anorectics. For example, there is considerable pharmacological evidence that the central release of 5-HT stimulates corticotrophin-releasing hormone (CRH) secretion [20] and that hypothalamic dopamine transmission appears to participate in regulating LH secretion [35]. The evidence for an effect of central dopamine and 5-HT pathways on other neuroendocrine systems is less conclusive. Disturbances in central dopamine or 5-HT function may contribute to neuroendocrine abnormalities in underweight anorectics. However, more specific conclusions will only be possible when further studies are done.

Chronic low weight and caloric deprivation might account for changes in monoamine metabolism. Studies in animals show that short-term caloric deprivation produces a mixture of changes in brain monoamine concentrations [35-43]. A possibility also exists that some disturbance in monoamine function drives weight loss, since animal studies support the concept that hypothalamic monoamine systems regulate appetitive behavior. It appears that monoamine metabolism is intimately linked with control of appetite and weight and that changes in one affect the other. An association between brain monoamine metabolism, appetitive behavior, and weight loss in anorexia nervosa appears feasible, although the causal relationship remains unknown.

ACCUMULATION OF CSF HVA AND 5-HIAA AFTER PROBENECID

Two methods are available to estimate brain dopamine and serotonin metabolism. The first method is to measure basal level of the serotonin metabolite, 5-HIAA, and of the dopamine metabolite, in CSF. The second method is to measure the accumulation of CSF 5-HIAA and HVA by blocking their transport from CSF to blood by the administration of probenecid.

Only one study [44] reports on accumulation of HVA and 5-HIAA after probenecid administration. This study found that after probenecid administration, a difference existed in accumulation of the serotonin metabolite, 5-HIAA, in CSF between anorectics that fasted and those that binged. This difference in serotonin metabolism between fasters and bingers was present only in weight-recovered anorectics, but not in the underweight anorectics. In contrast, CSF accumulation of the dopamine metabolite after probenecid was not different between weight-recovered fasters and bingers.

Patients with anorexia nervosa can be subdivided into two groups by appetitive behavior: those that fast and those that binge [45-48]. These subgroups of anorectics differ in other clinical dimensions, such as characterologic style, mood, and impulse control. These behavioral and appetitive differences between fasters and bingers are consistent with other data, suggesting specific influences of serotonin on mood and feeding. Alterations in brain serotonin metabolism have been found in other psychiatric populations. Decreased brain serotonin metabolism has been related to depression [49], suicide [50], and aggressive behavior [51]. Disturbances in brain serotonin pathways may serve to permit dysphoric or impulsive behavior to occur.

In animal studies, brain serotonin has been implicated in appetite suppression, particularly of carbohydrate intake [52,53]. Carbohydrate intake selectively increases tryptophan uptake by the brain, and consequently increases brain serotonin. Our data are consistent with this proposed carbohydrate/serotonin mechanism. Fasters have greater CSF 5-HIAA turnover after probenecid, and decreased appetites. Bulimics have lower 5-HIAA turnover after probenecid. Whether low 5-HIAA is responsible for carbohydrate craving is speculative, but may have heuristic value in suggesting new treatments. Possibly, bingeing on carbohydrates in an attempt to enhance brain serotonin and, in this manner, serves as a form of self-medication.

Alterations in serotonin metabolism may be a trait-related phenomenon, because it appears after weight recovery. Further investigations of brain serotonin metabolism in a larger sample are needed to answer questions raised by this preliminary study.

BRAIN NOREPINEPHRINE METABOLISM

As mentioned norepinephrine and MHPG are decreased in plasma and urine in all studies of underweight anorectics [8,54-60]. In contrast, two groups [31,34] have found that underweight anorectics have concentrations of CSF norepinephrine and MHPG that are similar to normal controls. Since there is usually a good correlation between peripheral and central values of norepinephrine and MHPG, this finding in underweight anorectics was surprising.

One explanation for this discrepancy may be that concentrations of norepinephrine or MHPG in underweight anorectics may relate to the nutritional state. A review of the anorexia nervosa literature suggests that investigations that reported decreased concentrations

of urinary MHPG or plasma norepinephrine in underweight anorectics had studied their subjects soon after admission [8,54,56]. Studies completed after some degree of nutritional rehabilitation had norepinephrine and MHPG values that were in the normal range [31,34]. Abraham [57] found a positive correlation between weight gain and urinary MHPG. Together these studies suggest that norepinephrine turnover decreases during starvation and increases with nutritional rehabilitation. A pattern of decrease in norepinephrine turnover with food restriction, and an increase of norepinephrine turnover with feeding is known to occur in animals and humans.

Of the brain monoamine systems investigated, brain norepinephrine pathways appear to demonstrate the clearest role in the normal regulation of each of the neuroendocrine systems that become disturbed in underweight anorectics. Norepinephrine appears to exert an excitatory influence on gonadotropin release [20,61], perhaps by stimulating the tonic secretion of the LH-releasing system [62,63]. Release of norepinephrine in the hypothalamus decreases CRH secretion [20] and appears to have an excitatory effect on the hypothalamic control of TSH secretion [64,65]. Central norepinephrine activity seems to inhibit vasopressin release [66], although some studies suggest norepinephrine stimulates vasopressin release [66]. Brain norepinephrine and opiate systems are intimately linked [68,69].

We have been interested in investigating anorectics who are weight recovered. Studies of long-term outcome find that many anorectics who return to a normal weight continue to have concerns with their weight and have appetite disturbances [70-75]. Since these women are at normal weight, if they have neurochemical disturbances, such disturbances might be trait related. We found [31,76] that anoectics who had been weight recovered for a mean of 20 months had decreased concentrations of CSF norepinephrine (figure 3), CSF and plasma MHPG, and plasma norepinephrine compared with healthy control women.

The decrease in norepinephrine and MHPG in long-term weight recovered anorectics suggests several interpretations. A decrease in norepinephrine activity might occur during the transition from recent weight recovery to long-term weight maintenance. Another possibility is that anorectics able to gain and maintain weight have a difference in SNS function compared with anorectics with a poor outcome. If decreases in norepinephrine activity occur in the interval between weight recovery and long-term weight maintenance, what might be the purpose? Other systems also slowly change during the transition from short- to long-term weight recovery. These include multiple neuroendocrine systems, physical activity, and caloric efficiency [77]. Since noradrenergtic

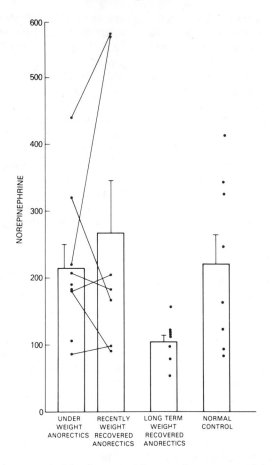

Figure 18.3 CSF norepinephrine concentrations demonstrated no consistent pattern of change between underweight anorectics and the same patients after weight recovery. Long-term weight recovered patients had significantly lower concentrations of CSF NE than normal controls (t = 2.60, p < .05) and underweight anorectics (t = 3.01, p < .02).

pathways contribute to regulating energy balance, perhaps altered norepinephrine metabolism in long-term weight recovered anorectics is one biologic adaptation that facilitates the maintenance of a relatively normal weight. It is also possible that some portion of continued symptoms in long-term weight-recovered anorectics are attributable to trait-dependent neurotransmitter alterations that may have been obscured by state-related changes while underweight or immediately after weight recovery.

CNS NEUROPEPTIDE METABOLISM

CSF Opiate Activity

Most data concerning endogenous opioids and appetite regulation [78-81] suggests that opioid agonists stimulate eating and antagonists diminish eating. Opiates are thought to influence other systems known to be disturbed in anorexia nervosa. Opiates, of course, have been implicated in modulation of mood. Opiates regulate and are regulated by monoamines and appear to influence some neuroendocrine systems, such as gonadotropins.

Two studies have measured CSF opiate concentrations in anorexia nervosa, but by quite different methodologies. Gerner and Sharp [82] found underweight anorectics had normal concentrations of CSF beta-endorphin-immunoreactivity. In contrast, our group [83] used a radioreceptor assay that measured total activity of all opiate compounds in CSF. We found the mean level of CSF opioid activity in beta-endorphin equivalents was significantly higher in the underweight anorectics than in the same patients after weight restoration or the long-term weight recovered anorectics.

In recent years a variety of opiates have been found in the brain. Thus, it is not surprising that there is a discrepancy between the measurement of one specific opiate, and all opiates together. It is unknown whether increased opiate activity at minimum weight reflects a specific opioid appetite stimulation that is a consequence of diminished weight or a stress effect that might serve as a biologic protective response to help the body decrease metabolic requirements when weight is lost. The peripheral endorphinergic system [84] may aid survival in famine by conserving nutrients and water and decreasing energy-expending activities.

CSF and Plasma Vasopressin Concentrations

Abnormalities of water balance in anorexia nervosa have been suggested by earlier work [18,19]. One important component of the regulation of water balance is arginine vasopressin (AVP), a peptide manufactured in the hypothalamus and released by the posterior pituitary to regulate free water. Underweight anorectics [85] have an abnormal release of AVP in response to an osmotic stimuli such as hypertonic saline. This defect takes two forms. The least common is a subnormal rise in AVP relative to the strength of the stimuli. The more common defect is erratic or osmotically uncontrolled AVP release. This pattern contrasts markedly to healthy adults who invariably show a smooth, progressive rise in plasma AVP that correlates closely with the rise in plasma sodium during the infusion of hypertonic saline. AVP osmoregulation returned to normal in most of the long-term weight recovered anorectics.

In healthy adults, daytime concentrations of CSF AVP ranges from 0.5 to 2.0 pg/ml [86]. In addition, the CSF levels tend to parallel but are almost always lower than those in plasma. In anorexia nervosa, some anorectics at any stage had elevated CSF AVP levels, and many anorectics had an abnormal ratio of CSF AVP to plasma AVP.

The pathophysiologic consequences of AVP disturbances in anorexia nervosa remain to be fully defined. We did find most subjects had increased urine output, but this finding is difficult to explain in patients who show erratic secretion without obvious deficiency of vasopressin. The possible significance of CSF abnormalities is speculative, because we do not know what role AVP plays in brain function.

CSF Somatostatin

The growth hormone release-inhibiting factor, somatostatin, has been found in multiple regions throughout the brain [87]. Malnourished anorectics have high basal plasma concentrations of growth hormone that normalize with nutritional rehabilitation without weight gain [16,17]. High levels of growth hormone could be due to decreased brain SRIF. Gerner and Yamada [88] found decreased CSF somatotropin-release inhibition factor (SRIF)-like immunoreactivity in underweight anorectics compared with controls. Whether SRIF alterations

are responsible for growth hormone or other disturbances in anorexia nervosa is an interesting question requiring further investigation.

OTHER CSF NEUROCHEMICALS

GABA

GABA is an inhibitory neurotransmitter [89] that has been implicated in Huntington's Disease [90,91] and epilepsy [92]. Animal studies suggest that GABA may have some modulatory effect on appetite [93]. Gerner and Hare [94] found underweight anorectics and normal control women had similar CSF levels of GABA. Since CSF GABA seems to adequately reflect brain GABA [95,96], this finding suggests that not all neurotransmitters are uniformly disturbed during low weight in anorexia nervosa.

Cortisol

In the underweight state, patients with anorexia nervosa have increased plasma cortisol secretion and nonsuppression to dexamethaxone [8]. Cortisol metabolism is disturbed in depression [9], and some investigators [98,99] have reported elevated CSF cortisol in depression. Gerner and Wilkins [100] found underweight anorectics had elevated CSF cortisol values. Depressed and nondepressed anorectics had similar CSF cortisol elevations. While elevated CSF cortisol may not be related to mood in anorexia nervosa, cortisol has a number of effects on catecholamine metabolism [101] and is, in turn, thought to be partially modulated by norepinephrine pathways. Thus, elevated cortisol may produce, or reflect, disturbances in other brain systems.

CONCLUSIONS

The questions we tried to answer in the studies reviewed in this chapter were: (1) Were abnormalities in brain neurotransmitters present in patients with anorexia nervosa, and if so (2) would abnormalities in brain neurotransmitters explain behavioral or physiologic disturbances in anorexia nervosa?

These studies have demonstrated that a number of changes occur in neurotransmitter and neuromodulator systems in anorexia nervosa. Whether any of these changes is a primary etiological event that occurs early in the illness or triggers the illness remains an open question. Some of the changes appear to occur predictably in each individual when underweight, such as the decrease in basal brain dopamine, serotonin, and somatostatin metabolism, and the increase in CSF cortisol and opioid activity. Some changes, such as those in vasopressin function, are prolonged and may last months after weight recovery. Some disturbances, such as in CSF norepinephrine in long-term weight recovered subjects, suggest that alterations in norepinephrine function may be necessary for sustaining weight restoration. Weight recovered fasting and bulimic anorectics appear to have differences in serotonin metabolism, data that is consistent with what is known about serotonergic influences on appetite and mood.

The past decade has produced a wealth of data about neuroendocrine disturbances in anorexia nervosa. These neuroendocrine studies have focused on peripheral hormonal systems. In general, these peripheral hormonal studies implicated disturbances of hypothalamic regulatory systems, which are in part regulated by the same neurotransmitters that are disturbed in anorexia nervosa. Furthermore, these neurotransmitter abnormalities could contribute to the disturbances of appetite, mood, motor activity, and metabolism described in anorexia nervosa. It is likely that there are other neurotransmitter system disturbances in anorexia nervosa. For example, many gastrointestinal peptides are also present in the brain [102]. The relationship of these peptides to appetite regulation needs to be elucidated. Our technology now permits more direct exploration of brain pathways and neurochemical dysfunction in anorexia nervosa and allows us to build on the foundation laid by previous investigators.

The discovery of neurochemical disturbances in anorexia nervosa may be most useful as a means of suggesting new neuropharmacologic treatments for this disease. At present there is no medication "magic bullet" that enhances weight restoration or weight maintenance. The possibility that there are trait-related disturbances of serotonin or norepinephrine metabolism in anorexia nervosa might suggest trials of specific agents.

In summary, we have come to accept that there are systematic disturbances of specific neuroendocrine systems in anorexia nervosa. Abnormalities in neurotransmitter metabolism are also part of the neurobiological syndrome of anorexia nervosa and may contribute to the characteristic changes in behavior and physiology.

REFERENCES

1. Mawson AR. Anorexia nervosa and the regulation of intake: A review. Psychol Med, 1974; 4:289-308.

2. Barry VC, Klawans HL. On the role of dopamine in the pathophysiology of anorexia nervosa. J Neural Transm, 1976; 38:107-22.

3. Redmond DE, Swann A, Heninger GR. Phenoxybenzamine in anorexia nervosa. Lancet, 1976; 2:307.

4. Crisp AH. Disturbances of transmitter metabolism in anorexia nervosa. Proc Nutr Soc, 1978; 37:201-9.

5. Stricker EM, Andersen AE. The lateral hypothalamic syndrome: comparison with the syndrome of anorexia nervosa. Life Sci, 1980; 26:1927-34.

6. Walsh BT, Katz JL, Levin J, et al. Adrenal activity in anorexia nervosa. Psychosom Med, 1978; 40:499-506.

7. Garfinkel PE, Brown GM, Darby PL. The role of neuroendocrine function in anorexia nervosa. Herdine PD, Singhal RL, ed. New York: Plenum Press, 1981: 279-293.

8. Gerner RH, Gwirstman HE. Abnormalities of dexamethasone suppression test and urinary MHPG in anorexia nervosa. Am J Psychiatry, 1981; 138:650-653.

9. Sherman BM, Halmi KA. Effects of nutritional rehabilitation on hypothalamic-pituitary function in anorexia nervosa. In: Vigersky RA, ed. Anorexia nervosa. New York: Raven Press, 1977; 225-241.

10. Nillus SJ, Wide L. A pituitary responsiveness to acute and chronic administration of gonadtropin-releasing hormone in acute and recovery stages of anorexia nervosa. In: Vigersky RA, ed. Anorexia nervosa. New York: Raven Press, 1977: 225-241.

11. Jueniewic N, Brown T, Garfinkle P, et al. Hypothalamic function as related to body weight and body function in anorexia nervosa. Psychosom Med, 1978; 40:187-98.

12. Brown G, Garfinkel PE, Jeuniewic N, et al. Endocrine profiles in anorexia nervosa. In: Vigersky RA, ed. Anorexia nervosa. New York: Raven Press, 1977: 123-136.

13. Mayai K, Yamamoto T, Iazukizawa M, et al. Serum tyroid hormones and throtropin in anorexia nervosa. J Clin Endocrinol Metabol, 1975; 40:334-8.

14. Vigersky RA, Loriaux DL, Andersen AE, et al. Delayed pituitary hormone response to LRF and TRF patients with anorexia nervosa and with secondary amenorrhea associated with simple weight loss. J Clin Endocrinol Metabol, 1976; 43:893-900.

15. Wakeling A, Desousa VFA, Gore MBR, et al. Amenorrhea, body weight and serum hormone concentrations with particular reference to prolactin and thyroid hormones in anorexia nervosa. Psychol Med, 1979; 9:265-72.

16. Kanis JA, Brown P, Fitzpatrick K, et al. Anorexia nervosa: a clinical, psychiatric, and laboratory study. O J Med, 1974; 170:321-38.

17. Casper RC, Davis JM, Pandel GN. The effect of nutritional status and weight changes on hypothalamic function tests in anorexia nervosa. In: Vigersky RA, ed. Anorexia nervosa. New York: Raven Press, 1977: 137-147.

18. Vigersky RA, Loriaux DL, Andersen AE, et al. Anorexia nervosa: Behavioral and hypothalamic aspects. J Clin Endocrinol Metabol, 1976; 5:518-38.

19. Meckenberg RS, Loriaux DL, Thompson RH, et al. Hypothalamic dysfunction in patients with anorexia nervosa. Medicine, 1974; 53:147-59.

20. Weiner RI, Gangong WF. Role of brain monamines and histamine in regulation of anterior pituitary secretion. Physiol Rev, 1978; 58:905-76.

21. Martin JB, Reichlin S, Brown GM, ed. Clinical neuroendocrinology. Philadelphia: F.A. Davis Company, 1977.

22. Cantwell DP, Sturzenberger KS, Burrought J, et al. Anorexia nervosa: An affective disorder. Arch Gen Psychiatry, 1977; 34:1087- 93.

23. Gershon ES, Hamovit JR, Schrieber JL, et al. Clincial findings in anorectics and affective illness in their relatives. Am J Psych, in press.

24. Liebowitz SF. Neurochemical systems of the hypothalamus. In: Morgane PJ, Ransapp J, eds. Handbook of the hypothalamus, vol 3. New York: Marcel Dekker, Inc, 1980: 299-437.

25. Ebert MH, Kartzinel R, Cowdry RW, et al. Cerebrospinal fluid amine metabilites and the probenecid test. In: Wood JH, ed. Neurobiology of Cerebrospinal Fluid. New York: Plenum Press, 1980: 97-112.

26. Kopin IJ, Gordon EK, Jimerson DC, et al. Relation between plasma and cerebrospinal fluid levels of 3-methoxy-4-hydroxyphenylgycol. Science, 1982; 219:73-5.

27. Fuxe K, Ungerstedt U. Localization of catecholamine uptake in rat brain after intraventricular injection. Life Sci, 1966; 5:1817-24.

28. Fuxe K, Ungerstedt U. Histochemical studies on the effect of (±) amphetamine, drugs of imipramine groups, and tryptamine on central catecholamine and 5-hydroxytryptamine neurons after intraventricular injection of catecholamines and 5-hydroxytryptamine. Eur J Pharmacol, 1968; 4:135-44.

29. Nygren LG, Olson L. A new major projection from locus coeruleus: The main source of noradrenergic nerve terminals in the ventral and dorsal columns of the spinal cord. Brain Res, 1977; 132:85-93.

30. Wurtman RJ. Effects of nutrients and circulating precursors on the synthesis of brain neurotransmitters. In: Garattini S, Samanin R, eds. Central Mechanisms of Anorectic Drugs. New York: Raven Press, 1967; 267-294.

31. Kaye WH, Ebert MH, Raleigh M, et al. Abnormalities in CNS monomine metabolism in anorexia nervosa. Arch Gen Psych, 1984; 41:350-5.

32. Russel GFM. The nutritional disorder in anorexia nervosa. J Psychosom Res, 1967; 11:141-9.

33. Coppen AJ, Gupta K, Eccleston EG, et al. Plasma tryptophan in anorexia nervosa. Lancet, 1976; 1:961.

34. Gerner RH, Cohen DJ, Fairbanks L, et al. CSF neurochemistry of women with anorexia nervosa and normal women. Am J Psychiatry, 1984; 141:1441-4.

35. Smythe GA. The role of serotonin and dopamine in hypothalamic- pituitary function. Clin Endocrinol, 1977; 7:325-41.

36. Curzon G, Joseph MH, Knott PH. Effects of immobilization and food deprivation on the rat brain tryptophan metabolism. J Neurochem, 1972; 19:1967-74.

37. Perez-Cruet J, Tagliamonte A, Tagliamonte P, et al. Changes in brain serotonin metabolism associated with fasting and satiation in rats. Life Sci, 1972; 2:31-9.

38. Knott PH, Curzon G. Effect of increased rat brain tryptophan on 5-hydroxytryptamine and 5-hydroxyindole acetic acid in the hypothalamus and other brain regions. J Neurochem, 1974; 22:1065-71.

39. Loullis CC, Felton DL, Shea PA. HPLC determination of biogenic amines in discrete brain areas in food deprived rats. Pharmacol Biochem Behav, 1979; 1:89-93.

40. Kantak KM, Wayner MJ, Tilson HA, et al. Turnover of 3H-5-hyroxyindoleacetic acid and the 3H-5-methoxyindoles in nondeprived and 24 hr food deprived rats. Pharmacol Biochem Behav, 1977; 6:221-5.

41. Kantak KM, Wayner MKJ, Stein JM. Effects of various periods of food deprivation on serotonin turnover in the lateral hypothalamus. Pharmacol Biochem Behav, 1978; 9:529-34.

42. Pirke KM, Spyra B. Catecholamine turnover in the brain and the regulation of luteinizing hormone and corticosterone in starved male rats. Endocrinology, 1982; 100:168-76.

43. Friedman E, Starr N, Gerhon S. Catecholamine synthesis and regulation of food intake in the rat.Life Sci, 1973; 12:317-26.

44. Kaye WH, Ebert MH, Gwirtsman HE, et al. Differences in brain Serotonergic metabolism between nonbulimic and bulimic patients with anorexia nervosa. Am J Psychiatry, 1984; 141:1598-1601.

45. Beaumont PVJ, George GCW, Smart DE. "Dieters" and "vomiters and purgers" in anorexia nervosa. Psychol Med, 1976; 6:617-22.

46. Russel G. Bulimia nervosa: an ominous variant of anorexia nervosa. Psychol Med, 1979; 9:429-48.

47. Garfinkel PE, Moldofsky H, Garner DM. The heterogeneity of anorexia nervosa. Arch Gen Psychiatry, 1980; 37:1036-40.

48. Casper RC, Eckert ED, Halmi KA, et al. Bulimia: its incidence and clinical importance in patients with anorexia nervosa. Arch Gen Psychiatry, 1980; 37:1030-5.

49. Van Praag HM. Depression, suicide and the metabolism of serotonin in the brain. J Affective Disord, 1982; 4:275-90.

50. Traskman L, Asberg M, Bertilsson L, et al. Monoamine metabolites in CSF and suicidal behavior. Arch Gen Psychiatry, 1981; 38:631-6.

51. Brown GI, Ebert MH, Goyer PF, et al. Aggression, suicide, and serotonin: relationship to CSF amine metabolites. Am J Psychiatry, 1982; 139:741-6.

52. Wurtman RJ. Behavioral effects of nutrients. Lancet, 1983; 1:1145-7.

53. Fernstrom JD, Wurtman RF. Brain serotonin content: increase following ingestion of carbohydrate diet. Science, 1971; 174:1023- 5.

54. Halmi KA, Dekirmenjian J, Davis JM, et al. Catecholamine metabolism in anorexia nervosa. Arch Gen Psych, 1978; 35:458-60.

55. Riederer P, Toifl K, Kruzik P. Excretion of biogenic amine metabolites in anorexia nervosa. Clin Chim Acta, 123:27-32.

56. Gross HA, Lake CR, Ebert MH, et al. Catecholamine metabolism in primary anorexia nervosa. J Clin Endocrinol Metab, 1979; 49:805-9.

57.	Abraham SF, Beumont PJV, Cobbin DM. Cate-cholamine metabolism and body weight in anorexia nervosa. Brit J Psych, 1981; 138:244-7.

58.	Biederman J, Herzog DB, Rivinus TM, et al. Urinary MHPG in anorexia nervosa patients with and without a concomitant major depressive disorder. J Psychiat Res, 1984; 18:149-60.

59.	Van Loon GR. Abnormal catecholamine mechanisms in hypothalamic- pituitary disease. Metabolism, 1980, 29(suppl.1):1198

60.	Luck P, Mikhailidis DP, Dashwood MR, et al. Platelet hyperaggregability and increased alpha-adrenoceptor density in anorexia nervosa. J Clin Endocrinol Metabl, 1983; 57:911-4.

61.	Sawyer CH, Hilliard J, Kanematsu S, et al. Effects of intraventricular infusions of norepinephrine and dopamine on LH release and ovulation in the rabbit. Neuroendocrinology, 1974; 15:328-37.

62.	Lofstrom A. Catecholamine turnover alterations in discrete areas of the medican eminence of the 4- and 5-day cytclic rat. Brain Res, 1977; 120:113-31.

63.	McCann SM. Neurohormonal correlates of ovulation. Fed Proc, 1970; 29:1888-970.

64.	Krulich LA, Giachetti A, Marchlewdkako JA, et al. On the role of the central noradrenergic and dopaminer-gic systems in the regulation of TSH secretion in the rat. Endocrinology, 1977; 100:496-505.

65.	Scapagnini U, Annaunziato L, Clememti G, et al. Chronic depletion of brain catecholamines and thy-rotropin secretion in the rat. Endocrinilogy, 1977; 101:1064-70.

66.	Blessing WW, Sved AF, Reis DJ. Destruction of nora-drenergic neurons in rabbit brainstem elevates plasma vasopressin, causing hypertension. Science, 1982; 217:661-3.

67.	Kimura T, Share L, Wang B, et al. The role of central adrenoreceptors in the control of vasopressin release and blood pressure. Endocrinology, 1981; 108:1829-36.

68.	Korf J, Bunney BS, Aghajanian GK. Noradrenergic neurons: morphine inhibition of spontaneous activity. Eur J Pharmacol, 1974; 25:165-9.

69.	Bird SJ, Kuhar MJ. Iontophoretic application of opieate to the locus coerleus. Brain Res, 1977; 122:523-33.

70.	Llorens C, Martres MP, Baudry M, et al. Hypersensi-tivity to noradrenaline in cortex after chronic mor-phine: relevance to tolerance and dependence. Nature, 1978; 274:603-5.

71.	Aghajanian GK. Central noradrenergic neurons: a locus for the functional interplay between alpha-2 adrenoceptors and opiate receptors. J Clin Psychiatry, 1982; 43:20-4.

72.	Gold MS, Redmond DE, Kleber, HD. Noradrenergic hyperactivity in opiate withdrawal supported by clonidine reversal of opiate withdrawal. Am J Psychi-atry, 1979; 136:100-2.

73.	Hsu LKG, Crisp AH, Harding B. Outcome of anorexia nervosa. Lancet, 1979; 1:61-5.

74.	Morgan H, Russel G. Value of family background and clinical features as predicators of long-term outcome in anorexia nervosa: four year follow-up study of 41 patients. Psychol Med, 1975; 5:355-71.

75.	Theander S. Anorexia nervosa. Acta Psychiatr Scand, 1970; 214:5- 194.

76.	Kaye WH, Jimerson DC, Lake CR, et al. Altered norepinephrine metabolism following long term weight recovery in patients with anorexia nervosa. Psy-chiatr Res, 1984; 14:333-42.

77.	Kaye WH, Gwirtsman HE, George T, et al. Caloric consumption and activity levels after weight recovery in anorexia nervosa: a prolonged delay in normaliza-tion. Int J Eating Disorder, 1986; 5:489-502.

78.	Grandison L, Guiddotti L. Stimulation of food intake by muscinol and beta endorphin. Neuropharmacology, 1977; 16:533-6.

79.	Baile CA, Della-Fera MA, McLaughlin CL, et al. Opiate antagonist and agonist and feeding in sheep. Fed Proc, 1980; 39:782.

80.	Holtzman SG. Behavioral effects of separate and com-bined administration of d-amphetamine. J Pharmacol Exp Ther, 1974; 189:51-60.

81.	Margules DL, Moisset B, Leewre MKJ, et al. B-En-dorphin is associated with overeating in genetically obese mice (ob/ob) and rats (fa/fa). Science, 1978; 202:988-91.

82.	Gerner RH. Sharp B. CSF beta-endorphin-im-munoreacivity in normal, schizophrenic, depressed, manic, and anorexic subjects. Brain Res, 1982; 237:244-5.

83.	Kaye WH, Pickar D, Naber D, et al. Cerebrospinal fluid opioid activity in anorexia nervosa. Am J Psych, 1982; 139:643-5.

84.	Margules DL. Beta-endorphin and endoloxone: hor-mones of the autonomic nervous system for the con-servation or expenditure of bodily resources and energy in anticipation of famine or feast. Neurosci Biobehav Rev, 1979; 3:155-62.

85.	Gold PW, Kaye WH, Robertson GL, et al. Abnormali-ties in plasma and cerebrospinal-fluid arginine vaso-pressin in patients with anorexia nervosa. N Engl J Med, 1983; 308:1117-23.

86.	Luerrson TB, Rovertson GL. Cerebrospinal fluid vasopressin and vasotocin in health and disease. In: Wood JH, ed. The Neurobiology of Cerebrospinal Fluid. New York: Plenum Publishing Co, 1980: 613-623.

87.	Woods JH. Neuroendocrinology of CSF: Peptides, steroids, and other hormones. Neuro Surgery, 1982; 11:293-305.

88.	Gerner RH, Yamada T. Altered neuropeptide concen-trations in cerebrospinal fluid of psychiatric patients. Brain Res, 1982; 238:298-302.

89.	Roberts E, Chase TN, Tower DB, ed. GABA in nerv-ous system function. New York: Raven Press, 1976.

90.	Manyam NV, Hare TA, Katz L, et al. Huntington's dis-ease: cerebrospinal fluid GABA levels in at-risk in-dividuals. Arch Neuro, 1978; 35:728-730.

91.	Perry TL, Hansen S, Kloster M. Huntington's chorea:

deficiency of gamma-aminobutyric acid in brain. N Engl J Med, 1973; 288:337-42.

92. Wood JD. The role of gamma-aminobutyric acid in the mechanism of seizures. Prog Neurobiol, 1975; 5:77-95.

93. Kimur AH, Kuriyama AK. Distribution of GABA in the rat hypothalamus: functional correlates of GABA with activities of appetite controlling mechanisms. J Neurochem, 1975; 24:903-7.

94. Gerner RH, Hare TA. CSF GABA in normal subjects and patients with depression, schizophrenia, mania, or anorexia nervosa. Am Psychiatry, 1981; 138:1098-101.

95. Enna SJ, Wood JH, Snyder SH. Gamma-aminobutyric acid (GABA) in human cereborspinal fluid: radiore-ceptor assy. J Neurochem, 1977; 28:1121-4.

96. Hare TA, Manyam, NV, Glaeser BS. Evaluation of cerebrospinal fluid gamma-aminobutyric acid content in neurological and psychiatric disorder. In: Wood JH, ed. Neurobiology of Cerebrospinal Fluid. New York: Plenum Publishing Co, 1980: 171-187.

97. Gwirtsman H, Gerner RH, Sternbach H. The over-night dexamethosone suppression test: clinical theoretical review. J Clin Psychiatry, 1982; 43:321-7.

98. Traskman L, Tybring G, Asberg M, et al. Cortisol in the CSF of depressed and suicidal patients. Arch Gen Psychiatry, 1980; 37:761-7.

99. Carroll BJH, Curtic GC, Mendels J, et al. Cerebrospi-nal fluid and plasma free cortisol concentrations in de-pression. Psychol Med, 1976; 6:235-44.

100. Gerner RH, Wilkins JN. CSF cortisol inpatients with depression, mania, or anorexia nervosa and in normal subjects. Am J Psychiatry, 1983; 140:92-4.

101. Schubert D, LaCorbine M, Klier GG, et al. The mod-ulation of neurotransmitter synthesis by steroid hor-mones and insulin. Brain Res, 1980; 190:67-9.

102. Gregory RA. Heterogeneity of gut and brain regula-tory peptides. Br Med Bull, 1982; 38:271-6.

Chapter 19

Pathophysiologic and Clinical Aspects of Medical, Endocrine, and Nutritional Abnormalities and Adaptations in Eating Disorders

James C. Sheinin

Anorexia nervosa, bulimia, and related eating disorders are a heterogeneous group of primary psychiatric disorders whose incidence has approached epidemic proportions in recent years [1,2]. Patients with eating disorders may have numerous secondary medical, hypothalamic, endocrine, metabolic, and nutritional abnormalities [2-38,58-60], some of which may be or become severe enough to be life-threatening. Further, it has been suggested that some of the psychologic abnormalities in patients with anorexia nervosa may be secondary to starvation and undernutrition rather than intrinsic to the syndrome of anorexia nervosa [39]. Response of the primary disorder to psychotherapy is associated with restoration of near-normal weight and reversal of the secondary medical, hypothalamic, endocrine, metabolic, and nutritional abnormalities. However, patients with bulimia may sustain irreversible damage to the gastrointestinal tract and the oral cavity as a result of emesis or laxative abuse.

This review will provide some general perspectives regarding the pathogenesis, incidence, severity,and evolution of the abnormalities in patients with anorexia nervosa, bulimia, and related eating disorders, and the adaptation to starvation, undernutrition, emesis, or laxative or diuretic abuse. Subsequently, those specific abnormalities that are most significant for the diagnosis,

evaluation, and management of these patients will be emphasized.

GENERAL PERSPECTIVES

Anorexia nervosa has been appropriately described as starvation in the midst of plenty. Unlike other settings where starvation and malnutrition occur, patients with anorexia nervosa have access to all foods and nutrients. They will selectively eat some things, albeit usually in meager quantities, and assiduously avoid others. Characteristically, they will eat little or no carbohydrate except as may be present in low-calorie fruits and vegetables, and little or no fat except as may be present in protein foods. However, their total caloric intake and relatively high protein intake further diminishes protein breakdown and conserves lean body mass (see below). The vitamin content of those foods they do eat, often supplemented by (calorie-free) vitamin supplements, militates against vitamin deficiency in all but the most severe cases. Most patients with eating disorders are young and otherwise medically well. Many tolerate severe and protracted undernutrition, severe fluid and electrolyte depletion, protracted emesis, or inordinate laxative or diuretic abuse with minimal or no detectable clinical or laboratory abnormalities. When findings in

227

older patients; patients with cardiac, gastrointestinal, neoplastic, or other systemic diseases; and patients with protein-calorie malnutrition are extrapolated to patients with eating disorders [38], the potential risks are exaggerated and exceed what is commonly observed [3,9].

The resilience of patients with anorexia nervosa further is facilitated by two prompt normal physiologic adaptations to starvation or to carbohydrate deprivation:

1. About 80% to 90% of the more active circulating throid hormone, triiodothyronine (T3), comes from extrathyroidal conversion of thyroxine (T4). Within days, peripheral conversion of T4 to T3 is inhibited, and T3 levels are decreased. In patients with anorexia nervosa, mean T3 levels are usually about half those of normal controls [4,9-12,17]. Findings such as cold intolerance, constipation, dry skin, bradycardia, carotenemia, hypercholesterolemia, and decreased basal metabolic rate provide further evidence for an apparent protective hypometabolic adaptation.

2. The needs of glucose-dependent tissues such as the CNS normally are met by food intake and by breakdown of liver glycogen to glucose. Within hours of starvation, glycogen stores are depleted, and glucose can be provided only by gluconeogenesis from the amino acid constituents of proteins. Within days, stimulation of lipolysis and ketogenesis provides ketones at levels high enough to be used by the CNS as an alternate fuel [40]. Glucose requirements and protein breakdown are diminished and lean body mass is conserved.

For young women, a reasonable general guideline for ideal body weight would be 100 lb for 5 ft plus 5 lb for each additional inch in height. Patients with eating disorders who are less than 20% below ideal body weight almost always are asymptomatic and have no clinical or laboratory abnormalities except as will be discussed. Patients between 20% and 40% below ideal body weight begin to have clinical and laboratory abnormalities that are infrequently life-threatening. Patients 40% or more below ideal body weight usually are symptomatic and have clinical and laboratory abnormalities that almost invariably are life-threatening [9]. Among other variables that may affect the incidence and severity of the abnormalities include the percent weight loss from premorbid weight, the rate of weight loss, the total weight loss, the duration of undernutrition, and the susceptibility of the individual patient [9].

Two specific exceptions to the above are:

1. Amenorrhea may occur before or concurrent with onset of weight loss in up to one third of patients

with anorexia nervosa and may persist following normalization of weight. These patients [14] exhibit an immature 24-hour pattern of luteinizing hormone (LH) secretion characteristic of prepubertal or pubertal girls, a physiologic as well as psychologic regression from adulthood to childhood.

2. Significant and sometimes life-threatening clinical and laboratory abnormalities due to emesis or laxative or diuretic abuse may occur in normal-weight or overweight patients.

Findings reported as individual values, range of values, or percent abnormal values, comparison of findings from different reports, and observation of large numbers of patients [9] indicate that the incidence and severity of clinical and laboratory abnormalities among patients are extremely variable. It should be emphasized that laboratory evaluation usually provides the initial evidence for these abnormalities.

The use of weight as the sole or primary criterion for assessment of medical and nutritional status has several significant limitations:

1. The patient has an overriding concern about weight and is extremely fearful of, threatened by, and resistant to weight gain.

2. Despite repeated explanations and reassurance, the patient almost invariably reacts adversely to the rapid and sizable weight gain that is associated with refeeding edema or cessation of purging (a quart of body fluid weighs 2 lb).

3. The patient can readily manipulate weight before weight-ins by eating, drinking, wearing heavy clothing, or loading clothing with heavy objects.

4. There may be little or no correlation between the absolute weight or the percentage below ideal or premorbid body weight and the presence, severity, and evaluation of clinical and laboratory abnormalities.

However, it must be emphasized to the patient with undernutrition that weight gain is a prerequisite for improvement of medical and nutritional status.

HYPOTHALAMIC, ENDOCRINE AND METABOLIC ABNORMALITIES IN PATIENTS WITH ANOREXIA NERVOSA

The protective hypometabolic adaptation of decreased peripheral conversion of T4 to T3 and the resultant marked diminution in T3 levels has been described. Total T4 levels (T4 is normally 99.96% bound to plasma proteins) usually have been found to be lower than in normal controls but within the normal range [3-6,9-13,17]. However, dialyzable free T4 levels, felt to be the most sensitive parameter of thyroid function, have been found to be normal [3,4,6,9,17]. That there is hypothalamic dysfunction or a protective hypothalamic hypometabolic adaptation has been suggested [4,5,8,10-13] by the findings of normal basal pituitary throid stimulating hormone (TSH) levels and quantitatively normal and temporally normal or delayed response to TSH to hypothalamic thyrotropin releasing hormone (TRH). In addition to the clinical and laboratory findings described, other hypothyroid-like alterations in glucocorticoid and androgen metabolism have been reported in patients with anorexia nervosa [15,17].

These perturbations in hypothalamic-pituitary-thyroid status may be seen in patients with other forms of caloric deprivation, with various severe nonthyroidal illnesses, with certain medications, and after major surgery [41], and have been dubbed the "euthyroid sick syndrome."

The physiologic regression of the 24-hour pattern of LH secretion to a prepubertal or pubertal pattern previously has been described. Basal LH and follicle stimulating hormone (FSH) levels have been found to be low [3-6,8,16]. FSH and LH responses to gonadotropin-releasing hormone (GnRH) have been reported to be normal, blunted, temporally delayed, and discordant [4,5,8,16]. As would be anticipated in amenorrheic women with low FSH and LH levels, plasma estradiol levels are low [4,8].

Although a critical body weight has been suggested as a prerequisite for maintenance or onset of menses [42], the clinical observation that women often become amenorrheic with little or no antecedent weight loss and may remain amenorrheic for months after restoration of a normal or near-normal weight suggests that factors other than weight are involved in the pathogenesis of amenorrhea in patients with anorexia nervosa. Stress-induced amenorrhea ("hypothalamic amenorrhea") in otherwise normal young women has long been recognized. That vigorous physical activity may be associated with delayed menarche and amenorrhea has been described more recently [43-45], but the significance is uncertain, since comparable vigorous physical activity ("obligatory" running) has been suggested to be an analogue of anorexia nervosa [46]. Finally, simple weight loss to about 20% below ideal body weight in nonanorectic women has been associated with amenorrhea and altered basal and post-GnRH, FSH, and LH levels [47].

Basal plasma cortisol levels have been found to be normal or elevated [3-6,17-19]. Diurnal variation of plasma cortisol levels has been found to be normal or absent [3-6,17,18]. Prolongation of the half-life of cortisol and decreased metabolic clearance rate of cortisol were thought to be responsible for the increased 24-hour mean cortisol level [17]. A subsequent study suggested that the cortisol production rate, initially thought to be normal [17], was elevated in proportion to body mass [19]. Dexamethasone suppression of plasma cortisol levels has been found to be impaired in patients with anorexia nervosa more than 20% below ideal body weight [20,21] and in patients with bulimia as well [22]. Bulimia was considered to be related to affective disorders and to be responsive to therapy with tricyclic antidepressants [48]. However, the clinical utility of the dexamethasone suppression test for psychiatric diagnosis and management has not been supported by recent critical evaluation [49,50].

Studies using recently available ovine corticotropin-releasing hormone (CRH) have shown marked basal hypercortisolism, normal basal corticotropin (ACTH) and marked reduction of the ACTH response to CRH in underweight women with anorexia nervosa [58]. However, hypercortisolism resolved and the ACTH response to CRH normalized respectively four weeks and six months after restoration of normal weight. This suggests that the abnormalities in the hypothalamic-pituitary-adrenal axis seen in anorexia nervosa are not intrinsic to the psychiatric disorder but rather are related to undernutrition. Further, normal weight bulimic women did not have significant hypercortisolism, and had a normal basal ACTH and a normal ACTH response to CRH.

The mean plasma concentration of the adrenal androgen dehydroisoandrosterone (DHA) recently was found to be similar to that of preadrenarcheal children. Like the immature 24-hour pattern of LH secretion, this represents another endocrine regression from adulthood to childhood [23].

Basal growth hormone (GH) levels have been found to be normal or increased [4-6]. An inverse relation between basal GH levels and dietary intake [5] and a direct relation between basal GH levels and severity of weight loss [4] have been noted. Both GH and cortisol are protective counterregulatory hormones that stimulate gluconeogenesis in response to the threat of hypoglycemia (see below). The presence of normal or elevated GH and cortisol levels readily distinguishes anorexia nervosa from hypopituitarism. Further, hypopituitarism now is known to be rarely associated with undernutrition.

Evidence for partial central diabetes insipidus using the fluid deprivation test with subsequent administration of exogenous antidiuretic hormone (ADH) has been found in one study [4] but not confirmed in another [7]. The distinction between diabetes insipidus and primary or psychogenic polydipsia may be difficult using the fluid deprivation test, and patients with anorexia nervosa frequently hoard and consume large amounts of noncaloric fluids. Abnormal levels of plasma and CSF arginine vasopressin recently were described in patients with anorexia nervosa, but the causes and consequences were not determined [24]. In addition, impaired concentration of urine in patients with bulimia may result from nephrogenic diabetes insipidus induced by hypokalemic nephropathy [51].

It is of interest that qualitatively similar but quantitatively less dramatic perturbations in hypothalamic and endocrine status have been found in nonanorectic women with secondary amenorrhea associated with simple weight loss [47].

Frequent mild to moderate and occasional marked fasting hypoglycemia is seen in patients with anorexia nervosa and apparently is asymptomatic [9]. The adaptive stimulation of lipolysis and ketogenesis, which provides ketone bodies as an alterante fuel and diminishes glucose requirements, and the stimulation of gluconeogenesis by GH and cortisol have been described. It has been found that total fasting for 72 hours in normal women results in similarly marked and asymptomatic hypoglycemia [52]. It is reasonable to anticipate, but it remains to be established, that these observations mitigate the clinical significance of hypoglycemia in patients with anorexia nervosa. Accordingly, it still seems prudent to be concerned about moderate to marked fasting hypoglycemia in these patients.

The association of hypercholesterolemia with anorexia nervosa is not commonly recognized but has been clearly demonstrated [25-27]. The elevation of total cholesterol was found to be related to an increase in low-density lipoprotein (LDL) cholesterol and to be reversible in patients who regained their original weight and began to menstruate [27]. Yet, patients with anorexia nervosa may have normal or low cholesterol levels as well [3,6,9,26,27]. The relative contributions of the protective hypometabolic adaptation of diminished peripheral conversion of T4 to T3 and of diet to the hypercholesterolemia and hypercarotenemia [28,29] of anorexia nervosa are not fully established.

No surprisingly, evidence for osteoporosis has been found in some women with anorexia nervosa [59,60], particularly after prolonged amenorrhea and undernutrition. Single photon absorptiometry has shown decreased cortical bone density in the distal forearm, and radiographs have shown vertebral compression fractures. A high level of physical activity may protect anorexic women against bone loss [59]. The effect of restoration of normal weight and resumption of menses on restitution of bone density is not yet known.

MEDICAL AND NUTRITIONAL ABNORMALITIES IN PATIENTS WITH ANOREXIA NERVOSA, BULIMIA AND RELATED EATING DISORDERS

Alterations in fluid status are common in patients with eating disorders [9]. Starvation or carbohydrate deprivation as well as emesis or laxative or diuretic abuse give rise to fluid depletion. Refeeding or cessation of purging are associated with fluid repletion and retention, and sometimes with dramatic edema. The effect of the accompanying rapid weight gain may be devastating to patients with eating disorders. Initial laboratory evaluation in patients with fluid depletion and decreased plasma volume frequently provides falsely high values, particularly for blood count and serum proteins. With fluid repletion and retention, laboratory values may fall precipitously, sometimes to falsely low levels. In such patients, some short-term weight loss usually is associated with ultimate restoration of normal fluid balance.

Patients with anorexia nervosa frequently have mild anemia and moderate to severe leukopenia with neutropenia or lymphopenia [3,9,30-32]. Thrombocytopenia has been found to be mild, infrequent, and asymptomatic [3,9,30-32]. The deficiency in all hematologic cellular elements appears to be a result of reversible bone marrow hypoplasia with increased gelatinous acid mucopolysaccharide ground substance in the marrow [30]. Sporadic cases of decreased granulocyte bactericidal activity and hypocomplementemia have been described in patients with anorexia nervosa and may contribute to increased susceptibility to infection [32]. In addition, significant lymphopenia may affect immune competence [53]. However, clinical observations do not support an increased susceptibility to infection [9,13], even in those patients with leukopenia, neutropenia, or lymphopenia.

Levels of serum proteins measured in routine multichannel automated chemistry profiles, ie, total protein and albumin, often are normal in patients with anorexia nervosa [9]. When present, significant hypoalbuminemia indicates severe or protracted undernutrition. However, because of its shorter half-life of six to eight days, serum transferrin levels, measured directly or calculated from measurement of total iron-binding capacity (TIBC), reflect significant protein deficiency much earlier than total protein or albumin levels [53]. Transferrin levels almost always are low in patients initially presenting with anorexia nervosa, and may be as low as half of normal values in patients with severe or protracted undernutrition [9].

Life-threatening potassium depletion and hypokalemia may occur as a result of emesis or laxative or diruetic abuse. Potent diuretics, eg, thiazides and furosemide, induce potassium depletion by increasing renal excretion of potassium as well as sodium. The potassium concentration of gastric fluid is relatively low, so only a small portion of the potassium depletion in patients with protracted emesis is a result of gastric potassium loss. However, loss of gastric fluid hydrochloric acid gives rise to metabolic alkalosis, and most of the potassium depletion in patients with protracted emesis is a result of increased renal potassium loss associated with chronic metabolic alkalosis. On the other hand, potassium depletion in patients with laxative abuse is a direct result of significant intestinal potassium losses in chronic diarrhea [51].

Small to moderate potassium loss usually is asymptomatic. Symptoms of moderate to severe potassium depletion and hypokalemia include skeletal and smooth muscle weakness and paralysis, cardiac arrhythmias and conduction abnormalities, and hypokalemic nephropathy, which may give rise to nephrogenic diabetes insipidus. When hypokalemia becomes significant and mandates treatment has been a subject of recent debate [54,55]. Even patients with emesis or laxative or diuretic abuse who have significant hypokalemia often have no symptoms or ECG abnormalities [9].

Surreptitious emesis or laxative or diuretic abuse may simulate Bartter's syndrome, a rare syndrome characterized by hypokalemic alkalosis, hyperaldosteronism, and hyperplasia of the renal juxtaglomerular apparatus. It may be differentiated from Bartter's syndrome by measuring serum or urinary laxative or diuretic levels and urinary chloride levels [56].

Renal function as measured by BUN and creatinine is affected by protein intake and catabolism and by fluid status as well as by intrinsic renal function in patients with eating disorders [9]. With normal fluid status and renal function, BUN, creatinine, and uric acid levels are normal or low. With significant fluid depletion, almost always associated with emesis or laxative or diuretic abuse, hypovolemia results in prerenal azotemia with BUN disproportionately more elevated than creatinine. Renal excretion of uric acid and of calcium may be compromised and hyperuricemia and hypercalcemia may ensue.

Orthostatic hypotension often is seen in patients with eating disorders. While reduction of plasma volume and significant electrolyte imbalance such as occurs in patients with emesis or laxative or diuretic abuse are known to induce orthostatic hypotension, the pathogenesis of orthostatic hypotension in patients with anorexia nervosa who have not purged is uncertain [57].

A variety of ECG changes have been observed in patients with eating disorders [3,9,33-35], some of which may be related to undernutrition, hypometabolic adaptation, and hypokalemia. The pathogenesis and significance of frequently nonspecific and occasional ischemic-like ST segment and T wave contour changes is uncertain. Arrhythmias and conduction abnormalities have caused the greatest concern. Prolongation of the QT interval has been observed [32,35] and recently was reported in an abstract [35] to be associated with the sud-

den death of three patients with anorexia nervosa. However, such ominous findings are most uncommon [3,9,34] in these patients.

Gastrointestinal symptoms and evidence for gastrointestinal dysfunction abnormalities are extremely common in patients with eating disorders. Symptoms and abnormalities may be related to undernutrition, hypometabolic adaptation, decreased food intake, binge eating, emesis, laxative abuse and hypokalemia. Irreversible damage to the gastrointestinal tract and to the oral cavity may ensur. Abnormal liver function tests, SGOT (AST) and SGPT (ALT) disproportionately more than GGTP are seen commonly [9] and presumably reflect hepatocellular injury as a result of moderate to severe undernutrition. Elevated serum amylase levels have been attributed to pancreatitis. However, salivary gland enlargement is seen occasionally in patients with bulimia [9,36] and is associated with elevated serum amylase levels [36]. The pathogenesis of the sialopathy is uncertain, but elevated serum amylase levels in untreated patients with eating disorders are more likely a result of sialopathy rather than of pancreatitis. Characteristic dental deterioration has been observed inpatients with eating disorders [37]. Dissolution of tooth enamel and altered caries response may occur as a result of emesis, abnormal diet, and alteration in the quality and composition of saliva.

SUMMARY

Patients with anorexia nervosa, bulimia, and related eating disorders have numerous secondary medical, hypothalamic, endocrine, metabolic, and nutritional abnormalities, some of which may be or become severe enough to be life-threatening. Some general perspectives regarding the pathogenesis, incidence, severity, and evolution of the abnormalities in these patients, and the adaptations that facilitate their resilience to starvation, undernutrition, emesis, or laxative or diuretic abuse have been provided. Specific abnormalities that are most significant for the diagnosis, evaluation, and management of these patients have been emphasized.

REFERENCES

1. Bruch H. Eating disorders. New York: Basic Books, 1973.

2. Vigersky RA, ed. Anorexia nervosa. New York: Raven Press, 1977.

3. Warren MP, Vande Wiele RL. Clinical and metabolic features of anorexia nervosa. Am J Obstet Gynecol, 1973; 117:435-49.

4. Vigersky RA, Loriaux DL, Anderson AE, Lipsett MB. Anorexia nervosa: behavioural and hypothalamic

aspects. Clin Endocrinol Metab, 1976; 5:517-35.

5. Brown GM, Garfinkel PG, Jeuniewic N et al. Endocrine profiles in anorexia nervosa. In: Vigersky RA, ed. Anorexia Nervosa. New York: Raven Press, 1977; 123-35.

6. Hurd HP II, Palumbo PJ, Gharib H. Hypothalamic-endocrine dysfunction in anorexia nervosa. Mayo Clin Proc, 1977; 51:711.

7. Fohlin L. Body composition, cardiovascular and renal fucntion in adolescent patients with anorexia nervosa. Acta Paediat Scand (Suppl), 1977; 268:1-20.

8. Beumont PJV, George GCW, Pimstone BL, Vinik AI. Body weight and the pituitary response to hypothalamic releasing hormones in patients with anorexia nervosa. J Clin Endocrinol Metab, 1976; 43:487-96.

9. Sheinin JC. Medical endocrine and nutritional abnormalities in over 300 patients with eating disorders. Unpublished observations.

10. Moshang T Jr, Parks JS, Baker L, et al. Low serum triiodothyronine in patients with anorexia nervosa. J Clin Endocrinol Metab, 1975; 40:470-73.

11. Miyai K, Yamamoto T, Azukizawa M et al. Serum thyroid hormones and thyrotropin in anorexia nervosa. J Clin Endocrinol Metab, 1975; 40:334-8.

12. Croxson MS, Ibbertson HK. Low serum triiodothyronine and hypothyroidism in anorexia nervosa. J Clin Endocrinol Metab, 1977; 44:167-74.

13. Casper RC, Frohman LA. Delayed TSH release in anorexia nervosa following injection of thyrotyropin-releasing hormone. Psychoneuroendocrinology, 1982; 7:59-68.

14. Boyar RM, Katz J, Finkelstein JW et al. Anorexia nervosa: Immaturity of the 24-hour luteinizing hormone secretory pattern. N Engl J Med, 1974; 291:861-5.

15. Bradlow HL, Boyar RM, O'Connor J et al. Hypothyroid-like alterations in testosterone metabolism in anorexia nervosa. J Clin Endocrinol Metab, 1976; 43:571-4.

16. Sherman BM, Halmi KA, Zamudio R. LH and FSH reponse to gonadotropin-releasing hormone in anorexia nervosa: effect of nutritional rehabilitation. J Clin Endocrinol Metab, 1975; 41:135-42.

17. Boyar RM, Hellman LD, Roffwang H et al. Cortisol secretion and metbolism in anorexia nervosa. N Engl J Med, 1977; 296:190-3.

18. Casper RC, Chatterton RJ Jr, Davis JM. Alterations in serum cortisol and its binding characteristics in anorexia. J Clin Endocrinol Metab, 1979; 49:406-11.

19. Walsh BT, Katz JL, Levin J et al. The production rate of cortisol declines during recovery from anorexia nervosa. J Clin Endocrinol Metab, 1981; 53:203-5.

20. Doerr P, Fichter M, Pirke KM, Lund R. Relationship between weight gain and hypothalamic function in patients with anorexia nervosa. J Steroid Biochem, 1980; 13:529-37.

21. Gerner RH, Gwirtsman HE. Abnormalities of dexamethasone suppression test and urinary MHPG in anorexia nervosa. Am J Psychiatry, 1981; 138:650-3.

22. Hudson JI, Pope HB Jr, Jonas JM, et al. Hypothalamic-pituitary- adrenal axis hyperactivity in bulimia. Psychiat Res, 1983; 8:111- 7.

23. Zumoff B, Walsh BT, Katz JL, et al. Subnormal plasma dehydroisoandrosterone to cortisol ratio in anorexia nervosa: a second hormonal parameter of ontogenic regression. J Clin Endocrinol Metab, 1983; 56:668-72.

24. Gold PW, Kaye W, Robertson GL, Ebert M. Abnormalities in plasma and cerebrospinal-fluid arginine vasopressin in patients with anorexia nervosa. N Engl J Med, 1983; 308:1117-23.

25. Klinefelter H. Hypercholesterolemia in anorexia nervosa. J Clin Endocrino, 1965; 25:1520-21.

26. Crisp AH, Blendix LM, Pawan GLS. Aspects of fat metabolism in anorexia nervosa. Metabolism, 1968; 17:1109-17.

27. Mordasini R, Klose G, Greten H. Secondary type II hyperlipoproteinemia in patients with anorexia nervosa. Metabolism, 1978; 27:71-9.

28. Pops MA, Schwabe AD: Hypercarotenemia in anorexia nervosa. J Am Med Assoc, 1968; 205:533-4.

29. Robboy MS, Sato AS, Schwabe AD. The hypercarotenemia in anorexia nervosa: A comparison of vitamin A and carotene levels in various forms of menstrual dysfunction and cachexia. Am J Clin Nutrit, 1974; 27:362-7.

30. Mant MJ, Faragher BS. The haematology of anorexia nervosa. Br J Haematol, 1972; 23:737-49.

31. Bowers TK, Eckert E. Leukopenia in anorexia nervosa: lack of increased risk of infection. Arch Intern Med, 1978; 138:1520-3.

32. Kay J, Stricker R. Hematologic and immunologic abnormalities in anorexia nervosa. South Med J, 1983; 76:1008-10.

33. Thurston J, Marks P. Electrocardiographic abnormalities in patients with anorexia nervosa. Br Heart J, 1974; 36:719-23.

34. Gottdiener JS, Gross HA, Henry WL et al. Effects of self-induced starvation on cardiac size and function in anorexia nervosa. Circulation, 1978; 58:425-33.

35. Isner JM, Roberts WC, Yagar J, Heymsfield S. Sudden death in anorexia nervosa: role of Q-T interval prolongation. Circulation, 1983; 68(Suppl III):426.

36. Levin PA, Falko JM, Dixon K et al. Benign parotid enlargement in bulimia. Ann Intern Med, 1980; 93:827-9.

37. Hurst PS, Lacey JH, Crisp AH. Teeth, vomiting and diet: A study of the dental characteristics of seventeen anorexia nervosa patients. Postgrad Med J, 1977; 53:298-305.

38. Harris RT. Bulimarexia and related serious eating disorders with medical complications. Ann Intern Med, 1983; 99:800-7.

39. Bruch H. Anorexia nervosa: therapy and theory. Am J Psychiatry, 1982; 139:1531-8.

40. Cahill GF Jr, Herrera MG, Morgan AP, et al. Hormone-fuel interrelationships during fasting. J Clin Invest, 1966; 45:1751-69.

41. Wartofsky L, Burman KD. Alterations in throid function in patients with systemic illness: The "euthyroid sick syndrome." Endocrine Reviews, 1982; 3:164-217.

42. Frisch RL, McArthur JW. Menstrual cycles: Fatness as a determinant of minimum weight for height necessary for their maintenance or onset. Science, 1974; 185:949-51.

43. Warren MP. The effects of exercise on pubertal progression and reproductive functIon in girls. J Clin Endocrinol Metab, 1980; 51:1150-7.

44. Frisch RL, Wyshak G, Vincent L. Delayed menarche and amenorrhea in ballet dancers. N Engl J Med, 1980; 303:17-19.

45. Frisch RL, Gotz-Welbergen AV, McArthur JW, et al. Delayed menarche and amenorrhea of college athletes in relation to age of onset of training. JAMA, 1981; 246:1559-63.

46. Yates A, Leehey K, Shisslak CM. Running—an analogue of anorexia? N Engl J Med, 1983; 308:251-5.

47. Vigersky RA, Anderson AE, Thompson RH, Loriaux DL. Hypothalamic dysfunction in secondary amenorrhea associated with simple weight loss. N Engl J Med, 297:1142-5.

48. Pope HG Jr, Hudson JI, Jonas JM, Yurgelun-Todd MSA. Bulimia treated with imipramine: a placebo-controlled double blind study. Am J Psychiatry, 1983;140:554-8.

49. Hirschfield RMA, Koslow SH, Kupfer DJ. The clincial utility of the dexamethasone suppression test in psychiatry. JAMA, 1983; 250:2172-4.

50. Health & Public Policy Committee, American College of Physicians: The dexamethasone suppression test for the detection, diagnosis and management of depression. Ann Intern Med, 1984; 100:307-8.

51. Cohen JJ. Disorders of potassium balance. Hospital Practice, 1979; 14(Jan):119-28.

52. Merimee TJ, Tyson JE. Stabilization of plasma glucose during fasting. N Engl J Med, 1974; 291:1275-8.

53. Blackburn GL, Thornton PA. Nutritional assessment of the hospitalized patient. Med Clin North Am, 1979; 63:1103-15.

54. Harrington JT, Isner JM, Kassirer JP. Our national obsession with potassium. Am J Med, 1982; 73:155-9.

55. Kaplan NM. Our appropriate concern about hypokalemia. Am J Med, 1984; 771:1-4.

56. Veldhuis JD, Bardin CW, Demers LM. Metabolic mimicry of Bartter's syndrome by covert vomiting: utility of urinary chloride determination. Am J Med, 1979; 66:361-3.

57. Schatz IJ. Orthostatic hypotension. I. Functional and neurogenic causes. Arch Intern Med,1984; 144:773-77.

58. Gold PW, Gwirtsman H, Avgerinos PC, et al. Abnormal hypothalamic-pituitary-adrenal function in anorexia nervosa. N Engl J Med 1986; 314:1335-42.

59. Rigotti NA, Nussbaum SR, Herzog DB, Neer RM. Osteoporosis in women with anorexia nervosa. N Engl J Med 1984; 311:1601-6.

60. Szmuckler GI, Brown SW, Parsons V, Darby A. Premature loss of bone in chronic anorexia nervosa. Br Med J 1985; 290:26-7.

Chapter 20

Classification and Diagnosis of the Eating Disorders

L.K. George Hsu

In the field of medicine the value of classification and diagnosis of diseases is generally unquestioned. Classification is the process whereby complex clinical phenomena are reduced to defined categories for the purpose of treatment and prevention, while diagnosis is the assignment of the patient's clinical features (eg, constrictive chest pain occurring on exertion in a 50-year-old man with exercise ECG changes and coronary atherosclerosis) to a particular category (eg, angina pectoris) for the purpose of treatment (eg, nitrates and beta-blockers) and secondary prevention (eg, weight reduction). However, in psychiatry, classification and diagnosis are often deemed irrelevant to the nature of the problem. Thus, for instance, a diagnosis of anorexia nervosa does not convey vital information such as why the patient needs to strive for control, who brought her to treatment, or how she relates to her family. Furthermore, in other branches of medicine treatment is usually directly related to diagnosis, whereas in psychiatry specific treatments are rare. Thus, classification and diagnosis are of less value for treatment planning in psychiatry. Finally, some psychiatrists feel that it is dehumanizing and harmful to fit a patient's symptoms into a classification scheme; they insist that a patient should be understood as an individual and treated as a person.

Why then are we concerned about classification and diagnostic criteria? Classification is based on the assumption that there are certain shared features between disorders that distinguish this particular category of disorder from others. A related assumption is that patients with this category of disorder can be distinguished from those without. Classification is therefore essential for delineating and defining the condition that we propose to treat. It is also essential for the purpose of communication, so that we can all know what particular mental disorder we are describing. A third reason is that it is essential for learning, for comparing with each other our experience of treating patients with the same disorder. The fourth is for developing specific prevention and treatments. While these are still rare in psychiatry, it is nevertheless essential that we should set the stage for the evaluation of such efforts by clearly defining the conditions.

However, to argue for the value of diagnosis in psychiatry is not to overlook its shortcomings. Thus, in clinical practice, the assignment of a diagnosis should always be accompanied by a detailed formulation of the patient's clinical features, personality features, personal and social history, family history and relationships, and previous treatments.

DIAGNOSES OF ANOREXIA NERVOSA AND BULIMIA NERVOSA

The emergence of the eating disorders as diagnostic categories have been hampered by two major difficulties. The first is a lack of agreement on how diagnostic criteria should be established. The traditional approach to establishing diagnostic categories is to provide brief descriptions of the characteristic featrures of each con-

Table 20.1 Comparison of Anorexia Nervosa and Bulimia Nervosa

| | Anorexia Nervosa | | Bulimia Nervosa |
	Restrictor Subgroup (60%)	Bulimic Subgroup (40%)	
Cardinal Features		Emaciation Drive for Thinness Behavior Directed to Weight Loss		Normal or Overweight Fear of Fatness Bulimic Episodes
Weight		Low		Normal or Overweight
Amenorrhea (female)		Present		Variable
Binge-eating	Absent		Present	Present
Vomiting/Purging	Usually Absent		Usually Present	Usually Present

dition. The problem related to this approach is a lack of precision, which severely limits the usefulness of classification schemes thus defined. A more recent approach is to provide adequate working (ie, operational) definitions of the various diagnostic categories. Examples of this approach are the Feighner et al criteria [1] and the American Psychiatric Association's DSM III [2]. The correct use of such operational criteria allows a clinician to make a fairly precise description of the patient sample.

A second hurdle is a lack of agreement and understanding among researchers as to the etiology, cardinal features, course, and outcome of the eating disorders. Thus, some clinicians still regard anorexia nervosa as an appetite disorder, when in fact many researchers have shown that the anorectic's refusal to eat is certainly not related to a loss of appetite. Despite these difficulties, the American Psychiatric Association [2] has produced succinct and useful descriptions of the disorders, which are contrasted in table 1.

DIAGNOSIS OF ANOREXIA NERVOSA

A list of diagnostic criteria for anorexia nervosa is decribed in table 2; it retains most of what is present in the DSM III. The cardinal feature of anorexia nervosa is the relentless pursuit of thinness [3], most commonly expressed by willful starvation and excessive exercising, less often by vomiting and laxative/diuretic abuse. Strictly speaking, anorexia nervosa is therefore not really an eating disorder, since the refusal to eat is related to the fear of weight gain. Amenorrhea is a recognized feature of the disorder and should be included. For operational purposes the degree of weight loss necessary to quality for a diagnosis of anorexia nervosa should be specified. Furthermore, simply relying on weight loss as a criterion may inadvertently classify normal or overweight subjects into the syndrome (eg, if a premorbidly obese subject weighing 100 kg loses weight to 60 kg and

displays all the other symptoms of anorexia nervosa, she could technically qualify for the diagnosis even though she is not emaciated) and thus destroy the classifical image of the emaciated patient. A low body weight as an additional criterion is thus proposed. An attempt is also made to include the less severe cases and to this end a staging of body weight is suggested. The distinction between the restrictor (or abstainer) and the bulimic (or vomiting) subgroups has been the subject of much recent research and should therefore be drawn. The presence of concurrent or previous Axis I and II diagnoses should be specified, since recent research has demonstrated that anorexia nervosa patients may also develop other psychiatric disorders such as a major depression or a schizophreniform disorder. Finally, disturbance of body image as a diagnostic criteria has been deleted, in part because the concept is difficult to define [4], and in part because all the recent studies suggest that overestimation of body width is not a characteristic feature of the illness [4,5,6]. The DSM-III-R has incorporated some but not all of these proposed changes.

Table 20.2 Diagnostic Criteria for Anorexia Nervosa

A. Intense fear of becoming obese, which does not diminish as weight loss progresses.

B. Emaciation as a result of weight loss of at least 15% of original body weight:
1. Grade 1: Body weight less than 85% of average weight for height
2. Grade 2: Body weight less than 75% of average weight for height

C. Behavior directed towards weight loss.

D. Amenorrhea in the female

E. Subgroup:
1. Bulimic: Presence of bulimic episodes
2. Restrictor: Absence of bulimic episodes

F. No known physical illness that could account for the weight loss and emaciation.

Table 20.3 Diagnostic Criteria for Bulimia Nervosa

A. Recurrent episodes of binge-eating (rapid consumption of a large amount of food in a discrete period of time, usually less than 2 hours), frequency of at least once a week over the previous four weeks.

B. Awareness that the eating pattern is abnormal and fear of not being able to stop eating voluntarily once the binge-eating begins.

C. Intense fear of fatness, depressed mood, and self-deprecatory thoughts following eating binges.

D. Termination of binge-eating episodes by abdominal pain, sleep, social interruption, self-induced vomiting, or use of cathartics or diuretics.

E. Repeated attempts to lose weight by severe dieting, self-induced vomiting, or use of cathartics or diuretics.

F. The bulimic episodes are not related to a concurrent anorexia nervosa of any known physical disorder.

DIAGNOSIS OF BULIMIA NERVOSA

The cardinal feature of bulimia (Greek for "ox appetite") is the presence of recurrent episodes of binge eating occurring with varying duration (from minutes to hours) and frequency (up to many times a day) (table 3). Initially the binge eating is almost always described as pleasurable and soothing, but depression and guilt soon follow, and the patient experiences a fear of loss of control. No clear demarcation exists between bulimia thus defined and eating binges or great variations in dietary intake [7,8]. Binge eating [9] occurs in nearly half of all anorexia nervosa patients [7,10,11] and in 30% of obese subjects who seek treatment [12]. Binges also occur sporadically in many normal-weight subjects, particularly in those dieting to control weight [13,14]. Thus in order to define bulimia nervosa as a syndrome, the frequency criterion has been included. In addition, the criterion for normal body weight is specified so that obese or anorectic subjects are excluded from the diagnosis. In the bulimic a relatively normal body weight is maintained by self-induced vomiting, laxative/diuretic abuse, prolonged fasting, or excessive exercising. A fear of fatness is always present, particularly after a binge, but bulimic patients do not seem to be striving for an unrealistically low weight. The term bulimia nervosa has been proposed for a diagnosable, severe form of the disorder [15] and will also be used in this chapter. The DSM-III-R has incorporated some but not all of these proposed changes.

Debate continues on whether the two eating disorders are separate, dichotomous syndromes [15-18]. Existing evidence suggests that the consistency of the association of the cardinal features, and the course and outcome of the two disorders, form relatively distinct aggregates. The treatment focus of the two disorders is also distinct: for anorexia nervosa the emphasis is on weight restoration, while for bulimia nervosa the emphasis is on the control of abnormal eating. Thus, from an operational and treatment point of view, it is best at this stage to regard them as separate conditions.

This proposed classification used body weight as the distinguishing feature between the two disorders. More recently researchers have suggested that bulimic behavior, rather than low body weight, may have greater diagnostic, prognostic, and etiological significance. For example, the bulimic patients, whether of normal or low body weight, more often are emotionally labile and impulsive, and are more likely to be premorbidly obese [11,19,20-24]. They are also more likely to have a family history of obesity, alcoholism and depression [20,23,25]. However, at this stage it seems premature to abandon the previous classification, because many issues remain unresolved (such as the fact that some normal-weight bulimics resemble closely the classic restricting anorectic in psychopathology [22]. It is to be expected, however, that as our understanding of the patients increases, the classification scheme will change.

REFERENCES

1. Feighner JP, Robins E, Guze SB, et al. Diagnostic criteria for use in psychiatric research. Arch Gen Psychiatry, 1972; 26:57.

2. American Psychiatric Association. Diagnostic and statistical manual of mental disorders, 3rd ed. Washington, DC: American Psychiatric Association, 1980:

3. Bruch H. Perceptual and conceptual disturbances in anorexia nervosa. Psychosom Med, 1962; 24:187-94.

4. Hsu LKG. Is there a disturbance of body image in anorexia nervosa. J Nerv Ment Dis, 1982; 170:305-7.

5. Garfinkel PE, Moldofsky H, Garner DM. The stability of perceptual disturbances in anorexia nervosa. Psychol Med, 1979; 9:703-8.

6. Touyz SW, Beumont PJ, Collins JK, et al. Body shape perception and its disturbance in anorexia nervosa. Br J Psychiat, 1984; 144:167-71.

7. Pyle RL, Mitchell JE, Eckert EE, et al. The incidence of bulimia in freshman college students. International J Eating Disorders, 1983; 2:61-74.

8. Lacey JK, Chadburd C, Crisp AH, et al. Variations in energy intake of adolescent schoolgirls. J Hum Nutr, 1978; 32:419-26.

9. Stunkard AJ. Eating patterns and obesity. Psychiatric Quarterly, 1959; 33:284-92.

10. Hsu LKG, Crisp AH, Harding B. Outcome of anorexia nervosa. Lancet, 1979; 1:61-5.

11. Casper RC, Eckert ED, Halmi KA, et al. Bulimia. Arch Gen Psychiatry, 1980; 37:1030-5.

12. Gormally J, Black S, Daston S, et al. The assessment of binge eating severity among obese persons. Addic-

tive Behaviors, 1982; 7:47-55.

13. Lucas AR. Pigging out. American Med Assoc, 1982; 247:82.

14. Hawkins RC II, Clement PF. Development and construct validation of a self-report measure of binge eating tendencies. Addictive Behaviors, 1980; 5:219-26.

15. Russell G. Bulimia nervosa: An ominous variant of anorexia nervosa. Psychol Med, 1979; 9:429-48.

16. Boskind-Lodahl M, White WC. The definition and treatment of bulimarexia in college women — a pilot study. JK Amer College Health Assoc, 1978; 27:84-97.

17. Palmer RL. The dietary chaos syndrome: A useful new term? Brit J Med Psychology, 1979; 52:187-90.

18. Abraham SF, Beumont PJ. How patients describe bulimia or binge- eating. Psycholog Med, 1982; 12:625-35.

19. Garfinkel PE, Moldofsky H, Garner DM. The heterogeneity of anorexia nervosa. Arch Gen Psychiatry, 1980; 37:1036-40.

20. Strober M, Salkin B, Burroughs J, et al. Validity of the bulimia- restricter distinction in anorexia nervosa. J Nerv Ment Disease, 1982; 170:345-51.

21. Beumont PJ, George GCW, Smart DE. Dieters and vomiters and purgers in anorexia nervosa. Psychol Med, 1976; 6:617-22.

22. Garner DM, Garfinkel PE, O'Shanghnessy M. Clinical and psychometric comparison between bulimia in anorexia nervosa and bulimia in normal weight women. Understanding anorexia nervosa and bulimia. Columbus: Ross Laboratories, 1983.

23. Pyle RL, Mitchell JE, Eckert ED. Bulimia: A report of 34 cases. J Clin Psychiatry, 1981; 42:60-4.

24. Johnson C, Larson R. Bulimia: An analysis of moods and behavior. Psychosom Med, 1982; 44:341-51.

25. Hudson JI, Pope HG, Jonas JM, et al. Family history study of anorexia nervosa and bulimia. Brit J Psychiatry, 1983; 142:133-8.

Chapter 21

The Etiology of Anorexia Nervosa

L.K. George Hsu

The valid question in a discussion on the etiology of anorexia nervosa is: what caused the willful starvation that stems from the fear of fatness? It is thus important to clarify two fundamental issues at the outset: First, starvation is the cause of many of the features of anorexia nervosa, such as amenorrhea; constipation; insomnia; preoccupation with food, dieting, and shape; bulimia; food fads; increased consumption of coffee, tea, and chewing gum; and diminished sexual desire [1,2]. To suggest, for instance, that a fear of sexuality is the *cause* of amenorrhea or that a need to withhold is the *cause* of constipation is absurd. Second, the cardinal feature of anorexia nervosa is a fear of fatness, or a pursuit of thinness. The food avoidance and the vomiting and purging stem from this fear. The disorder is not due to a loss of appetite (anorexia) or a primary fear of eating or food. Thus, for instance, to postulate a link between anorexia nervosa and Crohn's Disease is absurd, because in the latter condition there is a true loss of appetite. There are currently seven main theories organized along different conceptual levels that attempt to explain the etiology of anorexia nervosa. Logically, they are not mutually exclusive, and they overlap to some degree. However, their explanatory power varies and so does the strength of the evidence for each theory. This review will discuss each theory.

THE SOCIAL-CULTURAL THEORY

This theory in essence states that social-cultural pressures contribute to the development of the disorder.

Evidence that supports this theory will be summarized according to (1) the current emphasis on slimness, (2) the contradictory role of women in modern society, and (3) the vulnerability of the white upper-social-class adolescent female.

The importance of physical attractiveness in Western society is undeniable. In the female this attractiveness has taken the form of slimness. Several surveys indicated that the majority of young women are unhappy about their weight and want to be slimmer [3-5]. In contrast, men prefer to be bigger and heavier [3-5]. Garner et al [6], reviewing data from Playboy centerfolds and Miss America Pageant contestants in the last 20 years, found a significant trend toward slimness. All measurements of Playboy centerfold women, except for height and waist, decreased significantly. Thus, for instance, the average Playmate in 1959 weighted 91% of average, while in 1978 they weighted only 83.5% of average. Since 1970, Miss America Pageant winners had a mean weight of only 82.5% of average. Meanwhile, the number of diet articles in six women's magazines have increased substantially over the last 20 years.

However, Garner et al [6] found that this emphasis on thinness and dieting occurs in a population that is becoming heavier. Weight statistics from the Society of Actuaries over the last 20 years indicated an increase in average weight for women in all height categories below the age of 30 years. The pressure on women, particularly those of the upper social class, to diet and appear slim thus seem relentless [7,8]. That such pressure may precipitate the development of anorexia nervosa seems to be confirmed by the finding that the condition is much more common in women that must control rigorously their size and shape, such as ballerinas, modeling students, and athletes [9-11]. Competitiveness intensifies the pressure [11]. Under such circumstances it is perhaps not surprising that Branch and Eurman [12] found that the anorectic's friends and relatives actually admired her slimness, specialness, and control.

Boskind-Lodahl [13] regarded "the cultural heritage of sexual inequality" to be directly responsible for the development of eating disorders in women. However, since such inequlity presumably exists also in developing countries, it is difficult to see why the disorder is so rare in these countries [14]. Selvini Palazzoli [15,16] emphasized the complex and contradictory roles women have to play in modern society. Self-definition and achieving a feminine identity may be particularly problematic for the modern woman [17,18]. High-achieving women may experience low self-esteem [17] and a heightened fear of success, which revolve around fear of loss of femininity and of interpersonal rejection [18,19]. Dunn and Ondercin [20] suggested that eating disordered patients may have difficulty integrating "masculine" ideals, such as independence and assertiveness, with traditional concepts of femininity. Such role diffusion presumably increases insecurity and intensifies the striving for perfection and control.

The dilemma confronting the modern female may explain why adolescence tends to be a particularly difficult phase for the young white girl who is more likely to be biologically fatter, to have a poor self-image, low self-esteem, and high emotional instability and self-consciousness. The Ten State nutrition survey [21,22], which in 1968 to 1970 studied more than 40,000 individuals from all age-groups with respect to their nutritional status, has provided a good deal of insight into why current cultural emphasis on slimness has the greatest impact on the middle- and upper-class white adolescent female. The survey findings may be summarized as follows:

1. There is a tendency for females of all ages to be fatter (as measured by the triceps fat fold) than males.
2. There is prepubertal weight gain in both sexes, but during adolescence proper, the female gains fat, while the male loses fat.
3. High income is associated with greater fatness for males at all ages and for females through early adolescence. In the female, however, there is an income-related reversal of relative fatness during adolescence, ie, during adolescence, females in the lower-income families started out being leaner but ended up being fatter than those in the higher-income families. Garn and Clark [21,22] speculated that this reversal occurs as the result of conscious dieting on the part of the higher-income female.
4. White males tend to be fatter than black females at all ages. White females are also fatter than black females through early adolescence, but thereafter a reversal of relative fatness occurs similar to that for higher- and lower-income females. This differential fatness pattern between the two races, remains even after controlling for family income. Garn and Clark [21,22] again speculated that this reversal occurred as a result of conscious dieting on the part of the white female.

These findings suggest that fatness is related to being female, being white, and being from a high-income family. It is obvious that cultural emphasis on thinness has its most powerful impact on the white teenage girl from a higher-income family.

That such social-cultural pressure generates a greater likelihood for the development of anorexia nervosa in women is probably not in dispute. It is, however, obvious that not all women exposed to such pressure develop anorexia nervosa. Other factors must also occur to precipitate the final development of the illness.

FAMILY PATHOLOGY THEORY

The early investigators have all emphasized the family pathology in anorexia nervosa [23-25]. Charcot [23] advocated separation of the patient from family as part of treatment. Gull [24] found the relatives to be the worst attenders of the patient. Laseque [25] described the striking family enmeshment, and he urged clinicians not to overlook the family pathology. Other early investigators have likewise described the adverse influence of the family on the patient [26,27].

Attempts to identify a typical anorectic mother [28-30] or a typical anorectic father [30,32,33] have produced no consistent findings [34,35]. More recently, researchers have focused more on family interaction patterns that may be characteristic of the anorectic family. Bruch [36,37] emphasized the facade of happiness and stability that hid deep disillusionment and secret competition of the parents. She also found the parents to be enormously preoccupied with outward appearance and success. Palazzoli [15] studied 12 anorectic families and found rejection of communicated message, poor conflict resolution, covert alliance of family members, and blame shifting to be common. She also emphasized their rigidity in that they tried to preserve agricultural-patriarchal values and mores in an urban-industrial setting. Both Palazzoli [15] and Bruch [36,37] found the parents to be overprotective but also to involve the sick child in their covert competition and conflict. They seemed to use the child to discharge some of their own unfulfilled longings.

Minuchin and his co-workers have written extensively on the psychosomatic family [38-40]. They advocated an open-systems model for psychosomatic illness, anorexia nervosa included. This system included parts such as extrafamilial stress, family organization and functioning, the vulnerable child, physiological and biochemical meditating mechanisms, and the symptomatic child. The system could be activated at any point, and the parts could affect each other. Nevertheless, these authors have emphasized almost exclusively the family pathology in this sytem and stated that, "When significant family interaction patterns are changed, significant changes in the symptoms of the psychosomatic illness also occur," [40]. They further hypothesized that (1) certain family characteristics were related to the development and maintenance of psychosomatic symptoms in children, and (2) the child's psychosomatic symptoms played a major role in maintaining family homeostasis. The family characteristics identified were enmeshment, overprotectiveness, rigidity, and lack of conflict rsolution. Meanwhile, the child was used to maintain stability and avoid open conflict, and thus was often caught (triangulated) in the parents' covert conflict. The illness enabled the parents to submerge their conflicts in protecting or blaming the sick child, who was then defined as the sole family problem.

However, few studies confirm that such family interaction pathology occurs in anorexia nervosa. Crisp et al [41] used a standardized measure (the Middlesex Hosptial Questionnaire) and found that the psychoneurotic status of the parents worsened significantly as the patient's weight increased with treatment. This was particularly so if the marital relationship was poor. Six-month outcome for the patient's illness was significantly related to the initial parental psychoneurotic morbidity. Case selection factors and family therapy effects were, however, uncontrolled. Foster and Kupfer [42] telemetrically recorded the nocturnal motility of a female patient with anorexia nervosa and found that noctural activity was correlated with visits by specific family members during the previous day. Visits by the father and the identical twin led to a decrease in nocturnal motility, while visits by the mother and older sister led to an increase in such "arousal." The extent to which such findings can be generalized is, however, questionable.

Related to the issue of family environment is the role of genetic factors in the pathogenesis of anorexia nervosa. Several large-scale studies have found an increased incidence of anorexia nervosa in the family members of the patients [34,43-45]. Twin studies have found a concordance of about 50% for monozygotics and 10% for dizygotics [46-48]. Adoptive studies, however, are needed to tease out environmental versus genetic factors. In this connection, Crisp and Toms [49] described a remarkable case of a male chronic anorectic whose adoptive son as well as the girl who stayed with the family as a war evacuee both developed anorexia nervosa.

Crisp and his co-workers have suggested that family weight pathology may be specifically related to the pathogenesis of the illness [35,50]. In a well-controlled study of the parents of anorectic patients, Halmi et al [8] failed to confirm this.

Several detailed studies of affective disorders in the families of eating disordered patients have been published recently. Cantwell et al [51] reported an increase in the familial prevalence of depression in anorectics. Strober et al [52] compared the relatives of 35 bulimic with 35 restrictive anorectics, and they found that affective disorder, alcoholism, and substance abuse disorders were more prevalent among the first-and second-degree relatives of bulimics. In a study of 420 first-degree relatives of 89 eating disordered patients, Hudson et al [53] found an increased risk of affective disorder among the first-degree relatives of both anorectic and bulimic patients to a level similar to that of the families of bipolar disordered patients. Winokur et al [54] also found that there was a doubling of affective illness in the parents of anorectics in comparison with a controlled population. Thus, the familial prevalence of affective illness, and perhaps of alcoholism as well, appears to be increased in the eating disordered patients.

In summary, it remains to be substantiated that specific and abnormal family interaction patterns occurred in anorexia nervosa and that they are causally related to the development of the condition. Most of the studies quoted ignored the effect of this exasperating illness on family interaction, and the investigators failed to distinguish between family pathology occurring as stress reactions as opposed to pre-existing patterns [55]. Familial affective disorder and perhaps familial alcoholism and other impulse-controlled disorders may predispose an individual to develop anorexia nervosa [48,52,56]. The mechanism for such predisposition is, however, unclear.

INDIVIDUAL PSYCHODYNAMIC THEORY

Early psychoanalytic interpretation of anorexia nervosa considered it to be related to a rejection of female genital sexuality and oral impregnation fantasies by means of refusal to eat. This was accompanied by a regression to pregenital defense mechanism in the face of conflict revolving around primitive, sadistic, and cannibalistic oral fantasies [57,58]. Object relation theorists considered it to be related to the introjection and repression of a bad object consequent upon the early ambivalent relationship with an aggressively protective, unresponsive, castrating, domineering, and controlling mother [15,59,60]. On the more superficial level, it is generally recognized that starvation serves as an expression of hostility, control, and aggression toward the family [57,59]. In 1931 Brown [61] observed that anorexia nervosa was a pathological manifestation of the detachment of the growing individual from parental authority. Bruch [36,37,62,63] has repeatedly stated that anorexia nervosa was a struggle for a self-respecting identity. That such a struggle took the form of willful starvation suggested serious psychological developmental defects. Central to such defects was the failure of the parents to regard the patients as individuals in their own right; they failed to transmit a sense of competence and self-value to their children. The youngsters were instead treated as something to complement the parents' needs. Their sense of worth and value were thus derived from being needed by each parent. In short, they felt that they were the property of their parents. The illness thus represented an effort to escape from such a role and to establish control. Because of their disturbed perception of bodily sensation related to their lack of autonomy, and a paralyzing sense of ineffectiveness, such patients misinterpreted their biological functioning and social role, and came to interpret thinness and starvation as specialness and self-control in an exaggerated and concrete way. Palazzoli [15] and Boskind-Lodahl [13] echoed such views.

The individual psychodynamic theory is extremely plausible, but it has never been empircially tested; its emphasis on early parent-child interaction does not lend itself easily to such testing. A recent single case study [64] provided some evidence of abnormal mothering in a case of male anorexia nervosa.

THE DEVELOPMENTAL PSYCHOBIOLOGICAL THEORY

Brown [61] stated that a fear of growing up and assuming adult responsibility was highly characteristic of anorectics. Crisp has repeatedly stated [50,65,66] that anorexia nervosa was rooted in the biological and consequently experiential aspects of normal adult weight. Starvation in the anorectic represented a phobic avoidance of adolescent/adult weight. Anorexia nervosa was thus a disorder of weight pivoting around specific maturational changes of puberty, both biological and psychological. The psychobiological regression reflected the individual's need to avoid adolescent and related family turmoil. The severe dieting was reinforced by the relief that the control and the low weight brought, as biological and related psychological childhood was re-experienced and postpubertal experience was concurrently eliminated. Meanwhile, adolescence in the child threatened the rigid and experience-denying parents. The illness thus sometimes served to avert rekindling of buried and denied but unresolved parental conflicts and psychopathology. Needless to say, the illness brought its own problems, but they were deemed to be the price that the patient and her family had to pay to avoid deeper, more fundamental discord. Crisp has repeatedly emphasized that such maturational demands of adolescence and family pathology were not specific to the condition. Indirect and parital support for this view has come from several sources: 1. There is an immature pattern of gonadotrophin release in anorectics, which reverts to normal after weight gain [67,68], 2. Frisch [69,70] has found that puberty hinges on the individual attaining a critical amount of fatness, 3. Clinical experience suggests that anorectics will often agree to eat provided that weight gain does not occur, thereby indicating that weight rather than eating is involved in the issue of control, 4. Finally, Crisp et al [41] found that the parent's psychoneurotic status worsened after the patient's recovery, which seems to support the notion that the illness serves to reduce family tension. Nevertheless, this theory of "weight phobia" has never been empirically tested. One study found anorexia nervosa patients to be different from other phobic patients in terms of skin conductance changes [71].

PRIMARY HYPOTHALAMIC DYSFUNCTION THEORY

Russell [72-74] has repeatedly suggested that a primary hypothalamic dysfunction of unknown etiology and only partially dependent on weight loss and psychopathology occurred in anorexia nervosa.

Early onset of amenorrhea (sometimes before any appreciable weight loss), the incomplete recovery of hypothalamic function, and the persistence of amenorrhea despite weight gain have been cited as evidence for a primary hypothalamic disorder in anorexia nervosa [68,74]. Furthermore, several reports of hypothalamic tumor presenting as anorexia nervosa have appeared [47,75]. Finally, in animals the role of the ventromedical hypothalamic nucleus in the regulation of feeding and satiety appears to be well established [76].

However, the significance of all these findings remains controversial. An accurate dietary history is difficult to obtain in most eating disordered patients, and amenorrhea preceding the onset of eating disturbance probably occurs in only a small proportion of patients.

Furthermore, emotional disturbance, not specifically related to anorexia nervosa, may cause amenorrhea. Finally, patients who developed amenorrhea before appreciable weight loss do not seem to have a different outcome from those who develop the amenorrhea after the onset of weight loss. The incomplete recovery of hypothalamic function may be related to inadequate weight gain, abnormal eating habits, persistent preoccupation with food and weight, and the simple fact that recovery may take time. Simple weight loss without anorexia nervosa may lead to a functional hypothalamic disturbance [77]. The eating disorder that occurs in association with a hypothalamic tumor often has atypical features. Since the vast majority of anorectics have no demonstrable and antomical hypothalamic pathology, in those rare but typical cases, it remains possible that this infrequent association is entirely due to chance.

The noradrenergic system in the medial hypothalamus in rats seems to regulate intake and body weight directly [76]. Thus, for instance, a decrease of noradrenergic innervation to the paraventricular hypothalamus leads to a decrease of daily intake (particularly carbohydrates) and body weight. Food deprivation, which stimulates intake and carbohydrate preference in the animal, increases the turnover rate of endogenous norepinephrine in the medial hypothalamus. However, extrapolating animal data to human psychopathology is hazardous, and there is no direct evidence for the existence of a medial hypothalamic noradrenergic system dysfunction in anorexia nervosa. Urinary MHPG, an important end product of norepinephrine, is reduced in anorexia nervosa, but its level normalizes with weight gain [78]. Reduced plasma levels of dopamine and norepinephrine in anorexia nervosa are also weight related [47]. In summary, while it remains possible that there is a hypothalamic dysfunction in anorexia nervosa unrelated to the starvation and weight loss, the evidence is by no means compelling. Furthermore, this theory cannot easily explain why the disorder affects selected groups in the population and is apparently increasing in incidence.

COGNITIVE BEHAVIORAL THEORY

The cognitive behavioral theory on the etiology of anorexia nervosa emphasizes cognitions and behaviors rather than early childhood experience, family interaction, or biological processes [47,79]. However, it does draw on individual psychodynamic and psychobiological concepts. Garner and Bemis [79] and Garfinkel and Garner [47] set out their views systematically on this theory, but they were careful to point out that cognitive behavioral theory explains only one aspect of what they consider to be a multiply determined disorder. As they

see it, anorexia nervosa is the final common pathway of a pathological sequence of events beginning with the introverted, sensitive, and isolated adolescent arriving at the idea that weight loss will somehow alleviate her distress and dysphoria. The dieting that follows is therefore a means to achieve slimness as well as an expression of ascetic control. It is reinforced by a gratifying sense of success and by approval and concern from others. The negative reinforcement of avoiding food and weight gain gradually becomes more prominent, and the increasing isolation that occurs as a result of starvation decreases the youngster's responsiveness to other issues and considerations. Progressive weight loss secures a "safety margin," [80] and the anorectic cognitions and behaviors become autonomous.

This theory is intuitively familiar and consistent with the patients' own reports. However, the more crucial question may be why more dieters do not move toward this final common pathway. While this theory may explain how the illness perpetuates itself, it does not explain what distinguishes between a normal dieter and a committed anorectic. Garner et al [81] recently provided some evidence to suggest that anorectics score higher than normal dieters on several subscales of the Eating Disorder Inventory, which measures ineffectivenss, interpersonal distrust, and lack of interoceptive awareness. Thus, certain vulnerable individuals may choose to starve themselves in an attempt to gain confidence and control.

THE AFFECTIVE DISORDER THEORY

Cantwell et al [51] have recently stated that anorexia nervosa may be an atypical affective disorder occurring in an adolescent female at a time in her life when body image issues were important. Two findings in their study supported this view: there was an increased incidence of affective disorder in the family, and on long-term followup the anorectics were more prone to develop affective disorder than to suffer a relapse of the eating disorder.

The former finding is supported by several studies [53,54], and the relationship of familial affective disorder to anorexia nervosa has been discussed previously.

Biological marker studies in the two disorders have yielded inconclusive findings regarding their relationship. Plasma cortisol level [82], dexamethasone nonsuppression [83], and low urinary MHPG have been found in primary affective illness, and these changes are also seen in some anorectics. However, the abnormalities in the latter are apparently reversible with weight gain [78,84]. Moreover, severe weight loss per se is known to produce dexamethasone nonsuppression [83,85]. The characteristic sleep EEG findings seen in primary affec-

tive disorder [86] are different from those seen in anorexia nervosa [87].

Phenomenologic and outcome studies have likewise
been inconclusive. Anorectics are not as overtly or persistently depressed as patients with affective disorder
[88,89]. Depression may be associated with complex
changes in weight and appetite [90,91], and it remains
uncertain whether the dysphoria in anorexic nervosa is
primary or secondary to the eating disorder [56]. No
study exists to demonstrate that anorexia nervosa is
more common in the family of affective disorder probands; most follow-up studies indicate that anorexia
nervosa "breeds true" [92]. Finally anecdotal reports of
the usefulness of anti- depressants in treating anorexia
nervosa [93,94] have not been widely accepted
[47,72,80].

While the complex relationship between the two disorders requires further study, there is no compelling evidence at present to believe that anorexia nervosa is a
form of affective illness in an adolescent female.

CONCLUSION

While it is possible that anorexia nervosa has a single
discrete cause, it is equally possible that complex chains
of events interact to finally precipitate the illness. Kendell [95] clearly favored the latter view for psychiatric
diseases in general. He even stated that, "The very idea
of 'cause' has become meaningless, other than as a convenient designation for the point in the chain of event
sequences at which intervention is most practicable," (p.
64). The overlap of the theories reviewed in this chapter certainly suggests that this argument is at least
plausible in the case of anorexia nervosa. If this is so, the
challenge will be to identify such events and how they
interact. Needless to say, such events may include some
or all of the proposed etiological factors already reviewed—or none of them. A possible strategy may be
to prospectively study and follow a group of youngsters
considered to be at risk for developing the illness—for
example, professional dance and modeling students.
The logistical and ethical problems involved in such a
study may, however, be prohibitive.

REFERENCES

1. Keys A, Brozek J, Henschel A, et al. The biology of human starvation, vol 1 and 2. Minneapolis: University of Minnesota Press, 1950:
2. Franklin JC, Schiele BC, Brozek J, Keys A. Observa- tions on human behavior in experimental semi-starva- tion and rehabilitation. J Clin Psychol, 1948; 4:28-45.
3. Calden G, Lundy RM, Schlafer RJ. Sex differences in body concepts. Journal of Consulting Psychiatry, 1959; 23:378.
4. Huenemann RL, Shapiro LR, Hampton MC, Mitchell BW. A longitudinal study or gross body composition and body conformation and then association with food and activity in a teenage population. Am J Clin Nutri, 1966; 18:325-38.
5. Nylander I. The feeling of being fat and dieting in a school population. Acta Sociomedica Scandinavica, 1971; 3:17-26.
6. Garner DM, Garfinkel PE, Schwartz D, Thompson M. Cultural expectations of thinness in women. Psycholo- gical Reports, 1980; 47:483-91.
7. Goldblatt PB, Moore ME, Stunkard AJ. Social factors in obesity. JAMA, 1965; 192:97-102.
8. Halmi KA, Struss A, Goldberg SC. An investigation of weights in parents of anorexia nervosa patients. Nervous and Mental Dis, 1978; 166:358-61.
9. Druss RG, Silverman JA. Body image and perfection- ism of ballerinas. General Hospital Psychiatry, 1979; 2:115-21.
10. Frisch RE, Wyshak G, Vincent L. Delayed menarche and amenorrhea in ballet dancers. N Eng J Med, 1980; 303:17-9.
11. Garner DM, Garfinkel PE. Social cultural factors in the development of anorexia nervosa. Psychol Med, 1980; 10:647-56.
12. Branch CHH, Eurman LK. Social attitudes toward patients with anorexia nervosa. Psychiatry, 1980; 137:632-3.
13. Boskind-Lodahl M. Cinderella's stepsisters: A femi- nist perspective on anorexia nervosa and bulimia. Signs: Journal of Women In Culture and Society, 1976; 2:342-56.
14. Buhrich N. Frequency of presentation of anorexia in Malaysia. Aust. NZ Journal Psychia, 1981; 15:153-5.
15. Palazzoli MS. Self-starvation. New York: Jason Aron- son.
16. Palazzoli MS, Boscolo L, Cecchin GF. Family rituals: a powerful tool in family therapy. Family Process, 1977; 16:445-53.
17. Marcia JE, Freidman ML. Ego identity status in col- lege women. J Personal, 1970; 38:249-63.
18. Orlofsky JL. Identity formation, achievement, and fear of success in college men and women. J Youth Adol, 1978; 7:49-62.
19. Hoffman LW. Fear of success in males and females. J Consult Clin Psychol, 1974; 42:353-8.
20. Dunn PK, Ondercin P. Personality variables related to comprehensive eating in college women. J Clin Psy- chol, 1981; 37:43-9.
21. Garn SM, Clark DC. Nutrition, growth, development, and maturation — Findings from the ten state nutrition survey of 1968-1970. Pediatrics, 1975; 56:306-19.
22. Garn SM, Clark DC. Trends in fatness and the origins of obesity. Pediatrics, 1976; 57:443-56.
23. Charcot JM. Disorders of the nervous system. Lon- don: New Sydenham Society, 1889:
24. Gull W. Anorexia nervosa (apepsia hysterica, anorexia hysterica). London: Transactions of the Clinical

Society, 1874; 7:22-8.

25. Laseque C. On hysterical anorexia. Medical Times Gazette, 1873; 2:265-7.

26. Crookshank FG. Anorexia nervosa. In Brown WL, ed. Anorexia nervosa. London: CW Daniel, 1931:

27. Young JC. Anorexia nervosa. In Brown WL, ed. Anorexia nervosa. London: CW Daniel, 1931:

28. Cobb S. Emotions and clinical medicine. New York: Norton, 1950:

29. Kay DWK, Leigh D. The natural history, treatment and prognosis of anorexia nervosa, based on a study of 38 patients. Journal of Mental Science, 1954; 100:411-31.

30. King A. Primary and secondary anorexia nervosa. British Journal of Psychiatry, 1963; 109:470-9.

31. Nemiah JC. Anorexia nervosa. Medicine, 1950; 29:225-68.

32. Groen JJ, Feldman-Toledano Z. Educative treatment of patients and parents in anorexia nervosa. British Journal of Psychiatry, 1966; 112:671-81.

33. Sours JA. Depression and the anorexia nervosa syndrome. Pediatric Clinics of North America, 1981; 4:145-58.

34. Crisp AH, Hsu LKG, Harding B. The starving hoarder and voracious spender—Stealing in anorexia nervosa. J Psychosom Res, 1980; 24:225-31.

35. Kalucy R, Crisp AH, Harding B. A study of 56 females with anorexia nervosa. British Journal of Medical Psychology, 50:381.

36. Bruch H. Eating disorders. Harper, NY: Basic Books, 1973:

37. Bruch H. Psychological antecedents of anorexia nervosa. In Vigersky RA, ed. Anorexia nervosa. New York: Raven, 1977:

38. Minuchin S. Families and family therapy. Cambridge, Mass: Harvard University Press, 1974:

39. Minuchin S, Baker L, Rosman BL, et al. A conceptual model of psychosomatic illness in children. Archives of General Psychiatry, 32:1031-38.

40. Minuchin S, Rosman BL, Baker L. Psychosomatic families: Anorexia nervosa in context. Cambridge, Mass: Harvard University Press, 1978:

41. Crisp AH, Harding B, McGuinness B. Anorexia nervosa: Psychoneurotic characteristics of parents: Relationship to prognosis. Journal of Psychosomatic Research, 1974; 18:167-73.

42. Foster FG, Kupfer DJ. Anorexia nervosa: Telemetric assessment of family interactions and hospitals events. Journal of Psychosomatic Research, 1975; 12:19-35.

43. Halmi KA, Goldberg SC, Eckert E, et al. Pre-treatment evaluation in anorexia nervosa. In Vigersky RA, ed. Anorexia nervosa. New York: Raven Press, 1977:

44. Morgan HG, Russell GFM. Value of family background and clinical features as predictors of long-term outcome in anorexia nervosa: Four-year follow-up study of 41 patients. Psychological Medicine, 1975; 5:355-71.

45. Theander S. Anorexia nervosa: A psychiatric investigation of 94 female patients. Acta Psychiat Scand Suppl, 1970; 214:

46. Askevold F, Heiberg A. Anorexia nervosa: Two cases in discordant MZ twins. Psychotherapy and psychosmatics, 1979; 32:223-8.

47. Garfinkel PE, Garner DM. Anorexia nervosa: A multidimensional perspective. New York: Brunner/Mazel, 1982:

48. Hsu LKG, Holder D, Hindmarsh DJ, Phelps C. Bipolar affective disorders in identical twins preceded by anorexia nervosa. J Clin Psychiatry, 1984; 45:262-6.

49. Crisp AH, Toms DA. Primary anorexia nervosa or weight phobia in the male. British Medical Journal, 1972; i:334-8.

50. Crisp AH. Diagnosis and outcome of anorexia nervosa. Proceedings of the Royal Society of Medicine, 1977; 70:464-70.

51. Cantwell DP, Sturzenberger S, Borroughs J, et al. Anorexia nervosa—an affective disorder? Arch Gen Psychiatry, 1977; 34:1087-93.

52. Strober M, Salkin B, Burroughs J, Morrell W. Validity of the bulimia-restricter distinction in anorexia nervosa. J Nerv Ment Disease, 1982, 170:345-51.

53. Huson JI, Pope HG, Jonas JM, Yurgelun-Todd D. Family history study of anorexia nervosa and bulimia. Brit J Psychistry, 1983; 142:133-8.

54. Winokur A, March V, Mendels J. Primary affective disorder in relatives of patients with anorexia nervosa. American Journal of Psychiatry, 1980; 137:695-7.

55. Yager J. Family issues in the pathogenesis of anorexia nervosa. Psychosomatic Medicine, 1982; 44:43-60.

56. Cooper PJ, Fairburn CG. Are eating disorders forms of affective disorders? Br J Psychiatry, 1983; 148:96-7.

57. Waller J, Kaufman MR, Deutsch F. Anorexia nervosa: A psychosomatic study. Psychosom Med, 2:3-16.

58. Fenichel A. Anorexia. In the Collected Paper of Otto Fenichel, 1945; 2:288-95.

59. Szyrynski V. Anorexia nervosa and psychotherapy. Am J Psychotherapy, 1973; 27:492-505.

60. Sours JA. The anorexia nervosa syndrome. International Journal of Psychoanalysis, 1974; 55:567-76.

61. Brown WL. Anorexia nervosa. In Brown L, ed. Anorexia nervosa. London: CW Daniels, 1931:

62. Bruch H. Perceptual and conceptual disturbances in anorexia nervosa. Psychosom Med, 1962; 24:187-94.

63. Bruch H. Psychotherapy in primary anorexia nervosa. J Nerv Ment Dis, 1970; 150:51-67.

64. Rampling D. Abnormal mothering in the genesis of anorexia nervosa. J Nerv Ment Dis, 1980; 168:501-4.

65. Crisp AH. Anorexia nervosa. Hospital Medicine, 1967; 1:713-8.

66. Crisp AH. Anorexia nervosa: Feeding disorder, nervous malnutrition or weight phobia? World Review of Nutrition and Diet, 12:452-504.

67. Boyar RN, Katz J, Finkelstein JW, et al. Anorexia nervosa: Immaturity of the 24 hour luteinizing hormone secretory pattern. N Engl Med, 1974; 291:861-5.

68. Katz JL, Boyar R, Roffwarg H, et al. Weight and circadian luteinizing hormone secretory pattern in anorexia nervosa. Psychosomatic Medicine, 1978; 40:549-67.

69. Frisch RE. Weight in menarche. Pediatrics, 1972; 50:445-50.

70. Frisch RE. Food intake, fatness and reproductive ability. In Vigersky RA, ed. Anorexia nervosa. New York: Raven Press, 1977:

71. Salkind MR, Fincham J, Silverstone T. Is anorexia nervosa a phobic disorder? Biological Psychiatry, 1980; 15:803-8.

72. Russell GFM. Metabolic aspects of anorexia nervosa. Process of Royal Medicine, 1965; 58:811-4.

73. Russell GFM. Anorexia nervosa — Its identity as an illness and its treatment. In Price JH, ed. Modern trends in psychological medicine, vol 2. London: Butterworths, 1970:

74. Russell GFM. The present status of anorexia nervosa. Psychological Medicine, 1977; 7:353-67.

75. Mawson AR. Anorexia nervosa and the regulation of intake: A review. Psychological Medicine, 1974; 4:289-380.

76. Liebowitz SF. Hypothalamic noradrenergic system: Role in control of appetite and relation to anorexia nervosa. In Understanding anorexia nervosa and bulimia. Columbus: Ross Laboratories, 1983:

77. Vigersky RA, Anderson AE, Thompson RH, Loriaux L. Hypothalamic dysfunction in seconadary amenorrhea associated with simple weight loss. N Engl Med, 1977; 297:1141-5.

78. Gross HA, Lake CR, Ebert MHJ, et al. Catecholamine metabolism in primary anorexia nervosa. Journal of Clinical Endocrinological Metabolism, 1979; 49:805-9.

79. Garner DM, Bemis K. A cognitive behavioral approach to anorexia nervosa. Cognitive Therapy and Research, 1982; 6:1-27.

80. Crisp AH. Anorexia nervosa — Let me be. London: Plenum Press, 1980:

81. Garner DM, Olmsted MP, Garfinkel PE. Does anorexia nervosa occur on a continuum? Int J Eat Dis, 1983; 2:11-20.

82. Sachar EJ, Hellman L, Fukushima DK, Gallagher TF. Cortisol production in depressive illness. Archives of General Psychiatry, 1970; 23:289-98.

83. Carroll BJ. The dexamethasone suppression test for melancholia. Brit Journal of Psychiatry, 1982; 140:292-304.

84. Gerner RH, Gwirtsman HE. Abnormalities of dexamethasone suppression test and urinary MHPG in anorexia nervosa. American Journal of Psychiatry, 1981; 138:65-3.

85. Edelstein CK, Roy-Bryne P, Fawzy FI, Dornfeld L. Effects of weight loss on the dexamethasone suppression test. Am J Psychiat, 140:338-41.

86. Kupfer DJ, Thompson KS, Weiss B. EEG sleep changes as predictors in depression. American Journal of Psychiatry, 1976; 133:622-6.

87. Neil JF, Merikangas JR, Foster FG, et al. Waking and all night EEG in anorexia nervosa. Clincial Electroencephalography, 1980; 11:9- 15.

88. Bentovim DI, Marilov V, Crisp AH. Personality and mental state (P.S.E.) with anorexia nervosa. J Psycho-som Res, 1979; 23:321-5.

89. Eckert ED, Goldbert SC, et al. Depression in anorexia nervosa. Psychol Med, 12:115-122.

90. Crisp AH, & Stonehill E. Relation between aspects of nutritional disturbance and menstrual activity in primary anorexia nervosa. British Medical Journal, 1971; iii:149-151.

91. Polivy J, Herman CP. Clinical depression and weight change: A complex realtion. J Abn Psychol, 1976; 85:338-40.

92. Hsu LKG. Outcome of anorexia nervosa — a review of the literature. Arch Gen Psychiatry, 1980; 37:1041-6.

93. Mills IH. Amitriptyline therapy in anorexia nervosa. The Lancet, 1976; 687.

94. Needleman HL, Waber D. The use of amitriptyline in anorexia nervosa. In Vigersky RA, ed. Anorexia nervosa. New York: Raven Press, 1977:

95. Kendell RE. The role of diagnosis in psychiatry. Oxford, England: Blackwell.

Chapter 22

Anorexia Nervosa

David C. Sibley and Barton J. Blinder

INTRODUCTION

Anorexia nervosa as a clinical entity is an evolving concept [1]. Recognized as separate from pituitary failure for several decades, it is now also accepted to be distinct from other psychiatric disorders. Recently, bulimia has achieved recognition as a distinct nosologic category different from anorexia nervosa [2-4]. Refinements in classification will continue as pathophysiologic understanding expands. Additionally, social evolution continues to affect epidemiologic and clinical features. (See chapter by Gordon, this volume.)

Recognizing this continuous change, the aim of this chapter is to provide a description of the clinical features of anorexia nervosa at this point in its evolution. The patient population is currently defined by the diagnostic criteria in table 1 [5].

Following a historical overview, this chapter will consider premorbid factors, clinical features at presentation, cognitive and experiential aspects, differential diagnosis, and prognosis of anorexia nervosa. In conclusion, significant features in the assessment for treatment are discussed.

Many chapters in this volume relate to this one; those that expand on material specifically addressed in this chapter are cross-referenced in the text.

HISTORY

An early description of an anorexia-like syndrome, translated by Hajal [6], dates from the ninth century AD and describes the clinical history of a patient who is the teenaged son of the reigning Khalifah of the Islamic empire. An argument is made that he suffers from a primary refusal to eat or drink, with secondary medical complications. The royal physician, who has a psychological orientation, intervenes after the patient's resistant behavior has thwarted efforts by the family and local physicians to help. Behavioral techniques directed toward weight gain and increased eating are used, which begin the patient's recovery and cure.

Table 22.1 DSM-III-R Diagnosis of Anorexia Nervosa (5)

A. Refusal to maintain body weight over a minimal normal weight for age and height, e.g., weight loss leading to maintenance of body weight 15% below that expected; or failure to make expected weight gain during period of growth, leading to body weight 15% below that expected.

B. Intense fear of gaining weight or becoming fat, even though underweight.

C. Disturbance in the way in which one's body weight, size, or shape is experienced, e.g., the person claims to "feel fat" even when emaciated, believes that one area of the body is "too fat" even when obviously underweight.

D. In females, absence of at least three consecutive menstrual cycles when otherwise expected to occur (primary or secondary amenorrhea). (A woman is considered to have amenorrhea if her periods occur only following hormone, e.g., estrogen, administration).

While not identified as such, a condition resembling anorexia nervosa may have been recognized in the 16th century. Loudon [7] contends that the diagnosis of chlorosis, made from then until the mid-20th century, at first consisted of a symptom complex of food avoidance, weight loss, amenorrhea, and depression during adolescence. Some physicians reported the incidence to be predominantly among upper-class females, and it was said to be cured by the beginning of sexual activity. There were often reports of pica and bulimia in chlorotic patients. With the development of microscopic hematology, chlorosis came to be considered to be primarily a form of anemia, and Loudon [7] believes that two diseases were thus serially associated with that diagnostic label.

In a review that follows the elucidation of anorexia nervosa, Lucas [8] distinguishes five eras in its study. These correspond to the approach to medicine during each epoch and reflect current theoretical positions toward psychosomatic illness. In approximate chronological order the eras are:

1. Descriptive era. This era ended in 1914. At first consisting of case reports, including Morton's [9] of 1689, the descriptive period produced the disease entity with Gull's [10] and Lasegue's [11] independent presentations of "hysteric apepsia" and "anorexia hysterique," respectively, in 1868. Further English [12], French [13], and American [14] reports followed, and anorexia nervosa was established as a clinical diagnosis with emotional components and divisible into primary and secondary varieties.

2. Pituitary era. With Simmons [15] description of pituitary cachexia in 1914 applying Virchow's [16] concept of cellular pathology, anorexia nervosa was subsumed under pituitary failure, a rare condition.

3. Rediscovery era. Anorexia's revival as a separate entity began in the 1930s, when more clinical and psychological formulations were made. Refutation of claims that pituitary extracts had helped more patients and better understanding of starvation in anorexic patients allowed for separation from pituitary cachexia [17].

4. Psychoanalytic era. Concurrent with the rediscovery era and continuing through 1960, this orientation reflected the importance of psychoanalytic thinking in America. Freudians formulated anorexia as a rejection of unconscious wishes for oral impregnation. This has been viewed by some as a supportable dynamic, but of limited clincial utility. The analytically- influenced psychosomatic movement brought to attention such features as per-

sonality and conflict situations as potential contributors to the disease [1,18].

5. Modern era. Opened by Bruch in 1961, the modern era shows an attempt to synthesize previously opposing viewpoints [19,20]. Bruch accepted anorexia nervosa as a disease entity with the clinical features described in the early reports. She also distinguished anorexia syndromes secondary to other illnesses. For the primary disorder, she elaborated a specific intrapsychic experience, which consisted of body image distortion, disorderd perception of somatic stimuli, and a pervasive sense of ineffectiveness. Current thinking acknowledges hypothalamic and other neuroendocrine abnormalities, while continuing to explore a comprehensive biopsychosocial model. Constitutional factors, developmental events, and prevalent societal values act in concert to produce pathologic dieting, where-upon the effects of starvation worsen the clinical situation. This scheme of a multidetermined disorder accounts for the considerable clinical variations and for the advantages of a multidimensional approach to treatment [21,22].

PREMORBID FACTORS

An anorexic patient could be described as follows: She has been careful to please others, particularly authority figures in the family and at school. Her progress has been characterized by unquestioning adherence to age-appropriate expectations, and in transactions with others she quietly yields. She has sought and received praise, and her family finds her stubborn refusal to eat to be inconsistent with her previous behavior. At presentation she claims to have no control over most aspects of her life, and eating is the one area where she can have control.

While this description may apply to many patients with anorexia nervosa, there remains uncertainty as to the relative importance of constitution, developmental events, and social factors antecedent to the illness. Bruch [23] considers personality features and symptoms to have their roots in much earlier developmental challenges. Stating that the child's self-initiated cues weren't adequately confirmed, Bruch suggests that there is faulty discrimination of sensations such as hunger and other discomforts, which results in feelings of helplessness and discontrol. Throughout childhood, the future anorexic conforms excessively to rules, without exploring her own evolving capacities. This is met by uncritical praise, and the child remains at Piaget's stage of concrete operations. The incapacity for abstract thinking in patients is a cognitive deficit that reflects interference in mastery of prior developmental demands. In considering postpubertal personality features, Crisp [24] notes previous reports of obsessional and hysterical personalities in anorexic patients. Also, patients were described as egocentric, sensitive to rejection, timid, introspective, irritable, and hostile-dependent. While such traits might be used in developmental formulations of the patients, they were studied only near or at the time of hospitalization. Blinder [25] distinguishes three aspects of eating and psychopathology: (1) early feeding disturbances related to the mother-child interaction, (2) orality and its impact on personality organization and traits, and (3) specific eating disorders. With this distinction, developmental factors may have more of a role in the genesis of early feeding disturbances and personality traits than in eating disorders proper. These latter are distinguished by specific disturbances of appetite regulation, food preference, and consummatory pattern, with relatively more support for biological antecedents. Finally, Donohoe [26] presents a model for stress-induced anorexia, which acknowledges contributions from the developmental, constitutional, and social contexts, emphasizing intolerable stress experienced by the patient as the common pathway.

The families of anorexia patients have been repeatedly characterized. (See chapters by Liebman and Kramer, this volume.) Bruch [23] describes the family as materially successful, intact, and superficially happy. The family's communication style often minimizes parental and sibling problems, focusing almost exclusively on the anorexia patient's symptoms. There are both marital dissatisfaction and an underlying struggle for power. The father is older, somewhat passive, detached, and often overinvolved in his occupation. The anorexic's mother is omnipresent, allowing little room for individuation. She may show extreme concern for the patient while holding high, rigid expectations, with excessive concern for external appearances. Consistent with this family pathology orientation, Harper [27] revives the term "parentectomy" to emphasize a traditional protective-clinical approach. Citing cases where parents ignored severe deterioration of their daughter's health and examples of patients losing weight while on passes from the hospital, he states that certain parental behaviors actually sustain the illness. Using a family system approach, Liebman et al.[28], in reviewing work of Minuchin and others [29] from the Philadelphia Child Guidance Clinic, identify features of "psychosomatic families": enmeshment, overprotectiveness, rigidity, lack of conflict resolution, and involvement of the child in unresolved marital and family conflicts. The systems approach presumes the identified patient to belong to the family system and that family symptoms are expressed through the patient. Since the patient's illness represents a solution, albeit maladaptive, to family conflict, treatment can reactivate turmoil in the family. Experimental support for this is given by Crisp et al [30], who performed surveys of 44 anorexic patients and families both at evaluation and after combined nutritional-individual-family therapy. Mothers and fathers both scored higher than control parents in "somatic" and"hysteria" scales on the Middlesex Hospital Questionnaire. After restoration of weight, all scores increased, with significant rises in "anxiety" and "phobic" scales for both parents. In poor marriages, maternal "anxiety" and paternal "depression" scales rose significantly. This provides support for the "homeostatic" family model in which conflict is triangulated or routed through the patient.

In reviewing family studies, Yager [31] notes the pitfalls of generalizations. Many assessments are made when the family is in crisis and not in its best-adapted state. Studies have often included only intact families with younger patients and have suffered observer bias. The systems observations are not specific to anorexia families. Finally, a family explanation alone is inadequate in fully explaining the anorexic syndrome, including altered self-perceptions, early-onset amenorrhea, hyperactivity, desire for thinness, and other seemingly stereotypic signs. Case detection of anorexia nervosa in a broader demographic base (age level, social class, ethnic groups) adds to increasing evidence [24,32,33] for more heterogeneity in premorbid characteristics of individuals and families involved.

Precipitants of anorexia nervosa have been described both theoretically and phenomenologically, and stressors can be viewed as developmental stage-specific or nonspecific. As an early observer using the framework of revised psychoanalytic theory, Bruch [23] began with the still-prevalent view of anorexia as a retreat from adulthood, including its attendant responsibilities and sexuality. Crisp et al [34] support this in emphasizing the anorexic (and bulimic) weight "instability" at ranges where reproductive function is normal. The patient strives for a prepubertal state, which explains self-imposed weight barriers. Stressing psychobiologic regression, Blinder [25] speculates that the effectiveness of behavioral treatment reflects a regression to a stage where operant learning was especially important. Bodily preoccupation is viewed by Romeo [35] as a more primitive communication than the verbal skills required of developing adolescents.

Precipitants that have been observed without assertions of etiology include recent weight loss, obesity, teasing by peers or adults, object loss, family disgrace, illness, and sexual challenges [36,37].

PRESENTING FEATURES

Symptoms

A significant clinical feature of patients with anorexia nervosa is the minimization of symptoms and medical complications. Professional attention is sought usually after pressure from family, spouse, school, or employer. Thus, initial complaints may be first expressed by others.

Unusual behavior in proximity to and contact with food, such as food hoarding, food stealing, changed food handling, or very slow eating may be noticed. (See related chapter by Densmore-John, this volume.) The patient may show increased interest in cooking, become an expert chef, and assume most of the family's cooking duties while abstaining from meals. She may be inadvertently discovered while engaging in secretive binges, inducing vomiting or using laxatives, diuretics, or diet pills. Cuisine is usually restricted in range with progressive refusal of various types of foods, including carbohydrates, fats, and meats. Binge foods may be high-carbohydrate or fatty foods that the patient refuses publicly. Often, patients seek valid nutritional knowledge but use numerous rationalizations (including toxic fears, contemporary health concerns) for limiting their menu. There is increased exercise [38], sometimes amounting to hours each day. School studies may be pursued with increased intensity (but less efficiency), and social contacts may be progressively restricted.

The foregoing behavioral and attitudinal changes may be unnoticed, obscured, or actually praised by the family until the final common pathway of progressive weight loss becomes unavoidably apparent. All of the behaviors are then recognized as manifestations of the patient's perceived life's work, that is, an obsessional preoccupation with weight and appearance. When the marked incongruity between the patients' alleged concern about health and weight, and the reality of her cachetic state becomes painfully apparent, family and friends forcefully demand treatment.

Certain general features of patients at presentation deserve comment. It has been held that anorexics specifically avoid carbohydrate and that they usually have superior nutritional knowledge. Beumont et al [39], in studying diet composition in inpatient anorexics, found that they decreased carbohydrates only in proportion to total caloric reduction, and disproportionately reduced fat, while increasing protein. The mean nutritional knowledge was greater than controls, but 25% of patients knew less than controls. Halmi [40] found among 12 anorexic inpatients at the outset of treatment that the six "binge eaters" had a higher preference for very sweet solutions, while the "restrictors" showed more aversion to both sweets and fats, compared with controls. Huse and Lucas [41] assessed three parameters of diet in anorexics: regularity, quality, and quantity. Beyond noting that the largest such groups of patients (12 of 96) were disordered in all three parameters, no characteristic pattern of cuisine could be defined. There was considerable variety in the categories of vegetarianism, avoidance of red meats, and avoidance/preference of sweets and desserts. Similarly, the invariability of hyperactivity and its use as an indicator of poor prognosis has been questioned by Falk et al [42], who noted a quantitative increase in activity with weight gain in 20 improving hospitalized patients.

Recent reviews [36,43,44] have studied the prevalence of presenting symptoms and signs in anorexia patients by reviewing these in series of patients admitted to hospitals. While diagnostic criteria have been equivalent, the identification of symptoms is impaired, both by patient selection and by patients being unwilling or unable to report symptoms. This is reflected in wide ranges of prevalence, such as 10% to 45% for binge-eating, 31% to 62% for hyperactivity, and 11% to 43% for emesis. Within these limitations, common symptoms in anorexics are shown in table 2.

Table 22.2 Symptoms

Amenorrhea
Abdominal discomfort/constipation
Cold intolerance
Agitation/hyperactivity
Lethargy
Emesis
Binge eating
Insomnia
Dry skin
Brittle hair/nails
Musculoskeletal pain

As discussed in the next section, the patient's perceptions may be distorted, but there is considerable corroboration for many of the common symptoms. Amenorrhea, usually a sine qua non for the diagnosis, has varying onset in relation to severe dieting. Halmi [44] found 73% of patients had amenorrhea at the time of or before food refusal. This compares with 39% in the UCLA series [36] and 50% to 55% in previous studies [44]. Also noted in one follow-up study [45] was a correlation of disturbed psychological states with persistent amenorrhea in normal-weight patients. Hypothermia and cold intolerance have been attributed [46] to reduced tri-iodothyronine commonly found in anorexic patients, but hypothalamic thermoregulatory dysfunction has been proposed as well. Mecklenburg et al [47] found five anorexic patients unable to correct core temperatures to hot and cold challenges, and they could distinguish them from controls on this basis. Also, the patients failed to show normal autonomic responses of vasoconstriction and shivering. Luck and Wakeling [48] supported the hypothalamic etiology by showing reproducible elevations of preferred temperatures by patients compared with controls. Finally, there is a case report [49] of glucose- and thiamine-dependent hypothermia in an anorexic patient. Gastrointestinal complaints were studied by McCallum et al [50], who identified bloating, nausea, vomiting, heartburn, belching, bulimia, pain, and constipation in 16 anorexia patients. Employing the diagnostic technique of radionuclide gastrography, they demonstrated a significantly slowed gastric emptying time as measured by percent of food retained in the stomach (80% retained at 120 minutes versus 50% for controls, with significantly more retained continuously from 60 minutes onward). This difference was abolished with administration of metoclopramide. Dystrophic changes in the skin and nails, in addition to having a hypothyroid etiology, can be caused by zinc deficiency, as demonstrated by Casper [51] who found decreased serum zinc, copper and iron-binding capacity levels in 30 anorexia patients. Musculoskeletal pains should alert the clinician to the possibility of stress fractures secondary to the osteroporosis prevalent in anorexics [52].

Physical Findings

While many of the physical findings have been attributable to starvation, further elaboration is possible (table 3). The symptom complex of hypothermia, bradycardia, hypotension, skin changes, slowed relaxation phase of deep tendon reflexes, and hypercarotenemia correspond to the "euthyroid sick" state in anorexic and starving patients. In such cases, peripheral conversion of T4 to T3 is decreased without hypothalamic compensation, probably as an adaptation to starvation [36]. Hypotension and arrhythmias can result from decreased cardiac muscle mass and hypokalemia, the latter due to vomiting and laxative abuse [55]. Similarly, tetany, salivary gland enlargement, and dorsal hand scars are indirect complications in the subgroups of patients who induce vomiting [54,57]. Patients in this subgroup may be first seen by dentists, where they may present with irreversible erosion, decalcification, and severe caries [58]. (See chapter by Levinson, this volume).

Laboratory Findings

A number of abnormal laboratory results can be anticipated with the multiplicity of involved systems in anorexia patients. Much of the data is nonspecific. Noting that one might find a laboratory profile including

"...leukopenia, a relative lymphocytosis, a low serum potassium level, a low serum chloride level, a low fasting glucose level, an elevated SGOT, an elevated LDH, an elevated alkaline phosphatase, an elevated amylase, and an elevated serum cholesterol," [59]

in an anorexia patient, Halmi and Falk [59] reviewed laboratory results in 40 inpatient anorexics. When mean values were calculated, many of these findings were not prominent, but considerable ranges indicated some patients had abnormalities in nearly every category. Milner et al [60], in reviewing 47 inpatients, found a substantial incidence of abnormal laboratory values: decreased hematocrit (in 25% of patients), leukopenia (in 60%), increase SGOT and LDH (in 45% and 15%, respectively), increased total protein and albumin (in 33% and 25%), increased serum cholesterol (in 37%), decreased alkaline phosphatase (in 65%), and increased BUN and creatinine (in 33% and 25%).

Reviews [59,61] indicate that the hematologic/immunologic profile of leukopenia, anemia, mild thrombocytopenia, bone marrow hypoplasia, and decreased complement components (with *decreased* albumin and protein sometimes seen) are reversible responses to starvation and are not accompanied by an increased incidence of infection [62]. Increased liver enzymes seen on admission will sometimes become further increased during refeeding; this may represent fatty infiltration but may also mimic changes seen in kwashiorkor and marasmus [59]. Increased BUN and creatinine may be secondary to a combination of dehydration, a decreased glomerular filtration rate, and increased protein catabolism [55]. Sodium may be decreased or increased (due to polydipsia or dehydration/partial diabetes insipidus, respectively) [59,63] and increased sodium avidity accounts for refeeding-induced peripheral edema [55]. Hypokalemia results from vomiting, diarrhea, and renal losses; vomiting also causes the hypochloremic metabolic alkalosis [59]. ECGs reveal metabolic changes of hypokalemia and can also show low voltage, bradycardia, and nonspecific T-wave changes [46,53]. Finally, Lankenau et al [64] and Pirke and Ploog [65] note that both reversible and initially irreversible cerebral atrophy have been seen in some patients with anorexia nervosa.

COGNITIVE AND EXPERIENTIAL ASPECTS

Formal studies and case reports attempting to define characteristic personality profiles and cognitive deficits in patients with anorexia nervosa have not led to consensus in the interpretation of findings. Comparison of studies is difficult because of differences in stage of treatment, choice of controls, testing instruments, and self-reporting by patients (see below).

Table 22.3 Physical Findings

Halmi (44)	Provenzale (53)	Smith (46)	Andersen (54)	Herzog (55)	Schwabe (36)	Suematsu (56)
Weight loss Bradycardia 28% Lanugo 18% Dependent edema 18% Hypothermia 18%	Weight loss Bradycardia Dependent edema Hypothermia Hypotension Acrocyanosis	Weight loss Bradycardia Lanugo Hypothermia Dry, inelastic skin Loss of subcutaneous fat Petechiae Parotid swelling Increased caries	Weight loss Bradycardia Lanugo Hypothermia Hypotension Tetany seizures Arrhythmias Breast atrophy Dorsal hand scars Decreased muscle mass	Weight loss Bradycardia Slowed reflex relaxation Hypercarotenemia	Weight loss Bradycardia 36% Lanugo 28% Hypotension 22% Dry skin 22%	Weight loss Bradycardia 49% Lanugo 28% Dependent edema 26% Hypothermia 46% Hypotension 40% Pubic hair loss 5% Breast atrophy 21%

In a study of 12 anorexics, Skoog et al [66] showed pretreatment MMPI profiles to have peaks in depression, social introversion, and hypochondriasis, which improved significantly after treatment. The pretreatment profile was similar to that of an earlier study [66]. Vandereycken and Vanderlinden [67] showed overall heterogeneity in the MMPI profiles to 40 severely ill inpatient anorexics, but were able to identify certain profiles based on the Eating Attitudes Test (EAT) scores of these patients. Patients with false-negative (normal scores <30) EAT results showed significantly more ego strength and lower psychasthenia, schizophrenia, hysteria, and hypochondriasis on MMPI than those with high (>55) EAT scores. It was concluded that self-reporting studies must consider the effects of denial and also that there may be a subgroup of anorexics who have more severe neuropsychological deficits. This was studied by Fox [68], who compared testing results of 15 anorexic inpatients to those of 15 other psychiatric inpatients without eating disorders. Anorexics had significantly higher digit substitution, significantly lower general information, and significantly lower arithmetic than other psychiatric patients. The author attributes the improved digit substitution to increased mobilization of psychomotor activity and suggests that impaired arithmetic, like impaired body awareness and awareness of illness, could be related to right hemisphere dysfunction. Small et al [69] administered pre- and post-treatment WAIS and Rorschach tests to 27 hospitalized patients. Abnormal arithmetic and Digit Span results indicated poor potential for weight gain, while personality features and thought disturbances were not of prognostic significance. It was suggested that the inability to organize and sustain a cognitive focus made newly-admitted patients inaccessible to therapy. Witt et al [70] found associative learning as measured by the Symbol-Digit Learning Test to be significantly impaired in anorexics compared with matched depressed inpatients, diabetic outpatients, and healthy controls. The impairment correlated with duration of illness. Digit substitution, measured by the WAIS Digit Symbol subtest, was comparable to controls, in contrast to the study by Fox [68].

The intrapsychic experience of patients with anorexia nervosa was delineated by Bruch [71], who posited that patients are unable to acknowledge and identify their own affects and bodily sensations such as hunger. Both types of stimuli are perceived as externally-derived, and restrictive behavior is an autonomy-seeking response to perceived external threat (overwhelming hunger). Crisp [72] agrees that the anorexic's behavior may be experienced by her as adaptive to her needs, and adds that the sexual and maturational challenges of puberty may provide additional externally-perceived threats to the patient. Reliable body image identification could then be related to the extent of self-acceptance a patient has in areas such as autonomy and sexuality. As a measure of autonomy, Basseches and Karp [73] compared field dependence in 16 anorexics, 16 obese subjects and 16 matched controls. Both obese and anorexic patients showed significantly less capacity of autonomous functioning than controls. Leon et al [74] found significantly more negative self-assessment in sexuality, body state, and other parameters among 47 anorexic inpatients compared with controls. Responses indicated patients wanted to lose weight while knowing that they would be more sexually attractive at higher weights. Garner and Garfinkel [75], in reviewing the body image literature, note certain methodological issues, including reliability, construct validity, selection of patients and controls, and the effects of the experimental setting. (See also chapter by Meerman et al, this volume.) "Body image distortion" may refer to body misperception (visualization, unusual body experiences), or to body disparagement (evalaution) with normal perception. Measures of misperception, such as the Movable Caliper Technique, Image Marking Method, and Distorting Photograph Technique have shown considerable variability but have as a whole suggested body image overestimation by anorexics. Hsu [76] notes that body overestimation as an index of body image distortion is neither sensitive nor specific for anorexia nervosa and cannot be considered pathognomonic. Studies that assessed body disparagement [77,78,79], while showing a preference for thinness among both patients and controls, have been supportive of more body disparagement in anorexics.

DIFFERENTIAL DIAGNOSIS

Because of the weight-loss criterion required for the diagnosis of anorexia nervosa [5], bulimia cannot be diagnosed as a disorder in the presence of anorexia. However, the symptom of bulimia (binge-eating) is reported in 45% to 50% of patients with anorexia nervosa [43,80], and self-induced vomiting is present as frequently [43]. Also, 50% of patients with diagnosed bulimia have a history of anorexia nervosa, and it may

Table 22.4 Differential Diagnosis of Anorexia Nervosa

Bulimia	Hyperthyroidism
Affective disorders	Hypothyroidism
Schizophrenia	Adrenal insufficiency
Obsessive-compulsive disorder	Hypopituitarism
Conversion disorder	Inflammatory bowel disease
Personality disorders	Brain tumors

be ten times as prevalent as anorexia in the female population between ages 13 and 40 [82]. Evidence supporting diagnostic distinctions in the form of personality differences [83], family features [84], and parental personalities [85], as well as new similarities [86] continues to be defined. Current nosology would appear to favor at least two separate disorders, (restrictive) anorexia nervosa and (normal-weight) bulimia, with anorexics who binge-eat resembling patients with normal weight bulimia more than they resemble exclusively restrictive anorexics [85]. (See also chapters by Hsu, Pyle and Leichner, this volume.) Thus, Garner et al [85], using self-reporting of demographic, clinical, and psychometric variables in 59 patients with normal-weight bulimia, 59 with the bulimic subtype of anorexia nervosa, and 59 with restrictive anorexia, found the two bulimic groups to be more alike than either was to the restrictive group in the areas of impulse control, perceived family conflict, predisposition to obesity, and possibly proclivity toward affective disorder.

The relationship of affective disorders to eating disorders continues to be extensively studied, with new reports supporting correlations [87-90] as well as new criticism [91] of hypotheses linking affective and eating disorders. With more recognition of distinctions between anorexic and bulimic syndromes, bulimia appears more exclusively related to affective disorders, particularly major depression, than does anorexia. (See also chapters in this volume by Hsu, Chaitin, and Mitchell and Pyle for further discussion of classification, affective disorders, and bulimia, respectively.)

While other Axis I diagnoses can coexist with anorexia nervosa, they can be distinguished from anorexia when the characteristic pursuit of thinness and distorted body image are absent (as in cyclic conversion vomiting [92] and obsessive-compulsive disorder) or when thought disorder, delusions, or hallucinations predominate (as in schizophrenia). Personality disorder diagnoses such as schizoid, borderline, histrionic, and antisocial personality disorder are made in anorexic patients [45] and may be the primary diagnosis for patients in whom anorexia nervosa is only partially or occasionally manifest. (See also chapter by Sacher and Sporty relating eating disturbances to other psychiatric disorders.)

Medical diagnoses may account for some signs seen in anorexia nervosa and are excluded clinically and by laboratory examination. Hyperthyroid patients may show weight loss and hyperactivity, but they also have increased food intake, hyperthermia, heat intolerance, and increased serum thyroid hormones. Hypothyroidism mimics anorexia with symptoms of weakness, constipation, bradycardia, hypothermia, and cold intolerance, but hypothyroid patients often show weight gain, hypoactivity, and increased serum TSH. Adrenal insufficiency may cause bradycardia, hypotension, lethargy, and decreased oral intake, but it also causes hyperpigmentation, decreased intertriginous hair, hyperkalemia, and low serum cortisol. Rarely, pituitary dysfunction will cause amenorrhea, but there will often also be secondary hypothyroidism, adrenal insufficiency, or changes in prolactin if caused by a mass lesion. Inflammatory bowel disease and other causes of gastrointestinal dysfunction may be clinically similar to some manifestations of eating disorders but may be diagnosed by abnormal diarrhea and by laboratory and clinical indications of inflammation. Finally, chronic illnesses such as tuberculosis and malignancies may caused cachexia, but these are not accompanied by the desire for thinness and distorted body image and usually present other clinical signs [46].

PROGNOSIS

A critical comparison of anorexia nervosa outcome studies is difficult. Steinhausen and Glanville [93] reviewed 45 studies, and noted the methodological limitations: diagnostic criteria vary, follow-up duration is sometimes too short (less than four years), and treatment has usually been multimodal with few centers having enough subjects to compare one distinct consistently applied method with another. Data are usually by subjective report and often obtained by telephone or letter instead of by direct interview. Typically, only one or a few indices of improvement such as weight restoration or resumption of menses are used, while different outcome data are obtained if one includes such parameters as resolution of eating distubance and psychosocial improvement. There is variable inclusion of information regarding coexisting or subsequent other psychiatric diagnoses in the subjects. Often, there is a high dropout rate, and conclusions may be made based on atypical samples.

This is exemplified by Vandereycken and Pierloot's [94] observation of a differential outcome among patients who initially did not respond to follow-up inquiries, a group that accounted for 31% of a 128-patient study. They also found significant differences in demographics and outcome between patients who were followed more or less than five years, suggesting that the natural course of the illness can confound comparison of such subgroups. Halmi [45] confirms the above concerns and adds that more standardized forms of data collection are needed.

With these caveats, Steinhausen and Glanville [93] reviewed 45 studies from 1953 to 1981 and found general ranges of follow-up weight restoration and re-

Table 22.5 Outcome in Anorexia Nervosa

	Crisp (43)	Bassoe (95)	Morgan (96)	Hall (97)	Touyz (98)
Number of Patients	102	133	78	50	47
Treatment Population Treatment Modality	52% OP 48% IP Mulitmodal	34% OP 66% IP Educational-supportive	"normally outpatient" Multimodal & Medications	34% OP 66% IP Refeeding & Individual	25% OP 75% IP Refeeding & supportive
Follow-up duration (yr)	4-8	2-4 +	4-8.5	4-12	8.5
"Good" outcome (%)		58	58	36	37
Menstruating (%)	69				55
Normal body weight (%)	76				
"Intermediate" outcome (%)		28	19	36	18
No food preoccupation (%)	33				53
No weight preoccupation (%)	57				
"Poor" outcome (%)	20	14	19	26	10
Deaths (%)	2	0	1	2	2
Lost to follow-up (%)	0	0	0	0	33
Duration of illness among recovered (yr)	4.6				

OP: Outpatient
IP: Inpatient

sumption of menses to be 50% to 70%, with more return of menses after longer follow-up periods. Normalization of eating symptoms occurred in 30% to 70% of patients with the subjectivity of this parameter possibly accounting for the wide range. Recovery of social adjustment, another poorly defined measure, occurred in 50% to 80% of patients. Steinhausen and Glanville [93] considered the overall improvement rate of 30% to 50% to be conservative. Garfinkel and Garner [21], reviewing 724 patients included in relatively long follow-up studies, found 43% recovered, 28% improved, 20% unimproved, and 9% dead. Table 5 shows results in recent outcome studies.

Morgan and Russell [99] developed a 12-point average-outcome scale using self-rating of nutritional status, menstrual function, mental state, sexual adjustment, and socioeconomic state, and from this are derived the outcome categories of "good" (body weight 85% to 115% normal body weight), "intermediate" (body weight sometimes outside 85% to 115% and/or men-

strual irregularity), and "poor" (body weight below 85%, amenorrhea) used in the last three studies in table 5 [96,97,98].

The mortality rate in anorexia nervosa has ranged from 0% to 21%, with the majority of series showing rates below 10% [93]. The rate may be still lower in pediatric series [21]. Patients usually die of complications of starvation or suicide, but they may also die of complications of bulimia and other ingestive behavior, such as hypolkalemia-induced cardiac arrhythmias, gastric perforation [100], and ipecac poisoning [101].

Reviews of prognostic indicators [21,22] and recent outcome studies [84,96,97,102-104] show considerable variability in identifiable predictors of outcome. The factors most consistently associated with a good prognosis are early age of onset, short pretreatment duration of illness, and fewer previous hospitalizations. Less reproducible factors include higher socioeconomic class, good relationship with parents, premorbid hyperactivity as a primary means of weight loss, hysterical personality, improved body image after treatment, and post-treatment phobic symptoms. No indicators of poor prognosis are consistently found, but bulimia, vomiting laxative abuse, severe weight loss, depression, obsessive-compulsive symptoms, psychosis, somatization, and male gender have been suggested in some studies. Recently, early age of onset as a prognostic indicator has been questioned by Hawlay [105], who found similar menstruation, psychosocial adjustment, sexual adjustment, weight, and survival in 21 patients with onset age under 13, followed eight years, as compared with follow-up results in patients with onset at a later age. This may represent recent convergence of improved outcome for both adult and childhood-onset anorexics.

APPROACH TO TREATMENT

Bassoe and Eskeland [95] note:

Throughout the centuries many types of treatment have been advocated in the treatment of anorexia nervosa: psycotherapy, behavior modification, isolation, bedrest, drugs, acupuncture, endocrine therapy including pituitary transplantation, shock therapy, lobotomy, dialysis and exorcism.

The many therapies reflect the fact that patients with anorexia display disturbances in all of the areas of physical health, psychological and social functioning, family relationships, reproduction, and sexuality. Exclusive use of one treatment modality such as medications, refeeding, individual therapy, or family therapy will fail to address other aspects of the problem. Similarly, termination of treatment after short-term gains while hospitalized ("weight restored") does not comprise a good outcome. It is generally accepted [69,22] that nutritional rehabilitation is required at the outset of treatment to avoid medical complications and permit engagement in therapy. Establishment of a sound therapeutic alliance is important, although this should not be used as a rationale for permitting the patient to avoid refeeding. Regardless of one's assumptions as to the etiology of anorexia nervosa, the adolescent issues of separation and individuation will be present in this population and contribute to family interactions. In most cases, the family should be involved to effect adaptive separation. Although outpatient studies are lacking, recent-onset, mildly symptomatic anorexics may be treated without hospitalization, provided appropriate medical, behavioral, nutritional, and family interventions are possible [22].

REFERENCES

1. Kaufman M, Ralph, et al, ed. Evolution of psychosomatic concepts: Anorexia nervosa: a paradigm. Intl Univ Press, 1964.

2. Blinder B, Cadenhead K. Bulimia: An historical overview. Adoles Psych. Feinstein S, Sorosky A, eds. vol. 13, Developmental and clinical studies, Univ. of Chicago Press, 1986:231-240.

3. Boskind-Lodahl N, White WC. The definition and treatment of bulimarexia in college women—a pilot study. J Am College Health Assoc, 1978; 27:84-6.

4. Stunkard AJ. Eating patterns and obesity. Psych Quart, 1959; 33:289-94.

5. Diagnostic and Statistical Manual of Mental Disorders, Third Edition, REvised (DSM-III-R). Washington, D.C.: American Psychiatric Association, 1987:67.

6. Hajal F. Psychological treatment of anorexia: A case from the ninth century. Hist Med Allied Sci, 1982; 37:325-8.

7. Loudon I. The diseases called chlorosis. Psychol Med, 1984; 14:27-36.

8. Lucas AR. Toward the understanding of anorexia nervosa as a disease entity. Mayo Clin Proc, 1981; 56:254-64.

9. Morton R. Phthisiologia, seu excitationes de phthisi tribus libris comprehensae: totumque opus variis historiis illustratum. London: Samuel Smith, 1689.

10. Gull WW. Adress in medicine. Lancet, 1868; 2:171.

11. Lasegue CH. L'anorexie hysterique. Arch Gen Med, 1873; 21:385- 403.

12. Stephens L. Case of anorexia nervosa: necropsy. Lancet, 1895; 1:31-2.

13. Charcot JM. Clinical lectures on dieases of the nervous system, vol 3. (Trans by T. Savill.) London: New Sydenham Society, 1889.

14. Mitchell SW. Lectures on diseases of the nervous system especially in women. 2nd ed. Philadelphia: Lea Brothers, 1885.

15. Simmond M. Ueber Hypophysisschwund mit todlichem Ausgang Deutsch- Med-Wochenschr, 1940;40:322-3.

16. Virchow R. Die Cellularpathologie in ihrer Begrundung auf physiologische und pathologische Gewebelehre. Berlin: A. Hirschwald, 1858.

17. Berkman JM. Anorexia nervosa: The diagnosis and treatment of inanition resulting from functional disorders. Ann Int Med, 1945: 22:679-91.

18. Waller JV, Kaufman RN, Deutsch F. Anorxia nervosa: a psychosomatic entity. Psychosom Med, 1940; 2:3-16.

19. Bliss EL, Branch CHH. Anorexia nervosa: Its history, psychology and biology. New York: Paul B. Hoeber, 1960.

20. Nemiah JC. Anorexia nervosa: fact and theory. Am J Dig Dis, 1958; 33:249-74.

21. Garfinkel P, Garner D. Anroexia nervosa—a multidimensional perspective. New York: Brunner/Mazel, 1982.

22. Halmi K. Pragmatic information on the eating disorders. Psychiat Clin N Am, 1982; 5:371-7.

23. Bruch H. Developmental deviations in anorexia nervosa. Israel Ann Psychiatr, 1979; 17:255-61.

24. Crisp AH. Premorbid factors in adult disorders of weight, with particular reference to primary anorexia nervosa (weight phobia). A literature review. J Psychosom Res, 1970; 14:1-22.

25. Blinder BJ. Developmental antecedents of the eating disorders: a reconsideration. Psychiat Clin N Am, 1980; 3:579-92.

26. Donohoe TP. Stress-induced anorexia: implications for anorexia nervosa. Life Sciences, 1984; 34:203-18.

27. Harper G. Varieties of parenting failure in anorexia nervosa: protection and parentectomy revisited. J Am Acad Child Psychiat, 1983; 22:134-9.

28. Liebman R, Sargent J, Silver M. A family systems orientation to the treatment of anorexia nervosa. J Am Acad Child Psychiat, 1983; 22:128-33.

29. Minuchin S. Rosman B, Baker L. Psychosomatic families. Cambridge: Harvard University Press, 1978.

30. Crisp AH, Harding B, McGuiness B. Anorexia nervosa. Psychoneurotic characteristics of parents: relationship to prognosis. J Psychosom Res, 1974; 18:167-73.

31. Yager J. Family issues in the pathogenesis of anorexia nervosa. Psychosom Med, 1982: 44:43-60.

32. Hall A. Family structure and relationship of 50 female anorexia nervosa patients. Aust NZ J Psychiat, 1978; 12:263-8.

33. Silber T. Anorexia nervosa in black adolescents. J Natl Med Assoc, 1984; 76:29-32.

34. Crisp AH, Hsu LKG, Harding B. The starving hoarder and voracious spender: stealing in anorexia nervosa. J Psychosom Res, 1980; 24:225-31.

35. Romeo F. Adolescence, sexual conflict and anorexia nervosa. Adolescence, 1984; 19:551-5.

36. Schwabe A, Lippe B. Chang R, et al. Anorexia nervosa. Ann Int Med, 1981; 94:371-81.

37. Beumont P, Abraham S, Argall W, et al. The onset of anorexia nervosa. Aust NZ J Psychiatr, 1978; 12:145-9.

38. Blinder B, Freeman D, Stunkard A. Behavior therapy of anorexia nervosa: effectiveness of activity as a reinforcer of weight gain. Am J Psychiatr, 1970; 126:1093-8.

39. Beumont P, Chambers T, Rose L, et al. The diet composition and nutritional knowledge of patients with anorexia nervosa. J Hum Nutr, 1982; 35:265-75.

40. Halmi K. Satiety and taste in eating disorders. Presented at International Symposium — Disorders of Eating Behaviour — A psychoneuroendocrine approach. Pavia, Italy, Sept 12-15,1985.

41. Huse D, Lucas A. Dietary patterns in anorexia nervosa. Am J Clin Nutr, 1984; 40:251-4.

42. Falk J, Halmi K, Tryon W. Activity measures in anorexia nervosa. Arch Gen Psychiatr, 1985; 42:811-4.

43. Crisp A, Hsu L, Harding B, et al. Clinical features of anorexia nervosa. J Psychosom Res, 1980; 24:179-91.

44. Halmi K. Anorexia nervosa: demographic and clinical features in 94 cases. Psychosom Med, 1974; 36:18-26.

45. Halmi K. The state of research in anorexia nervosa and bulimia. Psychiatr Dev, 1983; 3:247-62.

46. Smith M. Anorexia nervosa and bulimia. J Fam Prac, 1984; 18:757- 66.

47. Mecklenburg R, Loraux DE, Thompson R, et al. Hypothalamic dysfunction in patients with anorexia nervosa. Medicine, 1971; 53:147-59.

48. Luck P, Wakeling A. Set-point displacement for behavioural thermoregulation in anorexia nervosa. Clin Sci, 1982; 62:677-82.

49. Smith D, Ovesen L, Chu R, et al. Hypothermia in a patient with anorexia nervosa. Metabolism, 1983; 32:1151-4.

50. McCallum, Gill B, Lange R, et al. Definition of a gastric emptying abnormality in patients with anorexia nervosa. Digest Dis Sci, 1985; 30:713-22.

51. Casper R. An evaluation of trace metals, vitamins and taste function in anorexia nervosa. Am J Clin Nutr, 1980; 33:1801-8.

52. Waldstreicher J. Anorexia nervosa presenting as morbid exercising. Lancet, 1985; (April 27):987.

53. Provenzale J. Anorexia nervosa — thinness as illness. Postgrad Med, 1983; 74:83-9.

54. Andersen A. Anorexia nervosa and bulimia: diagnosis and comprehensive treatment. Compt Ther, 1983; 9:9-17.

55. Herzog D, Copeland P. Eating disorders. N Engl J Med, 1985; 313:295-303.

56. Suematsu HJ, Ishikawa H, Kuboki, et al. Statistical studies on anorexia nervosa in Japan: Detailed clinical data on 1011 patients. Psychother Psychosom, 1985; 43:96-103.

57. Walsh BT, Croft C, Katz J. Anorexia nervosa and salivary gland enlargement. Int J Psychiat in Med, 1981; 11:255-61.

58. Stege P, Visco-Dangler L, Rye L. Anorexia nervosa: review including oral and dental manifestations. J Am Dent Assoc, 1982; 104:648-52.

59. Halmi K, Falk J. Common physiological changes in anorexia nervosa. Int J Eat Dis, 1981; 1:16-27.

60. Milner M, Mcanarney E, Klish W. Metabolic abnormalities in adolescent patients with anroexia nervosa. J Adol Health Care, 1985; 6:191-5.

61. Kay J, Strickler R. Hematologic and immunologic abnormalities in anorexia nervosa. South Med J, 1983; 76:1008-10.

62. Pertschuck MJ, Corsby LO, Barot L, et al. Immunocompetency in anorexia nervosa. Am J Clin Nutr, 1982; 35:968-72.

63. Gold P, Kaye W, Robertson G, et al. Abnormalities in plasma and cerebrospinal fluid arginine vasopressin in patients with anorexia nervosa. N Engl J Med, 1983; 308:1117-23.

64. Lankenau H, Swigar M, Bhimani S, et al. Cranial CT scans in eating disorder patients and controls. Comp Psychiat, 1985; 26:136-47.

65. Pirke K, Ploog D. Psychobiology of anorexia nervosa. In: Wurtman RJ, Wurtman JJ, eds. Nutrition and the Brain, vol 7. New York: Raven Press, 1986:167-198.

66. Skoog D, Andersen A, Laufer W. Personality and treatment effectiveness in anorexia nervosa. J Clin Psychol, 1984; 40:955-61.

67. Vandereycken W, Vanderlinden J. Denial of illness and the use of self-reporting measures in anorexia nervosa patients. Int J Eat Dis, 1983; 2:101-7.

68. Fox C. Neuropsychological correlates of anorexia nervosa. Int J Psychiatr In Med, 1981; 11:285-90.

69. Small A, Madero J, Teagno L, et al. Intellect, perceptual characteristics and weight gain in anorexia nervosa. J Clin Psychol, 1983; 39:780-2.

70. Witt E, Ryan C, Hsu LKG. Learning deficits in adolescents with anorexia nervosa. J Nerv Ment Dis, 1985; 173:182-4.

71. Bruch H. Anorexia nervosa: Therapy and theory. Am J Psychiatr, 1982; 139:1531-38.

72. Crisp AH. Anorexia nervosa. Br Med J, 1983; 287:855-8.

73. Basseches H, Karp S. Field dependence in young anorectic and obese women. Psychother Psychosom, 1984; 41:33-7.

74. Leon G, Lucas A, Colligan R, et al. Sexual, body-image and personality attitudes in anorexia nervosa. J Abnorm Child Psychol, 1985; 13:245-58.

75. Garner D, Garfinkel P. Body image in anorexia nervosa: measurement theory and clinical implications. Int J Psychiatr in Med, 1981; 11:263-84.

76. Hsu LKG. Is there a disturbance in body image in anorexia nervosa? J Nerv Ment Dis, 1982; 170:305-7.

77. Freeman D, Blinder B. Eating function and body image in anorexia nervosa: A comparative assessment utilizing underweight controls. Presented at APA annual meeting, May 15,1968.

78. Buree B, Papageorgis D, Solyom L. Body image perception and preference in anorexia nervosa. Can J Psychiatr, 1984; 27:157-71.

79. Touyz S, Beumont P, Collins J, et al. Body shape perception and its disturbance in anorexia nervosa. Br J Psychiatr, 1984; 144:167-71.

80. Casper R, Eckert E, Halmi K, et al. Bulimia: its incidence and clinical importance in patients with anorexia nervosa. Arch Gen Psychiatr, 1979; 37:1030-4.

81. Russell G. Bulimia nervosa: an ominous variant of anorexia nervosa. Psychol Med, 1979: 9:429-48.

82. Pope H, Hudson J, Yurgelon-Todd D. Anorexia nervosa and bulimia among suburban women shoppers. Am J Psychiatr, 1984; 141:292-4.

83. Strober M, Salkin B, Burroughts J et al. Validity of the bulimia- restrictor distinction in anorexia nervosa. Parental personality characteristics and family psychiatric morbidity. J Nerv Ment Dis, 1982; 170:345-51.

84. Halmi K, Falk J. Anorexia nervosa. A study of outcome discriminators in exclusive dieters and bulimics. J Am Acad Child Psychiatr, 1982; 21:369-75.

85. Garner D, Garfinkel P, O'Shaugnessy M. The validity of the distinction between bulimia with and without anorexia nervosa. A J Psychiartr, 1985; 142:5.

86. Pirke K, Pahl J. Schweiger U, et al. Metabolic and endocrine indices of starvation in bulimia: a comparison with anorexia nervosa. Psychiatr Res, 1984; 15:33-39.

87. Katz J, Kuperberg K, Pollack C, et al. Is there a relationship between eating disorder and affective disorder? New evidence from sleep recordings. Am J Psychiatr, 1984; 141:753-9.

88. Rivinus T, Biederman J, Herzog D, et al. Anorexia nervosa and affective disorders: a controlled family history study. Am J Psychiatr, 1984; 141:1414-18.

89. Gershon E, Schreiber J, Hamovit J, et al. Clinical findings in patients with anorexia nervosa and affective illness in their relatives. Am J Psychiatr, 1984; 141:1491-22.

90. Biederman J, Rivinus T, Kemper K, et al. Depressive disorders in relatives of anorexia nervosa patients with and without a current episode of nonbipolar major depression. Am J Psychiatr, 1985; 142:1495-7.

91. Altschuler K, Weiner M. Anorexia nervosa and depression: a dissenting view. Am J Psychiatr, 1985; 142:328-32.

92. Garfinkel P, Kaplan A, Garner D. The differentiation of vomiting/weight loss as a conversion disorder from anorexia nervosa. Am J Psychiatr, 1983; 140:1019-22.

93. Steinhausen H, Glanville K. Follow-up studies of anorexia nervosa: a review of research findings. Psychol Med, 1983; 13:239-49.

94. Vandereycken W, Pierloot R. Long-term outcome research in anorexia nervosa. The problem of patient selection and follow-up duration. Int J Eat Dis, 1983; 2:237-42.

95. Bassoe H, Eskeland I. A prospective study of 133 patients with anorexia nervosa. Treatment and outcome. Acta Psychiatr Scand, 1982; 65:127-33.

96. Morgan H, Purgold J, Welbourne J. Management and outcome in anorexia nervosa. A standardized prognotic study. Br J Psychiatr, 1983; 143:282-7.

97. Hall A, Slim E, Hawker, et al. Anorexia nervosa: long-term outcome in 50 female patients. Br J Psychiatr, 1984; 145:407-13.

98. Touyz S, Beumont P. Anorexia nervosa. A follow-up investigation. Med J Aust, 1984; 141:219-22.

99. Morgan H, Russell G. Value of family background and clinical features as predictors of long-term outcome in anorexia nervosa: four years followup study of 41 patients. Psychol Med, 1975; 5:355-71.

100. Saul S, Dekker A, Watson C. Acute gastric dilatation with infarction and perforation. Report of fatal outcome in patient with anorexia nervosa. Gut, 1981; 22:978-83.

101. Freidman E. Death from ipecac intoxication in a patient with anorexia nerovsa. Am J Psychiatr, 1984; 145:407-13.

102 Halmi K, Casper R. Eckert E, Goldberg J, Davis J. Unique features associated with age of onset of anorexia nervosa. Psychiat Res, 1979; 1:209-15.

103. Halmi K, Goldberg S, Casper R, et al. Pretreatment predictors of outcome in anorexia nervosa. Br J Psychiatr, 1979; 134:71-8.

104. Becker H, Korner P, Stoffler A. Psychodynamics and therapeutic aspects of anorexia nervosa. Psychother Psychosom, 1981; 36:8-16.

105. Hawley R. The outcome of anorexia nervosa in younger subjects. Br J Psychiatr, 1985; 146:657-60.

Chapter 23

The Epidemiology of Bulimia

Richard L Pyle and James E. Mitchell

Bulimia, as described in DSM-III [1], is characterized by an abnormal eating pattern of uncontrolled episodic binge eating usually accompanied by self-induced vomiting or laxative abuse to eliminate unwanted food. The bulimic episodes are followed by low mood and self-deprecatory thoughts. Food intake may be eliminated or greatly restricted between episodes. Patients who present for treatment are most often women in their mid-20s who developed the illness in their late teens [2-4]. The illness occurs primarily in white females of all socioeconomic classes [2-4].

While bulimia was included as a diagnostic category in DSM-III, research related to adequately describing and classifying the bulimia syndrome and the more narrowly defined sister syndrome, bulimia nervosa, is more recent [2-4]. Consequently, sophisticated epidemiologic studies have not yet been published. The purpose of this chapter is to examine our existing knowledge about the frequency of bulimic behaviors, the prevalence of the bulimia syndrome, and the factors that may be associated with the onset of that illness.

With increasing demand for more treatment resources for bulimia, the determination of the prevalence of bulimia in the general population is essential if we are to know what the potential needs for treatment might be. A related question of major importance is whether the incidence of bulimia is increasing.

Two problems that confound bulimia research in general are amplified in epidemiology research: the definition of binge eating and the selection of appropriate inclusion criteria to define the bulimia syndrome. While there is agreement that binge eating consists of eating an unusually large quantity of food over a brief period of time, researchers differ on whether the latter subjective definition of binge eating should be quantified in terms of amount of food consumed and whether the factor of loss of control should be introduced into the definition. Second, the present DSM-III criteria for classification of the bulimia syndrome are being challenged. This controversy further contributes to the difficulty of developing inclusion criteria for self-report questionnaires on prevalence. Interpretation of prevalence study results is even further complicated by the use of inclusion criteria for bulimia nervosa and bulimarexia in some prevalence studies.

DEFINITION AND FREQUENCY OF BULIMIC BEHAVIORS

Earlier studies [5-8] involving individuals who might now be diagnosed as having bulimia did not emphasize the high frequency of bulimic behaviors in the general population, as they were directed at differentiating between normal and compulsive eating [5], treating potential neurophysiological abnormalities [6,7], establishing inclusion criteria to define compulsive eating [7], or defining personality traits of compulsive eaters [8]. It wasn't until the studies of Hawkins and Clement in 1980 [9] and of Halmi et al in 1981 [10], that we became aware of the high frequency of bulimic behaviors in the popu-

Table 23.1

Diagnostic Criteria for Bulimia (DSM-III)

*A. Recurrent episodes of binge-eating (rapid consumption of a large amount of food in a discrete period of time, usually less than two hours).

B. At least three of the following:
1. consumption of high-caloric, easily ingested food during a binge
2. inconspicious eating during a binge
3. termination of such eating episodes by abdominal pain, sleep, social interruption, or self-induced vomiting
4. repeated attempts to lose weight by severely restrictive diets, self-induced vomiting, or use of cathartics or diuretics
5. frequent weight fluctuations greater than ten pounds due to alternating binges and fasts

*C. Awareness that eating pattern is abnormal and fear of not being able to stop eating voluntarily.

*D. Depressed mood and self-deprecating thoughts following eating binges.

E. The bulimic episodes are not due to Anorexia Nervosa or any known physical disorder.

*Essential features of Bulimia for the purposes of prevalence studies.

Diagnostic Criteria for Bulimia Nervosa

A. Powerful and intractable urges to overeat.

B. Attempts to avoid the fattening effects of food by inducing vomiting and/or abusing purgatives.

C. Have a morbid fear of being fat.

---

lation. In this section, we will review the frequency of the behaviors that are associated with the inclusion criteria for bulimia based on the diagnostic criteria specified by DSM-III [1], and the inclusion criteria for bulimia nervosa as defined by Russell [4]. Specific questions from self-report questionnaires that were used to operationalize DSM-III diagnostic criteria and bulimia nervosa criteria will be discussed. Finally, problems related to the use of self-report questionnaires designed to assess the prevalence of bulimia or bulimia nervosa will be discussed.

Inclusion criteria for prevalence studies may be designed to elicit the prevalence of bulimia or bulimia nervosa. The DSM-III criteria for bulimia [1] and Russell's criteria for bulimia nervosa [4] are listed in table 1. Those studies, which state that the prevalence of bulimia is based on all the essential features of bulimia, indicate that criteria A, C, and D have been included [10,11]. Criterion B may not considered to be an essential feature, since only three of five behaviors need to be endorsed.

Some researchers have reduced the number of subjects who meet the inclusion criteria by quantifying binge-eating behavior and adding other quantifying and qualifying statements such as weekly self-induced vomiting and/or laxative abuse [11,12]. This quantification may be important to more closely define the number of individuals who are potential treatment candidates. However, there is no assurance that the group of subjects identified by these more restrictive criteria desire treatment or view their behavior as problematic [13]. With this introduction, we will now consider the frequency of bulimic behaviors determined by responses to questions designed to operationalize DSM-III criteria for bulimia and criteria for bulimia nervosa.

Many researchers developing inclusion criteria for self-report questionnaires on bulimic behaviors introduce the element of loss of control into questions relevant to inclusion criteria for binge eating (DSM-III Criterion A). While the issue of quantifying the amount of food consumed during a binge remains, it has not been addressed by most researchers doing prevalence studies [13]. Hawkins and Clement, in their original study, used three statements, that of "uncontrolled excessive eating," "rapid eating," and "eating until painfully full" [9]. Two studies used "eating an enormous amount of food over a short period of time" and "uncontrollable urges to eat and then eating until physically ill" [10,11]. Our research group approached loss of control by adding to the binge-eating phrase, "in a way which would be embarrassing if others saw you" [12].

Table 2 summarizes binge-eating frequencies from several American studies [9-12]. These and other studies [14,15] support the premise that binge eating is a frequent behavior in both males and females with the frequency of binge eating reported by American women ranging between 57% and 79% [9-12] and by British women from 26% in a study of clinic patients [14] to 40% in a study of students [15]. Weekly binge eating has been reported by 7% to 14% of English women [14,15] and by 17% to 21% of American women [11,12]. Two American studies cite a lower frequency of binge eating for males [9,12], while one noted very little difference between males and females [10]. Weekly binge eating has been reported by 11% of males [12].

In studies based on DSM-III criteria, two questions have been asked to meet DSM-III Criterion C: "Do you consider yourself a binge-eater?" and "Are there times when you are afraid you cannot stop eating voluntarily?" [10,11]. In response to questions relevant to DSM-III Criterion C (table 2), women are much more apt than males (35% versus 8%) to consider themselves binge eaters [10]. Fifteen percent of female high school students endorsed this statement [11]. Fear of loss of

Table 23.2 Reported Frequency of Behaviors Associated with Inclusion Criteria for "Essential Features" of Bulimia

	Hawkins & Clement (9)		Halmi et al (10)		Pyle et al (12)		Johnson et al (11)
Population	College Students		College Summer School		College Freshman		High School Students
Sample	*Female*	*Male*	*Female*	*Male*	*Female*	*Male*	*Female*
	n=160	n=54	n=212	n=119	n=575	n=780	n=1268
Response Rate	88%	83%	66%		98%		98%
1. Criterion A (Binge-Eating)							
Binge-eating behavior	79%	45%	68%	60%	61%	42%	57%
Uncontrollable urge to binge-eat			54%	36%	17%	11%	19%
Weekly binge-eating							21%
2. Criterion C (problem eating/loss of control)							
See oneself as binge-eater	11%	0%	35%	8%			15%
Fear of loss of control over eating			29%	15%			24%
3. Criterion D (depressed/self-deprecatory)							
Depressed and self-deprecatory			62%	30%	45%	11%	42%
Depressed	29%	0%					
Self-deprecatory	21%	0%					

control over eating was reported by at least twice as many women as men [9,10]. One fourth of high school females reported a fear that they would lose control over their eating behavior [11].

DSM-III Criterion D, regarding depression and self-deprecatory thoughts, has been represented by one statement in three studies; being "miserable and annoyed after binge eating," [10,11] or being "depressed and down on yourself after binge eating" [12]. Hawkins and Clement [9] required endorsement of two statements to satisfy this criterion, "I hate myself after binge eating," and "I feel very depressed after binge eating." The feeling of being depressed and self- deprecatory after binge eating is much more common in women than men (table 2) [10,12]. Hawkins and Clement [9] found that while 29% of females endorsed being depressed after binge eating and 21% endorsed hating themselves after binge eating, neither statement was endorsed by any of the males (n=54) in the study.

Our group reported the frequency of nonessential features of bulimia (DSM-III Criterion B). It was found that 20% of female students reported binge eating on high-carbohydrate food; 8% preferred to eat in secret; 5% ate until interrupted by pain, self-induced vomiting, or other people; 51% used some form of weight control to lower their weight; and 20% had frequent weight fluctuations of 10 lb or more. These behaviors occurred at similar rates in males except for weight control measures and frequent weight fluctuations, which were approximately twice as frequent in women [12].

Studies of clinic patients with bulimia have shown that most patients use self-induced vomiting and/or laxative abuse as weight control measures [2,3]. For this reason, many prevalence studies include questions relative to one or more of the three criteria for bulimia nervosa. Cooper and Fairburn [14] have operationalized the criteria for bulimia nervosa by asking subjects if they have "uncontrollable episodes of binge eating," if they "vomit after binge eating," and if they are often "terrified by becoming fat." The latter criterion seems more specific than "I have a fear of becoming fat" [12]. Both American and English studies report the frequency of behaviors associated with bulimia nervosa. Six percent to 16% of the female population have reported self-induced vomiting [9-12,14,15), with 3% reporting that behavior on a current basis [14]. The 16% figure was somewhat alarming in that it occurred in high school females, which suggests that self-induced vomiting may be increasing relative to other bulimic behaviors [11]. The presence of self-inducing vomiting in males has been reported to be 6% [10,12]. Weekly self-induced vomiting has been reported in the range of 2% to 4% for females [11,12] and 1% for males [12] in

American studies. English studies indicate that a smaller percentage of weekly self-induced vomiting (from 0% to 1%) is reported by women [14,15]. We have far less data on the "morbid fear of being fat" [4], with our group noting that 63% of freshman college women and 32% of males reported a "fear of being fat." However, this was only slightly lower than that reported by "bulimic" female students (78%) [12]. In an English study, 21% of adult women endorsed a more restrictive statement, "often terrified of becoming fat" [14].

Ideally, prevalence studies involve the administration of a standardized, validated questionnaire to a sample, representative of the general population, through a structured interview. Unfortunately, such rigorous methodology has not been used thus far for bulimia research. Studies to date have been limited by the use of self-report questionnaires. Another limitation has been that most of the published questionnaire studies involve samples of high school or college students [9-12,15,16]. Only recently have other samples been surveyed [14,17]. A multitude of problems may confound results reported in questionnaire studies. Researchers must select wording that the surveyed population will understand, and at the same time correctly represent the diagnostic criteria on which the inclusion questions are based. Scope versus response rate must also be balanced in questionnaires. Questionnaires designed to operationalize DSM-III diagnostic criteria are often kept brief to maximize response rate [13,16]. However, this may preclude the detail necessary to measure lifetime prevalence for the disorder, and it may hinder the search for details about the psychopathological features of bulimia. The method of administration of a questionnaire can also greatly affect the response rate, with the lowest response rate usually obtained by direct mailings [16] and the highest by administration of the questionnaire by individuals who are in some way directly involved with the participants [11,12,14]. Many researchers prefer anonymous questionnaires, because the response rate is higher and the degree of honesty in response may also be greater [13]. With few exceptions [12,16], questionnaires used in reported studies were not validated by administration to eating disordered populations to determine their specificity for identifying that particular disorder. Also, controversy persists about whether bulimics overreport on questionnaires to please researchers [14,16] or underreport because they wish to keep their illness a secret [10,15,17,18].

To summarize, available studies clearly show that binge eating is a common problem. Self-induced vomiting to control weight is less common, with only a small percentage of people admitting to episodes of binge eating followed by self-induced vomiting. These behaviors are much less likely to occur on a weekly basis and rarely occur on a daily basis. Many behaviors and attitudes related to bulimia are more common in females, especially the pattern of feeling depressed and having self-deprecatory thoughts after binge-eating. Other attitudes more common in women are fear of loss of control over eating, seeing oneself as a binge eater, and fear of being fat. The feelings and cognitions of the individuals who engage in bulimic behavior merit further study, particularly the role of anxiety, which for the most part has been neglected. Having reviewed the process for development of operationalized criteria for the diagnosis of bulimia and for bulimia nervosa, we may proceed to our discussion of the prevalence of the bulimia syndrome.

THE PREVALENCE OF BULIMIA

Earlier work by Wermuth [7], which revealed that there was only one case of "compulsive eating" found in a retrospective chart review of 650 medical cases, illustrates the secretive nature of the bulimia syndrome and the ease with which cases may be overlooked. A study by Stangler and Printz in 1980 brought to our attention the high frequency of bulimia [18]. This retrospective chart review to check DSM-III diagnoses determined that 5.3% of 318 women and 1.4% of 282 men coming to a university student psychiatric clinic for treatment met the DSM-III diagnostic criteria for bulimia. The authors suggested that this figure was underreported, since a number of cases were revealed during treatment and were not diagnosed at evaluation. The same pattern was true of the development of interest in bulimia nervosa in England. Russell's original group of 30 cases was collected over a period of 6-1/2 years from 1972 to 1978 [4]. It wasn't until Fairburn and Cooper brought attention to the frequency of this problem and the small percentage of individuals who entered treatment that the high prevalence of this illness was suspected [19].

Table 3 summarizes much of the current work describing the prevalence of bulimia and bulimia nervosa using self-report questionnaires. The prevalence of bulimia, as defined in the questionnaires, ranges between 8% and 19% for students, with the higher percentage reported by studies involving eastern populations [10,16] and the lower percentage in two midwestern studies [11,12]. A recent survey of adult women demonstrated that 10% reported behaviors that met operationalized DSM-III criteria for bulimia [17]. The percentage of males with "bulimia" ranges from 0% to 6% [10,12,16], with less than 1 in 300 satisfying the more restrictive criteria of weekly binge eating and self-induced vomiting [12]. The prevalence of bulimia nervosa

in adult women in England was reported to be 2% using the criteria of uncontrollable binge eating, self-induced vomiting, and often terrified of being fat [14]. Fairburn [13] has observed that subjects meeting the diagnostic criteria for bulimia nervosa are also likely to meet the DSM-III diagnostic criteria for bulimia.

The use of more restrictive inclusion criteria, such as weekly binge eating and self-induced vomiting, has been advocated by our group as a method of identifying "bulimic" students who more closely resemble bulimic patients [12]. Our survey found that the sample defined as "bulimic" students without the restriction of weekly binge eating or self-induced vomiting differed from bulimic patients in that they tended to be overweight binge eaters who used fasting as a weight control measure. The clinic patients with bulimia who responded to the questionnaire, on the other hand, were more likely to be of normal weight, rather than overweight, and use self-induced vomiting as their primary method of weight control rather than fasting or restrictive dieting [12].

To summarize, the bulimia syndrome is more common in women. "Bulimic" students are different than bulimic patients unless restrictive criteria that include weekly binge eating and self-induced vomiting are applied to quantify the bulimic behavior. When these restrictive criteria are used, the prevalence of bulimia corresponds more closely to that of bulimia nervosa. Data also suggest that very few individuals with bulimia or bulimia nervosa seek treatment.

ETIOLOGY

A discussion of the factors contributing to the development of eating disorders is muddied by a lack of prospective studies regarding the development of bulimic behaviors. Information that we have available from bulimics and their families is retrospective and therefore colored by the effects of the eating disorder. The presence of specific personality traits in bulimic patients does not mean that they had these traits before their illness. Post-illness self-assessment of premorbid personality may be distorted. Depression, which is common in bulimics, will serve as an example. Severely depressed people may view themselves as having always been worthless, even though that is not the case. Similarly, we have seen bulimic patients who have stated that they always had low self-esteem and always needed to please others. These same patients may return for follow-up interviews a year after ending the behavior to tell us that they did not have either low self-esteem or the need to please others before their illness. A major need for future research is for a prospective longitudinal study that follows subjects from at least mid-high school

Table 23.3 The Reported Prevalence of Bulimia and Bulimia Nervosa

Source	Population	Response Rate	Inclusion Criteria[a]	Responding Sample	Prevalence for the Disorder	Bulimia with Weekly Binge-Eating	Bulimia & Weekly Binge-Eating Vomiting/Laxative Abuse
Halmi et al (10)	Eastern College Summer School	66%	DSM-III A, C & D	212 Female 119 Male	19% 6%	2%	
Pyle et al (12)	Midwestern College Freshman	98%	DSM-III A, B & D	575 Female 780 Male	8% 1%	4% 0.4%	1% 0.3%
Cooper and Fairburn (14)	Family Planning Clinic	96%	Bulimia Nervosa	369 Female	2%		
Johnson et al (11)[b]	Midwestern Public High School	98%	DSM-III A,C2,D	1268 Female	8%	5%	1%
Pope et al (19)[c]	Shopping Center Patrons	99%	DSM-III A,B,C1,D	300 Female	10%		
Pope et al (16)[c]	Urban Public College	50%	DSM-III A,B,C1,D	102 Female 47 Male	19% none		
	Private Women's College Seniors	64%	DSM-III A,B,C1,D	287 Female	13%		
	Surburban High School	84%	DSM-III A,B,C1,D	155 Female 107 Male	6% none		

[a]See Table 1
[b]Omits "awareness that the eating problem is abnormal" (Criterion C)
[c]Omits "fear of not being able to stop voluntarily" (Criterion C)

through mid-college and considers the psychopathologic parameters related to the development of bulimic behaviors as well as specific events that may be related to the onset. With this in mind, we will discuss the information available about the sociocultural, familial, characterological, and environmental factors that may contribute to the development of bulimia.

The current emphasis on thinness in our culture has been identified as a potential factor associated with the development of bulimia and bulimia nervosa [13,20]. There is mounting evidence of the increasing value placed on thinness in our society [20]. While the cultural dichotomy of exposure to unlimited amounts of food and an emphasis on thinness may contribute to eating disorders, there is at present little data to prove causality.

Information about families of bulimics is lacking. Herzog [21] has pointed out that 50% of the bulimics he studied came from homes broken by the death or severe physical illness of one parent. This is much higher than our own earlier findings of 9% of patients (3 of 34) who experienced death of parent, separation of parents, or were adopted [2]. We later found that 15% of 275 bulimics presenting at our eating disorder clinic had divorced parents (unpublished data).

Predisposing personality characteristics are even more difficult to evaluate. We are not aware of published studies that evaluate adult bulimics relative to predisposing personality traits. Consequently, the only studies available that provide clues to personality traits in bulimic individuals come from retrospective reports of subjects with bulimarexia [22] and bulimic anorectic adolescents [23] and adults [24]. Boskind-Lodahl pointed out that the bulimarectics that she saw had a high need for validation before the illness and felt that developing a better body would solve their problems [22]. Strober reported impulsiveness and weight control problems in bulimic anorectic adolescents before the onset of the illness [23]. Casper and associates [24] in comparing bulimic anorectics with restrictive anorectics noted that before the onset of the illness both groups were reported to have been industrious, achievement-oriented, and dichotomous thinkers. Bulimic anorectics, unlike restrictive anorectics, were outgoing, articulate, socially confident, sexually experienced, and had more dysphoria and less optimism about the future.

Neurological problems have been suggested as a possible factor in the onset of bulimic behaviors. Rau et al [6] and later Weumuth [7] reported on a series of "compulsive eaters" who demonstrated a high frequency of abnormal EEGs. While treatment with phenytoin was effective in some cases, improvement was not correlated with EEG findings. Our group has reported that the rate of abnormalities in EEG tracings

for bulimics probably is not different from the rate in the general population [25].

Russell's earlier findings [4] suggested to some that anorexia nervosa might be a cause for bulimia [26]. This suggestion has not been supported by Halmi's findings of only one case of anorexia nervosa in 355 students with a high prevalence of bulimia [10] and the recent survey findings of Pope et al [16] suggesting a relatively low prevalence of anorexia nervosa in student groups that have a higher prevalence of bulimia.

Considerable attention has been paid to precipitating events for bulimia, that is, those events that may be associated with the onset of the disorder. Voluntary dieting has been often associated with the onset of the disorder. Voluntary dieting before the onset of bulimia was reported by 88% of a small series of patients coming to our clinic [2]. Johnson et al [27] reported voluntary dieting in association with onset in 34% of a large series of bulimic subjects. On the other hand, concern over diet and weight also seems prominent in the typical student population. Johnson et al [11] reported that 52% of high school females reported dieting by the time they were 14, 37% were on a diet at the time of the survey, and 14% of the population reported being chronic dieters.

The high frequency of dieting behavior before the onset of bulimia has added to speculation that being overweight may contribute to the development of the bulimia syndrome [10]. Halmi et al [10] reported that the "bulimic" students had a history of being overweight and had more of a tendency to be overweight currently than nonbulimic students. Fairburn and Cooper [19] reported a high number of weight fluctuations, both above and below the norm, in those individuals who later developed symptoms of bulimia nervosa, but found no indication that a majority of patients had a history of being overweight. We are aware of no data to support the argument that a majority of bulimic patients are overweight before the onset of the illness, although they may view themselves as being overweight.

The presence of stressful events at the time of the onset of bulimia has been reported [2,27]. While studies at our center found that 88% of a series of bulimic patients reported some type of loss or stressful event [2], Johnson et al [27] reported that only 7% of their subjects reported conflict before the onset, with the same percentage reporting a significant loss. They found that a much higher percent of subjects (40%) reported the onset of bulimia at a time when there were a high number of unpleasant emotions present [27]. Reports of stress-induced onset would suggest that individuals who are prone to develop bulimia may have problems with coping skills or with cognitive style.

SUMMARY

While there have been several useful studies reported on the prevalence of bulimia in the general population, their research design has not been sufficiently rigorous to encourage definitive statements regarding the prevalence of bulimia in the general population. Taking these limitations into consideration, the bulimia syndrome as we see it in patients probably occurs in 1% to 2% of females in the target age of 18 to 30. This corresponds to the reported prevalence of bulimia nervosa. The higher prevalence figures reported may represent an earlier stage of the illness, may be identifying individuals who have a predisposition to develop the illness, or recording isolated symptoms that occur over time but never together in the person's life span. Prevalence studies may also be identifying a significant number of overeaters. Before the bulimic illness, individuals may be concerned about weight, with the bulimia syndrome developing after a combination of dieting and external or internal stress of undetermined severity. We must add to this limitied knowledge regarding the causes and prevalence of bulimia and bulimia nervosa to successfully develop programs for prevention and treatment of this debilitating syndrome.

REFERENCE

1. Diagnostic and Statistical Manual of Mental Disorders (DSM-III). American Psychiatric Association, Washington, D.C. 1980; 69.
2. Pyle RL, Mitchell JE, and Eckert ED. Bulimia: a report of 34 cases. J Clin Psychiatry, 1981; 42:60-4.
3. Mitchell JE, Pyle RL. The bulimia syndrome in normal weight in dividuals: a review. International Journal of Eating Disorders, 1982; 1:61-73.
4. Russell G. Bulimia nervosa: an ominous variant of anorexia nervosa. Psychol Med, 1979; 9:429-48.
5. Ondercin PA. Compulsive eating in college women. Jr of College Student Personnel, March 1979; 153-157.
6. Rau JH, Struve FA, Green RS. Electroencephalographic correlates of compulsive eating. Clin Electroencephalogr, 1979; 10:180-9.
7. Wermuth BM, Davis RL, Hollister LE, et al. Phenytoin treatment of the binge-eating syndrome. Am J Psychiatry, 1977; 134:1249-53.
8. Dunn PK, Ondercin PA. Personality variables related to compulsive eating in college women. Jr of Clin Psychol, 1980; 37:43-9.
9. Hawkins RC II, Clement PF. Development and construct validation of a self-report measure of binge-eating tendencies. Addictive Behaviors, 1980; 7:435-9.
10. Halmi KA, Falk JR, Schwartz E. Binge-eating and vomiting: A survey of a college population. Psychol Med, 1981; 11:697-706.
11. Johnson CL, Lewis C, Love S, et al. A descriptive survey of dieting and bulimic behavior in a female high school population. In Understanding Anorexia Nervosa and Bulimia. Columbus, Ohio: Ross Laboratories, 1983;14-18.
12. Pyle RL, Mitchell JE, Eckert ED, et al. The incidence of bulimia in freshman college students. International Journal of Eating Disorders, 1983; 2:75-85.
13. Fairburn CG. Bulimia: Its epidemiology and management. In Stunkard AJ, Steller E, eds. Eating and its Disorders. New York: Raven Press, 1983;
14. Cooper PJ, Fairburn CG. Binge-eating and self-induced vomiting in the community. A preliminary study. Brit J Psychiat, 1983; 142:139-44.
15. Clarke MG, Palmer RL. Eating attitudes and neurotic symptoms in University students. Brit J Psychiat, 1983; 142:299-304.
16. Pope HG, Hudson JI, Yurgelun-Todd D, et al. Prevalence of anorexia nervosa and bulimia in three student populations. International Journal of Eating Disorders, 1984; 3:45-51.
17. Pope HG, Hudson JI, Yurgelun-Todd D. Anorexia nervosa and bulimia among 300 surburban women shoppers. Am J Psychiatry, 1984; 141:292- 4.
18. Stangler RS, Printz AM. DSM-III: psychiatric diagnosis in a university population. Am J Psychiatry, 1980; 137:937-40.
19. Fairburn CG, Cooper PJ. Self-induced vomiting and bulimia nervosa: an undetected problem. Br Med J, 1982; 284:1153-5.
20. Garner DM, Garfinkel PE, Schwartz DM, et al. Cultural expectation of thinness in women. Psych Rep, 1980; 47:483-91.
21. Herzog DB. Bulimia: the secretive syndrome. Psychosomatics, 1982; 23:481-7.
22. Boskind-Lodahl M. Cinderella's step-sisters: A feminist perspective on anorexia nervosa and bulimia. Signs: Journal of Women in Culture and Society, 1976; 2:342-56.
23. Strober M. The significance of bulimia in juvenile anorexia nervosa: An exploration of possible etiologic factors. International Jorunal of Eating disorders, 1981; 1:28-43.
24. Casper RC, Eckert ED, Halmi KA, et al. Bulimia: Its incidence and clinical importance in patients with anorexia nervosa. Arch Gen Psychiatry, 1980; 37:1030-40.
25. Mitchell JM, Hosfield W, Pyle RL. EEG findings in patients with the bulimia syndrome. International Journal of Eating Disorders, 1983; 2:17-23.
26. Slade P. Towards a functional analysis of anorexia nervosa and bulimia. Brit J of Clin Psychol, 1982; 21:167-79.
27. Johnson CL, Stuckey MK, Lewis LD, et al. Bulimia: a descriptive survey of 316 cases. International Journal of Eating Disorders, 1983; 2:3-16.

Chapter 24

The Diagnosis and Clinical Characteristics of Bulimia

James E. Mitchell and Richard L. Pyle

The DSM-III-R category of bulimia nervosa describes an eating disorder characterized by binge-eating episodes as well as other abnormal eating-related behaviors. The choice of the term bulimia to label this syndrome in the DSM-III was in a sense unfortunate, since the term bulimia is also used simply to indicate binge eating episodes. However, this syndrome encompasses far more than binge eating episodes. Patients with this disorder usually demonstrate markedly abnormal eating patterns and eat little or no food when they are not binge eating. They also frequently self-induce vomiting or abuse laxatives in an attempt to control their weight.

This chapter will begin by discussing and contrasting the diagnostic systems for bulimia and bulimia nervosa that are in widespread clinical use. We will then turn to a discussion of the behavioral characteristics of the bulimic eating pattern, the psychological and family characteristics of this group of patients, and the medical complications and laboratory abnormalities associated with bulimia nervosa.

DIAGNOSTIC ISSUES

Several different systems have been suggested to diagnose the clinical syndrome of bulimia nervosa or clinical syndromes that appear to closely resemble it. The two systems most commonly used are the DSM-III-R and a system originally proposed by Russell in 1979, which describes a syndrome with considerable clinical overlap [1]. The former system is used commonly in the

United States and the latter system in England. Several other terms have been suggested to describe similar syndromes, including "bulimarexia" [2] and "the dietary chaos syndrome" [3]. However, most researchers and clinicians currently seem to favor bulimia nervosa.

The DSM-III criteria were recently revised, as follows:

1. Recurrent episodes of binge eating (rapid consumption of a large amount of food in a discrete period of time, usually less than two hours).
2. At least three of the following:
   i. consumption of high calorie, easily ingested food during a binge;
   ii. inconspicuous eating during a binge;
   iii. termination of such eating episodes by abdominal pain, sleep, social interruption, or self-induced vomiting;
   iv. repeated attempts to lose weight by severely restrictive diets, self-induced vomiting, or use of cathartics or diuretics; and
   v. frequent weight fluctuations greater than 10 lb because of alternating binges and fasts.
3. Awareness that the eating pattern is abnormal and fear of not being able to stop eating voluntarily.
4. Depressed mood and self-deprecating thoughts following eating binges.
5. The bulimic episodes are not due to anorexia nervosa or any known physical disorder.

An examination of the DSM-III criteria indicates quite clearly that the emphasis was on the binge-eating behavior itself. Such related problems as self-induced vomiting and laxative abuse are mentioned, but were not required for the diagnosis.

The syndrome of bulimia nervosa as originally described by Russell is diagnosed using the following criteria [1]:

1. The patient suffers from powerful and intractable urges to overeat.
2. The patient seeks to avoid "fattening" affects of food by inducing vomiting or abusing purgatives or both.
3. The patient has a morbid fear of becoming obese.

The criteria differ significantly from the DSM-III bulimia criteria in several ways, the most important of which may be that the presence of self-induced vomiting or laxative abuse is required for the diagnosis. The inclusion of the requirement for self-induced vomiting and/or laxative abuse in the bulimia nervosa criteria indicates that a more selective sample of patients will be identified. This is particularly important in view of research that has demonstrated that binge eating is a fairly common behavior in the general population [4-11]. The DSM-III bulimia criteria, when broadly interpreted, may therefore identify many individuals in the general population. The bulimia nervosa criteria of Russell probably are less likely to do so. Another essential point is that neither of these sets of criteria include frequency parameters. Since is is known that experimentation with bulimic behavior is common in young women [5-7], the lack of a frequency criterion suggests that people without clinically significant eating problems could be identified by either set of criteria. In defense of these criteria, it should be noted that both sets were proposed when little clinical work had been published concerning bulimic patients. Despite this, the authors showed considerable clinical accumen in delineating these syndromes.

In the recent revision of the DSM-III (DSM-III-R), bulimia is renamed bulmia nervosa, and the diagnostic criteria have been tightened up significantly, now including the following requirements:

1. Recurrent episodes of binge-eating (rapid consumption of a large amount of food in a discrete period of time).
2. A feeling of lack of control over eating behavior during the eating binges.
3. The person regularly engages in either self-induced vomiting, use of laxatives or diuretics, strict dieting or fasting, or vigorous exercise in order to prevent weight gain.
4. A minimum average of two binge-eating episodes a week for at least three months.
5. Persistent over concern about body shape and weight.

These criteria continue to emphasize binge-eating but now include a minimum frequency and duration of symptoms criterion. The last criterion beings the DSM-III-R into a closer alignment with the British criteria, and it appears that the DSM-III-R criteria will offer improved diagnostic guidepoints for clinicians, although they may be too broad for research purposes.

CLINICAL CHARACTERISTICS

Several series of patients with bulimia or bulimia nervosa have been reported in the literature. These series suggest that a variety of problems occur in these patients, some involving eating behavior and some involving other areas [1,12-19].

Available studies indicate that the usual age of onset is between 16 and 19 years of age [13,15,19]. Most patients are ill for several years before seeking treatment; the average age of first treatment contact is about age 24 [14-19]. Although bulimia and bulimia nervosa are primarily problems of young women, we have seen women in their 40s or 50s with this disorder who have been actively bulimic for more than 20 years. Less than 10% of the cases reported in the literature have been male [1,19].

As indicated previously, various abnormal eating-related behaviors have been reported by patients with bulimia [14-17,19]. The hallmark of the illness is binge eating, which is required for the diagnosis. Published frequency data indicate that most patients with bulimia binge eat once a day or more often [14-17,19]. The details concerning binge-eating episodes will be discussed later. Self-induced vomiting is also a prevalent and frequent behavior in this patient population. Prevalence data indicate that 70% to 95% of bulimic patients practice self-induced vomiting on a regular basis, and frequency data indicate that most who self-induce vomiting do so once a day or more often [14,16,17,19]. Another abnormal eating-related behavior commonly reported by these patients is laxative abuse [14,16,17,19]. Although this problem has been less intensively studied, published reports indicate that between 15% and 60% of patients with bulimia abuse laxatives in an attempt to rid themselves of excess food or to lose weight. A significant minority, perhaps as many as 20%, abuse laxatives on a daily basis [13,17,19]. The amounts of laxatives ingested are usually in excess of recommended dosage. Some patients who have become tolerant to the effects use amounts several hundred times the recommended dose.

A variety of other abnormal eating-related behaviors have been described in patients with bulimia, including diuretic abuse (33.1%), excessive use of enemas (7%), and chewing and splitting out food without swallowing it to prevent weight gain (64.5%). Although these behaviors have not been intensively studied, they are common enough to be considered as characteristics of the syndrome in some patients.

Meal intake patterns have also been studied in patients with bulimia. Most bulimic patients do not eat normally when they are not binge eating [14,15]. Their meal pattern is usually characterized by fasting or minimal food intake between binge-eating episodes. When these patients fast they become hungry, which may serve as a powerful stimulus for the next binge-eating episode. Therefore, in most cases the bulimic eating patterns should best be characterized as a pattern of alternating binge eating and fasting.

Our problem in discussing bulimia and bulimia nervosa concerns the definition, or the lack of definition, as to what actually constitutes a binge-eating episode or eating binge. DSM-III-R criteria suggest that binge eating involves the ingestion of a large amount of food, and available data indicates that patients usually do eat large amounts of food when binge eating [15,20]. Russell originally reported that some patients consumed between 5,000 and 20,000 calories during a binge-eating episode [1]. Other researchers have substantiated this finding [14,5,19,20]. However, not every patient with bulimia nervosa eats such large amounts of food during a binge-eating episode. A few patients, if asked to describe their behavior in detail, actually report an amount that many people would consider only slightly in excess of a normal meal. Patients tend to consume high-carbohydrate or high-fat foods during binge-eating episodes. Items such as ice cream, candy, bread, and doughnuts are commonly ingested [20,21]. These food choices are particularly interesting in view of the fact that these patients usually avoid such foods at other times because they consider them fattening. They eat them only when they are planning to "get rid" of the food through vomiting or laxative abuse. Binge-eating episodes are usually pursued in isolation. Although they can be temporally related to stressful life events, such as problems at work or interpersonal difficulties, for many patients binge eating eventually becomes an institutionalized part of the daily routine [13,15,21]. An example would be a bulimic individual who each day stops at a store on the way home from work, buys the foods necessary for binge eating, goes home, consumes the food over the period of an hour or so, and then self-induces vomiting. Although stress at work may have initially contributed to the development of this pattern, the pattern may continue even if the stress is no longer active. As this scenario suggests, binge-eating episodes tend to take place late in the day when individuals return home from work or school. Many patients state that they eat very rapidly when binge eating and don't really taste the food. They may read, watch TV, or engage in other activities while eating.

How does this disorder begin? Little is known about the onset of bulimia nervosa. Some work has suggested a possible link between the onset of bulimia nervosa and traumatic events, but the retrospective nature of such data makes the validity of the finding open to question [14]. Several authors have noted that bulimia nervosa tends to begin during a period of dieting [14,17,21]. However, it must be remembered that most patients with bulimia nervosa are chronically concerned about their weight, and many may have been dieting off and on much of the time during adolescence. A history of anorexia nervosa is not uncommon in these patients, with various series reporting that 30% to 80% of patients with bulimia nervosa have a history of weight loss sufficient to qualify for such a diagnosis [1,13-19]. This finding, coupled with the finding that the symptom of bulimia is relatively common in patients with anorexia nervosa, suggest that these two disorders represent parts of a spectrum of eating problems.

Another important point when considering the pathogenesis of this disorder is the apparent increasing incidence of this disorder in our culture. Why does our culture seem to predispose to significant eating problems such as anorexia nervosa and bulimia nervosa? It is interesting to speculate that the abundance of food combined with the cultural preoccupation with thinness as a model of attractiveness may be involved. However, such a simple cultural model does not explain why certain individuals develop this problem and others do not. This is a particularly intriguing question when one considers that experimentation with bulimic behaviors appears to be common among young people. Why does this behavior escalate out of control in a few individuals, while most give it up before it becomes an ongoing pattern of behavior? This is the crucial question that cannot yet be answered.

Unfortunately, the problem of bulimia nervosa is not only a problem of eating. A variety of other problems have been described in association with this condition, depression being one of the most common [1,14,19,21]. Patients with bulimia nervosa frequently have been noted to be depressed at the time of evaluation [13,14,18]. The prevalence of depressive symptoms in these patients has led several clinicians to investigate the possible associations between bulimia nervosa and primary affective disorder. Several lines of evidence suggest a close relationship between the two disorders, including a high rate of nonsuppression on the dexamethasone suppression test [22-26], an unexpectedly high rate of affective disorders in relatives of patients with bulimia nervosa [25,27], and the apparent utility of antidepressant compounds in the treatment of patients with bulimia [27-31]. Also, Hudson and associates found that the majority of patients with bulimia met DSM-III criteria for major affective disorders using the structured diagnostic interview schedule [23]. What has not been adequately studied is the course of depressive symptoms with improvement in eating behavior. Does depression improve if bulimic symptoms normalize? Or does the depressive component require separate treatment? These questions require further study.

Several other problems have been described in association with bulimia, including problems with impulse control [14], stealing behavior [32], and an unexpectedly high rate of chemical dependency problems [14,18]. Our group reported that 8 of 34 patients with bulimia previously had received chemical dependency treatment and that one additional patient was felt to have a diagnosis of a alcoholism [14]. Herzog found that 10 of 30 bulimic patients reported alcoholism in at least one first-degree family member [18]. Hatsukami and associates discussed the similarities between bulimic behavior and the behavioral pattern associated with drug abuse, including loss of control over the use of the substance, intense preoccupation with the substance, social isolation accompanying the behavior, and the reinforcing nature of the behavior [33]. It would appear that for some patients there is a relationship between the abuse of food and the abuse of alcohol or other drugs. Certainly the presence of chemical abuse problems should be evaluated in every patient with bulimia.

Several lines of evidence suggest significant psychological impairment in patients with bulimia nervosa. Weiss and Ebert [32] compared a sample of normal-weight female bulimic patients with a sample of normal-weight female controls matched for age, socioeconomic status, and IQ. Bulimic patients demonstrated higher levels of psychopathology on all the instruments used and consistently rated themselves as sicker on all psychometric scales. They also indicated more impulsive behavior and a history of more suicide attempts, more psychiatric hospitalizations, more episodes of stealing, and more problems with drug abuse. Two MMPI studies also suggested psychological impairment in this group of patients. Hatsukami and associates demonstrated that the MMPI profile of patients with bulimia were similar to the MMPI profiles of women with alcohol and drug abuse problems, the composite profiles for both groups demonstrating elevations on the scales for depression, impulsivity, anger, anxiety, and social withdrawal [33]. Norman and Herzog [34] found similar results. Taken together, these studies suggest that many patients with bulimia nervosa have significant emotional disturbances, at least when they are actively bulimic. To what extent these represent stable ongoing personality

characteristics that antedate the bulimia nervosa is unknown. However, clinical experience with bulimic patients suggests that no single type of personality pattern is invariably present and that many patients appear to be reasonably stable and well-adjusted after their eating pattern normalizes.

When patients with bulimia nervosa are seen for evaluation, there is also often evidence of significant social impairment. Using structured self-rating scales, Johnson and Berndt [35] showed that individuals with bulimia report increased impairment in social adjustment compared with a community sample control group. The bulimic patients demonstrated a response pattern similar to the response pattern of a group of alcoholic patients.

One of the social parameters most commonly disrupted by bulimia nervosa is social relationships. Patients with this disorder frequently report that they have experienced difficulties with family, friends, or other significant people in their lives since the development of the problem. They find that they frequently have to lie to others about why food has disappeared, why they can't go out, or why they fail to show up for an appointment. Many also report that their work or school performance suffers, and some report financial problems because of the costs involved. Some of the individuals we have evaluated have taken second jobs or have had to declare bankruptcy because of the attendant financial problems. Overall, most patients with this disorder report that bulimia nervosa interferes a great deal with other aspects of their life [14,21,35].

Little is known about the longitudinal course of this illness. Many patients apparently experience an initial period of weight loss at the onset of bulimic symptoms. However, as the illness progresses, this pattern is reversed and patients may eventually gain weight [13]. This may reflect changes in the binge eating pattern itself in that patients may begin to binge eat more frequently and to consume more food during each binge-eating episode as the illness progresses.

SIGNS AND SYMPTOMS

Bulimia nervosa is associated with several potentially serious physical complications. However, there is usually nothing apparent on physical examination to indicate the severity of the problem. Complaints are frequently vague, including such things as lethargy, impaired concentration, and nonfocal abdominal pain. Commonly patients with bulimia may undergo physical evaluations for such complaints or because electrolyte abnormalities were found on screening laboratory work during a general physical examination. If the patients never mention their bulimic symptoms, the evaluating physician will often not be able to uncover any etiology for the complaints or the laboratory results.

Of the medical complications, most commonly encountered are fluid and electrolyte abnormalities. Russell originally reported hypokalemia as a complicating factor of this disorder [1]. Our group [19] subsequently reported that nearly 50% of a series of 168 patients with bulimia or atypical eating disorder demonstrated fluid or electrolyte abnormalities. Most commonly encountered were metabolic alkalosis (27.4%), hypochloremia (23.8%), and hypokalemia (13.7%). This pattern of abnormalities results from the self-induced vomiting or laxative abuse pattern seen in these patients. Metabolic acidosis is less commonly seen and may result from prolonged fasting or the acute diarrhea that may follow laxative abuse [44].

Salivary gland swelling has been reported in patients with bulimia [36], the parotid glands being most commonly effected. The clinical picture is one of painless swelling at the lateral angle of the jaw and is sometimes referred to as "puffy cheeks" by patients. Biopsy studies have shown normal tissue or asymptomatic noninflammatory changes. The pathophysiology of this problem is unclear. In our experience this complication is fairly common. Interestingly, the problem may persist for several months beyond normalization of eating patterns.

A complication that is fortunately rare, but unfortunately quite serious when it occurs in association with bulimia, is gastric dilatation [37,38]. Although usually described in patients with anorexia nervosa who are undergoing refeeding, this condition can also be seen in patients of normal weight who binge eat. In a review of this problem, Saul and associates reported a case of a patient with a history of anorexia nervosa who excessively overate, developed gastric infarction, and subsequent perforation of the stomach [37]. Saul and associates reviewed 66 such cases of spontaneous rupture of the stomach and felt that approximately half of the cases were related to the ingestion of large amounts of food and/or gastric dilatation. Eleven of these patients had been diagnosed as having anorexia nervosa, and most of that subgroup were undergoing refeeding. We have also reported a case of gastric dilatation in a nonanorectic bulimic patient.

Dental complications are frequent in these patients. The pattern described most commonly is decalcification of the lingual, palatal, and posterior occlusal surfaces of the teeth, secondary to erosion of the enamel. This pattern is caused by exposure of the teeth to the acid gastric contents [39,45].

Several reports have suggested the possibility of underlying EEG abnormalities in patients with eating disorders, some of whom appear to have had bulimia nervosa. A series of studies reported by Rau, Green and their colleagues described certain EEG abnormalities in patients with compulsive eating disorders [40,41]. We subsequently examined EEGs in a series of patients diagnosed by DSM-III criteria as having bulimia and found a low rate of EEG abnormalities [42]. This area requires further research.

There has been considerable interest in recent years in the possibility of hypothalamic dysfunction in patients with eating disorders. Neuroendocrine regulatory systems that are under hypothalamic control have been studied to indirectly evaluate hypothalamic functioning. Most of the clinical work in this area on eating disorder patients has involved patients with anorexia nervosa or obesity. However, recent reports also suggest certain neuroendocrine abnormalities in patients with bulimia nervosa. The published studies have described pathological growth hormone responsiveness to TRH or glucose administration, elevated basal prolactin levels, and a high rate of nonsuppression on the dexamethasone suppression test but normal TRH responsiveness to TSH in most patients [24,25,46,47]. The clinical significance of these abnormalities is unclear. The medical complications of this disorder have recently been reviewed [48].

SUMMARY AND CONCLUSIONS

Bulimia nervosa, a disorder that is equated in the minds of many people with binge eating, actually is a syndrome characterized by a variety of abnormal eating-related behaviors as well as other problems. Patients with bulimia nervosa may demonstrate problems with self-induced vomiting, laxative abuse, diuretic abuse, excessive exercise, and abuse of diet pills and enemas. These patients rarely eat normal meals. Research indicates that this is a common problem and that it can be associated with serious psychological and medical consequences.

Unfortunately, we know little as to why certain people develop this disorder or about the longitudinal course of the illness once it is established. We do know that it usually begins late in adolescence. Stressful life events may precipitate the onset, as may a period of dieting behavior. There are several intriguing findings in the literature that suggest familial relationships between drug abuse problems, mood disorders, and bulimia. Clearly, further research is needed in this area.

REFERENCES

1. Russell G. Bulimia nervosa: an ominous variant of anorexia nervosa. Psychol Med, 1979; 9:429-48.

2. Boskind-Lodahl M, White WC. The definition and treatment of bulimarexia in college women: a pilot study. JACHA, 1978; 27:84-6.

3. Palmer RL. The dietary chaos syndrome: a useful new term? Br J Med Psychol, 1979; 52:187-190.

4. Hawkins II, Clement PF. Development and construct validation of a self-report measure of binge-eating tendencies. Addictive Behaviors, 1982; 7:435-9.

5. Halmi KA, Falk JR, Schwartz E. Binge-eating and vomiting: a survey of a college population. Psychol Med, 1981; 11:697-706.

6. Sinoway CG. The incidence and characteristics of bulimarexia in Penn State students. Paper presented at the American Psychological Association Meeting, Washington, DC, 1983:

7. Pyle RL, Mitchell JE, Eckert ED, et al. The incidence of bulimia in freshman college students. International Journal of Eating Disorders, 1983; 2:75-85.

8. Cooper PJ, Fairburn CG. Binge-eating and self-induced vomiting in the community—a preliminary study. Br J Psychiatry, 1983; 142:139-44.

9. Clark MG, Palmer RL. Eating attitudes and neurotic symptoms in university students. Br J Psychiatry, 1983; 142:299-304.

10. Johnson CL, Lewis C, Love S, et al. A descriptive survey of dieting and bulimic behavior in a female high school population. In Understanding Anorexia Nervosa and Bulimia. Columbus, Ohio: Ross Laboratories, 1983:

11. Pope HG Jr, Hudson JI, Yrgelun-Todd D. Anorexia nervosa and bulimi among 300 suburban women shoppers. Am J Psychiatry, 1984; 141:292-4.

12. Fairburn CG. Binge-eating and its management. Br J Psychiatry, 1982; 141:631-3.

13. Fairburn CG. Binge-eating and bulimia nervosa. SK and F Publications, 1982; 1:1-20.

14. Pyle RL, Mitchell JE, Eckert Ed. Bulimia: a report of 34 cases. J Clin Psychiatry, 1981; 42:60.

15. Abraham SF, Beumont PJV. How patients describe bulimia or binge- eating. Psychol Med, 1982; 12:625-35.

16. Fairburn CG, Cooper JP. Self-induced vomiting and bulimia nervosa: an undetected problem. Br Med J, 1982; 284:1153-5.

17. Johnson CL, Stuckey MK, Lewis LD, et al. Bulimia: a descriptive survey of 316 cases. International Journal of Eating Disorders, 1982; 2:3-16.

18. Herzog DB. Bulimia: the secretive syndrome. Psychosomatics, 1982; 23:481-7.

19. Mitchell JE, Pyle RL, Eckert ED, et al. Electrolyte and other physiological abnormalities in patients with bulimia. Psychol Med, 1983; 13:273-8.

20. Mitchell JE, Pyle RL, Eckert ED. Frequency and duration of binge-eating episodes in patients with bulimia. Am J Psychiatry, 1981; 138:835-6.

21. Johnson C, Larson R. Bulimia: an analysis of mood and behavior. Psychosom Med, 1982; 44:341-51.

22. Hudson JI, Laffer PS, Pope HG. Bulimia related to affective disorder by family history and response to the dexamethasone suppression test. Am J Psychiatry, 1982; 139:685-7.

23. Hudson JE, Pope HG, Jonas JM. Bulimia: a form of affective disorder? Paper presented at the American Psychiatric Association Meeting, New York, May 1983:

24. Hudson JI, Pope HG, Jonas JM, et al. Hypothalamic-pituitary- adrenal axia: Hyperactivity in bulimia. Psychiatry Research, 1983; 8:111-7.

25. Gwirtsman HE, Roy-Byrne P, Yager J, et al. Neuroendocrine abnormalities in bulimia. Am J Psychiatry, 1983; 140:559-63.

26. Mitchell JE, Pyle RL, Hatsukami D, et al. The dexamethasone suppression test in patients with the bulimia syndrome. J Clin Psychiatry, 1984; 45:508-11.

27. Hudson JE, Pope HG, Jonas JM, et al. Family history study of anorexia nervosa and bulimia. Br J Psychiatry, 1983; 142:133-8.

28. Pope HG, Hudson JI. Treatment of bulimia with antidepressants. Psychopharmacology, 1982; 78:176-9.

29. Pope HG, Hudson JI, Jonas JM. Antidepressant treatment of bulimia: preliminary experience and practical recommendations. J Clin Psychopharmacology, 1984; 3:274-81.

30. Pope HG, Hudson JI, Jonas JM, et al. Bulimia treated with imipramine: a placebo-controlled double-blind study. Am J Psychiatry, 1983; 140:544-58.

31. Mitchell JE, Groat R. A double-blind placebo-controlled trial of amitriptyline in bulimia. J Clin Psychopharmacology, 1984; 4:186- 93.

32. Weiss SR, Ebert MH. Psychological and behavioral characteristics of normal-weight bulimics and normal-weight controls. Psychosom Med, 1983; 45:293-303.

33. Hatsukami D, Own P, Pyle R, et al. Similarities and differences on the MMPI between women with bulimia and women with alcohol or drug abuse problems. Addictive Behaviors, 1982; 7:435-9.

34. Norman DK, Herzog DB. Bulimia, anorexia nervosa, and anorexia nervosa with bulimia: a comparative analysis of MMPI profiles. International Journal of Eating Disorders, 1983; 2:43-52.

35. Johnson C, Berndt DJ. Preliminary investigation of bulimia and life adjustment. Am J Psychiatry, 1983; 140:774-7.

36. Levin PA, Falko JM, Dixon K, et al. Benign parotid enlargement in bulimia. Ann Intern Med, 1980; 93:827-9.

37. Saul SH, Dekker A, Watson CG. Acute gastric dilatation with infarction and perforation. Gut, 1981; 22:978-83.

38. Mitchell JE, Pyle RL, Miner RA. Gastric dilatation as a complication of bulimia. Psychosomatics, 1982; 23:96-7.

39. Stege P, Visco-Dangler L, Rye L. Anorexia nervosa: review including oral and dental manifestations. JADA, 1982; 104:648-52.

40. Rau JH, Green RS. Compulsive eating: a neuropsychologic approach to certain eating disorders. Compr Psychiatry, 1975; 16:223-231.

41. Rau JH, Struve FA, Green RS. Electroencephalographic correlates of compulsive eating. Clin Electroencephalogr, 1979; 10:180-9.
42. Mitchell JE, Hostfield W, Pyle RL. EEG findings in patients with the bulimia syndrome. International Journal of Eating Disorders, 1983; 2:17-23.
43. Mitchell JE, Bantle JP. Metabolic and endocrine investigations in women of normal weight with the bulimia syndrome. Biol Psychiatry, 1983; 18:355-65.
44. Mitchell JE, Hatsukami D, Pyle RL, et al. Metabolic acidosis as a marker for laxative abuse in patients with bulimia. International Journal of Eating Disorders, 1987; 6:557-560.
45. Simmons MS, Grayden SK, Mitchell JE. The need for psychiatric-dental liaison in the treatment of bulimia. Am J Psychiatry, 1986; 143:783-4.
46. Lindy DC, Walsh BT, Roose SP, et al. The dexamethasone suppression test in bulimia. Am J Psychiatry, 1985; 142:1375-6.
47. Norris PD, O'Malley BP, Palmer RL. the TRH test in bulimia and anorexia nervosa: a controlled study. J Psychiatr Res, 1985; 19:215-9.
48. Mitchell JE, Seim HC, Colon E, et al. Medical complications and medical management of bulimia. Ann Int Med, 1987; 107:71-7.

Chapter 25

Eating Disorders in Infancy and Early Childhood

Joseph L. Woolston

INTRODUCTION

Eating disorders in infancy and early childhood have a number of unique characteristics that have inhibited our progress in understanding and diagnosing them. For example, their dyadic character has long been underemphasized [1]. To correct for this, pediatric textbooks refer to "feeding disoders" rather than "eating disorders of infancy." Another unique and confusing problem of the study of eating disorders of infancy is the linkage between eating disorders and growth disorders. At no other time in life will an aberration in eating have such a profound effect on growth and development. A third set of problems involves ethical and technical issues related to studying infants and young children. Informed consent, invasive procedures, prolonged hospitalizations, and blind research designs are all much more difficult with infants than with adolescents or adults. A fourth area of problems results from a persistent diagnostic confusion. The diagnostic blurring that has plagued investigation of eating disorders in infancy has greatly hindered meaningful research. For example, until recently no effort was made to distinguish nonorganic failure to thrive (NFTT) from psychosocial dwarfism (PSD), to separate rumination from gastroesophageal reflux (GER), or to delineate the relationship among NFTT, rumination, psychophysiological vomiting, and GER [1].

The *Diagnostic and Statistical Manual of Mental Disorders,* Third Edition (DSM-III) [2] exemplifies this confusion. It lists pica and rumination as the only eating disorders for this age-group. Obesity is considered a physical disorder. NFTT is described primarily as a problem of mother-infant attachment, and psychosocial dwarfism is not listed as a diagnosis.

A major contribution to this diagnostic confusion results from the multifactorial nature of eating disorders in this age-group. Virtually all of these disorders represent a final common pathway of diverse contributions at all levels of the human experience (figure 1). These contributions frequently include genetics, congenital vulnerabilies, intrapsychic disturbances between infant and parent, family dysfunction, and social stressors. In turn, the resultant eating disorder may well exacerbate some or all of the initiating problems, as well as cause new and even more maladaptive disturbances. Eating and growth disorders represent a closed system in which there is feedback between each "unit" of the system.

Although this conceptualization would seem to make any sort of diagnostic categorization hopeless, such nihilism is unwarranted. Rather, this systems approach to eating disorders should be kept in mind so that researchers and clinicians alike avoid becoming myopic in their search for "the cause" of eating disorders.

There are a number of different approaches to categorizing eating disorders of infancy and early childhood. Anna Freud [3] suggested one based on presumed theoretical etiology. She proposed that they could be divided into organic feeding disturbances, nonorganic disturbances of the instinctive process, and neurotic

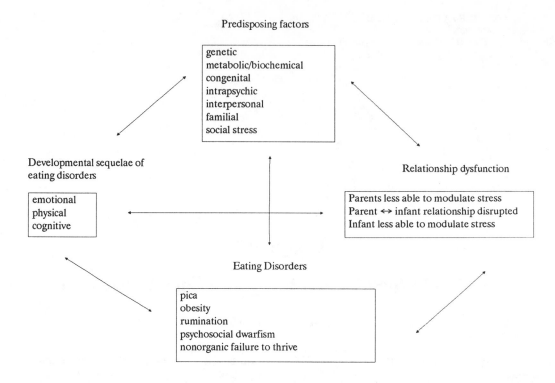

Predisposing factors

genetic
metabolic/biochemical
congenital
intrapsychic
interpersonal
familial
social stress

Developmental sequelae of
eating disorders

emotional
physical
cognitive

Relationship dysfunction

Parents less able to modulate stress
Parent ↔ infant relationship disrupted
Infant less able to modulate stress

Eating Disorders

pica
obesity
rumination
psychosocial dwarfism
nonorganic failure to thrive

Figure 25.1 Virtually all of these disorders represent a final common pathway of diverse contributions at all levels of the human experience.

feeding disturbances. Unfortunately, so little is known about eating disorders of this age-group that a phenomenological, rather than etiological, classification seems a necessary first step. One such schema would be to differentiate those eating disorders that result in intake of nonnutritive substances, from those that result in excessive weight gain, from those that result in insufficient weight gain and growth [1]. Using this schema, pica would be in the first group, simple obesity in the second, and nonorganic failure to thrive, rumination, and psychosocial dwarfism in the third group.

SPECIFIC SYNDROMES

Disorder of Nonnutritive Substances: Pica

The eating disorder of inappropriate food choice is represented by the syndrome of pica or geophagia. The DSM-III [2] defines pica as the persistent eating of nonnutritive substances such as paint, plaster, clay, and leaves. Age of onset is between 12 and 24 months. Pica usually remits in early childhood, although it may persist into adolescence. Little is known about the cause or the natural history of pica, although the common complications of lead poisoning and intestinal obstruction are well publicized. Pica appears to be a syndrome that

is the final common pathway of multiple interacting variables [1]. Wortis et al [4] reported that children manifesting pica tended to suffer more neonatal insults, to be slower in motor and mental development, to show more neurological defects, and to have more deviant behavior both before and at the time of the development of pica. Millican et al [5] examined pica from a psychoanalytic point of view. They proposed that pica might result from an identification with the mother's pica, the maternal fostering of oral activity as a defense against anxiety, or a regression of the oral stage in the face of frustration and deprivation. Although accidental poison ingestion is not pica, there seems to be a strong linkage between the two phenomena. Millican et al [5] reported that pica was found in 55% of children hospitalized for such accidental poisonings. Unfortunately, the existing studies are marred by methodological problems, so that understanding of the syndrome remains tentative. The differential diagnosis of pica includes vitamin and/or mineral deficiencies, infantile autism, mental retardation of a variety of etiologies, and certain physical disorders such as Klein-Levin syndrome (periodic somnolence, morbid hunger, and motor unrest) and Lesch-Nyhan syndrome (inherited abnormality or purine metabolism with associated mental retardation movement disorders and compulsive automutilation).

Research into the causes, prevention, or treatment of pica is still in its most rudimentary phases. No new research articles have appeared in the literature in the last 15 years. Obviously, basic phenomenological and epidemiological work must occur before more definitive research can proceed [1].

Disorder of Excessive Weight Gain: Simple Obesity

Obesity is the syndrome characterized by an excessive deposition and storage of fat. There are a variety of research definitions that use weight for age, weight for height, and skinfold thickness as arbitrary inclusionary criteria. One commonly accepted criterion is for body weight to exceed ideal body weight for height by 20% or more [6].

The prevalence of simple obesity is between 3% and 20%, depending on the group examined and exact definitions, methods, and standards used. Best estimates are that 5% to 10% of preschool-age children, 10% of schoolage children, 15% of adolescents, and 30% of American adults are obese [6]. There is a strong correlation between parental and sibling obesity and obesity of index child. Girls are about twice as likely as boys to be obese.

Like pica, simple obesity of infancy and early childhood is a complex syndrome, which is the final common pathway of the interplay of multiple factors, including genetics, prenatal experience, familial and cultural practices, emotional factors, activity levels, etc [1]. Perhaps because of the multiplicity of factors that contribute to obesity, the literature about etiology, prognosis, prevention, and treatment is contradictory [7-9]. The relative contributions of such basic variables as caloric intake, physical activity levels, and metabolic efficiency remain obscure. The role of such specific factors as cellularity of adipose tissue also remains controversial [10-13]. One issue that is quite clear is that obese infants more commonly become obese adolescents and adults than do nonobese infants [7,14]. From a slightly different perspective, once an infant or child has become significantly overweight, he or she is very likely to stay overweight into adulthood.

The differential diagnosis of simple obesity in infancy and childhood includes a variety of endocrine, genetic, and congenital disorders: hypothyroidism, Cushing's syndrome, Frolich's syndrome, Prader-Willi syndrome, disorders of glycogenosis, Klinefelter's syndrome, Laurence-Moon-Bidel syndrome, pseudohypothyroidism, Alstrom's syndrome, multiple X chromosome, Mauriac syndrome, CNS disease, or brain damage secondary to tumor, trauma, or infection [15]. One common clinical finding that characterizes obese children for

hormonal or genetic reasons is that they are short (usually less than the fifth percentile in height) and have delayed bone age, whereas children with simple obesity are almost always at the 50th percentile or greater and have a normal or advanced bone age [1].

Although there are numerous and well-defined etiologies for obesity secondary to other disorders, little research has been devoted to outlining specific subtypes of simple obesity. Such features as age of onset (eg, neonatal, infantile, toddler, preschool, school age), acuteness of onset, family history, presence of psychopathology in parents and/or child, and cultural practices or nutritional attitudes may all be quite important in clinically relevant categorization.

Forbes [16] is one of the few workers who has reported data that suggest that there are two groups of obese children. The first group is characterized by a definite increase in lean body mass as well as fat. In the second group, the excess body weight is due exclusively to the accumulation of fat. Subjects in the first group tend to be tall, to have advanced bone age, and to be obese since infancy. Subjects in the second group are, on the average, of normal height, are less apt to have accelerated bone age, and are more apt to have become obese during the mid- or late childhood years. Excess weight in this group is due entirely to fat accumulation. Forbes argued that these data suggest that "developmental" and "reactive" forms of obesity differ.

Several authors [17-19] have commented on the influence of dietary misinformation or changing cultural practices that have contributed to the development of infantile obesity. These authors reported that in England major changes have taken place in the feeding patterns of young infants, especially in the past 20 years. The incidence of breast feeding has declined, solid food is introduced at an increasingly early age, and artificial formulas are used in an excessively concentrated form. These practices have resulted in an increased incidence of obesity as a direct result of the excessive caloric intake of the infants.

An even more comprehensive diagnostic system for simple obesity would divide it into three categories: familial obesity, psychogenic obesity, and simple excessive caloric intake. In familial obesity, the onset of obesity starts in the neonatal or infantile period, and is gradual and progressive; there is a strong family history of obesity. Although there are no major areas of nutritional misinformation, there may be important cultural practices that favor a high-caloric diet. There is no major psychopathology in the family, parents, or child.

In psychogenic obesity, the onset may be either acute or more gradual and be at any age in childhood. There is no family history for obesity and no history of cultural or nutritional attitudes that support excessive caloric intake. The origin of the disorder is a significant disruption of the parent-infant relationship so that food is used to assuage psychological distress. There may or may not be evidence of formal psychopathology in the infant or parents.

Simple, excessive caloric intake obesity has an early age of onset and has no evidence of psychopathology in the parents, infant, or parent-infant relationship. The cause of the excessive caloric intake is secondary to relative well-defined and specific cultural practice or nutritional misinformation. There is a negative family history for obesity unless the same nutritional practices have been operating in previous generations.

Although this diagnostic classification system is supported by research and clinical findings, it can be viewed as helpful only if it is heuristically important. This system would lead researchers to readdress the basic assumption that there is a unity cause for a unitary syndrome of simple obesity. For example, we would expect metabolic and cellular contributions to familial-type obesity to be much more prominent than in psychogenic obesity or simple caloric intake. In addition, response to treatment would be predicted to be rapid in simple excessive caloric intake, variable in psychogenic obesity, and quite poor in familial obesity.

DISORDERS OF INSUFFICIENT GROWTH AND WEIGHT GAIN

Psychosocial Dwarfism

Psychosocial dwarfism (PSD), also called deprivational dwarfism, is a syndrome of deceleration of linear growth combined with characteristic behavior disturbances (sleep disorder and bizarre eating habits), both of which are reversible by a change in the psychosocial environment [20-23]. The most characteristic abnormal behaviors include polyphagia, gorging and vomiting, stealing and hoarding food, and eating from garbage pails and animals' dishes. Polydipsia, including drinking stagnant water, toilet bowl water, and dishwater was seen. Some have insomnia and night wandering [20]. PSD has its onset between 18 and 48 months of life. The long-term prognosis and prevalence rate of PSD are unknown.

The differential diagnosis for the organic causes of growth delay or failure include hypopituitarism from a variety of organic etiologies, primodial dwarfism, intrauterine growth failure with persistent small size, congenital hypopituitarism, constitutional delayed growth, Turner's syndrome (XO chromosome pattern), osteochondrodystophies, various chronic diseases, including congenital heart disease, chronic renal failure, chronic gastrointestinal disease, and chronic pulmonary disease [15].

Research in PSD has been hampered by the persistent confusion in the literature of PSD with nonorganic failure to thrive (NFTT). Although these two syndromes have quite distinct ages of onset, psychosocial characteristics and neuroendocrine correlates [24,25], the fact that they both involve psychosocial disruption and growth delay has caused considerable confusion. An example of the persistent nature of this diagnostic confusion between NFTT and PSD is presented in the most recent and comprehensive review article about PSD [20]. Although the authors concisely defined PSD as not including malnutrition as directly contributory to the disorder, and although they quoted Blizzard's clear distinction between PSD and NFTT, they used the term "failure to thrive" as a synonym for PSD in several places of their literature review, discussion of etiology, and summary.

Much of the research on PSD has focused on neuroendocrine abnormalities found in PSD in an attempt to unravel the relationship between growth rate and neuroendocrine changes. Unfortunately, these investigations have led to the discovery of no pathognomonic or consistently abnormal findings, with the possible exception of depressed somatomedian levels [20]. The abnormalities in hormonal levels or responses to provocation that have been found tend to normalize partially or completely following the subject's removal from the inimical environment. This normalization occurs from as quickly as a few days to as long as two years, depending on the specific endocrine disturbance, and with no specific medical, hormonal, or psychiatric treatment [20]. It also should be emphasized that none of the abnormal hormonal findings correlate on a one-to-one basis with growth failure. Growth failure has occurred with normal endocrine values, and catch-up growth has occurred with subnormal values [20]. The mechanisms causing the growth failure in PSD are thus, as yet, unknown.

Rumination

Rumination or merycism is a syndrome in which previously ingested food is voluntarily regurgitated, rechewed, and partially reswallowed [26]. In the process of this regurgitation, the infant loses a considerable amount of food and so becomes malnourished [26]. According to Cameron [27], "the infant appears withdrawn and apathetic except when in the act of ruminating. At these times, the infant lies with an expression of supreme satisfaction upon its face, sensing the regurgitated milk and subjecting it to innumerable sucking and chewing movements...It is very evident that achievement of his/her purpose produces a sense of beatitude while failure results in nervous unrest and imitation." In a review article, Flanagan [28] reported that predisposing factors, familial pattern, and prevalence are all unknown. The age of onset is usually between 3 weeks and 12 months of age in normal children, while in retarded children it may not occur until they are several years old [29]. The clinical course can range from a relatively benign, time-limited episode to a severe and chronic condition that causes severe malnutrition, growth failure, and even death [26,29].

Like many poorly understood syndromes, the spectrum of etiological explanations for rumination ranges from purely physiological [30] to purely psychological [26,27,29,30]. The literature on the psychological understanding of rumination has been sharply divided between psychodynamic and behavioral approaches, even though these two ways of viewing rumination are not necessarily mutually exclusive [29]. The psychodynamic explanation focus on an unsatisfactory mother-infant relationship [26,31-33], which causes the infant to seek an internal source of gratification. This turning inward by the infant has been proposed to occur either because the environment is more stimulating than the infant can tolerate [28], because the environment is not gratifying enough [26,31], or because the environment is too stimulating with negative effects [32,33].

Learning theory explanations focus on the reinforcing feedback responses that the rumination elicits. These proposed feedback mechanisms include positive reinforcement (a desired "event" such as pleasure or attention follows the rumination) and negative reinforcement (an undesired "event" such as anxiety is reduced or removed). A more sophisticated theory involves combining the concept of positive and negative reinforcement by proposing a change in the valence of the behavioral consequences. Consequences that are normally negative, behavior suppressing, may acquire positive, behavior-reinforcing characteristics if other, usually more positive, consequences are lacking [29].

From a very different perspective, some authors have argued that rumination is totally the result of physical disorders, including hiatal hernia and other esophageal abnormalities [30,34,35]. The relationship among the syndromes of rumination, gastroesophageal reflux (GER), psychophysiological vomiting [32] and NFTT is unknown. GER or chalasia is the syndrome of regurgitation of the stomach contents into the mouth and esophagus. New studies [36] indicate that this disorder may be caused by hypomobility of the gastric fundus and associated delayed gastric emptying rather than a weakened esophageal sphincter. Severe GER is associated with failure to thrive as well as specific behavioral abnormalities such as abnormal postures and torsion spasm of the neck [30,37]. A possible but untested hypothesis is that GER is the physiological substrate upon which various psychosocial disruptions act so that rumination syndrome develops.

The vociferousness with which each group of proponents argues in favor of their theory as the sole explanation for rumination is a testament to how much needs to be learned about this syndrome. A more realistic etiological approach would attempt to synthesize the various psychological and physical theories into a more coherent whole that recognizes that rumination probably has many "causes," some of which will be more prominent in different individuals. Three factors seem to be required for the development of rumination syndrome: an impaired ability by the infant to regulate his/her internal state of satisfaction, a physical propensity to regurgitate food, and a learned association that regurgitation helps relieve the internal state of dissatisfaction. Both research and clinical practice need to evaluate the relative importance of each one of these three factors in each patient if a better diagnostic understanding and treatment is to occur.

Nonorganic Failure to Thrive Syndrome (NFTT)

NFTT is a disorder of the first 24 months of life characterized by marked deceleration of weight gain and slowing of acquisition of developmental milestones. A deceleration of linear and head circumference growth is an associated but not a primary phenomenon. Failure to thrive is a common disorder, occurring at a rate of 1% to 5% of pediatric hospital admissions [38,39]. From 15% to 58% of these admissions have no demonstrable organic cause for their poor growth and are called NFTT [39,40].

The relative importance of hyponutrition versus psychosocial deprivation in the development of NFTT is a controversial issue. The DSM-III apparently has decided that the psychosocial deprivation is primary, since it calls the syndrome "Reactive Attachment Disorder of Infancy" rather than failure to thrive [2]. However, Whitten et al [41] have shown that even grossly understimulated infants with NFTT will gain weight rapidly if given enough food. Conceivably, both sides of the controversy may be correct. Psychosocial deprivation can cause infantile depression and developmental delay without deceleration of weight gain [42], and lack of nutrition may cause weight gain deceleration without developmental delay. Obviously these two separate processes are intimately interrelated, since starvation produces characteristic behavioral and developmental changes [43,44] and since behavioral and affective disturbances caused by psychosocial deprivation create problems for adequate feeding. In addition, the same type of psychosocial factors that lead to insufficient parental psychosocial stimulation of the infant may also contribute to parental inability to provide sufficient feeding of the infants [1].

A major weakness in research in NFTT has been the failure to investigate or even classify the degree of malnutrition that the infant is suffering [1]. Merely describing the infant as having fallen below a certain weight gain percentile curve does not describe the infant's nutritional status [45]. Partly because of the confusion with psychosocial dwarfism, numerous authors [46-48] have argued that the lack of weight gain in NFTT is not related to caloric intake but rather occurs as a result of metabolic/hormonal changes secondary to the psychosocial stress factors. Newer studies [1,41,49,50] strongly support the alternative hypothesis that weight gain recovery in NFTT is directly proportional to caloric intake. However, Bell and Woolston[49] described a group of infants with NFTT whose percentage of ideal body weight for length, age, and sex (% ideal body weight) was 81% or greater. In this group of infants there was no such linear correlation between caloric intake and weight gain, apparently because other factors such as activity level and metabolic state become more heterogeneous as an infant approaches the ideal body weight.

Since there are specific behavioral and hormonal changes that occur with certain levels of hyponutrition, the degree of protein-calorie malnutrition must be established if meaningful research is to be done. Such areas as special developmental characteristics of the infants and levels of psychosocial distress of the parents may be dependent variables to malnutrition.

One of the major issues that faces clinicians who treat infants with failure to thrive is how to differentiate organic failure to thrive from NFTT [1]. Although the literature on the special characteristics of infants with NFTT and their caretakers is voluminous (eg, review articles Cupoli et al [51] and Goldbloom [45]), it is not particularly helpful at providing nonexclusionary criteria to separate NFTT from other forms of FTT. Most of the articles are flawed by methodological weaknesses, and ways to easily differentiate NFTT from organic FTT are not yet available.

Infants with NFTT frequently have been found to display a variety of unusual behaviors such as "radar gaze" [52], unusual watchfulness [53] or unusual postures [54]. However, since only one study [55] that found special behavioral characteristics for NFTT used a control group of infants with organic FTT, it is unclear whether these special behaviors are really characteristic of NFTT in particular or rather are associated with all types of FTT. In this study of infants between 6 and 16 months of age, Rosenn et al [55] controlled for both the effects of weight loss and hospitalization. They used both hospitalized children with normal weight and children with organic FTT as controls. They found that they could reliably distinguish among these three groups by observing their response to a structured social interaction. Infants with NFTT predictably preferred distant social encounters and inanimate objects, while organic FTT infants and medically ill control patients consistently responded most positively to close personal interactions such as touching and holding.

Mother-infant interaction in NFTT has not been well studied [1]. In one of the few reports that examined mother-infant behavior, Vietze et al [56] used a prospective, multiple-parameter behavior frequency design. Their study was controlled for race, marital status, maternal age, level of education, parity, and gravidity, but not for infantile poor growth. They found no dyadic or infant behavior that differentiated infants who later became NFTT. The only difference between the two groups was that mothers of infants who were later diagnosed as NFTT spent less time in visually attending to their infants. The paucity of behavioral differences reported in this study is presumably due to studying newborns who were not yet failing to thrive.

The caretakers and families of NFTT infants have been found to have a variety of psychiatric, psychological, and psychosocial problems [1]. Many authors have found the mothers to be either acutely or chronically depressed and overwhelmed [53,57-59]. None of the studies was controlled for socioeconomic status, impact of hospitalization, rater bias, or nutritional status of the infant. Fishcoff et al [58] found mothers of children with NFTT to have histories of early childhood disturbance; poor performance in current day-to-day activities; desire for an anaclitic relationship; the use of denial, isolation, and projection as major mechanisms of defense; and a predisposition toward action as opposed to thought. However, they also found that 2 of the 16 mothers they studied had none of these characteristics.

Several studies have indicated that families of NFTT children are marked by many stigmata of psychosocial disruption [39,52,53,57]. However, Glaser et al [60] reported that most of the children in their study were members of intact, relatively stable families with steady incomes. Kotelchuck and Newberger [61] reported that three family/ecological factors differentiate NFTT families from families of control infants matched for race, age, and similar socioeconomic status. The parents perceived their child as sickly and themselves as more isolated from their neighborhood and had a larger discrepancy in their education. Demographic data, pregnancy, and contemporaneous stress factors were not significant. The authors used these findings to question whether previous reports of parental psychopathology and family dysfunction might be the effect of having an infant with NFTT, in addition to the cause of it.

Even the concept of the homogeneity of the syndrome of NFTT has been questioned [1]. Egan et al [62] have proposed that there is a second syndrome of weight gain failure of infancy that is quite distinct from "typical" NFTT. They suggested that some infants between 6 and 18 months of age develop such a struggle for autonomy with their caretakers that a vicious cycle is initiated that results in weight gain failure. They described this syndrome as characterized by overly intense mother-infant interaction and active food refusal by the infant.

Woolston [1] has proposed that various syndromes of NFTT should be defined by three axes: psychosocial characteristics of the mothers, behavioral/developmental disturbances of the infants, and specific abnormalities in the mother-infant interaction. Using this schema, NFTT might be divided into three subgroups types (table 1).

In Type I the mother both undernourishes and understimulates her infant. One would expect the mother to be emotionally unavailable, the infant to show developmental delays and an abnormal response to proximal interactions with others, and the mother-infant interactions to be characterized by a paucity of warmth and nurturance.

In Type II, the mother provides adequate stimulation for her infant but, as a result of misinformation or lack of resources, does not provide adequate nutrition. One would expect the mothers to appear within normal limits on psychological testing, the babies to show no abnormalities except in growth, and the mother-infant interaction to be within normal limits.

In Type III, the infant is struggling to create autonomy from the mother. One would expect the mothers to be angry or depressed, the babies to show specific behavioral disturbances focused on food refusal but without developmental abnormalities, and the mother-infant interaction to be characterized by negative and angry interchanges.

Although this subgrouping schema of the NFTT syndrome is compatible with the current available data, it must be regarded as tentative [1]. Empirical studies using controlled and blind methodologies will confirm, modify, or disprove the utility and accuracy of this schema.

The ultimate aim of refining our diagnostic work is to allow reliable classification of NFTT into homogeneous subgroups [1]. Once this subgrouping has been achieved, a variety of research questions about etiology, prognosis, and treatment can be vigorously pursued. The linkage between NFTT and major depressive disorder could be investigated on genetic, epidemiologic, endocrine, and neuroendocrine parameters. The relationship between protein-calorie malnutrition and be-

Table 25.1 Three Subgroups of NFTT

NFTT Type 1 (Reactive attachment disorder of infancy)

Infants
1. Significant developmental delays in motor, language, and adaptive areas
2. Lack of developmentally appropriate signs of social responsivity as defined by DSM-III in reactive attachment disorder of infancy
3. Onset of failure to thrive (FTT) before 8 months of age

Mothers
1. Perceive their infants as sick
2. Psychopathology characterized by depression and social isolation

Mother-Infant Interaction
1. Few interactions indicative of pleasure and mutual social responsivity
2. Infants prefer distal to proximal interaction
3. Infants show apathy and/or active withdrawal in proximal and feeding interactions

NFTT Type II (Simple calorie-protein malnutrition)

Infants
1. No or minimal developmental delays
2. Developmentally appropriate signs of social responsivity
3. Onset of FTT before 12 months

Mothers
1. Perceive their infants as sick
2. No characteristic psychopathology or psychosocial disruptions

Mother-Infant Interaction
1. Frequent interactions indicative of pleasure and mutual social responsivity
2. Infants prefer proximal to distal interactions
3. Infants cooperative and vigorous in proximal and feeding interactions

NFTT Type III (Pathological food refusal)

Infants
1. No or minimal developmental delays
2. Developmentally appropriate signs of social responsivity
3. Onset of FTT between 6 months and 16 months

Mothers
1. Do not perceive their infants as sick
2. Psychopathology characterized by depression and hostility

Mother-Infant Interaction
1. Few interactions indicative of mutual social responsivity and pleasure
2. Infants prefer distal to proximal interactions
3. Infants show angry withdrawal and active avoidance in proximal and feeding interactions

havioral/developmental and mother-infant interactional abnormalities could be explored. The effects of specific treatment interventions could be rigorously and scientifically evaluated.

As exemplified by NFTT syndrome, eating disorders of infancy and early childhood are complex and poorly understood phenomena, which are only just beginning to be described in detail. Research in this area is frought with many obstacles that continue to impede its progress. However, the application of more sophisticated research techniques should help to resolve some of the current confusion.

REFERENCES

1. Woolston JL. Eating disorders in infancy and early childhood. J Am Acad Child Psychiatry, 1983; 22:114-21.
2. American Psychiatric Association: Diagnostic and Statistical Manual of Mental Disorders, ed. III (DSM-III). Washington, DC: APA, 1980:
3. Freud A. The psychoanalytic study of infantile feeding disturbances. The psychoanalytic study of the child, 1946; 2:119-32.
4. Wortis H, Rae R, Heimer L, et al. Children who eat noxious substances. J Am Acad Child Psychiatry, 1962; 1:536-74.
5. Millican FK, Layman EM, Lourie RS, et al. Study of an oral fixation: Pica. J Am Acad Child Psychiatry, 1968; 7:49-107.
6. Maloney MJ, Klykylo WM. An overview of anorexia nervosa, bulimia and obesity in children and adolescents. J Am Acad Child Psychiatry, 1983; 22:99.
7. Golden MP. An approach to the management of obesity in childhood. Pediat Clin N Am, 1979; 26:187-97.
8. Knittle JL. Childhood obesity. Bull NY Acad Med, 1971; 47:579-89.
9. Taitz LS. Obesity in pediatric practice: Infantile obesity. Pediat Clin N Am, 1977; 24:107-22.
10. Brook CD, Lloyd JK, Wolf DH. Relation between age of onset of obesity and size and number of adipose cells. Br Med J, 1972; 2:25-7.
11. Bruch H, Voss WR. Infantile obesity and later weight control in the baboon. Nature, 1974; 250:268-9.
12. Hirsch J, Knittle JL. The cellularity of obese and non-obese human adipose tissue. Fed Proc, 1970; 29:1518-21.
13. Widdowson EM, Shaw WT. Full and empty fat cells. Lancet, 1974; 2:905.
14. Charney E, Chamblee H, McBride M, et al. The childhood antecedents of adult obesity: Do chubby infants become obese adults? N Engl J Med, 1976; 295:6-9.
15. Woolston JL. Eating disorders in childhood and adolescence. In Cavenar O, ed. Psychiatry. Philadelphia: Lippincott Co, 1985.
16. Forbes GB. Lean body mass and fat in obese children. Pediatrics, 1964; 34:308-14.
17. Oakes Rk. Infant-feeding practices. Br Med J, 1973; 2:762-4.
18. Shukla E, Forsyth HA, Anderson CM, et al. Infantile overnutrition in the first year of life: A field study in Dudley, Worcestershire. Br Med J, 1972; 4:507-15.
19. Taitz LS. Infantile overnutrition among artifically fed infants in the Sheffield region. Br Med J. 1971; 1:315-6.
20. Green WH, Campbell M, David R. Psychosocial dwarfism: A critical review of the evidence. J Am Acad Child Psychiatry, 1984; 23:39-48.
21. Money J, Wolff G. Late puberty, retarded growth, and reversible hyposomatotropinism (psychosocial dwarfism). Adolescence, 1974; 9:121-34.
22. Powell GF, Brasel JA, Blizzard RM. Emotional deprivation and growth retardation simulating idiopatic hypopituitarism. I and II. N Engl J Med, 1967; 276:1271-83.
23. Silver HK, Finkelstein M. Deprivation dwarfism. Pediatrics, 1967; 70:317-24.
24. Blizzard RM. Discussion in JL Van den Brande and MUL Du Caju, Plasma somatomedin activity in children with growth disturbances. In Raiti S, ed. Advances in Human Growth Hormone Research. Washington, DC: DHEW Publication No. (NIH) 74-612, 1973: 124-5.
25. Krieger I, Good MH. Adrenocortical and thyroid function in the deprivation syndrome. Am J Dist Child, 1970; 120:95-102.
26. Richmond JB, Eddy E, Green M, et al. Rumination: A psychosomatic syndrome of infancy. Pediatrics, 1958; 22:49-55.
27. Cameron HD. Forms of vomiting in infants. Br Med J, 1925; 1:872-6.
28. Flanagan CH. Rumination in infancy—past and present. J Am Acad Child Psychiatry, 1977; 16:140-9.
29. Winton A, Singh NN. Rumination in pediatric populations. J Am Acad Child Psychiatry, 1983; 22:269-75.
30. Herbst J, Friedland GW, Zboralske FF. Hiatal hernia and rumination in infants and children. J Pediat, 1971; 78:261-5.
31. Menking M, Wagnitz JG, Burton JJ, et al. Rumination: Near fatal psychiatric disease of infancy. N Engl J Med, 1969; 280:802-4.
32. Ferholt J, Provence S. Diagnosis and treatment of an infant with psychophysiological vomiting. The Psychoanalytic Study of the Child, 1976; 31:439-61.
33. Hollowell JG, Gardner LI. Rumination and growth failure in male fraternal twin: Association with disturbed family environment. Pediatrics, 1965; 36:565-71.
34. Astley R. Radiology of the alimentary tract in infancy. London: Arnold Press, 1956; 41,58-64.
35. Botha GS. The Gastro-esophagel function. Boston: Brown and Co, 1962; 5,59-65,184-206,301-337.
36. Hillemeier AC, Lange R, McCallum R, et al. Delayed gastric emptying in infants with gastroesophageal reflux. J Pediat, 1981; 98:190-3.
37. Sutcliffe J. Torsion spasms and abnormal postures in

children with hiatus hernia: Sandifer's syndrome. Progr Pediat Radiol, 1969; 2:190-7.

38. Hannaway P. Failure to thrive. A study of 100 infants and children. Clin Pediat, 1976; 9:69-99.

39. Shaheen E, Alexander D, Truskowsky M, et al. Failure to thrive: A retrospective profile. Clin Pediat, 1968; 7:255-60.

40. Sills RH. Failure to thrive: The role of clinical and laboratory evaluation. Am J Dis Child, 1978; 132:967-9.

41. Whitten CF, Pettit MH,Fischoff J. Evidence that growth failure from maternal deprivation is secondary to undereating. J Am Med Assn, 1969; 209:1675-82.

42. Provence S, Lipton RC. Infants and institutions. New York: International Universities Press, 1962.

43. Chavez A, Martinez C, Yaschine T. Nutrition, behavioral development, and mother-child interaction in young rural children. Fed Proc, 1975; 34:1574-82.

44. Pollitt E. Behavior of infant in causation of nutritional marasmus. Am J Clin Nutr, 1973; 26:264-70.

45. Goldbloom RB. Failure to thrive. Pediat Clin N Am, 1982; 29:151- 66.

46. Spitz RA. Hospitalism: An inquiry into the genesis of psychiatric conditions in early childhood. The Psychoanalytic Study of the Child, 1945; 1:53-74.

47. Talbot MR, Allen JE, Lelchach LA. Psychological exploration of the non-organic failure to thrive syndrome. Develpm Med Child Neurol, 1969; 11:601-7.

48. Fried A, Mayer MF. Socioeconomic factors accounting for growth failure in children living in an institution. J Pediat, 1948; 33:444-56.

49. Bell LS, Woolston JL. Weight gain and caloric intake in failure to thrive. J Am Acad Child Psychiatry, 1985; 24:447-452.

50. Frieger I, Chen YC. Calorie requirements of weight gain in infants with growth failure due to maternal deprivation, undernutrition, and congenital heart disease. Pediatrics, 1965; 44:647-54.

51. Cupoli JM, Hallock JA, Barness LA. Failure to thrive. Curr Prob Pediat, 1980; 10:3-42.

52. Barbero GE, Shaheen E. Environmental failure to thrive: A clinical interview. J Pediat, 1967; 73:690-8.

53. Leonard M, Rhymes J, Solnit A. Failure to thrive in infants. Am J Dis Child, 1966; 111:600-12.

54. Krieger I, Sargent DA. A postural sign in sensory deprivation syndrome in infants. J Pediat, 1967; 70:332.

55. Rosenn DW, Loeb LS, Jura MB. Differentiation of organic from nonorganic failure to thrive syndrome in infancy. Pediatrics, 1980; 66:698-704.

56. Vietze PM, Falsey S, O'Connor S. et al. Newborn beahavioral and interactional characteristics of nonorganic failure to thrive infants. In Field TM, Goldberg S, Stern D, et al. eds. High risk infants and children: adult and peer interactions. New York: Academic Press, 1980: pp 5-23.

57. Evans R, Reinhart J, Succop R. Failure to thrive: A study of 45 children and their families. J Am Acad Child Psychiatry, 1972; 11:440-57.

58. Fischoff J, Whitten D, Pettit M. A psychiatric study of mothers of infants with growth failure secondary to maternal deprivation. J Pediat, 1971; 79:209-15.

59. Togut M, Allen S, Helchuck L. A psychological exploration of the nonorganic failure to thrive syndrome. Develpm Med Child Neurol, 1969; 11:601-7.

60. Glaser H, Heagarty M, Gallard B, et al. Physical and psychological development of children with early failure to thrive. J Pediat, 1968; 73:690-8.

61. Kotelchuck M, Newberger EH. Failure to thrive: A controlled study of familial characteristics. J Am Acad Child Psychiatry, 1983; 22:322-8.

62. Egan J, Chatoor I, Rosen G. Nonorganic failure to thrive: Pathogenesis and classification. Clin Proc Child Hosp Natl Med Center, 1980; 34:173-82.

Chapter 26

Eating Disorders in Childhood
(Ages 4 Through 11 Years)

I. Lee Gislason

INTRODUCTION

Eating disorders in infancy, adolescence, and adulthood have been extensively described in the literature; however, eating disorders in childhood are reported with much less frequency. In order to restrict this chapter to eating disorders in childhood, I have focused on children aged 4 to 11 years old. This will avoid, as much as possible, disorders of infancy and disorders of adolescence. In 4- to 11-year-old children reviewed in the literature with eating disorders, as characterized in DSM-III, the major and almost exclusive category mentioned was anorexia nervosa. This chapter will therefore focus on anorexia nervosa.

Anorexia nervosa is considered to be of major importance because of its increasing frequency, its severity, and because it is one of the few psychiatric disorders of childhood that can progress to death.

In the literature examined, the diagnosis of anorexia nervosa is not made in children under age 4, and the diagnosis of bulimia is rarely mentioned [1,2].

This chapter will present a historical overview through an analysis of the literature describing children with eating disorders. Some of the articles reviewed will be set forth in tables, and comments will be made. Specific studies will then be discussed in greater detail. Later clinical issues, controversies, and future direction in this field will be explored.

DEFINITION

Eating disorders according to DSM-III are characterized by gross disturbances in eating behavior; they include anorexia nervosa, bulimia, pica, rumination disorder of infancy, and atypical eating disorder. Bulimia usually has a chronic, remitting course, whereas the other three specific disorders commonly are limited to a single episode. Two of these, anorexia nervosa and rumination disorder of infancy, may have an unremitting course that progresses to death due to malnutrition and medical complications.

Anorexia nervosa is defined in DSM-III using the following criteria: (1) An intense fear of becoming obese, which does not diminish as weight loss progresses; (2) disturbance of body-image, eg, claiming to "feel fat" even when emaciated; (3) weight loss of at least 25% of original body weight, or if under 18 years of age, weight loss of original body weight plus projected weight gain expected from growth charts may be combined to make the 25%; (4) refusal to maintain body weight or a minimal normal weight for age and height; and (5) no known physical illness that would account for the weight loss.

Puberty will now be defined, because it has particular relevance here in that children with prepubertal anorexia nervosa will be the major focus of this chapter. It is possible that puberty has a pivotal biopsychosocial role in this syndrome. Dorland's Medical Dictionary [3] defines puberty as the age at which the reproductive organs become functionally operative and secondary sex characteristics develop. Textbook of Pediatrics by Nelsons et al [4] indicates that puberty is an arbitrary point in the continuum of maturation: the menarche in girls (just under 13 years in the United States), and some less clearly defined event occurring approximately two years later in boys. Adolescence is defined as the period of time between puberty and maturity [5].

Normal developmental prepubescent changes are pertinent to weight problems in 4- to 11-year-olds. These changes precede the first secondary sex changes of adolescence and are integral elements of maturation, not simply preparatory ones. Boys have slightly less subcutaneous fat during the middle years of childhood. The fat in subcutaneous tissue, which showed a steady proportionate decrease in amount from the ages of 1 to 6 years in both sexes, begins to reaccumulate as early as 8 years in girls and 10 years in boys.

A HISTORICAL BACKGROUND OF ANOREXIA NERVOSA IN CHILDREN

Morton [6], in a book published in 1694 in England, was probably the first writer to refer to this symptom complex, as he does in the chapter entitled, "Of a Nervous Consumption." This description was followed by Lasegues' [7] in 1873 in France, under the name of "l'Anorexia Hysterique." Independently, Sir William Gull [8,9] described the same condition in England in 1874, giving the condition its current name, anorexia nervosa. Twenty years later in 1894, Collins [10] described in the Lancet a 7-1/2-year-old girl who was refusing all food. She was emaciated and exhibited "morbid egotism," selfishness, vanity, and self-absorption. One year later in 1895 Marshall [11] in England recorded a fatal case in a girl, 11 years of age, in which the autopsy revealed the same absence of lesions as was found in Gull's fatal case [12-14]. The early English literature [15-17] focused mainly on eating difficulties in infants and preschoolers and therefore included only a small number of children in the 4- to 11-year-old range. After Collin's and Marshall's description of prepubertal children the most frequent publications were not in the English but in the French and German literature [18-26].

Irwin [27] in 1984 reviewed 893 cases in which the authors claim to be dealing with anorexia nervosa. Of the 893 cases there were 29 children (3% of the total) aged 8 through 11 years. My review of the literature supports Irwin's findings regarding the paucity of case reports of preadolescent anorexia nervosa in the literature.

Two tables have been made to allow the reader an opportunity to compare and review many of the papers on eating disorders in childhood. Table 1 [28-34] describes epidemiological studies of children aged 4 to 11 years. Table 2 [1,2,27,12-14,35-45] gives brief clinical comments of cases reported in the literature.

EPIDEMIOLOGICAL SURVEYS OF CHILDREN WITH ANOREXIA NERVOSA

Table 1 reviews epidemiological surveys of 447 patients. The authors of these surveys state that the patients studied had anorexia nervosa. Unfortunately, the criteria for defining the disorder were not consistent. The articles were selected after excluding numerous studies that did not have any children younger than 12 years old. The studies often do not clearly relate what percentage of children are under 12 years old. In spite of the methodological problems, it is apparent that the frequency in children as compared with adolescents and adults is small. However, of children in the epidemiological studies, girls outnumber boys (86% girls to 14% boys), and onset of symptoms was often related to disappointments in object relations. Also in this population it was observed that sexual problems and suicidal behavior were minimal [19].

THIRTY-THREE CASE STUDIES OF ANOREXIA NERVOSA IN 4- TO 11-YEAR-OLDS

Table 2, titled "Thirty-three Case Studies of Anorexia Nervosa in 4- to 11-Year-Olds" gives an overview of this topic. Parameters such as age, sex, precipitant, personality, treatment, and follow-up are set forth in as much detail as each case report will allow. The case studies extracted from the literature were heterogeneous in composition. In addition, they are a reflection of the many adventitious influences to which referral policies are subject. Consequently, it is difficult to arrive at conclusions without qualification. However, some general comments can be made.

In the case studies of anorexia nervosa reported in 4- to 11-year-old children, as with other age-groups, there is a preponderance of females (23 females to 9 males, or 73% to 27%, respectively). In this review of the literature there are probably more males than would be expected, because anorexia nervosa in males in this age range is indeed a rare event and publishable. The female preponderance is of special interest, because in most psychiatric disorders of childhood there are more males than females.

In 23 (69%) of the 33 cases a precipitant is decribed. Five were related to a birth in the family, four began after the child was teased about being fat, three were to do with separation, and three related to bereavement.

Table 26.1 Epidemiological surveys of 4- to 11-year old children with anorexia nervosa

Author	Age of Onset	Sample
Anyan 1983	3 females age 10 and 1 male age 10	Sample of 137 females and 17 males with anorexia nervosa who were treated at the outpatient and inpatient services for adolescents at the Yale-New Haven Hospital.
Galdston 1972	50 patients 8 to 16. Those ages 11 and under not specified.	41 girls and 9 boys were all hospitalized on a childrens' psychiatric ward. Only 3 of 50 were suicidal. All were able to recall a disappointment in a valued relationship that had been invested with personal ambitions. No evidence of heterosexual activity. All compliant.
Goetz et al 1977	Details not given	Sample of 30 children between the ages of 9.5 and 16 years admitted to the Childrens Hospital of Pittsburgh between 1954 and 1970 (28 females and 2 males).
Hall 1978	Youngest child was 12	Sample consisted of the first 50 patients referred to a child psychiatrist from a defined geographic area in New Zealand
Halmi 1974	8% of sample were < 10	Sample of 94 divided into groups < 10, between 10 and 15 and > 25 years old. The sample was a retrospective study of the files of the Iowa General and Psychopathic Hospitals, 1920-1972.
Halmi et al 1979	2 children age 10 & 3 children age 11. Gender not given.	Sample consisted of 105 subjects who participated in a collaborative study. 1/3 had not reached puberty.
Pugliese 1983	14 children age 9 to 17. Those aged 11 was not delineated.	Authors state that the children had a fear of obesity resulting in short stature and delayed puberty. They claim that children did not have anorexia nervosa, which is controversial. The sample consisted of 14 of 201 patients who attended a pediatric endocrinology clinic.

Other precipitants are enumerated in table 2. The frequency of identification of external precipitants in adolescents and adults varies; for example, Theander [46] identified specific causes in 50%, Halmi [32] in 55%, Morgan and Russell [47] in 65%, while Casper and Davis [48] could identify precipitation factors in all their patients.

Two-thirds of the 33 children were hospitalized. Frequency of hospitalization, as with other diseases, is influenced by the patterns of practice in the community and other factors.

At follow-up there was information on 29 (89%) of the 33 cases. Of these 29, 18 (62%) were described as improved, three (10%) slightly improved, seven (24%) not improved, and one (4%) dead from anorexia nervosa. The 33 cases in my sample can be compared to Bruch's [49] series of 38 females with anorexia nervosa. The age of onset in her sample was from 10 to 26 years. Thirteen (36%) were reported to be recovered, and 23 (64%) as not recovered. Two had died, but the cause of death was not reported.

Premorbid personalities in the case studies examined are varied. Terms such as depressed, shy, schizoid, and hysterical are used. The idea that the child is either prepsychotic or has significant ego defects was alluded to in 6 (18%) of 33 children described.

Frequently in young adolescents with anorexia nervosa the term conscientious is used. Significantly, the term conscientious was mentioned in only two of the 33 childhood anorexia cases. In contrast, the adolescent anorexia nervosa patient is usually a high achiever, superficially compliant, and often described as conscientious.

Since table 2 was compiled, I discovered an article by Jacobs and Isaacs [56] which you will be well advised to review.

DESCRIPTIONS OF SPECIFIC STUDIES

Some of the early series, which reported preadolescent cases of anorexia nervosa, appeared in the late 1950s and the early 1960s. Falstein [1] in 1956 described one 9-year-old and two 10-year-old children. They were unique in that they were all males. One had a typical adolescent precipitant. Children at school began calling him "Fatso" and "Tubby," while the other two had more atypical precipitants. One precipitant was the death of a dog that was poisoned, and the other precipitant related to family arguments.

Blitzer et al [13] in 1961 reported seven children with onset of anorexia nervosa at age 11 or before and the sex ratio was two boys to five girls.

In 1968 Warren [44] described 20 cases of anorexia nervosa in girls. Three of the girls had onset of symptoms at age 11 or before. Girls aged 10 to 15 years were divided into three groups. Eight were prepubertal, four were pubertal, and eight were postpubertal. Warren does not give a precise definition of puberty in the paper, although he states that the postpubertal girls were menstruating before the onset of illness. It was Warren's observation regarding the 20 cases that, "as they showed

Table 26.2 33 Case Studies of Anorexia Nervosa in 4- to 11-years olds

Author	Age of Onset	Age When First Seen	Sex	Precipitant	Permorbid Personality	Hospitalized	Outpatient Therapy	Follow Up	Comment
Botella 1978	6	6-1/2	m	N.R.	depressed shy	no	several months	improved	mother wished him dead since birth
Blitzer 1961	7	10-1/2	f	N.R.	hysterical phobias	5 months	N.R.	recovered	pt. had magic idea of sacrifice in order to reunite separated parents
	8-1/2	11	f	N.R.	hysterical	1-1/2 years	N.R.	recovered	
	10-1/2	10-3/4	f	parents' separation	depressed	2-1/2 months	N.R.	died	
	10-1/2	10-3/4	f	N.R.	compulsive depressed	1 month	N.R.	slightly improved	
	11	11	f	N.R.	depressed	2 months	N.R.	recovered	
	11	16	m	N.R.	hysterical schizoid	2-1/2 years	N.R.	slightly improved	
	11-1/2	12-3/4	m	N.R.	schizoid compulsive phobic	2 years	N.R.	slightly improved	
Brown 1983	10-3/4	12-3/4	f	death of uncle, 2 friends moved	cheerful	no	3-1/2 yrs	improved	a lot of fathers' attention until late latency
	9-3/4	11-1/4	f	brother had 5 brain surgeries	paranoid schizoid	no	17 months	improved	a lot of father's attention until late latency
	9-1/4	9-3/4	f	best friend moved away	depressed	no	8 months	improved	father was a chronic alcoholic and was probably mildly psychotic
English 1937	4	6	f	father attempted vaginal intercourse and had child perform fellatio		no	2 years	did well	
Falstein 1956	7	N.R.	m	fear mother might have another child	shy depressed	8 months	N.R.	poor	residential placement suggested bulimic episodes; eating problems throughout childhood
	10	11	m	fear of fatness	prepsychotic demanding	14 days mother uncooperative	none		insisted he had a protuberant abdomen when it was scaphoid
	9-3/4	10	m	arguments between grandparents and parents	provocative hostile				
	10-1/2	11	m	death of dog that was poisoned		no	a few interviews	improved	distortion of body image; brief bulimic episode; mother rejecting & hostile
Forchheimer 1907	6	7	f	N.R.	oppositional	no	4 weeks	improved	child intelligent and suspicious parents neurotic
Irwin 1981	9-1/2	9-3/4	f	teased about being fat		yes	N.R.		mother was rejecting; bulimic episodes; claims abdomen protuberant when actually scaphoid exercised excessively; interest in preparing food
Irwin 1984	9	10	f	teased about being fat	compliant	yes			
	11	11-3/4	f	breast development	perfectionistic	yes			loss of interest in everything except cooking

Table 26.2 33 Case Studies of Anorexia Nervosa in 4- to 11-years olds (continued)

Author	Age of Onset	Age When First Seen	Sex	Precipitant	Permorbid Personality	Hospitalized	Outpatient Therapy	Follow Up	Comment
Lesser 1960	10	N.R.	f	viral illness	hysterical	1 month		uneventful recovery	
Mintz 1983	9-1/3	10	m	began just after aunt gave birth	depressed	no	3 times a week for 2 years	improved	fluids decreased; exercise increased; drank only milk; wished to be a baby
Reinhart et al 1972	8-1/3	8-2/3	f	birth of sibling	depressed	no	yes	2 years normal wt.	
	10-1/3	11	f	seemed to be reacting to her mothers urging her older sister to lose weight	depressed at times psychotic	1 year		fair to poor	6 years later she was heavy but not obese; psychologically fragile: in hospital had tube feeding and ECT
Shafii et al 1975	7-1/3	8	f	cry for help to liberate her from suppressive home environment	passive dependent depressed	6 months	refused	none	returned to normal weight in hospital but did not accept outpatient therapy tube feeding
Sperling 1978	6	7	f	birth of brother patient age 6	paranoid features	no	1-1/2 years	improved	followed into late adolescence and she did well; had fear of cats; suspicious mother wasn't giving her good food
Sylvester 1945	4	4	f	loss of mother's attention when father returned home & she became pregnant	shy depressed	7 months		3 years doing well	psychoanalytically oriented psychotherapy
Tridon et al 1983	11	11	m	experienced an injustice; suicide of relative	obsessive paranoid prepsychotic	no	12 months	poorly schizoid paranoid	possible schizophrenic evaluation; he defended a friend who was bullied by peers; he was excluded from his peers; he went on a hunger strike to protest the social injustice he perceived
Warren 1968	10-1/2	N.R.	f	N.R.	shy conscientious	yes		see comments	she was followed until age 20 and was healthy
	11-1/6	N.R.	f	N.R.	shy & anxious	yes		see comments	by age 14 she had not recovered
	11-1/2	N.R.	f	N.R.	shy & anxious	yes		see comments	by age 17 she had not recovered
Werman & Katz 1975	11-1/2	13	f	father said she was a walking garbage can	hysterical ego defects	3 weeks	5 weeks	see comments	homosexual orientation in late adolescence; father abusive and possibly sexually involved with neighborhood children
	11-1/2	13	f	same as above	ego defects	no	no	see comments	same as above except she did not have homosexual orientation

N.R. = not reported

no obvious differences in etiology, in features of their illness, and in the follow-up results, they were considered together." This study suggested that there is little differences between prepubertal and postpubertal anorexia nervosa.* It is not difficult to take issue with this hypothesis. The number in the sample is quite small and the age range of the girls is narrow (10 to 15 years). For example, two of the prepubertal girls were aged 11 years old, and two of the postpubertal girls were aged 12 and 13 years old. This study does not really compare children who are distinctly prepubertal to a group of postpubescent older adolescents who have completed all aspects of puberty. Nor does the paper clearly define puberty. Therefore, it is not surprising that differences were not found.

Sours [51] in 1979 indicated that latency-age girls tend to display besides the standard criteria for anorexia nervosa, defects in ego structure and organization along with pregenital instinctual fixation and infantile object dependency. In reference to boys, Sours mentions that these patients are usually prepubertal or early adolescent chubby boys who fear oedipal-genital feelings toward the mother. In wake of the regressive shift they experience a fear of maternal dependency and, sometimes, a merger with the inner object. They view their chubbiness as an indication of femininity, weakness, and homosexuality. A strong, negative, oedipal history and feminine identification is usually apparent. He also mentions that prepubertal onset, duration beyond five years, and persistence through adolescence are grave prognostic indicators. These areas are controversial.

Irwin [2,27] has written the only paper that presents a series of preadolescent and latency-age children. Fifteen cases of early-onset anorexia nervosa (age 12 and under) are identified based on records from Children's Memorial Hospital between 1960 and 1980. He describes the clinical characteristics and the possible connection to affective disorder (depression) of this early-onset variant of anorexia nervosa.

CASE ILLUSTRATION

Mary's family came to the University of California, Irvine, Child Study Center from a city about 800 miles away requesting treatment for their daughter. Mary, aged 10, had gone from 106 lb to 79 lb over about six months time. She had been unsuccessfully treated in her own area. Weight loss started as dieting to lose a few pounds but did not stop, becoming critical when her parents took a three-week vacation without her. Her best and only girlfriend had moved away, so she was left with adult friends of her parents.

Mary, who was depressed and obsessive, described her problem as follows: "I have a computer in my mind and stomach that says 'You dummy, don't eat that!'" It was an obsessive and driving voice that frightened her. She was fearful of eating, overeating, and not eating. She wanted to please her parents, but the voice inside her told her not to.

Her mother was 45 years old, overweight, serious, and dominating. Mary's parents had been married for 27 years. They became upset with the "rat race" in California and had moved three years before.

Her father was a 48-year-old, tall, extroverted man, with a deep voice, large hands, and a beard resembling that of a biblical prophet.

Although Mary was extremely thin and on the verge of being hospitalized, she saw herself as excessively obese. Her pediatric endocrinologist indicated that she had not had menarche.

Mary was born when her brother was 10. Her mother had not wanted another child. Throughout her childhood there were several separations. Mother returned to work when Mary was 3 months old. At 15 months the entire family left her with another family for three weeks when they went on vacation. At age 2 years she was sent to nursery school against her will. Generally during her life her parents took "adult" vacations.

Mary had never been able to oppose her parents nor the adult regime, which the family followed. Although not really overweight when her diet began, she was teased by boys about being fat. Her general helplessness led her to seek control of her life by controlling her weight. She shielded herself from budding sexuality by losing weight. Mary's depression and anorexia nervosa was contributed to by her mother's laissez-faire attitude toward her from the time of conception. Mary's parent's lack of empathy and inability to make contact with their daughter also happened with their son. He had experienced a marked depression, which lasted from the third through ninth grades. It wasn't until family therapy had started that they knew about it.

Mary received outpatient psychotherapy twice a week individually and family therapy once a week with her parents. Treatment continued for three months, when they decided to return home and resume with the former psychotherapist who was now obtaining consultation from a state facility. They telephoned a few months later to say that Mary was eating better and was happier.

DISCUSSION OF CLINICAL ISSUES

The course of illness in children with early-onset anorexia nervosa is different than in late adolescence and

---

* Similar ideas have been expressed about major depressive disorders in children. [59]

early adulthood, although there are phenomenological stimilarities.

Children in Piagets' [52] stage of concrete operations are more likely to generalize pathological food intake to fluid intake. In Irwins' study, three children stopped all food and fluid intake for an average of four days. At this stage of development they are less able to abstract, and even water is thought to be "food." Therefore, these children believe that water can cause them to gain weight and they abstain. In Warren's [44] series of 20 children, two prepubertal 12-year-olds died. In Blitzer's series of 15 children, one 10-year-old child died. These reports underlie the seriousness of anorexia nervosa.

Prepubertal adipose distribution differs from that found in postpubertal women. At average weight an 8-year-old girl will have a smaller percentage of total body fat than her 16-year-old counterpart. Having less total body fat initially, school girls will be more emaciated than young women who lose an equal percentage of total body weight.

In Irwin's [27] study of 15 preadolescent girls, two thirds of the patients required hospitalization less than six months after beginning dieting.

Children in the 4- to 11-year-old age range are, in Erikson's [53] terminology, developing initiative and industry as opposed to guilt and inferiority. In contrast, adolescents are developing identity as opposed to identity diffusion. Children are more dependent than adolescents on their families. Consequently, it might be expected that they would be influenced more by relationships within the family than by issues related to adolescence such as appearance, identity, and separation from the family. Children were profoundly affected by such stressors as birth of a sibling, poisoning of a dog, family arguments, divorce, and deaths. Fourteen (65%) of the 22 children for which a precipitant was given had stressors of this type. The more typical adolescent precipitant relating to being teased about being fat was mentioned in only 4 (18%) of the 22 children. This adolescent precipitant was less common in the younger children. This distinction is important in that an intense fear of becoming obese is a DSM-III diagnostic feature of anorexia nervosa. In future studies this diagnostic feature needs to be explored in more detail, because the case studies reported here did not provide enough detail to comment definitively on this point.

Children in the 4- to 11-year-old age range in Freudian terminology are in the oedipal and latency stages. Fantasies about pregnancy and avoidance of it could be of importance. In one girl the precipitant was being forced to perform fellatio [13]. The precipitant in several children was related to a birth in the family. In latency, the drives are quiescent in theory, which might help account for the apparent decreased incidence of anorexia nervosa.

Growth retardation in undernourished prepubertal children is a concern. Phillips [54] has emphasized that the impact of diet on growth is determined by the timing of altered nutrition. He points out that nutritional restrictions during tissue hyperplasia are likely to result in permanent limitation of growth. Lucas [55] in reviewing the records of a series of patients who began to lose weight before mid-adolescence found that of 35 girls and 12 boys, only 3 girls and 2 boys had an impairment of linear growth. It may be that once the chain of events initiating the pubertal growth spurt has been set into motion, only an extreme weight loss can stop it.

In 6 (17%) of the 33 cases in my sample, prepsychosis or significant ego defects were reported. This number seems high and needs to be examined in future studies.

Rapidity of deterioration characteristic of this age-group has important implications for treatment. There is little time for outpatient interventions to reverse the weight loss. It is especially important in the 4- to 11-year-olds to correctly identify the diagnosis at an early stage to implement treatment on an outpatient basis to avoid hospitalization.

CONTROVERSIES

There is some controversy over whether lean latency-age children need to lose 25% of their original body weight to be equivalent to a 25% weight loss in older adolescents or young adults. Irwin [2,27] has suggested that a 15% weight loss would be more appropriate as a diagnostic criteria for anorexia nervosa in prepubertal children.

Is early-onset anorexia nervosa merely a variant of the more usual presentation, or is it a different entity? Irwin [27] and Sours [51] intimate the latter possibility. In Irwin's [27] study and in the cases reviewed in this chapter, although none of the children could be diagnosed as suffering from a primary affective disorder, many of the children exhibited depressive symptoms. Could early-onset anorexia nervosa be a childhood form of affective disorder?

Six of the 33 cases demonstrated prepsychotic features or significant ego defects. This could indicate that these children have another psychiatric diagnosis with anorexia as a symptom, or it could indicate the children are more disturbed than adolescents or adults with anorexia nervosa.

Is prepububeral anorexia nervosa a different disorder than the adolescent or adult form? Developmental issues are different in childhood, which in part accounts for an altered clinical presentation. Organic factors related to hormonal homeostasis are also different before puberty. I think that anorexia nervosa does occur in younger childen and that there are both similarities and differences from the adolescent form.

FUTURE DIRECTION

It is possible that these younger children suffer in a different way than their adolescent counterparts because of the difference in developmental variables. Systematic biochemical, phenomenological, longitudinal, natural history, and family research on these children, separate from their older cohorts, will provide the basis for greater understanding.

REFERENCES

1. Falstein EI, Feinstein SC, Judas I. Anorexia nervosa in the male child. Am J Orthopsychiatry, 1956; 26:751-70.
2. Irwin M. Diagnosis of anorexia nervosa in children and the validity of DSM-III Am J Psychiatry, 1981; 138:1382-3.
3. Newman Dorland WA. Dorland's Illustrated Medical Dictionary, 23rd ed. Philadelphia and London: WB Saunders Company, November, 1962: 94.
4. Nelson EN, Vaughn VC, McKay JR. Textbook of pediatrics. Ninth edition. 1969: 28-9.
5. Merriam-Webster A. Webster's New Collegiate Dictionary. Springfield, Massachusetts: G & C Merriam Company, 1977: 47.
6. Morton R. Phtisiologica: On a treatise of consumption. London: Sam, Smith and Benj. Walford, 1694:202-203.
7. Lasegue EC. De l'anorexie hysterique. Arch Gen Med, 1873; 21:385- 403. Translation: On hysterical anorexia. Med Times & Gaz, 1873; 2:265-266, 367-369. New York: International University Press, 1964; 104-31.
8. Gull WW. Anorexia nervosa. Kaufman MR, Heiman M, ed. Evolution of psychosomatic concepts. New York: International University Press, 1964; 104-31.
9. Gull WW. Anorexia nervosa. Kaufman MR, Heiman M, ed. Evolution of psychosomatic concepts. New York: International Universities Press, 1964; 132-40.
10. Collins WJ. Anorexia nervosa. Lancet, 1894; 1:202-3.
11. Marshall CF. A fatal case of anorexia nervosa. Lancet, 1895; 1:817.
12. Botella C, Botella S. Two cases of anorexia nervosa. J Child Psychoatherpay (Paris), 1978; 4:119-29.
13. Blitzer JR, Rollins N, Blackwell A. Children who starve themselves: Anorexia nervosa. Psychosomatic Medicine, 1961; 23:369-83.
14. Brown SB. A retrospective study of six cases of primary anorexia nervosa in young females. Unpublished dissertation, Institute for Clinical Social Work, 1983:
15. Rose JA. Eating inhibition in children in relation to anorexia nervosa. Psychosomatic Medicine, 1943; 5:117-24.
16. Sherman JC, Sherman M. Birth fantasy in a young child. Psychoanalytic Review, 1929; 16:408-19.
17. Nemiah J. Anorexia nervosa—a clinical psychiatric study. Medicine (Baltimore), 1950; 19:225-68.
18. Comby J. Anorexie nerveuse. Arch Med Enf, 1909, 12:926.
19. Comby J. Anorexie nerveuse chez les nourissons. Arch med Enf, 1912; 15:697.
20. Comby J. Anorexia infantile et juvenile . Press Med, 1927; 1:40.
21. Lutz J. Kombination einer neurose der pubertatsmagersucht mit katatonerartigen zustandschild. A Kinderpsychiat, 1947-48; 14:68.
22. Ruegg M. Zum psycheschen bild der pubertatsmagersucht. Discussion Zurich, 1950. In Thoma H. Anorexia nervosa. New York; International University Press, 1967:
23. Trefzer C. Hungerstreik in Kindersalter. Discussion. Zurich, 1939. In Thoma H. Anorexia nervosa, New York: International University Press, 1967:
24. Wissler H. Die pubertatsmagersucht. Monatschrift Kinderheilklinic, 1941; 85:172.
25. Milner MA. A suicidal symptom in a child of three. International J Psychoanalysis, 1944; 25:53-61.
26. Rank B, Putnam MC, Rochlin G. The significance of the "emotional climate" in early feeding difficulties. Psychosomatic Medicine, 1943; 5:117-24.
27. Irwin M. Early onset of anorexia nervosa. Southern Medical Journal, May, 1984; 77:5.
28. Anyan WR Jr. Schowalter JE. A comprehensive approach to anorexia nervosa. Child Psychiatry, 1983; 22:122-7.
29. Galdston R. Mind over matter. Observations on 50 patients hospitalized with anorexia nervosa. J Am Academy of Child Psychiatry, 1972; 11:114-31.
30. Goetz PL, Succop RA, Reinhart JB, Miller A. Anorexia nervosa in children. A follow-up study. Am J Orthopsychiatry, 1977; 47:597- 603.
31. Hall A. Family structure and relationships of 50 female anorexia nervosa patients. Australian and New Zealand Journal of Psychiatrry, 1978; 12:263-8.
32. Halmi KA. Anorexia nervosa: Demographic and clinical features in 94 cases. Psychosomatic Medicine, 1974; 36:18-26.
33. Halmi KA, Casper RC, Eckert ED, Goldberg SC, Davis JM. Unique features associated with age of onset of anorexia nervosa. Elsevier North-Holland Biomedical Press. Psychiatry Research, 1979; I:209-15.
34. Pugliese MT, Lifshitz F, Grad G, Fort P, Marks-Katz M. Fear of obesity: A cause of short stature and delayed puberty. N Engl Med, 1983; 9:513-8.
35. English OS, Pearson GHJ. Common neurosis of children and adults. New York: Norton, 1937; 82-100.
36. Forchheimer F. Anroexia nervosa in children. Pediatrics half a century ago. Archives of Pediatrics, 1907; 24:801-10.
37. Lesser LI, Ashenden B. Debuskey M, Eisenberg L. Anorexia nervosa in children. Am J of Orthopsychiatry, 1960; 30:572-80.
38. Mintz IL. Fear of being fat: The treatment of anorexia nervosa and bulimia. In: Philip C, ed. Anorexia ner-

vosa and bulimia in males. New York: Wilson Aranson, 1983; 264-77.

39. Reinhart JB, Kenna MD, Succop RA. Anorexia nervosa in children: Outpatient management. J Am Academy Child Psychiatry, 1972; 11:114-31.

40. Shafii M, Salguero C, Finch SM. Psychopathology and treatments of anorexia nervosa in latency-age siblings. Anorexia a deux. J Am Child Psychiatry, 1975; 14:617-32.

41. Sperling M. Psychosomatic disorders in childhood: Case histories of anorexia nervosa. New York, London: Jason Aaronson, 1978; 142-149.

42. Sylvester E. Analysis of psychogenic anorexia and vomiting in a four-year-old-child. Psychoanalytic Study of the Child. New York: International Universities Press, 1945; 1:167-187.

43. Tridon P, Crombez Y, Marchand P, Prot F, Vidailhet C. L'anorexie mentale du garcon, Acta Paedopsychiat, Nancy, France, 1983; 49:311-9.

44. Warren W. A study of anorexia nervosa in young girls. J Child Psychol Psychiat, 1968; 9:27-40.

45. Weman DS, Katz J. Anorexia nervosa in a pair of identical twins. Child Psychiatry, 1975; 14:4.

46. Theander S. Anorexia nervosa: A psychiatric investigation of 94 female cases. Acta Psychiat Scand (Suppl), 1970; 214:1-194.

47. Morgan HG, Russell GFM. Value of family background and clinical featurees as predictors of long-term outcome in anorexia nervosa: Four year follow-up study of 42 patients. Psychol Med, 1975; 5:355-71.

48. Casper RC, Davos JM. On the course of anorexia nervosa. Am J Psychiatry, 1977; 134:974-8.

49. Bruch H. Eating disorders. New York: Basic Books, 1973; 274-286.

50. Kashani J. Current perspectives in childhood depression: An overview. Am J of Psych, 1981; 138(2): 143-153.

51. Sours GA. The primary anorexia nervosa syndrome. In Noshpitz JD, ed. Basic handbook of child psychiatry. New York: Basic Books, 1979; 2:568-580.

52. Piaget J. The child's conception of the world. New Jersey: Littlefield, Adams, 1975;1-33.

53. Erikson EH. Childhood and society, second edition. New York; WW Norton, 1963;247-274.

54. Phillips LS. Nutrition, metabolism and growth. In: Daughady WH, ed. Endocrine control of growth. New York: Elsevier Press, 1981: 121-73.

55. Lucas AR. Undernutrition and growth. N Engl J Med, 1983; 309:550-1.

56. Jacobs BW, Isaacs S. Pre-pubertal anorexia: A retrospective controlled study. J Child Psychol Psychiat, 1985; 27:237-250.

Chapter 27

Anorexia Nervosa in Adults

Walter Vandereycken

INTRODUCTION

Anorexia nervosa is no longer considered to be an exclusively adolescent disorder. Although many clinicians recognize its occurrence in adults, the literature on this subject is still very scarce, and research is almost inexistent.

Probably the most common form of adult anorexia nervosa is the continuation into the adult life of the syndrome that had begun in the patient's teens. In a yet unknown proportion of adult patients, however, a typical full-blown anorexia nervosa picture developed "de novo." But the question remains whether it is really "de novo," since the majority of cases demonstrate that some preoccupation with food or body shape preceded the actual establishment of the syndrome or that previous nonanorectic psychopathology clearly impinged on adult life [1].

In the present chapter we will focus first on the diagnostic problems raised by the occurrence of anorexia nervosa and related disorders in adults. The older patients face us with two major aspects that could be of great importance in clinical practice: the age at onset of the disorder and the duration of illness. Current research suggests that both factors might not only influence the form of the clinical picture the patient presents, but also determine to a great extent its long-term outcome. For this reason, the older and/or chronic patient represents a specific challenge to the clinician, particularly with regard to treatment efficacy and terti-

ary prevention. From a scientist-practitioner perspective it is argued that both researcher and therapist have to rely on a dynamic and dimensional conceptualization of eating disorders.

HISTORICAL BACKGROUND

Lasègue [2] based his classic paper "De 1'Anorexie Hystérique" (1873) on eight cases, all women, the youngest being 18 and the eldest 32. Very briefly, Lasègue noted some details on a married woman "hysterical for a long time and 30 years of age when the anorexia occurred." But, no doubt, this was a case of hysterical refusal of food that has nothing to do with the modern notion of anorexia nervosa. It is interesting to mention here that the few sentences Lasègue wrote on this elder woman have been omitted in the English translation of his paper [3].

Another case that is frequently mistaken for being a historical description of anorexia nervosa is the one reported by Naudeau [4] in 1789: It is about a 35-year-old woman who suddenly was suffering from pain attacks followed by a strong aversion to food, which was correctly diagnosed by Naudeau as being "une affection histérique." As these cases show, one has to be careful with the examples in the older literature claimed to be anorexia nervosa, especially when it concerns adult women.

The same applies to Ryle's [5] report on 51 cases seen during 16 years of consulting practice, including a series of 13 cases between 31 and 59 years (average 44 years). Though we may doubt the diagnosis in these cases, Ryle was the first to pay attention to these older-than-usual anorectics: "I have thought fit...to include a group of older women because the clinical picture seemed to me essentially similar and the patients equally deserving of proper understanding and treatment" (p. 894). "The physical and psychological stigmata were not to be distinguished from those encountered in the younger group excepting in so far as maturity and environmental influences modified the type or form of individual reaction" (p. 896).

The details Ryle gave on two cases of these "nervous, voluble, sparrowlike women with sparrow's appetite" do not seem to justify the diagnosis of anorexia nervosa according to modern criteria. Similar diagnostic doubts concern Berkman's [6] review of 117 patients diagnosed with anorexia nervosa at the Mayo Clinic between 1925 and 1932, including four postmenopausal women. This is equally true for the monograph by Bliss and Branch [7], who mentioned a woman in her 40s and two others who first lost weight in their 50s.

In France, Laboucarié and coworkers [8,9] reported on large series of so-called anorexia nervosa patients, but they included all types of weight loss or anorexia (loss of appetite) due to psychological reasons. Hence, no wonder that 10% of their cases were older than 30 years.

As King [10] rightly observed, most of the older cases (including women past their menopause) belong to a secondary atypical group. But, like in males, one might suppose that the diagnosis of primary anorexia nervosa is easily overlooked in adults because of one factor deviating from the classic picture of the syndrome: In boys the gender is misleading, in adults it is the age. Nevertheless, Garfinkel and Garner [11] argue that maybe the disorder has always been common in postadolescence, since studies by Kay and Leight [12] and Halmi [13] reported that 30% and 13%, respectively, of their patients were over age 25 at onset.

DIAGNOSTIC PROBLEMS

The syndrome method of diagnosis of anorexia nervosa has many strengths and weaknesses; it leads to several classes of qualitatively and quantitatively atypical presentations of the syndrome [14]. The Feighner criteria [15] exclude patients older than 25 years at the onset of the syndrome. But, as Andersen [14] emphasized, there arises a clinical problem of recognition of otherwise typical syndromes if such criteria are seen as defining criteria rather than as exclusionary criteria to be disregarded when appropriate. Probably because of

these problems, the age-of-onset factor has been deleted in the DSM-III criteria [16] for anorexia nervosa.

While it remains true that anorexia nervosa is overwhelmingly a disorder of adolescence (with a usual range from 12 to 25 years of age), several clinicians have the impression that it is developing more frequently in older women [11]. But due to a lack of epidemiological studies in this respect, the increase of reports on adult anorexia nervosa might equally well reflect a better and more accurate diagnostic assessment in an era of growing awareness of the disorder.

Interestingly enough, anorexia nervosa in young adults has not caught the attention in the literature, except for some casual reports [1], whereas more clinicians seem to have been struck by the occurrence of anorectic behavior in middle-aged females. Since 1970, several anecdotal case descriptions of women developing postmenopausal anorexia appeared in the literature:

1. Kellett et al. [17] described a 52-year-old woman with typical symptoms of anorexia nervosa including abuse of slimming tablets and purgatives and self-induced vomiting. The patient's previous medical history revealed periods of weight loss, bulimia, amenorrhea, and disturbed body image, which, however, were never diagnosed as anorexia nervosa or an anorectic-like condition.

2. Launer's [18] patient, a 70-year-old housewife, presented with weight loss of unexplained origin, fear of fatness, refusal to eat, and denial of her emaciated state. Though she was a lifelong consumer of laxatives and exhibited a limited food intake for many years, the absence of amenorrhea, pronounced weight loss, or marked anorectic behavior in her previous history justified the assumption that she had not developed the full clinical picture of anorexia nervosa before the actual episode.

3. Vecht-van den Bergh [19] reported on four cases of anorexia nervosa in women older than 35 years: in only one case (a 50-year-old married woman) the syndrome developed "de novo" without a previous history of weight/eating disturbances. In a 36-year-old woman it was clearly a relapse of a condition that started in the patient's teens, whereas in the two other cases (45 and 56 years old), it appeared to be an exacerbation of a rather chronic history of eating problems.

4. Andersen [14] discussed the case of a 53-year-old married female with a 22-year history of typical anorexia nervosa. This case combined both late onset and chronicity.

5. The case of a 47-year-old woman described by Maillot et al. [20] concerned, in fact, a typical ex-

ample of chronic anorexia nervosa that went undiagnosed for many years.

6. A variant of the latter example has been published by Oyewumi [21] who stresses that, especially in mild cases of long-standing and recurrent anorexia nervosa, the condition might go undiagnosed in adolescence and be picked up at a later age when the condition becomes worse.

7. Another variant is the case of a 67-year-old woman recorded by Böning [22]: Her anorexia nervosa appeared to be a relapse of a condition that first occurred in the patient's adolescence followed by a period of almost total remission during several years.

8. Finally, one of the rare examples of typical anorexia nervosa in a middle-aged man has been reported by Mintz [23].

Dally and Gomez [24] report on a number of cases beginning after the age of 40 and they called it "anorexia tardive" referring to the French author Carrier [25] who in his dissertation first used the term "forme tardive" to describe these older-than-usual patients. But Dally and Gomez are not clear as to the question whether the anorexia tardive is a variant of primary anorexia nervosa or just a secondary form. They report that virtually all patients with an age at onset of 19 years and older are atypical anorectics: "The older the patient the more likely she or he is to have atypical features, ie, to have secondary anorexia nervosa" (p. 18) [24]. The authors emphasize that especially in older patients other reasons of weight loss have to be excluded, in particular depression. But, "the patient with anorexia tardive has a bird-like alertness which belies serious depression" (p. 155). Hence, Dally and Gomez suggest that anorexia tardive is of primary nature, although it may be atypical in its presentation (see Andersen [14]).

Several cases of anorexia tardive in the literature are, in fact, atypical presentations of an atypical syndrome:

1. Bernstein [26] recorded a lady of 94 who stopped eating, but her prompt recovery with electroconvulsive therapy suggest the existence of an underlying affective disorder.

2. Lützenkirchen and Böning [27] extensively discussed the case of a 45-year-old woman in whom it was difficult to come to one diagnosis, because she suffered from both an anorectic syndrome and depression.

3. Three case reports of older men (28-30) concerned psychogenic weight loss without enough clinical evidence for the diagnosis of anorexia nervosa.

According to Sours [31], other examples of anorexia tardive are the thin spinster, emaciated for a lifetime and now in her fifth and sixth decade, and those anorectic individuals who conceal lifelong starvation behind a feigned malabsorption syndrome, which they claim resists treatment. Exceptionally, anorexia tardive may be preceded by other psychosomatic illnesses as in the case of a 40-year-old woman who manifested, in succession, bronchial asthma, peptic ulcer, regional ileitis, and finally, anorexia nervosa [32].

From a clinical point of view, the diagnosis of anorexia nervosa in late life faces two major problems: the definition of onset and the exclusion of previous episodes of anorectic-like conditions. Both aspects are, of course, interrelated. What is meant by onset of disorder? Does this mean the behavior leading to the loss of weight, or is it the onset of weight loss itself? Or, when does "normal" fasting end and when do pathological anorectic symptoms begin? [33] These questions are important in order to distinguish the cases with late-onset "de novo" from those with a previous history of mild, concealed, undiagnosed, or overt anorexia nervosa.

We have the impression that a real "de novo" development of anorexia nervosa after the age of 40 is very rare, whereas it may be more common in women between 25 and 35 years old. In the latter cases it is often linked to marital problems or pregnancy [34]. In most cases of anorexia tardive, a thorough clinical assessment (that has excluded other causes of emaciation) will reveal that the condition appears to be either an exacerbation of a chronic eating disorder or a relapse of anorexia nervosa after a period of (probably partial) remission.

According to Crisp [35], an anorexia nervosa syndrome supervening in older age is much more likely to be associated with a major degree of premorbid obesity: "The obese person is likely to have been struggling to reduce weight for years and may indeed have lost some down to near normal or normal levels, but only at the price of vigorous dietary control. Only later does anorexia nervosa emerge. Under such conditions it can be seen that, whatever age she may be at the time of onset, she has been wrestling with problems of an adolescent order" (p. 32). This clinical experience, however, forces us to reconsider the rather static way of diagnosing eating disorders, as we will discuss further on.

A final remark regarding clinical assessment in older-than-usual patients: the real age of onset is not always easy to establish when patients tend to deny or "forget" the occurrence of previous episodes of anorexia nervosa or related disorders [36]. For this reason, Bruch [37] warns that in some patients the reported age may be too high: "In three married women with a reported onset at age 25 or 26 years there was justified suspicion of an earlier episode, for which the information was vague and inaccurate" (p. 236). In some cases it is only during the course of treatment that patients come to "remember" having had similar symptoms in their youth. Sometimes an old history of anorexia nervosa is only discovered through the information from previous therapists or close relatives who have been a witness of the patient's behavior in that period.

THE CHANGING CLINICAL PICTURE

Comparing patients seen from 1970 to 1975 with those seen from 1976 to 1981, Garfinkel and Garner [11] found a trend toward increased average age of onset from 17 to 18 years. The same comparison showed that the age at presentation had significantly increased during the same period: from 19.3 to 22.2 years. This means, according to the authors, that the interval between onset and referral has increased despite the growing public awareness of the disorder. Garfinkel and Garner seem to overlook, however, that an important selection factor may have influenced these changes [38]. In specialized centers known for the treatment of anorexia nervosa patients, a "negative selection" may operate in such a way that patients with long and intractable illnesses tend to be referred.

This brings us to the question of whether there is a relationship between age at onset and/or duration of illness on the one hand, and form and/or severity of the clinical picture on the other. Such a relationship is suggested by the following three groups of clinical evidence:

1. Reports about unusual and severe cases (not necessarily anorexia nervosa patients) of purgative abuse [39], addiction to diuretics [40], or enema abuse [41] show that the patients concerned are mostly middle-aged (or even older) women, usually with a chronic disorder.

2. The majority of patients with bulimia or bulimia nervosa (excluding anorexia nervosa patients) are in their 20s; only a small minority are schoolchildren [42].

3. Most comparisons between the abstaining ("dieters") type of anorexia nervosa on the one hand, and the bulimic ("binge eaters") or related ("vomiters/purgers") type of anorexia nervosa on the other, demonstrate that patients of the second type are frequently older at onset or presentation and/or display a longer history of their eating disorder.

Since this chapter is about anorexia nervosa, we will discuss the research data that contribute to the third group of clinical evidence for the above mentioned relationship. Garfinkel et al. [43] reported no differences between the bulimia and the restrictor group of anorexia nervosa patients in age at onset or duration of illness, "arguing against bulimia simply representing a manifestation of chronicity." Beumont et al. [44] did not observe differences in age at onset between dieters and vomiters/purgers, but the latter displayed a longer delay from onset to presentation of symptoms (4.4 versus 1.1 years). This is very close to our own findings [45]: Comparing dieters to a combined group of binge eaters and vomiters/purgers, we found the latter were significantly older at admission (22.2 versus 18.4 years) and exhibited a significantly longer duration of illness (4.1 versus 2.0 years). According to Casper et al. [46], who similarly remarked an older age in their bulimic patients compared with dieters, this fact is "suggestive of bulimia as a sign of chronicity. An alternative, albeit hypothetical, explanation would be that a certain degree of physiological and psychological maturation is a necessary requirement for bulimia to develop."

Our own research on these variables revealed another interesting finding [45]: several anorexia nervosa patients develop bulimia during or after treatment and they seem to be characterized by the same features as those patients who already manifested bulimia at admission, namely older age and longer duration of illness. Moreover, our investigation showed a significantly higher proportion of previous treatment failures in both the binge eaters and vomiters/purgers in comparison with the dieters, of whom about 43% had received no previous specific treatment for anorexia nervosa. Although these findings do not prove a direct causal relationship between previous treatment (failures) and subsequent occurrence of bulimia or vomiting/purging, they at least suggest the possibility of iatrogenic influences on the development, exacerbation, or deterioration of an eating disorder.

The clinical evidence and assumptions we have discussed so far may be tested by comparing different age-groups within a sample of anorexia nervosa patients. Halmi et al. [47] examined the relationship between age of onset and a variety of personal characteristics in 105 anorectics. The patients whose onset of illness occurred at a later age (18 years and older) tended to have a greater weight loss during their illness, more "underweight problems" before the onset of illness, less of the typical anorectic behaviors and attitudes, greater body disparagement, more symptoms of depression, and a greater number of previous hospitalizations. These associations suggest that the disease process is somewhat different and clearly more severe in the older group. The authors concluded that an older age of onset of anorexia nervosa might predict a poor outcome.

Table 1 shows the results of our own investigation. We subdivided a consecutive series of 200 anorexia nervosa patients hospitalized at the University Psychiatric Center in Kortenberg according to the age of onset. We have chosen the age of 21 years as an arbitrary selection

Table 27.1 Comparison of adolescent and adult patients with anorexia nervosa

	Age at Onset		
	<21 N = 174	>21 N = 26	p*
Age at admission (yr)	20.0 ± 4.1	28.5 ± 5.4	.0001
Duration of illness (yr)	3.6 ± 3.5	3.3 ± 2.2	ns
Married (%)	12.6	44.0	.0001
Weight at admission (kg)	38.5 ± 6.0	35.8 ± 4.2	.008
Weight loss vs ideal weight (%)	29.7 ± 9.5	35.5 ± 9.4	ns
No previous hospitalization (%)	34.7	8.0	.001
Bulimia (%)	16.5	22.0	.01
Vomiting/purging (%)	28.7	52.4	.0004
Long-term outcome (%)**			.05
Excellent	38.8	25.0	
Much improved	18.4	12.5	
Symptomatic	20.4	12.5	
Poor outcome	22.4	50.0	

*Two-sample t-test or chi-square test in two-way frequency tables; ns = no significance.
**According to the Global Clinical Score (48); follow-up duration averaged 4.9 ± 3
  and 4.2 ± 2 years, respectively; follow-up data have been gathered in 66 and 10
  cases, respectively.

point, since this is the official and legal minimal limit for adulthood in Belgium. Most of the results confirm the assumptions discussed above as well as the trends found in Halmi's [47] study. One has to be careful, however, with the analysis of our follow-up data because of the limited number of patients involved and the problems encountered in this type of research as we have discussed elsewhere [38]. Nevertheless, although there was no significant difference in duration of illness, our older anorectics weighed less at admission, had been more often hospitalized before, displayed more frequently signs of bulimia and, especially, vomiting/purging behavior, and their long-term outcome was generally worse than in patients with an early onset of illness.

THE CONTINUUM OF EATING DISORDERS

The previous clinical considerations lead us to think that eating/weight disorders could be better approached and understood if we abandon a static system of diagnosis and use a more dynamic and dimensional model instead. By "dynamic" we mean that we wish to include an important time factor in our descriptive approach, indicating that clinical situations may change. Indeed, every classification is the product of a given assessment at a given moment, ie, a static picture, a snapshot, or cross-section of temporaily observed characteristics. A dynamic approach takes into account the fact that the clinical picture of an eating disorder or a "dysorectic" [49] patient may alter in the course of time while the core problem remains unchanged. We, therefore, also advocate a dimensional model that pays attention to the het-

erogeneity of anorexia nervosa and its relationship with other eating/weight disorders such as bulimia (nervosa) and psychosomatic obesity.

The dysorexia/dysponderosis continuum shown in figure 1 is an attempt to describe eating/weight disorders in a dynamic and dimensional way. If the core problem is labeled as disturbed eating behavior (disregulated appetite, hunger, and/or satiety), the disorder can be put on the dimension dysorexia (anorexia or food abstinence versus hyperorexia or overeating). When the disorder is mainly conceptualized as disturbed or dysfunctional weight regulation or distorted weight control, it seems more appropriate to speak about the dimension dysponderosis (pursuit of thinness or "Magersucht" versus obesity or "Fettsucht"). This is, of course, only an artificial distinction, since most cases in clinical practice display a cluster of combined or concomitant features of both dimensions.

At one end of the continuum we place the "classifical" picture of primary anorexia nervosa, namely the dieters or abstainers. The subgroups of vomiters/purgers are also those anorectics who show bulimic tendencies or behavior. The bulimia (nervosa) syndrome (defined as an entity in DSM-III [16]) occupies a somehow pivotal position between the bulimic anorexia nervosa patients on the one hand, and those overweight subjects who impulsively overeat on the other. The latter are (formerly) obese patients or "thin fat people" [36] in whom peculiar eating patterns may be observed, such as binge eating, night eating, and eating without satiation [50]. Finally, at the other pole of the continuum we may place the more or less stable psychosomatic obes-

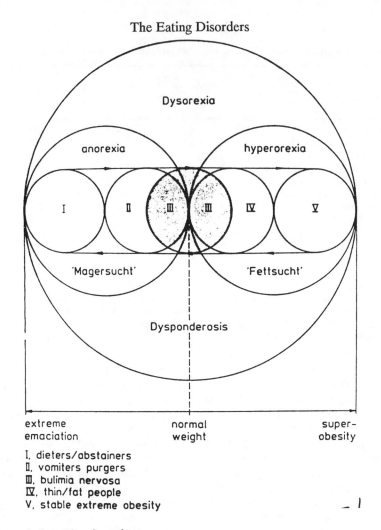

Figure 27.1 The dysorexia-dysponderosis continuum.

ity in which the overweight is the result of different factors (not merely caused by overeating).

These five identified clusters of symptoms have to be regarded as landmarks according to which we can subdivide a series of patients (eg, for comparative studies) and trace out the individual history of one patient [51]. Some cases may develop just one of these clinical forms, whereas others may move from one position to another. The interchangeability or alternation of symptoms is either a spontaneous phenomenon (eg, in the course of time an anorectic dieter may become a binge eater), or it is induced in an iatrogenic way (eg, forced feeding of the emaciated anorectic risks provoking vomiting).

In the case of the older patient, be it older with regard to age or to duration of disorder (the patient "career"), the dysorexia-dysponderosis problem may not only be different compared with younger patients, but may also show alterations in the clinical picture, either spontaneously or as a "complication" or side-effect of treatment (iatrogenic influences). This means that a special learning process is shaping the disorder into a more complicated form. Additional evidence for such a learning process is provided by the following findings: First, there seems to be a positive relationship between dietary restraint and binge eating, ie, chronic dieters are prone to bulimia through a mechanism of counterregulation [52]; second, vomiting as a weight-control method appears to be a learned maladaptive behavior, which is frequently inadvertently taught by well-meaning friends, relatives, and even professionals [53].

PROGNOSIS AND TREATMENT

When faced with chronic cases, one may be inclined to think of anorexia nervosa as an incurable illness with spontaneously occurring remission and exacerbation; here the aim of treatment is not cure but tertiary prevention, ie, limiting the "handicaps" of the disease the patient has to learn to live with. When faced with quick recoveries in young or "fresh" cases, anorexia nervosa may be viewed as a self-limited disorder from which almost all recover; here the follow-up question is not improvement but whether the course of the disease was milder as a result of treatment [54]. In view of the diversity of assessment methods used, it is not surprising that the published rates of recovery of anorexia nervosa vary between 10% and 86%, the majority falling between 30% and 50% [55].

Those studies with lengthy follow-up intervals and not restricted to young populations show similar results: About 40% of all patients are totally recovered, 30% are considerably improved, at least 20% are unchanged or seriously hampered, and about 10% have died as a result of anorexia nervosa [11]. As to the hard-fact type of data on which most researchers agree, long-term outcome of anorexia nervosa seems less favorable in cases showing a high age at onset, a long duration of illness, a very low body weight, and occurrence of bulimia, vomiting and/or laxative abuse. All these factors are not seldom combined in the older patients with a long illness history including treatment failures; this type of patient is clearly at risk for poor outcome and, therefore, in need of intensive, mostly residential treatment [54].

The chronic anorexia nervosa patient frequently elicits the analogy between eating disorders and addictions. Comparing excessive eating or pursuit of thinness to alcoholism, one has the impression that overeating and starving (together with vomiting and purging) may assume the character of hard drugs: Once present for some time, they show an apparent physical dependency and lead to social descent and physical ruin [56]. Perhaps one important consideration may explain the sometimes obstinate addiction to (non)eating: "Persons with eating disorders do not have the luxury of avoiding the problem substance as can be done for alcohol, drugs, or cigarettes. One has to eat, and difficulties in regulating food intake can remain a daily problem" [57] (p. 47).

Chronic patients with a long-standing illness of periodic and partial remissions and relapses or even less chronic cases with a history of treatment failures whereby "nutritional politics" has replaced psychotherapy (ie, repeated refeeding efforts without psychological understanding) are in danger that an irreversible automatization of the symptoms or a so-called "malignant autonomy" picture [58] may take over. Then, the symptoms that the anorectic patient has obstinately defended through the years come to be experienced as totally automatic, no longer the active expression of control over her body, but so dissociated from their original meaning and intention that the patient now feels controlled by the illness [59].

What eventually happens to those chronically dis-

abled anorexia nervosa patients who do not die from their condition? Crisp [35] called this an "elephants' graveyard" mystery: "Some remit at around the time of the menopause after having the condition since puberty—it has spanned their reproductive life and at the end of this time it is shed. Some others definitely remain 'ill' with it. Amenorrhoea is no longer a hallmark and they survive as isolated, eccentric and wizened old ladies" (p. 34).

What can we do for those patients who have "decided" to stay anorectic, who have "chosen" a life as an abstainer or a bulimic [60]? The life of the chronic abstainer is dominated by food both night and day; she feels safe in her rigid eating pattern and her routine and superficially satisfactory lifestyle in such a way that, although life is barren with anorexia, it becomes even more barren and painful without it. The chronic, "well-controlled" bulimic very often organizes her life around her bulimia; she no longer struggles to stop herself from bingeing, and she feels forced by the terror of weight gain to continue vomiting and purging." Bulimic episodes may become institutionalized, particularly with married patients, who can indulge in gourmet restaurants or at dinner parties, sustaining an otherwise empty but mutually dependent relationship with their spouse" [60] (p. 643).

Sometimes chronic anorectics may request treatment after many years of illness. Experienced clinicians all know some cases of chronic eating disorder who totally recovered after intensive treatment. In general, however, experience in treating chronic anorexia nervosa patients, who failed to maintain their weight after their index admission, was disappointing: At four- to eight-year follow-up most of them had a very low weight (below 75% of average) [61]. Treatment in these patients is a difficult and complex process not without serious risks, such as the precipitation of a psychotic reaction or a suicidal depression. "Perhaps we should abandon our so frequently unrealistic goal of a 'cure' and look towards supporting these individuals in their decision to remain anorectic, helping them to stabilize their anorexia nervosa and lead the fullest life possible with it" [60] (p. 641).

Chronic patients face us with the ethical question: When does the patient have the right to stay as she is? Opiate addicts are given the right to be maintained in an acceptable way by medically optimal prescription of their addictive drugs. In the same way, the anorexia nervosa patient may have at least the right to be helped to survive with her illness [34]. The problem remains of differentiating the treatable from the untreatable patient. The central questions are: Is this person likely to be better off without an eating disorder in the long-term? Has this person got the resources, both internal and external, to cope with the process of recovery? [60] In order to avoid overoptimistic or fatalistic reactions on the part of the therapist, the answers on these questions—the balance of advantages and disadvantages of the disorder and its eventual treatment—are, in fact, to be given during or after some treatment trial. In other words, the chronic patient has the right to stay anorectic if she has been offered an appropriate treatment, ie, the chance to change. And sometimes she will already change when being asked to keep her illness [62].

CONCLUSION

We know little or nothing substantial about anorexia nervosa in chronic cases or its course in adults. The limited knowledge we have seems to question our current approach to diagnosis and treatment of eating disorders, both of which have been based on the "typical" adolescent disorder. Maybe age and chronicity only shape the form of the clinical picture but not its real content. Dally and Gomez [24] divided the anorexia tardive into two groups: The hyperactive patients who pursue thinness at all costs, and the rather inactive ones who have sparrows' appetites and are afraid to eat much. The first type, less common, resembles the classical picture of adolescent anorexia nervosa, whereas the second type seems more close to the atypical or secondary forms of anorexia. Interestingly enough, in both types the crux of the problem, according to Dally and Gomez, is a resentful dependence on or a strongly ambivalent relationship with an important person the patient is living with: In the first type, this person usually is an adolescent daughter, while the husband seems to play the significant role in the second type (in unmarried patients this could also be the mother).

With regard to the form of eating disorders, we have advocated a dynamic and dimensional model in which the time factor (spontaneous life events and iatrogenic influences) plays an essential role. As to the content of the disorder, one may ask whether in some patients the anorexia is not engrained in their psychobiological development, whereas in others it could be rather an expression of interactional conflicts. In other words, it might be worthwhile to distinguish between the process type of anorexia nervosa and the reactive type. The former (more intrapersonal or endogenous?) seems difficult to cure in contrast to the latter (more interpersonal or exogenous?). We hypothesize that the first type, when occurring in adults, must have its roots in the patient's youth, and that the second type may develop "de novo" in later life.

Much of what has been said remains hypothetical. We need appropriate prospective studies on the long-term course of anorexia nervosa. Only this type of research may yield important information as to the factors—including therapeutic interventions—that determine the development and alteration (recovery, deterioration, relapse) of eating disorders.

REFERENCES

1. Wells LA. Anorexia nervosa: An illness of young adults. Psychiat, 1980; 52:270-82.
2. Lasègue C. De L'anorexie hystérique. Arch Gén Méd, 1873; 21:385-403.
3. Lasègue C. On hysterical anorexia. Med Tim Gaz, 1873; 2:265-266, 367-369. Reprinted in Kaufman MR, Heiman M, eds. Evolution of psychosomatic concepts. Anorexia Nervosa: A paradigm. New York: International Universities Press, 1964;143-155.
4. Naudeau J. Observation sur une maladie nerveuse accompagnée d'un dégoût extraordinaire pur les aliments (Observation on a nervous disease with an extraordinary aversion to food). J Méd Chir Pharmacol, 1789; 80:197-200.
5. Ryle JA. Anorexia nervosa. Lancet, 1936; 2:893-9.
6. Berkman JM. Anorexia nervosa, anorexia, inanition and low basal metabolic rate. Am J Med Sci, 1930; 180:411-24.
7. Bliss EL, Branch CHH. Anorexia nervosa: Its history, psychology and biology. New York: Hoeber, 1960.
8. Laboucarié J, Barrès P. Les aspects cliniques, pathogéniques et thérapeutiques de l'anorexie mentale (Clinical, pathogenic and therapeutic aspects of anorexia nervosa). Evol Psychiat, 1954; 1:119-46.
9. Laboucarié J, Rascol A, Karkous E, et al. L'anorexie mentale. Données resultant d'une expérience clinique et thérapeutique de 173 cas (Anorexia nervosa. Data from a clinical and therapeutic experience in 173 cases). Rev Méd Toulouse, 1966; 2193-210.
10. King A. Primary and secondary anorexia nervosa syndromes. Br J Psychiat, 1963; 109:470-9.
11. Garfinkel PE, Garner DM. Anorexia nervosa. A multidimensional perspective. New York: Brunner/Mazel, 1982.
12. Kay DWK, Leigh D. Natural history, treatment and prognosis of anorexia nervosa, based on study of 38 patients. J Ment Sci, 1954; 100:411-31.
13. Halmi KA. Comparison of demographic and clinical features in patient groups with different ages and weights at onset of anorexia nervosa. J Nerv Ment Dis, 1974; 158:222-5.
14. Andersen AE. Atypical anorexia nervosa. In Vigersky RA, ed. Anorexia nervosa. New York: Raven Press, 1977; 11-19.
15. Feighner JP, Robins E, Guze SB, et al. Diagnostic criteria for use in psychiatric research. Arch Gen Psychiat, 1972; 26:57-63.
16. American Psychiatric Association. Diagnostic and Statistical Manual of Mental Disorders (DSM-III). Washington DC: American Psychiatric Association,

1980.

17. Kellett J, Trimble M, Thorley A. Anorexia nervosa after the menopause. Br J Psychiat, 1976; 128:555-8.

18. Launer MA. Anorexia nervosa in late life. Br J Med Psychol, 1978; 51:375-7.

19. Vecht-van den Bergh R. Anorexia nervosa op oudere leeftijd (Anorexia nervosa in late life). Ned T Geneesk, 1979; 123:105-8.

20. Maillot S, Pras B, Perol JY, et al. Une anorexie mentale à l'âge de la ménopause (Anorexia nervosa at the menopause). Ann Méd-Psychol, 1979; 137:519-23.

21. Oyewumi LK. Is anorexia nervosa a disease of all ages? Psychiat J Univ Ottawa, 1981; 6:39-42.

22. Böning J. Psychogene Essstörungen und Anorexie im Senium (Psychogenic eating disorders and anorexia in old age). Prax Psychother, 1983; 28:170-80.

23. Mintz IL. Anorexia nervosa and bulimia in males. In Wilson CP, ed. Fear of being fat. The treatment of anorexia nervosa and bulimia. New York: Jason Aronson, 1983; 263-303.

24. Dally P, Gomez J. Anorexia nervosa. London: William Heinemann, 1979.

25. Carrier J. L'Anorexie Mentale. Paris: Librairie E. Le Francois, 1939.

26. Bernstein IC. Anorexia nervosa, 94-year-old woman treated with electroshock. Minn Med, 1972; 55:552-3.

27. Lützenkirchen J, Böning J. Anorektisches Syndrom und Depression (Anorectic syndrome and depression). Schweiz Arch Neurol Neurochir Psychiat, 1976; 118:175-84.

28. Carlberger G, Einarsson K, Felig P, et al. Severe malnutrition in a middle-aged man with anorexia nervosa. Nutr Metabol, 1971; 13:100-13.

29. Milberg WP, Hebben NA. Termination of self-monitoring as a negative reinforcer to increase weight gain in a 77-year-old anorexic male. Behav Therapist, 1979; 2(1):21-2.

30. Volmat R, Allers G, Vittouris N, et al. Statut actuel clinique et thérapeutique de l'anorexie mentale (Actual clinical and therapeutic state of anorexia nervosa). Ann Méd-Psychol, 1970; 128(2):161-84.

31. Sours J. Starving to death in a sea of objects. The anorexia nervosa syndrome. New York: Jason Aronson, 1980.

32. Levitan HL. Implications from an unusual case of multiple psychosomatic illness. Psychother Psychosom, 1978; 30:211-5.

33. Beumont PJV, Abraham SF, Argall WJ, et al. The onset of anorexia nervosa. Austr NZ J Psychiat, 1978; 12:145-9.

34. Vandereycken W. Uncommon eating/weight disorders related to amenorrhea, infertility and problematic pregnancy. In Prill HJ, Stauber M, eds. Advances in psychosomatic obstetrics and gynecology. Berlin-Heidelberg-New York: Springer Verlag, 1982; 124-128.

35. Crisp AH. Anorexia nervosa: Let me be. New York: Academic Press, 1981.

36. Mester H. Die anorexia nervosa. Berlin-Heidelberg-

New York: Springer Verlag, 1981.

37. Bruch H. Eating disorders. Obesity, anorexia nervosa, and the person within. New York: Basic Books, 1973.

38. Vandereycken W, Pierloot R. Long-term outcome research in anorexia nervosa. The problem of patient selection and follow-up duration. Int J Eat Dis, 1983; 2(4):237-42.

39. Levine D, Goode AW, Wingate DL. Purgative abuse associated with reversible cachexia, hypogammagolobulinaemia, and finger clubbing. Lancet, 1981; 1:919-20.

40. Love DR, Brown JJ, Fraser R, et al. An unusual case of self-induced electrolyte depletion. Gut, 1971; 12:284-90.

41. Barton JL, Terry JM, Barton ES. Enema abuse. Br J Psychiat, 1982; 141:621-3.

42. Fairburn CG. Bulimia: Its epidemiology and management. In Stunkard AJ, Stellar E, eds. Eating and its disorders. New York: Raven Press, 1984; 235-58.

43. Garfinkel PE, Moldofsky H, Garner DM. The heterogeneity of anorexia nervosa. Bulimia as a distinct subgroup. Arch Gen Psychiat, 1980; 37:1036-40.

44. Beumont PJV, George GCW, Smart DE. 'Dieters' and 'vomiters and purgers' in anorexia nervosa. Psychol Med, 1976; 6:617-22.

45. Vandereycken W, Pierloot R. The significance of subclassification in anorexia nervosa: A comparative study of clinical features in 141 patients. Psychol Med, 1983; 13:543-9.

46. Casper RC, Eckert ED, Halmi KA, et al. Bulimia. Its incidence and clinical importance in patients with anorexia nervosa. Arch Gen Psychiat, 1980; 37:1030-5.

47. Halmi KA, Casper RC, Eckert ED, et al. Unique features associated with age of onset of anorexia nervosa. Psychiat Res, 1979; 1:209- 15.

48. Garfinkel PE, Moldofsky H, Garner DM. The outcome of anorexia nervosa. In Vigersky RA, ed. Anorexia nervosa. New York: Raven Press, 1977; 315-29.

49. Guiora AZ. Dysorexia: A psychopathological study of anorexia nervosa and bulimia. Am J Psychiat, 1967; 124:391-3.

50. Stunkard AJ. Eating patterns and obesity. Psychiat Q, 1959; 33:284-95.

51. Holmgren S, Humble K, Norring C, et al. The anorectic bulimic conflict. An alternative diagnostic approach to anorexia nervosa and bulimia. Int J Eat Dis, 1983; 2(2):3-14.

52. Wardle J, Beinart H. Binge eating: A theoretical review. Br J Clin Psychol, 1981; 20:97-109.

53. Chiodo J, Latimer PR. Vomiting as a learned weight-control technique in bulimia. J Behav Ther Exp Psychiat, 1983; 14:131-5.

54. Vandereycken W, Meermann R. Anorexia nervosa. A clinician's guide to treatment. Berlin-New York: W. de Gruyter, 1984.

55. Steinhausen HC, Glanville K. Follow-up studies of anorexia nervosa: A review of research findings. Psychol Med, 1983; 13:239- 49.

56. Bachmann M, Röhr HP. Alkoholismus-Esssucht-

Magersucht. Ein Vergleich (alcoholism-overeating-anorexia nervosa. A comparison). Psychother Med Psychol, 1983; 33:111-6.

57. Leon GR. Treating eating disorders. Obesity, anorexia nervosa, and bulimia. Brattleboro (Vermont): Lewis Publ Co, 1983.

58. Story I. Anorexia nervosa and the psychotherapeutic hospital. Int J Psychoanal Psychother, 1982-83; 9:267-302.

59. Bruch H. Treatment in anorexia nervosa. Int J Psychoanal Psychother, 1982-83; 9:303-312.

60. Hall A. Deciding to stay an anorectic. Postgrad Med J, 1982; 58:641-7.

61. Hsu LKG, Harding B, Crisp AH. Outcome of anorexia nervosa. Lancet, 1979; 1:61-65.

62. Hsu LKG, Lieberman S. Paradoxical intention in the treatment of chronic anorexia nervosa. Am J Psychiat, 1982; 139:650-3.

Chapter 28

Nutritional Characteristics and Consequences of Anorexia Nervosa and Bulimia

Jean Densmore-John

INTRODUCTION

Abnormal patterns of behavior relating to food acquisition, selection, preparation, mental preoccupation, and dietary intake in anorexia nervosa and bulimia have been extensively documented in the literature [1-6]. Behavioral patterns may be viewed both as indicators of physiologic state and modes of psychosocial adaptation. Dysfunctional patterns of behavior can promote further deviations that may perpetuate an altered physical state. Anorexia nervosa and bulimia exemplify the latter. The overwhelming fear of fatness [3-8] alters food-related behaviors, which become progressively distorted with the worsening physical condition. A restrained or chaotic consumatory pattern along with the effects of sham eating and malnutrition warp the psychobiologic regulation of appetite and food selection.

The need for establishing differentiated criteria for the food-related behaviors and nutritional characteristics of anorexia nervosa and bulimia is important for early diagnosis and treatment of the disorders. A beginning differentiation and classification of the range of food-related behaviors in anorexia nervosa and bulimia is included in Table 1.

The classification may be useful (1) in assisting the clinician in assessing historical and observational diagnosis; (2) as a guide in confronting the patient with specific maladaptive behaviors, to heighten awareness

and motivation toward normalization of the behavior; and (3) to define social and environmental dimensions of human eating behavior that may be tested in animal eating behavior studies and serve as observational models to further our understanding of the effect of external conditions on eating behavior.

HISTORY

Early recognition of abnormal food-related behavior can benefit the treatment and prognosis of anorexia nervosa and bulimia.

The advantage of early diagnosis in the successful treatment, prevention of medical complications, and prognosis of anorexia nervosa was documented by Ryle 50 years ago [9]. He ascertained that anorexia nervosa was frequently unrecognized or treated inappropriately due to misdiagnosis [9]. Yet, the clinical characteristics of amenorrhea, bradycardia, weight loss, changes in temperament, and sustained physical and mental energy, despite the emaciated state, were recognized by Sir William Gull as early as 1868 [10].

Other physical features of the anorexia condition were noted subsequently. The characteristic reduction in basal metabolic rate in anorexia nervosa was first noted by Berkman in 1930 [11]. Damage to tooth enamel due to vomiting was reported by Bargen and Austin in 1937 [12].

Table 28.1 Differentiation and Classification of the Range of Food-Related Behaviors in Anorexia Nervosa and Bulimia

Food Preferences		Physical Experience	
Anorexia Nervosa	Bulimia	Anorexia Nervosa	Bulimia
Restrictive in fat and refined carbohydrate, as well as certain complex carbohydrates (bread and cereals) and protein (red meat).	Polyphagic or carbohydrate specific during a binge, however, when not in a binge-purge cycle specific "binge" foods, such as cereal, cakes, cookies, ice cream, bread, nuts, peanut butter, pasta and chips are restricted.	Cuts food into small pieces. Arranges food on plate.	Normal to large bites of food. May mix foods together.
Consumes most vegetables and specific fruits to control weight gain.	Consumes easily purged foods to control weight gain, such as ice cream, cheese, eggs, vegetables, cereal, milk.	Eats slowly with prolonged chewing time before swallowing. Prefers small containers of food.	Lifting food to mouth is generally more frequent with shortened chewing time before swallowing. Prefers large containers of food during a binge.
Observable increase in the amount of noncaloric condiments used to alter the flavor of food, possibly to make it less appealing (cinnamon, mustard, vinegar).	Craves foods that satisfy taste desires, usually for sweet or salty foods.	Throws away or hides food to avoid consumption.	Dislikes being responsible for food waste and will overeat or hoard food for an isolated binge experience.
Increased desire for diet drinks, coffee and/or tea.	Increased desire for diet drinks, coffee and/or tea. Consumes excess fluid to aid vomiting, attempt to suppress hunger and aid rehydration.	Does not self-induce vomiting to control food intake.*	Vomits to control food absorption by induced vomiting, spontaneous rumination or regurgitation.

*The exception is the anorectic who is also bulimic.

A presentation of case studies by Ryle in 1936 reveals the occurrence of self-induced vomiting in one anorexia nervosa patient and uncontrolled vomiting leading to severe weight loss in another [9]. The concept of vomiting and/or use of laxatives as a means of controlling weight was designated by Russell (1979) as "bulimia nervosa: an ominous variant of anorexia nervosa" [13].

Bliss and Branch (1960) refer to anorexia nervosa as "nervous malnutrition," contending that the behavior changes are primarily a result of the malnourished state [14]. Others oppose this view, considering it as a primary psychopathological disorder [15-20].

DEVELOPMENT IN THE FIELD

Crisp [3,15,21,22] regards anorexia nervosa as the result of a weight phobia that promotes restrictive dieting with the avoidance of carbohydrate foods, generally resulting in a "unique state of carbohydrate starvation."

Crisp [15] analyzed one day's diet of an anorexia patient on three occasions during the course of illness.

The analysis compares the total kilocalories and the grams of protein, carbohydrate, and fat consumed on each occasion.

Table 2 presents the percent of total kilocalories from protein, carbohydrate and fat, as calculated from Crisp's data. Table 2 represents a means of assessing and comparing the balance of macronutrients between the three days analyzed during the course of the anorexic condition.

Although the total amount of food decreased regardless of nutrient composition, the relative amounts of protein and fat increased in the period just prior to admission, while the percent of the kilocalories derived from carbohydrate decreased. During the inpatient treatment, the percentages of protein, carbohydrate, and fat represent a nutrient composition considered typical of average diets in developed countries [23]. The diet analyses at both one year and two months before admission indicated a low carbohydrate intake, supporting Crisp's carbohydrate avoidance theory.

In a subsequent controlled study of the diet composition, Crisp [24] again found the anorexia diet to be

Table 28.2 Percent Protein, Carbohydrate and Fat of an Anorexic's Diet on 3 Occasions*

	Calories	% Protein	% Carbohydrate	% Fat
1 yr. prior to admission	1180	22%	25%	50%
2 mo. prior to admission	470	27%	13%	57%
During in-patient treatment	3300-3500	16%	41-45%	41-42%

*adapted from: Crisp, A.H. Anorexia Nervosa "feeding disorder," "nervous malnutrition" or "weight phobia." World Reviews Nutrition and Dietetics, 1970; 12:452-504.

mainly restricted in carbohydrates. The study was based on three experimental groups of patients with anorexia nervosa. Group A consisted of 19 restrictive patients, and groups B and C were, respectively, made up of patients who binge and vomit, infrequently and frequently. Five dietary surveys from "normal" young females were used as the control group.

In looking at the mean daily intake, group A consumed fewer kilocalories than the control group, as expected. During binge periods, kilocalories consumed by groups B and C exceeded the intake of the control groups, as expected. It is of interest that the mean daily kilocalorie consumption during nonbinge periods for Groups B and C was similar in amount to that of the control group. The foregoing contrasts with Fairburn's [25,26] findings that bulimics are usually more restrictive in nonbinge periods, eating less than the average intake of normals.

It is also of interest that the experimental groups in Crisp's study have a relatively high proportion of the total kilocalories coming from fat, especially in groups B and C. This suggests that during nonbinge periods, anorexics with bulimia consume foods contributing significant amounts of fat to the diet. In the author's experience, however, anorexics and bulimics during nonbinge periods commonly have a subjective attitudinal aversion to dietary fats and to any other food they consider to be "fattening," regardless of actual fat content. (See chapters 10,11 in this volume for discussion of palatability and preference studies.)

It is also observed that bulimics' avoidance of food varies, being dependent on whether they have binged on the food in the past. The experience of binging and vomiting on a specific food instills a fear of overeating, which *inhibits consumption* during *nonbinge periods* and *promotes overconsumption* during *binge periods*. Psychobiologic homeostasis regulating variety and constancy of food selection may be interfered with or impaired.

In any diet, a balance of the energy-contributing nutrients (carbohydrate, protein, and fat) is important for two reasons: (1) any macronutrient alone cannot support growth, and (2) a relatively constant calorie intake can be maintained through balancing the propor-

tion of protein, carbohydrate, and fat [27].

An imbalance of the macronutrients in the diet may cause change in physiologic and behavioral response. Animal studies have been performed to show this effect. Rats given a glucogenic pattern of food intake (a mixed diet, with adequate carbohydrate as a percentage of total calories) show a heightened excitability (or tonus) level of CNS, whereas a reduced excitability level results from a gluconeogenic pattern of food intake [27]. An elevated excitability level causes the rats to learn better and makes them more resistant to stress. The inability of eating disorder patients to cope with stress is well documented in the literature [6,28,29], and an imbalance of carbohydrate, protein, and fat in the diet may contribute to these problems.

It was observed by Scott [30] that, given a choice of diet, rats will base their selection on "simple preference" when the choice is between diets containing differing protein concentrations that are balanced, but not abnormally high or low in protein content. However, when given the choice of a diet with an imbalance of amino acids (one containing a limiting amino acid and a surplus of all other amino acids) or an alternative that is protein-free, it was found by Sanahuja and Harper [31] that the rats usually chose the latter.

Various studies suggest that a diet with an imbalance of amino acids does not cause physiological or biochemical defects, as would a protein-free or amino acid-deficient diet. However, an imbalanced protein diet can cause a reduction in food consumption by an appetite-regulating mechanism [32,33].

In eating disorder patients, abnormal eating patterns, avoidance of meat, (1) and attempts to practice vegetarianism [34] may result in a diet that has a poor balance of amino acids. Based on the findings in animal studies, it may be possible that in humans a similar tendency toward a protein-free diet (ie, avoid protein) may result from consuming an imbalanced amino acid diet.

Reference has been made to carbohydrate-specific bingeing in bulimia [22,35] and carbohydrate craving in females with chronic, mild depression [36]. Wurtman et al [37] evaluated carbohydrate craving in obese subjects by the use of three drugs: tryptophan, fenfluramine, and a placebo (lactose). During the baseline period all subjects showed significant preference for carbohydrate food over protein food. Subsequently, fenfluramine was found to significantly decrease carbohydrate snacking in all subjects, while carbohydrate snacking was significantly decreased in three subjects with tryptophan. However, no subjects decreased carbohydrate snacking while taking the placebo.

The researchers concluded that a large quantity of dietary carbohydrate would be required to elevate serotonin neurotransmission and subsequently suppress carbohydrate craving. Increased intake of tryptophan, like carbohydrate, causes an increase in brain serotonin and therefore maybe useful in reducing carbohydrate bingeing. Wurtman et al [37] note that in treatment and diet therapy, the evaluation of a patient's food intake pattern is essential to determine whether the diet is overconsumption of all food or only certain macronutrients.

It is well known that delayed menarche, amenorrhea, and irregular periods are characteristic consequences of anorexia nervosa and bulimia [20,24,25,38,39]. Cause for the disturbed menstrual function has been attributed to a number of factors including psychological factors, reduced caloric intake, inadequate carbohydrate intake, and weight loss with reduced percentage of body fat [2]. A recent study and review has associated increased carotene intake (in the form of salads, vegetables, health diets) and intense exercise as important contributions to oligomenorrhea and amenorrhea in normal-weight women [40].

Frisch [41] compared seven-day food diaries in 13 premenarcheal trained athletes and 11 postmenarcheal trained athletes. The average dietary composition of the premenarcheal group was significantly lower in protein, in the percentage of kilocalories from fat, in total fat, in saturated fat, in calcium, and in total kilocalories than that of the postmenarcheal teammates. Although an eating disorder diagnosis was not applicable to this particular group, the relationship of diet composition to body fat composition and to menarche is of interest. (Vigorous athletic training in the prepubertal years may compromise the capacity of appetite regulatory mechanisms to compensate for both heightened energy expenditure and the beginning demands for skeletal growth and weight gain. A relative anorexia with growth retardation may result.)

Halmi and Falk [2] studied 40 menstruating female and amenorrheic anorexia nervosa patients one year after treatment. Both groups were assessed as to dietary and behavioral factors. The two groups were significantly different in response to variables measuring eating attitudes and behavior. For example, the amenorrheic group was assessed as feeling ill with eating, experiencing the feeling of bloating, fearful of fat, believ-

ing their food choices to be more nutritious, having a selective appetite, and having a fear of compulsive eating. The menstruating group was without all of the aforementioned behaviors and dietary attitudes [1].

Dietary attitudes contribute both to food selection and the experience of eating. The Eating Attitudes Test designed by Garner and Garfinkel [1] provides a rating scale for assessment of food related behaviors and attitudes applicable to varying populations of normal and eating disorder subgroups to assess similarities and differences.

Mental food preoccupation, food behavior rituals, interest in cooking for others (especially foods with high caloric density), gazing at recipes and food pictures, thinking about food, and calculating caloric intake have been consistently reported as characteristics of anorexia nervosa [15,17,20,24]. Food thought preoccupation is also characteristic of bulimia [13,26,42]. Bulimics will often plan food binges in advance, during hours of self-seclusion. Johnson and Larson [6] found that bulimics on the average spend 38% of the time thinking about food, food preparation, or eating compared with 14% for the control group. Mental and behavioral preoccupation with food may reflect a primary regulatory disorder further complicated by food restriction, chaotic eating schedule, and in some instances a state of relative starvation.

One major difference between anorexics and bulimics is the level of awareness of the problem. Anorexics will deny their eating habits and defiantly hide their fears of losing control [17,20,24]. Bulimics are aware of their abnormal behavior and may seek help to re-establish a sense of being in control, especially when vomiting ceases to be a successful mechanism for weight control or when vomiting becomes habitual and medically hazardous [28,43].

According to Fairburn [44] bulimics absorb a significant amount of each binge. Absorption and utilization are likely to be influenced by the macro and micro nutrient composition of the diet intake, factors inhibiting absorption (phytates, specific mineral and trace mineral ratios, coffee, tea, antacids, etc), biological availability, tissue depletion, the transport mechanism, extent of purgation, and the degree of emotional instability.

Dietary inadequacies in iron, calcium, zinc, thiamine, and vitamin B-6 are common in young women [45]. An unpublished study [46] of three-day dietary records from 23 bulimic subjects determined thiamine, niacin, calcium, iron and zinc to be less than 100% of the Recommended Dietary Allowance (RDA). Records analyzed from 24 controls found thiamine, iron, and zinc to be below the RDA, but not to the same extent as in the bulimic group with the exception of iron. The bulimic group consumed a higher percentage of vitamin A and iron, and a smaller percentage of vitamin C, thiamine, riboflavin, niacin, calcium, zinc and protein than the control group [46].

Thiamine is essential in energy metabolism, particularly in carbohydrate metabolism. Ingestion of large amounts of refined carbohydrates during a binge, or negligible amounts of thiamine during a starvation phase could rapidly deplete tissue stores of thiamine. The RDA for thiamine for an adult under normal conditions is 0.5 mg/1,000 kcal consumed [45]. Food sources of thiamine (whole grain cereals, nuts, dried beans and peas, beef, and pork) are usually restricted or consumed during a binge with the anticipation of vomiting the food before absorption.

Animal studies of food selection adaptation in response to thiamine deficiency are to be found in the literature [47]. In response to thiamine-deficient diets, rats will alter their diet composition by increasing total fats and decreasing protein and carbohydrates, a change in energy source that prolongs their survival. A similar shift by anorexics towards fat as an energy source was previously discussed based on findings of Crisp [15,24]. Rats with thiamine deficiency become hyperactive, seemingly related to food-seeking behavior and are observed to increase food hoarding activity [47]. Crisp et al [4] found that about 40% of a group of anorexics will binge and vomit and will also be more likely to hoard and steal food. Underweight patients with restriction and vomiting or normal-weight bulimic patients with high frequency bingeing and vomiting may develop symptoms and signs of peripheral neuropathy in association with malnutrition, high-carbohydrate load, and excess activity suggesting early state thiamine deficiency. A case of Wernicke's encephalopathy associated with anorexia nervosa has been reported [48].

The nutritional consequences of consistent vomiting are generalized malnutrition, fluid and electrolyte imbalance, impaired protein metabolism, and vitamin and mineral depletion [3]. Decreased serum potassium and chloride caused by repeated vomiting episodes will return to normal within 24 to 48 hours after cessation of vomiting and resumption of normal intake [49].

Crisp [24] states that anorexics do not become anemic or deficient in essential vitamins or minerals unless they binge and vomit. Nutrients such as vitamins A, D, E, K, and B_{12} in the liver, essential fatty acids in adipose tissue, amino acids in muscle, and minerals in bones and muscle are provided as needed by reserves stored in the body. Use of these stores is the first stage of nutritional depletion [50]. Plasma concentrations of electrolytes, protein, immunoglobulins, and total calcium, as well as serum B_{12}, folate, and iron are normal in restrictive anorexia [49] but may mask depletion of nutrient reserves. Certain laboratory findings may aid in early identification of deficiencies. For instance, falling C_3 complement and transferrin serum levels may reflect decline in circulating protein, and rising RDW index of the blood count may signify early RBC microcytosis reflecting iron deficiency prior to a decline in hemoglobin or serum iron [48].

It has been proposed that, due to the association of bingeing and vomiting with tension reduction, a subgroup of bulimic patients may have a predisposition to drug or alcohol abuse [52]. Alcohol may be consumed to end a food binge. Many bulimics seem unaware that alcohol is itself a source of calories. Alcohol contributes to poor utilization of vitamins and minerals and would further increase nutritional requirement for thiamine (B_1).

Other B vitamin requirements may be altered by physical stress or dietary imbalance. The need for riboflavin (B_2) may increase as a result of a negative nitrogen balance or a diet where carbohydrate isocalorically replaces fat [53]. B_2 allowances do not need to increase as energy intake increases [45]. Dietary tryptophan contributes significantly to fulfilling the RDA for niacin (B_3), through the conversion of tryptophan to niacin in the body. Inadequate amounts of vitamin B_6 impair this conversion [45]. The requirement for B_6 increases with a high-protein diet. Under acute emotional stress, vitamin C requirement increases to maintain normal plasma levels of vitamin C. Drugs, oral contraceptives, smoking, age, and sex may also alter vitamin C requirement [45]. Carotene, the vitamin A precursor, is often consumed in excessive amounts by eating disorder patients. This is in high concentration in orange fruits and vegetables. Excessive ingestion of carotene-containing foods and possible interference with metabolic enzymatic degradation can cause hypercarotenemia with its characteristic orange discoloration of the skin [21].

Minerals that may be of concern are calcium and zinc. High protein diets and intense physical activity increase calcium requirements. Under normal conditions, about 30% of dietary calcium is absorbed, and if the intake is suddenly reduced, the relative absorption may be insufficient. However, adaptation to lower calcium intake occurs in time [45]. A high intake ratio of phosphorus to calcium may inhibit absorption of calcium. Convenience foods, snack foods, and phosphate-based drinks contribute phosphorus to the diet, especially when diet drinks are taken as the primary fluid.

Zinc may be inadequate due to diet restriction; poor absorption due to chelation with phytates and fiber; geophagia; excess of calcium, magnesium, or copper in the diet; or alcohol intake that increases urinary excretion

Table 28.3 Clinical consequences of nutritional problems common to anorexia nervosa and bulimia

Area of Examination	Anorexia Nervosa	Bulimia
Hair	lack of lustre, thinness, sparseness, easy to pluck	dryness
Face	moon-face, sunken facial features, lanugo hair	naso-labial dysse-bacea, edema face and neck
Lips	angular stomatitis, angular scars, cheilosis	angular stomatitis, angular scars, cheilosis
Tongue	edema, scarlet or raw, atrophic papillae	
Teeth	depressed salivary flow	caries, enamel decalcification enamel erosion
Gums	recession of gum line, bleeding	recession of gum, bleeding
Glands	enlarged thyroid, enlarged parotid	enlarged parotid
Skin	darkening, rough lanugo hair, petechiae, ecchymoses, hypercarotenaemia	warm, clammy, hypercarotenemia
Nails	brittle, ridges	brittle, ridges
Subcutaneous	edema, low % body fat	dependent edema low to high % body fat
Muscular and skeletal systems	depleted lean body mass, atrophy of type 1 & 2 muscle fibers, bone marrow hypoplasia	low to normal lean body mass
Internal Systems		
Gastrointestinal	atrophy, delayed gastric emptying, constipation	esophagitis, esophageal tear, gastric rupture, abdominal distension, constipation
Nervous	peripheral neuropathy symptomatic epilepsy	stupor associated with fluid retention
Cardiovascular	bradycardia, low blood pressure, hypercholesterolemia, pericardial effusion	arrhythmia, temporary abnormal ECG

[55]. Smith et al [56] note that the protein source and amount, the caloric content of the diet, and the individual's energy expenditure all affect the body's zinc requirements. Zinc deficiency may occur in groups of vegetarians or those consuming a high intake of grains, legumes, fruits and vegetables with little or no meat or seafood [56]. The zinc from meat, eggs, and seafood, especially oysters, is more biologically available than that found in whole-grain products [46].

Changes in the concentration of copper, zinc, and magnesium have been observed in association with alterations in neurotransmitter concentrations in certain regions of the brain [57]. Zinc has a role at the receptor level in taste buds [58]. It acts as a cofactor in alkaline phosphate, which is found in highest concentration in taste bud membrane. The bitter quality of taste is affected first and most severely in zinc deficiency, while the sweet taste is affected last and least [58].

Table 3 summarizes the clinical consequences arising from possible nutritional problems common to anorexia

and/or bulimia. Not all of the characteristics mentioned are necessarily observed in all patients. Variations in the presenting clinical picture may be due to individual variation and ability to adapt to nutritional stress; the duration of the condition; the nutritional state of the individual before the onset of either condition; the actual diet intake; the use of self-induced vomiting; laxatives, diuretics, regurgitation, excessive exercise or fasting; and the rate of onset and extent of initial weight loss. An acute weight loss puts patients at greater risk than those with a slower chronic loss [49].

The reduced basal metabolic rate characteristic of anorexia nervosa [15,24,59] reflects the body's attempt to conserve energy and minimize or prolong the onset of biochemical lesions and observable anatomical changes [60].

Reduced salivation and disturbed electrolyte balance resulting from dehydration, starvation, vomiting, and antidepressant therapy decrease the buffering effect of saliva on acidic action on tooth enamel [35,61]. Changes in salivary flow also make the teeth of anorexics susceptible to acid. Typically, the restrictive anorexic may be consuming a large amount of citrus fruit or juices or sucking on hard candies, mints, or chewing gum to alleviate thirst.

The contact with acid or carbohydrate directly on the tooth surface enhances deterioration. Vomiting produces a low pH, and this causes decalcification of the tooth enamel [62]. Hurst et al [35] found tooth erosion to be worse in regurgitators compared with anorexic restrictors. However, the severity and frequency of dental caries was higher in carbohydrate bingers and vomiters [35]. Enlarged salivary and parotid glands are commonly found in bulimics [25]. A slowing down of body functions, a result of starvation, may contribute to delayed stomach emptying, constipation, and stomach distention [20,38]. Dehydration, irregular meals, and laxative abuse also contribute to these common complaints [63].

RESEARCH ISSUES

Extensive comprehensive surveys to evaluate parameters of the nutritional status in anorexia and bulimia have not been documented in the literature. A thorough assessment of vitamin and mineral status and anthropometric and physical data would contribute to the understanding of the metabolic and behavioral changes, as well as the unusual food preference and patterns of intake.

The possibility of specific nutrient deprivation, with respect to body weight, age, sex, and physical energy expenditure should be assessed. Comparison of the nutritional intake during nonbinge periods in eating disorder patients with that of normal subjects may be useful in evaluating the contribution of nutrient deprivation to a binge episode.

Nutritional analysis, based on a three- to seven-day dietary intake record from a sample of eating disorder patients during the course of treatment would be beneficial to menu and diet planning. One of the goals in nutritional rehabilitation is to plan diets that will provide the nutritive requirements, while gradually increasing the amount of food tolerated. Nutritional requirements need to be met with expediency. However, patient sensitivity to eating and physical discomfort from refeeding too quickly creates a meal-planning challenge. An evaluation of nutritional intake, as suggested, may provide a useful basis for planning incremented refeeding schedules that are better tolerated by eating disorder patients.

To understand the factors influencing dietary selection and motivation for change, the following are areas of possible investigation:
1. Comparison of cross-cultural food patterns
2. Composition of macronutrients associated with expansion and changes in food supply
3. Effect of the media's interest in "nutrition" promotion

A person's understanding of what should or should not be eaten is strongly influenced by these factors. In the United States, for example, emphasis on decreasing fat, cholesterol, sugar, and calories and increasing fiber in the diet has been pervasive in the advertising of food and health products over the past 10 to 15 years. Although this emphasis is appropriate for prevention and treatment of obesity and cardiovascular disease, an extreme response to trends in the media and food supply system may contribute to the diet restriction patterns observed with eating disorder patients.

Whether the observed changes in food preference in most eating disorder patients toward spicy foods (with often excessive use of mustard or cinnamon) is due to a taste sensitivity change, secondary to altered zinc availability, or some other factor has not been determined. The use of excessive spices on foods may simply be a mechanism to decrease the desirability of food or limit the appetite. Abnormal food practices on refeeding need to be further assessed in relation to the continuation and treatment of the disordered process.

Further assessment of alterations in body composition in anorexia and bulimia are needed. Bulimics appear to vary widely in the change in body fat resulting from vomiting and laxative abuse. The general lack of reduction in body fat may indicate metabolism of lean tissue during glyconeogenesis and/or shifts in fluid balance reflected by short-term weight fluctuation.

Lindboe et al [64] found type 1 and 2 muscle fiber atrophy in anorexics. The extent to which a restrictive diet effects anatomical change (and thus the body's capacity to tolerate physical exercise) needs to be assessed. This would benefit programs that use physical activity as a motivational tool in therapy. Activity scheduling in conjunction with dietary planning is essential for optimum rehabilitation.

CONCLUSION

The nutritional characteristics of the diet and the food-related patterns of behavior act conjointly to maintain, improve, or worsen psychobiologic integrity. The eating disorders are good examples of the impact that dietary factors have on the consequent physiological and behavioral functioning of the individual.

REFERENCES

1. Garner DM, Garfinkel PE. The eating attitudes test: an index of the symptoms of anorexia nervosa. Psychol Med, 1979; 9:273-9.

2. Halmi KA, Falk JR. Behavioral and dietary discriminators of menstrual function in anorexia nervosa. In Barby PK, Garfinkel PE, Garner DM, Coscina DV, eds. Anorexia nervosa: Recent developments in research. New York: Alan Liss, 1983; 323-9.

3. Crisp AH. The differential diagnosis of anorexia nervosa. Proc R Soc Med, 1977; 70:686-90.

4. Crisp AH, Hsu KG, Harding B. The starving hoarder and voracious spender stealing in anorexia nervosa. J Psychosom Res, 1980; 24:225-31.

5. Fairburn CG, Cooper PJ. The epidemiology of bulimia nervosa. Int J Eating Disorders, 1983; 2:61-7.

6. Johnson C, Larson R. Bulimia: An analysis of moods and behavior. Psycosom Med, 1982; 44:341-51.

7. Bosking-Lodahl M. Cinderella's stepsisters: A feminist perspective on anorexia nervosa and bulimia. Signs: J Women Culture Soc, 1976; 2:342-56.

8. Crisp AH. Some psychobiological aspects of adolescent growth and their relevance for the fat/thin syndrome (anorexia nervosa). Int J Obesity, 1977; 1:231-8.

9. Ryle J. Anorexia nervosa. Lancet, 1936; 2:893-9.

10. Gull WW. The address in medicine. Lancet, 1868; 2:171.

11. Berkman JM. Anorexia nervosa, anorexia, inanition and low basal metabolic rate. Am J Med Sci, 1930; 180:411-24.

12. Bargen JA, Austin LT. Decalcification of teeth as a result of obstipation with long continued vomiting: Report of a case. J Am Dent Assoc, 1937; 24:1271.

13. Russell GFM. Bulimia nervosa: An ominous variant of anorexia nervosa. Psychol Med, 1979; 9:429-48.

14. Bliss EL, Branch CHH. Anorexia nervosa: its history, psychology and biology. New York: Harper and Row, 1960.

15. Crisp AH. Anorexia nervosa "feeding disorder" "nervous malnutrition" or "weight phobia." World Rev Nutr Diet, 1970; 12:452-504.

16. Crisp AH. The psychopathology of anorexia nervosa: Getting the heat out of the system. In Stunkard AJ, Stellar E, eds. Eating and its disorders. New York: Raven Press, 1984; 209-34.

17. Bruch H. The golden cage: The enigma of anorexia nervosa. Cambridge MA; Harvard University Press, 1978.

18. Bruch H. Psychological antecedents of anorexia nervosa. In Vigersky RA, ed. Anorexia nervosa. New York: Raven Press, 1977; 1-10.

19. Russell GFM. General management of anorexia nervosa and difficulties in assessing the efficacy of treatment. In Vigersky RA, ed. Anorexia nervosa. New York: Raven Press, 1977; 277-90.

20. Dally P, Gomez J. Anorexia nervosa. London: Wm Heinemann, 1979; 11-24.

21. Crisp AH, Stonehill E. Hypercarotenaemia as a symptom of weight phobia. Postgrad Med J, 1967; 43:721-5.

22. Crisp AH. Disturbances of neurotransmitter metabolism in anorexia nervosa. Proc Nutr Soc, 1978; 37:201-9.

23. The Senate Select Committee on Nutrition and Human Needs. Dietary Goals for the United States. Washington DC: Superintendent of Documents, US Government Printing Office, 1977.

24. Crisp AH. Anorexia nervosa: Let me be. London: Academic Press, 1980; 12-30.

25. Fairburn CG. Bulimia nervosa. Br J Hosp Med, 1983; 29:537-42.

26. Fairburn CG, Cooper PJ. The clinical features of bulimia nervosa. Br J Psychiatry, 1984; 144:238-46.

27. Lat J. Self-selection of dietary components. In Code CF, ed. Handbook of physiology, 6:1. Washington DC: American Physiology Society, 1967; 367-87.

28. Fairburn CG. Binge eating and its management. Br J Psychiatry, 1982; 141:631-3.

29. Casper R. Some provisional ideas concerning the psychologic structure in anorexia nervosa and bulimia. In Barby PL, Garfinkel PE, Garner DM, Coscina DV, eds. Anorexia nervosa: Recent developments in research. New York: Alan Liss, 1983; 387-92.

30. Scott EM. Self selection of diet; IV: Appetite for protein. J Nutr, 1946; 32:293-301.

31. Sanahuja JC, Harper AE. Effect of amino acid imbalance on food intake and preference. Am J Physiol, 1962; 202:165-70.

32. Harper AE. Effects of dietary protein content and amino acid pattern on food intake and preference. In Code CF, ed. Handbook of physiology, 6:1. Washington DC: American Physiology Society, 1967; 399-410.

33. Morley JE, Levine AS. The central control of appetite. Lancet, 1983; 1:398-401.

34. Yager J. Family issues in the pathogenesis of anorexia nervosa. Psychosom Med, 1982; 44:43-60.

35. Hurst PS, Lacey JH, Crisp AH. Teeth, vomiting and diet: A study of the dental characteristics of seventeen anorexia nervosa patients. Postgrad Med J, 1977; 53:298-305.

36. Hopkinson G. A neurochemical theory of appetite and weight changes in depressive states. Acta Psychiatr Scand, 1982; 64:217-35.

37. Wurtman J, Wurtman RF, Growdon JH, et al. Carbohydrate craving in obese people suppression by treatments affecting serotoninergic transmission. Int J Eating Disorders, 1981; 1:2-16.

38. Halmi K. Pragmatic information on the eating disorders. Psychiatr Clin N Am, 1982; 5:371-7.

39. Frisch RE. Food intake, fatness and reproductive ability. In Vigersky RA, ed. Anorxia nervosa. New York: Raven Press, 1977: 149-161.

40. Kenmann E, Pasquale SA, Skaf R. Amenorrhea associated with carotenemia. JAMA, 1983; 249(7):926-9.

41. Frisch RE. What's below the surface? N Engl J Med, 1981; 305:1019-20.

42. Pyle RL, Mitchell JE, Elke DE. Bulimia: A report of 34 cases. J Clin Psychiatry, 1981; 42:60-4.

43. Spitzer RL, ed. Task force on nomenclature and statistics: Diagnostic and statistical manual of mental disorders, 3rd ed. Washington DC: American Psychiatric Association, 1980; 69-71.

44. Fairburn CG. Bulimia: its epidemiology and management. In Stunkard AJ, Stellar E, eds. Eating and its disorders. New York: Raven Press, 1984: 235-58.

45. National Research Council. Recommended Dietary Allowances, 9th ed. Washington, DC: National Academy of Science, 1980: 72-138.

46. Hazard CA. Nutritional status of bulimic women. Presented at the Int Conf on AN and Related Disorders, Swansea Wales, September 1984.

47. Rozin P. Thiamine specific hunger. In Code CF, ed. Handbook of physiology, 6:1. Washington DC: American Physiology Society, 1967: 411-31.

48. Handler CE, Perkin GD. Anorexia nervosa and Wernicke's encephalopathy: An underdiagnosed association. Lancet, 1982; 2:771-2.

49. Silverman JA. Medical consequences of starvation; the malnutrition of anorexia nervosa: Caveat medicus. In Barby PL, Garfinkel PE, Garner DM, Coscina DV, eds. Anorexia nervosa: Recent developments in research. New York: Alan Liss, 1983; 293-99.

50. Chipponi JX, Bleier JC, Santi MT, et al. Deficiencies of essential and conditionally essential nutrients. Am J Clin Nutr, 1982; 35:1112-6.

51. McClure S, Cluster E, Bessman JD. Improved detection of early iron deficiency in non-anemic subjects. JAMA, 1985; 253(7):1021-3.

52. Lacey JH. Compulsive eating. In Marks J, Glatt M, eds. Dependence phenomenon. Lancaster: MTP Press, 1982; 199-211.

53. Dakshinamurti K. B vitamins and nervous system function. In Wurtman RJ, Wurtman JJ, eds. Nutrition and the brain. New York: Raven Press, 1977; 251-318.

54. Evans DL, Edelsohn GA, Golden RN. Organic psychosis without anemia and spinal cord symptoms in patients with vitamin B_{12} deficiency. Am J Psychiatry, 1983; 140:218-20.

55. Abdulla M. How adequate is plasma zinc as an indicator of zinc status? In Prasad AS, ed. Zinc deficiency in human subjects. New York: Alan Liss, 1983; 171-83.

56. Smith CJ, Morris ER, Ellis R. Zinc requirements, bioavailabilities and recommended dietary allowances. In Prasad AS, ed. Zinc deficiency in human subjects. New York: Alan Liss, 1983; 147-69.

57. Donaldson J. The pathophysiology of trace metal: neurotransmitter interactions in the CNS. Trends Pharmacol Sci, 1981; 2:75-8.

58. Henkin RI, Patten BM, Re PK, et al. A syndrome of acute zinc loss. Arch Neurol, 1975; 32:745-51.

59. Pertschuk MJ, Crosby LO, Mullen JL. Nonlinearity of weight gain and nutrition intake in anorexia nervosa. In Barby PL, Garfinkel PE, Garner DM, Coscina DV, eds. Recent developments in research. New York: Alan Liss, 1983; 301-10.

60. Altschule MD. Calories, obesity, weight reduction, and starvation. In: Nutritional factors in general medicine, effects of stress and distorted diets. P. 5. Springfield, Ill: Charles Thomas, 1978; 5- 15.

61. Valentine AD, Anderson RJ, Bradnock G. Salivary pH and dental caries. Br Dent J, 1978; 144:105-7.

62. Allen DN. Dental erosion from vomiting. Br Dent J, 1969; 126:311-2.

63. Huse DM, Lucas AR. Dietary treatment of anorexia nervosa. J Am Diet Assoc, 1983; 83:687-90.

64. Lindboc CHF, Askevold F, Slettebo M. Changes in skeletal muscles of young women with anorexia nervosa. Acta Neuropathol, 1982; 56:299-302.

Chapter 29

Rumination: A Critical Review of Diagnosis and Treatment

Barton J. Blinder, Stanley L. Goodman, and Renée Goldstein

INTRODUCTION

Rumination, an uncommon disorder occurring from infancy throughout adulthood, is derived from the Latin *ruminare*, "to chew the cud." Merycism, derived from the Helenic, is the act of post-ingestive regurgitation of food from the stomach back into the mouth, followed by chewing and reswallowing [1]. The two terms are often used interchangeably. Rumination is associated with medical complications such as aspiration pneumonia, electrolyte abnormalities, and dehydration [2] and is considered in the differential diagnosis of vomiting [3] and failure to thrive [4] in infants and young children. From latency through adulthood, rumination frequently has a benign course [5]. Recently it has been associated with bulimia [6,7], anorexia nervosa, and depression [5,105,109]. Past studies have ascribed the disorder to lack of emotional reciprocity and attunement between mother and child stemming primarily from maternal depression and anxiety [8-10]. Medical disorders such as gastroesophageal reflux and hiatal hernia [2,8,11,12], also are present in the population of ruminating children. Applications of formal behavioral contingencies in treatment have led to describing ruminatory activity as a habit disorder [13-15].

In DSM III [16] rumination is designated as a disorder of infancy [307.53]. The infant shows "a characteristic position of straining and arching the back with sucking tongue movements and the gaining of satisfaction with rumination" [16]. Diagnostic criteria include repeated regurgitation without nausea or associated gastrointestinal illness for at least one month following a period of normal functioning. Weight loss or failure to make expected weight gain occur often [16]. Irritability is noted between regurgitations and hunger is often inferred by the observer. Although the disorder occurs most frequently after 3 months of age, it has been reported in a 3-week old infant [17] and in the neonatal intensive care unit [4]. Consequent failure to thrive with malnutrition may produce severe developmental delays [15]. Rumination has been described in families over four generations, and learning to ruminate by imitation has been suggested [18].

Rumination may be underreported, with only complicated cases (malnutrition, electrolyte disturbances, hiatal hernia) referred to a gastroenterologist and minor cases treated by parent or primary physician. Rumination in anorexia nervosa and bulimia may be underreported due to omission of inquiry in the systematic medical history and reluctance of patients to volunteer specific clinical information [5,6,7,109].

The course of rumination may depend on the age of the patient and the severity of the complications. Mortality can be as high as 25% to 40% in infants [19]. Although the infant may manifest hyperphagia, postingestive regurgitation leads to progressive malnutrition (ie, a sham eating sequence). In the ruminating adolescent bulimia and affective disorder may be present [7]. Rumination in adults has been associated with gastric

Table 29.1 Two vomiting syndromes of infancy

Characteristics	Nervous Vomiting	Infant Rumination
The nature of the vomiting	Involuntary Visceral Purposeless	Voluntary Behavioral Self-stimulation
Age of Onset	As early as newborn	After 3 months
Mothering	Attentive but dyssynchronous; increases rather than relieves tension.	Emotionally distant. Little reciprocal interaction.
Typical Circumstances of vomiting	During the baby's response to environmental stimulation	In the absence of environmental stimulation
Management	Lessening excessive stimulation. Alleviating the tension-producing quality of mother-infant interaction	Increasing environmental stimulation. Satisfying the infant's needs by mothering.

Fleisher, 1979

carcinoma [20] and anemia [21,22]. More frequent medical complications occur in the retarded [23], with a mortality rate of 12% to 20% [24].

Extended posttreatment evaluation of patients with rumination is rare. Investigators most often report a one- or two-year follow-up [3,4]. Kanner [19] stated that long-term follow-up of patients with rumination revealed a notable subsequent appearance of psychiatric disorder.

HISTORICAL PERSPECTIVES

Rumination was first discussed by Fabricius Ab Aquapendendente in an adult male with a hiatal hernia [25]. Lushka [26], and later Herbst et al [11], described rumination associated with hiatal hernia. Grulee [27] first suggested that attention be directed to the psychic condition of the child and that distracting the infant would diminish the rumination. Lourie [8] observed an abnormal mother-infant relationship and used a substitute caretaker for treatment. Since 1968, behavioral treatment techniques have included peripheral electric shock [14,28], lemon juice [29], and food satiation [24,30]. Chatoor and Dickson [31] proposed an integrated psychodynamic, biologic and behavioral etiology and treatment.

DEVELOPMENTAL AND PSYCHOSTRUCTURAL FACTORS FROM INFANCY THROUGH ADULTHOOD

Lourie [8] noted that both understimulation (maternal absence or neglect) and overstimulation (excessive inappropriate caretaking) were associated with rumination. These infants fail to develop basic trust in the maternal caretaker, resulting in a failure of attachment

[32]. Such children have been characterized by Lourie as passive and sensitive to rejection, with rumination serving to relieve inner tension states. Also, a physical source of irritability such as hiatal hernia has been associated with rumination [11]. From a psychodevelopmental perspective, rumination might be viewed as voluntary self-feeding compensating for an inadequate maternal-infant relationship. Rumination becomes a defensive habit pattern with both functional autonomy and a pleasurable self-reinforcing effect. Precursors of pleasurable swallowing and "libidinization" of the esophagus may date from prenatal experiences of the ingestive passage of amniotic fluid [33].

Infancy and Early Childhood

Cameron [34] has delineated the classical description of rumination in infancy. He noted purposeful movements of the abdomen, mouth, and tongue resulting in the pleasurable ejection of previously ingested food.

Rumination has been reported in infants with disorders including reflux esophagitis [2], hiatal hernia [11,12,35], necrotizing enterocolitis, malabsorption and malnutrition, failure to thrive, prematurity, severe bronchopulmonary dysplasia [4], growth failure [17], autism [31], infantile spasms [36], grand mal epilepsy [36], tuberous sclerosis [37], heroin withdrawal [38], barbiturate withdrawal [35], labile autonomic nervous system [31], object loss [8,39], and infection [18,35].

Repetitive self-stimulatory behavior (head banging, body rocking, and genital and anal-fecal play) resistant to maternal interruption has been observed in ruminating infants [10,31,35]. Rumination has been described in one member of a pair of both monozygotic [35] and dyzygotic [17] twins.

Fleisher [40] has differentiated rumination from nervous vomiting occurring in tense, anxious, labile infants (Table 1).

Latency

Rumination is rare in latency-age children who are not retarded. The few cases that have been documented have been described adequately elsewhere [5,18,31,39,41]. In general, infantile predisposition to rumination and variation in both symptom frequency and intesity with emotional arousal are notable.

Adolescence

In nonretarded adolescents, rumination associated with anorexia nervosa [5,18], bulimia [6,7], anxiety and depression [5], and iron deficiency [22] has been reported.

Adulthood

Adult rumination is a chronic disorder [5], except when associated with bulimia [7]. The individual episode is postprandial, without nausea, effortless, and predominately involuntary. It may occur spontaneously after a hastily eaten meal, causing embarrassment or may appear seemingly voluntary and pleasurable [1,5,20]. The symptomatic presence of active ruminatory behavior varies from as little as six months to a lifetime [5,18]. Patients may complain of food returning to the mouth, belching, precordial distress (possibly due to esophagitis), indigestion, halitosis, and excessive dental deterioration [5,105].

Long [20] notes two uses of rumination: (a) as a sham eating technique; and (b) to eat and dispose of foods contraindicated medically (fatty foods, meat) yet having strong palatability and preference for the patient. Thus a patient with gallbladder disease would regurgitate and extrude fatty foods, preventing painful cholecystitis.

The presence of specific psychiatric disorder in adult rumination is undefined. Diagnoses noted in prior reports include:

1. Neurasthenia [18]
2. Performance anxiety; somatic delusions of fatal illness [20]
3. Emotionally irritable, immature, and passive [45]
4. Schizophrenia hysterical traits [1]
5. Atypical personality [46]
6. Affective disorder [5]
7. Eating disorder-bulimia [5,6,7]

There were no structured psychiatric evaluations or uniformity of diagnostic criteria noted in the literature until Levine et al [5] evaluated nine patients with both psychiatric interview and questionnaire. Interviews revealed a family psychiatric history or disturbed family relationships in four of the patients; three patients had psychiatric histories (overdose, anorexia nervosa, brief reactive depression); patients had personalities that were anxious (seven of nine), obsessional (five of nine), or sensitive (six of nine); and four of five adult patients had

psychosexual and marital problems. However, on formal mental status exam, only one of the nine patients had current psychiatric symptoms.

The results of questionnaires revealed that mild traits of anxiety, hysteria, and neuroticism were present. In only one patient did symptoms interfere with psychosocial functioning, and the group revealed no evidence of a current psychiatric illness. The authors concluded that substantive psychiatric disorder was absent. However, the findings are suggestive of affective spectrum disorder (depression, anorexia nervosa, overdose) in three of five adults and significant family history of psychiatric disorder in four of eight patients whose family history was accessible. An instrument such as the SADS [47] might have been a more significant diagnostic tool for detecting psychiatric disorder in the adult ruminatory group studies [105].

Fairburn and Cooper [7] report rumination lasting at least 12 months in 7 of 35 female bulimic patients. Three patients had postprandial effortless daily regurgitation. The patients complained of losing control of eating with shame about their rumination. All patients had disturbed eating habits, abnormal attitudes toward body and shape, and high psychiatric morbidities. In the subgroup of bulimic ruminators, compared with the bulimic nonruminators, a history of both anorexia nervosa and psychiatric treatment for an eating disorder was more prevalent. The habit by itself was difficult to stop, but successful treatment of the bulimia led to cessation of the rumination. Blinder [6] reported a subgroup of normal-weight bulimic patients with primary ruminatory behavior antedating bulimic symptoms. The patients were more likely to be polyphagic during binge episodes rather than demonstrating the more usual specific carbohydrate preference. Ruminatory behavior shifted to regurgitation during adolescence to aid in weight control. Ruminators may not show the pattern of impulsive behavior, affective disturbance, or family history of alcoholism seen in other patients diagnosed as bulimic.

The only report of psychoanalytic treatment emphasized unconscious anger toward authority figures who were aggressively ejected representationally by the ruminatory behavior. Interpretation of unconscious conflict led to cessation of the ruminatory behavior [48].

There may be two adult subgroups of ruminators— one group with minimal psychiatric problems and the second subgroup with an associated eating disorder, such as anorexia nervosa and bulimia [109]. Since patients are reticent about their illness, a diagnosis of psychiatric disturbance may be undetected [110].

Rumination Associated with Central Nervous System Disorders and Retardation

Rumination is associated both with CNS disorders and mental retardation [49]. Eating disorders are prevalent in the institutionalized retarded (pica 25%, anorexia 7%, and rumination 2.7%) [23]. Frequently individuals with pica also exhibit rumination [49]. Postingestive gastroesophageal reflux has been associated with mental retardation, CNS lesions such as cerebritis, dilated ventricles, cerebral palsy, and sudden infant death syndrome, apnea, and laryngospasms [50]. Rumination has been associated with tuberose sclerosis [37], hypsarrhythmia [51], infantile spasms, and grand mal seizures [36].

Danford [23] summarized several clinical features in the retarded associated with the presence of rumination. These included male predominance, self-abuse, other food-related behaviors (pica, hyperphagia, anorexia), and medical complications.

Rumination in the retarded appears to be a self-stimulating behavior that relieves internal tension states that are blocked from social release because of marked communication deficit and inability to seek out external stimulation [51].

Although several recent reports of behavioral treatment of retarded ruminants have appeared using aversive conditioning (localized electroshock [14], and lemon juice [29]), there is little discussion of environmental changes that could have precipitated the rumination. A retarded child may suffer significant object losses both when being taken from the family to an institution and when staff changes occur within the institution [53]. A case report [54] described a 10-year-old boy who lost weight and started ruminating following institutionalization and separation from family. Treatment by increasing environmental stimulation abolished the disorder; thus, prompt social stimulation and reinforcement may abort or terminate the ruminatory disorder related to institutional adjustments.

THEORIES OF RUMINATION

Behavioral

Since 1968 there have been many reports documenting behavioral treatment of rumination [13]. Behaviorists report effective treatments that diminish rumination within two weeks, in contrast to psychodynamic treatments requiring four to five weeks [55].

Behavioral theory explains rumination as a habit pattern. Reinforcement enhances and maintains a specific behavior that is temporally linked to its consequences. A positive reinforcement such as food, increases the frequency of an antecedant behavior. Maternal attention (especially following rumination) to a child who is receiving inadequate nurturing may increase (reinforce) the rumination [54]. Rumination also allows the child to obtain increased attention in the form of medi-

cal treatment. Wright and Thalassino [56] consider rumination to be a "learned illness behavior." Remission of chronic ruminative vomiting occurs through a reversal of social contingencies. Behavioral theories focus on conditions that maintain rumination [13]. Lavigne and Burns [55] believe that rumination is an operant behavior maintained by its consequence and that it is a learned habit that can be extinguished.

A habitual response characteristic of rumination is suggested by a seeming voluntary quality, frequent waxing and waning with environmental stress, and extinction in response to aversive stimuli.

Association with Affective Disturbance

Four lines of evidence linking rumination and affective disorders will be presented. First, infants and children with rumination appear sad and withdrawn [8,9,31,35]. Lourie [8] described a ruminating child who developed features of an anaclitic depression due to the absence of a satisfactory love object (see section on Developmental and Psychodynamic Factors). Another child with rumination and hiatal hernia, age 7 months [8], was described as being withdrawn, expressionless, crying a great deal, irritable, and sleepless. Both cases demonstrate a passive (affective) reaction to helplessness in the face of psychic or physical pain. Several reports [8-10,17] described the emotional unavailability of a mother to her child because of maternal depression and feelings of rejection toward an unwanted infant. The child suffers a significant object loss (perceived or imagined) of the primary caretaker. This conceptualization also relates to Lourie's notion of understimulation in infants with ruminatory disorder [8]. An animal model has also been observed [108].

Lourie [8] noted passivity and diminished affective expression of needs in infants with rumination. Such behavior could foster parental confusion in responding to the child's immediate needs and lead to frustration, helplessness, and depressive affect. Lourie also noted that these children are markedly rejection-sensitive, a trait observed in atypical depression [57].

Second, there is a subgroup of children for whom object loss is a manifest onset condition for the appearance of ruminatory behavior [8,39,42,53,54,58-60]. *A review of the literature reveals that object loss is the most frequent psychosocial onset event associated with rumination* (Table 2).

A pleasurable self-stimulating component of ruminatory behavior may serve as a defense against the pain of object loss [33,61-63]. Protest, despair, and withdrawal, which are generally associated with object loss [32], may also be developmentally specific clinical features in the symptom context of rumination following loss.

Table 29.2 Onset of Rumination Associated with Object Loss

Age	Sex	Clinical Features	Reference
5-1/2 mo.	M	Ruminated from age 4 months. Separation from primary caretaker. (grandmother). Depressed mother	Chatoor and Dickson (31)
6 mo.	M	Mother initiated full time work. Failure to thrive and rumination.	Murray et al (59)
9 mo.	F	Monozygotic twin; mother returns to work.	Chatoor and Dickson(35)
11 mo.	M	Developed rumination after father left home abruptly; mother depressed.	Lourie (8)
5 yr.	M	Retarded; developed rumination following death of 8-year-old sibling.	Menolascino, personal communication (60)
7 yr.	M	Developed rumination at 18 months shortly after family moved away. from caretaking grandmother	Griffin (39)
8 yr.	M	Object loss upon institutionalization was followed by rumination which fluctuated in conjunction with presence or absence of substitute caretaker. Rumination ceased upon return home.	Menolascino (53)
11 yr.	M	Developed rumination at age 6 after multiple object losses occurred following transfer from home to institution.	Wright and Menolascino (54)
13 yr.	F	Rumination developed at age 9 within one year of mother's death and father's remarriage.	Chan, personal communication (42)

Third, observations linking ruminatory behavior in adults with depressive symptoms, anorexia nervosa, and bulimia have been described in the section on Biologic Determinants [5-7].

Fourth, maternal affective disorder may lead to *both* a *genetic factor* in the infant *and deprivation consequences to nurturance* contributing to increased risk to the infant for both mood vulnerability and ruminatory disorder. There may be a subgroup of infants and children with rumination who have an affective disturbance, rejection sensitivity, passivity, and increased incidence of psychiatric disorder [57].

Diagnostic procedures measuring biologic state and trait markers for affective disorders might be useful in further defining the relationship of rumination subgroups to other specific psychiatric disorders [64]. Prospective follow-up of ruminators, noting whether a greater-than-normal incidence of affective or other psychiatric disturbance occurs, would clarify this posited association.

BIOLOGICAL DETERMINANTS AND MEDICAL CONSEQUENCES

Reflux Subtypes

Proponents of a biological etiology of rumination equate rumination with gastroesophageal reflux. Winter [65] found abnormal gastroesophageal acid reflux, esophagitis, and normal or diminished lower esophageal sphincter pressure in infant and child ruminators. Why children with gastroesophageal reflux develop rumination remains a mystery, although the psychological context is considered important. Conversely, other gastroenterologists [3,66] have evaluated ruminators uncovering no significant gastrointestinal structural or motility disturbances. There may be two subgroups of ruminators; one with significant gastrointestinal problems such as reflux or hiatus hernia, and another with no significant gastrointestinal problems.

Up to 20% of children who spit up food or vomit during the first year of life have gastroesophageal reflux defined as "a failure of the sphincter mechanism at the junction of the esophagus and stomach that allows acidic gastric material to flow into the esophagus," (pg. 25) [12].

Reflux of acidic gastric material can cause peptic esophagitis with associated chronic blood loss, iron deficiency anemia, and possibly hematemesis. Esophagitis may diminish lower esophageal sphincter pressure and further increase reflux.

Reflux may be associated with vomiting and failure to thrive. Rumination is considered in the differential diagnosis of psychogenic vomiting and nonorganic failure to thrive (NFTT). Complications of gastroesophageal reflux, such as aspiration pneumonia and esophageal stricture, are often treated by surgery [2].

Reflux has also been associated with Sandifer's Syndrome [67]. This disorder is especially interesting to psychiatrists because the patient who displays headcocking, abnormal movements of the head and neck, and unusual postures may be misdiagnosed as having a tic or dystonic disorder. These abnormal postures occur during gastroesophageal reflux in the child with hiatus hernia. Surgical repair of the hernia abolishes reflux, terminating the abnormal movements within several days postsurgery.

Jolley et al [68] note three patterns of gastroesophageal reflux. Type I occurs in patients who have continuous postcibal reflux and large hiatal hernias, which frequently require antireflux surgical procedure. In type II, a functional motility disorder suggesting delayed gastric emptying appears to be important in infants with discontinuous reflux [69,70]. These infants had frequent gastroesophageal reflux for two hours postcibally, antral pylorospasm [69], increased lower esophageal sphincter pressures, high incidence of pulmonary symptoms, and nonspecific watery diarrhea. The mixed (type III) pattern of gastroesophageal reflux occurred in a small number of infants who exhibited features of both type I and II patterns. Dodds et al [71] noted the association of gastroesophageal reflux (GER) in adults with (1) continuous low esophageal sphincter pressure, (2) normal pressure with momentary drop in pressure, or (3) increased abdominal pressure.

Geffen [22] posited that rumination occurs because of an increased pleuroperitoneal gradient across the diaphragm with simultaneous relaxation of the cricopharyngeal and lower esophageal sphincters. Rapid gastric peristalsis with a contraction of the abdominal musculature, which is unconscious in certain patients, further increases this pressure gradient [106,107]. Incompetence of the lower esophageal sphincter, secondary to hiatus hernia, exacerbates this process. Herbst et al [11] discussed the mechanism of rumination observed during fluoroscopy in a 6-year-old child. The esophagus distended with barium up to the superior esophageal sphincter. When the child made sucking movements of the mouth and tongue, the superior esophageal sphincter opened and barium flowed into the mouth. Normal deglutition followed and initiated a peristaltic wave that emptied the esophagus [11]. The mechanism of rumination may not differ greatly from that of gaseous eructation [22].

Levine et al [5] speculated that an unconscious postprandial intraabdominal pressure occurs with coordinated relaxation of the upper and lower esophageal sphincter. Of the nine cases he reported, one patient had a large postprandial pressure wave starting first in her stomach, then spreading to the esophagus. He also posited that rumination was a benign habit disorder.

Esophageal motor dysfunction has been associated with reflux and rumination. A progressive esophageal peristaltic wave is normally present after the swallowing of food. In rumination, uncontrolled peristaltic movements are seen [72]. Esophageal contraction abnormalities [73] producing reflux are seen in children as well as adults [74]. Emotional stress in the infant or child may produce esophageal contraction abnormalities leading to reflux and rumination [75]. Prugh [76] finds a strong association between emotional stress, dyadic mother/infant disturbance, and upper gastrointestinal dysfunc-

tion [77].

Herbst et al [11] discussed three cases of hiatus hernia associated with rumination. The rumination terminated after surgical repair of the hiatal hernia. He suggests that the abnormal findings associated with rumination should be viewed as parts of an extended syndrome of presentation of gastroesophageal reflux [67].

A second type of gastrointestinal pathology in which the passage of food through the stomach to the duodenum is impaired is termed delayed gastric emptying (DGE) and is also associated with reflux. DGE, which is associated with antral dysmotility [69], pylorospasm, short segment pylorospasm [78], and pyloric stenosis has not been reported in association with rumination.

In two cases of adult rumination [79] no delay was noted in gastric emptying time as measured by radionuclide gastrography. The time course of gastric emptying did, however, affect the frequency and intensity of the ruminations. As gastric emptying progressed, rumination frequency diminished. Levine et al [5] also noted no delay in gastric emptying.

Increased pleuroperitoneal pressure gradient with incompetence or other abnormality of the lower esophageal sphincter may play a role in rumination with some adults. Rumination may lead to chronic esophageal irritation, the possibility of inducing metaplasia (Barrets esophagus) or frank neoplasia. A case of long-standing rumination reported with gastric carcinoma suggested that chronic irritation may have contributed to this malignancy [20]. Rumination associated with esophagitis [2] causes chronic bleeding, resulting in microcytic anemia.

Gastrointestinal Neurohormonal Substrate (Neuropeptides)

The role of neuropeptides (including opioids) in rumination remains to be precisely defined. Effects of upper gastrointestinal tract functions pertinent to postingestive rumination will be reviewed [80] (Table 3).

Gastrin and motilin elevate lower esophageal sphincter pressure (LESP). Glucagon, secretin, cholecystokinin (CCK) and vasoactive intestinal peptide (VIP) all lower LESP. VIP is considered the primary inhibitory gut neurotransmitter. VIP-containing nerve fibers, originating in the myenteric plexus of the lower esophageal sphincter, diminish LESP. VIP also promotes gastric emptying. In the stomach VIP inhibits gastrin release. Increased acetylcholine release from vagal stimulation is accompanied by increased VIP. Esophageal distention in animals increases VIP. Circulation clearance of VIP occurs within one minute of its release,

Table 29.3 Some agents influencing human lower esophageal sphincter pressure (LESP)

Agent	Raise	Lower	No Change
Neuropeptide Hormones	Gastrin	Estrogen	Prolactin
	Motilin	Progesterone	Somatostatin
	Prostaglandin (PGE)	Glucagon	
		Secretin	
		Cholecystokinin (CCK)	
		Prostaglandin (PGE)	
		Vasoactive intestinal peptide (VIP)	
Pharmacologic Agents	Sodium pentobarbital	Atropine	Diazepam
	Metoclopramide	Theophylline	
	Bethanechol	Meperidine	
	Histamine		
	Edrophonium		
	Indomethacin		
	Antacids		
Other (Nutrition, substance use)	Protein in diet	Smoking	
	Coffee	Fat in diet	
		Alcohol	

Adapted from Sleisenger, MH and Fordtran, JS (80)

supporting its role as a neurotransmitter. Also it may have a paracrine function effecting relaxation of circular muscle cells immediately adjacent to the neurofibers of origin. Although VIP is structurally identical in both the CNS and gut, CNS VIP has not yet been found to affect gut function [80].

Opioid-containing neurons innervate circular smooth muscle of the lower esophageal sphincter (LES). Dynorphin exhibits preferential agonist effects at kappa receptors, and metenkephalin is agnostic at delta receptors. Mu and kappa receptor stimulation produce LES relaxation, while delta and sigma receptor stimulation produce LES contraction [81]. Opioids diminish acetylcholine release, produce transient smooth circular muscle contraction, and block inhibitory transmission to circular muscle.

Blinder et al [79] have shown that an opioid agonist (paregoric) totally inhibited postingestive rumination in both a 33-year-old woman with a life-long history of rumination and a 23-year-old woman with rumination and bulimia. Naloxone administered intravenously inhibited this opioid agonist effect.

Premeal administration of both intravenous metochlorpramide (50 mg) and oral Haldol (3 mg) also abolished rumination. This effect was blocked by intravenous naloxone. Since dopamine receptor blocking agents (haloperidol and metoclopramide) increase endogenous opioid neurotransmission, their inhibition by naloxone *suggests a central or peripheral opioid mechanism in rumination characterized by opioid receptor insensitivity or reduction in endorphinergic neurotransmis-*

sion. Recent studies in sheep have demonstrated control of ruminant stomach motility by opioid inhibitory and stimulating neurotransmission in the CNS involving mu, delta (inhibition), and kappa (stimulation) receptors [82].

Herman and Panskeep [83] note that the brain circuit for separation distress may be the evolutionary elaboration of an endorphin-based pain network. The extension of opiate receptors into the limbic system suggests an additional affective role for the endorphins. Their data, which demonstrate the effects of morphine (decreases distress) and naloxone (increases distress) on separation distress and approach attachment, suggest that one function of this system may be to modulate emotions arising from social variables. Attachment may represent an endogenous cellular addiction process in which an infant becomes physiologically dependent on its mother for endorphin stimulation.

Chatoor and Dickson [35], acknowledging the finding of Blinder et al [79] and noting the hypothesis of Herman and Panksepp [83] suggesting that attachment behavior is mediated by endogenous opioids, hypothesize that *deficiency of attachment and the occurrence of separation may diminish endogenous opioid activity, thereby provoking rumination behavior in infancy.* Subsequently, the ruminating activity may act as a compensatory mechanism increasing endogenous opioid levels creating a type of self-stimulating addiction. Adjunctive autoerotic behaviors in infancy that persist after loss and detachment may entail a similar mechanism [84,85].

Rumination and vomiting have been reported during the postnatal withdrawal phase in infants born of narcotically addicted mothers [38,86]. Rumination has been noted in an infant born to a heroin-addicted mother. The child was small for a premature gestational age. Understimulation due to maternal deprivation and a hearing loss may have contributed to the ruminatory disorder along with the narcotic withdrawal [38,79]. Two infants who were in the intensive care unit with multiple medical and surgical problems did not terminate rumination in response to paregoric [4], which contrasts to the effectiveness of this drug in adults [79].

TREATMENT

Treatment in Infants and Children: Hospital Milieu and Family Collaboration

Since rumination in infants and young children may be life-threatening, a multidisciplinary approach is mandatory. The primary physician must decide whether hospitalization is indicated. The decision may be based on the chronicity of the rumination or the presence of significant medical complications (eg, failure to thrive, dehydration, electrolyte abnormalities) or gastrointestinal disturbances (eg, hiatal hernia). Hospitalization may also be indicated when the primary caretaker's ability is severely compromised. Since rumination often occurs in multiproblem families, careful evaluation of the child's psychosocial situation is mandatory. Although many authors have stressed deficient mother-infant interactions [8-10], recent reports [35,55] have noted a positive relationship between the mother and the infant. Rumination without severe weight loss or other physiologic alterations, in the context of a supportive family, may respond to outpatient treatment.

Hospitalization of the child is often a terrifying experience for the mother [9]. She may feel guilty, inadequate, and responsible for her infant's problem. She should be given permission to ventilate her fears and frustration that her child is not getting well immediately and to know that there are medical and psychological reasons for the rumination. An anatomical and physiologic description of reflux may be helpful.

Documentation of the staff's observations of the temperaments of mother and child and the degree of reciprocity should be obtained. Chess [87] suggests that a two- to three-hour home visit to determine the dyadic relationship of mother and child can be very helpful. Preferably, the observation period would be during a sleep and waking cycle. This amount of time is needed to put the patient at ease (as opposed to a brief structured laboratory observation, which could be stressful to both mother and infant and where the mother might present a facade of caring). The observer should refrain from taking notes and should be friendly and nonjudgmental. If the mother is the primary caretaker, she can be seen alone. However, if there are other caretakers, such as a father or grandmother, they can be present. Levy [88] gives an excellent review of the mother-infant relations during feeding. He discusses specific questions such as, for example, is the baby allowed to be an active participant in his feeding, how the foods are presented, who decides when the feeding will end, and how pleasurable feeding is for both mother and infant. Some obsessive mothers may become distraught when the infant vomits near them [3].

A structured interview with the mother, father, or other primary caretaker is crucial. The mother's own developmental and personal psychiatric history may often contain determinants of current conflictual attitudes and behavior toward the infant.

Dickson emphasizes minimizing the mother's guilt. Rumination can be attributed to babies who have a problem with homeostasis and withdrawing into a maladaptive habit. The mother should be told she is both an expert with her child and an important colleague in the treatment process. Her fantasies about the child's rumination, associated failure to thrive, and what techniques have either been helpful in reducing the rumination or what events seem to have precipitated the rumination should be explored. The mother's fragile self-esteem and her feelings of incompetence should be acknowledged and countered by designating her an important colleague in the child's treatment.

In the hospital, the baby should be placed near the nursing station to increase the child's visual and auditory stimulation. There should be a specific nurse on each shift who will give primary care to the child. Frequently, a competent social worker who is involved will be able to pick an empathetic nurse who will be emotionally available during an eight-hour shift to spend much of the time with the child.

A nurse acts as a substitute (surrogate) mother with whom the baby can develop an attachment [8]. Where there is a failure of attachment, substitution of primary care may be critical. As this attachment develops, the child restores a stable object relationship. Mother later will become more involved with feeding. The child will transfer its attachment and thus develop a restorative object relationship with mother. The next therapeutic task will be interruption of the rumination. The child's unique ruminative pattern should be recorded, eg, occurring when the baby is alone or occurring when the mother pushes the baby away [89]. The nurse who is aware of this pattern should be present to interrupt the possible anxiety-producing situation and frustration that may precede rumination. The fourth therapeutic task focuses on the relinquishing of maladaptive ruminative and self-stimulatory patterns.

Table 29.4 Suggested activities for a sensory stimulation program

---

Visual
- Place the infant in face-to-face contact with caretaker inside and outside of crib, particularly during feeding, diapering, etc.
- Place brightly colored mobiles about 7 to 12 inches above the infant's face.
- Place face patterns on the sides of the Isolette or crib.

Tactile
- Skin-to-skin contact while being held.
- Gentle stroking to back, legs, and arms.
- Gentle patting on the infant's back.

Auditory
- Frequent exposure to the human voice, particularly during routine care, and concomitant with eye contact with infant.
- Soft music from music box placed in Isolette or crib during alert periods.

Kinesthetic/vestibular
- Gentle rocking while cradled in caretaker's arms.
- Frequent changes in infant's body position, ie, sitting in infant seat, lying prone, lying on side.
- Carrying infant around room in various positions, ie, on shoulder, cradled in arms, etc.

Sheagren et al (4)

Lourie [8] has reported that a number of ruminators have hypersensitivity to touch and sound [90]. Placing the child on a pillow with minimal touching, but with visual or auditory stimulation would be helpful. In one child who was not interested in people, a relationship was started by a nurse who interested him with bright-colored clothing and jewelry. These auditory and visual stimuli, combined with the crib rocking, initiated the attachment process. In another infant who withdrew from any social contact, placement in a crib with another baby was helpful in starting an object attachment. Later, holding both children on a nurse's knee was useful in reinforcing the attachment process.

Hospital Milieu

Sheagren et al [4] discussed a multisensory stimulation approach (Table 4). He noted that in three cases using a limited number of nurses, and placing the child in an open crib, the children started to gain weight, developed a social smile, and had improved interaction with their caretakers.

The use of video tape may aid in analysis of the dyadic mother-child interactions by emphasizing tension states and separation-withdrawal in mother and infant and their link to ruminatory behavior.

The mother needs to recognize her child's strivings for autonomy and the baby's need to be a stimulated and active participant in the feeding process (many ruminant babies are quite passive). Feeding should terminate when the child is finished, and rigid schedules should be abandoned. The mother may need to stimulate the infant by increasing her eye contact, vocalizing, and smiling during feeding. She may have to work through her uncomfortable feelings that have been present during the feeding process [88].

Dickson and Chatoor [89] feel that the primary purpose of therapy is to break the ruminative habit. Problems in the family may exist after discharge, although rumination frequently will cease. The goal for the baby is to develop external object satisfaction by using a combination of negative and positive social reinforcers. As the child ruminates, the nurse will say "NO," gently touch the mouth, and place the baby down. In two minutes she will check the baby. If rumination has ceased she will again play with the patient. Ideally, the nurse will be able to play with and stimulate the baby during her entire shift, providing positive social reinforcement. At times the child may be pulled around and remain close to the nurse. This type of positive reinforcement may be more effective than the aversive behavioral techniques of squirting lemon juice and pepper sauce during rumination.

Maternal depression in association with infant rumination has been described frequently [8-10,31]. Therefore, a long-term goal may include individual treatment for a depressed mother. If the child continues to ruminate, placement outside the home may be necessary. As a part of discharge planning, home visits and increased support from mother's friends and family are advised. The mother should be seen after discharge both individually as indicated, with the child at least once a week for psychological interactive management, and at least once a week by the pediatrician.

Since rumination in young children can result in death, the resistant mother may have to be confronted about the poor prognosis if her emotional state and environmental conditions are not modified.

Treatment in Adolescence

In a 13-year-old patient with a three-year history of rumination, a multidimensional approach to treatment was necessary, including individual psychotherapy to work through a mother's death and the possible dissolution of a father's current marriage, and family treatment to resolve tensions of marital discord. Behavior monitoring documented three specific ruminatory patterns: food rising but not going to the mouth, food regurgitated and reswallowed, and food regurgitated and extruded. A relaxation technique using a personalized tape developed by the therapist was employed with the patient alternately tightening and relaxing parts of the body. Deep breathing and imagery were also used [42].

Biological Treatment: Medical-Surgical and Pharmocotherapy

Herbst [2] believes that many cases of rumination are primarily related to excessive gastroesophageal reflux. In this view, the management of rumination is essentially the same as the medical management of reflux [12]. The initial treatment includes elevation of the infant to the position of a 30 to 45 degree angle; avoidance of juices; and small, frequent, thickened feedings. A six-week medical course is usually instituted. After each meal, aluminum hydroxide, an antacid, can be alternated with magnesium hydroxide. If symptoms persist [12] in an infant over one year of age, cimetidine, which blocks H-2 receptors, diminishing gastric acid production, is given. Bethanchol also may be administered. In older children, administering a dopamine antagonist such as metoclopramide (acting centrally and peripherally), or domperidone (acting peripherally) increases LES pressure, gastric tone and peristalsis, and improves gastric emptying [91]. Side-effects such as extrapyramidal reactions may occur with metoclopramide but rarely with domperidone [92]. If a six-week trial of medical treatment is ineffective, surgery may be indicated [12].

Winter [65] evaluated five cases of rumination in infants and young children who displayed pathologic gastroesophageal acid clearance. Treatment of reflux and esophagitis by positional therapy, antacids, and cimetidine abolished rumination and suggested a medical etiology. Nasogastric tube feeding may be used in severe reflux to prevent dehydration and electrolyte abnormalities [35].

Criteria for surgery are persistent vomiting after vigorous medical management, failure to thrive with nutritional depletion, gastroesophageal bleeding from esophagitis, aspiration pneumonia, and esophageal stricture. The surgical procedure of choice is the Nissen fundoplication [93].

Treatment of Adults

Treatment of adult rumination presents a different context from that of the child. Family physicians may not recognize adult rumination as a discreet phenomenon. Often patients are confused by explanations of the behavior that allude to stress or emotional disorder. They become guilty about their problem and need reassurance. Pope's technique is to discuss gastroesophageal reflux using a diagram of the stomach and esophagus. Pictorial illustrations may be helpful. By explaining the mechanism of reflux to the patient, this problem is appropriately recognized, and the patient feels reassured and relieved [5,46].

Medical treatments with antispasmodics have been ineffective [1]. Because the esophageal contractile abnormalities producing reflux may be secondary to an agitated depression or anxiety disorder [73,74], some patients with rumination may have features of specific psychiatric disorder.

An experimental treatment using an opioid agonist (paregoric) and medications that enhance endogenous opioid transmission (metaclopramide, haloperidol) has been effective in diminishing ruminative behavior in two adult patients [79].

Preprandial hypnosis has been successful in an adult with chronic rumination [94].

Behavioral Therapy

Behavioral treatment to suppress rumination in the retarded encompasses physical aversive techniques including mild digital electroshock [14], oral application of pepper sauce [59,95] and lemon juice [29], and newer nonaversive modalities including food satiation [24], overcorrection [30,96], extinction [97], positive social reinforcement [31,35,98], withdrawal of music [99], or differential reinforcement of other behavior [100]. The general paradigm for behavioral treatment studies includes an analysis of the frequency, setting, duration and antecedent events of the behavior to the changed, followed by a procedural schedule of positive or negative reinforcement.

Behavioral treatment of rumination with physically aversive stimuli was first reported in 1968 [28]. Mild electroshock, an aversive stimulus to the finger, was successfully employed in a severely dehydrated child who did not respond to psychological management [14]. Winton and Singh concluded that "electroshock should be used only in life-threatening cases that have proved refractory to other forms of therapy and that its use should always be paired with positive reinforcement of appropriate behavior" [13].

Tart and bitter substances such as lemon juices [29] and pepper sauce [59] have been squirted into the mouth, diminishing rumination. Singh [95] found that pepper sauce was more effective than lemon juice (which can dissolve tooth enamel). Both substances, however, were difficult to apply effectively.

Subsequent approaches have deemphasized the physically aversive stimuli, which often led to staff resistance. For example, satiation techniques have been reported in which a subject is allowed to eat as much food as is desired, ultimately leading to suppression of rumination. A beneficial side-effect is an increase of weight for patients who are malnourished [24]. Duker and Seyes [101] used overcorrection, a procedure in which the patient is required to "clean up" after every episode of rumination. Fox et al [30] followed regurgitation with a mouth-cleansing punishment combined with satiation. Singh [96] suppressed rumination with oral hygiene contingent responses alone.

Negative punishment is a technique that deletes or delays a desirable event following rumination. Usually, food or staff attention is removed for a specific period of time. The efficacy depends on the potency of the reinforcement that has been removed. This technique was slower and produced less reduction than more aversive punishment. Wolf et al [97] used extinction where a positive reinforcer, specific for a child, was discontinued to abolish any favorable social consequence of rumination. An effective social aversive technique is to speak the word "no" as the child appears to ruminate and avoid physical and eye contact for five minutes [35].

Barman [98] employed a technique using positive reinforcers such as verbal praise and mild vibratory stimulation (from a vibrator worn on a special vest) as a reward for the absence of rumination. Contingent music to diminish both rumination and out-of-seat behavior has been used as an adjunct technique [99].

A differential reinforcement of other behavior (DRO procedure) has been reported. The patient was prompted to walk around a taped 5-ft square and eat a cracker every 30 seconds during rumination [100]. Daniel concluded that rapidity of the 30-second DRO procedure may have prevented rumination. However Winton and Singh [13] feel the patient was given a form of satiation.

Positive side effects of behavioral treatment are improved feeding skills, increased general motor activity and play, increased cognitive function, and decreased tantrum crying and stereotyped behavior. Behavior therapy promotes increased staff attention and social stimulation, which may provide adjunctive reinforcement of alternative acceptable behaviors. Negative side-effects reported by Becker et al [102] and Galbraith et al [103] included head slapping, rocking and weaving, self-mutilation, hair pulling, and masturbation.

Social reinforcement techniques may diminish rumination. Winton and Singh [13] concluded that rumination could be eliminated or effectively reduced by varied positive reinforcers such as attention and social interaction and changing stressful antecedent conditions associated with rumination.

In summary, each author advocates the efficacy of his own technique. However, methodologic inadequacies include small sample size, lack of comparison of different behavioral techniques in a given population, absence of control groups, and lack of long-term follow-up comparing relative effectiveness.

BIOPSYCHOSOCIAL SYNTHESIS IN RUMINATION

The etiology of rumination is unclear. Physiologic, psychodynamic, and behavioral theories have been discussed. Rumination is a psychobiological disorder in which psychological and physiological abnormalities combine in various degrees to produce the ruminatory behavior.

Rumination may be on a continuum wherein a patient might have maximal gastrointestinal pathophysiology such as severe reflux with hiatus hernia and minimal psychological concomitants, or the converse wherein a patient could have minimal gastrointestinal pathophysiology or reflux but severe psychopathology or psychosocial stress. Proponents of the biologic theories believe that psychological factors definitely influence rumination.

Multiple stresses in children can produce similar symptomatic behaviors [104]. For the child, irritability and discomfort may result in feeling overwhelmed, anxious, or depressed or may be manifest as severe reflux with esophagitis. Inferred reflux esophagitis, treated either medically or surgically, may result in a feeling of well being and a termination of rumination [72].

Psychodynamically oriented therapy using a substitute caregiver may reduce rumination for two reasons. First, the child receives increased stimulation, which aids in trust and attachment. Second, this additional care is effective because the child is held upright during the period of stimulation, diminishing both reflux and esophagitis. The esophagitis, which subsides, augments lower esophageal sphincter pressure, further diminishing reflux. Diminished esophagitis results in reduced psychological tension, promoting feelings of well being in both mother and infant.

Maternal anxiety may promote secondary physiologic changes in a child. For example, a mother feeling overwhelmed by a stressful situation or feeling anxious secondary to her child's persistent vomiting and weight loss may exhibit increased muscle tension. This is transmitted to the child, who becomes tense and develops a more rapid heart rate [77]. The increased autonomic response may alter neuroendocrine controls and VIP, producing lower esophageal sphincter relaxation and increased reflux. Thus, the tendency of the child to ruminate may be increased by an anxious mother. Psychiatric disorder has been associated with both reflux and esophageal contractility abnormalities [73]. Transmitted maternal stress could result in infant gastroesophageal contractile dysfunction, promoting reflux and rumination.

Two proposed biopsychosocial sequences of rumination in an infant are presented in Table 5 (predominance of interactive psychopathology or gastroesophageal abnormality). A close interrelation occurs between mother and infant with various pathophysiological and emotional stresses. Diagnosis and treatment based on evaluation of both the psychological state of the mother

Table 29.5 Biopsychosocial sequence in rumination with maternal infant interactive disturbance

I.   Child-natural tendency for vomiting and reflux.
II. Psychosocial stress.
  1. Understimulation — mother depressed.
  2. Maternal overstimulation — mother anxious or involves infant in excessive inappropriate involvement.
  3. Object loss of parent.
  4. Excessive family discord.
III. Neuroendocrine dysregulation related to II.
  1. Abnormal esophageal contractions.
  2. Endogenous opioid deficit (neurotransmission/receptor insensitivity central or peripheral).
IV. Increased reflux and rumination.
V.   Augmented maternal anxiety due to:
  1. Fear baby will die.
  2. Helplessness over an inability to feed baby.
  3. Further detachment due to mother's disgust with vomiting
VI. Increased rumination.
VII. Possible death due to dehydration, starvation, aspiration.

Biopsychosocial sequence in rumination with primary functional or anatomic pathophysiology

I.   Natural tendency toward vomiting and reflux.
II. Gastroesophageal reflux.
  A. Etiology #1 — Gastroesophageal pathology, eg:
    1. Hiatal hernia.
    2. Esophageal motor dysmotity — excess uncoordinated tertiary peristalic waves, esophageal contractural abnormalities, atonic distal esophagus.
    3. Congenital absence of distal esophageal sphincter.
    4. Excessive VIP (speculative).
    5. Subsensitive opioid-receptors or insufficent opioid gut transmission (speculative).
  B. Etiology #2 — Gastroduodenal pathology. Delayed gastric emptying due to:
    1. Antral dismotility.
    2. Pylorospasm.
    3. Short segment pyloric stenosis.
III. Rumination. Healthy mother becomes anxious due to loss of weight and vomiting of infant.
IV. Maternal anxiety transmitted to child.
V.   Increased rumination.

and infant and the infant's gastrointestinal function is indicated [111].

SUMMARY

Rumination is an uncommon disorder occurring from infancy through adult life. It consists of regurgitating and then reswallowing partially digested food. Rumination may result in considerable morbidity in infants and young children. Adult ruminators may have a benign course with embarrassing involuntary reflux or may have an associated eating disorder (bulimia or anorexia) or depression.

Biologic theories of etiology associate rumination with gastroesophageal reflux, hiatus hernia, and delayed gastric emptying. Psychological theories discuss infants who have severe failure to thrive and often appear depressed. Severe dysynchrony between mother and infant and maternal psychopathology consisting of anxiety, depression, and inability to adequately nurture the child may be present. Behavioral theory discusses the self-reinforcing aspect of the ruminatory behavior. Theories of neuropeptide and opioid regulation posit central and peripheral deficits of endorphinergic neurotransmission and receptor sensitivity. Rumination associated with interactive psychopathology may be an affective disorder variant.

Treatment approaches reveal pharmacologic or surgical treatment of reflux, psychological treatment of the infant-mother dysynchrony (with the use of substitute caretakers), and behavioral treatment using aversive stimuli (lemon juice, pepper sauce) or positive social reinforcement.

Since rumination may have a biologically or psychologically predominant context, a biopsychosocial theory and sequence have been elaborated. Therefore, a multidisciplinary approach to diagnosis and treatment that uses available appropriate treatment modalities is imperative to treat this disorder comprehensively and effectively.

REFERENCES

1. Brown WR. Rumination in the adult: A study of two cases. Gastroenter 1968; 54:933-9.
2. Herbst JJ. Diagnosis and treatment of gastroesophageal reflux in children. Ped Review 1983; 5:75-9.
3. Fleischer DR. Infant rumination syndrome. Am J Dis Child 1979; 133:266-90.
4. Sheagran TG, Mangurten HH, Brea F, Lutostanski S. Rumination a new complication of neonatal intensive care. Peds 1980; 66:551-5.
5. Levine DR, Wingate DL, Pfeffer JM. Habitual rumination: A benign disorder. Br Med J 1983; 287:255-6.
6. Blinder BJ. In: Cauwels JM, ed. Bulimia: The binge purge compulsion. New York, Doubleday, 1983: 77-79.
7. Fairburn CG, Cooper PJ. Rumination in bulimia nervosa. British Medical Journal 1984b; 288:826-7.
8. Lourie RS. Experience with therapy of psychosomatic problems in infants. In: Hoch PH, Zubin J, eds. Psychopathology of Childhood. New York: Grune and Stratton, 1954.

9. Gaddini RD, Gaddini E. Rumination in infancy. In: Jessner L, Pavenstedt E, eds. Dynamic Psychopathology in Childhood. New York: Grune & Stratton, 1959: pp. 166-185.

10. Richmond JB, Eddy E, Green M. Rumination: A psychosomatic syndrome of infancy. Peds 1958; 22: 49-55.

11. Herbst JJ, Friedland GW, Zboralske FF. Hiatal hernia and rumination in infants and children. J Peds 1971; 78:261-5.

12. Gryboski JD. Gastroesophageal reflux. In: Gryboski JD, Walker WA, eds. Gastrointestinal Problems in the Infant, second ed. Philadelphia: WB Saunders, 1983: pp. 30-39.

13. Winton ASW, Singh NN. Rumination in pediatric populations: A behavioral analysis. J Am Acad Child Psychiat 1983; 22:269-75.

14. Lang PJ, Melamed BG. Case report: Avoidance conditioning therapy of an infant with chronic ruminative vomiting. J Abnorm Psychol 1969; 74:1-8.

15. Halmi K. Eating disorders. In: Freeman AM, Kaplan HI, Sadock BJ, eds. Comprehensive Textbooks of Psychiatry, IV. Baltimore: William and Wilkins, 1985: 1735-6.

16. Diagnostic and Statistical Manual of Mental Disorders, 3rd edition, Washington DC: American Psychiatric Association, 1980.

17. Hollowell JG, Gardner LI. Rumination and growth failure in male fraternal twins: Association with disturbed family environment. Peds 1965; 36:565-7.

18. Brockbank EM. Merycism or rumination in man. Br Med J 1907; 1:421-7.

19. Kanner L. Rumination. In: Child Psychiatry, ed 3. Springfield Ill: Thomas, 1957: 484-7.

20. Long DF. Rumination in man. Am J Med Sci 1929; 178:814-22.

21. Djaldetti M, Pinkhas J, de Vries A. Rumination and cardioesophageal relaxation associated with pernicious anemia. Gastroenter 1962; 43:685-8.

22. Geffen M. Rumination in man. Am J Digest Dis 1966; 11:963-72.

23. Danford DE, Huber AM. Eating dysfunctions in an institutionalized mentally retarded population. Appetite 1981; 2:281-92.

24. Rast J, Johnston JM, Drum C, Conrin J. The relation of food quantity to rumination behavior. J Appl Behav Anal 1981; 14:121-30.

25. Fabricius A. Tractatus de gula ventriculoet intestinis. Padua 1618.

26. Lushka H. Das Antrum cardiac cum des menschlichen magens. Virchow Arch Path Anat 1857; 9:427-33.

27. Grulee CG. Rumination in the first year of life. Am J Dis Child 1917; 14:210-8.

28. Luckey RE, Watson CM, Musick JK. Aversive conditioning as a means of inhibiting vomiting and rumination. Am J Mental Defic 1968; 73:139-42.

29. Sajwaj T, Libet J, Agras S. Lemon-juice therapy: The control of life-threatening rumination in a six-month-old infant. J Appl Behav Anal 1974; 7:557-63.

30. Fox RM, Snyder MS, Schroeder F. A food satiation and oral hygiene punishment program to suppress chronic rumination by retarded persons. J Aut Developm Dis 1979; 9:399-412.

31. Chatoor I, Dickson L. Rumination: A maladaptive attempt at self-regulation in infants and children. Clin Proc CHNMC 1984; 40:107-16.

32. Bowlby E, Mostyn J. Attachment and Loss. New York: Basic Books, 1969.

33. Milakovic I. Hypothesis of a prenatal deglutative stage in libidinal development. Int J Psychoanalysis 1967; 48:76-8.

34. Cameron JC. Lumeian lectures: On some forms of vomiting in infancy. Br Med J 1925; I:872.

35. Chatoor I, Dickson L. Rumination: Etiology and treatment. Ped Ann December 1984.

36. O'Neil PM, White JL, King CR, Carek DJ. Controlling childhood rumination through differential reinforcement of other behavior. Behav Mod 1979; 3:355-72.

37. Marholin DII, Luiselli JK, Robinson M, Lott IT. Response contingent taste-aversion in treating chronic ruminative vomiting of institutionalized profoundly retarded children. J Ment Defic Res 1980; 24:47-56.

38. Vadapalli Maruthi. Personal communication, 1984.

39. Griffin JB Jr. Rumination in a 7-year-old child. So Med J 1977; 70:243-4.

40. Fleisher DR. Nervous vomiting in infancy. Unpublished paper presented at American Academy of Pediatrics, 1979.

41. Sargent. Personal communication, 1984.

42. Chan. Personal communication, 1984.

43. Wells. Personal communication, 1984.

44. Sorkin. Personal communication, 1984.

45. Dambassis JN. The clinical significance of rumination. Am Practit 1949; 3:309-13.

46. Pope C. Personal communication, 1984.

47. Spitzer R, Endicott J. Schedule for affective disorders and schizophrenia. New York: New York Psychiatric Institute, 1978.

48. Philippopoulus GS. The analysis of a case of merycism. In: Topics on Psychosomatic Research. Psychother, Psychosm 1973; 22:354-71.

49. Danford DE. Pica and nutrition. Ann Rev Nutr 1982; 2:303-22.

50. Lott I. Personal communication, 1984.

51. Renuart J. Personal communication, 1984.

52. Woolston JL. Eating disorders in infancy and early childhood. In this volume.

53. Menolascino FJ. Primitive, atypical and abnormal-psychotic behavior in institutionalized mentally retarded children. J Autism Childhood Schizophrenia 1972; 3:49-64.

54. Wright MM, Menolascino FJ. Nurturant nursing of mentally retarded ruminators. Am J Mental Def 1966; 71:451-9.

55. Lavigne JV, Burns WJ. Rumination in infancy: recent behavioral approaches. Int J Eating Dis 1981; 1:70-82.

56. Wright L, Thalassino PA. Success with electric shock in habitual vomiting: Report of two cases in young children. Clin Pediat 1973; 12:594-7.

57. Leibowitz MR, Quitkin FM. Psychopharmacologic validation of atypical depression. J Clin Psychiat 1984; 45:22-5.

58. Flanagan CH. Rumination in infancy past and present. JAACP 1977; 16(1):140-9.

59. Murray ME, Keele DK, McCarver JW. Behavioral treatment of rumination. Clinical Pediatrics 1976; 15:591-6.

60. Menolascino FJ. Personal communication, 1984.

61. Hoffer W. Mouth, hand, and ego integration. Psychoanalytic Study of the Child 1949; 3/4:4955.

62. Hoffer W. Development of the body ego. Psychoanalytic Study of the Child 1950; 5:18-23.

63. Kirs E. Some comments and observations on early autoerotic activities. Psychoanalytic Study of the Child 1951; 6:95-116.

64. Bunney W. Biologic markers. Psych Ann 1983; 13:366-427.

65. Winter H. Personal communication, 1984.

66. Berquist A. Personal communication, 1984.

67. Herbst JJ, Johnson DG, Oliveros MA. Gastroesophageal reflux with protein-losing enteropathy and finger clubbing. Am J Dis Child 1976; 130:1256-8.

68. Jolley SG, Herbst JJ, Johnson DG, Book LS, Matlak ME, Condon VR. Patterns of postcibal gastroesophageal reflux in symptomatic infants. Am J Surg 1979; 138:946-9.

69. Byrne WJ, Kangarloo H, Ament ME, Lo CW, Berquist W, Foglia R, Fonkalsrud EW. Antral dysmotility: An unrecognized cause of chronic vomiting during infancy. Ann Surg 1981; 193:521-4.

70. Bitar KN, Saffouri B, Makhlouf GM. Cholinergic and peptidergic receptors on isolated human antral smooth muscle cells. Gastroenter 1982; 82:832-7.

71. Dodds WJ, Dent J, Hogan WJ, Helm JF, Hauser R, Patel GK, Egide MS. Mechanisms of gastroesophageal reflux in patients with reflux esophagitis. N Eng J Med 1982; 307:1547-52.

72. Herbst J. Personal communication, 1984.

73. Clouse RE, Lustman PJ. Psychiatric illness and contraction abnormalities of the esophagus. N Eng J Med 1983; 309:1337-42.

74. Clouse R. Personal communication, 1984.

75. Leitch M, Escalona S. The reaction of infants to stress. In: Psychoanalytic study of the child. New York: Internat Univ Press, 1949; 3/4:121-5.

76. Prugh D, et al. Hypertrophic pyloric stenosis in infancy: Innate and experiential factors. In: Call J, Galenson E, Tyson RL, eds. Frontiers of Infant Psychiatry. New York: Basic Books, 1983: 301.

77. Kulka AM, Water RD, Fry CP. Mother-infant interaction as measured by simultaneous recording of physiological processes. J Am Acad Child Psych 1966; 5:496-503.

78. Swischuk LE, Hayden CK Jr, Tyson KR. Short segment pyloric narrowing: Pylorospasm or pyloric stenosis? Pediat Radiol 1981; 10:201-5.

79. Blinder BJ, Bain N, Simpson R. Evidence for an opioid neurotransmission mechanism in adult rumination.

80. Sleisenger MH, Fordtran JS. Gastrointestinal disease: Pathophysiology, diagnosis and management, third ed. Philadelphia, WB Saunders, 1983.

81. Goyal R. Personal communication, 1984.

82. Ruckebusch Y, Bardon TH, Pairet M. Opioid control of the ruminant stomach motility: Functional importance of mu, kappa and delta receptors. Life Sci 1984; 35:1731-8.

83. Herman BH, Panksepp J. Effects of morphine and naloxone on separation distress and approach attachment: Evidence for opiate mediation of social affect. Pharmacology, Biochemistry and Behavior 1978; 9:213-20.

84. Spitz RA, Wolf KM. Anaclitic depression: An inquiry into the genesis of psychiatric conditions in early infancy. In: The Psychoanalytic Study of the Child. New York, Internat Univ Press, 1946: 2:313-24.

85. Kris E. Notes on the development and on some current problems of psychoanalytic child psychology. Psychoanalytic study of the child, 1950; 5:24-46.

86. Mirin SM, Weiss RD. Abuse of opiate drugs. In: Bassuk EL, Schoonover SE, Galenburg AJ, eds. Practitioners Guide to psychoactive drugs. New York: Plenum Press, 1983: pp. 222-235.

87. Chess S. Personal communication, 1984.

88. Levy R. Mother-infant relations in the feeding situation. In: Lebanthal E, ed. Textbook of Gastroenterology and Nutrition in Infancy. New York: Raven Press, 1981.

89. Dickson L, Chatoor I. Personal communication, 1984.

90. Bergman P, Escalona SK. Unusual sensitivities in very young children. Psychoanal Study Child 1949; 314:333-52.

91. Brogden RN, Carmine AA, Heel RC, Speight TM, Avery GS. Domperidone. Drugs 1982; 24:360-400.

92. Sol P, Pelet B, Guignard JP. Extrapyramidal reactions due to domperidone. Lancet 1980; 2:802.

93. Randolph JG. Hiatal hernia and gastroesophageal reflux, the esophagus. In: Ravitch MM, Welch KJ, Benson DC, Aberdeen E, Randolph JG, eds. Pediatric Surg, third ed, vol 1. Chicago: Year Book Medical Publishers Inc, 1979.

94. Kahn D. Personal communication, 1984.

95. Singh NN. Aversive control of rumination in the mentally retarded. J Prac Approach Develpm Hand 1979; 3:2-6.

96. Singh NN, Manning PJ, Angell MJ. Effects of an oral hygiene punishment procedure on chronic rumination and collateral behaviors in monozygous twins. J Appl Behav Anal 1982; 15:309-14.

97. Wolf MM, Birnbrauer J, Lawler J, Williams T. The operant extinction, reinstatement and re-extinction of vomiting behavior in a retarded child. In Ulrich R, Statnik T, Mabry J, eds. Control of Human Behavior: From Cure to Prevention, vol 2. Glenview, Ill: Scott, Forseman, 1970: pp. 146-149.

98. Barmann BC. Use of contingent vibration in the treatment of self-stimulatory hand-mouthing and rumina-

Am J Psychiat 1986; 143:255.

tive vomiting behavior. J Behav Ther Exp Psychiat 1980; 11:307-11.

99. Davis WB, Weiseler NA, Hanzel TE. Contingent music in management of rumination and out-of-seat behavior in a profoundly mentally retarded institution-alized male. Mental Retardation 1980; 18:43-4.

100. Daniel WH. Management of chronic rumination with a contingent exercise procedure employing topo-graphically dissimilar behavior. J Behav Ther and Exp Psychiat 1982; 12(2):149-52.

101. Duker PC, Seys DM. Elimination of vomiting in a re-tarded female using restitutional overcorrection. Behav Ther 1977; 8:255-7.

102. Becker JV, Turner SM, Sajwaj TE. Multiple behavioral effects of the use of lemon juice with a ruminating toddler-age child. Behav Mod 1978; 2:267-78.

103. Galbraith DA, Bryick RJ, Rutledge JT. An aversive conditioning approach to the inhibition of chronic vomiting. Canad Psychiat Assn J 1970; 15:311-3.

104. Greenspan S. Personal communication, 1984.

105. Blinder BJ. Rumination: A benign disorder? Int J Eat-ing Disorders 1986; 5:385-6.

106. Amarnath RD, Abell TL, Malagelada JR. The rumi-nation syndrome in adults: A characteristic manometric pattern. Ann Intern Med 1986; 105:513-8.

107. Reynolds, RP, Lloyd DA. Manometric study of a rumi-nator. J Clin Gastroenterol 1986; 8:127-30.

108. Gould E, Bres M. Regurgitation in gorillas. Possible model for human eating disorders (rumina-tion/bulimia). J Dev Behav Pediatr 1986; 7:314-9.

109. Larocca FF, Della-Fera MR. Rumination: Its signifi-cance in adults with bulimia nervosa. Psychosomatics 1986; 27:209-12.

110. Collins JS, Brennan FN, Lee RJ, Love AH. Rumina-tion in adults — a rare cause of gastro-oesophageal re-gurgiation in two patients. Ulster Med J 1986; 55:176-80.

111. Rumination (Editorial) Lancet 1987; 1:200-01.

Chapter 30

Pica: A Critical Review of Diagnosis and Treatment

Barton J. Blinder, Stanley L. Goodman, and Phyllis Henderson

INTRODUCTION: OVERVIEW AND DEFINITION

Pica is defined as a pathological craving for either a food item or its constituents or for substances not commonly regarded as food [1]. DSM-III emphasizes repeated nonnutritive ingestion for a period of time as a habitual mode of response [2].

Pica must be viewed in a developmental context (age level, physiologic state, level of cognitive and intellectual development) and also related to sociocultural and historical patterns that may determine the food selection of a people or a region [1,3,4]. Animal studies suggest that pica may result from specific deficiencies or be part of a nutrient-specific appetite [1]. A similar pattern has been inferred in humans [5-12]. Nutrient deficiencies and medical consequences such as iron deficiency, lead intoxication, growth and cognitive impairment, and intestinal obstruction are freqently associated with the idiosyncratic dietary habits [13,14].

Pica has been reported in certain schizophrenic patients [15-18] and is frequently observed in the mentally retarded [19-21]. It has been attributed to delusional beliefs [18], behavioral lag [19,22], and the developmental chaos of autistic children [23].

Historical Perspectives

Cooper [24] extensively reviewed the existing historical literature concerning pica. Table 1 summarizes the varied ideas relating to presumed target patient populations, biological determinants and mechanisms, ecologic variables, and psychosocial correlations.

Etiology

Much of the early work is based on superstition and folklore. Early case studies are conspicuously absent. Most writers deal primarily with pica in pregnant women, although references to its occurrence in both sexes appear. Recommendations for dietary alteration and the empirical use of iron preparations as treatment appeared before iron deficiency was proposed as a factor in the development of pica [1]. Indeed, the empirical treatment most often deemed beneficial involved nutritional fortification [12]. Moral weakness, perverted instinct, and psychological factors are implicated. The ambiguity conveyed in early clinical descriptions continues to the modern era, although several lines of rational investigation have emerged. (see table 1, Historial Perspectives.)

Current efforts to define and explain the phenomenon of pica include (1) developmental studies (vestigial instinct); (2) psychodynamic theories (deprivation conflict); (3) need-state hypotheses that propose nutritional deficit and homeostatic compensation; (4) sociocultural determinants that involve ethnic group traditions and beliefs related to rites of passage, health, and fertility (see chapter in this volume by Freeman on Transcultural Descriptions of the Eating Disorders); (5) consequences of erratic reinforcement in a chaotic unstructured environment (adjunctive behavior model) [12];

Table 30.1 Historical perspectives on the etiology of pica

Cooper (24) and Danford (1982) extensively reviewed the existing literature concerning pica. A summary of the literature pertaining to etiology follows:

Date	Author	Etiology
10 BC	Thompson	Clay lozenges ingested to treat illness and poisoning.
1000	Boezo	Avicenna treated pica with iron.
1542	Aetius	In pregnant women, suppressed menstrual flow rises to the stomach and causes bizarre cravings.
1562	Hubrigkt	Adulterated stomach fluid. Occurs in both sexes, especially women who "yield too much to the state of mind."
1638	Boezo	a) Fetus attracts purer blood causing foul remainder to corrupt the stomach, producing pica. b) A "vitriolic tartar" clings to the stomach lining. c) Visceral obstruction d) Suppression of menses e) Heredity
1668	Ledelius	a) Remnants of food in stomach cause fermented humors to corrupt the appetite b) "Natural appetite" — First of the "need-determined" theorists c) Psychological factors: anger, fear, sadness
1684	Van der Burgh	Passions of the spirit cause nervous excitation in those not strong enough to resist, therefore more common in women
1687	Betten	a) The guardian of the senses is perverted by the lust of the body b) Transmitted in utero from pregnant mother with pica
1692	Maler	Conflict of the spirit as cause of pica
1698	Dehne	An interplay of heredity, "fermental humors" and psychopathology
1719	Schrey	In either sex, in the mind that "judges food badly" perversion of perception of taste and aroma predisposes to pica, as may tendency of infants to mouth inanimate objects
1811	Craigin	In slaves, mistreatment causes a depression, which causes an addiction to earth eating.
1833	Mason	Poor diet and iron lack. The first to suggest iron deficit a) Innate instinct b) Imitation c) Emotional — homesickness, separation from family d) Underlying disease such as worms, yaws, pregnancy e) Poor diet
1840	Dors	An instinctive impulse analogous to that in animals who because ignorance or need fail in each season to procure sufficient nourishment
1845	Hille	Splanchnic nervous dysfunction which at advanced stages becomes "a true condition of the psyche."
1849	Varga	Pica in the insane is the result of "not knowing what else to do with the things they pick up."
1867	Foote	Pica in Jamaicans as a crude remedy for gastrodynia
1876	Gould	Iron deficiency
1879	Kovatsch	Pica caused by worm infestation
1899	Baccarini	Heredity
1900	Simonini	CNS disease
1903	Gros	Instinctive action
1906	Hooper/Mann	Anemia — notes that anemic people eat clay, which paradoxically worsens their anemia
1909	Raynaud	Poor diet
1931	Smith	a) Nutritional. Pica occurs when an organism most stressed nutritionally, during pregnancy, lactation, growth b) Psychological — a change of environment helps
1935	Major	Pica a symptom of anemia and pinworms, disappears when underlying disease treated
1942	Dickins/Ford	Nutritional — noted pica to be higher in children with less iron-rich foods in their diet
1948	Kanner	a) Mental retardation b) Faulty habit training c) Parental neglect
1952	De Castro	Pica a manifestation of "specific hunger"
1955	Arieti	Pica in terminal schizophrenics a behavioral manifestation of lower levels of integration
1962	Gutelius	No relationship between pica and iron deficiency anemia
1969	Coltman	Pica a symptom of iron lack
1977	Youdim	Iron as a cofactor in hypothalmic neurotransmission regulating appetite

and (6) neurobiologic bases of food selection and ingestive behavior in animal investigations (iron deficiency leading to pagophagia, labyrinthine stimulation, and pica [26,27] and iron deficiency and decreased dopamine receptor neurotransmission as etiologic factors in spontaneous pica [28]).

Psychodynamic theorists describe childhood pica as either resulting from maternal and/or paternal deprivation and a maternal fostering of oral defenses against anxiety [29,30] or resulting from excess oral stimulation coupled with aggression toward the mother after the introduction of solid food [30]. A mother may foster oral defenses against anxiety by late weaning, using the bottle as a pacifier, displaying pica behavior herself, or seducing her child into eating nonnutritive substances [29].

In a study of 95 children with pica, Millican et al [29] found 31.2% had a positive history for maternal facilitation of pica concomitant with paternal deprivation. However, 21.4% of a psychiatric comparison group (but only 3.7% of a normal comparison group) also had this dyad. Millican et al [29] emphasize that the critical factor for determining the choice of pica as a symptom is the "shunting" of the child to oral satisfaction. Pueschel et al [31] confirmed these findings in a group of lead-poisoned children with a constellation of inadequate mother-child interaction, paternal deprivation, culturally dependent maternal oral interests, and significant stress factors leading to pica. The remaining normal oral drive may vary in intensity and may be exaggerated when "there are extra pressures in this direction" and there are "inadequate patterns of control for these oral activities" [30].

Frustration of oral drive as a cause of fixation was not seen in the pica group. Oral deprivation may lead to varied developmental and psychostructural deficits (affective, motor, characterologic) that are predominantly nonoral in nature [32,33].

In addition to poor parental supervision and oral overstimulation, maternal pica (63% in Millican's pica group) and cultural acceptance of pica—especially common in families with African lineage and in southern communities [24,29,34], may represent the extra pressures that allow pica to become manifest in a child prone to intense oral focus of drive satisfaction.

A study of children with iron deficiency anemia pica and anemic children without pica suggests that certain psychosocial stressors are significantly associated with pica: maternal deprivation, joint family, parental neglect, child beating, impoverished parent-child interaction, and disorganized family structure [3].

Psychological stress or conflict situations were present in a group with pica compared with matched controls. Education, socioeconomic level, and the presence of neuroses as evidenced by psychometric testing gave equivocal differential results. Ingelligence testing showed no significant difference between the pica and nonpica controls. Both pica cases and controls displayed hypochromic anemia. Psychological stress and environmental disturbances appeared to more specifically contribute to the development of pica behavior than anemia [4].

Lourie's belief that pica is a predictor of later addictive behavior [35], is supported by a longitudinal study by McCord and McCord [36], which showed that a significant number of children with pica later developed alcoholism. Mitchell et al noted the same association and proposed an underlying susceptibility to visceral conditioning as the prevailing mechanism in both pica and alcoholism [37]. Rats exhibit pica in response to gastrointestinal distress in much the same way as other animals display emesis. That this effect is separate from a substance-induced toxic response was shown by the development of geophagia in rats in response to rotational stimulation [26,27]. After pairing saccharin with cyclophosphamide (which induces pica in rats), pica was elicited by the presentation of saccharin alone. A visceral conditioning process was evidenced by the presence of loose stools both in geophagic rats receiving cyclophosphamide and geophagic rats receiving saccharin alone. A physiologic basis for geophagia is implicated, namely gastrointestinal malaise (suggested by Foote in 1867 [38] and by Laufer in 1930 [39]), which persists after the physiologic cause has been removed. Thus the pica persists as the result of the physiologic conditioning.

Animal Models of Pica

There are reports of pica induced in rats by iron deficiency [40], a low-calcium diet [41], various toxins [42], or stress [26,27,25,43].

In the albino rat made iron deficient by venopuncture, a preference for ice eating (pagophagia), rather than water drinking, occurs. With iron repletion, pagophagia disappears [40].

Also, rats ingesting a low-calcium diet voluntarily ingested greater proportions of lead acetate solutions than did iron-deficient or controlled rats. Therefore, calcium deficiency may promote lead pica in rats on a low-calcium diet. These rats showed an increased toxicity to lead exposure manifested by increased body lead [44]. Burchfield et al [43] reported that rats made arthritic by injection of Freund adjuvant subsequently increased their kaolin ingestion. Furthermore, the geophagic arthritic rats may transmit the pica behavior (kaolin ingestion) to naive rats housed with them. Additionally, Mitchell et al [42] reported that rats poisoned with lithium chloride, red squill or cyclophosphamide prefer kaolin to food, again suggesting a toxic stress-induced pica. Studies of potentially fertile rats engaging in amylophagia (starch eating) revealed lower conception rates. The amylophagic mothers neglected their offspring, contributing to a 100% 24-hour mortality [45]. Another stress, excessive turning (labyrinthine stimulation) of rats, also increased pica [26,27]. These mentioned dietary deficiencies, toxins, and stresses promoting animal pica acknowledge etiologies that may occur in human pica that deserve further experimental verification and replication.

Numerous writers have observed that the pica that is associated with iron-deficiency anemia ceases after treatment with iron [46]. In contrast, several authors have argued that the pica causes the iron deficiency [47-49]. Gutelius et al [50] proposes two types of pica that are recognizable syndromes: (1) children with severe anemia in whom the pica is terminated by treatment of the anemia, and (2) an anemic group with pica that persists after iron therapy. The existence of the latter group suggests the presence of a conditioned response similar to that in animal studies [37].

The theory that the eating of nonnutritive substances is a need-determined behavior is supported by studies of food selection in young infants. Of special interest is a child with rickets who selectively drank milk laced with cod liver oil until his blood calcium and phosphorus were normal and roentgenographic evidence of his rickets had disappeared [51]. Richter [52] demonstrated the ability of adrenalectomized rats to drink enough salt solution to remain symptom-free. This self-regulatory behavior was abolished by sectioning of the taste nerves, indicating the presumptive role of taste in dietary selection. In a later study, Richter [53] proposed that taste thresholds vary with internal needs, as adrenalectomized rats can distinguish far more dilute (1:33,000) solutions of salt than normals (1:2,000). Rolls's [54] studies of food selection suggest two adaptive mechanisms in the control of eating: (1) sensory specific satiety, a person's perception of a specific food as pleasant decreases with increasing intake of that food, while other foods not eaten increase in pleasantness as a function of time since last eaten. This parallels Richter's concept of changing taste thresholds. (2) Neophobia, the avoidance of food not in a person's current food repertoire. Both mechanisms have an adaptive value. Sensory specific satiety leads to increased variety, and neophobia insures against eating possibly dangerous or nonnutritive foods. Perhaps both mechanisms may be impaired or inoperative in pica.

An etiologic role for iron deficiency in clinical studies of pica has been long debated. Lanzkowsky [46] found cessation of pica after iron replacement in anemic dirt-eaters. Catzel [55] found cessation of pica with iron re-

placement before the peripheral manifestations of anemia and hemoglobin values had been corrected. Jolly [8] suggested that a rise in serum iron was "sufficient to remove the craving" found in pica. In 1984, Libnoch [56] described a woman with erythrocytosis requiring repeated therapeutic phlebotomy who developed pica (geomelophagia-raw potatoes) with normal hemoglobin values but low tissue iron stores. Upon administration of oral iron her serum ferritin, mean corpuscular volume, and serum iron returned to normal and her pica disappeared. The foregoing suggests a relationship between tissue iron depletion and pica. McDonald and Marshall [57] and McGehee and Buchanan [58] also support the role of iron therapy for relief of pica in anemic subjects.

Pica may be a cause of iron deficiency where the non-nutritive substance (clay, starch) interferes with dietary intake or absorption of iron [47,48,59]. However, iron deficit as a cause rather than a result of pica is most clearly seen in patients with iron deficiency and pagophagia (ice-eating). Ice displaces no known nutrients and does not alter the absorption of iron [9,10,60].

Olynyk and Sharpe [61], Von Bonsdorff [62], and Youdim and Greene [63] suggest CNS neurochemical iron-dependent appetite regulation. The studies of Quik and Sourkes [64] and Youdim and Greene [63,65] indicate that systemic iron deficiency results in no predictable alteration of iron-dependent enzymes or changes in CNS catechol neurotransmitter metabolites. Youdim et al [65,66] linked decreased brain iron specifically to decreased dopamine D2 receptors and consequent reduction of several CNS dopamine-driven behaviors. The foregoing studies suggest that further research on the neurobiologic basis of pica is clearly desirable.

Studies that cast doubt on iron deficiency in the etiology of pica include those by Morrow et al [67] and Gutelius et al [7]. Gutelius used a double-blind approach with well-matched, anemic controls and found that although pica decreased with iron replacement, hemoglobin levels rose in both the treated and non-treated subjects. Further, relapses of pica behavior were not associated with a drop in hemoglobin levels. Gutelius notes "the cure of pica, like the cause seems to be a complicated problem involving multiple factors in varying degrees" and "iron medication is not a specific therapy for pica," [7]. The attention shown the families during treatment and an increased awareness of the pica behavior and its antecedents may account for part of the ambiguity. The increase in hemoglobin levels in the nontreated subjects suggests that partaking in a study makes the mothers in both groups more conscious of nutrition despite the lack of any specific advice on the matter.

The Incidence of Pica

The incidence of pica is difficult to establish due to differences in definition and the reluctance of patients, both male and female, to admit to abnormal cravings and ingestion.

In pregnancy, 51% of patients described cravings for foods, especially sweet foods. In the past up to 50% of southern black women ate starch and clay [1]. Other studies reveal a 33% incidence of amylophagia (starch eating), and Bruhn and Pangborn [68] report 38% of pregnant women experience pica. McGanity [69] stated 20% of 800 pregnant women had a history of pica.

In children ages 1-1/2 to 3 years, pica is considered normal with an incidence greater than 50%. However, persistence of excessive hand-to-mouth movements as in pica is abnormal in children older than three [30]. There is a racial difference in the incidence of pica because 30% of black children ages 1 to 6 have nonfood pica, while only 10% to 18% of white children in this age-group engage in pica. The incidence of pica is highest in psychotic nonwhite children, reaching 50% [1]. Barltrop [70] felt pica decreased with age, indicating about 10% of children beyond age 12 engaged in pica.

It is estimated that lead poisoning may be present in 5% to 10% of all children ages 1 to 5 and in 30% of children with pica [1]. Of children who have lead poisoning, 70% to 90% traced the source of pica to paint chips [1].

In the institutionalized mentally retarded, Danford et al [71] reported a 26% incidence of pica [72]. In contrast, McAlpine and Singh [73] reported an incidence of only 8.4% in the same population. Although both Danford and Singh note the highest incidence of pica at ages 10 to 19, Danford noticed an increase in pica beyond age 70, while Singh noted no occurrence of pica past age 45.

Ethnic differences occur in pica. The majority of cases of lead poisoning in New York were of Puerto Rican extraction. The incidence increases in summer, as vitamin D elevation by sunlight induced synthesis may promote an increased lead absorption [74].

Pica is endemic among sedentary Australian aborigines. As diet and eating customs changed with colonization by the Europeans, and monotonous foods replaced the once varied diet, people wished to return to the traditional folkways and customs. For example, clay has been eaten as a fertility food [75,76]. In Turkey, young women were encouraged to eat clay to enhance their fertility. The similar ideas shared in a black culture encouraged pregnant females, both in Africa and later in the United States, to eat various types of clay to enhance childbearing [24].

Demographic incidence information reveals that pica has been associated with diets that are low in iron, zinc, and calcium compared with a balanced controlled diet [77].

In the mentally retarded, there are changes in incidence of pica with age, IQ, medication, and manifestations of behavior and appetite. The majority of patients with pica are moderately underweight. Pica increases as the IQ decreases. Increased incidence of pica occurred in patients with CNS congenital anomalies and associated medical problems, such as diabetes, deafness, and seizures [19]. Pica increased in incidence in patients taking neuroleptics, which may be related to diminished postsynaptic dopamine (DS) receptor changes [65,28].

Behavioral problems in the retarded associated with pica include stereotypic behavior (52%), hyperactivity (39%), self-abuse (39%), and food-related abnormal behaviors including eating off the floor (73%) and chewing of objects (73%). Pica coexisted with rumination (53%), hyperphagia (47%), and anorexia. There were no racial or sexual differences in pica in the mentally retarded group [19].

MEDICAL COMPLICATIONS

Clinical Description

Literature reports describe specific types of nonnutritive ingestion that occur in different age-groups and social and cultural contexts. Geography, sociocultural factors, and developmental considerations all have been significant in determining the type of pica. Lead poisoning, lead intoxication in children, and social and epidemiologic antecedents as well as complications for development and medical hazards will not be discussed extensively in this section because it is reviewed elsewhere and constitutes a special focused area of study.

Lead Poisoning and Pica

Lead poisoning continues to be a hazard in young children. Inner-city children residing in the 49 million homes with lead-based paint have an incidence of excessive blood lead of 18.6% [78]. The persistence of hand-to-mouth movements in young children, especially from the age of 18 months to 3 years, results in the ingestion of lead-based paint [70]. Lead may enter the bloodstream by inhalation of particulate lead from automobile fumes and from nearby factories using lead-based materials.

Whole blood lead levels greater than 25 μg/dl (Pb25 μg/dl) indicate the child is in a contaminated environment. Elevated blood levels have multiple effects on cognition (including learning impairment and behavior), diminished attention span, and impulsive behavior.

When whole blood lead levels reach 70 PbB μg/dl, an insidious onset of anorexia, apathy, and poor coordination may occur. At lead levels above 90 μg/dl, lead encephalopathy manifested by gross ataxia, vomiting, lethargy and intractable convulsions may occur. Some children with high lead levels may have no symptoms, while other children may be symptomatic.

Neurologic complications of chronic lead poisoning may present as mental retardation, convulsive disorders, peripheral neuropathy, behavioral disturbance, or any combination thereof.

Treatment of lead poisoning includes stringent dust control by damp cleaning methods, treating a coexisting underlying iron deficiency, assuring an adequate dietary intake of protein and minerals, and careful follow-up of children until blood levels diminish. Chelation therapy with edathamil calcium disodium (CaEDTA), 2,3-Dimercapto-1-Propanol (BAL), and Penicillamine (PCA) can rapidly lower, but not completely eliminate, the lead content in the CNS. In the treatment of acute encephalopathy, and when Pb90-100μg/dl whole blood, immediate treatment with both BAL and CaEDTA is mandatory.

Since the more severe lead poisoning originates in multiproblem families, Chisolm recommends consultation with medical social service departments. Reduction in exposure is the cornerstone of any treatment program. In addition, renovation of substandard housing and systematic screening of children in high-risk areas are imperative [79].

Special types of pica and their medical complications include paper pica, which may lead to mercury poisoning. Olynyk and Sharpe [61] reported a patient with paper pica who was found to have decreased serum iron and responded to iron therapy. In numerous clinical cases, pica was associated with occult iron deficiency, which resulted in the sudden appearance of eating nonnutritive objects such as match heads (cautopyreiophagia) [80] and raw potatoes (geomelophagia) [56]. Arcasoy and Cavdar [81] have shown decreased serum iron and zinc in association with geophagia in Turkish children who may manifest hypogonadism, hepatosplenomegaly and dwarfism. An identical syndrome has been described by Prasad [13] in Iranian children.

The term bezoar derives from the Persian word signifying antidote. These were concretions from the alimentary canal of animals and were thought to have both medicinal and magical properties [82]. Clinically, bezoars can be characterized as tricho (hair), phyto (plants), and gastroliths (mineral or chemical substances). Tricho and phyto bezoars account for over 90% of reported clinical cases [83]. Certain occupational situations (painters who swallow shellac, asphalt workers), medical procedures and treatments (oral contrast radiography, and medically prescribed special diets) may predispose to bezoar formation.

Grant et al [84] described a giant trichobezoar in a 17-year-old female with normal intelligence. The hair ball took up the entire stomach, and gastrostomy was required for its removal. McGehee and Buchanan [58] described trichophagia and trichobezoar in a 2-1/2-year-old female and a 19-month-old female, both with iron deficiency, and irritation and hemorrhage of the gastric mucosa. Singh [85] described severe fecal impaction in two school-age children resulting from sand eating. Gonzales-Espinosa et al [86] described trichophagia and trichobezoar resulting in blood loss, intestinal invagination, and the need for corrective surgery. Uretsky [87] described intestinal obstruction resulting from paper. Additional medical complications reported to result from nonnutritive eating have included intestinal perforation [88], dental complications [89], hyperkalemia associated with geophagia [90,91], hypokalemia and anemia [92], and parasitosis [93-97]. Nine of 23 children with toxocariasis had a history of pica [98]. Patients with pica should be screened for parasitism and other orally transmitted diseases.

Foreign body ingestion may be seen in delusional schizophrenic patients who may ingest glass, pins, or other nonnutritive items [16,18]. Arieti [16] noted that driven nonnutritive eating may be seen in disorganized schizophrenic patients.

Radiographic Diagnosis of Pica

Radiographic findings, which may assist in diagnosis, vary depending on the substance ingested. An abdominal flat plate may visualize chips of lead paint [99], radiopaque particles of clay or soil [100], or foreign objects.

If the ingested substance is sharp, intestinal perforation and the findings of both pneumoperitoneum and a radiopaque foreign body may be present [88]. In addition, a barium swallow may be useful in determining whether a large gastric mass is a larger bezoar, leiomyoma, or carcinoma [84]. Furthermore, of interest is a case of maternal pica of lead-based plaster resulting in an infant with radiographic findings of congenital lead poisoning [101].

Parotid hypertrophy occurs with starch eating [102]. Ulcerative colitis and iron deficiency have been described in an 8-year-old child who ingested masonry [103]. An interesting syndrome of nicotinism and myocardial infarction was described by Neil et al [21] in a psychotic delusional patient who ate tobacco. Neil notes that Kraeplin was the first to document an extraordinary array of inedible materials consumed by psychotic patients and felt that this behavior might be a vegatative sign of psychosis: "a perversion of the appetite."

Pica and Iron Deficiency

Numerous authors report pica associated with iron deficiency [46,104]. Ansell and Wheby [105] reviewed numerous studies and reaffirmed this association. Gutelius [7] concluded in a double-blind study that intramuscular iron was no more effective than saline injection in reducing pica. However, patients in this study were evaluated at two-month intervals. Since iron generally abolishes pica in less than seven days [46,104], the preferential effect of iron in abolishing pica might not be apparent. Also, the educative approach over the relatively long period of the study may have facilitated the mothers' prohibitions against pica and may have improved mother-child interaction, diminishing stress promotion of pica. The most compelling argument for the association of pica and iron deficiency is suggested by the studies of Reynolds et al [104] and Coltman [9] on pagophagia: the obligatory urge to eat at least one tray of ice daily for at least two months. Ice eating does not reduce iron levels and is not a culturally determined pica. Reynolds [104] found pagophagia associated with low serum iron levels. Iron repletion abolished pagophagia before correcting the anemia. Furthermore, Coltman [9] reported cessation of pagophagia in 19 of 25 women with iron deficiency after iron supplementation for five days with intramuscular injection and 11 days with oral iron administration.

Ambiguity in the sequence of pica and iron deficiency is partly due to the situation in geophagia (clay eating). In geophagia of Turkish clays, a culturally determined behavior, gastrointestinal adsorption of both iron and zinc occurs, producing iron and zinc deficiency. Although the Turkish diet is low in protein and also contains phytate (which binds iron and zinc), the patient may be also iron-and/or-zinc deficient before the geophagia [59].

Coltman [9] proposed that in iron deficiency, iron-dependent peripheral tissue enzymes such as catalase, or cytochrome-c, were deficient. However, he could not explain why the changes in these enzymes would promote pica. Youdim [65] using rats made iron deficient, reported a reduction of specific dopamine receptor (D2) binding sites leading to a down-regulation of dopaminergic activity similar to that found in neuroleptic treated animals. The behavioral response to both pre- and post-synaptic dopamine-acting drugs was diminished.

Another form of pica, amylophagia or starch eating, has been associated with iron deficiency. Thomas et al [106], found that starch inhibited mucosal iron uptake. Keith et al [107] found more severe iron deficiency in pregnant women who engaged in amylophagia.

Table 2 illustrates a number of clinical situations of iron deficiency in conjunction with various types of pica. There are reports of eating match heads or ashes in patients who became iron deficient as a result of colonic carcinoma [80,108]. Thus pica may be a presenting symptom that can alert the clinician to anticipate iron deficit and pursue a careful differential diagnosis [109]. Pica frequently ceases after a few days of iron repletion, suggesting a role for iron loss in initiating and promoting pica.

TREATMENT APPROACHES

Behavioral Treatment

Several behavioral techniques have been used to diminish pica behavior exhibited by mentally retarded patients in a residential setting. Ausman et al [124] reported a time-out procedure to interrupt the pica response. A verbal reprimand was given to a 14-year-old male patient who ate food wrappers, erasers, and string, resulting in intestinal obstruction requiring surgical correction. A paradigm consisting of verbal reprimand setting, response interruption, generalization, and reward resulted in discrimination training. Overcorrection as a procedure was employed by Foxx and Martin [125]. A patient was forced to spit out the pica item immediately followed by administration of oral hygiene consisting of mouth flush, tooth brushing, and wiping of the lips. This procedure was effective in decreasing the occurrence of parasitosis in patients with pica. Matsen et al [126] and Madden et al [127] reported the effective use of overcorrection procedures with a 57-year-old retarded female and three female retarded patients, respectively.

In a critical review of pica treatment, Albin [128] pointed out conceptual differences in the definition of pica: non-food items ingested in contrast to eating food on the floor. He noted that use of experimental tactics such as baiting the patient and the absence of data about generalization and maintenance of improvement made comparative evaluation of different treatment techniques difficult. Furthermore, primarily developmental factors, particularly the perpetuation of a finger-feeding stage interfering with the use of utensils in retarded patients, may be related to the persistence of pica.

Physical restraint alone can control pica, as demonstrated in a series of studies by Bitgood et al [129,130], Bucher et al [131], and Winton and Singh [132-134]. Ten seconds of physical restraint appeared more effective than either 30-second or 3-second restraint. Physical restraint was easy to use, required minimal staff training time, and no specific equipment. Initiation of treatment in the number of different settings was important in promoting generalization of the behavior. Singh and Winton [133] and McAlpine and Singh [73] showed that physical restraint was more efficacious than overcorrection for the treatment of pica. Since institutions are often understaffed, an easily employable brief treatment is desirable.

Table 30.2 Pica and Iron Deficiency Clinical Features and Response to Treatment

Patient Age/Sex	Type of Pica	Associated Clinical Features	Response to treatment	Source
43 YO F	Pagophagia	Anemia 2o to menorrhagia.	Iron Tx abolished pica in 3 wks.	Altafulla et al (115)
7 females & 5 males	Geophagia	Ingested sand and soil. 10 had worms (ascaris). Hb 3g to 10.9g severe anemia.	Intramuscular iron dextran (200-400 mg) cured pica 1-2 wks after treatment.	Lanzkowsky (46)
46 YO F	Geophagia	Ingested chalk and plaster for 2 yrs. Hemorrhages.	Pica abolished in 8 days by daily iron injections (100 mg)	Duc et al (121)
45 YO F	Geophagia	2 abortions, 23 blood donations. Snuffed clay dust every 10 min. and ate clay dust for 2 yrs. Hb 9.9 g.	Pica abolished after 20 iron injections. (1250 mg)	Hadnagy et al (122)
33 males & 35 females ages 3-24	History of geophagia 3-15 yrs.	Growth retardation & hypogonadism. Hb 5.7 + .2g hepatosplenomegoly	Iron deficiency anemia was corrected by intramuscular iron dextran. Of 68 patients 22 received additional zinc sulfate (120) mg) daily for 6 mo.	Cavdar et al (59)
17 YO F	Geophagia	Hb 4g, Hypokalemia	Anemia responded to intramuscular iron dextran Tx. Pica abolished after 8 mo. continued treatment.	Mengel et al (92)
32 YO F	Geophagia	Hb 10.5 2o menorrhaghia, soil ppt. asthmatic attack	Anemia responded to oral iron.	Krengel & Geyser (123)
53 YO F	Tomato seed craving	15 yrs ago partial gastrectomy, esophageal web. mechanical dilation relieving dysphagia. Hb 7 g. Hysterectomy for menometrorrhagia 4 yrs. ago.	Parental iron abolished pica	Coleman et al (119)
5 males ages 18-51	Pagophagia	Anemia due to GI bleeding	Iron Tx abolished pica in 3 of 4 men. Pica reappeared in 1 male due to bleeding ulcer. Iron Tx and surgery abolished pica.	Reynolds et al. (104)
18 females	Pagophagia	Ingested 2-11 glasses of ice daily. Anemia due to menorrhagia. Hb 5-10.2g Serum iron 0 to 52 mg.	Pica abolished by oral iron.	Reynolds et al. (104)
25 females	Pagophagia	Ingested at least 1 tray ice cubes daily. Severe menorrhagia except for 3 patients.	Completely resolved by treatment with iron insufficient in amount to correct either the anemia or iron lack.	Coltman (9)
46 YO F	Pagophagia	Ingested 20-40 ice cubes daily, anemia 2o gynecologic loss.	Iron abolished pica in 4 days.	Sacks (111)
35 YO F	Pagophagia	Ingested 6-8 trays of ice cubes daily for 5 months.	Oral iron abolished pica.	Coltman (10)
33 YO F	Pagophagia during pregnancy. Concurrent cigarette ash eating & geophagia.	Anemia 2o to carcinoma of ascending colon	Oral iron & blood transfusions abolished pica.	Desilva (113)
9 females ages 19-78 & 4 males	Amylophagia (in form of rice, potatoes & bread)	In women, anemia 2o to gynecologic loss. In 3 men, anemia 2o to GI bleeding. In 1 man anemia 2o to hemorrhoids. Hb 5.0-10.2g	Pica abolished by iron Tx.	Reynolds (104)

Table 30.2 Pica and Iron Deficiency Clinical Features and Response to Treatment (continued)

Patient Age/Sex	Type of Pica	Associated Clinical Features	Response to treatment	Source
41 YO F	Amylophagia (in form of cornflakes craving)	Anemia 2o to malnutrition & menorrhagias	Iron abolished pica	Altafulla (115)
44 YO F	Lectophagia	Ingested 4-5 heads lettuce daily for several months. Anemia	Oral iron Tx abolished pica in 1 mo. Hb14.0.	Marks (116)
78 YO F	Pagophagia to lectophagia	Hematocrit 27, enzyme changes consistent with MI. At discharge began to consume 3 trays ice cubes daily. Cut to 2 cups/day; began to eat many heads lettuce/day. Neoplasm and lesion of colon.	Responded to units of packed cells. Gave total remission of signs & symptoms	Moss et al. (108)
26 YO F	Geomelophagia (craving for raw chilled potatoes)	Symptomatic erythrocytosis requiring phlebotomy. Menorrhagia. Hb 17g Serum iron 67.	Oral iron Tx. Returned	Libnoch (56)
68 YO F	Geomelophagia	Anemia 2o to GI bleeding. Lung cancer. Hb 9.3g. Serum iron 13.	Iron Tx (3x300 mg/day) abolished pica after 1 wk.	Johnson and Stephens (117)
42 YO F	Olive craving	Ate approximately 5-7 jars green olives/wk for 4 mo.	Oral ferrous sulfate (3x300mg/day) diminished craving in 1 wk. In 2 wks down to 1 jar/wk. After 1 wk pica cured	Chandra and Rosner (118)
33 YO F	Sodium chloride craving	Hb 9.2 g. Serum iron 28	Iron Tx abolished pica in 2 wks.	Shapiro & Linas (110)
33 YO F	Tea leaves craving	Ingested 250g/day Anemia 2o to gynecologic loss	Iron Tx abolished pica after 6 days	Sacks et al. (111)
46 YO F 37 YO F	Paper craving Paper craving	Mercury poisoning. Blood level 251 ppb Hg Anemia 2o to chronic menorrhagia, ageusia, dysomia	Iron Tx abolished pica in 1 wk Oral iron sulfate (300mg) and zinc (24mg) abolished pica 1 mo. after treatment	Olynk & Sharpe (61) Chisholm and Martin (112)
48 YO F	Cautopyreiophagia	Ingested ashes of 15 burnt matchbooks daily. Hb 6.5g Serum iron 14. GI bleeding due to lesion in cecuma and adenocarcinoma of left lobe of liver.	Iron Tx, operations & transfusions abolished pica	Perry (80)
76 YO F	Magnesium carbonate	Micocytic hyperchromic anemia; consumed 60-80g/day 3 yrs prior to admission. Hb 5.7g	Repeat admissions about each mo. Given oral & parenteral iron. No blood loss site found. Only improved in hospital.	Leming et al. (47)
21 YO F	Paradichloro benzene craving	34 wks pregnant. Hb 6.6g	Treatment parenteral iron, folic acid abolished pica.	Campbell & Davidson (114)
17YO F & 34 YO F	aspirin craving	Ingested 4-6g aspirin/day. Anemia 2o to metrorrhagia and menorrhagic respectively	Pica abolished by iron Tx after 8 days	Sacks et al. (111)

Often the control of pica in mentally retarded adults with complicated histories presents a clinical problem that must be approached through individualized design and the presence of aversive consequences. Friedin and Johnson [135] described the treatment of copraphagia by linking it to aversive consequences such as delay of a shower. Most recently, Singh and Winton [134} have demonstrated that aversive oral hygiene when used alone was as effective as physical restraint and overcorrection. The oral hygiene technique was easily taught to staff and could be applied early in a variety of circumstances.

Behavioral treatment approaches in pica involve careful observational analyses and the application of consistent contingent responses by a trained staff.

Nutrient Approaches

Nutrient treatment of pica has been reported for almost 1,000 years. (Table 1) In the tenth century, Avicenna added iron to wine as a treatment for earth eating [1,24]. There are numerous case reports [46,104] indicating that iron treatment will abolish pica. Cavdar et al [59] reviewing a geophagia syndrome (iron-deficiency anemia, hepatosplenomegaly, hypogonadism, and dwarfism found in Turkey and Iran) reported that iron administration successfully treated both anemia and pica, but zinc was necessary for linear growth and pubertal advance. Zinc deficiency may also be associated with pica. Hambidge and Silverman [136] reported a 10-year-old boy with sickle cell disease who ate kitchen cleanser. Following oral administration of zinc, serum levels of the metal almost quadrupled, and pica was terminated [137]. A critical review of clinical reports reveals that the majority of authors verify the efficacy of iron repletion in abolishing both food and nonfood pica associated with iron deficiency states of different etiology. This suggests a common central pathway such as mediation by decreased CNS dopamine neurotransmission reported to be a specific result of iron deficiency states [65,28]. In animal studies Youdim [65] reported a 50% diminution of CNS dopamine (D2) receptors with iron depletion.

Pharmacologic Treatment of Pica

No specific pharmacologic treatment studies of pica exist. Jakab [138] reported that thioridazine reduced pica as well as a number of other problematic behaviors such as aggression in hospitalized mentally retarded patients. However, Danford and Huber [19] noted an increased pica incidence (39%) in a subgroup of institutionalized retarded patients receiving neuroleptic medication in contrast to a 25% incidence of pica in a medication-free group. Does diminished dopaminergic neurotransmission promote pica? Decreased dopamine transmission resulting from both iron deficiency and administration of neuroleptics may be a critical determinant in the appearance and maintenance of pica. A pharmacologic approach that increases dopaminergic transmission (bromocriptine, ritalin) may be worthy of investigation in a subgroup of patients in whom pica is both refractory and hazardous.

Psychosocial Treatment

Lourie [139] recommended a psychoeducation treatment approach. Mothers would be instructed about the danger of pica that could result in lead poisoning. Social workers would provide a social support system for mothers who may be depressed, meet their dependency needs, and help mothers be more available to the children. Strategies of prohibiting pica would be taught to mothers so that they would spend more time with their children and interrupt pica behavior. Lourie et al [30] suggested that identifying families at high risk for pica could function as a primary prevention.

CONCLUSION

Pica in man is indeed a complex behavior with multiple determinants ranging from demands of tradition and acquired tastes in the cultural context to presumptive neurobiologic mechanisms (iron deficiency, CNS neurotransmission, physiologic conditioning). Clinical consequences of pica may have broad epidemiologic implications as in lead intoxication and geophagia in children leading to severe impairment of intellectual and physical development. Acute and chronic medical complications may pose surgical emergencies (intestinal obstruction from bezoars) as well as more subtle encroaching symptoms in parasitosis, intoxications, and resulting nutritional deficits.

Although pica as a naturally occurring behavior in animals has apparent utility in aiding digestion or overcoming nutritional deficit, its presence in man appears to be the result of culturally contrived or pathophysiologic circumstances, and any adaptive value remains obscure. The occurrence of pica in pregnancy [40], mental retardation, schizophrenia, and autism suggests a psychobiologic significance to link a disturbance in food selection to other complex neuroendocrine medicated responses.

Treatment approaches have been primarily preventive, educational, and directed toward modification of pica behavior. Iron repletion has dramatically reversed pica for those patients whose clinical symptoms were more clearly coincident with iron deficiency from nutritional or covert medical causes [141,142,143].

Further investigation of pica may clarify the normal

psychobiology and developmental progression of food selection in man, the intricate role of sociocultural influences, and the significance of appetite and ingestive disturbances in neuropsychiatric disorders. Special focus should be given to the high incidence of pica in the mentally retarded and to the role of iron deficiency (the single most prevalent nutritional deficiency in world population studies) in the etilogy and perpetuation of eating disorders.

REFERENCES

1. Danford DE. Pica and nutrition. Am Rev Nutr 1982a; 2:303-22.

2. Spitzer R. American Psychiatric Association Diagnostic and Statistical Manual of Mental Disorders, third ed. Washington DC: American Psychiatric Association, 1980:

3. Singhi S, Singhi P, Adwani GB. Role of psychosocial stress in the cause of pica. Clin Peds 1981; 20:783-5.

4. Koptagel G, Reimann F. An investigation on the psychopathology of pica and hypochromic anemia. Ninth Europ Conf Psychosom Res, Vienna 1972; Psychother Psychosom 1973; 22:351-8.

5. Dickens D, Ford RM. Geophagy (dirt eating) among Mississippi Negro school children. Am Sociol Rev 1942; 7:59.

6. DeCastro J. Geography of hunger. Boston: Little. 1952:

7. Gutelius MF, Millican FK, Layman EH, et al. Children with pica: Treatment of pica with iron given intramuscularly. Ped 1962; 29:1018-23.

8. Jolly H. Advances in pediatrics. Practioner 1963; 191:417-25.

9. Coltman Jr CA. Pagophagia and iron lack. JAMA 1969; 207:513-6.

10. Coltman Jr CA. Pagophagia. Arch Intern Med 1971; 128:472-3.

11. Hunter JM. Geophagy in Africa and the US: a culture nutrition hypothesis. Geograph Rev 1973; 63:170.

12. Kilisz k, Ekvall S, Palmer S. Pediatric nutrition in developmental disorders. Springfield, Ill: Charles C Thomas, 1978:

13. Prasad AS, Halstead JA, Nadim M. Syndrome of iron deficiency anemia, hepatosplenomegaly hypogonadism, dwarfism and geophagia. Am J Med 1961; 31:532-46.

14. Mahaffey KR. Nutritional factors in lead poisoning. Nutr Rev 1981; 39:353-62.

15. Carp L. Foreign bodies in the gastrointestinal tracts of psychotic patients. Arch Surg 1950; 60:1055-75.

16. Arieti S. Interpretation of schizophrenia. New York: Bruner, 1955:

17. Teinourian B, Cigtay AS, Smyth NP. Management of ingested foreign bodies in the psychotic patient. Arch Surg 1964; 88:915-20.

18. Fishbain D, Rotondo D. Single case study: foreign body ingestion associated with delusional beliefs. J Nerv & Ment Dis 1983; 171:321-2.

19. Danford DE, Huber AM. Eating dysfunctions in an institutionalized mentally retarded population. Appetite 1981; 2:281-92.

20. Bitar DE, Holmes TR. Polybezoar and gastrointestinal foreign bodies in the mentally retarded. Am Surg 1975; 41:497-504.

21. Neil JF, Horn TL, Himmelhoch JM. Psychotic pica, nicotinism and complicated myocardial infarction. Dis Nerv Syst 1977; 38:724-6.

22. Robischon P. Pica practice and other hand-mouth behavior and children's developmental level. Nurs Res 1971; 20:4-16.

23. Cohen DF, Johnson WT, Caparulo BK. Pica and elevated blood lead level in autistic and atypical children. Am J Dis Child 1976; 130:47-8

24. Cooper M. Pica. Springfield, Ill: Charles Thomas, 1957:

25. Wetherington CL. Is adjunctive behavior a third class of behavior: Neurosci Biobehav Rev 1982; 6:329-50.

26. Mitchell D, Krusemark ML, Hafner E. Pica: a species relevant behavioral assay of motion sickness in the rat. Physiol & Behav 1977a; 18:125-30.

27. Mitchell D, Laycock JD, Stephens WF. Motion sickness induced pica in the rat. Am J Clin Nutr 1977b; 30:147-50.

28. Blinder BJ, Goodman S, Youdim S. Iron, dopamine receptors and tardive dyskinesia. Am J Psychiat 1986; 143:277-8.

29. Millican FK, Layman EM, Lourie AS, et al. Study of an oral fixation: pica. J Am Acad Child Psych 1968; 7:79-107.

30. Lourie RS, Layman EM, Millican FK. Why children eat things that are not food. Children 1963; 10:143-6.

31. Pueschel SM, Cullen SM, Howard RB, et al. Pathogenetic considerations of pica in lead poisoning. Int J Psych in Med 1977; 8:13-24.

32. Blinder BJ. Developmental antecedents of the eating disorders: a reconsideration. Psych Clin No. America 1980; 3:579-92.

33. Dowling S. Seven infants with esophageal atresia: a developmental study. Psycho Analyt Study Child 1977; 32:215-56.

34. Vermeer DE, Frate DA. Geophagia in rural Mississippi: environmental and cultural contexts and nutritional implications. Am J Clin Nutr 1979; 32:2129-35.

35. Lourie RS, Layman EM, Millican FK, et al. Study of the etiology of pica in young children, an early pattern of addiction. In: Hoch PH, Zubin J, eds. Problems of addiction and habituation. New York: Grune & Stratton, 1958:

36. McCord W, McCord J. Origins of alcoholism. Stanford: Stanford Univ Press, 1960:

37. Mitchell D, Winter W, Morsiaki C. Conditioned taste aversions accompanied by geophagia: evidence for the occurrence of psychological factors in the etiology of pica. Psychosom Med 1977; 39:402-11.

38. Foote, 1867 (cited in Cooper M) [24].

39. Laufer B. Field Mus Nat Hist Publ 280 Anthropol Ser 1930; 18:99.

40. Woods SC, Weisinger RS. Pagophagia in the albino rat. Science 1970; 169:1334-6.

41. Jacobson JL, Snowdon CT. Increased lead ingestion in calcium deficient monkeys. Nature 1976; 162:51-2

42. Mitchell D, Wells D, Hoch N, et al. Poison induced pica in rats. Physiol & Beh 1976; 17:691-7.

43. Burchfield WR, Elich MS, Woods SC. Geophagia in response to stress and arthritis. Physiol & Behav 1977; 19:265-7.

44. Snowdon CT, Sanderson BA. Lead pica-produced in rats. Science 1974; 183:92-4.

45. Keith L, Bartizal F, Brown E. Controlled amylophagia in female mice. Experientia 1971; 27:847-9.

46. Lanzkowsky P. Investigation into the etiology and treatment of pica. Arch Dis Child 1959; 34:140-8.

47. Leming PD, Reed DC, Martelo OJ. Magnesium carbonate pica: an unusual case of iron deficiency. Ann Int Med 1981; 94:660.

48. Roselle HA. Association of laundry starch and clay ingestion with anemia in New York City. Arch Int Med 1970; 125:57-61.

49. Cavdar AO, Arcasoy A. Hematologic and biochemical studies of Turkish children with pica. Clin Pediatr 1972; 11:215-23.

50. Gutelius MF, Millican FK, Layman EH, et al. Treatment of pica with a vitamin and mineral supplement. Am J Clin Nutr 1963; 12:388-93.

51. Davis CM. Self selection of diet by newly weaned infants: experimental study. Am J Dis Child 1928; 36:651-79.

52. Richter CP. Total self-regulatory functions in animals and human beings. Harvey Lecture Series 1942-43; XXXVIII:63-103.

53. Richter CP. Self-selection of diets. Essays in biology. Berkeley: Univ Cal Press, 1943;

54. Rolls BR. Palatability and preference: basic studies. This volume.

55. Catzel P. Pica and milk intake. Pediatrics 1963; 31:1056-7.

56. Libnoch JA. Geomelophagia. An unusual pica in iron-deficiency anemia. Am J Med 1984; 76:A69.

57. McDonald R, Marshall SR. Value of iron therapy in pica. Pediatr 1964; 34:558-62.

58. McGehee Jr FT, Buchanan GR. Tichophagia and trichobezoar: etiologic role of iron deficiency. J Ped 1980; 97:946-8.

59. Cavdar AO, Arcasoy A, Cin S, et al. Geophagia in Turkey: iron and zinc deficiency. Prog in Clin Biol Res 1983; 129:71-9.

60. Crosby WH. Food pica and iron deficiency. Arch Intern Med 1971; 127:960-1.

61. Olynyk F, Sharpe DH. Mercury poisoning in paper pica. N Engl J Med 1982; 306:1056-7.

62. Von Bonsdorff B. Pica: a hypothesis. Brit J Haematol 1977; 35:476-7.

63. Youdim MBH, Greene AR. Pica hypothesis. Br J Haematol 1977; 36:298.

64. Quik M, Sourkes TL. Iron: effect of chronic deficiency on an adrenal tyrosine hydroxylase activity. Can J Biochem 1977; 55:60-5.

65. Youdim MBH. Brain iron metabolism: biochemical aspects in relation to dopaminergic neurotransmission. In: Lajitha A, ed. Handbook of neurochemistry, Vol 10, Pathological chemistry. New York: Plenum Press, 1985:

66. Youdim MBH, et al. Brain iron and dopamine receptor function: molecular pharmacology. In: Mandell P, DeFeudis FV, eds. CNS receptors: from molecular pharmacology to behavior, vol 37. New York: Raven Press, 1983:

67. Morrow JF, Bass JH, Goldberg A. A continued trial of iron therapy in sideropenia. Scot Med J 1968; 13:79-83.

68. Bruhn CM, Pangborn RM. Reported incidence of pica among migrant families. J Amer Diet Assoc 1971; 58:417-20.

69. McGanity WJ, Little HM, Fogelman A, et al. Pregnancy in the adolescent. Am J Obstet & Gyn 1969; 103:773-88.

70. Barltrop D. The prevalence of pica. Am J Dis Child 1966; 112:116-23.

71. Danford DE, Huber AM. Pica and mineral status in the mentally retarded. Am J Clin Nutr 1982c; 35:958-67.

72. Danford DE, Smith Jr JC, Huber AM. Pica and mineral status in the mentally retarded. Am J Clin Nutr 1982c; 35:958-67.

73. McAlpine C, Singh NN. Pica in institutionalized mentally retarded persons. J Ment Def Res 1986; 30:171-8.

74. Jacobziner H, Raybin HW. Epidemiology of lead poisoning in children. Arch Pediatr 1962; 79:72-6.

75. Bateson EM, Lebroy T. Clay eating by aboriginals of the northern territory. Med J Australia 1978; 1:1-3.

76. Eastwell HD. A pica epidemic: a price for sedentarism among Australian ex-hunger-gatherers. Psychiatry 1979; 42:264-73.

77. Edwards CH. Clay and cornstarch eating women. J Am Diet Assoc 1959; 35:810-15.

78. Chisolm JJ. Continuous hazards of lead exposure and its effects in children. Neurotox 1984; 5:23-42.

79. Chisolm JJ. Management of increased lead absorption in children: illustrative cases. In: Chisolm JJ, O'Hara DM, eds. Lead absorption in children: management, clinical and environmental aspects. Baltimore and Munich: Urbin and Schwarzenberg, 1982:

80. Perry MC. Cautopyreiophagia. N Engl J Med 1977; 296:824.

81. Arcasoy A, Cavdar AP, Babacan E. Decreased iron and zinc absorption in Turkish children with iron deficiency geophagia. Acta Haemat 1978; 60:76-84.

82. Allan JD, Woodruff J. Starch gastrolith: report of a case of obstruction. N Engl J of Med 1964; 268:776-8.

83. DeBakey M, Ochsner A. Bezoars and concretions: comprehensive review of literature with analysis of 303 collected cases and presentation of 8 additional cases. Surg 1938; 4:934-64.

84. Grant JA, Murray WR, Patel AR. Giant trichobezoar: an unusual case. Scot Med J 1979; 24:83-6.

85. Singh M. Sandy fecal impaction caused by severe pica. Trop Geogr Med 1983; 35:393-4.

86. Gonzales-Expinoza C, Hernandez N, Santisteben M, et al. Trichophagia, trichobezoar, intestinal invagination, condition deficiency. An Esp Pediatr 1983; 19:337-8.

87. Uretsky BF. Paper bezoar causing intestinal obstruction. Arch Surg 1974; 109:123.

88. Harrison RA. Pica: an unusual cause of intestinal perforation. Brit J Clin Pract 1980; 34:155-6.

89. Abbey CM, Lombard JA. The etiological factors and clinical implications of pica: report of a case. J Am Dent Assoc 1973; 87:885-7.

90. Gelfand MC, Zarate A, Knepshield JH. Geophagia: a cause of life-threatening hyperkalemia in patients with chronic renal failure. JAMA 1975; 234:738-40.

91. Gonzales JJ, Ownns W, et al. Clay ingestion: a rare case of hypokalemia. Ann Int Med 1982; 97:656.

92. Mengel CE, Carter WA, Horton ES. Geophagia with iron deficiency and hypokalemia. Arch Int Med 1964a; 114:470-4.

93. Padmanabhan AS, Ramesh S, Gunasekaran M. A rare case of scarabaeusis. Indian Peds 1982; 19:807.

94. Glickman LT. Toxocara infection and epilepsy in children. J Ped 1979; 94:75-8.

95. Marcus LC, Stambler M. Visceral larva migrans and eosinophilia in an emotionally disturbed child. J Clin Psych 1979; 40:139-46.

96. Jones WE, Schantz PM, Foreman K, et al. Human toxocariasis in a rural community. Am J Dis Child 1980; 134:967-9.

97. Berger OG, Hornstein MD. Eosinophilia and pica: lead or parasites. Lancet 1980; 1:553.

98. Stagno S, Dykes AC, Amos CS, et al. An outbreak of toxoplasmosis linked to cats. Peds 1980; 65:706-12.

99. Maravilla AM, Berk RN. The radiology corner: the radiographic diagnosis of pica. Am J Gastro 1978; 70:94-9.

100. Mengel CE, Carter WA, Durham NC. Geophagia diagnosed by roentgenograms. JAMA 1964b; 187:955-6.

101. Pearl M, Boxt LM. Radiographic findings in congenital lead poisoning. Ped Rad 1980; 136:83-4.

102. Merkatz IR. Medical intelligence: parotid enlargement resulting from excessive eating of starch. N Engl J Med 1961; 265:1304-6.

103. DiCagno L, Castello D, Savio MT. Un caso di colite ulcerosa associata a pica. Min Ped 1974; 26:1768-77.

104. Reynolds RD, Binder HJ, Miller MB, et al. Pagophagia and iron deficiency anemia. Ann of Int Med 1968; 69:435-40.

105. Ansell JE, Wheby MS. Pica: its relation to iron deficiency: a review of the recent literature. Virg Med Monthly 1972; 99:951-4.

106. Thomas CW, Rising JL, Moore JK. Blood lead concentrations of children and dogs from 83 Illinois families. J Am Vet Med Assoc 1976; 169:1237-40.

107. Keith L, Brown ER, Rosenberg C. Pica: the unfinished story background: correlations with anemia and pregnancy. Persp Biol and Med 1970; Summer:626-32.

108. Moss J, Nissenblatt MJ, Inui TS. Successive picas. Ann Int Med 1974; 80:425.

109. Ackerman L. Surgical pathology. St. Louis: C.V. Mosby Co, 1981:

110. Shapiro MO, Linas SL. Sodium chloride pica secondary to iron deficiency anemia. Am J Kidney Dis 1985; 5:67-8.

111. Sacks S, Tapia A, Nycor V, et al. Perversion of appetite (pica) a strange, curious symptom of sideropenia. Revista Medica de Chile 1971; 99:848-51.

112. Chisolm JC, Martin HI. Hypozincemia, ageusia, dysosmia and toilet tissue pica. J Nat Med Assoc 1981; 73:163-4.

113. Desilva RA. Eating cigarette ashes in anemia. Ann Int Med 1974; 80:115-6.

114. Campbell DM, Davidson RJ. Toxic hemolytic anemia in pregnancy due to a pica for parachlorobenzene. J Obst Gyn 1970; 77:657-9.

115. Altafulla M, Vasquez de Bernal J. Pica. Revista Medica de Panama 1982; 7:176-80.

116. Marks JW. Lettuce craving and iron deficiency. Ann Int Med 1973; 79:612.

117. Johnson BE, Stephens RL. Geomelophagia: an unusual pica in iron-deficiency anemia. Am J Med 1982; 73:931-2.

118. Chandra P, Rosner F. Olive craving in iron deficiency anemia. Ann of Intern Med 1973; 78:973-4.

119. Coleman DL, Greenberg CS, Ries CA. Iron deficiency anemia and pica for tomato seeds. N Engl J Med 1981; 304:848.

120. Ber R, Valero A. Pica and hyperchronic anemia. Harefuah J Is Med Assoc 1961; 61:35-8.

121. Duc M, Leichtmann G, Lucas P, et al. Que lien entre pica et anemie ferriprive (what is the relationship between pica and iron anemia). La Nouvelle Presse Medicale 1980; 9:3362.

122. Hadnagy CS, et al. Durch eisenmangel verursachte psychische aberration: Tonschnuphfen (Pulverem argillae in nasan ducit). Psychiatr Neurol Med Leipzig 35 Marz. 1983; 3:S172-4.

123. Krengel B, Geyser F. Chronic pica in an adult. S Afr Med Tyclsk 1978; 53:480.

124. Ausman J, Ball TS, Alexander D. Behavior therapy of pica with a profoundly retarded adolescent. Mental Retard 1974; 12:16-8.

125. Foxx RM, Martin ED. Treatment of scavenging behavior (coprophagy and pica) by overcorrection. Beh Res & Ther 1975; 13:153-62.

126. Matsen JL, Stephens RM, Smith C. Treatment of self injurious behaviour with overcorrection. J Ment Def Res 1977; 22:175-8.

127. Madden NA, Russo DC, Cataldo MF. Behavioral treatment of pica in children with lead poisoning. Child Behav Ther 1980; 2:67.

128. Alvin JB. The treatment of pica (scavenging) behavior in the retarded: a critical analysis and implications for research. Mental Retard 1977; 15:14-7.

129. Bitgood SC, et al. Immobilization: effects and side effects of stereotyped behavior in children. Behav Modif 1980; 4:187.

130. Bitgood SC, et al. Reducing out of seat behavior in developmentally disabled children through brief immobilization. Educ Treat Child 1982; 5:249.

131. Bucher B, Reykdal B, Albin J. Brief restraint to control pica in retarded children. J Behav Ther Exper Psychiat 1976; 7:137-42.

132. Winton ASW, Singh NN. Suppression of pica using brief duration physical restraint. J Ment Def Res 1983; 27:93-105.

133. Singh NN, Winton AS. Effects of a screening procedure on pica and collateral behaviors. J Beh Ther Exp Psychia 1984; 15:59-65.

134. Singh NN, Winton AS. Controlling pica by components of an overcorrection procedure. Am J Ment Def 1985; 90:40-5.

135. Friedin BD, Johnson HK. Treatment of a retarded child's feces smearing and coprophagic behaviour. J Ment Def Res 1979; 23:55-61.

136. Hambidge KM, Silverman A,. Pica with rapid improvement after dietary zinc supplementation. Arch Dis Child 1973; 48:567-8.

137. Karayalcin G, Lanzkowsky P. Letter: pica with zinc deficiency. Lancet 1976; 2:687.

138. Jakab I. Short term effect of thioridazine tablets versus suspension on emotionally disturbed retarded children. J Clin Psychopharm 1984; 4:210-5.

139. Lourie RS. Pica and poisoning. Am J Orthopsych 1977; 41:697-9.

140. Edwards AA, Mathura CV, Edwards CH. Effects of maternal geophagia on infant and juvenile rats. J Nat Med Assoc 1983; 75:895-902.

141. Reimann F, Koplagel G. Geophagia in iron deficiency disease. New Istanbul Contri to Clin Sci 1980; 13:63-79.

142. Snowdon CT. A nutritional basis for lead pica. Physiol & Beh 1977; 18:885-93.

143. McLoughlin IJ. The picas. Brit J Med 1987; 37:289-90.

Chapter 31

The Relationship of the Eating and Affective Disorders

Barry F. Chaitin

INTRODUCTION

At the turn of the century, Freud [1] speculated about the relationship between anorexia nervosa and melancholia. Abraham, in writing of a patient suffering from excessive hunger and binge eating, was impressed with the addictive intoxicating aspect of the behavior, which he interpreted as substitute libidinal gratification [2]. Over the ensuing years, much of the psychoanalytic focus in anorexia nervosa in adolescent females revolved around fear of oral impregnation, denial of genitality, and the concept of organ neurosis in which the ego is fixated at the oral phase and produces secondary hormonal changes. Fenichel, in his psychoanalytic compendium, points out that anorexia nervosa can be the result of a variety of dynamic processes and may be an affective equivalent of a depression that antedates other signs of depression [3]. He also mentions cyclic food addiction in woman and its relationship to manic depressive illness as well as the relationship of bulimia to mourning. Working from an existential framework, Binswanger detailed the case history of his anorexic patient, Ellen West, and described her overwhelming sense of despair and alienation [4]. Bruch, also in moving beyond the standard psychoanalytic conflict formulations, emphasized the self-despair and pervasive sense of personal ineffectiveness in patients with anorexia nervosa [5]. From a phenomenologic orientation, these depictions may equate with a depressive illness.

In recent years, growing theoretical and clinical interest in the eating disorders has led to increased precision in diagnosis. As the eating disorders have been more carefully studied, more distinct subtypes have been defined [6-9]. Now it is perhaps more correct to talk of primary restrictive anorexia nervosa, bulimia nervosa, and normal-weight bulimia. It is also important to recognize that these syndromes are not completely static, and the clinical course for any particular patient may cross diagnostic boundaries. However, with this fractionation of the eating disorders and the emergence of bulimia as a diagnostic entity, the relationship to the affective disorders has become more visible.

At the same time, the boundaries of the affective disorders have come under new scrutiny and revision. What was previously passed off as personality and character, and ergo not susceptible to biological intervention, is being reexamined—albeit with a high-resolution clinical microscope. Akiskal, in his study of subaffective disorders, has uncovered many treatable conditions that formerly were ascribed to personality [10]. Keller and Shapiro's work on "double depression" has also been enlightening by recognizing the coexistence of a depressive personality core with a superimposed affective episode [11]. The borderline quality of many patients with eating disorders has been frequently observed and may rivet the clinician's attention. Carroll et al caution that the presence of dramatic psychopathology may mask the more traditional signs and symptoms of major depressive disorders [12].

345

As in all diagnostic schema, how hard one looks and where one draws the line determines the yield. It is extremely important to take a careful and detailed history from the patient and, when possible, obtain corroborative history from family members, as the compelling nature of the eating disorder symptoms may indeed obscure other pathology. If one insists on full DSM-III criteria for a major affective disorder in eating disorder patients before considering a codiagnosis and pharmacologic intervention, a number of treatable patients may be missed.

In this chapter, I will briefly review the current lines of inquiry and data concerning an affective disorder-eating disorder linkage without attempting a thorough critique of research strategies.

STUDIES OF PSYCHOPATHOLOGY

In an often-cited study, Cantwell followed 26 patients who had been hospitalized as adolescents for anorexia nervosa [13]. The distinction was not made between pure restricters and bulimics. Almost 50% of the patients, by parent and self-report, were diagnosed as having an affective disorder at follow-up. In a retrospective evaluation of premorbid psychiatric symptomatology, 61% of the patients reported dysphoric mood, and 71% reported being fearful. These findings agree with three earlier studies by Dally [14], Theander [15], and Morgan and Russell [16], who reported significant psychiatric morbidity at initial presentation and follow-up.

Stonehill and Crisp found that anorexia nervosa patients scored significantly higher than healthy female students on the anxiety, obsessional somatic, and depression scales of a standardized instrument [17]. When patients who vomited were separated out, the depression scores were even higher. However, the anorexic group scored significantly lower on the anxiety, somatic, phobic, and depression scales than a matched group of depressed outpatients. Stonehill and Crisp felt that this lent support to the view that anorexia nervosa is not a simple variant of depression. They ascribed the high level of scores on the depression scale to the overrepresentation of early morning awakening, which is quite prominent in anorexia nervosa supposedly apart from any affective disorder.

In discussing what he termed "bulimia nervosa" as an ominous variant of anorexia nervosa, Russell reported on 30 patients (28 females and 2 males), 24 of whom suffered at least moderate depression [8]. Russell doubted that there were primary depressives, because the eating disorder did not appear to improve with the relief of depressive symptoms, and the depressive symptoms did not seem to be of an endogenous variety.

Ben-Tovin et al used the Present State Examination to evaluate the mental status of 21 anorexics and found that they did not closely resemble any other published group [18]. The predominant affect was depressive, which differentiated them from patients with anxiety states. There was some similarity to an inpatient sample of depressives in terms of the mixture of symptoms, but the anorexic group could be separated by the absence of depressive delusions, ideas of reference, and retardation. Out of this anorexic group, which included 12 abstainers and nine vomiters, a case for a clinical depression using operational criteria could be made for certain in only three patients, with seven patients seen as probable cases of depression. In a depressive sample of 23 patients, 16 definites and three probable cases were identified. The spread and diagnostic frequency between these two groups was significant and lead the authors to conclude that the findings they uncovered were possibly related to starvation states and their secondary effects, the ongoing existential struggles of the anorexic, a reflection of underlying personality, or a coincidental finding. Despite the differences in depressive symptoms reported by anorexics and depressives, Ben-Tovin et al were impressed by the qualitative depressive feelings identified by their patients and suggested that the measures of depression used were not able to tap the existential despair and guilt of the anorexic with its focus on the loathing of the body and fear of losing control over eating and resultant weight gain.

In their comprehensive study of 105 female inpatient anorexics, Casper et al gave further support to the notion that bulimics constitute a subgroup of anorexia highly impacted by depression, obsessionalism, and somatization [6]. They make the point that bulimia is not simply a disorder of appetite but a highly complex symptom with depression, anxiety, and guilt interwoven within its matrix. To some degree, their conclusions are at variance with Russell [8] and Stonehill and Crisp [17], who tended to minimize the affective linkage of the illness.

Using the same 105 patient sample, Eckert et al concluded that anorexia nervosa patients manifest a clinically significant level of depression as measured by symptoms and mood [19]. The severity of the depression correlated with other features of the illness felt to be indicative of greater severity, such as more bulimic vomiting, greater disturbance in body image, greater denial, more impairment in relationship with their fathers, and sexual disturbance. Depression was observed to be reduced but not eliminated over time, and patients who gained more weight were observed to experience a greater reduction in depression. While clearly recognizing that weight loss and depression exist together, the authors did not feel that their data allowed them to draw any etiological conclusions.

Using DSM-III criteria, Strober was able to assign a diagnosis of major depression to 41% of his bulimic patients but to only 9% of the restricters [20]. Premorbid personality characteristics differed between the two groups, with the bulimic patients often described as unhappy, fearful, clinging, and quarrelsome during childhood. Strober saw these qualities as implying affective instability.

Pyle et al studied 34 bulimic patients of whom most reported feelings of depression and problems with interpersonal relationships and self concept [21]. Mean MMPI scores on the D, Pd, Pt, and Sc scales were at least two standard deviations above the norm. There also appeared to be a high rate of substance abuse in these patients. Over 75% of them reported a decrease in sexual interest since the start of their illness, and 90% identified some traumatic event being associated with the onset of the bulimia, with the most frequent event being a loss or separation. This latter finding may be retrospective elaboration or could truly represent the beginning of a depressive episode.

Hendren reviewed the case records of all patients diagnosed as having anorexia nervosa at the Mayo Clinic over a seven-year period [22]. From the 230 cases with an anorexia nervosa diagnosis, 84 women were eventually evaluated on the basis of research diagnostic criteria (RDC) for major depressive disorder and endogenous major depressive disorder. Fifty-six percent met the RDC criteria for a major depressive disorder and 35% met RDC criteria for an endogenous depression. MMPI data was also reviewed and agreed in large part with the results reported above.

The trend of the above studies is in the direction of a significant relationship between eating disorders—particularly bulimia and affective illness. The lack of consistency in defining depression from study to study makes the drawing of general conclusions difficult.

FAMILY STUDIES

The idea that affective disorders run in families has received greater credence over the last 20 years. Recently, the Yale-NIMH collaborative family study of depression reported on a study of psychiatric disorders in 2,003 first-degree relatives of 335 probands and found considerable support for a familial relationship with differential rates and types of illness observed depending on the diagnosis of the proband [23]. Of additional possible significance for our discussion was the finding of Leckman and his colleagues that appetite disturbance and excessive guilt in depressed probands was associated with increased rates of major depression among family members with a 2.5 times greater risk for the same subtype [24]!

While not directly addressing the relationship of eating disorders to affective illness, Crisp et al studied the relationship of parental psychoneurotic characteristics to the prognosis of patients with anorexia nervosa [25]. They found that after the patient's weight restoration, maternal anxiety and paternal depression increased if the marital relationship was judged to be poor. Also, in patients who demonstrated bulimic symptoms, the fathers were seen as having an undue preoccupation with discipline and self-control and having a propensity for developing affective illness. Increased levels of anxiety and depression emerged with the daughter's recovery. Poor outcome was associated with high levels of parental psychiatric morbidity particularly in respect to depression. This study, while seeming to make a strong statement about anorexia nervosa in adolescents and its dynamic relationship to parental psychopathology, could also be interpreted as supporting the idea that affective loading and a particularly severe form of eating disorder may be related.

Cantwell et al reported a high degree of affective illness in the families of the anorexic patients he studied [13]. Out of 26 patients studied, 2 fathers, 15 mothers, 6 siblings, and 3 maternal grandparents were given a diagnosis of affective disorder. Four of the mothers had made suicide attempts. After affective disorders, alcohol abuse was diagnosed most frequently, appearing in 16 relatives.

Winokur et al studied the presence of primary affective disorders in the relatives of 25 patients with anorexia nervosa and 25 normal controls according to RDC criteria [26]. Affective disorders were present in 22% of the relatives of the anorexic patients and in only 10% of controls. Of the 43 relatives of anorexics who had an affective disorder, 34 were given a diagnosis of unipolar depression, and 9 were given a bipolar diagnosis. In both groups, more female than male relatives had a history of affective disorder, but the rate was significantly higher in female relatives of anorexic patients. Seventy-six percent of the anorexic families had at least one relative with affective disorder compared to 48% in the control group.

In an attempt to further validate the bulimia-restriction distinction in anorexia nervosa, Strober et al analyzed MMPI scores of parents of bulimics and restricters [27]. Their data suggested that the severity of bulimia in anorexia nervosa is associated with more pronounced affective disturbance in both parents along with greater impulsivity in fathers. The morbid risk of affective disorder in first- and second-degree relatives of the combined group was computed to be 15% which is more than two times the average expected lifetime risk for affective disorder in the general population. Seventy-one percent of the bulimic group versus 40% of the restricter group had positive family histories. Affective disorder was almost four times greater in the mothers of the bulimic group and was more prevalent in the fathers of the bulimics, but not at a statistically significant level. Alcoholism was shown to be present in 83% of the families of bulimics and 49% of the restricters, which may also point to a linkage with affective disorders.

Hudson and his group evaluated ten normal-weight nonanorexic bulimic patients for familial affective disorder [28]. Their results were similar to other investigators and revealed a risk factor for major depression of about 22% in first-degree relatives of the bulimic patients. In another study, Hudson et al evaluated 420 first-degree relatives of 14 patients with anorexia nervosa, 55 patients with bulimia, and 20 patients with both disorders [29]. The found the prevalence of familial affective disorder to be significantly greater in patients with anorexia nervosa and/or bulimia than in patients with bipolar disorder. The morbid risk of affective disorders in relatives of the total eating disorder group was 27%.

In a prospective study of 40 anorexic patients, Rivinus et al [30] found significantly more depression in the relatives of the patient group compared with a control group. When substance abuse diagnoses were added to depression, the familial impact of impairment was even greater. An increase in multigenerational impairment and increased frequency of affected relatives within families was also observed in the patient group.

Gershon et al [31] attempted to ascertain the presence of an identifiable subgroup of anorexic patients with a higher risk of affective illness in their relatives as a way of further evaluating the data that suggest anorexia nervosa and major affective disorder may share etiological factors. The presence of affective disorder, self-induced vomiting, or bulimia in the patient did not predict affective illness in the relatives, which suggested the absence of clinically observable genetic heterogeneity with anorexia nervosa defined by these features. The data seemed to support the idea of a shared genetic vulnerability between anorexia nervosa and affective disorders.

The idea that familially mediated variables play a crucial role in the pathogenesis of the eating disorders was further advanced by a recent report by Strober et al [32]. They found a five-fold increased risk of eating disorders in the female relatives of anorexics compared with relatives of controls. Subclinical anorexia nervosa was the most frequent disorder observed in the relatives of anorexics, with a greater total transmission of eating disorders occurring in the families of bulimic anorexics. Interestingly, all diagnoses of severe restrictive anorexia nervosa were made in relatives of restricter probands, whereas the preponderance of bulimic diagnoses were made in the relatives of anorexic/bulimic probands—suggesting familial segregation of the disorders. The authors offered several hypotheses for the familial transmission of which the cotransmission of an affective disorder or other psychopathology may be one. However, they caution that the data do not support any conclusions.

A recent study by Stern et al questions the relationship of familial affective disorder to normal-weight bulimia [33]. Their findings, which used strict diagnostic criteria, direct family interview, and blind raters, were at odds with the above. They only found a 9% prevalence of affective disorder in the relatives of bulimic probands, compared with 10% in the relatives of controls. However, a history of affective disorder was considerably more common among the bulimic patients, but it did not reach statistical significance and their study was limited to normal-weight bulimia.

Again, the differing methodologies may account for the variance in results, ie, patient report, family questionnaire, and direct interview. However, the trend of most of the data is consistently in the same direction except for the last study cited—namely, that there does seem to be some connection between eating disorders and affective illness.

BIOLOGICAL STUDIES

For convenience, under this heading are subsumed the neuroanatomical, neurophysiologic, neuroendocrine, neurochemical, and psychopharmacologic data that have been forthcoming in relating the eating disorders to the affective disorders.

That such relationships should exist biologically should not be very surprising when one considers the overlap of systems involved in the maintenance of eating and mood. The hypothalamus has been implicated as being an important structure in the regulation of both appetite and mood. Opioid peptides, neuropeptides, and monoamines are increasingly being suggested as important neuroregulators of both systems [34,35].

Catecholamine metabolism has been thought to be integral to the understanding of affective illness for some time. Though the limitations of this hypothesis have become more apparent, the monoamines are still thought to be important neuroregulators even if not solely responsible for affective illness [36-38]. Halmi et al studied MHPG during treatment in a group of 25 anorexics with secondary depressive symptoms [39].

MHPG is a major metabolite of brain norephinphrine and may correlate with central noradrenergic activity. An increase in MHPG correlated with a decrease in depression on two of three measures of depression. Gerner and Gwirtsman found that 24-hour urinary MHPG was low for all 11 female anorexic patients tested compared with control subjects [40]. This finding appeared to be independent of depression.

Abraham et al measured urinary MHPG in seven anorexics during a bed rest and refeeding program and found a positive relationship between MHPG and body weight, but no correlation between body weight and depression [41]. They interpreted their findings as reflecting a general metabolic effect. In an attempt to resolve some of the confusing findings concerning the significance of low urinary MHPG levels in anorexia nervosa, Biederman et al studied a group of anorexia nervosa patients before and after five weeks of treatment and a group of matched controls [42]. A subgroup of the patients who met RDC criteria for a concomitant major depressive disorder was found to have lower pre- and posttreatment mean urinary MHPG levels than both normal controls and nondepressed anorexia nervosa patients, both of whom had similar values. The median value of all urinary MHPG samples was used as a cutoff point to assess the distribution of values. They reported that significantly more depressed patients excreted low MHPG compared with nondepressed patients and normal controls.

Kaye et al studied CNS dopamine and serotonin metabolites and norepinephrine in underweight anorectics, recently weight-recovered anorectics, and long-term weight-recovered anorectics [43]. They found that the dopamine metabolite homovanillic acid (HVA) and the serotonin metabolite 5-hydroxyindolacetic acid (5-HIAA) were reduced in underweight anorectics but returned to normal shortly after weight was normalized. Norepinephrine levels, on the other hand, were similar to normals in underweight anorectics and after weight restoration. However, long-term weight-recovered anorectics had a 50% decrease in CSF norepinephrine levels compared with controls. The investigators felt that these changes in neurotransmitter metabolism are an integral part of the neurobiology of anorexia nervosa and may influence the changes in mood, behavior, and neuroendocrine function that have been observed. A longstanding disturbance in CNS norepinephrine may certainly point to a coexisting affective disturbance.

Monoamine oxidase (MAO) is an important enzyme in the degradation of many biogenic amines and thus has been the subject of studies attempting to link biochemical disturbances with a variety of psychiatric illness. The data generated from these studies appear inconclusive. Biederman et al studied platelet MAO activity prospectively in a group of young anorexia nervosa patients with and without an RDC major depressive disorder along with a matched control group [44]. They found that the depressed anorexics had lower MAO activity compared with nondepressed anorexics and controls. This finding led them to conclude that MAO activity may be useful in identifying a depressed subtype of anorexia nervosa that may be etiologically related to other low-platelet MAO conditions such as bipolar affective disorder and alcoholism.

Over the last 15 years, there has been great activity in the exploration of the neuroendocrine basis of depression [45,46]. The development of the dexamethasone suppression test (DST) for depression was enthusiastically greeted initially as a long-awaited biological marker of psychiatric illness [47,48]. This neuroendocrine line of inquiry has been naturally extended to the eating disorders as a way of establishing a connection to the affective disorders.

As part of the study cited above, Gerner and Gwirtsman studied 21 female primary anorexics and one male anorexic [40]. The 21 women demonstrated a uniform and marked abnormal DST. Interestingly, the male anorexic had a normal DST. No correlation was observed between depression and abnormal DST leading the investigators to conclude that the abnormality was a product of primary anorexia nervosa but not solely of weight loss, because the patients were not starving. In addition, three drug-free schizophrenic patients who had starved themselves to 75% of their ideal weight had normal DST. The findings of low MHPG and abnormal DST led the authors to the speculation that low hypothalamic norepinephrine, via its tonic inhibition of corticotrophin-releasing factor, might be responsible for the abnormal DST and point to an adrenergic vulnerability in anorexic patients, which might explain the strong familial association of affective illness and high degree of risk for depression in recovered anorexics.

Beside nonsuppression of cortisol by dexamethasone, there are other measures of adrenocortical activity that are disturbed in anorexia nervosa. Walsh et al studied a group of anorexic women and reported an increased absolute cortisol production rate adjusted for body size and weight, increased plasma cortisol concentration, and increased urinary free cortisol [49]. All of these findings were statistically significant when compared with controls matched for age and sex. The above findings, while similar to those observed in malnutrition, are different on several measures of adrenocortical function. Walsh speculated that the increased adrenal activity in anorexia nervosa is out of proportion to the malnutrition and might reflect response to any number of stresses—depressive illness being one.

Given the fact that the malnourished state in anorexia

nervosa confounds much of the data generated, the normal-weight bulimic population became a promising group for study. Hudson et al reported abnormal DST results in five of nine normal-weight bulimics without a history of anorexia nervosa [28]. This percentage compared favorably with the results obtained by Carroll and coworkers on patients with major depression [46]. In an expanded study, Hudson and coworkers reported on a slightly more mixed group of normal weight bulimics, some of whom were on psychotropic medication, and found 47% nonsuppression on the DST [50].

More evidence is provided by Gwirtsman et al, who reported that 67% of 18 normal-weight bulimic patients had abnormal DST [51]. These findings lead the authors to adjust their previous conclusion that neuroendocrine abnormalities previously found in anorexics were solely an artifact of low weight. They now suggested that weight may only be a partial determinant of cortisol nonsuppression. Though the neuroendocrine abnormalities observed were not associated with diagnosable major depressive disorder, a diagnosis of dysthymic disorder could be made in 50% of their patients, with over half of the dysthymic patients also carrying a borderline personality diagnosis. Thus, the neuroendocrine abnormalities observed could be seen as a result of disorders in the affective and borderline spectrum rather than purely as a result of the bulimia itself.

Gadpaille et al studied amenorrheic and menstruating runners and found that the amenorrheic runners had an overwhelming representation of affective disorders, eating disorders and affectively ill relatives when compared to menstruating runners. Their findings raise the possibility of a shared neuroendocrine vulnerability in the eating and affective disorders [82].

In a study of 29 normal-weight bulimic women, Blinder et al found that there was a significantly greater incidence of prior history of anorexia nervosa and current clinical diagnosis of depression among the DST positive subgroup [52]. This data suggested to them that appetite disturbance may be closely linked to affective disturbance in certain patient subgroups and that perhaps the ingestive dysfunction may be a phasic manifestation of an underlying affective disorder.

The response of thyroid stimulating hormone (TSH) to thyroid releasing hormone (TRH) is thought to be blunted in depression, with generally normal circulating thyroxin (T_4) and triiodothyronine (T_3). In anorexia nervosa, the TSH response to TRH is normal, although the peak response is most often delayed [53]. Gwirtsman et al found eight of ten normal weight bulimic patients to have blunted TRH tests [51]. Unlike the situation in depression, T_3 is significantly decreased in anorexia nervosa, which is probably secondary to a

diminished rate of conversion of T_4 to T_3, which also may be partially responsible for the decreased breakdown of cortisol. Also, anorexics have a lower mean T_4 than normals [54,55]. Whybrow and Prange have suggested that thyroid hormones may be important in regulating noradrenergic receptors in the brain and as a result may influence the development of and recovery from affective illness [56].

Activation is a fundamental neurophysiologically determined state of living organisms. In the affective disorders this state can be both underactive and overactive. It has been known for some time that hyperactivity is a clinical feature of anorexia nervosa [57]. This observation has been used to design an operant conditioning paradigm for the treatment of this condition [58]. Winokur et al were impressed by the presence of racing thoughts in their patients and felt that this suggested similarity to bipolar affective disorder, particularly when considered along with a history of distinct episodes of both depression and hypomania [26]. Mills and Medlicott [59] in exploring the theoretical basis of naloxone treatment in anorexia nervosa, make some extremely interesting points relating arousal, perfectionism, compulsivity, and anorexia. The mechanism they posit is that anorexia enhances arousal, which serves perfectionism and compulsivity. In their view, the depression observed in anorexia is related to the exhaustion produced from fighting compulsion.

Crisp and Stonehill pointed out in a rather complicated study that there is a relationship between weight loss, reduced sleep time, sleep discontinuity on one hand and weight gain, longer sleep time, sleep continuity and later waking on the other [60]. These changes appeared to transcend psychiatric diagnosis and to be primarily related to nutritional factors. The findings are similar to those uncovered in relationship to anorexia nervosa and suggest a common hypothalamic disruption in anorexia nervosa and other psychiatric illness. Though the authors did not observe a relationship between early morning awakening and depression, this is still felt to be a cardinal sign of endogenous depression.

Rapid eye movement (REM) latency has been thought to be a psychobiologic marker for primary depression [61]. Katz et al studied a mixed group of eating disorder patients with all-night sleep recordings and found a significantly reduced REM latency in the eating disorders group, which was approximately midway between previously established values for normal controls and primary depressives [62]. When the eating disorders group was divided into short versus long REM latency subgroups, Hamilton scores for depression were significantly higher in the former group; bulimia was a part of the clinical picture in the short latency group and

DSM-III criteria for major depression were met by all the short REM latency patients. Mean urinary cortisol was higher in the short latency REM group, but because of a wide distribution of values, this finding did not reach statistical significance.

The application of psychopharmacology to the eating disorders became a logical step as the affective components of the eating disorders began to be better appreciated. As of this writing, almost every class of psychotropic agent has been used in the eating disorders. Many of the studies of psychotropic agents in the treatment of eating disorders are of an anecdotal or open experimental structure, which mitigates the positive effects reported. However, the experience of the investigators is important from a clinical empirical standpoint.

L-dopa was utilized in a group of six anorexics because of what appeared to be clinical similarity to patients with Parkinson's Disease [63]. Four of the patients were noted to be improved with this medication. Amitriptyline was reported to promote weight gain, decrease weight focus and improve mood in six young anorexics admitted to a pediatric ward [64]. The effects of the amitriptyline were noted between the sixth to twelfth day, and weight change was felt to be preceeded by a brightening of mood and improved sociability. The authors questioned the representative nature of their sample, as it was a young sample with an eight-month average length of illness—all factors which auger well for a good prognosis. The also questioned other treatment factors that might have been operative, because the response to the tricyclic medication was quite rapid.

In one of the few double-blind studies, Pope et al treated 11 chronically bulimic women with imiprimine and assigned a similar group of 11 patients to placebo [65]. Eventually 19 patients completed the six-week study with a 70% decrease in bingeing observed in the imipramine treated group and virtually no change in the placebo group. After the six-week blind study period was completed, patients in the placebo group were offered antidepressant treatment and changes were made in antidepressant medications in treated patients who were not responding. Eventually 20 of 22 patients received a complete course of therapy with at least one antidepressant. On follow-up of one to eight months, 90% of treated patients reported a moderate or marked decrease in binge eating. Also, decrease in Hamilton Depression Scale scores and reduction in binge eating were significantly correlated, suggesting a connection between antibulimic and antidepressant drug effects. Mitchell and Groat in a double-blind controlled study using amitriptyline observed similar results [66].

Brotman et al reported on an uncontrolled retrospective study of 22 bulimics treated with at least one therapeutic trial of antidepressants [67]. Of 17 depressed bulimics, 10 achieved a remission in depressive symptoms. Only 4 of these 17 depressed bulimics maintained both a decrease in binge eating and remission of depression at follow-up. The patients who decreased their bingeing after the drug trial were less often depressed than those patients whose bingeing did not decrease. This study suggests that antidepressant medication may have independent antibinge and antidepressant effects, which would imply a less direct linkage between bulimia and affective illness. However, the fact that four of five true responders had an underlying depression that was successfully treated argues for a more intimate relationship.

In a recent controlled double-blind crossover study, Hughes et al found desipramine to be of value in the treatment of nondepressed bulimics. Sixty-eight percent of their patients were eventually able to completely eliminate their bulimic behaviors within the ten weeks of treatment. Whether this effect could be sustained over a longer time frame is open to question. The desipramine blood levels did not seem to completely predict response but seemed to indicate a group of patients in which response could be enhanced by more aggressive treatment and more rational management of side-effects and compliance. A prior history of anorexia nervosa did not predict response to desipramine, which led the authors to regard the distinction between anorexia nervosa and bulimia with less certainty. This study, while seeming to make a strong statement concerning the independence of antibulimic antidepressant drug effects, and perhaps the independence of bulimia and affective illness, is confounded by the fact that over 50% of the patients had a history consistent with a major affective disorder. In addition, the Zung scores (though not in the depressed range) improved significantly in the desipramine-treated group, pointing to a more general effect [68].

The follow-up report of Pope et al based on the patients cited above sheds some more light on this issue. They reported 95% partial improvement in bulimia and 50% complete remission after two years. The improvement was noted not just on measures of bulimia but in a marked reduction in depressive symptoms as well. This suggested to them that antidepressants provide an overall therapeutic effect for bulimmic patients [69].

A double blind study of pheytoin versus placebo in bulimia produced moderate to marked improvement in only 42% of treated patients [70]. However, this was significant compared with placebo. On follow-up of four phenytoin responders, two were observed to relapse after two months while continuing the medication.

Of related interest is a recent case report of the successful usage of another anticonvulsant, carbamazepine, in bulimia [71]. This agent is finding increased applicability in the treatment of bipolar affective disorder. The one bulimic patient who responded, out of the six treated, had a history of brief dramatic mood swings. The observation of mood instability in the eating disorder population has also led others to employ lithium [72,73]. Hsu recently reported on 14 normal weight bulimics who were treated in an uncontrolled fashion with lithium and a cognitive behavioral psychotherapeutic approach [74]. Twelve of these patients improved markedly or moderately, including four of six patients who relapsed or failed to improve with behavior therapy alone. Hsu raises the possibility that lithium achieved its effectiveness as an antidepressant acting on a variant of affective illness perhaps by dampening the dysphoria that precipitates a binge. Indeed, over 70% of his patients had elevated Beck inventories. Hsu was clinically impressed by the mood swings and emotional instability of his patients and suggests that lithium may have provided a general calming effect in emotionally labile patients.

Atypical depression is a classification that has been offered to describe a group of depressives who have a reactive mood and reversal of some of the typical neurovegetative signs of depression. This group seems to respond more effectively to monoamine oxidase inhibitors (MAOI) [75]. The overeating of bulimics and their mood disturbance suggested to investigators that they might indeed also respond to MAOIs. Walsh and coworkers studied six patients who met both criteria for bulimia and atypical depression [76]. All of the patients were reported to respond dramatically to MAOIs. The usefulness of MAOIs in bulimia was further reinforced by Walsh et al in a double-blind controlled study of phenelzine with significant positive effect reported [77].

Pope et al reported on their extensive experience in treating 65 consecutive bulimics with a variety of antidepressants and found promising results with tricyclics, trazadone, and MAOIs, which produced by far the best response [78]. The structure of this study in using tricyclics as the initial drug probably led to the underestimation of the effectiveness of the nontricyclic antidepressants. The authors felt that they could safely conclude that antidepressant medications have a clear place in the treatment of bulimia.

CONCLUSIONS

Certainly the preponderance of data would allow one to conclude that the eating disorders carry with them, at the minimum, an increased risk for developing an affective disorder. The difference in risk between pure restrictive anorexia and bulimia and the heavy loading for affective illness in the families of bulimics point to the

potential importance of biologic endowment in this disorder. Still, the nature of the relationship between the eating disorders and affective disorders remains to be clarified.

Hudson et al feel that their data suggest that bulimia may indeed be a forme fruste of an affective disorder [28]. In more recent work, they studied a group of active and remitted bulimics and found high lifetime rates of major affective disorders as well as anxiety and substance abuse disorders. They interpreted their results as providing further support for the existence of a phenomenologic relationship between bulimia and major affective disorder [83]. Strober, in reviewing his data, speculated that some adolescent cases of bulimia nervosa might represent a "phenotypically unique phasebound manifestation of the affective disorder spectra" or that bulimia nervosa is the product of and final common pathway for different but overlapping etiologic factors of which affective biologic endowment is but one [20]. Gerner and Gwirtsman leaned toward an adrenergic vulnerability model to explain the strong familial association of affective dysfunction in anorexic patients [40].

The successful treatment of some eating disorders with antidepressant agents have led some to conclude that the eating disorders are manifestations of affective illness, but this view may be somewhat overzealous. Walsh et al observed the close variation of bulimic symptoms and depression but backed away from concluding that they are one and the same [75]. Glassman and Walsh caution against equating bulimia with an affective disorder on the basis of response to antidepressants and make the point that everything that improves with an antidepressant is not necessarily depression [79]. They suggest that both conditions may arise from a unitary biological matrix with environmnental and intrapsychic factors determining the final outcome.

In a recent commentary, Altshuler and Weiner strongly question the relationship between anorexia nervosa and depression and raise some troublesome issues concerning reliability of diagnosis, research methodology, and epidemiology [80]. However, they do not distinguish between restrictive anorexia nervosa, bulimia nervosa, and normal-weight bulimia. Also their diagnostic focus was on major depression rather than a broader notion of affective impairment. Both of these factors could certainly contribute to underestimating the potential for linkage between the eating disorders and affective disorders.

Swift et al have concluded that affective disorders and eating disorders are related but in an unclear way. They have proposed an interactive, multidetermined model for understanding this complex relationship [84].

Hinz and Williamson argue that the data does not yet justify the conclusion that bulimia is a variant of an affective disorder. They view bulimia as a chronic psychiatric disorder which, like other chronic disorders, may be accompanied by depression [85].

Even if eating disorders are not manifestations of affective disorders, the high incidence of affective impairment in eating disorder patients must be explained. The issues are sufficiently complex that a multi-axial biopsychosocial approach is necessary for perspective. Garner et al have studied the question of the continuity of anorexia nervosa and have concluded that there are qualitative differences between true anorexia nervosa and weight preoccupation in supposed normals [81]. Despite a culturally reinforced "drive for thinness," many young women flirt with anorexia nervosa and bulimia without succumbing. This leads one to speculate about predisposing factors. Certainly episodic or chronic affective dysregulation could provide a fertile ground for the growth of maladaptive culturally reinforced coping strategies, as may other factors. The affective dysregulation serves to deprive the individual of the emotional stability necessary to surrender maladaptive behaviors and establish less self-destructive defenses.

That there should be greater representation of affectively disordered individuals among bulimics than restricting anorexics should not be all that surprising when one considers the instability created by mood swings and poor impulse control. The bulimia itself represents the shifting internal environment that may be attempting to cope with pubertal body changes, individuation, and autonomy. In addition, the bulimic behaviors are sufficiently complex that they can become self-perpetuating and addicting, particularly when they are seen as providing mood change. Restrictive anorexia, on the other hand, would seem to require different constitutional factors, parenting experiences, and ego defenses.

The clinical encounter requires continuous reformulation as new information is uncovered and new impressions registered. In the treatment of patients with eating disorders, this process is magnified because of the many problems that present simultaneously. Addressing the biological underpinnings is just one factor in what must be a comprehensive rehabilitative effort. However, it is important to appreciate how disorganizing an affective disorder can be—particularly in a young individual who is attempting to consolidate a sense of self. The successful treatment of the underlying affective disorder allows new learning to proceed.

In conclusion, it would seem reasonable for a prudent clinician to maintain a high index of suspicion for a concurrent affective disorder when evaluating or treating a patient with one of the eating disorders, particularly in the context of mood instability, substance abuse, or a family history of affective dysfunction.

REFERENCES

1. Freud S. On the origins of psychoanalysis: Letters to Wilhelm Fleiss. New York: Basic Books, 1954.
2. Abraham K. The first pregenital stage of the libido (1916). Selected Papers of Karl Abraham. New York: Basic Books, 1954: 262-85.
3. Fenichel O. The psychoanalytic theory of neurosis. New York: WW Norton & Co, 1945.
4. Binswanger L. The case of Ellen West. In: May R, Angel E, Ellenberger H, eds. Existence. New York: Basic Books, 1958.
5. Bruch H. Eating disorders: obesity, anorexia nervosa and the person within. New York: Basic Books, 1973.
6. Casper RC, Eckert ED, Halmi KA, et al. Bulimia: its incidence and clinical importance in patients with anorexia nervosa. Arch Gen Psychiatry 1980; 37:1030-5.
7. Garfinkel PA, Moldofsky H, Garner DM. The heterogeneity of anorexia nervosa: bulimia as a distinct subgroup. Arch Gen Psychiatry 1980; 37:1037-40.
8. Russell G. Bulimia nervosa: an ominous variant of anorexia nervosa. Psychol Med 1979; 9:429-48.
9. Vandereycken W, Pierloot R. The significance of subclassification in anorexia nervosa: a comparative study of crucial features in 141 patients. Psychol Med 1983; 13:543-9.
10. Akiskal HS. Dysthymic disorder: psychopathology of proposed chronic depressive subtypes. Am J Psychiatry 1983; 140:11-20.
11. Keller MB, Shapiro RW. "Double Depression": superimposition of acute depressive episodes on chronic depressive disorders. Am J Psychiatry 1982; 139:438-42.
12. Carroll BJ, Greden JF, Feinberg MD, et al. Neuroendocrine evaluation of depression in borderline patients. Psychiatr Clin North Am 1981; 4(1):88-99.
13. Cantwell DP, Sturzenberger S, Burrought J, et al. Anorexia nervosa—an affective disorder? Arch Gen Psychiatry 1977; 34:1087-93.
14. Dally P. Anorexia nervosa. London: William Heileman Medical Books, 1969.
15. Theander S. Anorexia nervosa. Acta Psychiatr Scand 1970; Suppl 213.
16. Morgan H, Russell G. Value of family background and clinical features as predictors of long-term outcome in anorexia nervosa: four year follow-up study of 41 patients. Psychol Med 1975; 5:355-71.
17. Stonehill E, Crisp AH. Psychoneurotic characteristics of patients with anorexia nervosa before and after treatment and at follow-up 4-7 years later. J Psychosomatic Res 1977; 21:127-93.
18. Ben-Tovin DI, Maricov V, Crisp AH. Personality and mental state within anorexia nervosa. J Psychosom Res 1979; 23:321-5.
19. Eckert ED, Goldberg SC, Halmi KA, et al. Depression in anorexia nervosa. Psychol Med 1981; 12:115-22.

20. Strober M. The significance of bulimia in juvenile anorexia nervosa: an exploration of possible etiologic factors. Int J Eating Disorders 1981; 1:28-43.

21. Pyle RL, Mitchell JE, Eckert ED. Bulimia: a report of 34 cases. J Clin Psychiatry 1981; 42:60-4.

22. Hendren RL. Depression in anorexia nervosa. J Amer Acad Child Psychiatry 1983; 22:59-62.

23. Weissman MM, Gershon ES, Kidd KK, et al. Psychiatric disorders in the relatives of probands with affective disorders. Arch Gen Psychiatry 1984; 41:13-21.

24. Leckman JF, Caruso KA, Prosoff BA, et al. Appetite disturbance and excessive guilt in major depression: the use of family study data to define depressive subtypes. Arch Gen Psychiatry 1984; 41:839-44.

25. Crisp AM, Harding B, McGuinness B. Anorexia nervosa. Psychoneurotic characteristics of patients: relationship to prognosis. J Psychosom Res 1974; 18:167-73.

26. Winokur A, March V, Mendels J. Primary affective disorder in relatives of patients with anorexia nervosa. Am J Psychiatry 1980; 137:695-8.

27. Strober M, Salkin B, Burroughs J, et al. Validity of the bulimia-restricter distinction in anorexia nervosa — parental personality characteristics and family psychiatric morbidity. J Nerv Ment Dis 1982; 170:345-51.

28. Hudson JI, Laffer PS, Pope Jr HG. Bulimia related to affective disorder by family history and response to the dexamethasone suppression test. Am J Psychiatry 1982; 139:685-7.

29. Hudson JI, Pope HG, Jonas JM, et al. Family history study of anorexia nervosa and bulimia. Brit J Psychiat 1983; 142:133-8.

30. Rivinus TM, Biederman J, Herzog DB, et al. Anorexia nervosa and affective disorders: a controlled family history study. Am J Psychiatry 1984; 141:1414-8.

31. Gershon ES, Schreiber JL, Hamovit JR, et al. Clinical findings in patients with anorexia nervosa and affective illness in their relatives. Am J Psychiatry 1984; 141:1419-22.

32. Strober M, Morrell W, Burroughs J, et al. A controlled family study of anorexia nervosa. J Psychiat Res 1985; 19:239-46.

33. Stern SL, Dixon KN, Nemzer E, et al. Affective disorder in the families of women with normal weight bulimia. Am J Psychiatry 1984; 141:1224-7.

34. Morley JE, Levine AS. The central control of appetite. Lancet: Feb 19, 1983; 398-401.

35. Kaye WH, Pickar D, Naber D, et al. Cerebrospinal fluid opioid activity in anorexia nervosa. Am J Psychiatry 1982; 139:643-5.

36. Bunney WE, Garland BL. A reevaluation of the catecholamine hypothesis in affective disorders. In: Usdin E, Carlson A, Dahlstrom A, Engel J, eds. Catecholamines: neuropharmacology and the central nervous system — therapeutic aspects. New York: Alan R Liss, 1984.

37. Bunney WE, Garland BL. Selected aspects of amine and receptor hypothesis of affective illness. J Clin Psychopharmacol 1981; 1:3S-11S.

38. Siever LJ, Davis KL. Overview: toward a dysregulation hypothesis of depression. Am J Psychiatry 1985; 142:1017-31.

39. Halmi KA, Dekirmenjian H, Davis JM, et al. Catecholamine metabolism in anorexia nervosa. Arch Gen Psychiatry 1978; 35:458-60.

40. Gerner RH, Gwirtsman HE. Abnormalities of dexamethasone suppression test and urinary MHPG in anorexia nervosa. Am J Psychiatry 1981; 138:650-3.

41. Abraham SF, Beumone PJV, Cobbin DM. Catecholamine metabolism and body weight in anorexia nervosa. Br J Psychiatry 1981; 138:244-7.

42. Biederman J, Rivinus T, Herzog D. Urinary MHPG in anorexia nervosa patients. In: Abstracts of the 137th Annual Meeting of the American Psychiatric Association. Los Angeles, 1984.

43. Kaye WM, Ebert JH, Raleigh M, et al. Abnormalities in CNS monoamine metabolism in anorexia nervosa. Arch Gen Psychiatry 1984; 41:350-5.

44. Biederman J, Rivinus TM, Herzog DB, et al. Platelet MAO activity in anorexia nervosa patients with and without a major depressive disorder. Am J Psychiatry 1984; 141:1244-7.

45. Sachar EJ, Hellman L, Fukushima D, et al. Cortisol production in depressive illness. Arch Gen Psychiatry 1970; 23:289-98.

46. Carroll BJ, Curtis GC, Mendels J. Neuroendocrine regulation in depression, II: discrimination of depressed from nondepressed patients. Arch Gen Psychiatry 1976; 33:1051-7.

47. Asnis GM, Sachar EJ, Halbreich V, et al. Cortisol secretion and dexamethasone response in depression. Am J Psychiatry 1981; 138:1218-21.

48. Carroll BJ, Feinberg M, Greden JF. A specific laboratory test for the diagnosis of melancholia: standardization, validation and clinical utility. Arch Gen Psychiatry 1981; 38:15-22.

49. Walsh BT, Katz JL, Levin J, et al. Adrenal activity in anorexia nervosa. Psychosom Med 1978; 40:499-506.

50. Hudson JI, Pope HG, Jonas JM, et al. Hypothalamic-pituitary-adrenal-axis hyperactivity in bulimia. Psychiatry Research 1983; 8:111-7.

51. Gwirtsman HE, Roy-Byrne P, Yager J, et al. Neuroendocrine abnormalities in bulimia. Am J Psychiatry 1983; 140:559-63.

52. Blinder BJ, Chaitin BF, Hagman J. Two diagnostic correlates of dexamethasone non suppression in normal weight bulimia. Hillside Journal of Clinical Psychiatry, 1987; 9:211-216.

53. Loosen PT, Prange AJ. Serum thyrotropin response to thyrotropin releasing hormone in psychiatric patients: a review. Am J Psychiatry 1982; 139:405-16.

54. Walsh BT. Endocrine disturbances in anorexia nervosa and depression. Psychosom Med 1982; 44:85-01.

55. Moshang T, Utiger RD. Low triiodothyronine euthyroidison in anorexia nervosa. In: Vigersky RA, ed. Anorexia nervosa. New York: Raven Press, 1977.

56. Whybrow PC, Prange AF. A hypothesis of thyroid-catecholamine-receptor interaction. Arch Gen Psychi-

atry 1981; 38:106-13.

57. Kron L, Katz JL, Gorzynski G, et al. Hyperactivity in anorexia nervosa: a fundamental clinical feature. Compr Psychiatry 1978; 19:433-40.

58. Blinder BJ, Freeman DM, Stunkard AJ. Behavior therapy of anorexia nervosa: effectiveness of activity as a reinforcer of weight gain. Am J Psychiatry 1970; 126:1093-8.

59. Mills IH, Medlicott L. The basis of naloxone treatment in anorexia nervosa and the metabolic responses to it. In: Pirke KM, Ploog D, eds. The psycholbiology of anorexia nervosa. Berlin: Springer-Verlag, 1984.

60. Crisp AH, Stonehill E. Aspects of the relationship between sleep and nutrition: a study of 375 psychiatric outpatients. Brit J Psychiat 1973; 122:379-94.

61. Kupfer DJ. REM latency: A psychobiological marker for primary depression. Biol Psychiatry 1976; 11:154-74.

62. Katz JL. Kuperberg A, Pollack CP, et al. Is there a relationship between eating disorder and affective disorder? New evidence from sleep recordings. Am J Psychiatry 1984; 141:7653-9.

63. Johansen AJ, Knorr NJ. Treatment of anorexia nervosa by levodopa. Lancet 1974; 1:591.

64. Needleman HL, Waber D. The use of amitriptyline in anorexia nervosa. In: Vigersky RA, ed. Anorexia nervosa. New York: Raven Press, 1977.

65. Pope HG, Hudson JI, Jonas JM, et al. Bulimia treated with imipramine a placebo-controlled, double-blind study. Am J Psychiatry 1983; 140:554-8.

66. Mitchell JE, Groat R. A placebo-controlled, double-blind trial of amitriptyline in bulimia. J Clin Psychopharmacol 1984; 4:186-93.

67. Brotman AW, Herzog DV, Woods SW. Antidepressant treatment of bulimia: the relationship between bingeing and depressive symptomatology. J Clin Psychiatry 1984; 45:7-9.

68. Hughes PL, Wells LA, Cunningham CJ, et al. Treating of bulimia with desipramine. Arch Gen Psychiatry 1986; 43:182-6.

69. Pope HG, Hudson JI, Jonas JM, et al. Antidepressant treatment of bulimia: a two-year follow-up study. J Clin Psychopharmacol 1985; 5:320-7.

70. Wermuth BM, Davis KL, Hollister LE, et al. Phenytoin treatment of the binge-eating syndrome. Am J Psychiatry 1977; 134:1249-53.

71. Kaplan AS, Garfinkel PD, Darby PL, et al. Carbamazepine in the treatment of bulimia. Am J Psychiatry 1983; 140:1225-6.

72. Barcai A. Lithium in anorexia nervosa: a prior report on two patients. Acta Psychiatr Scand 1977; 55:97-101.

73. Stein GS, Hartshorn S, Jones J, et al. Lithium in a case of severe anorexia nervosa. Brit J Psychiatry 1982; 140:526-8.

74. Hsu LK. Treatment of bulimia with lithium. Am J Psychiatry 1984; 141:1260-2.

75. Liebowitz MR, Quitkin F, Stewart JW, et al. Phenelzine and imipramine in atypical depression. Psychopharmacol Bull 1981; 17:159-61.

76. Walsh BT, Steward JW, Wright L, et al. Treatment of bulimia with monoamine oxidase inhibitors. Am J Psychiatry 1982; 139:1629-30.

77. Walsh BT, Stewart JW, Roose SP, et al. Treatment of bulimia with phenelzine: a double-blind, placebo-controlled study. Arch Gen Psychiatry 1984; 41:1105-9.

78. Pope HG, Hudson JI, Jonas JM. Antidepressant treatment of bulimia: preliminary experience and practical recommendations. J Clin Psychopharmacol 1983; 3:274-81.

79. Glassman A, Walsh BT. Link between bulimia and depression (letter). J Clin Psychopharm 1983; 3:203.

80. Altschuler KZ, Weiner MF. Anorexia nervosa and depression: a dissenting view. Am J Psychiatry 1985; 142:328-32.

81. Garner DM, Olmsted MP, Garfinkel PE. Does anorexia nervosa occur on a continuum? Int J Eating Disorders 1983; 2:11-20.

82. Gadpaille WJ, Sanborn CF, Wagner Jr WW. Athletic amenorrhea, major affective disorders and eating disorders. Am J Psychiatry 1987; 144:939-942.

83. Hudson JI, Pope Jr HG, Yugelun-Todd et al. A controlled study of lifetime prevalence of affective and other psychiatric disorders in bulimic outpatients. Am J Psychiatry 1987; 144:1283-1287.

84. Swift WJ, Andrews D, Barklage NF. The relationship between affective disorder and eating disorders: a review of the literature. Am J Psychaitry 1986; 143:290-299.

85. Hinz DL, Williamson DA. Bulimia and depression: a review of the affective variant hypothesis. Psychol Bulletin 1987; 102:150-158.

Chapter 32

Nutrition in Schizophrenia and Major Depressive Illness: A Review of the Research

S. Mark Sacher and Lawrence D. Sporty

INTRODUCTION

Eating disorders are categorized in DSM III as five distinct clinical entities: anorexia nervosa, bulimia, pica, rumination disorder of infancy, and atypical eating disorder [1]. Peculiar eating patterns have been observed in patients with schizophrenia and affective disorders; however, such eating disturbances are not considered primary determinants of the active phase of the illness [2]. Instead, the eating disturbances seen in schizophrenia are viewed as secondary manifestations of hallucinations or psychotic delusions, eg, an acutely decompensated patient who is paranoid and delusional about his food being poisoned may seriously restrict his caloric intake [3]. After recompensation with the return of improved reality testing, the schizophrenic patient may increase his caloric intake to more stable levels. Depressive episodes have been associated with appetite disturbances resulting in predominantly decreased appetite and weight loss. Less frequently, depressed patients may experience increased appetite with carbohydrate craving leading to a weight gain [4-6]. Like the schizophrenic eating disorders mentioned above, these appetite disturbances are also seen as state dependent; the appetite will return to normal as the depressive illness is resolved. Therefore, the appetite disturbance is seen as a secondary manifestation of the active phase of the illness and not causally related to the onset of the depression.

A question arises concerning appetite disturbance or altered dietary patterns seen in major psychiatric illness. Is it really a secondary manifestation of the disease in all instances, or is it primary to the disease process itself in some instances? Leckman et al [7], using a post hoc analysis of 810 first-degree relatives of 133 depressed and 82 normal probands, found that relatives of depressed individuals who reported symptoms of appetite disturbance and excessive guilt were at 2.5 times greater risk for a major depressive episode than relatives of depressed individuals lacking either or both of these symptoms. Furthermore, Leckman et al state, "The finding that appetite disturbance is a powerful predictor of risk in first-degree relatives suggests that the neurochemical and neurophysiological mechanisms that regulate appetite may be closely linked to some forms of depressions." [7]

Additional support for the relationship between appetite regulation, food consumption, and psychiatric illness comes from the animal studies of Wurtman and his associates on dietary precursor control of brain neurotransmitter metabolism [8-12]. The brain synthesis of the neurotransmitter serotonin has been shown to be influenced by the plasma availability of its dietary precursor tryptophan; the plasma availability of tryptophan has been shown to be influenced by the ratio of carbohydrate to protein consumed in the diet. Conversely, serotonergic mechanisms have been implicated in the control of food choice: specifically, the ratio of carbohydrate to protein consumed during each meal. Serotonin has also been associated with depressive illnesses and less frequently with schizophrenia. There are other neurotransmitters that are also influenced by dietary precursors: acetylcholine, the catecholamines (dopamine and norepinephrine), histamine, and glycine [8,9]. Abnormalities in dopamine metabolism have been linked to schizophrenia [13,14], norepinephrine to depression and mania [15,16], and acetylcholine to affective illnesses, tardive dyskinesia, and several neurological diseases [8,9].

Wurtman and his group have also demonstrated that brain neurotransmitter synthesis in animals can be altered by dietary manipulations. The administration of megadoses of normal dietary constituents such as tryptophan and tyrosine with carbohydrates have resulted in increased levels of CNS serotonin and catecholamines. These two findings, that dietary precursors exert control over brain neurometabolism, and that dietary manipulations can effectively alter brain neurometabolism refute (with the exception of glucose) the previously held theory of the independence of brain function from dietary intake. The new theory documented by Wurtman and his associates proposes that brain neurometabolism is dependent on the plasma availability of ingested nutrients [8,9,17].

Abnormalities in the synthesis of brain monoamines (serotonin, dopamine, and norepinephrine) have been implicated in psychiatric illness: dopamine in schizophrenia and serotonin and norepinephrine in affective illness. As Wurtman and others have shown, measurable changes in brain monoamine synthesis may be influenced by the plasma availability of tryptophan and tyrosine, the substrates for monoamine synthesis.

Other nutrients that are required for the synthesis of brain monoamines are the amino acid methionine, the vitamins pyridoxine and ascorbic acid, the metals iron and copper, and oxygen [18]. The nutrients methionine, folic acid, and vitamin B_{12} interrelated with s-adenosylmethionine (SAM) in transmethylation reactions have been implicated in influencing monoamine synthesis [19]. These nutrients have also been associated with psychotic and affective disorders [20-23].

A large body of research on the biochemistry of schizophrenia has evolved from the "dopamine hypothesis". The "biogenic amine hypothesis" has also stimulated much research on the biochemistry of major affective illness. Nutrients that are involved in the metabolism of the brain monoamines may influence brain monoamine synthesis and thereby play an important role in the biochemical substrate of schizophrenia and major affective illness [8,9,18,24].

The fact that brain function can be affected by ingested nutrients gives importance to an investigation of nutrition and brain function. Currently, dietary and nutritional factors have been given little significance in major psychiatric illness. The literature is devoid of any body of research concerning dietary intake and pattern in humans, and its relationship to mental illness outside of work done on the medical complications of anorexia nervosa and bulimia. The typical clinical, medical, and psychiatric history usually does not include dietary history. Furthermore, accurate clinical assessment of dietary intake of nutrients by history is problematic. Much of the research has focused on correlative studies of serum vitamin coenzyme deficiencies in psychiatric populations: the data have been interesting but inconclusive [24]. The claims of successful treatment of schizophrenia by orthomolecular psychiatrists, through their use of megavitamin therapy, have met with much skepticism because of the absence of double-blind clinical investigations [25].

This chapter will synthesize the literature on the role of some of the more thoroughly investigated nutrients in the biochemistry of schizophrenia and major depression. Other associated biochemical factors, including disturbances of water metabolism and wheat gluten enteropathy, will also be reviewed.

Only schizophrenia and major depression will be considered. These two illnesses seem to have strong genetic loading with biochemical abnormalities that are the most thoroughly investigated to date. Alcoholism and its effects on brain functions has been extensively studied elsewhere [26] and will not be covered in this chapter.

SECTION I: SCHIZOPHRENIA

WEIGHT CHANGES AND DISTURBANCES OF WATER METABOLISM IN SCHIZOPHRENIA

Weight Changes

Schizophrenia has been associated with eating disturbances, weight fluctuations, and disturbances of water metabolism. In the era preceding the introduction of phenothiazines in 1954, there were numerous reports concerning the organic findings present in schizophrenia [27-31]. Bleuler [28] described the course of dementia praecox (schizophrenia) as characterized by weight fluctuations from "extreme marasmus to excessive obesity and the reverse. In acute disease the bodily weight usually diminishes, and increases during convalescence." Mayer-Gross and Walker [32] stated, "schizophrenics sometimes refuse food, others devour everything they can get hold of regardless of taste." Freeman [33] describes acute psychosis as being preceded by a weight loss and clinical improvement by a weight gain. Freeman associated the psychiatric symptoms and weight changes as being caused by some "central mechanism."

Crammer [34] investigated the relationship between mental changes and rapid weight fluctuations in three medication-free patients with periodic catatonia, a rare form of schizophrenia. Clinically, these patients cycle through acute stuporous or excited catatonia at approximately regular intervals, and then recompensate between periods to near "normal behavior." For example, one case reported was of a 38-year-old man hospitalized for five years with periods of decompensation lasting ten days, characterized by unpredictable, excited, hostile behavior and stereotypic speech, followed by periods of recompensation and stability occurring at 23- to 30-day intervals.

The study data revealed cyclical weight fluctuations that corresponded to the course of the psychosis: rapid weight loss within a 24-hour period (maximum 9 lb per 24 hours) preceded the development of acute psychosis, the regaining of the lost weight was associated with clinical improvement. Crammer considered the weight loss as a physical sign of the pathological process of the illness and he explained the pathophysiology of the rapid weight loss as probably related to fluid and electrolyte imbalance. He recommended further study on the regulatory glands controlling fluid and electrolyte balance.

Holden and Holden [35] investigated weight changes in 22 chronic schizophrenic males taking psychotropic medications and placebo at eight-week intervals, employing a double-blind crossover design. Behavior assessment was done by rating scales including the BPRS. The data for the placebo period revealed a significant correlation between weight fluctuations and psychosis: weight loss preceded worsening of psychosis and weight gain predicted clinical improvement. There was also some significant correlation between weight change and psychosis during some of the drug periods. The authors suggested that changes in weight may be primary to the psychotic disease process. In addition, hypothalamic-pituitary function may be involved in this process.

In summary, central mechanisms [33], hormonal regulation of fluid and electrolytes [34], and the hypothalamic-pituitary axis [35] all have been implicated in the weight change observed in schizophrenia.

Fluid and Electrolyte Balance

Fluid and electrolyte disturbances have been reported in schizophrenia. Hoskins and Sleeper [31] reported on the 24-hour urine volume of 92 male schizophrenic patients. The authors found a larger (2602 ml versus 1328 ml) average daily urine volume in the schizophrenic patients compared with the male control subjects. A recent report by Lawson et al [36] found similar results while comparing the 24-hour urine volumes of 35 medication-free chronic schizophrenic patients, 31 control subjects, and 7 medication-free nonschizophrenic patients with various diagnoses. The schizophrenic patients' mean urine volumes were significantly higher than the other two groups (2319 ml versus 1054 ml).

Polyuria has been associated with psychogenic polydipsia (compulsive water drinking) in the schizophrenic population [37-41]. Smith and Clark [40] reported on 21 schizophrenic patients developing water intoxication secondary to polydipsia. The authors also cited 25 other cases in the literature of water intoxication with the majority of these cases having a diagnosis of schizophrenia. Water intoxication causes severe dilution of the body fluids resulting in hyponatremia. Early symptoms include nausea, vomiting, headaches, increased perspiration, difficulties in coordination, and excitability. Late symptoms are tetany, delirium, seizures, and coma [41].

Dopaminergic neurons implicated in the biochemistry of schizophrenia may also be implicated in the abnormalities of body weight and water metabolism. The hypothalamus regulates thirst as well as appetite [42]. Dopaminergic neurons have been located in the hypothalamus [43]. Dopaminergic neurons have been shown to influence thirst in rats: Dopaminergic agonists increase water intake in rats while the dopaminergic antagonists decrease water intake in rats [44]. Dopaminergic neurons have also been shown to influence feeding in rats: Dopaminergic agonists decrease feeding in rats while dopaminergic antagonists increase feeding [43,45,46}. Psychotropic drugs shown to alter brain dopaminergic activity may also affect appetite in humans [47,48].

Some cases of polydipsia and secondary polyuria haven been associated with the syndrome of inappropriate antidiuretic hormone (SIADH) secretion [40]. Dopamine has also been implicated in neural antidiuretic hormone regulation [40,49].

Cooles and Borthwick [50] reported a case of SIADH in association with Wernicke's encephalopathy that showed an improved clinical response of both Wernicke's encephalopathy and SIADH to intravenous therapy with vitamin B complex. Kremen and Kremen [51] reported a case of SIADH in association with hypomagnesemia that was responsive to magnesium repletion. The role of these agents in the abnormalities of water metabolism in these two cases is interesting. Some cases of anorexia nervosa have also been linked to ADH abnormalities [52].

Rapid weight changes have been observed in schizophrenic patients in the preneuroleptic era. As Crammer [34] suggested in 1957, such rapid weight losses were probably due "to losses of body water and its associated salt; ...the loss was probably urinary." Schizophrenic medication-free patients have also been reported to have disorders of water metabolism manifested by polydipsia and polyuria. The underlying mechanism may involve neural-hormonal regulation of thirst and water metabolism mediated by dopamine. Weight fluctuations in schizophrenic patients may also involve neural-hormonal mechanisms affecting appetite regulation mediated by dopamine. The interrelationship between abnormalities in dopamine and appetite and water metabolism in schizophrenia warrants further scientific delineation.

OTHER BIOCHEMICAL THEORIES OF SCHIZOPHRENIA

The principal biological hypotheses for the pathogenesis of schizophrenia implicate neurotransmitters, neurotransmitter imbalances, neurotransmitter binding site densities, and toxic metabolites forming endogenous hallucinogens [53-55] (the psychological theories will not be covered here).

The dopamine hypothesis of schizophrenia postulates an increased dopaminergic activity in the brains of schizophrenic patients [13,14,53]. The presumptive defect occurs at the nerve synapse either presynaptically or postsynaptically at dopamine receptors. Evidence supporting the dopamine hypothesis comes from pharmacological studies [53]. Neuroleptic agents that alleviate schizophrenic psychotic symptoms also reduce brain dopaminergic activity. This has been demonstrated in human and animal studies [13,14,52]. In addition, the more potent the antipsychotic agent, the greater the dopamine receptor blockade [56-57]. Conversely, agents that increase cerebral dopaminergic activity (such as amphetamine or cocaine) can cause psychosis indistinguishable from acute paranoid schizophrenia [58].

A major flaw in the dopamine hypothesis, however, is a lack of substantial direct evidence of altered dopamine concentrations or their metabolites in the central nervous system of schizophrenic patients [53]. It has been reported that amphetamines, L-dopa, apomorphine, and monoamine oxidase inhibitors, substances that should, according to the dopamine hypothesis, always aggravate schizophrenic symptoms, have in some cases resulted in clinical improvement [55].

As a consequence of these inconsistencies in the dopamine hypothesis in satisfactorily describing the eti-

ology of schizophrenia, other neurotransmitters have been investigated and implicated. These other neurotransmitters are norepinephrine, gamma-aminobutyric acid (GABA), and acetylcholine. Norepinephrine is a product of the hydroxylation of dopamine by an enzyme, dopamine beta-hydroxylase. GABA is an inhibitory neurotransmitter that is believed to affect dopaminergic activity.

Acetylcholine is a neurotransmitter postulated to be in dynamic balance with dopamine in the brain [53,55]. Enzymes significant in the metabolism of these neurotransmitters such as dopamine beta hydroxylase (DBH) and monoamine oxidase (MAO) have also been investigated. DBH, as already mentioned, is an important enzyme in the conversion of dopamine to norepinephrine. MAO is an important enzyme in the metabolism of both dopamine and norepinephrine.

Investigations of these neurotransmitters and enzymes have resulted in suggestive but inconclusive evidence [53,55] of their role in schizophrenia. What is apparent, however, is the complexity of the interrelationship of these few neurotransmitters and enzymes and how an imbalance in any one component may affect the whole system because of their dynamic interactions. Cooper et al [59] describe the direction of future research on neurotransmitters in the introduction of their book *The Biochemical Basis of Neuropharmacology*, "...to explain the function of integration of the approximately three dozen classical neurotransmitters, neuroactive peptides and the unclassifiable items, such as adenosine, in eliciting behavioral changes." The few neurotransmitters investigated thus far may only delineate a small portion of the complex interrelationship. However, it is a necessary step toward increasing the understanding of the biochemistry of schizophrenia.

The formation of endogenous hallucinogens by toxic metabolites is another hypothesis long under investigation as a possible factor in the pathogenesis of schizophrenia. Naturally occurring hallucinogens, such as LSD or mescaline, are known to produce symptoms of psychosis in otherwise normal individuals. The putative formation of endogenous hallucinogens by some inborn defect in neurotransmitter metabolism was first investigated in 1952 by Osmond and Smythies [60]. They were impressed with the similarity of structure between mescaline and epinephrine. Hoffer et al [61] suggested that adrenochrome, an oxidation product of epinephrine, was the highly toxic, mescaline-like metabolite present in schizophrenia. It supposedly resulted from an abnormal methylation of epinephrine in schizophrenic patients. The abnormal methylation process, according to the investigators, could be inhibited by a strong methyl acceptor, such as niacin or nicotinic acid [62].

Niacin was employed in megadoses of greater than 3 grams daily (RDA 18 mg per day) [63]. In 1957, Hoffer et al [62] tested the clinical efficacy of niacin in reversing schizophrenic symptoms. Dramatic claims of success were made, but other researchers employing double-blind measurements could not replicate the original claims of success [24,64].

In the 1960s and 1970s the "methylation hypothesis" evolved from the sole use of nicotinic acid as a therapeutic agent to a variety of vitamins and nutrients. These included nicotinamide adenine dinucleotide (NAD), a coenzyme derived from vitamin B_3 to megadoses of multiple vitamins: vitamin C, B_6, folic acid, B_{12}, pantothenic acid, other vitamins, hormones, minerals, diets, etc [29,64].

The megavitamin therapies were given added support by Pauling in 1968 [65]. Pauling subsequently defined orthomolecular psychiatry as "the achievement of preservation of mental health by varying the concentrations in the human body of substances that are normally present, such as the vitamins" [66]. Schizophrenia, theorized Pauling, was caused by an abnormal enzyme that leads to a defective coenzyme-apoenzyme system. This results in the formation of an inactive enzyme, leading to a cerebral avitaminosis. Pauling stated that the decreased affinity of the apoenzyme to the defective coenzyme can be overcome by increasing the amount of coenzyme (vitamin): this would lead to an active holo-enzyme. Pauling's hypothesis that schizophrenia is a vitamin-dependency illness provided a rational basis for the use of megavitamin therapy. Principles of ortho-molecular psychiatry have been viewed as plausible and reasonable, but without sufficient scientific evidence to support this hypothesis or treatment modality [64,67]. Furthermore, the orthomolecular group has been cited for failure to use adequate research methodology, including lack of double-blind studies, nonrandom use of subject and experimental design, inaccuracy of measuring instruments, and lack of a testable hypothesis [24].

Megavitamin therapy or orthomolecular psychiatry has been very controversial but it should be noted that Osmond and Smythies, in 1952, put forth the first modern biochemical hypothesis of the etiology of schizophrenia [68]. The current transmethylation hypothesis, according to Shulman, states that "Abnormal methylation of the neurotransmitted biogenic amines might result in the formation of endogenous hallucinogens" [69].

Some other examples of proposed endogenous hallucinogens formed by abnormal methylation are 3,4-dimethoxyphenylethylamine (DMPEA) and kryptopyrrole. DMPEA was initially found in the urine of schizophrenics but not normal controls. It was detected by chromatography, which revealed a "pink spot" [70]. Similarly, kryptopyrrole was found in the urine of schi-zophrenics; it was also detected by chromatography, which revealed a mauve-colored spot. The phenomenon was referred to as malvaria [71]. The pink-spot hypothesis of schizophrenia and malvaria were believed to be invalid because of the absence of these chemicals in many schizophrenics and their presence in normals [54,55].

Phenylethylamine (PEA), structurally and functionally similar to amphetamine, is another possible endogenous hallucinogen. It is formed by the decarboxylation of the amino acid phenylalanine. (Phenylalanine is also hydroxylated to tyrosine, which is a catecholamine precursor.) Potkin et al [72] found higher urinary concentrations of PEA in paranoid-schizophrenics than in other nonparanoid types of schizophrenic patients. Further investigation on PEA and its relation to schizophrenia is currently underway.

It is interesting that the work on PEA distinguishes a subgroup of schizophrenic patients, the paranoid-type, from the other subgroups of schizophrenics as to possible difference in pathogenesis. This is consistent with Bleuler's [27,28] original view of schizophrenia in 1911 as having multiple etiologies, as well as current studies in clinical phenomenology, genetics, and biochemistry, which support the concept of schizophrenia being a complex disorder with multiple etiologies [53].

NUTRITIONAL AND DIETARY FACTORS IN SCHIZOPHRENIA

Folic acid is a vitamin that is part of the vitamin "B-complex" group. A deficient state in humans has been associated with a variety of psychiatric disturbances, including depression, organic mental states, psychosis, delirium, dementia, mental retardation, and sleep disturbance [24,73]. Freeman et al [74] reported an interesting syndrome in a 15-year-old girl with homocystinuria who developed schizophrenic-like behavior that responded to folate supplementation. Homocystinuria is an autosomal recessive disorder of amino acid metabolism. The disease is commonly caused by a deficiency of cystathionine synthase; several hundred cases have been reported. In the case of the patient with schizophrenic-like symptoms reported by Freeman et al, the biochemical defect was a deficiency in a folate-containing enzyme, 5,10- methylene-tetra-hydro-folate-reductase (methylene THF reductase). This enzyme is needed for the remethylation of homocysteine to methionine. The deficiency of methylene THF reductase results in the accumulation of homocysteine, which may be converted to homocysteic acid, a potentially excitotoxic substance on the nervous system [75]. Megadoses of folic acid (eg, 20 mg/day, RDA [63] 400 mcg/day) appear to alleviate this type of homocystinuria.

According to the current literature there have been only four cases of methylene THF reductase deficiency resulting in homocystinuria. The clinical manifestations result in neurological symptoms including mental retardation, seizure disorder, electroencephalographic abnormalities, and musculoskeletal abnormalities [74-76]. One of these cases, as reported by Freeman [74] was a 15-year-old girl who exhibited a thought disorder with hallucinations, delusions, and catatonic posturing. When given folate supplementation psychotic symptomatology disappeared. Upon the discontinuation of folate the psychotic symptoms would return. However, the patient had a sister who also had methylene THF reductase deficient homocystinuria who did not exhibit psychotic symptoms. Further investigation revealed that the psychotic sister had low platelet levels of monoamine oxidase while the nonpsychotic sister had normal MAO levels. Low levels of monoamine oxidase have been reported in schizophrenic patients [53,54], suggesting that the patient with psychotic symptomatology may have had increased vulnerability to schizophrenia. Furthermore, the abnormality of folate metabolism, leading to schizophrenic-like symptoms, may be hypothesized as representing only a part of polygenetic predisposition to schizophrenia [74].

The precise role of folate in improving the psychotic symptoms is unclear. The excessive accumulation of homocysteine resulting in homocystinemia is the unlikely causative agent, because homocystinemia patients with cystathionine synthase deficiency are rarely psychotics; several hundred cases have been reported with only a few cases with psychotic symptoms [75]. Reynolds [77] · has stressed the organic factors present in the psychotic sister, which included a diffusely slow EEG that is more consistent with a metabolic encephalopathy, an organic psychosis rather than functional psychosis. However, the development of schizophrenic-like symptoms in a 15-year-old girl with an abnormality of folate metabolism responsive to folate supplementation is an interesting finding, especially since schizophrenia may be an illness with multiple etiologies.

Carney and Sheffield [78,79] surveyed 432 psychiatric patients for serum folate and vitamin B_{12} levels. Twenty-three percent or 105 patients had low folate levels. Of these 105 patients, 20% were diagnosed as schizophrenics, 24% organic psychotics, 30% depressive, and 86% epileptics. A retrospective examination of the results of treatment with folic acid and vitamin B_{12} was undertaken [79]. Among the low-folate groups, 39 were given folic acid and 63 were not. The folate-treated patients with schizophrenia, endogenous depression, and organic psychosis showed significant clinical improvement on discharge. However, external factors

were present that may have resulted in the lowered folate levels: 14% also had decreased B_{12} levels, 75% were taking various drugs for three weeks prior to the survey, 23% were malnourished, 17% were physically ill, and 44% chronically ill for more than three years. Furthermore, 86% of the low-folate group were diagnosed as epileptic and were probably on anticonvulsants, which are folate-depleting [24,80].

Carney did another survey on 272 newly admitted patients in 1972- 1973. He found the proportion of patients with low folate levels to be 21%, similar to the previous study, and to be highly represented by depressives and organic psychotics. Similar to the previous study, preadmission drugs, malnutrition, and physical illness were more frequent among the low-folate group than among the normal-folate group. As Carney states, "Whether the observed folate deficiency is an effect or cause of the mental symptoms has not been established beyond doubt, but evidence has been advanced to support the hypothesis that in some patients folate deficiency can produce mental symptoms" [79].

Thornton and Thornton [73] reviewed the serum folate values of 269 psychiatric hospital admissions controlling for dietary habits, medications, and gastrointestinal illness. The psychiatric patients, compared with the 40 control subjects, demonstrated a greater incidence of low serum folate that could not be explained by poor diet alone. The authors concluded that other explanations should be investigated.

Cyanocobalamin, vitamin B_{12}, acts as a coenzyme in several reactions including the methylation of homocysteine to methionine (folate and B_{12} cofactors), oxidation-reduction reactions, isomerization reactions, and methylation of soluble RNA [24,81]. Psychiatric symptoms reported with B_{12} deficiency include dementia, confusional states, depression, and psychosis with hallucinations, delusions, and paranoia [24,82].

Zucker et al [83] reviewed the literature and found 15 cases including one of their own that met specific criteria for B_{12} responsive psychosis. Ten of the patients reviewed had paranoid delusions, seven had hallucinations, seven were depressed, and six had some degree of organic impairment. The authors reviewed the hematologic and neurologic findings, which were variable. Neurological and psychiatric symptoms were present in some cases in the absence of anemia. Psychiatric symptoms were variable; the most common in this review were paranoia, violence, depression, and organic brain syndrome. The authors asserted that symptoms of psychotic depression with organic mental impairment were factors that should increase the level of suspicion for a B_{12} deficiency. Other important historical and physical findings present may include subacute combined degeneration of the spinal cord, anemia, prior gastrointestinal surgery, parasitic infection, malabsorption syndromes, or patients on a strict vegetarian diet. Other authors have recommended testing of serum B_{12} levels on all patients with organic psychiatric symptoms [84].

Skaug [85], screening for serum B_{12} levels on 396 admissions to Lier Mental Hospital in Norway, found a higher incidence of B_{12} deficiency in the psychiatric population than in the general population. In this study, the lower limit of normal for B_{12} was determined at less than 150 pg/ml, while the severely deficient B_{12} level was determined at less than 100 pg/ml. Sixty-one patients (15.4%) had B_{12} levels less than 150 pg/ml, while 23 patients (5.85%) had B_{12} levels less than 100 pg/ml. According to Skaug, poor nutritional status could not account for the prevalence of hypovitaminosis in the psychiatric population. The severely deficient B_{12} group included nine schizophrenic patients, three manic-depressive patients, three patients with senile dementia, and seven with various psychoses. No specific psychiatric syndrome was present, although paranoid symptoms were common. B_{12} treatments for this severely deficient B_{12} group resulted in one complete recovery, seven moderately improved, and four mildly improved.

Coggans [86] reported the case of an 81-year-old male who developed a manic syndrome without delirium associated with vitamin B_{12} deficiency. Following vitamin B_{12} replacement, the patient recovered rapidly. The psychiatric symptoms in this case preceded neurological and hematological manifestations of pernicious anemia.

Though no direct link has been established between schizophrenia and vitamin B_{12} deficiency, it appears that perceptual, affective, and cognitive changes present in schizophrenia may be associated or aggravated by B_{12} deficiency or subclinical B_{12} deficient states. Further investigations may be warranted, as there may be a subgroup of schizophrenics who respond to B_{12} supplementation.

Pyridoxine (vitamin B_6) functions in the nervous system as a required coenzyme in the formation of GABA, serotonin, norepinephrine, dopamine, and epinephrine, in the regulation of sulfur-containing amino acids including methionine, and the formation of nicotinic acid (niacin) from the amino acid tryptophan [24].

Isoniazid (antituberculin drug), hydralazine (antihypertensive drug), oral contraceptive usage, and pregnancy have been associated with vitamin B_6 deficiency [63]. Reported psychiatric symptoms of B_6 deficiency are psychosis (primarily paranoia), euphoria, depression with suicidal ideation and acts, and poor impulse control. The symptoms are heterogenous, as we might expect with the multiple effects B_6 has on neurometabolism [24].

Rimland [87], in a nonblind study of 191 autistic children, identified a subgroup of 20 autistic children who responded favorably to megadoses of vitamin B_6 and apparently relapsed upon withdrawal of B_6. In a follow-up study [88] on 16 of these autistic children who were positive responders to B_6 supplementation, vitamin B_6 and placebo trials were double-blinded to determine if significant deterioration of behavioral gains would occur upon withdrawal of pyridoxine in these patients. Behavior was determined by an individualized target symptom checklist rated by teacher and parent. Analysis of the data revealed a significant deterioration of behavior upon withdrawal of pyrid-oxine. Lelord et al [89] investigated the effects of B_6 therapy on the urinary homovanillic acid (HVA) levels of 33 autistic children. HVA is the principal metabolite of dopamine. The data revealed a decrease in the urinary HVA of the autistic children compared with an increase in the urinary HVA of the normal children acting as controls. Behavioral gains were reported in 15 of the autistic children. The reduction of the urinary HVA in the autistic children treated with pyrid-oxine indicates an abnormality of dopamine neurometabolism in autistic children. As previously discussed, disorders of dopamine metabolism are implicated in schizophrenia [12,13].

Abnormalities in averaged evoked potentials have been reported in autistic children [90,91]. A study by Martineau et al [92] on 12 autistic and 11 normal children administered B_6 therapy revealed a tendency in the autistic group toward clinical improvement accompanied by the normalization of both the averaged evoked potentials and urinary homovanillic acid levels. (Magnesium was added to the B_6 regime to decrease reported incidences of irritability and enuresis associated with high doses of pyridoxine.)

Other neurotransmitter abnormalities, including serotonin and norepinephrine, have been reported in autism [93-95]. Interrelated neurometabolic pathways may be involved. Pyridoxine's involvement as a coenzyme in reactions affecting the serotonergic, catecholaminergic, and GABAergic systems may play an important role in the etiology of childhood autism for a subgroup of genetically susceptible children. Further investigation appears to be indicated.

Niacin (nicotinic acid, vitamin B_3) in its active coenzyme form, nicotinamide adenine dinucleotide (NAD) and nicotinamide adenine dinucleotide phosphate (NADP) is involved, as Lipton et al [24] state, "in glycolysis, the tricarboxylic acid cycle, electron transport reactions of mitochondria, and the hexose monophosphate shunt (pentose phosphate pathway). NADPH, formed by a reaction involving malic enzyme, is utilized in fatty acid synthesis, steroid hydroxylases, phenylalanine hydroxylases and glutathione reductase." Tryptophan is a dietary precursor of niacin as well as a precursor of the neurotransmitter serotonin. Dietary tryptophan is converted to niacin in limited amounts in the liver via the kynurenine pathway, but probably not in the brain [24].

Niacin, when deficient, results in a condition known as pellagra, usually characterized by the "three Ds"— dermatitis, diarrhea, and dementia [63]. Psychiatric symptoms are diffuse and depend on the degree of deficiency. Mild deficiencies may present with apathy, depression, emotional lability, hyperirritability, anxiety, and memory deficits. Severe and chronic niacin deficiency may present as mania and delirium [24].

It was previously mentioned that in 1952 Osmond and Smythies [60] put forth the first modern biochemical hypothesis of the etiology of schizophrenia, the methylation hypothesis. This hypothesis proposed that schizophrenia was caused by an endogenous hallucinogen, adrenochrome, the result of abnormal methylation of epinephrine. Niacin was postulated to be a strong methyl acceptor that could inhibit the formation of adrenochrome from epinephrine. Early trials were promising with dramatic claims of success made for niacin. However, as previously stated, the original claims of success were never replicated and scientific evidence is currently lacking for niacin deficiency as an etiologic factor in schizophrenia or for the efficacy of niacin in the treatment of schizophrenia.

WHEAT GLUTEN ENTEROPATHY AND SCHIZOPHRENIA

Gluten, the protein part of certain grains including wheat, barley, rye, and oats, has been implicated in the etiology of schizophrenia by some investigators [96,97]. Gluten is the known pathogenic agent in celiac sprue. According to Trier [98], "Celiac sprue is a disease in which there is (1) actual or potential intestinal malabsorption of virtually all nutrients, (2) a characteristic though not specific lesion of the small intestinal mucosa, and (3) prompt clinical improvement following withdrawal of certain gluten-containing cereal grains from the diet."

In 1969, Dohan et al [96] investigated the effects of eliminating gluten from the diets of acute schizophrenics. One hundred and two acute schizophrenic patients admitted to a locked psychiatric unit were randomly assigned to two dietary groups. The control group was on a high-cereal (high-gluten) diet and the experimental group on a diet free of cereal and milk (gluten-free). Milk was omitted from the gluten-free group because some celiac patients experience exacerbation of symptoms after ingesting milk and dairy products, probably

secondary to an associated lactase deficiency [98]. All patients received the usual prescribed treatment for this disorder including antipsychotics. Clinical improvement was assessed by how rapidly (measured in days) it took for a patient to be transferred to an open unit. In this study, transfer to an open unit occurred significantly faster in the gluten-free group. In the second part of the study, patients and staff were blind to the addition of gluten to the cereal-free group. The data indicated no significant difference in time of transfer to the open unit between cereal-free plus gluten and high-cereal groups. The authors concluded that the clinical improvement seen in the gluten-free group was not due to a placebo effect. In a follow-up double-blind study, Dohan and Grassberger [99] investigated 115 male schizophrenic patients admitted to a locked ward at a Veteran's Administration Hospital. The experimental group given a diet free of milk and cereal grains was discharged about two times faster than the control group on a high-cereal diet.

Singh and Kay [97], employing a double-blind crossover design, investigated 14 schizophrenic patients treated with neuroleptics on a locked research ward for the clinical effect of wheat gluten on the schizophrenic symptoms. Three types of independent rating assessments were obtained: a psychopathology rating schedule, social participation and avoidance behavior scales, and psychiatric interviews. The data indicated that schizophrenic patients on a cereal grain-free and milk-free diet showed clinical improvement but when wheat gluten was added to their diet, an exacerbation of the schizophrenia occurred. The authors concluded that gluten may be a pathogenic factor in schizophrenia.

Rice et al [100] investigated the clinical response of 16 chronic schizophrenic patients treated with neuroleptics to the addition and elimination of wheat gluten from their diets. Two of the patients showed clinical improvement as measured by the Brief Psychiatric Rating Scales (BPRS) on a gluten-free and milk-free diet. One of these two patients, a 29-year-old chronic paranoid schizophrenic hospitalized for 15 years, decompensated during the gluten challenge phase of the study. The patient became severely agitated, uncooperative, and paranoid. The other patient, hospitalized for 13 years, showed such significant improvement that she was discharged to her family. Potkin et al [101] in a double-blind study of eight chronic schizophrenic patients, found no evidence of clinical deterioration or improvement on the BPRS to gluten challenge or withdrawal.

In 1966 Dohan [102,103] did an epidemiologic investigation of schizophrenic admissions during World War II because, in various parts of the world, cereal grains were scarce and the consumption of wheat was greatly reduced. In countries such as Finland, Norway, and Sweden, where wheat shortages were present, Dohan found a marked decrease in admissions for schizophrenia. However, in the United States, where wheat was abundant, schizophrenic admissions were increased. Dohan et al [104] investigated tribal populations of the South Pacific Islands, where cereal grains were scarce, for the incidence of schizophrenia. Public Health Medical Officers and anthropologists observed only two florid schizophrenics in more than 65,000 adults examined in Papua, New Guinea (1950-1967), Malaita, Solomon Islands (1980-1981), and Yap, Micronesia (1947-1948). The prevalence rate expected by the author would have been 2/1,000 adults or 130.

These figures are based on the prevalence of schizophrenia in Europe prior to the neuroleptic era from 7/1,000 to 2/1,000. This modification was necessary because flagrant observable schizophrenic-psychosis was a necessary criterion for identification of schizophrenia, (a conservative estimate according to the authors) in this anthropological survey. When these tribal populations became partially Westernized with a dietary change to wheat, barley, and rice, the prevalence rates changed to European proportions.

Dohan [105] proposed that there is a partial genetic relationship between schizophrenia and celiac disease. He supports his celiac disease model for schizophrenia by citing the work by Zioudrou et al [106] on the discovery of exorphins (endorphin-like peptides) in enzymatic digests of several glutens. It has been suggested that the exorphins from gluten may be antagonists to the body's endorphins [107]. He further cites a discovery by Mycroft et al [108] that the gliadin fraction of gluten contains a neuropeptide, melanocyte-stimulating-hormone-release-inhibiting factor (MIF). MIF has been shown in animals to increase CNS dopaminergic activity [108]. Ashkenazi et al [109] demonstrated in approximately 50% (10 of 21) of schizophrenic patients tested, a lymphocytic reaction to gluten similar to lymphocytic reactions occurring in celiac disease patients.

In 1982 Hallert and Derefeldt [110,111] investigated an area of Sweden where the prevalence rate for celiac disease was high at 1/1,000. The authors, in a retrospective examination of celiac patients for psychiatric morbidity, found a high incidence of depressive illness with no cases of schizophrenia encountered. In addition, those with prolonged depressive illness were the largest group to receive disability pensions. Hallert and Astrom [112] proposed that there is a strong correlation between celiac disease and depressive illness.

Depression was hypothesized to result from decreased central monoamine levels secondary to nutrient deficiencies. Nutrient deficiencies were the result of intestinal malabsorption present in celiac patients. Hallert et al [113] reported reduced lumbar cerebrospinal fluid (CSF) monoamine metabolites in untreated celiac patients. As stated previously, Sourkes [18] described the required dietary nutrients for monoamine synthesis (serotonin and catecholamines) as (1) the amino acids, phenylalanine or tyrosine, tryptophan, and methionine, (2) the vitamins, pyridoxine (B_6) and ascorbic acid (C), and (3) the minerals, iron and copper. Decreased central nervous system levels of monoamines (serotonin and catecholamines) have been implicated in depressive illness [15,16].

In 1983, Hallert and Sedvall [113] determined the metabolites of central nervous system (CNS) monoamines from seven untreated adult celiac patients. Concentrations of 5-hydroxyindoleacetic acid (5-HIAA), homovanillic acid (HVA), and 4-hydroxy-3-methoxyphenylethylene glycol (MOPEG) (3-methoxy-4-hydroxy-phenylethylene glycol [MHPG]) metabolites of serotonin, dopamine, and norepinephrine, respectively, were determined by lumbar studies. In addition, the concentration of CSF tryptophan, the dietary precursor of serotonin, was measured. All patients were placed on gluten-free diets and when jejunal biopsies revealed the evidence of remission of the celiac disease, CSF studies of monoamine metabolites were repeated.

Approximately one year (range 7 to 18 months) elapsed between the initial and final CSF studies. The results were significant for a mean increase of 33% in the concentrations of CSF monoamine metabolites, indicating increased central metabolism of serotonin, dopamine, and norepinephrine. CSF tryptophan levels showed an insignificant increase of 10%. The simultaneous improvement in the jejunal mucosa, together with significantly elevated CSF levels of monoamine metabolites in treated adult celiac patients indicated, according to the authors, that reduced central monoamine levels in untreated adult celiac patients may not be genetically determined. Instead, environmental factors such as a nutrient malabsorption may be involved.

Hallert et al [112], employing the MMPI, evaluated the psychopathology of 12 untreated celiac patients diagnosed by history, biochemical signs of malabsorption, and jejunal biopsy. The celiac patients were tested on the MMPI (1) at the beginning of the study following diagnostic assessment for celiac disease, (2) after approximately one year on a gluten-free diet plus vitamin supplements (folic acid, three patients also on vitamin B_{12} and iron) with morphological evidence of improvement in the jejunal mucosa, and (3) after approximately three years on a gluten-free diet with 80 mg pyridoxine hydrochloride (B_6) added 6 months before testing. The control subjects in this study were 12 surgical patients scheduled for elective cholecystectomy. Celiac patients exhibited a high score (greater than 70) on the depression scale of the MMPI on initial testing (70 ± 12.5), and retesting on the MMPI one year following a gluten-free diet revealed no significant change on the depression scale (68 ± 14.0). No significant abnormalities were present in the other subscales including the schizophrenia scale in comparison matched with the control group. The third MMPI testing which occurred three years following the initial evaluation and included six months of B_6 supplementation revealed a significant drop in the depression scale to 56 ± 8.5 ($p < 0.01$).

The authors suggested a possible association between pyridoxine deficiency and the symptoms of depression reported in untreated celiac patients. Pyridoxine is a required nutrient in monoamine synthesis. It has been shown to be poorly absorbed in children with acute celiac disease [114]. Paradoxically, Hallert et al [110] found increased levels of pyridoxal phosphate (active B_6 coenzyme) in the CSF of untreated celiac patients; furthermore, an insignificant correlation between changes in both CSF serotonin and its dietary precursor tryptophan was reported in the previous study [113]. Further investigation into the role of the malabsorption of nutrients in the etiology of depressive illness seen in untreated celiac patients is needed.

It is possible that there may be two subgroups of celiac patients, one with a genetic vulnerability to develop schizophrenia secondary to gluten neurotoxins or exorphins, and another subgroup of celiacs with a genetic vulnerability to depressive illness who are predisposed to develop intestinal lesions resulting in the malabsorption of required nutrients for brain neurometabolism.

SECTION II: MAJOR DEPRESSIVE ILLNESS

INTRODUCTION

Depressive disorders have been recognized for many centuries. The term melancholia itself is Greek for "black bile" and is itself an ancient humoral hypothesis put forth to describe a severe form of this disorder. There have been multiple hypotheses proposed for the origin of this disorder, ranging the gamut of human experience and imagination. It is certainly not possible to review the history of the theories of this disorder. Indeed, it is most likely not a unitary disorder, but a spectrum of disorders with similar resultant symptomatologies. Thus, biologically homogenous experimental human populations of depression do not exist. Differing etiological theories derive not only from experimental design, but also from the nature of the populations studied and the definition of the disorder used in selection of experimental subjects [115].

The past 30 years have seen a major expansion of our knowledge and understanding of the biochemistry of

these disorders. The resulting neurochemical theories and neuroendocrine correlates of depressive disorders will be briefly reviewed by way of background for the main topic of this section, the nutrients and cofactors that may be involved in depressive disorders.

THE BIOGENIC AMINE HYPOTHESIS OF DEPRESSION

It has been known since the 1950s that certain drugs used in the treatment of hypertension can produce depression in certain individuals [116]. Reserpine precipitates depression in 15% to 20% of hypertensive human patients when given in doses of more than 0.5 mg daily. In a third of these patients the depression is serious enough to require psychiatric hospitalization. Similar depressive states have been produced by administering alpha methyl dopa [116].

Laboratory studies have shown that reserpine depletes normal stores of norepinephrine and 5HT by impairing their storage in intraneuronal granules and thus impairing their protection from degradation by MAO enzymes. Furthermore, alpha methyl dopa induces depletion of central catecholamines and 5HT through synthesis inhibition [116].

In 1952 iproniazide was found to produce mood elevation in tuberculosis patients receiving the drug experimentally as a potentially new antituberculosis agent [117]. Subsequent trials of this drug in depressed patients showed it to be effective in alleviating their depressions. This drug was found to inhibit MAOs, the degradative enzymes that deaminate the biogenic amines norepinephrine, dopamine, and 5HT. Since then many more MAO-inhibitors (MAO-I) have been developed and are used as antidepressants; the degree of inhibition of MAO activity appears to be related to their clinical antidepressant efficacy [117].

Imipramine, another drug with antidepressant properties, was originally developed in the late 1940s as a possible antihistamine sedative or hypnotic. In 1958 during clinical investigation of this drug, Kuhn discovered that, unlike the phenothiazines to which it is chemically related, it was relatively ineffective in quieting agitated psychotic patients. Instead, it was found effective in some depressed patients. A subsequent search for additional chemically related antidepressant compounds led to the discovery of a number of new antidepressants in this group, the tricyclic antidepressants (TCAs) [118]. Further investigation revealed that imipramine and other antidepressants in this class block biogenic amine (dopamine, norepinephrine, 5HT) reuptake by the presynaptic neuron, a major mechanism of inactivation of biogenic amines at neuron synapses.

By the 1960s, the biogenic amine hypothesis was put forward as an experimental model based on the clinical effects of MAO-Is, the TCAs and alpha methyl dopa. This biogenic hypothesis stated that some depressions may be associated with an absolute or relative insufficiency of monoamines, principally norepinephrine or 5HT, at functionally important neural synapses in the brain [119-121].

This model was recognized as a probable oversimplification of the disorder at the outset, but it provided a useful heuristic model for further study. Since then, the evidence in support of this model has continued to accumulate.

We now know that in some depressions, urinary MHPG levels are abnormally low [122]. This compound is a metabolite of norepinephrine. Further, 5-HIAA (a metabolite of 5HT) is abnormally low in the CSF of some patients who have committed suicide by violent means that brain 5-HIAA has been found abnormally low in some patients who have committed suicide [123].

Not all depressed patients have low 5-HIAA or low MHPG levels, and the exact interrelationship between 5HT and norepinephrine is complex; therefore, it is not always possible to predict which antidepressant will work best based on urinary MHPG or CSF 5-HIAA levels [116]. Not only are absolute quantities of catecholamines at neuronal synapses implicated in the development of depressive disorders, but receptor sensitivities at these same synapses may also be involved. Neuronal receptors can be affected by a host of recently investigated factors in the CNS neurons, which we are only beginning to understand.

ACETYLCHOLINE

Acetylcholine in the CNS has also been implicated in some depressions [121,124]. It has been noted that physostigmine, a cholinesterase inhibitor in the CNS, can produce depressions in susceptible individuals, and there is mounting evidence of acetylcholine receptor supersensitivity in some individuals who are prone to depression. Further, physostigmine and other CNS cholinergic drugs can produce neuroendocrine changes similar to those seen in some depressions [121,124].

DEPRESSION AND THE ENDOCRINE SYSTEM

A number of endocrine system abnormalities appear to be present in certain patients with depressive disorders. The existence of depressive-like states in hypothyroidism and Cushing's disease and the recognition of postpartum depressions and the involutional depressions all suggest an important linkage between the endocrine system and depressive disorders.

Cortisol hypersecretion, reflected in 24-hour urinary-free cortisol levels, has been found in approximately half of depressed patients [125,126]. This abnormality resolves when the depression clears; depressed patients showing this disorder fail to suppress cortisol when dexamethasone is administered. This nonsuppression points to central endocrine abnormality. Similarly, some depressed patients fail to increase TSH output from the pituitary when THRH is exogenously administered, as would normally be expected. It has been suggested that this nonresponse is due to chronic intrinsic hypersecretion of THRH, leading to down-regulation of the neuronal receptor sites responsible for TSH secretion [121,125].

Some investigators have reported abnormalities in the hypothalamic-pituitary growth hormone axis, including a reduced growth hormone response to insulin induced hypoglycemia in some depressed patients [121,125]. These results and their interpretation are actively being debated in the literature, and the significance of this finding remains uncertain at this time.

NEUROTRANSMITTER-ENDOCRINE RELATIONSHIPS

The neurotransmitters 5HT, dopamine, norepinephrine, and acetylcholine are also found in neurons that innervate the hypothalamus [43,125,127]. This may be of significance in furthering the understanding of the association between major depressive illness and the frequent depressive symptoms of appetite and weight changes.

Appetite regulation by the hypothalamic feeding and satiety center has been demonstrated in animal studies by stimulation and ablation of the hypothalamic nuclei representing these centers [42]. Changes in brain levels of monoamines, already implicated in depression, have also been implicated in appetite regulation of feeding and satiety states [128,129].

Therefore, it may not be necessary to see the endocrine abnormalities in depressive disorders as separate or distinct from the neurotransmitter abnormalities already described. It may be that the endocrine abnormalities are secondary to the neurotransmitter defects in some depressive disorders. The appetite disturbances seen in depressive illness, which are usually viewed as secondary manifestations, may in some instances be primary determinants of the disease process (see introduction). Currently, there is much controversy in the literature concerning anorexia and bulimia as separate and distinct diagnostic entities or variants of affective illness [130]. (See Chaitin et al, this volume.)

The interrelationship between depression and eating behavior needs further delineation. However, the important role played by the brain monoamines appears evident. Nutrients influencing the synthesis of the monoamines and acetylcholine (dietary precursors, vitamin coenzymes, and associated biochemical factors) may be of heuristic value in the understanding of the biochemistry of depression and of clinical value in the use of a new treatment modality. This will be the topic of the next section.

NUTRITIONAL AND DIETARY FACTORS IN MAJOR DEPRESSIVE ILLNESS

A subgroup of patients with endogenous depression or major depressive illness may have functional deficits in brain monoamine (MA) metabolism, thereby involving serotonergic and catecholaminergic neurotransmission [16,121,125]. The amino acids tryptophan and tyrosine are dietary precursors for the synthesis of the central monoamines. Tryptophan is the substrate for 5HT synthesis; tyrosine is the substrate for dopamine synthesis. In neurons containing the enzyme dopamine-beta hydroxylase, dopamine is metabolized to norepinephrine [8-12,131,132]. The role of the dietary precursors tryptophan and tyrosine in influencing the synthesis of the central MAs and thereby altering behavior and mood has been investigated [131,133-138]. The mechanism coupling the brain concentration of tryptophan and tyrosine to the plasma availability of these nutrients has been determined largely from animal research [8-12,139], and this mechanism will be described briefly.

The brain uptake of the dietary precursors tryptophan and tyrosine depends on a low-affinity type transport system in which there is competition among the large neutral amino acids (LNAA) including tryptophan, tyrosine, phenylalanine, leucine, isoleucine, and valine for uptake into the brain. The factor facilitating the flux of tryptophan into the brain is an increased plasma ratio of tryptophan in relation to the other competing LNAA. The factor that increases the plasma concentration of tryptophan in comparison to other competing LNAA is the secretion of insulin, which is stimulated by a carbohydrate-rich meal. Approximately 80% of tryptophan is loosely bound to albumin, while 20% is free in the circulation. Insulin secretion shifts the LNAA to the peripheral tissues except for albumin-bound tryptophan, which then becomes more concentrated in the plasma than the other LNAA. This tryptophan, because of the relative depletion of the competing LNAA, becomes more available for uptake into the brain. Once across the blood-brain barrier, tryptophan can enhance serotonin synthesis, because the enzyme tryptophan hydroxylase is not usually fully saturated and readily reacts with the available amino acid substrate. Dietary

manipulations employing tryptophan supplements taken together with a carbohydrate snack may act as a treatment strategy to increase brain serotonin production [11,140].

Tyrosine uptake into the brain is by the same low-affinity type transport system used by tryptophan. The enzyme tyrosine hydroxylase is also not saturated by its amino acid substrate, allowing for enhanced catecholamine (CA) synthesis. However, unlike tryptophan, where there is no known cerebral extracellular feedback mechanism to inhibit the synthesis of 5HT, CA synthesis and release is modulated by neuronal firing rates and amine turnover [8-12]. As stated by Gelenberg et al [131] "...in disease states characterized by deficiencies in norepinephrine or dopamine, in which neurons may be firing more rapidly (in an attempt to compensate for the deficiencies), there could be greater sensitivity of CA neurons to tyrosine administration." Theoretically, a subtype of endogenous depression mediated by decreased synthesis of norepinephrine may result in increased firing of catecholaminergic neurons as a compensatory mechanism. Under this condition of increased noradrenergic neuronal firing, tyrosine supplements may be employed to enhance norepinephrine synthesis.

Gelenberg et al [131] and Van Praag [133] reviewed the numerous controlled studies of tryptophan in depression over the previous decade. The results of these studies were inconclusive. The equivocal findings were explained by the following arguments:

1. The putative heterogeneity of depressive illness. Theoretically, only those patients with decreased brain serotonergic activity should be positive responders to tryptophan supplementation.

2. A therapeutic window may exist for tryptophan in which certain limits of plasma tryptophan must be present for therapeutic effect. Exceeding or going below these limits may result in therapeutic failure. Tryptophan in a dosage above the therapeutic window may result in diminished plasma levels of its competitor tyrosine, which would lead to reduced CA synthesis [139]. Furthermore, a dosage of tryptophan above the therapeutic window may result in the greater induction of the liver enzyme tryptophan pyrrolase, which would increase the catabolism of tryptophan and, therefore, decrease the plasma levels of tryptophan.

Other possible factors for the inconclusive results obtained in earlier trials using tryptophan may involve the frequent lack of the administration of a carbohydrate-rich meal with tryptophan. As stated previously, a carbohydrate-rich meal or snack will facilitate the uptake of tryptophan into the brain. Also, there may be a subgroup of patients with a dysfunction in the transport carrier system that transports tryptophan across the blood-brain barrier [141]. The dysfunction of tryptophan transport into the brain may lead to depleted levels of brain tryptophan and, theoretically, tryptophan supplementation would be ineffective in elevating brain tryptophan levels.

A study by De Meyer et al [135] compared the plasma Try/LNAA ratio in 18 depressed patients and 10 normal controls matched for age, sex, and nutritional status over a six-day period. All patients were medication-free at least three weeks prior to the study and no psychoactive medication was employed during this study. The Hamilton Depression Rating Scale was given to all patients daily by independent raters. On days 2, 3, and 5, plasma samples for LNAA analysis were taken. Patients were allowed to choose freely from a hospital diet and their daily dietary intake of carbohydrates, protein, fat, and amino acids was assessed by a dietician from standard reference tables. The patients were seen daily by staff psychiatrists for counseling and allowed to participate in group and milieu activities.

The results indicated a significantly lower Try/LNAA ratio in the most severely depressed group (N=14). Further data indicated that improvement in depression determined by change in the Hamilton score was significantly correlated with an increase in the Try/LNAA ratio. No significant mean differences were reported between the depressed group and controls in daily dietary intake. The findings, according to the authors, are consistent with the hypothesis correlating brain tryptophan levels and its effect on brain serotonin activity to the plasma availability of tryptophan. In this study, daily dietary intake was not significantly correlated with the biochemical changes in the Try/LNAA plasma ratio as would be expected by the interrelationship of dietary intake to plasma availability of tryptophan. An explanation may be that the depressed patients had a different diet the weeks before the study. Further investigation is needed.

An investigation in a diagnostically mixed group of 87 depressives by Moller et al [136] of the relationship between the Try/LNAA ratio and the treatment response to Try supplementation revealed an 80% frequency of remission in depressives with Try/LNAA ratios below the 15th percentile of control matched norms. Moller et al [137] reviewed their own studies comparing Try and Tyr to LNAA plasma ratios in depressives in relationship to clinical response to various antidepressant medications including imipramine, clomipramine, amitriptyline, and lithium plus tryptophan. The authors concluded that Try/LNAA ratio may be a useful predictor of response to antidepressant pharmacotherapy; a low ratio indicating a probable good response to antidepressants and a high Try/LNAA indicating a probable poor response to antidepressants.

Further evidence in human studies of brain serotonin mediated behavioral changes associated with altered plasma availability of Try was addressed by Branchey et al in 1984 [142] in which the Try/LNAA plasma ratio was found to be significantly decreased in a subgroup of depressed alcoholics with a history of suicide and/or aggression. The relationship between decreased 5HT levels in depressives with a history of suicide and/or aggression has been reported previously [143].

Tyrosine, the precursor of dopamine and norepinephrine has been scantily investigated as a pharmacological treatment in depression. This may have been due to the former belief that tyrosine administration would not affect CA synthesis [131,138]. However, animal studies indicate that tyrosine may enhance CA synthesis under circumstances of increased neuronal firing and amine turnover (as previously discussed). Some initial data indicate a correlation between Tyr plasma levels and changes in depression, as determined by Hamilton Depression Rating Scale (HAM-D) [138]. Further investigation is needed.

The synthesis of acetylcholine, another neurotransmitter implicated in depression, may also be affected by its dietary precursor. Choline is a nutrient found in eggs, meat, and legumes in the form of lecithin and in milk in the form of sphingomyelin. Increasing brain choline levels by the administration of its dietary precursor lecithin may affect acetylcholine synthesis under circumstances of increased cholinergic neuronal firings similar to the mechanism proposed for tyrosine precursor control of the catecholamines [8]. The therapeutic employment of lecithin for precursor enhancement of acetylcholine synthesis is currently under investigation in the treatment of tardive dyskinesia, depression, mania, and several neurological diseases [8,140].

As Gelenberg et al [131] state in their review of neurotransmitter precursors in depression "...future studies on these substances would do well to incorporate important biochemical markers such as plasma amino acid levels, urine and possibly CSF amine metabolites, careful control of diet, and attention to optimal levels of drug dosages." In future studies on dietary precursor treatment response in depression, biochemical measures of the tryptophan and tyrosine to plasma amino acid ratios would be efficacious in treatment strategy; a low tryptophan/LNAA ratio may indicate selection of tryptophan, a low tyrosine/LNAA ratio may indicate selection of tyrosine, and a possible low plasma level of both tryptophan and tyrosine may indicate a combination of the two agents as a treatment strategy in depression. Correlating the tryptophan and tyrosine plasma neutral amino acid ratios with the urine and CSF amine metabolites to treatment response may provide additional supportive evidence for the dietary precursor control of monoaminergic synthesis and additional support to the monoaminergic theory of depression.

Pyridoxine, vitamin B_6, among its diverse functions, is required as a coenzyme (pyridoxal phosphate) with the apoenzyme L-aromatic amino acid decarboxylose in monoamine synthesis [18]. Pyridoxine deficiency has been implicated in depressive symptomatology reported in females using oral contraceptives [24,63,144]. Adams et al [145], employing a double-blind crossover design, investigated 22 depressed women taking oral contraceptives for biochemical indices of vitamin B_6 deficiency and clinical response to B_6 treatment. In order to better correlate the symptoms of depression with the use of oral contraceptives, patients with a previous psychiatric history of endogenous depression and patients with current psychosocial stressors were excluded from the study. Patients with moderate to severe depression, as judged by a score equal to or greater than 23 on the Beck self-rated depression questionnaire were included in the study. The results indicated 55%, or 11 of the 20 depressed women, had biochemical evidence of an absolute (as opposed to relative) B_6 deficiency, and this subgroup showed significant improvement to the administration of pyridoxine. The proposed biochemical mechanism of the depression observed in women taking oral contraceptives involved a possible alteration in amine metabolism as a consequence of B_6 depletion. Pyridoxal phosphate depletion may arise as a result of estrogen conjugates competitively inhibiting pyridoxal phosphate binding to its apoenzyme. In addition, estrogen may stimulate increased cortisol production, which may induce increased activation of tryptophan oxygenase in the liver, thereby shifting tryptophan away from the brain to the peripheral tryptophan-kynurenine-niacin pathway [144,145].

Isoniazid (antituberculin drug), hydralazine (antihypertensive drug), and pregnancy have also been associated with vitamin B_6 deficiency [63]. Neurobiological and psychiatric symptoms of B_6 deficiency have been numerous, including depressive symptomatology (see section on Nutritional and Dietary Factors in Schizophrenia).

Depressed psychiatric patients have also been surveyed for vitamin B_6 deficiencies [146-148]. Nobbs [146] found only 1 of 23 depressed patients to have conclusive evidence of pyridoxal phosphate deficiency and three additional patients to have suggestive evidence of deficiency. Stewart et al [147] assessed the plasma B_6 levels in 101 consecutive outpatient psychiatric patients placed on depression treatment protocols; he found that 21 patients (21%) had abnormally low B_6 values. Patients were medically cleared before the study. Possible neurological symptoms associated with B_6 defi-

ciency including numbness, paresthesias, and subjective feelings of electric shock were also evaluated. Of 75 patients assessed for these specific neurological symptoms, 14 (19%) revealed neurological findings positively correlated with the B_6 deficient group. As the authors state, "These data do not tell us whether diet, depression, or some other etiology accounts for the B_6 deficits found. Other vitamin deficiencies should also be investigated in order to determine whether low B_6 is an isolated finding in these patients or part of a larger picture of panhypovitaminemia." Other researchers have proposed that pyridoxine may be associated with endogenous depression [148]. Multiple vitamin deficiencies in psychiatric patients have also been reported [149]. (For the role of wheat gluten and pyridoxine in depression, please see section on Schizophrenia and Wheat Gluten Enteropathy.)

Folic acid deficiency has also been associated in the literature with depression [78-80. 149-151]. There is evidence that folate-deficient rats and humans have decreased brain 5HT activity. Botez et al [152,153] found lowered levels of CSF 5-HIAA, the major metabolite of 5HT, in the folate-deficient patients who exhibited neuropsychiatric symptoms consisting of organic mental changes, polyneuropathy, and depression that were responsive to folate supplementation. The group unresponsive to folate supplementation did not show lowered levels of CSF 5-HIAA. Furthermore, in the folate-responsive group CSF 5-HIAA reverted to normal following folate treatment, indicating increased activity of 5HT. (Paradoxically, rats given excess folic acid also showed decreases in 5HT activity [152].) Exacerbation of psychiatric illness with excesses of folic acid has also been reported [154].

Folic acid-deficient rats have also demonstrated decreased levels of s-adenosylmethionine (SAM) [155], a physiological substance found in mammals interrelated with folic acid in transmethylation reactions [21]. SAM is the major "methyl donor" in methylation reactions involving brain neurotransmitters including monoamines [19]. SAM has been shown to have antidepressant properties [156,157].

The interrelationship between SAM and folic acid suggests an important metabolic link between folic acid and brain monoamine synthesis. It was mentioned in a previous section (see section on Other Biochemical Theories of Schizophrenia) that Osmond and Smythies in 1952 put forward the first modern biochemical hypothesis of the etiology of schizophrenia, the "methylation hypothesis." The interrelationships between the folate cycle, s-adenosylmethionine, transmethylation, and the brain monoamines suggest that methylation processes may be implicated in affective disorders

[21,158].

Folate deficiencies have been associated with the use of diphenylhydantoin (dilantin), oral contraceptives, barbiturates, and ethanol [21,73]. Reynolds and Stramentinoli [21], reviewing previous surveys since 1967 of the serum folate levels of inpatient psychiatric populations, found 10% to 30% may have low serum folate levels most often associated with depression. Other reported symptoms of folate deficiency are organic mental states, psychosis, sleep disturbance, and mental retardation [24,73].

A study by Thornton and Thornton [73] on serum folate values in 269 psychiatric hospital admissions controlling for dietary habits, medications, and gastrointestinal illness revealed a greater incidence of low serum folate in the psychiatric population. Chadirian et al [151] investigated folate values in 16 depressed patients, 13 nondepressed psychiatric patients, and 19 medical patients. Excluded from the study were patients with cancer, anemia, and gastrointestinal illness as well as patients taking medication known to affect folate levels. For one week before the study patients were placed on a standard hospital diet and were medication free. Results indicated that the depressed group had significantly lower serum folic acid levels than the other two groups. The authors suggested that depression due to folic acid deficiency may be a distinct entity, but further investigation is needed.

CONCLUSION

Brain neurometabolism can be dependent on the plasma availability of ingested nutrients. The fact that brain function can be affected by dietary factors gives importance to an investigation of nutrition, brain neurometabolism, and human behavior. Brain monoamine synthesis of the neurotransmitters serotonin, dopamine, and norepinephrine has been implicated in psychiatric illness through the "dopamine hypothesis" of schizophrenia and the "biogenic amine hypothesis" of major depressive illness.

Required nutrients in monoamine synthesis and other nutrients affecting monoamine synthesis through metabolic interactions were reviewed in the literature for their relationship to schizophrenia and major depressive illness—two psychiatric illnesses that seem to have strong genetic loading and investigated biochemical abnormalities. Other associated biochemical factors affecting appetite and body water regulation were also examined.

The data suggest that nutrients may be important factors in schizophrenia and major depressive illness. The role of eating behavior and body water regulation may also play an integral part, as the same neurotransmitters implicated in schizophrenia and major depressive illness are implicated in the neural-hormonal regulation of appetite and body water.

The role of nutrients in affecting human behavior and the effective use of these nutrients as a treatment or adjunctive modality in medical and psychiatric illness is as yet to be determined.

While this chapter has focused on certain specific nutrients, it is certainly possible that other chemical compounds currently known or as yet to be discovered may also play a major role in these disorders; certainly, the investigations reviewed in this chapter indicate that further research in the role of nutrition and human behavior should be actively pursued.

In addition to expanding this research into other chemical compounds, other neurobehavioral disorders may involve the same neurotransmitter systems already outlined in this chapter. For example, the authors are currently investigating the efficacy of tyrosine, an amino acid precursor to catecholamine synthesis, as a possible treatment for Attention Deficit Disorder of Childhood. In this pilot study, the response to treatment with tyrosine of ten prepubertal males diagnosed with this disorder will be correlated with biochemical measures (plasma amino acid levels and urinary MHPG levels), cognitive measures (Paired-Associate Learning Test), and behavioral measures (Conner's Rating Scale).

REFERENCES

1. American Psychiatric Association. DSM III: Diagnostic and statistical manual of mental disorders, third edition. Washington DC: American Psychiatric Association, 1980:

2. Halmi KA. Eating disorders. In: Comprehensive textbook of psychiatry/III, vol 2. Baltimore/London: Williams and Wilkins, 1980: 2598-2605.

3. Lyketsos GC, Paterkis P, Beis A, et al. Eating disorders in schizophrenia. Br J Psychiatry 1985; 146:255-61.

4. Hopkinson G. A neurochemical theory of appetite and weight changes in depressives states. Acta Psychiat Scand 1981; 64:217-25.

5. Smith SL, Sauder C. Food craving, depression, and premenstrual problems. Psychosom Med 1969; 31:281-7.

6. Paykel ES. Depression and appetite. J Psychosom Res 1977; 21:401-7.

7. Leckman JF, Caruso KA, Prusoff BA, et al. Appetite disturbance and excessive guilt in major depression: the use of family study data to define depressive subtypes. Arch Gen Psychiatry 1984; 41(9):839-44.

8. Growdon JH. Neurotransmitter precursors in the diet: their use in the treatment of brain diseases. In: Wurtman RJ, Wurtman JJ, eds. Nutrition and the brain, vol 3. New York: Raven Press, 1979:

9. Wurtman RJ, Hefti F, Melamed E. Precursor control

of neurotransmitter synthesis. Pharmacological Reviews 1981; 32(4):315-35.

10. Wurtman RJ. Nutrients that modify brain function. Scientific American 1982; 246:42-51.

11. Wurtman RJ. Food consumption, neurotransmitter synthesis, and human behavior. Experentia (Suppl) 1983; 44:356-69.

12. Fernstrom JD, Wurtman RJ. Brain serotonin content: physiological regulation by plasma amino acids. Science 1972; 176:414-16.

13. Meltzer HY, Stahl SM. The dopamine hypothesis of schizophrenia (review). Schizophrenia Bull 1976; 2:19-76.

14. Snyder SH, Banerjee SP, Yamamura HI, et al. Drugs, neurotransmitters and schizophrenia. Science 1974; 184: 1243-53.

15. Mendels J, Frazer A. Brain biogenic amine depletion and mood. Arch Gen Psychiatry 1974; 30:447-51.

16. Van Praag HM. Neurotransmitters and CNS disease. Lancet 1982; 2:1259-64.

17. Strain GW. Nutrition, brain function and behavior. Psychiatric Clinics of North America 1981; 4(2):253-68.

18. Sourkes TL. Nutrients and the cofactors required for monoamine synthesis in nervous tissue. In: Wurtman RJ, Wurtman JJ, eds. Nutrition and the brain, vol 3. New York: Raven Press, 1979:

19. Bottiglieri T, Laundy M, Martin R, et al. S-adenosyl-methionine influences monoamine metabolism. Lancet 1984; 2:224.

20. Shulman R. An overview of folic acid deficiency and psychiatric illness. In: Botez MI, Reynolds EH, eds. Folic acid in neurology, psychiatry and internal medicine. New York: Raven Press, 1979:

21. Reynolds EH, Stramentinoli G. Folic acid, s-adenosyl-methionine and affective disorder. Psychological Medicine 1983; 13:705-10.

22. Carney JWP, Sheffield BF. Association of subnormal serum folate and vitamin B-12 values and effects of replacement therapy. The Journal of Nervous and Mental Disease 1970; 150(5):404-12.

23. Evans DL, Edelsohn GA, Golden RN. Organic psychosis without anemia or spinal cord symptoms in patients with vitamin B-12 deficiency. American Journal of Psychiatry 1983; 140(2):218-20.

24. Lipton MA, Mailman RB, Nemeroff CB. Vitamins, megavitamin therapy, and the nervous system. In: Wurtman RJ, Wurtman JJ, eds. Nutrition and the brain, vol 3. New York: Raven Press, 1979:

25. APA Task Force Report 7. Megavitamin and orthomolecular therapy in psychiatry. Library of Congress Catalogue No. 73-78890, Washington DC: American Psychiatric Association, 1973:

26. Tabahoff B, Noble EP, Warren KR. Alcohol, nutrition and the brain. In: Wurtman RJ, Wurtman JJ, eds. Nutrition and the brain, vol 4. New York: Raven Press, 1979:

27. Bleuler E. Textbook of psychiatry. New York: MacMillan Company, 1924:

28. Bleuler E. Dementia praecox. New York: Grune and Stratton, 1948:

29. Bellak L. Schizophrenia: a review of the syndrome. New York: Grune and Stratton, 1958:

30. Kraepelin E. Dementia praecox and paraphrenia. Edinburg: Livingstone, 1919:

31. Hoskins RG, Sleeper FH. Organic functions in schizophrenia. Archives of Neurology and Psychiatry 1933; 30:123-32.

32. Mayer-Gross W, Walker JW. Taste and selection of food in hypoglycemia. British Journal of Experimental Pathology 1946; 27:297-305.

33. Freeman H. Physiological studies in schizophrenia: a review of the syndrome. In: Bellak L, ed. New York: Grune and Stratton, 1958:

34. Crammer JL. Rapid weight changes in mental patients. Lancet 1957; 2:259-62.

35. Holden JMC, Holden UP. Weight changes with schizophrenia psychosis and psychotropic drug therapy. Psychosomatics 1970; 11:551-60.

36. Lawson WB, Karson CN, Llewellyn BB. Psychogenic polydipsia in chronic schizophrenic patients. Paper presented at Winter Conference on Brain Research, 1983.

37. Sleeper FH, Jellinck EM. A comparative physiologic, psychologic, and psychiatric study of polyuric and nonpolyuric schizophrenic patients. Annals of Internal Medicine 1933; 7:445-56.

38. Jose CJ, Perez-Cruet. Incidence and morbidity of self-induced water intoxication in state mental hospital patients. Am J Psychiatry 1979; 136(2):221-2.

39. Blum A, Friedland GW. Urinary tract abnormalities due to chronic psychogenic polydipsia. Am J Psychiatry 1983; 140(7):915-6.

40. Smith WO, Clark ML. Self-induced water intoxication in schizophrenic patients. Am J Psychiatry 1980; 137(9):1055-60.

41. Chinn TA. Compulsive water drinking: a review of the literature and an additional case. The Journal of Nervous and Mental Disease 1974; 158:78-80.

42. Guyton AC. Textbook of medical physiology (sixth edition). Philadelphia: Saunders, 1980:

43. Kolata G. Brain receptors for appetite discovered. Science 1982; 218:460-1.

44. Fitzsimons JT, Setler PE. The relative importance of central nervous catecholaminergic and cholinergic mechanisms in drinking response to angiotension and other thirst stimuli. J Physiol 1975; 250:613-31.

45. Leibowitz SF, Miller NE. Unexpected adrenergic effect of chlorpromazine: eating elicited by injection into rat hypothalamus. Science 1969; 165:609-10.

46. Stolerman IP. Eating, drinking and spontaneous activity in rats after the administration of chlorpromazine. Neuropharmacology 1970; 9:405.

47. Rockwell WJ, Everett HE, Trader DW. Psychotropic drugs promoting weight gain: health risks and treatment implications. Southern Medical Journal 1983; 76(11):1407-12.

48. Doss FW. The effect of antipsychotic drugs on body

weight: a retrospective review. J Clin Psychiatry 1979; 40:528-30.

49. Raskind MA, Orenstein H, Christopher GT. Acute psychosis, increased water ingestion, and inappropriate antidiuretic hormone secretion. Am J Psychiatry 1975; 132(9):907-10.

50. Cooles PE, Borthwick LJ. Inappropriate antidiuretic hormone secretion in Wernicke's encephalopathy. Postgrad Med J 1982; 58:173-4.

51. Kremen AF, Kreman AJ. Hypomagnesemia and inappropriate secretion of antidiuretic hormone. Minnesota Medicine 1980; 63:385-7.

52. Gold PW, Kaye W, Robertson GL, et al. Abnormalities in plasma and cerebrospinal fluid arginine vasopressin in patients with anorexia nervosa. N Engl J Med 1983; 308(19):1117-23.

53. Berger PA. Biochemistry and the schizophrenias: old concepts and new hypotheses. The Journal of Nervous and Mental Disease 1981; 169:90-9.

54. Weiner H. Schizophrenia: etiology. In: Kaplan HI, Sadock BJ, eds. Comprehensive textbook of psychiatry/IV. Baltimore/London: Williams and Wilkins, 1985:

55. Thakar J. Biochemical studies in schizophrenia. The Psychiatric Journal of the University of Ottawa 1983; 8(1):44-50.

56. Snyder SH. Dopamine receptors, neuroleptics, and schizophrenia. Am J Psychiatry 1981; 138:460-4.

57. Bernstein JG. Handbook of drug therapy in psychiatry. Littleton MA: John Wright, 1983:

58. Snyder SH. Amphetamine psychosis, a "model" of schizophrenia mediated by catecholamines. Am J Psychiatry 1974; 130:61-7.

59. Cooper JR, Bloom FE, Roth RH. The biochemical basis of neuropharmacology. New York: Oxford University Press, 1982:

60. Osmond H, Smythies J. Schizophrenia: a new approach. Journal of Mental Sciences 1952; 98:309-15.

61. Hoffer A, Osmond H, Smythies J. Schizophrenia: a new approach II. Results of a year's research. J Ment Sci 1954; 100:29-54.

62. Hoffer A, Callbeck MJ, Kahan I, et al. Treatment of schizophrenia with nicotine acid and nicotinamide. J Clin Exp Psychopathol 1957; 18:131-58.

63. Danford ED, Munro HN. The vitamins. In: Gilman AG, Goodman LS, Gilman A, eds. The pharmacological basis of therapeutics, sixth edition. New York: MacMillan Publishing Co, 1980:

64. APA Task Force Report 7. Megavitamin and orthomolecular therapy in psychiatry. Library of Congress Catalogue No. 73-78890, Washington DC: American Psychiatric Association, 1973:

65. Pauling L. Orthomolecular psychiatry. Science 1968; 160:265-71.

66. Pauling L. On the orthomolecular environment of the mind: orthomolecular theory. Am J Psychiatry 1974; 131(11):1251-7.

67. Wyatt RJ. Commentary on, On the orthomolecular environment of the mind: orthomulecular theory by Pauling L. Am J Psychiatry 1974; 131(11):1258-62.

68. Bourdillon RE, Ridges PA. Catecholamines and schizophrenia. In: Himwick HE, ed. Biochemistry, schizophrenias and affective illnesses. Baltimore: Wilkins Co, 1970:

69. Shulman R. An overview of folic acid deficiency and psychiatric illness. In: Botez MI, Reynolds EH, eds. Folic acid in neurology, psychiatry and internal medicine. New York: Raven Press, 1979:

70. Friedhoff AJ, VanWinkle E. Conversion of dopamine to 3,4-dimethoxyphenylacetic acid in schizophrenic patients. Nature 1963; 199:1271-2.

71. Hoffer A, Osmond H. Malvaria: a new psychiatric disease. Acta Psychiatrica Scandinavia 1963; 39:335-66.

72. Potkin SG, Karoum F, Chuang LW. Phenylethylamine in paranoid chronic schizophrenia. Science 1979; 206:470-1.

73. Thornton WE, Thornton BP. Folic acid, mental function, and dietary habits. Journal of Clinical Psychiatry 1978; 7:315-22.

74. Freeman JM, Finkelstein JD, Mudd SH. Folate-responsive homocystinuria and schizophrenia. N Engl J Med 1975; 292(10):491-6.

75. Grieco AJ. Homocystinuria: pathogenic mechanisms. Am J Medical Sciences 1977; 273(2):120-32.

76. Nutritional Reviews. Folate-responsive homocystinuria and shizophrenia. 1982; 40(8):242-3.

77. Reynolds EH. Folate-responsive schizophrenia (letter). Lancet 1975; 2:189-90.

78. Carney MWP. Serum folate values in 423 psychiatric patients. Brit Med J 1967; 4:512-6.

79. Carney MWP. Psychiatric aspects of folate deficiency. In: Botez MI, Reynolds EH, eds. Folic acid in neurology, psychiatry and internal medicine. New York: Raven Press, 1979:

80. Trimble MR, Corbett JA, Donaldson D. Folic acid and mental symptoms in children with epilepsy. Journal of Neurology, Neurosurgery and Psychiatry 1980; 43:1030-4.

81. Girdwood RH. Abnormalities of vitamin B-12 and folic acid metabolism: their influence on the nervous system. Proc Nutr Soc Eng Scot 1968; 27:101.

82. Geagea K, Ananth J. Response of a psychiatric patient to vitamin B-12 therapy. Diseases of the Nervous System 1975; 36(6):343-4.

83. Zucker DK, Livingston RL, Nakra R, et al. B-12 deficiency and psychiatric disorders: case report and literature review. Biological Psychiatry 1980; 16(2):197-204.

84. Evans DL, Edelsohn GA, Golden RN. Organic psychosis without anemia or spinal cord symptoms in patients with vitamin B-12 deficiency. Am J Psychiatry 1983; 140(2):218-20.

85. Skaug OE. Vitamin B-12 deficiency in mental disease. In: Walass O, ed. Molecular basis of some aspects of mental activity. New York: Academic Press, 1967:

86. Goggans FC. A case of mania secondary to vitamin B-12 deficiency. Am J Psychiatry 1984; 141:300-1.

87. Rimland B. An orthomolecular study of psychotic children. Orthomolecular Psychiatry 1974; 3(4):371-7.

88. Rimland B, Callaway E, Dreyfus P. The effect of high doses of vitamin B-6 on autistic children: a double-blind crossover study. Am J Psychiatry 1978; 135(4):472-5.

89. Lelord G, Callaway E, Muh JP, et al. Modifications in urinary homovanillic acid after ingestion of vitamin B-6; functional study in autistic children. Revue Neurologic (Paris) 1978; 134(2):797-801.

90. Small JG. Sensory evoked responses of autistic children. In: Churchill DW, Alpern GD, DeMyer M, eds. Infantile autism. Proceedings of the Indiana University Colloquium, Springfield: Charles C. Thomas, 1971:

91. Lelord G, Laffont F, Jusseaume P, et al. Comparative study of conditioning of averaged evoked responses by coupling sound and light in normal and autistic children. Psychophysiology 1973; 10:415-25.

92. Martineau J, Garreau B, Barthelemy C, et al. Effects of vitamin B-6 on average evoked potentials in infantile autism. Biological Psychiatry 1981; 16(7):627-41.

93. Ritvo ER, Yuwiler A, Geller E, et al. Increased blood serotonin and platelets in early infantile autism. Arch Gen Psychiatry 1970; 23:566-72.

94. Lake CR, Ziegler MG, Murphy DL. Increased norepinephrine levels and decreased dopamine-beta-hydroxylase activity in primary autism. Arch Gen Psychiatry 1977; 34:553-6.

95. Goldstein M, Muhanand D, Lee J, et al. Dopamine-beta-hydroxylase and endogenous total 5-hydroxyindoles levels in autistic patients and controls. In: Coleman M, ed. The autistic syndromes. North Holland Publishing Company, 1976:

96. Dohan FC, Grasberger JC, Lowell FM, et al. Relapsed schizophrenics: more rapid improvement on a milk and cereal-free diet. Brit J Psychiatry 1969; 115:595-6.

97. Singh MM, Kay SR. Wheat gluten as a pathogenic factor in schizophrenia. Science 1976; 191:401-2.

98. Trier JS. Celiac sprue. In: Sleisenger MH, Fordtran JS, eds. Gastrointestinal disease: Pathophysiology diagnosis management, third edition. Philadelphia/London: WB Saunders, 1983:

99. Dohan FC, Grasberger JC. Relapsed schizophrenics: earlier discharge from the hospital after cereal-free, milk-free diet. Am J Psychiatry 1973; 130(6):685-8.

100. Rice JR, Ham CH, Gore WE. Another look at gluten in schizophrenia. Am J Psychiatry 1978; 135(11):1417-8.

101. Potkin SG, Weinberger D, Kleinman J. Wheat gluten challenge in schizophrenic patients. Am J Psychiatry 1981; 138(9):1208-11.

102. Dohan FC. Wartime changes in hospital admissions for schizophrenia. Acta Psychiatrica Scandinavia 1966; 42:1-23.

103. Dohan FC. Cereals and schizophrenia — data and hypotheses. Acta Psychiatrica Scandinavia 1966; 42:125-52.

104. Dohan FC, Harper EH, Clark MH. Is schizophrenia rare if grain is rare? Biological Psychiatry 1984; 19(3):385-99.

105. Dohan FC. More on celiac disease as a model for schizophrenia (commentary). Biological Psychiatry 1983; 18(5):561-4.

106. Zioudrou C, Streaty RA, Klee WA. Opioid peptides derived from food proteins: the exorphins. The Journal of Biological Chemistry 1979; 254(7):2446-9.

107. Klee WA, Zioudrou C, Streaty RA. Exorphins, peptides with opioid activity, isolated from wheat gluten, and their possible role in the etiology of schizophrenia. In: Usdin E, ed. Endorphins in mental health research. New York: MacMillan Publishing Co, 1978:

108. Mycroft FJ, Wei ET, Bernardin JE, et al. MIF-like sequences in milk and wheat proteins (correspondence). N Engl J Med 1982; 307:895.

109. Ashkenazi A, Krasilowsky D, Levin S, et al. Immunologic reaction of psychotic patients to fractions of gluten. Am J Psychiatry 1979; 136(10):1306-9.

110. Hallert C, Derefeldt T. Psychic disturbances in adult celiac disease. I. Clinical observations. Scandinavian Journal of Gastroenterology 1982; 17:17-9.

111. Hallert C. Psychiatric illness, gluten, and celiac disease (editorial). Biological Psychiatry 1982; 17(9):959-60.

112. Hallert C, Astrom J, Walan A. Reversal of psychopathology in adult celiac disease with the aid of pyridoxine (vitamin B-6). Scandinavian Journal of Gastroenterology 1983; 18:299-304.

113. Hallert C, Sedvall G. Improvement in central monoamine metabolism in adult celiac patients starting a gluten-free diet. Psychological Medicine 1983; 13:267-71.

114. Reinken L, Zieglauer H. Vitamin B-6 absorption in children with acute celiac disease and in control subjects. Journal of Nutrition 1978; 108:1562-5.

115. Akiskal H, McKinney W. Depressive disorders: toward a unified hypothesis. Science 1973; 182:20-9.

116. Garver DL, Davis JM. Biogenic amine hypothesis of affective disorders. Life Sciences 1979; 24(5):383-94.

117. Weiner N. Drugs that inhibit adrenergic nerves and block adrenergic receptors. In: Gilman AG, Goodman LS, Gilman A, eds. The pharmacological basis of therapeutics, sixth edition. New York: MacMillan Publishing Co, 1980:

118. Baldessarini RJ. Drugs and the treatment of psychiatric disorders. In: The pharmacological basis of therapeutics, sixth edition, as above.

119. Bunney WE, Davis JM. Norepinephrine in depressive reactions. Arch Gen Psychiatry 1965; 13:483-94.

120. Schildkraut JJ. The catecholamine hypothesis of affective disorders: a review of supporting evidence. Am J Psychiatry 1965; 122:509-22.

121. Schildkraut JJ, Green A, Mooney J. Affective disorders: biochemical aspects. In: Kaplan HI, Sadock BJ, eds. Comprehensive textbook of psychiatry/IV, fourth edition. Baltimore/London: Williams and Wilkins, 1985:

122. Charney DS, Menkes DV, Phil M, et al. Receptor sensitivity and the mechanism of action of antidepressant treatment: implications for the etiology and therapy of depression. Arch Gen Psychiatry 1981; 38:1160-79.

123. McClure DJ. Biochemistry of depression (review). Canad Psychiatric Assn J 1971; 16:247-52.

124. Snyder SH, Yamamura HI. Antidepressants and the muscarinic acetylcholine receptor. Arch Gen Psychiatry 1977; 34:236-9.

125. Post RM, Ballenger JC. Neurobiology of mood disorders. In: Wood JH, Brooks BR, eds. Frontiers of clinical neuroscience, vol 1. Baltimore: 1984:

126. Carroll BJ, Feinberg M, Greden JF, et al. A specific laboratory test for the diagnosis of melancholia: standardization, validation, and clinical utility. Arch Gen Psychiatry 1981; 38:15-22.

127. Risch SC, Kalin NH, Murphy DL. Neurochemical mechanisms in the affective disorders and neuroendocrine correlates. J Clinical Psychopharmacology 1981; 1(4):180-5.

128. Leibowitz SF. Brain catecholaminergic mechanisms for control of hunger. In: Novin D, Wyrwicka W, Bray GA, eds. Hunger: Basic mechanisms and clinical implications. New York: Raven Press, 1976:

129. Hopkinson G. A neurochemical theory of appetite and weight changes in depressive states. Acta Psychiatrica Scandinavia 1981; 64:217-25.

130. Hatsukami DK, Mitchell JE, Eckert ED. Eating disorders: a variant of mood disorders. Psychiatric Clinics of North America 1984; 7(2):349-65.

131. Gelenberg AJ, Gibson CJ, Wojcik JD. Neurotransmitter precursors for the treatment of depression. Psychopharmacology Bulletin 1982; 18(1):7-18.

132. Axelrod J. Dopamine-beta-hydroxylase: regulation of its synthesis and release from nerve terminals. Pharmacological Review 1972, 24:233-43.

133. Van Praag HM. Management of depression with serotonin precursors. Biological Psychiatry 1981; 16:291-310.

134. Van Praag HM. In search of the mode of action of antidepressants: 5 HTP/tyrosine mixtures in depression. In: Usdin E, et al, eds. Frontiers in biochemical and pharmacological research in depression. New York: Raven Press, 1984:

135. DeMyer MK, Shea PA, Hendrie JC, et al. Plasma tryptophan and five other amino acids in depressed and normal subjects. Arch Gen Psychiatry 1981; 38:642-6.

136. Moller SE, Kirk L, Honore P. Relationship between plasma ratio of tryptophan to competing amino acids and the response to L-tryptophan treatment in endogenously depressed patients. Journal of Affective Disorders 1980; 2:47-59.

137. Moller SE, Larsen OB. Tryptophan and tyrosine availability: reaction to clinical response to antidepressive pharmacotherapy. In: Usdin E, et al, eds. Frontiers in biochemical and pharmacological research in depression. New York: Raven Press, 1984:

138. Gelenbert AJ, Wojcik JD, Gibson CJ, et al. Tyrosine for depression. Journal of Psychiatric Research 1982/83; 17:175-80.

139. Wurtman RJ, Larin F, Mostafapour S, et al. Brain catechol synthesis: controlled by brain tyrosine concentration. Science 1974; 185:183-4.

140. Wurtman RJ. Behavioral effects of nutrients. Lancet 1983; 1:1145-7.

141. Spano PF, Andreoli V, Tonon GC, et al. Plasma tryptophan transport in normal and depressed subjects. Medical Biology 1975; 53:489-92.

142. Branchey L, Branchey M, Shaw S, et al. Depression, suicide and aggression in alcoholics and their relationship to plasma amino acids. Psychiatry Reserach 1984; 12:219-26.

143. Brown GL, Ebert MH, Goyer PF, et al. Aggression, suicide and serotonin: relationship to CSF amine metabolites. Am J Psychiatry 1982; 139:741-6.

144. Winston F. Oral contraceptives, pyridoxine, and depression. Am J Psychiatry 1973; 130(11):1217-21.

145. Adams PW, Rose DP, Folkard J, et al. Effect of pyridoxine hydrochloride (vitamin B-6) upon depression associated with oral contraception. Lancet 1973;1:897-904.

146. Nobbs BT. Pyridoxal phosphate status in clinical depression. Lancet 1974; 1:405-6.

147. Stewart JW, Harrison W, Quitkin F, et al. Low B-6 levels in depressed outpatients. Biological Psychiatry 1984; 19(4):613-6.

148. Carney MWP, Wilhams DG, Sheffield BF. Thiamine and pyridoxine lack in newly-admitted psychiatric patients. Brit J Psychiatry 1979; 135:249-54.

149. Carney MWP, Ravindran A, Rinsler MG, et al. Thiamine, riboflavin, and pyridoxine deficiency in psychiatric in-patients. Brit J Psychiatry 1982; 141:271-2.

150. Shovron SD, Carney MWP, Chanarin I, et al. The neuropsychiatry of megaloblastic anemia. Brit Medical Journal 1980; 281:1036-42.

151. Ghadirian AM, Ananth J, Engelsmann F. Folic acid deficiency and depression. Psychosomatics 1980;21:926-9.

152. Botez MI, Young SN, Bachevalier J, et al. Effect of folic acid and vitamin B-12 deficiencies on 5-hydroxyindoleacetic acid in human cerebrospinal fluid. Annals of Neurology 1982:12(5):479-84.

153. Botez MI, Young SN, Bachevalier J, et al. Folate deficiency and a decreased brain 5-hydroxythryptamine synthesis in man and rat. Nature 1979; 278:182-3.

154. Prakash R, Petrie WM. Psychiatric changes associated with an excess of folic acid. Am J Psychiatry 1982; 139(9):1192-3.

155. Ordonez LA, Wurtman RJ. Folic acid deficiency and methyl group metabolism in rat brain: effects of L-dopa. Archives of Biochemistry and Biophysics 1974; 160:372-6.

156. Agnoli A, Andreoli V, Casacchia M, et al. Effect of s-adenosyl-l-methionine (SAMe) upon depressive symptoms. J Psychiatric Research 1976; 13:43-54.

157. Miccoli L, Pooro V, Bertolino A. Comparison between the antidepressant activity of s-adenosyl-l-methionine (SAMe) and that of some tricyclic drugs. Acta Neurologica 1978; 33:243-55.

158. Reynolds EH, Carney MWP, Toone BK. Methylation and mood. Lancet 1984; 2:196-8.

Chapter 33

Menstrual Cycle Variation in Food Intake

Douglas G. Kahn

INTRODUCTION

Variations in a number of human behaviors during the menstrual cycle are well known. The luteal phase, compared with the follicular phase, has a well-documented increase in the incidence of depression, accidents, hospital admission, suicidal thinking, and suicide. The immediate premenstrual and menstrual period in women is associated with an increased frequency of examination failure, work absenteeism, development of acute psychiatric symptoms, commission of crimes, accidents, attempted suicide, and death by accident or suicide [1,2].

The effect of food intake and body weight, lean mass/fat ratio and emotional stress on the menstrual cycle is well known (for example, the suppression of menstruation with anorexia nervosa or other starvation) [3-9]. Less well known and less frequently studied is the effect of the menstrual cycle on food intake and eating behavior. In mammals studied to date, including humans, there is a significant cyclic variation in food intake and taste preference during the menstrual cycle.

This chapter reviews the literature of the past 30 to 40 years on menstrual cycle variation in food intake and eating behavior. Studies on lower mammals (hamsters, gerbils, rats, mice, pigs, goats, and sheep) as well as subhuman primates and human studies are reported. These variations are considered significant for treatment planning in patients with eating disorders and for research on mechanisms of eating behavior and taste preference.

SUBPRIMATE MAMMALS

Most studies on variation in food intake during the estrus cycle (which lasts 4 to 5 days) have been done in the laboratory rat. Since the 1940s numerous reports have demonstrated that endogenous ovarian estrogens reduce food intake and body weight in a cyclic fashion correlated with vaginal estrus, decreased body temperature, and increased activity [10-16]. Ovariectomy results in increased food intake and body weight more than in sham-operated animals and this effect is reversed by exogenous estradiol replacement [17].

Dalvit [18] summarizes the most important findings in laboratory rats as follows:

1. Estradiol appears to be the principal ovarian hormone for regulating body weight.
2. During proestrus, when estradiol is at its peak, food intake and body weight decrease.
3. During diestrus, when progesterone is high and estrogen is low, food intake and weight increase.
4. Female rats have a higher saccharin preference than males due to the stimulatory effect of ovarian hormones.
5. After ovariectomy, meal size increases, but treatment with estradiol causes a return to control level.
6. In intact female rats, treatment with progesterone causes an increase in feeding and body weight.
7. There is no change in feeding following progesterone administration to ovariectomized rats.

Coling and Herberg [19] found increased food hoarding activity after ovariectomy paralleling the increased body weight. Injection of estradiol benzoate (EB) counteracted the increases in body weight and hoarding activity as did normal estrus; progesterone and testosterone were without effect. They concluded that "estrogen-dependent changes in body weight were caused, at least in part, by a lowering of the regulated level of body weight, and that circulating estrogen (was) responsible for this." They also observed the direct non-regulating restriction of food caused by endogenous estrogen in free feeding normally cycling female rats.

Sandberg et al [20] found the injection of EB in ovariectomized (OVX) rats led to an immediate but transient suppression in both food and ethanol intake, with almost identical magnitude and time course.

The mechanism by which the preovulatory estrogen increase at proestrus proves anorexic is not known, but is presumed to be, at least in part, an intensification of short-term satiation of hunger. Drewett [10] reported that anorectic effect of the estrogen peak was limited to a reduction in meal size. Meal size on the night of estrus was reduced about 40% and associated with this was a reduction in intrameal intervals—both differences were statistically significant. Because food intake was reduced by estradiol doses too low to stimulate sexual receptivity, this decrease in food intake is not caused by the correlative increase in sexual receptivity of proestrus.

Dalvit [21] cites Wurtman, who found that rats reduce total food intake and carbohydrate intake at estrus but not their protein intake, a finding replicated in OVX rats injected with estradiol. Gray and Greenwood [22] found that progesterone attenuated estrogen-induced effects on OVX rats (including decreased body weight and carcass lipid content). Mueller and Hsiao [12] reported that estrogenic regulation of body weight was the result of two mechanisms: decreased food intake (a direct effect) and modulation of anonasal growth. They found that induced weight gain in OVX rats is largely independent of food intake, thus challenging the hypothesis that estradiol decreased body weight by lowering the set point for body weight. Since their OVX animals gained weight independent of changes in food intake, they postulated that estrogen also alters metabolic processes by direct action on peripheral tissues or by action on areas of the brain regulating metabolic processes in addition to its short-term feeding-related effect (explained by a model whereby circulating estrogens bind to hypothalamic receptors to decrease food intake and indirectly lower body weight).

Nance [13] suggested that estrogen modulated feeding behavior by both hypothalamic and extrahypothalamic mechanisms. He suggested that fats and proteins may modify feeding behavior independent of

the hypothalamus and supported a primary role in neural regulation of feeding by carbohydrate mechanisms. Young et al [15] found that the factor determining response to estradiol could be altered in magnitude and dissociated from body weight by feeding different diets. Rats fed high-fat diets responded more to estradiol benzoate than did rats given chow or high-dextrose diets, and these responses were not the result of increased body weight.

Bartness and Waldbillig [23] studied intact estrus cycling rats, OVX rats, OVX rats given EB, and found no variation in total caloric intake or body weight during the estrus cycle in intact cycling rats given access to an isocaloric diet triplet of fat, carbohydrate, and protein. They did find a change in diet selection: fat intake increased, while carbohydrate and protein (to a lesser extent) decreased during estrus ... the opposite selection occurred during diestrus.

HAMSTERS AND GERBILS

Morin and Fleming [24] found a similar systematic variation of food intake and body weight with the normal estrus cycle, OVX, and EB treatment in the hamster (and noted that the same has been reported in rats, guinea pigs, and mice). They found food intake and body weight were lowest when endogenous estrogen levels were elevated. They also found a greater fluctuation in body weight than could be predicted solely by the weight of food consumed (consistent with work they cited in female rats), thus supporting studies suggesting that estradiol may in part decrease body weight independent of the direct restriction in food intake. Zucker and Wade [25] reported that estradiol failed to affect eating and body weight in female hamsters.

Observing the conflict between their study and others (including that of Zucker and Wade), Morin and Fleming suggest that rats are more sensitive than hamsters to the effect of estradiol benzoate and that subthreshold doses of estradiol benzoate may have been used in other hamster studies. They also criticized the statistical measures used in other studies.

In concurrence with the studies of Morin and Fleming, Miceli and Fleming [26] found that estrogenic effects on food intake in hamsters were the same as those described in the rat, but were limited to specific dietary constituents. Thus estradiol decreased fat consumption without a strong effect on protein intake. However, in contrast to rats, hamsters did not show cyclic ovarian-dependent variations in carbohydrate intake.

In the only available study on gerbils, Roy found that estrogen increases body weight and food intake [27].

PRIMATES

Female primates also show a cyclic variation in food intake systematically associated with ovarian changes (levels of endogenous estrogen) during the menstrual cycle [18]. A significant decrease in food intake occurred midway through the menstrual cycle (periovulatory) and during the preovulatory phase (follicular) as compared with the postovulatory (luteal) phase, in Rhesus monkeys [27,18,28] and Chacma baboons [30].

Rosenblatt [31] found that the significant decrease in amount of food consumed correlated well with the midcycle estrogen surge, and that the amount of food consumed during the luteal phase was greater than that of the earlier follicular phase. This resulted mainly from a change in meal size. The injection of estradiol into OVX primates causes a similar depression of food intake [18].

Czaja [28] studied 202 female Rhesus monkeys for completion of meals and incidence of food rejection during nonpregnant menstrual cycles and during pregnancy. He found that food rejection incidence was greatest around the expected time of ovulation and that food rejection also "rose sharply during the third through the fifth weeks of pregnancy and tapered off during the next six weeks." He observed a positive correlation between the incidence of food rejection and the levels of circulating estrogens but not of progesterone. The similarity of food rejection during early Rhesus pregnancy to feeding changes that accompany morning sickness during early human pregnancy was noted. Morning sickness in humans is more frequently reported while estrogen levels are rising and progesterone levels declining in a time course parallel to that seen in the Rhesus monkey in early pregnancy.

Bielert and Busse [30] studied the effects of ovarian hormones on the food intake and feeding of normal, captive, wild, and OVX captive Chacma baboons. They found a significant decrease in follicular phase (preovulatory) food intake versus luteal phase (postovulatory) food intake. Exogenous estradiol benzoate inhibited food intake in OVX females. No effects of progesterone were demonstrated. These effects were independent of mating activity.

Both Dalvit [18] and Czaja [28] comment on prior studies done by Gilbert and Gilman [32] in baboons, in which Gilbert and Gilman hypothesized that progesterone in the luteal phase acted as a appetite stimulant. Czaja [28] cites more recent work refuting such a progesterone effect. He notes that progesterone antagonizes estrogen effects, and that exogenous EB (but not progesterone) has a significant influence on feeding levels in OVX Rhesus monkeys.

HUMANS (NORMAL MENSTRUAL CYCLE)

The normal physiology and neuroendocrine regulation of the human menstrual cycle is well documented. The circulating levels of hormones of the hypothalamic-pituitary axis are well known during all phases of the menstrual cycle [33-39]. Only a very few studies, however, describe the variation in food intake during the menstrual cycle in humans.

Dalvit [18] studied the self-reported dietary intakes of eight human females for 60 days (two menstrual cycles). She found that food intake averaged approximately 500 calories more per day during the ten days following ovulation than during the ten days before ovulation. This variation in food intake correlates with the estrogen levels that begin to rise at menstruation, and begin to fall after ovulation.

Dalvit-McPhillips [21] published an analysis of more of her data from this same study, looking at the differences in carbohydrate, fat, and protein consumption. She found significant and consistent variation during the menstrual cycle only in carbohydrate consumption, not in fat or protein. Her data showed that women consumed more carbohydrate per day in the postovulatory phase than in the preovulatory phase. The mean preovulatory carbohydrate intake was between 51.6% and 56.4% of the mean postovulatory consumption. Noting the parallel variation in basal metabolic rates (increased postovulation, sudden drop with onset of menses, preovulatory rise), she postulated this increased carbohydrate intake may be an attempt to compensate for the change in basal metabolic rate. She also noted the well-described anorectic effect of estrogen levels in other mammalian species. She suggested that increased carbohydrate intake elevated blood glucose levels, inducing increased levels of serotonin in the brain.

Dalvit suggested that a more useful diet strategy in the treatment of eating disorders would be to increase carbohydrate and caloric consumption seven to ten days before menstruation rather than "rigidly adhere to a sub-optimal caloric level at the time when the body's physiological needs are increased" [21].

Pliner and Fleming [17] studied self-reported food intake, body weight, and sweetness preference in 34 women. Both food intake and body weight were significantly higher during the luteal phase than during the follicular phase as measured at the midpoint of each phase. The mean caloric intake in the luteal phase was approximately 223 calories greater than the mean caloric intake of the follicular phase. Sixty-six percent of their women showed an increase in food intake in the luteal phase (independent of premenstrual fluid retention); 71% showed an increase in body weight.

Weizenbaum et al [40] found that short menses females (menstrual periods less than or equal to five days) had increased food intake during the luteal phase, whereas long menses females (menstrual period greater than five days) did not.

Abraham et al [3] reported a study of variations in self-reported nutrient intake (carbohydrate, fat, protein, and calories) during the menstrual cycle in 23 normal women over a 35-day period. They found that "the relationship between day of cycle and intake was most obvious in respect to protein." Protein intake decreased most three days before the onset of menses. Phillips and Phillips [41] severely criticized the manipulation and adjustment of data in Abraham's study, however, and felt that the statistical measures used were inadequate.

Psychosocial factors may also cause menstrual cycle variations in food preference (and thus perhaps in intake). Snow and Johnson [42] in an article about folkloric beliefs about menstruation, report that a number of women prefer to alter their diet during the menstrual cycle. Some Central and South American women and black and southern white women believe that ingesting certain foods at the time of menstruation will result in impeded blood flow, as these foods cause blood clotting and thus disease (arthritis, being "run down").

Latin American women designate foods (and medications) as "hot" or "cold" (properties unrelated to temperature, texture, or spiciness) and avoid "cold" foods and medications on the basis of cultural beliefs at different times. The avoidance of cold foods during "la dieta"—a 40-day period of postpartum restriction—may lead to vitamin deficiency during a period of nutritional stress, since "cold" foods include citrus, tomatoes, and leafy greens. Similar cultural food avoidance has been described in Haitian, Puerto Rican, and Malaga women as well as in Cubans and Caribbean Island subcultures [42,43]. No attempt was made in either of these studies to determine whether overall food intake varied as a result of these belief-stimulated alterations in food preference.

HUMANS: VARIATION WITH PREMENSTRUAL TENSION SYNDROME

Since the 1940s several investigators have reported alterations in food preference and food intake associated with premenstrual tension syndrome (PMS) [14,18,26,28,43-46].

Smith and Sauder [47] studied a group of 300 nurses by self-report questionnaire. They found an association between a craving for food and/or sweets and premenstrual feelings of depression or tension. They also found "an association between craving at specific times (ie, during menstrual periods or depression) and the occurrence of premenstrual fluid retention" and "the desire

to eat compulsively and the tendency to be depressed more frequently." Their "sweets-craving group" differed from 30% of the subjects, who developed a craving for spicy foods and tomatoes but not for sweets. Both Smith and Sauder and Dalvit [18] reviewed prior studies done by Morton, who found that 37% of the women complaining of PMS had a craving for sweets and 23% had increased appetite at this time, and by Fortin, Wittkower, and Katz, who studied 45 women, 25 of whom had premenstrual symptoms and listed a craving for sweets as one of the most frequently reported phenomena. In summary, most studies report an increased craving for sweets in association with PMS.

A brief review article in the British Medical Journal [2] cited excessive thirst and appetite as among the symptoms of premenstrual syndrome and noted that PMS may persist after the menopause and is unaffected by age or parity. Endicott [45] noted that "...within a group of women with premenstrual full depressive syndrome, 35% described themselves as hypersomnic and tending to overeat."

Abraham [48] divided the premenstrual syndrome into several symptom-complex subgroups. His subgroup PMT-C is characterized by "the premenstrual craving for sweets, increased appetite and indulgence in eating refined sugar followed by palpitations, fatigue, fainting spells, headaches and sometimes the shakes." He reviewed Moo's menstrual stress questionnaire, which asked about changes in eating habits. Abraham asked about increased appetite, craving for sweets, and craving for salt. He found that 35% of premenstrual tension symptom patients could be classified as Group PMT-C. Budoff [44] mentioned that premenstrual symptoms are known to include food cravings.

Hamilton et al [49] noted that changes in appetite, including food cravings or avoidance, episodes of bulimia or binge-purge cycles, and altered patterns of drug or alcohol abuse have been reported premenstrually.

Price and Giannini [46] reported a 26-year-old woman whose two-to four-day menstrual period binge eating extended over all menses for a 12-year period, with a resultant weight gain of 2 to 4 kg in each episode. Their patient reported that binge eating alleviated feelings of anxiety, cramping, and restlessness. They also cited a report by Billiard, who described a 13-year-old girl with menstruation-linked hypersomnia and hyperphagia beginning three days before the onset of menstruation.

Price and Giannini postulated an endorphin withdrawal-mediated etiology of PMS based on their finding that a decline in beta endorphin levels correlated with severity of premenstrual symptoms. In possible support of an endogenous opiate-mediated mechanism for stress-induced premenstrual (or other) increased food intake is a study by Roland and Antelman and a correlative study by Morley and Levine. Roland and Antelman [29] induced mild nonspecific stress in the laboratory rat by mild tail pinching. Tail pinch predictably elicited the syndrome of eating, gnawing, and licking in sated rats, with short latency and without obvious pain. These rats preferred highly palatable fluids and familiar foods. Furthermore, such stress elicited a generalized responsiveness to the environmental stimuli at hand (rat pups precipitated maternal behavior; receptive females precipitated mounting; absence of stimulus object precipitated washing, grooming, and nail pulling). Stress-induced hyperphagia and resultant obesity were consistent outcomes of tail-pinching when food was available ad libitum. The similarity between this rat behavior and stress-induced hyperphagia and obesity in humans (premenstrual, depressed, or other) is recognized. Morley and Levine [50] demonstrated the inhibition of tail-pinch-induced eating by the opiate antagonist naloxone. This inhibition of tail-pinch-induced eating was not replicated by saline or Diazepam, both of which increased the amount of food ingested.

Budoff [44] suggested that prostaglandins may play a part in the regulation of food intake (as well as body water content and body temperature). Budoff noted that several prostaglandins have affected the food intake of rats when they were given systematically, and prostaglandin E-1 had been reported to inhibit food intake when injected into specific sites in the rat hypothalamus. In sheep the prostaglandin E-1 both suppressed and stimulated food intake depending on injection site [44]. Abraham [48] suggests that the deficiency of prostaglandin and prostaglandin E-1 might be involved in the PMT-C subgroup of women with increased sweet and food cravings.

Giannini and Price, in a recent publication [56], reported finding "a relationship between caloric intake and severity of premenstrual tension symptoms. Women who reported more severe symptoms recorded higher caloric intake." They also found that caloric intake during the premenstrual period increased with age. They did not report the magnitude of the increased caloric intake. Their method was to divide their subjects into high and low intake groups according to whether they fell above or below the median level of caloric intake for the study groups. The median level was derived from the arithmetic difference between the caloric intake 10 days premenstrually and 10 days post-menstrually. Subjects with greater change tended to have more severe PMS (CHI^2 = 5.20, p < .05). They found no relationship between caloric intake and progression of the menstrual cycle in their study.

MENSTRUAL CYCLE VARIATION IN TASTE PERCEPTION

Generally, female laboratory rats are known to have a higher saccharin preference than male rats because of the stimulatory effects of ovarian hormones [11,18,26]. This phenomenon is more pronounced in young rats than in old rats [30]. Similar sex differences in the preference for, or consumption of, sweet solutions have been demonstrated in hamsters and in human infants [25].

Sweetness preference in adult human females during the menstrual cycle has been observed in the fasting state and before and after glucose loads. Weizenbaum et al [40] studied sucrose pleasantness ratings in 25 females and five males studied over a five-week period. They found that males and long-menses (greater than five days menstrual period) females exhibited similar patterns, and their patterns were significantly different than that of the short-menses (menstrual period less than or equal to five days) females. Short menses females rated sucrose pleasantness significantly higher overall but did not vary during phases of the menstrual cycle.

Pliner and Fleming [17] measured sucrose sweetness preference before and after a glucose load in 41 women. They found that during the luteal phase of the menstrual cycle there was a marked decrease in pleasantness ratings following the glucose load (negative alliesthesia), and no such decrease in the follicular phase. They explained this by citing evidence that following a glucose load, glucose clearance from the blood is slower during the luteal phase than during the follicular phase, and since blood glucose levels are correlated with preferences for sugar solutions, this negative alliesthesia would be expected.

Wright and Crow [37] studied 94 normal, nonobese women. They found that the affective response (pleasantness ratings) to sugar varied significantly over the course of the menstrual cycle. They found that in the luteal phase (postovulatory), but not including the immediate premenstrual period, subjects found sugar solutions significantly less pleasant than subjects tested at other phases of the cycle (menses, preovulatory, ovulatory, and premenstrual). They also found that a significant postglucose load decrease in perceived sweetness pleasantness occurred in all subjects except those in the ovulatory phase. They note that their observed luteal decrease in sugar preference corresponds to the mid-luteal progesterone peak, and the postglucose load ovulatory decrease corresponds to the high estrogen levels. They conclude that further research in taste preference, food intake, weight gain, and hormone levels in the menstrual cycle needs to be done. Their work has been supported by Aaron's study [51].

Studies of salt preference have been performed in two species. Salt preference was studied during the estrus cycle of sheep by Michell [52], who found a maximum sodium preference six days before estrus (luteal phase), which was statistically significant when compared with six days postestrus. Kumanyika and Jones [53] studied ad lib table salt use in 24 men on a fixed daily menu constant caloric diet and 13 women on a fixed daily menu but varied caloric diet (varied with cookies only). They found "a high degree of intraindividual consistency in salt use week to week and among the women, across menstrual phases." This consistency across menstrual cycle phases in women was unexpected. They caution that if variation does occur, it may only occur in women eating ad libitum and may vary with caloric intake or diet composition, which have known menstrual cycle phase variation.

Taste sensitivity to quinine and 6-N-propylthiouracil (PROP) was studied in 19 women during one or more menstrual cycles by Glanville and Kaplan [54]. They measured taste thresholds (the lowest concentrations of the compounds that could be distinguished from water) and compared three phases of the cycle: premenstrual, menstrual, and postmenstrual. They found that in the majority of women thresholds tended to be significantly lower (more sensitive) during the menstrual period.

Henkin [55] studied sensory detection acuity for taste, smell, hearing, light, touch, and two-point discrimination during the menstrual cycle in five normal women. He found that sensory detection acuity was greater for all studied senses during the follicular phase than during the luteal phase whether cycles were long (greater than 28 days) or short (less than 28 days). He posited that "the relative increase in sensory detection acuity may be related to the effects of estrogen or progesterone on either receptor, nerve, or central nervous system activity."

SUMMARY

Almost all studies in mammalian species (humans, primates, and subprimate mammals) show systematic variation in food intake, diet selection, and/or taste preference during the menstrual cycle. The empirical evidence describes a luteal phase increase in caloric consumption. Further research is indicted in humans to validate this phenomenon, and to identify alterations in taste preference and nutrient appetites (carbohydrates vs fats vs proteins) in both the normal menstrual cycle and premenstrual tension syndrome.

Dietary strategies that respect and reflect this luteal phase increase in food intake should decrease demoralization, enhance dietary compliance and thus foster success.

REFERENCES

1. Wetzel RD, et al. Premenstrual symptoms in self-referrals to a suicide prevention service. Brit J Psychiat 1971; 119:525-6.
2. Premenstrual symptoms. British Medical Journal, London 1973; 33:689-90.
3. Abraham JF, et al. Nutrient intake and the menstrual cycle. Aust N Z J Med 1981; 11:210-1.
4. Calloway DH, Kurzer MS. Menstrual cycle and protein requirements in women. J Nutrition 1982;112:356-66.
5. Check J. Emotional aspects of menstrual dysfunction. Psychosomatics 1978; 19:178-84.
6. Frisch RE, McArthur JW. Menstrual cycles: Fatness as a determinant of minimum weight for height necessary for their maintenance or onset. Science 1974; 185:949-51.
7. Garfinkel PE, Garner DM. Menstrual disorders and anorexia nervosa. Psychiatric Annals 1984; 14:442-6.
8. Hill P, et al. Diet, lifestyle and menstrual activity. Am J Clin Nutri 1980; 33:1192-8.
9. Russell GFM. Psychological and nutritional facts in disturbances of menstrual function and ovulation. Postgraduate Med J 1972; 48:10-3.
10. Drewett RF. The meal patterns of oestrous cycle and their motivational significance. J Exp Psychol 1974; 26:489-94.
11. Lfau H-P, Peng M-T. Suppressive effects of estrogen on food intake and body weight in senile female rats. J Formosan Med Assoc 1982; 81:848-56.
12. Mueller K, Hsaio S. Estrus- and ovariectomy-induced body weight changes: evidence for two estrogenic mechanisms. J Compara and Pysiol Psychol 1980; 94:1126-34.
13. Nance DM. The developmental and neural determinants of the effects of estrogen on feeding behavior in the rat: A theoretical perspective. Neurosci & Biobehav Rev 1983; 7:189-211.
14. Sfikakis A, et al. Implication of the estrous cycle on conditioned avoidance behavior in the rat. Physiol & Behav 1978; 21:441-6.
15. Young JK, et al. Dietary effects upon food and water intake and responsiveness to estrogen, 2-deoxy-glucose and glucose in female rats. Physiol & Behav 1978; 21:395-403.
16. Young JK, et al. Effects of estrogen upon feeding inhibition produced by intragastric glucose loads. Physiol & Behav 1978; 21:423-30.
17. Pliner P, Fleming AS. Food intake, body weight, and sweetness preferences over the menstrual cycle in humans. Physiol & Behav 1983; 30:663-6.
18. Dalvit SP. The effect of the menstrual cycle on patterns of food intake. Am J Clin Nutri 1981; 34:1811-5.
19. Coling JG, Herberg LJ. Effect of ovarian and exogenous hormones on defended body weight, actual body weight, and the paradoxical hoarding of food by female rats. Physiol & Behav 1982; 29:687-91.
20. Sandberg D, et al. Effects of estradiol benzoate on the pattern of eating and ethanol consumption. Physiol &

Behav 1982; 29:61-5.

21. Dalvit-McPhillips SP. The effect of the human menstrual cycle on nutrient intake. Physiol & Behav 1983; 31:209-12.

22. Gray JM, Greenwood MRC. Time course of effects of ovarian hormones on food intake and metabolism. Am J Physiol 1982; 243:E407-12.

23. Bartness TV, Waldbillig RJ. Dietary self-selection in intact, ovariectomized and estradiol-treated female rats. Behav Neuros 1984; 98:125-37.

24. Morin LP, Fleming AS. Variation of food intake and body weight with estrous cycle, orariectomy, and estradiol benzoate treatment in hamsters (mesocritus auratus). J Compar and Physiol Psychol 1978; 92:1-6.

25. Zucker I, Wade et al. Sexual and hormonal influences on eating, taste preference, and body weight of hamsters. Physiol & Behav 1972; 8:101-1.

26. Miceli MO, Fleming AS. Variation of fat intake with estrous cycle, ovariectomy and estradiol replacement in hamsters (mesocritus auratus) eating a fractionated diet. Physiol & Behav 1983; 30:415-20.

27. Roy EJ, et al. Central action and a species comparison of the estrogenic effects of an antiestrogen on eating and body weight. Physiol & Behav 1977; 18:137-40.

28. Czaja JA. Food rejection by female Rhesus monkeys during the menstrual cycle and early pregnancy. Physiol & Behav 1975; 14:579-87.

29. Rowland NE, Antelman SM. Stress-induced hyperphagia and obesity in rats: A possible model for understanding human obesity. Science 1976; 191:310.

30. Bielert C, Busse C. Influences of ovarian hormones on the food intake and feeding of captive and wild female chacma baboons (Papio Ursinus). Physiol & Behav 1983; 30:103-11.

31. Rosenblatt H, et al. Food intake and the menstrual cycle in Rhesus monkeys. Physiol & Behav 1980; 24:447-9.

32. Gilbert C, Gillman J. The changing pattern of food intake and appetite during the menstrual cycle of the baboon (Papio Ursinus) with a consideration of some of the controlling endocrine factors. S Afr J Med Sci 1956; 21:75-88.

33. Hirsch J. Hypothalamic control of appetite. Hospital Practice 1984; 2:131-8.

34. Katz JL. Psychiatric and endocrinology: An expanding interface. Psychiatric Quarterly 1979; 51:198-208.

35. Kennedy CG. The regulation of food intake. Adv Psychosomatic Med 1972; 7:91-9.

36. Stevenson JS. Paramenstrual craving and hormone levels. ANA Publ 1978; 23: 679-84.

37. Wright P, Crow RA. Menstrual cycle: Effects on sweetness preferences in women. Hormones and Behavior 1973; 4:387-91.

38. Yen SSC. Neuroendocrine regulation of the menstrual cycle. Hospital Practice 1979; 3:83-97.

39. Yen SSC, et al. Hormonal relationships during the menstrual cycle. JAMA 1970; 211:1513-7.

40. Weizenbaum F, et al. Relationship among reproductive variables, sucrose taste reactivity and feeding be-

havior in humans. Physiol & Behav 1980; 24:1053-6.

41. Phillips PR, Phillips PJ. Nutrient intake and the menstrual cycle. Aust N Z J Med 1982; 12:211.

42. Snow LF, Johnson SM. Modern day menstrual folklore—Some clinical implications. JAMA 1977; 237:2736-9.

43. Snow LF. Traditional health beliefs and practices among lower class Black Americans. West J Med 1983; 139:820-8.

44. Budoff PW. The use of prostaglandin inhibitors for the premenstrual syndrome. J Reprod Med 1983; 28:469-78.

45. Endicott J. PMS studies explore depression links. In: Psychiatric News. June 1984.

46. Price WA, Giannini AJ. Binge eating during menstruation (letter). J Clin Psych 1983; 44:431.

47. Snmith SL, Sauder C. Food cravings, depression, and premenstrual problems. Psychosomatic Med 1969; XXXI:281-7.

48. Abraham G. Nutritional factors in the etiology of the premenstrual tension syndromes. Journal of Reproductive Medicine 1983; 28:446-64.

49. Hamilton JA, et al. Premenstrual mood changes: A guide to evaluation and treatment. Psychiatric Annals 1984; 14:426-36.

50. Morley JE, Levine AS. Stress-induced eating is mediated through endogenous opiates. Science 1980; 209:1259-60.

51. Aaron M. Effect of the menstrual cycle on subjective ratings of sweetness. Perceptual and Motor Skills 1974; 40:974.

52. Michell AR. Changes in sodium appetite during the estrous cycle of sheep. Physiol & Behav 1975; 14:223-6.

53. Kumanyika SK, Jones EY. Patterns of week-to-week table salt use by men and women consuming constant diets. Human Nutri: Appl Nutri 1983; 37A:348-56.

54. Glanville EW, Kaplan AR. Taste perception and the menstrual cycle. Nature 1965; 205:930-1.

55. Henkin RI. Sensory changes during the menstrual cycle. In: Ferin M, ed. Biorhythms in human reproduction. 1974: 277-85.

56. Giannini AJ, Price WA et al. Hyperphagia in Premenstrual Tension Syndrome. J Clin Psyuchiatry 1985; 46:10:436-438.

Chapter 34

Significance of Eating Disorders in Oncologic Diagnosis and Treatment

Rowan T. Chlebowski*

INTRODUCTION

Weight loss in patients with advanced cancer has been recognized clinically for many years. More recently the development of weight loss prior to treatment has been shown to be an important factor prognostic of decreased survival in patients with this disease. DeWys and colleagues [1] reported a study involving more than 3,000 patients entered on protocols of the Eastern Cooperative Oncology Group with advanced cancer. In this experience the frequency of significant weight loss varied from 40% in breast cancer patients to more than 80% in patients with pancreatic or gastric cancer. The median survival of patients with weight loss was significantly shorter than that of patients with no weight loss for tumors originating from a variety of sites including lung, colon, prostate, gastric, breast, and sarcomas [1]. The influence of weight loss on survival was independent of tumor extent and performance status as well. In lung cancer, the leading cause of cancer death in the United States, several studies have reported that approximately 50% of patients experience weight loss at the time of their initial presentation [1-3]. In both small cell and nonsmall cell lung cancer, the median survival of patients with weight loss was half that of patients who were within 5%

of their usual weight [2]. Even when stage, histologic factors, and treatment were taken into account, weight loss significantly influenced lung cancer patient survival. In one report, anthropometric assessment of nutritional status was an even more sensitive prognostic factor in this population [4]. Thus, accumulating data supports the concept that pretreatment weight loss, representing an alteration in nutritional status, is an important, independent factor prognostic of decreased survival in patients with a variety of cancers.

Taken from a somewhat different perspective, weight loss as a clinical presentation is commonly associated with a diagnosis of cancer. In a series of 91 patients presenting with involuntary weight loss as a major clinical problem, a diagnosis of underlying malignancy was found in 19% [5]. Cancer represented the most common diagnosis in 65% of patients found to have a physical cause for weight loss in this report. However, almost all patients with cancer were detected during initial evaluation, and occult cancer as a cause of weight loss was rare. Thus, weight loss is not only prognostic of a poor outcome in patients with proven cancer but may well be an indicator of the presence of cancer in an adult population as well.

The factors underlying the development of weight loss in the patient with cancer (cancer cachexia) are mul-

* Studies reported in this chapter were supported in part by the General Clincal Research Center Grant RR-00425, NIH, Grant CA-37320 from the NCI, NIH, and Grant RD-163 from the American Cancer Society.

tifactorial [6-9] and incompletely understood at the present time. Simplistically stated, the cause of cancer cachexia may be related to a failure of the patient to ingest sufficient nutrients to meet the host metabolic requirements. In fact, cancer patient populations have been demonstrated to have reduced caloric intakes, an increased energy requirement, and a variety of abnormal metabolic processes [6-9]. Details of such changes seen in the cancer-bearing host are outlined in this chapter.

ANOREXIA

Anorexia leading to a decreased caloric intake has been recognized clinically for many years in patients with cancer [10]. Suggested factors [8,11-14] contributing to anorexia in this situation include: alterations of taste sensation, psychological influence of a cancer diagnosis, metabolic products and hypothetical tumor toxins, as well as direct effects on the appetite center. Once treatment for cancer is under way, anorexia may result from complications of chemotherapy or radiation treatment as well [6,8,15].

The older concept that the weight loss in cancer patients is related to the "tumor feeding on the host" can be severely challenged when one considers that in the usual clinical situation, tumor burdens rarely exceed 1% of a host body mass [16,17]. Thus, the suggestion that changes in tumor metabolism are of sufficient magnitude to alter overall host energy balance cannot be easily supported. Only limited information on the CNS food intake control mechanism in patients with cancer and weight loss is available. In animal models, the hypothalamic components of control of food intake appear not to be affected by the presence of tumor [10,14]. Hypotheses implicating derangements in the serotoninergic system in the regulation of feeding behavior in the cancer-bearing host have been proposed but have undergone limited clinical evaluation [18]. At present then, little direct evidence suggests a major role for central control of weight loss development in the patient with cancer.

TASTE ABNORMALITIES IN CANCER PATIENTS

Alteration in taste perception is one factor that has undergone considerable evaluation in the cancer patient population. Cancer patients have reported a general reduction in the pleasant taste of food and negative taste sensations related to specific foods [19,20]. More quantitative efforts in this area have included determination of taste recognition and detection thresholds for salt, sweet, sour, and bitter taste sensations.

Although most trials in this area have been small, involving fewer than 50 patients, several characteristic abnormalities have been described [20-25]. Although some investigators reported the increased taste recognition threshold for bitter taste [20,25,26], the most consistent abnormality seen is an increased taste recognition for sweet substances, occurring in approximately one third of patients tested with a variety of tumors [9,20]. In several of these studies, the presence of abnormal taste sensation has been associated with decreased caloric intake [20,27]. DeWys and Walters [20] reported, in addition, a correlation between tumor extent and sensitivity of taste sensation abnormality in cancer patients. Patients determined to have only a limited tumor burden had no taste threshold abnormalities (in nine cases) compared with patients determined to have extensive tumor involvement where 15 of 20 patients had abnormalities of taste detected. Similar abnormalities of taste can be independently reproduced by radiation therapy as well. Mossman and coworkers [28] serially assessed taste sensation in a series of patients who had received radiation one to seven years previously for tumors of the head and neck. Sixty-nine percent of patients had measurable taste loss. The authors estimated that the maximal tolerance doses resulting in a 50% complication rate five years after treatment was between 50 and 65 gy for taste loss. Such changes may reflect direct damage to taste receptors as well as interference with salivary function, since in another prospective study over 80% of radiation-treated patients with tumors of the oral cavity noted complications of taste loss and/or dry mouth. Of interest was the observation that 25% of patients experienced similar complications before initiation of radiation therapy as a consequence of their tumor [29].

An intriguing but unexplained observation in patients receiving radiation treatment is the relatively common development of appetite perversions and taste changes triggered or abolished by radiotherapy given at sites distant from the oropharynx. Brewin [30] has reported that 147 of 819 oncology patients questioned reported that local tumor radiation, regardless of tumor type, site, or volume radiated, either triggered (in 97 cases) or abolished (in 50 cases) an isolated appetite perversion. These changes occurred early in the treatment course at a time when little if any tumor regression was apparent. The same association with the cravings or aversions for food noted during pregnancy in some cases were reported [31].

Only limited information on the influence of chemotherapy on taste sensation in patients with cancer is available. A combination chemotherapy regimen that included bleomycin, actinomycin-D, vindisine, and

DTIC diminished patients' ability to discriminate between the highest and lowest concentration for sweet, sour, and bitter tastes [32]. In another study, therapy with 5-FU resulted in a decrease in elevated sweet recognition thresholds to the normal range after two weeks of treatment [33].

Changes in cancer-associated taste abnormalities appear to be reversible, at least under some circumstances. Improvement in taste parameters have been noted in patients responding to antineoplastic therapy, parenteral nutritional support, and tumor excision [19,34,35]. In successfully treated patients with laryngeal carcinoma, recovery of taste sensation was noted to occur for up to six months after completion of treatment. It is noteworthy that recurrence of taste abnormalities was seen in patients demonstrating tumor recurrence in this same trial [34].

The true relationship among taste sensation abnormalities, the presence of cancer, and the development of weight loss remains to be clearly defined. That is, are these taste sensation abnormalities a specific and direct consequence of the tumor resulting in a decreased caloric intake and weight loss, or are such taste abnormalities themselves the result of other factors commonly seen in a cancer patient population? A smoking history and/or advancing age have been shown to profoundly influence taste sensation thresholds in cancer-free populations [36-38]. Obviously, these parameters are also associated with the development of a variety of cancers as well. In an attempt to determine the relative importance of such factors influencing taste sensation thresholds in patients with cancer, we have recently evaluated taste recognition thresholds in 93 patients with malignancy, including 18 patients with lung carcinoma, and compared our results with a 61-patient control population free of cancer [24]. Sucrose (sweet) and urea (bitter) taste thresholds were determined by a forced choice technique. Albumin, transferrin, anthropometrics, caloric intake, and protein intake were used to assess nutritional status. Sweet and bitter taste thresholds were significantly higher ($p < 0.05$) for smokers compared with nonsmokers. In cancer patients, no cases of decreased threshold of bitter tastes were detected. Thirty-eight percent of cancer patients had an increased threshold for sweet substances, a proportion significantly greater than that seen in control patients without cancer ($p < 0.01$). However, when correction using a multivariant analysis was made for smoking history and age of study patients, no differences in taste test parameters were seen between cancer patients and control patients without malignancy. In addition, we did not find an association between caloric intake and taste test abnormalities in our cancer patient population. Therefore, the altered taste sensation threshold found in these cancer patient populations may be related to factors such as age and smoking history rather than cancer per se. In any event, it is possible that the combination of cancer-associated malnutrition and taste sensation abnormalities can set up a vicious cycle, since disturbance of regeneration of chemoreceptors for taste can result from general malnutrition by itself [39].

One possible consequence of malnutrition in cancer populations that may contribute to the development of taste sensation abnormalities is relative zinc deficiency. Early studies suggested that zinc deficiency may be associated with taste sensation threshold elevation [37,40]. However, Bolze and coworkers [21] could not demonstrate a significant correlation between the taste thresholds and plasma zinc levels in 35 patients who were undergoing radiotherapy, nor could Trant and colleagues [33] correlate hair zinc levels with taste perception in 62 patients. In a somewhat larger population reported by Silverman and Thompson [41], 75 patients with oropharyngeal carcinoma were studied to assess the relationship between serum zinc levels and radiation-induced taste loss. Thirty patients who did not experience spontaneous postradiation taste recovery were subsequently supplemented with zinc sulfate daily for at least one month. In 11 cases, improvement in taste sensation was reported with markedly increased serum zinc levels seen in the patients with taste improvement [41]. Thus, further study of zinc sulfate supplementation in treatment of taste sensation abnormalities in other cancer-bearing populations would seem warranted.

The common occurrence of increased thresholds to such tastes in patients with cancer has led to recommendations for adding more highly sweet foods to the cancer patient's diet [9]. However, taste threshold data did not correlate with taste preference data in an anorectic cancer patient population reported by Trant [33]. In fact, preference data suggested a favored reduction of sweet foods in some subsets [33]. Such apparently conflicting information points to the complexity of factors influencing food intake in the cancer population. Taken together the current data suggest that information obtained from individual patients [42] is needed to outline the optimal dietary composition needed to maximize caloric intake in the patient with cancer.

Another factor potentially influencing caloric intake and development of weight loss in cancer patients that has received surprisingly limited evaluation is the influence of psychological factors such as depression. In a population of 72 advanced solid tumor patients receiving chemotherapy, Bruera and coworkers [43] examined for associations among caloric intake, psychological depression, glucose taste threshold, and tumor burden. An equivalent number of malnourished patients and patients with normal nutritional status were

Table 34.1 Factors potentially contributing to the development of anorexia in the patient with cancer

Taste abnormalities
Food aversions
Psychological factors (depression)
Abnormal host metabolism
Effects of treatment:
   Radiotherapy
   Chemotherapy

included. In the malnourished group, a significantly lower caloric intake and higher incidence of depression (59% versus 20%; p<0.03) was seen. Interestingly, although abnormal glucose taste thresholds occurred in over 60% of patients, the percentage showing this abnormality were equivalent in the malnourished and well-nourished cancer patient groups. As in many of the previously described studies, once again the question of association rather than causation must be raised. Prospective studies involving patients either at high risk for cancer development or cancer recurrence following primary treatment of their initial localized disease will be needed to definitively address these problems.

Factors potentially contributing to the development of anorexia in the patient with cancer are outlined in table 1. Regardless of specific etiology, anorexia and decreased caloric intake represent a major problem confronting patients with a diagnosis of cancer.

ENERGY BALANCE AND ABNORMAL METABOLISM

Although, as outlined above, caloric intake is clearly decreased in cancer cachexia, an increasing body of evidence suggests that other factors may play a role in the weight loss seen in the cancer patient population as well. A large study has compared quantitative food intakes of 205 normal individuals with 198 ambulatory cancer patients using a 24-hour recall technique [3]. Although the caloric intake of normal males free of cancer significantly exceeded that of males with lung cancer (2,358 kcal versus 1,778 kcal, p.05), essentially no difference in caloric intake between normal females and females with lung cancer was seen. Furthermore, the caloric intake for cancer patients who had lost body weight compared with those who had been able to maintain their body weight was nearly identical (1,776 kcal versus 1,780 kcal). Thus, anorexia or reduced caloric intake alone could not account for the weight loss experienced by these lung cancer patients. In further support of the concept that factors other than a decreased caloric intake play a major role in the development of weight loss in lung cancer is the failure of the provision of calories

via force feeding [44] or hyperalimentation [33] to uniformly increase lean body mass in patients with cancer. Such observations suggest that weight loss may be related to altered host metabolism brought about by the presence of malignancy.

Recent studies involving basal metabolic rate determinations using the technique of indirect calorimetry have reported a relatively consistent pattern of a moderate increase in energy expenditure in patients with various tumor types [45-47]. In some diseases such as gastrointestinal malignancies, only a minority (26%) of patients appear to be hypermetabolic [45]. In other diseases such as small cell carcinoma of the lung, a more consistent increase in resting energy expenditure has been found [47]. Chemotherapeutic administration alone or use of nutritional support [36,45] did not reduce the elevations of resting energy expenditure. However, either tumor resection or complete response to chemotherapy resulted in reduced resting energy expenditure in these reports [47,48]. Such data suggest that in some cases the cancer patient may manifest a characteristically increased energy demand that contributes to the weight loss. The underlying mechanism of such an increase in energy expenditure is poorly understood at the present time. However, a wide range of metabolic changes have been described in the cancer-bearing host including abnormalities of carbohydrate, protein, and lipid metabolism [49-52].

CANCER CACHEXIA: THERAPEUTIC IMPLICATIONS

While the impact of malnutrition on survival in cancer patients is evident, the ability of existing methods of nutritional intervention to influence this adverse clinical outcome is not established. Early trials with forced feeding [44] and enteral supplements [53] achieved only mixed results. The introduction of total parenteral nutrition (TPN) has permitted the physician to provide nutritional support without using the gastrointestinal tract. Early clinical experience in nonrandomized trials have suggested TPN to be beneficial in converting skin tests and decreasing toxic effects associated with chemotherapeutic regimens [54]. However, in a series of investigations supported by the Diet, Nutrition, and Cancer program of the National Cancer Institute, no significant improvement in either response or survival was associated with TPN use in patients with lymphoma, metastatic colon cancer, adenocarcinoma of the lung, or metastatic testicular carcinoma [55]. Similar conclusions have been drawn from randomized TPN trials involving pediatric patients as well [56]. It is worth noting that these studies have not directly tested the hy-

Table 34.2 Metabolic treatment strategies for cancer cachexia under evaluation

Metabolic abnormality seen in cancer cachexia providing rationale	Treatment Approach	References
Abnormal protein metabolism	Prednisolone	Willox et al (61)
	Medroxylprogesterone	Lelli et al (64)
Hypogonadism	Nandrolone decanoate	Chlebowski et al (63)
Abnormal glucose metabolism	Hydrazine sulfate	Gold (67)
		Gershanovich (69)
		Chlebowski et al (65)
	Insulin	Schein et al (84)

pothesis that nutritional repletion of a malnourished patient with cancer will improve clinical outcome, since sequential improvement in lean body mass has not been reported in these trials. As they currently stand, the data from these studies has been recently reviewed and the consensus is that provision of increased calories alone does not significantly alter the clinical course of patients with advanced cancer and weight loss [54,55,57].

Although pre- and perioperative TPN has demonstrated benefit in the cancer patient undergoing curative resection in terms of decreasing operative morbidity and mortality in several reports [58-60], this result may well represent the influence of nutritional status on surgical outcome rather than reversal of a specific cancer-related abnormality.

The failure of increased calories alone to alter the clinical course of patients with cancer and weight loss suggests that consideration of the mechanism underlying the development of cancer·cachexia may be needed to develop more successful nutritional strategies in this population. Based on observed metabolic disturbances in the cancer population with weight loss, a number of nutritional-metabolic therapeutic interventions are under investigation (table 2).

The weight gain associated with corticosteroid use in a variety of clinical situations is well established. Based on this rationale, investigators have evaluated the impact of prednisolone in a 5 mg, three-times-a-day dose compared with placebo administration in advanced cancer patients [61]. Study endpoints included subjective parameters of sense of well-being and appetite and objective parameters of caloric intake and weight change. A statistically significant improvement in appetite without change in caloric intake or weight was noted in the prednisolone-treated population, which was associated with an improvement in sense of well-being as well. Thus, prednisolone treatment may be considered to represent a symptomatic approach to the problem of cancer cachexia.

The recent identification of hypogonadism or low testosterone levels in male patient populations with advanced cancer, which was correlated with weight loss and adverse outcome [49,62], has led to a trial of replacement therapy with androgen in this condition. Chlebowski and coworkers [63] have recently conducted a randomized prospective clinical trial in which short-term addition of nandrolone decanoate to chemotherapy treatment in patients with non-small cell lung cancer was evaluated. Patients received a standard platinum-containing combination chemotherapy regimen plus or minus the addition of nandrolone decanoate at 200 mg dose given intramuscularly every week for four doses. This short term androgen therapy was associated with a decreased rate of weight loss, which was of borderline statistical significance. However, since pretreatment androgen levels were not identified in this trial, further prospective studies of such agents using pretreatment testosterone levels to guide administration will be needed to definitively evaluate its role in lung cancer cachexia treatment. The recent report that high-dose medroxyprogesterone acetate had anabolic effect in advanced cancer patients in a small trial represents a similar approach using a currently available agent that bears further evaluation [64].

Finally, abnormal glucose metabolism has been frequently seen in patients with cancer cachexia. The increase in total glucose production [50,65,66] which has likewise been observed, has led to the suggestion that inappropriate activation of such pathways could lead to futile cycling and host energy loss [67]. Since hydrazine sulfate is an inhibitor of gluconeogenesis in animals, this agent has undergone preliminary clinical trials as a potential therapeutic approach to cancer cachexia in humans as well [65,68,69]. Randomized trials have demonstrated an ability of hydrazine sulfate administration in a 60 mg, three-times-a-day dosage to favorably influence abnormal glucose metabolism seen in patients with advanced cancer [65]. More recent studies in Russia [69] and the United States [68] have suggested a role for this agent in weight stabilization as well. Further clinical trials, some of which are under way currently at our institution, will define whether such changes in metabolic parameters and nutritional indices will be associated with any change in clinical outcome.

LEARNED TASTE AVERSION AND BEHAVIORAL INTERVENTION

Another potential factor that may influence the development of anorexia in a cancer patient population is the phenomenon of learned taste aversion [70-72]. In both animal and preliminary clinical observations in pediatric populations, an aversion to specific tastes are learned after even the single pairing of the taste with gastrointestinal symptomatology related to radiation therapy or chemotherapy [70,73,74]. It is interesting that in animal models, learned food aversions may occur apparently as a result of the discomfort induced by tumor growth itself [74]. In these circumstances, it is postulated that tumor growth may suppress appetite indirectly by producing chronic symptoms that act as unconditioned stimuli leading to subsequent food avoidance. In a pediatric population studied by Bernstein [73], foods eaten up to five hours after administration of a chemotherapy regimen that was associated with nausea and vomiting were subsequently identified as disliked foods. This observation may have important therapeutic implications, especially in terms of maintaining caloric intake in patients undergoing chemotherapy administration.

A comprehensive discussion of the treatment of nausea and vomiting in a cancer patient population is beyond the scope of this chapter but has recently been extensively reviewed [75,76]. Two relatively recent developments in this area appear to be related to the phenomenon of learned food aversion. In patients receiving chemotherapy as adjuvant to their primary breast surgery, anticipatory nausea and vomiting (patients developing gastrointestinal toxicity before the actual administration of the emetogenic chemotherapeutic agent) has been observed to be a major problem in several reports [77,78]. An opposite extreme of the same spectrum is the increasing attention given to behavioral intervention for reduction of nausea and vomiting in cancer patient populations receiving chemotherapy [79]. Behavioral intervention strategies have included hypnosis with guided imagery for relaxation [80], electromyographic biofeedback combined with relaxation training imagery [81], and systematic desensitization [81].

In adult patient programs largely aimed at anticipatory nausea and vomiting, some effectiveness has been seen [82]; however, symptoms control has largely been dependent on continuation of the intervention, with symptoms returning after termination [21,74,83].

Recently, however, considerable success has been described in a program involving hypnosis and supportive counseling in a pediatric population in which a favorable impact on gastrointestinal symptomology was maintained after the active behavioral intervention program had been discontinued [79]. These studies are of special interest, since they may help elucidate further the role of psychological factors in cancer-associated anorexia.

In summary, weight loss is commonly seen in patients with cancer and is associated with an adverse prognosis. Anorexia contributes to the relative caloric insufficiency that results in weight loss in this population. The anorexia associated with cancer is almost certainly multifactoral, and precise elucidation of the relative contributions of such factors as taste sensation abnormalities, learned food aversions, psychological factors including depression, and metabolic abnormalities will require further study. Although intensive nutritional support by providing calories via TPN can be safely administered to patients with cancer, only limited therapeutic benefit has been seen with this approach. Consideration of the underlying mechanisms associated with weight loss in this population has led to a variety of new nutritional and metabolic approaches directed at improving the poor prognosis of a cancer patient with anorexia and weight loss. Increasing attention is being directed at behavioral intervention strategies in such populations as well.

REFERENCES

1. DeWys WD, Begg C, Lavin PT, et al. Prognostic effect of weight loss prior to chemotherapy in cancer patients. Am J Med 1980; 69:491-8.
2. Costa G, Bewley P, Aragon M, Siebold J. Anorexia and weight loss in cancer patients. Cancer Treat Rep 1981; 65(5):3-7.
3. Costa G, Lane WW, Vincet RG, Siebold JA, Aragon M, Bewley PT. Weight loss and cachexia in lung cancer. Nutr Cancer 1981; 2:98-103.
4. Freeman M, Frankmann C, Beck J, Valdivieso M. Prognostic nutrition factors in lung cancer patients. J Parent Ent Nutr 1982; 6:122-7.
5. Martin KI, Sox HC, Krupp JR. Involuntary weight loss: diagnostic and prognostic significance. Ann Int Med 1981; 95:568-74.
6. Barry RE. Malignancy, weight loss, and the small intestinal mucosa. Gut 1974; 15:562-70.
7. Cohen A, Heymesfield S, Kuck K, et al. Mechanism of weight loss in hospitalized cancer patients (abst). Clin Res 1978; 26:36.
8. Costa G, Donaldson SS. Effects of cancer and cancer treatment on the nutrition of the host. N Engl J Med 1979; 300:1471-3.
9. DeWys WD, Hoffman FA. Pathophysiology of anorexia and disturbances of taste in cancer patients. In:

Levin B, Riddell RH, eds. Frontiers in gastrointestinal cancer. New York: Elsevier, 1984:81-90.

10. Morrison SD. Control of food intake in cancer cachexia: a challenge and a tool. Physiol Behav 1976; 17:705-8.

11. Chlebowski RT. Effect of nutritional support on the outcome of antineoplastic therapy. Clin Oncol 1986; 5:365-79.

12. Garattini S, Guaitani A. Animal models for the study of cancer-induced anorexia. Cancer Treat Rep 1981; 65(5):23-35.

13. Mordes JP, Rossini AA. Tumor-induced anorexia in the Wistar rat. Science 1981; 213:565-7.

14. Morrison SD. Control of food intake during growth of a Walker 256 carcinosarcoma. Cancer Res 1973; 33:526-8.

15. Kokal WA. The impact of antitumor therapy on nutrition. Cancer 1985; 55:273-8.

16. Schein PS, MacDonald JS, Waters C, et al. Nutritional complications of cancer and its treatment. Semin Oncol 1975; 2:337-47.

17. Young VR. Energy metabolism and requirements in the cancer patient. Cancer Res 1977; 37:2336-41.

18. Krause R, Humphrey C, Von Meyenfeldt M, James H, Fischer JE. A central mechanism for anorexia in cancer: a hypothesis. Cancer Treat Rep 1981; 65:15-21.

19. DeWys WD. Changes in taste sensation and feeding behavior in cancer patients: A review. J Hum Nutr 1978; 32:447-53.

20. DeWys WD, Walters K. Abnormalities of taste sensation in cancer patients. Cancer 1975; 36:1888-96.

21. Bolze MS, Fosmire GJ, Stryker JA, Chung CK, Flipse BG. Taste acuity, plasma zinc levels and weight loss during radiotherapy: a study of relationships. Radiology 1982; 144:163-9.

22. Carson JAS, Gormican A. Taste acuity and food attitudes of related patients with cancer. J Am Diet ASsoc 1977; 70:361-4.

23. Gorshein D. Posthypophysectomy taste abnormalities: their relationship to remote effects of cancer. Cancer 1977; 39:1700-3.

24. Larsen C, Byerley L, Heber D, Chlebowski R. Factors contributing to altered taste sensation in cancer patients. JPEN 1983; 6:575.

25. Williams LR, Cohen MH. Altered taste thresholds in lung cancer. Am J Clin Nutri 1978; 31:122-5.

26. Hall JC, Staniland JR, Giles I. Altered taste thresholds in gastrointestinal cancer. Clin Oncology 1980; 6:137-42.

27. DeWys WD, Costa G, Henkin R. Clinical parameters related to anorexia. Cancer Treat Rep 1981; 65(5):49-52.

28. Mossman K, Shatzman A, Chencharick J. Long term effects of radiotherapy on taste and salivary function in man. Int J Radiat Oncol Biol Phys 1982; 8:991-7.

29. Chencharick JD, Mossman KL. Nutritional consequences of the radiotherapy of head and neck cancer. Cancer 1983; 51:811-5.

30. Brewin TB. Can a tumor cause the same appetite perversion or taste change as a pregnancy. Lancet 1980; 2:907-8.

31. Brewin TB. Appetite perversions and taste changes triggered or abolished by radiotherapy. Clin Radiol 1982; 33:471-5.

32. Mulder NH, Smith JM, Krevmer WM, Bouman J, et al. Effect of chemotherapy on taste sensation in patients with disseminated malignant melanoma. Oncology 1983; 40:36-8.

33. Trant AS, Serin J. Douglass HO. Is taste related to anorexia in cancer patients. Am J Clin Nutr 1982; 36:45-58.

34. Kashima HK, Kalinowski B. Taste impairment following laryngectomy. Ear Nose Throat 1979; 58:88-92.

35. Russ J, DeWys WD. Correction of taste abnormality of malignancy with hyperalimentation. Arch Int Med 1977; 138:799-800.

36. Conger AD, Wells MA. Radiation and aging effects on taste structure and function. Radiation Res 1969; 37:31-8.

37. Henkin R. Taste loss in aging. In: Davis HJ, Neithmeimer R, St. Petersburg R, eds. The biomedical role of trace elements in aging. Echerd College Gerontology Center, 1976:221-36.

38. Kaplan AR. The effect of cigarette smoking on malnutrition and digestion. Gastroenterology 1963; 61:208.

39. Schiffman SS. Taste and smell in disease. N Engl J Med 1983; 308:1337-43.

40. Henkin RI, Schechter PJ, Hoye R, Mattern FCT. Idiopathic hypoguesia with dysgeusia, hyposmia and dysosmia: a new syndrome. JAMA 1971; 217:434-40.

41. Silverman S Jr, Thompson JS. Serum zinc and copper in oral/oropharyngeal carcinoma. Oral Surg 1984; 57:34-6.

42. Vickers ZM, Nielsen SS, Theologides A. Food preferences of patients with cancer. J Am Diet Assoc 1981; 79:441-5.

43. Bruera E, Carraro S, Roca E, Cedaro L, Chacon R. Association between malnutrition and caloric intake, emesis, psychological depression, glucose taste and tumor mass. Cancer Treat Rep 1984; 68:873-6.

44. Terepka AR, Waterhouse C. Metabolic observations during forced feeding of patients with cancer. Am J Med 1956; 20:225-38.

45. Dempsey DT, Feurer ID, Knox LS, Corsby LO, Buzby GP, Mullen JL. Energy expenditure in malnourished gastrointestinal cancer patients. Cancer 1984; 53:1265-73.

46. Knox LS, Crosby LO, Fuerer ID, et al. Energy expenditure in malnourished cancer patients. Ann Surg 1983; 197:152-62.

47. Russell DM, Shike M, Marliss EB, et al. Effects of total parenteral nutrition and chemotherapy on the metabolic derangements in small cell lung cancer. Cancer Res 1984; 44:1700-11.

48. Arbeit JM, Lee SDE, Corsey R, Brennen MF. Resting energy expenditure in controls and cancer patients with localized and diffuse disease. Ann Surg 1984; 200:292-

8.

49. Chlebowski RT, Heber D, Block JB. Lung cancer cachexia. In: Greco FA, ed. Biology and Management of Lung Cancer. Boston: Martinus Nijhoff Publishers, 1983:125-42.

50. Holyrode CP, Gabuzda G, Putnam RC, et al. Altered glucose metabolism in metastatic cancer. Cancer Res 1975; 35:3710-4.

51. Heber D, Chlebowski RT, Ishibashi DE, Herrold JN, Block JB. Metabolic abnormalities in lung cancer patients. Cancer Res 1982; 42:2495-8.

52. Jeevanandam M, Horowitz GD, Lowry SF, Brennan M. Cancer cachexia and protein metabolism. Lancet 1984; 1:1423-6.

53. Aker SN. Oral feedings in the cancer patient. Cancer 1979; 43:2103-7.

54. Copeland EM. Intravenous hyperalimentation and chemotherapy: an update. J Parent Ent Nutr 1982; 6:236-9.

55. Nixon DW. Hyperalimentation in the undernourished cancer patient. Cancer Res 1982; 42 (Suppl):727-8.

56. Van Eye J, Copeland EM, Cangin, et al. A randomized controlled clinical trial of hyperalimentation in children with metastatic malignancies. Med Ped Oncol 1980 1980; 8:63-73.

57. Chlebowski RT. Critical evaluation of the role of nutritional support with chemotherapy. Cancer 1985; 35:268-72.

58. Muller JM, Dienst C, Brenner U, Pichlmaier H. Preoperative parenteral feeding in patients with gastrointestinal carcinoma. Lancet 1982; 1:68-71.

59. Silberman H. The role of preoperative parenteral nutrition in cancer patients. Cancer 1985; 55:254-7.

60. Smale BF, Mullen JE, Buzby GP, Rosato EF. The efficacy of nutritional assessment and support in cancer surgery. Cancer 1981; 47:2375-81.

61. Willcox JC, Corr J, Shaw J, Richardson M, Calman KC, Drennan M. Prednisolone as an appetite stimulant in patients with cancer. Brit Med J 1984; 288:27.

62. Chlebowski RT, Heber D. Hypogonadism in male patients with metastatic cancer prior to treatment. Cancer Res 1982; 42:2495-8.

63. Chlebowski RT, Herrold J, Richardson B, Block JB. Effects of decadurabolin in patients with non-small cell lung cancer. Clin Res 1982; 23:541.

64. Lelli G, Angellelli B, Giambasi ME, et al. The anabolic effect of high dose medroxyprogesterone acetate in oncology. Pharm Res Com 1983; 15:561-8.

65. Chlebowski RT, Heber D, Richardson B, Block JB. Influence of hydrazine sulfate in abnormal carbohydrate metabolism in cancer patients with weight loss. Cancer Res 1984; 44:857-61.

66. Eden E, Edstrom S, Bennegard K, Schersten T, Lundhold K. Glucose flux in relation to energy expenditure in malnourished patients with and without cancer during periods of fasting and feeding. Cancer Res 1984; 44:1717-24.

67. Gold J. Cancer cachexia and gluconeogenesis. Ann NY Acad Sci 1979; 230:103-10.

68. Chlebowski RT, Bulcavage L, Grosvenor M et al. Hydrazine sulfate in cancer patients with weight loss: a placebo-controlled clinical experience. Cancer 1987; 59:406-10.

69. Gershanovich ML. Clinical effects of hydrazine sulfate in patients with advanced malignant disease. In: Filov VA, Evin BA, Gershanovich ML, eds. Medical therapy of tumors. Leningrad: USSR Ministry of Health, 1983: 91-138.

70. Bernstein IL. Learned taste aversions in children receiving chemotherapy. Science 1978; 200:1300-3.

71. Smith JC, Blumsack JT. Learned taste aversion as a factor in cancer therapy. Cancer Treat Rep (Suppl) 1981; 65:37-42.

72. Smith JC, Birkle RA. Conditioned aversion to sucrose in rats using xrays. Psychonomic Science 1666; 5:271-2.

73. Bernstein IL, Bernstein ID. Learned food aversions and cancer anorexia. Cancer Treat Rep 1981; 65(5):43-7.

74. Bernstein IL, Fenner DP. Learned food aversions: heterogeneity of animal models of tumor induced anorexia. Appetite: J for Intake Res 1983; 4:79-86.

75. Frytak S, Moertel CG. Management of nausea and vomiting in the cancer patient. JAMA 1981; 245:393-6.

76. Laszlo J, Lucas VS. Emesis as a critical problem in chemotherapy. N Engl J Med 1981; 305:948-9.

77. Morrow GR. Clinical characteristics associated with the development of anticipatory nausea and vomiting in cancer patients undergoing chemotherapy treatment. J Clin Onc 1984; 2:1170-4.

78. Wilcox PM, Fetting JH, Nettesheim KM, et al. Anticipatory vomiting in women receiving cyclophorphamide, methotrexate, and 5-FU (CMF) adjuvant chemotherapy for breast carcinoma. Cancer Treat Rep 1982; 66:1601-4.

79. Zeltzer L, LeBaron S, Zelter PM. The effectiveness of behavioral intervention for reduction of nausea and vomiting in children and adolescents receiving chemotherapy. J Clin Oncol 1984; 2:683-90.

80. Redd WH, Andersen GV. Conditioned aversion in cancer patients. Behav Res Ther 1981; 4:34.

81. Burish TG, LYles JN. Effectiveness of relaxation training in reducing adverse reactions to cancer chemotherapy. J Behav Med 1981; 4:65-78.

82. Morrow GR, Morrell C. Behavioral treatment for the anticipatory nausea and vomiting induced by cancer chemotherapy. N Engl J Med 1982; 307:1476-80.

83. Redd WH, Andrykowski MA. Behavioral intervention in cancer treatment: controlled aversion reactions to chemotherapy. J Consult Clin Psychol 1982; 50:1018-29.

84. Schein PS, Kisner D, Haller D, Blecher M, Hamosh M. Cachexia of malignancy: potential role of insulin in nutritional management. Cancer 1979; 43:2070-6.

Chapter 35

Atypical Eating Disorders

Stanley Goodman, Barton J. Blinder, Barry F. Chaitin, and Jennifer Hagman

ATYPICAL EATING DISORDERS

Atypical eating disorders are classified in DSM III-R as disorders of eating that do not meet the criteria for a specific eating disorder due to absence of particular clinical criteria (frequency of symptom, clinical sign, and in special instances gender or age).

This chapter discusses the presence of anorexia nervosa and bulimia nervosa in children, males, and females beyond age 25 and in the elderly are also presented. In addition, cultural presentations of anorexia nervosa in Blacks and Hispanics, anorexia nervosa in neuropsychiatric conditions, and eating disorders associated with medical conditions, hyperphagic conditions, and eating disturbance in various endocrine disorders are also reviewed. Core psychological conflicts, etiologic considerations, precipitating events, prognosis, and treatment specific to these unusual and atypical presentations are also discussed.

ANOREXIA NERVOSA IN CHILDREN

Anorexia nervosa has been reported to occur as early as age four [1]. Childhood anorexia should fulfill criteria for adolescent- or adult-onset anorexia nervosa, except that in children, due to a diminished amount of body fat, a 25 percent weight loss is not necessary. In female childhood cases, primary amenorrhea occurs. The incidence of prepubertal anorexia nervosa is three percent in a series of 600 consecutive patients of all ages evaluated for

anorexia nervosa at the Mayo clinic [2]. Females comprise 73 percent of all reported children with anorexia nervosa [1]. However, in one subgroup of anorectics (see below), 50 percent were males [3].

Developmental antecedents of childhood anorexia have not been systematically researched [4]. Delaney and Silber [5] evaluated approximately 30 patients and noted lack of stage-specific negativism at age two, anxious clinging behavior upon commencement of school, and difficulty maintaining peer relations, leading to a degree of social isolation. In infants ages nine to twenty-six months, Chatoor and Egan [6] described a developmental eating disturbance which they consider to be both a separation disorder and a form of infantile anorexia. Latency-age children, at the Piagetian stage of concrete thinking, conceptualize food and water together as one entity, resulting in global ingestive restriction. This may lead to rapid weight loss and serious dehydration. In addition, prepubertal children, especially girls, have less body fat than their adolescent counterparts and become more quickly emaciated [7]. In Irwin's series, over two-thirds of the children with anorexia were hospitalized within six months of the onset of the anorexia. Gislason [1] noted one death in 33 children with prepubertal anorexia nervosa.

Sargent [3] described three subgroups of prepubertal anorectics. The first group similar to one described by Pugliese, et al. [8] severely restricted their food intake, resulting in short stature. They had fears of becoming obese, and by their deficient weight gain they maintained both a physical and psychological immaturity. The second group consisted primarily of prepubertal females, ages ten to twelve, who were psychologically pseudo-precocious, engaging in overt behavior more characteristics of that of a pubescent 14-year old. Their parents discouraged age-appropriate behavior and strongly encouraged their pseudo-adolescent behavior. This female subgroup is most similar to pubertal-onset anorexia nervosa. The third subgroup consisted of an equal number of male and female anorectics who were more psychologically impaired, having major ego deficits with the occasional presence of psychotic episodes [9].

Gislason [1] noted premorbid personality characteristics of dependency, timidity, and schizoid traits, with features of depression. Significant disturbances of ego development, prepsychotic personality traits, and psychotic episodes have been reported [1]. Moreover, premorbid eating disturbances, including a history of being a finicky eater, have been noted [7]. Family structural characteristics found in adolescent anorexia nervosa, consisting of *rigidity, lack of conflict resolution,* and *triangulation,* appear to be present in the families of children with the disorder [7]. In childhood anorexia, Sargent [3] noted increased divorce among families, as contrasted to adolescent anorexia where the family divorce rate is approximately equal to the general population.

The clinical manifestation of childhood anorexia nervosa should fulfill most DSM III-R criteria. However, since prepubertal children, especially girls, have less body fat than their adolescent counterparts, a 15-percent reduction in body weight should be sufficient for diagnosis [7,10]. It is unclear if there is a body image distortion equivalent to that of older anorectics. The child may be more concerned with separation-individuation issues than fears of sexuality [7,11]. They frequently demonstrate alexithymia, the inability to translate one's feelings into words [12].

Irwin [7] feels psychodynamics in childhood anorexia nervosa are similar to those of adolescent onset and include identity disturbance, failure of separation/individuation with fears of growing up, maladaptive attempts to be in control, and failure of parents to resolve marital or family conflicts. Precipitating events associated with the onset of childhood anorexia nervosa include: the birth of a sibling, bereavement over the death of a parent or relative, a disappointment in object relations, family discord, viral illness, peer criticism about being fat, the fear of becoming obese, the onset of breast development, sexual abuse, sustained fear of choking while eating, anticipated fear of parental loss related to an ill or depressed parent, and the coincident onset of a psychophysiologic disorder such as ulcerative

colitis [1] or ileitis [13].

In the treatment of the childhood anorectic, the therapist should work closely with a pediatrician to rule out medical and psychological conditions producing anorexia. A physical examination and laboratory studies are mandatory to monitor the child's physical condition. The prognosis in childhood anorexia is unclear. Sargent feels that his group II females have less individual and family psychopathology, and have the most favorable outcome as contrasted to group III, where both individual and parental psychopathology are more severe. The group I prognosis is intermediate between groups II and III. Gislason [1] summarized and reported cases of prepubertal anorexia and noted that 63 percent improved, 21 percent did not improve, and 3 percent died. Russell [14] found prolonged delay of puberty (a later menarche) and possible permanent interference with growth in stature and breast development in children with prepubertal anorexia nervosa. In contrast, Pfeiffer, et al. [15] noted relatively minimal growth retardation on follow-up of treatment. He stresses the importance of identifying childhood anorexia nervosa and returning the children to an optimum weight to safeguard their puberty.

ATYPICAL BULIMIA NERVOSA DISORDERS IN CHILDREN

There have been no extensive published reports of childhood bulimia in association with purging. The appearance of bulimia nervosa in latency may be rare. Prepubertal children were thought to be insufficiently sophisticated to purge; and latency-age girls were thought to be less vulnerable to the social pressure to be thin. However, Herzog, et al. [16] noted a ten-year old male, and Goodman [17] noted a fourteen-year old female, each hospitalized with an affective disturbance with both binging and purging initiated in latency. Moreover, Walsh [18] has identified adolescent female bulimics who admitted to purging while in latency.

Two cases of bulimia and/or purging (vomiting) beginning in latency are reported. One patient had a severe affective disorder with mood lability and frequent wrist cutting when seen as an adolescent. Two case reports of male bulimia occurred in association with object loss featuring global impulsiveness, learning disability, and in one case, possible Attention Deficit Disorder [19].

There may be a subgroup of mildly obese, impulsive children (especially males) who have a variant of bulimia. A complete evaluation, including the way stressful events modify eating, the presence and frequency of binging, fluctuations in weight, depression, and delineation of individual and family psychodynamics, is warranted in obese children. Bulimia in latency, while probably rare, does occur in atypical forms. Primary physicians and school nurses need to recognize these symptoms and carefully evaluate eating patterns of latency-age obese and impulsive children.

ANOREXIA NERVOSA IN MALES

Anorexia nervosa was first described in males by both Morton [20] and Gull [21]. Anorexia in males accounted for approximately 6 percent of cases seen in an eating disorder clinic [16,22]. The mean age of onset of male anorexia has been reported ranging from as young as 17 years in a British series by Crisp and Burns [23] to 24 years [16,24]. Crisp found that the illness was present an average of three-and-one half years and that most patients were mildy obese (127.3 percent of ideal body weight, IBW) prior to the onset of illness. Minimal weight dropped to 67.3 percent of IBW during the acute phase of illness.

Apparently contrasting socioeconomic groups of origin for male anorectics may represent specific populations, seen in various programs. Andersen and Mickalide [25] found a high socioeconomic group at Johns Hopkins, while Herzog [16] in Boston and Vandereycken and Van den Broucke [22] in Belgium found an equal socioeconomic distribution.

Clinical manifestations of male anorexia were reported in several series to be similar to female anorexia [22,23,26,27,28,29,30]. However, in a minority of reports [31,32] differences were noted; patients were from lower socioeconomic groups, feared competition and were not successful either academically or in their vocation. Yates et al. [33] compared male marathon runners to anorectics and found many similar sociocultural and personality characteristics. Runners were found to have a bizzare preoccupation with food, and even when they would achieve a lean body mass of 95 percent with only 5 percent body fat, they would aim for 4 percent body fat. Many have lost greater than 25 percent of their original weight and show a relentless pursuit of thinness or a disturbance of body image. Male anorectic characteristics include perfectionism and obsession [25]. Vandereycken and Van den Broucke [22] noted a high incidence of schizoid/introversion features as well as obsessional, passive/dependent and anti-social features. A comparison to female anorectics showed a higher percentage of undifferentiated- immature psychological structure, hysterical/histrionic features, and anti-social features, but an equal number of schizoid/introversion traits [22].

The etiology of male anorexia is unclear, but Crisp and Burns [23] hypothesize that it is related to gender identity problems in the premorbid personality, since the male desire is to be bigger and stronger as compared to the female preference for slimness. Herzog [16] found male anorexic patients experiencing sexual isolation, sexual inactivity, and conflicted homosexuality. He posited that the cultural pressure on the homosexual male to be thin and attractive places him at a greater risk for eating disorders. Hall [26] in a series of nine male patients whose personal family history was reviewed, noted attention directed to bodily concerns caused by being overweight, having close contact with an eating disordered patient, attempting to identify with a thin family member, attempting to treat acne through a stringent diet, and attempting to deal with the fear of having cancer.

Endocrine disturbances present in male anorexia include decreased testosterone and gonadotrophins (luteinizing hormone-LH and follicle stimulating hormone-FSH) in proportion to weight loss. With weight gain, both terstosterone and gonadotrophins increase to normal levels [25,34,35]. Anderson and Mickalide [25] noted that two of ten patients studied were infertile.

BULIMIA NERVOSA IN MALES

Bulimia has been reported in male patients [16,36,37,38]. Herzog et al. [16] noted an incidence in males of approximately 4 to 5 percent of a total population of bulimic patients. Gwirtsman found that 10 to 13 percent of male students met DSM-III criteria for bulimia. The mean age of onset ranged from 21 [16] to 24 years [36]. Duration of illness prior to treatment ranged from six years [36] to 7.4 years [16]. This duration is significantly longer than the 4.2 year's duration of illness prior to treatment for bulimic females [16].

Approximately two-thirds of bulimic males had a history of being overweight as compared to one-third of bulimic females. Socioeconomic classes were equally distributed in one series [16]. Mitchell's [36] study noted that patients were employed, that they were functioning well, and that 11 of 12 were married. Mitchell and Goff [36] noted that 11 of 12 bulimics were satisfied with their weight which ranged from 81 percent to 100 percent of ideal body weight (IBW).

The clinical manifestations of male bulimia are comparable to female bulimia. Preoccupation with weight control and associations with the cultural pressures of professional life regarding personal performance (especially in sports, fashion, and music) have been related to the onset of bulimia in some male patients [37]. Psychiatric and drug histories in Mitchell and Goff's [36] series of 12 patients reveal that five patients admitted to alcohol or drug abuse problems in the past and that four had received chemical-dependency treatment. Two of the five developed problems with alcohol prior to the onset of bulimia, and another did so after the onset. One patient reported the simultaneous onset of alcohol abuse and bulimia during a stressful period in his life. Four of these five patients reported a history of chemical abuse problems in at least one first-degree relative, and one had a family history of drug abuse, affective disorder, and anxiety disorder. That patient periodically substituted alcohol abuse for this bulimic behavior. Gwirtsman and associates [37] noted that two of three patients engaged in drug and alcohol abuse, and that all demonstrated some degree of impulsive antisocial behavior.

Herzog [16] discussed sexual isolation, diminished sexual activity, and conflicted homosexuality in bulimic and anorexic males, but he did not specifically subgroup the sexual difficulties in bulimia. Gwirtsman and associates [37] mentioned anecdotally that bulimia may be more common in the male gay community than among heterosexuals. Mitchell and Goff [36] noted that three out of twelve patients had a history of depression, and that most patients had markedly disrupted social situations and were depressed when first seen, but their mood improved as their bulimia came under control.

ATYPICAL EATING DISORDERS IN MALES

Andersen and Mickalide [24] noted that 21 percent of male patients who were referred to Johns Hopkins eating disorders clinic had an eating disturbance with weight loss or abnormal eating patterns in the absence of criteria of DSM III anorexia nervosa.

One group had a swallowing phobia (fear of choking) with significant weight loss, previously misdiagnosed as anorexia nervosa. An earlier choking episode (often vaguely recalled) and a second, more recent choking episode resulted in a sustained fear of choking associated with severe dietary restriction of solid food. (Blinder [39] noted that this syndrome may be a variant of anorexia occurring in a post-traumatic context; he found patients who exhibited similar fears after mouth injury or dental surgery. Choking and aspiration, associated with a rare chronic ruminatory disorder, may also lead to food restriction [40]).

Andersen and Michalide [24] also noted patients who had a classic panic disorder with an associated preoccupation with fears of public vomiting, leading to food restriction and diminished weight. In contrast, a patient with general anxiety had specific overeating episodes unassociated with the fear of obesity [24].

These atypical eating disorders may be defined as a mild form of anorexia and are differentiated from anorexia nervosa since full DSM III criteria for anorexia

nervosa are not present.

ANOREXIA NERVOSA IN FEMALES OVER AGE TWENTY-FIVE

Anorexia nervosa may occur after age 25 in females [41,42,43]. The oldest reported patient was a 68-year old woman with no prior history of eating disturbance. While the incidence of anorexia in the general population is 0.37 per 100,000 [44] the incidence of anorexia nervosa in old age is unknown. Less than 100 older patients, both male and female, have been reported in the world's literature [25,41,43,45,46,47]. Adult-onset causes usually come from upper-middle class families [41]. Anorexia nervosa in susceptible patients include those with multiple surgical procedures or illnesses [45], stress secondary to childbirth or marriage [46], or death of a spouse [42]. Sloan and Leichner [48] recently described six anorectic women, first hospitalized as adults, who were sexually abused in childhood or adolescence. In married anorectics whose dependency needs have been shifted to their children, the child's absence resulting from moving or marriage has been associated with an acute onset of anorexia [41].

Numerous onset patterns have been described. The most common pattern is one in which the patient has a chronic eating disturbance or peculiar eating habits and a stress produces a full-blown clinical expression of anorexia nervosa. In other patients, an anorexia episode may have occurred as an adolescent, followed by a long remission, with stressful events serving to precipitate anorexia at a later time in young adulthood. The most uncommon pattern is an adult patient who develops anorexia nervosa de novo [43]. The therapist must obtain a very detailed history of the patient's early eating patterns to determine if a prior episode occurred.

Some patients who exhibit pure restrictive anorexia develop bulimia during or after treatment. Failure of symptomatic restraint may first be manifested in bulimic episodes. Vandereycken [43] suggests that some anorectics who fail treatment develop vomiting, purging, or frank bulimia. Kellett [46] described a 52-year old woman who purged and vomited in addition to the anorexia.

In a study of fifty married patients, Dally [41] divided anorectics into four groups. In group I, onset of anorexia started during the engagement period prior to marriage. In group II, onset occurred while subjects were married and prior to a pregnancy. Onset in group III occurred within three years of becoming pregnant. The period after menopause marked the onset of anorexia in group IV. Dally felt that the anorexia that developed in groups I and II was a maladaptive solution to an emerging marital crisis. Dally [41] notes that Group IV post-menopausal-onset anorectics are markedly depressed and suicidal and may have a more ominous course than their younger counterparts.

The course of anorexia nervosa in later life is variable. Crisp [49] notes that some chronic anorexic patients who have the illness throughout their reproductive life (puberty to menopause) shed the illness at menopause, while others remain ill, surviving as "isolated, eccentric, and wizened old ladies." Vandereycken [43] conceptualizes anorexia as an incurable illness in some patients with spontaneously occurring remissions and exacerbations. This chronic course seen in older patients is a form of "process" anorexia nervosa, as differentiated from a more "reactive," self-limited disorder seen in younger, mainly adolescent patients.

Though some patients with late onset or chronic anorexia nervosa may recover after intensive treatment, patients failing to maintain their weight at four- to eight-year follow-ups may have to inevitably recognize their decision to remain anorectics. In these cases, the goal of treatment is to minimize the physical and emotional handicaps of the disease. Vandereycken [43] raises ethical questions concerning treatment of chronic anorectics and bulimics. Although the patients may feel life is barren with anorexia, life may become even more barren and painful without it. Furthermore, chronic bulimics can organize their life around the bulimia, with bulimic episodes becoming "institutionalized."

BULIMIA IN FEMALES BEYOND AGE THIRTY

Bulimia may be underreported in women over age 30. Population surveys have uncovered few older bulimic patients. Jonas [50] reported a 56-year old woman with rapid-cycling bipolar disorder and unexplained vomiting. She had no prior history of an eating disorder, and during hospitalization the staff discovered surreptitious vomiting. Bulimia disappeared with individual medication trials, first with imipramine, and then phenelzine. Older patients with affective disorder and unexplained vomiting not secondary to psychotropic drug toxicity should be screened for bulimia. Lithium use may be hazardous, therapeutically unpredictable, or lethal in patients with self-induced, surreptitious vomiting, due to electrolyte disturbance. Patients taking lithium for bipolar disorder, emotionally unstable character disorder, or recurrent unipolar depression should be screened for bulimia. Bipolar patients with bulimia may respond to carbamazepine [51] as an alternative to lithium carbonate.

CULTURAL PRESENTATIONS OF ANOREXIA NERVOSA

Anorexia Nervosa in Blacks

Anorexia nervosa has been reported in American Blacks [52,53,54,55] and in Blacks of Afro-Caribbean extraction from the West Indies [56]. The incidence of black anorexic patients in a total population of patients with anorexia nervosa is less than five percent [53]. Case reports from lower socioeconomic groups of West Indian patients living in England [56] and middle-to upper-class patients [52] are noted.

Anorexia Nervosa in Hispanics

Hispanic females, described by Silber [52], experienced significant disruption moving from South America to Washington, D.C. with resultant object losses of friends and family, including grandparents. The onset of anorexia nervosa in these cases was associated with family disturbance and sexual abuse. Family dynamics in the Hispanic cases included severe disruption, infidelity by the father, alcoholism, depression, suicide attempts, and parental separation, creating a chaotic environment for the patient.

Silber [52] noted the Hispanic females had high personal ideals. Being raised in a more traditional Latin culture, they may have had difficulty when expected to assimilate into the American culture, where thinness and academic achievement were highly valued. In addition, they had to contend with contrasting sexual attitudes, which may have exacerbated their own conflicts. Development of anorexia nervosa, with its regression to a prepubertal psychological structure, served as a maladaptive attempt to cope with issues of identity and cultural and sexual conflict.

ANOREXIA NERVOSA IN NEUROPSYCHIATRIC DISORDERS

Anorexia Nervosa in Tourette's Syndrome

Anorexia has been seen in association with Tourette's Syndrome (TS) [57,58,59]. Blinder et al. [57] described a 14-year old female anorectic with Tourette's Syndrome diagnosed at age nine. The development of anorexia was associated with a family move, a change of schools, and a demanding social environment. The use of haloperidol, with consequent weight gain, may have been an additional provocative factor in initiating a restrictive eating pattern. Larocca [59] reported a 12-year old male with obsessive-compulsive symptomatology who developed TS near the time of weight gain one year previously. For unexplained reasons, the patient exercised excessively and severely restricted his dietary intake. In Tourette's Syndrome, inadequate impulse inhibition places an overwhelming stress on the ego which is weakened by this neurophysiologic disorder. In adolescence, these patients may need to cope with both heightened sexual and aggressive conflicts, separation-individuation and identity issues. Anorexia nervosa may be a maladaptive attempt at homeostasis. In the 12-year old male, and in the case of a 22-year old female with both Tourette's Syndrome and anorexia nervosa, described by Yayura-Tobias [58] severe depression with overdose or self-mutilation occurred. The coexistence of anorexia nervosa and Tourette's created an overwhelming sense of ineffectiveness resulting in helplessness and depression.

A common central nervous system mechanism may underlie both Tourette's and anorexia nervosa. In addition, Yayura-Tobias [58] hypothesizes that both entities share a common CNS (hypothalmic, caudate) locus, since TS and anorexia nervosa present with a high incidence of associated obsessive-compulsive symptoms. Although neurotransmitter levels have not been studied in patients with both Tourette's Syndrome and anorexia nervosa, Cohen et al [60] found increased 5-hydroxyindole acetic acid (5-HIAA) in the cerebral spinal fluid of TS patients, suggesting increased serotonin turnover. Serotonin has been implicated in eating inhibition and a shift away from carbohydrate consumption [61].

Neurotransmitter labeled positron emission tomography may be helpful in determining shared neurotransmitter dysfunction, and CNS localization in these coexisting disorders. Further research into common psychodynamic, cognitive, and neurotransmitter determinants, including cerebral mechanisms, are indicated.

Anorexia Nervosa in Schizophrenia

Anorexia nervosa has been reported in patients with schizophrenia [24,62,63,64]. Hsu [62] described six patients who had paranoid delusions and auditory hallucinations in which several heard people stating, "You're so fat and ugly." Prior to the onset of overt psychosis, depressive and suicidal symptoms were present. In addition, major depression but not schizophrenia, was found in the families. Hsu [62] concluded that these patients would be better diagnosed as schizoaffective disorder than schizophrenia. Treatment with phenothiazines was effective in diminishing psychosis, and one patient became psychotic again with refeeding. Another patient with schizoaffective disorder and borderline mental retardation (IQ) was reported [65]. Similar developmental conflicts concerning separation, individuation, autonomy, and control issues may occur in both disorders [66,44].

Anorexia Nervosa in Post-traumatic Stress Disorder

Anorexia nervosa has been reported in patients with post-traumatic stress disorder. In three patients, an accident caused physical injury, disfigurement, and preoc-

cupation with their bodies. Damlounji and Ferguson [67] posit that physical injury and placement in a stressful hospital environment resulted in body image distortion, which may have been etiologic in the development of anorexia nervosa. Similarly a patient developed anorexia after prolonged use of the Milwaukee Brace [68] which restricted physical activity and may have promoted undesired weight gain.

Anorexia Nervosa in Depression

Fichter et al [69] reported a 15-year old male presenting with depression, hyperactivity and fasting who lost 35 percent of body weight, but did not have other criteria of anorexia nervosa.

Anorexia Nervosa in Obsessive-Compulsive Disorders

In some patients with severe obsessive-compulsive disorders, not fulfilling DSM III Criteria for anorexia nervosa, obsessive-compulsive traits such as spending hours cutting and eating small amounts of food in a ritualized manner are present [32].

Anorexia Nervosa in Mental Retardation

Anorexia nervosa has been described in patients with mental retardation [70,71]. A 15-year old patient with agitated, withdrawn behavior and an IQ of 62 had a distorted body image and anorexia. This patient was treated with behavior therapy. Anorexia nervosa in the retarded may go undiagnosed because of the misconception that mentally retarded individuals do not develop this disorder [70]. Anorexia nervosa has been reported in a 35-year old female with Down's Syndrome [71]. Due to the developmental and cognitive delays of retardation the patient only recently experienced adolescent issues (e.g., separation individuation) associated with the onset of anorexia nervosa. Treatment approach involved modification of environment combined with family therapy.

ANOREXIA NERVOSA IN ASSOCIATION WITH MEDICAL DISORDERS

Crohn's disease has been reported coexisting with anorexia nervosa [72,73,74]. Hershman and Hershman [72] reported a 27-year old anorectic female with diarrhea and increasing lower abdominal pain who developed a palpable cecal mass with inflamed appendix. At surgery a diagnosis of Crohn's disease was made. Diagnostic confusion can arise between patients with Crohn's disease, atypical anorexia and anorexia nervosa because of the similar symptoms of nausea, anorexia and abdominal pain. In addition these two disorders can coexist.

Blinder et al. [40] noted that a 34-year old patient following right temporal lobectomy for post-traumatic intractable motor seizures developed anorexia nervosa. Central nervous system disorders have been reported in anorexia nervosa. A 25-year old female presenting with complaints of poor memory, nausea, ataxia, diploplia and dysarthria was later diagnosed to have Wernicke's encephalopathy. The anorexia, producing a thiamine deficiency, may have caused this disorder. However thiamine levels were not performed because she presented six months after resuming a normal diet. Anorexia patients developing mental status changes with ataxia and nystagmus should be screened for Wernicke's encephalopathy [75]. A 19-year old female who presented with both acute, severe depression and anorexia nervosa syndrome subsequently developed petechial skin hemorrhages, suddenly collapsed and died. At postmortem disseminated herpes simplex infection with massive intra-cerebral hemorrhage was noted. The sudden onset of depression was due to the herpes simplex infection. The patient's malnutrition contributed to a lowered immunological defense and other susceptibility to herpes simplex [76]. Symptoms of anorexia nervosa have been reported in the initial stage of multiple sclerosis [77].

Anorexia Nervosa in Genetic Disorders

Anorexia nervosa has been reported in genetic disease such as Turner's Syndrome [59] and Gaucher's disease [78]. There are thirteen case reports of patients with the coexistence of anorexia nervosa with Turner's Syndrome, a disorder manifesting a 45-chromosome XO genotype, webbed neck, and gonad hypodevelopment. Endocrine treatment with estrogen at pubertal age may induce sufficient body and weight changes in the Turner Syndrome patient to provoke attempts at dieting or restrictive eating.

Anorexia Nervosa with Autophonia

An interesting report associates anorexia nervosa with autophonia, the perception of one's own voice and breathing. Rapid weight loss seen in a variety of wasting disorders including anorexia nervosa has been associated with autophonia. The therapist should not confuse a patient's complaint of hearing her own voice with transitory psychotic phenomena occasionally seen in anorexic patients [79].

EATING DISORDERS IN ENDOCRINE DISTURBANCE

There have been no systematic studies of abnormal eating attitudes or behavior in classical endocrine diseases such as excess or insufficient thyroid or adrenal states. Excess cortisol levels can be associated with depression, mania and organic mental syndromes and may result in a moderate weight gain. Patients with restrictive anorexia nervosa may have high blood cortisol levels related to increased corticotropic releasing factor (CRF) [80,81]. Recent findings demonstrating GABA neuronal receptor activation by cortisol suggest CNS inhibitory and stimulatory potential for cortisol with implications for neurobiologic consequences in Cushing's Syndrome, depression, and anorexia nervosa (hypercortisol states) [82]. Cushing's patients may not manifest overtly abnormal eating behavior, however their eating habits may be similar to patients with mild obesity. A slight increase in appetite may be present. In Cushing's disease, there may also be increased urinary-free cortisol which may not be present in either anorexia nervosa or depression. Cortisol, which has a catabolic effect and destroys tissues may possibly have a role in increased appetite to augment protein intake, restoring lost tissue and muscle mass.

A woman age 27-years-old, with a prior diagnosis of anorexia nervosa and a 54 percent loss of body weight, subsequently developed a pituitary corticotrophic cell adenoma with Cushing's Syndrome alleviated by transsphenoidal surgery. Within two years of surgery in the absence of hypercortisolism, anorexia features reappeared [83] suggesting a common CRF-inducing mechanism.

In contrast to Cushing's disease, cortisol insufficiency is found in Addison's disease. These patients may have a seemingly normal appetite, but satiety occurs with minimal food ingestion. Exogenous steroids, when abruptly withdrawn, can produce a similar effect. Delayed gastric emptying seen in eating disorder patients, may produce early satiety and feelings of fullness [84,85]. These effects may persist after renutrition and may be related to gut neuroendocrine dysfunction.

Diabetes Mellitus coexisting with anorexia nervosa and bulimia has been frequently reported [86,87,88,89,90]. The prevalence of anorexia nervosa with Diabetes Mellitus ranged from zero percent [88] to 6.5 percent [91]. The presence of bulimia ranged from 6.5 percent [111] to 35 percent [143]. Rodin et al. [91] noted a six-fold increase for anorexia nervosa and a two-fold increase for bulimia over the expected prevalence for nondiabetic individuals. Patients who failed to take their insulin developed glucosoria and thereby effected an indirect chemical method of "purging" [86]. The treatment of Diabetes Mellitus offers patients numerous opportunities to pursue their morbid goal of weight loss by dangerous maneuvers including surreptitious vomiting after bulimic episodes, adjustment of the insulin dose, failure to inject insulin and failure to provide urine samples [86,92,93]. Fairburn and Steel [94] noted that girls with anorexia nervosa could skillfully adjust their insulin dosage to match their reduced carbohydrate consumption.

Patients with growth hormone deficiency, which may occur in panhypopituitarism, may have diminished appetite [95]. This syndrome has been identified with nonorganic failure to thrive and with maternal deprivation and may simulate idiopathic hypopituitarism. These children may show pica, eat from unusual places such as garbage cans and drink from toilets. They may steal food and polyphagia and polydipsia may alternate with vomiting and self-starvation. Patients may be overweight or underweight for their dwarfed height, but not emaciated. In contrast increased growth hormone levels may occur in malnutrition syndromes including kwashiorkor, marasmus and anorexia nervosa. When the patient is placed in a more normal environment, eating and drinking patterns normalize [96].

EATING DISORDERS IN THE ELDERLY

Morley and Castle [97] have reported atypical anorexia syndromes in the elderly. Anorexia in the elderly was first described in 1890 in Guy's Hospital when it was termed "senile marasmus." Patients were anorexic and died with no apparent cause of death [97].

A spectrum of anorexia occurs in the elderly. In bereavement appetite can be markedly diminished and overt depression may not be apparent. A second anorexic pattern occurs in the elderly where patients decide to stop eating. Denying hunger and refraining from eating, they may become emaciated and die. A distortion of body image is present as they do not consider themselves thin. They deny suicidal ideation and, if asked, wish to be resuscitated in the event of cardiac arrest [97]. One atypical patient engaged in sham eating in that he would chew and then spit out most ingested food. Inspite of weight loss, he felt his body size was "just right" [97].

Morley [98] has not seen bulimia in the elderly manifested by binging or purging. However, he considers the almost universal laxative use in the elderly a possible iatrogenic form of purging.

Diminished olfactory sensitivity, appetite disorders and impaired taste sensation may contribute to eating disorders in the elderly. Zinc deficiency, sometimes present in the elderly, produces dysguesia and may also have a role in decreasing enjoyment of food [97].

HYPERPHAGIA

Hyperphagia is defined as excessive ingestion of food beyond that needed for basic energy requirements. Ingestion may occupy unusual amounts of time. Eating may be obligatory and disrupt normal activity. In contrast, bulimia usually occurs surreptitiously in defined episodes and is terminated by abdominal pain, guilt or sleepiness.

Hyperphagic conditions may occur in association with central nervous system (CNS) disorders including gangliocytoma of the third ventricle [99], hypothalmic astrocytoma [100], Kleine-Levin Syndrome [101,102,103], Froehlich's Syndrome [104], Parkinson's Disease [105], genetic disorders including Praeder-Willi Syndrome (deletion of the long arm of chromosome 15) [105,106,107,108], major psychiatric disorders including anxiety, major depressive disorder [44], depressive phase of bipolar disorder [109], seasonal affective disorder [110,111,112] and schizophrenia [113,114], psychotropic medication, including delta-9 tetrahydrocannabinol [109], antidepressants and neuroleptics [115,116] and sleep disorders including sleep apnea [117]. Recent evidence evaluating episodic hormone secretion during sleep in Klein-Levin syndrome reveals an abnormality in the hypothalamic regulation of pituitary hormones [114].

Hyperphagia Associated with Sleep Disorders

Sasson [117] has noted that in patients with sleep apnea who are somnolent during the day, there is obligatory eating to induce alertness, thus reducing daytime drowsiness. This hyperphagia has produced markedly increased body weights in such patients. Binge eating behavior and morning anorexia have been described by Stunkard [118] in the contex of a "night eating" syndrome, suggesting a component of sleep disturbance. In the Kleine-Levine Syndrome [101] hyperphagia is associated with hypersomia.

Recent evidence evaluating episode hormone secretion dorms sleep in Kleine-Levin Syndrome reveals an abnormality in the hypothalamic regulation of pituitary hormes [119].

Hyperphagia Associated with Psychiatric Disorder

Hyperphagia may occur in psychiatric disorders such as depression, anxiety [44] and schizophrenia [113]. A subgroup of patients with anxiety overeat and gain weight [44] as do some patients with unipolar depression [44] and the depressive phase of a bipolar disorder [119].

Rosenthal [110,112] reported patients with seasonal affective disorder who appeared to have an atypical depression with hypersomnia, compulsive hyperphagia, carbohydrate craving, and weight gain, a syndrome which recurred beginning in the fall of the year and lasting through the winter months, with resolution during the increasing daylight hours in spring and summer.

Lyketsos et al. [113] noted that schizophrenic women

were found to give too much time and thought to food and to be preoccupied with food or they were perceived by nursing staffs as becoming anxious and greedy at mealtimes. In addition, it was noted that 60-percent of schizophrenic women were overweight, in contrast to 33 percent of schizophrenic men. The hyperphagic effects of phenothiazines appear to have only a minor role in increasing appetite.

Arieti [114] noted unusual eating patterns and described a terminal stage of schizophrenia wherein food selectivity was lost and indiscriminate eating, including pica (non-nutritive eating), occurred. A number of medications, including psychotropics and antidepressants, specifically amytriptiline [115,116], neuroleptics [115] and many other medications [115] increase appetite. Furthermore, Vaupel and Morton [109] noted that a number of abused substances, such as marijuana (Delta-9 tetrahydrocannabinol) increased appetite. Eating disorder syndromes may be found in increasing association with substance abuse with more extensive clinical and diagnostic delineation.

REFERENCES

1. Gislason LI. Eating disorder in childhood ages 4 through 11 years. Blinder BJ, Chaitin BF, et al: The eating disorders: Diagnosis, treatment, research. Great Neck (NY): PMA Publishing Corp. 1988.
2. Lucas 1985 (p.c.)
3. Sargent 1985 (p.c.)
4. Blinder BJ. Developmental antecedents of the eating disorders: A reconsideration. Psychiatr Clin North Am, 1980; 3(3):579-92.
5. Delaney DW, Silber TJ. Treatment of anorexia nervosa in a pediatric program. Pediatr Ann, 1984; 13:860-4.
6. Chatoor I, Egan J. Nonorganic failure to thrive and dwarfism due to food refusal: A separation disorder. J Am Acad Child Psychiatry, 1983; 22:294-301.
7. Irwin M. Early onset anorexia nervosa. South Med J, 1984; 77:611- 614.
8. Pugliese MT, Lifshitz F, Grad G, et al. Fear of obesity. A cause of short stature and delayed puberty. N Engl J Med, 1983; 309:513-518.
9. Falstein EI, Feinstein SC, Judas I. Anorexia nervosa in the male child. Am J Orthopsychiatry, 1956; 26:751-772.
10. Boileau RA, Lohman TG, Slaughter MH, et al. Hydration of the fat-free body in children during maturation. Hum Biol, 1984; 56:651-66.
11. Irwin M. Diagnosis of anorexia nervosa in children and the validity of DSM III. Am J Psychiatry, 1981; 138:1382-1383.
12. Panikar 1986 (p.c.)
13. Piazza 1985 (p.c.)
14. Russell GFM. Permenarchal anorexia nervosa and its sequelae. J Psychiatr Res, 1985; 19:363-369.
15. Pfeiffer RJ, Lucas AR, Ilstrup DM. Effect of anorexia nervosa on linear growth. Clin Pediatr, 1986; 25:7-12.
16. Herzog, DB, Norman DK, Gordon C, et al. Sexual conflict and eating disorders in 27 males. Am J Psychiatry, 1984; 141:989-990.
17. Goodman 1986 (p.c.)
18. Walsh 1986 (p.c.)
19. Atkinson 1985 (p.c.)
20. Morton R. Phthisiologica: or a treatise of consumptions. London: S. Smith & B. Walford, 1694.
21. Gull WW. Anorexia nervosa (apepsia hystreria, anorexia hysteria). Transactions of the Clinical Society of London, 1894; 7:22-28.
22. Vandereycken W, Van den Broucke S. Anorexia nervosa in males. Acta Psychiatr Scand, 1984; 70:447-454.
23. Crisp AH, Burns T. The clinical presentation of anorexia nervosa in males. Int J Eat D; 1983; 2(4):5-10.
24. Anderson AE, Michalide AD. Anorexia nervosa and bulimia: Their differential diagnoses in 24 males referred to an eating and weight disorders clinic. Bull Menninger Clin, 1985; 49:227-35.
25. Andersen AE, Michalide AD. Anorexia nervosa in the male: An underdiagnosed disorder. Psychosomatics, 1983; 24:1066-9, 1072-5.
26. Hall A, Delahunt JW, Ellis PM. Anorexia nervosa in the male: Clinical features and follow-up of nine patients. J Psychiatr Res, 1985; 19:315-321.
27. LaGrone DM. Primary anorexia nervosa in an adolescent male. South Med J, 1979; 72:501-502.
28. Hasan MK, Tibbetts RW. Primary anorexia nervosa (weight phobia) in males. Postgrad Med J, 1977; 53:146-151.
29. Beumont PJV, Beardwood CJ, and Russell GFM. The occurrence of the syndrome of anorexia nervosa in male subjects. Psychol Med, 1972; 2:216-231.
30. Hogan WM, Huerta E, Lucas AR. Diagnosing anorexia nervosa in males. Psychosomatics, 1974; 15:122-26.
31. Kiecolt-Glaser J, Dixon K. Postadolescent onset male anorexia. J Psychosoc Nurs Ment Health Serv, 1984; 22(1):11-13,17-20.
32. McFarlane AH, Bellisimo A, Upton E. "Atypical" anorexia nervosa: Treatment and management on a behavioral medicine unit. Psychiatr J Univ Ottawa, 1982; 7:158-162.
33. Yates A, Leehey K, Shisslak CM. Running - An analogue of anorexia? N Engl J Med, 1983; 308:251-255.
34. Wheeler MJ, Crisp AH, Hsu LKG, et al. Reproductive hormone changes during weight gain in male anorectics. Clin Endocrinol, 1983; 18:423-9.
35. Crisp AH, Hsu LG, Chen CL, et al. Reproductive hormone profiles in male anorexia nervosa before, during and after restoration of body weight to normal: A study of twelve patients. Int J Eat D, 1982; 1(3):3-9.
36. Mitchell JE, Goff G. Bulimia in male patients. Psychosomatics, 1984; 25:909-913.
37. Gwirtsman HE, Roy-Byrne P, Lerner L, et al. Bulimia in men: Report of three cases with neuroendocrine findings. J Clin Psychiatry, 1984; 45:78-81.
38. Russell G. Bulimia nervosa: an ominous variant of an-

orexia nervosa. Psychol Med, 1979; 9:429-48.

39. Blinder 1985 (p.c.)

40. Blinder BJ, Goodman SL. Atypical eating disorders. New Dir Ment Health Serv, San Francisco: Jossey-Bass, 1986 (31) pp 29-37.

41. Dally P. Anorexia tardive-late onset marital anorexia nervosa. J Psychosom Res, 1984; 28:423-428.

42. Price WA, Giannini AJ, Colella J. Anorexia nervosa in the elderly. J Am Geriatr Soc, 1985; 33:213-215.

43. Vandereycken W. Anorexia nervosa in adults. Blinder BJ, Chaitin BF & Goldstein R. (Eds): The eating disorders: Diagnosis, treatment, research. Great Neck (NY): PMA Publishing Corp., 1988.

44. Kaplan HI, Sadock BJ. Comprehensive textbook of psychiatry IV, Baltimore: Williams & Wilkins, 1985.

45. Ryle JA. Anorexia nervosa. Lancet, 1936; 2:893-9.

46. Kellett J, Trimble M, Thorley A. Anorexia nervosa after the menopause. Br J Psychiatry, 1976; 128:555-558.

47. Launer MA. Anorexia nervosa in late life. Br J Med Psychol, 1978; 51:375-377.

48. Sloan G, Leichner P. Is there a relationship between sexual abuse or incest and eating disorders? Can J Psychiatry, 1986; 31:656-60.

49. Crisp AH. Anorexia nervosa at normal body weight! - The abnormal normal weight control syndrome. Int J Psychiatry Med, 1981; 11:203-33.

50. Jonas JM, Pope Hg Jr, Hudson JJ, et al. Undiagnosed vomiting in an older woman: Unsuspected bulimia. Am J Psychiatry, 1984; 141:902-3.

51. Kaplan AS, Garfinkel PE, Darby PL, et al. Carbamazepine in the treatment of bulimia. Am J Psychiatry, 1983; 140:1225-1226.

52. Silber TJ. Anorexia nervosa in blacks and hispanics. Int J Eat D, 1986; 5:121-8.

53. Robinson P, Andersen A. Anorxia nervosa in American Blacks. J Psychiatr Res, 1985; 19:183-188.

54. Pumariega AJ, Edwards P, Mitchell CB. Anorexia nervosa in Black adolescents. J Am Acad Child Psychiatry, 1984; 23:111-4.

55. Silber TJ. Anorexia nervosa in Black adolescents. J Natl Med Assoc, 1984; 76:29-32.

56. Thomas JP, Szmukler GI. Anorexia nervosa in patients of Afro- Caribbean Extraction. Br J Psychiatry, 1985; 146:653-666.

57. Blinder BJ, Caswell-Papillon L, Sukin PJ. Anorexia nervosa and Tourette's Syndrome, 1984. Paper presented Internat'l Conference on the Eating Disorders. New York. 1984.

58. Yayura-Tobias JA. Gilles de la Tourette Syndrome: Interactions with other neuropsychiatric disorders. Acta Psychiatr. Scand, 1979; 59:9-16.

59. Larocca FEF. Concurrence of Turner's Syndrome, anorexia nervosa, and mood disorders: Case report. J Clin Psychiatry, 1985; 46:296-7.

60. Cohen DJ, Lechman JF, Shaywitz BA. Tourette's Syndrome: Assessment and treatment. In: Shaffer D, Khoharot AA & Greenhill L (eds). Diagnosis and treatment in pediatric psychiatry. New York: MacMil-lan Free Press, 1983.

61. Wurtman JJ, Wurtman RJ, Growden JH, et al. Carbohydrate craving in obese people: Suppression by treatments affecting serotonergic transmission. Int J Eat D, 1981; 1(1):2-15.

62. Hsu LKG, Meltzer ES, Cirsp AH. Schizophrenia and anorexia nervosa. J Nerv Ment Dis, 1981; 169:273-276.

63. Frighner JP, Robins E, Guze SB. Diagnostic criteria for use in psychiatric research. Arch Gen Psychiatry, 1972; 26:57-63.

64. Crisp AH. Differential diagnosis of anorexia nervosa. Proc R Soc Med, 1977; 70:686-690.

65. Mohl PC, McMahon T. Anorexia nervosa associated with mental retardation and schizoaffective disorder. Psychosomatics, 1980; 21:602-603,606.

66. Bruch H. Developmental considerations of anorexia nervosa and obesity. Can J Psychiatry, 1981; 26:212-7.

67. Damlouji NF, Ferguson JM. Three cases of posttraumatic anorexia nervosa. Am J Psychiatry, 1985; 142:362-363.

68. Bernstein AE, Warner, GM. Onset of anorexia nervosa after prolonged use of the Milwaukee brace. Psychosomatics, 1983; 24:1033-1034.

69. Fichter MM, Daser C, Postpischil F. Anorexic syndromes in the male. J Psychiatr Res, 1985; 19:305-313.

70. Hurley AD, Sovner R. Anorexia nervosa and mental retardation: A case report. J Clin Psychiatry, 1979; 40:480-482.

71. Cottrell DJ, Crisp AH. Anorexia nervosa in Down's Syndrome — a case report. Br J Psychiatry, 1984; 145:195-196.

72. Hershman MJ, Hershman M. Anorexia nervosa and Crohn's disease. Br J Clin Pract, 1985; 39:157-9.

73. Metcalfe-Gibson C. Anorexia nervosa and Crohn's disease. Br J Surg, 1978; 65:231-233.

74. Wellmann W, Pries K, Freyberger H. Die Kombination von Morbus Crohn und Anorexia-Nervosa-Symptomatik. Dtsch Med Wochenschr, 1981; 106:1499-1502.

75. Handler CE, Perkin GD. Anorexia nervosa and Wernicke's encephalopathy: An underdiagnosed Association. Lancet, 1982; 2:771-2.

76. George GCW. Anorexia nervosa with herpes simplex encephalitis. Postgrad Med, 1981; 57:366-7.

77. Wender M. Case of multiple sclerosis with the symptoms of anorexia nervosa in the intial stage of the disease. Pol Tyg Lek, 1982; 37:1361-1362.

78. Erman MK, Murray GB. A case report of anorexia nervosa and Gaucher's Disease. Am J Psychiatry, 1980; 137:858-9.

79. Dally P, Gomez J, Isaacs AJ. Anorexia nervosa. London: William Heinemann Medical Books Ltd, 1979.

80. Gold PW, Gwirtsman H, Avgerinos PC, et al. ACTH responses to corticotropin releasing hormone (CRH) are abnormal in anorexia nervosa: Implications for a defect in hypothalmic CRH secretion in this disorder. Acta Endocrinol (Suppl), 1985; 270:27.

81. Gold PW, Gwirtsman H, Avgerinos PC, et al. Abnormal hypothalmic-pituitary-adrenal function in ano-

rexia nervosa: Pathophysiologic mechanisms in underweight and weight-corrected patients. N Engl J Med, 1986; 314:1335-42.

82. Majewska MD, Harrison NL, Schwartz RD, et al. Steroid hormone metabolites are barbiturate-like modulators of the GABA receptor. Science, 1986; 232:1004-7.

83. Kontula K, Mustajoki P, Paetau A, et al. Development of Cushing's Disease in a patient with anorexia nervosa. J Endocrinol Invest, 1984; 7:35-40.

84. Blinder BJ. Gastroesophageal function in anorexia nervosa and bulimia—Delayed gastric emptying and rumination paper presented at the International Conference on Eating Disorders in Adolescents and Young Adults. Jerusalem: May 1987.

85. Barrett J, Clarke M, Robinson PH, et al. Delayed gastric emptying in patients with anorexia nervosa. J Physiol, 1987; 387:92P.

86. Szmukler GI. Anorexia nervosa and bulimia in diabetics. J Psychosom Res, 1984; 28:365-9.

87. Roland JM, Bhanji S. Anorexia nervosa occurring in patients with diabetes mellitus. Postgrad Med J, 1982; 58:354-356.

88. Hudson JI, Wentworth SM, Hudson MS, et al. Prevalence of anorexia nervosa and bulimia among young diabetic women. J Clin Psychiatry, 1985; 46:88-9.

89. Hardoff D, Shenker IR, and Nussbaum M. Anorexia nervosa in a patient with juvenile diabetes. NY St J Med, 1984; 84(2):61.

90. Dally P, Gomez J, Isaacs AJ. Anorexia nervosa in diabetes mellitus. Br Med J, 1980; 281:61-2.

91. Rodin GM, Daneman D, Johnson LE, et al. Anorexia nervosa and bulimia in female adolescents with insulin dependent diabetes mellitus: A systematic study. J Psychiatr Res, 1985; 19:381-384.

92. Powers PS, Malone JI, Duncan JA. Anorexia nervosa and diabetes mellitus. J Clin Psychiatry, 1983; 44:133-135.

93. Szmukler GI, Russell GFM. Diabetes mellitus, anorexia nervosa and bulimia. Br J Psychiat, 1983; 142:305-308.

94. Fairburn CG, Steel JM. Anorexia nervosa in diabetes mellitus. Br Med J, 1980; 280:1167-8.

95. Sodeman WA Jr, Sodeman TM. Sodeman's pathologic physiology, 11th edition. Philadelphia: W.B. Saunders Co., 1985.

96. Money J, Annecillo C, Werlwas J. Hormonal and behavioral reversals in hyposomatotropic dwarfism. In: Hormones behavior and psychopathology (ed.) Edward J. Sachar. New York: Raven Press, 1976.

97. Morley JE, Castele SC. Death by starvation: The Sepulveda Grecc Method No. 6. Geriatric Medicine Today, 1985; 4(11):76-8,83.

98. Morley 1986 (p.c.)

99. Beal MF, Kleinman GM, Ojemann RG, et al. Gangliocytoma of third ventricle: Hyperphagia, somnolence, and dementia. Neurology, 1981; 31:1224-8.

100. Haugh RM, Markesbery WR. Hypothalamic astrocytoma, syndrome of hyperphagia, obesity, and distur-

bances of behavior and endocrine and autonomic function. Arch Neurol, 1983; 40:560-3.

101. Orlosky MJ. The Kleine-Levin Syndrome: A review. Psychosomatics, 1982; 23:609-10,15-17,21.

102. Carpenter S, Yassa R, Ochs R. A pathologic basis for Kleine-Levin Syndrome. Arch Neurol, 1982; 39:25-28.

103. Critchley M, Hoffman HL. The syndrome of periodic somnolence and morbid hunger (Kleine-Levin Syndrome). Br Med J, 1942; 1(4230):137-9.

104. Magalini SI, Scrascia E. Dictionary of medical syndromes 2nd ed, 1981. Philadelphia: JB Lippincott.

105. Rosenberg P, Herishanu Y, Beilin B. Increased appetite (bulimia) in Parkinson's Disease. J Am Geriatr Soc, 1977; 25:277-278.

106. Holm VA, Pipes PL. Food and children with Prader-Willi Syndrome. Am J Dis Child, 1976; 130:1063-1067.

107. Kyriakides M, Silverstone T, Jeffcoate W, et al. Effect of nalaxone on hyperphagia in Prader-Willi Syndrome. Lancet, 1980; 1:876-7.

108. Donlon TA, Lalande M, Wyman A, et al. Molecular diagnosis and analysis of chromosome #15 microdeletion and lability in the Prader-Willi Syndrome. Am J Hum Genet, 1985; 37:A91.

109. Vaupel DB, Morton EC. Anorexia and hyperphagia produced by five pharmacologic classes of hallucinogens. Pharmacol Biochem Behav, 1982; 17:539-545.

110. Rosenthal NE, Sack DA, Gillin JC, et al. Seasonal affective disorder—A description of the syndrome and preliminary findings with light therapy. Arch Gen Psychiatry, 1984; 41:72-80.

111. Rosenthal NE, Sack DA, Carpenter CJ, et al. Antidepressant effects of light in seasonal affective disorder. Am J Psychiatry, 1985; 142:163-70.

112. Rosenthal NE, Carpenter CJ, James SP, et al. Seasonal affective disorder in children and adolescents. Am J Psychiatry, 1986; 143:356-8.

113. Lyketsos GC, Paterakis P, Beis A, et al. Eating disorders in schizophrenia. Br J Psychiatry, 1985; 146:255-261.

114. Arieti S. Interpretation of schizophrenia. New York: Robert Brunner Publisher of Psychiatric Books, 1955.

115. Stolar M. The effect of psychopharmacologic agents upon appetite and eating in The eating disorders: Diagnosis, treatment, research. Great Neck (NY): PMA Publishing Corp, 1988.

116. Winston F, McCann ML. Antidepressant drugs and excessive weight gain. Br J Psychiatry, 1972; 120:693-694.

117. Sasson 1986 (p.c.)

118. Stunkard AJ, Grace WJ, Wolff HG. The night-eating syndrome: A pattern of food intake among certain obese patients. Am J Med, 1955; 19:78-86.

119. Goodwin FK. Special issues in lithium treatment of recurrent affective illness in Lithium Clinical Considerations. Excepta Medica 1982.

120. Gorloth N, Dickerman Z, Bechar M. et al. Episodic hormone secretion during sleep in Kleine-Levin syndrome: Evidence of hypothalamic dysfunction. Brain Dev 1987; 9:309-315.

Chapter 36

Oral Manifestations of Eating Disorders: Indications for a Collaborative Treatment Approach

Nadine A. Levinson

INTRODUCTION

The effects of self-induced starvation and chronic vomiting can cause significant and often irreversible changes of the dentition and oral cavity, besides the complex medical and psychiatric symptoms. A dental emergency may be the patient's first confrontation of damage and deleterious sequelae caused by the eating disorder. The dental complications can cause crumbling teeth, loss of restorations, abscesses, and pain, which can intensify the patient's narcissistic vulnerability. With the aim of facilitating optimal patient care for the eating disorder patient, this paper will review the dental literature on the oral and dental manifestations, describe current dental management, and finally, discuss the guidelines for consultation liaison between dentistry and psychiatry.

REVIEW OF LITERATURE

Dentists are becoming more interested in the multidetermined psychologic and physiologic origins of eating disorders, which in the United States involve more than 500,000 individuals [1]. Although the first recorded case of anorexia nervosa appeared in the medical literature in 1694 [2], the first case in the dental literature did not appear until 1937 [3]. The article vividly described a young school teacher who looked like a "walking skeleton" and vomited, causing extensive decalcification of her teeth. However, there was no recognition that the woman had an eating disorder or a serious psychiatric condition stemming from a fear of weight gain, a relentless pursuit of thinness, or disturbance in body sensations and body image [4].

In 1939, Holst and Lange [5] first used the word perimylolysis to describe decalcification of the dentition due to chronic regurgitation. The authors noted that "gastric dysfunction" with vomiting produced a smooth and polished appearance of some "wasted teeth." The tooth erosion was caused by both the acidic composition of the vomitus and the acid retention within the filliform papillae of the tongue, which mechanically polished the teeth. There was no appreciation of the etiology of the bizarre food behaviors and/or vomiting that caused the dental erosion.

Perimylolysis and perimolysis are used in the dental literature with the same frequency and have a similar meaning. Hellström [6] gives a graphic definition by describing perimylolysis as "a loss of enamel and dentin on the lingual surfaces as a result of chemical and mechanical effects caused mainly by regurgitation of gastric contents and aggravated by the movements of the tongue." Perimolysis, a simpler term, is used more often in the American literature and is preferred by the author.

A review of the Index Medicus between 1968 and 1978 shows a fourfold increase in medical publications on anorexia nervosa, but with no discussion of the oral and dental manifestations [7]. As a notable exception, a team of two psychiatrists and a dentist systematically studied 17 randomly selected anorectic patients [8]. Medical, dental, and dietary examinations were completed. The patients were separated into three groups: a group who vomited for more than three years, a group who regurgitated for more than three years, and a nonvomiting group. Differences between vomitting and regurgitating groups were not explained in the article. Dental erosion was the most common and deleterious symptom for the vomiting and regurgitating groups. Caries incidence was increased and atypical compared with the normal population. Dental plaque was reduced in the vomiting group. In addition to reported high carbohydrate consumption, patients in the vomiting group showed an increase in the consumption of citrus fruits.

In two studies of anorectic and bulimic patients, Hellström [6,9] demonstrated the typical dental manifestations of altered caries rate and dental erosion. The relationship of dental plaque to caries and erosion between the two studies showed inconsistent findings. An exact differential diagnosis among the various subtypes of eating disorders was not yet appreciated.

Many articles [7,10-18] discussing diagnosis, treatment, and case histories have recently appeared in the dental literature, thus paralleling the increase in incidence of the disorder. An updated differential diagnosis of eating disorders based on a description of symptoms has only appeared in the most recent articles [16-18]. Levinson [17] has discussed the importance of understanding the development and psychodynamic meaning of the symptom for each individual patient. However, some of the articles fail to recognize the important and diversified psychologic and psychodynamic factors. In two cases reported, dental treatment was undertaken before psychiatric referral [11,12].

The oral and dental manifestations resulting from eating disorders involve six areas of pathology:

Perimolysis, or erosion of enamel

Erosion can take place on all surfaces of the teeth. The most frequent sites are the lingual surfaces of the maxillary and mandibular anterior teeth (figure 1) and buccal and occlusal aspects of the posterior teeth (figure 2). The teeth appear smooth, dished-out, and have rounded margins. The anterior teeth can become thinned out and shortened, appearing as if there were an open bite causing a space between the upper and lower teeth. The exposed dentin causes thermal sensitivity and is one of the chief dental complaints. Several of the patients treated by the author have discussed fan-

tasies of having "dirty and scummy teeth after vomiting." They would fastidiously and overzealously clean their teeth with a toothbrush after each vomiting episode. This accompanying ritual worsens the erosion process. In some cases, the teeth crumble away, leaving silver fillings that stand out on the deteriorating tooth (figure 3).*

Caries incidence

Caries or tooth decay is multidetermined by diet, heredity, and hygiene. Bulimics with a high-carbohydrate diet, poor hygiene, and a predisposition to decay will have increased caries. A mixed atypical clinical picture is seen in several of the dental studies, because the eating disorder groups that were studied did not differentiate the various subtypes [6,8,9]. Further systematic research is needed to study the diverse subtypes of eat-

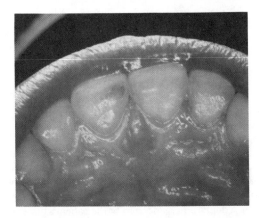

Figure 36.1 Palatal erosion of maxillary teeth with thinning and rounding of edges from chronic vomiting.

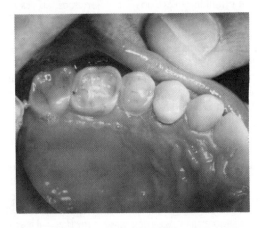

Figure 36.2 Severe erosion of occlusal surfaces of teeth causing a dished out appearance.

* The pictures in Figures 1-4 were provided by Robert Wolcott, DDS.

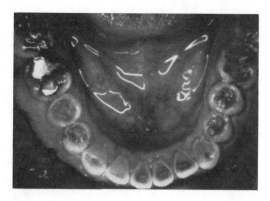

Figure 36.3 Severe perimolysis of mandibular teeth with silver fillings standing away from teeth in a patient who was bulimic for four years

ing disorders and correlate them with the different oral and dental manifestations.

Periodontium

Deleterious effects on the gingival and supporting bone (periodontium) reflect some of the insidious metabolic and neuroendocrinologic changes that may not show up for years. Bleeding gums are usually caused by poor hygiene and/or a vitamin deficiency secondary to the cachectic state. Stege et al [14] have noticed periodontal changes in anorexic and bulimic patients with extensive decay. However, many bulimic patients also demonstrate excellent periodontal health with increased erosion.

Saliva

Laxatives, diuretics, bingeing and starvation, leading to electrolyte imbalance, have serious dental implications by affecting the saliva. The saliva of bulimics at rest and when stimulated is reduced in quantity and decreased in pH [6]. Quantitative and qualitative changes of saliva decreases its buffering and remineralizing capacity [8,9]. The saliva, which normally ranges between a pH of 5.5 and 8.0, loses its buffering capacity and cannot neutralize the contents of the stomach, which ranges between a pH of 1.0 and 5.0 [19]. Blinder and Hagman [28] found differential levels of salivary isoamylase in a pilot study of 35 women with eating disorders. Salivary isoamylase was elevated in patients with bulimia nervosa and bulimia and depressed in patients with anorexia nervosa. Psychiatrists should also be aware that antidepressants will complicate the decreased quantity of saliva, thus increasing the risk for decay and erosion. Many patients will suck citrus flavored candies to help the xerostomia and unknowingly increase caries potential. Other psychophysiological concomitants such as malnutrition, anxiety, depres-

sion, and hormonal disorders can influence the saliva [9]. Reversible salivary gland enlargement (particularly of the parotid gland) secondary to starvation has been reported in the literature [18,20,21]. The pathophysiology to explain the salivary gland enlargement has not been proposed and is another area in need of research.

Oral mucous membranes

It is well accepted that saliva is important as a lubricator of the mucous membranes of the mouth. There have been no studies of the change, quality, quantity, and buffering capacity of saliva on the mucous membranes that can be correlated with the different eating disorders. These changes can reflect metabolic and neuroendocrinologic effects in addition to the direct contact of acidic contents on the mucous membranes, which causes chronic irritation.

Mandibular dysfunction

There have been no reports in the dental literature of any relationship between temporomandibular joint disorders and eating disorders. However, the author has treated several patients who first presented with symptoms typical of mandibular dysfunction (having chronic myofascial pain, muscle hyperactivity, and restricted opening) who later announced that they had a secret eating disorder. Acknowledgment of the eating disorder took place after the oral dysfunction was resolved and in the context of a positive treatment alliance. An assessment of the patient's personality, including an understanding of the underlying meaning of the symptom formation, was crucial for dental and psychiatric treatment.

Other eating disorders and miscellaneous dental manifestations

Not only does the carbohydrate consumption and acid from bulimics affect the dentition, but interestingly, the teeth can cause calluses on the dorsum of the fingers. Russell [22] described abrasions on the backs of the hands, which can be used as an early sign of bulimia from self-induced vomiting.

Persistent eating of lead can cause stains in the mucous membranes of the mouth. A mentally retarded adult with pica who consumed lead was diagnosed by the presence of a "lead line" on the patient's gingiva. Dentists need to be on the lookout for lead poisoning in children and retarded patients [23]. Rumination, which is characterized by repeated regurgitation, can also cause erosion of the dentition. The first anorexic case in the dental literature [3] was also reported to be a ruminator. There have been no systematic studies of the differences of the oral manifestations of bulimics compared with ruminators. More observational studies comparing the different dental and oral effects are needed.

CONSULTATION LIAISON AND DENTAL TREATMENT

Pain caused by decay, a pulpitis or thermal sensitivity are the most common dental symptoms presented by patients with bulimia, with or without anorexia. It takes approximately two years of frequent vomiting to induce this damage. Vomiting of longer duration will eventually cause crumbling and ugly teeth, which add to a negative self-image. The insidious effects from anorexia without vomiting are far more subtle and not distinguishable from the effects of malnutrition. A collaborative treatment approach requiring dental and psychiatric skills is indicated.

Interdisciplinary seminars for discussing the nature of the disorder and practical guidelines for confrontation are necessary. The psychiatrist can be available to advise the dentist of the complex psychologic and physiologic origins of the eating disorder so that an empathic confrontation can be facilitated. It must be emphasized to the dentist that the patient has no volitional control over his or her behavior. Psychologic and subjectively experienced data can be elicited in an empathic and sensitive manner during the dental emergency and diagnostic phases. Helping the patient identify and discuss current and surface emotional difficulties related to friendships, school, or family can often enhance the rapport necessary for the encounter. Treating a patient as if she has conscious control or can be shamed or frightened out of her "surreptitious" habit is contraindicated and can worsen the condition.

The patient should be reassured that dental treatment will continue while the patient is in psychotherapy so he or she does not feel rejected or abandoned. However, the usual dental procedures to restore form and function must wait. Some individuals are resistant to acknowledging their eating disorder and are reluctant to accept treatment. The prognosis depends on the nature and extent of the personality disorder, which can be mild to severe. Any extensive dental treatment undertaken without psychiatric treatment of the underlying problem is obviously doomed to failure.

The dentist should be prepared for obstinate behavior that might temporarily compromise "perfect" dental care. Sometimes anger, despair, or even depression may be provoked in the dentist who treats eating disorder patients. The psychiatrist can use this opportunity to illustrate the concepts of transference and countertransference, which are useful for understanding the eating disorder patient. The dentist then learns that his or her feelings are responses to those feelings of the patient that are provoked by parents, authority, or parent-like individuals. These involuntary, unconscious, psychologic mechanisms are the primary means by which the patient maintains control of people, activities, food, and his or her own body.

The psychiatrist can alert the dentist about the important dynamics around the issues of control. With the right approach, the dental setting can be a situation where the dentist can help the patient feel in control of his or her mouth and body. Oral hygiene instruction, fluoride mouthrinses (using a 0.05% concentration of sodium fluoride twice daily) [14] and sodium bicarbonate rinses to neutralize acid in vomitus can be suggested. Emergency dental problems can be treated in the usual ways, using temporary procedures such as preformed crowns, calcium hydroxide, and composite resin on the teeth. Plastic splints lined with magnesium hydroxide can be made to protect the teeth (figure 4). Artificial saliva for bulimics with decreased salivary output may be beneficial, as well as vitamin supplements for gingival bleeding. Any permanent restorations are contraindicated until the eating disorder is under control.

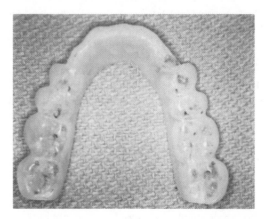

Figure 36.4 A splint that can be used to restore bite and that can be lined with a basic liner to neutralize the acid.

An illustration of the extensive and potentially traumatic procedures that may be eventually required for permanent restoration of oral health can be seen in figures 5 through 10.* Because of the severe loss of tooth structure, the collapsed bite has to be opened (figures 5 and 6). The crown-to-root ratios must be increased so that the new restorations will have adequate retention. Electrosurgery (figure 7) is used to remove and lower the level of gingival tissue. The crowns are prepared with a diamond stone, and a model is made for the lab work (figure 8). Using models of the teeth, waxups are made and then cast into gold copings (figure

---

*   The patient was treated by John Flocken, DDS, who provided the pictures.

9) and cemented in the mouth. Afterward, the teeth are reprepared for porcelain crowns (figure 10). These procedures are expensive, time-consuming, and potentially traumatic, so it is imperative that the patient be in a healthy mental state before extensive dental treatment.

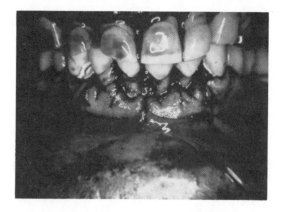

Figure 36.7 Electrosurgery was necessary to increase the crown-to-root ratio for better crown retention.

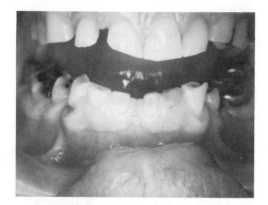

Figure 36.5 Preoperative photos of case before restorations. Loss of tooth structure has caused bite to severely close down. (See also Figure 36.6)

Figure 36.8 A work model with wax coping preparations.

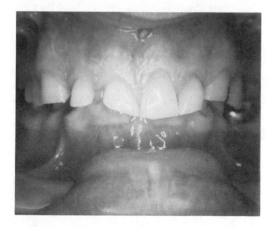

Figure 36.6

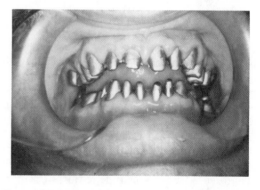

Figure 36.9 Gold copings in place and with final preparation for porcelain crowns.

DISCUSSION

DSM-III [24] clearly differentiates between bulimia and anorexia, although recognizing that both conditions may exist together. The same patients may fulfill the criteria for differentiation at various times [22]. However, physiologic studies of the changes in the metabolic, hemopoietic, and endocrine systems have not revealed specific diagnostic criteria for anorexia or bulimia that can be differentiated from starvation secondary to other causes [25].

Just as there may be psychiatric differences such as impulse control or levels of psychopathology [26,27], there are also differences that will show up in the oral cavity due to the different weight and food consumption patterns. The early dental studies [6,8,9], while being excellent observational studies, took place before careful differentiation between the eating disorders were recognized. The validity for the distinction between bulimia

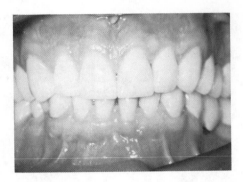

Figure 36.10 Final postoperative porcelain crowns.

with and without anorexia needs to be ascertained for the oral manifestations. For example, there is no differentiation of oral sequelae between: (1) the bulimic who has a high carbohydrate consumption, but no emaciation; (2) the bulimic who has abnormal eating habits, including increased citric juices; (3) the anorexic who has self-induced starvation; or (4) the bulimic who has high-carbohydrate binges and is also malnourished and emaciated.

As a result, some of the dental manifestations of malnutrition, such as periodontal disease, gingivitis, or increased caries may be due to changes from starvation rather than from the profound effects of acid on the dentition resulting from persistent vomiting. Specific changes of the salivary flow and content due to the separate or combined effects of vomiting, malnutrition, and high carbohydrate uptake still remain unclear and in need of study.

SUMMARY

Eating disorders have been on the rise for the last 15 to 20 years. Often, the dentist may be one of the first health care professionals to recognize the eating disorder because of the extensive deterioration and mutilation that can occur in the mouth. The acid from the vomitus causes severe damage to the teeth and surrounding tissues, and the condition is progressive unless the psychiatric problem is understood and treated. Individuals who shamefully and secretly guard their obsessive habit must be empathically and nonjudgementally confronted by the dentist and referred for psychiatric diagnosis and treatment before any permanent of extensive dental procedures. This perplexing behavior, which has plagued and intrigued physicians for years, has now become a concern of dentists that challenges their technical and interpersonal skills. The dentist can be crucial in facilitating an effective psychiatric referral and must be included as a part of the multidisciplinary team involved in the management of eating disorders.

REFERENCES

1. Sours JA. The primary anorexia syndrome. In: Nospitz J, ed. Basic handbook of child psychiatry, vol II. New York: Basic Books, 1979: 568-580.

2. Morton R. Phthisiologica — or a treatise of consumptions. London, 1694:

3. Bargen JA, Austin LT. Decalcification of teeth as a result of obstipation with long continued vomiting: report of a case. J Am Dent Assoc 1937; 24:1271-3.

4. Bruch H. Eating disorders: Obesity, anorexia and the person within. New York; Basic Books, 1973:

5. Holst JJ, Lange F. Perimylolysis. A contribution towards the genesis of tooth wasting from non-mechanical causes. Acta Odontol Scand 1939; 1:37-48.

6. Hellström I. Oral complications in anorexia nervosa. Scand J Dent Res 1977; 85:71-86.

7. Brady WF. The anorexia nervosa syndrome. Oral Surg 1980; 50:509-16.

8. Hurst PS, Lacey JH, Crisp AH. Teeth, vomiting and diet: a study of the dental characteristics of 17 anorexia nervosa patients. Postgrad Med J 1977; 53:298-305.

9. Hellström I. Anorexia nervosa-odontologiska problem. Swed Dent J 1974; 67:253-69.

10. House RC, Bliziotes MM, Licht JH. Perimolysis: unveiling the surreptitious vomiter. Oral Surg 1981; 51:152-5.

11. Sweeney EA, Swanson LT, Kaban LB. Erosion of dental enamel by acids: report of a case. J Dent Child 1977; 44:457-9.

12. White DK, Hayes RC, Benjamin RN. Loss of tooth structure associated with chronic regurgitation and vomiting. J Am Dent Assoc 1978; 97:833-5.

13. Linkon JJ, Roper RE, Wiedlen RA. Perimolysis: report of a case. S Calif Dent J 1968; 36:65-8.

14. Stege P, Visco-Dangler L, Rye L. Anorexia nervosa: review including oral and dental manifestations. J Am Dent Assoc 1982; 104:648-52.

15. Kleier JK, Aragon SB, Averbach RE. Dental management of the chronic vomiting patient. J Am Dent Assoc 1984; 108:618-21.

16. Wolcott RB, Yager J, Gordon G. Dental sequelae to the binge-purge syndrome (bulimia): report of cases. J Am Dent Assoc 1984; 109:723-5.

17. Levinson NA. Anorexia and bulimia: an eating function gone awry. Calif Dent Assoc J 1985; 13:18-22.

18. Harrison JL, George LA, Cheatham JL, et al. Dental effects and management of bulimia nervosa. Gen Dent 1985; 33:65-8.

19. Valentine AD, Anderson RJ, Bradnock G. Salivary pH and dental caries. Brit Dent J 1978; 144:105-7.

20. Ahola SJ. Unexplained parotid enlargement: a clue to occult bulimia. Conn Med 1982; 46:185-6.

21. Laudenbach P, Mauvais P, Simon D, et al. The dysorexia-sialomegaly-amenorrhea syndrome. Rev Stomatol Chir Maxillofac 1978; 79:451-65.

22. Russell G. Bulimia nervosa: an ominous variant of anorexia nervosa. Psychol Med 1979; 9:429-48.

23. Lockhart PB. Gingival pigmentation as the sole pre-

senting sign of chronic lead poisoning in a mentally retarded adult. Oral Surg, Oral Med, Oral Path 1981; 52:143-9.

24. American Psychiatric Association. Diagnostic and statistical manual of mental disorders, (DSM-III). Washington DC: American Psychiatric Association, 1980: 67-73.

25. Halmi KA: Anorexia nervosa and bulimia. Psychosomatics 1984; 24:111-29.

26. Garner DM, Garfinkel PE, O'Shaughnessy M. The validity of the distinction between bulimia with and without anorexia nervosa. Am J Psych 1985; 142:581-6.

27. Garfinkel PE, Moldofsky H, Garner DM. The heterogeneity of anorexia nervosa. Arch Psych 1980; 37:1036-8.

28. Blinder BJ, Hagman J. Serum salivary isoamylase levels in patients with anorexia nervosa, bulimia or bulimia nervosa. Hillside J Clin Psychiatry 1986; 8:152-163.

Section III

Treatment

Barton J. Blinder, Barry F. Chaitin, and Renée Goldstein

At this point in the history of modern psychiatry, the only reasonable model is the biopsychosocial. While this is espoused by many, its actual effective application requires vigilance, effort, and integration at the highest level of knowledge and professional communication. In the eating disorders, this perspective is even more fundamental because of the multiple presentations, in often dramatic ways, of somatic, intrapsychic, and social manifestations.

In our experience, application of a comprehensive general rehabilitation philosophy insures the appropriate balanced attention to all sectors of dysfunction. Historically, past treatment approaches have focused on unitary aspects of the disorder and applied singular treatment modalities. Early interventions in the eating disorders were characterized primarily by physician authority conveyed to family and patient and were directed toward renutrition while attempting to challenge mental distortions about food and health. Psychoanalytic views of treatment were based on an intrapsychic conflict model of oral psychosexual conflict, which subordinated the pragmatic significance of the eating disorders, their tenacity, resistance to change, and the often severe medical consequences. The advent of behavioral approaches resulted in rapid in-hospital weight gain, which often distracted attention from significant deficits in ego development and interpersonal relation ships that required a long-term psychotherapeutic focus.

The cornerstone of our therapeutic approach is the establishment of a psychotherapeutic alliance with patient and family. Within this framework, diagnostic evaluation can proceed both within and outside of a hospital setting, and a treatment plan can be formulated. This must include thorough medical and dental evaluation, laboratory and radiologic evaluation, and nutrition consultation. The special resistances posed by eating disorder patients and their families often frustrate and defeat the most carefully constructed treatment plans. Since control and its consequences are a core issue for virtually every patient, recognition of the impediments to smooth and unencumbered progress must be identified and processed at key junctures in the treatment program. The hazardous course these patients travel is beset with denial and neglect of self as they impose on others the worry and concern for their survival and the hope for their future growth and development.

While there are no modalities of treatment specific for the eating disorders, there are indeed special clinical challenges. In this section, the contributors emphasize the relevance and special modifications of established medical and psychological treatments for eating disorder patients and their families.

Chapter 37

Nutritional Rehabilitation and Normalization of Eating Pattern

Jean Densmore-John

The most important component in the initiation of a nutritional rehabilitation program is the establishment of trust and rapport with the eating disorder patient. The importance of the need for a therapeutic alliance has been discussed in the literature [1,2]. The eating disorder patient usually has her or his own views on what is "nutritious" and what can or cannot be consumed. Treatment is often difficult, being adversely influenced by (1) the pervasive goal of weight reduction and the avoidance of weight gain [3], (2) dichotomous thinking patterns [2], and (3) an overwhelming fear of losing control [4]. Working within a framework of trust, the patient and clinician create a basis for change that promotes self-assurance in the patient's own food choices as treatment progresses.

The response to nutritional restructuring, as observed by the author, may be differentiated in patients presenting with anorexia nervosa or bulimia in the following ways. In anorexia nervosa, the patient desires control of the diet plan during a rehabilitation program and generally resists dietary treatment; whereas in bulimia, the patient desires to help in planning a diet, and may want to be told specifically what and how much to eat during a rehabilitation program. The anorexic is preoccupied with the pursuit of a thinner appearance and a lower weight on the scale, while the bulimic patient is usually more intent on achieving an aesthetically "perfect" figure as well as a low weight on the scale. The an-

orexic avoids eating as a means of producing a sense of lightness and energy and will avoid food to suppress the anxiety created by choosing what to eat to prevent weight gain. Bulimics resist the urge to binge to stimulate the feeling of being in control of food intake and external pressures. However, they may commence a binge as a psychological means of coping with anxiety, depression, boredom, and/or dealing with relationships or situations.

A characteristic similarity that both groups have in common is their food preoccupation, which may become very disturbing to both restrictive anorexics and bulimics as they seek to resist the need to eat. It is frequently the food preoccupation that brings them to treatment.

Selecting what to eat when given a range of food choices becomes an overwhelmingly difficult task for the undernourished anorexic and bulimic. To restore the ability to make food choices, which will provide for the individual's nutritional requirements over time, professional guidance in the selection and planning of food intake is necessary. The patient should be encouraged to be an active participant in the process of food selection and planning. Involving the patient with her/his own diet during the course of treatment will counter the anorexic's battle to control food intake by discouraging the avoidance and diminishing the fear of certain foods. The bulimic patient will learn to trust herself/himself around food through learned principles of selection and planning of a healthy diet.

Both anorexia and bulimia are characterized by a morbid fear of fatness [3-5]. The two conditions usually differ in respect to the desired or "idealized" body shape, as noted previously. The "fear of fat" is transferred to the food, and the food is then viewed as a source of potential fatness. The food takes on a negative connotation, which must be changed to a positive association during treatment to re-establish normal eating patterns. The dichotomous manner of thinking creates a tendency for the patient to view food as being either good or bad, making education toward a more realistic viewpoint regarding food selection challenging.

Learning about what their individual nutritional needs are and how to meet those needs through food selection and meal planning is an involved process that should start with an initial nutrition assessment. This assessment is essential for making the original diagnosis, organizing treatment plans, predicting long- and short-range goals, and in evaluating the subsequent response to treatment. Mutually agreed upon goals direct the patient from her previous single goal-oriented, weight conscious approach to life.

Rehabilitation begins at the stage of renourishment of the patient. A certain degree of nutritional rehabilitation must occur before psychotherapy can begin to be effective [6]. The nutritional restructuring of the diet involves not only renourishing the patient and achieving the desired weight gain, but also supporting and re-educating the patient toward more positive and realistic expectations regarding food and feelings about bodily needs and shape.

HISTORY

Sir William Gull (1868) described his dietary treatment plan for anorexia nervosa as the institution of a feeding schedule of "regular intervals" during which the patient is surrounded by people who could exert the most control over the patient. The patient was not consulted during the treatment process [7]. Ryle (1936) noted the tendency for hiding and disposing of food by anorexic patients and advocated that initial control over the patient was necessary to see that food, a mixed diet, was consumed. His treatment included bed rest and warmth to conserve energy [8].

All dietary programs seem to meet with difficulties with the resistant patient. With the onset of tube-feeding and later parenteral hyperalimentation in 1968 [9], even the most resistant patient could be force-fed and made to achieve the "goal" weight. Infection and metabolic complications associated with the use of hyperalimentation [10,11] and the rapid weight gain deter its use as a preferred means of therapy today. Psychological adjustment to changes in body shape do not have time to occur with the rapid weight gain produced by force-feeding techniques, and weight loss may follow after force-feedings are discontinued [12]. When hyperalimentation is used as a life-saving procedure in anorexia nervosa, it should be instituted along with psychiatric therapy.

More recently, Huse and Lucas [12] have recommended basing the initial kilocalorie allowance on the estimated basal or resting energy expenditure (BEE or REE) of the individual and then gradually increasing the level of kilocalories as the patient's energy requirements and physical and psychological acceptance of food increases. As the metabolic alterations and the anorexic psyche become more clearly understood, the dietary program may be more individualized.

The recognition of bulimia as a clinical entity has occurred within the past decade [5,13]. Treatment programs that include nutritional counseling have recently been reported in the literature [14-17].

DEVELOPMENTS IN THE FIELD OF NUTRITIONAL REHABILITATION

Classic studies by Keys et al [18] on the behavioral response to starvation have given insight to the importance of the nutritional adequacy of the diet. In these studies, the following changes in behavior were observed in normal male subjects starved to 25% of normal body weight: social isolation, decreased verbalization, depressed affect, food preoccupation, compliance, apathy, and unusual eating behavior when re-fed. Two of the observed behaviors from this study—food preoccupation and unusual eating behavior when re-fed—are of particular importance to anorexia nervosa patients and poorly nourished bulimic patients. It is not clear whether these behaviors are due to the effect of starvation or perhaps more primary to the problem. Normalization of both behavior characteristics is benefited by nutritional rehabilitation.

Maloney et al [19] used 18 adolescent anorexic patients on total parenteral nutrition to assess changes in behavior with weight gain. It was found that a weight increase of three to four kg was necessary for behavioral change, and that this increase also allowed the patients to benefit more from psychotherapy.

The therapeutic alliance is enhanced by establishing a weight range, rather than a single specific weight goal for a patient to achieve [20]. A weight range gives a more realistic view of weight, as daily fluctuations do occur, even under normal conditions. The thought of striving for a weight range is more acceptable to the anorexic who is in fear of gaining beyond a specific point [20].

The charts prepared by Frisch [21] are useful in establishing a weight range for female patients. These charts can be used to estimate the minimal weight for height necessary for the onset of menstrual cycles in primary amenorrhea or the minimal weight for height necessary to restore menstrual cycles in secondary amenorrhea due to weight loss. Frisch [21] reports that women of 16 or older with amenorrhea secondary to weight loss will require a weight about 10% heavier than the observed minimal weight for the same height at menarche. Using the Frisch chart, the 25th percentile for weight to height ± 3 lb is recommended as being the most acceptable to the patient, as well as effective in re-establishing menstruation [21]. A loss of body weight of 10% to 15% of normal weight for height will stop menstrual function and represents a loss of one third body fat [21].

Depletion of adipose tissue can be assessed indirectly with standardized procedures [22,23] using a caliper to measure triceps skinfold. It has been estimated [22] that 75% to 80% of anorexia nervosa patients are in less than the fifth percentile for body fat (reference standards based on triceps skinfold, age- and sex-specific) indicating severe depletion and that another 10% to 15% are in less than the 15th percentile, indicating depleted reserves of body fat. Bulimics seem to vary widely in changes in body fat although body composition studies have not been specifically performed on this population group. Bulimic patients may have triceps skinfold measurements that range over the 50th percentile for age and sex, despite consistent vomiting episodes.

Tables of percentiles for upper arm circumference, arm muscle circumference, and triceps skinfold, age- and sex-specific, have been reported in the literature [24]. The arm muscle circumference (AMC) may be determined from the triceps skinfold and the arm circumference (AC) indices using a nomogram for arm anthropometry [25], or estimated using the formula [22,24]:

AMC (cm) = (AC (cm)-(triceps skinfold (mm)) x .314

Arm muscle circumference is below the fifth percentile (reference standards based on age and sex) for more than 80% of patients with anorexia nervosa, while 90% are lower than the 15th percentile [22]. This represents a loss of somatic protein. The extent of the loss of lean body mass (LBM) or adipose tissue is a factor of age, nutritional state prior to weight loss, the rate of weight loss, and the amount of physical activity in which the patient has engaged [22,26].

Another indirect measure of somatic protein stores is the creatinine height index (CHI). As creatinine is a normal waste product of muscle metabolism, the amount of creatinine excreted in the urine is a reflection of lean body tissue. Thus, as LBM decreases, the amount of creatinine excreted in the urine also decreases. CHI is the ratio of actual 24-hour creatinine excretion to ideal creatinine excretion, with ideal levels of creatinine excretion being 18 mg per kg of ideal body weight (IBW) per day for females, and 23 mg per kg of IBW per day for males [22]. A CHI less than 75% indicates a depletion of somatic protein.

Laboratory values for serum albumin and serum transferrin are indicators of visceral protein [22]. Serum albumin values are usually within normal range but may be elevated with dehydration or depressed with edema. Rehydration of the dehydrated patient is suggested for an accurate assessment of serum albumin. Serum transferrin values are normal to mildly depleted in the patient with anorexia nervosa. Visceral protein status provides evidence of the body's ability to endure and manage with physical stress. Depressed serum albumin and transferrin measurements are a good indicator of generalized malnutrition, rather than protein malnutrition specifically [27].

The degree of depletion of total body mass should be assessed by considering not only the percentage of usual or predicted weight, but also the percentage of IBW. The percentage of usual or predicted weight is calculated as

$$\frac{\text{current weight x 100}}{\text{predicted or usual weight}}$$

where predicted weight is determined using past weight-for-height records if the patient is under 18 years of age, and usual weight is used if the patient is 18 or over. The percentage of IBW is calculated as:

$$\frac{\text{current weight x 100}}{\text{IBW}}$$

where the IBW is obtained by use of standardized pediatric growth grids for patients under 18 years of age and standard reference tables of desired weight-for-height-and-sex for patients 18 years and older.

The percentage of usual or predicted weight is an indication of the amount of actual weight lost, while the percentage IBW indicates the degree of underweight compared with the reference standard. Thus, by comparing the two calculated values, an overall picture of body depletion may be established. This is of great importance, as the premorbid weight may have been initially unsatisfactory or consistently undesirable for a period of time. Severe depletion of total body mass is commonly noted in anorexic patients [22], but not necessarily in bulimic patients, who are generally within an acceptable range of body weight-for-height [23].

Weight gain during therapy is dependent on the consumption and absorption of a kilocalorie intake greater than energy requirements over a period of time. The composition of body tissue formed during this period will influence the rate of weight gain [28].

Pertschuk et al [29] examined weight change in five anorexia nervosa subjects in relation to kilocalorie intake and energy requirement on a day-to-day and a long-term basis. Actual REE and total body potassium were used as measures to assess the change in body cell mass or lean body mass in the subjects. An important finding of this study was that, for all subjects, the actual REE was unusually low compared with the calculated REE based on the Harris and Benedict formula [30]. The REE (or BEE as it is often referred to) is calculated as:

Male REE = 66 + (13.7 x W) + (5 x H) - (6.8 x A)

Female REE = 655 + (9.6 x W) - (1.7 x H) - (4.7 x A)

where W = current weight in kg; H = height in cm; and A = age in years.

The number of kilocalories in excess was determined from energy intake from oral and parenteral feedings minus the 24-hour energy expenditure (estimated as 1.1 x REE). On a daily basis there was no significant correlation between excess kilocalories and weight gain. However, long-term assessment showed a highly significant correlation between total weight gained and total kilocalorie excess. The authors found that a mean excess of 10,918 ± 5,634 kilocalories was required to achieve a 1-kg body weight gain. Intake and weight gain data also indicated that weight plateauing for a period of five days or more may occur several times during the rehabilitation process [29].

Use of the Harris and Benedict formula [30] to calculate REE is likely to overestimate the actual REE, at least during the initial stage of treatment. However, use of the calculated REE to determine kilocalorie requirements should stop further weight loss and will not overwhelm the patient with large amounts of food to consume [12]. As weight gain increases, the REE will need to be recalculated for accurate determination of the energy intake required to promote weight gain.

Metabolic requirements are further increased by anabolism, physical exercise, fever, and stress. Ambulation will increase the patient's metabolic rate by about 20%. Recommendations have been reported for the calculation of anabolic and maintenance requirements with regard to kilocalories, nitrogen, and protein, for both parenteral and enteral feeding [31,32].

Knowledge of the factors influencing weight gain will relieve some of the frustration and anxiety associated with eating meals and snacks. Upon refeeding eating disorder patients, an initial rapid weight gain may occur as a result of water retention in extracellular spaces, retention of electrolytes, and/or repletion of liver and muscle glycogen reserves [12]. Patients need to be informed of the possibility of an initial short-term rapid weight gain due to these factors. If the patient does not understand that this is due to the body's response to the original starvation state, the weight gain and uncomfortable "feeling" of fatness may stimulate the urge to purge and/or refuse food intake. Reassurance must be given to the patient that the rapid rate of weight gain will not continue. The assurance that the gain in weight is not a gain in fat alone will benefit compliance to the dietary program. Due to the inconsistency in the rate of weight gain, it is prudent to reinforce food intake rather than weight gain.

Reduced gastric emptying may occur in starvation [33]. Dehydration and reduced gastrointestinal (GI) motility can cause constipation in anorexics and bulimics. GI bloating is a frequent complaint on refeeding and may be due to stomach atrophy [3,34]. Normally the feeling of stomach distention will subside as the stomach capacity for more food returns [12]. The bulk content of meals may precipitate bloating and should be monitored. Constipation and motility problems should resolve as the patient begins to consume greater amounts of food at more regular intervals [12].

Dogs, rabbits, and rats maintained on total parenteral nutrition (TPN) are observed to exhibit small bowel hypoplasia, changes in gastrointestinal hormone secretion, and decreased intestinal enzyme activity [32]. It was concluded that direct contact with food may be necessary to maintain the normal morphologic and functional ability of the GI tract [32]. Thus, careful planning of refeeding after periods of starvation, restrictive eating, or vomiting is essential to reduce physiologic stress and optimize the restoration of normal function and absorptive efficiency of the GI tract.

To ease GI complaints during refeeding, a gradual increase in kilocalories and amount and types of food is recommended. Fat and milk products should be given with care to anorexics, as they may have lost some digestive capacity to handle these types of foods [20].

Anorexics never actually lose their hunger drive [4]. The characteristic behavior patterns are similar to those of starving people [34] and can inevitably lead a restrictive anorexic into a food binge, which is estimated to occur in 40% of reported cases of anorexia nervosa [35].

A study of the psychological effects of TPN on 30 patients failed to reveal depression secondary to the loss of the capacity to eat [10]. However, 6 of the 30 patients went on intermittent eating binges, even though they were aware that illness and GI problems would result [10]. This suggests that in some people, the urge to eat will lead to a binge rather than eating small or normal amounts of food. Many anorexics and bulimics report feeling that they have lost the ability to determine what is a normal amount to eat in respect to specific portion sizes and the amount of total food consumed/meal/day.

Fairburn [36] notes that it is not the quantity of food eaten that is critical in defining a binge, but instead the subject's experience of the eating. He contends a binge should meet two criteria: (1) that the subject regards the food intake as excessive, and (2) that the episode is experienced by the patient as being outside her control [36]. Fairburn [37] uses the diet diary recording method and a prescribed eating pattern emphasizing meal and snack regularity, rather than what to eat, as part of a comprehensive three-stage treatment program for bulimia.

Lacey [17] studied 30 bulimic subjects to assess improvement based on a specific treatment approach using a diet diary recording method. A prescribed diet was structured into meals, specifying the type and amount of carbohydrate to eat. All other foods could be eaten freely. Contracts between patient and therapist were established and individual and group therapy were also part of the treatment program. The treatment program had positive results on patient outcome as measured by long-term follow-up. The diet diary was assessed as an important tool, as it became a highly personal record, which provided control and discipline as well as an emotional outlet [17].

In keeping a diet diary, the patient records the date, time, type of food eaten, the amount (in household measures), mood state, and situation at the time of the eating activity. A diet diary may be useful in assessing dietary patterns and habits such as: the length of time between each eating experience; the tendency to restrict eating prior to a binge; the patient's concept of the amount of food that constitutes a binge; the patient's experience of the binge and degree of hunger awareness; the type, variety, and palatability of food sources; the basic nutritional composition of the diet; and the situation, circumstance, place, and time a binge is likely to occur.

A diet diary may be most useful in evaluating the variability of food sources in the diet. The best way to ensure nutritional adequacy in a diet is to maintain variety in the types of food consumed over a period of time. The problem incurred by the eating disorder patient, by nature of their restrictive food selection pattern, is a general lack of variety of foods in the diet. Therapeutic supplementation of vitamins and minerals is suggested.

All patients have their own specific food avoidances; usually whatever the individual considers to be "fatten-ing." It is important to note that no one food is "fatten-ing" unless too much of it is eaten and total kilocalorie intake exceeds energy expenditure. What makes a specific food considered "fattening" needs to be understood, as the results may indicate how attitudes toward food are established and can be altered.

Investigations by Rolls et al [38] indicate that in normal subjects food is eaten until it no longer tastes pleasant so that eating food never becomes adverse. This "mechanism" of control appears not to be operating in binge eating where eating beyond the point of enjoyment leads to aversions toward the food, the eating experience, their own body, and self-conception. Feelings of being out of control emerge and often become associated with particular foods. The food or foods are avoided unless a binge period arises, which breaks down the controls against eating the "avoided" foods.

Food aversions, due to bingeing experiences and preconceived ideas about certain foods, need to be separated from normal food dislikes when planning a program for introducing the "avoided" foods back into the diet. Gradual and consistent additions of "avoided" foods need to be reintroduced into the diet. The patient needs to be positively reinforced when a previously avoided food is eaten. Positive reinforcement has been used to encourage the patient's acceptance of the food and stimulate eating enjoyment [15].

In normalizing eating patterns, regular meals (snacks if necessary) are advocated. The meal plan may be easier for the eating disorder patient to accept if it is slightly lower in fat, about 25% to 30% of the total kilocalories; with 50% to 60% of the total kilocalories from complex carbohydrates and 10% to 20% from protein. A balance of carbohydrate, protein, and fat should be provided at each meal. "Diet food" or special low-calorie products should not be allowed in the diet plan. High-bulk, low-calorie foods should not be eaten in large amounts, because they act to satiate the hunger urge while minimizing caloric intake. Drinking large amounts of water or other fluid should also be discouraged because this reduces appetite and aids vomiting.

Unusual food habits should be discouraged such as excessive use of condiments, prepared mustard, and cinnamon. In food preparation, cooking with moderate amounts of certain herbs and spices may help to stimulate the appetite. This effect is likely to depend on individual taste preferences. In normal subjects, Rolls et al [38,39] found that the palatability and satiety of the meal are affected by the order in which food is presented and also by the sensory properties of foods such as flavor, color, and shape. It may be of interest to experiment with eating disorder patients to see whether an increase or decrease in food intake is effected by manipulation of these factors. Such investigations could prove enlightening and beneficial to dietary treatment programs.

Rigid diet plans should be avoided. The patient should adjust to and learn portion sizes. This may be done by confrontation with various sizes of food containers or service and types of service (such as individual trays, family style, or cafeteria style). A guide to eating, such as the food group plan or the American Dietetic Association food exchange plans, may be useful for estimating the portion size to be consumed for a particular type of food. Calorie counting should be discouraged. Knowledge of how many servings to consume from each group per day may be useful to replace or de-emphasize preoccupation with counting calories.

Once the goal weight range is achieved, it should be emphasized that diet variety, portion size, and regularity of eating are the important factors in maintaining weight and emotional stability. As the patient gains more trust in the dietary treatment and in her own ability to make food choices and accept normal fluctuations in body weight, a more spontaneous manner of choosing what to eat will ensue.

Supportive counseling as a follow-up to maintain treatment results is necessary. Fairburn [16,37] notes bulimic patients may experience binge-vomiting urges again, and they should be prepared that this may occur, especially under stressful conditions. Relaxation exercises or other techniques to reduce the feeling of tension and anxiety associated with the act of eating and digestion may be beneficial. Similarly, the effect of a relaxed pleasant atmosphere on eating attitudes and hedonic enjoyment of foods is an area for further experimentation. Many eating disorder programs feed patients under controlled, disciplined, and pressured situations without any emphasis on the encouragement of food appreciation and enjoyment. It is the author's view that a more positive approach to ensuring a conducive feeding environment may influence long-term success in treatment outcome.

CONCLUSION

The escape into a binge-purge cycle and the self-denial of food will cease to occur as the patient becomes able to deal directly with uncomfortable moods and trust in her own decision-making ability. The patient needs to deal with food appropriately through the following learned techniques: (1) planning nutritionally balanced diets; (2) identifying standard portion sizes for foods; (3) knowledge of nutritional needs for health and body weight maintenance; (4) food sources to meet nutritional needs; (5) self-confidence in making food selections to satisfy taste desires, as well as emotional

and nutritional needs; and (6) an understanding of the factors influencing normal fluctuation in body weight, growth, and composition.

A diet diary will aid patient awareness of her food intake and behavior. It is beneficial to refeed the eating disorder patient gradually with a diet composition at each meal which includes carbohydrate, protein, and fat in order to ease physical complications and psychological stress. Specific food avoidances need to be reintroduced into the diet to relieve the "fear" associated with those foods which contribute to the fear of body fatness. Patient understanding of bodily needs will contribute to willing participation in the dietary treatment program and greater self-assurance in making appropriate food choices.

REFERENCES

1. Russell GFM. General management of anorexia nervosa and difficulties in assessing the efficacy of treatment. In: Vigersky RA, ed. Anorexia nervosa. New York: Raven Press, 1977: 277-90.

2. Garner DM, Garfinkel PE, Bemis KM. A multidimensional psychotherapy for anorexia nervosa. Int J Eating Disorders 1981; 2:3-45.

3. Crisp AH. The differential diagnosis of anorexia nervosa. Proc R Soc Med 1977; 70:686-90.

4. Bruch H. Obesity and eating disorders. In: Sholevar P, Benson R, Blinder BJ, eds. Treatment of emotional disorders in children and adolescents. New York: Spectrum, 1980: 353-61.

5. Russell GFM. Bulimia nervosa: an ominous variant of anorexia nervosa. Psychol Med 1979; 9:429-48.

6. Bruch H. The golden cage: The enigma of anorexia nervosa. Cambridge MA: Harvard University Press, 1978.

7. Gull WW. The address in medicine. Lancet 1868; 2:171.

8. Ryle J. Anorexia nervosa. Lancet 1936; 2:893-9.

9. Dudrick SJ, Wilmore DW, Vars HM, et al. Long-term total parenteral nutrition with growth, development, and positive nitrogen balance. Surgery 1968; 64:134-42.

10. Hall RC, Stickney SK, Gardner ER, et al. Psychiatric reactions to long-term intravenous hyperalimentation. Psychosomatics 1981; 22:428-43.

11. Chiulli R, Grover M, Steiger E. Total parenteral nutrition in anorexia nervosa. In: Gross M, ed. Anorexia nervosa. Indianapolis: Collamore Press, 1982: 141-52.

12. Huse DM, Lucas AR. Dietary treatment of anorexia nervosa. J Am Diet Assoc 1983; 83:687-90.

13. Spitzer RL, ed. Diagnostic and statistical manual of mental disorders, Third edition. Washington DC: American Psychiatric Association, 1980: 69-71.

14. Willkard SG, Anding RH, Winstead DK. Nutritional counseling as an adjunct to psychotherapy in bulimia treatment. Psychosomatics 1983; 24:545-51.

15. Long CG, Cordle CJ. Psychological treatment of binge

eating and self-induced vomiting. J Med Psychol 1982; 55:139-45.

16. Fairburn C. A cognitive behavioral approach to treatment of bulimia. Psychol Med 1981; 11:707-11.

17. Lacey HJ. Bulimia nervosa, binge-eating and psychogenic vomiting: a controlled treatment study and long term outcome. Br Med J 1983; 286:1609-13.

18. Keys A, Brozek J, Henschel A, et al. The biology of human starvation, vol 2. Minneapolis: University of Minnesota Press, 1950: 819-53.

19. Maloney MJ, Brunner R, Winget C, et al. Hyperalimentation as a research model for studying the cognitive, behavioral and emotional effects of starvation and nutrition rehabilitation. In: Barby PL, Garfinkel PE, Garner DM, Coscina DV, eds. Anorexia nervosa: Recent developments in research. New York: Alan R Liss, Inc, 1983: 311-21.

20. Paige DM, ed. Anorexia nervosa. In: Manual of clinical nutrition. John Hopkins University, Pleasantville, NJ: Nutrition Publications, Inc, 1983; 26:6.

21. Frisch RE. Menstrual cycles: fatness as a determinant of minimum weight for height necessary for their maintenance or onset. Science 1974; 185:949-52.

22. Kovach KM. The assessment of nutritional status in anorexia nervosa. In Gross M, ed. Anorexia nervosa. Indianapolis: Collamore Press, 1982: 69-79.

23. Fairburn CG, Cooper PJ. The clinical features of bulimia nervosa. Br J Psychiatry 1984; 144:238-46.

24. Frisancho AR. Triceps skinfold and upper arm muscle size norms for assessment of nutritional status. Am J Clin Nutr 1974; 27:1052-8.

25. Gurney JM, Jelliffe DB. Arm anthropometry in nutritional assessment: nomogram for rapid calculation muscle circumference and cross-sectional muscle and fat areas. Am J Clin Nutr 1973; 26:912-5.

26. Silverman JA. Medical consequences of starvation; the malnutrition of anorexia nervosa: caveat medicus. In: Barby PL, Garfinkel PE, Garner DM, Coscina DV, eds. Anorexia nervosa: Recent developments in research. New York: Alan R Liss, Inc,, 1983: 293-9.

27. Harper AE, Simopoulos AP. Summary, conclusions, recommendations. Am J Clin Nutr 1982; 35:1098-107.

28. Russell GFM, Mezey AG. An analysis of weight gain in patients with anorexia nervosa treated with high calorie diets. Clin Sci 1962; 23:449-61.

29. Pertschuk MJ, Crosby LO, Mullen JL. Nonlinearity of weight gain and nutrition intake in anorexia nervosa. In: Barby PL, Garfinkel PE, Garner DM, Coscina DV, eds. Anorexia nervosa: Recent developments in research. New York: Alan R Liss, Inc, 1983: 301-10.

30. Harris J, Benedict F. Biometric studies of basal metabolism in man. Carnegie Institute of Washington DC: Publication No 279, 1919.

31. Blackburn GL, Hopkins BS, Bistrian BR. The nutrition support service in hospital practice. In: Schneider H, Anderson C, Coursin D, eds. Nutrition support of medical practice. Philadelphia: Harper and Row, 1983: 111-39.

32. Meng HC. Parenteral nutrition — principles, nutrient requirements, techniques and clinical applications. Philadelphia: Harper and Row, 1983: 184-224.

33. Dally P, Gomez J. Anorexia nervosa. London: Wm Heinemann, 1979: 54-5.

34. Crisp AH. Disturbances of neurotransmitter metabolism in anorexia nervosa. Proc Nutr Soc 1978; 37:201-9.

35. Crisp AH, Hsu KG, Harding B. The starving hoarder and voracious spender stealing in anorexia nervosa. J Psychosom Res 1980; 24:225-31.

36. Fairburn CG. Bulimia nervosa. Br J Hosp Med 1983; 29:537-42.

37. Fairburn CG. Bulimia: its epidemiology and management. In: Stunkard AJ, Stellar E, eds. Eating disorders. New York: Raven Press, 1984: 235-58.

38. Rolls BJ, Rolls ET, Rowe EA, et al. Sensory specific satiety in man. Physiol Beh 1981; 27:137-42.

39. Rolls BJ. Palatability and food preference. In Gioffi LA, James WPT, Van Itallie TE, eds. The body weight regulatory system: Normal and disturbed mechanisms. New York: Raven Press, 1981: 271-8.

Chapter 38

Learning and Behavioral Approaches to the Treatment of Anorexia Nervosa and Bulimia

James Kuechler and Robert Hampton

INTRODUCTION

Many signs and symptoms observed in patients with anorexia nervosa resemble those seen in non-self-induced starvation states; namely, personality changes, difficulty with concentration, memory disturbances, irritability, and apathy [1,2]. Indeed, actual cerebral atrophy may occur in the anorexia nervosa patient [3].

Accordingly, many anorexia nervosa patients in the initial stages of treatment do not respond or appreciate the traditional forms of insight-oriented psychotherapeutic interventions [4]. Active treatment is necessary. While parenteral nutrition (or enteral intubation techniques) may be indicated in life-threatening circumstances, more commonly (structured) behavioral methods may be useful when applied in a hospital setting where observation, measurement, and stepwise informal feedback is possible. The purpose of this active treatment is to physically prepare the patient for a more comprehensive psychiatric treatment program, which might include individual dynamic psychotherapy, group therapy, and family therapy.

HISTORICAL BACKGROUND AND DEFINITIONS

The behavioral approach to psychiatry has its origin in experimental animal studies exemplified by the works of Thorndike and Pavlov [5]. Emphasis is placed on ob-

servable behavioral events and related antecedent and consequent conditions and responses.

In the strictest sense, behavior can be defined as an individual's skeletal muscle activity, which includes verbal expression [5]. Overt behavior is considered to be events that are directly observable. Relevant examples might include vomiting, amount of time spent exercising, time spent eating, food choices, weight change, etc. This is to be distinguished from covert behaviors, which, while still observable, require indirect techniques. This includes affective and cognitive processes that could be indirectly observed by body posture, limb movements, or facial expressions. For example, clenched fists might indicate the cognitive (covert) behavior of tension or anxiety, and crying could similarly imply the affective behavior of sadness. Inferring the behavior by indirect observations, of course, would increase the possibility of error. Observed crying, while often signifying sadness, could also imply tears of joy—for example, at a wedding. Thus, a degree of caution is advised to discourage overgeneralization.

The concept of "behavior therapy" is more difficult to define, because different investigators have used it in a variety of ways. Some feel there is no universal definition of this term [6], but in general it can be considered as a group of treatment techniques based to some extent on learning theory, conditioning techniques, and empirical evaluation of results. We will describe four distinct subsections of behavior therapy, although the distinction often blurs in clinical application.

1. Classical conditioning, also referred to as respondent conditioning, involves the pairing of previously neutral stimuli with an innate response evoked by an unconditioned stimulus. The subject eventually "learns" to react to the neutral stimulus with the same response (now termed conditioned response) in the absence of the unconditioned stimulus. Clinical applications include systematic desensitization, flooding, and graded exposure.

2. Operant (instrumental) conditioning is based on work by Thorndike and B.F. Skinner [5]. It essentially consists of selectively rewarding and/or punishing specified "target behavior" to increase or decrease, respectively, their frequency of emission by the organism. This "shaping" of desired behaviors is often referred to as "behavior modification," although the authors feel this definition is too restrictive.

3. Cognitive behavioral conditioning was described by Beck [7,8] and operates under the premise that cognitions (ie, thoughts, belief systems) precede and are causally related to feelings, mood, and behavior. Therapeutic intervention would be aimed at modifying the antecedent thought to effect clinical change.

4. Social learning theory is based on vicarious experiences causing change in an individual's behavior. This concept, also referred to as "modeling" [5], suggests that a subject learns a behavior by observing another person engaged in that behavior and seeing whether the observed person is rewarded (or punished).

Behavior therapy in the mental health setting is generally recognized as having begun with Ayllon et al in 1964 [9]. They used attention by staff to modify eating behavior in chronic schizophrenic inpatients. Ward observers had noted that patients who were unwilling or unable to eat received increased staff attention. It was hypothesized that this increased attention was a positive social reinforcer. By changing the contingencies (ie, staff was subsequently instructed to simply ignore problem eaters), problem eating became unrewarding and decreased significantly. In other words, the target behavior (poor eating) was extinguished by withdrawal of reinforcement (social attention).

Note should be taken, however, that when Leitenberg et al (1968) tried this strategy in 1968 in patients with anorexia nervosa, it was ineffective [10].

SPECIFIC STUDIES

Behavioral techniques applied to eating disorders began in the 1960s. Hallsten and Lang in 1965 reported single case studies of female anorectics using systematic

desensitization to decrease both fears of weight gain and feelings of self-consciousness [11,12]. Although there were numerous methodological flaws, both authors reported some success.

Also in 1965, Bachrach et al used socialization (ie, attention and praise by staff) as a reward in an operant conditioning paradigm to reinforce improved eating behavior in a 37-year-old anorectic patient [13]. The patient gained weight initially, but this soon leveled off. At this point the contingency was changed to weight gain (as opposed to eating) when the possibility of secretive vomiting became apparent. The patient then resumed increasing her weight and was discharged after a two-month period, having gained approximately 17 lbs.

Leitenberg et al essentially repeated this procedure using two patients and reported similar success [10]. They attempted to refine the methodology by having the patients individually be their own controls, measuring weight gain in reinforcement versus non-reinforcement phases, but results were not clear-cut. Although both patients gained significant amounts of weight during reinforcement, one patient continued to show weight increase after reinforcement was stopped—thus the predicted extinction effect did not occur.

In 1970, Blinder et al studied six hospitalized anorectic patients and applied operant conditioning using access to activity contingent on weight gain [14]. Noting the patients' proclivity toward motor hyperactivity during the initial observation period, they were given six hours of unrestricted access to physical activity on any day that weight increased 1/2 lb over the previous day. The first three patients gained a mean of 4.8 lbs. per week during the initial three weeks after behavior therapy was started. As they approached more normal proportions, their rate of increase decreased and averaged 3.9 lbs. per week for the whole treatment period. Medication and limited psychotherapy were also used during this period.

A fourth patient did not respond to limited activity as a reinforcer but did complain about the sedative side-effects of her medication (chlorpromazine). This suggested a new source of reinforcement—decreasing dosage contingent on weight gain—and this was successfully used. The fifth and sixth patients were treated with the different contingencies (an initial 6-lbs. weight gain and then a further 10-lbs. increase before hospital discharge) while using the same reinforcements as patients one, two, and three (activity). This paradigm was also successful for short-term weight gain.

The significance of this study is that reinforcers were specifically tailored to individual patients.

In 1975, Brady and Rieger reported a 1972 University of Pennsylvania study involving 16 anorectic patients treated with operant conditioning combined with other treatment modalities (medication, group therapy, occupational therapy, etc) [15]. Behavior analysis was conducted during an initial four- to five-day observation period, and reinforcers were individualized for each patient. These included increased activity privileges, access to textbooks, personal hygiene materials, other patients for socialization, and reduction of medication dosage. Reinforcement was given daily, contingent on a weight increase of 1/2 lb. All patients gained weight, averaging 4.07 lbs. per week. This study is significant for more refined diagnostic criteria, including greater than a 30% weight loss and amenorrhea greater than six months in female patients. However, the authors note the absence of exclusion criteria and the possibility that two schizophrenics were part of the sample. The study is also notable for a relatively long-term follow-up in a fairly large sample, ranging from four to five months after discharge. The results were extremely variable and included two deaths and several other patients who "did poorly after discharge."

Pertschuk, continuing the work of Brady and Rieger, reported a follow-up study of 29 patients, 27 of whom were treated with operant conditioning for weight gain in addition to medications [16]. Behavior therapy was shown effective in 25 of the 27 patients. The study, ranging from 3 to 45 months after discharge, was also significant for the finding that bulimia developed in ten patients who did not report this as a problem on admission.

Agras et al reported a 1974 study using five single case studies to investigate the relative importance of three variables on weight gain using an A-B-A design [17]. They were reinforcement, size of meals, and informational feedback.

Reinforcement of daily weight gain was proved effective as in prior studies, but they also noted that weight continued to increase during nonreinforcement phases—although at a decreased rate. At this point, the hypothesis of hospitalization as a negative reinforcer was introduced. This was tested by having the patient remain for a 12-week period, regardless of weight change, to remove the "discharge contingent on weight gain" effect. As predicted, the rate of weight increase declined, and food intake greatly declined.

Informational feedback consisted of the patient receiving exact information regarding the number of calories consumed and mouthfuls of food taken after each meal plus exact body weight every morning. Under conditions of informational feedback plus reinforcement versus reinforcement alone, weight clearly improved under the former.

Size of meal presented versus weight gain was also tested using a 3,000-calorie-per-day diet versus 6,000 calories, but only a weak treatment effect was noted.

While not demonstrated definitively, the authors felt that informational feedback was more important than positive reinforcement, but that combining all three variables was the most efficacious.

Agras and Werne published a subsequent report in 1977 on the first 25 patients treated at Stanford University [18]. They used a similar protocol and noted that only three of the 25 patients did not gain weight at discharge.

Bhanji and Thompson [19] studied 11 anorectic patients using operant conditioning often combined with medications. Patients were allowed to specify their own hierarchy of reinforcers, and these were made contingent on progressively more stringent criteria—initially a complete meal but later modified to account for actual weight gain. All but one patient gained significant weight at discharge. Long-term (2 to 27 months) follow-up was attempted using mailed questionnaires, but only seven were returned, and only three contained a weight update. The authors concluded that, based on limited follow-up, operant techniques were useful for initial weight gain, but were inadequate for long-term maintenance of normal eating and weight. However, it is unclear whether operant techniques were adequately maintained after discharge.

Parker et al (1977) reported on ten anorectic females treated with a combination of psychotherapy and operant conditioning, and in some cases medication [20]. Reinforcement consisted of giving the patient a variable number of chips contingent on both cooperation with staff (which was individualized) and weight gain. For example, one chip was given for simply coming to weigh-in, one for maintaining weight, and ten for each 1/2 lb gained. These could be used to "purchase" passes, social activities, and other reinforcements that the patient selected. Additionally, the patients received novelty gifts at 1-lb weight-gain intervals. All patients are reported to have gained weight during hospitalization. The authors also emphasized the need to educate the staff that (1) a behavioral approach to therapy did not imply a totalitarian ideology, and (2) any comment on a patient's eating behavior (as opposed to weight) was unproductive.

In 1977 Garfinkel et al studied 42 inpatients and outpatients [21]. Of the 26 inpatients, 17 received operant conditioning with other therapies and nine received only other therapies. No outpatient received behavior therapy. All patients were followed a minimum of one year after discharge. Results showed that patients treated with behavioral methods were statistically similar in final weight to the remainder of the group. The authors also attempted to design a scale, the "Global Clinical Score," to measure parameters other than weight. They concluded that behavior therapy, while not superior to other methods, was also not harmful, as had been implied [22].

In 1979 Eckert et al [23] did a randomized prospective study involving 81 patients assigned to either behavioral or nonbehavioral treatment. The behavioral program was similar to prior protocols using privileges to reinforce weight gain. However, reinforcement was not individualized and was given in five-day increments. Both groups received individual psychotherapy, and half the patients in each group also received cyproheptadine. Results showed no difference in weight gain over a 35-day period between the behavior versus nonbehavior groups. In our opinion, this would tend to underscore the need for individualizing reinforcement and suggests there may be a more optimal frequency of reinforcement. The authors also attempted to identify specific subgroups of patients who would benefit more from behavioral treatment by using psychiatric and social history pretreatment variables. Although no variable was statistically significant, it appeared that patients with little or no prior outpatient treatment gained more weight with behavioral treatment. Possibly more naive patients may be more responsive and less resistant to structure.

A large study was reported by Pierloot et al [24] using a group of 145 patients with a minimum one-year follow-up on 88 of them during 1967 to 1969. Patients were generally treated with operant conditioning for weight gain along with other treatment modalities. An unspecified number of "early patients" received "enforced feeding" and medications—a protocol later discontinued.

Of the follow-up group, 11.4% died, including four suicides and four deaths secondary to malnutrition. Using the "Global Clinical Score" of Garfinkel et al [21], the authors described only one third as having fully recovered. Because of the 49% drop-out rate, it is difficult to assess from this study the effectiveness or dangers of behavioral treatment.

Reese and Gross published a 1982 report in support of operant conditioning with positive reinforcement to facilitate weight gain [25]. Rewards were individualized and both patient and staff agreed on a behavior contract. An interesting variation of informational feedback was used. The patient's daily weight was visually displayed on a graph, along with a second line indicating weight expectations to gain privileges. This was designed to decrease confrontation with staff and give the patient an increased sense of control, and it also appeared to be effective.

Halmi [26] proposed another variation in treating anorectic patients with operant methods, using a general hospital instead of a psychiatric setting. The stated advantages included immediate access to medical treatment—which is often necessary for patients severely emaciated and/or engaged in self-induced vomiting or laxative abuse. Additionally, there was a postulated increase in willingness of patients to enter "medical treatment" as opposed to "psychiatric" due to a presumed decrease in denial regarding a "medical condition." The author's protocol included restriction to bed until a target weight is achieved and use of bedpans (instead of bathroom to reduce surreptitious food disposal) until normal weight is achieved along with other less-severe deprivation. The goal is immediate restoration of weight to enable the patient to be more available to more definitive psychiatric treatment at a later date. Results of this variation are not clear-cut at the present time.

In addition to standard operant techniques aimed at promoting weight gain, some authors have suggested additional behavioral strategies to deal with the cognitive distortions and irrational beliefs in anorexia nervosa and bulimia [11,27,28].

For example, fear of weight gain or eating certain foods has been conceptualized as similar to a phobia and vomiting as similar to an obsessive-compulsive ritual.

In 1976, Williams treated six anorectic patients with a multifaceted behavioral approach [29]. In addition to reinforcement of weight gain, he also attempted to systematically desensitize patients to fears of putting on weight, disapproval by others, eating, and sexual activities. He also used aversion techniques (mild electrical shocks) to decrease pleasure at being thin and engaging in abnormal eating, along with other "miscellaneous techniques." No patient gained weight and the author described the overall results as a "resounding failure."

Perhaps trying to desensitize so many variables resulted in desensitization to the whole program. The study is, however, significant for its novelty, and it probably served as a stimulus for refinement of the technique by subsequent investigators.

In 1977 Monti et al reported a single case study of an anorectic female with bulimic traits [30]. The treatment consisted of standard positive reinforcement for weight gain using contingency contracting and feedback. In addition, a behavioral analysis revealed "maladaptive thoughts" (feeling she was a "bad person"), which often preceded bulimic episodes. These were treated with deep muscle relaxation and systematic desensitization. Both reinforcement and desensitization were continued on a weekly outpatient basis. Results showed that the patient gained a significant amount of weight during the inpatient phase, and this continued to a lesser extent during the six-month outpatient follow-up. Unfortunately, the results are confounded by development of edema early in treatment. Because of the nature of the experimental design, it was not possible to assess the effect of adding desensitization to other treatment modalities.

In 1982 Mavissakalian reported a study of two anorectic patients [27]. Inpatient treatment used procedures specifically aimed at reducing the apparent "weight phobia" and "ritualistic exercising" components of the illness in addition to the more common behavioral methods of reinforcing weight gain based on Agras and Werne [18]. Compulsive exercise was decreased by using response prevention by requiring the patients to spend one hour resting after each 30-minute meal period. Thus, the patient was prevented from neutralizing (ie, "undoing" by exercise) the obsessionally feared consequences of eating—weight gain. The investigator also noted that this had the effect of exposing the patient to phobic stimuli (food, weight gain, feelings of fullness) for 90 minutes per session. During a 30-day treatment period, this "...exceeds the 20-30 hours of programmed exposure required in the successful treatment of phobias and obsessive-compulsive behavior."

Both patients gained significant amounts of weight during hospitalization. Modified behavioral treatment continued by family members for the patients after discharge. Weight was not only maintained during the three- to five-month follow-up, but increased. Both patients became overweight without development of bulimia. The reasons for them becoming overweight are unclear. Perhaps this was an exaggerated response to behavior therapy. The author suggests chance and notes this occurs in an approximate 5% of anorectics. But he also calls for further study of behavioral treatment aimed at the special nature of the phobic and obsessive-compulsive components in anorexia nervosa. He states that patients with a simple phobic or obsessive-compulsive disorder are aware of the irrationality of their behavior, whereas anorectics usually deny this.

Cinciripini et al [28] reported on two anorectic patients with bulimic traits in a 1983 study designed to deal with cognitive aspects of the illness via behavioral methods in addition to operant conditioning for weight gain. After an initial four-day baseline period, patient #1 was put on a contingency management program for weight gain and continued to self-monitor urges and episodes of bingeing and emesis. After day 25, thought stopping was added to provide a cognitive control for these urges. This procedure used ten 60-minute sessions consisting of slides depicting binge behavior with the patient instructed to signal the therapist when the scenes became vivid and distressing. The therapist would then present a loud (distracting) noise with the word "stop" and instruct the patient to repeat "stop" to herself while imagining a relaxing scene after the binge urge declined.

After 28 days, flooding was added to the protocol for a two-week period. This consisted of (1) having the patient taste, smell, and handle various "binge foods" while the therapist vividly described the bulimic act; (2) exposing the patient to binge items both before and after meals in the hospital; and (3) exposing the patient to binge items in the community (restaurants and supermarkets) both with and later without supervision.

Results showed that (1) patient #1 gained weight with reinforcement alone, and binge episodes stopped during this phase; (2) with addition of thought stopping, weight continued to increase, but both binge and vomiting episodes also increased while the frequency of these urges declined; and (3) toward the end of flooding and through discharge, binge and vomiting episodes were gradually eliminated, while some vomiting urges continued to be reported. Over a two-year follow-up period, weight was maintained. Although some binge activity was reported, brief outpatient therapy using flooding techniques "successfully suppressed immediate binge activity."

In patient #2, therapy consisted mainly of reinforcement for weight gain and response prevention for vomiting. Response prevention eliminated both emesis urges and episodes and these remained extinguished after this aspect of treatment was discontinued. The patient successfully achieved weight gain at discharge but required brief rehospitalization two months later after losing 10 lbs. and resuming emesis. She was discharged after two weeks and had maintained ideal weight at one-year follow-up. After two years, the patient reported by telephone a slight weight decrease but no vomiting and was "functioning well."

The authors concluded that contingency management, flooding, and response prevention but not thought stopping were effective.

Goldberg et al [31] studied a group of 105 female anorectic inpatients to evaluate treatment effects on attitudinal dimensions of the illness in addition to the more common weight gain/calorie intake criteria. Prior to assignment to a given treatment mode (eg, cyproheptadine, behavior modification, etc), patients responded to 63 attitude statements using a four-point scale ranging from agreement to disagreement. Initially hypothesized significant attitudinal dimensions included: denial of illness, loss of appetite, manipulativeness, ambivalence toward parents, fear of fatness, high achievement goals, cooking as a hobby, decreased sexual desire, and subjective feeling of hypothermia.

A factor analysis of the 63 items yielded 19 factors accounting for 76.6% of the variance. Of these, 15 were considered interpretable and 11 were deemed useful as prognostic indicators. These included: feeling exploited by staff, fear of fatness, parents at fault, denial of illness, appetite loss, hypothermia, poor self-care, efforts required for achievement goals, the illness is due to mysterious physical causes, hobby cooking, and decreased sexual interest.

Attitudes useful as prognostic indicators of weight restoration included: less fear of fatness, less denial of illness, and a lesser feeling that food is sickening to the stomach. Behavior modification appeared to decrease fear of fatness, decrease interest in cooking, and make the patient feel that decreased effort is needed for achievement.

Although the identification of a given factor in an analysis does not automatically imply validity and reliability, this study is significant for its demonstration that attitudes can be prognostic indicators of weight gain and useful measurements of behavioral treatment effects. The evaluation of pretreatment variables may also be important in individualizing behavioral strategies in future studies.

In a 1982 study Fichter et al [32] examined attitude change (along with other variables) in 24 anorectic inpatients, 21 of which received behavior therapy consisting of reinforcement or systematic desensitization. Attitudes and "anorectic behavior" were measured by having patients use the "Anorexia Nervosa Inventory for Self-Rating" [32].

Weight increased steadily during the reinforcement phase to above 80% of ideal body weight on the average. Specific "anorectic attitudes" (figure consciousness, adverse effect of meals, and bulimia) seemed to change significantly, but not those of a "general neurotic" nature (feelings of insufficiency, obsessional traits, and sexual anxieties). While neither Fichter nor Goldberg attempted to actively change attitudes as part of their treatment program (ie, cognitive therapy), it would seem a reasonable course of action in future trials in view of the previously described beneficial changes in attitude secondary to "traditional" treatment methods.

In 1982 Garner and Bemis [33] published a basic set of guidelines for cognitive behavioral treatment of anorexia nervosa based on Beck's model for cognitive treatment of depression. They emphasized the finding of persistent "distorted attitudes and beliefs" even in weight-recovered anorexia nervosa patients and suggested a theoretical model involving the role of cognitions in the development of the illness.

Their treatment protocol emphasizes (1) the need to develop motivation for treatment in these patients (compared with patients with depression), (2) the need for patient education on both the illness and the theory of cognitive therapy, and (3) the need for early weight stabilization using behavioral methods that include role playing, scheduling pleasant events to enhance the set

of reinforcers beyond the pleasures of weight loss, diversion techniques (eg, response prevention to decrease bulimic behavior), social skills training, desensitization to phobic-like responses to eating and/or weight gain, and "standard operant technology" to reinforce desirable behavior.

Cognitive techniques are described separately but in reality are difficult to separate in an effective treatment program. The idea is to teach patients to examine the validity of their belief systems on a moment-to-moment basis. The therapist is then in a position to introduce the element of doubt regarding the basic (distorted) beliefs in a nonjudgemental fashion. To facilitate this process, the authors suggested several procedures including (1) operationalizing beliefs as precisely as possible, (2) decentering (ie, ask, "Do your rules apply to others as well as yourself?"), (3) "What if" technique to reduce the imagined consequences of feared events, and (4) evaluation of automatic thoughts by teaching patients to ask themselves: What is the evidence, what are alternative explanations, and what are the realistic consequences if the analysis is correct? Patients could then test their conclusions and expectations in an ongoing manner. In addition, underlying assumptions (ie, the principles that organize irrational beliefs) need to be identified to enable modification using many of the above techniques.

The authors conclude that cognitive therapy is compatible with other treatment modalities, that the affective component of the illness must be addressed during treatment (but not necessarily at the beginning), and by stating the need for systematic studies to support or refute their treatment approach.

The behavioral treatment of bulimia as an isolated entity (ie, without anorexia nervosa or other psychopathology) has received much less attention in the literature. Factors related to this include a blurring of diagnostic criteria with anorexia nervosa in the past and the fact that the mortality rate for bulimia is much lower than that reported for anorexia nervosa.

In 1982 Rosen and Leitenberg reported on a single case of "bulimia nervosa" (defined as bingeing, self-induced vomiting, and fear of weight gain in a normal-weight person) using behavioral methods [34]. They hypothesized that the binge/purge cycle was linked by a "vicious circle of anxiety" regarding weight gain. Eating was seen as the cause of anxiety and purging was the anxiety reducer. Since reduction of anxiety is self-reinforcing, the treatment was aimed at reducing the purging behavior, which the author hypothesized would then lead to extinction of binge eating and fear of weight gain.

The protocol included obtaining a history of overeating behavior: types of food, amounts eaten, duration of episodes, and also subjective feelings following an episode. Such feelings included feeling bloated, lightness around the mouth, worry over poor health, and "contamination" from food consumed. The next step consisted of exposing the patient to the "problem foods" under staff supervision and preventing the typical response (vomiting). The patient was given a detailed explanation of the treatment program and was instructed to eat an amount of food sufficient to cause vomiting urges during each session—knowing she would not be allowed to vomit. The therapist would help the patient focus on her subjective discomfort until the urge to vomit disappeared. The duration of the vomiting urge initially was greater than 90 minutes but decreased over time as did anxiety ratings. After this phase, the patient was then instructed to follow a schedule at home of gradually increasing the number of days per week with no vomiting. This part of the treatment lasted 44 days, and the rate of vomiting decreased from 3 to 1.25 times per day. During ten months of follow-up, there was only one episode of vomiting. Of interest, the patient also eventually stopped bingeing—without explicit instructions by the therapist to do so. It is also noted that the patient reported that the urge to vomit after eating was never eliminated but rather was described as much less distressing and of shorter duration.

Long and Cordle [35] reported on two patients with bulimia successfully treated with behavioral techniques on an outpatient basis. After a two-week baseline assessment, with patients keeping a daily record of food intake and vomiting, one-hour weekly sessions were started. Treatment concentrated on four main areas: (1) behavioral self-control, (2) dietary education, (3) cognitive restructuring, and (4) resocialization. The behavioral methods included self-monitoring of binge/purge episodes, self-targeting of frequency of binge/purge episodes, visual display of progress on a graph, positive verbal reinforcement by therapist, relaxation training, and response prevention (ie, increasing intervals after eating without vomiting). The cognitive restructuring included "cognitive modeling of covert assertion and thought management exercises."

Patient "A" required 40 sessions over ten months, and patient "B" required 12 sessions over three months. At the end of treatment, both patients were able to eat "normal" meals without vomiting or laxative use and were less preoccupied with their own body weight. Follow-up at nine months for patient "A" showed improvement was maintained. Patient "B" at 12 months described only two episodes of induced vomiting. The length of illness may be a crucial factor—the longer vomiting exists and the increasing frequency over years may make it a secondary autonomous behavior, which is reinforcing and will not disappear without special effort.

Fairburn [36] reported on a group of 11 patients with "bulimia nervosa." This included six patients with a history suggestive of anorexia nervosa, which complicates interpretation of the study. Patients were treated on an outpatient basis in two phases. The first part included self-monitoring, restricting eating to meal times only, and setting limited goals at the end of each session. This generally was accomplished in eight weeks or less. In the second phase (with bingeing and vomiting now decreased to an intermittent frequency) antecedent conditions to loss of control over food were identified, with the therapist suggesting more adaptive coping mechanisms. Systematic desensitization was also employed to decrease anxiety over intake of "forbidden" (ie, high-calorie) foods.

Results showed nine patients decreased the frequency of bingeing and vomiting to less than one per month without significant change in body weight. The mean duration of treatment was seven months.

The authors noted (in contrast to Rosen and Leitenberg) that control over food intake seemed to be the important factor in the binge/purge cycle and that once this was managed it was not necessary to focus on the vomiting.

CRITICISMS AND CONTROVERSIES

There have been many critics of behavioral techniques applied to eating disorders since its inception. Bruch has long been a critic of behavior therapy and considers it damaging [22]. Indeed, death has been reported following an inpatient behavioral regimen [14]. But even Bruch feels that psychotherapy is ineffective until the malnourished patient can assimilate and process new information [37]. Blinder pointed out [14] that weight gain achieved in behavioral therapy should not be treated as equivalent to comprehensive treatment in the eating disorders; in fact, the very potency of behavioral techniques may be a hazard in leading to change in one clinical feature (weight) dissociated from other clinical improvement. Thus, while it is true that sometimes behaviorally oriented therapists focus on weight gain as the sole criterion for improvement, it need not necessarily be so, nor is it desirable.

Recently Touyz et al [38] compared a strict and lenient operant conditioning protocol for weight gain in 65 inpatients with anorexia nervosa and found no significant difference between them. However, they did find that in the lenient program the patients were better motivated and accessible to psychotherapy and other aspects of treatment. Behavior therapy should be viewed as but one aspect of the total treatment plan and is consistent with human concern [16].

Specific criticisms of studies in behavioral and cognitive therapy of eating disorders are shared by those in the basic sciences and medicine as a whole: (1) Do all the investigators use the same diagnostic criteria? (2) Is the selection of the sample and its size sufficient to discount bias? (3) Are other variables held constant so as not to contaminate the variable(s) being studied? (4) How is treatment effectiveness to be evaluated? (5) What is appropriate follow-up time? (6) Are the results reproducible?

Generally, many of the early investigators suffered from not consistently addressing these questions, but as the field has evolved, later studies have improved.

Accounting for appropriate variables and holding them constant is an often difficult and subtle exercise, but necessary to avoid spurious conclusions. For example, Goldberg et al [31] initially designed a study to evaluate the effects of behavior modification and a drug on weight gain in 105 patients with a diagnosis of anorexia nervosa. Three different hospitals participated, using the same protocol, and at first there appeared to be a positive correlation between weight gain and increasing milieu structure. The investigators point out, however, that when patient prognostic characteristics were used in the analysis of the data, an entirely different conclusion was reached. Their results showed that differences in weight gain among the hospitals were due to the kinds of patients admitted to the various hospitals rather than any differences among the hospitals themselves.

Studies with a small sample size are common in the literature and have been criticized. Bemis [39] points out that many single case studies haven't used an "A-B-A-B" design, and therefore, specific interventions cannot be assigned to successful results. For example, both Rosen et al and Fairburn report positive results stopping or greatly reducing bingeing and purging in a small number of patients [34,36]. However, Fairburn focused on food intake while Rosen felt vomiting was more important and similar to an obsessive-compulsive neurosis.

While such disparity precludes generalization, it may obliquely address the question of homogeneity in eating disorders. How discreet are the entities of anorexia nervosa and bulimia? Some investigators describe them as being linked with other psychiatric disorders [20,33,40]. Such a finding may have strong implications for behavior therapy. It seems reasonable that once a patient's specific problems other than anorexia nervosa or bulimia are identified, a behavior therapy protocol could be designed for them. Thus, the behavior therapy for an eating disorder patient with a phobic component might involve desensitization or flooding, and a patient

with a depressive component might receive cognitive therapy [33,39]. Specific treatment tailored to the individual patient and systematic long-term follow-up to evaluate such treatment are both clearly needed.

FUTURE DIRECTIONS

Traditionally, treatment of eating disorders has focused on patients and their immediate environment (eg, the hospital, family, etc) with little effort going to the enormous cultural pressures for thinness. As exemplified by the "Venus de Milo" and the paintings of Rubens, it is clear that the ideal cultural shape is ephemeral.

In 1980 Garner et al [41] quantified a shift toward a thinner cultural ideal for females over the last 20 years using data from Miss America Pageant contestants and Playboy centerfolds. They noted an increase in diet articles in six women's magazines during the same period and also an increase in population weight norms for young women using statistics from the Society of Actuaries. The authors also felt that these trends were linked to "the apparent increasing prevalence of anorexia nervosa and related eating disorders."

Designing an effective behavioral therapy program that addresses these issues might include desensitization or cognitive components awaits future investigation.

REFERENCES

1. Keys A, Brozek J, Henschel A, Mickelson O, Taylor HL. The biology of human starvation, (2 vols). Minneapolis: University of Minnesota Press, 1950:

2. McLaren DS. Nutrition and its disorders. New York: Churchill Livingstone, 1981:

3. Nussbaum M, Shenker R, Marc J, et al. Cerebral atrophy in anorexia nervosa. Journal of Pediatrics 96(5):867-9.

4. Bruch H. Anorexia nervosa: Therapy and theory. Am J Psychiatry 1982; 139:1531-8.

5. Brady JP. Behavior therapy. In: Kaplan HI, Freedman AM, Sadock FJ, eds. Comprehensive textbook of psychiatry/III. Baltimore: Williams and Wilkins, 1980:

6. O'Neill GW, Gardner R. Behavior therapy: An overview. Hospital and Community Psychiatry 1983; 34:709-15.

7. Beck AT. Thinking and depression. 2. Theory and therapy. Arch Gen Psychiatry 1964; 10:561.

8. Beck AT. Cognitive therapy: Nature and relation to behavior therapy. Behav Ther 1970; 1:184.

9. Ayllon T, Haughton E, Osmond HO. Chronic anorexia: A behavioral problem. Canadian Psychiatric Association Journal 1964; 9:147-54.

10. Leitenberg H, Agras WS, Thompson LE. A sequential analysis of the effect of selective positive reinforce-

ment in modifying anorexia nervosa. Behaviour Research & Therapy 1968; 6:211-8.

11. Hallsten EA. Adolescent anorexia nervosa treated by desensitization. Behaviour Research & Therapy 1965; 3:87-91.

12. Lang PJ. Behavior therapy with a case of nervous anorexia. In: Ullsmann LP, Krasner L, eds. Case studies in behaviour modification. New York: Holt, Rinehart & Winston, 1965:

13. Bachrach AJ, Erwin SW, Mohr JP. The control of eating behavior in an anorexic by operant conditioning techniques. In: Ullmann LP, Krasner L, eds. Case studies in behavior modification. New York: Holt, Rinehart & Winston, 1965:

14. Blinder BJ, Freeman DMA, Stunkard AJ. Behavior therapy of anorexia nervosa: Effectiveness of activity as a reinforcer of weight gain. Amer J. Psychiatry 1970; 126:1093-8.

15. Brady JP, Rieger W. Behavioral treatment of anorexia nervosa. In: Thompson T, Dockens WS, eds. Applications of behavior modification: International symposium on behavior and modification at Minneapolis, 1972. New York: Academic Press, 1975:

16. Pertschuk MJ. Behavior therapy: Extended follow-up in anorexia nervosa. In: Vigersky RA, ed. Anorexia nervosa. New York: Raven Press, 1977:

17. Agras WS, Barlow DH, Chapin HN, et al. Behavior modification of anorexia nervosa. Arch Gen Psychiatry 1974; 30:279-86.

18. Agras S, Werne J. Behavior modification in anorexia nervosa: Research foundations in anorexia nervosa. In: Vigersky RA, ed. Anorexia nervosa. New York: Raven Press, 1977:

19. Bhanji S, Thomson J. Operant condition in the treatment of anorexia nervosa: A review & restrospective study of 11 cases. Brit J Psychiatry 1974; 124:166-72.

20. Parker JB, Balzer D, Wyrick L. Anorexia nervosa: A combined therapeutic approach. Southern Medical Journal 1977; 70:448-52.

21. Garfinkel PE, Moldofsky H, Garner DM. The outcome of anorexia nervosa: Significance of clinical features, body image & behavioral modification. In: Vigersky RA, ed. Anorexia nervosa. New York: Raven Press, 1977:

22. Bruch H. Perils of behavior modification in treatment of anorexia nervosa. JAMA 1974; 230:1419-22.

23. Eckert ED, Goldberg SC, Halmi KA, et al. Behavior therapy in anorexia. Brit J Psychiatry 1979; 134:55-9.

24. Pierloot R, Vandereycken W, Verhaest S. An inpatient treatment program for anorexia nervosa patients. Acta Psychiat Scand 1982; 66:1-8.

25. Reece BA, Gross M. A comprehensive milieu program for treatment In: Gross M, ed. Anorexia nervosa, a comprehensive approach. Collamore Press, 1982:

26. Halmi KA. Anorexia nervosa: Treatment in the general hospital. Current Psychiatric Therapies, Vol 21, 1982: 181-184.

27. Mavissakalian M. Anorexia nervosa treated with response prevention & prolonged exposure. Behavior Research & Therapy, 1982; 20:27-31.

28. Cinciripini PM, Karnblith SJ, Turner SM et al. A behavioral program for the management of anorexia & bulimia. The Journal of Nervous & Mental Disease 1983; 171:186-9.

29. Williams W. A comprehensive behavior modification programme for the treatment of anorexia nervosa: Results in six cases. Australian & New Zealand Journal of Psychiatry 1976; 10:321-4.

30. Monti PM, McCrady BS, Barlow DH. Effect of positive reinforcement, informational feedback & contingency contracting on a bulimic anorexic female. Behavior Therapy 1977; 8:258-63,

31. Goldberg SC, Halmi KA, Eckert ED, et al. Attitudinal dimensions in anorexia nervosa. J Psychiat Res 1980; 15:239-51.

32. Fichter MM, Doerr P, Pirke KM, et al. Behavioral, attitude, nutrition & endocrinology in anorexia nervosa. Acta Psychiat Scand 1982; 66:429-44.

33. Garner DM, Bemis KM. A cognitive-behavioral approach to anorexia nervosa. Cognitive Therapy & Research 1982; 6:123-50.

34. Rosen JC, Leitenberg H. Bulimia nervosa: Treatment with exposure & response prevention. Behavior Therapy 1982; 13:117-24.

35. Long CG, Cordle CJ. Psychological treatment of binge eating & self-induced vomiting. British Journal of Medical Psychology 1982; 55:139-55.

36. Fairburn C. A cognitive behavioural approach to the treatment of bulimia. Psychological Medicine 1981; 11:707-11.

37. Bruch H. Anorexia nervosa: Therapy & theory. Am J Psychiatry 1982; 139:1531-8.

38. Touyz SW, Beumont PJV, Glaun D, et al. A comparison of lenient & strict operant conditioning programmes in refeeding patients with anorexia nervosa. British Journal of Psychiatry 1984; 144:517-20.

39. Bemis KM. Current approaches to the etiology & treatment of anorexia nervosa. Psychological Bulletin 1984; 85:593-617.

40. Herzog DB. Are anorexic & bulimic patients depressed? Am J Psychiatry 1984; 141:1594-7.

41. Garner DM, Garfinkel PE, Schwartz D, et al. Cultural expectations of thinness in women. Psychological Reports 1980; 47:483-91.

Chapter 39

The Psychoanalytic Treatment of Anorexia Nervosa and Bulimia

C. Philip Wilson

During the past 30 years there has been increasing evidence that anorexia nervosa is a psychosomatic disorder [1-5]. From the psychoanalytic point of view, both historically and currently, anorexia nervosa is a generic term that includes the bulimic as well as the restrictor syndromes [1-5].

Since the beginning of the century, the psychoanalytic literature on this illness has been voluminous. In 1918 Freud [6] noted a neurosis in pubertal and adolescent girls that "expresses aversion to sexuality by means of anorexia." Anna Freud [7] noted the resistance aspect of the anorexic's self-starvation. Extensive bibliographic studies can be found in Sperling [2], Sours [4], Wilson et al [5,88], Bliss and Branch [8], Bruch [9], Dally [10], Kaufman and Heiman [11], and Palazzoli [12]. Deutsch [13] has explored the neglect of psychodynamics in his comprehensive book review of biochemical, endocrinological, ecological, sociological, and psychological research in psychosomatics. Summarizing current psychoanalytic theories of somatization, he underscores the crucial importance of psychoanalysis in research and treatment. I [14] recently noted that the technique of analysis of psychosomatic patients is similar to that of analysts Boyer and Giovacchini [15], Kernberg [16], and Volkan [17], who treat nonpsychosomatic patients suffering from a preponderance of preoedipal conflicts. Sperling largely based her hypotheses on the treatment of children and adolescents [2]. Her findings have been confirmed, refined, and expanded in the analyses of adolescents [18,19] and adults [5,20-25]. The structure of the ego, the split in the ego, the archaic superego, separation-individuation, and the defense of projective identification are among the many areas of research that have been explored since Sperling's death in 1973.

There is a heterogeneous range of anorexic patients with great dynamic structural and genetic variability under the coating of a relatively uniform symptomatology. While constitutional factors of infancy, variations in drive endowment, and gender differences affect each child's development, it is the domineering and controlling personality of the mother (and/or the father) that profoundly warps and inhibits the normal development of the anorexia-prone child [5,88]. All the phases of separation- individuation described by Mahler [26,27] are profoundly affected by parental attitudes. In no clinical case have we observed the constitutional lack of aggression suggested by Kramer [28] in anorexia-prone children. On the contrary, ample clinical evidence demonstrates excess drive repression in these patients, which causes the frequent appearance of habits such as teeth-grinding, head-banging, nail-biting, and thumb-sucking.

As far as psychiatric diagnosis is concerned, anorexia nervosa is a neurotic symptom complex that occurs in a variety of character disorders: hysterical, obsessive compulsive, borderline, and in some cases, conditions close to psychoses. However, even in the most disturbed cases

433

there is a split in the ego, with areas of relatively intact ego functioning and a capacity for a transference relationship [5,88].

We concur in Thoma's [1] delineation of the syndrome: (1) the age of onset is usually puberty; (2) the patients are predominantly female (although male cases have been reported by Falstein et al [29], Wilson et al [5,88], and Sours [4]; (3) the reduction in nutritional intake is psychically determined; (4) spontaneous or self-induced vomiting can occur, usually in secret; (5) amenorrhea (which is psychically caused) generally appears either before, or more rarely, after the beginning of the weight loss; (6) constipation, sometimes an excuse for excessive consumption of laxatives, speeds up weight loss; (7) the physical effects of undernourishment are present, and in severe cases, death may ensue (7% to 15% die [30]). Wilson et al [5,88] added three further observations: (8) there is commonly a tendency toward hyperactivity, which may be extreme; (9) in females there is often a disproportionate loss of breast tissue early in the disease; and (10) the symptom complex is often accompanied by or alternates with other psychosomatic symptoms (or psychogenic equivalents such as depressions, phobias, or periods of self-destructive acting out that may include impulsive sexual behavior, stealing, or accident-prone behavior). In agreement with Sours [4], we have found that all the physical signs and symptoms of anorexia nervosa, including hypothermia, lanugo hair, hypotension, bradycardia, anemia, and leukocytosis, subside when patients resume normal eating as a result of psychodynamic treatment; however, menstruation may not resume, even though the patient's weight returns to normal limits, if significant unconscious psychosexual conflicts have not been resolved [5,88].

My research and that of my colleagues [88] correlates with that of Halmi and Falk [31] who recently noted that a variety of physiologic abnormalities are associated with anorexia nervosa, all of them caused by self-starvation. In a study of 40 anorexic patients for hematologic, electrolyte, lipid, and serum enzyme aberrations when they entered a treatment study in the emaciated state and again after nutritional rehabilitation, all of the metabolic findings reverted to normal with nutritional rehabilitation. Blood studies show that changes are the result of starvation. Anorexic patients do have a leukopenia but are no more subject to infections than control groups with normal white cells and lymphocytes. Bulimic anorexics are subject to hypokalemic alkalosis. Because of the physiological effects of self-starvation on normal metabolism, these patients induce liver, kidney,

and heart disease, which can result in death.

I recently [5,24,25,32,88] presented major new hypotheses about the diagnosis, etiology, psychodynamics, and technique of treatment of anorexia nervosa. My research [5,33,88] indicates that fat phobia should replace anorexia nervosa as a diagnostic term. These patients do not suffer from lack of hunger, but from the opposite, a fear of insatiable hunger as well as of impulses of many other kinds [1,2,4,5,88].

Psychoanalytic work with restrictor and bulimic anorexics [5,24,25,32,34,88] focused on their intense fear of being fat, body-image disturbance and their fear-of-being-fat complex. Neurotic analysands also evidenced less intensely cathected but clear-cut fear of being fat obsessions and body-image disturbances [5,88]. These findings could with nonanalytic research lead to the conclusion that in our culture most women and certain men, those with unresolved feminine identifications, have a fear of being fat. Normal women readily admit to the fear. No matter how "perfect" a woman's figure may be, if she is told she is fat she will have an emotional reaction out of all proportion to reality. On the other hand, if she is told she looks thin or has lost weight, she will be inordinately pleased.

It is a central hypothesis of my research [5,24,25,88] that restrictor and bulimic anorexia symptoms are caused by an overwhelming terror of being fat, which has been primarily caused by an identification with a parent or parents who have a similar fear of being fat, and that anorexia (fat phobia) is secondarily reinforced by the general irrational fear of being fat of most other women and many men in our culture.

THE FAMILY PSYCHOLOGICAL PROFILE AND ITS THERAPEUTIC IMPLICATIONS

Psychoanalytic reserch with the families of 100 anorexia nervosa patients* revealed a parental psychological profile that appears to be etiologic in establishing a personality disorder in the children, which later manifests itself as anorexia nervosa. Melitta Sperling's analysis [2] of anorexic children and their mothers laid the groundwork for this research with her finding that the predisposition for anorexia nervosa is established in early childhood by a disturbance in the mother-child symbiosis. Four of the six features of the psychological profile correlate with parental attitudes and behavior described by Bruch [3] in 50 cases and by Minuchin et al [35] in 53 cases. Sours [4] confirms these features in his family research. The two features of the profile not described by these authors are usually only uncovered

* I am particularly indebted to Drs. Otto Sperling, Lawrence Deutsch, Ira Mintz, Cecilia Karol, Charles Hogan, Gerald Freiman, Anna Burton, Robert Grayson, and Leonard Barkin for their contributions.

by psychoanalysis, a modality they do not use [5,88].

THE PSYCHOLOGICAL PROFILE OF THE ANOREXIC FAMILY

Although the psychiatric diagnosis in anorexia nervosa cases ranges from neurosis to psychosis and the symptoms offer dramatic evidence of conflict, usually anorexic girls vehemently deny their conflicts. Most often the unhappy parents bring them in for consultation. These parents are usually highly motivated, well-meaning people who will do everything they can for their sick child. It is healthy for a child to grow up in a home where there are rules, limits, and a parental example of impulse control, responsibility, and ethical behavior; however, in their overconscientiousness, the parents of anorexics overcontrol their child. The adolescent anorexic girl is in a situation of realistic and neurotic dependence on her family, so that changes in the parents' behavior and attitudes toward her can be crucial for therapeutic success. Parents may try to withdraw their daughter from treatment prematurely because they cannot tolerate the rebelliousness and antisocial behavior that surfaces when the anorexic symptoms are resolved. They may need therapy themselves to accept the emotional changes in their daughter and to understand certain pathological interactions they have with her. Research on the anorexic families yielded the following six-part anorexic family psychological profile:*

1. All the families showed *perfectionism*. The parents were overconscientious and emphasized good behavior and social conformity in their children. Most were successful people who gave time to civic, religious, and charitable activities. Many were physicians, educators, business executives, or religious leaders, ie, pillars of society.

   Parental overconscientiousness was reflected in the exemplary childhood behavior and performance of the anorexic children. Divorce was infrequent, and when it occurred the parents who were conscientious people established residences near each other and continued to be caring, concerned parents.

   Two mothers were addicts (one to alcohol, the other to morphine), but their addictions were family secrets and both women were compulsive, perfectionistic college professors who tried to be perfect mothers. Their addictions expressed a rebellion against their hypermoral character structure. Both these addicted mothers had bulimic daughters. My research and that of Sours [4] shows that the compulsively perfectionistic parents of bulimics have more personal and marital conflict than do the parents of abstaining anorexics.

2. *Repression* of emotions was found in every family group; it was caused by the hypermorality of the parents. In several cases, parents kept such strict control over their emotions that they never quarreled in front of the children. Aggressive behavior in the children was not permitted, and aggression in general was denied (eg, one father's volunteer military service was disdained by his family). Most families laughed at the father's assertive male behavior and saw him as the "spoiler" in the sexual relation; the mother was the superior moral figure. The father's authority was diminished further by his busy schedule, which left him little time for his children.

3. The overconscientious perfectionism of the parents in these families resulted in *infantilizing decision-making* and overcontrol of the children. In some of the families, fun for fun's sake was not allowed. Everything had to have a noble purpose, the major parental home activity was intellectual discussion and scholarly reading. It was no surprise that the anorexic daughters hated the long hours of study they felt compelled to do. In therapy, it was difficult for them to become independent and mature and to get rid of the humiliating feeling that they were puppets whose strings were pulled by mother and father.

The last two features of the profile are usually uncovered only by psychoanalysis.

4. Parental overconcern with *fears of being fat and dieting* was apparent in every case. In two families, the mothers dieted and were afraid of being fat; in one of these families, the father was also afraid of being fat and dieted because of colitis.

   My research [5,25,32,88] has confirmed Sperling's observations [2] that specific conflicts and attitudes of the mother and/or father predispose a child for the development of psychosomatic symptoms (eg, a mother's overconcern with bowel functions may predispose a child for ulcerative colitis). The specific etiological factor in anorexia is the parental preoccupation with dieting and the fear of being fat, which is transmitted to the daughter by identification. The other features of this profile are also found in the parents of patients suffering from psychosomatic symptoms such as asthma, migraine, headaches, and colitis.

5. *Exhibitionistic parental sexual and toilet behavior,* whose significance was completely denied, was found in every family. Doors in these homes were not locked, and bedroom and toilet doors often

---

* A useful acronym for the profile is PRIDES. P = perfectionism, R = repression of emotion, I = infantilizing decision-making, D = dieting and fears of being fat, E = sexual and toilet exhibitionism, S = the emotional selection of a child.

were left open, which facilitated the curious child's viewing of sexual relations and toilet functions. The children frequently witnessed parental sexual intercourse. Such experiences, coupled with parental hypermorality and prudishness, caused an inhibition in normal psychosexual development in the anorexic daughters. Many were virginal, sexually repressed girls who feared boys.

Sours[4] does not observe as much exhibitionistic behavior in families of self-starving young anorexics. However, he notes exhibitionistic parental behavior in families of gorging, vomiting anorexics, including frequent seductive sexual behavior by the fathers.

6. In these families, there was an *emotional selection of one child* by the parents for the development of anorexia. This child was treated differently than the other children. Such a choice may result from (1) the carryover of an unresolved emotional conflict from the parents' childhood (eg, the infant may represent a hated parent or brother or sister); (2) an intense need to control the child, so that the child is treated almost as a part of the body of one parent; (3) a particular psychological situation and emotional state of the parent(s) at the time of the child's birth that seriously damaged the parent-child relationship (eg, the child may be infantilized because he or she is the last baby or may be over-cathected by a parent who has suffered a recent loss).

The psychoanalysis of the mother's fear-of-being-fat complex can result in the clearing of anorexic (fat phobic) symptoms in an adolescent child, as the following case exemplifies:*

Margaret, a married businesswoman, came to analysis for sexual conflicts and phobias of airplanes, elevators, and subways. A fat-phobic dietician, she was obsessed with weight and dieting and fantasies of being young and beautiful. She kept her figure zealously on the thin side, 10 lb. underweight. Her mother had been chronically 15 lb. overweight, whereas the father, a beautician, had been obsessed with dieting and weight control. In associating to the scales that she weighed herself on daily, Margaret referred to them as her "conscience" and "the law of her father." With the analysis of the transference neurosis in the context of a strong therapeutic alliance, her severe phobic symptoms subsided, but she reported that her 12-year-old daughter was amenorrheic and had symptoms of intense fat phobia (anorexia nervosa).

The analysis of the mother's fear of being fat revealed

many conflicts, a most important one being her inability to tolerate any aggression in her daughter. Associations to fat led to a childhood memory of her father telling her she had a "fat lip"; he used to slap her for "sassing him." By the defense of identification with the aggressor, she was repeating the same harsh discipline with her daughter. All roundings of the female breast, buttocks, or "tummy" in herself or her daughter repelled her. As these and other conflicts that had been displaced onto the fear of being fat were analyzed and the mother could accept her own as well as her daughter's femininity, the latter's anorexic symptoms disappeared.

PSYCHODYNAMICS

Much has been written about the psychodynamics of anorexia nervosa. It generally has been observed by analytic authors that there is a flight from adult sexuality accompanied by a regression to more primitive defenses [1,2,5,12,36-44,88]. This regression involves conflict around primitive sadistic and cannibalistic oral fantasies [2,12,41-43]; typical pregenital defense mechanisms are at work [2,5,17,36,42,43,45,46,88].

Sperling [2] notes that unresolved preoedipal fixations to the mother contribute to difficulties in psychosexual development. She feels that anorexic girls displace sexual and masturbatory conflicts from the genitals to the mouth, thus equating food and eating with forbidden sexual objects and activities.

Most analytic authors agree that the regression of anorexic patients is a flight from their own insatiable instinctual needs, which are defended against with primitive defenses of equal force. Sperling [2] has labeled anorexia nervosa "an impulse disorder."

The role of unconscious pregnancy fantasies in the genesis of this illness is almost universally recognized by psychoanalytic authors. The anorexic patient fears and denies these fantasies.

I and my colleagues [5,88] along with Sperling [2] do not agree with Bruch [3,47,48,49], Crisp [50,52], Dally [10], and Selvini Palazzoli [12,41] that a psychoanalytic approach to these patients should be avoided. The experience of our group agrees with Mushatt [53], Blitzer et al [54], Jessner and Abse [55], Lorand [38], Mushat [56], Sperling [2,42,43], Thoma [1], Waller et al [44], Sours [4], Mogul [57], Risen [46], and others, that psychoanalytic investigation is of the utmost importance in understanding this illness, as well as the treatment of choice in most cases.

---

*   This case with minor changes is reprinted from Wilson et al [5,88].

PSYCHODYNAMICS OF ANOREXIA NERVOSA*

In psychodynamic terms, this complex is rooted in unresolved sadomasochistic oral-phase conflicts that result in an ambivalent relationship with the mother. Fixation to this phase of development, with its accompanying fears of object loss, is caused by maternal and/or paternal overcontrol and overemphasis on food and eating functions as symbols of love. This unresolved conflict influences each subsequent maturational phase so that anal, oedipal, and later developmental conflicts also are unresolved.

The unresolved preoedipal fixation on the mother contributes to the difficulty in psychosexual development and the intensity of the oedipal development. As Serpling noted [2] anorexia nervosa fat phobia can be considered a specific pathological outcome of unresolved oedipal conflicts in a child whose preoedipal relationship to the mother has predisposed her to this particular reaction under precipitating circumstances.

The genetic influences on this complex are parental conflicts about weight and food specifically, and about aggressive and libidinal expression generally. In addition, the parents tend to be compulsive, moralistic, and perfectionistic, significantly denying the impact on the developing child of their exhibitionistic toilet, bedroom, and other behavior. Other genetic factors are cultural, societal, and general medical influences, as well as secondary identification with women and/or men who share the fear-of-being-fat complex.

From an economic point of view, the unremitting pressure in bulimic and restrictor anorexics of repressed, unsublimated, aggressive, and libidinal drives, conflicts, and fantasies is a central issue. In the bulimic anorexics the attempt to control drive is manifested by the fear-of-being-fat complex but defective ego functioning results in a giving in to voraciousness as well as to impulse gratifications of other kinds. Then intense guilt inflicted by the archaic superego causes attempts at undoing by self-induced vomiting and laxative use as well as other masochistic behavior. In the restrictor anorexic the same feared drive eruptions are masked by the fear of being fat complex but intact ego controls result in total impulse control brought about by the restrictor's archaic superego.

From a structual point of view, ego considerations are central. In the preoedipal years, the ego of the bulimic anorexia-prone (fat-phobic) child becomes split. One part develops in a pseudonormal fashion: cognitive functions, the self-observing part of the ego, adaptive capacities, and other ego functions appear to operate normally. While the restrictor anorexics in childhood are most often described as "perfect" and have excellent records in school, the bulimic anorexics have more evidence of disobedience and rebellion at home and school. In adolescence there is more antisocial behavior, sexual promiscuity, and addiction. The ego represses, denies, displaces, externalizes, and projects conflicts onto the fear-of-being-fat complex. In many cases, conflicts are displaced onto habits such as thumbsucking, enuresis, encopresis, nailbiting, headbanging, and hairpulling. In other cases, there is a concomitant displacement and projection of conflict onto actual phobic objects. In some patients, anorexia nervosa alternates with other psychosomatic disease syndromes, such as ulcerative colitis [2,5,88]. This split in the ego manifests itself in the intense, psychotic-like denial of the displaced wishes, conflicts, and fantasies. In other words, the split-off neurotic part of the personality is denied in the fear-of-being-fat complex.

From an adaptive point of view, conflicts at each maturational and libidinal phase are denied, displaced, and projected onto the fear-of-being-fat. Conflicts in separation-individuation [53,56] are paramount and are denied by the parents and developing child. Normal adaptive conflict is avoided and denied. Many parents of anorexics raise them in an unreal, overprotected world. Perfectionistic parents impair the ego's decision-making functions with their infantilizing intrusions into every aspect of their child's life. In each case a focus of analysis is on the pregenital object relations, which have been caused by the unresolved parental relationship and the conflicts in separation-individuation.

Unlike Sperling [2], I along with Hogan [5] and Mintz [5,19,34,88] include males under the diagnostic category of anorexia nervosa. Mintz and Welsh [5] have shown that male anorexics have oedipal and preoedipal fixations and unresolved problems in separation-individuation, severe latent homosexual conflicts and a feminine identification, and the same fear-of-being-fat complex seen in the females, which is caused by an identification with the mother and/or the father's fear-of-being-fat.

BODY IMAGE

Anorexic self-starvation, an extreme of asceticism [57], is rooted in a massive preoedipal repression of sadomasochistic oral-phase conflicts that have been elaborated by the ego with new defensive structures at each subsequent libidinal and maturational phase of development. It is the surface of the mother's breast,

---

* I am indebted to Dr. Howard Schwartz who restated my findings in a metapsychological framework that I have elaborated on in these formulations.

and by extension the figure, that has been projected in the anorexic's body image [Freud 58]. The fear of being fat reflects the terror of oral sadistic incorporation of the breast of mother and later of other objects [5,88].

A few restrictors and a number of bulimics do not evidence a clear-cut body-image disturbance [5,88], although they are all fat phobic. In these cases the ego is healthier, and the psychopathology primarily oedipal.

SPLIT IN THE EGO

To further understand the anorexic ego structure, one has to keep in mind the split in the ego. In 1983 I [88] noted that from a structural point of view, ego considerations are central. In the preoedipal years, the ego of the anorexia-prone child becomes split. One part develops in a pseudonormal fashion; cognitive functions, the self-observing functions of the ego, adaptive capacities, and other ego functions appear to operate normally. The ego suppresses, represses, denies, displaces, externalizes, and projects conflicts onto the fear of being fat complex. *The pseudonormal part of the ego of the abstaining (restrictor) anorexic evidences many of the characteristics seen in compulsion neuroses.* The pseudonormal part of the bulimic ego is an admixture of hysterical and compulsive traits.

Strober's conclusions [59,60] about the differences between restrictors and bulimics correlate with my research. His type-1 and type-2 anorexics, the restrictors, evidence "obsessionality," whereas his type-3 patients, the bulimics, present "a distinctive profile of low ego strength, impulsivity, proneness to addictive behaviors and more turbulent interpersonal dynamics."

FUNCTIONING OF THE EGO

While the restrictor anorexic is capable of controlling the impulse to eat, the bulimic patient is not and consumes tremendous quantities of food. The patient gorges, becomes so frightened of gaining weight that she feels forced to vomit to regurgitate her caloric intake.

The clinical and psychodynamic relevance of gorging deserves some consideration, because it permits an additional perspective in viewing the patient's feelings, psychodynamics, and personality structure. The restrictor anorexic is able to contain (and overcontrols) the wish to gorge and impulse gratifications of other kinds because of intact ego controls. In a series of publications, I [5,25,34,88] noted that the bulimic patient has strict but ineffective ego controls that are unable to regulate the impulse to eat. This defect in self-control is so threatening to the patient that the slightest gain in weight produces panic, exercising, starving, and vomit-

ing. The bulimic patient who is unable to control eating is also unable to control other impulses, so that one sees sexual promiscuity, delinquency, stealing, lying, and running away much more frequently than in the starving anorexic patient. This defect in ego and superego controls arises in part from identifying with the parents who frequently argue, fight, and act out destructively more often than the parents of the starving anorexics. Thus the superego structure of the bulimic is not as rigid and strict as that of the restrictor.

Restrictor and bulimic anorexia nervosa are symptom complexes that occur in a variety of character disorders: hysterical, obsessive-compulsive, borderline, and in some cases conditions close to psychoses. However, even in the most disturbed cases, there is a split in the ego with areas of selectively intact ego functioning and a capacity for a transference relationship. I have worked analytically with ten bulimic patients and have seen many more in consultation and supervision. Four patients who completed their treatment are illustrative. One adolescent, who alternately abstained, gorged, and vomited, resolved her conflicts in a year's analysis. She was neither amenorrheic nor dangerously underweight. The treatment prevented the development of phobic fear of being fat (anorexic nervosa). Both the second and third cases abstained, gorged, and vomited, but they did not use laxatives. Neither brought their weight down to dangerous levels. Diagnostically, they suffered from mixed neuroses with severe preoedipal conflicts. Both patients, unlike the typical restrictor anorexic, had an abundant psychosexual fantasy life and had masturbated in childhood. Doubts have been expressed to me by experienced analysts about the possibility of analyzing any bulimic. Cases I've analyzed and supervised have experienced a full resolution of their fear-of-being-fat body-image and their obsession with being thin. Long-term follow-up studies in certain cases showed that they were able to face and master the conflicts of self-fulfillment in a career, pregnancy, childbirth, and motherhood. In my experince, if the bulimic anorexic process can be analyzed in *statu nascendi* as in my first case, the prognosis is excellent. However, a longer and more complicated treatment is necessary for the analysis of the rigid layered defenses of the chronic bulimic anorexic [5,88]. Of course, statements about prognosis must be qualified by the psychodynamic diagnosis of the individual case and by the presenting situation. Obviously, if the addicted bulimic is seen when acutely alcoholic and/or under the influence of drugs, all the technical problems involved in the management and treatment of such cases confront the therapist.

What follows is a simplied diagram of the split in the ego in anorexia.

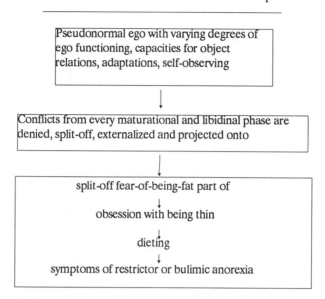

Pseudonormal ego of the restrictor
resembles compulsive neurotic

Pseudonormal ego of the bulimic is a
mixture of compulsive and hysterical
neurotic complexes

Pseudonormal ego with varying degrees of
ego functioning, capacities for object
relations, adaptations, self-observing

↓

Conflicts from every maturational and libidinal phase are
denied, split-off, externalized and projected onto

↓

split-off fear-of-being-fat part of

↓

obsession with being thin

↓

dieting

↓

symptoms of restrictor or bulimic anorexia

TECHNIQUE

The technique of analysis or analytic psychotherapy is discussed with extensive case histories in our recent volumes [5,88]. Although some cases can be analyzed with classical technique, in regressed cases in the first phase of treatment the transference is handled along the principles set forward by Kernberg [16] and summarized by Boyer [15] in regard to borderline cases:

1. The predominantly negative transference is systematically elaborated only in the present without initial efforts directed toward full genetic interpretations.

2. The patient's typical defensive constellations are interpreted as they enter the transference (see discussion of particular defensive constellations below).

3. Limits are set in order to block acting out in the transference insofar as this is necessary to protect the neutrality of the therapist (but with many limitations, see below).

4. The less primitively determined aspects of the positive transference are not interpreted early, since their presence enhances the development of the therapeutic and working alliances (only if we look at these alliances as part of the positive transference—see discussion of limiting transference above), although the primitive idealizations that reflect the splitting of "all good" from "all bad" object relations are systematically interpreted as part

of the effort to work through those primitive defenses.

5. Interpretations are formulated so that the patient's distortions of the therapist's interventions and of present reality, especially the patient's perceptions during the hour, can be systematically clarified.

6. The highly distorted transference, at times psychotic in nature and reflecting fantastic internal object relations pertaining to early ego disturbances, is worked through first in order to reach the transferences related to actual childhood experiences (p.176).

The early interpretation of the denial of suicidal behavior (masochism) parallels the technique of Sperling [2] and Hogan [5,88] with psychosomatic patients and correlates with the therapeutic technique used in the therapy of schizophrenic, borderline, and character disorders by Boyer and Giovacchini [15], Kernberg [16], and Volkan [17].

First, one interprets anorexic patients' masochism—their archaic superego and the guilt they experience at admitting to any conflicts. Next, one interprets defenses against facing masochistic behavior; then, when the ego is healthier, defenses against aggressive impulses are interpreted. Such interpretations are inexact; frequently, patients' associations do not confirm the interpretation. These patients have an archaic, punitive superego and a relatively weak ego. The analyst provides auxiliary ego strength and a rational superego [5,15,21,61,88]. Interpretations should be made in a firm, consistent manner [15]. With such patients, the analyst needs to have authority.

These patients' behavioral responses can be interpreted. Patients' dreams have to be used in the context of their psychodynamics. Early in treatment, patients do not usually offer useful associative verbal material, as is also the case in the analyses of children and patients with character disorders [15]. At this stage of treatment, the analyst uses construction and reconstruction to respond to patients' silences.

Because anorexic patients in their projective identifications can pick up almost imperceptible nuances in the tone of voice, facial expression, movements, and even feelings of the analyst, they provoke intense countertransference reactions [5,62,88].

There is a special technique in the analysis of anorexics. The analyst must demonstrate to the patient the need for immediate gratification (the impulse disorder, ie, the primary narcissism) early in treatment [2,5,62,88]. Thus, the patient is shown that the symptoms of restrictor and bulimic anorexia are manifestations of a split-off impulsive part of the ego; ie, the fear-of-being-fat complex.

EGO STRUCTURE AND TRANSFERENCE INTERPRETATION

Analytic technique has to be adapted to the varying defenses of the ego. The bulimic patients use acting out, rationalization, denial, withholding, and lying more intensely and persistently than the restrictors. In many cases once the restrictor's anorexic crisis subsides, the course of analysis is in some way similar to that of a compulsive neurotic. There are of course many varieties of ego structure in anorexic patients. Analytic technique varies with different patients and with the degree of regression encountered. Technique also varies according to the individual style and experience of the analyst. Most of my colleagues and I tend to see the patient vis-a-vis in the first dyadic phase of treatment. However, some restrictor and bulimic anorexics can be analyzed along more classical lines with the couch being used from the beginning [5,88].

The technique of interpretation is determined by multiple factors such as the transference and the quality of object relationships. A crucial consideration is the split in the anorexic's ego and the extent to which this split is comprehended by the self-observing functions of the patient's ego. The first phase of analysis involves making the healthier part of the patient's ego aware of the split-off, primitive-impulse-dominated part of the ego and its modes of functioning.

In this early phase effective technique with restrictor anorexics is to interpret defenses (rationalization, denial, etc.) that mask masochistic behavior whereas with bulimics the multiple functions of the patient's gorging, vomiting, and laxative use are interpreted as acting out defenses against the experiencing of affects such as guilt, anxiety, depression, anger, or sexual feelings.

Typical anorexic defenses are: (1) denial and splitting; (2) belief in magic; (3) feelings of omnipotence; (4) demand that things and people be all perfect—the alternative is to be worthless; (5) need to control; (6) displacement and projection of conflict; (7) ambivalence; (8) masochistic perfectionism that defends against conflicts, particularly those around aggression; (9) pathological ego ideal of beautiful peace and love; (1); fantasied perfect, conflict-free mother-child symbiosis.

Both the restrictor and bulimic anorexic make extensive use of the defense of projective identification [15,63-77]. As Wilson et al [5,88] demonstrated, the anorexic projects unacceptable aspects of the personality—impulses, self-images, superego introjects—onto other people, particularly the analyst, with a resulting identification based on these projected self-elements. The extreme psychotic-like denial of conflict of the anorexic is caused by primitive projective identification onto others of archaic destructive superego introjects.

Sperling [2] noted that part of the anorexic's conflicts are conscious. Wilson et al [5,88] emphasize that conscious withholding, rationalization, distortion, and lying are characteristic defenses of the restrictor and bulimic anorexics. This pseudopsychopathic behavior is analyzable [5].

THIRST, HUNGER, AND SAND SYMBOLISM IN ANOREXIA NERVOSA

The anorexic's defensive asceticism stressed by Mogul [57] and Risen [46] is represented in the dreams of these patients by sand symbols. The analysis of sand symbols in the dreams of anorexics is of great importance. Spitz [78] emphasized that infants feel thirst, but not hunger, in the hallucinatory state. I have emphasized [5,79,88] that sand can be used as a pregenital symbol in which repressed oral and anal conflicts are regressively represented. Sand symbolizes oral-phase thirst and/or the formless stool of the infant (diarrhea). Antithetically, it depicts a characteristic anorexic attitude, asceticism—the ability to do without mother's milk, to control impulse gratification.

Sand representations in dreams can symbolize aspects of conflicts and processes that are involved in addictions such as smoking, substance abuse, alcohol, or food as in the eating disorders. Anorexic self-starvation and dehydration mask and express an Isakower-like phenomenon in that they induce a dry (thirsty) mouth.

For example,* a bulimic anorexic who was becoming aware of the oral phase meanings of her sand dreams reported the following clinical material when she was mourning the recent death of her mother. She had just paid the bill for her mother's funeral and had expressed weary resignation at paying her analytic bill. In her analysis she was trying to analyze three habits—vomiting, laxative taking, and cigarette smoking. She stated: "I have a dry mouth. Yesterday I was so thirsty I drank a quart of orange juice, but it did not help. For years while I have been anorexic I have been thirsty. I would just take a sip of water. When I am depressed I am more thirsty. I was crying yesterday: I miss my mother so much. Why couldn't I make everything up to her? Why did we have to fight so much?"

An interpretation was made that she not only wanted her mother's love but wished the analyst would love her, baby her, and give her gifts as her mother had done. This included not charging her for his services, but giving them as a "present." The patient cried and said, "Yes mother gave me so much—she'd say, 'My money is yours.' I used to try to refuse her gifts, which I do not need, but she made me take them."

The "Little Person" Phenomenon

Volkan [17] described an anorexic patient with a split-off, archaic part of her ego—a "little person." He related this pathological ego structure to the "little man" phenomenon described by Kramer [28] and Niederland [81,82]. In my experience, all psychosomatic patients, including anorexics, have a split-off, archaic, primtive ego. A conscious manifestation of this split-off ego is represented by the fear-of-being-fat complex.

Susan, an impulsive anorexic high school student brought in a series of dreams containing images of an innocent, wide-eyed little girl that reminded her of current sentimental oil paintings that depicted an innocent, raggedly dressed child with tears in her enormous eyes. Susan was beginning to understand that these paintings showed how she tried to come across to people and to the analyst. After these dreams were analyzed, she had a dream of a little prince whom she wanted to control. Analysis showed this little prince to be her "little person"—the archaic split-off ego. The little prince was narcissistic, omnipotent, and magical. That he was male was a reflection of her secret wish to be a boy. For her, males were aggressive and magical while females were innocent, passive, and masochistic. The split-off part of her ego was filled with murderous rage and hatred.

CLINICAL CASES

A Restrictor Anorexic and Her Family**

The R. family came for consultation about their 17-year-old daughter Sally who recently had lost 30 lb and became amenorrheic. Sally's history was typical of the majority of restrictor anorexics. A "good" girl, she was obsessed with the proper behavior, studying, and social achievement. Her father, a very idealistic man, disapproved of his successful business career and always wished that he had been a physician. A workaholic, he delegated the care of his children to his wife, Mrs. R., who divided her time between a social work career and her family. She was overconcerned with lady-like behavior, manners, and proper behavior for her daughter.

Sally's brother Robert, two years her senior, was an easygoing adolescent boy who had a succession of girlfriends, smoked, drank, and enjoyed parties, dancing, and rock music. Although the mother weakly argued with Robert and chided him for his poor performance in school, most of her attention was focused on her daughter. She did everything she could for Sally, helping her with her studies, reviewing her homework, and barraging her with advice and criticism.

The Rs followed a strict routine: meals were always on time, television was rationed to one hour a day, and the major form of relaxation for the parents was intellectual discussion and reading of a serious nature. They never quarreled in front of their children, and in general, they shared the same ethical, social, and political views.

Memories of having witnessed parental intercourse (primal scene) emerged in the course of Sally's analysis. At three years of age, she woke up screaming with nightmares, and in order to quiet her, her mother had her sleep the rest of the night in the parents' bed. It was then that Sally overheard the heavy breathing of intercourse, which she fantasied was an attack by her father on her mother. Other occasions of her witnessing parental intercourse, at 5 and 6 years of age, increased Sally's fear of sexuality. There were no operable locks on the doors in the Rs home. Parental nudity and toilet activities also were observed frequently by Sally, who became inhibited and afraid of boys.

Analysis. As with all anorexics, many different conflicts were displaced onto and masked by Sally's anorectic symptoms. The focus of therapy was upon showing Sally the nature of her overly strict conscience, which demanded perfect behavior in herself and others. In her

---

* This material is reprinted from Wilson, Hogan and Mintz [5,88] (p. 252-253).

** This case of Dr. Wilson's with minor changes is reprinted from Wilson et al [5,88], p. 36-37.

treatment behavior she was hypercritical; memories and dreams revealed that she had developed this attitude by identifying with her mother's perfectionism.

Both Mr. and Mrs. R. were referred for psychotherapy. Mrs. R. came to understand that she was treating Sally very differently from Robert and that she had been pressuring her daughter to carry out certain of her own unfulfilled aspirations in life. The Rs moderated their overconcern with dieting and weight loss, and they learned how to tolerate and understand the emerging rebellious, critical, adolescent behavior that Sally manifested when her anorectic symptoms subsided. Mrs. R. interrupted her intrusive controlling attitude toward her daughter. The parents also took some vacations without their children for the first time and began to quarrel in front of their children. Operable locks on the bedroom and bathroom doors were installed, and Sally was given a degree of privacy appropriate to her age.

Sally's anorectic symptoms cleared up in six weeks, and she resumed eating, achieved normal weight levels, and began to menstruate again. Two years of analysis were required to resolve her underlying personality disorder.

A Bulimic Anorexic*

Nancy was a 19-year-old student who had been gorging and vomiting for the past five years. She was 5 ft 4 inches and currently weighed 115 lb, although her weight varied between 160 and 98 lb. She stated that when she began gorging she could gain 30 lbs in two weeks. She felt that she could not stop and would eat a gallon of ice cream, an entire chocolate cake, sandwiches, and almost everything in the refrigerator. She ate whatever she found on the shelves, including raw dough. Starving and vomiting resulted in an equally dramatic weight loss. Regular exercise, which included 45 minutes of daily jogging, helped to maintain the weight loss. Menstrual periods were irregular but present.

The patient came from a fat-phobic food-and-weight-conscious family. The father was a rigid, controlling engineer who would slap the patient when he became angry with her. The mother was obese, unable to maintain her own reasonable weight but prone to making insulting remarks about the patient's weight gain. The patient stated that the mother was so fanatic about the patient's weight that she would accuse her of still being fat when she weighed 115 lb. Distortion in the mother's view of her child is not an uncommon finding. The patient had a 15-year-old acting-out sister who fought constantly with the parents. The patient noted urges to stuff the sister with food, and experienced enjoyment watching the sister eat, "as if I was eating." Junk food was never allowed in the house. When the patient began gaining weight, the entire family found themselves on a diet, because the mother limited the food brought into the house.

Early in the treatment the patient realized that when she was upset or depressed she began to eat. As she became increasingly preoccupied and disturbed with eating, her previous worries disappeared. She began to see that eating served to cover up anxieties. Her excessive attachment to the parents became apparent as she recounted dropping out of college in her first year because of stomach aches and feelings of depression. During her bouts of bulimia, the parents would never go out in the evenings. She saw that the gorging kept them close to her. As the months passed she became increasingly aware that she was unable to assert herself with either parent and that she harbored many feelings of resentment toward them. This anger was expressed indirectly against her father by not studying and against her mother by gaining weight. Weight gain was also unconsciously used to terminate relationships with boyfriends when feelings of closeness and sexuality became too threatening.

Analysis achieved a resolution to the patient's bulimic symptoms and insight into the underlying adolescent maturational conflicts.

PROGNOSTIC DIFFERENCES IN RESTRICTOR AND BULIMIC ANOREXICS

Many bulimic anorexics, those who would diagnostically be termed neurotic, give an appearance of healthier (pseudonormal) ego functioning. Since they evidence an admixture of hysterical traits, their emotions are under less repression. They develop a seemingly good therapeutic alliance. Wilson and Mintz [5,34,88] as well as Bruch [3] feel that the prognosis is poorer for the chronic bulimic. Hogan [5,88] sees little difference. In general, because of the lesser degree of acting out and the stronger ego, the prognosis would appear better for the restrictor anorexic; however, in some bulimic cases where the symptoms are of recent development and limited to gorging and vomiting, the prognosis may be favorable because there is a readiness for the expression of affect. It is still felt by many analysts that the hysterical neurotic is easier to analyze than the compulsive neurotic. However, the degree of preoedipal psychopathology is the limiting factor in both the hysterical and compulsive neurotic and the bulimic and restrictor anorexic.

---

* This case of Dr. Mintz's is reprinted from Wilson and Mintz [33] p. 29.

CURRENT STUDIES

Currently there is a widespread application of psychoanalysis to the treatment of anorexia nervosa. Long-term research is being conducted by the members of the Psychoanalytic Study Group of the Psychoanalytic Association of New York, Inc, an Affiliate Society of The American Psychoanalytic Association, which is composed of psychoanalytically trained psychiatrists specializing in the treatment of psychosomatic disorders. This group was led by Dr. Melitta Sperling from 1965 until her death in 1973; since that time the chairman has been Dr. C. Philip Wilson.

This research has provided a unique opportunity to review and discuss numerous anorexic cases. Particularly important has been the presentation of the psychodynamic treatment of the mother, the father, the siblings, and the spouses of these patients. The combined experience of this study group was recently published in a book: *Fear of Being Fat: The Treatment of Anorexia Nervosa and Bulimia,* edited by C. Philip Wilson, MD, with the assistance of Drs. Charles C. Hogan and Ira L. Mintz [5,88].

Other important ongoing research is being conducted by The Psychosomatic Discussion Group of The American Psychoanalytic Association.* The topic since 1982 has been anorexia nervosa. Technical and theoretical aspects of the psychoanalysis of restrictor and bulimic anorexics have been presented to this group by Mintz [83], Hogan [84], Keith [85], and Hitchcock [86].

Recent psychoanalytic studies have included focus on asceticism [57], the pathologic sense of self [87] and the analysis of an adolescent girl [46]. The use of pharmacotherapy and behavioral techniques pose hazards that may limit their effectiveness in the absence of sustained and careful psychotherapeutic effort with the individual patient and family [88,89,90].

SUMMARY

A review of the extensive psychoanalytic literature shows that most psychoanalysts view anorexia nervosa as an emotional disturbance that emerges as a retreat from developing adult sexuality via a regression to the prepubertal relation to the parents. I presented a number of new hypotheses about the psychodynamics and technique of treatment:

1. Restrictor or bulimic fat phobia should replace anorexia nervosa as a diagnostic term, because these patients do not suffer from a lack of appetite but the opposite, a struggle to avoid being overwhelmed by their impulses, including voraciousness.

2. While the underlying conflicts, their fear of being fat complexes, are similar, the ego of the bulimic is not as perfectionistic and controlling as that of the restrictor, so that it is periodically overwhelmed by not only impulses to gorge but impulses of other kinds.

3. Family psychodynamics, which are viewed as etiologic, were detailed.

4. I summarized new techniques of treatment that focus in the first phase of analysis on the dyadic transference, the failure to free associate, the patient's impulsivity, and the use of denial and projective identification. The importance of understanding sand symbolism in anorexia was emphasized, because it reveals these patients' conflicts over thirst, impulse control, and asceticism. Psychoanalysis or analytic psychotherapy are the treatments of choice for anorexia nervosa. Most patients are seen vis-a-vis in the first dyadic phase of treatment. The parents of adolescent anorexics are usually seen in conjoint therapy by a collegue. The analyst is in charge of treatment, with hospitalization reserved for true emergencies. Medication is contraindicated if analysis is feasible. Our technique of treatment has similarities to the methods used by Boyer and Giovacchini [15] and Kernberg [16] in the analysis of patients with borderline and narcissistic disorders.

REFERENCES

1. Thoma H. Anorexia nervosa. New York: International Universities Press, 1967:4-20.

2. Sperling M. Psychosomatic disorders in childhood. New York: Jason Aronson, 1978:139-173.

3. Bruch H. The golden cage: The enigma of anorexia nervosa. Cambridge, Massachusetts: Harvard University Press, 1978:1-150.

4. Sours J. Starving to death in a sea of objects: The anorexia nervosa syndrome. New York: Jason Aronson, 1980:206-266.

5. Wilson CP, Hogan CC, Mintz IL. Fear of being fat: The treatment of anorexia nervosa and bulimia. New York: Jason Aronson, 1983: 1985:1-366.

6. Freud S. From the history of an infantile neurosis, in Standard Edition 17, 7:122. London: Hogarth Press, 1955:106.

7. Freud A. Indications for child analysis and other papers. 1945- 1956. vol 4: Writings of Anna Freud. New York: International Universities Press, 1968:386-391.

8. Bliss EL, Branch CHH. Anorexia nervosa: Its history,

---

* The research of this discussion group is being published in a book that is in press: *Eating to Live or Living to Eat: The Anorexic Dilemma,* ed. C.P. Wilson, C.C. Hogan, and I.L. Mintz. Riverside, N.J.: Jason Aronson, p. 38.

psychology, and biology. New York: Hoeber, 1960:1-210.

9. Bruch H. Eating disorders: Obesity, anorexia nervosa and the person within. New York: Basic Books, 1973:1-396.

10. Dally PJ. Anorexia nervosa. New York: Grune and Stratton, 1969:1-137.

11. Kaufman MR, Heiman M, (eds). Evolution of psychosomatic concepts. Anorexia nervosa: A paradigm. New York: International Universities Press, 1964:1-399.

12. Selvini Palazzoli M. Self-starvation: From individual to family therapy in the treatment of anorexia nervosa. New York: Jason Aronson, 1978:1-296.

13. Deutsch L. Psychosomatic Medicine from a psychoanalytic viewpoint. J Amer Psychoanalytic Assoc 1980; 28:653-702.

14. Wilson CP. Parental overstimulation in asthma. Internat J Psychoanalytic Psychotherapy 1980; 8:601-21.

15. Boyer LB. Working with a borderline patient. In: Boyer LB, Giovacchini PI (eds). Psychoanalytic treatment of schizophrenic, borderline and characterological disorders. New York: Jason Aronson, 1980:171-208.

16. Kernberg OF. Borderline conditions and pathological narcissism. New York: Jason Aronson, 1975:1-361.

17. Volkan VD. Primitive internalized object relations: A clinical study of schizophrenic, borderline, and narcissistic patients. New York: International Universities Press, 1976:1-337.

18. Karol C. The role of primal scene and masochism in asthma. Internat J Psychoanalytic Psychotherapy 1980; 8:577-92.

19. Mintz IL. Multideterminism in asthmatic disease. Internat J Psychoanalytic Psychotherapy 1980; 8:593-600.

20. Wilson CP. Psychosomatic asthma and acting out: A case of bronchial asthma that developed de novo in the terminal phase of analysis. Internat J Psycho-Analysis 1968; 49:330-5.

21. Wilson CP. On the limits of the effectiveness of psychoanalysis: early ego and somatic disturbances. J Amer Psychoanalytic Assoc 1971; 19:552-64.

22. Wilson CP. The psychoanalytic treatment of hospitalized anorexia nervosa patients. Paper presented at the meeting of the Psychoanalytic Association of New York: November 19, 1973.

23. Wilson CP. The psychoanalysis of an adolescent anorexic girl. Discussion group on "Late Adolescence," S Ritvo, Chairman. Meeting of the American Psychoanalytic Association: December 12, 1974.

24. Wilson CP. On the fear of being fat in female psychology and anorexia nervosa patients. Journal Bulletin of the Psychoanalytic Association of New York 1980; 17:8-9.

25. Wilson CP. The fear of being fat and anorexia nervosa. Internat J of Psychoanalytic Psychotherapy 1982; 9:233-55.

26. Mahler MS, Furer M. On human symbiosis and the vicissitudes of individuation. New York: International Universities Press, 1968:1-271.

27. Mahler MS. On the first three subphases of the separation-individuation process. Internat J of Psycho-Analysis 1972; 53:333-8.

28. Kramer S. A discussion of Sours's paper on "The anorexia syndrome." Internat J of Psycho-Analysis 1974; 55:577-9.

29. Falstein EI, Feinstein, SC, Judas I. Anorexia nervosa in the male child. Amer J Orthopsychiat 1956; 26:751-72.

30. Sours J. Anorexia nervosa: nosology, diagnosis, developmental patterns, and power-control dynamics, in Adolescence. In: Caplan G, Lebovici S (eds). Psychosocial perspectives. New York: Basic Books, 21969:185-212.

31. Halmi K, Falk J. Common physiologic changes in anorexia nervosa. Internat J of Eating Disorders 1981; 1:28.

32. Wilson CP. The family psychological profile of anorexia nervosa patients. Journal of the Medical Society of New Jersey 1980; 77:341-4.

33. Wilson CP, Mintz IL. Abstaining and bulimic anorexics: two sides of the same coin. Primary Care 1982; 9:459-72.

34. Wilson CP. Fat phobia as a diagnostic term to replace a medical misnomer: "Anorexia nervosa." American Academy of Child Psychiatry. G Harper, M.D., Chairman. Tape #96 and 97, by Instant Replay, 760 South 23rd Street, Arlington, VI 22202, Oct 25, 1983.

35. Minuchin S, Rosman BL, Baker l. Psychosomatic families: Anorexia nervosa in context. Cambridge, Mass: Harvard University Press, 1978:1-351.

36. Fenichel O. Anorexia. In: The collected papers of Otto Fenichel. New York: Norton, 1954; 2:288-295.

37. Gero G. An equivalent of depression: Anorexia. In: Greenacre P (ed). Affective disorders: Psychoanalytic contributions to their study. New York: International Universities Press, 1953:117-189.

38. Lorand S. Anorexia nervosa: Report of a case. Psychosomatic Medicine 1943; 5:282-92.

39. Masserman JH. Psychodynamics in anorexia nervosa and neurotic vomiting. Psychoanalytic Quarterly 1942; 10:211-42.

40. Moulton R. Psychosomatic study of anorexia nervosa including the use of vaginal smears. Psychosomatic Medicine 1942; 4:62-72.

41. Selvini Palazzoli M. Emaciation as magic means for the removal of anguish in anorexia mentalis. Acta Psychotherapica 1961; 9:37-45.

42. Sperling M. Food allergies and conversion hysteria. Psychoanalytic Quarterly 1953; 22:525-38.

43. Sperling M. Trichotillomania, trichophagy, and cyclic vomiting: A contribution to the psychopathology of female sexuality. International Journal of Psycho-Analysis 1968; 49:682-690.

44. Waller JV, Kaufman MR, Deutsch F. Anorexia nervosa: A psychosomatic entity. Psychosomatic Medicine 1940; 2:3-16.

45. Masterson J. Primary anorexia in the borderline adolescent—an object relations review. In: Horticollis P

(ed). Borderline Personality disorders: the concept, the syndrome, the patient. New York: International Universities Press, 1977:475-494.

46. Risen SE. The psychoanalytic treatment of an adolescent with anorexia nervosa. The Psychoanalytic Study of the Child 1982; 37:433-59.

47. Bruch HP. Perceptual and conceptual disturbances in anorexia nervosa. Psychosomatic Medicine 1962; 24:187-94.

48. Bruch H. Anorexia nervosa and its differential diagnosis. Journal of Nervous and Mental Disease 1965; 141:555-66.

49. Bruch H. Psychotherapy in primary anorexia nervosa. Journal of Nervous and Mental Disease 1970; 150:51-67.

50. Crisp AH. Clinical and therapeutic aspects of anorexia nervosa: A study of 30 cases. Journal of Psychosomatic Research 1965; 9:67.

51. Crisp AH. Anorexia nervosa. Hospital Medicine 1967; 1:713-8.

52. Crisp AH. Primary anorexia nervosa. Gut 1968; 9:370-2.

53. Mushatt C. Anorexia nervosa: A psychoanalytic commentary. International Journal of Psychoanalytic Psychotherapy 1982; 9:257-65.

54. Blitzer JR, Rollins N, Blackwell A. Children who starve themselves: Anorexia nervosa. Psychosomatic Medicine 1961; 23:369-83.

55. Jessenr L, Abse DW. Regressive forces in anorexia nervosa. British Journal of Medical Psychology 1960; 33:301-11.

56. Mushatt C. Mind-body environment: Toward understanding the impact of loss on psyche and soma. Psychoanalytic Quarterly 1975; 44:81-106.

57. Mogul SL. Asceticism and anorexia nervosa. The Psychoanalytic Study of the Child 1980; 35:155-75.

58. Freud S. The ego and the id. Standard Edition. London: Hogarth Press 1961; 19:13-66.

59. Strober M. The significance of bulimia in juvenile anorexia nervosa: An exploration of possible etiologic factors. International Journal of Eating Disorder 1981; 1:28-43.

60. Strober M. An empirically derived typology of anorexia nervosa. In: Dally PL, Garfinkel PE, Garney D, Coscina D. (eds). Anorexia nervosa: Recent development in research. New York: Alan R Liss, Inc, 1983:185-196.

61. Wilson CP. Theoretical and clinical considerations in the early phase of treatment of patients suffering from severe psychosomatic symptoms. Bulletin of the Philadelphia Association of Psychoanalysis 1970; 20:71-4.

62. Sperling M. Transference neurosis in patients with psychosomatic disorders. Psychoanalytic Quarterly 1967; 36:342-55.

63. Bion WR. Development of schizophrenic thought. International Journal of Psycho-Analysis 1956; 37:344-6.

64. Carpinacci JA, Liberman D, Schlossberg N. Perturbaciones de la commuinicacion y neurosis de contra-transferencia. Revista de Psicoanalisis 1963; 20:63-9.

65. Carter L, Rinsley DB. Vicissitudes of "empathy" in a borderline patient. International Review of Psycho-Analysis 1977; 4:317-26.

66. Cesio FR. La communicacion extraverbal en psico-analisis: transferencia, contratransferencia e inter-pretacion. Revista de Psicoanalisis 1963;20:124-7.

67. Cesio FT. Los fundamentos de la contratransferencia: el yo ideal y las identificaciones directas. Revista de Psicoanalisis 1973; 30:5-16.

68. Giovacchini PL. Self-projections in the narcissistic transference. International Journal of Psychoanalytic Psychotherapy 1975; 4:142-66.

69. Grinberg L. Practicas Psicoanaliticas Comparadas en las Psicosis. Buenos Aires: Editoral Paidos, 1972.

70. Grinberg L. Teoria de la Identificacion. Buenos Aires: Editorial Paidos, 1976.

71. Grinberg L. Countertransference and projective counter identification. Contemporary Psychoanalysis 1979; 15:226-47.

72. Klein M. On identification. In: Klein M, Heimann P, Money-Kyle R (eds). New directions in psychoanalysis. London: Tavistock 1955:309-45.

73. Ogden TH. A developmental view of identifications resulting from maternal impingements. International Journal of Psychoanalytic Psychotherapy 1978; 7:486-506.

74. Perestrello M. Um cao de intensa identifacao projetiva. Journal Brasileiro de Psiquiatria 1963; 12:425-41.

75. Rosenfeld D, Mordo E. Fusion, confusion, simbiosis e identificacion. Revista de Psicoanalisis 1973; 30:413-23.

76. Rosenfeld HA. Notes on the psychoanalysis of the superego conflict of an acute schizophrenic patients. International Journal of Psycho-Analysis 1952; 33:111-31.

77. Searles HF. Collected papers on schizophrenia and related subjects. New York: International Universities Press, 1965:654-716.

78. Spitz RA. The primal cavity: A contribution to the genesis of perception and its role for psychoanalytic theory. The Psychoanalytic Study of the Child 1955; 10:215-40.

79. Wilson CP. Sand symbolism: The primary dream representation of the Isakower phenomenon and of smoking addictions. In: Orgel S, Fine BD (eds). Clinical Psychoanalysis. New York: Jason Aronson, 1981:45-55.

80. Gero G. Book review of Sours J: Starving to death in a sea of objects: The anorexia nervosa syndrome. New York: Jason Aronson, 1984:187-191.

81. Niederland WG. Clinical observations on the "little man" phenomenon. The Psychoanalytic study of the Child 1956; 11:381-95.

82. Niederland WG. Narcissistic ego impairment in patients with early physical malformations. The Psychoanalytic Study of the Child 1965; 20:518-34.

83. Mintz IL. Psychoanalytic treatment of a regressed restrictor anorexic. Psychosomatic Discussion Group. Meeting of the American Psychoanalytic Association,

December 15, 1982, New York. Chairman, Wilson CP.

84. Hogan CC: Psychoanalytic treatment of a bulimic anorexic woman. Psychosomatic Discussion Group. Meeting of the American Psychoanalytic Association, April 27, 1983, Philadelphia, PA. Chairman, Wilson CP.

85. Keith C. Psychoanalytic treatment of bulimic anorexia. Psychosomatic Discussion Group. Meeting of the American Psychoanalytic Association, December 14, 1983, New York. Chairman, Wilson CP.

86. Hitchcock J. Psychoanalytic treatment of restrictor anorexia nervosa. Psychosomatic Discussion Group. Meeting of the American Psychoanalytic Association, May 2, 1984. Chairman, Wilson CP.

87. Rizzuto AM, Petersen RK, Reed M. The pathological sense of self in anorexia nervosa. Psychiatric Clinics of North America 1981; 4(3):471-482.

88. Wilson, CP, Hogan CC, Mintz IL. Fear of being fat: The treatment of anorexia nervosa and bulimia. Revised edition with a new chapter by Wilson CP: Psychodynamic and/or psychopharmacologic treatment of bulimic anorexia nervosa. Riverside, NJ: Jason Aronson, 1985:52.

89. Brotman AW, Herzog DB, Woods SW. Antidepressant treatment of bulimia: The relationship between binging and depressive symptomatology. Journal of Clinical Psychiatry 1984; 45(1):7-9.

90. Bruch H. Perils of behavior modification in the treatment of anorexia nervosa. Journal of the American Medical Association 1974; 230:1409-22.

Chapter 40

Family Therapy for Eating Disorders

John Sargent and Ronald Liebman

INTRODUCTION

Family therapy was first described as a primary psychotherapeutic modality for anorexia nervosa by Minuchin in 1970 [1]. In that description and subsequent work, Minuchin and colleagues have identified dysfunctional aspects of family interaction in families with anorectic members and formulated specific family-centered interventions to respond to symptoms of the anorexia and alter family behavior [1-12]. Minuchin's work was highlighted by a strong therapeutic presence, specific attention to family behavior within therapeutic sessions, and the creation and assignment of tasks that would help change family relationships and establish control over the symptoms of the anorexia. Family therapy for anorexia, as described by Minuchin, was based on structural family therapy that he had originated and described [13,14]. Minuchin's therapeutic efforts for anorexia include (1) establishing parental hierarchy within the family, (2) clarifying and resolving conflict between parental figures, (3) establishing boundaries between family subsystems and between individual family members to reduce parental overinvolvement with the anorectic patient, and finally (4) involving the entire family to enhance the development of the young person with anorexia while she achieves autonomy appropriate for her age and developmental level. Liebman and colleagues, while working with Minuchin, amplified the techniques of family therapy for anorexia by integrating a behavioral

paradigm for weight gain within the family therapy [2,3,8,15]. Rosman [6] has described lunch sessions in which the anorectic patient and her family have a meal with the therapist. During these sessions, the cycle of family interaction concerning food is made apparent and directly altered.

Minuchin, Rosman, and colleagues also reviewed the treatment of a cohort of 53 patients with anorexia nervosa followed for at least five years after completion of family therapy for the anorexia. They found the treatment to be effective in inducing resolution of the anorectic symptoms and improvement in psychosocial functioning in 83% of the cases [4,5,7,9]. Sargent and colleagues have recently described the entire course of family therapy for anorexia including an outline of the integration of family treatment into hospitalization [16]. Sargent and Liebman have also recently reviewed a family-oriented approach to outpatient therapy [17] as well as family treatment for both anorexia and bulimia [18].

Other descriptions of family therapy for anorexia have included (1) a description of the role of hospitalization in catalyzing and supporting family therapy [19], (2) an elucidation of the family ties of loyalty across three generations in families of anorectic members, with specific interventions aimed at diluting and altering the impact of loyalty conflicts and trans-generational coalitions [20]. and (3) Selvini-Palazzoli's work in identifying family patterns of control and the influence of the larger culture upon the family with an anorectic member at times of transition [21]. A more strategic approach to family therapy has been advocated by Madanes in her description of marital therapy for a couple in which the woman was chronically bulimic [22]. Schwartz and colleagues have outlined an integration of structural and strategic techniques of family therapy for families with bulimic members in which positive connotation of the symptom and flexible participation in therapy sessions with fluctuating attention to bulimic symptoms and family interaction have been successful in reducing bulimic symptoms [23,24].

This chapter will describe the guiding concepts of family therapy for eating disorders and outline a family approach to the treatment of anorexia nervosa and bulimia. Specific interventions appropriate for the treatment of each of these disorders will be reviewed, and family therapy approaches to the problems particular to each disorder will be identified.

A CONCEPTUAL FRAMEWORK FOR FAMILY THERAPY FOR EATING DISORDERS

Family therapy as a set of psychotherapeutic techniques is based on a conceptualization of the family as a biopsychosocial system. Family systems theory becomes a way of understanding both a particular family and the symptoms that are presented for treatment. This conceptualization points out the role of family interaction in the maintenance of eating disorder symptoms and also identifies the role of these symptoms in maintaining family stability and integrity [4,5]. The behavior of the family member with the eating disorder affects other family members. Their behavior, in turn, affects the symptomatic identified patient. Dysfunctional family relationships and family interaction patterns apparent in families of patients with anorexia nervosa and bulimia have been described previously (Chapter 14). The therapist treating the eating disorder, therefore, should recognize that his role is to identify ways for the family to respond more effectively to the eating disorder symptoms, and to improve family relationships while facilitating the family's role in the growth and development of the individual with the eating disorder.

Several key concepts form the underpinnings of family treatment for eating disorders. The therapist's initial efforts are directed at reframing the eating disorder symptoms in relation to family interaction and not solely as the problems of a disturbed individual. As that belief takes hold within the family, the therapist can enhance family members' responsibility to react differently to the eating disorder symptoms and to relate to the individual with the eating disorder in a more productive manner. The eating disorder symptoms themselves

become communications within family interaction, and individuals are encouraged to communicate more directly verbally, without using the symptoms or predictable responses to them. The family therapist focuses on problems apparent in dyadic relationships as he or she identifies cross-generational coalitions in which a parent and child join together against the other parent or important adult. As these problems are highlighted, the therapist should reinforce supportive family relationships, thus creating productive communication between family members within the therapy sessions.

The family therapist appreciates the strong loyalty and interdependency in families with eating disorders and uses individual and family strengths to create alternative relationships between people. Individual autonomy is possible while a sense of mutual responsibility and interrelatedness are supported. The family therapist also enhances and reinforces family problem-solving and family development. This occurs especially in relationship to difficulties inherent in adolescent and young adult development. As the family therapist develops a holistic approach that unites the physical and psychosocial needs of the eating disordered individual, he will also be able to help the family balance individual and family needs. Finally, the family therapist, through his focus on disordered family interaction, will be able to recognize the vulnerability of all family members, appreciate each individual's pain and difficulty in his or her current situation, and assist the family to be more supportive for each individual throughout the course of treatment. The family therapist's focus on the present and the future can create an approach to therapy that is growth-oriented and that will transform the rigidity and resistance of the family, which views change and growth as particularly threatening and difficult.

FAMILY TREATMENT FOR EATING DISORDERS

Medical Evaluation

Any approach to an individual with an eating disorder and her family requires an evaluation of the individual's physical and psychosocial status as well as an understanding of the family's response to the symptoms and other important aspects of family interaction. Prior to the inception of family therapy, we strongly recommend that the individual with an eating disorder have a complete physical evaluation that identifies the appropriate diagnosis, current nutritional status, and any physical complications secondary to the symptoms of the eating disorder. The physical evaluation should be done on an outpatient basis if possible. Specific diagnostic concerns or the patient's physical status may warrant medical hospitalization. In our view, it is essential for parental figures to participate in the medical evaluation with the young person with an eating disorder so that any questions concerning either the etiology, physical status, or recommended nutritional or medical treatment may be answered directly. In addition, the individual with the eating disorder experiences parental concern about the physical effects of her symptoms. This will also insure that the parents and the young person hear the same facts concerning the eating disorder, so there is little opportunity for further conflict concerning the physician's statements. The therapist also should understand the physician's impression of the patient's physical status and his recommendations for nutritional and medical treatment so that he/she can further reinforce the physician's statements through the initial phases of family therapy. The physician who performs the physical evaluation should understand the physical and metabolic symptoms associated with eating disorders and be able to make a straightforward statement to the family and patient concerning the patient's condition. It is important also that the physician not become embroiled with the patient in discussions or arguments about potential complications of the eating disorder or goals with respect to weight gain or weight maintenance. Frequently, the parents or involved adults will expect that the physician convince the patient of the correctness of his/her statements, which the physician must resist.

It is also essential for the physician and family therapist to coordinate their plan for monitoring the patient's weight, physical status, and body chemistries as directed by the nature of the patient's condition. This will enable the family to recognize that treatment is coordinated and enable the therapist to know the patient's physical status through the course of treatment. It is also important that the physician appreciate that the changes necessary for resolution of the eating disorder will be taking place in therapy sessions and that he or she will need to communicate directly with the therapist if he has concerns about lack of progress in treatment or about deterioration of the patient's physical condition. Effective collaboration between the physician and family therapist will lead to greater organization within the family as members respond to the individual with the eating disorder and to more control for the therapeutic team over the family's level of anxiety and motivation for change. Physician-therapist coordination requires frequent communication and clear identification of appropriate boundaries. The family therapist encourages the family and patient to take medical questions directly to the physician, and the physician encourages them to bring questions about the direction or efficacy of therapy to the therapist. Especially early in treatment, the family may identify frustration with or

confusion about the approach taken in family therapy and may bring this to the physician's attention. It is important that the physician encourage the family to direct their concerns and questions to the therapist for resolution.

The potential for confusion and splitting of the treatment team also exists when additional health professionals are involved with family members on a regular basis in the course of treatment. In some treatment programs, a nutritionist provides nutritional guidance and a nurse or nurse practitioner weighs the patient regularly. It is essential that these professionals coordinate their efforts with those of the physician and family therapist and also that all professionals develop an approach that is directed at the entire family and not purely at the individual with the eating disorder symptoms. It may be possible in some circumstances for the nutritionist or nurse practitioner to meet individually with the young person with the eating disorder; however, it is important that these meetings be goal-directed, informational in content, and encourage personal responsibility on the part of the patient and not act as substitutes for individual or family psychotherapy. These professionals need to frequently remind the patient to bring important issues up in therapy sessions.

The physician can also, at times, be of immeasurable assistance to the therapist if the family should discontinue psychotherapy prematurely. At that point, the therapist can inform the physician of this difficulty and encourage the physician to also discuss this decision with the family. He or she can inform the family of the risks that they are incurring by prematurely discontinuing treatment, and strongly advise them to continue therapy. If the physician determines that the family is displeased with therapy or mistrusting of the therapist, he/she can help the family outline their concerns and questions and support the family in bringing these questions directly to the therapist for resolution. Often the support of the physician, another trusted professional, or an individual within the family's community enables a family to persevere with therapy to resolution of symptoms and improvement of family relationships.

Individual and Family Assessment

Strober has described the heterogeneity of patients with anorexia nervosa [25]. Descriptions of individuals with bulimic symptoms also highlighted the varieties of psychosocial adaptation, impulse control, and symptom frequency in large groups of patients [26,27]. It has been our impression that there is also marked heterogeneity in family interaction, with many families demonstrating markedly more functional interaction and relationships and being more responsive to therapeutic interventions. Therefore, an assessment of individual and family psychosocial functioning at the inception of treatment is essential for planning therapeutic interventions and to determine prognosis.

The assessment of the patient with anorexia or bulimia includes an evaluation of impulsivity and self-care by identifying the level of eating disorder symptoms, as well as noting the patient's ability to take an independent position verbally by stating her goals concerning eating and weight control. Her independent academic, occupational, and social adaptation help form a picture of her development, extrafamilial success, and her self-esteem. The young person's ability to relate to both the therapist and family members during the initial family interview is also identified. The therapist pays particular attention to the patient's ability to relate, to speak in an assertive and goal-directed fashion, to project herself into the future, to recognize and experience both success and failure, and to cope effectively with disappointments and emotional upset. The patient's openness and her ability to disagree and state her own position directly are also important. Her ability to reason abstractly can be identified through noting her understanding of the positive and negative consequences of the eating disorder symptoms and her goals for treatment. The degree of denial and difficulty entering trusting relationships can also be determined by the therapist through direct questioning and through observation of family interaction. It is our impression that relating ability and degree of impulse control are among the most important individual psychosocial features of the patient in determining prognosis. The therapist will need to be attentive to clues about these qualities throughout the initial evaluation phase.

The therapist, in evaluating the family, will attend especially to the availability of individual family members for a relationship with the therapist and their personal flexibility as they approach treatment. The therapist also monitors relationships within the family and carefully notes both intrusiveness and abandonment between family members, especially as problems are discussed or need to be resolved. It is our impression that the psychological availability of family members to participate in treatment and their ability to take responsibility for the therapeutic process—together with the therapist—have most prognostic significance for successful resolution of the eating disorder. If parents are totally focused on their own individual efforts with the patient and her symptoms and not able to maintain a stable relationship with the therapist in the early phases of family therapy, then treatment is likely to be more difficult and require greater intensity on the part of the family therapist.

It is also extremely important for the therapist to identify difficulties with impulse control for the parents. Impulse control problems may involve substance abuse, poor frustration tolerance, or explosive responses to conflict or disagreement. The more impulsive family members are, the less flexible their relationships are, and the less available they are to assist the eating disordered individual.

Finally, it is important for the therapist to pay attention to family members' appreciation of the effectiveness of their efforts. In eating disordered families, individuals often care more about the perceived correctness of their actions and less about whether the actions are effective. This can lead to significant defensiveness on family members' parts and relationships that are characterized by repeated criticisms and attacks. There is a marked lack of mutuality within these relationships, which then leads to an inability of people to support one another, especially when distressed. The degree to which there is a lack of mutuality and inflexibility in family relationships will also need to be defined and altered during the course of treatment. Finally, the structure of the family, including who takes a leadership position, how effectively parents encourage mature behavior on the part of their children, and the level of power of the symptomatic member, will also need to be examined. If family relationships are continually defined by marked disrespect and a significant lack of cooperation between the parents, often the symptomatic individual is involved in an intense relationship with one parent to the exclusion of the other parent. Treatment will also need to define and address these difficulties while providing more autonomy for the symptomatic individual and creating more satisfying relationships for the parents both together and separately.

The Family in the Hospital

The use of the hospital for the treatment of symptoms related to anorexia nervosa and bulimia has been described at length elsewhere in this volume. (See Chapters 19,22,37,38) It is our strong impression that hospitalization should be identified to the family as an intervention with potential helpful effects not only for the eating disordered individual, but for the family as a whole. We create this orientation by helping the family to see hospitalization not as a sign of their failure and need to relinquish responsibility for the patient, but rather as an opportunity for the family as a whole to gain new skills and learn new ways of responding to the symptoms and supporting the patient's recovery. We promote this effort by requiring that the entire family participate in the initial assessment prior to hospitalization and that the family, as a whole, identify goals that are to be achieved during the hospitalization both for the individual and for her family. Hospitalizations are short-term (30 to 40 days) and the family is actively involved in the hospital program. Thus, the family as well as the staff develop methods of responding to the eating disorder symptoms and psychosocial difficulties. In our experience, 15% of patients with anorexia or bulimia require hospitalization.

Medical hospitalization in our program is used to rectify severe nutritional deficiencies and metabolic difficulties. Once patients are medically stable, they are transferred to our family-oriented psychiatric inpatient unit. The psychiatric hospitalization is directed toward creating a sense of momentum and participation in the treatment of the entire family as well as an appreciation of the role of family change in resolving the eating disorder. The hospital staff enlist the parents into the treatment team at the same time as the hospitalized individual is encouraged to participate in defining her own program. The parents and staff together take responsibility for identifying appropriate and effective behavioral responses to eating disorder symptoms. A program emphasizing weight gain for anorectic patients and a contract to ensure monitoring to prevent purging for bulimic individuals is chosen for a particular family and patient because it is successful. Renegotiation of the treatment contract is possible. Family therapy sessions through the course of hospitalization are essential to define the most appropriate method of using the hospital successfully.

The patient is strongly supported to obtain autonomy by demonstrating physical and psychological responsibility for herself. She is encouraged to define her own needs with the help of the peer group within the hospital and the hospital staff in order to present her wishes to her family in an assertive and forthright fashion. The hospital environment also can provide a sense of control for the entire family, thereby reducing everyone's anxiety. At the same time, it can help people develop new forms of relating to one another. By reducing family anxiety, impatience, perfectionism, and impulsivity also can be diminished and treatment can proceed in a patient, measured fashion oriented to developmental change for the patient and her family. The father may participate with his daughter in some hospital activities, while the mother participates in others. The father and mother together may be encouraged, during the daughter's hospitalization, to do different things together as they begin to resolve differences concerning their own relationship as well as concerning the eating disorder.

Discharge from the hospital is contingent upon the achievement of individual and family psychosocial goals as well as on the achievement of weight gain and improvement in symptoms. If the hospitalization has been successful, there will have been an introduction of greater interpersonal flexibility among family members as well as greater autonomy for individuals. Family members also should have a greater sense of mutual support and mutual understanding. If the outpatient therapist is able to be actively involved in treatment during the hospitalization, the hospitalization can enhance his/her relationship with the patient and her family and build the level of trust and support between family and outpatient therapist. This involvement can also further the working relationship of the family and therapist for future outpatient therapy.

We have found that in extremely difficult situations, multiple hospitalizations may be necessary; however, it is important that each hospitalization be identified as a positive step to resolve limited, important difficulties in treatment at the present time. By involving the entire family in the course of hospitalization, we attempt to decrease the parents' sense of helplessness and family dependency upon the hospital when things are difficult. In addition, we enhance the entire family's appreciation of responsibility for resolution of the eating disorder symptoms. The patient's age and developmental status are important in outlining the course of treatment as well as highlighting the goals of a hospitalization and the responsibility of family members. The younger the patient is both chronologically and developmentally, the more the parents will need to be involved in a way that emphasizes their responsibility for their daughter's symptoms. On the other hand, developmentally older patients who are more autonomous require parental involvement that is collaborative and supportive rather than controlling. Therapist and hospital staff need to be highly flexible in their understanding of individual situations and assist parents to react in ways that support the young person's experience of control and developmental gains. This may be extremely difficult, because the parents' attempts to control the young person and her symptoms reflects not only their sense of their child's ineffectiveness, but also the parents' own need to be actively involved with her and their need to reduce their own anxiety as they experience her difficulties.

Outpatient Treatment of Anorexia Nervosa

The family therapist carries out outpatient therapy for anorexia with assurance of the patient's physical stability, an impression of the physiological and psychosocial status of the identified patient, and an appreciation of the family's style of interacting and of responding to the eating disorder symptoms. The initial phase of treatment, whether hospitalization is required or not, is a phase in which clear and defined responses to weight-related symptoms are identified and in which the therapist creates strong relationships between him or herself and all family members. In so doing, the therapist alters the family's experience by requiring that they attend to his/her expectations as well as their own preferred responses to difficult situations. The therapist also identifies each family member's strengths and competencies and develops a relationship with each of them based on mutual respect and consideration. A transformation of the family takes place based on the therapist's presence and input. The therapist then gains initial control over the therapeutic process and begins to define, with the family, problems to be solved and to create shared approaches to these problems. The therapist maintains a holistic approach to treatment by retaining the dual goals of greater interpersonal space and further differentiation and more effective and satisfying support and mutual connectedness.

A consistent, nonimpulsive response to eating and weight can be identified early on and maintained throughout the course of treatment. For significantly low-weight individuals, steady, slow (1 to 2 lb per week) weight gain can be reinforced on a regular basis while parents are advised to leave to the young person the problem of determining what to eat in order to meet the weight-related goals. If the anorectic individual claims helplessness and ineffectiveness as the cause of poor weight gain, then she can be encouraged to ask her parents and other potential support people for assistance in defining the food intake necessary to gain the required weight. The therapist guides the parents to help the young person with anorexia to recognize her responsibility for meeting weight goals while helping the parents to limit their intrusiveness and ineffective attempts to control food intake. Potential parental responses to lack of weight gain should be agreed upon and consistently enforced. These responses should limit the eating disordered individual while the parents are encouraged not to become involved with her disappointment at experiencing these consequences of failure to gain weight. Such responses as a limitation of exercise or activities or an inability to participate in a desired event may be stipulated as consequences. It is important, though, that the parents experience the primary responsibility to reinforce her success. The therapist constantly attends to this process of building interpersonal boundaries and personal autonomy. Helplessness is transformed into competence and enmeshment into individuation. The parents are helped to recognize that the young person will need to gain weight and become more mature for herself, while the parents are encouraged to identify goals for themselves as individuals and for their relationship instead of relying solely on their daughter's improvement to enhance their self-esteem.

As treatment proceeds, the therapist identifies further issues for the therapeutic agenda, including psychosocial goals for the patient such as increased flexibility, greater patience, more effective friendships, and potential for intimacy. The parents' individual concerns about job, personal success, growing older, and adjusting to the increasing maturity of their children as well as marital dissatisfaction also become issues for therapy.

As these items are added to the treatment agenda, the therapist creates an experience of continuity for the treatment and remains its guiding force until the family as a whole trusts both the therapist and the changes that are slowly taking place in treatment. It is not unusual for families with anorexia to return for treatment on a weekly basis for several months, acting in the beginning of each therapy session as though they were just beginning treatment, having not understood or experienced previous sessions. The therapist must be patient and appreciate that this rigidity is a reflection of the family's anxiety, pre-existing resentments, their concern that effective change is not possible, and their fear that treatment will be significantly disruptive to the family. As the therapist maintains a sense of patience, continuity, and support, as well as a sense of humor and a sense of optimism about the possibilities of all family members for the future, the family increasingly comes to experience therapy as a welcomed and desired situation and see that change and growth are valuable for all of them. Therapists make two common errors with families with anorectic members: first, the therapist maintains a stance of impatience and criticism of the family if the therapist thinks they are responding too slowly to treatment; and second, the therapist develops too much closeness to one family member, creating isolation from other family members and often not believing in their ability to change. The therapist must be able to develop a respectful relationship with each family member and then help build family relationships. The therapist can share the responsibility for the course and pacing of treatment with the family by expecting them to identify issues for resolution and to demonstrate greater flexibility and more mutual concern.

The therapist also addresses the quality of the anorectic individual's relationship with each of her parents and helps her develop effective but different relationships with her father and with her mother. These relationships should be based on mutual respect, with opportunities for individual assertiveness and clear communication on the part of parent and young person. The father often is demanding and impatient. First the therapist and then the anorectic patient will need to challenge this. The therapist can help her expect that he be supportive of her and recognize both her abilities and her inabilities. The patient and her mother also will need to learn to cooperate more effectively with one another and become truly connected in a less competitive and critical fashion. This often requires that the mother recognize her inability to totally protect her daughter from hardship and her need to be available to her daughter when distressed, but in a genuinely calm and supportive fashion. As the therapist works on the anorectic patient's relationship with each parent, it is important that he or she help the other parent to support that process and not find increasing closeness between his or her daughter and spouse threatening. This often depends on the development of a more respectful and less antagonistic and resentful relationship between the parents, which the therapist is encouraging throughout the course of treatment.

As treatment progresses and there is greater differentiation of individuals and enhanced mutual respect within the family, sessions should be planned to include appropriate family members according to the issues worked on at that time. At times, individual sessions for the patient or sessions for both parents may be necessary, and sessions that involve father and daughter or mother and daughter may be appropriate. We generally recommend that one outpatient therapist continue the treatment and work with smaller subgroupings as well as with the entire family. This is often very helpful, because the therapist then not only works with the family members present at a particular session, but also creates ways in which his work with those individuals further facilitates his and the family's overall goals for treatment.

Anorexia occurs in families of varied composition and with varied levels of flexibility. Problems occur in treatment based on the history of the family, the chronicity of the symptoms, and previous ineffective treatment. In situations where the anorectic's parents have separated or divorced prior to the inception of treatment, we believe that it is essential that both natural parents be involved in therapy as well as other important family members. This may require sessions that include both natural parents without the young person to establish methods of effective collaboration and consistent approaches to the eating disorder symptoms. In remarried families step-parents should also be involved so that all adults are collaborating in an appropriate way. The therapist generally has the ability to bring important family members into the treatment process early in treatment based on concern for the young person's safety and for the severity of the symptoms. In some situations, significant resentment may exist between ex-spouses, and the therapist will need to be forceful in arranging that both natural parents collaborate effectively in limiting their disagreements and developing a unified

approach to treatment.

In situations where chronicity and treatment failure have led to marked helplessness on the part of all family members, it is often helpful for the therapist to begin with a somewhat detached, inquisitive approach, letting the family know that this treatment will only be effective if it includes all members in an active way. The therapist can define everyone's participation in ways that are different from previous treatments and, thus, avoid previous pitfalls. It is common for families who have been faced with chronic symptoms to hope that the next treatment will be effective and also to be impatient and impulsive in their approach to the therapeutic process. In these situations, a systemic approach using the techniques of Selvini-Palazzoli and colleagues [28] is often very helpful in appreciating the nature of family interconnectedness and in identifying reasons for previous treatment failure. As the therapist resists the family's attempt to get him/her to take full responsibility for the patient's recovery, he or she then will have the authority to move the family's participation in the desired fashion. The therapist's approach should be genuinely friendly, interested, and humane while also remaining questioning of the family's ability to actively collaborate in a different way with treatment. He should convey his belief that recovery is possible, but it is a choice which the entire family must make.

Termination of treatment can occur at different times for different family subsystems. We generally hold follow-up sessions monthly with the patient and with the family for two to four months when the patient, spouses, and entire family are functioning effectively. We may maintain phone contact with patient and family for some time after that. We try to help family members to experience their own resources in dealing with stresses and transitions. We move to decrease our therapeutic involvement as these stresses are negotiated by family members with little disruption in other family members or subsystems.

Outpatient Treatment of Bulimia

Much of outpatient psychotherapy for bulimia will be similar to treatment for anorexia nervosa. The therapist will identify family relationships and determine when the symptoms occur, what events precipitate binges, and the role of family members in bringing on episodes of bingeing and purging. Difficulties in treatment can arise due to the lack of objective markers of symptomatic behavior. The therapist will need to define with the family and patient appropriate medical surveillance, depending upon the degree of purging, which limits the acute risks of purging behavior. This medical monitoring can take place on a weekly or biweekly basis and provide a sense of safety for the patient and her family. Monitoring can be reduced as the patient demonstrates reduced impulsivity and greater control over symptoms. A treatment plan is developed that identifies the need for all family members to collaborate in the resolution of the symptoms and identifies alternative means for the patient to respond to the stress and emotional upset that have led to episodes of bingeing and purging. The patient often expresses a desire to work on resolving the symptoms independently without her parents. The therapist resists this as he supports family collaboration in resolution of the bulimia. The therapist will need to identify positive features of the symptoms for the patient and her family and help them determine ways of establishing and encouraging alternative methods of satisfaction and release of tension. Together the family and the therapist will help the patient to eat when she is physically hungry and manage her diet appropriately to reduce episodes of weight gain and periods of anxiety leading to purging behavior. The therapist may suggest collecting data concerning the symptoms (ie, a record containing what the patient eats and what she is feeling and doing when she eats) before helping the family reduce the symptomatic behavior. The parents are instructed not to attempt to interfere with the symptoms during this time. Restraining the family from changing rapidly reduces everyone's anxiety that the symptoms will be gone without positive change in family behavior and family relationships [24]. Throughout the treatment of bulimia, the therapist actively encourages individuation and independent control as he encourages parents to establish a foundation of self-acceptance and appropriate response to food and weight for the patient. Patient and family members learn to express and resolve conflict while the parents learn to provide genuine support to the patient. Other difficulties with impulse control are addressed directly in treatment.

The major problems in the treatment of bulimia include abrupt cessation of symptoms, leading to premature termination of treatment, and the tendency of family members to become frustrated if symptom resolution does not occur rapidly. The therapist will reinforce the family's participation in a gradual process of resolving the symptoms of bulimia and encouraging appropriate support within the family as well as differentiation and development for both patient and parents. As in the treatment of anorexia, therapy proceeds from family sessions to individual therapy for the patient and marital therapy for the parents. The development of themes and issues to be pursued occurs as described above. Antidepressant medication, relaxation training, group therapy, and self-help groups may assist the patient significantly in dealing with depressed affect and anxiety and decrease loneliness and social isolation,

which lead to repetitive episodes of bingeing and purging. We feel strongly, however, that these treatment modalities should be used only when patient and family are actively engaged in the therapeutic process. Any additional treatment modalities should also help family members, through the therapist's support, to provide increased support for one another and assist the patient to develop friendships and effective social relationships, and to improve self-esteem and contentment with herself.

Family therapy for bulimia should continually recognize and support the patient's degree of autonomy and her increasing psychological and physical self-control. This can be carried out in individual and family therapy sessions. However, the therapist must also recognize the importance of effective family relationships for the patient and steadily counteract family members' tendency to abandon the patient and be unavailable to her when she is stressed and in need of support.

CONCLUSION

Family therapy addresses the individual and family difficulties associated with eating disorders. It provides assistance that balances need for autonomy and need for supportive relationships through changes in family interactions. Family treatment offers hope that the patient can be independent, competent, and self-satisfied, and that her family can respond to the eating disorder successfully. The therapist is an active catalyst of treatment and is responsible for the quality of her relationship with all family members. His or her concern for the patient and her family should be addressed directly and humanely. With patience and persistence—and with thoughtful planning and a clear conceptualization of the role of family interaction in the maintenance of the eating disorder symptoms—the family therapist can help the family support individual and collective development and effectiveness.

REFERENCES

1. Minuchin S. The use of an ecological framework in the treatment of a child. In: Anthony J, Koupernik C, eds. The child in his family. New York: Wiley, 1970:
2. Liebman R, Minuchin S, Baker L. An integrated treatment program for anorexia nervosa. Am J Psychiatry 1974; 131:432-6.
3. Liebman R, Minuchin S, Baker L. The role of the family in the treatment of anorexia nervosa. J of Am Acad of Child Psychiat 1974; 13:264-74.
4. Minuchin S, Baker L, Rosman B, et al. A conceptual model of psychosomatic illness in children: family organization and family therapy. Arch of Gen Psychiat 1975; 32:1031-3.

5. Minuchin S, Rosman B, Baker L. Psychosomatic families: Anorexia nervosa in context. Cambridge, MA: Harvard University Press, 1978:

6. Rosman B, Minuchin S, Liebman R. Family lunch session: an introduction to family therapy in anorexia nervosa. Am J Orthopsychiatry 1975; 45(5):846-53.

7. Rosman B, Minuchin S, Liebman R, et al: Input and outcome of family therapy in anorexia nervosa. In: Claghorn J, ed. Successful Psychotherapy. New York: Bruner/Mazel, 1976:

8. Liebman R, Minuchin S, Baker L, et al. The treatment of anorexia. In: Masserman JH, ed. Current psychiatric therapies. New York: Grune & Stratton, 1975:

9. Rosman BL, Minuchin S, Baker L, et al. A family approach to anorexia nervosa: study, treatment, outcome. In Vigersky RA, ed. Anorexia nervosa, New York: Raven Press, 1977:

10. Aponte H, Hoffman L. The open door: a structural approach to a family with an anorectic child. Fam Proc 1973; 12:1-44.

11. Fishman HC. Family considerations in liaison psychiatry. Psych Clinics of NA 1979; 2:249-63.

12. Minuchin S. Families and family therapy. Cambridge MA: Harvard University Press, 1974:

13. Minuchin S, Fishman HC. Family therapy techniques.. Cambridge MA: Harvard University Press, 1981:

14. Minuchin S. Family kaleidoscope. Cambridge MA: Harvard University Press, 1985:

15. Liebman R, Sargent J, Silver M. A family systems orientation to the treatment of anorexia nervosa. J Am Acad of Child Psychiat 1983; 22:2:128-33.

16. Sargent J, Liebman R, Silver M. Family therapy for anorexia. In: Garner DM, Garfinkel P, eds. Treatment of anorexia nervosa and bulimia. New York: Guilford Press, 1984:

17. Sargent J, Liebman R. Outpatient treatment of anorexia nervosa. Psych Clinics of NA 1984:7:235-45.

18. Sargent J, Liebman R. Eating disorders. In: Henao S, Grose N, eds. Principles of family systems in family medicine. New York: Bruner/Mazel, 1985:

19. Stern S, Whitaker CA, Hagemann NJ, et al. Anorexia nervosa: the hospital's role in family treatment. Fam Proc 1981; 20:395-408.

20. White M. Anorexia nervosa: a transgenerational system persepective. Fam Proc 1983; 22:255-73.

21. Selvini-Palazzoli M. Self-starvation. New York: Jason Aronson, 1978:

22. Madanes C. Strategic family therapy . San Francisco: Jossey/Bass, 1981:

23. Schwartz RC. Bulimia and family therapy: a case study. Int J of Eating Disorders 1982; 2:75-82.

24. Schwartz R, Barrett MJ, Saba G. The family therapy of bulimia. In: Garner DM, Garfinkel PE, eds. The treatment of anorexia and bulimia. New York: Guilford Press, 1984:

25. Strober M. An empirically derived typology of anorexia nervosa. In: Anorexia nervosa: Recent developments in research. New York: Alan R Liss, 1983: 185-96.

26. Cauwels JM. Bulimia: The binge-purge compulsion. New York: Doubleday and Co, 1983:

27. Johnson, The syndrome of bulimia. Psych Clinics of NA (7); 2:247-74.

28. Selvini-Palazzoli M, Boscolo L, Cecchin G, et al. Paradox and counter paradox. New York: Jason Aaronson, 1978:

Chapter 41

Group Psychotherapy for Anorexia Nervosa and Bulimia

Katharine N. Dixon

INTRODUCTION

Few other psychiatric disorders have spawned a sizable patient population as rapidly as did anorexia nervosa and bulimia during the 1970s and 1980s. Feminism, unisex fashions, emphasis on youthfulness, and a culture of narcissism contributed to women's increasing focus on their bodies and need for a feeling of control in their lives. These culturally fueled syndromes were further fanned by the media through advertising trends for women's products, descriptions of celebrity dieting and bulimia, and a proliferation of medically unsound diets in women's magazines.

The mental health profession was largely unprepared for the numbers of eating disordered women who often needed extensive diagnostic and treatment services. The professional community's lack of understanding or inexperience with these usually difficult and complex disorders further hampered effective delivery of treatment services. Over time, the trend for specialized eating disorders centers has increased the number of qualified professionals through clinical and training programs. Nevertheless, a group-therapy approach came to be frequently used, in part to ration experienced therapists. It appeared to be at least a cost-effective modality, if not also treatment-effective.

Group therapy has been used widely in the treatment of psychosomatic illness [1] and other specific problems, eg, alcoholism, gambling, weight control, and smoking [2]. Prior to the recent increase in reports describing group treatment of eating disorders, self-help and support organizations already had begun to offer group meetings for individuals with eating disorders and their family members or friends [3]. Moreover, because bulimic patients often are spontaneous, outgoing, gregarious, and socially adept, it is not surprising that group treatments would be readily considered for patients with these particular personality traits and that these patients would be attracted to a group setting.

Therapy in groups offers unique opportunities for altruism, social skills practice, peer reinforcement, and peer feedback and advice that are unavailable in an individual therapy setting. Further, the homogenous format of eating disorder groups provides a potentially powerful framework within which the patient's behavioral symptoms and associated distress can receive maximal attention, both through shared experiences with other group members and a concrete focus on the problems that brought the group together.

GROUP THERAPY WITH BULIMIC PATIENTS

The current interest in group treatment of bulimia is reflected in the increase in published studies over the past three to four years. In early reports, only Boskind-Lodahl and White [4] and White and Boskind-White [5] had described experience treating bulimic women in a group setting. Since 1983, more than 20 reports, including five controlled studies, have related the effects of group treatment on bulimic behavior and associated symptoms in these patients. By far, the majority of studies report experience with time-limited, closed-membership groups using an eclectic combination of treatment techniques. Thirteen studies [5-17] include follow-up data on maintenance of change.

Group Orientation and Strategies

A few group treatment studies use primarily a psychodynamic approach [18-20], but the majority of groups report using a combination of strategies, with [4,8,9,17,21-24] or without [6,10-16,25,26] a psychodynamic or experiential component (table 1). Most frequently, group studies reported in the literature employ a combination of cognitive, behavioral, and educational methods. The trend toward a cognitive-behavioral-educational orientation in the group treatment of bulimia has been created by a number of influences. Clinicians became aware early that traditional insight-oriented psychotherapy with bulimic patients either avoided the issue of eating behavior or was insufficient to bring about significant symptom change and elimination of bulimic behaviors in many patients [27]. Prior research in the treatment of obesity showed that behavior modification techniques effectively shaped eating behavior and could be applied in group settings [28]. Similarities in problems with eating control between bulimic patients and some patients with obesity, thus, led to the application of techniques used for eating restraint in the obese population to the bulimic population. Likewise, the major role played by cognition in allowing unrestrained eating to occur in bulimia led to an interest in cognitive therapy techniques for these patients.

Cognitive-behavioral techniques focus on current problematic behavior and underlying faulty cognitions, actively changing the bulimic behavior and introducing new, more adaptable behaviors and thinking. Treatment tends to be relatively brief, progress measurable, and the methods potentially applicable by a more inexperienced therapist than would be required for more traditional methods.

Fairburn [29] first described the systematic application of cognitive-behavioral techniques in the individual treatment of 11 bulimic patients, with remission of symptoms in nine patients after 28 weeks of treatment and maintenance of change in most patients over one year. While a number of studies include cognitive-behavioral techniques as one of several methods, only three studies [11,13,14] have examined the effects of cognitive-behavioral treatment of bulimic patients. Schneider and Agras [14] reported symptom remission in 7 of 13 women with 16 weeks of cognitive-behavioral group treatment based on Fairburn's model. Five patients (38%) in this study continued to be symptom free at six-month follow-up. Kirkley et al [13] compared cognitive-behavioral and nondirective approaches during 12 weeks of group treatment and found a greater change in bulimic symptoms and lower dropout rate in the cognitive-behavioral group. Yates and Sambrailo [11] examined the differences between two groups, both of which were cognitive-behavioral, but only one included specific behavioral recommendations, over a treatment interval of six weeks. Both groups with and without specific instruction had a 33% dropout rate, no patients were abstinent in the group without specific instruction, and only two of eight patients in the cognitive-behavioral with instructions group were abstinent at six month follow-up. Whether cognitive-behavioral techniques as the only or primary approach in group treatment, particularly brief treatment, will uphold the promise of Fairburn's work remains to be seen and has not been supported by evidence to date. Indeed, Fairburn [30] questions whether the patient-therapist relationship and interaction necessary for the success of cognitive restructuring can occur in a group setting. To date, no study of cognitive-behavioral group treatment for bulimia has approached the four to six month duration of Fairburn's individual treatment of 82% post-treatment remission of symptoms. Clearly, symptom outcome in bulimic groups may be related not only to treatment approach but also to other variables, such as treatment length and format.

Behavioral principles used in bulimic groups are similar to those shown to be effective in the treatment of obesity, ie, record-keeping, identification of stimuli leading to binge-eating, techniques to gain control of eating, and development of alternate strategies. Relaxation and assertiveness training are sometimes included in bulimic group strategies to address the problems of anxiety and low self-assertion commonly seen in bulimic patients. No group studies report the use of behavior modification techniques alone in the treatment of bulimic patients, although nearly every study, other than those from primarily psychodynamic groups, indicates incorporation of behavior techniques in the group approach.

The educational component of most groups furnishes information about bulimia, medical consequences, nutrition, set-point theory, and sociocultural influences through the use of lectures, handouts, and structured discussions. Even Fairburn's [29] model for individual cognitive-behavioral treatment of bulimia incorporates education in the initial weeks. Although a valuable addition and perhaps therapeutic, education about bulimia cannot be construed as therapy and is always combined with other therapy techniques.

A psychodynamic or experiential approach used

Table 41.1 Group treatment studies in bulimia

Study	Subjects		Treatment Length	Group Approaches
	Entered	Completed		
Psychodynamic				
Weinstein & Richman (1984)	32	7 (10 wks)		
		16 (20 weeks)	10 & 20 weeks	Psychodynamic
Reed & Sech (1985)	5	4	26 weeks	Psychodynamic
Barth & Wurman (1986)	40	not reported	3 years	Psychodynamic
Eclectic with psychodynamics or experiential component				
Boskind-Lodahl & White (1978)	13	12	11 weeks, including 6 hr marathon	Experiential
Hornak (1983)	8	8	6 months	Encounter/peer support
Dixon & Kiecolt-Glaser (1984)	30	11	10 weeks	Behavioral/cognitive Psychodynamic/behavioral
Roy-Byrne et al. (1984)	19	9	1 year	Psychodynamic/educational/ cognitive/behavioral
Stevens & Salisbury (1984)	8	6	16 weeks	Psychodynamic/behavioral
Fernandez (1984)	6	6	12 weeks	Psychodynamic/educational/ cognitive/behavioral
Freeman et al. (1986)	--	--	15 weeks	Psychodynamic/behavioral
Johnson et al. (1983)	13	10	12 sessions/ 9 wks	Educational/ cognitive/behavioral
Connors et al. (1983)	26	20	12 sessions/ 9 wks	Educational/ cognitive/behavioral
Weiss & Katzman (1984)	5	5	7 wks	Educational/behavioral/ experiential
Yates & Sambrailo (1984)	24	16	6 wks	Cognitive/behavioral, directive and non-directive
Wolchik et al. (1986)	13	11	7 wks	Educational/behavioral/ experiential
Huon & Brown (1985)	45	40	12 sessions/ 6 and 12 wks	Educational/structured discussion/relaxation and assertion training
Kirkley et al. (1985)	28	22	16 wks	Cognitive/behavioral, directive & non-directive
Schneider & Agras (1985)	13	13	16 wks	Cognitive/behavioral
Lee & Rush (1986)	15	11	12 sessions/ 6 wks	Cognitive/ behavioral/educational
Intensive and combined modality treatment with group emphasis				
White & Boskind-White (1981)	14	14	5 hrs daily/ 5 days	Experiential/behavioral
Lacey (1983)	30	30	10 weeks	Psychodynamic/behavioral
Mitchell et al. (1985)	104	86	8 weeks	cognitive/behavioral/ educational/self-help
Brisman & Siegel (1985)	114	114	15 weeks	Behavioral/educational/ self-help
Wooley & Kearney-Cooke (1986)	18	18	3.5 weeks	Psychodynamic/experiential/ eductional/behavioral

alone or with other treatment orientations is described by several authors [4,18-20,22,31]. Various levels of "insight" occur in a group setting [32]: (1) how group members are seen by other people (interpersonal), (2) what they are doing to and with other people (behavioral), (3) why they do what they do to other people (motivational), and (4) how they got to be the way they are (genetic). Since persistent psychosocial factors play a role in the etiology and perpetuation of bulimia, it could be hoped that durable treatment effects would come about through the patient's increased understanding of the intrapsychic and interpersonal contribution to symptomatic behavior and maladaptive coping and, further, that group interaction would augment opportunities for such insight to occur.

Combined and Intensive Treatment Modalities

Multicomponent and multidimensional treatment programs are commonly used in the treatment of anorexia nervosa. Although bulimia group therapy studies report the process, content, or outcome of a group format, in reality patients often receive other concurrent treatment modalities. That multimodal and intensive treatment is increasingly described for bulimic patients reflects an improved understanding of the complex, difficult, and enduring problems these patients present. The role, value, and intensity of each component varies among clinical settings, so that individual, group, family, or drug treatment modalities may each be considered as primary or adjunctive in the patient's treatment depending on therapist or treatment setting orientation. Five combined or intensive outpatient treatment programs with emphasis on group treatment have been described in published studies [5,15,27,31,33]. That concurrent outpatient modalities are beginning to be combined into a larger unit of treatment rather than used in parallel fashion marks a step forward in the treatment of bulimia.

White and Boskind-White [5] first reported an intensive group treatment format using an experiential/behavioral approach with 14 bulimic women five hours daily for five days. Follow-up at six months showed three women binge-free, seven improved, and four unchanged. Mitchell et al [27] describe an eight-week intensive outpatient group treatment program conducted during evening hours at the University of Minnesota. Groups meet three hours nightly in the first week, diminishing to weekly meetings in the second month. Lectures, group therapy, and eating together are supplemented with three individual sessions and regular support group meetings. The Minnesota intensive program evolved to treat patients with severe eating problems following the observation that these patients often failed to maintain change after hospitalization. Reported results indicate that 47% of these patients with severe disturbance are able to be abstinent from the onset of the program [34]. Brisman and Siegel [15] initiate treatment with a 15-hour weekend marathon followed by six bimonthly group meetings and support groups on alternate weeks. Thirty-three percent of 114 women attending the marathon weekend were symptom free at follow-up, which ranged from one month to two years.

Lacey [7] used a combined individual and group format over a ten- week period in a controlled treatment study of 30 bulimic women, 28 of whom had symptom remission at the end of treatment and 24 of whom remained symptom-free over two years. Patients were seen by the same therapist for a weekly 1/2-hour be-

haviorally-oriented individual session and a 1 1/2-hour five-member, insight-oriented group session held on the same half-day.

Wooley and Wooley [31] describe a unique 3 1/2-week intensive treatment program with special emphasis on body image. Following a two-day evaluation, patients receive six to eight hours of therapy daily while housed in a nearby hotel. While an emphasis is placed on the group modality, treatment intensity approximates or exceeds that of inpatient treatment. Patients are involved in educational seminars and body image therapy as well as individual, group, and family therapy. Patients are urged to continue treatment after completion of the intensive program. A one-year follow-up of 18 patients showed 39% symptom-free and 44% with maintenance of at least 50% symptom reduction [17].

Prescription of Group Therapy

While homogenous for problem and usually gender, the bulimic patient population is heterogenous for age, psychopathology, psychodynamics, and severity of impairment. It goes without saying, then, that the prescription and timing of treatment modalities should take into consideration various aspects of the patient's presentation.

Mitchell et al [27] have outlined guidelines for prescription of treatment modalities within the University of Minnesota program following a detailed clinical assessment of the bulimic patient. Those with mild eating problems are referred to weekly psychotherapy groups, those with more severe problems to an intensive outpatient group program, and those with medical or psychiatric instability to the inpatient program. Individual psychotherapy and antidepressant medication are used sparingly.

The Eating Disorders Program at Ohio State University has seen an evolution in timing and orientation of individual and group treatment modalities. After observing the apparent ineffectiveness of traditional individual insight-oriented psychotherapy with bulimic patients early in the development of clinical services, patients were assigned in the initial phases of their treatment to groups using a cognitive-behavioral orientation to address the problems with eating control. The high attrition rate from these groups led to re-evaluation of the prescription and timing of the components of the patient's treatment plan. Following a clinical assessment, bulimic outpatients in our program presently begin treatment in individual psychotherapy. Vigorous efforts are made by individual therapists to recapture patients who miss appointments or fail to show. Individual sessions have an initial cognitive-behavioral emphasis to bring the eating behavior under control, followed by a gradual transition to a more psychodynamically oriented approach to help the patient gain awareness of associated interpersonal and intrapsychic issues. Assignment to group psychotherapy is reserved for those patients who have been engaged in the psychotherapeutic process and would further benefit from the interaction of a treatment group. Since substantial education and cognitive-behavioral work has already been accomplished in individual sessions, groups tend to be primarily insight-oriented in approach. Whenever possible, patients are assigned to groups led by their individual therapist.

A number of group treatment studies conducted with patients solicited through articles or newspaper advertisements [4,5,11-13,16,26] have improved knowledge about the applicability of treatment techniques in a group setting for bulimics. However, even though careful screening of respondents eliminates unqualified subjects, the use of solicited subjects for a group treatment study does not substantially increase our understanding of the prescription of group treatment within a comprehensive treatment plan. Moreover, the effectiveness of the group treatment modality may be underestimated unless the timing of entry into specific treatment modalities is done under clinical conditions and as part of an overall clinical plan.

GROUP THERAPY WITH ANOREXIA NERVOSA PATIENTS

There are far fewer reports in the literature of group psychotherapy with anorexia nervosa patients than with bulimia patients, and all reports are largely descriptive. Individual and family psychotherapy and, in the very low-weight patient, hospitalization have been the main interventions used to bring about weight restoration and repair of the developmental and psychological deficits in the anorexia nervosa patient. Even though successful weight restoration may be accomplished through behavioral methods or hospitalization, the anorexia nervosa patient's recovery occurs within the context of the patient-therapist relationship. What, then, is the role of group psychotherapy in the treatment of the patient with anorexia nervosa?

Several authors relate experience with outpatient groups for anorexia nervosa [35-40] as an adjunct to the patient's primary treatment method. Group therapists, as a rule, are different from therapists working with the individual or family, except for Hall [38], who was at least the family therapist for all her group patients. One group [36] used a recovered anorexic as a group cotherapist, a practice generally reserved for self-help groups.

The anorexia nervosa patient is likely to have an initial group psychotherapy experience during an acute hospitalization, more so since the development of eating disorder units in many general and psychiatric hospitals over the last decade. Inpatient groups may include all anorexic patients on the ward, or they may allow the low-weight patient to attend only after significant nutrition restoration. Such groups are also more likely to include both anorexia nervosa and bulimia patients, whereas outpatient groups almost always segregate by present diagnosis. Only Lieb and Thompson [41] describe experience with a group composed solely of inpatients, a closed-ended group of four adolescents on a medical ward. Polivy [35] and Piazza et al [36] report experience with mixed inpatient/outpatient groups for anorexia nervosa patients.

Whether inpatient or outpatient, the anorexia nervosa patient will not be able to participate meaningfully in group therapy until the starvation process is reversed. Inpatient settings with separate treatment modalities for insuring adequate nutrition and weight restoration are thus better able to accommodate low-weight patients in group therapy than can outpatient groups. Too, the captive nature of inpatient settings eliminates the problem of sporadic attendance and premature termination frequently seen with anorexia nervosa patients in outpatient settings.

With weight loss and progression of the disorder, the anorexic becomes increasingly withdrawn from relationships, bodily preoccupied, and constricted in outside interest. Even with weight restoration, many patients continue to have significant problems with self-esteem, assertiveness, independence, and expressiveness compounded by a set of distorted thoughts and beliefs. While these issues are addressed in individual and family therapy, the group setting has advantages of peer feedback, support, and social interaction under the direction of a psychotherapist, an opportunity not available within other modalities.

Goals in group therapy for anorexia nervosa patients are generally directed toward the psychological and social aspects of the illness, ie, issues of self-worth, adequacy, control, family relationships, intimacy, and expression of feelings. In some instances, secondary motives may be to decrease social isolation and treatment resistance [41], provide a forum for discussion of common concerns [37], and to extend treatment options when individual and family therapy modalities have been insufficient to reverse chronicity [38]. Most reports emphasize the supportive role of group therapy for these patients. Although food and weight concerns are reported as issues for discussion, no groups for anorexia nervosa report using cognitive-behavioral techniques or focus on weight gain or maintenance as a group therapy goal. Inbody and Ellis [40] indicate that all group members attained normal body weight over the eight-month life of the group, although the group was psychodynamically oriented and weight gain was not a primary focus of the group. Outpatient groups for anorexia nervosa tend, in fact, to require that the anorexia nervosa patient be within at least 20% of normal body weight before entry into group therapy [35,39].

Although group therapy is preferred by many group therapists as the sole treatment modality for many psychiatric problems and problems of living, other prior or concurrent treatment modalities are prerequisites for anorexia nervosa patients due to the complex and chronic nature of the disorder. Thus, it is not surprising that most reports to date used group treatment as an adjunctive modality, including that of Lieb and Thompson [35], who treated four adolescents on a medical ward.

MIXED ANOREXIC AND BULIMIC GROUPS

Eating disorder groups in an outpatient setting tend to be homogenous for current diagnosis, ie, anorexia nervosa or bulimia. A poorer outcome for currently bulimic patients with a past history of anorexia nervosa has been noted in several outpatient bulimia group therapy studies [7,9,23]. Inbody and Ellis [40] discuss the eight-month group treatment of seven anorexia nervosa patients, five of whom also had bulimic behavior. In this psychodynamically oriented group, all patients gained to a pre-agreed weight and those five patients who were binge-vomiting had a decrease in bulimic behavior over the course of eight months.

Mixed-composition groups are more likely to be conducted in an inpatient setting and, as such, are more likely to have a greater degree of individual psychopathology. The open-ended nature of hospital groups prevents the use of structured sessions found to be useful in short-term, closed outpatient groups for bulimics. Nevertheless, the mixed composition of inpatient groups presents the opportunity for patients to understand the similarities in underlying psychological and social issues associated with anorexia nervosa and bulimia.

SPECIAL PROBLEMS IN EATING DISORDERS GROUPS

Coexisting Psychiatric Disturbance

Personality disorder features and depressive symptoms are common among anorexia nervosa and bulimia patients. The relationship between eating disorders and other psychiatric syndromes has not had sufficient systematic study to warrant classification of anorexia nervosa or bulimia as variants of other psychiatric disorders or co-existing illnesses in some patients. However, subgroups of eating disorder patients may fulfill diagnostic criteria for coexisting psychiatric disorders. For example, Levin and Hyler [42] noted that 63% of bulimic patients enrolled in a drug study met DSM-III criteria for histrionic or borderline personality disorder.

Several authors [7,22,38-40] have noted that patients with serious characterological or affective disturbance often do poorly in outpatient eating disorder groups. Roy-Byrne et al [22] recommend limiting the number of patients with borderline personality organization to no more than three per group. Prior or concurrent individual psychotherapy should be a strong consideration for the borderline patient whose impulsivity, low frustration tolerance, hostility, and shifting alliances are particular liabilities in a group setting. These patients may be able to benefit from a short-term, structured group directed specifically toward eating control, but even under these conditions, strict limits for attendance, punctuality, and compliance often need to be enforced. Maher [39] describes an outpatient group experience with anorexia nervosa patients in which the depression and despair within the group substantially interfered with the group process, even though most patients were within a normal weight range.

Pregroup assessment for coexisting personality or affective disorder in eating disorder patients is important to determine whether the patient may need longer or more intense treatment than the group therapy alone can provide. Adequate screening and planning for these patients will increase their chance of effective utilization of group treatment and the group's chance for constructive work.

Noncompliance

Noncompliance with group rules, including erratic attendance, has been noted as a problem in eating disorder groups [18,22,26,27]. Late arrivals in one group [22] led to establishment of firm ground rules, including locking the door five minutes after start of the group and loss of membership after two unexplained absences. Missing sessions and failing to complete homework assignments results in dismissal from the University of Minnesota program, and approximately 6% of entering group patients are asked to leave the program before completion [27].

Premature Termination

Patients who drop out from group treatment both fail to benefit from the group and have a negative effect on group morale and cohesiveness. Premature termination from group therapy is a common occurrence in many types of groups, usually in the early phase of treatment [32]. Failure to complete group treatment has been reported as a problem in both anorexic and bulimic groups [8,22,24,27,35,39].

A number of factors have been reported to be associated with premature termination in eating disorder groups. Polivy [35] found that dropouts from an anorexia nervosa group were younger and more likely to be still living in their family of origin than group completers. In a comparison study of individual and group therapy for bulimic patients, Freeman [24] observed a dropout rate twice as high in group therapy as individual therapy, noting that reasons for premature termination from group seemed related to lack of improvement or dissatisfaction with the group treatment modality. Kirkley et al [13] found a higher dropout rate in a bulimic group using a nondirective approach than in a cognitive behavioral group; and dropouts tended to be younger, more angry and depressed, and have a shorter duration of bulimia than completers. At least two of the six dropouts in bulimic groups studied by Conners et al [10] had problems with alcohol abuse. Dixon and Kiecolt-Glaser [8] also found that patients with alcohol or substance abuse did poorly in bulimic groups or dropped out prematurely. Further, this study reported that premature terminators had higher social desirability scores on the Marlowe-Crowne Social Desirability scale than did group completers. In an eclectic group treatment for bulimics described by Lee and Rush [26], dropouts had higher hostility scores on the SCL-90 and more depression at follow-up than did completers.

One hundred percent completion of group therapy was accomplished by Fernandez [23] with a requirement for prepayment of the entire fee to cover the 12-session group treatment, a strategy used in behavioral groups for obese patients. All members attended all sessions and were punctual.

In a previous study in which group therapy was offered to bulimic patients without a requirement for concurrent or substantial prior individual treatment [8[], we found that 63% of group members failed to complete ten sessions in a group using both behavioral and insight-oriented techniques. The group was open-ended, and pregroup preparation did not emphasize the importance of attending a specified number of sessions. Some group members left because of external factors (geographic distance, end of school year). However, we were impressed that reasons for premature termination seemed related to the inadequacy of group treatment alone to provide the time or opportunity to address adequately both behavioral change and the complex underlying intrapsychic and interpersonal issues associated with anorexia nervosa and bulimia.

This led, then, to a patient selection process that required that the patient be referred for group therapy by an individual therapist who felt the patient was ready for and would benefit from group treatment. Since our groups by this time were primarily insight-oriented and ongoing, patients were considered to be completers after they successfully met treatment objectives determined by the patient's individual therapist before beginning group therapy. An effort was made to assign patients to a group led or co-led by their individual therapist.

In a study of 38 eating disorder patients (34 bulimic, 4 anorexic) who were seen in insight-oriented group therapy under conditions providing pregroup preparation and requiring concurrent individual therapy [Scheuble, 46], the overall premature termination rate dropped to 44%, considerably less than our experience with open-membership groups not requiring concurrent individual therapy. Premature terminators were most likely to leave group treatment within the first five sessions. Four of five patients with alcohol or substance abuse left group prematurely, even though they were concurrently in individual treatment. Only one of four patients with a diagnosis of anorexia nervosa left group therapy prematurely. Interestingly, of the 19 patients who participated in a group led or co-led by their individual therapist (combined psychotherapy), only four patients (21%) dropped out early, while 68% of patients in a group led by a therapist other than their individual therapist (conjoint psychotherapy) left prematurely. It appears, then, that the establishment of a working alliance with an individual psychotherapist enables some eating disorder patients to persist in a group treatment setting, more so if the individual and group therapists are the same. Similar findings have been described by Wong [43] and Slavinska-Holy [44] in the treatment of patients with borderline personality organization.

Only Lee and Rush [26] have attempted to obtain follow-up information on patients who left group therapy prematurely. These investigators found that premature terminators reported more depressive symptoms before group entry and had a higher binge frequency at three to four month follow-up than did group completers.

Patients who discontinue group therapy prematurely not only do not benefit from the brief exposure to the group, but they also may be harmed by the treatment failure [32]. In addition, irregular attendance and early dropouts interfere with cohesiveness and motivation among the remaining group members. For these reasons, pregroup identification of factors that are related to the patient's likelihood of successful or failure in group therapy are important, both to the individual patient and the group.

Selection of patients and pregroup preparation are two factors within the control of the group therapist that can mitigate the high drop-out rates associated with eating disorder groups. In addition to the usual exclusionary criteria for entry into a group, specific factors may need to be considered before placing an eating disorder patient in group therapy. Patients with alcohol and substance abuse appear to fare poorly in eating disorder groups, even with concurrent individual treatment. Indeed, the current trend is to exclude patents with alcohol and substance abuse from bulimic groups. Hostile, angry, and depressed patients may have difficulty with a group setting until these problems are moderated through other modes of treatment. Patients with a high need for social approval may experience difficulty in open or goal-directed groups that require honesty and self-disclosure for optimal benefit. Since many bulimic groups are time-limited and rely heavily on completion of homework assignments, patients with chaotic interpersonal relationships, uneven school or employment histories, or other indications of unreliability may need to demonstrate evidence of regular attendance in individual sessions before placement in a group.

At least three group-related factors may influence group completion for some patients and warrant further systematic study. These include (1) the use of structured, directive techniques in brief, time-limited groups; (2) incorporation of cognitive-behavioral techniques in individual psychotherapy sessions before or concurrent with assignment to a group whose orientation is psychodynamic or experiential, and (3) placement of the patient in a group led or co-led by the patient's individual therapist.

Maintenance of Change

The literature on bulimia treatment is replete with studies demonstrating the short-term effectiveness of cognitive-behavioral techniques in a group setting. Both symptom reduction and remission occurs immediately post-group in the majority of patients completing a course of group therapy. It is not surprising to find those aspects of the patient's distress related to demoralization—eg, feelings of low self-esteem, hopelessness, or inadequacy—improved along with a decrease or elimination of bulimic behaviors. However, long-term postgroup outcome is less favorable and indicates that some patients lose the progress obtained during the group treatment period

The final treatment phase in Fairburn's model for individual cognitive therapy includes specific strategies for relapse prevention. Varying degrees of attention are given to the issue of relapse prevention in reports of time-limited bulimic groups. Except for two reports [23,34] indicating inclusion of relapse prevention strategies within the group format, minimal time seems to be devoted to anticipating post-group problems. Further,

except for reports from intensive or combined treatment programs, little or no information is provided on how recommendations for additional, ongoing treatment are made.

CONTROLLED STUDIES

Five studies [4,7,16,24,26] using waiting-list controls have been reported. Boskind-Lodahl and White [4] nonrandomly assigned advertisement respondents to experimental and control groups. Few significant effects of group treatment as assessed by psychological measures were noted between experimental and no-treatment groups, and differences were even less at follow-up. Comparisons of bulimic behaviors between the treatment and non-treatment groups were not reported. In another study [7], however, 15 patients alternately assigned to a waiting-list control group had no significant change in bulimic frequency compared with an overall remission rate of 80% (93% by four weeks later) at the end of ten weeks of combined group and individual treatment for the 30 subjects in the study. Wolchik et al [16] reported that 11 women who were in a behavioral/educational/experiential group program, including two individual sessions, for ten weeks had a greater decrease in bulimic behaviors and improvement in depression and self-esteem post-group than did seven women who received no treatment. Patients were nonrandomly assigned to treatment or no-treatment groups, however, based on scheduling conflicts or time of response to news announcements. Thirty respondents to a newspaper advertisement were randomly assigned to treatment or a waiting-list control group by Lee and Rush [26]. Seventy-one percent of patients who received twice weekly cognitive-behavioral group therapy for six weeks had greater than 50% decrease in binge frequency post-group compared with 21% of no-treatment subjects. However, only half of treated patients had a 50% decrease in vomiting, suggesting that vomiting behavior may be more resistant to treatment than binge-eating. Freeman [24] outlines a comparison study with random assignment of subjects to cognitive-behavioral individual psychotherapy, educational, insight-directed group therapy, and a no-treatment group. Preliminary results indicated that all treatment conditions produced significant changes in bulimic behaviors, that cognitive therapy produced greater change in depression, and that patients were more likely to drop out of group therapy than individual therapy.

Although aggregate data of these four studies reporting individual outcomes immediately post-group [4,7,16,26] show that 54% of patients were symptom free and 28% had 50% or greater improvement, the largest study [7] combined individual and group treatment modalities, and the study by Wolchik et al [16] included two individual sessions. Thus, whether group or individual treatment primarily accounted for symptom improvement cannot be determined. Nevertheless, in these controlled studies in which the only treatment condition was psychosocial, 82% of bulimic patients had 50% or greater improvement in bulimic behavior in the immediate post-group period.

OUTCOME

Few patients with anorexia nervosa or bulimia receive only group therapy as treatment of their eating disorder. On the contrary, many patients receive other concurrent and/or post-group treatment. In this light, most immediate outcome reports are contaminated by other concurrent treatment. Thus, long-term follow-up of group treatment more accurately reflects the outcome of a treated eating disorder rather than the efficacy of the group treatment modality itself.

Bulimia

Composite results from 13 studies of group therapy for bulimics [4,6-9,11,12,14,16,18,22,26,34] that provide individual immediate outcome data (N = 201), indicate that 62% of patients were symptom-free postgroup, 18% had at least 50% symptom reduction, and 20% were less than 50% improved or had no change. Follow-up information at intervals ranging from one month to two years is also available on 338 individual patients in the reports of 13 studies (table 2). Of these 338 patients, 36% were symptom free, 36% were at least 50% improved, and 28% had less than 50% improvement, no change, or were unavailable for follow-up. It should be noted that outcome data is reported only on patients who are group completers, thus excluding dropouts, who are likely to continue to be symptomatic [26].

From available information in the bulimia group therapy literature, then, it appears that fewer patients are symptom-free at follow-up (36%) than immediately post-group (62%), with a substantial number of patients resuming bulimic behavior. Nevertheless, 72% of bulimic patients who met requirements for completion of group therapy, usually time-based, continue to be at least 50% improved over time.

All group therapy studies with bulimic patients reporting either immediate or follow-up data, regardless of orientation or treatment duration, can demonstrate a significant reduction in binge-purging frequency for the study sample post-group and over time, albeit to varying degrees. For many patients, maintenance of

change poses a greater problem. Indeed, Mitchell et al [45] describe a fluctuating, chronic course of illness for many bulimic patients. While a single outcome variable is insufficient to gauge the efficacy of treatment, it is disturbing that many patients have continued bulimic symptoms, sometimes unchanged, even with specific and/or intensive treatment.

Anorexia Nervosa

No systematic outcome measures, immediate or long-term, are available in the literature of group psychotherapy for anorexia nervosa. The multimodal nature of the treatment plan of most anorexia nervosa patients is an obstacle in the objective assessment of the relative values of each component of the treatment plan. Subjective impressions of six of seven authors [35-38,40,41], however, support the usefulness of group therapy as an adjunctive treatment modality for some patients with anorexia nervosa. Hall [38] reported that six of ten chronic anorexia nervosa patients were able to gain and maintain close to a target weight, and three resumed menstruation by the end of 13 months of group therapy. Lieb and Thompson [41] found that all four anorexics in group therapy during a medical hospitalization maintained their discharge weight at follow-up several months later.

Maher [39], however, felt that group therapy had little or no usefulness in the anorexia nervosa patient's treatment. Unrelenting despair, dependency on the group therapists, inability to reach out to other group members, and a high dropout rate were problems encountered during the nine-month period of Maher's outpatient group. That 75% of the group members also had a diagnosis of borderline personality disorder was recognized as a potential source of difficulty for this group.

Since group therapy for anorexia nervosa is adjunctive in nature and has primarily psychodynamic, experiential, or supportive orientations, its efficacy and role in the treatment of these patients is difficult to determine. Six of seven descriptive reports [35-37,39-41] indicate positive treatment effects, mostly psychosocial, for some anorexia nervosa patients in group treatment after acute starvation has been reversed. One report [39], however, indicates negative effects from outpatient group treatment. Most reports suffer from limited descriptions of the patient population, unspecified or vague objectives of the group modality, and absence of outcome measures relevant to the type of group. Before generalizations can be made regarding the efficacy or nonefficacy of group therapy for anorexia nervosa patients, more systematic research is needed to identify better the relationship between specific group interventions and specific effects with specific sub-

Table 41.2 Outcome in Group Treatment of Bulimia

Study	% Dropout	# Completers	Follow-up Interval	Follow-Up Outcome		
				Symptom free	Improved 50+%	No change or no data
Eclectic approach with psychodynamic/experiential component						
Dixon & Kiecolt-Glaser (1981)	63%	11	1 yr	45%	55%	0%
Stevens & Salisbury (1984)	25%	6	10 mo	83%	17%	0%
Eclectic approach without psychodynamic component						
Johnson et al.(1983)	23%	10	8 wks	10%	70%	20%
Connors et al. (1983)	23%	20	10 wks	15%	40%	45%
Yates & Sambrailo (1984)						
Directive approach	33%	8	6 wks	25%	25%	50%
Non-directive	33%	8		0%	50%	50%
Kirkley et al. (1985)						
Directive approach	7%	13	12 wks	38%	39%	23%
Non-directive	35%			11%	69%	21%
Huon & Brown (1985)	12.5%	40	6,12, & 18 mo	68%	22%	5%
Schneider & Agras (1985)	0%	13	6 mo	38%	31%	15%
Wolchik et al. (1986)	15%	11	10 wks	9%	45%	45%
Intensive or combined treatment modalities						
White & Boskind-White (1981)	0%	14	6 mo	21%	50%	29%
Lacey (1983)	0%	30	1 mo, 3 mo and q 3 mo for 2 yrs	67%	27%	6%
Brisman & Siegel (1985)	0%	114	1 mo-2yrs	33%	38%	29%
Wooley & Kearney-Cooke (1986)	0%	18	1 yr	39%	44%	17%

groups of these patients.

CONCLUSION

Although no systematic investigations of group therapy for anorexia nervosa patients have been published, the few available descriptive reports give evidence of limited benefit for some patients. On the other hand, the group treatment of bulimia has a high level of patient acceptance and permits high-volume delivery of service, with a short-term, cognitive-behavioral approach, which seems to be the emerging trend. Whether this trend is representative overall of the group psychotherapy practice for bulimia patients is unclear since behavioral psychotherapy is more conducive to systematic research than psychodynamic or experiential psychotherapy.

In spite of the apparent effectiveness of brief, behaviorally oriented psychotherapy as an initial intervention, high attrition and relapse rates continue to be significant problems for the bulimic patient in group therapy. Future research needs to identify the concurrent or sequential combinations of different formats optimal for specific patients, develop screening and intervention techniques to prevent premature termination from treatment, and address the issue of durability of change in these potentially persistent, disabling psychiatric disorders.

REFERENCES

1. Stein A. Group psychotherapy with psychosomatically ill patients. In: Kaplan HI, Saddock BJ, eds. Comprehensive group psychotherapy. Baltimore: Williams & Wilkins, 1983:
2. Lowison JH. Group psychotherapy with substance abusers and alcoholics. In: Kaplan HI, Saddock BJ, eds. Comprehensive group psychotherapy. Baltimore: Williams & Wilkins, 1983:
3. Enright AB, Butterfield P, Berkowitz B. Self-help and support groups in the management of eating disorders. In: Garner DM, Garfinkel PE, eds. Handbook of psychotherapy for anorexia nervosa and bulimia. New York: Guilford Press, 1985:
4. Boskind-Lodahl M, White WC. The definition and treatment of bulimarexia in college women—a pilot study. J Am Coll Health Assoc 1978; 27:84-97.
5. White WC, Boskind-White M. An experiential behavioral approach to the treatment of bulimarexia. Psychotherapy: Theory, Research and Practice 1981; 18:501-7.
6. Johnson C, Connors ME, Stuckey MK. Short-term group treatment of bulimia: a preliminary repoort. Int J Eating Disorders 1983; 2:199-208.
7. Lacey JH. Bulimia nervosa, binge eating and psychogenic vomiting: a controlled treatment study and long term outcome. Brit Med J 1983; 286:1609-13.
8. Dixon KN, Kiecolt-Glaser J. Group therapy for bulimia. Hillside J Clin Psychiatry 1984; 6:156-70.
9. Stevens EV, Salisbury JD. Group therapy for bulimic adults. Am J Orthopsychiatry 1984; 54:156-61.
10. Connors ME, Johnson CL, Stuckey MK. Treatment of bulimia with brief psychoeducational group therapy. Am J Psychiatry 1984; 141:1512-6.
11. Yates AJ, Sambrailo F. Bulimia nervosa: a descriptive and therapeutic study. Behav Res Ther 1984; 5:503-17.
12. Huon GH, Brown LB. Evaluating a group treatment for bulimia. J Psychiatr Res 1985; 19:479-83.
13. Kirkley BG, Schneider JA, Agras WS, Bachman JA. Comparison of two group treatments for bulimia. J Consult Clin Psychol 1985; 53:43-8.
14. Schneider JA, Agras WS. A cognitive behavioural group treatment of bulimia. Brit J Psychiatry 1985; 146:66-9.
15. Brisman J, Siegel M. The bulimia workshop: a unique integration of group treatment approaches. Int J Group Psychother 1985; 35:585-600.
16. Wolchik SA, Weiss L, Katzman MA. An empirically validated, short-term psychoeducational group treatment program for bulimia. Int J Eating Disorders 1986; 5:21-34.
17. Wooley SC, Kearney-Cooke A. Intensive treatment of bulimia and body image disturbance. In: Brownell K, Foreyt J, eds. Physiology, psychology, and the treatment of eating disorders. New York: Basic Books, 1986:
18. Weinstein HM, Richman A. The group treatment of bulimia. J Amer Coll Health 1984; 32:208-15.
19. Reed G, Sech EP. Bulimia: a conceptual model for group treatment. J Psychosocial Nursing and Mental Health Services 1985; 23:16-22.
20. Barth D, Wurman V. Group therapy with bulimic women: a self- psychological approach. Int J Eating Disorders 1986; 5:735-45.
21. Hornak NJ. Group treatment for bulimia: bulimics anonymous. J Coll Student Personnel 1983; 24:461-3.
22. Roy-Byrne P, Lee-Benner K, Yager J. Group therapy for bulimia. Int J Eating Disorders 1984; 3:97-116.
23. Fernandez RC. Group therapy of bulimia. In: Powers PS, Fernandez RC, eds. Current treatment of anorexia nervosa and bulimia. Basel: Karger, 1984:
24. Freeman C, Sinclair F, Turnbull J, Annadale A. Psychotherapy for bulimia: a controlled study. J Psychiatr Res 1986; 19:473-8.
25. Weiss L, Katzman M. Group treatment for bulimic women. Arizona Med 1984; 41:100-4.
26. Lee NF, Rush AJ. Cognitive-behavioral group therapy for bulimia. Int J Eating Disorders 1986; 5:599-615.
27. Mitchell JE, Hatsukami D, Goff G, Pyle RL, Eckert ED, Davis LE. Intensive outpatient group treatment for bulimia. In: Garner DM, Garfinkel PE, eds. Handbook of psychotherapy for anorexia nervosa and bulimia. New York: Guilford Press, 1985:
28. Wollersheim JP. Effectiveness of group therapy based upon learning principles in the treatment of overweight women. J Abnorm Psychol 1970; 76:462-74.

29. Fairburn CG. A cognitive behavioral approach to the treatment of bulimia. Psychol Med 1981; 11:707-11.

30. Fairburn CG. Cognitive-behavioral treatment for bulimia. In: Garner DM, Garfinkel PE, eds. Handbook of psychotherapy for anorexia nervosa and bulimia. New York: Guilford Press, 1985:

31. Wooley SC, Wooley OW. Intensive outpatient and residential treatment for bulimia. In: Garner DM, Garfinkel PE, eds. Handbook of psychotherapy for anorexia nervosa and bulimia. New York: Guilford Press,, 1985:

32. Yalom ID. The theory and practice of group psychotherapy. New York: Basic Books, 1970:

33. Lacey JH. An outpatient treatment program for bulimia nervosa. Int J Eating Disorders 1983; 2:209-14.

34. Pyle RL, Mitchell JE, Eckert ED, Hatsukami DK, Goff G. The interruption of bulimic behaviors: a review of three treatment programs. Psychiatr Clin North Am 1984; 7:275-86.

35. Polivy J. Group therapy as an adjunctive treatment for anorexia nervosa. J Psychiat Treatment & Evaluation 1981; 3:279-82.

36. Piazza E, Carni JD, Kelly J, et al. Group psychotherapy for anorexia nervosa. J Am Acad Child Psychiatry 1983; 22:276-8.

37. Huerta E. Group therapy for anorexia nervosa patients. In: Gross M, ed. Anorexia nervosa. Lexington: Collamore Press, 1982:

38. Hall A. Group psychotherapy for anorexia nervosa. In: Garner DM, Garfinkel PE, eds. Handbook of psychotherapy for anorexia nervosa and bulimia. New York: Guilford Press, 1985:

39. Maher MS. Group therapy for anorexia nervosa. In: Powers P, Fernandez R, eds. Current treatment of anorexia nervosa and bulimia. Basel: Karger, 1984:

40. Inbody DR, Ellis JJ. Group therapy with anorexic and bulimic patients: implications for therapeutic intervention. Am J Psychother 1985; 34:411-20.

41. Lieb RC, Thompson TL. Group psychotherapy of four anorexia nervosa inpatients. Int J Group Psychotherapy 1984; 34:639-42.

42. Levin AP, Hyler SE. DSM-III personality diagnosis in bulimia. Comp Psychiatr 1986; 27:47-53

43. Wong N. Combined group and individual treatment of borderline and narcissistic patients; heterogenous versus homogenous groups. Int J Group Psychotherapy 1980; 30: 389-404.

44. Slavinska-Holy N. Combining individual and homogenous group psychotherapies for borderline conditions. Int J Group Psychotherapy 1983; 33:297-312.

45. Mitchell JE, Hatsukami D, Pyle RL, Eckert ED. The bulimia syndrome: course of the illness and associated problems. Comp Psychiatry 1986; 27:165-70.

46. Scheuble KJ, Dixon KN, Levy AB, Kagan-Moore L. Premature termination: a risk in eating disorder groups. Group 1987; 11:85-93.

Chapter 42

Pharmacotherapy of Eating Disorders

B. Timothy Walsh

ANOREXIA NERVOSA

Anorexia nervosa is a potentially life-threatening illness that, in some cases, seems resistant to all forms of therapeutic intervention. For this reason, virtually every type of somatic treatment known to psychiatry has been employed at some time in the treatment of patients with anorexia nervosa and has been described as being effective. Currently, the limited number of controlled studies of pharmacological treatment in this illness suggest that medication can play, at most, a secondary role as one component of a comprehensive treatment strategy. In this chapter, I will briefly review the major approaches that have been taken in the use of medication in anorexia nervosa, and what the outcome of such attempts has been.

Antipsychotic Medication

Twenty-five years ago, soon after the introduction of antipsychotic medication into psychiatry, British clinicians described a treatment program using chlorpromazine and insulin to produce rapid weight gain among patients with anorexia nervosa [1]. Chlorpromazine was given in doses of 150 to 1000 mg daily combined with subcutaneous insulin, which was used to induce hypoglycemia in an attempt to increase appetite. In a follow-up report in 1966, these authors reviewed their experience [2]. They compared the outcome of 48 women with anorexia nervosa who had been hospitalized and treated with chlorpromazine and insulin to a series of 48 similar patients who had been admitted over the preceding 20 years and treated in the same hospital but without the use of chlorpromazine. They found that the patients treated with chlorpromazine gained weight substantially faster and left the hospital significantly sooner than the patients who had been treated without medication. However, on follow-up there was no advantage for the chlorpromazine-treated group. After two years, approximately 30% of each group required readmission, and 45% of the patients treated with chlorpromazine had developed bulimia compared with 12% of the patients treated without medication. Furthermore, the chlorpromazine treatment was associated with significant side effects, including grand mal seizures in 5 of the 48 patients. In a more recent review of the treatment of anorexia nervosa [47], Dally noted that although chlorpromazine had once been used for all patients with anorexia nervosa on his service, less than one third of such patients received chlorpromazine in 1981 and usually only for brief periods. The use of insulin had been abandoned entirely.

In recent years, Dutch investigators have explored the utility of antipsychotic medication in a controlled fashion. In 1982, Vandereycken and Pierloot reported a study of the antipsychotic drug pimozide in 18 patients with anorexia nervosa [3]. Patients were all hospitalized and were also treated in a behavior modification program. Patients received three weeks of either pimozide or placebo followed by three weeks of the alternative drug. Unfortunately, the group that was randomized to begin pimozide was lower in weight at initiation of treatment than the group that started on placebo. The patients who began on pimozide gained weight faster than those who began on placebo, but this difference continued after drug crossover. Overall, there was a trend favoring weight gain on pimozide, but the difference from placebo was not statistically significant. The staff's rating of the patients' attitudes detected no significant effect of drug treatment.

In 1984, Vandereycken reported a study of similar design of the antipsychotic drug sulpiride [4]. Once again, there was a slight trend favoring the drug compared with placebo, but no statistically significant effect was demonstrated either on weight gain or on the staff's rating of the patients' attitudes or behavior.

In summary, although there was significant enthusiasm for the possible utility of antipsychotic medication in anorexia nervosa in the early 1960s, this enthusiasm has not been borne out by controlled study. In addition, the severity of potential side-effects of antipsychotic medication, including not only the grand mal seizures noted by Dally and his co-workers, but also hypotension and the long-term risk of tardive dyskinesia limit the utility of neuroleptics in this syndrome. Despite these limitations, a number of experienced clinicians believe that antipsychotic medications can be of assistance in the management of particularly physically active or particularly compulsive patients who may respond to the sedative properties of antipsychotic drugs. It is interesting to note that although the distortion of body image characteristic of anorexia nervosa at times approaches delusional proportions, there is no indication that antipsychotic medications reduce these cognitive disturbances.

Antidepressant Medication

Although some degree of mood disturbance has long been noted among patients with anorexia nervosa, the possibility that there is a link between anorexia nervosa and major affective illness has attracted significant attention only in recent years and has led to a number of attempts to explore the utility of antidepressant medication. Several case reports suggest that some patients with anorexia nervosa obtain impressive benefit from antidepressants [5-7]. However, other reports imply that substantial benefit is uncommon [8,9].

Several recent controlled studies have attempted to assess the utility of antidepressant medication in anorexia nervosa. In 1980 Lacey and Crisp reported a study of the tricyclic antidepressant clomipramine in 16 hospitalized patients [10]. Clomipramine is widely used in Europe for the treatment of depression and, in addition, has been found in several studies to be of significant

benefit in the treatment of patients with obsessive compulsive disorder. For these reasons, clomipramine would appear to be a particularly attractive medication for patients with anorexia nervosa who frequently exhibit both mood disturbance and compulsive symptoms. In this trial, however, the clomipramine-treated patients did no better than the patients receiving placebo. The implications of this study are limited by the small patient sample (a total of 16) and by a low dose of drug (50 mg/day) even allowing for the low weight of the patients.

The two other controlled studies of antidepressant medication in anorexia nervosa have used amitriptyline. Beiderman et al examined the usefulness of amitriptyline in a sample of 43 patients [11]. Twenty-five of these 43 patients elected to participate in a double-blind, placebo-controlled trial, and 11 were randomized to receive amitriptyline and 14 to receive placebo. The 18 patients who refused participation in the trial were used as a comparison group. Patients were treated at one of two institutions for five weeks; five were outpatients and 38 were inpatients. The mean dose of medication was 115 mg/day (2.8 mg/kg). This study was unable to detect any advantage for the amitriptyline-treated group compared with the placebo group or with the group of patients who had refused to participate in the study. Like the previous study of Lacey and Crisp, this study is limited by its small sample size and also by the fact that two of the patients taking amitriptyline had very low plasma levels of drug, suggesting poor compliance.

The third double-blind, placebo-controlled trial of antidepressant medication in anorexia nervosa was conducted by Halmi et al [12]. In this study, 72 female inpatients with anorexia nervosa were treated at one of two centers and, in addition, were randomly assigned to receive one of three medications for up to six weeks: placebo, amitriptyline, or cyproheptadine. There were indications of a marginal advantage for the amitriptyline-treated group in reaching target weight faster than patients treated with placebo. This study is notable for its large sample size and the rigorous analysis of the treatment response; however, plasma level data have not yet been reported, so there is some question about the adequacy of the pharmacological intervention.

In summary, despite the indications of significant mood disturbances associated with the syndrome of anorexia nervosa, there are few rigorous data to suggest a major role for antidepressant medication in this syndrome. There are several potential explanations for this finding. First, it is possible that the depression associated with anorexia nervosa is distinct from those forms of major depressive illness that respond to antidepressant medication [13]. Second, the physiological disruptions induced by starvation might conceivably make patients refractory who might otherwise respond to antidepressant treatment. Third, it is possible that only a subset of patients with anorexia nervosa are drug-responsive, and the positive drug effect in these patients is obscured by the results of other patients who are not drug-responsive. Finally, it should be noted that only three controlled studies involving only two antidepressant agents have been reported.

From a clinical perspective, the role of antidepressant medication in anorexia nervosa must, at this point, be viewed as an adjunct to a comprehensive and multifaceted treatment approach. The relatively limited benefits of antidepressant medication must be weighed against the potential side-effects in this medically ill population, including orthostatic hypotension and cardiac conduction disturbances.

Cyproheptadine

Cyproheptadine is a serotonin and histamine antagonist that is primarily used to treat allergic conditions. It was noted that patients receiving cyproheptadine for such problems sometimes gained weight, and several studies have explored whether this effect might be usefully applied to underweight patients with anorexia nervosa.

The first double-blind, placebo-controlled trial of cyproheptadine in anorexia nervosa was reported by Vigersky and Loriaux in 1977 [14]. They treated 24 outpatients with cyproheptadine, 12 mg daily, or placebo for eight weeks and were unable to detect a significant drug/placebo differences. They noted difficulties in interpreting this negative result because of uncertainty about patient compliance with medication and recommended further assessment of cyproheptadine.

In 1979 Goldberg et al reported the results of a multicenter trial of cyproheptadine in hospitalized patients with anorexia nervosa [15]. Cyproheptadine was given in doses of 12 to 32 mg/day for 35 days. The cyproheptadine-treated patients gained slightly more weight than the placebo-treated patients, but this difference was not statistically significant.

In the study of Halmi et al previously described, cyproheptadine was compared with amitriptyline and placebo in 72 patients hospitalized for anorexia nervosa. Cyproheptadine was slightly more effective than placebo in inducing weight gain and in relieving depression. It was of interest that there was a differential drug effect related to the presence of bulimia, so that cyproheptadine significantly increased treatment efficiency in the nonbulimic patients and impaired treatment efficiency in the bulimic patients. Although there have been consistent reports of differences between bulimic and nonbulimic subgroups of patients with anorexia ner-

vosa, it is unclear why cyproheptadine should affect these two subgroups differentially.

In sum, there are indications that cyproheptadine in relatively large doses may have some mild effect in promoting weight gain and relieving depression in anorexia nervosa. However, these therapeutic effects appear to be modest. One major advantage of cyproheptadine is that it appears to have few side-effects, even in the relatively large doses used.

Other Pharmacological Agents

A variety of other pharmacological agents have been used in the treatment of patients with anorexia nervosa, and some have been subjected to double-blind, placebo-controlled trials. A few open trials suggested that lithium might be of benefit [16,17]. In 1981 Gross et al reported a double-blind, placebo-controlled trial of lithium in the treatment of 16 women hospitalized for anorexia nervosa [18]. Over the four-week trial, the lithium-treated patients gained slightly more weight than the placebo-treated patients. However, the difference was not statistically significant. Because of baseline differences between the drug-and placebo-treated groups, because both groups did improve over this brief trial, and because of the small sample size, this study cannot be taken to exclude definitively the use of lithium in patients with anorexia nervosa. However, at present, except for the rare patient who has both bipolar affective illness and anorexia nervosa, there is no clear indication for the use of lithium in anorexia nervosa.

Gross et al also conducted a controlled trial of delta-9-tetrahydrocannabinol (THC), which is the active ingredient of marijuana [19]. The rationale was that since smoking marijuana is known to increase appetite, THC might be useful in assisting patients with anorexia nervosa to gain weight. In fact, the THC had a negative therapeutic impact; it produced a significant amount of dysphoria and had no detectable effect on weight.

Another avenue for the treatment of anorexia nervosa with medication has focused on a known physiological abnormality of patients with this illness, namely that gastric emptying is slowed [20]. Because many patients with anorexia nervosa complain of feeling bloated after meals, it has been suggested that drugs that increase gastric emptying may relieve symptoms and assist in the normalization of eating. Several authors have reported that gastric emptying is increased by the administration of drugs such as metoclopramide, bethanechol, and domperidon [20- 22]. In these uncontrolled trials, patients have had fewer complaints of bloating after meals, but the overall utility of the drugs was not clear. Furthermore, the use of metoclopramide was associated with significant depression and with hormonal changes, potentially limiting its use in anorexia nervosa.

Finally, a number of other drugs and hormonal preparations have been described in case reports as being of benefit to patients with anorexia nervosa. The drugs used include glycerol, phenoxybenzamine, L-DOPA, and anabolic steroids [23-26]. None of these drugs has been evaluated by controlled trial, and there is little evidence for their utility in anorexia nervosa.

Summary

In short, despite the multitude of biological abnormalities described in patients with anorexia nervosa, there is no compelling evidence that somatic treatments other than weight restoration are of dramatic benefit in this syndrome. As noted above, occasional patients, particularly agitated ones, may benefit from low doses of antipsychotic medications, and there are suggestions that some patients may benefit from antidepressant medication or from the serotonin antagonist cyproheptadine. However, at the moment, medication must be viewed as playing only a secondary role in the treatment of anorexia nervosa.

BULIMIA

Although the syndrome of bulimia in normal-weight individuals has only recently gained the attention of the mental health professions, an impressive amount of effort has already been devoted to the evaluation of pharmacological methods of treatment. These pharmacological interventions have been based on one of two conceptual models. The first model is that bulimia is a manifestation of a seizure disorder and could be treated effectively with anticonvulsant medication. The second model that has been explored more recently is that bulimia is in some way linked to disturbances of mood and can be approached through the use of antidepressant medication.

Anticonvulsant treatment

In the mid-1970s Green and Rau suggested a relationship between binge eating and seizure disorders [27-30]. They noted that patients with binge eating typically described the binges as episodic, uncontrollable, and ego-dystonic. The episodes were also frequently preceded by a change in mental state that could be interpreted as an aura. Green and Rau were struck by the similarity of these features to those of patients with seizure disorders. Over several years they obtained EEGs in patients with "compulsive eating" and found that a majority had abnormal EEGs, most frequently the occurrence of 14- and 6-per-second spikes. These findings led them to propose that "compulsive eaters

have a *primary* neurologic disorder similar to epilepsy." On the basis of this formulation they treated patients with phenytoin and described impressive results in a series of uncontrolled trials.

There has been a limited amount of additional work pursuing this hypothesis. However, the work that has been done generally does not suggest that bulimia is a form of seizure disorder. In 1977 Wermuth et al reported a controlled study of phenytoin in bulimia [31]. As was true of the patients described by Green and Rau, the patients in the study of Wermuth et al were more heterogeneous in terms of body weight and eating behavior than patients who have been studied with bulimia in the last five years. Wermuth et al obtained EEGs from 20 patients and found definite abnormalities in only three, a far smaller fraction than that reported in the original studies of Green and Rau. One reason for this discrepancy is that electroencephalographers became more skeptical that the 14- and 6-per-second spike pattern was of any significance. Wermuth et al compared phenytoin to placebo in a double-blind crossover experiment in which patients received either phenytoin for three weeks followed by placebo for three weeks or the opposite sequence. The ten patients who began on phenytoin improved in comparison to their baseline, but when they were switched to placebo, there was no deterioration. The nine patients who received the placebo/phenytoin sequence did not improve on placebo, but reduced their bingeing somewhat on phenytoin. Overall, the difference between placebo and phenytoin treatment was not statistically significant. Contrary to what one would predict if bulimia were a form of seizure disorder, there was no relationship between pretreatment EEG abnormality and the response to phenytoin, or between the plasma level of phenytoin and the clinical response. In addition, the efficacy of treatment with phenytoin was modest even in those patients who did obtain some benefit.

Greenway et al obtained EEGs in seven patients with obesity associated with compulsive overeating [32]. No significant abnormalities were detected. Four patients were treated with phenytoin in a controlled fashion and no evidence of therapeutic efficacy was obtained.

There is only one other study that may bear on the idea that bulimia is a form of seizure disorder. Kaplan et al reported that one of six normal-weight patients with bulimia responded impressively to treatment with carbamazepine in a double-blind, placebo-controlled crossover trial [33]. None of the other five patients had significant therapeutic responses. The patient who did respond had, in addition to bulimia, a mood disturbance that may have been a mild form of bipolar disorder. Carbamazepine is an anticonvulsant drug that is widely used in the treatment of seizure disorders but that also appears to be effective in the treatment of some patients with bipolar mood disturbance. Therefore, the efficacy of carbamazepine in this single patient with bulimia cannot be clearly interpreted as evidence of a seizure disturbance.

In sum, little compelling evidence has been gathered to support the hypothesis of Green and Rau that bulimia is a form of seizure disorder. There are hints that phenytoin may be of use for the treatment of some patients with bulimia, but additional controlled studies of phenytoin in eating disorders will be required to clarify its potential role.

Antidepressant Treatment

The relationship between bulimia in normal-weight individuals and mood disturbance has generated a great deal of interest and some controversy. There is general agreement that patients with bulimia are more anxious, depressed, and irritable than control subjects. Most studies that have used structured rating instruments have also found an elevated lifetime frequency of major depression among patients with bulimia. However, it is far from clear whether bulimia should be viewed as an unusual manifestation of an underlying affective illness or whether the mood disturbances of bulimia are best regarded as a secondary consequence of the eating disorder.

While this controversy concerning the significance of the mood disturbance in bulimia remains unsettled, the recognition of depression and anxiety among patients with bulimia has lead to a series of trials of antidepressant medications. The first clear description is that of Rich, who in 1978 described a 21-year-old woman with bulimia and depression who failed to respond to a tricyclic antidepressant but had an impressive response to the monoamine oxidase inhibitor (MAOI) phenelzine [34]. In 1982 Pope et al described a series of normal-weight patients with bulimia who responded to open treatment with tricyclic antidepressants, and our own group published similar results using MAOIs [35,36]. These series of patients treated openly were followed by reports of seven double-blind, placebo-controlled trials of antidepressants in normal-weight patients with bulimia.

The first study reported was that of Sabine et al, who examined the use of mianserin, an antidepressant drug available in Europe [37]. Twenty patients were randomized to receive mianserin, 60 mg per day, and 30 to receive placebo. Both groups improved somewhat over the eight-week trial, but there was no significant difference between the drug-and placebo-treated groups. A major limitation of the study is that the dose of mianserin used was low compared with that sometimes required for treatment of depression. In addition, this study may have treated a group of patients who are less severely ill than those who were treated in subsequent studies.

Pope et al followed their initial report with a double-blind, placebo-controlled trial of imipramine in 22 normal-weight patients with bulimia [38]. The placebo-treated group improved minimally, while the group receiving imipramine reduced their binge frequency about 75%, a statistically significant result. Hughes et al conducted a similar study of patients with bulimia using the tricyclic antidepressant desipramine [39]. In a dose of 200 mg daily, desipramine was strikingly superior to placebo, and 15 of the 22 patients (68%) who received desipramine either during the study or later during follow-up achieved symptomatic remission.

Mitchell and Groat reported a controlled study of amitriptyline in which both the drug- and placebo-treated groups improved [40]. It is interesting that the therapeutic effect of amitriptyline in this study was similar to the effect of the active drug in the controlled studies of Pope et al and Hughes et al. The major difference between the studies is that in the amitriptyline study the placebo-treated patients improved substantially, while the placebo-treated groups did not improve in the other two studies. The procedures used to treat the patients receiving placebo were similar in all three studies, and the reason for the discrepant outcome of placebo treatment is not clear. While the patients in these studies were similar in simple clinical terms such as age, percent of ideal weight, and frequency of bulimic behavior, it is possible that these similarities camouflage important differences between patient groups treated at different centers.

Agras et al recently reported the results of a controlled trial of imipramine in 20 bulimic women [48]. This study differs from the preceding tricyclic antidepressant trials in its longer length (16 weeks vs. 6 to 8 weeks) and in its rigorous attempt at restricting therapeutic interventions other than medication. The imipramine-treated group obtained greater reductions in the frequency of binge eating and of purging than the placebo-treated group, but the differences between drug and placebo were not as impressive as in the studies of Pope et al [38] and Hughes et al [39]. For example, in the Agras et al study, there was a 72% reduction in binge frequency in the imipramine group after 16 weeks, similar to the reduction at 6 weeks reported by Pope et al in their imipramine group. However, at 16 weeks, the placebo-treated group of Agras et al obtained a reduction of 43% in binge eating frequency compared to virtually no change in the placebo-group in the study of Pope et al. In sort, the study of Agras et al supports the efficacy of tricyclic antidepressant treatment compared to placebo, but, like the study of Mitchell & Groat, raises questions about the reasons for differences in outcome in different centers.

We have conducted a controlled study of the MAOI phenelzine in the treatment of normal-weight patients with bulimia. We embarked on this investigation several years ago because of our impression that many bulimic patients presented symptoms of anxiety and depression similar to those of patients with "atypical" depression, which has been thought to respond particularly well to treatment with MAOIs. An analysis of the first 30 patients completing our double-blind, placebo-controlled trial indicated a significant advantage for phenelzine. Six of 14 phenelzine-treated patients were in remission at the completion of the study, compared with none of the 16 placebo-treated patients (p<.01) [41]. Our data, like those of three of the four studies using tricyclic antidepressants, suggest that antidepressant medications are of benefit to some patients with bulimia.

We were initially concerned about the potential risks of giving bulimic patients, who by definition cannot control their eating, MAOIs, which demand that patients avoid certain foods or risk a hypertensive reaction. We have carefully screened patients for their ability to comply with a tyramine-free diet and have not had a serious hypertensive reaction because of patient noncompliance. However, we have been impressed that, in this population, other side-effects of phenelzine such as postural hypotension and sleep disturbance caused significant difficulty and are a major impediment to the use of MAOIs in many patients.

Kennedy et al have reported the preliminary results of a controlled trial of another MAOI in buliomia [49]. They examined the utility of isocarboxazid in a double-blind, placebo-controlled crossover trial in 18 patients. As in our study of phenelzine, there was a significant advantage for the MAOI compared to placebo.

In addition to these controlled trials, therapeutic response has been reported on the basis of open trial experience with a variety of tricyclic antidepressants, MAOIs, trazodone, bupropion, nomifensine, and lithium carbonate [42-46]. The data are now reasonably convincing that, at least for some patients of normal body weight with bulimia, antidepressant medications have significant therapeutic effect. However, some important questions about the use of medication in such patients remain unanswered. First, it is unclear which patients are most likely to respond. Most of the controlled trials of antidepressant medications have studied patients who are chronically and moderately-to-severely ill. It is not clear if the same drug-placebo difference would be found in less severely ill patients. Although one could anticipate that depressed bulimic patients would be particularly likely to respond to antidepressant medication, the study of Hughes et al [39] explicitly excluded patients with major depressive disorder and yet found impressive results with desipramine. Similarly, in a preliminary analysis of our patients treated with MAOIs, nondepressed patients appear to derive benefit as well as depressed patients. Thus it appears that the clinician cannot rely on the presence of depression to indicate which patients with bulimia will respond to antidepressant medication. Of more concern is the fact that we know very little about the long-term outcome of the drug treatment of bulimia or how best to combine drug treatment with other forms of therapy. It should be noted that all of the controlled studies of antidepressant medication in bulimia are of relatively short duration and there is no knowledge of how long patients who respond to medication need to remain on it or of what the relapse rate is when the drug is discontinued. Answers to these questions will demand the attention of investigators in this field for the next several years.

ACKNOWLEDGEMENTS

This work was supported in part by NIH grants AM-28150, MH-30906, and MH-00383, and by the Communities Foundation of Texas, Inc.

REFERENCES

1. Dally PJ, Sargant W. A new treatment of anorexia nervosa. Br Med J 1960; 1:1770-3.
2. Dally P, Sargant W. Treatment and outcome of anorexia nervosa. Br Med J 1966; 2:793-5.
3. Vandereycken W, Pierloot R. Pimozide combined with behavior therapy in the short-term treatment of anorexia nervosa. A double-blind, placebo-controlled, cross-over study. Acta Psychiat Scand 1982; 66:445-50.
4. Vandereycken W. Neuroleptics in the short-term treatment of anorexia nervosa. A double-blind placebo-controlled study with sulpiride. Br J Psychiatry 1984; 144:288-92.
5. Needleman HL, Waber D. Amitriptyline therapy in patients with anorexia nervosa (letter). Lancet 1976; 2:580.
6. White JH, Schnaultz NL. Successful treatment of anorexia nervosa with imipramine. Dis Nerv Sys 1977; 38:567-8.
7. Hudson JI, Pope HG, Jonas JM, et al. Treatment of anorexia nervosa with antidepressants. J Clin Psychopharmacol 1985; 5:17-23.
8. Mills IH. Amitriptyline therapy in anorexia nervosa (letter). Lancet 1976; 2:687.
9. Kendler K. Amitriptyline-induced obesity in anorexia nervosa. Am J Psychiatry 1978; 135:1107-8.
10. Lacey JH, Crisp AH. Hunger, food intake and weight:

the impact of clomipramine on a refeeding anorexia nervosa population. Postgraduate Medical Journal 1980; 56(Supplement);79-85.

11. Biederman J, Herzog DB, Rivinus TM, et al. Amitriptyline in the treatment of anorexia nervosa: a double-blind, placebo-controlled study. J Clin Psychopharmacol 1985; 5:10-6.

12. Halmi KA, Eckert E, LaDu TJ, et al. Anorexia nervosa: treatment efficacy of cyproheptadine and amitriptyline. Arch Gen Psychiatry 1986; 43:177-81.

13. Altshuler KZ, Weiner MF. Anorexia nervosa and depression: a dissenting view. Am J Psychiatry 1985; 142:328-32.

14. Vigersky RA, Loriaux DL. The effect of cyproheptadine in anorexia nervosa. A double-blind trial. In: Vigersky RA, ed. Anorexia nervosa. New York: Raven Press, 1977: 349-56.

15. Goldberg SC, Halmi KA, Eckert ED, et al. Cyproheptadine in anorexia nervosa. Br J Psychiatry 1979; 134:67-70.

16. Barcai A. Lithium in adult anorexia nervosa. A pilot report on two patients. Acta Psychiat Scand 1977; 55:97-101.

17. Stein GS, Hartshorn S, Jones J, et al. Lithium in a case of severe anorexia nervosa. Br J Psychiatry 1982; 140:526-8.

18. Gross HA, Ebert MH, Faden VB, et al. A double-blind controlled trial of lithium carbonate in primary anorexia nervosa. J Clin Psychopharmacol 1981; 1:376-81.

19. Gross H, Ebert MH, Faden VB, et al. A double-blind trial of delta-9-tetrahydrocannabinol in primary anorexia nervosa. J Clin Psychopharmacol 1983; 3:165-71.

20. Dubois A, Gross HA, Richter JE, et al. Effect of bethanechol on gastric functions in primary anorexia nervosa. Dig Dis Sc 1981; 26:598-600.

21. Moldofsky H, Jeuniewic N, Garfinkel PE. Preliminary report on metoclopramide in anorexia nervosa. In Vigersky RA, ed. Anorexia nervosa. New York: Raven Press, 1977:373-6.

22. Saleh JW, Lebwohl P. Metoclopramide-induced gastric emtying in patients with anorexia nervosa. Am J Gastroenterology 1980; 74:127-32.

23. Caplin H, Ginsburg J, Beaconsfield P. Glycerol and treatment of anorexia. Lancet 1973; 1:319.

24. Tec L. Nandrolone in anorexia nervosa (letter). JAMA 1974; 229:1423.

25. Redmond DE, Swann A, Heninger GR. Phenoxybenzamine in anorexia nervosa. Lancet 1976; 2:307.

26. Johanson AJ, Knorr NJ. L-dopa as treatment for anorexia nervosa. In: Vigersky RA, ed. Anorexia nervosa. New York: Raven Press, 1977:363-72.

27. Green RS, Rau JH. Treatment of compulsive eating disturbances with anticonvulsant medication. Am J Psychiatry 1974; 131:428-32.

28. Rau JH, Green RS. Compulsive eating: a neuropsychologic approach to certain eating disorders. Comprehensive Psychiatry 1975;16:223-31.

29. Green RS, Rau JH. The use of diphenylhydantoin in compulsive eating disorders: Further studies. In:

30. Rau JH, Struve FA, Green RS. Electroencephalographic correlates of compulsive eating. Clinical Electroencephalography 1979; 10:180-9.

31. Wermuth BM, Davis KL, Hollister LE, et al. Phenytoin treatment of the binge-eating syndrome. Am J Psychiatry 1977; 134:1249-53.

32. Greenway FL, Dahms WT, Bray GA. Phenytoin as a treatment of obesity associated with compulsive eating. Curr Ther Res 1977; 21:338-42.

33. Kaplan AS, Garfinkel PE, Darby PL, et al. Carbamazepine in the treatment of bulimia. Am J Psychiatry 1983; 140:1225-6.

34. Rich CL. Self-induced vomiting. Psychiatric consideration. JAMA 1978; 239:2688-9.

35. Pope HG, Hudson JI. Treatment of bulimia with antidepressants. Psychopharmacology 1982; 78:176-9.

36. Walsh BT, Stewart JW, Wright L, et al. Treatment of bulimia with monoamine oxidase inhibitors. Am J Psychiatry 1982; 139:1629-30.

37. Sabine EJ, Yonace A, Farrington AJ, et al. Bulimia nervosa: a placebo-controlled, double blind therapeutic trial of mianserin. Br J Clin Pharmac 1983; 15:195S-202S.

38. Pope HG, Hudson JI, Jonas JM, et al. Bulimia treated with imipramine: a placebo-controlled, double-blind study. Am J Psychiatry 1983; 140:554-8.

39. Hughes PL, Wells LA, Cunningham CJ et al. Treating bulimia with desipramine. A double-blind, placebo-controlled study. Arch Gen Psychiatry 1986; 43:182-6.

40. Mitchell JE, Groat R. A placebo-controlled, double-blind trial of amitriptyline in bulimia. J Clin Psychopharmacol 1984; 4:186-93.

41. Walsh BT, Stewart JW, Roose SP, et al. A double-blind trial of phenelzine in bulimia. J of Psychiatric Research 1985; 19:485- 9.

42. Pope HG, Hudson JI, Jonas JM. Antidepressant treatment of bulimia: preliminary experience and practical recommendations. J Clin Psychopharmacol 1983; 3:274-81.

43. Hsu LKG. Treatment of bulimia with lithium. Am J Psychiatry 1984; 141:1260-2.

44. Horne RL. Bupropion in the treatment of bulimia. Paper presented at the 138th Meeting of the American Psychiatric Association, Dallas, Texas, 1985.

45. Brotman A, Herzog DB, Woods SW. Antidepressant treatment of bulimia: The relationship between bingeing and depressive symptomatology. J Clin Psychiatry 1984; 45:7-9.

46. Pope HG, Heridge PL, Hudson JI, Fontaine R, Yurgelun-Todd D. Treatment of bulimia with nomifensine. Presented in the New Research Program. 138th Meeting of the American Psychiatric Association, Dallas, Texas, 1985.

47. Dally P. Treatment of Anorexia nervosa. Br J Hosp Med 1981; 25:434-40.

48. Agras WS, Dorian B, Kirkley BG et al. Imipramine in the treatment of bulimia: a double-blind controlled

study. Int J Eat Dis 1987; 6:29-38.

49. Kennedy S, Piran N, Garfinkel PE. Isocarboxazid in
     the treatment of bulimia (letter). Am J Psychiatry
     1986; 143:1495-6.

Chapter 43

Self-Help in Anorexia and Bulimia: Principles of Organization and Practice

Félix E.F. Larocca

INTRODUCTION

Этhis chapter will cover the important aspects of organizing self-help groups (focusing on those that apply to treating eating disorders). Although literature abounds with theories and hypotheses on self-help in general [1-3], there are few theories on how self-help groups are formed and conducted in the treatment of anorectic and bulimic patients [4].

Bulimia Anorexia Self-Help, Inc., started in April of 1981. The idea for such a self-help organization began when more and more patients asked to meet with the therapist in a group rather than individually. Soon relatives and other members of the community became involved. A specific format was then designed to incorporate self-help groups with informational lectures aimed at educating patients and families alike. After several well-received meetings of this kind (dubbed BASH meetings), BASH began publishing a monthly newsletter. As BASH grew and the self-help format evolved, a facilitator's program was started and resulted in the publication of a formal training manual [5]. A summary of the evolution of 'BASH has been given elsewhere [6].

The self-help format of BASH was chosen by Rubel as a model self-help organization in structure and philosophy [4]. Additional literature on the effectiveness of the BASH format can be found in articles by Fauri and Larocca [6,7]. This chapter will outline the principles of organization and the method of practice of self-help groups using the BASH format as a model.

HISTORY OF MODERN CONCEPTS OF THE SELF-HELP GROUP

Alcoholics Anonymous (AA), the first known modern health-related self-help group was founded in 1935 [8]. Other self-help groups, each with a different purpose and founder, soon followed. Recover, Inc., was started in 1937 by Abraham Low for former mental patients. In 1955 Integrity Groups were founded to help people realize a better psychological life [9]. An Australian self-help group, GROW, was founded to help ex-mental patients lead a more normal life [10]. Synanon, Compassionate Friends, Parents Anonymous, and Epilepsy Self-Help are only some of the many other health-related self-help groups founded between 1950 and 1975 [11-14]. The first eating disorder self-help group, Anorexia Aid Society, was formed in 1974 in England.

Self-help thrived throughout the 1970s and continued to grow in this decade. Gussow and Tracey estimated that self-help groups must grow at a rate of 3% a year to survive [15]. A successful self-help group must generate growth in order to keep operating. AA and Parents Anonymous (PA) both surpassed the 3% rate of growth between 1972 and 1978 when the number of

AA chapters doubled and PA chapters grew from 40 to 1,000 [16].

To keep pace with the necessary growth, other aspects of the self-help group must also change. Borman was correct when he suggested that the group's organizational structure will need to take diverse forms while continuing to reflect the stable ideology and philosophy of the group [17]. The group's energy may need to be redirected as it becomes more concerned with recruitment, organizational maintenance, chapter development, and public education [17,18].

The nature of group membership and leadership may also change [10]. Though many members of self-help groups join during a time of crisis, they can remain vital participants even after the crisis has subsided. Some can take on group leadership or administrative roles [4,6,19]. Others can work in community awareness [4]. For example, the efforts of GROW members to share their group with the community resulted in an increase in members who were not ex-mental patients but needed GROW's kind of help [17].

Most self-help groups have had to develop mutually beneficial relationships with affiliated professionals, institutions, and voluntary fund-raising associations. The Heart Association, for example, donates funds to Mended Hearts, a self-help group for heart patients. Hospitals and detoxification centers have special ties with AA groups. And some hospitals are now working in tandem with eating disorder self-help groups [4,7].

Although many self-help groups benefit financially from these relationships, a systematic means of acquiring financial support is found in all successful self-help groups [17,20].

CHARACTERISTICS OF THE MODERN SELF-HELP GROUP

Because self-help cannot be studied by the use of a control group, current studies of them often prove unreliable. There are other problems, too, that make the scientific study of self-help groups difficult: Membership cannot be denied to those in need of help; persons afflicted with the disorder who do not seek help are impossible to detect; most members are multiple-help seekers; and outcome studies fail to determine which type of help was the most significant in the patient's recovery [21]. Despite these obstacles, a number of studies have attempted to answer some questions about the characteristics of self-help groups [21-23].

Some researchers divide health-related self-help groups into two types [17,22]. The first type (like AA) is devoted to changing each member's behavior—group members view their membership as permanent. The second type is a coping group (like Parents Without Partners), where members view membership as temporary. Members of this type of group usually join during a time of crisis. Frane et al [23] and Levy [24] concluded that in both types of groups the support and mutual disclosure offered by the group often encourages members' continued participation.

Membership in a self-help group extends the size and depth of the members' social network. Lieberman studied help-seeking behavior in members of self-help groups and in individuals who enter psychotherapy [25]. He hypothesized that social networks:

1. Buffer the experience of stress,
2. Decrease the need for professional help by replacing it with instrumental and affective support,
3. Act as screening and referral agents for professional services, and
4. Transmit positive attitudes, values, and norms about help-seeking.

Sidel and Sidel believe the growth of self-help groups is a response to inadequate and unequal distribution of professional resources [26]. The view self-help groups as products of "cop-out" by professionals who blame the victim instead of working to change the deeper problems in society that contribute to members' frustrations. They write, "The groups can exacerbate the very symptoms which caused members to seek help... [and] we now speak of *coping* to refer to what was once called *living*" [26].

Katz and Bender agree that proliferation of self-help groups is a response to inadequate resources, but they view this as a positive response [2]. They see the growth of self-help groups as a "grass-roots" consumer response consistent with the spirit of change and adaptation throughout American history. Reissman also agrees. He believes that on a micro-level self-help groups encourage members to live effectively, and on macro-level they shift members' attitudes to a "consumer-based approach." Reissman believes that participating as an equal member of a group instead of seeking help alone is a major benefit of self-help groups [27]. Levy is correct when he writes, "Self-help represents an effective and inexpensive alternative to the purchased friendship of psychotherapy" [28].

Mutual need, commitment, and sharing are often not enough, however, to sustain a self-help group. Strong leadership is required. Eating disorder self-help groups are no exception.

Rubel suggests the dynamics of anorexia and bulimia prevent long-term commitment to self-help groups and, unless some of those involved have above-average interpersonal skills, the groups usually disband [4]. What then are the mechanisms and interactions in self-help groups that allow leaders to arise and members to be helped?

PROCESSES AT WORK IN SELF-HELP GROUPS

Levy divides the processes that take place in self-help groups into two types: behavior-oriented and cognitive-oriented [29]. Behavior of members of self-help groups is changed by group participation in various ways, such as social reinforcement of desirable behaviors, training in self-control, modeling of coping methods, and devising a program of action.

Cognitive processes serve to remove members' mystification of their experience, increase their expectancy of change, and provide a rationale for their problem. Normative and practical information is shared among participants. Most importantly, the "range of alternative perceptions of members' problems and circumstances and the actions they may take to cope with them broadens" [29]. Members essentially learn to discriminate for themselves between what works and what does not.

There are many similarities between self-help groups and psychotherapy groups. However, certain features distinguish them from each other. Hurvitz [30] concluded that mutual-aid groups use more subjective, peer-initiated approaches than orthodox psychotherapy. Instead of the private disclosures of psychotherapy, experiences are shared in group therapy. Where the psychotherapist is trained to use distance and objectivity, group participants are more judgemental with each other. In psychotherapy, objectivity is the goal. This objectivity has limitations—the patient may come to rely on the therapist instead of assuming more responsibility for himself or herself. Self-help groups can counterbalance the limitations of psychotherapy [30].

Thus, it can be seen that the professional is an important part of a successful self-help group, but is just that—a part. A balance is needed between professional and member responsibility. BASH is one example of a self-help organization with a balanced format. Along with psychotherapy, facilitator training and supervision is used to ensure that the quality of group interaction is high. Because the facilitators are chosen from among membership, the self-help premise of "equal status" relationships is preserved.

Health professionals also can contribute to the evaluative, educational, organizational, and community outreach components of self-help groups. Larocca and Kolodny write, "In the area of self-help such partnership and colleague complementarity can be particularly effective" [31].

RESEARCH ISSUES AND CURRENT HYPOTHESES

The use of self-help groups in the treatment of eating disorders is a recent innovation. The newness of this approach is reflected in the lack of significant study and research on the effectiveness of self-help in the treatment of eating disorders [13]. The use of self-help groups in general, however, has matured to the point of instigating serious research [17,31]. In this section four major issues in general self-help research will be discussed that could be applied to self-help groups for eating disorders.

The first and most important issue is evaluating the impact of self-help groups on group members. Devices must be developed to measure the effectiveness of a chosen self-help group. This is problematic, however, because certain factors inherent in the self-help group format make it difficult to study outcome. These problems can be summarized as follows:

1. Many participants in self-help groups are multiple help-seekers, making it difficult to determine the effect on their well-being of the self-help group experience alone [21,25].

2. It is difficult to establish an effective control group against which the self-help group can be measured. Should the controls be persons who chose another type of therapy for their problem: Or should the control group be composed of persons who have chosen no method of treatment [32]?

3. Many participants of self-help groups attend intermittently. When assessing the group's impact on a person's recovery, how should attendance be figured into the research protocol? A person may attend one of every three meetings but be more involved in those meetings than the person who attends every time [32].

4. The issue of participant involvement is complex and difficult to measure. One would hypothesize that the person who is more involved in the self-help process would receive more benefits, but factors that make up involvement are hard to pinpoint. Involvement could be measured by persistence of attendance, support of the organization, the volunteering of services, or any number of other outward signs of interest in and devotion to the group process.

Another issue in need of further research is how self-help groups are started. What set of circumstances in the initial organization of the group will give that group the best chance for survival? Leadership, group charter, recruitment of members, frequency of meetings and affiliation with other organizations are some of the specific characteristics of the group that need to be researched and delineated.

And still another issue needing to be researched is who participates in self-help groups. By finding patterns in the types of people who are likely to be attracted to these groups, one might be able to better assess who would most benefit from this approach.

A final issue also needs to be researched: How do self-help groups work to aid their members? What are the specific change mechanisms in the group process? How important is an ideology in giving the group a character and personality that can help its members? What activities does the group support? What training and supervision should group leaders undergo? This research should try to pinpoint the major, dynamic factors that give the group its life and its salutary power [28]. If these factors can be determined and the other research issues settled, new and existing self-help groups would have a successful model after which to pattern their own organization.

FUTURE DIRECTIONS

After a successful campaign that was launched in the summer of 1984 by BASH in St. Louis, the St. Louis community was the beneficiary of the by-products of a $300,000 significant grant for the purpose of community awareness and education and the formation of the Mary Anne Richardson Memorial BASH Assistance and Information Center.

The prediction was that with the community's greater awareness of the significance and importance of early detection and intervention on eating disorders a substantially greater number of individuals would seek assistance and find treatment resources early in the development of the eating disorder. Categorically, the BASH organization has moved in this direction and the number of its meetings have been augmented fivefold, reaching approximately 30,000 persons a year.

BASH has also developed a network of further community resources emphasizing transgenerational efforts, including the older (gentry) adult generation and children. In addition, BASH has instigated the development of groups for support of family members who do not necessarily suffer from an eating disorder.

The rising costs of medical treatment and hospitalization are forcing many people to consider alternative forms of therapy [7,33]. This cooperation should enhance the efficacy of self-help as an adjunct to medical treatment.

This efficacy would also enhance another trend that is developing: the greater emphasis on scientific and research material in self-help. Self-help organization, when structured on the BASH format, can provide needed services to the general public by translating complex technical information into easily understood articles and presentations. Thus, self-help groups can educate the public and gain credibility in the eyes of the community [34].

Finally, a development yet to take place: a national registry of self-help groups, which should evolve in the next few years. Just as persons seeking medical or psychiatric care have the benefit of several types of referral services, those seeking self-help therapy deserve information on the kinds of help available. This registry should include evaluation of the type of care, perhaps by a national board yet to be created [35], numbers of years in existence, fees, curriculum for training group leaders, format of meetings, and other pertinent information.

However, as Larocca [36] lamented in his editorial on the Tower of Babel, the issues confronting the development of such a therapist registry are dwarfed by the obstacles arising from such undertaking. As in any new or growing field, the quality of services can vary drastically. A national referral service would help ensure, if properly monitored by supervising agencies, that every person who seeks self-help will find the best program for his or her needs.

Finally, with the instigation of National Eating Disorders Awareness Week by BASH in 1981, and with the mailings of many thousands of packages of free information to every state of the union, its possessions and other countries, BASH has helped insure the realization this year by the American Psychiatric Association, for the first time, of its observation of a Mental Illness Awareness Week, with all its important derivations.

CONCLUSION

In this chapter the present state of self-help has been summarized in relation to the study of a model self-help group. Historically, the self-help movement for anorexia and bulimia is relatively new. But because of its effectiveness in treating eating disorders, it has grown by quantum leaps. The time has come for a more systematic and scientific point of view to be taken in the study of self-help for the treatment of eating disorders. As Rubel asserts, the success and survival of self-help groups for eating disorders depends on systematic structuring and direction by a professional committed to the group's continuance [7]. BASH has been fortunate enough to have evolved in this manner, resulting in its current position as a thriving self-help organization [4].

REFERENCES

1. Evans G. The Family Circle guide to self-help. New York: Ballantine Books, 1979: 198-199, 224.
2. Katz AH, Bender EI. The strength in us: Self-help groups in the modern world. New York: New Viewpoints, 1976: 113-114.
3. Weber GH. Self-help and beliefs. In: Weber GH, Cohen LM, eds. Beliefs and self-help. New York: Human Sciences Press Inc, 1982: 13-30.
4. Rubel JR. The function of self-help groups in recovery for anorexia and bulimia. In: Larocca FEF, ed. Psychiatric clinics of North America: Symposium on eating disorders. 1984; 7:2.
5. Larocca FEF, Kolodny NJ. A facilitator's training manual: A primer: The BASH approach. St. Louis: Midwest Medical Publications, 1983.
6. Larocca FEF. The relevance of self-help in the management of anorexia and bulimia. Res Medica (medical magazine published by St. John's Mercy Medical Center, St. Louis, Missouri, USA) 1983; 1:16-9.
7. Fauri DP. The use of self-help groups with persons and family members facing anorexia nervosa. BASH Newsletter 1983; 2:4.
8. Powell TJ. Self-help organizations and professional practice. Silverspring, Maryland: National Association of Social Workers, 1987: 11.
9. Mowrer OH. Integrity groups: Basic principles and procedures. Couns Psych 1972; 2:7-33.
10. Wood M. The road to mental recovery. Aust Fam Phys 1981; 10:858-859.
11. Borman LD. Characteristics of development and growth. In: Lieberman MA, Borman LD, eds. Self-help groups for coping with crisis. San Francisco: Jossey-Bass, 1979: 22-23.
12. Pitch L. What a show. Health Visitor 1981; 8:21.
13. Tapia F. Self-help on an individual basis. In: Larocca FEF, editor. Eating disorders: Effective care and treatment. St. Louis: Isyiyakyu EuroAmerica Inc, 1986: 247-257.
14. Lieber LL. Mothers anonymous: New directions against child abuse. Paper presented at the First Biennial Conference of the Society for Clinical Social Work, San Francisco, 1971.
15. Gussow A, Tracy GS. The role of self-help clubs in adaption to chronic illness and disability. Soc Science and Med 1976; 10:407-14.
16. Parents Anonymous Frontiers, Torrance, California, Parents Anonymous, 1979.
17. Borman LD. Characteristics of development and growth. In: Lieberman MA, Borman LD, eds. Self-help for coping with crisis. San Francisco: Jossey-Bass, 1979:13-42.
18. Gartner A. Self-help and mental health. Soc Pol 1976; 7:20-40.
19. Larocca FEF, Stern J. Eating disorders: Self-help and treatment in Missouri. Mo Med 1984; 81(12):764-73.
20. Gartner A, Reissman F. The self-help revolution, vol. X. New York: Human Services Inc., 1984: 243-248.
21. Rosenblatt A, Mayer JE. Help-seeking for family problems: A survey of utilization and satisfaction. Am J of Psych 1972; 28:126-30.
22. Wollert RW, Levy LH, Knight BG. Help giving in behavioral control and stress coping self-help groups. Sm Gr Beh 1982; 13:204-18.
23. Frane CC, Knight B, Levy LH, et al. Self-help groups: The members' perspectives Am J of Comm Psych 1980; 8:53-65.
24. Levy LH. Self-help groups viewed by mental health professionals: A survey and comments. Am J of Comm Psych 1973; 6:305-15.
25. Lieberman MA. Help seeking and self-help groups. In: Lieberman MA, Borman LP, eds. Self-help groups for coping with crisis. San Francisco: Jossey-Bass, 1979:116-150.
26. Sidel VW, Sidel R. Beyond coping. Soc Pol 1976; 7:67-70.
27. Riessman F. The helper therapy principle. Social Work, April 1965; 10:27.
28. Levy LH. Self-help groups: Types and psychological processes. J of App Beh Science 1976; 12:310-22.
29. Levy LH. Process and activities in groups. In: Lieberman MA, Borman LD, eds. Self-help groups for coping with crisis. San Francisco: Jossey-Bass, 1979: 234-271.
30. Hurvitz N. Characteristics of orthodox (professional) psychotherapy and self-help group therapy conference. Sixty-Sixth Annual Conference of the American Psychological Association, San Francisco, California, September 1968.
31. Larocca FEF, Kolodny NJ. Treating depression in adolescence: The psychiatric and social work connection. In: Munoz RA, ed. New directions for mental health services. San Francisco: Jossey-Bass, 1984: 51-8.
32. Lieberman MA, Bond GR. Self-help groups: Problems and measuring outcome. Sm Gr Beh 1978; 9:221-41.
33. Mantell JE, Alexander ES, Kleiman MA. Social work and self-help groups. Health and Soc Work 1976; 1:80-100.
34. Larocca FEF, Goodner SA. Eating disorders and self-help revisited. Clinical Psychiatric Quarterly 1987; 10(2):6-9.
35. Fink PJ. Mental illness awareness week (editorial). American Journal of Psychiatry 1987; 144(10):1298, 1300.
36. Larocca FEF. Tower of babel—a therapist registry (editorial). BASH Newsletter 1983; 2(1):3.

Index